PETERSON'S LEARNING *Adventures* AROUND THE WORLD

Peter Greenberg

Editor

Peterson's
Princeton, New Jersey

Editorial inquiries concerning this book should be addressed to the editor at Peterson's, P.O. Box 2123, Princeton, New Jersey 08543-2123.

ISSN 1089-246X
ISBN 1-56079-701-0

Cover design by Susan Newman Design, Inc.

Visit Peterson's Education Center on the Internet (World Wide Web) at http://www.petersons.com

Printed in the United States of America

10 9 8 7 6 5 4 3 2 1

CONTENTS

Introduction

BY PETER S. GREENBERG

It's not surprising that I love every chance I have to travel. It's a job I love. But I'm also fascinated with the process of travel—the logistics, the machinery, and, ultimately, the finesse of getting from point A to point B.

I remain infatuated, and some would say obsessed, with the temptation—almost always fulfilled—of adventure and romance each journey brings. Each time I sit in an airline seat, the plane roars down the concrete, and we defy gravity yet again I am excited by who I might meet, what I might see, and perhaps most important, what I will learn along the way.

If you approach the concept of travel as the introductory course toward becoming a citizen of the world, then every trip is an amazing voyage of discovery in the global village of which you are a member.

This book is not just a compilation of interesting and different holidays. Instead, it is about the fastest-growing segment in the travel business—the brave new and mind-expanding world of learning vacations.

These are trips designed to test, challenge, and enrich; journeys that take you to—and often beyond—what you thought were your limits of conditioning, understanding, and acceptance.

Learning vacations strongly reflect the growing trend toward socially and ecologically responsible tourism. One of my favorite sayings is that I never wanted to let school interfere with my education, or allow work to interfere with my life.

Learning vacations only enhance both.

Some are physically challenging; others teach you a skill or help you master a craft; there are study tours, arts programs, language courses, university programs, and one of my favorite learning vacations—voluntary service.

If you're tired of taking the same old holiday to the same resort or hotel, or you're bored spending time by the same pool sipping the same tired semitropical drink, then you need a vacation—from your traditional vacation thinking.

No, I'm not talking about some bizarre time-share idea, or the latest all-inclusive couples resort. Instead, there's a whole new approach to the feel-good vacation. It is an entirely different kind of travel, with different destinations, different cultures, and most important, different expectations and goals.

A majority of these trips are proactive. They add meaning and depth to the travel experience. They enrich as well as simply entertain; they

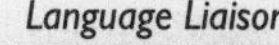
Language Liaison

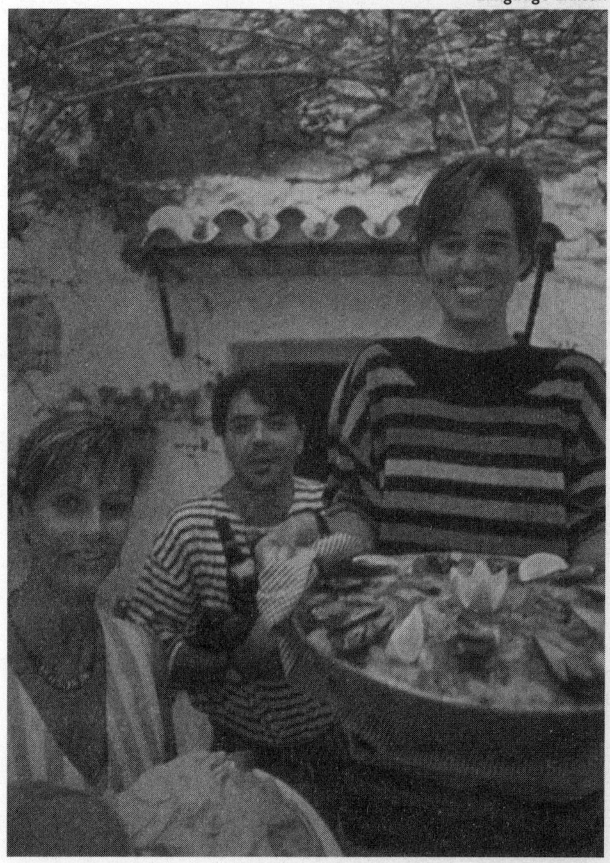

recharge as well as simply relax. And they offer the perfect combination of energy, fulfillment... and *knowledge.*

Learning vacations don't just take you to the threshold of discovery—they take you *across* it. You're not a tourist but a participant. Welcome to the expanding universe of the learning vacation, where you can become a part of an archaeological dig in Central America, help scientists studying the effects of beach erosion in Trinidad, teach English on the southern coast of central Java in Indonesia, or work in the colonies of rural Mexico.

You are rewarded with knowledge or a mastery of a skill, the refinement of a craft or the best—and usually unexpected—benefit: in many cases, you are helped to realize goals you never even knew you had.

These learning vacations can be as small as six people or two hundred folks at a time. Many of the programs and trips are sponsored or led by museums, universities, or nonprofit volunteer organizations. If you're looking to be fulfilled instead of just fed, if you want to learn instead of just lay around, and if you want to help other people instead of just helping yourself, these are fantastic alternative vacations.

First, a few minor words of historical perspective and caution. Travel for personal and spiritual enrichment is not new, nor are trips that focus more on learning than on leisure activity.

What *is* new is that the new global opportunities for learning vacations are rapidly expanding.

Some learning vacations are purely hands-on experiences. Cook with some of the great chefs of the world; build your own wooden canoe; fly a real Mig jet fighter in the skies over Moscow. Others test your physical limits, not to mention your own thrill-seeking threshold: ice and rock climbing, parachuting, bicycling in the Alps. But all learning vacations challenge your mind.

One of the greatest things about learning vacations is that they know no boundaries; in most cases they are not affected by political disputes between countries.

You can learn Spanish in Spain or Guatemala, or go to language school in Cuba; work alongside archaeologists at a fascinating dig under the main streets of Istanbul, or study the ruins near Damascus or Tunisia; or study folk medicine and traditional healing techniques in India and Nepal. You can sail up the Amazon looking for rare birds, swim with dolphins in the Bahamas, or participate in an up-close and personal environmental program to save sea turtles in Trinidad.

Many tourists have visited the incredible ruins in Petra in Jordan and Luxor in Egypt. But now, a cruise ship dedicated to the fields of history, archaeology, and architecture is sailing to the tenth century and the port of Hodeidah in the once forbidden country of the real Arabian nights, Yemen.

There are dozens of museum-sponsored affordable trips, ranging from a Smithsonian learning vacation to South Africa and the villages of the Zulus, to rain forest workshops, to specially designed-to-be-fun cultural learning vacations geared for families with children whose global views may have only extended as far as Disney World.

Learning vacations can also have a greater, deeper purpose.

Instead of staying at another recognizable chain hotel in a foreign country, live with a family in a small town devastated by a natural disaster and help them rebuild their community.

Learning vacations don't simply teach you understanding as much as they confirm it; they don't instruct you in compassion as much as they encourage you to enthusiastically practice it.

Many of my friends have returned from these specialized trips angry—that they had to come home. "It is truly a selfish act," one of them told me. "I received so much more than I gave."

There are a number of potential side benefits. For some travelers, many of these trips—or at least a portion of each one—may be tax deductible.

Indeed, with some programs, you can earn credit toward a degree. With *all* programs, you earn life experience.

It's one thing to witness a beautiful sunset in Bali or take in the view from a hilltop restaurant overlooking the small magical harbor in Villefranche. You return from your experience with beautiful memories.

It's another thing to learn a language, a skill, or immerse yourself in a foreign culture. You still get the sunsets, but you return from your trip with knowledge you can apply forever, and usually at times when you least expect it.

It is, to say the least, one of the best definitions of responsible tourism. There's a learning vacation for every age group, budget, and physical ability.

As opposed to intense adventure travel itineraries, where many of us "learn" not to do THAT again, these are trips that pay knowledge and experience dividends in near perpetuity.

I first learned about learning vacations a few years ago when I spent $300 to join a diverse group of my fellow citizens for a nine-day voluntary service program sponsored by Global Volunteers of St. Paul, Minnesota (800-487-1074). The experience took us to a place many Americans consider foreign.

There was no color brochure. Just the facts:

Population: 1,476.
Ninety-five percent black.
Eighty-five percent unemployed.
And one of the poorest counties in America.

Welcome to Jonestown, Mississippi. To get there, you drive south from Memphis down Highway 61, the road made famous by Bob Dylan. But don't drive too fast, or you'll miss it.

This is a place that time forgot, or, perhaps more accurately, ignored.

Most of the stores on Main Street have been shuttered. Broken beer bottles and garbage litter the empty town playground, and a cold wind rips at frayed sheets of thin plastic that barely cover the open holes of most of the homes where glass windows used to be.

There's nobody in line at the teller windows at the bank, which closed last year for lack of money. But you can always find three local dogs lying in their regular afternoon place in front of the small brick building that is now being used as the town hall.

If you didn't know any better, you might think Jonestown was a ghost town—with people.

So who goes there on vacation? And why?

There's Susan, a nurse from New York; Pat, a retired judge from Oregon; and Laura, a college student from Minnesota. They all took their vacation time and came to Jonestown, not to relax, but to work.

The nurse, the judge, and the college student bypassed their beach or golf vacations for something much more enriching. They came to Jonestown to learn, and to help.

My $300 covered basic costs and materials. How I got to Jonestown was my responsibility. Once there, I participated in community projects ranging from painting, planting gardens, and cleaning yards to rebuilding the town's community center.

At first, the locals didn't know quite what to make of this unusual group of vacationers. "Let's face it," one resident told me. "Black people down here aren't used to being helped by white people. They figure if we want to help them, there's got to be a catch."

At the first town meeting, only three residents showed up.

Still, work began immediately on fixing some of the houses and cleaning up some of the abandoned buildings.

But by the end of the first week, the volunteers found themselves outnumbered by the locals, three to one.

The group attacked some of the more pressing problems first. Only two of the town's thirty-four fire hydrants worked. Abandoned buildings were being used as garbage dumps. And the town lacked street signs.

All the hydrants were fixed. The garbage was removed, and the buildings renovated. And, for the first time in its history, Jonestown finally got the much-needed street signs.

By the end of my first week there, we had virtually become a part of the town. I played touch football games with the children, shot pool (badly) in the local pool hall, and had a close gastronomic encounter with everything from mustard greens and grits to spicy barbecue.

When I returned from my "vacation," I knew I couldn't—and wouldn't—trade that experience for anything. My trip to Jonestown was arguably more fulfilling for me than any vacation I've ever had, because I wasn't just visiting a place. I'd become a part of it. A traveler with a purpose. I'd become *involved*.

That experience inspired me to explore other learning vacations around the world. And thus, this book.

Think of the possibilities to learn something new, or pursue one of your passions in-depth. Quite simply, learning vacations will never interfere with your education. And, given the wide range of programs offered by these—and hundreds of other organizations—I can't say enough about the special "vacations" they offer. They are, to say the very least, worth writing home about. And come to think of it, I just did.

Peter S. Greenberg is an authority on travel. He is travel editor for the NBC Today Show *and hosts a weekly call-in radio show on KABC, a top-rated radio station in Southern California. He also writes a syndicated travel column for the* Los Angeles Times, *which appears in 60 newspapers.*

How to Use This Guide

Browse freely. Read often. *Peterson's Learning Adventures Around the World* can help you discover the learning vacation of a lifetime.

All of the programs in the guide offer opportunities to learn a new skill, master a craft, or enrich your understanding of another land or people. But the learning experiences they offer can be as different as a classroom lecture, a rugged field expedition, or a luxurious museum-hopping tour. You'll need to decide the type of program that best suits your needs, pocketbook, and interests before you can narrow your choices. For a quick view of the possibilities, consult the index of Program Types on page 559.

The 1997 edition profiles 2,000 learning adventures, arranged by region and country and alphabetized by sponsor name. These are mainly scheduled group courses and trips held outside the United States that last between one and six weeks. Keep in mind that in addition to these programs, there are others that sponsors may schedule as the year goes on. Some program directors may even design a special tour just for you or your group. For a more complete list of options or the latest program additions, write or call sponsors directly using the contact information found at the end of each profile.

An open book appearing before the sponsor name indicates that the program may result in college credit. Because no program sponsor can promise that your college or university will award you credit, you'll want to talk to your adviser before making any decisions. A good place to start is the index of programs offering credit on page 594.

To obtain the profiles in this guide, we surveyed over 400 universities and colleges, organizations, museums, and travel outfitters during the summer of 1996. All information has been submitted by program directors. All usable data received in time for publication have been included. Because of the comprehensive editorial review that takes place in our offices and because all materials come directly from the sponsoring organizations, we have every reason to believe that the information in this guide is accurate. But program specifics—including dates and costs—are subject to change so check with sponsors.

Updated annually, *Peterson's Learning Adventures Around the World* with Contributing Editor Peter S. Greenberg will only grow larger in subsequent editions. We'll continue to dig for new programs. And we welcome your help in identifying learning adventures that you have discovered. To contact the editor, write to *Learning Adventures*, Peterson's, P.O. Box 2123, 202 Carnegie Center, Princeton, NJ 08543-2123, or on the Web at www.petersons.com/adventures/tellus.html

WORLDWIDE ORGANIZATIONS

With 2,000 programs to choose from, *Peterson's Learning Adventures Around the World* can help you find the vacation you've always dreamed about. But since some organizations sponsor hundreds of programs that they add throughout the year, you'll want to contact them for their most recent catalogs. Here's a list of organizations that operate worldwide:

The Catholic Network of Volunteer Services
4121 Harewood Road, NE
Washington, DC 20017-1593
800-543-5046; Fax: 202-526-1094
E-mail: cnvs@ari.net

Earthwatch
Field Operations
680 Mount Auburn Street
Watertown, MA 02272
800-776-0188; Fax: 617-926-8532
E-mail: info@earthwatch.org

Elderhostel
75 Federal Street
Boston, MA 02110-1941
World Wide Web: http://www.elderhostel.org

Journeys International, Inc.
4011 Jackson Road
Ann Arbor, MI 48103
313-665-4407; Fax: 313-665-2945

Language Liaison
20533 Biscayne Boulevard-Station 4-162
Miami, FL 33180
305-682-9909; Fax; 305-682-9907
E-mail: langstudy@aol.com

National Geographic Society
Journeys Abroad
Reservation Center
347 Congress Street
Boston, MA 02210
800-866-3270

Smithsonian Institution
Smithsonian Study Tours and Seminars
1100 Jefferson Drive, SW (MRC 702)
Washington, DC 20560
202-357-4700; Fax: 202-633-9250

TraveLearn
P.O. Box 315
Lakeville, PA 18438
800-235-9114; Fax: 717-226-9114
E-mail: travelearn@aol.com

COUNTRY TO COUNTRY

PROGRAMS

If your idea of the perfect learning adventure is to roam from one country to another, you've come to the right place. The sponsors in this section offer programs in destinations around the world. Interested in art? One program lets you tour Paris, Prague, and Antibes while you study painting. Is music your passion? There are programs that send you to performances in leading venues throughout Europe. Want to get ahead in international business? One course lets you study global business trends in the world's major markets. And if nothing less than an around-the-world odyssey will do, you'll find tours that will take you to all corners of the globe.

To start your search for the perfect globetrotting itinerary, look through the programs listed in this section. But don't stop here. You'll also want to check out the program listings for those countries and regions in which you're most interested. You may be able to work with the sponsor to put together your own dream tour. Happy hunting.

Programs in this section are listed alphabetically by the name of the sponsoring institution.

COUNTRY TO COUNTRY

PROGRAMS

AMERICAN UNIVERSITY IN BULGARIA

BALKAN POLITICAL CULTURE

General Information • Academic study program in Albania (Tirana), Bulgaria (Blagoevgrad), Greece (Thessaloniki), Turkey (Istanbul), Yugoslavia (Skopje). Classes are held on the campus of American University in Bulgaria.
Learning Focus • Courses in political science, history. Instruction is offered by professors from the sponsoring institution.
Accommodations • Dormitories, hotels. Single rooms are available. Meals are taken in central dining facility, in local restaurants.
Program Details • Program offered once per year. Session length: 6 weeks. Departures are scheduled in May. The program is open to undergraduate students, graduate students, adults. Most participants are 16-65 years of age. 15 participants per session. Application deadline: March 1.
Costs • $2800 (includes tuition, housing, some meals, books and class materials, ground transportation). A $500 deposit is required.
Contact • Jenny Pendeva, Educational Outreach Coordinator, American University in Bulgaria, Blagoevgrad 2700, Bulgaria; +359 73-64-735; Fax: +359 73-20-603; E-mail: jenny@nws.aubg.bg

ART TREK

AN ARTIST'S TRAVEL WORKSHOP: PARIS, PRAGUE, AND ANTIBES

General Information • Arts program with visits to Czech Republic (Prague), France (Antibes, Paris); excursions to Monet's garden at Giverny, Musée d'Orsay Paris, Nice, Prague Castle. Once at the destination country, participants travel by train, bus, foot, airplane. Program is affiliated with University of California Santa Cruz Extension.
Learning Focus • Instruction in watercolor painting and printmaking. Escorted travel to France and the Czech Republic. Museum visits (Orsay, Picasso, Matisse, Chagall, Maeghi). Attendance at performances (music and theater). Instruction is offered by professors, artists. This program would appeal to people interested in fine arts, education, art therapy.
Accommodations • Hotels. Single rooms are available for an additional $520.
Program Details • Program offered once per year. Session length: 17 days. Departures are scheduled in June. Most participants are 35-55 years of age. Participants must be 14 years or older to enroll. 16 participants per session. Application deadline: April 20. Reservations are recommended at least 4-6 months before departure.
Costs • $4550 (includes tuition, housing, some meals, excursions, international airfare, instruction and leadership). A $450 deposit is required.
Contact • Carol Duchamp, Director, Art Trek, PO Box 807, Bolinas, CA 94924; 415-868-9558; Fax: 415-868-9033

THE CATHOLIC NETWORK OF VOLUNTEER SERVICES

CATHOLIC NETWORK OF VOLUNTEER SERVICES

General Information • Volunteer service program with visits to Africa, East Asia and Pacific, Middle East, Western Europe, Western Hemisphere.
Learning Focus • Volunteer work (education, health care, social service). Instruction is offered by clergy, volunteer support staff, project leaders. This program would appeal to people interested in the Catholic faith.
Program Details • Session length: contact sponsor. Departures are scheduled throughout the year. Program is targeted to seniors, college graduates. Most participants are 18-70 years of age. Participants must be 18 years or older to enroll.
Costs • Contact sponsor for information.
Contact • Phyllis Scaridge, Office Coordinator, The Catholic Network of Volunteer Services, 4121 Harewood Road, NE, Washington, DC 20017-1593; 800-543-5046; Fax: 202-526-1094; E-mail: cnvs@ari.net; World Wide Web: http://www2.ari.net/home3/cnvs

EARTHWATCH

EARTHWATCH EXPEDITIONS

General Information • Research expedition with visits to Africa, East Asia and Pacific, Eastern Europe, Middle East, Russia and Central Asia, Western Europe, Western Hemisphere. Once at the destination country, participants travel by bus, foot, boat, bicycle. Program is affiliated with Drexel University.
Learning Focus • Instruction in biodiversity, ecology, wildlife management, health and nutrition. Field research in animal behavior, sustainable development, global change. Escorted travel to coral reefs, rainforests, dinosaur and other fossils. Museum visits (art and architecture museums). Nature observation (birds, marine mammals, endangered

species). Other activities include camping, hiking. Instruction is offered by professors, researchers, naturalists, scientists. This program would appeal to people interested in photography, sketching, data collection, data management, culture, traditions, archaeology, resource management.

Accommodations • Homestays, dormitories, locally-rented apartments, hotels, campsites, inns, lodges.

Program Details • Session length: 1-12 weeks. Departures are scheduled throughout the year. Most participants are 16-80 years of age. Participants must be 16 years or older to enroll. Participants must be members of the sponsoring organization (annual dues: $35). Other requirements: good health, an open mind and a sense of humor. 5-10 participants per session. Reservations are recommended at least 3 months before departure.

Costs • $700-$2300 (includes housing, all meals, books and class materials, registration fees, park fees). A $250 deposit is required.

Contact • Earthwatch, Field Operations, 680 Mount Auburn Street, Watertown, MA 02272; 800-776-0188; Fax: 617-926-8532; E-mail: info@earthwatch.org

ELDERHOSTEL

ELDERHOSTEL

General Information • Tour programs of all types with visits to China (Shandong Province), England (London), Indonesia (Ubud, Bali), Israel (Jerusalem), Italy (Florence), Scotland (Glasgow) among other destinations; excursions to areas of historical, cultural, and natural history interest. Once at the destination country, participants travel by train, bus, foot, boat, airplane, bicycle.

Learning Focus • Instruction in liberal arts and sciences. Field research in archaeology, ecology, ornithology. Museum visits (museums of cultural and historical importance). Nature observation (whale research, ornithology). Volunteer work (human services, ecological and archaeological work). Other activities include camping, hiking. Instruction is offered by professors, researchers, naturalists, artists, historians, scientists.

Accommodations • Homestays, dormitories, hotels, campsites, sailing vessels, youth hostel bunkrooms, conference center lodgings.

Program Details • Session length: 1- 4 weeks. Departures are scheduled throughout the year. Program is targeted to seniors 55 and older. Most participants are 50-100 years of age. Participants must be 55 years or older to enroll. Other requirements: must be accompanied by age eligible spouse if under 55. 20-45 participants per session. Reservations are recommended at least May 17 before departure.

Costs • $1900-$5000 (includes tuition, housing, all meals, books and class materials, insurance, excursions, international airfare). A $250 deposit is required.

Contact • Elderhostel International Catalog, Elderhostel, 75 Federal Street, Boston, MA 02110-1941; World Wide Web: http://www.elderhostel.org

FOLKWAYS INSTITUTE

GRAND TOUR PROJECT

General Information • Cultural tour with visits to Austria (Vienna), Czech Republic (Prague), England (London), France (Paris), Italy (Rome). Once at the destination country, participants travel by train, foot, car.

Learning Focus • Escorted travel to major cities. Museum visits (local museums). Instruction is offered by historians. This program would appeal to people interested in European culture.

Accommodations • Hotels. Single rooms are available.

Program Details • Program offered once per year. Session length: 6 weeks. Departures are scheduled in May. 16 participants per session. Application deadline: November 1. Reservations are recommended at least 6 months before departure.

Costs • Contact sponsor for information. A $50 deposit is required.

Contact • David Christopher, Director, Folkways Institute, 14600 Southeast Aldridge Road, Portland, OR 97236-6518; 503-658-6600; Fax: 503-658-8672

FOLKWAYS INSTITUTE

SYMPHONIC PROJECT

General Information • Cultural tour with visits to Austria (Vienna), Czech Republic (Prague), Hungary (Budapest). Once at the destination country, participants travel by train, foot.

Learning Focus • Museum visits (local cities). Attendance at performances (symphonies). Instruction is offered by artists. This program would appeal to people interested in art, classical music.

Accommodations • Hotels. Single rooms are available.

Program Details • Program offered once per year. Session length: 12 days. Departures are scheduled in April. 16 participants per session. Application deadline: October 1. Reservations are recommended at least 6 months before departure.

Costs • $3100 (includes housing, all meals, books and class materials, international airfare, performances). A $50 deposit is required.

Contact • David Christopher, Director, Folkways Institute, 14600 Southeast Aldridge Road, Portland, OR 97236-6518; 503-658-6600; Fax: 503-658-8672

FORUM TRAVEL INTERNATIONAL

PRAGUE TO PASSAU: CASTLES OF BOHEMIA

General Information • Bicycle tour with visits to Czech Republic (Hluboka, Prague), Germany (Passau). Once at the destination country, participants travel by bicycle.

Learning Focus • Instruction in culture and art, history. Escorted travel to castles. Other activities include cycling. Instruction is offered by professional guides. This program would appeal to people interested in castles, bicycling.

Accommodations • Hotels. Single rooms are available.

Program Details • Session length: 8 days. Departures are scheduled in May-September. Most participants are 20-60 years of age. Participants must be 16 years or older to enroll. 10 participants per session. Application deadline: 60 days prior to departure. Reservations are recommended at least 3-5 months before departure.

Costs • $605-$980 (includes housing, some meals). A $200 deposit is required.

Contact • Jeannie Graves, Operations Manager, Forum Travel International, 91 Gregory Lane #21, Pleasant Hill, CA

94525; 510-671-2900; Fax: 510-671-2993; E-mail: forum@ix.netcom.com; World Wide Web: http://www.ten-io.com/forumtravel

GEORGE MASON UNIVERSITY

HOLOCAUST STUDY TOUR

General Information • Academic study program in Austria (Vienna), Czech Republic (Prague), Germany (Berlin), Hungary (Budapest), Israel (Jerusalem), Poland (Cracow, Warsaw).

Learning Focus • Courses in history, sociology, Judaic studies, international studies. Instruction is offered by professors from the sponsoring institution and local teachers.

Accommodations • Hotels. Meals are taken as a group, in local restaurants.

Program Details • Program offered once per year. Session length: 3 weeks. Departures are scheduled in May. The program is open to undergraduate students, graduate students. Most participants are 18-65 years of age. Other requirements: minimum 2.25 GPA. 10-20 participants per session. Application deadline: April 1.

Costs • $3500 for George Mason University students, $4000 for other students (includes tuition, housing, some meals, insurance, excursions, international airfare). Application fee: $35. A $500 deposit is required.

Contact • Dr. Yehuda Lukacs, Director, George Mason University, 4400 University Drive, 235 Johnson Center, Fairfax, VA 22030; 703-993-2156; Fax: 703-993-2153; E-mail: ylukacs@gmu.edu; World Wide Web: http://www.gmu.edu/departments/oie

 GLOBAL CITIZENS NETWORK

GLOBAL CITIZENS NETWORK

General Information • Volunteer service program with visits to Belize (Pueblo Viejo), Guatemala (San Juan), Kenya (Charuru), Mexico; excursions to game park, Mayan ruins, local markets. Once at the destination country, participants travel by bus, foot.

Learning Focus • Instruction in local crafts and customs. Attendance at performances (cultural events). Volunteer work (building a health clinic, teaching in a school). Instruction is offered by Peace Corps volunteers. This program would appeal to people interested in people, carpentry, nature studies, service, education, engineering, children, cultural immersion.

Accommodations • Homestays, community building. Single rooms are available.

Program Details • Session length: 1, 2, or 3 weeks. Departures are scheduled throughout the year. Most participants are 18-80 years of age. Other requirements: students under 16 must be accompanied by an adult. 6-8 participants per session. Reservations are recommended at least 8-10 weeks before departure.

Costs • $400-$1300 (includes housing, some meals, donation to the project that the team is working on in the village). A $200 deposit is required.

Contact • Kim Regnier, Program Director, Global Citizens Network, 1931 Iglehart Avenue, St. Paul, MN 55104; 800-644-9292; Fax: 612-644-0960; E-mail: gcn@mtn.org

GLOBAL FITNESS ADVENTURES

GLOBAL FITNESS ADVENTURES

General Information • Adventure/spa program with visits to Dominica, Indonesia (Bali), Italy (Lake Como), Kenya. Once at the destination country, participants travel by foot.

Learning Focus • Instruction in health, fitness, yoga and meditation. Other activities include hiking. Instruction is offered by naturalists, sports professionals, health educators. This program would appeal to people interested in yoga, meditation, nutrition, longevity, wellness, spirituality, empowerment, hiking, rafting, bicycling, skiing, horseback riding, scuba diving.

Accommodations • Hotels, private islands, ranches, estates, homes. Single rooms are available for an additional $400.

Program Details • Departures are scheduled throughout the year. Program is targeted to professionals. Most participants are 16-70 years of age. Participants must be 16 years or older to enroll. Other requirements: must be willing to be challenged in hiking and enjoy health advancements. 8-16 participants per session. Application deadline: 2 weeks prior to departure. Reservations are recommended at least 2 weeks before departure.

Costs • $2175 (includes tuition, housing, all meals, excursions, massage, all activities, evening cultural and motivational programs). A $500 deposit is required.

Contact • Kristina Hurrell, Director, Global Fitness Adventures, PO Box 1390, Aspen, CO 81612; 800-488-8747; Fax: 970-927-4793

HOLBROOK TRAVEL INC.

GUIDED NATURAL HISTORY TOURS

General Information • Nature study tour with visits to Costa Rica, Ecuador (Galapagos Islands), Guatemala, Honduras, Kenya, Peru; excursions to national parks, forest reserves. Once at the destination country, participants travel by bus, boat, airplane. Program is affiliated with Caribbean Conservation Corporation.

Learning Focus • Escorted travel to national parks and forest reserves. Museum visits (local museums). Nature observation (indigenous flora and fauna). Volunteer work (turtle tagging in Costa Rica). Instruction is offered by professors, naturalists, scientists. This program would appeal to people interested in ecotourism, natural history.

Accommodations • Hotels, lodges. Single rooms are available.

Program Details • Session length: 8-19 days. Departures are scheduled throughout the year. Most participants are 30-90 years of age. 10-15 participants per session. Reservations are recommended at least 60 days before departure.

Costs • $1200-$5000 (includes housing, all meals, excursions). A $300 deposit is required.

Contact • Philip Lovejoy, Director of Marketing, Holbrook Travel Inc., One World, Inc., 264 Beacon Street, Boston, MA 02116; 617-262-8044; Fax: 617-262-8389; E-mail: travel@holbrook.usa.com

MARINE EXPEDITIONS

ISLANDS OF THE SOUTH ATLANTIC

General Information • Wilderness/adventure program with visits to England (Plymouth, St. Helena, Tristan da

Cunha), Falkland Islands (Malvinas), Spain (Canary Islands, Madeira); excursions to Falkland Islands, South Georgia Island, Ascension Island, Cape Verde Islands, Canary Islands, Madeira Islands. Once at the destination country, participants travel by boat.

Learning Focus • Instruction in biology, ornithology and history. Field research in biology, ornithology and history. Nature observation (penguins, albatrosses, seals, volcanoes, turtles, seabirds). Instruction is offered by naturalists, historians, scientists. This program would appeal to people interested in nature studies, photography, ornithology.

Accommodations • Boat. Single rooms are available.

Program Details • Program offered once per year. Session length: 50 days. Departures are scheduled in March. Most participants are 20–90 years of age. Participants must be 10 years or older to enroll. 80 participants per session. Reservations are recommended at least 6 months before departure.

Costs • $5000 (includes tuition, housing, all meals, excursions, international airfare). A $500 deposit is required.

Contact • Anne Lex, Sales Manager, Marine Expeditions, 13 Hazelton Avenue, Toronto, ON M5R 2E1, Canada; 800-263-9147; Fax: 416-964-9069

MOZART'S EUROPE TOURS

MOZART'S EUROPE–VARIATION #1

General Information • Cultural tour with visits to Austria (Salzburg, Vienna), Czech Republic (Prague), Germany (Berlin, Dresden, Leipzig); excursions to Esterhazy Palaces, Vienna Woods, Zwinger Palace, Cecilienhof, Gewandhaus Orchestra, Sinfonietta Chamber Orchestra. Once at the destination country, participants travel by bus, foot.

Learning Focus • Escorted travel to Melk Monastery and Strahov Monastery. Museum visits (Schloss Klessheim, Albertina Gallery). Attendance at performances (Vienna State Opera Company, Salzburger Marionette Theater). Instruction is offered by professors, artists, historians. This program would appeal to people interested in music, opera, Mozart.

Accommodations • Hotels. Single rooms are available for an additional $590.

Program Details • Program offered once per year. Session length: 16 days. Departures are scheduled in May. Program is targeted to music lovers. Most participants are 30–75 years of age. 25 participants per session. Reservations are recommended at least 6 months before departure.

Costs • $3728 (includes housing, some meals, excursions, concert and opera performances). A $200 deposit is required.

Contact • Norman Eagle, President, Mozart's Europe Tours, Deer Lane, Pawlet, VT 05761; 802-325-3656; Fax: 802-325-3656

MOZART'S EUROPE TOURS

MOZART'S EUROPE–VARIATION #2

General Information • Cultural tour with visits to Austria (Salzburg, Vienna), Czech Republic (Prague), Germany (Munich); excursions to Augsburg, Strahov Monastery, Austerlitz, Vienna Woods. Once at the destination country, participants travel by bus, foot.

Learning Focus • Escorted travel to Residenz Palace. Museum visits (Deutsches Museum, Schloss Klessheim). Attendance at performances (Salzburg Marionette Theater, Vienna Volksoper, Wiener Symphoniker). Instruction is offered by professors, researchers, artists, historians. This program would appeal to people interested in music, opera.

Accommodations • Hotels. Single rooms are available for an additional $438.

Program Details • Program offered once per year. Session length: 13 days. Departures are scheduled in June. Program is targeted to music lovers. Most participants are 30–75 years of age. 25 participants per session. Reservations are recommended at least 6 months before departure.

Costs • $2898 (includes housing, some meals, excursions, concert and opera performances). A $200 deposit is required.

Contact • Norman Eagle, President, Mozart's Europe Tours, Deer Lane, Pawlet, VT 05761; 802-325-3656; Fax: 802-325-3656

MOZART'S EUROPE TOURS

MOZART'S EUROPE–VARIATION #3

General Information • Cultural tour with visits to Austria (Innsbruck, Salzburg, Vienna), Czech Republic (Prague), Italy (Milan, Rovereto); excursions to Esterhazy Palaces, Vienna Woods, Salzkammergut, Salzburg, Mozartsolisten, Verona, Lake Garda. Once at the destination country, participants travel by bus, foot.

Learning Focus • Escorted travel to Austerlitz and the Strahov Monastery. Museum visits (Schloss Klossheim, Sforza Castle Museum). Attendance at performances (Vienna Volksoper, Marionette Theater, Mozart Festival Concerts). Instruction is offered by professors, artists, historians. This program would appeal to people interested in music, opera, history.

Accommodations • Hotels. Single rooms are available for an additional $440.

Program Details • Program offered once per year. Session length: 15 days. Departures are scheduled in September. Program is targeted to music lovers. Most participants are 30–75 years of age. 25 participants per session. Reservations are recommended at least 6 months before departure.

Costs • $2898 (includes housing, some meals, excursions, concert and opera performances). A $200 deposit is required.

Contact • Norman Eagle, President, Mozart's Europe Tours, Deer Lane, Pawlet, VT 05761; 802-325-3656; Fax: 802-325-3656

MOZART'S EUROPE TOURS

MOZART'S EUROPE–VARIATION #4

General Information • Cultural tour with visits to Austria (Salzburg), Czech Republic (Prague), Germany (Berlin, Dresden, Leipzig), Italy (Milan, Rovereto); excursions to Rovereto Mozart Festival, Lake Como, Verona, Lake Garda, Zwinger Palace, Gewandhaus Orchestra, Cecilienhof. Once at the destination country, participants travel by bus, foot.

Learning Focus • Escorted travel to Teatro Scientifico, Strahov Monastery and Sans Souci. Museum visits (Haydn Museum, Schloss Klossheim, Albertina Gallery). Attendance at performances (The Orpheus Ensemble, Semper Opera,

University of Delaware Archives

University of Delaware Archives

Color Your World

In 1923, the University of Delaware pioneered Study Abroad for American students.

Today, we offer one of the broadest and most affordable arrays of programs available.

Our semester abroad programs take you to England, Italy, France, Spain, Costa Rica, Germany and Scotland. (See program listings.)

Our Winter and Summer Session programs, among the most extensive University-sponsored offerings in the country, take you to places like Paris and London, but also offer the mystique of Martinique, Israel, China, South Africa, Russia, Tanzania, Japan, and others.

Develop real-world skills in a new environment. Taste the flavor of other customs and heritages.

Learn and grow through enriching study with faculty knowledgeable about the host country and its ways of life.

University of Delaware

For more information contact:
International Programs & Special Sessions
4 Kent Way, Room 103
University of Delaware
Newark, DE 19716-1450
(302) 831-2852. Ask for Study Abroad
or dial toll-free 1-888-UD1-INTL (1-888-831-4685)
Fax: (302) 831-6042
e-mail: studyabroad@mvs.udel.edu
http://www.udel.edu/IntlProg/studyabroad/contents.htm

concerts, operas). Instruction is offered by professors, artists, historians. This program would appeal to people interested in music, opera, history.
Accommodations • Hotels. Single rooms are available for an additional $539.
Program Details • Program offered once per year. Session length: 18 days. Departures are scheduled in September. Program is targeted to music lovers. Most participants are 30–75 years of age. 25 participants per session. Reservations are recommended at least 6 months before departure.
Costs • $3639 (includes housing, some meals, excursions, concert and opera performances). A $200 deposit is required.
Contact • Norman Eagle, President, Mozart's Europe Tours, Deer Lane, Pawlet, VT 05761; 802-325-3656; Fax: 802-325-3656

NATIONAL GEOGRAPHIC SOCIETY

JOURNEYS ABROAD WITH NATIONAL GEOGRAPHIC

General Information • Cultural tour with visits to Australia, Costa Rica, England, Ireland, New Zealand, Scotland, Turkey, Wales. Once at the destination country, participants travel by bus, boat, airplane. Program is affiliated with National Geographic Society.
Learning Focus • Escorted travel to local sites of historic, natural or National Geographic interest. Instruction is offered by professors, naturalists, photographers and geographers. This program would appeal to people interested in geography, history, archaeology, art, photography, culture, nature studies.
Accommodations • Hotels. Single rooms are available.
Program Details • Program offered 16 times per year. Session length: 3 weeks. Departures are scheduled throughout the year. Program is targeted to adults and seniors. Most participants are 50–80 years of age. Participants must be 21 years or older to enroll. Participants must be members of the sponsoring organization (annual dues: $25). 30 participants per session. Reservations are recommended at least 90 days before departure.
Costs • $2000–$5000 (includes tuition, housing, some meals, books and class materials, excursions, international airfare). A $250 deposit is required.
Contact • Journeys Abroad, National Geographic Society, Reservation Center, 347 Congress Street, Boston, MA 02210; 800-866-3270

NATIONAL GEOGRAPHIC SOCIETY

ON TOUR WITH NATIONAL GEOGRAPHIC

General Information • Cultural tour with visits to Belize, Brazil (Amazon River), China (Yangtze River), France (Provence), Guatemala, Kenya, Mexico, Tanzania. Once at the destination country, participants travel by bus, boat, airplane. Program is affiliated with National Geographic Society.
Learning Focus • Escorted travel to historical sites. Museum visits (local museums). Nature observation (local wildlife parks). Instruction is offered by professors, naturalists, historians, archaeologists, geographers and National Geographic photographers. This program would appeal to people interested in geography, archaeology, history, art, photography, nature and environmental studies, culture.
Accommodations • Hotels. Single rooms are available.
Program Details • Program offered 10 times per year. Session length: 12 days. Departures are scheduled throughout the year. Program is targeted to adults and seniors. Most participants are 40–65 years of age. Participants must be 21 years or older to enroll. Participants must be members of the sponsoring organization (annual dues: $25). 20 participants per session. Reservations are recommended at least 120 days before departure.
Costs • $2000–$6000 (includes tuition, housing, some meals, books and class materials, excursions, international airfare). A $500 deposit is required.
Contact • National Geographic Society, On Tour with National Geographic, PO Box 96097, Washington, DC 20090; 202-857-7500

PEOPLE TO PEOPLE INTERNATIONAL

INTERNATIONAL BUSINESS AND INTERNATIONAL RELATIONS

General Information • Academic study program in Czech Republic (Prague), England (London), France (Paris), Germany (Munich).
Learning Focus • Courses in business, international relations, economics. Instruction is offered by professors from the sponsoring institution.
Accommodations • Dormitories, hotels. Single rooms are available. Meals are taken as a group, on one's own.
Program Details • Program offered once per year. Session length: 5 weeks. Departures are scheduled in June. The program is open to undergraduate students, graduate students, pre-college students, adults. Most participants are 20–40 years of age. Other requirements: good academic standing. 20–30 participants per session. Application deadline: April 25.
Costs • $3900 (includes tuition, housing, some meals, books and class materials, insurance, excursions, some local transportation, cultural events, all group travel in Europe). A $300 deposit is required.
Contact • Dr. Alan M. Warne, Vice President for Programs, People to People International, 501 East Armour Boulevard, Kansas City, MO 64109; 816-531-4701; Fax: 816-561-7502; E-mail: ptpi@cctr.umkc.edu

SANTA BARBARA MUSEUM OF ART

SPAIN AND MOROCCO: MOORISH GARDENS AND ARCHITECTURE

General Information • Cultural tour with visits to Morocco (Tangier), Portugal (Lisbon, Madeira), Spain (Canary Islands, Granada, Seville); excursions to Alhambra. Once at the destination country, participants travel by bus, boat, airplane.
Learning Focus • Escorted travel to Alhambra Palace and the Arab Palace. Museum visits (Museum of Fine Arts, Archives, Malcolm Forbes Museum, American Museum). Instruction is offered by art historians. This program would appeal to people interested in art, photography, architecture, gardening, history.
Accommodations • Boat. Single rooms are available.

Program Details • Program offered once per year. Session length: 13 days. Departures are scheduled in April. Most participants are 30–80 years of age. Participants must be members of the sponsoring organization (annual dues: $40). 15–20 participants per session. Application deadline: January.

Costs • Contact sponsor for information. A $1000 deposit is required.

Contact • Shelley Ruston, Director of Special Programs, Santa Barbara Museum of Art, 1130 State Street, Santa Barbara, CA 93101; 805-963-4364, ext. 336; Fax: 805-966-6840

SMART TRAVEL

FOLLOW THE FOOTSTEPS

General Information • Cultural tour with visits to Austria (Vienna), France (Paris, Provence), Greece (Athens), Hungary (Budapest), Italy (Rome), Switzerland (Geneva), Turkey (Istanbul). Once at the destination country, participants travel by train, bus, foot, boat, airplane, bicycle.

Learning Focus • Instruction in history and art. Escorted travel to eastern and western Europe. Museum visits (art history). Attendance at performances (opera, theater). Other activities include hiking. Instruction is offered by professors, artists, historians. This program would appeal to people interested in history, art.

Accommodations • Locally-rented apartments, hotels. Single rooms are available.

Program Details • Session length: 3 weeks. Departures are scheduled in April–September. Program is targeted to students of any age. Most participants are 14–70 years of age. Participants must be 14 years or older to enroll. 20 participants per session. Reservations are recommended at least 6 months before departure.

Costs • Contact sponsor for information. A $450 deposit is required.

Contact • Erica Blatt Harkins, Manager, Smart Travel, 1728 Union Street #309, San Francisco, CA 94941; 415-381-4031; Fax: 415-381-4031

TRAVELEARN

AN AROUND THE WORLD ODYSSEY

General Information • Cultural tour with visits to China (Shanghai), Egypt (Port Said), Greece (Piraeus), India (Madras), Japan (Kobe), Turkey (Istanbul). Once at the destination country, participants travel by bus, foot, boat. Program is affiliated with the nationwide TraveLearn network of 290 universities and colleges.

Learning Focus • Instruction in major scholastic disciplines. Escorted travel to cultural sites in ports-of-call. Attendance at performances (music and dance). Nature observation (national parks, reserves). Instruction is offered by

professors, researchers, naturalists, artists, historians, scientists. This program would appeal to people interested in international education, cross-cultural study, global economics.
Accommodations • Boat. Single rooms are available for an additional $3000.
Program Details • Program offered 2 times per year. Session length: 100 days. Departures are scheduled in September, February. Program is targeted to adults and traditional students. Most participants are 18–75 years of age. Participants must be 18 years or older to enroll. 70–400 participants per session. Application deadline: 2 months prior to departure. Reservations are recommended at least 6–8 months before departure.
Costs • $14,880 (includes housing, all meals, books and class materials, cruise ship). A $300 deposit is required.
Contact • Keith Williams, Director of Marketing, TraveLearn, PO Box 315, Lakeville, PA 18438; 800-235-9114; Fax: 717-226-6912; E-mail: travelearn@aol.com

UNIVERSITY OF RICHMOND

SUMMER STUDY ABROAD PROGRAMS

General Information • Academic study program in Australia, Austria, Belgium, Ecuador, England, France, Germany, Honduras, Japan, Luxembourg, Russia, Spain.
Learning Focus • Courses in biology, German language, Spanish language, French language, Russian language. Instruction is offered by professors from the sponsoring institution.
Accommodations • Homestays, dormitories, campsites. Meals are taken as a group, on one's own, with host family, in central dining facility, in local restaurants, in residences.
Program Details • Program offered 10 times per year. Session length: 3–6 weeks. Departures are scheduled in May, June, July. The program is open to undergraduate students. Most participants are 18–21 years of age. Other requirements: approval of the program director. 10–25 participants per session. Application deadline: March 1.
Costs • $4000–$6000 (includes tuition, housing, some meals, excursions, international airfare). A $150 deposit is required.
Contact • Dr. Patricia Brown, Associate Dean, School of Continuing Studies, University of Richmond, School of Continuing Studies, Richmond, VA 23173; 804-289-8133; Fax: 804-289-8138; E-mail: pbrown@urvax.urich.edu

PROGRAM DESCRIPTIONS

In this main section of the guide, programs are listed by the region in which they are held. You'll find sections for Africa, Arctic and Antarctic, East Asia and Pacific, Eastern Europe, the Middle East, Russia and Central Asia, Western Europe, and the Western Hemisphere (outside the United States). Within regions, programs are listed by country alphabetically under the sponsor's name.

Be sure to consult the indexes at the back of the guide if you are looking for a particular type of program (for instance, an archaeological tour), if you're interested in seeing the listings of a particular sponsor, or if you'd like to target your search to only those programs that may result in college credit.

AFRICA

REGIONAL

Botswana
Cameroon
Ghana
Ivory Coast
Kenya
Madagascar
Mali
Morocco
Namibia
Senegal
South Africa
Tanzania
Tunisia
Uganda
Zambia
Zimbabwe

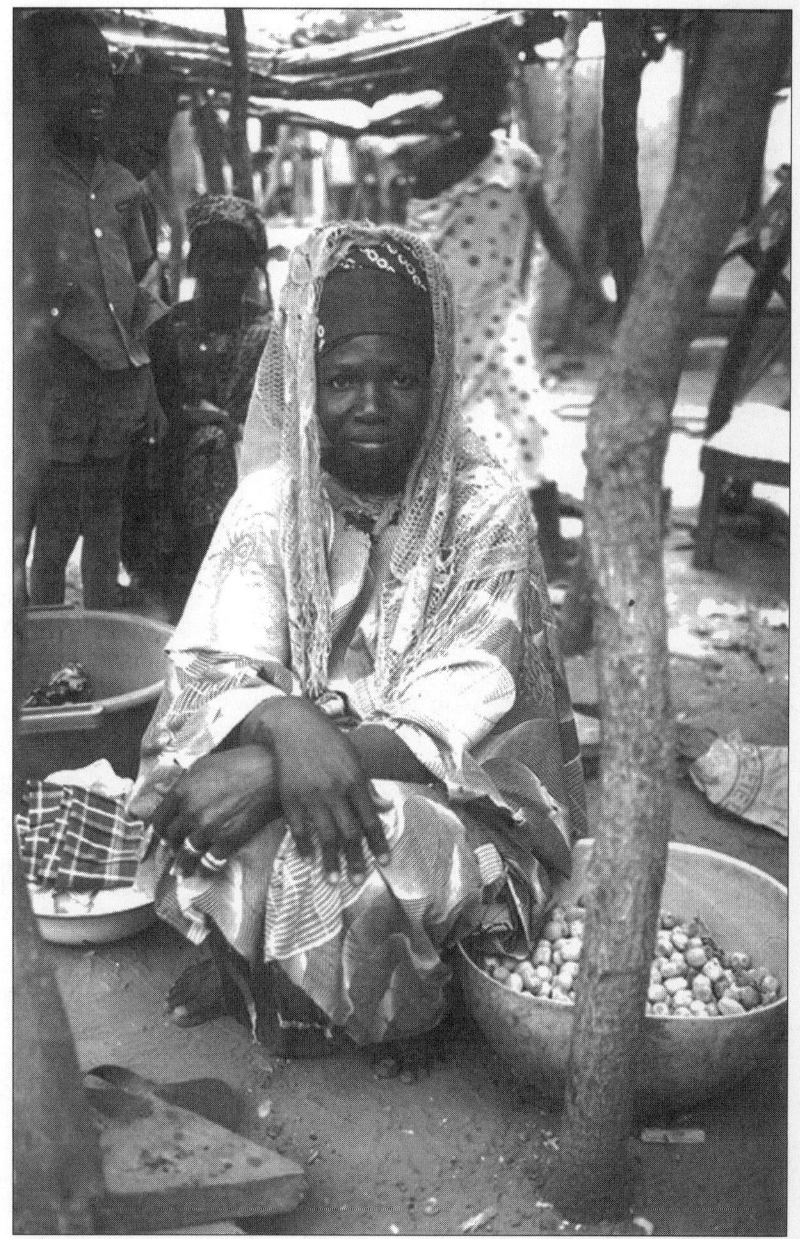

REGIONAL

ARCHAEOLOGICAL TOURS

ERITREA AND ETHIOPIA

General Information • Cultural tour with visits to Eritrea (Asmara), Ethiopia (Addis Ababa, Axum, Bahar Dar, Gondar, Harar, Lalibela, Mekele); excursions to Senafe, Matara, Yeha, Tigray churches, Simien Mountains, Lake Tana, Tiya, Melka Kunture. Once at the destination country, participants travel by bus.
Learning Focus • Museum visits (Asmara, Axum, Addis Ababa, Harar). Attendance at performances (dance and music shows). Instruction is offered by professors, historians. This program would appeal to people interested in history, art, archaeology, architecture.
Accommodations • Hotels. Single rooms are available for an additional $610.
Program Details • Program offered once per year. Session length: 22 days. Departures are scheduled in January. Program is targeted to adults. Most participants are 30–80 years of age. 18 participants per session. Application deadline: 1 month prior to departure.
Costs • $4290 (includes housing, some meals, excursions, internal flights). A $500 deposit is required.
Contact • Archaeological Tours, 271 Madison Avenue, Suite 904, New York, NY 10016; 212-986-3054; Fax: 212-370-1561

CENTER FOR GLOBAL EDUCATION AT AUGSBURG COLLEGE

AFRICA TRAVEL SEMINAR

General Information • Academic study program with visits to South Africa (Durban, Johannesburg), Uganda (Entebbe, Kampala); excursions to South Africa (Soweto Township). Once at the destination country, participants travel by foot, airplane, van. Program is affiliated with Bread for the World.
Learning Focus • Instruction in current issues facing South Africa and Uganda. Escorted travel to local communities. Other activities include meetings with community representatives, development workers, human rights workers. Instruction is offered by in-country coordinators. This program would appeal to people interested in Africa, democracy, international aid policies, hunger issues, social justice, development.
Accommodations • Guest houses.
Program Details • Program offered once per year. Session length: 17 days. Departures are scheduled in March. Most participants are 20–70 years of age. Participants must be 18 years or older to enroll. Other requirements: accompaniment by an adult if under 18 years of age. 15 participants per session. Application deadline: February 4. Reservations are recommended at least 6 weeks before departure.
Costs • $4495 (includes housing, all meals, books and class materials, excursions, international airfare, translation). A $100 deposit is required.
Contact • International Travel Seminars, Center for Global Education at Augsburg College, Center for Global Education, 2211 Riverside Avenue, Minneapolis, MN 55454; 800-299-8889; Fax: 612-330-1695; E-mail: globaled@augsburg.edu; World Wide Web: http://www.augsburg.edu/global

FORUM TRAVEL INTERNATIONAL

SPECIAL INTEREST SAFARIS IN SOUTHERN AFRICA

General Information • Wilderness/adventure program with visits to Botswana (Kalahari Desert, Moremi Game Reserve, Okavango Delta), Namibia (Damaraland), South Africa (Namaqualand); excursions to major ecosystems of southern Africa. Once at the destination country, participants travel by bus, foot, boat, airplane. Program is affiliated with International Ecosystems University.
Learning Focus • Instruction in natural history and ornithology. Escorted travel to Botswana. Other activities include camping. Instruction is offered by professors, researchers, naturalists, artists, sports professionals. This program would appeal to people interested in nature studies, photography, overlanding.
Accommodations • Program-owned houses, hotels, campsites, lodges. Single rooms are available.
Program Details • Program offered 12 times per year. Session length: 2 weeks. Departures are scheduled throughout the year. Program is targeted to nature-oriented adventurers of all ages. Participants must be 16 years or older to enroll. Other requirements: must be in good health.
Costs • $989 (includes tuition, housing, some meals, excursions). A $300 deposit is required.
Contact • Jeannie Graves, Operations Manager, Forum Travel International, 91 Gregory Lane #21, Pleasant Hill, CA 94525; 510-671-2900; Fax: 510-671-2993; E-mail: forum@ix.netcom.com; World Wide Web: http://www.ten-io.com/forumtravel

GEO EXPEDITIONS

BOTSWANA WILDLIFE SAFARI

General Information • Nature study tour with visits to Botswana (Chobe National Park, Kalahari Desert, Okavango Delta), Zimbabwe (Victoria Falls); excursions to Zambezi River. Once at the destination country, participants travel by landcruiser.
Learning Focus • Nature observation (naturalist-led safari). Instruction is offered by naturalists. This program would appeal to people interested in wildlife, ecology.
Accommodations • Hotels, campsites. Single rooms are available for an additional $145.
Program Details • Session length: 18 days. Departures are scheduled in March–October. Most participants are 30–70 years of age. Participants must be 10 years or older to enroll. 10 participants per session. Reservations are recommended at least 6 months before departure.
Costs • $2995–$3395 (includes housing, all meals, excursions). A $300 deposit is required.
Contact • David Risard, President, GEO Expeditions, PO Box 3656, Sonora, CA 95370; 800-351-5041; Fax: 209-532-1979; E-mail: geoexped@mlode.com

INTERNATIONAL BICYCLE FUND

ETHIOPIA AND ERITREA: ABYSSINIAN ADVENTURE

General Information • Cultural tour with visits to Eritrea (Asmara), Ethiopia (Addis Ababa, Axum, Debre Birham, Lalibela, Mekele); excursions to Lalibela, Axum. Once at the destination country, participants travel by bicycle.
Learning Focus • Instruction in culture, history, economics, environment and development. Escorted travel to cultural, religious and historical sites. Museum visits (National Museum). Instruction is offered by African studies specialists. This program would appeal to people interested in African culture, bicycling, economic development, photography.
Accommodations • Hotels.
Program Details • Program offered once per year. Session length: 22 days. Departures are scheduled in October. Most participants are 20–60 years of age. 8 participants per session. Reservations are recommended at least 3 months before departure.
Costs • $1290 (includes housing, some meals, excursions). A $300 deposit is required.
Contact • David Mozer, Director, International Bicycle Fund, 4887 Columbia Drive, S, Seattle, WA 98108; 206-767-0848; Fax: 206-767-0848; E-mail: intlbike@scn.org; World Wide Web: http://www.halcyon.com/fkroger/bike/homepage.html

INTERNATIONAL BICYCLE FUND

WEST AFRICA PEOPLE TO PEOPLE

General Information • Cultural tour with visits to Benin (Abomey, Natitingou), Burkina Faso (Ouagadougou, Tenkodogo), Togo (Dapaong, Lome); excursions to Fon Palace, Abomey, Tatasomba village. Once at the destination country, participants travel by train, bus, foot, bicycle.
Learning Focus • Instruction in culture, history, economics, environment and development. Escorted travel to historical and cultural sites and villages. Museum visits (National Museum). Instruction is offered by African studies specialists. This program would appeal to people interested in African culture, bicycling, economic development, photography.
Accommodations • Hotels.
Program Details • Program offered once per year. Session length: 14 days. Departures are scheduled in November. Most participants are 20–60 years of age. 8 participants per session. Reservations are recommended at least 3 months before departure.
Costs • $1090 (includes housing, some meals, excursions). A $300 deposit is required.
Contact • David Mozer, Director, International Bicycle Fund, 4887 Columbia Drive, S, Seattle, WA 98108; 206-767-0848; Fax: 206-767-0848; E-mail: intlbike@scn.org; World Wide Web: http://www.halcyon.com/fkroger/bike/homepage.html

JOURNEYS INTERNATIONAL, INC.

THE BEST OF AFRICA

General Information • Wilderness/adventure program with visits to Malawi, South Africa (Johannesburg), Tanzania (Mbeya), Zambia (Lusaka), Zimbabwe (Bulawayo, Victoria Falls). Once at the destination country, participants travel by airplane, small vehicle.
Learning Focus • Escorted travel to national parks. Nature observation (wildlife). Other activities include camping. Instruction is offered by a professional English-speaking safari guide. This program would appeal to people interested in photography, wildlife, nature studies.
Accommodations • Hotels.
Program Details • Program offered 12 times per year. Session length: 24 days. Departures are scheduled in January–December. Program is targeted to adventurous travelers. Most participants are 25–45 years of age. Participants must be 12 years or older to enroll. Other requirements: excellent health. 10–16 participants per session. Application deadline: 60 days prior to departure. Reservations are recommended at least 60 days before departure.
Costs • $2375 (includes housing, some meals, park fees). A $300 deposit is required.
Contact • Michelle Gervais, Africa Sales Director, Journeys International, Inc., 4011 Jackson Road, Ann Arbor, MI 48103; 313-665-4407; Fax: 313-665-2945; E-mail: michelle@journeys-intl.com; World Wide Web: http://www.journeys-intl.com

JOURNEYS INTERNATIONAL, INC.

THE SOUTHERN CROSS SAFARI

General Information • Wilderness/adventure program with visits to Botswana (Maun), Namibia (Swakopmund, Windhoek), South Africa (Johannesburg, Kalahari Gemsbok National Park), Zimbabwe (Bulawayo); excursions to Victoria Falls, Zambezi River. Once at the destination country, participants travel by airplane.
Learning Focus • Escorted travel to national parks. Nature observation (wildlife). Other activities include camping, river rafting. Instruction is offered by professional English-speaking safari leader. This program would appeal to people interested in wildlife, nature studies, photography.
Accommodations • Hotels, campsites.
Program Details • Program offered 12 times per year. Session length: 24 days. Departures are scheduled in January–December. Program is targeted to active campers. Most participants are 25–55 years of age. Participants must be 12 years or older to enroll. 15 participants per session. Application deadline: 60 days prior to departure. Reservations are recommended at least 60 days before departure.
Costs • $2125 (includes housing, some meals, park fees). A $300 deposit is required.
Contact • Michelle Gervais, Africa Sales Director, Journeys International, Inc., 4011 Jackson Road, Ann Arbor, MI 48103; 313-665-4407; Fax: 313-665-2945; E-mail: michelle@journeys-intl.com; World Wide Web: http://www.journeys-intl.com

MICHIGAN STATE UNIVERSITY

EDUCATION, SOCIETY, AND LEARNING

General Information • Academic study program in South Africa, Zimbabwe (Harare).
Learning Focus • Courses in education, anthropology, English language, history, sociology. Instruction is offered by professors from the sponsoring institution.

Accommodations • Hotels. Meals are taken on one's own, in local restaurants.
Program Details • Program offered once per year. Session length: 6 weeks. Departures are scheduled in June. The program is open to undergraduate students, graduate students. Most participants are 18–24 years of age. Other requirements: good academic standing and the approval of the instructor. 12 participants per session. Application deadline: March 14.
Costs • $1900 (includes housing, some meals, excursions). Application fee: $75. A $250 deposit is required.
Contact • Cynthia Chalou, Educational Programs Coordinator, Michigan State University, Office of Study Abroad, 109 International Center, East Lansing, MI 48824-1035; 517-353-8920; Fax: 517-432-2082; E-mail: chalouc@pilot.msu.edu; World Wide Web: http://study-abroad.msu.edu

MICHIGAN STATE UNIVERSITY

FOOD, AGRICULTURE, AND NATURAL RESOURCES SYSTEMS IN SOUTHERN AFRICA

General Information • Academic study program in South Africa (Lesotho), Swaziland.
Learning Focus • Courses in food, natural resources, agriculture. Instruction is offered by professors from the sponsoring institution.
Accommodations • Hotels. Meals are taken on one's own, in local restaurants.
Program Details • Program offered once per year. Session length: 4 weeks. Departures are scheduled in May. The program is open to undergraduate students, graduate students. Most participants are 18–26 years of age. Other requirements: good academic standing and the approval of the director. 12 participants per session. Application deadline: March 14.
Costs • $2193 (includes housing, some meals, excursions). Application fee: $75. A $250 deposit is required.
Contact • Cynthia Chalou, Educational Programs Coordinator, Michigan State University, Office of Study Abroad, 109 International Center, East Lansing, MI 48824-1035; 517-353-8920; Fax: 517-432-2082; E-mail: chalouc@pilot.msu.edu; World Wide Web: http://study-abroad.msu.edu

NATURAL HABITAT ADVENTURES

THE BEST OF KENYA AND TANZANIA

General Information • Nature study tour with visits to Kenya (Abedere, Lake Nakuru, Masai Mara, Mount Kenya), Tanzania (Lake Manyara, Ngorongoro Crater, Serengeti). Once at the destination country, participants travel by land rover or minivan.
Learning Focus • Nature observation (animals in the wild). Instruction is offered by naturalists. This program would appeal to people interested in nature studies, photography, wildlife.
Accommodations • Hotels, campsites, lodges. Single rooms are available for an additional $585.
Program Details • Session length: 13 days. Departures are scheduled throughout the year. Most participants are 20–65 years of age. 6 participants per session. Reservations are recommended at least 1 year before departure.
Costs • $2330 (includes housing, all meals, excursions, park fees). A $500 deposit is required.
Contact • Planet Expeditions, Natural Habitat Adventures, 2945 Center Green Court, Suite H, Boulder, CO 80301; 800-233-2433; Fax: 303-449-3712; E-mail: nathab@worldnet.att.net

NATURAL HABITAT ADVENTURES

BOTSWANA AND NAMIBIA FLY-IN SAFARI

General Information • Nature study tour with visits to Botswana (Chobe National Park, Okavango Delta), Namibia (Etosha National Park, Soussesvlei Sand Dunes, Windhoek). Once at the destination country, participants travel by airplane, land rover or minivan.
Learning Focus • Nature observation (animals in the wild). Instruction is offered by naturalists. This program would appeal to people interested in nature studies, photography, wildlife.
Accommodations • Hotels, campsites, lodges. Single rooms are available for an additional $750.
Program Details • Session length: 15 days. Departures are scheduled throughout the year. Most participants are 20–65 years of age. 2 participants per session. Reservations are recommended at least 1 year before departure.
Costs • $4300 (includes housing, all meals, excursions). A $500 deposit is required.
Contact • Planet Expeditions, Natural Habitat Adventures, 2945 Center Green Court, Suite H, Boulder, CO 80301; 800-233-2433; Fax: 303-449-3712; E-mail: nathab@worldnet.att.net

NATURAL HABITAT ADVENTURES

BOTSWANA AND ZIMBABWE

General Information • Nature study tour with visits to Botswana (Chobe National Park, Linyanti Savuti Channel), Zimbabwe (Hwange National Park, Kariba Lake, Victoria Falls). Once at the destination country, participants travel by boat, airplane, four-wheel drive vehicle.
Learning Focus • Nature observation (elephants, lions, cheetahs, impalas, zebras and buffaloes from camps, vehicles, boats, and guided walks). Instruction is offered by naturalists. This program would appeal to people interested in nature studies, photography, wildlife.
Accommodations • Hotels, campsites, safari lodges. Single rooms are available for an additional $1090.
Program Details • Program offered 2 times per year. Session length: 13 days. Departures are scheduled in July, September. 10 participants per session. Reservations are recommended at least 6–12 months before departure.
Costs • $5895 (includes housing, all meals, air transportation within Botswana and Zimbabwe). A $500 deposit is required.
Contact • Natural Habitat Adventures, 2945 Center Green Court, Suite H, Boulder, CO 80301; 800-543-8917; Fax: 303-449-3712; E-mail: nathab@worldnet.att.net

NATURAL HABITAT ADVENTURES

FAMILY KENYA AND TANZANIA

General Information • Nature study tour with visits to Kenya (Great Rift Valley, Masai Mara, Nairobi), Tanzania (Arusha, Ngorongoro Crater, Tarangire); excursions to a

Masai village. Once at the destination country, participants travel by airplane, safari cruiser.
Learning Focus • Museum visits (Natural History Museum, Arusha). Nature observation (elephant, rhinoceros, buffalo, leopard, cheetah, lion, wildebeest, hippo, zebra, gazelle, giraffe, impala, waterbuck and warthog). Instruction is offered by naturalists, photographers. This program would appeal to people interested in nature studies, photography, wildlife.
Accommodations • Campsites, safari lodges. Single rooms are available for an additional $695.
Program Details • Session length: 12 days. 12 participants per session. Reservations are recommended at least 6–12 months before departure.
Costs • $3595 for adults, $2195 for children under 12 (includes housing, some meals, all national park fees, membership in the Flying Doctor Society). A $500 deposit is required.
Contact • Natural Habitat Adventures, 2945 Center Green Court, Suite H, Boulder, CO 80301; 800-543-8917; Fax: 303-449-3712; E-mail: nathab@worldnet.att.net

NATURAL HABITAT ADVENTURES

HIDDEN KENYA AND TANZANIA

General Information • Nature study tour with visits to Kenya (Lake Elementieta, Lake Nakuru, Masai Mara, Mount Kenya, Nairobi), Tanzania (Arusha, Serengeti, Tarangire); excursions to a Masai village. Once at the destination country, participants travel by airplane, safari cruiser.
Learning Focus • Museum visits (Natural History Museum, Arusha). Nature observation (elephant, rhinoceros, buffalo, leopard, cheetah, lion, wildebeest, hippo, zebra, gazelle, giraffe, impala, waterbuck and warthog). Instruction is offered by naturalists. This program would appeal to people interested in nature studies, photography, wildlife.
Accommodations • Campsites, safari lodges. Single rooms are available for an additional $695.
Program Details • Session length: 16 days. Departures are scheduled in February, July, August. Participants must be 14 years or older to enroll. 12 participants per session. Reservations are recommended at least 6–12 months before departure.
Costs • $4595 (includes housing, some meals, all national park fees, membership in the Flying Doctor Society). A $500 deposit is required.
Contact • Natural Habitat Adventures, 2945 Center Green Court, Suite H, Boulder, CO 80301; 800-543-8917; Fax: 303-449-3712; E-mail: nathab@worldnet.att.net

NATURAL HABITAT ADVENTURES

KENYA AND TANZANIA BY AIR

General Information • Nature study tour with visits to Kenya (Masai Mara, Mount Kenya, Nairobi, Samburu), Tanzania (Arusha, Ngorongoro Crater, Serengeti, Tarangire). Once at the destination country, participants travel by land rover or minivan.
Learning Focus • Nature observation (animals in the wild). Instruction is offered by naturalists. This program would appeal to people interested in nature studies, photography, wildlife.
Accommodations • Hotels, campsites, lodges. Single rooms are available for an additional $1350.
Program Details • Session length: 15 days. Departures are scheduled throughout the year. Most participants are 20–65 years of age. 6 participants per session. Reservations are recommended at least 1 year before departure.
Costs • $6500 (includes housing, all meals, excursions, park fees). A $500 deposit is required.
Contact • Planet Expeditions, Natural Habitat Adventures, 2945 Center Green Court, Suite H, Boulder, CO 80301; 800-233-2433; Fax: 303-449-3712; E-mail: nathab@worldnet.att.net

NATURAL HABITAT ADVENTURES

KENYA AND TANZANIA EXPLORER

General Information • Nature study tour with visits to Kenya (Amboseli, Lake Elementieta, Lewa Downs, Masai Mara, Mount Kenya, Samburu), Tanzania (Ngorongoro Crater, Serengeti). Once at the destination country, participants travel by foot, airplane, land rover.
Learning Focus • Nature observation (animals in the wild). Instruction is offered by naturalists. This program would appeal to people interested in nature studies, photography, wildlife.
Accommodations • Hotels, campsites, lodges. Single rooms are available for an additional $890.
Program Details • Session length: 22 days. Departures are scheduled throughout the year. Most participants are 20–65 years of age. 12 participants per session. Reservations are recommended at least 1 year before departure.
Costs • Contact sponsor for information. A $500 deposit is required.
Contact • Planet Expeditions, Natural Habitat Adventures, 2945 Center Green Court, Suite H, Boulder, CO 80301; 800-233-2433; Fax: 303-449-3712; E-mail: nathab@worldnet.att.net

NATURAL HABITAT ADVENTURES

SOUTHERN AFRICA EXPLORER

General Information • Nature study tour with visits to Botswana (Chobe National Park, Kalahari Desert, Okavango Delta), Namibia (Etosha National Park), South Africa (Johannesburg), Zimbabwe (Hwange National Park, Victoria Falls). Once at the destination country, participants travel by boat, airplane, safari vehicle.
Learning Focus • Nature observation (elephant, lion, cheetah, leopard, oryx, zebra, giraffe, monkey, impala, sable, springbok and bird life). Instruction is offered by naturalists, photographers. This program would appeal to people interested in nature studies, photography, wildlife.
Accommodations • Hotels, campsites, lodges. Single rooms are available for an additional $1985.
Program Details • Session length: 21 days. Participants must be 14 years or older to enroll. 10 participants per session. Reservations are recommended at least 6–12 months before departure.
Costs • $8895 (includes housing, all meals, airfare within Africa, all park and permit fees). A $500 deposit is required.
Contact • Natural Habitat Adventures, 2945 Center Green Court, Suite H, Boulder, CO 80301; 800-543-8917; Fax: 303-449-3712; E-mail: nathab@worldnet.att.net

NATURAL HABITAT ADVENTURES

SOUTHERN AFRICA EXPLORER

General Information • Nature study tour with visits to Botswana (Chobe National Park, Okavango Delta), Namibia (Etosha National Park, Skeleton Coast, Windhoek), South Africa (Cape Town), Zimbabwe (Victoria Falls). Once at the destination country, participants travel by foot, boat, airplane, land rover or minivan.

Learning Focus • Nature observation (animals in the wild). Instruction is offered by naturalists. This program would appeal to people interested in nature studies, photography, wildlife.

Accommodations • Hotels, campsites, lodges. Single rooms are available for an additional $950.

Program Details • Session length: 20 days. Departures are scheduled throughout the year. Most participants are 20-65 years of age. 2 participants per session. Reservations are recommended at least 1 year before departure.

Costs • $5800 (includes housing, all meals, excursions, park fees). A $500 deposit is required.

Contact • Planet Expeditions, Natural Habitat Adventures, 2945 Center Green Court, Suite H, Boulder, CO 80301; 800-233-2433; Fax: 303-449-3712; E-mail: nathab@worldnet.att.net

NATURAL HABITAT ADVENTURES

SOUTHERN AFRICA PHOTOGRAPHY SAFARI

General Information • Nature study tour with visits to Botswana (Chobe National Park), Namibia (Etosha National Park, Soussesvlei Sand Dunes, Windhoek), Zimbabwe (Hwange National Park, Victoria Falls). Once at the destination country, participants travel by boat, airplane, four-wheel drive vehicle.

Learning Focus • Nature observation (elephant, rhino, lion, cheetah, leopard, giraffe, zebra, buffalo, monkey, oryx, sable, impala, kudu and bird life). Instruction is offered by naturalists, photographers. This program would appeal to people interested in nature studies, photography, wildlife.

Accommodations • Hotels, safari lodges. Single rooms are available for an additional $745.

Program Details • Session length: 14 days. Participants must be 14 years or older to enroll. 11 participants per session. Reservations are recommended at least 6-12 months before departure.

Costs • $6295 (includes housing, some meals, airfare within Africa, airport transfers, all park and permit fees). A $500 deposit is required.

Contact • Natural Habitat Adventures, 2945 Center Green Court, Suite H, Boulder, CO 80301; 800-543-8917; Fax: 303-449-3712; E-mail: nathab@worldnet.att.net

NATURAL HABITAT ADVENTURES

ULTIMATE EAST AFRICA

General Information • Nature study tour with visits to Kenya (Great Rift Valley, Masai Mara), Tanzania (Lake Manyara, Ngorongoro Crater, Serengeti), Uganda (Bwindi, Entebbe, Olduvai Gorge). Once at the destination country, participants travel by foot, airplane, safari cruiser. Program is affiliated with Dian Fossey Gorilla Fund.

Learning Focus • Nature observation (mountain gorilla, colobus monkey, elephant, rhino, buffalo, leopard, cheetah, lion, wildebeest, hippo, zebra, gazelle, giraffe and birds). Instruction is offered by professors, researchers, naturalists. This program would appeal to people interested in nature studies, photography, wildlife.

Accommodations • Campsites, lodges. Single rooms are available for an additional $695.

Program Details • Program offered 2 times per year. Session length: 18 days. Departures are scheduled in May, June. Participants must be 14 years or older to enroll. 9 participants per session. Reservations are recommended at least 6-12 months before departure.

Costs • $6995 (includes housing, all meals, airfare within Africa, national park fees, membership in the Flying Doctor Society). A $500 deposit is required.

Contact • Natural Habitat Adventures, 2945 Center Green Court, Suite H, Boulder, CO 80301; 800-543-8917; Fax: 303-449-3712; E-mail: nathab@worldnet.att.net

NATURE EXPEDITIONS INTERNATIONAL

LAND OF THE MASAI: EAST AFRICA WILDLIFE SAFARI

General Information • Nature study tour with visits to Kenya (Masai Mara, Nairobi, Ngorongoro Crater, Samburu), Tanzania (Amboseli, Arusha); excursions to Uganda, Zaire. Once at the destination country, participants travel by airplane, jeep.

Learning Focus • Nature observation (wildlife, gorillas). Other activities include camping. Instruction is offered by professors, naturalists. This program would appeal to people interested in wildlife, native cultures, nature studies.

Accommodations • Hotels, campsites. Single rooms are available.

Program Details • Program offered 3 times per year. Session length: 18 or 23 days. Departures are scheduled in January, July, September. Most participants are 25-75 years of age. Other requirements: doctor's permission for participants 70 years and older. Reservations are recommended at least 6 months before departure.

Costs • $4290 for 18 days, $6280 for 23 days (includes housing, some meals, excursions, all guiding). A $400 deposit is required.

Contact • Christopher Kyle, President, Nature Expeditions International, 6400 East El Dorado Circle, Suite 210, Tucson, AZ 85715; 800-869-0639; Fax: 520-721-6719; E-mail: naturexp@aol.com

PHOTO ADVENTURE TOURS

AFRICAN SAFARI

General Information • Photography tour with visits to Botswana (Gaborone, Kalahari Desert), Namibia (Swakopmund, Windhoek), South Africa (Cape Town, Johannesburg). Once at the destination country, participants travel by train, bus, foot, boat, airplane.

Learning Focus • Instruction in photography. Nature observation (wildlife). Instruction is offered by researchers, naturalists, artists, historians, photographers. This program would appeal to people interested in photography, wildlife, history, culture, adventure.

Accommodations • Hotels. Single rooms are available for an additional $1250.
Program Details • Program offered 2 times per year. Session length: 24 days. Departures are scheduled in January–February. Most participants are 18–80 years of age. Participants must be 18 years or older to enroll. Other requirements: good health. 12 participants per session. Application deadline: 2 months prior to departure. Reservations are recommended at least 6 months before departure.
Costs • $5895 (includes housing, all meals, international airfare). A $400 deposit is required.
Contact • Richard Libbey, General Partner, Photo Adventure Tours, 2035 Park Street, Atlantic Beach, NY 11509-1236; 516-371-0067; Fax: 516-371-1352

SMITHSONIAN INSTITUTION

SMITHSONIAN STUDY TOURS AND SEMINARS IN AFRICA

General Information • Nature study, cultural, and wilderness programs with visits to Botswana, Kenya, Morocco, South Africa, Tanzania, Tunisia. Once at the destination country, participants travel by train, bus, foot, boat, airplane.
Learning Focus • Instruction in history, culture, and natural history. Escorted travel to special sites off limits to most tourists. Museum visits (major museums, important small collections). Attendance at performances (traditional music and dance). Nature observation (wildlife safari). Instruction is offered by professors, researchers, naturalists, artists, historians, scientists. This program would appeal to people interested in archaeology, religious history, photography, natural history.
Accommodations • Hotels. Single rooms are available.
Program Details • Session length: 9–17 days. Departures are scheduled throughout the year. Most participants are 25–85 years of age. Participants must be 18 years or older to enroll. Participants must be members of the sponsoring organization (annual dues: $24). 15–30 participants per session.
Costs • $1999 and up (includes tuition, housing, some meals, excursions, international airfare).
Contact • Customer Service Representative, Smithsonian Institution, Smithsonian Study Tours and Seminars, 1100 Jefferson Drive, SW (MRC 702), Washington, DC 20560; 202-357-4700; Fax: 202-633-9250

SPECIAL INTEREST TOURS

GRAND EAST AFRICAN SAFARI

General Information • Nature study tour with visits to Kenya (Masai Mara Game Reserve, Nairobi, Samburu Game Reserve), Tanzania (Lake Manyara National Park, Ngorongoro Crater, Serengeti National Park); excursions to Arusha National Park, Tanzania, Lake Nakuru, Aberdare National Park, Olduvai Gorge. Once at the destination country, participants travel by mini-van.
Learning Focus • Instruction in animal behavior. Nature observation (trees, plants, herbs). Instruction is offered by naturalists, professional photographers. This program would appeal to people interested in wildlife, natural history, photography, adventure.
Accommodations • Hotels, safari lodges.
Program Details • Session length: 19 days. Departures are scheduled throughout the year. Most participants are 30–60 years of age. Participants must be 12 years or older to enroll. 10–12 participants per session. Application deadline: 60 days prior to departure. Reservations are recommended at least 6 months before departure.
Costs • $4300 (includes housing, all meals, excursions, international airfare). A $450 deposit is required.
Contact • Nancy Koch, Vice President, Special Interest Tours, 10220 North 27 Street, Phoenix, AZ 85028; 800-525-6772; Fax: 602-493-3630; E-mail: GoSafari@usa.net

SPECIAL INTEREST TOURS

SOUTH AFRICA NATURE AND WILDLIFE QUEST

General Information • Nature study tour with visits to South Africa (Cape Town, Eastern Transvaal, Garden Route, Kruger National Park, Kwazulu Natal), Swaziland (Piggs Peak); excursions to Kirsten Bofch Botanical Gardens, Cape of Good Hope Nature Reserve. Once at the destination country, participants travel by bus, foot, airplane.
Learning Focus • Instruction in flora and fauna. Instruction is offered by naturalists. This program would appeal to people interested in nature studies, wildlife, photography.
Accommodations • Hotels. Single rooms are available for an additional $395.
Program Details • Session length: 16 days. Departures are scheduled throughout the year. Most participants are 30–65 years of age. 6 participants per session. Application deadline: 60 days prior to departure. Reservations are recommended at least 6 months before departure.
Costs • $2195 (includes housing, some meals, excursions). A $450 deposit is required.
Contact • Nancy Koch, Vice President, Special Interest Tours, 10220 North 27 Street, Phoenix, AZ 85028; 800-525-6772; Fax: 602-493-3630; E-mail: GoSafari@usa.net

SPECIAL INTEREST TOURS

ZIMBABWE ADVENTURE TRAIL

General Information • Wilderness/adventure program with visits to Zambia (Lower Zambezi River), Zimbabwe (Chizarira National Park, Hwange National Park, Kariba Lake, Victoria Falls). Once at the destination country, participants travel by foot, boat, four-wheel drive vehicle.
Learning Focus • Nature observation (wildlife and birds). Other activities include camping, hiking, canoeing on Zambezi River. Instruction is offered by naturalists. This program would appeal to people interested in camping, natural history, wildlife, photography, adventure.
Accommodations • Campsites.
Program Details • Program offered 15 times per year. Session length: 17 days. Departures are scheduled in March–December. Most participants are 20–50 years of age. Participants must be 15 years or older to enroll. 8 participants per session. Application deadline: 60 days prior to departure. Reservations are recommended at least 6 months before departure.
Costs • $2930 (includes housing, all meals, excursions). A $450 deposit is required.
Contact • Nancy Koch, Vice President, Special Interest Tours, 10220 North 27 Street, Phoenix, AZ 85028; 800-525-6772; Fax: 602-493-3630; E-mail: GoSafari@usa.net

SYRACUSE UNIVERSITY

FACES OF INDEPENDENCE IN SOUTHERN AFRICA

General Information • Academic study program in Mozambique, Swaziland, Zimbabwe (Harare).
Learning Focus • Courses in African politics, sociology, geography, African-American studies, history. Instruction is offered by professors from the sponsoring institution.
Accommodations • Hotels. Single rooms are available. Meals are taken as a group, in local restaurants.
Program Details • Program offered once per year. Session length: 6 weeks. Departures are scheduled in June. The program is open to undergraduate students, graduate students, adults. Most participants are 19-30 years of age. Other requirements: minimum 2.7 GPA. 18 participants per session. Application deadline: March 15.
Costs • $5500 (includes tuition, housing, some meals, books and class materials, excursions). Application fee: $40. A $350 deposit is required.
Contact • Ms. Daisy Fried, Associate Director, Syracuse University, 119 Euclid Avenue, Syracuse, NY 13244; 315-443-9419; Fax: 315-443-4593; E-mail: dsfried@summon3.syr.edu; World Wide Web: http://sumweb.syr.edu/dipa/dipa9.htm

UNIVERSITY OF TOLEDO

TRADITIONS OF PROTEST AND RESISTANCE IN LESOTHO AND SOUTHERN AFRICA

General Information • Academic study program in Lesotho (Roma), South Africa (Alexandra, Natal, Soweto, Transvaal). Classes are held on the campus of National University of Lesotho. Excursions to Sharpville.
Learning Focus • Courses in political science, history, economics. Instruction is offered by professors from the sponsoring institution and local teachers.
Accommodations • Dormitories, program-owned apartments, hotels. Meals are taken as a group, in central dining facility.
Program Details • Program offered once per year. Session length: 4 weeks. Departures are scheduled in July. The program is open to undergraduate students. Most participants are 22-30 years of age. 10 participants per session. Application deadline: March 25.
Costs • $3400 (includes housing, some meals, excursions, international airfare). Application fee: $25. A $100 deposit is required.
Contact • Joel A. Gallegos, Coordinator of Study Abroad, University of Toledo, SWAC 2357, Toledo, OH 43606-3390; 419-530-1240; Fax: 419-530-1245; E-mail: jgalleg@utnet.utoledo.edu; World Wide Web: http://www.utoledo.edu/www/cisp/study-abroad/

VOYAGERS INTERNATIONAL

PHOTOGRAPHIC TOUR AND WORKSHOP IN AFRICA

General Information • Photography tour with visits to Kenya, Tanzania. Once at the destination country, participants travel by foot, small vehicle.
Learning Focus • Instruction in photography. Escorted travel to the Serengeti Plains, Ngorongoro Crater and Manyara. Nature observation (wildlife and scenery). Instruction is offered by photographers. This program would appeal to people interested in photography, culture, nature studies.
Accommodations • Hotels, lodges. Single rooms are available.
Program Details • Program offered 10 times per year. Session length: 17 days. Departures are scheduled throughout the year. Program is targeted to photography enthusiasts. Most participants are 30-70 years of age. 8-10 participants per session. Reservations are recommended at least 6-12 months before departure.
Costs • $5000 including airfare from New York (includes tuition, housing, all meals, excursions, international airfare). A $400 deposit is required.
Contact • David Blanton, Managing Director, Voyagers International, PO Box 915, Ithaca, NY 14851; 800-633-0299; Fax: 607-273-3873; E-mail: voyint@aol.com

WILDLAND ADVENTURES

BOTSWANA LUXURY SAFARI

General Information • Nature study tour with visits to Botswana (Maun, Okavango Delta), South Africa (Johannesburg, Victoria Falls); excursions to Okavango Delta. Once at the destination country, participants travel by bus, foot, boat, airplane.
Learning Focus • Escorted travel to wildlife reserves. Nature observation (African wildlife). Other activities include hiking. Instruction is offered by naturalists. This program would appeal to people interested in photography, wildlife, hiking.
Accommodations • Hotels, campsites. Single rooms are available.
Program Details • Program offered 20 times per year. Session length: 13 days. Departures are scheduled throughout the year. Participants must be 8 years or older to enroll. 12 participants per session. Application deadline: 30 days prior to departure. Reservations are recommended at least 3-6 months before departure.
Costs • Contact sponsor for information. A $300 deposit is required.
Contact • Wildland Adventures, 3516 Northeast 155th Street, Seattle, WA 98155; 800-345-4453; Fax: 206-363-6615; E-mail: wildadve@aol.com; World Wide Web: http://www.wildland.com

WILDLAND ADVENTURES

BOTSWANA OKAVANGO CAMPING SAFARI

General Information • Nature study tour with visits to Botswana (Maun), South Africa (Johannesburg, Victoria Falls); excursions to Okavango Delta, Chobe. Once at the destination country, participants travel by bus, foot, boat, airplane.
Learning Focus • Escorted travel to national parks. Other activities include hiking, canoeing. Instruction is offered by naturalists. This program would appeal to people interested in photography, wildlife, bird watching.
Accommodations • Hotels, campsites. Single rooms are available.
Program Details • Program offered 20 times per year. Session length: 12 days. Departures are scheduled throughout the year. Most participants are 30-60 years of age. Participants must be 12 years or older to enroll. 8

participants per session. Application deadline: 30 days prior to departure. Reservations are recommended at least 3-6 months before departure.

Costs • $1695 (includes housing, some meals, excursions, complete pre-departure dossier). A $300 deposit is required.

Contact • Wildland Adventures, 3516 Northeast 155th Street, Seattle, WA 98155; 800-345-4453; Fax: 206-363-6615; E-mail: wildadvc@aol.com; World Wide Web: http://www.wildland.com

Botswana

JOURNEYS INTERNATIONAL, INC.

THE BOTSWANA EXPLORER

General Information • Wilderness/adventure program with visits to Botswana (Chobe National Park, Maun, Moremi Wildlife Reserve, Okavango Delta), Zimbabwe (Victoria Falls). Once at the destination country, participants travel by foot, canoe.
Learning Focus • Escorted travel to national parks and wildlife reserves. Other activities include camping, canoeing. Instruction is offered by professional English-speaking guides. This program would appeal to people interested in bird watching, nature studies, wildlife, photography.
Accommodations • Hotels, campsites.
Program Details • Program offered 23 times per year. Session length: 12 days. Departures are scheduled in January–December. Program is targeted to persons interested in nature. Most participants are 25–55 years of age. 8–13 participants per session. Application deadline: 60 days prior to departure. Reservations are recommended at least 60 days before departure.
Costs • $1925 (includes housing, some meals). A $300 deposit is required.
Contact • Michelle Gervais, Africa Sales Director, Journeys International, Inc., 4011 Jackson Road, Ann Arbor, MI 48103; 313-665-4407; Fax: 313-665-2945; E-mail: michelle@journeys-intl.com; World Wide Web: http://www.journeys-intl.com

JOURNEYS INTERNATIONAL, INC.

LUXURY OKAVANGO SAFARI

General Information • Wilderness/adventure program with visits to Botswana (Chobe National Park, Moremi Wildlife Reserve), Zambia (Victoria Falls). Once at the destination country, participants travel by foot, canoe.
Learning Focus • Escorted travel to national parks and game reserves. Other activities include camping, hiking, canoeing. Instruction is offered by local English-speaking guides. This program would appeal to people interested in wildlife, photography, nature studies.
Accommodations • Lodges. Single rooms are available for an additional $500.
Program Details • Program offered 10 times per year. Session length: 9 days. Departures are scheduled in March–December. Program is targeted to persons interested in wildlife observation. Most participants are 25–55 years of age. 15 participants per session. Application deadline: 60 days prior to departure. Reservations are recommended at least 60 days before departure.
Costs • $1825 (includes housing, some meals, park fees). A $300 deposit is required.
Contact • Michelle Gervais, Africa Sales Director, Journeys International, Inc., 4011 Jackson Road, Ann Arbor, MI 48103; 313-665-4407; Fax: 313-665-2945; E-mail: michelle@journeys-intl.com; World Wide Web: http://www.journeys-intl.com

NATURAL HABITAT ADVENTURES

BOTSWANA FLY-IN SAFARI

General Information • Nature study tour with visits to Chobe National Park, Okavango Delta. Once at the destination country, participants travel by airplane, land rover.
Learning Focus • Nature observation (animals in the wild). Instruction is offered by naturalists. This program would appeal to people interested in nature studies, photography, wildlife.
Accommodations • Hotels, campsites, lodges. Single rooms are available for an additional $555.
Program Details • Session length: 8 days. Departures are scheduled throughout the year. Most participants are 20-65 years of age. 2 participants per session. Reservations are recommended at least 1 year before departure.
Costs • $1950 (includes housing, all meals, excursions, park fees). A $500 deposit is required.
Contact • Planet Expeditions, Natural Habitat Adventures, 2945 Center Green Court, Suite H, Boulder, CO 80301; 800-233-2433; Fax: 303-449-3712; E-mail: nathab@worldnet.att.net

NATURAL HABITAT ADVENTURES

BOTSWANA SAFARI

General Information • Nature study tour with visits to Botswana (Chobe National Park, Kalahari Desert, Moremi Wildlife Reserve, Okavango Delta, Savuti), Zimbabwe (Victoria Falls). Once at the destination country, participants travel by foot, boat, airplane, four-wheel drive vehicle.
Learning Focus • Nature observation (lions, leopards, hippos, crocodiles, sables, cheetahs, giraffes, zebras, elephants). Other activities include camping. Instruction is offered by researchers, naturalists. This program would appeal to people interested in nature studies, photography, wildlife.
Accommodations • Hotels, campsites, lodges. Single rooms are available for an additional $495.
Program Details • Program offered 6 times per year. Session length: 16 days. Departures are scheduled in June–October. 8 participants per session. Reservations are recommended at least 6–12 months before departure.
Costs • $4495 (includes housing, all meals, air transportation within Botswana). A $500 deposit is required.
Contact • Natural Habitat Adventures, 2945 Center Green Court, Suite H, Boulder, CO 80301; 800-543-8917; Fax: 303-449-3712; E-mail: nathab@worldnet.att.net

NATURAL HABITAT ADVENTURES

INTIMATE BOTSWANA

General Information • Nature study tour with visits to Chobe National Park, Okavango Delta. Once at the destination country, participants travel by airplane, land rover.

Learning Focus • Nature observation (animals in the wild). Instruction is offered by naturalists. This program would appeal to people interested in nature studies, photography, wildlife.

Accommodations • Hotels, campsites. Single rooms are available for an additional $315.

Program Details • Session length: 13 days. Departures are scheduled in March–January. Most participants are 20–65 years of age. Other requirements: maximum age of 70. 8 participants per session. Reservations are recommended at least 1 year before departure.

Costs • $3600 (includes housing, all meals, park fees). A $500 deposit is required.

Contact • Planet Expeditions, Natural Habitat Adventures, 2945 Center Green Court, Suite H, Boulder, CO 80301; 800-233-2433; Fax: 303-449-3712; E-mail: nathab@worldnet.att.net

SPECIAL INTEREST TOURS

BOTSWANA: THE LAST EDEN

General Information • Wilderness/adventure program with visits to Botswana (Chobe National Park, Moremi Wildlife Refuge, Okavango Delta), Zimbabwe (Victoria Falls). Once at the destination country, participants travel by boat, airplane, four-wheel drive vehicle.

Learning Focus • Nature observation (animal and bird behavior). Other activities include camping, hiking, special emphasis on elephant herds. Instruction is offered by naturalists. This program would appeal to people interested in wildlife, natural history, photography, adventure.

Accommodations • Campsites.

Program Details • Program offered 16 times per year. Session length: 16 days. Departures are scheduled in March–December. Most participants are 20–50 years of age. Participants must be 15 years or older to enroll. 8 participants per session. Application deadline: 60 days prior to departure. Reservations are recommended at least 6 months before departure.

Costs • $3105 (includes housing, all meals, excursions, charter flights). A $450 deposit is required.

Contact • Nancy Koch, Vice President, Special Interest Tours, 10220 North 27 Street, Phoenix, AZ 85028; 800-525-6772; Fax: 602-493-3630; E-mail: GoSafari@usa.net

CAMEROON

DICKINSON COLLEGE

FIELD SCHOOL IN CULTURAL ANTHROPOLOGY

General Information • Academic study program in Buea, Limbe.

Learning Focus • Courses in cultural anthropology. Instruction is offered by professors from the sponsoring institution.

Accommodations • Field quarters. Meals are taken as a group.

Program Details • Program offered once per year. Session length: 6 weeks. Departures are scheduled in May. The program is open to undergraduate students. Most participants are 18–20 years of age. 10 participants per session. Application deadline: February 15.

Costs • $5200 (includes tuition, housing, all meals, excursions, international airfare). Application fee: $15. A $300 deposit is required.

Contact • Dr. John S. Henderson, Director of Off-Campus Studies, Dickinson College, PO Box 1773, Carlisle, PA 17013-2896; 717-245-1341; Fax: 717-245-1688; E-mail: ocs@dickinson.edu; World Wide Web: http://www.dickinson.edu

GHANA

 JAMES MADISON UNIVERSITY

JMU IN WEST AFRICA–GHANA

General Information • Academic study program in Legon. Classes are held on the campus of University of Ghana, Legon. Excursions to Elmina, Cape Coast castles, Kumase, Aburi Botanical Gardens.

Learning Focus • Courses in history, African experiences. Instruction is offered by professors from the sponsoring institution.

Accommodations • Hotels. Meals are taken as a group, in local restaurants.

Program Details • Program offered once per year. Session length: 4 weeks. Departures are scheduled in May. The program is open to undergraduate students, graduate students, adults. Most participants are 18 years of age and older. Other requirements: minimum 2.5 GPA. 15 participants per session. Application deadline: February 1.

Costs • $2500 (includes tuition, housing, some meals, excursions). A $400 deposit is required.

Contact • Dr. David Owusu-Ansah, Professor of History, James Madison University, Harrisonburg, VA 22807; 540-568-6132; Fax: 540-568-6556; E-mail: owusuadx@jmu.edu; World Wide Web: http://www.jmu.edu/intl-ed/

 TEMPLE UNIVERSITY

TEMPLE IN WEST AFRICA: GHANA

General Information • Academic study program in Accra.

Learning Focus • Courses in African-American studies, African history, African civilization. Instruction is offered by professors from the sponsoring institution.

Accommodations • Dormitories. Meals are taken as a group, in central dining facility.

Program Details • Program offered once per year. Session length: 6 weeks. Departures are scheduled in July. The program is open to undergraduate students. Other requirements: minimum 2.5 GPA. 20–25 participants per session. Application deadline: March 15.

Costs • $2360–$2966 (includes tuition, housing, all meals, excursions). Application fee: $30. A $100 deposit is required.

Contact • Denise A. Connerty, Interim Director of International Programs, Temple University, Conwell Hall, 5th Floor, Suite 501, Philadelphia, PA 19122; 215-204-4684; Fax: 215-204-5735; E-mail: intlprog@vm.temple.edu; World Wide Web: http://www.temple.edu/intlprog/

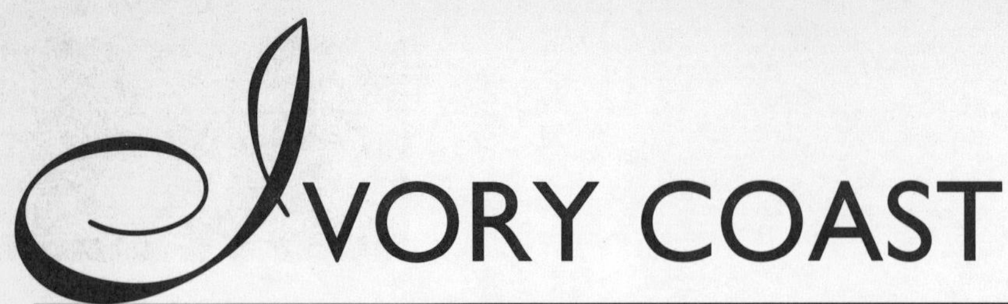

IVORY COAST

STATE UNIVERSITY OF NEW YORK COLLEGE AT BROCKPORT

DRUMMING AND DANCE IN THE IVORY COAST

General Information • Academic study program in Abidjan. Classes are held on the campus of Foundation Guiraud School of Dance and Cultural Exchange.

Learning Focus • Courses in dance, cultural studies, drumming.

Accommodations • Dormitories, hotels. Single rooms are available. Meals are taken as a group, in central dining facility, in local restaurants.

Program Details • Program offered once per year. Session length: 3 weeks. Departures are scheduled in July. The program is open to undergraduate students, graduate students, people seeking continuing education credit. Most participants are 19 years of age and older. Other requirements: minimum 2.5 GPA, junior or senior status preferred. 6–12 participants per session. Application deadline: May 1.

Costs • $3400 (includes tuition, housing, some meals, excursions, international airfare). A $100 deposit is required.

Contact • Dr. John J. Perry, Director, International Education, State University of New York College at Brockport, Rakov Center, 350 New Campus Drive, Brockport, NY 14420; 800-298-7866; Fax: 716-637-3218; World Wide Web: http://www.brockport.edu/study_abroad

KENYA

JOURNEYS INTERNATIONAL, INC.

FAMILY MILLION ANIMAL SAFARI

General Information • Family tour with visits to Buffalo Springs, Hell's Gate, Lamu Island, Loita Plains, Masai Mara, Nairobi. Once at the destination country, participants travel by foot, small vehicle.
Learning Focus • Escorted travel to national parks and wildlife reserves. Other activities include camping, hiking. Instruction is offered by Kenyan naturalists. This program would appeal to people interested in culture, photography, wildlife, hiking.
Accommodations • Hotels, campsites.
Program Details • Program offered once per year. Session length: 15 days. Departures are scheduled in July. Program is targeted to families interested in adventure travel. Most participants are 5–55 years of age. Participants must be 5 years or older to enroll. 18 participants per session. Application deadline: 60 days prior to departure. Reservations are recommended at least 60 days before departure.
Costs • $2345 for adults, $995 for children under 12 (includes housing, some meals, park fees). A $300 deposit is required.
Contact • Michelle Gervais, Africa Sales Director, Journeys International, Inc., 4011 Jackson Road, Ann Arbor, MI 48103; 313-665-4407; Fax: 313-665-2945; E-mail: michelle@journeys-intl.com; World Wide Web: http://www.journeys-intl.com

JOURNEYS INTERNATIONAL, INC.

MILLION ANIMAL SAFARI

General Information • Wilderness/adventure program with visits to Hell's Gate, Lake Nakuru, Loita Plains, Masai Mara, Mount Kenya, Nairobi. Once at the destination country, participants travel by foot, small vehicle.
Learning Focus • Escorted travel to national parks and wildlife reserves. Other activities include camping. Instruction is offered by Kenyan naturalists. This program would appeal to people interested in wildlife, culture, nature studies, photography.
Accommodations • Campsites, lodges. Single rooms are available for an additional $225.
Program Details • Program offered 10 times per year. Session length: 17 days. Departures are scheduled in January–April, June–October, December. Program is targeted to persons interested in wildlife and culture. Most participants are 25–55 years of age. Participants must be 12 years or older to enroll. 4–15 participants per session. Application deadline: 60 days prior to departure. Reservations are recommended at least 60 days before departure.
Costs • $2445 (includes housing, some meals, park fees). A $300 deposit is required.
Contact • Michelle Gervais, Africa Sales Director, Journeys International, Inc., 4011 Jackson Road, Ann Arbor, MI 48103; 313-665-4407; Fax: 313-665-2945; E-mail: michelle@journeys-intl.com; World Wide Web: http://www.journeys-intl.com

 MICHIGAN STATE UNIVERSITY

WILDLIFE AND ECOLOGY MANAGEMENT

General Information • Academic study program in Nairobi.
Learning Focus • Courses in wildlife management, conservation, ecological studies. Instruction is offered by professors from the sponsoring institution.
Accommodations • Dormitories, lodges. Meals are taken on one's own, in local restaurants.
Program Details • Program offered once per year. Session length: 5 weeks. Departures are scheduled in May. The program is open to undergraduate students, graduate students. Most participants are 18–26 years of age. Other requirements: good academic standing. 15 participants per session. Application deadline: March 14.
Costs • $2100 (includes housing, some meals, excursions). Application fee: $75. A $250 deposit is required.
Contact • Cynthia Chalou, Educational Exchange Coordinator, Michigan State University, Office of Study Abroad, 109 International Center, East Lansing, MI 48824-1035; 517-353-8920; Fax: 517-432-2082; E-mail: chalouc@pilot.msu.edu; World Wide Web: http://study-abroad.msu.edu

NATURAL HABITAT ADVENTURES

HIGHLIGHTS OF KENYA

General Information • Nature study tour with visits to Amboseli, Delemere's Camp, Lewa Downs, Masai Mara, Mount Kenya, Nairobi, Samburu. Once at the destination country, participants travel by foot, airplane, land rover.
Learning Focus • Nature observation (animals in the wild). Instruction is offered by naturalists. This program would appeal to people interested in nature studies, photography, wildlife.
Accommodations • Hotels, campsites, lodges. Single rooms are available for an additional $610.
Program Details • Session length: 15 days. Departures are scheduled throughout the year. Most participants are 20–65 years of age. 12 participants per session. Reservations are recommended at least 1 year before departure.
Costs • $3190 (includes housing, all meals, excursions, park fees). A $500 deposit is required.
Contact • Planet Expeditions, Natural Habitat Adventures, 2945 Center Green Court, Suite H, Boulder, CO 80301; 800-233-2433; Fax: 303-449-3712; E-mail: nathab@worldnet.att.net

NATURAL HABITAT ADVENTURES

KENYA LODGE AND CANVAS SAFARI

General Information • Nature study tour with visits to Amboseli, Lake Nakuru, Masai Mara, Mount Kenya, Nairobi, Samburu. Once at the destination country, participants travel by minivan or four-wheel drive land rover.
Learning Focus • Escorted travel to game parks. Nature observation (animals in the wild). Instruction is offered by naturalists. This program would appeal to people interested in nature studies, photography, wildlife.
Accommodations • Campsites, lodges. Single rooms are available for an additional $350.
Program Details • Program offered 8 times per year. Session length: 13 days. Departures are scheduled in January-March, July-September. Most participants are 20-65 years of age. Participants must be 12 years or older to enroll. 18 participants per session. Reservations are recommended at least 6-12 months before departure.
Costs • $2800 (includes housing, all meals, excursions, park fees, taxes, guide services). A $500 deposit is required.
Contact • Planet Expeditions, Natural Habitat Adventures, 2945 Center Green Court, Suite H, Boulder, CO 80301; 800-233-2433; Fax: 303-449-3712; E-mail: nathab@worldnet.att.net

NATURAL HABITAT ADVENTURES

KENYAN COAST

General Information • Nature study tour with visits to Malindi. Once at the destination country, participants travel by foot, boat, airplane.
Learning Focus • Nature observation (coral reef and animals in the wild). Instruction is offered by naturalists. This program would appeal to people interested in nature studies, photography, wildlife.
Accommodations • Ocean lodge. Single rooms are available for an additional $40 per day.
Program Details • Session length: 3-5 weeks. Departures are scheduled throughout the year. Most participants are 20-65 years of age. 2 participants per session. Reservations are recommended at least 1 year before departure.
Costs • $160 per day (includes housing, all meals, excursions, park fees). A $500 deposit is required.
Contact • Planet Expeditions, Natural Habitat Adventures, 2945 Center Green Court, Suite H, Boulder, CO 80301; 800-233-2433; Fax: 303-449-3712; E-mail: nathab@worldnet.att.net

NATURAL HABITAT ADVENTURES

KENYA PHOTOGRAPHY SAFARI

General Information • Nature study tour with visits to Lake Nakuru, Masai Mara, Nairobi, Samburu, a Masai village. Once at the destination country, participants travel by airplane, safari cruiser.
Learning Focus • Instruction in safari photography. Nature observation (elephant, rhinoceros, buffalo, leopard, cheetah, lion, wildebeest, hippo, zebra, gazelle, giraffe, impala, waterbuck and warthog). Instruction is offered by naturalists, photographers. This program would appeal to people interested in nature studies, photography, wildlife.
Accommodations • Campsites, safari lodges. Single rooms are available for an additional $795.
Program Details • 12 participants per session. Reservations are recommended at least 6-12 months before departure.
Costs • Contact sponsor for information. A $500 deposit is required.
Contact • Natural Habitat Adventures, 2945 Center Green Court, Suite H, Boulder, CO 80301; 800-543-8917; Fax: 303-449-3712; E-mail: nathab@worldnet.att.net

RAMAPO COLLEGE OF NEW JERSEY

SUMMER STUDY IN KENYA

General Information • Academic study program in Nairobi. Excursions to Lake Victoria, Kisumu, Homa Bay, Kericho, Kisii, Kakamega.
Learning Focus • Courses in Kenyan culture. Instruction is offered by professors from the sponsoring institution.
Accommodations • Homestays, hotels. Meals are taken as a group, in central dining facility.
Program Details • Program offered 2 times per year. Session length: 3 or 6 weeks. Departures are scheduled in July. The program is open to undergraduate students, graduate students, pre-college students, adults. Most participants are 18 years of age and older. Other requirements: minimum 2.0 GPA and a minimum of 18 years old.
Costs • $2250 (includes tuition, housing, all meals, excursions, international airfare, miscellaneous fees and tips). A $300 deposit is required.
Contact • Mrs. Robyn Perricelli, Coordinator, Study Abroad, Ramapo College of New Jersey, 505 Ramapo Valley Road, Mahwah, NJ 07430; 201-527-7463; Fax: 201-529-7508; E-mail: rperrice@ramapo.edu

SPECIAL INTEREST TOURS

HEMINGWAY AUTHENTIC CAMPING SAFARI

General Information • Wilderness/adventure program with visits to Lake Nakuru, Masai Mara Game Reserve, Samburu Game Reserve, Masai Manyatta. Once at the destination country, participants travel by four-wheel drive vehicle.
Learning Focus • Nature observation (animal and bird behavior). Other activities include camping, hiking. Instruction is offered by naturalists. This program would appeal to people interested in wildlife, natural history, photography, adventure.
Accommodations • Campsites.
Program Details • Session length: 14 days. Departures are scheduled in January, February, March, July, September, October. Most participants are 20-60 years of age. Participants must be 12 years or older to enroll. 12 participants per session. Application deadline: 60 days prior to departure. Reservations are recommended at least 6 months before departure.
Costs • $3450 (includes housing, all meals, excursions, international airfare). A $450 deposit is required.
Contact • Nancy Koch, Vice President, Special Interest Tours, 10220 North 27 Street, Phoenix, AZ 85028; 800-525-6772; Fax: 602-493-3630; E-mail: GoSafari@usa.net

TRAVELEARN

A KENYA ADVENTURE

General Information • Nature study and cultural tour with visits to Aberdares, Amboseli, Lake Nakuru, Masai Mara, Mount Kenya, Mount Kilimanjaro, Nairobi, Naivasha, Samburu, Tanzania (Mombasa). Once at the destination country, participants travel by foot, special safari vehicles. Program is affiliated with the nationwide TraveLearn network of 290 universities and colleges.

Learning Focus • Instruction in natural history, ecology and cultural history. Museum visits (National Museum and African Heritage). Attendance at performances (dances at Bomas of Kenya). Nature observation (national parks and reserves). Other activities include "people-to-people" experience in Nairobi and Masai Mara. Instruction is offered by professors, researchers, naturalists. This program would appeal to people interested in natural history, pre-history, ecology, cultural history and understanding.

Accommodations • Campsites, safari lodges. Single rooms are available for an additional $695.

Program Details • Program offered 5 times per year. Session length: 17–21 days. Departures are scheduled in January, June, July, August, October. Program is targeted to mature adults. Most participants are 40–75 years of age. Participants must be 18 years or older to enroll. 14–20 participants per session. Application deadline: 60 days prior to departure. Reservations are recommended at least 4–8 months before departure.

Costs • $4495 (includes housing, all meals, books and class materials, excursions, international airfare). A $300 deposit is required.

Contact • Keith Williams, Director of Marketing, TraveLearn, PO Box 315, Lakeville, PA 18438; 800-235-9114; Fax: 717-226-9114; E-mail: travelearn@aol.com

WILDLAND ADVENTURES

KENYA TRAILS SAFARI

General Information • Nature study tour with visits to Masai Mara, Nairobi, national parks. Once at the destination country, participants travel by bus, foot, airplane. Program is affiliated with East African Wildlife Society.

Learning Focus • Nature observation (African wildlife observation and photography). Instruction is offered by naturalists, native Masai. This program would appeal to people interested in photography, bird watching, hiking.

Accommodations • Single rooms are available.

Program Details • Program offered 12 times per year. Session length: 13 days. Most participants are 30–65 years of age. Participants must be 8 years or older to enroll. 2–12 participants per session. Application deadline: 30 days prior to departure. Reservations are recommended at least 3–6 months before departure.

Costs • $2180 (includes housing, some meals, excursions, complete pre-departure dossier). A $300 deposit is required.

Contact • Wildland Adventures, 3516 Northeast 155th Street, Seattle, WA 98155; 800-345-4453; Fax: 206-636-6615; E-mail: wildadve@aol.com; World Wide Web: http://www.wildland.com

MADAGASCAR

JOURNEYS INTERNATIONAL, INC.

MADAGASCAR NATURE ODYSSEY

General Information • Wilderness/adventure program with visits to Antananarivo, Berenty Reserve, Nosy Be, Nosy Komba, Perinet, Tana. Once at the destination country, participants travel by foot, airplane, small vehicle.

Learning Focus • Escorted travel to game reserves. Other activities include hiking. Instruction is offered by naturalists. This program would appeal to people interested in bird watching, nature studies, wildlife, photography.

Accommodations • Hotels, lodges. Single rooms are available for an additional $350.

Program Details • Program offered 8 times per year. Session length: 10 days. Departures are scheduled in March–October. Program is targeted to persons interested in nature and wildlife. Most participants are 25–55 years of age. Participants must be 12 years or older to enroll. 2–10 participants per session. Application deadline: 60 days prior to departure. Reservations are recommended at least 60 days before departure.

Costs • $2000 (includes internal airfare). A $300 deposit is required.

Contact • Michelle Gervais, Africa Sales Director, Journeys International, Inc., 4011 Jackson Road, Ann Arbor, MI 48103; 313-665-4407; Fax: 313-665-2945; E-mail: michelle@journeys-intl.com; World Wide Web: http://www.journeys-intl.com

MALI

INTERNATIONAL BICYCLE FUND

MALI: SAHEL JOURNEY

General Information • Cultural tour with visits to Bamatco, Djenné, Dogon Country, Mopti, Timbuktu. Once at the destination country, participants travel by bus, foot, boat, airplane, bicycle.

Learning Focus • Instruction in culture, history, economics, environment and development. Escorted travel to a village and historic sites. Museum visits (National Museum). Nature observation (sahel and desert). Instruction is offered by African studies specialists. This program would appeal to people interested in African culture, bicycling, economic development, Sahel history, photography.

Accommodations • Homestays, dormitories, hotels.

Program Details • Program offered once per year. Session length: 15 days. Departures are scheduled in November. Most participants are 20–60 years of age. 8 participants per session. Reservations are recommended at least 3 months before departure.

Costs • $1290 (includes housing, some meals, excursions). A $300 deposit is required.

Contact • David Mozer, Director, International Bicycle Fund, 4887 Columbia Drive, S, Seattle, WA 98108; 206-767-0848; Fax: 206-767-0848; E-mail: intlbike@scn.org; World Wide Web: http://www.halcyon.com/fkroger/bike/homepage.html

AMERICAN JEWISH CONGRESS, INTERNATIONAL TRAVEL PROGRAM
MOROCCAN DISCOVERY

General Information • Cultural tour with visits to Beni Mellal, Casablanca, Fez, Marrakech, Meknés, Rabat, Tomb of Mohammed V, Royal Palace, Dar Alkabira, Arab Medina, Nejjarine Square, Atlas Mountains, Saadian Tombs. Once at the destination country, participants travel by bus, foot.
Learning Focus • Escorted travel to synagogues, tanneries and Majorelle Gardens. Museum visits (Handicrafts Museum, Moroccan Arts Museum). Attendance at performances (Moroccan Fantasia, storytellers, snake charmers). Instruction is offered by historians. This program would appeal to people interested in Jewish history.
Accommodations • Hotels. Single rooms are available for an additional $500.
Program Details • Program offered 8 times per year. Session length: 11 days. Departures are scheduled in February, March, May, August-December. Program is targeted to Jewish-American adults. Most participants are 40-75 years of age. Participants must be 15 years or older to enroll. Participants must be members of the sponsoring organization (annual dues: $50). 30 participants per session. Reservations are recommended at least 6 months before departure.
Costs • $3045-$3145 (includes housing, some meals, excursions, international airfare, travel bag, documents portfolio, travel journal). A $200 deposit is required.
Contact • Betty Van Dyke, Worldwide Operations Manager, American Jewish Congress, International Travel Program, 18 East 84th Street, New York, NY 10028; 212-360-1571; Fax: 212-717-1932

ARCHAEOLOGICAL TOURS
MOROCCO

General Information • Archaeological tour with visits to Fez, High Atlas, Marrakech, Meknés, Rabat, Volubilis, Erfoud, Zagora, Ouarzazate, Tamgrout, Tin-Mal. Once at the destination country, participants travel by bus.
Learning Focus • Escorted travel to Islamic monuments, Berger villages, Sahara Desert and the Atlas Mountains. Museum visits (Rabat, Fez, Marrakech). Attendance at performances (music). Instruction is offered by professors, historians. This program would appeal to people interested in history, architecture, archaeology.
Accommodations • Hotels. Single rooms are available for an additional $472.
Program Details • Program offered once per year. Session length: 15 days. Departures are scheduled in October. Program is targeted to adults. Most participants are 30-80 years of age. 22 participants per session. Application deadline: 1 month prior to departure.
Costs • $3140 (includes housing, some meals, excursions). A $500 deposit is required.
Contact • Archaeological Tours, 271 Madison Avenue, Suite 904, New York, NY 10016; 212-986-3054; Fax: 212-370-1561

CRAFT WORLD TOURS
MOROCCO

General Information • Cultural tour with visits to Casablanca, Chechaoen, Essaouira, Marrakech, Ouarzazate, Rabat. Once at the destination country, participants travel by bus.
Learning Focus • Escorted travel to Kasbah Oudayas, Andalusian Garden, Kings Palace and ruins. Museum visits (Museum of Moroccan Art, Dar Batha Museum). Instruction is offered by artists. This program would appeal to people interested in handicrafts, folk arts, village life.
Accommodations • Hotels. Single rooms are available for an additional $379.
Program Details • Program offered once per year. Session length: 17 days. Departures are scheduled in October. Most participants are 30-80 years of age. Other requirements: appreciation of handcrafts and folk arts. 18 participants per session. Application deadline: September 14. Reservations are recommended at least 6 months before departure.
Costs • $3387 (includes housing, some meals, excursions, international airfare). A $250 deposit is required.
Contact • Tom Wilson, President, Craft World Tours, 6776 Warboys Road, Byron, NY 14422; 716-548-2667; Fax: 716-548-2821

 DUKE UNIVERSITY
DUKE IN MOROCCO

General Information • Academic study program in Marrakech, Rabat. Classes are held on the campus of University Cadi Ayyad Marrakech, Mohammed V University. Excursions to Aghmat Ourika, Tin Mallal, Almohads, Fez.
Learning Focus • Courses in North African culture, history, religion. Instruction is offered by professors from the sponsoring institution.
Accommodations • Hotels. Meals are taken as a group, in local restaurants.
Program Details • Program offered once per year. Session length: 6 weeks. Departures are scheduled in June. The program is open to undergraduate students. Most participants are 19-21 years of age. Other requirements: minimum 2.7 GPA. 15 participants per session. Application deadline: February 21.
Costs • $4888 (includes tuition, housing, some meals, excursions, international airfare).

Contact • Foreign Academic Programs, Duke University, 121 Allen Building, Box 90057, Durham, NC 27708-0057; 919-684-2174; Fax: 919-684-3083; E-mail: abroad@mail01.adm.duke.edu; World Wide Web: http://www.mis.duke.edu/study_abroad/study_abroad.html

INTERHOSTEL, UNIVERSITY OF NEW HAMPSHIRE

MOROCCO

General Information • Cultural tour with visits to Casablanca, Fez, Marrakech, Ouarzazate, Rabat, Volubilis, Meknes, Glaoui Kasbah, High Atlas Mountains, Ait Benhaddou, Tifoultoute, Todra Gorge, Zagora. Once at the destination country, participants travel by bus, foot, airplane. Program is affiliated with American University of Paris and University of Fez.
Learning Focus • Instruction in history and culture. Escorted travel to mountains and cities. Museum visits (Archaeology Museum, Oudayas). Attendance at performances (belly dancing). Instruction is offered by professors, city guides. This program would appeal to people interested in history, culture.
Accommodations • Hotels. Single rooms are available for an additional $450.
Program Details • Program offered once per year. Session length: 2½ weeks. Departures are scheduled in October. Program is targeted to seniors over 50. Most participants are 60–80 years of age. Participants must be 50 years or older to enroll. 40 participants per session. Reservations are recommended at least 6 months before departure.
Costs • $2975 (includes tuition, housing, all meals, excursions, international airfare, entrance fees). A $200 deposit is required.
Contact • Janice Pierson, Office Supervisor, Interhostel, University of New Hampshire, 6 Garrison Avenue, Durham, NH 03824-3529; 800-733-9753; Fax: 603-862-1113; World Wide Web: http://www.learn.unh.edu/

NATURAL HISTORY MUSEUM OF LOS ANGELES COUNTY

THE NATURAL HISTORY AND MYSTERY OF MOROCCO

General Information • Cultural tour with visits to Casablanca, Erfoud, Fez, Marrakech, Ouarzazate, Rabat, Bouknadel Garden, Azrou, Erg Chebbi, Dadis Gorge, Zagora, Essaouira, Isle of Mogador. Once at the destination country, participants travel by bus, foot, boat, land rover.
Learning Focus • Attendance at performances (Fantasia in Marrakech). Nature observation (bird watching in Sidi Boughaba, land rover to the Erg Chebbi, High Altar Mountains). Other activities include hiking. Instruction is offered by naturalists. This program would appeal to people interested in natural history, archaeology, culture, geology.
Accommodations • Hotels. Single rooms are available for an additional $950.
Program Details • Program offered once per year. Session length: 15 days. Departures are scheduled in February. Most participants are 40–75 years of age. Participants must be 12 years or older to enroll. 20 participants per session. Application deadline: December 20. Reservations are recommended at least 2 months before departure.
Costs • $3095 (includes housing, some meals, excursions, airfare from New York). A $500 deposit is required.
Contact • Karen Hovanitz, Travel Program Manager, Natural History Museum of Los Angeles County, 900 Exposition Boulevard, Los Angeles, CA 90007; 213-744-3350; Fax: 213-747-6718; E-mail: khovanit@mizar.usc.edu; World Wide Web: http://www.lam.mus.ca.us/lacmnh

OUACHITA BAPTIST UNIVERSITY

MOROCCO STUDY PROGRAM

General Information • Academic study program in Morocco (Casablanca, Fez, Ifrane, Rabat), Spain (Gibraltar). Classes are held on the campus of Al Akhawayn University.
Learning Focus • Courses in Arabic language, Arabic culture, comparative religion, Arabic business. Instruction is offered by local teachers.
Accommodations • Dormitories. Single rooms are available. Meals are taken on one's own, in central dining facility, in local restaurants.
Program Details • Program offered 3 times per year. Session length: 14 weeks. Departures are scheduled in January, June, August. The program is open to undergraduate students. Most participants are 18–23 years of age. Other requirements: minimum 2.5 GPA. 2 participants per session. Application deadline: April 1.
Costs • $4990 (includes tuition, housing, all meals, international airfare). A $500 deposit is required.
Contact • Dr. Trey Berry, Director of International Programs, Ouachita Baptist University, OBU Box 3777, Arkadelphia, AR 71998; 501-245-5197; Fax: 501-245-5312; E-mail: berryt@alpha.obu.edu; World Wide Web: http://www.obu.edu

 TRAVELEARN

A MOROCCO ADVENTURE

General Information • Cultural tour with visits to Casablanca, Fez, Marrakech, Ouarzazate, Rabat, Sahara. Once at the destination country, participants travel by bus, foot. Program is affiliated with the nationwide TraveLearn network of 290 universities and colleges.
Learning Focus • Instruction in history, cultural understanding and religion. Other activities include "people-to-people" experience in Fez. Instruction is offered by professors, historians, social scientists. This program would appeal to people interested in history, cultural history, religion.
Accommodations • Hotels. Single rooms are available for an additional $595.
Program Details • Program offered 4 times per year. Session length: 15 days. Departures are scheduled in February, March, July, October. Program is targeted to mature adults. Most participants are 40–75 years of age. Participants must be 18 years or older to enroll. 14–20 participants per session. Application deadline: 60 days prior to departure. Reservations are recommended at least 4-8 months before departure.
Costs • $2995 (includes housing, all meals, books and class materials, excursions, international airfare). A $300 deposit is required.

Contact • Keith Williams, Director of Marketing, TraveLearn, PO Box 315, Lakeville, PA 18438; 800-235-9114; Fax: 717-226-9114; E-mail: travelearn@aol.com

UNIVERSITY OF FLORIDA

ARABIC LANGUAGE INSTITUTE OF FEZ

General Information • Language study program in Fez. Classes are held on the campus of Arabic Language Institute in Fez. Excursions to cultural sites.

Learning Focus • Courses in Arabic language. Instruction is offered by local teachers.

Accommodations • Homestays, dormitories, locally-rented apartments, hotels. Meals are taken on one's own, with host family, in central dining facility, in local restaurants, in residences.

Program Details • Program offered once per year. Session length: 6 weeks. Departures are scheduled in June. The program is open to undergraduate students, graduate students. Most participants are 18–40 years of age. Other requirements: minimum 2.5 GPA and one year of Arabic or the equivalent. Application deadline: March 1.

Costs • $5600 (includes tuition, housing, books and class materials, international airfare, living expenses, administration fee). Application fee: $250.

Contact • Overseas Studies, University of Florida, 123 Tigert Hall, PO Box 113225, Gainesville, FL 32611-3225; 352-392-5206; Fax: 352-392-5575; E-mail: ovrseas@nervm.nerdc.ufl.edu

UNIVERSITY OF WISCONSIN–MADISON

RABAT, MOROCCO PROGRAM

General Information • Academic study program in Rabat. Classes are held on the campus of Mohammed V University. Excursions to Casablanca-Sale, Quarzazate Region, Atlas Mountains.

Learning Focus • Courses in Arabic language, cultural studies, history. Instruction is offered by local teachers.

Accommodations • Homestays, dormitories. Meals are taken as a group, in central dining facility.

Program Details • Program offered once per year. Session length: 8 weeks. Departures are scheduled in May. The program is open to undergraduate students. Other requirements: sophomore standing. 3–13 participants per session. Application deadline: first Friday in February.

Costs • $4450 (includes tuition, housing, all meals, excursions, international airfare, personal and miscellaneous expenses). A $100 deposit is required.

Contact • Peer Advisors, Office of International Studies and Programs, University of Wisconsin–Madison, 261 Bascom Hall, 500 Lincoln Drive, Madison, WI 53706; 608-265-6239; Fax: 608-262-6998; E-mail: abroad@macc.wisc.edu; World Wide Web: http://www.wisc.edu/uw-oisp/

NAMIBIA

JOURNEYS INTERNATIONAL, INC.

THE NAMIBIA EXPLORER

General Information • Wilderness/adventure program with visits to Damaraland, Etosha National Park, Namib Desert, Seal Colony, Twyfelfontein, Windhoek.
Learning Focus • Escorted travel to national parks. Nature observation (lions, elephants, zebras, Namib Desert). Other activities include camping, swimming. Instruction is offered by professional English-speaking safari leader. This program would appeal to people interested in wildlife, photography, nature studies, bird watching.
Accommodations • Campsites.
Program Details • Program offered 18 times per year. Session length: 15 days. Departures are scheduled in January–December. Program is targeted to adventurous travelers. Most participants are 25–45 years of age. Participants must be 12 years or older to enroll. Other requirements: must be in excellent health and physical condition. 8–13 participants per session. Application deadline: 60 days prior to departure. Reservations are recommended at least 60 days before departure.
Costs • Contact sponsor for information. A $300 deposit is required.
Contact • Michelle Gervais, Africa Sales Director, Journeys International, Inc., 4011 Jackson Road, Ann Arbor, MI 48103; 313-665-4407; Fax: 313-665-2945; E-mail: michelle@journeys-intl.com; World Wide Web: http://www.journeys-intl.com

NATURAL HABITAT ADVENTURES

BEST OF NAMIBIA

General Information • Nature study tour with visits to Etosha National Park, Soussesvlei Sand Dunes, Swakopmund. Once at the destination country, participants travel by airplane, land rover or minivan.
Learning Focus • Nature observation (animals in the wild). Instruction is offered by naturalists. This program would appeal to people interested in nature studies, photography, wildlife.
Accommodations • Hotels, campsites, lodges. Single rooms are available for an additional $300.
Program Details • Session length: 16 days. Departures are scheduled in March–January. Most participants are 20–65 years of age. Other requirements: maximum age of 70. 7–8 participants per session.
Costs • $3500 (includes housing, all meals, excursions, park fees). A $500 deposit is required.
Contact • Planet Expeditions, Natural Habitat Adventures, 2945 Center Green Court, Suite H, Boulder, CO 80301; 800-233-2433; Fax: 303-449-3712; E-mail: nathab@worldnet.att.net

NATURAL HABITAT ADVENTURES

NAMIBIA FLY-IN SAFARI

General Information • Nature study tour with visits to Etosha National Park, Namib Desert, Skeleton Coast, Swakopmund, Windhoek. Once at the destination country, participants travel by foot, airplane, land rover or minivan.
Learning Focus • Nature observation (animals in the wild). Instruction is offered by naturalists. This program would appeal to people interested in nature studies, photography, wildlife.
Accommodations • Hotels, lodges. Single rooms are available for an additional $175.
Program Details • Session length: 8 days. Departures are scheduled throughout the year. Most participants are 20–65 years of age. 2 participants per session. Reservations are recommended at least 1 year before departure.
Costs • $2200 (includes housing, all meals, excursions, park fees). A $500 deposit is required.
Contact • Planet Expeditions, Natural Habitat Adventures, 2945 Center Green Court, Suite H, Boulder, CO 80301; 800-233-2433; Fax: 303-449-3712; E-mail: nathab@worldnet.att.net

SPECIAL INTEREST TOURS

NAMIBIA KALEIDOSCOPE

General Information • Wilderness/adventure program with visits to Damaraland Wilderness, Etosha National Park, Fish River Canyon, Hardap Dam, Namib Desert, Swakopmund, Twyfelfontein Rock Paintings. Once at the destination country, participants travel by bus, foot.
Learning Focus • Nature observation (wildlife, birds, desert). Other activities include camping, hiking. Instruction is offered by naturalists. This program would appeal to people interested in natural history, biology, photography, wildlife.
Accommodations • Hotels, campsites.
Program Details • Program offered 12 times per year. Session length: 18 days. Departures are scheduled throughout the year. Most participants are 20–55 years of age. Participants must be 15 years or older to enroll. 8 participants per session. Application deadline: 60 days prior to departure. Reservations are recommended at least 6 months before departure.
Costs • $1910 (includes housing, all meals, excursions). A $450 deposit is required.
Contact • Nancy Koch, Vice President, Special Interest Tours, 10220 North 27 Street, Phoenix, AZ 85028; 800-525-6772; Fax: 602-493-3630; E-mail: GoSafari@usa.net

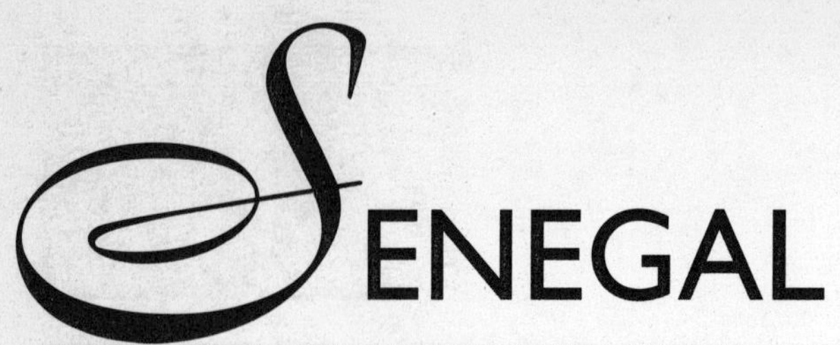

SENEGAL

GLOBAL EXCHANGE REALITY TOURS

SENEGAL

General Information • Community development program with visits to Dakar, Goree Island, Kaolack, Somone. Once at the destination country, participants travel by bus, airplane.
Learning Focus • Instruction in West African history, culture and politics. Museum visits (Dakar). Other activities include meeting with grassroots women's rights groups, youth and development groups. Instruction is offered by researchers, naturalists. This program would appeal to people interested in history, culture, grassroots development.
Accommodations • Hotels, guest houses. Single rooms are available for an additional $200–$500.
Program Details • Program offered once per year. Session length: 16 days. Departures are scheduled in August. Program is targeted to seniors, students and professionals. Participants must be 18 years or older to enroll. 10 participants per session. Application deadline: 1 month prior to departure. Reservations are recommended at least 2 months before departure.
Costs • $2800 (includes housing, some meals, books and class materials, international airfare). A $200 deposit is required.
Contact • Reality Tours Coordinator, Global Exchange Reality Tours, 2017 Mission Street, Room 303, San Francisco, CA 94110; 415-255-7296; Fax: 415-255-9498; E-mail: globalexch@igc.apc.org

SOUTH AFRICA

CENTER FOR GLOBAL EDUCATION AT AUGSBURG COLLEGE

CHANGE AND CHALLENGE IN THE NEW SOUTH AFRICA

General Information • Academic study program with visits to Cape Town, Durban, Johannesburg. Once at the destination country, participants travel by foot, airplane, van.
Learning Focus • Instruction in current issues facing South Africa. Escorted travel to local communities. Other activities include visits to development projects, meeting with local community representatives. Instruction is offered by in-country coordinators. This program would appeal to people interested in South African development, anti-racism, social justice, democracy.
Accommodations • Guest houses.
Program Details • Program offered 2 times per year. Session length: 2 weeks. Departures are scheduled in February, June. Most participants are 20–70 years of age. Participants must be 18 years or older to enroll. Other requirements: accompaniment by an adult if under 18 years of age. 15 participants per session. Application deadline: 3 weeks prior to departure. Reservations are recommended at least 6 weeks before departure.
Costs • $3650 (includes housing, all meals, books and class materials, excursions, international airfare). A $100 deposit is required.
Contact • International Travel Seminars, Center for Global Education at Augsburg College, Center for Global Education, 2211 Riverside Avenue, Minneapolis, MN 55454; 800-299-8889; Fax: 612-330-1695; E-mail: globaled@augsburg.edu; World Wide Web: http://www.augsburg.edu/global

EASTERN MICHIGAN UNIVERSITY

AFRICAN-AMERICAN STUDIES IN TRANSKEI

General Information • Academic study program in Umtata. Classes are held on the campus of University of Transkei. Excursions to Johannesburg.
Learning Focus • Courses in African-American studies, contemporary Africa. Instruction is offered by professors from the sponsoring institution.
Accommodations • Dormitories. Meals are taken on one's own, in central dining facility.
Program Details • Program offered once per year. Session length: 6 weeks. Departures are scheduled in July. The program is open to undergraduate students, graduate students. Most participants are 18–25 years of age. Other requirements: minimum 2.0 GPA and 18 years of age. Application deadline: March 1.
Costs • $4000 (1997 cost) (includes tuition, housing, some meals, excursions, international airfare, travel in South Africa). A $200 deposit is required.
Contact • Academic Programs Abroad, Eastern Michigan University, 332 Goodison Hall, Ypsilanti, MI 48197; 800-777-3541; Fax: 313-487-2316; E-mail: programs.abroad@emich.edu; World Wide Web: http://www.emich.edu/public/cont_ed/abroad.html

GEORGE MASON UNIVERSITY

SOUTH AFRICA: MULTICULTURAL ISSUES IN THE NEW SOUTH AFRICA

General Information • Academic study program in Cape Town, Durban, Johannesburg, Pretoria.
Learning Focus • Courses in education. Instruction is offered by professors from the sponsoring institution.
Accommodations • Hotels. Meals are taken as a group.
Program Details • Program offered once per year. Session length: 3 weeks. Departures are scheduled in July. The program is open to undergraduate students, graduate students, adults. Most participants are 18–65 years of age. Other requirements: minimum 2.25 GPA. 10–15 participants per session. Application deadline: April 26.
Costs • $3514 for George Mason University students, $4064 for other students (includes tuition, housing, some meals, insurance, excursions, international airfare). Application fee: $35. A $500 deposit is required.
Contact • Dr. Yehuda Lukacs, Director, Center for Global Education, George Mason University, 4400 University Drive, 235 Johnson Center, Fairfax, VA 22030; 703-993-2155; Fax: 703-993-2153; E-mail: ylukacs@gmu.edu; World Wide Web: http://www.gmu.edu/departments/oie

GLOBAL EXCHANGE REALITY TOURS

SOUTH AFRICA

General Information • Academic study program with visits to Cape Town, Johannesburg. Once at the destination country, participants travel by bus, airplane.
Learning Focus • Instruction in politics and grassroots organizations. Museum visits (African Museum). Instruction is offered by researchers, naturalists. This program would appeal to people interested in grassroots development, history, politics, culture.
Accommodations • Hotels, guest houses. Single rooms are available for an additional $200–$500.
Program Details • Program offered 3 times per year. Session length: 15 days. Departures are scheduled in April, July, October. Program is targeted to seniors, students and professionals. Participants must be 18 years or older to

enroll. 10–15 participants per session. Application deadline: 1 month prior to departure. Reservations are recommended at least 2 months before departure.
Costs • $3300 (includes housing, some meals, international airfare). A $200 deposit is required.
Contact • Lisa Russ, Reality Tours Coordinator, Global Exchange Reality Tours, 2017 Mission Street, Room 303, San Francisco, CA 94110; 415-255-7296, ext. 229; Fax: 415-255-7498; E-mail: globalexch@igc.apc.org

LEXIA EXCHANGE INTERNATIONAL

LEXIA SUMMER PROGRAM IN CAPETOWN

General Information • Academic study program in Cape Town. Classes are held on the campus of University of the Western Cape. Excursions to Durban, Port Elizabeth, Windhoek, Umtata, Pretoria, Johannesburg.
Learning Focus • Courses in history, development studies, theater, fine arts, economics, race relations, Xhosa language, political science. Instruction is offered by local teachers.
Accommodations • Homestays, dormitories. Single rooms are available. Meals are taken on one's own, with host family, in central dining facility, in local restaurants.
Program Details • Program offered once per year. Session length: 8 weeks. Departures are scheduled in June. The program is open to undergraduate students, graduate students, adults. Most participants are 18–35 years of age. Other requirements: minimum 2.5 GPA. 5–10 participants per session. Application deadline: April 15.
Costs • $4495 (includes tuition, housing, books and class materials, excursions). Application fee: $30. A $300 deposit is required.
Contact • Justin Meilgaard, Program Coordinator, LEXIA Exchange International, 378 Cambridge Avenue, Palo Alto, CA 94306-1544; 800-775-3942; Fax: 415-327-9192; E-mail: lexia@rquartz.stanford.edu; World Wide Web: http://www.lexiaintl.org

NATURAL HABITAT ADVENTURES

SOUTH AFRICA FLY-IN SAFARI

General Information • Nature study tour with visits to Cape Town, Johannesburg, Kruger, Maputuland. Once at the destination country, participants travel by foot, airplane, land rover or minivan.
Learning Focus • Nature observation (animals in the wild). Instruction is offered by naturalists. This program would appeal to people interested in nature studies, photography, wildlife.
Accommodations • Hotels, campsites, lodges. Single rooms are available for an additional $375.
Program Details • Session length: 10 days. Departures are scheduled throughout the year. Most participants are 20–65 years of age. 2 participants per session. Reservations are recommended at least 1 year before departure.
Costs • $2300 (includes housing, all meals, excursions, park fees). A $500 deposit is required.
Contact • Planet Expeditions, Natural Habitat Adventures, 2945 Center Green Court, Suite H, Boulder, CO 80301; 800-233-2433; Fax: 303-449-3712; E-mail: nathab@worldnet.att.net

NATURAL HISTORY MUSEUM OF LOS ANGELES COUNTY

SOUTH AFRICA

General Information • Nature study tour with visits to South Africa (Durban, Johannesburg, Kruger National Park, Maputaland, Timbavati), Swaziland; excursions to St. Lucia Lake, Dumazulu cultural village, Hluhluwe, Ubizane. Once at the destination country, participants travel by bus, foot, boat, airplane.
Learning Focus • Museum visits (Museum Africa). Attendance at performances (Zulu kraal living museum). Nature observation (big game). Other activities include hiking. Instruction is offered by researchers, naturalists. This program would appeal to people interested in wildlife.
Accommodations • Hotels, lodges. Single rooms are available for an additional $675.
Program Details • Program offered once per year. Session length: 2 weeks. Departures are scheduled in October. Most participants are 35–75 years of age. Participants must be 12 years or older to enroll. 20 participants per session. Reservations are recommended at least 4 months before departure.
Costs • $4995 (includes housing, all meals, excursions, international airfare). A $500 deposit is required.
Contact • Karen Hovanitz, Travel Program Manager, Natural History Museum of Los Angeles County, 900 Exposition Boulevard, Los Angeles, CA 90007; 213-744-3350; Fax: 213-747-6718; E-mail: khovanit@mizar.usc.edu; World Wide Web: http://www.lam.mus.ca.us/lacmnh

SYRACUSE UNIVERSITY

ARCHAEOLOGY IN SOUTH AFRICA

General Information • Academic study program in Cape Town, French Hook, Stellenbosch. Classes are held on the campus of University of Cape Town.
Learning Focus • Courses in archaeology. Instruction is offered by professors from the sponsoring institution.
Accommodations • Dormitories, hotels. Meals are taken on one's own, in local restaurants.
Program Details • Program offered once per year. Session length: 6 weeks. Departures are scheduled in June. The program is open to undergraduate students, graduate students. Most participants are 19–30 years of age. Other requirements: minimum 2.7 GPA. 12 participants per session. Application deadline: March 15.
Costs • $6000 (includes tuition, housing, some meals, books and class materials, excursions). Application fee: $40. A $350 deposit is required.
Contact • Ms. Daisy Fried, Associate Director, Syracuse University, 119 Euclid Avenue, Syracuse, NY 13244; 315-443-9419; Fax: 315-443-4593; E-mail: dsfried@summon3.syr.edu; World Wide Web: http://sumweb.syr.edu/dipa/dipa9.htm

TEMPLE UNIVERSITY

TEMPLE IN SOUTH AFRICA

General Information • Academic study program in Durban. Classes are held on the campus of University of Durban-Westville. Excursions to Johannesburg.

Learning Focus • Courses in African studies, history, political science. Instruction is offered by professors from the sponsoring institution.
Accommodations • Homestays, dormitories. Meals are taken as a group, with host family, in residences.
Program Details • Program offered once per year. Session length: 5 weeks. Departures are scheduled in July. The program is open to undergraduate students. Other requirements: minimum 2.5 GPA. 10 participants per session. Application deadline: March 1.
Costs • $2960–$3566 (includes tuition, housing, all meals, excursions). Application fee: $30. A $100 deposit is required.
Contact • Denise A. Connerty, Interim Director of International Programs, Temple University, Conwell Hall, 5th Floor, Suite 501, Philadelphia, PA 19122; 215-204-4684; Fax: 215-204-5735; E-mail: intlprog@vm.temple.edu; World Wide Web: http://www.temple.edu/intlprog/

TRAVELEARN

THE NEW SOUTH AFRICA

General Information • Nature study and cultural tour with visits to Cape Town, Durban, Johannesburg, Kruger National Park, Rocktail Bay, Zululand, Victoria Falls, Botswana. Once at the destination country, participants travel by bus, foot, airplane. Program is affiliated with the nationwide TraveLearn network of 290 universities and colleges.
Learning Focus • Instruction in natural history, ecology and cultural history. Attendance at performances (Zulu tribal dances). Nature observation (national parks, reserves). Instruction is offered by researchers, naturalists, social scientists. This program would appeal to people interested in natural history, cultural history, ecology.
Accommodations • Hotels, safari lodges. Single rooms are available for an additional $995.
Program Details • Program offered 4 times per year. Session length: 18 days. Departures are scheduled in January, April, July, September. Program is targeted to mature adults. Most participants are 40–75 years of age. Participants must be 18 years or older to enroll. 14–20 participants per session. Application deadline: 60 days prior to departure. Reservations are recommended at least 4–8 months before departure.
Costs • $5995 (includes housing, all meals, books and class materials, excursions, international airfare). A $300 deposit is required.
Contact • Keith Williams, Director of Marketing, TraveLearn, PO Box 315, Lakeville, PA 18438; 800-235-9114; Fax: 717-226-9114; E-mail: travelearn@aol.com

UNIVERSITY OF DELAWARE

WINTER SESSION IN SOUTH AFRICA

General Information • Academic study program in Johannesburg, Pretoria. Excursions to Kruger National Park, Cape Town.
Learning Focus • Courses in education, history, women's studies. Instruction is offered by professors from the sponsoring institution.
Accommodations • Homestays, hotels. Meals are taken on one's own, in local restaurants.
Program Details • Program offered once per year. Session length: 5 weeks. Departures are scheduled in January. The program is open to undergraduate students. Other requirements: minimum 2.0 GPA. Application deadline: October.
Costs • $3832 (includes tuition, housing, some meals, excursions, international airfare). A $200 deposit is required.
Contact • International Programs and Special Sessions, University of Delaware, 4 Kent Way, Newark, DE 19716-1450; 888-831-4685; Fax: 302-831-6042; E-mail: studyabroad@mvs.udel.edu

TANZANIA

ALPINE ASCENTS, INTERNATIONAL

MOUNT KILIMANJARO

General Information • Wilderness/adventure program with visits to Mount Kilimanjaro, Ngorongoro Crater, Lake Manyara, Tarangire National Park. Once at the destination country, participants travel by bus, foot, land rover.

Learning Focus • Escorted travel to Shira Plateau, Marangu Route and Machame Trail. Nature observation (wildlife, jungles, coffee fields). Other activities include camping, hiking, interaction with Masai tribe. Instruction is offered by naturalists, sports professionals, guides. This program would appeal to people interested in wildlife, adventure, walking.

Accommodations • Hotels, campsites. Single rooms are available.

Program Details • Program offered once per year. Session length: 13 days. Departures are scheduled in August. Most participants are 15-64 years of age. Other requirements: good physical condition, able to walk up to eight hours per day. 7 participants per session. Reservations are recommended at least 6 months before departure.

Costs • $3595 (includes housing, some meals, group equipment, porters, guides, permits). A $500 deposit is required.

Contact • Gordon Janow, Program Coordinator, Alpine Ascents, International, 16615 Saybrook Drive, Woodinville, WA 98072; 206-788-1951; Fax: 206-788-6757; E-mail: aaiclimb@accessone.com

FORUM TRAVEL INTERNATIONAL

ROOF OF AFRICA: KILIMANJARO!

General Information • Wilderness/adventure program with visits to Mount Kilimanjaro, Ngorongoro Crater, Ruaha, Selous, Serengeti, Zanzibar, major Tanzanian/African ecosystems, cultures and peoples. Once at the destination country, participants travel by bus, foot, airplane, four-wheel drive vehicle. Program is affiliated with International Ecosystems University.

Learning Focus • Instruction in natural history, biology and ecology. Nature observation (wildlife ethology, anthropology, biology). Other activities include camping. Instruction is offered by researchers, naturalists, tribal elders. This program would appeal to people interested in natural history, biology, ecology.

Accommodations • Program-owned houses, hotels, campsites, lodges. Single rooms are available.

Program Details • Program offered 8 times per year. Session length: 8 days. Departures are scheduled throughout the year. Program is targeted to people interested in wildlife, ecology, anthropology and history. Most participants are 16-84 years of age. 6-20 participants per session. Application deadline: 2 weeks prior to departure.

Costs • $1175 (includes tuition, housing, all meals, excursions). A $300 deposit is required.

Contact • Jeannie Graves, Operations Manager, Forum Travel International, 91 Gregory Lane #21, Pleasant Hill, CA 94525; 510-671-2900; Fax: 510-671-2993; E-mail: forum@ix.netcom.com; World Wide Web: http://www.ten-io.com/forumtravel

GEO EXPEDITIONS

TANZANIA UNDER CANVAS

General Information • Nature study tour with visits to Lake Nampra National Park, Ngorongoro Crater, Serengeti National Park, Tarangire National Park, Mount Kilimanjaro, Bwindi Impenetrable Forest Reserve. Once at the destination country, participants travel by landcruiser.

Learning Focus • Instruction is offered by naturalists. This program would appeal to people interested in wildlife, ecology.

Accommodations • Hotels, campsites. Single rooms are available for an additional $450.

Program Details • Session length: 17 days. Departures are scheduled in December-March, July-October. Most participants are 30-70 years of age. Participants must be 10 years or older to enroll. 10 participants per session. Reservations are recommended at least 6 months before departure.

Costs • $3595 (includes housing, some meals, excursions). A $300 deposit is required.

Contact • David Risard, President, GEO Expeditions, PO Box 3656, Sonora, CA 95370; 800-351-5041; Fax: 209-532-1979; E-mail: geoexped@mlode.com

INTERNATIONAL BICYCLE FUND

TANZANIA: SURF TO SUMMIT

General Information • Cultural tour with visits to Lushoto, Moshi, Mount Kilimanjaro, Tanga, Zanzibar, Mount Kilimanjaro. Once at the destination country, participants travel by bus, foot, boat, bicycle.

Learning Focus • Instruction in culture, history, economics, environment and development. Escorted travel to spice plantations, villages and climb at Mount Kilimanjaro. Museum visits (history museum). Nature observation (vegetation zones from sea level to 18,000 feet). Other activities include hiking, bicycling. Instruction is offered by African studies specialists. This program would appeal to people interested in African culture, bicycling, economic development, hiking, climbing, photography.

Accommodations • Dormitories, hotels.

Program Details • Program offered once per year. Session length: 16 days. Departures are scheduled in February. Most participants are 20-60 years of age. 8 participants per session. Reservations are recommended at least 3 months before departure.

Costs • $1390 (includes housing, some meals, excursions, climb at Mount Kilimanjaro). A $300 deposit is required.
Contact • David Mozer, Director, International Bicycle Fund, 4887 Columbia Drive, S, Seattle, WA 98108; 206-767-0848; Fax: 206-767-0848; E-mail: intlbike@scn.org; World Wide Web: http://www.halcyon.com/fkroger/bike/homepage.html

JOURNEYS INTERNATIONAL, INC.

TANZANIA SELOUS SAFARI

General Information • Wilderness/adventure program with visits to Dar es Salaam, Dodoma, Morogoro, Selous, Selous-Rufiji River, Tarangire National Park, Zanzibar. Once at the destination country, participants travel by boat.
Learning Focus • Escorted travel to national parks and game reserves. Other activities include camping, hiking. Instruction is offered by Tanzanian guides. This program would appeal to people interested in wildlife, hiking, photography.
Accommodations • Hotels, campsites. Single rooms are available for an additional $300.
Program Details • Program offered 12 times per year. Session length: 8 days. Departures are scheduled throughout the year. Program is targeted to active persons interested in wildlife observation. Most participants are 25-55 years of age. Participants must be 12 years or older to enroll. Other requirements: must be in good health and physical condition. 2-10 participants per session. Application deadline: 60 days prior to departure. Reservations are recommended at least 60 days before departure.
Costs • $1950 (includes housing, some meals). A $300 deposit is required.
Contact • Michelle Gervais, Africa Sales Director, Journeys International, Inc., 4011 Jackson Road, Ann Arbor, MI 48103; 313-665-4407; Fax: 313-665-2945; E-mail: michelle@journeys-intl.com; World Wide Web: http://www.journeys-intl.com

JOURNEYS INTERNATIONAL, INC.

TANZANIA WILDLIFE WEEK

General Information • Wilderness/adventure program with visits to Kenya (Kenya (Nairobi)), Tanzania (Arusha, Lake Manyara, Ngorongoro Crater, Serengeti, Tarangire). Once at the destination country, participants travel by foot, small vehicle.
Learning Focus • Escorted travel to the plains and reserves. Museum visits (Homo habilis and zinjanthropus). Nature observation (Ngorongoro crater). Instruction is offered by Tanzanian guides. This program would appeal to people interested in wildlife, photography, nature studies.
Accommodations • Campsites, lodges. Single rooms are available for an additional $125.
Program Details • Program offered 12 times per year. Session length: 7 days. Departures are scheduled in February-December. Program is targeted to persons interested in wildlife observation. Most participants are 25-55 years of age. Participants must be 12 years or older to enroll. 2-10 participants per session. Application deadline: 60 days prior to departure. Reservations are recommended at least 60 days before departure.
Costs • $1650 (includes housing, some meals, park fees). A $300 deposit is required.
Contact • Michelle Gervais, Africa Sales Director, Journeys International, Inc., 4011 Jackson Road, Ann Arbor, MI 48103; 313-665-4407; Fax: 313-665-2945; E-mail: michelle@journeys-intl.com; World Wide Web: http://www.journeys-intl.com

MOUNTAIN MADNESS

MOUNT KILIMANJARO CLIMB AND SAFARI

General Information • Wilderness/adventure program with visits to Arusha, Mount Kilimanjaro, safari in various locations in Tanzania, national parks, game viewing areas. Once at the destination country, participants travel by bus, foot, mini-van.
Learning Focus • Escorted travel to summit of Mount Kilimanjaro. Nature observation (African wildlife safari). Other activities include camping, hiking. Instruction is offered by naturalists, sports professionals, professional mountaineering guides. This program would appeal to people interested in climbing, wildlife, hiking, photography.
Accommodations • Hotels, campsites. Single rooms are available.
Program Details • Program offered 7 times per year. Session length: 2 weeks. Departures are scheduled in January, March, June, August, September, October, December. Most participants are 16-60 years of age. Participants must be 16 years or older to enroll. Other requirements: good physical fitness. 6-10 participants per session. Reservations are recommended at least 60 days before departure.
Costs • $4195 (includes housing, some meals, excursions, guides, camp equipment). A $1000 deposit is required.
Contact • Tom Nickels, Africa Manager, Mountain Madness, 4218 Southwest Alaska Street #206, Seattle, WA 98116; 206-937-8389; Fax: 206-937-1772; E-mail: mountmad@aol.com

NATURAL HABITAT ADVENTURES

KILIMANJARO: AFRICA'S HIGHEST PEAK

General Information • Nature study tour with visits to Arusha, Mount Kilimanjaro. Once at the destination country, participants travel by foot, mini-van.
Learning Focus • Nature observation (animals en route). Other activities include camping, hiking. Instruction is offered by expedition leaders. This program would appeal to people interested in nature studies, photography, wildlife.
Accommodations • Hotels, campsites. Single rooms are available for an additional $80.
Program Details • Session length: 8 days. Departures are scheduled throughout the year. Most participants are 20-65 years of age. 6 participants per session. Reservations are recommended at least 1 year before departure.
Costs • $1470 (includes housing, all meals, excursions, park fees). A $500 deposit is required.
Contact • Planet Expeditions, Natural Habitat Adventures, 2945 Center Green Court, Suite H, Boulder, CO 80301; 800-233-2433; Fax: 303-449-3712; E-mail: nathab@worldnet.att.net

NATURAL HABITAT ADVENTURES

TOTAL TANZANIA

General Information • Nature study tour with visits to Ngorongoro Crater, Selous Game Park, Serengeti, Zanzibar. Once at the destination country, participants travel by airplane, land cruiser, land rover, or minivan.
Learning Focus • Nature observation (animals in the wild). Instruction is offered by naturalists. This program would appeal to people interested in nature studies, photography, wildlife.
Accommodations • Hotels, campsites, lodges. Single rooms are available for an additional $610.
Program Details • Session length: 15 days. Departures are scheduled throughout the year. Most participants are 20-65 years of age. Participants must be 12 years or older to enroll. 10 participants per session. Reservations are recommended at least 6-12 months before departure.
Costs • $3900 (includes housing, all meals, excursions, park fees). A $500 deposit is required.
Contact • Planet Expeditions, Natural Habitat Adventures, 2945 Center Green Court, Suite H, Boulder, CO 80301; 800-233-2433; Fax: 303-449-3712; E-mail: nathab@worldnet.att.net

UNIVERSITY OF DELAWARE

WINTER SESSION IN TANZANIA

General Information • Academic study program in Tanzania. Excursions to safari, Mweska Wildlife College, Mkomazi Park, Arusha Park, Mount Kilimanjaro, Serengeti Park.
Learning Focus • Courses in wildlife conservation. Instruction is offered by professors from the sponsoring institution.
Accommodations • Safari camps. Meals are taken as a group.
Program Details • Program offered once per year. Session length: 5 weeks. Departures are scheduled in January. The program is open to undergraduate students, graduate students, adults. Most participants are 18-21 years of age. Other requirements: minimum 2.0 GPA. 15 participants per session. Application deadline: October.
Costs • $6610 (includes tuition, housing, all meals, excursions, international airfare). A $200 deposit is required.
Contact • International Programs and Special Sessions, University of Delaware, 4 Kent Way, Newark, DE 19716-1450; 888-831-4685; Fax: 302-831-6042; E-mail: studyabroad@mvs.udel.edu

WILDLAND ADVENTURES

TANZANIA SERENGETI SAFARI

General Information • Nature study tour with visits to Arusha, Ngorongoro Crater, Serengeti. Once at the destination country, participants travel by bus, foot. Program is affiliated with East African Wildlife Society.
Learning Focus • Nature observation (African wildlife, life history). Other activities include camping, hiking. Instruction is offered by naturalists, Native Maasai. This program would appeal to people interested in photography, hiking, cultural encounters, wildlife.
Accommodations • Hotels, campsites. Single rooms are available for an additional $300.
Program Details • Program offered 8 times per year. Session length: 17 days. Departures are scheduled in May-December. Most participants are 30-60 years of age. Participants must be 12 years or older to enroll. 2-10 participants per session. Application deadline: 30 days prior to departure. Reservations are recommended at least 3-6 months before departure.
Costs • $2500 (includes housing, all meals, excursions, complete pre-departure dossier). A $300 deposit is required.
Contact • Wildland Adventures, 3516 Northeast 155th Street, Seattle, WA 98155; 800-345-4453; Fax: 206-363-6615; E-mail: wildadve@aol.com; World Wide Web: http://www.wildland.com

TUNISIA

ARCHAEOLOGICAL TOURS

TUNISIA

General Information • Archaeological tour with visits to Ain Draham, Matmata, Sbeitla, Sousse, Tozeur, Tunis, Cathage, Kerkouane, Thuburbo Majus, Zaghouan, Dougga ruins, Bulla Regia, Maktar, Nefta, Douz, Kariouan. Once at the destination country, participants travel by bus.

Learning Focus • Escorted travel to major Roman, Byzantine, and Islamic sites. Museum visits (historical landmarks). Attendance at performances (dance and music shows). Instruction is offered by professors, historians. This program would appeal to people interested in history, archaeology.

Accommodations • Hotels. Single rooms are available for an additional $465.

Program Details • Program offered once per year. Session length: 15 days. Departures are scheduled in May. Program is targeted to adults. Most participants are 30–80 years of age. 22 participants per session. Application deadline: 1 month prior to departure.

Costs • $2820 (includes housing, some meals, excursions). A $500 deposit is required.

Contact • Archaeological Tours, 271 Madison Avenue, Suite 904, New York, NY 10016; 212-986-3054; Fax: 212-370-1561

COUNCIL ON INTERNATIONAL EDUCATIONAL EXCHANGE

COUNCIL STUDY CENTER IN TUNISIA

General Information • Academic study program in Monastir. Classes are held on the campus of National Heritage Institute. Excursions to El Jem, Kairouan, Dougga, Sbeitla, Bulla Regia.

Learning Focus • Courses in art history, archaeology. Instruction is offered by local teachers.

Program Details • Program offered once per year. Session length: 6 weeks. Departures are scheduled in May. The program is open to undergraduate students, graduate students, adults. Most participants are 20–25 years of age. Other requirements: minimum 2.75 GPA and one semester of college studies. 10 participants per session. Application deadline: April 1.

Costs • $2995 (includes tuition, housing, some meals, International Student Identification card). Application fee: $30. A $300 deposit is required.

Contact • Council on International Educational Exchange, College and University Division, 205 East 42nd Street, New York, NY 10017-5706; 888-268-6245; Fax: 212-822-2699; E-mail: weuropereg@ciee.org; World Wide Web: http://www.ciee.org

INTERNATIONAL BICYCLE FUND

TUNISIA: EDEN TO OASIS

General Information • Cultural tour with visits to Cap Bon, Djerba, Douz, Medenine, Tozeur, Tunis, Ghorfas. Once at the destination country, participants travel by train, foot, airplane, bicycle.

Learning Focus • Instruction in culture, history, economics and environment. Escorted travel to historic and cultural sites. Museum visits (culture and history museums). Nature observation (limestone formations and desert). Other activities include bicycling. Instruction is offered by African studies specialists. This program would appeal to people interested in North African culture, bicycling, Mediterranean history, economic development, photography.

Accommodations • Hotels. Single rooms are available for an additional $100.

Program Details • Program offered once per year. Session length: 16 days. Departures are scheduled in April. Most participants are 20–60 years of age. 8 participants per session. Reservations are recommended at least 3 months before departure.

Costs • $1190 (includes housing, some meals, excursions). A $300 deposit is required.

Contact • David Mozer, Director, International Bicycle Fund, 4887 Columbia Drive, S, Seattle, WA 98108; 206-767-0848; Fax: 206-767-0848; E-mail: intlbike@scn.org; World Wide Web: http://www.halcyon.com/fkroger/bike/homepage.html

INTERNATIONAL BICYCLE FUND

TUNISIA: HISTORIC NORTH

General Information • Cultural tour with visits to El Jem, El Kef, Kairouan, Tabarca, Teboursouk, Tunis, Dougga ruins, Bella Regia ruins, Kairouan, El Jem Amphitheater. Once at the destination country, participants travel by bus, foot, bicycle.

Learning Focus • Instruction in culture, history, economics, environment and development. Escorted travel to several historic sites. Museum visits (Bando [National Museum]). Nature observation (cork forests, sahel). Other activities include bicycling. Instruction is offered by African studies specialists. This program would appeal to people interested in North African culture, bicycling, Mediterranean history, economic development, photography, archaeology, Islam.

Accommodations • Homestays, hotels. Single rooms are available for an additional $100.

Program Details • Program offered once per year. Session length: 14 days. Departures are scheduled in April. Most participants are 20–60 years of age. 8 participants per session. Reservations are recommended at least 3 months before departure.

Costs • $1090 (includes housing, some meals, excursions). A $300 deposit is required.

Contact • David Mozer, Director, International Bicycle Fund, 4887 Columbia Drive, S, Seattle, WA 98108; 206-767-0848; Fax: 206-767-0848; E-mail: intlbike@scn.org; World Wide Web: http://www.halcyon.com/fkroger/bike/homepage.html

RUSSIAN AND EAST EUROPEAN PARTNERSHIPS

TUNISIAN LANGUAGE AND CULTURAL IMMERSION PROGRAM

General Information • Language study program in Tunis. Classes are held on the campus of Center of International Languages, University of Letters, Arts and Human Sciences (Tunis I)–Bourgiba Institute of Modern Languages. Excursions to Carthage, Oases of Tozeur and Nefta, Sousse, Sidi Bou Said, Safax.

Learning Focus • Courses in Arabic language, Farsi language, French language, North African history, North African culture and art. Instruction is offered by professors from the sponsoring institution and local teachers.

Accommodations • Homestays, locally-rented apartments. Single rooms are available. Meals are taken on one's own, with host family, in local restaurants, in residences.

Program Details • Program offered 11 times per year. Session length: 4 or more weeks. Departures are scheduled in January–November. The program is open to undergraduate students, graduate students, adults. Most participants are 18 years of age and older. Other requirements: in good health and 18 or older unless chaperoned by an adult. 6 participants per session. Application deadline: 45 days prior to departure.

Costs • $4150 (includes tuition, housing, some meals, books and class materials, excursions, international airfare, local transportation, airport transfers). A $1500 deposit is required.

Contact • Kenneth Fortune, President, Russian and East European Partnerships, PO Box 227, Fineview, NY 13640; 888-873-7337; Fax: 800-910-1777; E-mail: reep@fox.nstn.ca

UGANDA

CHEESEMANS' ECOLOGY/BIRDING

AFRICA: AN IN-DEPTH SAFARI TO UGANDA

General Information • Nature study tour with visits to Ugandan National parks and reserves, Murchison Falls National Park, Queen Elizabeth National Park. Once at the destination country, participants travel by foot, boat, land cruiser.
Learning Focus • Nature observation (field observations of birds, mammals, reptiles). Instruction is offered by researchers, naturalists, scientists. This program would appeal to people interested in photography, bird watching.
Accommodations • Hotels, lodges and tented camps. Single rooms are available for an additional $35 per day.
Program Details • Program offered once per year. Session length: 21 days. Departures are scheduled in July. Program is targeted to wildlife enthusiasts. Most participants are 25-65 years of age. Participants must be 11 years or older to enroll. Other requirements: non-smokers only. 15 participants per session.
Costs • $5730. A $300 deposit is required.
Contact • Gail Cheeseman, Co-Owner, Cheesemans' Ecology/Birding, 20800 Kittredge Road, Saratoga, CA 95070; 800-527-5330; Fax: 408-741-0358; E-mail: cheesemans@aol.com; World Wide Web: http://www.cheesemans.com

INTERNATIONAL BICYCLE FUND

UGANDA: PEARL OF AFRICA

General Information • Cultural tour with visits to Fort Portal, Kabale, Kampala, Kesse, Muko, Rukungiri. Once at the destination country, participants travel by bus, foot, bicycle.
Learning Focus • Instruction in culture, history, economics, environment and development. Escorted travel to Kibale National Park, development projects, tea factory and a Catholic mission. Museum visits (National Museum). Nature observation (Kibale National Park, Queen Elizabeth National Park, chimpanzees, baboons, monkeys, water bucks, impalas). Other activities include bicycling. Instruction is offered by African Studies specialists. This program would appeal to people interested in African culture, bicycling, economic development, wildlife, primates, photography.
Accommodations • Homestays, dormitories, hotels.
Program Details • Program offered once per year. Session length: 15 days. Departures are scheduled in January. Most participants are 20-60 years of age. 8 participants per session. Reservations are recommended at least 3 months before departure.
Costs • $990 (includes housing, some meals, excursions). A $300 deposit is required.
Contact • David Mozer, Director, International Bicycle Fund, 4887 Columbia Drive, S, Seattle, WA 98108; 206-767-0848; Fax: 206-767-0848; E-mail: intlbike@scn.org; World Wide Web: http://www.halcyon.com/fkroger/bike/homepage.html

JOURNEYS INTERNATIONAL, INC.

UGANDA GORILLA VIEWING

General Information • Wilderness/adventure program with visits to Entebbe, Kampala, Mbarara, Nuwenzoria, Kibale National Forest, Queen Elizabeth Falls, Murchison Falls. Once at the destination country, participants travel by foot, hiking.
Learning Focus • Escorted travel to national parks and wildlife reserves. Other activities include camping, hiking. Instruction is offered by Ugandan guides. This program would appeal to people interested in wildlife, hiking, photography.
Accommodations • Hotels, campsites. Single rooms are available for an additional $150.
Program Details • Session length: 6 days. Departures are scheduled throughout the year. Program is targeted to active persons interested in wildlife observation. Most participants are 25-55 years of age. Participants must be 12 years or older to enroll. Other requirements: must be in good health and physical condition. 2-10 participants per session. Application deadline: 60 days prior to departure. Reservations are recommended at least 60 days before departure.
Costs • $2095 (includes housing, some meals, park fees). A $300 deposit is required.
Contact • Michelle Gervais, Africa Sales Director, Journeys International, Inc., 4011 Jackson Road, Ann Arbor, MI 48103; 313-665-4407; Fax: 313-665-2945; E-mail: michelle@journeys-intl.com; World Wide Web: http://www.journeys-intl.com

NATURAL HABITAT ADVENTURES

PRIMATE WATCH

General Information • Nature study tour with visits to Bwindi, Entebbe, Kibale, Queen Elizabeth National Park, a gorilla family group. Once at the destination country, participants travel by foot, minivan or land cruiser. Program is affiliated with Dian Fossey Gorilla Fund.
Learning Focus • Instruction in gorilla behavior, African wildlife. Nature observation (mountain gorilla, chimpanzee, colobus monkey, buffalo, hippo, elephant, and bird life). Other activities include hiking. Instruction is offered by researchers, naturalists, photographers. This program would appeal to people interested in nature studies, photography, wildlife.
Accommodations • Hotels, campsites. Single rooms are available for an additional $395.
Program Details • Program offered 8 times per year. Session length: 11 days. Departures are scheduled in

January–October. 9 participants per session. Reservations are recommended at least 6–12 months before departure.
Costs • $4795 (includes housing, all meals, all national park and permit fees, membership in the Flying Doctor Society).
Contact • Natural Habitat Adventures, 2945 Center Green Court, Suite H, Boulder, CO 80301; 800-543-8917; Fax: 303-449-3712; E-mail: nathab@worldnet.att.net

 UNIVERSITY OF FLORIDA

MAKERERE UNIVERSITY, BIOLOGICAL FIELD STATION, KIBALE FOREST, UGANDA

General Information • Academic study program in Makerere. Classes are held on the campus of Makerere University. Excursions to Kibale Forest.
Learning Focus • Courses in biology, conservation, ecology. Instruction is offered by professors from the sponsoring institution and local teachers.
Accommodations • Dormitories, field stations. Meals are taken as a group, in central dining facility.
Program Details • Program offered once per year. Session length: 8 weeks. Departures are scheduled in June. The program is open to undergraduate students, graduate students, adults, faculty. Most participants are 20–35 years of age. Other requirements: completed junior year and two years in biological subjects. 10 participants per session. Application deadline: March 15.
Costs • $2900 (includes tuition, housing, all meals, excursions, orientation). Application fee: $200.
Contact • Overseas Studies, University of Florida, 123 Tigert Hall, PO Box 113225, Gainesville, FL 32611-3225; 352-392-5206; Fax: 352-392-5575; E-mail: overseas@nervm.nerdc.ufl.edu

ZAMBIA

JOURNEYS INTERNATIONAL, INC.

THE WILDERNESS ADVENTURE: FIFTEEN-DAY ZAMBIA SAFARI

General Information • Wilderness/adventure program with visits to Zambia (Kariba Lake, Livingstone, Lusaka, Zambezi River), Zimbabwe (Victoria Falls).

Learning Focus • Escorted travel to national parks. Other activities include camping, canoeing. Instruction is offered by a professional English-speaking safari guide. This program would appeal to people interested in culture, photography, wilderness, wildlife, nature studies.

Accommodations • Campsites.

Program Details • Program offered 8 times per year. Session length: 15 days. Departures are scheduled in April–November. Program is targeted to persons interested in nature. Most participants are 25–55 years of age. Participants must be 12 years or older to enroll. 6–12 participants per session. Application deadline: 60 days prior to departure.

Costs • $1875 (includes housing, some meals). A $300 deposit is required.

Contact • Michelle Gervais, Africa Sales Director, Journeys International, Inc., 4011 Jackson Road, Ann Arbor, MI 48103; 313-665-4407; Fax: 313-665-2945; E-mail: michelle@journeys-intl.com; World Wide Web: http://www.journeys-intl.com

NATURAL HABITAT ADVENTURES

UNTOUCHED ZAMBIA

General Information • Nature study tour with visits to Kapisha Hot Springs, Kasanka, South and North Luangwe. Once at the destination country, participants travel by foot, boat, land rover.

Learning Focus • Nature observation (animals in the wild). Instruction is offered by naturalists. This program would appeal to people interested in nature studies, photography, wildlife.

Accommodations • Hotels, campsites, lodges. Single rooms are available for an additional $400.

Program Details • Session length: 15 days. Departures are scheduled in July–October. Most participants are 20–65 years of age. 6 participants per session. Reservations are recommended at least 1 year before departure.

Costs • $3200 (includes housing, all meals, excursions, park fees). A $500 deposit is required.

Contact • Planet Expeditions, Natural Habitat Adventures, 2945 Center Green Court, Suite H, Boulder, CO 80301; 800-233-2433; Fax: 303-449-3712; E-mail: nathab@worldnet.att.net

ZIMBABWE

ARCHAEOLOGICAL TOURS

ZIMBABWE

General Information • Archaeological tour with visits to Bulawayo, Harare, Hwange National Park, Mashvingo, Nyanga Hills, Victoria Falls, Great Zimbabwe, caves, archaeological sites, game drives. Once at the destination country, participants travel by bus.

Learning Focus • Museum visits (Harare, Mutare). Attendance at performances (dance and music). Nature observation (safari, Victoria Falls). Instruction is offered by professors, historians. This program would appeal to people interested in history, nature studies, archaeology.

Accommodations • Hotels. Single rooms are available for an additional $510.

Program Details • Program offered once per year. Session length: 18 days. Departures are scheduled in April. Most participants are 30–80 years of age. 20 participants per session. Application deadline: 1 month prior to departure.

Costs • $5790 (includes housing, some meals, excursions, international airfare). A $500 deposit is required.

Contact • Archaeological Tours, 271 Madison Avenue, Suite 904, New York, NY 10016; 212-986-3054; Fax: 212-370-1561

INTERNATIONAL BICYCLE FUND

ZIMBABWE: MASHONALAND SOJOURN

General Information • Cultural tour with visits to Birchenough Bridge, Great Zimbabwe, Harare, Nyanga, Rusape, Vumba. Once at the destination country, participants travel by bus, foot, bicycle.

Learning Focus • Instruction in culture, history, economics, environment and development. Escorted travel to historic sites, farms, schools and development projects. Museum visits (National Gallery, National Archives). Nature observation (land use patterns, wildlife, vegetation zones). Other activities include bicycling. Instruction is offered by African studies specialists. This program would appeal to people interested in African culture, bicycling, economic development, wildlife, photography.

Accommodations • Homestays, dormitories, hotels.

Program Details • Program offered 2 times per year. Session length: 15 days. Departures are scheduled in June, July. Most participants are 18–60 years of age. 8 participants per session. Reservations are recommended at least 3 months before departure.

Costs • $1090 (includes housing, some meals, excursions). A $300 deposit is required.

Contact • David Mozer, Director, International Bicycle Fund, 4887 Columbia Drive, S, Seattle, WA 98108; 206-767-0848; Fax: 206-767-0848; E-mail: intlbike@scn.org; World Wide Web: http://www.halcyon.com/fkroger/bike/homepage.html

INTERNATIONAL BICYCLE FUND

ZIMBABWE: MATABELELAND SOJOURN

General Information • Cultural tour with visits to Balawayo, Binga, Harare, Hwange National Park, Matopos, Victoria Falls, Victoria Falls. Once at the destination country, participants travel by train, bus, foot, boat, bicycle, canoe or raft.

Learning Focus • Instruction in culture, history, economics, environment and development. Escorted travel to ruins, factories, a training centerand a village. Museum visits (Nature History Museum, galleries). Attendance at performances (music and dance). Nature observation (wildlife, inselberg geology). Other activities include canoeing, rafting, bicycling. Instruction is offered by African studies specialists. This program would appeal to people interested in African culture, bicycling, economic and social development, wildlife, photography.

Accommodations • Homestays, dormitories, hotels.

Program Details • Program offered 2 times per year. Session length: 14 days. Departures are scheduled in July, August. Most participants are 18–60 years of age. 8 participants per session. Reservations are recommended at least 3 months before departure.

Costs • $1290 (includes housing, some meals, excursions). A $300 deposit is required.

Contact • David Mozer, Director, International Bicycle Fund, 4887 Columbia Drive, S, Seattle, WA 98108; 206-767-0848; Fax: 206-767-0848; E-mail: intlbike@scn.org; World Wide Web: http://www.halcyon.com/fkroger/bike/homepage.html

JOURNEYS INTERNATIONAL, INC.

THE ZIMBABWE EXPLORER

General Information • Wilderness/adventure program with visits to Harare, Hwange, Matopos, Victoria Falls, Zambezi River. Once at the destination country, participants travel by small vehicle.

Learning Focus • Escorted travel to national parks and game reserves. Other activities include camping, rafting. Instruction is offered by professional English-speaking guides. This program would appeal to people interested in wildlife, photography, nature studies.

Accommodations • Hotels, campsites.

Program Details • Program offered 10 times per year. Session length: 15 days. Departures are scheduled in March–December. Most participants are 30–65 years of age. Participants must be 12 years or older to enroll. 6–12 participants per session. Application deadline: 60 days prior to departure. Reservations are recommended at least 60 days before departure.

Costs • $2175 (includes housing, some meals, park fees). A $300 deposit is required.

Contact • Michelle Gervais, Africa Sales Director, Journeys International, Inc., 4011 Jackson Road, Ann Arbor, MI 48103; 313-665-4407; Fax: 313-665-2945; E-mail: michelle@journeys-intl.com; World Wide Web: http://www.journeys-intl.com

NATURAL HABITAT ADVENTURES

ZIMBABWE ACTIVE SAFARI

General Information • Nature study tour with visits to Chizarira, Hwange National Park, Lake Kanbo, Victoria Falls. Once at the destination country, participants travel by foot, airplane, land rover.
Learning Focus • Nature observation (animals in the wild). Instruction is offered by naturalists. This program would appeal to people interested in nature studies, photography, wildlife.
Accommodations • Hotels, campsites, lodges. Single rooms are available for an additional $250.
Program Details • Program offered 9 times per year. Session length: 13 days. Departures are scheduled in April–December. Most participants are 20–65 years of age. Other requirements: maximum age of 70. 7 participants per session. Reservations are recommended at least 1 year before departure.
Costs • $3200 (includes housing, all meals, excursions, park fees). A $500 deposit is required.
Contact • Planet Expeditions, Natural Habitat Adventures, 2945 Center Green Court, Suite H, Boulder, CO 80301; 800-233-2433; Fax: 303-449-3712; E-mail: nathab@worldnet.att.net

ROCKLAND COMMUNITY COLLEGE

ART IN AFRICA

General Information • Academic study program in Harare. Excursions to Harare, Victoria Falls.
Learning Focus • Courses in art history, photography. Instruction is offered by professors from the sponsoring institution.
Accommodations • Hotels. Single rooms are available. Meals are taken on one's own, in local restaurants.
Program Details • Program offered once per year. Session length: 2 or more weeks. Departures are scheduled in June. The program is open to undergraduate students, adults, professional artists. Most participants are 18–65 years of age. 15 participants per session. Application deadline: April 15.
Costs • $2600 (includes tuition, housing, some meals, excursions, international airfare). A $200 deposit is required.
Contact • Jody Dudderar, Coordinator, Study Abroad, Rockland Community College, Suffern, NY 10907; 914-574-4205; Fax: 914-574-4423; E-mail: jdudderar@sunyrockland.edu

SYRACUSE UNIVERSITY

LAW IN ZIMBABWE

General Information • Internship program in Harare. Classes are held on the campus of University of Zimbabwe. Excursions to Great Zimbabwe.
Learning Focus • Courses in legal studies. Instruction is offered by professors from the sponsoring institution.
Accommodations • Dormitories. Single rooms are available. Meals are taken as a group, in residences.
Program Details • Program offered once per year. Session length: 7 weeks. Departures are scheduled in June. The program is open to graduate students. Most participants are 23–35 years of age. Other requirements: completion of one year of law school. 15 participants per session. Application deadline: February 15.
Costs • $5415 (includes tuition, housing, all meals, books and class materials, excursions). Application fee: $40. A $350 deposit is required.
Contact • Ms. Daisy Fried, Associate Director, Syracuse University, 119 Euclid Avenue, Syracuse, NY 13244; 315-443-9419; Fax: 315-443-4593; E-mail: dsfried@summon3.syr.edu; World Wide Web: http://sumweb.syr.edu/dipa/dipa9.htm

WILDLAND ADVENTURES

ZIMBABWE ZAMBEZI SAFARI

General Information • Nature study tour with visits to Hwange, Victoria Falls, Hwange National Park, Victoria Falls, Lake Kariba, Mana Pools. Once at the destination country, participants travel by bus, foot, boat, airplane.
Learning Focus • Escorted travel to national parks. Nature observation (African wildlife). Instruction is offered by naturalists. This program would appeal to people interested in photography, wildlife.
Accommodations • Hotels, campsites. Single rooms are available.
Program Details • Program offered 20 times per year. Session length: 12 days. Departures are scheduled throughout the year. Most participants are 30–60 years of age. Participants must be 8 years or older to enroll. 8 participants per session. Application deadline: 30 days prior to departure. Reservations are recommended at least 3–6 months before departure.
Costs • $1950 (includes housing, some meals, excursions, complete pre-departure dossier). A $300 deposit is required.
Contact • Wildland Adventures, 3516 Northeast 155th Street, Seattle, WA 98155; 800-345-4453; Fax: 206-363-6615; E-mail: wildadve@aol.com; World Wide Web: http://www.wildland.com

ARCTIC AND ANTARCTIC

REGIONAL

Antarctica
Falkland Islands
Greenland
South Sandwich Islands

REGIONAL

ALPINE ASCENTS, INTERNATIONAL

MOUNT GUNNBJORNSFJELD

General Information • Mountain climbing tour with visits to Greenland (Mount Gunnbjornsfjeld). Once at the destination country, participants travel by bus, foot.
Learning Focus • Instruction in mountain climbing. Nature observation (rivers, glaciers, fjords). Other activities include camping, hiking. Instruction is offered by sports professionals. This program would appeal to people interested in mountain climbing.
Accommodations • Hotels, campsites. Single rooms are available.
Program Details • Program offered 2 times per year. Session length: 15 days. Departures are scheduled in June. Program is targeted to intermediate/advanced mountain climbers. Reservations are recommended at least 6 months before departure.
Costs • $12,000 (includes housing, some meals, group equipment).
Contact • Gordon Janow, Program Coordinator, Alpine Ascents, International, 16615 Saybrook Drive, Woodinville, WA 98072; 206-788-1951; Fax: 206-788-6757; E-mail: aaiclimb@ascentone.com

ALPINE ASCENTS, INTERNATIONAL

MOUNT VINSON EXPEDITION

General Information • Mountain climbing tour with visits to Antarctica (Mount Vinson); excursions to Punta Arenas. Once at the destination country, participants travel by foot, airplane.
Learning Focus • Instruction in mountain climbing. Escorted travel to Patriot Hills and Branscomb Glacier. Nature observation (Ellsworth Mountains). Other activities include camping, hiking. Instruction is offered by sports professionals. This program would appeal to people interested in mountain climbing.
Accommodations • Hotels, campsites. Single rooms are available.
Program Details • Program offered once per year. Session length: 15 days. Departures are scheduled in January. Program is targeted to mountain climbers. Other requirements: excellent physical condition. Reservations are recommended at least 6 months before departure.
Costs • $25,750 (includes housing, some meals, group equipment, guides, fees). A $5000 deposit is required.
Contact • Gordon Janow, Program Coordinator, Alpine Ascents, International, 16615 Saybrook Drive, Woodinville, WA 98072; 206-788-1951; Fax: 206-788-6757

COUNTRY WALKERS

ARCTIC GARDEN

General Information • Cultural, gourmet cooking, nature study and walking tour with visits to Canada (Iqaluit); excursions to Lake Harbor, Livingstone Falls. Once at the destination country, participants travel by foot, boat, airplane.
Learning Focus • Escorted travel to Cascade Falls and Soper Falls. Nature observation (falcons, horned lark, caribou). Other activities include walking. Instruction is offered by professors, researchers, naturalists, historians. This program would appeal to people interested in walking, nature studies, food and wine.
Accommodations • Hotels. Single rooms are available for an additional $300–$600.
Program Details • Program offered 2 times per year. Session length: 8 days. Departures are scheduled in July, August. Program is targeted to adults 35 to 65 years old. Most participants are 35–65 years of age. Participants must be 18 years or older to enroll. 18 participants per session. Reservations are recommended at least 5–6 months before departure.
Costs • $2300 (includes housing, all meals, excursions). A $400 deposit is required.
Contact • Heather Kellingbeck, Vice President, Country Walkers, PO Box 180, Waterbury, VT 05176; 800-464-9255; Fax: 802-244-5661; E-mail: ctrywalk@aol.com

JOURNEYS INTERNATIONAL, INC.

ANTARCTICA WILDLIFE CRUISE

General Information • Wilderness/adventure program with visits to Antarctica. Once at the destination country, participants travel by foot, boat.
Learning Focus • Nature observation (penguins, fur seals). Instruction is offered by naturalists. This program would appeal to people interested in photography, wildlife, nature studies.
Accommodations • Boat. Single rooms are available.
Program Details • Program offered 11 times per year. Session length: 11 days. Departures are scheduled in November, January, February. Most participants are 15–75 years of age. Reservations are recommended at least 60 days before departure.
Costs • $4865 (includes housing, some meals, excursions). A $300 deposit is required.
Contact • Michelle Gervais, Latin America Sales Director, Journeys International, Inc., 4011 Jackson Road, Ann Arbor, MI 48103; 313-665-4407; Fax: 313-665-2945; E-mail: michelle@journeys-intl.com; World Wide Web: http://www.journeys-intl.com

MARINE EXPEDITIONS

EXPEDITION ANTARCTICA

General Information • Wilderness/adventure program with visits to Antarctica (Antarctic Peninsula, South Shetland Islands), Argentina (Ushuaia), Chile (Santiago); excursions to penguin rookeries, seal colonies and bases in Antarctica. Once at the destination country, participants travel by boat.
Learning Focus • Instruction in history, biology and goegraphy. Field research in history, biology and geography. Nature observation (glaciers, whales, penguins, seals). Other activities include hiking. Instruction is offered by naturalists, historians, scientists. This program would appeal to people interested in nature studies, photography, ornithology.
Accommodations • Boat. Single rooms are available for an additional $1250.
Program Details • Program offered 40 times per year. Session length: 2 weeks. Departures are scheduled in November–March. Most participants are 20–90 years of age. Participants must be 10 years or older to enroll. 80

participants per session. Reservations are recommended at least 6 months before departure.
Costs • $2500 (includes tuition, housing, all meals, excursions, international airfare). A $500 deposit is required.
Contact • Anne Lex, Sales Manager, Marine Expeditions, 13 Hazelton Avenue, Toronto, ON M5R 2E1, Canada; 800-263-9147; Fax: 416-964-9069

MARINE EXPEDITIONS

EXPEDITION ANTARCTICA AND FALKLANDS

General Information • Wilderness/adventure program with visits to Antarctica (Antarctic Peninsula, South Shetland Islands), Argentina (Ushuaia), Chile (Santiago), Falkland Islands (Malvinas); excursions to penguin rookeries, seal colonies and bases in Antarctica. Once at the destination country, participants travel by boat.
Learning Focus • Instruction in history, geology and biology. Field research in history, geology and biology. Nature observation (glaciers, whales, penguins, seals). Other activities include hiking. Instruction is offered by naturalists, historians, scientists. This program would appeal to people interested in nature studies, photography, ornithology.
Accommodations • Boat. Single rooms are available for an additional $1750.
Program Details • Program offered 4 times per year. Session length: 3 weeks. Departures are scheduled in March. Most participants are 20–90 years of age. Participants must be 10 years or older to enroll. 80 participants per session. Reservations are recommended at least 6 months before departure.
Costs • $3500 (includes tuition, housing, all meals, excursions, international airfare). A $500 deposit is required.
Contact • Anne Lex, Sales Manager, Marine Expeditions, 13 Hazelton Avenue, Toronto, ON M5R 2E1, Canada; 800-263-9147; Fax: 416-964-9069

MARINE EXPEDITIONS

EXPEDITION ANTARCTICA, FALKLANDS, AND SOUTH GEORGIA

General Information • Wilderness/adventure program with visits to Antarctica (Antarctic Peninsula, South Shetland Islands), Falkland Islands (Malvinas), South Georgia and the South Sandwich Islands; excursions to penguin rookeries, seal colonies and research bases. Once at the destination country, participants travel by boat.
Learning Focus • Instruction in history, geology and biology. Field research in history, geology and biology. Nature observation (glaciers, whales, penguins, seals). Other activities include hiking. Instruction is offered by naturalists, historians, scientists. This program would appeal to people interested in nature studies, photography, ornithology.
Accommodations • Boat. Single rooms are available for an additional $1750.
Program Details • Program offered 4 times per year. Session length: 3 weeks. Departures are scheduled in November. Most participants are 20–90 years of age. Participants must be 10 years or older to enroll. 80 participants per session. Reservations are recommended at least 6 months before departure.
Costs • $3500 (includes tuition, housing, all meals, excursions, international airfare). A $500 deposit is required.
Contact • Anne Lex, Sales Manager, Marine Expeditions, 13 Hazelton Avenue, Toronto, ON M5R 2E1, Canada; 800-263-9147; Fax: 416-964-9069

MARINE EXPEDITIONS

GREENLAND, BAFFIN, AND CHURCHILL

General Information • Wilderness/adventure program with visits to Canada (Baffin Island, Churchill), Greenland; excursions to archaeological sites, areas of high wildlife concentration. Once at the destination country, participants travel by boat.
Learning Focus • Instruction in history, ornithology and biology. Field research in history, ornithology and biology. Escorted travel to Panghirtung, Kekerten Island and Digges Cove. Nature observation (whales, fjörds, bergs, caribou, falcons, foxes, walruses, polar bears). Other activities include hiking. Instruction is offered by naturalists, historians, scientists. This program would appeal to people interested in nature studies, photography, ornithology.
Accommodations • Boat. Single rooms are available.
Program Details • Program offered 2 times per year. Session length: 2 weeks. Departures are scheduled in July, August. Most participants are 20–90 years of age. Participants must be 10 years or older to enroll. 80 participants per session.
Costs • $1995 (includes tuition, housing, all meals, excursions, international airfare). A $500 deposit is required.
Contact • Anne Lex, Sales Manager, Marine Expeditions, 13 Hazelton Avenue, Toronto, ON M5R 2E1, Canada; 800-263-9147; Fax: 416-964-9069

MARINE EXPEDITIONS

ICELAND AND GREENLAND

General Information • Wilderness/adventure program with visits to Greenland, Iceland; excursions to archaeological sites, areas of high wildlife concentration. Once at the destination country, participants travel by boat.
Learning Focus • Instruction in history, ornithology and biology. Field research in history, ornithology and biology. Escorted travel to Breidafjördur Islands, Nanortalik and Herjolfsnaes. Nature observation (whales, seabirds, seals, hot springs). Other activities include hiking. Instruction is offered by naturalists, historians, scientists. This program would appeal to people interested in nature studies, photography, ornithology.
Accommodations • Boat. Single rooms are available.
Program Details • Program offered once per year. Session length: 2 weeks. Departures are scheduled in July. Most participants are 20–90 years of age. Participants must be 10 years or older to enroll. 80 participants per session. Reservations are recommended at least 6 months before departure.
Costs • $1995 (includes tuition, housing, all meals, excursions, international airfare). A $500 deposit is required.
Contact • Anne Lex, Sales Manager, Marine Expeditions, 13 Hazelton Avenue, Toronto, ON M5R 2E1, Canada; 800-263-9147; Fax: 416-964-9069

MARINE EXPEDITIONS

THE NORTHWEST PASSAGE

General Information • Wilderness/adventure program with visits to Canada (Baffin Island, Canadian Arctic), Greenland; excursions to archaeological sites, areas of high wildlife concentration. Once at the destination country, participants travel by boat.
Learning Focus • Instruction in history, geology and ornithology. Field research in history, geology and ornithology. Escorted travel to Sondre Stromfjord, Baffin Island and Resolute Bay. Nature observation (glaciers, fjords, seabirds, whales). Other activities include hiking. Instruction is offered by naturalists, historians, scientists. This program would appeal to people interested in nature studies, photography, ornithology.
Accommodations • Boat. Single rooms are available.
Program Details • Program offered 3 times per year. Session length: 1 week. Departures are scheduled in July, August. Most participants are 20–90 years of age. Participants must be 10 years or older to enroll. 80 participants per session. Reservations are recommended at least 6 months before departure.
Costs • $1995 (includes tuition, housing, all meals, excursions, international airfare). A $500 deposit is required.
Contact • Anne Lex, Sales Manager, Marine Expeditions, 13 Hazelton Avenue, Toronto, ON M5R 2E1, Canada; 800-263-9147; Fax: 416-964-9069

NATURAL HABITAT ADVENTURES

ANTARCTICA

General Information • Nature study tour with visits to Antarctica (Antarctic Peninsula), Argentina (Ushuaia), Chile (Santiago). Once at the destination country, participants travel by boat.
Learning Focus • Instruction in Antarctic wildlife. Escorted travel to research stations, Antarctic Peninsula, islands. Nature observation (seals, whales, penguins). Instruction is offered by researchers, naturalists, photographers. This program would appeal to people interested in nature studies, photography, wildlife.
Accommodations • Hotels, boat. Single rooms are available.
Program Details • Program offered once per year. Session length: 14 days. Departures are scheduled in January. 98 participants per session. Reservations are recommended at least 6–12 months before departure.
Costs • $5665–$7465 (includes housing, some meals, excursions, shore excursions, transfers in Ushuaia and Santiago).
Contact • Natural Habitat Adventures, 2945 Center Green Court, Suite H, Boulder, CO 80301; 800-543-8917; Fax: 303-449-3712; E-mail: nathab@worldnet.att.net

NATURAL HABITAT ADVENTURES

ARCTIC WATCH

General Information • Nature study tour with visits to Canada (Calgary, Somerset Island). Once at the destination country, participants travel by airplane, all-terrain vehicle.
Learning Focus • Nature observation (narwhals, polar bears, muskox, caribou and arctic fox). Instruction is offered by researchers, naturalists, scientists, Inuits. This program would appeal to people interested in nature studies, photography, wildlife.
Accommodations • Wilderness lodge. Single rooms are available.
Program Details • Program offered 3 times per year. Session length: 8 days. Departures are scheduled in July. Participants must be 14 years or older to enroll. Reservations are recommended at least 6–12 months before departure.
Costs • Contact sponsor for information. A $500 deposit is required.
Contact • Planet Expeditions, Natural Habitat Adventures, 2945 Center Green Court, Suite H, Boulder, CO 80301; 800-233-2433; Fax: 303-449-3712; E-mail: nathab@worldnet.att.net

PHOTO ADVENTURE TOURS

ICELAND AND GREENLAND

General Information • Photography tour with visits to Greenland (Angmagssalik, Kulusuk), Iceland (Blue Lagoon, Geysir, Hekla, Jokulsarlon, Keflavik, Reykjavik, Skaftafell). Once at the destination country, participants travel by bus, foot, boat, airplane, helicopter.
Learning Focus • Instruction in photography. Escorted travel to Iceland and Greenland. Museum visits (folk museum in Skogar). Nature observation (waterfalls, geysers, glaciers, birds and wildlife, hot springs, geologic formations). Other activities include hiking. Instruction is offered by naturalists, artists, historians, photographers. This program would appeal to people interested in photography, geology, adventure, hiking, ornithology.
Accommodations • Hotels. Single rooms are available for an additional $615.
Program Details • Program offered once per year. Session length: 10 days. Departures are scheduled in August. Most participants are 18–80 years of age. Participants must be 18 years or older to enroll. Other requirements: a positive attitude and an open mind. 12 participants per session. Application deadline: 60 days prior to departure. Reservations are recommended at least 60 days before departure.
Costs • $4494 (includes housing, all meals, excursions, international airfare, round-trip airfare to Reykjavik and Kulusuk, round-trip helicopter from Kulusuk and Angmagssalik). A $400 deposit is required.
Contact • Richard Libbey, General Partner, Photo Adventure Tours, 2035 Park Street, Atlantic Beach, NY 11509-1236; 516-371-0067; Fax: 516-371-1352

VOYAGERS INTERNATIONAL

PHOTOGRAPHIC TOUR AND WORKSHOP IN ANTARCTICA

General Information • Photography tour with visits to Antarctica, Falkland Islands (Malvinas). Once at the destination country, participants travel by foot, small vehicle.
Learning Focus • Instruction in photography. Nature observation (wildlife and scenery). Instruction is offered by photographers. This program would appeal to people interested in photography, culture, nature studies.
Accommodations • Hotels, lodges. Single rooms are available.

Program Details • Program offered 3 times per year. Session length: 18–20 days. Departures are scheduled in November–February. Program is targeted to photography enthusiasts. Most participants are 30–70 years of age. 8–10 participants per session. Reservations are recommended at least 6–12 months before departure.
Costs • $5000 (includes tuition, housing, all meals, excursions). A $400 deposit is required.
Contact • David Blanton, Managing Director, Voyagers International, PO Box 915, Ithaca, NY 14851; 800-633-0299; Fax: 607-273-3873; E-mail: voyint@aol.com

WILLARDS ADVENTURE CLUB

ANTARCTICA EXPEDITION CRUISE

General Information • Nature study tour with visits to Antarctica. Once at the destination country, participants travel by foot, boat.
Learning Focus • Escorted travel to the Antarctic Pennisula. Nature observation (wildlife, birds, glaciers, mammals). Instruction is offered by naturalists, wilderness guides. This program would appeal to people interested in wildlife, nature studies.
Accommodations • Hotels, boat. Single rooms are available.
Program Details • Program offered once per year. Session length: 14 days. Departures are scheduled in January. Most participants are 9–80 years of age. Participants must be members of the sponsoring organization (annual dues: $5). 15 participants per session. Reservations are recommended at least 6 months before departure.
Costs • $3490–$5090 (includes housing, some meals, international airfare). A $300 deposit is required.
Contact • Willard Kinzie, President, Willards Adventure Club, Box 10, Barrie, ON L4M 4S9, Canada; 705-737-1881; Fax: 705-737-5123

EAST ASIA AND PACIFIC

REGIONAL

Australia
Bhutan
Burma
Cambodia
China
Hong Kong
India
Indonesia
Japan
Korea
Laos
Malaysia
Midway Islands
Nepal
New Zealand
Papua New Guinea
Phillippines
Singapore
Taiwan
Thailand
Tibet
Vietnam

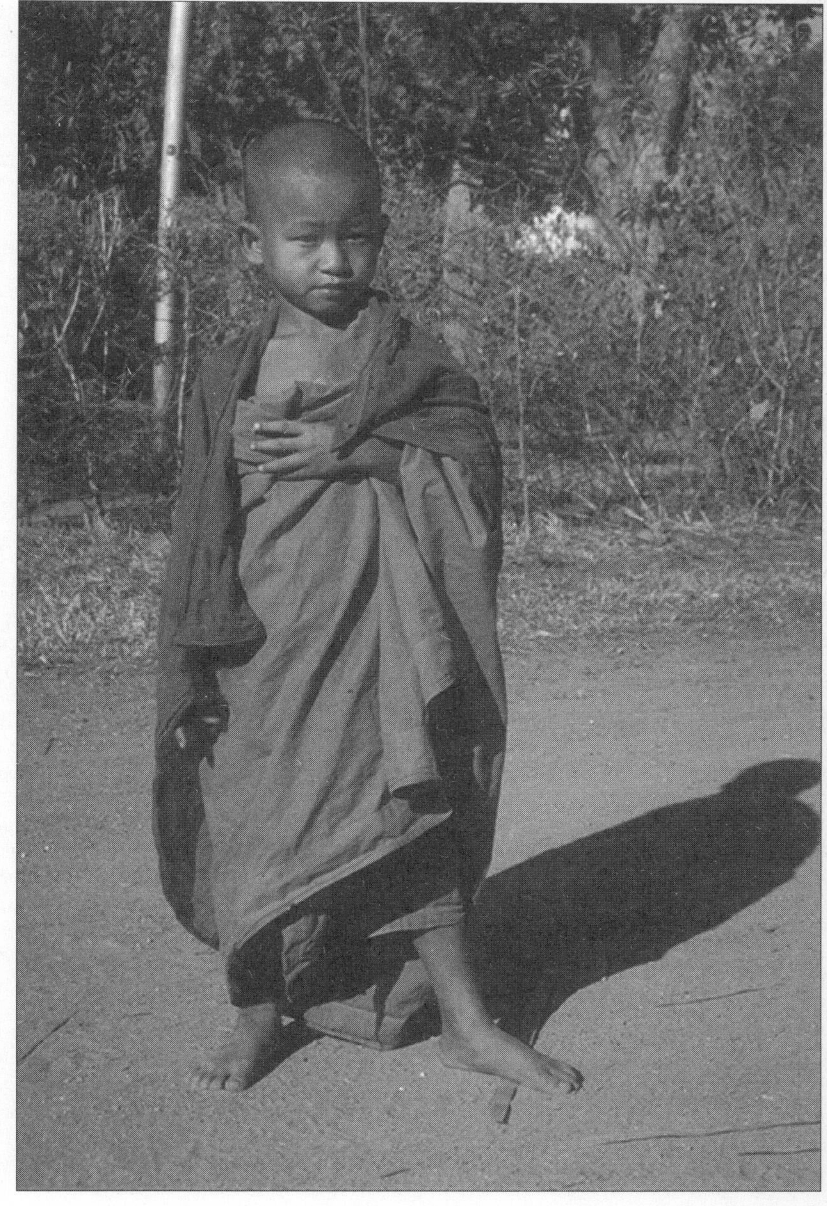

REGIONAL

ALPINE ASCENTS, INTERNATIONAL

CHO-OYU

General Information • Mountain climbing tour with visits to China (Mount Cho-Oyu), Nepal (Kathmandu); excursions to Thame, Tengboche, Nangpa-La Pass, Khumbu Region. Once at the destination country, participants travel by bus, foot, helicopter.

Learning Focus • Instruction in mountain climbing. Escorted travel to monasteries and local homes. Nature observation (Himalayan mountains). Other activities include camping, hiking. Instruction is offered by sports professionals. This program would appeal to people interested in mountain climbing.

Accommodations • Hotels, campsites. Single rooms are available.

Program Details • Program offered once per year. Session length: 37 days. Departures are scheduled in September. Program is targeted to mountain climbers. Other requirements: intermediate to advanced climbers. 12 participants per session. Reservations are recommended at least 6 months before departure.

Costs • $15,000-$18,000 (includes housing, some meals, helicopter transport, group equipment, fees, sherpa, yaks, porters, guides). A $2000 deposit is required.

Contact • Gordon Janow, Program Coordinator, Alpine Ascents, International, 16615 Saybrook Drive, Woodinville, WA 98072; 206-788-1951; Fax: 206-788-6757; E-mail: aaiclimb@accessone.com

AMERICAN INSTITUTE FOR FOREIGN STUDY (AIFS)

SOUTHEAST ASIA: INTERNATIONAL RELATIONS AND BUSINESS

General Information • Academic study program in Hong Kong, Thailand (Bangkok), Vietnam (Ho Chi Minh City). Classes are held on the campus of Richmond College.

Learning Focus • Courses in international relations, international business. Instruction is offered by local teachers.

Accommodations • Dormitories, hotels. Single rooms are available. Meals are taken in residences.

Program Details • Program offered once per year. Session length: 28 days. Departures are scheduled in July. The program is open to undergraduate students, graduate students, adults, high school graduates. Other requirements: minimum 2.0 GPA. Application deadline: March 15.

Costs • $2739 (includes tuition, housing, some meals). A $400 deposit is required.

Contact • Carmela Vigliano, Director of Admissions, College Summer Programs, American Institute for Foreign Study (AIFS), 102 Greenwich Avenue, Greenwich, CT 06830; 800-727-2437, ext. 6087; Fax: 203-869-9615; E-mail: info@aifs.org

AMERICAN JEWISH CONGRESS, INTERNATIONAL TRAVEL PROGRAM

AUSTRALIA AND NEW ZEALAND

General Information • Cultural tour with visits to Australia (Cairns, Melbourne, Sydney), New Zealand (Auckland, Christchurch, Queenstown); excursions to Great Barrier Reef, Whakarewarewa Thermal Reserve, Glow Worm Caves. Once at the destination country, participants travel by train, bus, foot, boat, airplane.

Learning Focus • Escorted travel to Royal Botanical Gardens, synagogues and Mount Cook. Attendance at performances (sheep-shearing, Maori folklore). Nature observation (rain forests, alps, glaciers, fjords, volcanoes). Instruction is offered by naturalists, historians. This program would appeal to people interested in Jewish history.

Accommodations • Hotels. Single rooms are available for an additional $995.

Program Details • Program offered 7 times per year. Session length: 19 days. Departures are scheduled in January–March, May, October–December. Program is targeted to Jewish-American adults. Most participants are 40–75 years of age. Participants must be 15 years or older to enroll. Participants must be members of the sponsoring organization (annual dues: $50). 30 participants per session. Reservations are recommended at least 6 months before departure.

Costs • $4795-$4995 (includes housing, some meals, excursions, international airfare, travel bag, documents portfolio, travel journal). A $200 deposit is required.

Contact • Betty Van Dyke, Worldwide Operations Manager, American Jewish Congress, International Travel Program, 18 East 84th Street, New York, NY 10028; 212-360-1571; Fax: 212-717-1932

AMERICAN JEWISH CONGRESS, INTERNATIONAL TRAVEL PROGRAM

THE EXOTIC ORIENT

General Information • Cultural tour with visits to Hong Kong (Kowloon), Indonesia (Bali), Singapore, Thailand (Bangkok); excursions to Damnern Saduak Floating Market, Parliament House, Sri Mariamman Hindu Temple, Wanchai Gap. Once at the destination country, participants travel by bus, foot, boat, airplane.

Learning Focus • Escorted travel to the Grand Palace and synagogues. Attendance at performances (traditional arts and customs). Nature observation (volcanoes). Instruction is offered by naturalists, historians. This program would appeal to people interested in Jewish history, Oriental culture.

Accommodations • Hotels. Single rooms are available for an additional $950.

Program Details • Program offered 7 times per year. Session length: 14 days. Departures are scheduled in March, May–October. Program is targeted to Jewish-American adults. Most participants are 40–75 years of age. Participants must be 15 years or older to enroll. Participants must be members of the sponsoring organization (annual dues: $50). 30 participants per session. Reservations are recommended at least 6 months before departure.

Costs • $4095-$4335 (includes housing, some meals, excursions, international airfare, travel bag, documents portfolio, travel journal). A $200 deposit is required.

Contact • Betty Van Dyke, Worldwide Operations Manager, American Jewish Congress, International Travel Program, 18 East 84th Street, New York, NY 10028; 212-360-1571; Fax: 212-717-1932

ARCHAEOLOGICAL TOURS

KHMER KINGDOMS: MYANMAR (BURMA), THAILAND, LAOS, AND CAMBODIA

General Information • Archaeological tour with visits to Cambodia (Phnom Penh, Siem Reap), Laos (Pakge, Vientiane), Burma (Mandalay, Pagan, Yangon), Thailand (Korat, Ratchathau, Ubon); excursions to Amarapura, Sagaing, Ayutthaya, Pimai, Phnom Rung, Wat Phou, Angkor Wat. Once at the destination country, participants travel by bus, airplane.
Learning Focus • Escorted travel to Rangoon, Mandalay, Khmer ruins and Angkor ruins. Museum visits (historical landmarks). Attendance at performances (dance and puppet shows). Instruction is offered by professors, historians. This program would appeal to people interested in history, art, archaeology.
Accommodations • Hotels. Single rooms are available for an additional $840.
Program Details • Program offered once per year. Session length: 22 days. Departures are scheduled in January. Program is targeted to adults. Most participants are 30–80 years of age. 19 participants per session. Application deadline: 1 month prior to departure.
Costs • $4860 (includes housing, some meals, excursions, internal flights). A $500 deposit is required.
Contact • Archaeological Tours, 271 Madison Avenue, Suite 904, New York, NY 10016; 212-986-3054; Fax: 212-370-1561

ARCHAEOLOGICAL TOURS

VIETNAM AND CAMBODIA

General Information • Archaeological tour with visits to Cambodia (Phnom Penh, Siem Reap), Vietnam (Da Lat, Da Nang, Hanoi, Ho Chi Minh City, Hue, Nha Trang); excursions to Hoa Binh, Angkor Wat, Laos. Once at the destination country, participants travel by bus, airplane.
Learning Focus • Museum visits (Hanoi, Danang, Ho Chi Minh, Phnom Penh). Attendance at performances (dance, music, water puppets). Instruction is offered by professors, historians. This program would appeal to people interested in history, anthropology, archaeology.
Accommodations • Hotels. Single rooms are available for an additional $985.
Program Details • Program offered once per year. Session length: 21 days. Departures are scheduled in November. Most participants are 30–80 years of age. 18 participants per session. Application deadline: 1 month prior to departure.
Costs • $4695 (includes housing, some meals, excursions, internal flights). A $500 deposit is required.
Contact • Archaeological Tours, 271 Madison Avenue, Suite 904, New York, NY 10016; 212-986-3054; Fax: 212-370-1561

BOLDER ADVENTURES, ASIA TRANSPACIFIC JOURNEYS

LAOS AND CAMBODIA

General Information • Cultural tour with visits to Cambodia (Angkor Wat, Phnom Penh), Laos (Luang Prabang, Vientiane); excursions to Vietnam, Thailand. Once at the destination country, participants travel by foot, boat, airplane.
Learning Focus • Escorted travel to Laos, Cambodia, Angkor Wat. Museum visits (Angkor Wat). Instruction is offered by professors, researchers, historians.
Accommodations • Hotels. Single rooms are available for an additional $325.
Program Details • Program offered 2 times per year. Session length: 16 days. Departures are scheduled in January, March. Most participants are 35–65 years of age. 8–10 participants per session. Reservations are recommended at least 4 months before departure.
Costs • $2795 (includes housing, all meals, excursions, internal airfare). A $500 deposit is required.
Contact • Bolder Adventures, Asia Transpacific Journeys, 3055 Center Green Drive, Boulder, CO 80301; 800-642-2742; Fax: 303-443-7078; World Wide Web: http://www.southeastasia.com/

COLORADO STATE UNIVERSITY

AUSTRALEARN: COMMUNICATION SKILLS FOR INTERNATIONAL BUSINESS IN ASIA

General Information • Academic study program in Hong Kong, Indonesia (Jakarta), Singapore, Thailand, Vietnam. Excursions to Philippines.
Learning Focus • Courses in communications, international business.
Accommodations • Hotels. Meals are taken on one's own, in local restaurants.
Program Details • Program offered once per year. Session length: 4 weeks. Departures are scheduled in July. The program is open to undergraduate students, graduate students, adults. Most participants are 18–23 years of age. Other requirements: minimum 2.5 GPA and approval by university. 10–20 participants per session. Application deadline: April 1.
Costs • $6700 (includes tuition, housing, some meals, books and class materials, excursions, international airfare). Application fee: $30. A $300 deposit is required.
Contact • Cynthia Flannery-Banks, Director, US Office, Colorado State University, 315 Aylesworth Hall, Fort Collins, CO 80523; 800-980-0033; Fax: 970-491-5501; E-mail: cflannery@vines.colostate.edu

CRAFT WORLD TOURS

BHUTAN AND SIKKIM

General Information • Cultural tour with visits to Bhutan (Bumthang, Paro, Punakha, Thimphu, Tongsa), India (Darjeeling, Delhi, Gangtok, Jaldapara). Once at the destination country, participants travel by bus.
Learning Focus • Escorted travel to Buddhist monasteries, Paro Valley, palaces and festivals. Museum visits (Delhi Crafts Museum, National Museum). Instruction is offered by artists. This program would appeal to people interested in handicrafts, folk arts, village life.
Accommodations • Hotels. Single rooms are available for an additional $395.
Program Details • Program offered once per year. Session length: 22 days. Departures are scheduled in October. Most

participants are 30–80 years of age. Other requirements: appreciation of handcrafts and folk arts. 18 participants per session. Application deadline: August 12. Reservations are recommended at least 6 months before departure.
Costs • $5498 (includes housing, some meals, excursions, international airfare). A $250 deposit is required.
Contact • Tom Wilson, President, Craft World Tours, 6776 Warboys Road, Byron, NY 14422; 716-548-2667; Fax: 716-548-2821

CRAFT WORLD TOURS

THAILAND AND LAOS

General Information • Cultural tour with visits to Laos (Luang Prabang, Vientiane), Thailand (Bangkok, Chiang Mai, Chiang Rai, Khon Kaen, Nong Khai). Once at the destination country, participants travel by bus.
Learning Focus • Escorted travel to Doi Suthep temple, Thaton, Nog Khai. Museum visits (Tribal Research Center Museum, Ban Chiang Museum). Instruction is offered by artists. This program would appeal to people interested in handicrafts, folk arts, village life.
Accommodations • Hotels. Single rooms are available for an additional $695.
Program Details • Program offered once per year. Session length: 21 days. Departures are scheduled in January. Most participants are 30–80 years of age. Other requirements: interest in folk arts and an appreciation of handicrafts. 18 participants per session. Application deadline: November 22. Reservations are recommended at least 6 months before departure.
Costs • $4499 (includes housing, some meals, excursions, international airfare). A $250 deposit is required.
Contact • Tom Wilson, President, Craft World Tours, 6776 Warboys Road, Byron, NY 14422; 716-548-2667; Fax: 716-548-2821

FOLKWAYS INSTITUTE

SILK ROAD PROJECT

General Information • Cultural tour with visits to China, Pakistan. Once at the destination country, participants travel by train, bus, foot, airplane.
Learning Focus • Museum visits (local museums). Nature observation (wildlife). Instruction is offered by professors, historians. This program would appeal to people interested in Chinese culture, Silk Road history.
Accommodations • Hotels. Single rooms are available.
Program Details • Program offered once per year. Session length: 25 days. Departures are scheduled in September. Program is targeted to seniors. Most participants are 55–80 years of age. 12–16 participants per session. Application deadline: March 1. Reservations are recommended at least 6 months before departure.
Costs • $5500 (includes housing, all meals, books and class materials, excursions, international airfare, instruction). A $50 deposit is required.
Contact • David Christopher, Director, Folkways Institute, 14600 Southeast Aldridge Road, Portland, OR 97236-6578; 503-658-6600; Fax: 503-658-8672

FORUM TRAVEL INTERNATIONAL

HIMALAYAS: BHUTAN, NEPAL, INDIA, AND TIBET

General Information • Nature study and cultural tour with visits to Bhutan (Bumthang, Paro, Punakha, Thimphu, Ura Valley), India (Garwhal, Rajasthan), Nepal (Chitwan, Kathmandu, Pokhara), Tibet (Lhasa, Manasarowar). Once at the destination country, participants travel by bus, foot, airplane. Program is affiliated with International Ecosystems University and International Outreach University.
Learning Focus • Escorted travel to natural and cultural sites. Nature observation (altitude ecosystems). Instruction is offered by professors, naturalists, artists. This program would appeal to people interested in nature studies, culture.
Accommodations • Homestays, dormitories, program-owned houses, hotels, campsites.
Program Details • Program offered 6 times per year. Session length: 2 weeks. Departures are scheduled throughout the year. Most participants are 18–76 years of age. Other requirements: must be in good health due to high altitude. 2–16 participants per session. Application deadline: 2 weeks prior to departure.
Costs • $1867 (includes tuition, housing, all meals, excursions). A $300 deposit is required.
Contact • Jeannie Graves, Operations Manager, Forum Travel International, 91 Gregory Lane #21, Pleasant Hill, CA 94525; 510-671-2900; Fax: 510-671-2993; E-mail: forum@ix.netcom.com; World Wide Web: http://www.ten-io.com/forumtravel

GEORGE MASON UNIVERSITY

THE ENTREPOTS OF EAST ASIA

General Information • Academic study program in China (Beijing, Guyangzhou, Shanghai, Xi'an), Hong Kong. Excursions to South Korea (Seoul), Great Wall of China.
Learning Focus • Courses in business, government, trade. Instruction is offered by professors from the sponsoring institution.
Accommodations • Hotels. Single rooms are available. Meals are taken as a group.
Program Details • Program offered once per year. Session length: 4 weeks. Departures are scheduled in June. The program is open to graduate students, adults. Most participants are 22–65 years of age. Other requirements: minimum 2.25 GPA. 10–20 participants per session. Application deadline: April 12.
Costs • $5835 for George Mason University students, $6385 for other students (includes tuition, housing, all meals, insurance, excursions, international airfare). Application fee: $35. A $500 deposit is required.
Contact • Dr. Yehuda Lukacs, Director, Center for Global Education, George Mason University, 4400 University Drive, 235 Johnson Center, Fairfax, VA 22030; 703-993-2155; Fax: 703-993-2153; E-mail: ylukacs@gmu.edu; World Wide Web: http://www.gmu.edu/departments/oie

HIMALAYAN HIGH TREKS

TIBET AND MOUNT KAILAS

General Information • Cultural tour with visits to Nepal (Kathmandu), Tibet (Gyawtse, Lhasa, Shigatse). Once at the destination country, participants travel by foot, land rover.

Learning Focus • Escorted travel to monasteries. Other activities include camping, hiking. Instruction is offered by trip leader and local guides. This program would appeal to people interested in Tibet, Buddhism.
Accommodations • Hotels, campsites. Single rooms are available for an additional $200.
Program Details • Program offered once per year. Session length: 4 weeks. Departures are scheduled in September. Participants must be 18 years or older to enroll. Other requirements: must be active, fit, and in good health. Application deadline: July. Reservations are recommended at least 4-6 months before departure.
Costs • $4600 (includes housing, some meals). A $250 deposit is required.
Contact • Effie Fletcher, Director and Founder, Himalayan High Treks, 241 Dolores Street, San Francisco, CA 94103-2211; 800-455-8735; Fax: 415-861-2391; E-mail: effie@well.com; World Wide Web: http://www.well.com/user/effie

MICHIGAN STATE UNIVERSITY

MODERN ASIA PROGRAM

General Information • Academic study program in Singapore. Excursions to Micronesia, Indonesia.
Learning Focus • Courses in family and child ecology, social sciences. Instruction is offered by professors from the sponsoring institution.
Accommodations • Hotels. Meals are taken on one's own, in local restaurants.
Program Details • Program offered once per year. Session length: 4 weeks. Departures are scheduled in May. The program is open to undergraduate students. Most participants are 18-22 years of age. Other requirements: good academic standing and the approval of the director. 12 participants per session. Application deadline: March 14.
Costs • $2800 (includes housing, some meals, excursions). Application fee: $75. A $250 deposit is required.
Contact • Brenda S. Sprite, Educational Programs Coordinator, Michigan State University, Office of Study Abroad, 109 International Center, East Lansing, MI 48824-1035; 517-353-8920; Fax: 517-432-2082; E-mail: sprite@pilot.msu.edu; World Wide Web: http://study-abroad.msu.edu

NORTHERN ILLINOIS UNIVERSITY

BUSINESS AND CULTURE IN KOREA AND CHINA

General Information • Academic study program in China (Shanghai), Korea (Seoul). Classes are held on the campus of Kyung Hee University Seoul, Shanghai University of Finance and Economics.
Learning Focus • Courses in operations management, information systems. Instruction is offered by professors from the sponsoring institution.
Accommodations • Dormitories. Single rooms are available. Meals are taken as a group, in local restaurants.
Program Details • Program offered once per year. Session length: 3 weeks. Departures are scheduled in May. The program is open to undergraduate students, graduate students. Most participants are 21-30 years of age. 12 participants per session. Application deadline: March 15.
Costs • $3950 (includes tuition, housing, some meals, insurance, excursions, international airfare). A $200 deposit is required.
Contact • Anne Seitzinger, Program Coordinator, Short-Term Study Abroad, Northern Illinois University, Study Abroad Office-WI 417, DeKalb, IL 60115; 815-752-0700; Fax: 815-753-0825; E-mail: aseitz@niu.edu; World Wide Web: http://www.niu.edu/depts/intl_prgms/intl.html

PHOTO ADVENTURE TOURS

INDIA: HIMALAYAN KINGDOMS

General Information • Photography tour with visits to Bhutan (Phontsoliug, Thimphu), India (Darjeeling, Delhi, Enugton, Kalimpong), Nepal (Kathmandu). Once at the destination country, participants travel by train, bus, foot, boat, airplane, rickshaw.
Learning Focus • Instruction in photography. Escorted travel to India. Nature observation (wildlife parks). Other activities include hiking. Instruction is offered by professors, researchers, naturalists, artists, historians, photographers. This program would appeal to people interested in photography, culture, history, art, ornithology, adventure.
Accommodations • Hotels. Single rooms are available for an additional $875.
Program Details • Program offered 3 times per year. Session length: 23 days. Departures are scheduled in February, March, October, November. Most participants are 18-80 years of age. Participants must be 18 years or older to enroll. Other requirements: accompaniment by an adult if under 18 years of age. 12 participants per session. Application deadline: 2 months prior to departure. Reservations are recommended at least 6 months before departure.
Costs • $4875 (includes housing, all meals, excursions, international airfare). A $400 deposit is required.
Contact • Richard Libbey, General Partner, Photo Adventure Tours, 2035 Park Street, Atlantic Beach, NY 11509-1236; 516-371-0067; Fax: 516-371-1352

PHOTO ADVENTURE TOURS

ROOF OF THE WORLD

General Information • Photography tour with visits to China (Beijing, Chengdu, Golmud, Xigaze, Xining), Tibet (Lhasa); excursions to Qinghai - Tibet Highway. Once at the destination country, participants travel by train, bus, foot, airplane.
Learning Focus • Instruction in photography. Instruction is offered by researchers, naturalists, artists, historians, photographers. This program would appeal to people interested in photography, culture, history, adventure, hiking, geology.
Accommodations • Homestays, hotels, campsites. Single rooms are available for an additional $995.
Program Details • Program offered 2 times per year. Session length: 20 days. Departures are scheduled in June, July. Most participants are 18-80 years of age. Participants must be 18 years or older to enroll. Other requirements: good health. 12 participants per session. Application deadline: 2 months prior to departure. Reservations are recommended at least 6 months before departure.
Costs • $5995 (includes housing, all meals, excursions, international airfare). A $400 deposit is required.

Contact • Richard Libbey, General Partner, Photo Adventure Tours, 2035 Park Street, Atlantic Beach, NY 11509-1236; 516-371-0067; Fax: 516-371-1352

PHOTO EXPLORER TOURS

BURMA (MYANMAR)

General Information • Photography tour with visits to Burma (Mandalay), Thailand (Chiang Mai); excursions to Valley of Pagodas, Lake at Inle, Chiang Mae. Once at the destination country, participants travel by bus, foot, boat.
Learning Focus • Instruction in photography. Escorted travel to Pagan, Rangoon and Mandalay. Instruction is offered by professional photographers. This program would appeal to people interested in photography.
Accommodations • Hotels. Single rooms are available.
Program Details • Program offered once per year. Session length: 12 days. Departures are scheduled in November. Program is targeted to amateur and professional photographers. Most participants are 35–85 years of age. Other requirements: good physical condition. 8–16 participants per session. Application deadline: 60 days prior to departure. Reservations are recommended at least 3 months before departure.
Costs • Contact sponsor for information. A $500 deposit is required.
Contact • Dennis Cox, Director, Photo Explorer Tours, 22111 Cleveland, #211, Dearborn, MI 48124; 800-315-4462; Fax: 313-561-1842; E-mail: decoxphoto@aol.com; World Wide Web: http://www.apogeephoto.com/photo_explorer.html

SENIORS ABROAD INTERNATIONAL HOMESTAY

SENIORS ABROAD

General Information • Homestay learning tours with visits to Australia, Japan, New Zealand. Once at the destination country, participants travel by train, bus, airplane.
Learning Focus • Instruction in alternative ways to stay active in older years. Instruction is offered by hosts. This program would appeal to people interested in active aging.
Accommodations • Homestays.
Program Details • Program offered 2 times per year. Session length: 4 weeks. Program is targeted to seniors over 50. Most participants are 50–82 years of age. Participants must be 50 years or older to enroll. 25–30 participants per session. Reservations are recommended at least 10 months before departure.
Costs • $2575–$3200 (includes housing, all meals, international airfare). A $100 deposit is required.
Contact • Evelyn Zivetz, Director, Seniors Abroad International Homestay, 12533 Pacato Circle North, San Diego, CA 92128; 619-485-1696; Fax: 619-487-1492

SMITHSONIAN INSTITUTION

SMITHSONIAN STUDY TOURS AND SEMINARS IN ASIA AND THE PACIFIC

General Information • Nature study and cultural tours with visits to Australia, China, Hong Kong, India, Nepal, New Zealand, Tibet, Vietnam. Once at the destination country, participants travel by bus, foot, boat, airplane.
Learning Focus • Instruction in Asian history, religion, and culture. Escorted travel to special sites off limits to most tourists. Museum visits (major museums, important collections, and private collections). Attendance at performances (traditional performances of music, dance, and theater). Nature observation (wildlife in remote Australia, thermal areas of New Zealand). Instruction is offered by professors, researchers, naturalists, artists, historians, scientists. This program would appeal to people interested in archaeology, religious history, photography, natural history.
Accommodations • Hotels. Single rooms are available.
Program Details • Session length: 9–17 days. Departures are scheduled throughout the year. Most participants are 25–85 years of age. Participants must be 18 years or older to enroll. Participants must be members of the sponsoring organization (annual dues: $24). 15–30 participants per session.
Costs • $1999 and up (includes tuition, housing, some meals, excursions, international airfare).
Contact • Customer Service Representative, Smithsonian Institution, Smithsonian Study Tours and Seminars, 1100 Jefferson Drive SW (MRC 702), Washington, DC 20560; 202-357-4700; Fax: 202-633-9250

UNIVERSITY OF MIAMI

SUMMER PROGRAM IN SOUTHEAST ASIA

General Information • Academic study program in Thailand (Bangkok), Vietnam (Ho Chi Minh City).
Learning Focus • Courses in Vietnamese language, intercultural communications, Vietnamese culture, Thai culture. Instruction is offered by professors from the sponsoring institution.
Accommodations • Dormitories, locally-rented apartments. Single rooms are available. Meals are taken on one's own, in local restaurants.
Program Details • Program offered once per year. Session length: 5 weeks. Departures are scheduled in June. The program is open to undergraduate students, graduate students, adults, non-degree university students. Most participants are 18–21 years of age. Other requirements: minimum 2.5 GPA. 7–10 participants per session. Application deadline: April 15.
Costs • $3500–$4400 for credit, $2550–$2750 non-credit (includes tuition, housing, excursions). Application fee: $30. A $500 deposit is required.
Contact • Glenda H. Hayley, Manager and Advisor, International Education and Exchange Programs, University of Miami, PO Box 248005, Coral Gables, FL 33124-1610; 800-557-5421; Fax: 305-284-6629; E-mail: ieep@cstudies.msmail.miami.edu; World Wide Web: http://www.miami.edu/cstudies/ieep.html

UNIVERSITY OF NORTH CAROLINA AT CHARLOTTE

EDUCATION AND CULTURE

General Information • Academic study program in Malaysia, Singapore, Thailand.

Learning Focus • Courses in counseling, human services. Instruction is offered by professors from the sponsoring institution.
Accommodations • Hotels. Single rooms are available. Meals are taken as a group, in local restaurants.
Program Details • Program offered once per year. Session length: 2 weeks. Departures are scheduled in July. The program is open to undergraduate students, graduate students, adults. Most participants are 20–60 years of age. 15 participants per session. Application deadline: May.
Costs • $3500 (includes tuition, housing, books and class materials, insurance, excursions, international airfare). Application fee: $10. A $400 deposit is required.
Contact • Elizabeth A. Adams, Director, Education Abroad Programs, University of North Carolina at Charlotte, Office of International Programs, 9201 University City Boulevard, Charlotte, NC 28223-0001; 704-547-2464; Fax: 704-547-3168; E-mail: eaadams@email.uncc.edu; World Wide Web: http://unccvm.uncc.edu

UNIVERSITY OF SOUTHERN MISSISSIPPI

AUSTRALIAN AND NEW ZEALAND EXPEDITION

General Information • Academic study program in Australia (Brisbane, Cairns, Canberra, Sydney), New Zealand (Auckland).
Learning Focus • Courses in geography, anthropology, sociology.
Accommodations • Hostels, motels.
Program Details • Program offered once per year. Session length: 3 weeks. Departures are scheduled in May. The program is open to undergraduate students, graduate students. Other requirements: minimum 2.0 GPA and good academic standing. 12 participants per session. Application deadline: April 6.
Costs • $3499 for undergraduates, $3749 for graduate students (includes tuition, housing, excursions, international airfare). A $200 deposit is required.
Contact • Director, Australian Studies, University of Southern Mississippi, Box 10047, Hattiesburg, MS 39406-0047; 601-266-4344; Fax: 601-266-5699; E-mail: m_ravencraft@bull.cc.usm.edu

UNIVERSITY OF TOLEDO

SOUTH EAST ASIA STUDY ABROAD

General Information • Academic study program in Malaysia, Singapore.
Learning Focus • Courses in marketing. Instruction is offered by professors from the sponsoring institution.
Accommodations • Hotels. Single rooms are available. Meals are taken as a group, in local restaurants.
Program Details • Program offered once per year. Session length: 3 weeks. Departures are scheduled in August. The program is open to undergraduate students. Most participants are 20–30 years of age. 10–15 participants per session. Application deadline: March 1.
Costs • $2700 (includes housing, some meals, books and class materials, excursions, international airfare). Application fee: $25. A $100 deposit is required.
Contact • Joel A. Gallegos, Coordinator of Study Abroad, University of Toledo, SWAC 2357, Toledo, OH 43606-3390; 419-530-1240; Fax: 419-530-1245; E-mail: jgalleg@utnet.utoledo.edu; World Wide Web: http://www.utoledo.edu/www/cisp/study-abroad/

AUSTRALIA

APPALACHIAN STATE UNIVERSITY

AUSTRALIA

General Information • Academic study program in Brisbane. Classes are held on the campus of The University of Queensland. Excursions to Lamington, Border Ranges, Stadbrooke Island.

Learning Focus • Courses in management. Instruction is offered by professors from the sponsoring institution.

Program Details • Program offered once per year. Session length: 4 weeks. Departures are scheduled in June. Most participants are 18 years of age and older. 20 participants per session.

Costs • $3400 (includes tuition, housing, insurance, international airfare, International Student Identification card).

Contact • Dr. Jeremy Fox, Study Abroad Trip Leader, Appalachian State University, Department of Management, Boone, NC 28608; 704-262-2163; Fax: 704-262-4037

BEAVER COLLEGE

ACTING FOR THE CAMERA

General Information • Academic study program in Sydney. Classes are held on the campus of University of New South Wales. Excursions to Blue Mountains, Cairns, Gold Coast.

Learning Focus • Courses in acting, drama. Instruction is offered by local teachers.

Accommodations • Hotels. Meals are taken in residences.

Program Details • Program offered once per year. Session length: 6 weeks. Departures are scheduled in June. The

program is open to undergraduate students, graduate students, adults. Other requirements: minimum 3.0 GPA and three or four semesters of college-level course work. 15 participants per session. Application deadline: March 31.
Costs • $4250 (includes tuition, housing, all meals, excursions, International Student Identification card, predeparture materials, host country support, some ground transportation). Application fee: $35. A $500 deposit is required.
Contact • Christopher Hennessy, Program Coordinator, Beaver College, Center for Education Abroad, 450 South Easton Road, Glenside, PA 19038; 888-232-8379; Fax: 215-572-2174; E-mail: hennessy@turret.beaver.edu

 BEAVER COLLEGE

AUSTRALIAN ENVIRONMENT: CASE STUDIES AND PERSPECTIVES

General Information • Academic study program in Sydney. Classes are held on the campus of University of New South Wales. Excursions to Blue Mountains, Australian desert, Uluru (Ayers Rock), Cairns.
Learning Focus • Courses in environmental studies. Instruction is offered by local teachers.
Accommodations • Hotels. Meals are taken in residences.
Program Details • Program offered once per year. Session length: 6 weeks. Departures are scheduled in June. The program is open to undergraduate students, graduate students, adults. Other requirements: minimum 3.0 GPA and three or four semesters of college-level course work. 15 participants per session. Application deadline: March 31.
Costs • $3700 (includes tuition, housing, all meals, excursions, International Student Identification card, predeparture materials, host country support, some ground transportation). Application fee: $35. A $500 deposit is required.
Contact • Christopher Hennessy, Program Coordinator, Beaver College, Center for Education Abroad, 450 South Easton Road, Glenside, PA 19038; 888-232-8379; Fax: 215-572-2174; E-mail: hennessy@turret.beaver.edu

 BOSTON UNIVERSITY

AUSTRALIAN CINEMA PROGRAM

General Information • Academic study program in Sydney.
Learning Focus • Courses in film studies. Instruction is offered by professors from the sponsoring institution.
Accommodations • Dormitories. Single rooms are available. Meals are taken on one's own, in local restaurants, in residences.
Program Details • Program offered once per year. Session length: 6 weeks. Departures are scheduled in May. The program is open to undergraduate students, adults. Most

participants are 19–22 years of age. Other requirements: minimum 3.0 GPA, good academic standing and a background in film studies recommended. 15 participants per session. Application deadline: March 15.

Costs • $3950 (includes tuition, housing, excursions, entrance pass to Sydney Film Festival). Application fee: $35. A $300 deposit is required.

Contact • Division of International Programs, Boston University, 232 Bay State Road, Boston, MA 02215; 617-353-9888; Fax: 617-353-5402; E-mail: abroad@bu.edu; World Wide Web: http://web.bu.edu/abroad

CHARLES STURT UNIVERSITY

GENERAL ENGLISH–BEGINNERS TO ADVANCED IN SYDNEY, AUSTRALIA

General Information • Language study program in Sydney. Excursions to Sydney Harbour.

Learning Focus • Courses in study skills. Instruction is offered by professors from the sponsoring institution.

Accommodations • Homestays, locally-rented apartments, lodges. Single rooms are available. Meals are taken with host family, in local restaurants, in residences.

Program Details • Program offered 13 times per year. Session length: 4 weeks. Departures are scheduled in January-December. The program is open to pre-college students, adults. Most participants are 18–30 years of age. 20 participants per session. Application deadline: one week prior to departure.

Costs • Contact sponsor for information.

Contact • Melissa Yeung, Secretary, Charles Sturt University, 210 Clarence Street, 10th Floor, Sydney 2000, Australia; +61 2-9320-7878; Fax: +61 2-93-20-78-77; E-mail: myeung@csu.edu.au

CHARLES STURT UNIVERSITY

GENERAL ENGLISH–BEGINNERS TO ADVANCED IN WAGGA WAGGA, AUSTRALIA

General Information • Language study program in Wagga Wagga. Classes are held on the campus of Charles Sturt University. Excursions to Melbourne, Canberra.

Learning Focus • Courses in study skills. Instruction is offered by professors from the sponsoring institution.

Accommodations • Homestays, dormitories, program-owned houses. Single rooms are available. Meals are taken with host family, in central dining facility, in residences.

Program Details • Program offered 13 times per year. Session length: 4 weeks. Departures are scheduled in January-December. The program is open to pre-college students, adults. Most participants are 18–50 years of age. 60 participants per session. Application deadline: one week prior to departure.

Costs • Contact sponsor for information.

Contact • Jackie Hunt, Secretary, Charles Sturt University, Locked Bag 669, Wagga Wagga 2678, Australia; +61 6933-2602; Fax: +61 69-33-27-99; E-mail: jhunt@csu.edu.au

CHEESEMANS' ECOLOGY/ BIRDING

AUSTRALIA 1997

General Information • Nature study tour with visits to Australia. Once at the destination country, participants travel by bus, foot, boat, airplane.
Learning Focus • Nature observation (bird watching, night spotting, snorkeling, photography, walking). Instruction is offered by naturalists. This program would appeal to people interested in nature studies, wildlife, photography, bird watching.
Accommodations • Hotels. Single rooms are available for an additional $25 per day.
Program Details • Program offered once per year. Session length: 31 days. Departures are scheduled in September. Other requirements: participants should be non-smokers. Reservations are recommended at least 6 months before departure.
Costs • $6200 (includes housing, some meals, excursions). A $300 deposit is required.
Contact • Gail Cheeseman, Co-Owner, Cheesemans' Ecology/Birding, 20800 Kittredge Road, Saratoga, CA 95070-6302; 800-527-5330; Fax: 408-741-0358; E-mail: cheesemans@aol.com; World Wide Web: http://www.cheesemans.com

CHEESEMANS' ECOLOGY/ BIRDING

AUSTRALIA: IN-DEPTH WILDLIFE TOUR

General Information • Nature study tour with visits to Kangaroo Island, Queensland, Tasmania. Once at the destination country, participants travel by bus, foot, boat, airplane.
Learning Focus • Nature observation (field wildlife observation). Instruction is offered by researchers, naturalists, scientists. This program would appeal to people interested in photography, bird watching.
Accommodations • Hotels, national park lodges. Single rooms are available for an additional $30 per day.
Program Details • Program offered once per year. Session length: 25 days. Departures are scheduled in October. Program is targeted to wildlife enthusiasts. Most participants are 25–65 years of age. Participants must be 11 years or older to enroll. Other requirements: non-smokers only. 14 participants per session. Reservations are recommended at least 6 months before departure.
Costs • $5160. A $300 deposit is required.
Contact • Gail Cheeseman, Co-Owner, Cheesemans' Ecology/Birding, 20800 Kittredge Road, Saratoga, CA 95070; 800-527-5330; Fax: 408-741-0358; E-mail: cheesemans@aol.com; World Wide Web: http://www.cheesemans.com

COLORADO STATE UNIVERSITY

AUSTRALEARN: ENVIRONMENTAL STUDIES AND AUSTRALIAN HISTORY (BELOIT COLLEGE)

General Information • Academic study program in Brisbane, Cairns, Canberra, Lady Elliott Island, Stradbroke Island, Sydney. Classes are held on the campus of The University of Queensland. Excursions to Brisbane, Lady Elliott Island, Sydney, Cairns, Stradbroke Island, Canberra.
Learning Focus • Courses in environmental studies, Australian history. Instruction is offered by professors from the sponsoring institution and local teachers.
Accommodations • Homestays, dormitories, hotels. Meals are taken as a group, on one's own, in central dining facility, in local restaurants, in residences.
Program Details • Program offered once per year. Session length: 5½ weeks. Departures are scheduled in July. The program is open to undergraduate students, graduate students, adults. Most participants are 18–23 years of age. Other requirements: minimum 2.5 GPA and approval by Beloit College. 15–25 participants per session. Application deadline: April 1.
Costs • $4900 (includes tuition, housing, some meals, books and class materials, insurance, excursions). Application fee: $30. A $300 deposit is required.
Contact • Cynthia Flannery-Banks, Director, US Office, Colorado State University, 315 Aylesworth Hall, Fort Collins, CO 80523; 800-980-0033; Fax: 970-491-5501; E-mail: cflannery@vines.colostate.edu

COLORADO STATE UNIVERSITY

AUSTRALEARN: INTERNATIONAL BUSINESS (GEORGETOWN COLLEGE)

General Information • Academic study program in Sydney.
Learning Focus • Courses in international business. Instruction is offered by professors from the sponsoring institution.
Accommodations • Dormitories, hotels. Meals are taken as a group, on one's own, in local restaurants.
Program Details • Program offered once per year. Session length: 3 weeks. Departures are scheduled in December. The program is open to undergraduate students, graduate students. Most participants are 18–23 years of age. Other requirements: approval by Georgetown College. 15 participants per session. Application deadline: November.
Costs • $3050 (includes tuition, housing, some meals, excursions, international airfare). Application fee: $30. A $300 deposit is required.
Contact • Cynthia Flannery-Banks, Director, US Office, Colorado State University, 315 Aylesworth Hall, Fort Collins, CO 80523; 800-980-0033; Fax: 970-491-5501; E-mail: cflannery@vines.colostate.edu

COLORADO STATE UNIVERSITY

AUSTRALEARN: INTERNSHIPS

General Information • Internship program in New South Wales, Northern Territory, Queensland, South Australia, Tasmania, Victoria, Western Australia.
Learning Focus • Courses in business, legal studies, arts, biology, communications, political science, social work, ecotourism.
Accommodations • Homestays, locally-rented apartments. Single rooms are available. Meals are taken on one's own, with host family, in residences.

Program Details • Session length: 6 weeks–one year. The program is open to undergraduate students, graduate students, pre-college students, adults. Most participants are 17–35 years of age. Application deadline: 4 months prior to departure.
Costs • $3250–$11,000 (includes tuition, housing, some meals, books and class materials). A $500 deposit is required.
Contact • Cynthia Flannery-Banks, Director, US Office, Colorado State University, 315 Aylesworth Hall, Fort Collins, CO 80523; 800-980-0033; Fax: 970-491-5501; E-mail: cflannery@vines.colostate.edu

COLORADO STATE UNIVERSITY

AUSTRALEARN: INTERNSHIP–STUDY IN ENVIRONMENT AND TOURISM

General Information • Internship program in North Queensland, Sydney. Classes are held on the campus of University of Western Sydney, Hawkesbury. Excursions to north Queensland.
Learning Focus • Courses in environmental studies, tourism. Instruction is offered by local teachers.
Accommodations • Homestays, dormitories. Single rooms are available. Meals are taken on one's own.
Program Details • Program offered once per year. Session length: 10 weeks. Departures are scheduled in June. The program is open to undergraduate students, graduate students. Most participants are 19–23 years of age. Other requirements: minimum 2.5 GPA. 8–10 participants per session. Application deadline: April 1.
Costs • $3300 (includes tuition, housing, some meals, excursions). Application fee: $30. A $300 deposit is required.
Contact • Cynthia Flannery-Banks, Director, US Office, Colorado State University, 315 Aylesworth Hall, Fort Collins, CO 80523; 800-980-0033; Fax: 970-491-5501; E-mail: cflannery@vines.colostate.edu

COLORADO STATE UNIVERSITY

AUSTRALEARN: INTERNSHIP–STUDY IN NATURAL RESOURCES AND SUSTAINABLE DEVELOPMENT

General Information • Internship program in Sydney. Classes are held on the campus of University of Western Sydney, Hawkesbury. Excursions to Australian outback.
Learning Focus • Courses in natural resources, sustainable development. Instruction is offered by local teachers.
Accommodations • Homestays, dormitories. Single rooms are available. Meals are taken on one's own.
Program Details • Program offered once per year. Session length: 10 weeks. Departures are scheduled in June. The program is open to undergraduate students, graduate students. Most participants are 18–23 years of age. Other requirements: minimum 2.5 GPA. 5–10 participants per session. Application deadline: April 1.
Costs • $3300 (includes tuition, housing, some meals, excursions). Application fee: $30. A $300 deposit is required.
Contact • Cynthia Flannery-Banks, Director, US Office, Colorado State University, 315 Aylesworth Hall, Fort Collins, CO 80523; 800-980-0033; Fax: 970-491-5501; E-mail: cflannery@vines.colostate.edu

COLORADO STATE UNIVERSITY

AUSTRALEARN: RURAL FIELD STUDIES

General Information • Academic study program in Brisbane, rural Australia. Excursions to New Zealand, Cairns.
Learning Focus • Courses in animal science, agriculture. Instruction is offered by professors from the sponsoring institution.
Accommodations • Homestays, dormitories, hotels. Meals are taken as a group, on one's own, in central dining facility, in local restaurants, in residences.
Program Details • Program offered once per year. Session length: 3 weeks. Departures are scheduled in May. The program is open to undergraduate students, graduate students, adults. Most participants are 18–25 years of age. Other requirements: minimum 2.5 GPA and a background or interest in rural studies. 15–25 participants per session. Application deadline: March 1.
Costs • $3300 (includes tuition, housing, all meals, excursions, international airfare). Application fee: $30. A $300 deposit is required.
Contact • Cynthia Flannery-Banks, Director, US Office, Colorado State University, 315 Aylesworth Hall, Fort Collins, CO 80523; 800-980-0033; Fax: 970-491-5501; E-mail: cflannery@vines.colostate.edu

COLORADO STATE UNIVERSITY

AUSTRALEARN: TROPICAL MARINE SCIENCE ON THE GREAT BARRIER REEF

General Information • Academic study program in Rockhampton. Classes are held on the campus of Central Queensland University. Excursions to Brisbane, Heron Island, Central Queensland University, Cairns, Stradbroke Island.
Learning Focus • Courses in marine science. Instruction is offered by professors from the sponsoring institution and local teachers.
Accommodations • Dormitories, motels, hotels. Meals are taken as a group, in central dining facility, in local restaurants, in residences.
Program Details • Program offered once per year. Session length: 4 weeks. Departures are scheduled in May. The program is open to undergraduate students, graduate students, adults. Most participants are 18–23 years of age. Other requirements: minimum 2.5 GPA and a background or interest in science. 15–25 participants per session. Application deadline: April 1.
Costs • $3500 (includes tuition, housing, some meals, books and class materials, insurance, excursions). Application fee: $30. A $300 deposit is required.
Contact • Cynthia Flannery-Banks, Director, US Office, Colorado State University, 315 Aylesworth Hall, Fort Collins, CO 80523; 800-980-0033; Fax: 970-491-5501; E-mail: cflannery@vines.colostate.edu

COOPERATIVE CENTER FOR STUDY ABROAD

AUSTRALIA

General Information • Academic study program in Cairns, Sydney. Excursions to Great Barrier Reef, rain forests.

Learning Focus • Courses in anthropology, business, nursing, education, biology, geology, sociology, history. Instruction is offered by professors from the sponsoring institution.
Accommodations • Dormitories, hotels. Meals are taken as a group, on one's own, in central dining facility, in local restaurants.
Program Details • Program offered 2 times per year. Session length: 2 weeks. Departures are scheduled in December, July. The program is open to undergraduate students, graduate students, adults. Most participants are 18–60 years of age. Other requirements: minimum 2.0 GPA. 70 participants per session. Application deadline: October 21, March 20.
Costs • $3295 (includes housing, some meals, insurance, excursions, international airfare). A $100 deposit is required.
Contact • Dr. Michael A. Klembara, Executive Director, Cooperative Center for Study Abroad, NKU, BEP 301, Highland Heights, KY 41099; 800-319-6015; Fax: 606-572-6650; E-mail: ccsa@nku.edu

DUKE UNIVERSITY

DUKE IN AUSTRALIA

General Information • Academic study program in Sydney. Classes are held on the campus of University of New South Wales. Excursions to Lady Elliott Island, Blue Mountains, Queensland.
Learning Focus • Courses in botany, biogeography, history. Instruction is offered by professors from the sponsoring institution and local teachers.
Accommodations • Dormitories. Meals are taken on one's own, in local restaurants.
Program Details • Program offered once per year. Session length: 6 weeks. Departures are scheduled in June. The program is open to undergraduate students. Most participants are 19–21 years of age. Other requirements: minimum 2.7 GPA. 25 participants per session. Application deadline: February 21.
Costs • $5451 (includes tuition, housing, some meals, excursions, international airfare).
Contact • Foreign Academic Programs, Duke University, 121 Allen Building, Box 90057, Durham, NC 27708-0057; 919-684-2174; Fax: 919-684-3083; E-mail: abroad@mail01.adm.duke.edu; World Wide Web: http://www.mis.duke.edu/study_abroad/study_abroad.html

FLINDERS UNIVERSITY OF SOUTH AUSTRALIA

AUSTRALIAN ARCHAEOLOGY SHORT COURSES

General Information • Academic study program in Adelaide. Classes are held on the campus of The Flinders University of South Australia. Excursions to Ayers Rock, Kakadu National Park, Great Barrier Reef.
Learning Focus • Courses in Aboriginal archaeology, historical archaeology, maritime archaeology. Instruction is offered by local teachers.
Accommodations • Dormitories, campsites, hostels. Single rooms are available. Meals are taken as a group, in central dining facility.
Program Details • Program offered 2 times per year. Session length: 6 weeks. Departures are scheduled in June, August. The program is open to undergraduate students, graduate students. Most participants are 20–28 years of age. Other requirements: must be an undergraduate or graduate of archaeology, history, geology or anthropology. 15 participants per session.
Costs • $4345 (includes tuition, housing, all meals, excursions, travel expenses pertaining to course). Application fee: $39.
Contact • Ms. Ann Wadsworth, Study Abroad Advisor, Flinders University of South Australia, International Office, GPO Box 2100, Adelaide SA 5001, Australia; +61 8-201-2727; Fax: +61 8-201-3177; E-mail: ann.wadsworth@flinders.edu.au; World Wide Web: http://adminwww.flinders.edu.au/intloff/home.html

FOREIGN LANGUAGE STUDY ABROAD SERVICE

INTERNATIONAL LANGUAGE STUDY HOMESTAYS IN AUSTRALIA

General Information • Language study program in Australia.
Learning Focus • Courses in English language. Instruction is offered by local teachers.
Accommodations • Homestays. Single rooms are available. Meals are taken with host family, in residences.
Program Details • Session length: varies. Departures are scheduled in January–December. The program is open to undergraduate students, graduate students, pre-college students, adults. Most participants are 12 years of age and older. Other requirements: students must be at least 12 years old. 1 participant per session.
Costs • Contact sponsor for information. A $300 deposit is required.
Contact • Louise Harber, Coordinator, Foreign Language Study Abroad Service, Department IH, Box 903, 5935 Southwest 64th Avenue, South Miami, FL 33143; 800-282-1090; Fax: 305-662-2907; E-mail: flsas@netpoint.net; World Wide Web: http://www.netpoint.net/~flsas

FORUM TRAVEL INTERNATIONAL

AUSTRALIA BUSHWALKING ADVENTURES

General Information • Wilderness/adventure program with visits to Kakadu, Kimberley, Red Centre. Once at the destination country, participants travel by foot, airplane. Program is affiliated with International Outreach University.
Learning Focus • Nature observation (ecosystems). Other activities include camping, hiking. Instruction is offered by local guides. This program would appeal to people interested in nature studies, culture.
Accommodations • Hotels, campsites.
Program Details • Program offered 24 times per year. Session length: 2 weeks. Departures are scheduled throughout the year. Most participants are 18–80 years of age. Participants must be 18 years or older to enroll. Other requirements: must be in good physical and mental health. 8–16 participants per session.
Costs • $500–$1850 (includes all meals, excursions). A $200 deposit is required.

Contact • Jeannie Graves, Operations Manager, Forum Travel International, 91 Gregory Lane #21, Pleasant Hill, CA 94525; 510-671-2900; Fax: 510-671-2993; E-mail: forum@ix.netcom.com; World Wide Web: http://www.ten-io.com/forumtravel

GEORGE MASON UNIVERSITY

HISTORY AND CULTURE

General Information • Academic study program in Brisbane. Classes are held on the campus of The University of Queensland.
Learning Focus • Courses in history, cultural studies. Instruction is offered by professors from the sponsoring institution and local teachers.
Accommodations • Homestays. Single rooms are available. Meals are taken as a group, in central dining facility, in local restaurants.
Program Details • Program offered once per year. Session length: 3 weeks. Departures are scheduled in December. The program is open to undergraduate students, graduate students, adults. Most participants are 18–65 years of age. Other requirements: minimum 2.25 GPA. 15–20 participants per session. Application deadline: October 11.
Costs • $3995 (includes tuition, housing, some meals, books and class materials, insurance, excursions, international airfare, administrative fees). Application fee: $35. A $500 deposit is required.
Contact • Dr. Yehuda Lukacs, Director, George Mason University, 4400 University Drive, 235 Johnson Center, Fairfax, VA 22030; 703-993-2155; Fax: 703-993-2153; E-mail: ylukacs@gmu.edu; World Wide Web: http://www.gmu.edu/departments/oie

GEORGETOWN UNIVERSITY

GEORGETOWN IN SYDNEY, AUSTRALIA–COMPARATIVE HISTORY AND LITERATURE

General Information • Academic study program in Sydney. Classes are held on the campus of University of New South Wales. Excursions to Norfolk Island, Fraser Island, Queensland coast, Cairns.
Learning Focus • Courses in comparative history, comparative literature. Instruction is offered by professors from the sponsoring institution and local teachers.
Accommodations • Dormitories. Single rooms are available. Meals are taken as a group, on one's own, in central dining facility.
Program Details • Program offered once per year. Session length: 6 weeks. Departures are scheduled in June. The program is open to undergraduate students, graduate students, adults. Most participants are 18–25 years of age. 15 participants per session. Application deadline: March.
Costs • $3000 (includes tuition, housing, all meals, books and class materials, insurance). A $100 deposit is required.
Contact • Marianne T. Needham, Director, International Programs, Georgetown University, 306 ICC, Box 571012, Washington, DC 20057-1012; 202-687-6184; Fax: 202-687-8954; E-mail: sscefps1@gunet.georgetown.edu; World Wide Web: http://guweb.georgetown.edu/ssce

INTERHOSTEL, UNIVERSITY OF NEW HAMPSHIRE

AUSTRALIA

General Information • Cultural tour with visits to Adelaide, Andamooka, Melbourne, Sydney, Blue Mountains, Katoomba, Healesville, Great Ocean, Werribee Park, Port Fairy, Barossa Valley. Once at the destination country, participants travel by bus, foot, airplane. Program is affiliated with Council of Adult Education, Victoria.
Learning Focus • Instruction in history and culture. Escorted travel to the Blue Mountains and Werribee Park. Museum visits (National Gallery of Victoria, South Australia Museum). Attendance at performances (Australian Bush ballads). Instruction is offered by historians, city guides. This program would appeal to people interested in history, culture.
Accommodations • Hotels. Single rooms are available for an additional $350.
Program Details • Program offered once per year. Session length: 2 weeks. Departures are scheduled in February. Program is targeted to seniors over 50. Most participants are 60–80 years of age. Participants must be 50 years or older to enroll. 35 participants per session. Reservations are recommended at least 6 months before departure.
Costs • $4595 (includes tuition, housing, all meals, excursions, international airfare, entrance fees). A $200 deposit is required.
Contact • Janice Pierson, Office Supervisor, Interhostel, University of New Hampshire, 6 Garrison Avenue, Durham, NH 03824; 800-733-9753; Fax: 603-862-1113; World Wide Web: http://www.learn.unh.edu/

JOURNEYS INTERNATIONAL, INC.

AUSTRALIA FAMILY ODYSSEY

General Information • Family tour with visits to Alice Springs, Ayers Rock and Olgas, Cape Tribulation Rain Forest, Great Barrier Reef, Queensland, Sydney. Once at the destination country, participants travel by foot, airplane.
Learning Focus • Other activities include snorkeling, swimming. Instruction is offered by regional experts. This program would appeal to people interested in culture, nature studies.
Accommodations • Hotels.
Program Details • Program offered once per year. Session length: 13 days. Departures are scheduled in August. Program is targeted to active families. Most participants are 25–55 years of age. Participants must be 4 years or older to enroll. 12–22 participants per session. Application deadline: 60 days prior to departure. Reservations are recommended at least 60 days before departure.
Costs • $2595 for adults, $995 for children under 12 (includes housing, some meals). A $300 deposit is required.
Contact • Joan Weber, Family Trips Director and Owner, Journeys International, Inc., 4011 Jackson Road, Ann Arbor, MI 48103; 313-665-4407; Fax: 313-665-2945; E-mail: joan@journeys-intl.com; World Wide Web: http://www.journeys-intl.com

NATURAL HABITAT ADVENTURES

UNTOUCHED AUSTRALIA

General Information • Nature study tour with visits to Cairns, Eungella National Park, Great Barrier Reef, Kangaroo Island, Lakefield National Park, Sydney. Once at the destination country, participants travel by foot, boat, airplane, four-wheel drive vehicle.
Learning Focus • Instruction in snorkeling, natural history. Attendance at performances (Tjapukai Aboriginal Dance Theater). Nature observation (kangaroos, koalas, emus, platypus, giant saltwater crocodiles, wallabies, echnidas, lizards, Australian possums, coral reefs and bird life). Other activities include hiking. Instruction is offered by professors, researchers, naturalists. This program would appeal to people interested in nature studies, photography, wildlife.
Accommodations • Campsites, lodges. Single rooms are available for an additional $795.
Program Details • Program offered 2 times per year. Session length: 18 days. Departures are scheduled in June-July, November, December. Participants must be 14 years or older to enroll. 12 participants per session. Reservations are recommended at least 6-12 months before departure.
Costs • $5995 (includes housing, some meals, airfare within Australia, park fees and service charges). A $500 deposit is required.
Contact • Natural Habitat Adventures, 2945 Center Green Court, Suite H, Boulder, CO 80301; 800-543-8917; Fax: 303-449-3712; E-mail: nathab@worldnet.att.net

NORTH CAROLINA STATE UNIVERSITY

GREAT BARRIER REEF OF AUSTRALIA

General Information • Academic study program in Queensland.
Learning Focus • Courses in ecology, marine science, environmental studies.
Accommodations • Boat. Meals are taken as a group.
Program Details • Program offered once per year. Session length: 10 days. Departures are scheduled in July. The program is open to undergraduate students, graduate students, adults. Most participants are 18-50 years of age. 6-10 participants per session. Application deadline: contact sponsor.
Costs • $1300 (includes tuition, housing, all meals, excursions). Application fee: $65.
Contact • Ingrid Schmidt, Study Abroad Director, North Carolina State University, 2118 Pullen Hall, Box 7344, Raleigh, NC 27695-7344; 919-515-2087; Fax: 919-515-6021; E-mail: study_abroad@ncsu.edu; World Wide Web: http://www2.ncsu.edu/ncsu/chass/intstu/abroad.html

SYRACUSE UNIVERSITY

CULTURE AND ENVIRONMENT IN AUSTRALIA

General Information • Academic study program in Alice Spring, Ayers Rock, Great Barrier Reef, New South Wales, Sydney. Excursions to Cairns, Canberra.
Learning Focus • Courses in geography, environmental studies, cultural studies. Instruction is offered by professors from the sponsoring institution.
Accommodations • Dormitories, hotels. Meals are taken on one's own, in local restaurants, in residences.
Program Details • Program offered once per year. Session length: 5 weeks. Departures are scheduled in June. The program is open to undergraduate students, graduate students, adults. Most participants are 19-30 years of age. Other requirements: minimum 2.5 GPA. 12 participants per session. Application deadline: March 15.
Costs • $6500 (includes tuition, housing, some meals, books and class materials, excursions). Application fee: $30. A $350 deposit is required.
Contact • Ms. Daisy Fried, Associate Director, Syracuse University, 119 Euclid Avenue, Syracuse, NY 13244; 315-443-9419; Fax: 315-443-4593; E-mail: dsfried@summon3.syr.edu; World Wide Web: http://sumweb.syr.edu/dipa/dipa9.htm

BHUTAN

HIMALAYAN HIGH TREKS

BHUTAN: LAND OF THE THUNDER DRAGON

General Information • Cultural tour with visits to Paro, Thimphu, Taksang Gompa (Tiger's Nest). Once at the destination country, participants travel by foot.
Learning Focus • Escorted travel to ruins in Paro and the monastery of Taktsang Gompa. Nature observation (Kanchenjunga). Other activities include hiking. Instruction is offered by local guides with a western leader. This program would appeal to people interested in Buddhism.
Accommodations • Hotels, campsites. Single rooms are available for an additional $200.
Program Details • Program offered 2 times per year. Session length: 2-4 weeks. Departures are scheduled in March, April. Most participants are 40-60 years of age. Participants must be 18 years or older to enroll. Other requirements: must be active, fit, and in good health. 6-8 participants per session. Application deadline: January or February. Reservations are recommended at least 4-6 months before departure.
Costs • $2900 (includes housing, all meals). A $250 deposit is required.
Contact • Effie Fletcher, Director and Founder, Himalayan High Treks, 241 Dolores Street, San Francisco, CA 94103-2391; 800-455-8735; Fax: 415-861-2391; E-mail: effie@well.com; World Wide Web: http://www.well.com/user/effie

JOURNEYS INTERNATIONAL, INC.

BHUTAN CULTURAL EXPLORATION

General Information • Cultural tour with visits to Jakar, Paro, Thimphu, Tongsa. Once at the destination country, participants travel by foot, small vehicle.
Learning Focus • Attendance at performances (cultural dances and festivals). Other activities include camping. Instruction is offered by naturalists. This program would appeal to people interested in culture, photography.
Accommodations • Hotels, campsites. Single rooms are available for an additional $800.
Program Details • Session length: 6-8 days. Departures are scheduled throughout the year. Most participants are 25-55 years of age. Participants must be 12 years or older to enroll. 2-8 participants per session. Application deadline: 60 days prior to departure. Reservations are recommended at least 60 days before departure.
Costs • $800 (includes housing, some meals). A $300 deposit is required.
Contact • Pat Ballard, Asia Sales Director, Journeys International, Inc., 4011 Jackson Road, Ann Arbor, MI 48103; 313-665-4407; Fax: 313-665-2945; E-mail: pat@journeys-intl.com; World Wide Web: http://www.journeys-intl.com

BURMA

BOLDER ADVENTURES, ASIA TRANSPACIFIC JOURNEYS

BURMA: LAND OF THE GOLDEN PAGODA

General Information • Cultural tour with visits to Burma. Once at the destination country, participants travel by train, foot, boat, airplane.
Learning Focus • Escorted travel to Burma. Museum visits (Pagan historical sites). Instruction is offered by professors, historians.
Accommodations • Hotels. Single rooms are available for an additional $525.
Program Details • Program offered 5 times per year. Session length: 16 days. Departures are scheduled in November–February. Most participants are 35–65 years of age. Participants must be 18 years or older to enroll. 10–12 participants per session. Reservations are recommended at least 4 months before departure.
Costs • $2895 (includes housing, all meals, excursions). A $500 deposit is required.
Contact • Bolder Adventures, Asia Transpacific Journeys, 3055 Center Green Drive, Boulder, CO 80301; 800-642-2742; Fax: 303-443-7078; World Wide Web: http://www.southeastasia.com/

CALIFORNIA ACADEMY OF SCIENCES

BURMA: THE ROAD TO MANDALAY

General Information • Wilderness/adventure program with visits to Burma (Kalaw, Mandalay, Pagan, Rangoon), Thailand (Thailand (Bangkok)); excursions to Maymyo, Amarapura, Sagaing, Inle Lake, Pindaya Caves. Once at the destination country, participants travel by bus, foot, boat, airplane.
Learning Focus • Escorted travel to Shwedagon Pagoda, School of Art, Music and Drama and Botanical Gardens. Museum visits (National Museum). Attendance at performances (traditional puppet show). Instruction is offered by researchers, naturalists, scientists. This program would appeal to people interested in natural history, Buddhism, culture, Burmese history.
Accommodations • Hotels. Single rooms are available for an additional $680.
Program Details • Program offered once per year. Session length: 2 weeks. Departures are scheduled in November. Most participants are 35–80 years of age. Participants must be 12 years or older to enroll. Participants must be members of the sponsoring organization. 15–20 participants per session.
Costs • $5105–$5320 (includes housing, some meals, insurance, excursions, international airfare, entrance fees, tour leaders, local guides). A $500 deposit is required.
Contact • Nancy Fuller, Travel Assistant, California Academy of Sciences, San Francisco, CA 94118; 415-750-7348; Fax: 415-750-7346

CRAFT WORLD TOURS

MYANMAR (BURMA)

General Information • Cultural tour with visits to Burma (Bagan, Inle Lake, Mandalay, Yangon), Thailand (Thailand (Bangkok)). Once at the destination country, participants travel by bus.
Learning Focus • Escorted travel to Shwedagon Pagoda, a bronze foundry and archeological site of Bagan. Museum visits (National Museum, Archaeological Museum). Instruction is offered by artists. This program would appeal to people interested in handicrafts, folk arts, village life.
Accommodations • Hotels. Single rooms are available for an additional $590.
Program Details • Program offered once per year. Session length: 18 days. Departures are scheduled in January. Most participants are 30–80 years of age. Other requirements: appreciation of handcrafts and folk arts. 16 participants per session. Application deadline: December 2. Reservations are recommended at least 6 months before departure.
Costs • $3797 (includes housing, some meals, excursions, international airfare). A $250 deposit is required.
Contact • Tom Wilson, President, Craft World Tours, 6776 Warboys Road, Byron, NY 14422; 716-548-2667; Fax: 716-548-2821

FOLKWAYS INSTITUTE

MYANMAR (BURMA) PROJECT

General Information • Cultural tour with visits to Burma. Once at the destination country, participants travel by bus, foot, airplane.
Learning Focus • Nature observation (wildlife). Instruction is offered by professors, historians. This program would appeal to people interested in history, cultural heritage.
Accommodations • Hotels. Single rooms are available.
Program Details • Program offered once per year. Session length: 22 days. Departures are scheduled in October. Program is targeted to seniors. 16 participants per session. Application deadline: April 1. Reservations are recommended at least 6 months before departure.
Costs • $3600 (includes housing, all meals, books and class materials, excursions, international airfare, instruction). A $50 deposit is required.
Contact • David Christopher, Director, Folkways Institute, 14600 Southeast Aldridge Road, Portland, OR 97236-6518; 503-658-6600; Fax: 503-658-8672

JOURNEYS INTERNATIONAL, INC.

BURMA: EIGHT DAY ODYSSEY

General Information • Cultural tour with visits to Bagan, Mandalay, Yangon. Once at the destination country, participants travel by train, boat, small vehicle.

Learning Focus • Escorted travel to markets, temples, monasteries and small villages. Museum visits (National Museum). Instruction is offered by local English-speaking guides. This program would appeal to people interested in religion, nature studies, culture, photography.

Accommodations • Hotels. Single rooms are available for an additional $125.

Program Details • Program offered 12 times per year. Session length: 8 days. Departures are scheduled throughout the year. Program is targeted to persons interested in religion and culture. Most participants are 25–55 years of age. Participants must be 12 years or older to enroll. 2–8 participants per session. Application deadline: 60 days prior to departure. Reservations are recommended at least 60 days before departure.

Costs • $1395 (includes housing). A $300 deposit is required.

Contact • Pat Ballard, Asia Sales Director, Journeys International, Inc., 4011 Jackson Road, Ann Arbor, MI 48103; 313-665-4407; Fax: 313-665-2945; E-mail: pat@journeys-intl.com; World Wide Web: http://www.journeys-intl.com

CAMBODIA

HIMALAYAN TRAVEL

ESSENTIAL CAMBODIA TOUR

General Information • Archaeological tour with visits to Phnom Penh, Siem Reap. Once at the destination country, participants travel by bus, airplane.

Learning Focus • Escorted travel to Phnom Penh, Angkor Wat ruins. Instruction is offered by government-trained guides and experts. This program would appeal to people interested in archaeology.

Accommodations • Hotels. Single rooms are available for an additional $110.

Program Details • Program offered 24 times per year. Session length: 4 days. Departures are scheduled throughout the year. Most participants are 25–55 years of age. 8 participants per session. Reservations are recommended at least 2 months before departure.

Costs • $885 (includes housing, all meals, excursions). A $250 deposit is required.

Contact • James Faubel, President, Himalayan Travel, 110 Prospect Street, Stamford, CT 06901; 800-225-2380; Fax: 203-359-3669

HINA

AMERICAN JEWISH CONGRESS, INTERNATIONAL TRAVEL PROGRAM

HIGHLIGHTS OF CHINA

General Information • Cultural tour with visits to China (Beijing, Shanghai, Xi'an), Hong Kong; excursions to Tiananmen Square, Forbidden City, Summer Palace, Ming Tombs, Temple of Heaven, Hua Qing Hot Springs, Wanchai Gap. Once at the destination country, participants travel by bus, foot, boat, airplane.

Learning Focus • Escorted travel to the Beijing Zoo, Great Wall of China and synagogues. Museum visits (Shaanxi Provincial Museum). Attendance at performances (circus, acrobatics show). Instruction is offered by naturalists, historians. This program would appeal to people interested in Oriental culture, Jewish history.

Accommodations • Hotels. Single rooms are available for an additional $825.

Program Details • Program offered 6 times per year. Session length: 13 days. Departures are scheduled in April–September. Program is targeted to Jewish-American adults. Most participants are 40–75 years of age. Participants must be 15 years or older to enroll. Participants must be members of the sponsoring organization (annual dues: $50). 30 participants per session. Reservations are recommended at least 6 months before departure.

Costs • $3995–$4195 (includes housing, some meals, excursions, international airfare, travel bag, documents portfolio, travel journal). A $200 deposit is required.

Contact • Betty Van Dyke, Worldwide Operations Manager, American Jewish Congress, International Travel Program, 18 East 84th Street, New York, NY 10028; 212-360-1571; Fax: 212-717-1932

AMERICAN JEWISH CONGRESS, INTERNATIONAL TRAVEL PROGRAM

THE SPLENDORS OF CHINA

General Information • Cultural tour with visits to China (Beijing, Shanghai, Xi'an), Hong Kong; excursions to Tiananmen Square, Forbidden City, Temple of Heaven, Ming Tombs, Yangtze River, Wanchai Gap. Once at the destination country, participants travel by bus, foot, boat, airplane.

Learning Focus • Escorted travel to the Great Wall of China, Hua Qing Hot Springs, Fengdu and synagogues. Museum visits (Shaanxi Provincial Museum, Jingzhou Museum). Instruction is offered by naturalists, historians. This program would appeal to people interested in Oriental culture, Jewish history.

Accommodations • Hotels, boat. Single rooms are available for an additional $1200.

Program Details • Program offered 5 times per year. Session length: 19 days. Departures are scheduled in May–September. Program is targeted to Jewish-American adults. Most participants are 40–75 years of age. Participants must be 15 years or older to enroll. Participants must be members of the sponsoring organization (annual dues: $50). 30 participants per session. Reservations are recommended at least 6 months before departure.

Costs • $5495 (includes housing, some meals, excursions, international airfare, travel bag, documents portfolio, travel journal). A $200 deposit is required.

Contact • Betty Van Dyke, Worldwide Operations Manager, American Jewish Congress, International Travel Program, 18 East 84th Street, New York, NY 10028; 212-360-1571; Fax: 212-717-1932

APPALACHIAN STATE UNIVERSITY

CHINA

General Information • Academic study program in Beijing, Guilin, Shenyang, Suzhou, Xi'an.

Learning Focus • Courses in history. Instruction is offered by professors from the sponsoring institution.

Program Details • Program offered once per year. Session length: 4–5 weeks. Departures are scheduled in May. Most participants are 18 years of age and older. 20 participants per session.

Costs • $3500 (includes tuition, housing, insurance, international airfare, International Student Identification card).

Contact • Dr. Robert A. White, Professor, Appalachian State University, Department of History, Boone, NC 28608; 704-262-2282; Fax: 704-262-4037

ARCHAEOLOGICAL TOURS

ANCIENT CAPITALS OF CHINA

General Information • Cultural tour with visits to Beijing, Guilin, Kaifeng, Luoyang, Shanghai, Suzhou, Xi'an. Once at the destination country, participants travel by bus.

Learning Focus • Museum visits (Beijing, Xian, Kaifeng, Shanghai). Attendance at performances (shows). Instruction is offered by professors, historians. This program would appeal to people interested in history, archaeology.

Accommodations • Hotels. Single rooms are available for an additional $700.

Program Details • Program offered once per year. Session length: 21 days. Departures are scheduled in October. Program is targeted to adults. Most participants are 30–80 years of age. 20 participants per session. Application deadline: 1 month prior to departure.

Costs • $4500 (includes housing, some meals, excursions, internal flights). A $500 deposit is required.

Contact • Archaeological Tours, 271 Madison Avenue, Suite 904, New York, NY 10016; 212-986-3054; Fax: 212-370-1561

ARCHAEOLOGICAL TOURS

CHINA SILK ROAD

General Information • Cultural tour with visits to Beijing, Dunhuang, Kashgar, Lanzhou, Turpan, Urumgi, Xi'an, Hami Oases, Labrang Monastery, Binglingsi. Once at the destination country, participants travel by bus.
Learning Focus • Museum visits (Xian, Dunhuang, Urungi, Turpan). Attendance at performances (dance and music shows). Instruction is offered by professors, historians. This program would appeal to people interested in history, art, archaeology.
Accommodations • Hotels. Single rooms are available for an additional $863.
Program Details • Program offered once per year. Session length: 25 days. Departures are scheduled in May, September. Program is targeted to adults. Most participants are 30–80 years of age. 19 participants per session. Application deadline: 1 month prior to departure.
Costs • $4785 (includes housing, some meals, excursions, internal flights). A $500 deposit is required.
Contact • Archaeological Tours, 271 Madison Avenue, Suite 904, New York, NY 10016; 212-986-3054; Fax: 212-370-1561

BOSTON UNIVERSITY

BEIJING SUMMER PROGRAM

General Information • Language study program in Beijing. Classes are held on the campus of Capital Normal University of Foreign Language. Excursions to Qingdao, local farm.
Learning Focus • Courses in Chinese language. Instruction is offered by professors from the sponsoring institution and local teachers.
Accommodations • Dormitories. Meals are taken as a group, on one's own, in central dining facility.
Program Details • Program offered once per year. Session length: 8 weeks. Departures are scheduled in June. The program is open to undergraduate students. Most participants are 19–22 years of age. Other requirements: minimum 3.0 GPA and good academic standing. 18 participants per session. Application deadline: March 15.
Costs • $4500 (includes tuition, housing, all meals, books and class materials, insurance, visa fees and departure taxes). Application fee: $35. A $300 deposit is required.
Contact • Division of International Programs, Boston University, 232 Bay State Road, Boston, MA 02215; 617-353-9888; Fax: 617-353-5402; E-mail: abroad@bu.edu; World Wide Web: http://web.bu.edu/abroad

CENTER FOR GLOBAL EDUCATION AT AUGSBURG COLLEGE

FROM MAOISM TO MARKETISM: CHINA AND HONG KONG IN TRANSITION

General Information • Academic study program with visits to China (Beijing, Guilin, Shanghai), Hong Kong. Once at the destination country, participants travel by train, foot, boat, airplane.
Learning Focus • Instruction in current issues facing China and Hong Kong. Escorted travel to The Great Wall and the Forbidden City. Other activities include meetings with community leaders, political representatives. Instruction is offered by local resource persons. This program would appeal to people interested in education, economics, social justice.
Accommodations • Hotels.
Program Details • Program offered once per year. Session length: 2 weeks. Departures are scheduled in April. Most participants are 20–70 years of age. Participants must be 18 years or older to enroll. Other requirements: accompaniment by an adult if under 18 years of age. 15 participants per session. Application deadline: March 1. Reservations are recommended at least 6 weeks before departure.
Costs • $3900 (includes housing, all meals, books and class materials, excursions, international airfare, translation). A $100 deposit is required.
Contact • Kathryn Inofeno, Director of Asia Programs, Center for Global Education at Augsburg College, Center for Global Education, 2211 Riverside Avenue, Minneapolis, MN 55454; 800-299-8889; Fax: 612-330-1695; E-mail: globaled@augsburg.edu; World Wide Web: http://www.augsburg.edu/global

COLLEGE OF WILLIAM AND MARY

SUMMER IN BEIJING

General Information • Academic study program in Beijing, Yantai. Classes are held on the campus of Beijing Normal University, Yantai University. Excursions to major cities.
Learning Focus • Courses in Chinese language, anthropology, Tai Chi, history, calligraphy. Instruction is offered by professors from the sponsoring institution and local teachers.
Accommodations • Dormitories. Meals are taken on one's own, in central dining facility, in local restaurants.
Program Details • Program offered once per year. Session length: 10 weeks. Departures are scheduled in June. The program is open to undergraduate students, graduate students. Most participants are 20–26 years of age. Other requirements: minimum of 2 years of Chinese and good academic standing. 19 participants per session. Application deadline: February 15.
Costs • $5000 (includes tuition, housing, some meals, books and class materials, excursions, international airfare, two week study tour including travel,). Application fee: $40. A $1500 deposit is required.
Contact • Dr. Ann M. Moore, Head of Programs Abroad, College of William and Mary, Reves Center, PO Box 8795, Williamsburg, VA 23187-8795; 757-221-3594; Fax: 757-221-3597; E-mail: ammoo2@facstaff.wm.edu

COUNCIL ON INTERNATIONAL EDUCATIONAL EXCHANGE

COUNCIL STUDY CENTER AT PEKING UNIVERSITY

General Information • Language study program in Beijing. Classes are held on the campus of Peking University. Excursions to Great Wall of China, Ming Tombs, Temple of Heaven, Summer Palace, Forbidden City, Jietai Temple.
Learning Focus • Courses in Mandarin Chinese language. Instruction is offered by local teachers.
Accommodations • Dormitories. Meals are taken on one's own, in central dining facility, in local restaurants.
Program Details • Program offered once per year. Session length: 8 weeks. Departures are scheduled in June. The program is open to undergraduate students, graduate students. Most participants are 19–30 years of age. Other requirements: 1 year of Chinese, 1 Asian studies course, and a minimum 2.75 GPA. 35–40 participants per session. Application deadline: April 1.
Costs • $3500 (includes tuition, housing, all meals, insurance, excursions, orientation, International Student Identification card). Application fee: $30. A $300 deposit is required.
Contact • Alyssa McCloud, Program Registrar, Council on International Educational Exchange, College and University Division, 205 East 42nd Street, New York, NY 10017-5706; 212-822-2699; Fax: 212-822-2779; E-mail: info@ciee.org; World Wide Web: http://www.ciee.org

COUNCIL ON INTERNATIONAL EDUCATIONAL EXCHANGE

SHANGHAI SUMMER LANGUAGE AND CULTURE PROGRAM AT FUDAN UNIVERSITY

General Information • Academic study program in Shanghai. Classes are held on the campus of Fudan University Shanghai. Excursions to Pudong economic zone, stock market, site of first meeting of the Communist Party, Jiading rural area, Shanghai museum, neighborhoods of Shanghai.
Learning Focus • Courses in Mandarin Chinese language, Chinese area studies. Instruction is offered by professors from the sponsoring institution and local teachers.
Accommodations • Dormitories. Meals are taken on one's own, in central dining facility, in local restaurants.
Program Details • Program offered once per year. Session length: 8 weeks. Departures are scheduled in June. The program is open to undergraduate students, graduate students. Most participants are 19–25 years of age. Other requirements: minimum 2.75 GPA. 15–20 participants per session. Application deadline: April 1.
Costs • $3500 (includes tuition, housing, all meals, insurance, excursions, International Student Identification card). Application fee: $30. A $300 deposit is required.
Contact • Alyssa McCloud, Program Registrar, Council on International Educational Exchange, College and University Division, 205 East 42nd Street, New York, NY 10017-5706; 212-822-2766; Fax: 212-822-2779; E-mail: info@ciee.org; World Wide Web: http://www.ciee.org

CRAFT WORLD TOURS

CHINA SILK AND CRAFT ROUTE

General Information • Cultural tour with visits to Beijing, Dunhuang, Kashgar, Khotan, Turpan, Urumgi, Xi'an. Once at the destination country, participants travel by bus.
Learning Focus • Escorted travel to Tiananmen Square, Silk Road, Forbidden City, Great Wall, Mogao Grottoes and bazaars. Museum visits (Museum of National Minorities). Attendance at performances (Beijing Opera). Instruction is offered by artists, historians. This program would appeal to people interested in handicrafts, folk arts, village life.
Accommodations • Hotels. Single rooms are available for an additional $550.
Program Details • Program offered once per year. Session length: 22 days. Departures are scheduled in October. Most participants are 30–80 years of age. Other requirements: appreciation of handcrafts and folk arts. 18 participants per session. Application deadline: August 3. Reservations are recommended at least 6 months before departure.
Costs • $4896 (includes housing, some meals, excursions, international airfare). A $250 deposit is required.
Contact • Tom Wilson, President, Craft World Tours, 6776 Warboys Road, Byron, NY 14422; 716-548-2667; Fax: 716-548-2821

CROSS-CULTURE

EXPLORING NORTHERN CHINA

General Information • Cultural tour with visits to Beijing, The Forbidden City, The Great Wall, Chengde, Xi'an, Banpo Neolithic Village, Shanghai. Once at the destination country, participants travel by bus, foot, airplane.
Learning Focus • Instruction in Tibetan Buddhism and other religious influences on Chinese culture, architecture, and traditions. Escorted travel to The White Dagoba, Temple of Heaven and the Children's Palace. Museum visits (Shaanxi Historical Museum). Attendance at performances (traditional entertainers, Shanghai Acrobatic Troupe). Instruction is offered by highly educated guides. This program would appeal to people interested in culture, history, nature studies, arts, traditions, food and wine.
Accommodations • Hotels. Single rooms are available for an additional $450.
Program Details • Program offered once per year. Session length: 14 days. Departures are scheduled in October. Program is targeted to adults of all ages. Most participants are 40–70 years of age. Participants must be 12 years or older to enroll. Other requirements: good health, accompaniment of an adult if under 18. 20–25 participants per session. Application deadline: 1 month prior to departure. Reservations are recommended at least 3–12 months before departure.
Costs • $3520 from Los Angeles, $3710 from New York (includes tuition, housing, all meals, books and class materials, excursions, international airfare). A $300 deposit is required.
Contact • Cross-Culture, 52 High Point Drive, Amherst, MA 01002-1224; 413-256-6303; Fax: 413-253-2303; E-mail: xculture@javanet.com; World Wide Web: http://www.empiremall.com/cross-culture

CROSS-CULTURE

EXPLORING SOUTHERN CHINA

General Information • Cultural tour with visits to China (Guilin, Kunming, Shanghai, Suzhou), Hong Kong; excursions to Wuxi, Hangzhou, Guilin, Kunming. Once at the destination country, participants travel by train, foot, boat, airplane.
Learning Focus • Escorted travel to Feilei Feng, Jade Buddha Temple and Reed Flute Cave. Museum visits (Shanghai Museum, Tea Museum, Ethnic Minorities Institute Museum). Attendance at performances (tribal music). Instruction is offered by highly educated guides. This program would appeal to people interested in culture, history, nature studies, arts, traditions, food and wine.
Accommodations • Hotels. Single rooms are available for an additional $675.
Program Details • Program offered once per year. Session length: 17 days. Departures are scheduled in October. Program is targeted to adults of all ages. Most participants are 40–70 years of age. Participants must be 12 years or older to enroll. Other requirements: good health, accompaniment of an adult if under 18. 20–25 participants per session. Application deadline: 1 month prior to departure. Reservations are recommended at least 3–12 months before departure.
Costs • $4170 from Los Angeles, $4370 from New York (includes tuition, housing, all meals, books and class materials, excursions, international airfare). A $300 deposit is required.
Contact • Cross-Culture, 52 High Point Drive, Amherst, MA 01002-1224; 413-256-6303; Fax: 413-253-2303; E-mail: xculture@javanet.com; World Wide Web: http://www.empiremall.com/cross-culture

 GEORGE MASON UNIVERSITY

CHINA AND INNER MONGOLIA

General Information • Academic study program in Beijing, Hohhot, Nanjing, Shanghai, Xi'an.
Learning Focus • Courses in history, cultural studies. Instruction is offered by professors from the sponsoring institution.
Accommodations • Dormitories, hotels. Single rooms are available. Meals are taken as a group, in central dining facility.
Program Details • Program offered once per year. Session length: 4 weeks. Departures are scheduled in June, July. The program is open to undergraduate students, graduate students, adults. Most participants are 18-65 years of age. Other requirements: minimum 2.25 GPA. 10–15 participants per session. Application deadline: May 31.
Costs • $3995 for George Mason University students, $4495 for other students (includes tuition, housing, all meals, insurance, excursions, international airfare). Application fee: $35. A $500 deposit is required.
Contact • Dr. Yehuda Lukacs, Director, Center for Global Education, George Mason University, 4400 University Drive, 235 Johnson Center, Fairfax, VA 22030; 703-993-2156; Fax: 703-993-2153; E-mail: ylukacs@gmu.edu; World Wide Web: http://www.gmu.edu/departments/oie

INSTITUTE OF EUROPEAN STUDIES/INSTITUTE OF ASIAN STUDIES

BEIJING SUMMER PROGRAM

General Information • Language study program in Beijing. Classes are held on the campus of Hydro-Ecology Institute.
Learning Focus • Courses in Chinese language. Instruction is offered by local teachers.
Accommodations • Dormitories. Meals are taken on one's own, in local restaurants.
Program Details • Program offered once per year. Session length: 6 weeks. Departures are scheduled in July. The program is open to undergraduate students, graduate students, adults. Most participants are 18–40 years of age. Other requirements: no more than one semester of Chinese. 12 participants per session. Application deadline: April 15.
Costs • $2500 (includes tuition, housing, books and class materials). Application fee: $25. A $500 deposit is required.
Contact • Department of Admissions, Institute of European Studies/Institute of Asian Studies, 223 West Ohio Street, Chicago, IL 60610-4196; 800-995-2300; Fax: 312-944-1448; E-mail: recruit@iesias.org; World Wide Web: http://www.iesias.org

INTERHOSTEL, UNIVERSITY OF NEW HAMPSHIRE

SHANGHAI, HANGZHOU, XI'AN AND BEIJING, CHINA

General Information • Cultural tour with visits to Beijing, Hangzhou, Shanghai, Xi'an, Great Wall, Ming Tombs, Ban Po, Big Goose Pagoda, Lingyin Temple, Six Harmonies Pagoda. Once at the destination country, participants travel by train, bus, foot, boat, airplane. Program is affiliated with Hangzhou University.
Learning Focus • Instruction in history, culture and tai ji. Museum visits (Shanghai Museum, Shanxi Museum). Attendance at performances (Beijing Opera). Instruction is offered by professors, city guides. This program would appeal to people interested in history, culture.
Accommodations • Hotels. Single rooms are available for an additional $375.
Program Details • Program offered 2 times per year. Session length: 2½ weeks. Departures are scheduled in October, May. Program is targeted to seniors over 50. Most participants are 60–80 years of age. Participants must be 50 years or older to enroll. 40 participants per session. Reservations are recommended at least 6 months before departure.
Costs • $3325 (includes tuition, housing, all meals, excursions, international airfare, entrance fees). A $200 deposit is required.
Contact • Janice Pierson, Office Supervisor, Interhostel, University of New Hampshire, 6 Garrison Avenue, Durham, NH 03824-3529; 800-733-9753; Fax: 603-862-1113; World Wide Web: http://www.learn.unh.edu/

NORTHERN ILLINOIS UNIVERSITY

CHINA COOPERATIVE LANGUAGE AND CULTURE PROGRAM

General Information • Language study program in Beijing. Classes are held on the campus of Peking University.
Learning Focus • Courses in Chinese language. Instruction is offered by local teachers.
Accommodations • Dormitories. Meals are taken on one's own, in central dining facility.
Program Details • Program offered once per year. Session length: 7 weeks. Departures are scheduled in June. The program is open to undergraduate students. Most participants are 20–26 years of age. Other requirements: 1 year college Mandarin Chinese, 1 Chinese area study course and a minimum 2.75 GPA. 25 participants per session. Application deadline: March 15.
Costs • $3735 (includes tuition, housing, some meals, insurance, excursions). A $200 deposit is required.
Contact • Anne Seitzinger, Program Coordinator, Short-Term Study Abroad, Northern Illinois University, Study Abroad Office-WI 417, DeKalb, IL 60115; 815-752-0700; Fax: 815-753-0825; E-mail: aseitz@niu.edu; World Wide Web: http://www.niu.edu/depts/intl_prgms/intl.html

OUACHITA BAPTIST UNIVERSITY

CHINA STUDY PROGRAM

General Information • Academic study program in Beijing. Classes are held on the campus of Peking University. Excursions to Hong Kong.
Learning Focus • Courses in Chinese language, Tai Chi, Chinese culture. Instruction is offered by professors from the sponsoring institution.
Accommodations • Hotels. Single rooms are available. Meals are taken on one's own, in central dining facility, in local restaurants.
Program Details • Program offered once per year. Session length: 4 weeks. Departures are scheduled in July. The program is open to undergraduate students. Most participants are 18–23 years of age. Other requirements: minimum 2.5 GPA. 15 participants per session. Application deadline: April 1.
Costs • $2950 (includes tuition, housing, some meals, excursions, international airfare). A $500 deposit is required.
Contact • Dr. Trey Berry, Director of International Programs, Ouachita Baptist University, OBU Box 3777, Arkadelphia, AR 71998; 501-245-5197; Fax: 501-245-5312; E-mail: berryt@alpha.obu.edu; World Wide Web: http://www.obu.edu

PHOTO ADVENTURE TOURS

GRAND CANAL

General Information • Photography tour with visits to Qufu, Shanghai, Suzhou, Wuxi, Yangzhou, Zhenjiang. Once at the destination country, participants travel by train, bus, foot, boat, airplane.
Learning Focus • Instruction in photography. Instruction is offered by researchers, naturalists, artists, historians, photog-

raphers. This program would appeal to people interested in photography, culture, history, adventure.
Accommodations • Hotels, boat. Single rooms are available for an additional $650.
Program Details • Program offered 4 times per year. Session length: 20 days. Departures are scheduled in April, May, September, October. Most participants are 18–80 years of age. Participants must be 18 years or older to enroll. 12 participants per session. Application deadline: 2 months prior to departure. Reservations are recommended at least 6 months before departure.
Costs • $3475 (includes housing, all meals, excursions, international airfare, photo guide). A $400 deposit is required.
Contact • Richard Libbey, General Partner, Photo Adventure Tours, 2035 Park Street, Atlantic Beach, NY 11509-1236; 516-371-0067; Fax: 516-371-1352

PHOTO ADVENTURE TOURS

SOUTHWEST CHINA EXPLORER

General Information • Photography tour with visits to Chengdu, Dali, Dukou, Emei Mountain, Shanghai, Xi'an, Kunming, Dianchi Lake, Stone Forest. Once at the destination country, participants travel by train, bus, foot, airplane.
Learning Focus • Instruction in photography. Instruction is offered by researchers, naturalists, artists, historians, photographers. This program would appeal to people interested in photography, culture, history, adventure, geology.
Accommodations • Hotels, boat, train. Single rooms are available for an additional $875.
Program Details • Program offered 2 times per year. Session length: 19 days. Departures are scheduled in April, May. Most participants are 18–80 years of age. Participants must be 18 years or older to enroll. Other requirements: good health. 12 participants per session. Application deadline: 2 months prior to departure. Reservations are recommended at least 6 months before departure.
Costs • $4395 (includes housing, all meals, excursions, international airfare, photo guide). A $400 deposit is required.
Contact • Richard Libbey, General Partner, Photo Adventure Tours, 2035 Park Street, Atlantic Beach, NY 11509-1236; 516-371-0067; Fax: 516-371-1352

PHOTO EXPLORER TOURS

MOUNTAINS AND WATERS OF CHINA

General Information • Photography tour with visits to Beijing, Huangshan, Yellow Mountain, Li River, West Lake, Beijing. Once at the destination country, participants travel by bus, foot, boat.
Learning Focus • Instruction in photography. Escorted travel to Huangshan, Guilin, Longji and Hangzhou. Nature observation (wildlife and scenery). Instruction is offered by professional photographers. This program would appeal to people interested in photography.
Accommodations • Hotels. Single rooms are available for an additional $550.
Program Details • Program offered once per year. Session length: 17 days. Departures are scheduled in October. Program is targeted to amateur and professional photographers. Most participants are 35–85 years of age. Other requirements: good physical condition. 8–16 participants per session. Application deadline: 60 days prior to departure. Reservations are recommended at least 3 months before departure.
Costs • $3895 (includes housing, all meals, excursions, international airfare). A $500 deposit is required.
Contact • Dennis Cox, Director, Photo Explorer Tours, 22111 Cleveland, #211, Dearborn, MI 48124; 800-315-4462; Fax: 313-561-1842; World Wide Web: http://www.apogeephoto.com/photo_explorer.html

PHOTO EXPLORER TOURS

SOUTHWEST CHINA EXPLORER

General Information • Photography tour with visits to China (Yunnan), Hong Kong; excursions to water-splashing festival, Stone Forest, Li River. Once at the destination country, participants travel by bus, foot, boat.
Learning Focus • Instruction in photography. Escorted travel to Lake Erhai and Lijiang. Nature observation (jungle, mountains). Instruction is offered by professional photographers. This program would appeal to people interested in photography.
Accommodations • Hotels. Single rooms are available for an additional $475.
Program Details • Program offered once per year. Session length: 17 days. Departures are scheduled in April. Program is targeted to amateur and professional photographers. Most participants are 35–85 years of age. Other requirements: good physical condition. 8–16 participants per session. Application deadline: 60 days prior to departure. Reservations are recommended at least 3 months before departure.
Costs • $3990 (includes housing, all meals, excursions, international airfare). A $500 deposit is required.
Contact • Dennis Cox, Director, Photo Explorer Tours, 22111 Cleveland, #211, Dearborn, MI 48124; 800-315-4462; Fax: 313-561-1842; E-mail: decoxphoto@aol.com; World Wide Web: http://www.apogeephoto.com/photo_explorer.html

 RAMAPO COLLEGE OF NEW JERSEY

SUMMER STUDY IN CHINA

General Information • Academic study program in Shanghai. Classes are held on the campus of Shanghai Teacher's University. Excursions to The Forbidden City, Emperor's Tombs, Tiananmen Square, the Summer Palace, Great Wall of China.
Learning Focus • Courses in history, political science, cultural studies, international business, Mandarin Chinese language. Instruction is offered by professors from the sponsoring institution.
Accommodations • Dormitories. Single rooms are available. Meals are taken as a group, in central dining facility.
Program Details • Program offered once per year. Session length: 3 weeks. Departures are scheduled in June. The program is open to undergraduate students, graduate students, adults. Most participants are 19 years of age and older. Other requirements: minimum 2.0 GPA and a minimum of 19 years old. 18 participants per session.

Costs • $3300 (includes tuition, housing, all meals, excursions, international airfare). A $300 deposit is required.
Contact • Mrs. Robyn Perricelli, Coordinator, Study Abroad, Ramapo College of New Jersey, 505 Ramapo Valley Road, Mahwah, NJ 07430; 201-529-7463; Fax: 201-529-7508; E-mail: rperrice@ramapo.edu

RUSSIAN AND EAST EUROPEAN PARTNERSHIPS

CHINESE LANGUAGE AND CULTURAL IMMERSION PROGRAM

General Information • Language study program in Beijing. Classes are held on the campus of Universal Ideas. Excursions to Tiananmen Square, Antique Market: Liuli Chaing, Great Wall of China, Shanghai, Forbidden City, The Temple of Heaven, Ming Tombs.
Learning Focus • Courses in Chinese language, Chinese culture and art, Chinese history. Instruction is offered by professors from the sponsoring institution and local teachers.
Accommodations • Homestays, locally-rented apartments. Single rooms are available. Meals are taken on one's own, with host family, in local restaurants, in residences.
Program Details • Program offered 11 times per year. Session length: 4 or more weeks. Departures are scheduled in January–November. The program is open to undergraduate students, graduate students, adults. Most participants are 18 years of age and older. Other requirements: in good health and 18 or older unless chaperoned by an adult. 6 participants per session. Application deadline: 45 days prior to departure.
Costs • $3995 (includes tuition, housing, some meals, books and class materials, excursions, international airfare, local transportation, airport transfers). A $1500 deposit is required.
Contact • Kenneth Fortune, President, Russian and East European Partnerships, PO Box 227, Fineview, NY 13640; 888-USE-REEP; Fax: 800-910-1777; E-mail: reep@fox.nstn.ca

ST. JOHN'S UNIVERSITY

CHINESE PROGRAM

General Information • Academic study program in Beibei. Classes are held on the campus of Southwest Normal University. Excursions to Hong Kong.
Learning Focus • Courses in Chinese language, art, sociology. Instruction is offered by local teachers.
Accommodations • Dormitories. Meals are taken as a group, on one's own, in central dining facility, in local restaurants.
Program Details • Program offered once per year. Session length: 12 weeks. Departures are scheduled in September. The program is open to undergraduate students. Most participants are 20–22 years of age. Other requirements: minimum 2.5 GPA. 25 participants per session. Application deadline: March.
Costs • $9200 (includes tuition, housing, all meals, excursions). Application fee: $100.
Contact • Stephen Burmeister-May, Director, Center for International Education, St. John's University, Collegeville, MN 56321; 320-363-2082; Fax: 320-363-2013; E-mail: intleduc@csbsju.edu

SANTA BARBARA MUSEUM OF ART

CHINA AND THE YANGTZE RIVER

General Information • Cultural tour with visits to Beijing, Shanghai, Xi'an, Yangtze River. Once at the destination country, participants travel by bus, boat, airplane.
Learning Focus • Escorted travel to Beijing, Xian, the Forbidden City, the Summer Palace and tombs. Museum visits (Arthur Sackler Museum, Hong Kong Museum of Art, Tsui Museum). Instruction is offered by art historians. This program would appeal to people interested in art, archaeology, photography.
Accommodations • Hotels, boat. Single rooms are available.
Program Details • Program offered once per year. Session length: 16 days. Departures are scheduled in September. Most participants are 30–80 years of age. Participants must be members of the sponsoring organization (annual dues: $40). 15–20 participants per session. Application deadline: June.
Costs • $5695 (includes housing, some meals, excursions, international airfare). A $500 deposit is required.
Contact • Shelley Ruston, Director of Special Programs, Santa Barbara Museum of Art, 1130 State Street, Santa Barbara, CA 93101; 805-963-4364, ext. 336; Fax: 805-966-6840

SANTA BARBARA MUSEUM OF ART

HEAVENLY LANDSCAPES OF CHINA: CLASSICAL AND TRIBAL CHINA

General Information • Cultural tour with visits to Dali, Guilin, Guiyang, Hangzhou, Kaili, Kunming, Shanghai. Once at the destination country, participants travel by train, bus, airplane.
Learning Focus • Escorted travel to Stone Bell Mountain, caves and landscapes. Instruction is offered by art historians. This program would appeal to people interested in art, archaeology, gardening, history, photography, architecture.
Accommodations • Hotels. Single rooms are available.
Program Details • Program offered once per year. Session length: 16 days. Departures are scheduled in May. Most participants are 30–80 years of age. Participants must be members of the sponsoring organization (annual dues: $40). 15–20 participants per session. Application deadline: February.
Costs • $5200 (includes housing, some meals, excursions, international airfare). A $500 deposit is required.
Contact • Shelley Ruston, Director of Special Programs, Santa Barbara Museum of Art, 1130 State Street, Santa Barbara, CA 93101; 805-963-4364, ext. 336; Fax: 805-966-6840

SYRACUSE UNIVERSITY

EMERGING MARKETS IN CHINA

General Information • Academic study program in Beijing, Shanghai. Classes are held on the campus of East China University of Chemical Technology.
Learning Focus • Courses in finance, international business. Instruction is offered by professors from the sponsoring institution.
Accommodations • Guest houses. Single rooms are available. Meals are taken as a group, in central dining facility.
Program Details • Program offered once per year. Session length: 5 weeks. Departures are scheduled in May. The program is open to undergraduate students, graduate students. Most participants are 19–25 years of age. Other requirements: minimum 2.5 GPA. 10 participants per session. Application deadline: March 15.
Costs • $5201 (includes tuition, housing, all meals, books and class materials, excursions). Application fee: $40. A $350 deposit is required.
Contact • Ms. Daisy Fried, Associate Director, Syracuse University, 119 Euclid Avenue, Syracuse, NY 13244-4170; 315-443-9419; Fax: 315-443-4593; E-mail: dsfried@summon3.syr.edu; World Wide Web: http://sumweb.syr.edu/dipa/dipa9.htm

TRAVELEARN

A CHINA ODYSSEY

General Information • Cultural tour with visits to Beijing, Qufu, Shanghai, Suzhou, Xi'an, Guilin, Hong Kong, Yangtze River. Once at the destination country, participants travel by train, bus, foot, boat, airplane. Program is affiliated with the nationwide TraveLearn network of 290 universities and colleges.
Learning Focus • Instruction in history, sociology, and the culture of China. Museum visits (Forbidden City, Confucian Mansion). Attendance at performances (Beijing Opera, a Shanghi Circus). Other activities include "people-to-people" experience in a farm village in Weifang and Shanghai. Instruction is offered by professors, artists, historians, social scientists. This program would appeal to people interested in history, cultural understanding.
Accommodations • Hotels. Single rooms are available for an additional $695.
Program Details • Program offered 5 times per year. Session length: 20–25 days. Departures are scheduled in April, July, September, October. Program is targeted to mature adults. Most participants are 40–75 years of age. Participants must be 18 years or older to enroll. 14–20 participants per session. Application deadline: 45 days prior to departure. Reservations are recommended at least 6 months before departure.
Costs • $3395 (includes housing, all meals, books and class materials, excursions, international airfare). A $300 deposit is required.
Contact • Keith Williams, Director of Marketing, TraveLearn, PO Box 315, Lakeville, PA 18438; 800-235-9114; Fax: 717-226-9114; E-mail: travelearn@aol.com

UNIVERSITY OF FLORIDA

SHAANXI TEACHERS UNIVERSITY, XIAN, CHINA–CHINESE CULTURE AND LANGUAGE

General Information • Language study program in Xi'an. Classes are held on the campus of Shaanxi Teacher's University. Excursions to local cultural sites/events.
Learning Focus • Courses in Chinese language, Chinese culture. Instruction is offered by local teachers.
Accommodations • Dormitories. Meals are taken on one's own, in central dining facility, in local restaurants.
Program Details • Program offered 3 times per year. Session length: 12 weeks. Departures are scheduled in May. The program is open to undergraduate students, graduate students, adults. Most participants are 18–40 years of age. Other requirements: minimum 2.5 GPA. Application deadline: March 15.
Costs • $5200 (includes tuition, housing, some meals, books and class materials, international airfare, administrative fee, living expenses). Application fee: $250.
Contact • Overseas Studies, University of Florida, 123 Tigert Hall, PO Box 113225, Gainesville, FL 32611-3225; 352-392-5206; Fax: 352-392-5575; E-mail: ovrseas@nervm.nerdc.ufl.edu

UNIVERSITY OF MINNESOTA, THE GLOBAL CAMPUS

CHINESE IN TIANJIN

General Information • Language study program in Tianjin. Classes are held on the campus of Nankai University. Excursions to Inner Mongolia, Beijing, Bedhaie, Ming Tombs.
Learning Focus • Courses in Chinese language, calligraphy, Chinese opera. Instruction is offered by local teachers.
Accommodations • Dormitories. Single rooms are available. Meals are taken as a group, in central dining facility.
Program Details • Program offered once per year. Session length: 9 weeks. Departures are scheduled in June. The program is open to undergraduate students, graduate students, pre-college students, adults. Most participants are 16–45 years of age. Other requirements: minimum 2.5 GPA. 15 participants per session. Application deadline: March 15.
Costs • $3350 (includes tuition, housing, all meals, excursions). Application fee: $40. A $400 deposit is required.
Contact • Chinese in Tianjin, University of Minnesota, The Global Campus, 106 P2 Nicholson Hall, 216 Pillsbury Drive, SE, Minneapolis, MN 55455-0138; 612-625-3379; Fax: 612-626-8009; E-mail: globalc@maroon.tc.umn.edu; World Wide Web: http://www.isp.umn.edu/tgchome/tgchome.html

UNIVERSITY OF SOUTHERN MISSISSIPPI

CHINESE HISTORY AND CULTURE

General Information • Academic study program in Beijing.
Learning Focus • Courses in history, international studies.
Program Details • Program offered once per year. Session length: 3 weeks. Departures are scheduled in May. The program is open to undergraduate students, graduate students. Other requirements: minimum 2.0 GPA and good academic standing.

Costs • $2499 for undergraduates, $2799 for graduate students (includes tuition, housing, international airfare). A $100 deposit is required.
Contact • Director, Chinese History and Culture, University of Southern Mississippi, Box 10047, Hattiesburg, MS 39406-0047; 601-266-4344; Fax: 601-266-5699

VOYAGERS INTERNATIONAL

PHOTOGRAPHIC TOUR AND WORKSHOP IN CHINA

General Information • Photography tour with visits to China. Once at the destination country, participants travel by foot, small vehicle.
Learning Focus • Instruction in photography. Nature observation (wildlife and scenery). Instruction is offered by photographers. This program would appeal to people interested in photography, culture, nature studies.
Accommodations • Hotels, lodges. Single rooms are available.
Program Details • Program offered 2 times per year. Session length: 2 weeks. Departures are scheduled in Fall, Spring. Program is targeted to photography enthusiasts. Most participants are 30–70 years of age. 8–10 participants per session. Reservations are recommended at least 6–12 months before departure.
Costs • $4000 (includes tuition, housing, some meals, excursions, international airfare). A $400 deposit is required.
Contact • David Blanton, Managing Director, Voyagers International, PO Box 915, Ithaca, NY 14851; 800-633-0299; Fax: 607-273-3873; E-mail: voyint@aol.com

HONG KONG

COOPERATIVE CENTER FOR STUDY ABROAD

HONG KONG

General Information • Academic study program in Hong Kong.
Learning Focus • Courses in art, political science. Instruction is offered by professors from the sponsoring institution.
Accommodations • Hotels. Single rooms are available. Meals are taken as a group, on one's own, in central dining facility, in local restaurants.
Program Details • Program offered once per year. Session length: 2 weeks. Departures are scheduled in May. The program is open to undergraduate students, graduate students, adults. Most participants are 18–60 years of age. Other requirements: minimum 2.0 GPA. Application deadline: March 1.
Costs • $3395 (includes housing, some meals, insurance, excursions, international airfare). A $100 deposit is required.
Contact • Dr. Michael A. Klembara, Executive Director, Cooperative Center for Study Abroad, NKU, BEP 301, Highland Heights, KY 41099; 800-319-6015; Fax: 605-572-6650; E-mail: ccsa@nku.edu

GEORGETOWN UNIVERSITY

COMPARATIVE BUSINESS: THE ASIA-PACIFIC PERSPECTIVE

General Information • Academic study program in Hong Kong. Classes are held on the campus of Chinese University of Hong Kong. Excursions to China Free Enterprize Zones.
Learning Focus • Courses in comparative business policy, international marketing. Instruction is offered by professors from the sponsoring institution and local teachers.
Accommodations • Dormitories. Meals are taken on one's own, in central dining facility, in local restaurants.
Program Details • Program offered once per year. Session length: 5 weeks. Departures are scheduled in July. The program is open to undergraduate students. Most participants are 21 years of age. Other requirements: minimum 3.0 GPA and rising senior status only. 22 participants per session. Application deadline: March.
Costs • $3800 (includes tuition, housing, some meals, books and class materials, insurance, excursions). A $100 deposit is required.
Contact • Marianne T. Needham, Director, International Programs, Georgetown University, 306 ICC, Box 571012, Washington, DC 20057-1012; 202-687-6184; Fax: 202-687-8954; E-mail: sscefps1@gunet.georgetown.edu; World Wide Web: http://guweb.georgetown.edu/ssce

LEXIA EXCHANGE INTERNATIONAL

LEXIA SUMMER PROGRAM IN HONG KONG

General Information • Academic study program in Hong Kong. Classes are held on the campus of University of Hong Kong. Excursions to China (Shanghai), Singapore, Taiwan (Taipei), Myanmar.
Learning Focus • Courses in civilizations, fine arts, economics, history, business, Chinese language, environmental studies, cultural studies. Instruction is offered by local teachers.
Accommodations • Homestays, dormitories. Single rooms are available. Meals are taken on one's own, with host family, in central dining facility, in local restaurants.
Program Details • Program offered once per year. Session length: 8 weeks. Departures are scheduled in June. The program is open to undergraduate students, graduate students, adults. Most participants are 18–35 years of age. Other requirements: minimum 2.5 GPA. 5–10 participants per session. Application deadline: April 15.
Costs • $4495 (includes tuition, housing, books and class materials, excursions). Application fee: $30. A $300 deposit is required.
Contact • Justin Meilgaard, Program Coordinator, Overseas Study, LEXIA Exchange International, 378 Cambridge Avenue, Palo Alto, CA 94306-1544; 800-775-3942; Fax: 415-327-9192; E-mail: lexia@rquartz.stanford.edu; World Wide Web: http://www.lexiaintl.org

SANTA BARBARA MUSEUM OF ART

HONG KONG 1997

General Information • Cultural tour with visits to Hong Kong. Once at the destination country, participants travel by bus, airplane. Program is affiliated with Tucson Museum of Art and the World Affairs Council of Northern California.
Learning Focus • Escorted travel to historical landmarks. Museum visits (Hong Kong Arts Festival). Instruction is offered by art historians. This program would appeal to people interested in art, current events, history, music, economics.
Accommodations • Hotels. Single rooms are available.
Program Details • Program offered once per year. Session length: 1 week. Departures are scheduled in February. Most participants are 30–80 years of age. Participants must be members of the sponsoring organization (annual dues: $40). 15–20 participants per session.
Costs • $3000 (includes housing, some meals, international airfare). A $400 deposit is required.
Contact • Shelley Ruston, Director of Special Programs, Santa Barbara Museum of Art, 1130 State Street, Santa Barbara, CA 93101; 805-963-4364, ext. 336; Fax: 805-966-6840

 SYRACUSE UNIVERSITY

GRADUATE MANAGEMENT INTERNSHIPS IN HONG KONG

General Information • Internship program in Hong Kong. Excursions to Southern China.

Learning Focus • Courses in international business, marketing. Instruction is offered by professors from the sponsoring institution.

Accommodations • Hotels. Meals are taken on one's own, in local restaurants.

Program Details • Program offered once per year. Session length: 7 weeks. Departures are scheduled in May. The program is open to graduate students. Most participants are 22–35 years of age. Other requirements: minimum 2.7 GPA. 15 participants per session. Application deadline: February 15.

Costs • $6000 (includes tuition, housing, some meals, books and class materials, excursions). Application fee: $40. A $350 deposit is required.

Contact • Ms. Daisy Fried, Associate Director, Syracuse University, 119 Euclid Avenue, Syracuse, NY 13244; 315-443-9419; Fax: 315-443-4593; E-mail: dsfried@summon3.syr.edu; World Wide Web: http://sumweb.syr.edu/dipa/dipa9.htm

 SYRACUSE UNIVERSITY

RETAILING AND FASHION INTERNSHIPS IN HONG KONG

General Information • Internship program in Hong Kong.

Learning Focus • Courses in retailing, fashion design. Instruction is offered by professors from the sponsoring institution.

Accommodations • Hotels. Single rooms are available. Meals are taken on one's own.

Program Details • Program offered once per year. Session length: 5 weeks. Departures are scheduled in May. The program is open to undergraduate students. Most participants are 19–25 years of age. Other requirements: background and courses in retailing or fashion design. 15 participants per session. Application deadline: February 15.

Costs • $4856 (includes tuition, housing, some meals, books and class materials, excursions). Application fee: $40. A $350 deposit is required.

Contact • Ms. Daisy Fried, Associate Director, Syracuse University, 119 Euclid Avenue, Syracuse, NY 13244-4170; 315-443-9419; Fax: 315-443-4593; E-mail: dsfried@summon3.syr.edu; World Wide Web: http://sumweb.syr.edu/dipa/dipa9.htm

CRAFT WORLD TOURS

INDIA PUSHKAR CAMEL FAIR

General Information • Cultural tour with visits to Agra, Bombay, Delhi, Jaipur, Jaisalmer, Jodhpur, Pushkar, Udaipur. Once at the destination country, participants travel by bus.
Learning Focus • Escorted travel to Gandhi Memorial, Taj Mahal, City Palace and Jagmandir Island. Museum visits (Craft Museum, Lok Kala Mandel Museum). Instruction is offered by artists. This program would appeal to people interested in handicrafts, folk arts, village life.
Accommodations • Hotels. Single rooms are available for an additional $595.
Program Details • Program offered once per year. Session length: 19 days. Departures are scheduled in November. Most participants are 30–80 years of age. Other requirements: appreciation of handcrafts and folk arts. 18 participants per session. Application deadline: October 1. Reservations are recommended at least 6 months before departure.
Costs • $4176 (includes housing, some meals, excursions, international airfare). A $250 deposit is required.
Contact • Tom Wilson, President, Craft World Tours, 6776 Warboys Road, Byron, NY 14422; 716-548-2667; Fax: 716-548-2821

CRAFT WORLD TOURS

SOUTH INDIA AND ORISSA

General Information • Cultural tour with visits to Bhubaneswar, Bombay, Calcutta, Cochin, Mysore, Bangalore, Madras, Madurai, Pondicherry. Once at the destination country, participants travel by bus.
Learning Focus • Escorted travel to Sun Temple of Konarak and coir weaving factory. Attendance at performances (Bharat Natyam, Kathakali dance-drama). Instruction is offered by artists. This program would appeal to people interested in handicrafts, folk arts, village life.
Accommodations • Hotels. Single rooms are available for an additional $510.
Program Details • Program offered once per year. Session length: 24 days. Departures are scheduled in January. Most participants are 30–80 years of age. Other requirements: appreciation of handcrafts and folk arts. 18 participants per session. Application deadline: November. Reservations are recommended at least 6 months before departure.
Costs • $4495 (includes housing, some meals, excursions, international airfare). A $250 deposit is required.
Contact • Tom Wilson, President, Craft World Tours, 6776 Warboys Road, Byron, NY 14422; 716-548-2667; Fax: 716-548-2821

CROSS-CULTURAL SOLUTIONS

PROJECT INDIA

General Information • Volunteer service program with visits to New Delhi, Taj Mahal. Once at the destination country, participants travel by rickshaw.
Learning Focus • Volunteer work (health, education, development, arts and recreation). Instruction is offered by professional cultural educators and social workers.
Accommodations • Homestays, program-owned apartments. Single rooms are available.
Program Details • Session length: 3 weeks. Departures are scheduled throughout the year. Program is targeted to seniors and students. Most participants are 21–70 years of age. Participants must be 18 years or older to enroll. 5 participants per session. Application deadline: 60 days prior to departure. Reservations are recommended at least 90 days before departure.
Costs • $1650 (includes housing, all meals, all Indian-based expenses, training, supervision, orientation). A $275 deposit is required.
Contact • Steve Rosenthal, Executive Director, Cross-Cultural Solutions, 6 Aurum Street, PO Box 625, Ophir, CO 81426; 970-728-5551; Fax: 970-728-4577; E-mail: ccsmailbox@aol.com; World Wide Web: http://emol.org/emol/projectindia

CROSS-CULTURAL SOLUTIONS

SAHELIN WOMAN'S ISSUES TOUR PROGRAM IN INDIA

General Information • Women's tour with visits to Agra, New Delhi, Rajasthan. Once at the destination country, participants travel by train, bus.
Learning Focus • Instruction in women's issues. Escorted travel to the Taj Mahal and palaces. Attendance at performances (Indian dance). Nature observation (nature preserve). Volunteer work (visiting many social service organizations). Other activities include camel trekking. Instruction is offered by naturalists, artists, social service leaders. This program would appeal to people interested in cultural travel, women's travel.
Accommodations • Hotels. Single rooms are available.
Program Details • Program offered 2 times per year. Session length: 3 weeks. Departures are scheduled in October, February. Most participants are 18–85 years of age. Participants must be 18 years or older to enroll. 15 participants per session. Application deadline: 30 days prior to departure. Reservations are recommended at least 60 days before departure.
Costs • $3500 (includes housing, all meals, excursions). A $300 deposit is required.
Contact • Steve Rosenthal, Executive Director, Cross-Cultural Solutions, PO Box 625, Ophir, CO 81426; 970-728-5551; Fax: 970-728-4577; E-mail: ccsmailbox@aol.com; World Wide Web: http://emol.org/emol/projectindia

FOLKWAYS INSTITUTE

TIGER PROJECT

General Information • Nature study tour with visits to India. Once at the destination country, participants travel by bus.

Learning Focus • Museum visits (local museums). Nature observation (wildlife, scenery). Instruction is offered by researchers, naturalists. This program would appeal to people interested in wildlife, botany, conservation.

Accommodations • Hotels. Single rooms are available.

Program Details • Program offered once per year. Session length: 18 days. Departures are scheduled in February. Program is targeted to seniors 55 years and older. Most participants are 55–78 years of age. 16 participants per session. Application deadline: September 20. Reservations are recommended at least 6 months before departure.

Costs • $3800 (includes housing, all meals, books and class materials, excursions, international airfare, instruction). A $50 deposit is required.

Contact • David Christopher, Director, Folkways Institute, 14600 Southeast Aldridge Road, Portland, OR 97236-6518; 503-658-6600; Fax: 503-658-8672

GEORGE MASON UNIVERSITY

INDIA: AN EMERGENT MARKET–PAST, PRESENT AND FUTURE

General Information • Academic study program in Agra, Delhi, Kerala, New Delhi. Classes are held on the campus of Cochin University of Science and Technology.

Learning Focus • Courses in cultural studies, arts, history. Instruction is offered by professors from the sponsoring institution and local teachers.

Accommodations • Dormitories. Meals are taken as a group, in central dining facility.

Program Details • Program offered once per year. Session length: 3 weeks. Departures are scheduled in December. The program is open to undergraduate students, graduate students, adults. Most participants are 18–50 years of age. Other requirements: minimum 2.25 GPA. 10–20 participants per session. Application deadline: October 11.

Costs • $3933 for George Mason University students, $4433 for other students (includes tuition, housing, some meals, insurance, excursions, international airfare). Application fee: $35. A $500 deposit is required.

Contact • Dr. Yehuda Lukacs, Director, Center for Global Education, George Mason University, 4400 University Drive, 235 Johnson Center, Fairfax, VA 22030; 703-993-2155; Fax: 703-993-2153; E-mail: ylukacs@gmu.edu; World Wide Web: http://www.gmu.edu/departments/oie

HIMALAYAN HIGH TREKS

MARKHA VALLEY TREK

General Information • Wilderness/adventure program with visits to Leh, New Delhi, Gandaha, Markha Valley, Indus Valley. Once at the destination country, participants travel by foot.

Learning Focus • Escorted travel to monasteries. Other activities include camping, hiking. Instruction is offered by local guides with a western leader. This program would appeal to people interested in Buddhism.

Accommodations • Hotels, campsites. Single rooms are available for an additional $200.

Program Details • Program offered once per year. Session length: 3 weeks. Departures are scheduled in August. Most participants are 18–40 years of age. Other requirements: must be very fit and active. 6–8 participants per session. Application deadline: June. Reservations are recommended at least 4–6 months before departure.

Costs • $1900 (includes housing, all meals, excursions). A $250 deposit is required.

Contact • Effie Fletcher, Director and Founder, Himalayan High Treks, 241 Dolores Street, San Francisco, CA 94103-2211; 800-455-8735; Fax: 415-861-2391; E-mail: effie@well.com; World Wide Web: http://www.well.com/user/effie

HIMALAYAN HIGH TREKS

SIKKIM AND THE BLUE SHEEP TRAIL

General Information • Cultural tour with visits to Darjeeling, New Delhi, Sikkim. Once at the destination country, participants travel by foot.

Learning Focus • Museum visits (Institute of Tibetology). Other activities include camping, hiking, visits to monasteries and other cultural institutions. Instruction is offered by American group leader and local guide. This program would appeal to people interested in Buddhism, mountains.

Accommodations • Hotels, campsites. Single rooms are available for an additional $200.

Program Details • Program offered once per year. Session length: 2 weeks. Departures are scheduled in October. Most participants are 30–60 years of age. Participants must be 12 years or older to enroll. Other requirements: must be an active, healthy person. 6–8 participants per session. Application deadline: August 6. Reservations are recommended at least 4–6 months before departure.

Costs • $1600 (includes all meals, excursions). A $250 deposit is required.

Contact • Effie Fletcher, Director and Founder, Himalayan High Treks, 241 Dolores Street, San Francisco, CA 94103-2211; 800-455-8735; Fax: 415-861-2391; E-mail: effie@well.com; World Wide Web: http://www.well.com/user/effie

HIMALAYAN HIGH TREKS

ZANSKAR AND LADAKH TREK

General Information • Wilderness/adventure program with visits to Kulu, Ladakh, Leh, Manali, New Delhi, Zanskar, Darcha, Lamrayuru. Once at the destination country, participants travel by foot.

Learning Focus • Escorted travel to Buddhist monasteries. Other activities include camping, hiking. Instruction is offered by American group leader and local guide. This program would appeal to people interested in Buddhism.

Accommodations • Homestays, hotels, campsites. Single rooms are available for an additional $200.

Program Details • Program offered once per year. Session length: 4 weeks. Departures are scheduled in July. Most participants are 16–40 years of age. Other requirements: must be very fit and active. 8 participants per session.

Application deadline: April. Reservations are recommended at least 6 months before departure.
Costs • $2400 (includes housing, all meals, excursions). A $250 deposit is required.
Contact • Effie Fletcher, Director and Founder, Himalayan High Treks, 241 Dolores Street, San Francisco, CA 94103-2211; 800-455-8735; Fax: 415-861-2391; E-mail: effie@well.com; World Wide Web: http://www.well.com/user/effie

ILLINOIS STATE UNIVERSITY

SUMMER PROGRAM IN INDIA

General Information • Academic study program in Pune. Classes are held on the campus of Simbioisis International Cultural and Education Center.
Learning Focus • Courses in business, business culture and practices, Indian history, contemporary Indian culture and civilization, contemporary Indian political, economic, and social issues.
Accommodations • Hotels.
Program Details • Program offered once per year. Session length: 4 weeks. Departures are scheduled in May. The program is open to undergraduate students, graduate students. Other requirements: minimum 2.5 GPA and a minimum of sophomore status. 15 participants per session. Application deadline: March 15.
Costs • $1320 (includes housing, all meals, excursions, fees).
Contact • Dr. Sharad Chitgopekar, Illinois State University, Campus Box 5580, Normal, IL 61790-5580; 309-438-7993; Fax: 309-438-3987; E-mail: oisp@rs6000.cmp.ilstu.edu; World Wide Web: http://www.orat.ilstu.edu/

JOURNEYS INTERNATIONAL, INC.

GREAT SIGHTS OF INDIA

General Information • Cultural tour with visits to Agra, Jaipur, Khajuraho, Varanasi. Once at the destination country, participants travel by foot, boat.
Learning Focus • Escorted travel to sites and cities of India. Other activities include boat ride on Ganges River. Instruction is offered by local English-speaking guides. This program would appeal to people interested in culture, nature studies, wildlife, photography, bird watching.
Accommodations • Hotels. Single rooms are available for an additional $375.
Program Details • Session length: 8 days. Departures are scheduled throughout the year. Program is targeted to people interested in culture. Most participants are 25–55 years of age. Participants must be 12 years or older to enroll. 2–8 participants per session. Application deadline: 60 days prior to departure. Reservations are recommended at least 60 days before departure.
Costs • $1195 (includes housing). A $300 deposit is required.
Contact • Pat Ballard, Asia Sales Director, Journeys International, Inc., 4011 Jackson Road, Ann Arbor, MI 48103; 313-665-4407; Fax: 313-665-2945; E-mail: pat@journeys-intl.com; World Wide Web: http://www.journeys-intl.com

JOURNEYS INTERNATIONAL, INC.

INDUS VALLEY ODYSSEY

General Information • Religion/spirituality program with visits to Delhi, Temisgam. Once at the destination country, participants travel by foot, small vehicle.
Learning Focus • Escorted travel to monasteries of Ladakh. Other activities include hiking. Instruction is offered by Tsering guides. This program would appeal to people interested in culture, religion, nature studies.
Accommodations • Hotels. Single rooms are available for an additional $100.
Program Details • Session length: 8 days. Departures are scheduled throughout the year. Most participants are 25–55 years of age. Participants must be 12 years or older to enroll. 2–12 participants per session. Application deadline: 60 days prior to departure. Reservations are recommended at least 60 days before departure.
Costs • $1095 (includes housing, some meals). A $300 deposit is required.
Contact • Pat Ballard, Asia Sales Director, Journeys International, Inc., 4011 Jackson Road, Ann Arbor, MI 48103; 313-665-4407; Fax: 313-665-2945; E-mail: pat@journeys-intl.com; World Wide Web: http://www.journeys-intl.com

JOURNEYS INTERNATIONAL, INC.

LADAKH WOMEN'S TREK

General Information • Cultural tour with visits to Delhi, Dharamsala, Leh, Likir, Nimo, Temisgam. Once at the destination country, participants travel by foot, hiking or small vehicle.
Learning Focus • Escorted travel to villages and monasteries of Ladakh. Other activities include camping, hiking. Instruction is offered by senior staff. This program would appeal to people interested in religion, nature studies, culture, photography.
Accommodations • Homestays, hotels, campsites. Single rooms are available for an additional $200.
Program Details • Program offered once per year. Session length: 20 days. Departures are scheduled in July. Program is targeted to active women interested in cultures. Most participants are 25–55 years of age. Participants must be 12 years or older to enroll. Other requirements: must be in good health and physical condition. 2–12 participants per session. Application deadline: 60 days prior to departure. Reservations are recommended at least 60 days before departure.
Costs • $2595 (includes housing, some meals). A $300 deposit is required.
Contact • Pat Ballard, Asia Sales Director, Journeys International, Inc., 4011 Jackson Road, Ann Arbor, MI 48103; 313-665-4407; Fax: 313-665-2945; E-mail: pat@journeys-intl.com; World Wide Web: http://www.journeys-intl.com

JOURNEYS INTERNATIONAL, INC.

NORTHERN LADAKH TREK

General Information • Religion/spirituality program with visits to Delhi, Likir Monastery, Nimo, Ridzong Monastery, Temisgam. Once at the destination country, participants travel by foot.
Learning Focus • Escorted travel to monasteries of Ladakh. Other activities include camping, trekking. Instruction is

offered by Ladakhi guides. This program would appeal to people interested in trekking, nature studies, culture, religion.
Accommodations • Hotels, campsites. Single rooms are available for an additional $200.
Program Details • Program offered 3 times per year. Session length: 17 days. Departures are scheduled in May–July. Program is targeted to active hikers with an interest in cross-cultural contact. Most participants are 25–55 years of age. Participants must be 12 years or older to enroll. Other requirements: must be in good health and physical condition. 12 participants per session. Application deadline: 60 days prior to departure. Reservations are recommended at least 60 days before departure.
Costs • $1095 (includes housing, some meals). A $300 deposit is required.
Contact • Pat Ballard, Asia Sales Director, Journeys International, Inc., 4011 Jackson Road, Ann Arbor, MI 48103; 313-665-4407; Fax: 313-665-2945; E-mail: pat@journeys-intl.com; World Wide Web: http://www.journeys-intl.com

JOURNEYS INTERNATIONAL, INC.

SOUTH INDIA NATURAL HISTORY EXPLORATORY

General Information • Cultural tour with visits to Allepey, Kurumba Village, Madras, Nilgiri Grassland Plateau, Ooty, Thoda Village. Once at the destination country, participants travel by foot, boat.
Learning Focus • Escorted travel to small villages. Attendance at performances (Hindu rituals). Nature observation (national parks). Other activities include camping, canoeing. Instruction is offered by local English-speaking experts. This program would appeal to people interested in wildlife, culture, bird watching, nature studies.
Accommodations • Hotels, campsites. Single rooms are available for an additional $350.
Program Details • Program offered once per year. Session length: 15 days. Departures are scheduled in January. Program is targeted to active persons interested in cultures. Most participants are 25–55 years of age. Participants must be 12 years or older to enroll. 15 participants per session. Application deadline: 60 days prior to departure. Reservations are recommended at least 60 days before departure.
Costs • $2595 (includes housing). A $300 deposit is required.
Contact • Pat Ballard, Asia Sales Director, Journeys International, Inc., 4011 Jackson Road, Ann Arbor, MI 48103; 313-665-4407; Fax: 313-665-2945; E-mail: melissa@journeys-intl.com; World Wide Web: http://www.journeys-intl.com

NATURE EXPEDITIONS INTERNATIONAL

SANCTUARIES OF THE SUBCONTINENT: INDIA WILDLIFE EXPEDITION

General Information • Nature study tour with visits to India (Agra, Bharatpur, Delhi, Jaipur, Ranthambhor), Nepal (Nepal (Royal Chitwan)); excursions to Kazaringa, Katmandu Valley.
Learning Focus • Escorted travel to game parks. Museum visits (Taj Mahal). Nature observation (wildlife). Instruction is offered by professors, naturalists. This program would appeal to people interested in wildlife, culture, nature studies, bird watching.
Accommodations • Hotels, lodges. Single rooms are available for an additional $400.
Program Details • Program offered 3 times per year. Session length: 16 days. Departures are scheduled in February, March, November. Most participants are 25–75 years of age. Other requirements: doctor's permission for participants 70 years and older. Reservations are recommended at least 6 months before departure.
Costs • $2690 (includes housing, some meals, excursions, all guiding). A $400 deposit is required.
Contact • Christopher Kyle, President, Nature Expeditions International, 6400 East El Dorado Circle, Suite 210, Tucson, AZ 85715; 800-869-0639; Fax: 520-721-6719; E-mail: naturexp@aol.com

NORTHERN ILLINOIS UNIVERSITY

DISCOVER THE ROLE OF ADULT EDUCATION IN INDIA

General Information • Academic study program in India. Excursions to Mansingh, Taj Mahal, Bombay, Agra, Bangalore.
Learning Focus • Courses in adult education. Instruction is offered by professors from the sponsoring institution.
Accommodations • Hotels. Single rooms are available. Meals are taken as a group, in local restaurants.
Program Details • Program offered once per year. Session length: 2 weeks. Departures are scheduled in December. The program is open to undergraduate students, graduate students. Most participants are 30–55 years of age. 12 participants per session. Application deadline: November 1.
Costs • $2600 (includes tuition, housing, some meals, insurance, excursions). A $200 deposit is required.
Contact • Program Coordinator, Short-Term Study Abroad, Northern Illinois University, Study Abroad Office-WI 417, DeKalb, IL 60115; 815-752-0700; Fax: 815-753-0825; E-mail: aseitz@niu.edu; World Wide Web: http://www.niu.edu/depts/intl_prgms/intl.html

THE PARTNERSHIP FOR SERVICE-LEARNING

INDIA INTERSESSION

General Information • Academic study and volunteer service program in Calcutta. Excursions to Delhi, Agra (Taj Mahal).
Learning Focus • Courses in history, sociology, religion, literature.
Accommodations • Locally-rented apartments. Meals are taken as a group, in local restaurants, in residences.
Program Details • Program offered once per year. Session length: 3 weeks. Departures are scheduled in December. The program is open to undergraduate students, graduate students, pre-college students, adults. Most participants are 19–24 years of age. 11 participants per session. Application deadline: 2 months prior to departure.
Costs • $3400 (includes tuition, housing, some meals, books and class materials, excursions, international airfare,

service placement and supervision, pre-departure and orientation materials). A $250 deposit is required.
Contact • Maureen Lowney, Coordinator of Student Programs, The Partnership for Service-Learning, 815 Second Avenue, Suite 315, New York, NY 10960; 212-986-0989; Fax: 212-986-5039; E-mail: pslny@aol.com

PHOTO ADVENTURE TOURS

INDIA: THE PASSAGE

General Information • Photography and cultural tour with visits to Jaipur, Jaisalmer, Jodhpur, Pushkar Camel Fair, Ranthambhor Wildlife Park, Varanasi, bird sanctuary, tiger sanctuary. Once at the destination country, participants travel by bus, car, rickshaw, camel, or elephant.
Learning Focus • Instruction in Hinduism and Buddhism. Escorted travel to archaeological sites, Pushkar Camel Fair, the Taj Mahal and the University of Benares. Instruction is offered by researchers, naturalists, artists, historians, photographers. This program would appeal to people interested in culture, history, photography, adventure.
Accommodations • Hotels. Single rooms are available for an additional $850.
Program Details • Program offered once per year. Session length: 23 days. Departures are scheduled in October. Most participants are 18–83 years of age. Participants must be 18 years or older to enroll. 12 participants per session. Application deadline: 2 months prior to departure. Reservations are recommended at least 6 months before departure.
Costs • $4575 (includes housing, some meals, excursions, international airfare). A $400 deposit is required.
Contact • Richard Libbey, General Partner, Photo Adventure Tours, 2035 Park Street, Atlantic Beach, NY 11509-1236; 516-371-0067; Fax: 516-371-1352

PHOTO ADVENTURE TOURS

SAFARI IN INDIA

General Information • Nature study tour with visits to India (Corbett National Park, Delhi, Keolateo Bird Sanctuary, Varanasi), Nepal (Nepal (Kathmandu, Royal Chitwan Park)); excursions to game park. Once at the destination country, participants travel by train, bus, foot, airplane, rickshaw.
Learning Focus • Instruction in photography. Field research in wildlife (Project Tiger). Nature observation (wildlife, large and small birds). Instruction is offered by naturalists, artists, historians, photographers. This program would appeal to people interested in photography, mountain climbing, wildlife, ornithology, culture, adventure.
Accommodations • Hotels, campsites. Single rooms are available for an additional $975.
Program Details • Program offered once per year. Session length: 21–25 days. Departures are scheduled in January. Most participants are 50–60 years of age. 10 participants per session. Reservations are recommended at least 3 months before departure.
Costs • $4995 (includes housing, some meals, excursions, international airfare). A $400 deposit is required.
Contact • Richard Libbey, General Partner, Photo Adventure Tours, 2035 Park Street, Atlantic Beach, NY 11509-1236; 516-371-0067; Fax: 516-371-1352

PHOTO ADVENTURE TOURS

SOUTH INDIA

General Information • Photography tour with visits to Bombay, Cochin, Madras, Madurai, Mahabalipuram, Mysore. Once at the destination country, participants travel by bus, foot, boat, airplane, rickshaw.
Learning Focus • Instruction in photography. Nature observation (wildlife). Instruction is offered by professors, naturalists, artists, historians, photographers. This program would appeal to people interested in photography, culture, temples, art, adventure, wildlife.
Accommodations • Hotels. Single rooms are available for an additional $995.
Program Details • Program offered once per year. Session length: 24 days. Departures are scheduled in February. Most participants are 18–80 years of age. Participants must be 18 years or older to enroll. 12 participants per session. Application deadline: 2 months prior to departure. Reservations are recommended at least 6 months before departure.
Costs • $4995 (includes housing, all meals, excursions, international airfare). A $400 deposit is required.
Contact • Richard Libbey, General Partner, Photo Adventure Tours, 2035 Park Street, Atlantic Beach, NY 11509-1236; 516-371-0067; Fax: 516-371-1352

SANTA BARBARA MUSEUM OF ART

INDIA: LEGENDARY RAJASTHA

General Information • Cultural tour with visits to Agra, Delhi, Jaipur, Jaisalmer, Jodhpur, Udaipur. Once at the destination country, participants travel by bus, airplane. Program is affiliated with Scripps College Alumnae.
Learning Focus • Escorted travel to forts, palaces, tombs, gardens, castles and bazaars. Museum visits (National Museum in Delhi, Crafts Museum, Gandhi Memorial). Attendance at performances (music, concerts and dance recitals). Instruction is offered by art historians. This program would appeal to people interested in art, photography, architecture, gardening.
Accommodations • Hotels. Single rooms are available for an additional $1190.
Program Details • Program offered once per year. Session length: 18 days. Departures are scheduled in November. Most participants are 30–80 years of age. Participants must be members of the sponsoring organization (annual dues: $40). 15–20 participants per session.
Costs • $5395 including airfare, $3930 without airfare (includes housing, all meals, excursions, international airfare). A $500 deposit is required.
Contact • Shelley Ruston, Director of Special Programs, Santa Barbara Museum of Art, 1130 State Street, Santa Barbara, CA 93101; 805-963-4364, ext. 336; Fax: 805-966-6840

SANTA BARBARA MUSEUM OF ART

INDIA: THE EXOTIC SOUTH

General Information • Cultural tour with visits to Ayderabad, Bangalore, Bombay, Cochin, Madras, Mysore. Once at the destination country, participants travel by bus, airplane.

Learning Focus • Escorted travel to temples, tombs, palaces and historical sites. Museum visits (National Museums, J. K. Mittall Museum). Instruction is offered by art historians. This program would appeal to people interested in art, music, architecture, dance.
Accommodations • Hotels. Single rooms are available.
Program Details • Program offered once per year. Session length: 18 days. Departures are scheduled in January. Most participants are 30–80 years of age. Participants must be members of the sponsoring organization (annual dues: $40). 15–20 participants per session. Application deadline: October.
Costs • $5200 (includes housing, all meals, excursions, international airfare). A $500 deposit is required.
Contact • Shelley Ruston, Director of Special Programs, Santa Barbara Museum of Art, 1130 State Street, Santa Barbara, CA 93101; 805-963-4364, ext. 336; Fax: 805-966-6840

UNIVERSITY OF PENNSYLVANIA

PENN-IN-INDIA

General Information • Academic study program in Pune. Classes are held on the campus of University of Poona.
Learning Focus • Courses in economics, religion, performing arts, folk medicine. Instruction is offered by professors from the sponsoring institution and local teachers.
Accommodations • Homestays. Meals are taken with host family, in residences.
Program Details • Program offered once per year. Session length: 6 weeks. Departures are scheduled in June. The program is open to undergraduate students, graduate students. Most participants are 18–35 years of age. 23 participants per session. Application deadline: March 1.
Costs • $4424 (includes tuition, housing, excursions, international airfare). Application fee: $35. A $300 deposit is required.
Contact • Elizabeth Sachs, Director, Penn Summer Abroad, University of Pennsylvania, 3440 Market Street, Suite 100, Philadelphia, PA 19104-3335; 215-898-5738; Fax: 215-573-2053; E-mail: esachs@mail.sas.upenn.edu

UNIVERSITY OF WISCONSIN–MADISON

KERALA SUMMER PERFORMING ARTS PROGRAM

General Information • Performing arts program in Thiruvananthapuram. Classes are held on the campus of University of Kerala.
Learning Focus • Courses in performing arts, Malayalam language, martial arts, meditational arts. Instruction is offered by local teachers.
Accommodations • Program-owned houses. Meals are taken as a group, in residences.
Program Details • Program offered once per year. Session length: 10–11 weeks. Departures are scheduled in June. The program is open to undergraduate students, graduate students. Other requirements: sophomore standing. 3–18 participants per session. Application deadline: first Friday in February.
Costs • $4120 (includes tuition, housing, some meals, books and class materials, excursions). A $100 deposit is required.
Contact • Gwen Mueller, Office of International Studies and Programs, University of Wisconsin–Madison, 261 Bascom Hall, 500 Lincoln Drive, Madison, WI 53706; 608-265-6329; Fax: 608-262-6998; E-mail: abroad@macc.wisc.edu; World Wide Web: http://www.wisc.edu/uw-oisp/

ALPINE ASCENTS, INTERNATIONAL

CARSTENSZ PYRAMID

General Information • Mountain climbing tour with visits to Bali, Carstensz Pyramid, Irian Jaya. Once at the destination country, participants travel by foot, airplane, helicopter.
Learning Focus • Instruction in rock climbing. Escorted travel to Nasidomeh, Larson Lake and Ilaga. Nature observation (flora, jungle, rain forest). Other activities include camping, hiking. Instruction is offered by sports professionals. This program would appeal to people interested in mountain climbing, rock climbing.
Accommodations • Hotels, campsites. Single rooms are available.
Program Details • Program offered once per year. Session length: 19 days. Departures are scheduled in November. Program is targeted to mountain and rock climbers. Other requirements: basic rock climbing skills and good physical condition. 10 participants per session. Reservations are recommended at least 6 months before departure.
Costs • $9500 (includes housing, some meals, local airfare, helicopter transport, group equipment, guides, porters). A $2500 deposit is required.
Contact • Gordon Janow, Program Coordinator, Alpine Ascents, International, 16615 Saybrook Drive, Woodinville, WA 98072; 206-788-1951; Fax: 206-788-6757; E-mail: aaiclimb@accessone.com

ARCHAEOLOGICAL TOURS

INDONESIA

General Information • Cultural tour with visits to Hong Kong, Indonesia (Bali, Jakarta, Solo, Tana Toraja, Yogyakarta). Once at the destination country, participants travel by bus, airplane.
Learning Focus • Museum visits (Jakarta, Solo). Attendance at performances (dance, music, puppet shows). Instruction is offered by professors, historians. This program would appeal to people interested in history, art, crafts, archaeology, music.
Accommodations • Hotels. Single rooms are available for an additional $985.
Program Details • Program offered once per year. Session length: 21 days. Departures are scheduled in August. Program is targeted to adults. Most participants are 30–80 years of age. 20 participants per session. Application deadline: 1 month prior to departure.
Costs • $3690 (includes housing, some meals, excursions). A $500 deposit is required.
Contact • Archaeological Tours, 271 Madison Avenue, Suite 904, New York, NY 10016; 212-986-3054; Fax: 212-370-1561

BOLDER ADVENTURES, ASIA TRANSPACIFIC JOURNEYS

INDONESIA: CULTURE AND WILDLIFE

General Information • Cultural and nature study tour with visits to Bali, Borneo, Java, Komodo Islands, Sumba, Sumatra, New Guinea, Bandas, Sulawesi. Once at the destination country, participants travel by foot, boat, airplane.
Learning Focus • Attendance at performances (dances in Bali and Java). Nature observation (Komodo Dragons, orangutan). Instruction is offered by professors, researchers, naturalists, artists, historians. This program would appeal to people interested in culture, wildlife.
Accommodations • Hotels. Single rooms are available for an additional $375.
Program Details • Program offered 7 times per year. Session length: 17 days. Departures are scheduled in April–October. Most participants are 35–65 years of age. Participants must be 18 years or older to enroll. 12–14 participants per session. Reservations are recommended at least 4 months before departure.
Costs • $3495 (includes housing, all meals, excursions). A $500 deposit is required.
Contact • Bolder Adventures, Asia Transpacific Journeys, 3055 Center Green Drive, Boulder, CO 80301; 800-642-2742; Fax: 303-443-7078; World Wide Web: http://www.southeastasia.com/

BOLDER ADVENTURES, ASIA TRANSPACIFIC JOURNEYS

ORANGUTAN RESEARCH AND STUDY TOUR

General Information • Nature study tour with visits to Borneo, Bali, Java, New Guinea, Sumatra. Once at the destination country, participants travel by foot, boat, airplane, mini-van. Program is affiliated with Orangutan Foundation International.
Learning Focus • Instruction in primate research and conservation. Field research in primate behavior. Nature observation (orangutans). Volunteer work (supporting work of Orangutan Foundation International). Instruction is offered by professors, researchers, naturalists, scientists. This program would appeal to people interested in wildlife, natural history, conservation, rain forest ecology.
Accommodations • Dormitories, guest houses. Single rooms are available for an additional $220.
Program Details • Program offered 10 times per year. Session length: 10 days. Departures are scheduled in June–December. Most participants are 25–55 years of age. 10 participants per session. Reservations are recommended at least 6 months before departure.
Costs • $2000 (includes tuition, housing, some meals, excursions). A $500 deposit is required.

Contact • Robin Van Norman, OFI Program Director, Bolder Adventures, Asia Transpacific Journeys, 3055 Center Green Drive, Boulder, CO 80301; 800-642-2742; Fax: 303-443-7078; E-mail: bolder@southeastasia.com; World Wide Web: http://www.southeastasia.com/

It is the 10th year that Bolder Adventures–Asia Transpacific Journeys is offering trips to Thailand, Indonesia, Laos, Vietnam, Cambodia, Philippines, Papua, New Guinea, Malaysia, Burma, and Nepal. Featuring close-up cultural interaction, wildlife, and natural history encounters. Small group trips feature leadership by world authorities such as Dr. Birute Galdikas, orangutan expert; Bill Dalton, author of the *Indonesia Handbook*; Joe Cummings, southeast Asia scholar and author of *Lonely Planet* guides to Laos, Thailand, and Burma. Also offered are custom independent travel services. Activities include elephant safaris, visits with indigenous people, wildlife viewing of orangutans and Komodo dragons, sailing, sea kayaking, snorkeling, scuba diving, and hiking.

CRAFT WORLD TOURS

INDONESIA

General Information • Cultural tour with visits to Bali, Irian Jaya, Kalimantan (Borneo), Sulawesi. Once at the destination country, participants travel by bus.
Learning Focus • Escorted travel to Mother temple of Besakih and the Balien Valley. Museum visits (Jayapuran local museum). Instruction is offered by artists. This program would appeal to people interested in handicrafts, folk arts, village life.
Accommodations • Hotels. Single rooms are available for an additional $395.
Program Details • Program offered once per year. Session length: 22 days. Departures are scheduled in May. Most participants are 30–80 years of age. Other requirements: appreciation of handcrafts and folk arts. 18 participants per session. Application deadline: March. Reservations are recommended at least 6 months before departure.
Costs • $4787 (includes housing, some meals, excursions, international airfare). A $250 deposit is required.
Contact • Tom Wilson, President, Craft World Tours, 6776 Warboys Road, Byron, NY 14422; 716-548-2667; Fax: 716-548-2821

FOREIGN LANGUAGE STUDY ABROAD SERVICE

INTERNATIONAL LANGUAGE STUDY HOMESTAYS IN INDONESIA

General Information • Language study program in Indonesia.
Learning Focus • Courses in Indonesian language. Instruction is offered by local teachers.
Accommodations • Homestays. Single rooms are available. Meals are taken with host family, in residences.
Program Details • Session length: varies. Departures are scheduled in January–December. The program is open to undergraduate students, graduate students, pre-college students, adults. Most participants are 12 years of age and older. Other requirements: students must be at least 12 years old. 1 participant per session.
Costs • Contact sponsor for information. A $300 deposit is required.
Contact • Louise Harber, Coordinator, Foreign Language Study Abroad Service, Department IH, Box 903, 5935 Southwest 64th Avenue, South Miami, FL 33143; 800-282-1090; Fax: 305-662-2907; E-mail: flsas@netpoint.net; World Wide Web: http://www.netpoint.net/~flsas

FORUM TRAVEL INTERNATIONAL

IMAGES OF INDONESIA

General Information • Wilderness/adventure program with visits to National Parks, Bali, Kalimantan, Sumatra, Nusa Tenggara, Sulawesi, Spice Islands. Once at the destination country, participants travel by bus, foot, boat, airplane. Program is affiliated with International Ecosystems University.
Learning Focus • Instruction in natural and cultural history. Escorted travel to Bali, Kalimantan, Sumatra, Nusa Tenggara, Sulawesi and the Spice Islands. Nature observation (rain forests, marine, pelagic, montane ecosystems). Instruction is offered by professors, naturalists. This program would appeal to people interested in nature studies, culture.
Accommodations • Program-owned houses, hotels, campsites.
Program Details • Program offered 6 times per year. Session length: 2 weeks. Departures are scheduled throughout the year. Most participants are 16–85 years of age. Participants must be 16 years or older to enroll. 12–20 participants per session.
Costs • $1988 (includes tuition, housing, all meals, excursions, international airfare). A $300 deposit is required.
Contact • Jeannie Graves, Operations Manager, Forum Travel International, 91 Gregory Lane #21, Pleasant Hill, CA 94525; 510-671-2900; Fax: 510-671-2993; E-mail: forum@ix.netcom.com; World Wide Web: http://www.ten-io.com/forumtravel

JOURNEYS INTERNATIONAL, INC.

GRAND INDONESIAN ODYSSEY

General Information • Cultural tour with visits to Bali, Can, Denpasar, Java, Komodo, Camp Leakey.
Learning Focus • Escorted travel to small villages of Indonesia. Attendance at performances (dance concert). Other activities include hiking. Instruction is offered by Indonesian experts. This program would appeal to people interested in culture, photography, nature studies, wildlife.
Accommodations • Lodges. Single rooms are available for an additional $275.

Program Details • Session length: 15 days. Departures are scheduled throughout the year. Most participants are 25–55 years of age. Participants must be 12 years or older to enroll. 2–8 participants per session. Application deadline: 60 days prior to departure. Reservations are recommended at least 60 days before departure.
Costs • $1495 (includes housing, some meals). A $300 deposit is required.
Contact • Pat Ballard, Asia Sales Director, Journeys International, Inc., 4011 Jackson Road, Ann Arbor, MI 48103; 313-665-4407; Fax: 313-665-2945; E-mail: pat@journeys-intl.com; World Wide Web: http://www.journeys-intl.com

JOURNEYS INTERNATIONAL, INC.

ORANGUTANS OF CAMP LEAKEY

General Information • Wilderness/adventure program with visits to Camp Leakey. Once at the destination country, participants travel by boat.
Learning Focus • Attendance at performances (a traditional Hornbill Dance). Instruction is offered by Indonesian experts. This program would appeal to people interested in nature studies, culture, wildlife, photography.
Accommodations • Homestays, hotels, lodges. Single rooms are available for an additional $50.
Program Details • Program offered 12 times per year. Session length: 8 days. Departures are scheduled throughout the year. Most participants are 25–55 years of age. Participants must be 12 years or older to enroll. 2 participants per session. Application deadline: 60 days prior to departure. Reservations are recommended at least 60 days before departure.
Costs • $1295 (includes housing, some meals). A $300 deposit is required.
Contact • Pat Ballard, Asia Sales Director, Journeys International, Inc., 4011 Jackson Road, Ann Arbor, MI 48103; 313-665-4407; Fax: 313-665-2945; E-mail: pat@journeys-intl.com; World Wide Web: http://www.journeys-intl.com

 TRAVELEARN

AN INDONESIAN ODYSSEY

General Information • Cultural tour with visits to Bali, Borobudur, Lombok, Prambanan, Ubud, Yogyakarta, Toraja Highlands. Once at the destination country, participants travel by bus, foot, airplane. Program is affiliated with the nationwide TraveLearn network of 290 universities and colleges.
Learning Focus • Instruction in history, art, religion and cultural understanding. Museum visits (Palace Museum in Yogyakarta). Attendance at performances (Barong Dance, Kecak Fire Dance). Other activities include "people-to-people" experience in Yogyakarta and Bali. Instruction is offered by professors, artists. This program would appeal to people interested in history, religion, art, cultural understanding.
Accommodations • Hotels. Single rooms are available for an additional $595.
Program Details • Program offered 4 times per year. Session length: 15 days. Departures are scheduled in February, May, August, October. Program is targeted to mature adults. Most participants are 40–75 years of age. Participants must be 18 years or older to enroll. 14–20 participants per session. Application deadline: 60 days prior to departure. Reservations are recommended at least 4–8 months before departure.
Costs • $2895 (includes housing, all meals, books and class materials, excursions, international airfare). A $300 deposit is required.
Contact • Keith Williams, Director of Marketing, TraveLearn, PO Box 315, Lakeville, PA 18438; 800-235-9114; Fax: 717-226-9114; E-mail: travelearn@aol.com

JAPAN

AMERICAN INSTITUTE FOR FOREIGN STUDY (AIFS)

RICHMOND COLLEGE IN SHIZOUKA

General Information • Academic and language study program in Shizouka. Excursions to Kyoto, Tokyo.
Learning Focus • Courses in Japanese language, Japanese art, Japanese culture.
Accommodations • Homestays. Single rooms are available.
Program Details • Program offered once per year. Session length: 3 weeks. Departures are scheduled in June. The program is open to undergraduate students, graduate students, adults, high school graduates. Other requirements: minimum 2.0 GPA. Application deadline: March 15.
Costs • $3879 (includes tuition, housing, all meals). A $400 deposit is required.
Contact • Carmela Vigliano, Director, Summer Programs, American Institute for Foreign Study (AIFS), 102 Greenwich Avenue, Greenwich, CT 06830; 800-727-2437, ext. 6087; Fax: 203-869-9615; E-mail: info@aifs.org

BENTLEY COLLEGE

BUSINESS STUDY TOUR TO JAPAN

General Information • Academic study program in Tokyo.
Learning Focus • Courses in business. Instruction is offered by professors from the sponsoring institution.
Accommodations • Asian Center. Single rooms are available. Meals are taken as a group, in local restaurants.
Program Details • Program offered once per year. Session length: 2 weeks. Departures are scheduled in May. The program is open to undergraduate students, graduate students. Most participants are 19–35 years of age. Other requirements: minimum 3.0 GPA. 15 participants per session. Application deadline: March 15.
Costs • $4500 (includes tuition, housing, excursions, international airfare, International Student Identification card). Application fee: $35. A $1500 deposit is required.
Contact • Jennifer L. Scully, Director of Study Abroad, Bentley College, International Center, 175 Forest Street, Waltham, MA 02154; 617-891-3474; Fax: 617-891-2819; E-mail: inprinfo@bentley.edu

CROSS-CULTURE

JOURNEY TO OLD JAPAN

General Information • Cultural tour with visits to Kyoto, Nara, Tokyo, Miyama-cho, Kurotani, Horyuji, Temple Rengejoin. Once at the destination country, participants travel by train, foot.
Learning Focus • Instruction in the history of Japan. Escorted travel to Kiyomizu Temple and Himeji Castle. Museum visits (Reihokan Museum, Tokyo National Art Museum, Ota Museum of Art). Attendance at performances (Kabuki-za Theater). Instruction is offered by highly educated guides. This program would appeal to people interested in culture, history, nature studies, arts, traditions, food and wine.
Accommodations • Hotels. Single rooms are available for an additional $570.
Program Details • Program offered once per year. Session length: 15 days. Departures are scheduled in November. Program is targeted to adults of all ages. Most participants are 40–70 years of age. Participants must be 12 years or older to enroll. Other requirements: good health, accompaniment of an adult if under 18. 20–25 participants per session. Application deadline: 1 month prior to departure. Reservations are recommended at least 3–12 months before departure.
Costs • $5910 from Los Angeles, $6090 from New York (includes tuition, housing, all meals, books and class materials, excursions, international airfare). A $300 deposit is required.
Contact • Cross-Culture, 52 High Point Drive, Amherst, MA 01002-1224; 413-256-6303; Fax: 413-253-2303; E-mail: xculture@javanet.com; World Wide Web: http://www.empiremall.com/cross-culture

EUROCENTRES

LANGUAGE IMMERSION IN JAPAN

General Information • Language study program in Kanazawa. Classes are held on the campus of Eurocentre Kanazawa. Excursions to Noto Peninsula, Gokayama, Takayama.
Learning Focus • Courses in Japanese language, Japanese culture. Instruction is offered by professors from the sponsoring institution.
Accommodations • Homestays. Single rooms are available. Meals are taken with host family, in residences.
Program Details • Program offered 20 times per year. Session length: 2–12 weeks. Departures are scheduled in January–December. The program is open to undergraduate students, graduate students, pre-college students, adults. Most participants are 16–80 years of age. 15 participants per session.
Costs • Contact sponsor for information.
Contact • Marketing, Eurocentres, 101 North Union Street, Suite 300, Alexandria, VA 22314; 800-648-4809; Fax: 703-684-1495; E-mail: 100632.141@compuserve.com; World Wide Web: http://www.clark.net/pub/eurocent/home.htm

FOREIGN LANGUAGE STUDY ABROAD SERVICE

INTERNATIONAL LANGUAGE STUDY HOMESTAYS IN JAPAN

General Information • Language study program in Japan.

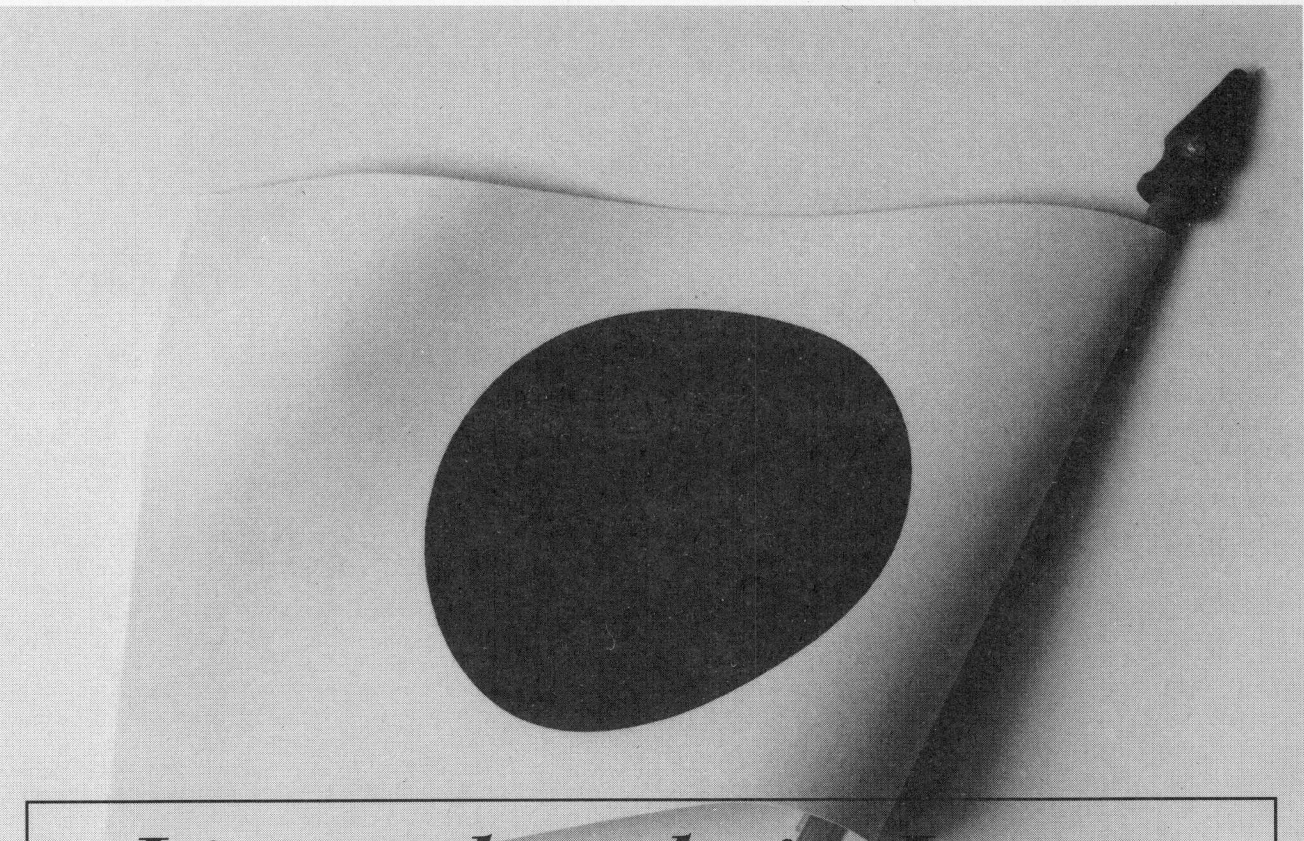

Live and study in Japan

Study Japanese amid the natural beauty of mountainous central Japan. Live in Shizuoka in carefully selected Japanese households that provide breakfast and dinner. Lunches are at Prospera Language Institute where classes in Japanese are offered (no previous study required). An optional Japanese art and culture course offers an overview of literary, dramatic, applied art and cultural traditions. Two full-day excursions are included. Optional three-day field trips go to Kyoto and Tokyo. The AIFS Resident Director organizes cultural activities.

American Institute For Foreign Study®
Dept. PLA 102 Greenwich Ave.
Greenwich, CT 06830
Phone (800) 727-2437
E-mail info@aifs.org
http://www.aifs.org

Learning Focus • Courses in Japanese language. Instruction is offered by local teachers.
Accommodations • Homestays. Single rooms are available. Meals are taken with host family, in residences.
Program Details • Session length: varies. Departures are scheduled in January–December. The program is open to undergraduate students, graduate students, pre-college students, adults. Most participants are 12 years of age and older. Other requirements: students must be at least 12 years old. 1 participant per session.
Costs • Contact sponsor for information. A $300 deposit is required.
Contact • Louise Harber, Coordinator, Foreign Language Study Abroad Service, Department IH, Box 903, 5935 Southwest 64th Avenue, South Miami, FL 33143; 800-282-1090; Fax: 305-662-2907; E-mail: flsas@netpoint.net; World Wide Web: http://www.netpoint.net/~flsas

GEORGETOWN UNIVERSITY

PACIFIC RIM: BUSINESS MANAGEMENT, POLITICS, AND MARKETS

General Information • Academic study program in Tokyo. Classes are held on the campus of Waseda University.
Learning Focus • Courses in government relations, business, public policy, international relations, marketing. Instruction is offered by professors from the sponsoring institution and local teachers.
Accommodations • Dormitories, locally-rented apartments. Single rooms are available. Meals are taken on one's own, in local restaurants.
Program Details • Program offered once per year. Session length: 6 weeks. Departures are scheduled in June. The program is open to graduate students, adults. Most participants are 23–30 years of age. 12 participants per session. Application deadline: February.
Costs • $4600 (includes tuition, housing, books and class materials). A $100 deposit is required.
Contact • Marianne T. Needham, Director, International Programs, Georgetown University, Box 571012 - ICC 306, Washington, DC 20057-1012; 202-687-6184; Fax: 202-687-8954; E-mail: sscefps1@gunet.georgetown.edu; World Wide Web: http://guweb.georgetown.edu/ssce

INTERNATIONAL COUNCIL FOR CULTURAL EXCHANGE (ICCE)

SUMMER SESSION IN ASIAN STUDIES

General Information • Language study program in Tokyo. Excursions to local city sites.
Learning Focus • Courses in Asian studies, Japanese language.
Accommodations • Locally-rented apartments. Single rooms are available. Meals are taken on one's own, in local restaurants.
Program Details • Program offered once per year. Session length: 26 days. Departures are scheduled in July. The program is open to undergraduate students, graduate students, teachers. Application deadline: June 1.
Costs • $4369 (includes tuition, housing, excursions, international airfare). A $300 deposit is required.
Contact • Dr. Stanley I. Gochman, Program Coordinator, International Council for Cultural Exchange (ICCE), 5 Bellport Lane, Bellport, NY 11713; 516-286-5228

JAMES MADISON UNIVERSITY

SUMMER STUDY IN JAPAN

General Information • Academic study program in Kyoto, Tokyo. Excursions to Osaka, Nagoya, Kamakura, Hiroshima, Nikko.
Learning Focus • Courses in Japanese history. Instruction is offered by professors from the sponsoring institution.
Accommodations • Locally-rented apartments. Meals are taken on one's own, in local restaurants.
Program Details • Program offered once per year. Session length: 4 weeks. Departures are scheduled in May, June. The program is open to undergraduate students, graduate students, adults. Most participants are 18–22 years of age. Other requirements: minimum 2.0 GPA. 10 participants per session. Application deadline: February 1.
Costs • $3888 for Virginia residents, $4296 for non-residents (includes tuition, housing, some meals, excursions). A $400 deposit is required.
Contact • Dr. Chong Yoon, Professor and Coordinator, Study Abroad in Asia, James Madison University, Office of International Education, Harrisonburg, VA 22807; 540-568-3607; Fax: 540-568-6556; E-mail: yoonck@jmu.edu; World Wide Web: http://www.jmu.edu/intl-ed/

JAPAN-AMERICA STUDENT CONFERENCE

JAPAN-AMERICA STUDENT CONFERENCE

General Information • Academic study and cultural exchange program in Kyoto, Tokyo.
Learning Focus • Courses in arts, cultural studies, business, political science, economics, science, international relations, philosophy, religion. Instruction is offered by professors from the sponsoring institution.
Accommodations • Homestays, dormitories. Meals are taken as a group, on one's own, with host family, in central dining facility, in local restaurants, in residences.
Program Details • Program offered once per year. Session length: 4 weeks. Departures are scheduled in July. The program is open to undergraduate students, graduate students. Other requirements: must be a U.S. citizen or permanent resident. 80 participants per session. Application deadline: February 14.
Costs • $1900 (includes housing, all meals, international airfare). Application fee: $15.
Contact • Mrs. Gretchen Hobbs Donaldson, Executive Director, Japan-America Student Conference, 606 18th Street, NW, 2nd Floor, Washington, DC 20006; 202-289-4231; Fax: 202-789-8265; E-mail: jascinc@access.digex.net

JAPAN CENTER FOR MICHIGAN UNIVERSITIES

SUMMER PROGRAM

General Information • Language study program in Hikone.

Learning Focus • Courses in Japanese language. Instruction is offered by professors from the sponsoring institution.
Accommodations • Homestays, program-owned apartments. Single rooms are available. Meals are taken on one's own, with host family, in residences.
Program Details • Program offered once per year. Session length: 10 weeks. Departures are scheduled in May. The program is open to undergraduate students, graduate students, adults. Most participants are 18–70 years of age. Other requirements: minimum 2.5 GPA. 40 participants per session. Application deadline: March 1.
Costs • $5500 (includes tuition, housing, books and class materials, excursions, international airfare). Application fee: $25. A $500 deposit is required.
Contact • Mr. John Hazewinkel, Program Coordinator, Japan Center for Michigan Universities, International Center, East Lansing, MI 48824; 517-353-1680; Fax: 517-432-2659; E-mail: jcmu@pilot.msu.edu; World Wide Web: http://study-abroad.msu.edu/japan.html

JOURNEYS EAST

BRUSHES WITH INNER JAPAN

General Information • Cultural tour with visits to Izu Peninsula, Kurashiki, Kyoto, Tokyo. Once at the destination country, participants travel by train, foot, boat.
Learning Focus • Escorted travel to off the beaten track spots. Museum visits (local museums). Attendance at performances (local shows, festivals of theater, dance, music). Other activities include hiking. Instruction is offered by social anthropologists. This program would appeal to people interested in traditional arts, contemporary arts.
Accommodations • Hotels, ryokans, local inns. Single rooms are available.
Program Details • Program offered once per year. Session length: 2 weeks. Departures are scheduled in October. Program is targeted to people with culture and adventure oriented interests. Most participants are 30–70 years of age. 17 participants per session. Reservations are recommended at least 12 months before departure.
Costs • $4085 (includes housing, some meals, excursions, museum admissions, local tips, gifts). A $300 deposit is required.
Contact • Debra Loomis, Co-Director, Journeys East, 2443 Fillmore Street, #289, San Francisco, CA 94115; 800-527-2612; Fax: 510-601-1977

JOURNEYS EAST

FROM FARMHOUSE TO TEAHOUSE

General Information • Cultural tour with visits to Kyoto, Niigata, Takayama, Tokyo. Once at the destination country, participants travel by train, foot.
Learning Focus • Escorted travel to off the beaten track spots. Museum visits (local museums). Attendance at performances (local shows, festivals of dance, theater, music). Other activities include hiking. Instruction is offered by social anthropologists. This program would appeal to people interested in folk architecture.
Accommodations • Hotels, ryokans, local inns. Single rooms are available.
Program Details • Program offered once per year. Session length: 2 weeks. Departures are scheduled in May. Program is targeted to people with culture and adventure oriented interests. Most participants are 30–70 years of age. 17 participants per session. Reservations are recommended at least 12 months before departure.
Costs • $3985 (includes housing, some meals, excursions, museum admissions, local tips, gifts). A $300 deposit is required.
Contact • Debra Loomis, Co-Director, Journeys East, 2443 Fillmore Street, #289, San Francisco, CA 94115; 800-527-2612; Fax: 510-601-1977

JOURNEYS INTERNATIONAL, INC.

JAPAN CULTURAL ODYSSEY

General Information • Cultural tour with visits to Dewa Sanzan, Hiraizumi, Kakunodate, Narita, Tokyo, Tono. Once at the destination country, participants travel by train, foot, small vehicle.
Learning Focus • Escorted travel to cities in Japan. Instruction is offered by Asian specialists. This program would appeal to people interested in culture, photography.
Accommodations • Hotels. Single rooms are available for an additional $225.
Program Details • Program offered once per year. Session length: 16 days. Departures are scheduled in July. Most participants are 25–55 years of age. Participants must be 12 years or older to enroll. 12 participants per session. Application deadline: 60 days prior to departure. Reservations are recommended at least 60 days before departure.
Costs • $2895 (includes housing, some meals, Japan rail pass). A $300 deposit is required.
Contact • Pat Ballard, Asia Sales Director, Journeys International, Inc., 4011 Jackson Road, Ann Arbor, MI 48103; 313-665-4407; Fax: 313-665-2945; E-mail: pat@journeys-intl.com; World Wide Web: http://www.journeys-intl.com

KCP INTERNATIONAL LANGUAGE INSTITUTE

INTENSIVE JAPANESE AND CULTURE PROGRAM

General Information • Language study program in Tokyo. Classes are held on the campus of KCP International Language Institute. Excursions to Mount Fuji, Hakone, Nikko, kabuki and bunraku theaters, Tsukiji Fish Market.
Learning Focus • Courses in Japanese language, Japanese culture. Instruction is offered by local teachers.
Accommodations • Homestays, dormitories. Single rooms are available. Meals are taken with host family.
Program Details • Program offered 4 times per year. Session length: 9 weeks. Departures are scheduled in January, April, July, October. The program is open to undergraduate students, graduate students, adults. Most participants are 18–32 years of age. Other requirements: minimum 2.75 GPA. Application deadline: 1 month prior to departure.
Costs • $4500 (includes tuition, housing, some meals, books and class materials, insurance, excursions). Application fee: $150. A $150 deposit is required.
Contact • Michael Anderson, Director, KCP International Language Institute, 304 36th Street, Suite 223, Bellingham, WA 98225; 888-KCP-7020; Fax: 360-647-0736; E-mail: kcp@kcp-usa.com

 LANGUAGE LIAISON

LIC KOKUSAI KAWA GAKUIN–LEARN JAPANESE IN JAPAN

General Information • Language study program with visits to Tokyo, prominent companies.
Learning Focus • Instruction in the Japanese language. Instruction is offered by professors. This program would appeal to people interested in language.
Accommodations • Guest houses. Single rooms are available.
Program Details • Session length: unlimited. Departures are scheduled throughout the year. Most participants are 18–70 years of age. Participants must be 16 years or older to enroll. Reservations are recommended at least 35 days before departure.
Costs • Contact sponsor for information.
Contact • Nancy Forman, President, Language Liaison, 20533 Biscayne Boulevard-Station 4-162, Miami, FL 33180; 305-682-9909; Fax: 305-682-9907; E-mail: langstudy@aol.com; World Wide Web: http://languageliaison.com

 LANGUAGE LIAISON

LIVE 'N' LEARN (LEARN IN A TEACHER'S HOME)–JAPAN

General Information • Language study program with visits to Japan.
Learning Focus • Instruction in the Japanese language. Instruction is offered by professors. This program would appeal to people interested in language.
Accommodations • Homestays. Single rooms are available.
Program Details • Session length: unlimited. Departures are scheduled throughout the year. Most participants are 18–70 years of age. Participants must be 16 years or older to enroll. Reservations are recommended at least 35 days before departure.
Costs • Contact sponsor for information.
Contact • Nancy Forman, President, Language Liaison, 20533 Biscayne Boulevard-Station 4-162, Miami, FL 33180; 305-682-9909; Fax: 305-682-9907; E-mail: langstudy@aol.com; World Wide Web: http://languageliaison.com

NATIONAL REGISTRATION CENTER FOR STUDY ABROAD

EUROCENTRE: JAPAN

General Information • Language study program in Kanazawa.
Learning Focus • Courses in Japanese language, contemporary Japan.
Accommodations • Homestays. Single rooms are available. Meals are taken with host family.
Program Details • Program offered 7 times per year. Session length: 4 weeks. Departures are scheduled in April–September. The program is open to undergraduate students, graduate students, adults. 7–10 participants per session. Application deadline: 40 days prior to departure.
Costs • $3432 (includes tuition, housing, some meals, insurance). Application fee: $40. A $100 deposit is required.
Contact • Reuel Zielke, Coordinator, National Registration Center for Study Abroad, 823 North Second Street, Milwaukee, WI 53203; 414-278-0631; Fax: 414-271-8884; E-mail: inquiries@nrcsa.com; World Wide Web: http://www.nrcsa.com

NATIONAL REGISTRATION CENTER FOR STUDY ABROAD

LANGUAGE AND CULTURE IN JAPAN

General Information • Language study program in Tokyo.
Learning Focus • Courses in Japanese language.
Accommodations • Students make own arrangements. Meals are taken on one's own.
Program Details • Program offered 4 times per year. Session length: 5 weeks. Departures are scheduled in January, April, July, October. The program is open to undergraduate students, graduate students, adults. 10–12 participants per session. Application deadline: 40 days prior to departure.
Costs • $1782 (includes tuition, insurance). Application fee: $40. A $100 deposit is required.
Contact • Reuel Zielke, Coordinator, National Registration Center for Study Abroad, 823 North Second Street, Milwaukee, WI 53203; 414-278-0631; Fax: 414-271-8884; E-mail: inquiries@nrcsa.com; World Wide Web: http://www.nrcsa.com

 OREGON PARTNERSHIP FOR INTERNATIONAL EDUCATION

WASEDA / OREGON SUMMER PROGRAM

General Information • Academic study program in Tokyo. Classes are held on the campus of Waseda University.
Learning Focus • Courses in economics, business, art, design, cultural studies, society. Instruction is offered by local teachers.
Accommodations • Homestays, dormitories. Meals are taken as a group, in central dining facility.
Program Details • Program offered once per year. Session length: 9 weeks. Departures are scheduled in June, July. The program is open to undergraduate students, graduate students. Most participants are 18–26 years of age. Other requirements: minimum 2.5 GPA. 90 participants per session. Application deadline: April 15.
Costs • $4400 (includes tuition, housing, some meals, books and class materials, excursions, international airfare, wilderness program). A $200 deposit is required.
Contact • Sally Strand, Coordinating Officer, Oregon Partnership for International Education, 222 Southwest Columbia Street #1750, Portland, OR 97201; 503-223-7938; Fax: 503-223-7946; E-mail: opiejapan@aol.com

The Oregon/Japan Summer Program is sponsored by Waseda University, Tokyo, and a consortium of Oregon colleges and universities. This unique program brings 45 Japanese and 45 US students together in Oregon for 5 weeks of Japanese language and cross-cultural immersion. Waseda/Oregon team-taught courses examine "Tradition and Innovation," the 1997 program theme. Tuition, meals, housing, textbooks, and a wilderness trip are approximately $1700. Scholarships are available.

RUSSIAN AND EAST EUROPEAN PARTNERSHIPS

JAPANESE LANGUAGE AND CULTURAL IMMERSION PROGRAM

General Information • Language study program in Osaka. Classes are held on the campus of Wexle Japanese School. Excursions to Tokyo.
Learning Focus • Courses in Japanese language, Japanese history, Japanese culture and art. Instruction is offered by local teachers.
Accommodations • Homestays. Single rooms are available. Meals are taken on one's own, with host family, in local restaurants, in residences.
Program Details • Program offered 11 times per year. Session length: 4 or more weeks. Departures are scheduled in January–November. The program is open to undergraduate students, graduate students, adults. Most participants are 18 years of age and older. Other requirements: in good health and 18 or older unless chaperoned by an adult. 6 participants per session. Application deadline: 45 days prior to departure.
Costs • $4850 (includes tuition, housing, some meals, books and class materials, excursions, international airfare, local transportation, airport transfers). A $1500 deposit is required.
Contact • Kenneth Fortune, President, Russian and East European Partnerships, PO Box 227, Fineview, NY 13640; 888-873-7337; Fax: 800-910-1777; E-mail: reep@fox.nstn.ca

STATE UNIVERSITY OF NEW YORK AT BUFFALO

JAPANESE LANGUAGE AND CULTURE

General Information • Language study program in Kobe. Classes are held on the campus of Konan University.
Learning Focus • Courses in Japanese language, Japanese culture.
Accommodations • Homestays, houses.
Program Details • Program offered once per year. Session length: 4 weeks. Departures are scheduled in June. The program is open to undergraduate students, graduate students, adults. Other requirements: minimum 2.67 GPA and one or two years language experience. Application deadline: April 1.
Costs • $2450 (includes tuition, housing, all meals, excursions). A $250 deposit is required.
Contact • Sandra J. Reinagel, Interim Study Abroad Coordinator, State University of New York at Buffalo, 210 Talbert Hall, Box 601604, Buffalo, NY 14260-1604; 716-645-3912; Fax: 716-645-6197; E-mail: studyabroad@acsu.buffalo.edu; World Wide Web: http://wings.buffalo.edu/academic/provost/intl/studyabroad

TEMPLE UNIVERSITY

TEMPLE UNIVERSITY–JAPAN

General Information • Academic study program in Tokyo. Classes are held on the campus of Temple University Japan.
Learning Focus • Courses in Asian studies, liberal arts, Japanese language. Instruction is offered by local teachers.
Accommodations • Studio apartments. Meals are taken on one's own, in residences.
Program Details • Program offered once per year. Session length: 6 weeks. Departures are scheduled in June. The program is open to undergraduate students. Most participants are 19–25 years of age. Other requirements: minimum 2.5 GPA. 10 participants per session. Application deadline: April 1.
Costs • $4625 (includes tuition, housing). Application fee: $30. A $150 deposit is required.
Contact • Denise A. Connerty, Interim Director of International Programs, Temple University, Conwell Hall, 5th Floor, Suite 501, Philadelphia, PA 19122; 215-204-4684; Fax: 215-204-5735; E-mail: intlprog@vm.temple.edu; World Wide Web: http://www.temple.edu/intlprog/

UNIVERSITY OF ARIZONA

TRIDENT SCHOOL OF LANGUAGES

General Information • Language study program in Nagoya. Classes are held on the campus of Trident School of Languages.
Learning Focus • Courses in language study, cultural studies. Instruction is offered by local teachers.
Accommodations • Homestays. Single rooms are available. Meals are taken with host family, in residences.
Program Details • Program offered once per year. Session length: 6 weeks. Departures are scheduled in May. The program is open to undergraduate students. Most participants are 20–26 years of age. Other requirements: minimum 2.5 GPA, sophomore standing and 1 year Japanese language. 8–10 participants per session. Application deadline: March 1.
Costs • $2800 (includes tuition, housing, all meals, books and class materials, excursions). Application fee: $35. A $300 deposit is required.
Contact • Stephanie Bleecker, Study Abroad Advisor, University of Arizona, Center for Global Student Programs, 915 North Tyndall, Tucson, AZ 85721; 520-621-4627; Fax: 520-621-4069

UNIVERSITY OF CALIFORNIA, RIVERSIDE

INTENSIVE JAPANESE PROGRAM

General Information • Language study program in Fukuyama. Classes are held on the campus of Fukuyama University.
Learning Focus • Courses in Japanese language. Instruction is offered by local teachers.
Accommodations • Homestays. Meals are taken with host family.
Program Details • Program offered once per year. Session length: 4 weeks. Departures are scheduled in June. The program is open to undergraduate students, graduate students, pre-college students, adults, people at least 17

years old. Most participants are 17–25 years of age. 12 participants per session. Application deadline: April 30.
Costs • $3300 (includes tuition, housing, some meals, books and class materials, insurance, international airfare, some local transportation). A $500 deposit is required.
Contact • Dr. Sheila Dwight, Director, University of California, Riverside, 1200 University Avenue, Riverside, CA 92507-4596; 909-787-4346; Fax: 909-787-5796; E-mail: ucriep@ucx.ucr.edu; World Wide Web: http://www.unex.ucr.edu/iephomepage.html

UNIVERSITY OF DELAWARE

WINTER SESSION IN JAPAN

General Information • Language study program in Kobe. Classes are held on the campus of Shoin Women's University. Excursions to Osaka, Nara, Kyoto, Himeji castle.
Learning Focus • Courses in Japanese language. Instruction is offered by professors from the sponsoring institution.
Accommodations • Dormitories. Single rooms are available. Meals are taken in central dining facility, in local restaurants.
Program Details • Program offered once per year. Session length: 5 weeks. Departures are scheduled in January. The program is open to undergraduate students, graduate students, adults. Most participants are 18–21 years of age. Other requirements: minimum 2.0 GPA. 20 participants per session. Application deadline: October.
Costs • $4810 (includes tuition, housing, all meals, international airfare). A $200 deposit is required.
Contact • International Programs and Special Sessions, University of Delaware, 4 Kent Way, Newark, DE 19716-1450; 888-831-4685; Fax: 302-831-6042; E-mail: studyabroad@mvs.udel.edu

UNIVERSITY OF KANSAS

MODERN JAPAN: CONTINUITY AND CHANGE

General Information • Language, culture and business study program in Hiratsuka. Classes are held on the campus of Kanagawa University. Excursions to Kyoto, Nara, Tokyo.
Learning Focus • Courses in business, East Asian languages and cultures, Japanese language. Instruction is offered by professors from the sponsoring institution and local teachers.
Accommodations • Homestays, guest houses. Meals are taken on one's own, with host family, in local restaurants, in residences.
Program Details • Program offered once per year. Session length: 5 weeks. Departures are scheduled in June. The program is open to undergraduate students, graduate students. Most participants are 20–28 years of age. 20 participants per session. Application deadline: March 1.
Costs • $2100 (includes tuition, housing, some meals, excursions, 3-day excursion to Kyoto, group cultural events, city transportation). Application fee: $15. A $300 deposit is required.
Contact • Susan MacNally, Coordinator of Summer Institutes, University of Kansas, Office of Study Abroad, 203 Lippincott Hall, Lawrence, KS 66045; 913-864-3742; Fax: 913-864-5040; E-mail: osa@falcon.cc.ukans.edu; World Wide Web: http://kuhub.cc.ukans.edu/~intlstdy/osa/osamain.html

UNIVERSITY OF MASSACHUSETTS AMHERST

SUMMER PROGRAM IN JAPAN

General Information • Language study and cultural program in Sapporo. Classes are held on the campus of Hokkaido University. Excursions to Hokkaido.
Learning Focus • Courses in Japanese society. Instruction is offered by local teachers.
Accommodations • Homestays. Meals are taken with host family, in residences.
Program Details • Program offered once per year. Session length: 4 weeks. Departures are scheduled in June. The program is open to undergraduate students, graduate students, adults. Most participants are 18–40 years of age. 10 participants per session. Application deadline: April 1.
Costs • $1400 (includes tuition, housing, some meals, books and class materials, excursions). A $300 deposit is required.
Contact • Laurel Foster-Moore, Study Abroad Coordinator, University of Massachusetts Amherst, International Programs, William S. Clark International Center, Amherst, MA 01003; 413-545-2710; Fax: 413-545-1201; E-mail: abroad@ipo.umass.edu; World Wide Web: http://www.umass.edu/ipo/

UNIVERSITY OF MIAMI

INTENSIVE JAPANESE SUMMER PROGRAM AT KAGOSHIMA UNIVERSITY

General Information • Language study program in Kagoshima. Classes are held on the campus of Kagoshima University. Excursions to countryside.
Learning Focus • Courses in Japanese language. Instruction is offered by local teachers.
Accommodations • Homestays, dormitories. Single rooms are available. Meals are taken on one's own, in central dining facility, in local restaurants.
Program Details • Program offered once per year. Session length: 5 weeks. Departures are scheduled in June. The program is open to undergraduate students, graduate students. Most participants are 18–27 years of age. Other requirements: minimum 2.75 GPA. 8–10 participants per session. Application deadline: March 1.
Costs • $3200 (includes tuition, housing, excursions, field trips). Application fee: $30. A $500 deposit is required.
Contact • Glenda H. Hayley, Manager and Advisor, International Education and Exchange Programs, University of Miami, PO Box 248005, Coral Gables, FL 33124-1610; 800-557-5421; Fax: 305-284-6629; E-mail: ieep@cstudies.msmail.miami.edu; World Wide Web: http://www.miami.edu/cstudies/ieep.html

UNIVERSITY OF MIAMI

SUMMER PROGRAM AT SOPHIA UNIVERSITY

General Information • Academic study program in Tokyo. Classes are held on the campus of Sophia University Tokyo.
Learning Focus • Courses in business, religion, political science, history, literature, art, sociology. Instruction is offered by local teachers.

Accommodations • Dormitories, locally-rented apartments, hotels. Single rooms are available. Meals are taken on one's own, in central dining facility, in local restaurants.
Program Details • Program offered once per year. Session length: 4–5 weeks. Departures are scheduled in July. The program is open to undergraduate students, graduate students. Most participants are 18–25 years of age. Other requirements: minimum 2.75 GPA. 150 participants per session. Application deadline: April 15.
Costs • $3350 (includes tuition, housing, excursions). Application fee: $30. A $500 deposit is required.
Contact • Glenda H. Hayley, Manager and Advisor, International Education and Exchange Programs, University of Miami, PO Box 248005, Coral Gables, FL 33124-1610; 800-557-5421; Fax: 305-284-6629; E-mail: ieep@cstudies.msmail.miami.edu; World Wide Web: http://www.miami.edu/cstudies/ieep.html

 UNIVERSITY OF TOLEDO

COMPARATIVE EDUCATION AND JAPANESE CULTURE

General Information • Academic study program in Nagoya, Tokyo. Classes are held on the campus of Nagoya Gakuin. Excursions to Takayama, Gero.
Learning Focus • Courses in cultural understanding. Instruction is offered by professors from the sponsoring institution and local teachers.
Accommodations • Homestays, dormitories, campsites. Meals are taken as a group, with host family, in central dining facility, in residences.
Program Details • Program offered once per year. Session length: 3½ weels. Departures are scheduled in July, August. The program is open to undergraduate students, graduate students, pre-college students, adults. Most participants are 18–80 years of age. 8–15 participants per session. Application deadline: April 1.
Costs • Contact sponsor for information. A $250 deposit is required.
Contact • Joel A. Gallegos, Study Abroad Coordinator, University of Toledo, C.I.S.P. 1400 SE, Toledo, OH 43606; 419-530-3527; Fax: 419-537-3526; World Wide Web: http://www.utoledo.edu/www/cisp/study-abroad/

EASTERN CONNECTICUT STATE UNIVERSITY

KOREAN TRADITIONAL MUSIC SUMMER PROGRAM

General Information • Academic study program in Seoul. Classes are held on the campus of Seoul National University. Excursions to folk village in Yong-In.

Learning Focus • Courses in Korean traditional music, Korean culture.

Accommodations • Dormitories. Meals are taken in central dining facility, in local restaurants.

Program Details • Program offered once per year. Session length: 4 weeks. Departures are scheduled in June. The program is open to undergraduate students, graduate students. Other requirements: recent academic transcript or resumé. 20 participants per session. Application deadline: March 1.

Costs • Contact sponsor for information. A $887 deposit is required.

Contact • Dr. Okon Hwang, Associate Professor of Music, Eastern Connecticut State University, Fine Arts Department, Willimantic, CT 06226; 860-465-5109; Fax: 860-465-4652; E-mail: hwango@ecsuc.ctstateu.edu

FOREIGN LANGUAGE STUDY ABROAD SERVICE

INTERNATIONAL LANGUAGE STUDY HOMESTAYS IN KOREA

General Information • Language study program in Korea.

Learning Focus • Courses in Korean language. Instruction is offered by local teachers.

Accommodations • Homestays. Single rooms are available. Meals are taken with host family, in residences.

Program Details • Session length: varies. Departures are scheduled in January–December. The program is open to undergraduate students, graduate students, pre-college students, adults. Most participants are 12 years of age and older. Other requirements: students must be at least 12 years old. 1 participant per session.

Costs • Contact sponsor for information. A $300 deposit is required.

Contact • Louise Harber, Coordinator, Foreign Language Study Abroad Service, Department IH, Box 903, 5935 Southwest 64th Avenue, South Miami, FL 33143; 800-282-1090; Fax: 305-662-2907; E-mail: flsas@netpoint.net; World Wide Web: http://www.netpoint.net/~flsas

RUSSIAN AND EAST EUROPEAN PARTNERSHIPS

KOREAN LANGUAGE AND CULTURAL IMMERSION PROGRAM

General Information • Language study program in Seoul. Classes are held on the campus of Korea World University Service. Excursions to Independence Hall, Korean folk village, Secret Garden, Demilitarized Zone Tour, Insadong (antique store alley), City Tour of Seoul, National Museum, Mount Keryoug Temples.

Learning Focus • Courses in Korean language, Korean culture and art, Korean history. Instruction is offered by professors from the sponsoring institution and local teachers.

Accommodations • Homestays. Single rooms are available. Meals are taken on one's own, with host family, in local restaurants, in residences.

Program Details • Program offered 11 times per year. Session length: 4 or more weeks. Departures are scheduled in January–November. The program is open to undergraduate students, graduate students, adults. Most participants are 18 years of age and older. Other requirements: in good health and 18 or older unless accompanied by a chaperone. 6 participants per session. Application deadline: 45 days prior to departure.

Costs • $4050 (includes tuition, housing, some meals, books and class materials, excursions, international airfare, local transportation, airport transfers). A $1500 deposit is required.

Contact • Kenneth Fortune, President, Russian and East European Partnerships, PO Box 227, Fineview, NY 13640; 888-873-7337; Fax: 800-910-1777; E-mail: reep@fox.nstn.ca

UNIVERSITY AT ALBANY, STATE UNIVERSITY OF NEW YORK

KOREA SUMMER PROGRAM

General Information • Academic study program in Seoul. Classes are held on the campus of Yonsei University Seoul.

Learning Focus • Courses in Korean language, international business, Korean culture, philosophy, Korean history. Instruction is offered by local teachers.

Accommodations • Dormitories, boarding houses. Meals are taken on one's own, in central dining facility, in local restaurants.

Program Details • Program offered once per year. Session length: 6 weeks. Departures are scheduled in June. The program is open to undergraduate students. Application deadline: April 1.

Costs • $3234 (includes housing, all meals, books and class materials, insurance, in-state tuition and fees).

Contact • Dr. Alex M. Shane, Director, University at Albany, State University of New York, Office of International Programs, LI 85, Albany, NY 12222; 518-442-3525; Fax: 518-442-3338; E-mail: oipua@csc.albany.edu; World Wide Web: http://www.albany.edu/~oipwebua

UNIVERSITY OF MIAMI

INTERNATIONAL SUMMER SESSION AT YONSEI UNIVERSITY IN SEOUL, KOREA

General Information • Academic study program in Seoul. Classes are held on the campus of Yonsei University Seoul. Excursions to countryside.

Learning Focus • Courses in Korean language, art, economics, literature, business, history, legal studies, political science, sociology, philosophy, communications. Instruction is offered by local teachers.

Accommodations • Dormitories. Single rooms are available. Meals are taken on one's own, in central dining facility, in local restaurants.

Program Details • Program offered once per year. Session length: 7 weeks. Departures are scheduled in June. The program is open to undergraduate students, graduate students. Most participants are 18–27 years of age. Other requirements: minimum 2.75 GPA. 250 participants per session. Application deadline: April 15.

Costs • $3610 (includes tuition, housing, some meals, excursions). Application fee: $30. A $500 deposit is required.

Contact • Glenda H. Hayley, Manager and Advisor, International Education and Exchange Programs, University of Miami, PO Box 248005, Coral Gables, FL 33124-1610; 305-284-3434; Fax: 305-284-6629; E-mail: ieep@cstudies.msmail.miami.edu; World Wide Web: http://www.miami.edu/cstudies/ieep.html

UNIVERSITY OF PENNSYLVANIA

PENN-IN-SEOUL

General Information • Academic study program in Seoul. Classes are held on the campus of Kyung Hee University Seoul.

Learning Focus • Courses in economics, social sciences. Instruction is offered by professors from the sponsoring institution and local teachers.

Accommodations • Dormitories. Meals are taken as a group, in central dining facility.

Program Details • Program offered once per year. Session length: 9 weeks. Departures are scheduled in June. The program is open to undergraduate students, graduate students. Most participants are 19–25 years of age. 15 participants per session. Application deadline: March 7.

Costs • $3484 (includes tuition, housing, some meals). Application fee: $35. A $300 deposit is required.

Contact • Elizabeth Sachs, Director, Penn Summer Abroad, University of Pennsylvania, 3440 Market Street, Suite 100, Philadelphia, PA 19104-3335; 215-898-5738; Fax: 215-573-2053; E-mail: esachs@mail.sas.upenn.edu

YONSEI UNIVERSITY SEOUL

INTERNATIONAL SUMMER SESSION IN KOREA

General Information • Academic study program in Seoul. Classes are held on the campus of Yonsei University Seoul. Excursions to folk village, Kyung-ju, Sorak Mountains, industry visits.

Learning Focus • Courses in Korean language, Asian studies, Korean studies, international business, international affairs, economics, history, intercultural studies. Instruction is offered by local teachers.

Accommodations • Dormitories. Meals are taken on one's own, in local restaurants.

Program Details • Program offered once per year. Session length: 6 weeks. Departures are scheduled in June. The program is open to undergraduate students, adults. Most participants are 19–25 years of age. Other requirements: minimum 2.5 GPA and a fluency in English. 400 participants per session. Application deadline: May 15.

Costs • $1750 (includes tuition, housing). Application fee: $60.

Contact • Dr. Horace H. Underwood, Director, Yonsei University Seoul, Division of International Education, Seoul 120-749, Korea; +82 2-361-3485; Fax: +82 2-393-7272; E-mail: ysid@bubble.yonsei.ac.kr; World Wide Web: http://www.yonsei.ac.kr

LAOS

JOURNEYS INTERNATIONAL, INC.

LAOS ROAD AND RIVER ODYSSEY

General Information • Wilderness/adventure program with visits to Pakbeng, Prabang, Vientiane. Once at the destination country, participants travel by foot, boat.

Learning Focus • Other activities include boat rides. Instruction is offered by Lao English-speaking guides. This program would appeal to people interested in culture, photography, nature studies.

Accommodations • Single rooms are available for an additional $100.

Program Details • Session length: 5 days. Departures are scheduled throughout the year. Program is targeted to active persons interested in cultures. Most participants are 25–55 years of age. Participants must be 12 years or older to enroll. Other requirements: must be in good health and physical condition. 2–8 participants per session. Application deadline: 60 days prior to departure. Reservations are recommended at least 60 days before departure.

Costs • $995 (includes housing, some meals, boat ride). A $300 deposit is required.

Contact • Pat Ballard, Asia Sales Director, Journeys International, Inc., 4011 Jackson Road, Ann Arbor, MI 48103; 313-665-4407; Fax: 313-665-2945; E-mail: pat@journeys-intl.com; World Wide Web: http://www.journeys-intl.com

MALAYSIA

BOLDER ADVENTURES, ASIA TRANSPACIFIC JOURNEYS

WILDS OF BORNEO

General Information • Cultural and nature study tour with visits to Borneo. Once at the destination country, participants travel by foot, boat, airplane.
Learning Focus • Escorted travel to Sabah and Sarawak, Borneo. Nature observation (orangutans, underwater life). Other activities include snorkeling, optional scuba diving. Instruction is offered by professors, naturalists.
Accommodations • Hotels. Single rooms are available for an additional $400.
Program Details • Program offered 4 times per year. Session length: 16 days. Departures are scheduled in March, April, September, October. Most participants are 35–65 years of age. Participants must be 18 years or older to enroll. 10–12 participants per session. Reservations are recommended at least 4 months before departure.
Costs • $2995 (includes housing, all meals, excursions). A $500 deposit is required.
Contact • Bolder Adventures, Asia Transpacific Journeys, 3055 Center Green Drive, Boulder, CO 80301; 800-642-2742; Fax: 303-443-7078; World Wide Web: http://www.southeastasia.com/

NATURAL HISTORY MUSEUM OF LOS ANGELES COUNTY

NATURAL HISTORY OF BORNEO

General Information • Nature study tour with visits to Kota Kinabalu, Kuala Lumpur, Kuching, Mulu, Bako National Park, Gunung Mulu National Park, Kinabalu National Park, Mount Kinabalu. Once at the destination country, participants travel by bus, foot, boat, airplane.
Learning Focus • Instruction in botany. Museum visits (Sarawak Museum). Attendance at performances (cultural performance in Kuala Lumpur). Nature observation (botany, birds, primates). Other activities include hiking. Instruction is offered by researchers, naturalists, scientists. This program would appeal to people interested in botany, ornithology, anthropology.
Accommodations • Hotels, cabins. Single rooms are available for an additional $575.
Program Details • Program offered once per year. Session length: 2 weeks. Departures are scheduled in June. Most participants are 35–75 years of age. Participants must be 10 years or older to enroll. 15 participants per session. Reservations are recommended at least 3 months before departure.
Costs • $3275 (includes housing, some meals, excursions, international airfare). A $300 deposit is required.
Contact • Karen Hovanitz, Travel Program Manager, Natural History Museum of Los Angeles County, 900 Exposition Boulevard, Los Angeles, CA 90007; 213-744-3350; Fax: 213-747-6718; E-mail: khovanit@mizar.usc.edu; World Wide Web: http://www.lam.mus.ca.us/lacmnh

NATURE EXPEDITIONS INTERNATIONAL

ORANGUTANS AND THE IBAN: BORNEO EXPEDITION

General Information • Nature study and cultural tour with visits to Kota Kinabalu, Kuching, Lambir Hills National Park, Mount Kinabalu, Nanga, Sampa, Semengoah Reserve. Once at the destination country, participants travel by foot, boat, airplane.
Learning Focus • Other activities include hiking, wildlife observation. Instruction is offered by naturalists. This program would appeal to people interested in wildlife, native cultures, rain forest habitats, nature studies, ecology.
Accommodations • Single rooms are available for an additional $400.
Program Details • Program offered 3 times per year. Session length: 15 days. Departures are scheduled in July, August, October. Most participants are 25–75 years of age. Other requirements: doctor's permission for participants 70 years and older. Reservations are recommended at least 6 months before departure.
Costs • $2690 (includes housing, some meals, excursions, all guiding). A $400 deposit is required.
Contact • Christopher Kyle, President, Nature Expeditions International, 6400 East El Dorado Circle, Suite 210, Tucson, AZ 85715; 800-869-0639; Fax: 520-721-6719; E-mail: naturexp@aol.com

MIDWAY ISLANDS

OCEANIC SOCIETY EXPEDITIONS

MIDWAY ATOLL–HAWAIIAN MONK SEAL MONITORING AND RECOVERY PROJECT

General Information • Research expedition with visits to Midway Atoll. Once at the destination country, participants travel by foot, boat.
Learning Focus • Instruction in field research methods. Field research in monk seal recovery and monitoring. Escorted travel to the eastern island. Nature observation (beach walks and surveys). Other activities include evening discussions and presentations on monk seal biology, island ecology and the maritime and natural history of Midway. Instruction is offered by researchers, naturalists. This program would appeal to people interested in marine mammals, seal rehabilitation, wildlife conservation.
Accommodations • Restored military barracks. Single rooms are available.
Program Details • Program offered 15 times per year. Session length: 8 days. Departures are scheduled throughout the year. Most participants are 16–80 years of age. Participants must be 16 years or older to enroll. Other requirements: good health. 6 participants per session. Application deadline: 60 days prior to departure. Reservations are recommended at least 6 months before departure.
Costs • $2130 (includes housing, all meals, excursions, research leadership, round trip air from Kauai, HI). A $300 deposit is required.
Contact • Jennifer Austin, Expedition Manager, Oceanic Society Expeditions, Fort Mason Center, Building E, #230, San Francisco, CA 94123; 415-441-1106; Fax: 415-474-3395

OCEANIC SOCIETY EXPEDITIONS

MIDWAY ATOLL–SEABIRD MONITORING PROJECT

General Information • Research expedition with visits to Midway Atoll. Once at the destination country, participants travel by foot, boat.
Learning Focus • Instruction in field research methods. Field research in seabird monitoring and nesting habitats. Escorted travel to the eastern island. Nature observation (seabird distribution). Volunteer work (assisting with data collection). Instruction is offered by researchers, naturalists. This program would appeal to people interested in bird watching.
Accommodations • Restored military barracks. Single rooms are available.
Program Details • Program offered 15 times per year. Session length: 8 days. Departures are scheduled throughout the year. Program is targeted to birders. Most participants are 16–80 years of age. Participants must be 16 years or older to enroll. Other requirements: good health. 6 participants per session. Application deadline: 60 days prior to departure. Reservations are recommended at least 6 months before departure.
Costs • $2190 (includes housing, all meals, excursions, research leadership, round trip air from Kauai, HI). A $300 deposit is required.
Contact • Jennifer Austin, Expedition Manager, Oceanic Society Expeditions, Fort Mason Center, Building E, #230, San Francisco, CA 94123; 415-441-1106; Fax: 415-474-3395

OCEANIC SOCIETY EXPEDITIONS

MIDWAY ATOLL–SPINNER DOLPHIN RESEARCH PROJECT

General Information • Research expedition with visits to Midway Atoll. Once at the destination country, participants travel by boat.
Learning Focus • Instruction in research techniques. Field research in spinner dolphin ecology, behavior and social organization. Volunteer work (assisting with data collection). Instruction is offered by researchers, naturalists. This program would appeal to people interested in dolphin ecology, dolphin behavior, dolphin communication.
Accommodations • Restored military barracks. Single rooms are available.
Program Details • Program offered 15 times per year. Session length: 8 days. Departures are scheduled throughout the year. Most participants are 16–80 years of age. Participants must be 16 years or older to enroll. Other requirements: swimming and snorkeling experience, general good health. 6 participants per session. Application deadline: 60 days prior to departure. Reservations are recommended at least 6 months before departure.
Costs • $2190 (includes housing, all meals, excursions, research leadership, round trip air from Kauai, HI). A $300 deposit is required.
Contact • Jennifer Austin, Expedition Manager, Oceanic Society Expeditions, Fort Mason Center, Building E, #230, San Francisco, CA 94123; 415-441-1106; Fax: 415-474-3395

OCEANIC SOCIETY EXPEDITIONS

MIDWAY HABITAT RESTORATION–NATIVE PLANT PROJECT

General Information • Research expedition with visits to Midway Atoll. Once at the destination country, participants travel by foot.

Learning Focus • Volunteer work (collecting and transplanting seedlings). Other activities include swimming, island exploration and relaxation. Instruction is offered by researchers. This program would appeal to people interested in gardening, horticulture.
Accommodations • Restored military barracks. Single rooms are available.
Program Details • Program offered 7 times per year. Session length: 8 days. Departures are scheduled in January, March, May, July, September, November. Most participants are 16–80 years of age. Participants must be 16 years or older to enroll. Other requirements: good health. 8 participants per session. Application deadline: 60 days prior to departure. Reservations are recommended at least 6 months before departure.
Costs • $2130 (includes housing, all meals, excursions, researcher leadership, round trip air from Kauai, HI). A $300 deposit is required.
Contact • Jennifer Austin, Expedition Manager, Oceanic Society Expeditions, Fort Mason Center, Building E, #230, San Francisco, CA 94123; 415-441-1106; Fax: 415-474-3395

NEPAL

ALPINE ASCENTS, INTERNATIONAL

MOUNT EVEREST EXPEDITION CLIMB

General Information • Mountain climbing tour with visits to Kathmandu, Mount Everest, Namche, Tengpoche, Pheriche, Lobuche. Once at the destination country, participants travel by foot, airplane, climbing.
Learning Focus • Instruction in mountain climbing. Escorted travel to South Col Route. Nature observation (Himalayan mountains). Other activities include camping, hiking. Instruction is offered by sports professionals. This program would appeal to people interested in mountain climbing.
Accommodations • Hotels, campsites. Single rooms are available.
Program Details • Program offered once per year. Session length: 65 days. Departures are scheduled in March. Program is targeted to advanced climbers. Other requirements: excellent physical condition. Reservations are recommended at least 6 months before departure.
Costs • $65,000 (includes housing, all meals, local airfare, oxygen canisters, group equipment, sherpa, porters, guides, doctor, fees). A $20,000 deposit is required.
Contact • Gordon Janow, Program Coordinator, Alpine Ascents, International, 16615 Saybrook Drive, Woodinville, WA 98072; 206-788-1951; Fax: 206-788-6757

ALPINE ASCENTS, INTERNATIONAL

MOUNT EVEREST TREK

General Information • Wilderness/adventure program with visits to Kathmandu, Mount Everest Base Camp, Pushupathineth Temple, Phakding, Swamayambhu Temple, Namche, Tengboche. Once at the destination country, participants travel by foot, airplane.
Learning Focus • Escorted travel to monasteries and research centers. Nature observation (Himalayan mountains). Other activities include camping, hiking. Instruction is offered by sports professionals. This program would appeal to people interested in hiking.
Accommodations • Hotels, campsites. Single rooms are available.
Program Details • Program offered once per year. Session length: 21 days. Departures are scheduled in March. Program is targeted to adventurous hikers. Other requirements: excellent physical condition. 6–10 participants per session. Reservations are recommended at least 6 months before departure.
Costs • $2700 (includes housing, some meals, group supplies, park fees, local airfare). A $500 deposit is required.
Contact • Gordon Janow, Program Coordinator, Alpine Ascents, International, 16615 Saybrook Drive, Woodinville, WA 98072; 206-788-1951; Fax: 206-788-6757

BOLDER ADVENTURES, ASIA TRANSPACIFIC JOURNEYS

ADVENTURER'S NEPAL

General Information • Cultural tour with visits to Nepal Himalaya. Once at the destination country, participants travel by bus, foot, airplane.
Learning Focus • Escorted travel to Himalayas. Other activities include camping, hiking, river rafting, elephant riding, mountain trekking. Instruction is offered by professors, naturalists.
Accommodations • Hotels, campsites. Single rooms are available for an additional $300.
Program Details • Program offered 2 times per year. Session length: 17 days. Departures are scheduled in March–May. Program is targeted to active, fit people. Most participants are 25–50 years of age. 8–10 participants per session. Reservations are recommended at least 4 months before departure.
Costs • $2595 (includes all meals, excursions). A $500 deposit is required.
Contact • Bolder Adventures, Asia Transpacific Journeys, 3055 Center Green Drive, Boulder, CO 80301; 800-642-2742; Fax: 303-443-7078; World Wide Web: http://www.southeastasia.com/

HIMALAYAN HIGH TREKS

ANNAPURNA TREK

General Information • Cultural tour with visits to Annapurna Region, Kathmandu, Pokhara, Annapurna Himal. Once at the destination country, participants travel by foot.
Learning Focus • Escorted travel to Tatopani and Jomsom. Nature observation (Kali Gandaki river gorge). Other activities include hiking. Instruction is offered by a local cultural guide with an American leader. This program would appeal to people interested in hiking, mountains.
Accommodations • Homestays, hotels. Single rooms are available for an additional $200.
Program Details • Program offered 3 times per year. Session length: 2–4 weeks. Departures are scheduled in October, December, March. Most participants are 30–60 years of age. Participants must be 12 years or older to enroll. Other requirements: must be active, fit, and in good health. 4–6 participants per session. Application deadline: August 17, October 15, January 15. Reservations are recommended at least 4–6 months before departure.
Costs • $1700 (includes all meals, international airfare). A $250 deposit is required.
Contact • Effie Fletcher, Director and Founder, Himalayan High Treks, 241 Dolores Street, San Francisco, CA 94103; 800-455-8735; Fax: 415-861-2391; E-mail: effie@well.com; World Wide Web: http://www.well.com/user/effie

 HIMALAYAN HIGH TREKS

DOLPO TREK

General Information • Cultural tour with visits to Dolpo Area, Kathmandu, Pokhara. Once at the destination country, participants travel by foot.
Learning Focus • Other activities include hiking. Instruction is offered by local guides with a German group leader. This program would appeal to people interested in hiking, Buddhist culture.
Accommodations • Hotels, campsites. Single rooms are available for an additional $200.
Program Details • Program offered once per year. Session length: 4 weeks. Departures are scheduled in May. Most participants are 18–40 years of age. Participants must be 18 years or older to enroll. Other requirements: must be active, fit, and in good health. 6 participants per session. Application deadline: February 26. Reservations are recommended at least 4–6 months before departure.
Costs • $1900 (includes housing, all meals). A $250 deposit is required.
Contact • Effie Fletcher, Director and Founder, Himalayan High Treks, 241 Dolores Street, San Francisco, CA 94103; 800-455-8735; Fax: 415-861-2391; E-mail: effie@well.com; World Wide Web: http://www.well.com/user/effie

HIMALAYAN HIGH TREKS

EVEREST TREK

General Information • Cultural tour with visits to Kathmandu, Namche Bazaar, Tengboche Monastary, Mount Everest area. Once at the destination country, participants travel by foot.
Learning Focus • Escorted travel to Namche and Buddhist monasteries. Nature observation (Khumbu Ice Fall, Chukkung Lake, Gokyo Lake). Other activities include hiking. Instruction is offered by local guides with an American leader. This program would appeal to people interested in mountains, Buddhism, hiking.
Accommodations • Homestays, hotels. Single rooms are available for an additional $200.
Program Details • Program offered 3 times per year. Session length: 2–4 weeks. Departures are scheduled in October, November, April. Most participants are 12–50 years of age. Participants must be 12 years or older to enroll. Other requirements: must be active, fit, and in good health. 6–8 participants per session. Application deadline: 2 months prior to departure. Reservations are recommended at least 4–6 months before departure.
Costs • $1400–$1750 (includes housing, all meals). A $250 deposit is required.
Contact • Effie Fletcher, Director and Founder, Himalayan High Treks, 241 Dolores Street, San Francisco, CA 94103-2211; 800-455-8735; Fax: 415-861-2391; E-mail: effie@well.com; World Wide Web: http://www.well.com/user/effie

 HIMALAYAN HIGH TREKS

MUSTANG TREK

General Information • Cultural tour with visits to Kathmandu, Mustang Region, Mustang. Once at the destination country, participants travel by foot.
Learning Focus • Instruction in traditional Tibetan culture. Escorted travel to Kagbeni. Other activities include hiking. Instruction is offered by trek leader and local guides. This program would appeal to people interested in Tibet, hiking, Buddhism.
Accommodations • Hotels, campsites. Single rooms are available for an additional $200.
Program Details • Program offered once per year. Session length: 2½ weeks. Departures are scheduled in May, June. Most participants are 18–40 years of age. Participants must be 18 years or older to enroll. Other requirements: must be active, fit, and in good health. 6 participants per session. Application deadline: April 1. Reservations are recommended at least 4–6 months before departure.
Costs • $2400 (includes housing, all meals). A $250 deposit is required.
Contact • Effie Fletcher, Director and Founder, Himalayan High Treks, 241 Dolores Street, San Francisco, CA 94103-2211; 800-455-8735; Fax: 415-861-2391; E-mail: effie@well.com; World Wide Web: http://www.well.com/user/effie

INTERHOSTEL, UNIVERSITY OF NEW HAMPSHIRE

NEPAL

General Information • Cultural tour with visits to Kathmandu, Pokhara, Royal Chitwan, Pashopatinath, Bodhnath, Bhaktapur, Tharu Village. Once at the destination country, participants travel by bus, foot, airplane. Program is affiliated with Folkways Institute.
Learning Focus • Instruction in history and culture. Escorted travel to Nepalese cities and villages. Museum visits (National Museum, Nepal Association of Fine Arts). Attendance at performances (Tharu dancers). Instruction is offered by professors, city guides. This program would appeal to people interested in history, culture.
Accommodations • Hotels. Single rooms are available for an additional $580.
Program Details • Program offered once per year. Session length: 2 weeks. Departures are scheduled in January. Program is targeted to seniors over 50. Most participants are 60–80 years of age. Participants must be 50 years or older to enroll. 35 participants per session. Reservations are recommended at least 6 months before departure.
Costs • $4075 (includes tuition, housing, all meals, excursions, international airfare, entrance fees). A $200 deposit is required.
Contact • Janice Pierson, Office Supervisor, Interhostel, University of New Hampshire, 6 Garrison Avenue, Durham, NH 03824; 800-733-9753; Fax: 603-862-1113; World Wide Web: http://www.learn.unh.edu/

JOURNEYS INTERNATIONAL, INC.

ANNAPURNA FAMILY TREK

General Information • Family tour with visits to Birthanti, Dhampus, Ghandrung, Hyangja, Kathmandu, Pokhara. Once at the destination country, participants travel by foot, trekking.
Learning Focus • Escorted travel to Nepali sites and villages. Other activities include hiking, trekking. Instruction

is offered by Sherpa staff. This program would appeal to people interested in hiking, nature studies, culture, photography.
Accommodations • Hotels, campsites.
Program Details • Program offered 2 times per year. Session length: 16 days. Departures are scheduled in March, December. Program is targeted to active families with an interest in culture. Most participants are 5–75 years of age. Participants must be 3 years or older to enroll. 15 participants per session. Application deadline: 60 days prior to departure. Reservations are recommended at least 60 days before departure.
Costs • $1345 for adults, $890 for children under 12 (includes housing, some meals, excursions, porters, cooks). A $300 deposit is required.
Contact • Joan Weber, Family Trips Director and Owner, Journeys International, Inc., 4011 Jackson Road, Ann Arbor, MI 48103; 313-665-4407; Fax: 313-665-2945; E-mail: joan@journeys-intl.com; World Wide Web: http://www.journeys-intl.com

JOURNEYS INTERNATIONAL, INC.

ANNAPURNA LODGE TREK

General Information • Wilderness/adventure program with visits to Birthanti, Ghandruk, Hampus, Pokhara. Once at the destination country, participants travel by foot, trekking.
Learning Focus • Nature observation (Himalayas). Other activities include hiking, trekking. Instruction is offered by Nepalese staff. This program would appeal to people interested in photography, culture, hiking.
Accommodations • Lodges. Single rooms are available for an additional $100.
Program Details • Session length: 8 days. Departures are scheduled throughout the year. Program is targeted to active persons with an interest in culture. Most participants are 25–55 years of age. 4–12 participants per session. Application deadline: 60 days prior to departure. Reservations are recommended at least 60 days before departure.
Costs • $995 (includes housing, some meals). A $300 deposit is required.
Contact • Pat Ballard, Asia Sales Director, Journeys International, Inc., 4011 Jackson Road, Ann Arbor, MI 48103; 313-665-4407; Fax: 313-665-2945; E-mail: pat@journeys-intl.com; World Wide Web: http://www.journeys-intl.com

JOURNEYS INTERNATIONAL, INC.

ANNAPURNA SANCTUARY TREK

General Information • Wilderness/adventure program with visits to Annapurna Sanctuary, Chomro, Ghandrung, Hinko, Kathmandu, Pokhara. Once at the destination country, participants travel by bus, trekking.
Learning Focus • Escorted travel to regions of the Himalayas. Nature observation (Himalayas). Other activities include trekking. Instruction is offered by Nepalese staff. This program would appeal to people interested in trekking, culture, nature studies, photography.
Accommodations • Campsites. Single rooms are available for an additional $100.
Program Details • Program offered 3 times per year. Session length: 21 days. Departures are scheduled in March, October, November. Program is targeted to active persons with an interest in nature and culture. Most participants are 25–55 years of age. Participants must be 12 years or older to enroll. Other requirements: must be in good health and physical condition. 4–12 participants per session. Application deadline: 60 days prior to departure. Reservations are recommended at least 60 days before departure.
Costs • $1545 (includes housing, some meals, porters, cooks). A $300 deposit is required.
Contact • Pat Ballard, Asia Sales Director, Journeys International, Inc., 4011 Jackson Road, Ann Arbor, MI 48103; 313-665-4407; Fax: 313-665-2945; E-mail: pat@journeys-intl.com; World Wide Web: http://www.journeys-intl.com

JOURNEYS INTERNATIONAL, INC.

EVEREST MONASTERY TREK

General Information • Religion/spirituality program with visits to Jorsale, Kathmandu, Lukla, Namche, Taksindho, Thangboche Monastery. Once at the destination country, participants travel by foot, hiking.
Learning Focus • Escorted travel to monasteries. Other activities include hiking. Instruction is offered by Sherpa guides. This program would appeal to people interested in religion, nature studies, trekking, culture.
Accommodations • Campsites. Single rooms are available.
Program Details • Program offered once per year. Session length: 24 days. Departures are scheduled in September. Program is targeted to active persons interested in Buddhist religion. Most participants are 25–50 years of age. Participants must be 12 years or older to enroll. Other requirements: must be in excellent health and physical condition. 4–12 participants per session. Application deadline: 60 days prior to departure. Reservations are recommended at least 60 days before departure.
Costs • $2095 (includes housing, some meals, porters and cooks). A $300 deposit is required.
Contact • Pat Ballard, Asia Sales Director, Journeys International, Inc., 4011 Jackson Road, Ann Arbor, MI 48103; 313-665-4407; Fax: 313-665-2945; E-mail: pat@journeys-intl.com; World Wide Web: http://www.journeys-intl.com

JOURNEYS INTERNATIONAL, INC.

EVEREST SHERPA COUNTRY TREK

General Information • Wilderness/adventure program with visits to Jiri, Kasrokash, Kathmandu, Kenja, Tasindo, Thaktor. Once at the destination country, participants travel by foot, airplane, hiking.
Learning Focus • Escorted travel to the Himalaya region. Nature observation (Himalayan region). Other activities include camping, hiking, cultural contact. Instruction is offered by Sherpa guides. This program would appeal to people interested in culture, photography, hiking.
Accommodations • Campsites. Single rooms are available for an additional $100.
Program Details • Program offered 4 times per year. Session length: 18–30 days. Departures are scheduled in March–December. Program is targeted to active hikers with an interest in Nepali culture. Most participants are 25–55 years of age. Participants must be 12 years or older to enroll. Other requirements: must be in excellent health and physical condition. 4–12 participants per session. Application dead-

line: 60 days prior to departure. Reservations are recommended at least 60 days before departure.
Costs • $1995–$2295 (includes housing, some meals). A $300 deposit is required.
Contact • Pat Ballard, Asia Sales Director, Journeys International, Inc., 4011 Jackson Road, Ann Arbor, MI 48103; 313-665-4407; Fax: 313-665-2945; E-mail: pat@journeys-intl.com; World Wide Web: http://www.journeys-intl.com

JOURNEYS INTERNATIONAL, INC.

HIMALAYAN DISCOVERY SAFARI

General Information • Wilderness/adventure program with visits to Kathmandu. Once at the destination country, participants travel by foot, trekking.
Learning Focus • Nature observation (Himalayas). Other activities include hiking, rafting, elephant rides. Instruction is offered by Nepali guide. This program would appeal to people interested in bird watching, culture, nature studies, photography, hiking.
Accommodations • Hotels, campsites. Single rooms are available for an additional $100.
Program Details • Program offered 6 times per year. Session length: 20 days. Departures are scheduled in February, March, May, October, November, December. Program is targeted to active persons interested in Nepali culture. Most participants are 25–55 years of age. Participants must be 12 years or older to enroll. 4–12 participants per session. Application deadline: 60 days prior to departure. Reservations are recommended at least 60 days before departure.
Costs • $1995 (includes housing, some meals, porters, cooks). A $300 deposit is required.
Contact • Pat Ballard, Asia Sales Director, Journeys International, Inc., 4011 Jackson Road, Ann Arbor, MI 48103; 313-665-4407; Fax: 313-665-2945; E-mail: pat@journeys-intl.com; World Wide Web: http://www.journeys-intl.com

 JOURNEYS INTERNATIONAL, INC.

HIMALAYAN HEALTH

General Information • Medical expedition with visits to Ampipal, Dhulikhel, Gampesal, Gorkha, Kathmandu, Sirendanda. Once at the destination country, participants travel by bus, foot.
Learning Focus • Escorted travel to Nepali villages. Volunteer work (possibility for work in Nepali clinics). Other activities include camping, trekking. Instruction is offered by scientists, physicians, local healers. This program would appeal to people interested in medicine, nature studies, culture.
Accommodations • Hotels, campsites. Single rooms are available for an additional $100.
Program Details • Program offered 2 times per year. Session length: 23 days. Departures are scheduled in October, January. Program is targeted to medical students and professionals. Most participants are 25–55 years of age. 4–12 participants per session. Application deadline: 60 days prior to departure. Reservations are recommended at least 60 days before departure.
Costs • $2595 (includes housing, some meals, porters, cooks). A $300 deposit is required.
Contact • Pat Ballard, Asia Sales Director, Journeys International, Inc., 4011 Jackson Road, Ann Arbor, MI 48103; 313-665-4407; Fax: 313-665-2945; E-mail: pat@journeys-intl.com; World Wide Web: http://www.journeys-intl.com

JOURNEYS INTERNATIONAL, INC.

NEPAL CULTURE WEEK

General Information • Cultural tour with visits to Bhaktapur, Dhulikhel, Kathmandu, Patan. Once at the destination country, participants travel by foot, trekking.
Learning Focus • Escorted travel to villages of Nepal. Other activities include hiking. Instruction is offered by Nepalese guides. This program would appeal to people interested in culture, photography, nature studies.
Accommodations • Hotels, lodges. Single rooms are available.
Program Details • Departures are scheduled throughout the year. Most participants are 25–55 years of age. Participants must be 12 years or older to enroll. 1–8 participant per session. Application deadline: 60 days prior to departure. Reservations are recommended at least 60 days before departure.
Costs • $1095 (includes housing, some meals). A $300 deposit is required.
Contact • Pat Ballard, Asia Sales Director, Journeys International, Inc., 4011 Jackson Road, Ann Arbor, MI 48103; 313-665-4407; Fax: 313-665-2945; E-mail: pat@journeys-intl.com; World Wide Web: http://www.journeys-intl.com

JOURNEYS INTERNATIONAL, INC.

NEPAL WOMEN'S CULTURAL TREK

General Information • Cultural tour with visits to Kumjang, Lukla, Namche, Thame, Thami, Thangboche. Once at the destination country, participants travel by foot.
Learning Focus • Escorted travel to Nepali villages. Other activities include trekking. Instruction is offered by female Nepalese staff members. This program would appeal to people interested in culture, bird watching, nature studies.
Accommodations • Hotels, campsites. Single rooms are available for an additional $200.
Program Details • Program offered once per year. Session length: 20 days. Departures are scheduled in June. Program is targeted to active women with an interest in cross cultural contact. Most participants are 25–55 years of age. Participants must be 12 years or older to enroll. 4–12 participants per session. Application deadline: 60 days prior to departure. Reservations are recommended at least 60 days before departure.
Costs • $2195 (includes housing, some meals, porters, cooks). A $300 deposit is required.
Contact • Pat Ballard, Asia Sales Director, Journeys International, Inc., 4011 Jackson Road, Ann Arbor, MI 48103; 313-665-4407; Fax: 313-665-2945; E-mail: pat@journeys-intl.com; World Wide Web: http://www.journeys-intl.com

MOUNTAIN MADNESS

TREKKING IN NEPAL

General Information • Wilderness/adventure program with visits to Himalayan Mountains, Kathmandu, temples. Once at the destination country, participants travel by foot, airplane.
Learning Focus • Escorted travel to Himalayan mountain destinations and villages. Other activities include camping, hiking. Instruction is offered by sports professionals, professional trekking guides. This program would appeal to people interested in Asian culture, mountains, trekking, photography.
Accommodations • Hotels, campsites. Single rooms are available.
Program Details • Program offered 2 times per year. Session length: 3 weeks. Departures are scheduled in April, September. Most participants are 20–60 years of age. Participants must be 16 years or older to enroll. Other requirements: good physical fitness. 4–6 participants per session. Reservations are recommended at least 60 days before departure.
Costs • $2950 (includes housing, some meals, guides, porters, camp equipment). A $1000 deposit is required.
Contact • Manomi Fernando, Program Coordinator, Mountain Madness, 4218 Southwest Alaska Street #206, Seattle, WA 98116; 206-937-8389; Fax: 206-937-1772; E-mail: mountmad@aol.com

NEW COLLEGE OF CALIFORNIA, WORLD COLLEGE INSTITUTE

HIMALAYAN FIELD STUDIES PROGRAM

General Information • Cultural tour in Kathmandu. Excursions to Pokhara, Chitwan National Park, sacred sites in the Kathmandu valley.
Learning Focus • Courses in Himalayan cultures, Hinduism, hiking, Buddhism, adventure, wildlife.
Accommodations • Hotels, guest houses. Single rooms are available. Meals are taken in central dining facility, in local restaurants.
Program Details • Program offered 3 times per year. Session length: 3 weeks. Departures are scheduled in May, September, December. Most participants are 25–45 years of age. 15 participants per session. Application deadline: 60 days prior to departure.
Costs • $2550 (includes housing, some meals, excursions, international airfare). A $300 deposit is required.
Contact • Jerry Dekker, Director of Himalayan Field Studies Program, New College of California, World College Institute, 777 Valencia Street, San Francisco, CA 94110; 800-335-6262, ext. 406; Fax: 415-776-7160; E-mail: jerryd@ncgate.newcollege.edu; World Wide Web: http://www.newcollege.edu

SANN RESEARCH INSTITUTE

SEMESTER IN NEPAL

General Information • Cultural tour in Kathmandu. Excursions to mountains of Nepal, villages, Chitwan Jungle National Park, Tibetan Buddhist Monasteries.
Learning Focus • Courses in anthropology, Nepali language, economics, religion, philosophy, political science, geology, history.
Accommodations • Homestays. Single rooms are available. Meals are taken with host family, in central dining facility, in residences.
Program Details • Program offered 3 times per year. Session length: 12 weeks. Departures are scheduled in January, September, December. The program is open to undergraduate students, pre-college students. Other requirements: minimum 2.5 GPA for college students and a 3.0 minimum GPA for high school students. Application deadline: December 1, August 1, November 15.
Costs • $8500 (includes tuition, housing, all meals, books and class materials, excursions, international airfare). A $1500 deposit is required.
Contact • Mr. Narayan Shrestha, President, Sann Research Institute, 948 Pearl, Boulder, CO 80302; 303-440-0331; Fax: 303-440-6958; E-mail: nshresth@carbon.cudenver.edu

BRITISH COASTAL TRAILS SCENIC WALKING

NEW ZEALAND'S SOUTH ISLAND

General Information • Cultural tour with visits to Christchurch, Fox Glacier Township, Hanmer Springs, Lake Moeraki, Queenstown, Wanaka, Arrowtown, Haast Pass, Munro Beach, Hanmer Basin. Once at the destination country, participants travel by bus, foot.
Learning Focus • Escorted travel to Makarora Valley and the Pororari River gorge. Nature observation (sheep, rain forests, glaciers, lakes, wildlife, waterfalls, seals, penguins). Other activities include hiking. Instruction is offered by naturalists, historians, professional guides. This program would appeal to people interested in nature studies, walking, culture, photography, history.
Accommodations • Hotels. Single rooms are available.
Program Details • Program offered 2 times per year. Session length: 12 days. Departures are scheduled in January, March. Most participants are 40–65 years of age. Participants must be 13 years or older to enroll. Other requirements: physician's approval and signed release form. 18 participants per session. Application deadline: 30 days prior to departure. Reservations are recommended at least 6 months before departure.
Costs • $2895 (includes housing, some meals, excursions, full-time guide). A $250 deposit is required.
Contact • Tour Manager, British Coastal Trails Scenic Walking, 7777 Fay Avenue, Suite 100, La Jolla, CA 92037; 800-473-1210; Fax: 619-456-2277; E-mail: lajolla@bctwalk.com; World Wide Web: http://www.bctwalk.com/lajolla

COUNTRY WALKERS

NATURE'S TREASURE BOX

General Information • Cultural, gourmet cooking, nature study and walking tour with visits to Christchurch, Greymouth, Haast River Valley, Queenstown, Marvia Springs. Once at the destination country, participants travel by foot, boat.
Learning Focus • Escorted travel to the alpine bog, Truman Track and the Fox Glacier. Nature observation (tui, river eels, "dinosaur trees," banded dottorels). Other activities include walking. Instruction is offered by professors, researchers, naturalists, historians. This program would appeal to people interested in walking, nature studies, food and wine.
Accommodations • Hotels. Single rooms are available for an additional $300–$600.
Program Details • Program offered 4 times per year. Session length: 12 days. Departures are scheduled in January, February, November, December. Program is targeted to adults 35 to 65 years old. Most participants are 35–65 years of age. Participants must be 18 years or older to enroll. 18 participants per session. Reservations are recommended at least 5–6 months before departure.
Costs • $2650 (includes housing, all meals, excursions). A $400 deposit is required.
Contact • Heather Kellingbeck, Vice President, Country Walkers, PO Box 180, Waterbury, VT 05176; 800-464-9255; Fax: 802-244-5661; E-mail: ctrywalk@aol.com

FOREIGN LANGUAGE STUDY ABROAD SERVICE

INTERNATIONAL LANGUAGE STUDY HOMESTAYS IN NEW ZEALAND

General Information • Language study program in New Zealand.
Learning Focus • Courses in English language. Instruction is offered by local teachers.
Accommodations • Homestays. Single rooms are available. Meals are taken with host family, in residences.
Program Details • Session length: varies. Departures are scheduled in January–December. The program is open to undergraduate students, graduate students, pre-college students, adults. Most participants are 12 years of age and older. Other requirements: students must be at least 12 years old. 1 participant per session.
Costs • Contact sponsor for information. A $300 deposit is required.
Contact • Louise Harber, Coordinator, Foreign Language Study Abroad Service, Department IH, Box 903, 5935 Southwest 64th Avenue, South Miami, FL 33143; 800-282-1090; Fax: 305-662-2907; E-mail: flsas@netpoint.net; World Wide Web: http://www.netpoint.net/~flsas

INTERHOSTEL, UNIVERSITY OF NEW HAMPSHIRE

NEW ZEALAND

General Information • Cultural tour with visits to Christchurch, Dunedin, Paihia, Rotorua, Te Anao, Wellington, Waitangi, Russell, Auckland, Akaroa, Milford Sound, Hokitika, Haast Pass, Arrowtown. Once at the destination country, participants travel by bus, foot, boat, airplane. Program is affiliated with University of Canterbury.
Learning Focus • Instruction in history and culture. Escorted travel to cities and landmarks. Museum visits (popular attractions). Attendance at performances (local theater). Other activities include a Maori welcome. Instruction is offered by professors, historians. This program would appeal to people interested in history, culture.
Accommodations • Hotels. Single rooms are available for an additional $1450.

Program Details • Program offered once per year. Session length: 3 weeks. Departures are scheduled in January. Program is targeted to seniors over 50. Most participants are 60–80 years of age. Participants must be 50 years or older to enroll. 35 participants per session. Reservations are recommended at least 6 months before departure.
Costs • $4795 (includes tuition, housing, all meals, excursions, international airfare, entrance fees). A $200 deposit is required.
Contact • Janice Pierson, Office Supervisor, Interhostel, University of New Hampshire, 6 Garrison Avenue, Durham, NH 03824; 800-733-9753; Fax: 603-862-1113; World Wide Web: http://www.learn.unh.edu/

SYRACUSE UNIVERSITY

INCLUSIVE EDUCATION IN NEW ZEALAND

General Information • Academic study program in Auckland, Christchurch, Dunedin, Hamilton, Rotorua, Queenstown. Classes are held on the campus of University of Waikato.
Learning Focus • Courses in special education. Instruction is offered by professors from the sponsoring institution.
Accommodations • Hotels. Meals are taken as a group, in central dining facility.
Program Details • Program offered once per year. Session length: 5 weeks. Departures are scheduled in June. The program is open to undergraduate students, graduate students. Most participants are 19–25 years of age. Other requirements: two years of special education coursework. 15 participants per session. Application deadline: March 15.
Costs • $5081 (includes tuition, housing, some meals, books and class materials, excursions). Application fee: $40. A $350 deposit is required.
Contact • Ms. Daisy Fried, Associate Director, Syracuse University, 119 Euclid Avenue, Syracuse, NY 13244-4170; 315-443-9419; Fax: 315-443-4593; E-mail: dsfried@summon3.syr.edu; World Wide Web: http://sumweb.syr.edu/dipa/dipa9.htm

PAPUA NEW GUINEA

BOLDER ADVENTURES, ASIA TRANSPACIFIC JOURNEYS

PAPUA NEW GUINEA ODYSSEY

General Information • Cultural and nature study tour with visits to Papua New Guinea. Once at the destination country, participants travel by foot, boat, airplane.
Learning Focus • Escorted travel to tribal villages, cultural sites. Museum visits (National Museum). Attendance at performances (highlands cultural show). Nature observation (birding, wildlife). Instruction is offered by professors, researchers, naturalists. This program would appeal to people interested in photography.
Accommodations • Hotels. Single rooms are available for an additional $750.
Program Details • Program offered once per year. Session length: 20 days. Departures are scheduled in August. Most participants are 35–65 years of age. Participants must be 18 years or older to enroll. 10–12 participants per session. Reservations are recommended at least 4 months before departure.
Costs • $6000 (includes housing, all meals, excursions, international airfare, internal flights in Papua New Guinea). A $500 deposit is required.
Contact • Bolder Adventures, Asia Transpacific Journeys, 3055 Center Green Drive, Boulder, CO 80301; 800-642-2742; Fax: 303-443-7078; World Wide Web: http://www.southeastasia.com/

JOURNEYS INTERNATIONAL, INC.

REMOTE LODGE ODYSSEY

General Information • Wilderness/adventure program with visits to Karawani, Madang, Tari. Once at the destination country, participants travel by foot, trekking.
Learning Focus • Nature observation (rain forest). Other activities include snorkeling. Instruction is offered by English-speaking guides. This program would appeal to people interested in nature studies, wildlife, culture.
Accommodations • Lodges. Single rooms are available for an additional $250.
Program Details • Session length: 7 days. Departures are scheduled throughout the year. Program is targeted to persons interested in culture. Most participants are 25–55 years of age. Participants must be 12 years or older to enroll. 2–16 participants per session. Application deadline: 60 days prior to departure. Reservations are recommended at least 60 days before departure.
Costs • $1445 (includes housing, some meals). A $300 deposit is required.
Contact • Pat Ballard, Asia Sales Director, Journeys International, Inc., 4011 Jackson Road, Ann Arbor, MI 48103; 313-665-4407; Fax: 313-665-2945; E-mail: pat@journeys-intl.com; World Wide Web: http://www.journeys-intl.com

JOURNEYS INTERNATIONAL, INC.

SEPIK HIGHLAND ODYSSEY

General Information • Cultural tour with visits to Papua New Guinea.
Learning Focus • Escorted travel to northern highlands, the Sepik River and the coastline. Nature observation (wildlife, birdwatching). Instruction is offered by naturalists. This program would appeal to people interested in culture, nature studies.
Accommodations • Inns, lodges.
Program Details • Program offered 4 times per year. Session length: 17 days. Departures are scheduled throughout the year. Most participants are 25–55 years of age. 15 participants per session. Application deadline: 60 days prior to departure. Reservations are recommended at least 60 days before departure.
Costs • $2295 (includes housing, some meals). A $300 deposit is required.
Contact • Pat Ballard, Asia Sales Director, Journeys International, Inc., 4011 Jackson Road, Ann Arbor, MI 48103; 313-665-4407; Fax: 313-665-2945; E-mail: pat@journeys-intl.com; World Wide Web: http://www.journeys-intl.com

PHILIPPINES

BOLDER ADVENTURES, ASIA TRANSPACIFIC JOURNEYS

ADVENTURER'S PHILIPPINES

General Information • Wilderness/adventure program with visits to Phillippines. Once at the destination country, participants travel by foot, boat, airplane, sea kayak.
Learning Focus • Escorted travel to Phillippines. Other activities include camping, hiking, sea kayaking. Instruction is offered by naturalists, sports professionals. This program would appeal to people interested in snorkeling, scuba diving.
Accommodations • Hotels, campsites. Single rooms are available for an additional $400.
Program Details • Program offered 3 times per year. Session length: 16 days. Departures are scheduled in March–May. Program is targeted to active, fit people. Most participants are 25–50 years of age. Participants must be 18 years or older to enroll. 8–10 participants per session. Reservations are recommended at least 4 months before departure.
Costs • $2795 (includes housing, all meals, excursions). A $500 deposit is required.
Contact • Bolder Adventures, Asia Transpacific Journeys, 3055 Center Green Drive, Boulder, CO 80301; 800-642-2742; Fax: 303-443-7078; World Wide Web: http://www.southeastasia.com/

GLOBAL EXCHANGE REALITY TOURS

PHILIPPINES

General Information • Cultural tour with visits to Luzón, Manila, Mindanao. Once at the destination country, participants travel by bus, airplane.
Learning Focus • Instruction in current political, economic and social situations. Escorted travel to province of Mindanao and Muslim areas. Instruction is offered by researchers, naturalists. This program would appeal to people interested in globalization, environmental issues, culture, health.
Accommodations • Homestays, hotels, guest houses. Single rooms are available for an additional $200–$500.
Program Details • Program offered 2 times per year. Session length: 2 weeks. Departures are scheduled in November, March. Program is targeted to seniors, students and professionals. Participants must be 18 years or older to enroll. 10 participants per session. Application deadline: 1 month prior to departure. Reservations are recommended at least 2 months before departure.
Costs • $2500 (includes housing, some meals, international airfare). A $200 deposit is required.
Contact • Jennifer Cariño, Reality Tours Coordinator, Global Exchange Reality Tours, 2017 Mission Street, Room 303, San Francisco, CA 94110; 415-255-7296; Fax: 415-255-7498; E-mail: globalexch@igc.apc.org

THE PARTNERSHIP FOR SERVICE-LEARNING

PHILIPPINES

General Information • Academic study and volunteer service program in Manila. Classes are held on the campus of Trinity College. Excursions to Manila, Mount Pinatubo.
Learning Focus • Courses in history, sociology, literature, Filipino language. Instruction is offered by local teachers.
Accommodations • Guest houses. Single rooms are available. Meals are taken on one's own, in central dining facility, in local restaurants.
Program Details • Program offered once per year. Session length: 11 weeks. Departures are scheduled in June. The program is open to undergraduate students, graduate students, pre-college students, adults. Most participants are 19–24 years of age. Other requirements: sophomore standing. 5 participants per session. Application deadline: 2 months prior to departure.
Costs • $4400 (includes tuition, housing, some meals, excursions, service placement and supervision, pre-departure and orientation materials). A $250 deposit is required.
Contact • Maureen Lowney, Coordinator of Student Programs, The Partnership for Service-Learning, 815 Second Avenue, Suite 315, New York, NY 10960; 212-986-0989; Fax: 212-986-5039; E-mail: pslny@aol.com

SINGAPORE

SYRACUSE UNIVERSITY

INTERNATIONAL BUSINESS INTERNSHIPS IN SINGAPORE

General Information • Internship program in Singapore. Excursions to Malaysia (Kuala Lumpur).

Learning Focus • Courses in international business, marketing. Instruction is offered by professors from the sponsoring institution.

Accommodations • Hotels. Single rooms are available. Meals are taken on one's own, in local restaurants.

Program Details • Program offered once per year. Session length: 6 weeks. Departures are scheduled in June. The program is open to undergraduate students, graduate students. Most participants are 19-30 years of age. Other requirements: minimum 2.8 GPA. 15 participants per session. Application deadline: March 15.

Costs • $5976 (includes tuition, housing, some meals, books and class materials, excursions). Application fee: $40. A $350 deposit is required.

Contact • Ms. Daisy Fried, Associate Director, Syracuse University, 119 Euclid Avenue, Syracuse, NY 13244; 315-443-9419; Fax: 315-443-4593; E-mail: dsfried@summon3.syr.edu; World Wide Web: http://sumweb.syr.edu/dipa/dipa9.htm

TAIWAN

FOREIGN LANGUAGE STUDY ABROAD SERVICE

INTERNATIONAL LANGUAGE STUDY HOMESTAYS IN TAIWAN

General Information • Language study program in Taiwan.
Learning Focus • Courses in Mandarin Chinese language. Instruction is offered by local teachers.
Accommodations • Homestays. Single rooms are available. Meals are taken with host family, in residences.
Program Details • Session length: varies. Departures are scheduled in January–December. The program is open to undergraduate students, graduate students, pre-college students, adults. Most participants are 12 years of age and older. Other requirements: students must be at least 12 years old. 1 participant per session.
Costs • Contact sponsor for information. A $300 deposit is required.
Contact • Louise Harber, Coordinator, Foreign Language Study Abroad Service, Department IH, Box 903, 5935 Southwest 64th Avenue, South Miami, FL 33143; 800-282-1090; Fax: 305-662-2907; E-mail: flsas@netpoint.net; World Wide Web: http://www.netpoint.net/~flsas

INTER-UNIVERSITY BOARD FOR CHINESE LANGUAGE STUDIES

INTERNATIONAL CHINESE LANGUAGE PROGRAM

General Information • Language study program in Taipei. Classes are held on the campus of National Taiwan Normal University.
Learning Focus • Courses in Mandarin Chinese language. Instruction is offered by professors from the sponsoring institution and local teachers.
Accommodations • Students make own arrangements. Meals are taken on one's own.
Program Details • Program offered once per year. Session length: 8 weeks. Departures are scheduled in June. The program is open to undergraduate students, graduate students, adults. Most participants are 20–40 years of age. Other requirements: previous college-level Chinese study of 2 years. 30 participants per session. Application deadline: March 1.
Costs • $3000 (includes tuition). Application fee: $55. A $200 deposit is required.
Contact • Janet Sclar, Program Administrator, Inter-University Board for Chinese Language Studies, 300 Lasuen Street, Littlefield Center Basement, Stanford, CA 95128; 415-725-2575; Fax: 415-723-9972; E-mail: iub.cls@forsythe.stanford.edu

LANGUAGE LIAISON

LIVE 'N' LEARN (LEARN IN A TEACHER'S HOME)–TAIWAN

General Information • Language study program with visits to Taiwan.
Learning Focus • Instruction in Chinese. Instruction is offered by professors. This program would appeal to people interested in language.
Accommodations • Homestays. Single rooms are available.
Program Details • Session length: unlimited. Departures are scheduled throughout the year. Most participants are 18–70 years of age. Participants must be 16 years or older to enroll. Reservations are recommended at least 35 days before departure.
Costs • Contact sponsor for information.
Contact • Nancy Forman, President, Language Liaison, 20533 Biscayne Boulevard-Station 4-162, Miami, FL 33180; 305-682-9909; Fax: 305-682-9907; E-mail: langstudy@aol.com; World Wide Web: http://languageliaison.com

LANGUAGE LIAISON

MANDARIN IN TAIWAN

General Information • Language study program with visits to Taipei.
Learning Focus • Instruction in Chinese language. Instruction is offered by professors. This program would appeal to people interested in Chinese language.
Accommodations • Students make their own arrangements.
Program Details • Session length: unlimited. Departures are scheduled throughout the year. Program is targeted to students of any age. Most participants are 18–70 years of age. Participants must be 16 years or older to enroll. Reservations are recommended at least 35 days before departure.
Costs • Contact sponsor for information.
Contact • Nancy Forman, President, Language Liaison, 20533 Biscayne Boulevard, Sta. 4-162, Miami, FL 33180; 305-682-9909; Fax: 305-682-9907; E-mail: langstudy@aol.com; World Wide Web: http://languageliaison.com

NATIONAL REGISTRATION CENTER FOR STUDY ABROAD

TAIPEI LANGUAGE INSTITUTE

General Information • Language study program in Koahsiung, Shihlin, Taichung, Taipei.
Learning Focus • Courses in Taiwanese language, Mandarin Chinese language.
Accommodations • Hostels.
Program Details • Program offered 50 times per year. Session length: 4 weeks. Departures are scheduled in

January–December. The program is open to undergraduate students, graduate students, adults. Application deadline: 40 days prior to departure.
Costs • $1070 (includes tuition, insurance). Application fee: $40. A $100 deposit is required.
Contact • Reuel Zielke, Coordinator, National Registration Center for Study Abroad, PO Box 1393, Milwaukee, WI 53201; 414-278-0631; Fax: 414-271-8884; E-mail: inquiries@nrcsa.com; World Wide Web: http://www.nrcsa.com

UNIVERSITY OF FLORIDA

MANDARIN TRAINING CENTER, TAIWAN NORMAL UNIVERSITY, TAIPAI, TAIWAN

General Information • Language study program in Taipei. Classes are held on the campus of National Taiwan Normal University.
Learning Focus • Courses in Mandarin Chinese language. Instruction is offered by local teachers.
Accommodations • Dormitories. Meals are taken on one's own.
Program Details • Program offered once per year. Session length: 8 weeks. Departures are scheduled in July. The program is open to undergraduate students, graduate students, adults. Most participants are 18–40 years of age. Other requirements: minimum 2.5 GPA and 2 semesters of Chinese language. Application deadline: March 15.
Costs • $4500 (includes housing, books and class materials, insurance, international airfare, administration fees). Application fee: $250.
Contact • Overseas Studies, University of Florida, 123 Tigert Hall, PO Box 113225, Gainesville, FL 32611-3225; 352-392-5206; Fax: 352-392-5575; E-mail: ovrseas@nervm.nerdc.ufl.edu

UNIVERSITY OF MASSACHUSETTS AMHERST

INTENSIVE CHINESE LANGUAGE PROGRAM

General Information • Language study program in Taichung. Classes are held on the campus of Tunghai University.
Learning Focus • Courses in Chinese language. Instruction is offered by local teachers.
Accommodations • Dormitories. Meals are taken in central dining facility.
Program Details • Program offered once per year. Session length: 8 weeks. Departures are scheduled in June. The program is open to undergraduate students. Most participants are 18–28 years of age. Other requirements: minimum 3.0 GPA and 1 year college-level Mandarin or equivalent. 25 participants per session. Application deadline: March 1.
Costs • $2400 (includes tuition, housing, some meals, books and class materials). A $30 deposit is required.
Contact • Director, University of Massachusetts Amherst, Asian Languages and Literatures, Thompson Hall, Box 37505, Amherst, MA 01003; 413-545-4350; Fax: 413-545-4975; E-mail: abroad@ipo.umass.edu; World Wide Web: http://www.umass.edu/ipo/

THAILAND

BOLDER ADVENTURES, ASIA TRANSPACIFIC JOURNEYS

THAILAND

General Information • Cultural tour with visits to Thailand. Once at the destination country, participants travel by train, foot, boat, airplane, sea kayak or elephant.
Learning Focus • Escorted travel to Thailand. Instruction is offered by professors, naturalists, historians. This program would appeal to people interested in culture, natural history.
Accommodations • Hotels. Single rooms are available.
Program Details • Program offered 7 times per year. Session length: 16 days. Departures are scheduled in January–December. Most participants are 30–60 years of age. Other requirements: spirit of adventure. 10–12 participants per session. Reservations are recommended at least 4 months before departure.
Costs • $1995 (includes housing, all meals, excursions). A $500 deposit is required.
Contact • Bolder Adventures, Asia Transpacific Journeys, 3055 Center Green Drive, Boulder, CO 80301; 800-642-2742; Fax: 303-443-7078; World Wide Web: http://www.southeastasia.com/

COUNCIL ON INTERNATIONAL EDUCATIONAL EXCHANGE

DEVELOPMENT AND ENVIRONMENT PROGRAM AT KHON KAEN UNIVERSITY

General Information • Academic study program in Khon Kaen. Classes are held on the campus of Khon Kaen University. Excursions to Bangkok.
Learning Focus • Courses in development studies, public health, Thai language, environmental studies. Instruction is offered by professors from the sponsoring institution and local teachers.
Accommodations • Dormitories. Meals are taken on one's own, in central dining facility, in local restaurants.
Program Details • Program offered 2 times per year. Session length: 7 weeks. Departures are scheduled in June. The program is open to undergraduate students, graduate students. Most participants are 19–25 years of age. Other requirements: minimum 2.75 GPA and 1 Asian studies course. 10–15 participants per session. Application deadline: April 1.
Costs • $2850 (includes tuition, housing, all meals, insurance, excursions, International Student Identification card, orientation in Bangkok). Application fee: $30. A $300 deposit is required.
Contact • Alyssa McCloud, Program Registrar, Council on International Educational Exchange, College and University Division, 205 East 42nd Street, New York, NY 10017-5706; 212-822-2766; Fax: 212-822-2779; E-mail: info@ciee.org; World Wide Web: http://www.ciee.org

INTERHOSTEL, UNIVERSITY OF NEW HAMPSHIRE

THAILAND

General Information • Cultural tour with visits to Ayutthaya, Bangkok, Chiang Mai, Lampang, Sukhothai, Doi Inathon Royal Project, Doi Suthep, Khong River, Damnern Saduak, Wat Phra That Lampang Luang. Once at the destination country, participants travel by bus, foot, boat, airplane. Program is affiliated with Bangkok University.
Learning Focus • Instruction in history and culture. Escorted travel to villages and landmarks. Instruction is offered by professors, historians. This program would appeal to people interested in history, culture.
Accommodations • Hotels. Single rooms are available for an additional $700.
Program Details • Program offered once per year. Session length: 2 weeks. Departures are scheduled in January. Program is targeted to seniors over 50. Most participants are 60–80 years of age. Participants must be 50 years or older to enroll. 35 participants per session. Reservations are recommended at least 6 months before departure.
Costs • $3250 (includes tuition, housing, all meals, excursions, international airfare). A $200 deposit is required.
Contact • Janice Pierson, Office Supervisor, Interhostel, University of New Hampshire, 6 Garrison Avenue, Durham, NH 03824; 800-733-9753; Fax: 603-862-1113; World Wide Web: http://www.learn.unh.edu/

JOURNEYS INTERNATIONAL, INC.

ANCIENT CULTURES ODYSSEY

General Information • Cultural tour with visits to Akha Village, Ayutthaya, Bangkok, Chiang Mai, Lampang, Mal Salong. Once at the destination country, participants travel by foot, boat.
Learning Focus • Attendance at performances (Hill Tribe Show). Other activities include an elephant ride. Instruction is offered by English-speaking local guides. This program would appeal to people interested in culture, photography, nature studies.
Accommodations • Hotels. Single rooms are available for an additional $75.
Program Details • Session length: 7 days. Departures are scheduled throughout the year. Program is targeted to persons interested in culture. Most participants are 25–55 years of age. Participants must be 12 years or older to enroll. 2–8 participants per session. Application deadline: 60 days prior to departure. Reservations are recommended at least 60 days before departure.

Costs • $1125 (includes housing, some meals, boat ride). A $300 deposit is required.
Contact • Pat Ballard, Asia Sales Director, Journeys International, Inc., 4011 Jackson Road, Ann Arbor, MI 48103; 313-665-4407; Fax: 313-665-2945; E-mail: pat@journeys-intl.com; World Wide Web: http://www.journeys-intl.com

NORTHERN ILLINOIS UNIVERSITY

ENVIRONMENT, ECOLOGY, AND DEVELOPMENT: THE HUMAN PERSPECTIVE

General Information • Academic study program in Khon Kaen. Classes are held on the campus of Khon Kaen University.
Learning Focus • Courses in geography, Thai language. Instruction is offered by local teachers.
Accommodations • Dormitories. Meals are taken on one's own, in central dining facility.
Program Details • Program offered once per year. Session length: 9 weeks. Departures are scheduled in June. The program is open to undergraduate students. Most participants are 20–24 years of age. Other requirements: minimum 2.75 GPA. Application deadline: March 15.
Costs • $3085 (includes tuition, housing, some meals, insurance, excursions). A $200 deposit is required.
Contact • Anne Seitzinger, Program Coordinator, Short-Term Study Abroad, Northern Illinois University, Study Abroad Office-WI 417, DeKalb, IL 60115; 815-752-0700; Fax: 815-753-0825; E-mail: aseitz@niu.edu; World Wide Web: http://www.niu.edu/depts/intl_prgms/intl.html

RUSSIAN AND EAST EUROPEAN PARTNERSHIPS

THAI LANGUAGE AND CULTURAL IMMERSION PROGRAM

General Information • Language study program in Bangkok. Classes are held on the campus of Nisa Thai Language School. Excursions to Sam Pran, seaside resorts, Khon Kaen.
Learning Focus • Courses in Thai language, Thai culture and art, Thai history. Instruction is offered by local teachers.
Accommodations • Dormitories. Single rooms are available. Meals are taken on one's own, in central dining facility, in local restaurants.
Program Details • Program offered 11 times per year. Session length: 4 or more weeks. Departures are scheduled in January–November. The program is open to undergraduate students, graduate students, adults. Most participants are 18 years of age and older. Other requirements: in good health and 18 or older unless chaperoned by an adult. 6 participants per session. Application deadline: 45 days prior to departure.
Costs • $4850 (includes tuition, housing, some meals, books and class materials, excursions, international airfare, local transportation, airport transfers). A $1500 deposit is required.
Contact • Kenneth Fortune, President, Russian and East European Partnerships, PO Box 227, Fineview, NY 13640; 888-873-7337; Fax: 800-910-1777; E-mail: reep@fox.nstn.ca

UNIVERSITY STUDIES ABROAD CONSORTIUM

SOUTHEAST ASIAN STUDIES: RANGSIT, THAILAND

General Information • Academic study program in Rangsit. Classes are held on the campus of Rangsit University. Excursions to Ayutthaya, Kanchanaburi, Huahin, Malaysia, Singapore.
Learning Focus • Courses in Buddhism, international finance, Thai language, philosophy, hospitality marketing, international marketing. Instruction is offered by local teachers.
Accommodations • Dormitories, locally-rented apartments. Single rooms are available. Meals are taken on one's own, in central dining facility.
Program Details • Program offered once per year. Session length: 8 weeks. Departures are scheduled in June. The program is open to undergraduate students, graduate students, pre-college students, adults. Most participants are 18–50 years of age. Other requirements: minimum 2.5 GPA. 15 participants per session. Application deadline: April 15.
Costs • $1100 (includes tuition, insurance, International Student Identification card). Application fee: $50. A $150 deposit is required.
Contact • Dr. Carmelo Urza, Director, University Studies Abroad Consortium, University of Nevada Library/323, Reno, NV 89557-0093; 702-784-6569; Fax: 702-784-6010; E-mail: usac@equinox.unr.edu; World Wide Web: http://www.scs.unr.edu/~usac

TIBET

JOURNEYS INTERNATIONAL, INC.

TIBET OVERLAND ODYSSEY

General Information • Wilderness/adventure program with visits to Drepung, Jhokhang, Lhasa, Norbulingka, Potala, Sera. Once at the destination country, participants travel by bus, airplane.

Learning Focus • Escorted travel to monasteries. Nature observation (Mount Everest). Instruction is offered by Tibetan and Chinese guides. This program would appeal to people interested in culture, photography, nature studies.

Accommodations • Hotels.

Program Details • Session length: 8 days. Departures are scheduled throughout the year. Most participants are 25–55 years of age. Participants must be 12 years or older to enroll. 4–15 participants per session. Application deadline: 60 days prior to departure. Reservations are recommended at least 60 days before departure.

Costs • $1295 (includes housing, some meals, airfare from Kathmandu to Lhasa). A $300 deposit is required.

Contact • Pat Ballard, Asia Sales Director, Journeys International, Inc., 4011 Jackson Road, Ann Arbor, MI 48103; 313-665-4407; Fax: 313-665-2945; E-mail: pat@journeys-intl.com; World Wide Web: http://www.journeys-intl.com

PHOTO EXPLORER TOURS

TIBET AND PANDA RESERVE

General Information • Photography tour with visits to Tibet, Sholdon Festival, Sichuan Province. Once at the destination country, participants travel by bus, foot.

Learning Focus • Instruction in photography. Escorted travel to Lhasa and Wolong Nature Preserve. Attendance at performances (Tibetan opera). Nature observation (pandas, wildlife). Instruction is offered by professional photographers. This program would appeal to people interested in photography.

Accommodations • Hotels. Single rooms are available for an additional $600.

Program Details • Program offered once per year. Session length: 15 days. Departures are scheduled in August. Program is targeted to amateur and professional photographers. Most participants are 35–85 years of age. Other requirements: good physical condition. 8–16 participants per session. Application deadline: 60 days prior to departure. Reservations are recommended at least 3 months before departure.

Costs • $4000 (includes housing, all meals, excursions, international airfare). A $500 deposit is required.

Contact • Dennis Cox, Director, Photo Explorer Tours, 22111 Cleveland, #211, Dearborn, MI 48124; 800-315-4462; Fax: 313-561-1842; E-mail: decoxphoto@aol.com; World Wide Web: http://www.apogeephoto.com/photo_explorer.html

VIETNAM

BOLDER ADVENTURES, ASIA TRANSPACIFIC JOURNEYS

VIETNAM DISCOVERY

General Information • Cultural tour with visits to Dien Bien Phu, Hanoi, Hue, My Son, Saigon. Once at the destination country, participants travel by train, bus, foot, boat, airplane.

Learning Focus • Instruction in hill tribe customs. Escorted travel to Vietnam. Other activities include hiking. Instruction is offered by professors, researchers, naturalists.

Accommodations • Homestays, hotels. Single rooms are available for an additional $325.

Program Details • Program offered 4 times per year. Session length: 17 days. Departures are scheduled in February-June. Program is targeted to active people. Most participants are 35-65 years of age. Participants must be 18 years or older to enroll. 10-12 participants per session. Reservations are recommended at least 4 months before departure.

Costs • $2695 (includes housing, all meals, excursions, internal airfare). A $500 deposit is required.

Contact • Bolder Adventures, Asia Transpacific Journeys, 3055 Center Green Drive, Boulder, CO 80301; 800-642-2742; Fax: 303-443-7078; World Wide Web: http://www.southeastasia.com/

 GEORGE MASON UNIVERSITY

CONTEMPORARY VIETNAM

General Information • Academic study program in Hanoi, Ho Chi Minh City, Hue.

Learning Focus • Courses in history, trade, economics, ecology. Instruction is offered by professors from the sponsoring institution.

Accommodations • Dormitories. Meals are taken as a group, in central dining facility.

Program Details • Program offered once per year. Session length: 4 weeks. Departures are scheduled in May. The program is open to undergraduate students, graduate students, adults. Most participants are 18-65 years of age. Other requirements: minimum 2.25 GPA. 10-15 participants per session. Application deadline: April 12.

Costs • $4660 for George Mason University students, $5210 for other students (includes tuition, housing, all meals, insurance, excursions, international airfare). Application fee: $35. A $500 deposit is required.

Contact • Dr. Yehuda Lukacs, Director, Center for Global Education, George Mason University, 4400 University Drive, 235 Johnson Center, Fairfax, VA 22030; 703-993-2155; Fax: 703-993-2153; E-mail: ylukacs@gmu.edu; World Wide Web: http://www.gmu.edu/departments/oie

GLOBAL EXCHANGE REALITY TOURS

VIETNAM

General Information • Cultural tour with visits to Da Nang, Hanoi, Hue, Lang Co, Mekong Delta, Saigon. Once at the destination country, participants travel by bus, boat, airplane.

Learning Focus • Instruction in current issues in politics and the economy. Escorted travel to historical sites and development projects. Instruction is offered by researchers, naturalists. This program would appeal to people interested in history, agriculture, culture.

Accommodations • Hotels, guest houses. Single rooms are available for an additional $200-$500.

Program Details • Program offered 3 times per year. Session length: 17 days. Departures are scheduled in January, November. Program is targeted to seniors, students and professionals. Participants must be 18 years or older to enroll. 10 participants per session. Application deadline: 1 month prior to departure. Reservations are recommended at least 2 months before departure.

Costs • $3100 (includes housing, some meals, books and class materials, international airfare). A $200 deposit is required.

Contact • Reality Tours Coordinator, Global Exchange Reality Tours, 2017 Mission Street, Room 303, San Francisco, CA 94110; 415-255-7296; Fax: 415-255-7498; E-mail: globalexch@igc.apc.org

 JAMES MADISON UNIVERSITY

SUMMER STUDY IN VIETNAM

General Information • Academic study program in Hanoi. Excursions to Hue, Nha Trang, Saigon, Da Nang, Da Lat, rural area excursions.

Learning Focus • Courses in business, management. Instruction is offered by professors from the sponsoring institution.

Accommodations • Hotels. Meals are taken as a group, in local restaurants.

Program Details • Program offered once per year. Session length: 2½-3 weeks. Departures are scheduled in May, June. The program is open to undergraduate students. Most participants are 18-22 years of age. Other requirements: minimum 2.8 GPA. 10-20 participants per session. Application deadline: February 1.

Costs • $3400 (includes tuition, housing, some meals, excursions, international airfare). A $400 deposit is required.

Contact • Dr. Roger Ford, Professor, Management, James Madison University, Office of International Education, Harrisonburg, VA 22807; 540-568-3228; Fax: 540-568-3275; E-mail: fordrh@jmu.edu; World Wide Web: http://www.jmu.edu/intl-ed/

JOURNEYS INTERNATIONAL, INC.

VIETNAM EXPLORER

General Information • Cultural tour with visits to China Beach, Da Lat, Ha Long Bay, Hanoi, Hoi An, Saigon. Once at the destination country, participants travel by foot, boat.
Learning Focus • Escorted travel to small villages and cities of Vietnam. Other activities include boat ride. Instruction is offered by English-speaking guides. This program would appeal to people interested in culture, history, nature studies.
Accommodations • Hotels. Single rooms are available for an additional $250.
Program Details • Program offered 36 times per year. Session length: 22 days. Departures are scheduled in September–May. Program is targeted to persons interested in culture. Most participants are 25–55 years of age. Participants must be 12 years or older to enroll. 6–15 participants per session. Application deadline: 60 days prior to departure. Reservations are recommended at least 60 days before departure.
Costs • $1925 (includes housing, some meals, excursions, boat rides). A $300 deposit is required.
Contact • Pat Ballard, Asia Sales Director, Journeys International, Inc., 4011 Jackson Road, Ann Arbor, MI 48103; 313-665-4407; Fax: 313-665-2945; E-mail: pat@journeys-intl.com; World Wide Web: http://www.journeys-intl.com

RUSSIAN AND EAST EUROPEAN PARTNERSHIPS

VIETNAMESE LANGUAGE AND CULTURAL IMMERSION PROGRAM

General Information • Language study program in Ho Chi Minh City. Classes are held on the campus of Vietnamese Language School for Foreigners. Excursions to Cu Chi Tunnels.
Learning Focus • Courses in Vietnamese language, Vietnamese culture and art, Vietnamese history. Instruction is offered by local teachers.
Accommodations • Dormitories. Single rooms are available. Meals are taken on one's own, in central dining facility, in local restaurants.
Program Details • Program offered 11 times per year. Session length: 4 or more weeks. Departures are scheduled in January–November. The program is open to undergraduate students, graduate students, adults. Most participants are 18 years of age and older. Other requirements: good health and 18 or older unless chaperoned by an adult. 6 participants per session. Application deadline: 45 days prior to departure.
Costs • $4550 (includes tuition, housing, some meals, books and class materials, excursions, international airfare, local transportation, airport transfers). A $1500 deposit is required.
Contact • Kenneth Fortune, President, Russian and East European Partnerships, PO Box 227, Fineview, NY 13640; 888-873-7337; Fax: 800-910-1777; E-mail: reep@fox.nstn.ca

STATE UNIVERSITY OF NEW YORK AT BUFFALO

SUMMER IN VIETNAM: LANGUAGE AND CULTURE PROGRAM

General Information • Language study program in Hanoi. Classes are held on the campus of Dong Do University. Excursions to Ho Chi Minh City, northern Vietnamese villages.
Learning Focus • Courses in cultural studies, economics, arts, history, political science, language study. Instruction is offered by professors from the sponsoring institution and local teachers.
Accommodations • Homestays, guest houses, hotels. Single rooms are available. Meals are taken as a group, in central dining facility, in local restaurants.
Program Details • Program offered once per year. Session length: 6 weeks. Departures are scheduled in June. The program is open to undergraduate students, graduate students, adults. Most participants are 18–58 years of age. Other requirements: minimum 2.67 GPA and a minimum age of 18. 8 participants per session. Application deadline: April 15.
Costs • $1982 (includes housing, some meals, excursions, fees). A $125 deposit is required.
Contact • Sandra J. Reinagel, Interim Study Abroad Coordinator, State University of New York at Buffalo, 210 Talbert Hall, Box 601604, Buffalo, NY 14260-1604; 716-645-3912; Fax: 716-645-6197; E-mail: studyabroad@acsu.buffalo.edu; World Wide Web: http://wings.buffalo.edu/academic/provost/intl/studyabroad

EASTERN EUROPE

REGIONAL

Belarus
Bulgaria
Croatia
Czech Republic
Estonia
Hungary
Moldova
Poland
Ukraine

REGIONAL

 ACTR/ACCELS

ACCELS 1997 CZECH AND SLOVAK SUMMER LANGUAGE PROGRAMS

General Information • Language study program in Czech Republic (Brno, Olomouc, Prague), Slovakia (Bratislava). Classes are held on the campus of Charles University, Masaryk University, Palacky University, Comenius University in Bratislava. Excursions to Bohemia, Moravia, Slovakia.
Learning Focus • Courses in language study, literature, linguistics, contemporary society. Instruction is offered by local teachers.
Accommodations • Dormitories. Single rooms are available. Meals are taken as a group, in central dining facility.
Program Details • Program offered once per year. Session length: 4-5 weeks. Departures are scheduled in July. The program is open to undergraduate students, graduate students, adults, young faculty members at US institutions. Most participants are 20-30 years of age. Other requirements: at least 1 semester to 1 year of prior Czech or Slovak language study. 4-10 participants per session. Application deadline: March 1.
Costs • $2200 (includes tuition, housing, all meals, books and class materials, insurance, excursions, international airfare). Application fee: $35. A $100 deposit is required.
Contact • Michael Kuban, Senior Program Officer, ACTR/ACCELS, 1776 Massachusetts Avenue, NW, Suite 700, Washington, DC 20036; 202-833-7522; Fax: 202-833-7523; E-mail: general@actr.org

AMERICAN JEWISH CONGRESS, INTERNATIONAL TRAVEL PROGRAM

EASTERN EUROPE DISCOVERY

General Information • Cultural tour with visits to Czech Republic (Prague), Hungary (Budapest), Lithuania (Vilna), Poland (Cracow, Warsaw); excursions to Oscar Schindler's factory, Majdanek, Auschwitz, and Birkenan death camps, Wawel Castle, Holocaust Monument, Charles Bridge, Heroes Square, Raoul Wallenberg Memorial. Once at the destination country, participants travel by train, bus, foot, airplane.
Learning Focus • Escorted travel to synagogues, Gediminas Square and Strahov Monastery Library. Museum visits (Jewish Historical Institute, Museum of Jewish History). Attendance at performances (Laterna Magika Theater). Instruction is offered by historians. This program would appeal to people interested in Jewish history.
Accommodations • Hotels. Single rooms are available for an additional $700.
Program Details • Program offered 3 times per year. Session length: 18 days. Departures are scheduled in July-September. Program is targeted to Jewish-American adults. Most participants are 40-75 years of age. Participants must be 15 years or older to enroll. Participants must be members of the sponsoring organization (annual dues: $50). 30 participants per session. Reservations are recommended at least 6 months before departure.
Costs • $4495-$4825 (includes housing, some meals, excursions, international airfare, travel bag, documents portfolio, travel journal). A $200 deposit is required.
Contact • Betty Van Dyke, Worldwide Operations Manager, American Jewish Congress, International Travel Program, 18 East 84th Street, New York, NY 10028; 212-360-1571; Fax: 212-717-1932

AMERICAN JEWISH CONGRESS, INTERNATIONAL TRAVEL PROGRAM

THE SPLENDORS OF CENTRAL EUROPE

General Information • Cultural tour with visits to Austria (Vienna), Czech Republic (Prague), Hungary (Budapest), Slovakia (Bratislava); excursions to Old Town Square, Theresienstadt, Heroes Square, Bratislava Castle, Innerestadt. Once at the destination country, participants travel by bus, foot, airplane.
Learning Focus • Escorted travel to synagogues and Palace Eskels. Museum visits (Jewish State Museum, National Museum). Attendance at performances (Laterna Magika Theater). Instruction is offered by historians. This program would appeal to people interested in Jewish history.
Accommodations • Hotels. Single rooms are available for an additional $650.
Program Details • Program offered 5 times per year. Session length: 12 days. Departures are scheduled in May-September. Program is targeted to Jewish-American adults. Most participants are 40-75 years of age. Participants must be 15 years or older to enroll. Participants must be members of the sponsoring organization (annual dues: $50). 30 participants per session. Reservations are recommended at least 6 months before departure.
Costs • $3095 (includes housing, some meals, excursions, international airfare, travel bag, documents portfolio, travel journal). A $200 deposit is required.
Contact • Betty Van Dyke, Worldwide Operations Manager, American Jewish Congress, International Travel Program, 18 East 84th Street, New York, NY 10028; 212-360-1571; Fax: 212-717-1932

APPALACHIAN STATE UNIVERSITY

CENTRAL EUROPE

General Information • Academic study program in Hungary, Poland, Slovakia.
Learning Focus • Courses in health, leisure, and exercise science, political science. Instruction is offered by professors from the sponsoring institution.
Program Details • Program offered once per year. Session length: 3 weeks. Departures are scheduled in June. Most participants are 18 years of age and older. 20 participants per session.
Costs • $2938 (includes tuition, housing, insurance, international airfare, International Student Identification card).
Contact • Dr. Paul Gaskill, Professor, Appalachian State University, Department of Health, Leisure, and Exercise Science, Boone, NC 28608; 704-262-3140; Fax: 704-262-4037

CRAFT WORLD TOURS

ROMANIA AND HUNGARY

General Information • Cultural tour with visits to Hungary (Budapest, Debrecen, Kecskemét), Romania (Brasov, Bucharest, Cimpulung, Sibiu, Sighet Marmatiei). Once at the destination country, participants travel by bus.
Learning Focus • Escorted travel to Transylvania, Horezu pottery workshops and the Black Church. Museum visits (Village and Folk Art Museum, Outdoor Folk Museum, Bran Castle). Instruction is offered by artists. This program would appeal to people interested in handicrafts, folk arts, village life.
Accommodations • Hotels. Single rooms are available for an additional $495.
Program Details • Program offered once per year. Session length: 23 days. Departures are scheduled in August. Most participants are 30–80 years of age. Other requirements: appreciation of handcrafts and folk arts. 18 participants per session. Application deadline: June. Reservations are recommended at least 6 months before departure.
Costs • $3996 (includes housing, some meals, excursions, international airfare). A $250 deposit is required.
Contact • Tom Wilson, President, Craft World Tours, 6776 Warboys Road, Byron, NY 14422; 716-548-2667; Fax: 716-548-2821

INTERHOSTEL, UNIVERSITY OF NEW HAMPSHIRE

CZECH REPUBLIC AND SLOVAKIA

General Information • Cultural tour with visits to Czech Republic (High Tatra Mountains, Novemesto, Prague), Slovakia (Bratislava); excursions to Dobrosov, Olomouc, Spis, Levoca, Banska Bystrica. Once at the destination country, participants travel by bus, foot. Program is affiliated with Akademie J. A. Komenskeho.
Learning Focus • Instruction in history and culture. Escorted travel to a village and landmarks. Museum visits (National Gallery, Glass Museum). Attendance at performances (opera or ballet, Slovak folk music). Instruction is offered by historians. This program would appeal to people interested in history, culture.
Accommodations • Hotels. Single rooms are available for an additional $325.
Program Details • Program offered once per year. Session length: 2 weeks. Departures are scheduled in September. Program is targeted to seniors over 50. Most participants are 60–80 years of age. Participants must be 50 years or older to enroll. 30 participants per session. Reservations are recommended at least 3 months before departure.
Costs • $2625 (includes tuition, housing, all meals, excursions, international airfare). A $200 deposit is required.
Contact • Janice Pierson, Office Supervisor, Interhostel, University of New Hampshire, 6 Garrison Avenue, Durham, NH 03824-3529; 800-733-9753; Fax: 603-862-1113; World Wide Web: http://www.learn.unh.edu/

JAMES MADISON UNIVERSITY

SUMMER STUDY IN MOLDOVA AND ROMANIA

General Information • Academic study program in Romania (Bucharest). Classes are held on the campus of Romanian American University. Excursions to Dniester Republic.
Learning Focus • Courses in former Soviet Union. Instruction is offered by professors from the sponsoring institution.
Accommodations • Homestays, hotels. Meals are taken as a group, with host family, in central dining facility.
Program Details • Program offered once per year. Session length: 15 days. Departures are scheduled in May. The program is open to undergraduate students. Most participants are 18–22 years of age. Other requirements: minimum 2.8 GPA. Application deadline: February 1.
Costs • $1650 for Virginia residents, $2084 for non-residents (includes tuition, housing, all meals, excursions, international airfare). A $400 deposit is required.
Contact • Dr. Stephen Bowers, Professor, Department of Political Science, James Madison University, Office of International Education, Harrisonburg, VA 22807; 540-568-3605; Fax: 540-568-6920; E-mail: bowerssr@jmu.edu; World Wide Web: http://www.jmu.edu/intl-ed/

MICHIGAN STATE UNIVERSITY

INTERNATIONAL RELATIONS–EASTERN EUROPE

General Information • Academic study program in Czech Republic (Prague), Hungary (Budapest).
Learning Focus • Courses in international policy, political systems in developing countries, economics. Instruction is offered by professors from the sponsoring institution.
Accommodations • Dormitories. Meals are taken on one's own, in central dining facility, in local restaurants.
Program Details • Program offered once per year. Session length: 4 weeks. Departures are scheduled in June. The program is open to undergraduate students. Most participants are 18–22 years of age. Other requirements: good academic standing and the approval of the director. 12 participants per session. Application deadline: March 14.
Costs • $900 (includes housing, some meals, excursions). Application fee: $75. A $250 deposit is required.
Contact • Brenda S. Sprite, Educational Programs Coordinator, Michigan State University, Office of Study Abroad, 109 International Center, East Lansing, MI 48824; 517-353-8920; Fax: 517-432-2082; E-mail: sprite@pilot.msu.edu; World Wide Web: http://study-abroad.msu.edu

SANTA BARBARA MUSEUM OF ART

BUDAPEST, PRAGUE, AND THE BOHEMIAN COUNTRYSIDE

General Information • Cultural tour with visits to Czech Republic (Prague), Hungary (Budapest); excursions to Bohemian Countryside, Vienna (optional). Once at the destination country, participants travel by bus, airplane.
Learning Focus • Instruction in art and history. Escorted travel to castles and landmarks. Museum visits (Budapest, Prague). Attendance at performances (opera, concerts).

Instruction is offered by art historians. This program would appeal to people interested in art, photography, music, architecture.
Accommodations • Hotels. Single rooms are available for an additional $690.
Program Details • Program offered once per year. Session length: 10 days. Departures are scheduled in October. Most participants are 30–80 years of age. Participants must be members of the sponsoring organization (annual dues: $40). 15–20 participants per session.
Costs • $4790 including air from West Coast; $3880, land only (includes housing, some meals, excursions, international airfare). A $500 deposit is required.
Contact • Shelley Ruston, Director of Special Programs, Santa Barbara Museum of Art, 1130 State Street, Santa Barbara, CA 93101; 805-963-4364, ext. 336; Fax: 805-966-6840

SMITHSONIAN INSTITUTION

SMITHSONIAN STUDY TOURS AND SEMINARS IN EASTERN EUROPE

General Information • Garden, nature study, cultural, cooking and wilderness programs with visits to Hungary, Poland, Russia. Once at the destination country, participants travel by train, bus, foot, boat, airplane.
Learning Focus • Instruction in art history, Western civilization, Italian cuisine, and other subjects. Escorted travel to special sites off limits to most tourists. Museum visits (major museums, small galleries, and private collections). Attendance at performances (opera, symphony, theater, dance, traditional folk and private recitals). Nature observation (birding, horticulture). Other activities include hiking. Instruction is offered by professors, researchers, naturalists, artists, historians, scientists. This program would appeal to people interested in archaeology, religious history, photography, natural history, trains.
Accommodations • Hotels, campsites. Single rooms are available.
Program Details • Session length: 9–17 days. Departures are scheduled throughout the year. Most participants are 25–85 years of age. Participants must be 18 years or older to enroll. Participants must be members of the sponsoring organization (annual dues: $24). 15–30 participants per session.
Costs • $1999 and up (includes tuition, housing, some meals, excursions, international airfare).
Contact • Customer Service Representative, Smithsonian Institution, Smithsonian Study Tours and Seminars, 1100 Jefferson Drive SW (MRC 702), Washington, DC 20560; 202-357-4700; Fax: 202-633-9250

BELARUS

ACTR/ACCELS

CIS REGIONAL LANGUAGE TRAINING PROGRAM–BELARUS

General Information • Language study program in Belarus. Excursions to museums, churches, sites of historical interest.
Learning Focus • Courses in history, literature, cultural studies, Russian language, language study.
Accommodations • Homestays, dormitories. Single rooms are available. Meals are taken on one's own, with host family, in residences.
Program Details • Program offered once per year. Session length: 7 weeks. Departures are scheduled in June. The program is open to undergraduate students, graduate students, adults. Most participants are 19–28 years of age. Other requirements: intermediate-level Russian or target language. 1–3 participant per session. Application deadline: March 1.
Costs • $3400 (includes tuition, housing, some meals, books and class materials, insurance, excursions, visa processing fee, mandatory orientation in Washington, DC). Application fee: $35. A $500 deposit is required.
Contact • Margaret Stephenson, Program Officer, ACTR/ACCELS, 1776 Massachusetts Avenue, NW, Suite 700, Washington, DC 20036; 202-833-7522; Fax: 202-833-7523; E-mail: stephens@actr.org

RUSSIAN AND EAST EUROPEAN PARTNERSHIPS

BELARUS LANGUAGE AND CULTURAL IMMERSION PROGRAM

General Information • Language study program in Minsk. Classes are held on the campus of Economic Information. Excursions to Russia (Moscow, St. Petersburg).
Learning Focus • Courses in Russian language, Belarussian language, Russian history, Belarussian culture and art. Instruction is offered by professors from the sponsoring institution and local teachers.
Accommodations • Homestays. Single rooms are available. Meals are taken on one's own, with host family, in local restaurants, in residences.
Program Details • Program offered 11 times per year. Session length: 4 or more weeks. Departures are scheduled in January–November. The program is open to undergraduate students, graduate students, adults. Most participants are 18 years of age and older. Other requirements: in good health and 18 or older unless chaperoned by an adult. 6 participants per session. Application deadline: 45 days prior to departure.
Costs • $2995 (includes tuition, housing, some meals, books and class materials, excursions, international airfare, local transportation, airport transfers). A $1500 deposit is required.
Contact • Kenneth Fortune, President, Russian and East European Partnerships, PO Box 227, Fineview, NY 13640; 888-USE-REEP; Fax: 800-910-1777; E-mail: reep@fox.nstn.ca

BULGARIA

AMERICAN UNIVERSITY IN BULGARIA

INSTITUTE FOR SOUTHEASTERN EUROPEAN COOPERATION AND DEVELOPMENT

General Information • Academic study program in Blagoevgrad. Classes are held on the campus of American University in Bulgaria. Excursions to Sofia, Plovdiv, Rila and Pirin Mountains.

Learning Focus • Courses in political science, economics, Balkan issues. Instruction is offered by professors from the sponsoring institution.

Accommodations • Dormitories. Single rooms are available. Meals are taken in central dining facility.

Program Details • Program offered once per year. Session length: 4 weeks. Departures are scheduled in July. The program is open to undergraduate students, graduate students. Most participants are 20–28 years of age. 70 participants per session.

Costs • $1150 (includes tuition, housing, all meals, books and class materials, excursions, ground transportation). A $250 deposit is required.

Contact • Irena Dryankova-Bond, Administrative Assistant, American University in Bulgaria, Blagoevgrad 2700, Bulgaria; +359 73-23-652; Fax: +359 73-25-218; E-mail: irena@nws.aubg.bg

AMERICAN UNIVERSITY IN BULGARIA

SUMMER ARCHAEOLOGICAL FIELD SCHOOL

General Information • Academic study program in Blagoevgrad. Classes are held on the campus of American University in Bulgaria. Excursions to Greece (Thessalonik), Macedonia (Skopje).

Learning Focus • Courses in archaeology, field techniques. Instruction is offered by professors from the sponsoring institution.

Accommodations • Dormitories. Single rooms are available. Meals are taken in central dining facility.

Program Details • Program offered once per year. Session length: 8 weeks. Departures are scheduled in June. The program is open to undergraduate students, graduate students, adults. Most participants are 20–35 years of age. Other requirements: good health. 30–50 participants per session. Application deadline: April 2.

Costs • $2312 (includes tuition, housing, all meals, excursions, ground transportation). A $350 deposit is required.

Contact • Mark Stefanovich, Associate Professor, Anthropology and Archaeology, American University in Bulgaria, Blagoevgrad 2700, Bulgaria; +359 73-23-927; Fax: +359 73-23-927; E-mail: mark@nws.aubg.bg

AMERICAN UNIVERSITY IN BULGARIA

SUMMER PROGRAM

General Information • Academic study program in Blagoevgrad. Classes are held on the campus of American University in Bulgaria. Excursions to Greece, Turkey, Republic of Macedonia, Albania.

Learning Focus • Courses in business administration, international relations, computer science, language study, mathematics, philosophy, sociology, political science, journalism, economics, history, anthropology. Instruction is offered by professors from the sponsoring institution.

Accommodations • Dormitories. Meals are taken on one's own, in central dining facility, in residences.

Program Details • Program offered 3 times per year. Session length: 2–6 weeks. The program is open to undergraduate students. Most participants are 18–22 years of age. Other requirements: minimum 2.75 GPA. 20–70 participants per session. Application deadline: April 1.

Costs • $750 per 3 credits (includes tuition, housing, all meals, insurance). A $200 deposit is required.

Contact • Lydia Grim, Director of Student Services, American University in Bulgaria, Blagoevgrad 2700, Bulgaria; +359 73-23-652; Fax: +359 73-25-168; E-mail: lydia@sa.aubg.bg

---

The fall of communist governments in southeastern Europe was widely hailed as the dawn of a new era of prosperity and integration into the world community. However, the following years have seen economic contractions, halting reforms, and heightened tensions and violence from resurgent national, ethnic, and religious interests. This program brings together students and faculty members from within and outside of the region to examine the causes of the current situation and explore approaches for constructive resolutions and cooperation. Students will examine the process of individual and community identity formation and its implications for regional conflict and cooperation.

COLLEGE CONSORTIUM FOR INTERNATIONAL STUDIES–TRUMAN STATE UNIVERSITY

SUMMER STUDY ABROAD PROGRAM IN BULGARIA

General Information • Academic study program in Veliko Tarnovo. Classes are held on the campus of Veliko Tarnovo University. Excursions to Black Sea Coast.

Learning Focus • Courses in Bulgarian language, ethnography, fine arts, history, music. Instruction is offered by local teachers.

Accommodations • Dormitories. Meals are taken as a group, in central dining facility.

Program Details • Program offered once per year. Session length: 4 weeks. Departures are scheduled in August. The program is open to undergraduate students, adults. Most participants are 19–30 years of age. Other requirements: minimum 2.5 GPA. 6 participants per session.

Costs • $780 (includes tuition, housing, all meals, books and class materials, excursions).

Contact • Jane C. Evans, Executive Director, College Consortium for International Studies, 2000 P Street, NW, Suite 503, Washington, DC 20036; 800-453-6956; Fax: 202-223-0999; E-mail: ccis@intr.net

RUSSIAN AND EAST EUROPEAN PARTNERSHIPS

BULGARIAN LANGUAGE AND CULTURAL IMMERSION PROGRAM

General Information • Language study program in Sofia. Classes are held on the campus of Bulgarian Language School. Excursions to Varna.

Learning Focus • Courses in Bulgarian language, Bulgarian culture and art, Bulgarian history. Instruction is offered by professors from the sponsoring institution and local teachers.

Accommodations • Homestays. Single rooms are available. Meals are taken on one's own, with host family, in local restaurants, in residences.

Program Details • Program offered 11 times per year. Session length: 4 or more weeks. Departures are scheduled in January–November. The program is open to undergraduate students, graduate students, adults. Most participants are 18 years of age and older. Other requirements: in good health and 18 or older unless chaperoned by an adult. 6 participants per session. Application deadline: 45 days prior to departure.

Costs • $4650 (includes tuition, housing, some meals, books and class materials, excursions, international airfare, local transportation, airport transfers). A $1500 deposit is required.

Contact • Kenneth Fortune, President, Russian and East European Partnerships, PO Box 227, Fineview, NY 13640; 888-USE-REEP; Fax: 800-910-1777; E-mail: reep@fox.nstn.ca

CROATIA

RUSSIAN AND EAST EUROPEAN PARTNERSHIPS

SERBIAN AND CROATIAN LANGUAGE AND CULTURAL IMMERSION PROGRAM

General Information • Language study program in Zagreb. Classes are held on the campus of University of Zagreb. Excursions to Slovenia (Bled, Ljuljana).

Learning Focus • Courses in Serbian and Croatian language, Serbian and Croatian culture and art, Southern Slavic history. Instruction is offered by local teachers.

Accommodations • Homestays. Single rooms are available. Meals are taken on one's own, with host family, in local restaurants, in residences.

Program Details • Program offered 11 times per year. Session length: 4 or more weeks. Departures are scheduled in January–November. The program is open to undergraduate students, graduate students, adults. Most participants are 18 years of age and older. Other requirements: in good health and 18 or older unless chaperoned by an adult. 6 participants per session. Application deadline: 45 days prior to departure.

Costs • $3895 (includes tuition, housing, some meals, books and class materials, excursions, international airfare, local transportation, airport transfers). A $1500 deposit is required.

Contact • Kenneth Fortune, President, Russian and East European Partnerships, PO Box 227, Fineview, NY 13640; 888-USE-REEP; Fax: 800-910-1777; E-mail: reep@fox.nstn.ca

CZECH REPUBLIC

AMERICAN INSTITUTE FOR FOREIGN STUDY (AIFS)

PRAGUE UNIVERSITY OF ECONOMICS SUMMER PROGRAM

General Information • Academic and language study program in Prague. Classes are held on the campus of University of Economics. Excursions to Germany (Berlin).
Learning Focus • Courses in business, economics, political science, Czech language.
Accommodations • Dormitories.
Program Details • Program offered once per year. Session length: 5 weeks. Departures are scheduled in June. The program is open to undergraduate students, graduate students, adults, high school graduates. Other requirements: minimum 2.0 GPA. Application deadline: March 15.
Costs • $2699 (includes tuition, housing, all meals). A $400 deposit is required.
Contact • Carmela Vigliano, Director, Summer Programs, American Institute for Foreign Study (AIFS), 102 Greenwich Avenue, Greenwich, CT 06830; 800-727-2437, ext. 6087; Fax: 203-869-9615; E-mail: info@aifs.org

CROSS-CULTURE

PRAGUE: ITS CASTLES AND COUNTRYSIDE

General Information • Cultural tour with visits to Prague. Once at the destination country, participants travel by bus, foot, boat.
Learning Focus • Escorted travel to Royal Palace, St. Vitus Cathedral and Tyl Theater. Attendance at performances (concerts). Instruction is offered by highly educated guides. This program would appeal to people interested in culture, history, nature studies, arts, traditions, food and wine.
Accommodations • Hotels. Single rooms are available for an additional $220.
Program Details • Program offered 2 times per year. Session length: 9 days. Departures are scheduled in July, August. Program is targeted to adults of all ages. Most participants are 40–70 years of age. Participants must be 12 years or older to enroll. Other requirements: good health, accompaniment of an adult if under 18. 20–25 participants per session. Application deadline: 1 month prior to departure. Reservations are recommended at least 3–12 months before departure.
Costs • $2240 (includes tuition, housing, all meals, books and class materials, excursions, international airfare). A $300 deposit is required.
Contact • Cross-Culture, 52 High Point Drive, Amherst, MA 01002-1224; 413-256-6303; Fax: 413-253-2303; E-mail: xculture@javanet.com; World Wide Web: http://www.empiremall.com/cross-culture

FOREIGN LANGUAGE STUDY ABROAD SERVICE

INTERNATIONAL LANGUAGE STUDY HOMESTAYS IN THE CZECH REPUBLIC

General Information • Language study program in Czech Republic.
Learning Focus • Courses in Czech language. Instruction is offered by local teachers.
Accommodations • Homestays. Single rooms are available. Meals are taken with host family, in residences.
Program Details • Session length: varies. Departures are scheduled in January–December. The program is open to undergraduate students, graduate students, pre-college students, adults. Most participants are 12 years of age and older. Other requirements: students must be at least 12 years old. 1 participant per session.
Costs • Contact sponsor for information. A $300 deposit is required.
Contact • Louise Harber, Coordinator, Foreign Language Study Abroad Service, Department IH, Box 903, 5935 Southwest 64th Avenue, South Miami, FL 33143; 800-282-1090; Fax: 305-662-2907; E-mail: flsas@netpoint.net; World Wide Web: http://www.netpoint.net/~flsas

INTERHOSTEL, UNIVERSITY OF NEW HAMPSHIRE

CZECH REPUBLIC

General Information • Cultural tour with visits to Moravia, Prague, Chateau Konopiste, Chateau Veltrusy, Terezin, Podebrady, Litomysl, Brno, Telc, Buchlov Castle, Velehrad. Once at the destination country, participants travel by bus, foot. Program is affiliated with Akademie J. A. Komenskeho.
Learning Focus • Instruction in history and culture. Escorted travel to castles, villages and landmarks. Museum visits (Dvorak Museum, Museum of Moravian Folklore). Attendance at performances (opera or ballet). Instruction is offered by professors, historians, city guides. This program would appeal to people interested in history, culture.
Accommodations • Hotels. Single rooms are available for an additional $310.
Program Details • Program offered once per year. Session length: 14 days. Departures are scheduled in June. Program is targeted to seniors over 50. Most participants are 60–80 years of age. Participants must be 50 years or older to enroll. 35 participants per session. Reservations are recommended at least 6 months before departure.
Costs • $2675 (includes tuition, housing, all meals, excursions, international airfare, entrance fees). A $200 deposit is required.
Contact • Janice Pierson, Office Supervisor, Interhostel, University of New Hampshire, 6 Garrison Avenue, Durham,

Study in the Czech Republic

Prague is at the heart of democratic and cultural revolutions taking place in Europe. Prague's University of Economics Central and East European Studies Program offers courses in English—comparative government, managerial systems and environmental economics. Czech language is optional. You live in a residence hall room with private bath and kitchenette and use the meal allowance for cafés, cafeterias or cooking. A three-day field trip in the Czech Republic visits spa towns, castles and other historic sites. An optional weekend trip goes to Berlin. The AIFS Resident Director plans on-going cultural activities.

American Institute For Foreign Study®
Dept. PLA 102 Greenwich Avenue
Greenwich, CT 06830
Phone (800) 727-2437
E-mail info@aifs.org
http://www.aifs.org

NH 03824; 800-733-9753; Fax: 603-862-1113; World Wide Web: http://www.learn.unh.edu/

LEXIA EXCHANGE INTERNATIONAL

LEXIA IN PRAGUE

General Information • Academic study program in Prague. Classes are held on the campus of Charles University, Prague College of Studies in Art and Architecture. Excursions to Southern Bohemia, Brataslava, Austria (Vienna), Poland (Cracow), Hungary (Budapest), Germany (Berlin).
Learning Focus • Courses in civilizations, political science, fine arts, theater, business, economics, Czech language, literature, cultural studies. Instruction is offered by local teachers.
Accommodations • Homestays, dormitories. Single rooms are available. Meals are taken on one's own, with host family, in central dining facility, in local restaurants.
Program Details • Program offered once per year. Session length: 8 weeks. Departures are scheduled in June. The program is open to undergraduate students, graduate students, adults. Most participants are 18–35 years of age. Other requirements: minimum 2.5 GPA. 5–7 participants per session. Application deadline: April 15.
Costs • $3495 (includes tuition, housing, some meals, books and class materials, excursions). Application fee: $30. A $300 deposit is required.
Contact • Justin Meilgaard, Program Coordinator, LEXIA Exchange International, 378 Cambridge Avenue, Palo Alto, CA 94306-1544; 800-775-3942; Fax: 415-327-9192; E-mail: lexia@rquartz.stanford.edu; World Wide Web: http://www.lexiaintl.org

LOS ANGELES COMMUNITY COLLEGE DISTRICT

SUMMER SESSION IN PRAGUE

General Information • Academic study program in Prague.
Learning Focus • Courses in creative writing, music. Instruction is offered by professors from the sponsoring institution.
Accommodations • Dormitories. Single rooms are available. Meals are taken as a group, in local restaurants.
Program Details • Program offered once per year. Session length: 3–6 weeks. Departures are scheduled in July. The program is open to undergraduate students, pre-college students, adults. Most participants are 17–65 years of age. 25 participants per session. Application deadline: May 1.
Costs • $1674 for 3 weeks (includes tuition, housing, some meals, insurance, excursions, international airfare). A $400 deposit is required.
Contact • International Education Program, Los Angeles Community College District, 770 Wilshire Boulevard, Los Angeles, CA 90017; 213-891-2282; Fax: 213-891-2150; E-mail: intered@laccd.cc.ca.us; World Wide Web: http://laccd.cc.ca.us

NEW YORK UNIVERSITY

NEW YORK UNIVERSITY IN PRAGUE

General Information • Academic study program in Prague. Classes are held on the campus of Charles University. Excursions to Southern Bohemia, Slovakia.
Learning Focus • Courses in Czech language, European literature, European cinema, art history, European politics. Instruction is offered by professors from the sponsoring institution and local teachers.
Accommodations • Dormitories. Single rooms are available. Meals are taken on one's own, in local restaurants.
Program Details • Program offered once per year. Session length: 4½ weeks. The program is open to undergraduate students, graduate students, pre-college students, adults, non-US students. Most participants are 16–25 years of age. Other requirements: minimum 2.75 GPA. 30 participants per session. Application deadline: May 15.
Costs • $3020 (includes tuition, housing, some meals, excursions). Application fee: $20.
Contact • Jenny M. Gibbs, Director, New York University, Arts and Science Summer Programs, 6 Washington Square North, Room 41, New York, NY 10003; 212-998-8175; Fax: 212-995-4177; E-mail: abroad@nyu.edu; World Wide Web: http://www.nyu.edu/studyabroad

NORTH CAROLINA STATE UNIVERSITY

DESIGN PROGRAM IN PRAGUE, CZECH REPUBLIC

General Information • Academic study program in Prague. Classes are held on the campus of Academy of Fine Arts.
Learning Focus • Courses in architecture, drawing, graphic arts, painting, urban studies, art, fashion, architecture, printmaking, Czech language. Instruction is offered by local teachers.
Accommodations • Dormitories. Meals are taken on one's own, in local restaurants.
Program Details • Program offered once per year. Session length: 6½ weeks. Departures are scheduled in June. The program is open to undergraduate students, graduate students. Most participants are 18–50 years of age. 12–15 participants per session. Application deadline: March 15.
Costs • $2700 (includes tuition, housing, excursions, cultural events). Application fee: $25. A $600 deposit is required.
Contact • Ingrid Schmidt, Study Abroad Director, North Carolina State University, 2118 Pullen Hall, Box 7344, Raleigh, NC 27695-7344; 919-515-2087; Fax: 919-515-6021; E-mail: study_abroad@ncsu.edu; World Wide Web: http://www2.ncsu.edu/ncsu/chass/intstu/abroad.html

RAMAPO COLLEGE OF NEW JERSEY

WINTER SESSION IN PRAGUE, CZECH REPUBLIC

General Information • Academic study program in Prague. Classes are held on the campus of Czech Technical University. Excursions to Hradcany, St. Vitus Cathedral, Mala Strana, Stare Mesto, Nove Mesto, Vysehard, Prazkynrad, Strahov Monastery, Karlov Most, Kutra Hora, Cesky Krumlov.

Learning Focus • Courses in Eastern European politics, Eastern European business. Instruction is offered by professors from the sponsoring institution.
Accommodations • Hotels. Meals are taken as a group, in central dining facility.
Program Details • Program offered once per year. Session length: 3 weeks. Departures are scheduled in January. The program is open to undergraduate students, graduate students, pre-college students, adults. Most participants are 18 years of age and older. 20 participants per session. Application deadline: November 1.
Costs • $1575 (includes tuition, housing, some meals, excursions, international airfare). A $300 deposit is required.
Contact • Mrs. Robyn Perricelli, Coordinator, Study Abroad, Ramapo College of New Jersey, 505 Ramapo Valley Road, Mahwah, NJ 07430; 201-529-7463; Fax: 201-529-7508; E-mail: rperrice@ramapo.edu

RUSSIAN AND EAST EUROPEAN PARTNERSHIPS

CZECH LANGUAGE AND CULTURAL IMMERSION PROGRAM

General Information • Language study program in Pilsen. Classes are held on the campus of LuWell Cultural Center. Excursions to Prague.
Learning Focus • Courses in Czech language, Czech culture and art, Czech history. Instruction is offered by professors from the sponsoring institution and local teachers.
Accommodations • Homestays. Single rooms are available. Meals are taken on one's own, with host family, in local restaurants, in residences.
Program Details • Program offered 11 times per year. Session length: 4 or more weeks. Departures are scheduled in January–November. The program is open to undergraduate students, graduate students, adults. Most participants are 18 years of age and older. Other requirements: in good health and 18 or older unless chaperoned by an adult. 6 participants per session. Application deadline: 45 days prior to departure.
Costs • $3595 (includes tuition, housing, some meals, books and class materials, excursions, international airfare, local transportation, airport transfers). A $1500 deposit is required.
Contact • Kenneth Fortune, President, Russian and East European Partnerships, PO Box 227, Fineview, NY 13640; 888-USE-REEP; Fax: 800-910-1777; E-mail: reep@fox.nstn.ca

UNIVERSITY OF MIAMI

SUMMER FILM PROGRAM IN PRAGUE

General Information • Academic study program in Prague. Excursions to St George's Convent, Vysehrad castle, South Moravia, Wenceslas Square, Barrandov Film Studio, Terezin Concentration Camp.
Learning Focus • Courses in film studies. Instruction is offered by professors from the sponsoring institution.
Accommodations • Dormitories. Meals are taken as a group, in central dining facility, in local restaurants.
Program Details • Program offered once per year. Session length: 4 weeks. Departures are scheduled in July. The program is open to undergraduate students, graduate students. Most participants are 18–25 years of age. Other requirements: minimum 3.0 GPA and some film studies background. 15 participants per session. Application deadline: April 1.
Costs • $3500 (includes tuition, housing, books and class materials). Application fee: $30. A $500 deposit is required.
Contact • Peggy Ting, Study Abroad Program, University of Miami, PO Box 248005, Coral Gables, FL 33124-1610; 305-557-5421; Fax: 305-284-6629; E-mail: ieep@cstudies.msmail.miami.edu; World Wide Web: http://www.miami.edu/cstudies/ieep.html

UNIVERSITY OF NEW ORLEANS

PRAGUE WRITERS WORKSHOP

General Information • Academic study program in Prague. Classes are held on the campus of Charles University.
Learning Focus • Courses in writing, literature, fiction. Instruction is offered by professors from the sponsoring institution and local teachers.
Accommodations • Dormitories. Single rooms are available. Meals are taken as a group, in central dining facility.
Program Details • Program offered once per year. Session length: 4 weeks. Departures are scheduled in July. The program is open to undergraduate students, graduate students, adults, the general public. Most participants are 19–79 years of age. 100 participants per session. Application deadline: April 1.
Costs • $1750 (includes tuition, some meals, books and class materials, insurance). A $100 deposit is required.
Contact • Trevor Top, Coordinator, University of New Orleans, PO Box 1171, New Orleans, LA 70148; 504-280-6143; Fax: 504-280-7317; World Wide Web: http://www.uno.edu/~inst/Welcome.html

UNIVERSITY OF PENNSYLVANIA

PENN-IN-PRAGUE

General Information • Academic study program in Prague. Classes are held on the campus of Charles University. Excursions to Hungary (Budapest), Austria (Vienna).
Learning Focus • Courses in Czech language, political science, folklore, Jewish studies, European civilization. Instruction is offered by professors from the sponsoring institution and local teachers.
Accommodations • Dormitories. Single rooms are available. Meals are taken on one's own, in local restaurants.
Program Details • Program offered once per year. Session length: 5½ weeks. Departures are scheduled in July. The program is open to undergraduate students, graduate students. Most participants are 19–35 years of age. 12 participants per session. Application deadline: March 15.
Costs • $3384 (includes tuition, housing, excursions). Application fee: $35. A $300 deposit is required.
Contact • Elizabeth Sachs, Director, Penn Summer Abroad, University of Pennsylvania, 3440 Market Street, Suite 100, Philadelphia, PA 19104-3335; 215-898-5738; Fax: 215-573-2053; E-mail: esachs@mail.sas.upenn.edu

ESTONIA

RUSSIAN AND EAST EUROPEAN PARTNERSHIPS

ESTONIAN LANGUAGE AND CULTURAL IMMERSION PROGRAM

General Information • Language study program in Tallinn. Classes are held on the campus of Economic Information. Excursions to Russia (St. Petersburg).

Learning Focus • Courses in Russian language, Estonian language, Estonian art, Russian history, Estonian culture. Instruction is offered by professors from the sponsoring institution and local teachers.

Accommodations • Homestays. Single rooms are available. Meals are taken on one's own, with host family, in local restaurants, in residences.

Program Details • Program offered 11 times per year. Session length: 4 or more weeks. Departures are scheduled in January–November. The program is open to undergraduate students, graduate students, adults. Most participants are 18 years of age and older. Other requirements: in good health and 18 or older unless accompanied by a chaperone. 6 participants per session. Application deadline: 45 days prior to departure.

Costs • $2995 (includes tuition, housing, some meals, books and class materials, excursions, international airfare, local transportation, airport transfers). A $1500 deposit is required.

Contact • Kenneth Fortune, President, Russian and East European Partnerships, PO Box 227, Fineview, NY 13640; 888-873-7337; Fax: 800-910-1777; E-mail: reep@fox.nstn.ca

HUNGARY

 ACTR/ACCELS

ACCELS 1997 SUMMER HUNGARIAN LANGUAGE PROGRAM

General Information • Language study program in Budapest. Classes are held on the campus of Eötvös Lorand University Budapest.
Learning Focus • Courses in language study, literature, linguistics, contemporary society. Instruction is offered by local teachers.
Accommodations • Dormitories. Single rooms are available. Meals are taken as a group, in central dining facility.
Program Details • Program offered once per year. Session length: 4–5 weeks. Departures are scheduled in July. The program is open to undergraduate students, graduate students, adults, young faculty members at US institutions. Most participants are 22–35 years of age. Other requirements: at least 1 semester to 1 year of prior Hungarian language study. 3–4 participants per session. Application deadline: March 1.
Costs • $2200 (includes tuition, housing, all meals, insurance, excursions, international airfare). Application fee: $35. A $100 deposit is required.
Contact • Michael Kuban, Senior Program Officer, ACTR/ACCELS, 1776 Massachusetts Avenue, NW, Suite 700, Washington, DC 20036; 202-833-7522; Fax: 202-833-7523; E-mail: general@actr.org

CROSS-CULTURE

HUNGARIAN HOLIDAY

General Information • Cultural tour with visits to Budapest. Once at the destination country, participants travel by bus, foot.
Learning Focus • Instruction in Hungarian history. Escorted travel to Matthias Church, Castle Hill and the Danube Bend. Museum visits (Open-Air Ethnographical Museum, Museum of Primitive Painting). Attendance at performances (gypsy fiddlers, traditional folk dances). Instruction is offered by historians, scientists, highly educated guides. This program would appeal to people interested in culture, history, nature studies, arts, traditions, food and wine.
Accommodations • Hotels. Single rooms are available for an additional $185.
Program Details • Program offered 2 times per year. Session length: 9 days. Departures are scheduled in July, September. Program is targeted to adults of all ages. Most participants are 40–70 years of age. Participants must be 12 years or older to enroll. Other requirements: good health, accompaniment of an adult if under 18. 20–25 participants per session. Application deadline: 1 month prior to departure. Reservations are recommended at least 3–12 months before departure.
Costs • $2180 (includes tuition, housing, all meals, books and class materials, excursions, international airfare). A $300 deposit is required.
Contact • Cross-Culture, 52 High Point Drive, Amherst, MA 01002-1224; 413-256-6303; Fax: 413-253-2303; E-mail: xculture@javanet.com; World Wide Web: http://www.empiremall.com/cross-culture

FOREIGN LANGUAGE STUDY ABROAD SERVICE

INTERNATIONAL LANGUAGE STUDY HOMESTAYS IN HUNGARY

General Information • Language study program in Hungary.
Learning Focus • Courses in Hungarian language. Instruction is offered by local teachers.
Accommodations • Homestays. Single rooms are available. Meals are taken with host family, in residences.
Program Details • Session length: varies. Departures are scheduled in January–December. The program is open to undergraduate students, graduate students, pre-college students, adults. Most participants are 12 years of age and older. Other requirements: students must be at least 12 years old. 1 participant per session.
Costs • Contact sponsor for information. A $300 deposit is required.
Contact • Louise Harber, Coordinator, Foreign Language Study Abroad Service, Department IH, Box 903, 5935 Southwest 64th Avenue, South Miami, FL 33143; 800-282-1090; Fax: 305-662-2907; E-mail: flsas@netpoint.net; World Wide Web: http://www.netpoint.net/~flsas

 GEORGE MASON UNIVERSITY

BUDAPEST POLITICAL ECONOMY OF TRANSITION IN HUNGARY AND EAST CENTRAL EUROPE

General Information • Academic study program in Budapest. Classes are held on the campus of Budapest University of Economic Sciences. Excursions to Transylvania, Romania.
Learning Focus • Courses in economics, foreign trade. Instruction is offered by local teachers.
Accommodations • Dormitories, hotels. Single rooms are available. Meals are taken as a group.
Program Details • Program offered once per year. Session length: 4 weeks. Departures are scheduled in July, August. The program is open to undergraduate students, graduate students, adults. Most participants are 18–65 years of age. Other requirements: minimum 2.25 GPA. 10–15 participants per session. Application deadline: April 12.

Costs • $2740 for George Mason University students, $3290 for other students (includes tuition, housing, some meals, insurance, excursions). Application fee: $35. A $500 deposit is required.
Contact • Dr. Yehuda Lukacs, Director, Center for Global Education, George Mason University, 4400 University Drive, 235 Johnson Center, Fairfax, VA 22030; 703-993-2155; Fax: 703-993-2153; E-mail: ylukacs@gmu.edu; World Wide Web: http://www.gmu.edu/departments/oie

INTERHOSTEL, UNIVERSITY OF NEW HAMPSHIRE

BUDAPEST, HUNGARY

General Information • Cultural tour with visits to Budapest, Kecskemét, Rackeve, Szentendre, Gyor, Sopron, Koskeg, Visegrad, Esztergom, Kalocsa. Once at the destination country, participants travel by bus, foot. Program is affiliated with Hungarian Academy of Sciences.
Learning Focus • Instruction in history and culture. Escorted travel to cities. Museum visits (Royal Palace, Margit Kovacs). Attendance at performances (folk dance, opera or concert). Instruction is offered by professors. This program would appeal to people interested in history, culture.
Accommodations • Hotels. Single rooms are available for an additional $350.
Program Details • Program offered once per year. Session length: 2 weeks. Departures are scheduled in October. Program is targeted to seniors over 50. Most participants are 60–80 years of age. Participants must be 50 years or older to enroll. 35 participants per session. Reservations are recommended at least 3 months before departure.
Costs • $2585 (includes tuition, housing, all meals, excursions, international airfare, entrance fees). A $200 deposit is required.
Contact • Janice Pierson, Office Supervisor, Interhostel, University of New Hampshire, 6 Garrison Avenue, Durham, NH 03824-3529; 800-733-9753; Fax: 603-862-1113; World Wide Web: http://www.learn.unh.edu/

 LANGUAGE LIAISON

LIVE 'N' LEARN (LEARN IN A TEACHER'S HOME)–HUNGARY

General Information • Language study program with visits to Hungary.
Learning Focus • Instruction in the Hungarian language. Instruction is offered by professors. This program would appeal to people interested in language.
Accommodations • Homestays. Single rooms are available.
Program Details • Session length: unlimited. Departures are scheduled throughout the year. Most participants are 18–70 years of age. Participants must be 16 years or older to enroll. Reservations are recommended at least 35 days before departure.
Costs • Contact sponsor for information.
Contact • Nancy Forman, President, Language Liaison, 20533 Biscayne Boulevard-Station 4-162, Miami, FL 33180; 305-682-9909; Fax: 305-682-9907; E-mail: langstudy@aol.com; World Wide Web: http://languageliaison.com

 LEXIA EXCHANGE INTERNATIONAL

LEXIA IN BUDAPEST

General Information • Academic study program in Budapest. Classes are held on the campus of Eötvös Collegium, Pázmány University. Excursions to Transylvania, Slovakia, Britaslava, Poland (Cracow), Austria (Vienna).
Learning Focus • Courses in civilizations, Hungarian language, fine arts, political science, business, theater, economics, literature, cultural studies. Instruction is offered by local teachers.
Accommodations • Homestays, dormitories. Single rooms are available. Meals are taken on one's own, with host family, in central dining facility, in local restaurants.
Program Details • Program offered once per year. Session length: 8 weeks. Departures are scheduled in June. The program is open to undergraduate students, graduate students, adults. Most participants are 18–35 years of age. Other requirements: minimum 2.5 GPA. 5–7 participants per session. Application deadline: April 15.
Costs • $3495 (includes tuition, housing, books and class materials). Application fee: $30. A $300 deposit is required.
Contact • Justin Meilgaard, Program Coordinator, LEXIA Exchange International, 378 Cambridge Avenue, Palo Alto, CA 94306-1544; 800-775-3942; Fax: 415-327-9192; E-mail: lexia@rquartz.stanford.edu; World Wide Web: http://www.lexiaintl.org

RUSSIAN AND EAST EUROPEAN PARTNERSHIPS

HUNGARIAN LANGUAGE AND CULTURAL IMMERSION PROGRAM

General Information • Language study program in Debrecen. Classes are held on the campus of University of Debrecen. Excursions to Lake Balaton, Budapest.
Learning Focus • Courses in Hungarian language, Hungarian history, Hungarian culture, Hungarian art. Instruction is offered by professors from the sponsoring institution and local teachers.
Accommodations • Homestays. Single rooms are available. Meals are taken on one's own, with host family, in local restaurants, in residences.
Program Details • Program offered 11 times per year. Session length: 4 or more weeks. Departures are scheduled in January–November. The program is open to undergraduate students, graduate students, adults. Most participants are 18 years of age and older. Other requirements: in good health, 18 or older unless chaperoned by an adult. 6 participants per session. Application deadline: 45 days prior to departure.
Costs • $3895 (includes tuition, housing, some meals, books and class materials, excursions, international airfare, local transportation, airport transfers). A $1500 deposit is required.
Contact • Kenneth Fortune, President, Russian and East European Partnerships, PO Box 227, Fineview, NY 13640; 888-873-7337; Fax: 800-910-1777; E-mail: reep@fox.nstn.ca

MOLDOVA

ACTR/ACCELS

CIS REGIONAL LANGUAGE TRAINING PROGRAM–REPUBLIC OF MOLDOVA

General Information • Language study program in Moldova. Excursions to museums, churches, sites of historical interest.

Learning Focus • Courses in language study, Russian language, history, literature, cultural studies.

Accommodations • Homestays, dormitories. Single rooms are available. Meals are taken on one's own, with host family, in residences.

Program Details • Program offered once per year. Session length: 7 weeks. Departures are scheduled in June. The program is open to undergraduate students, graduate students, adults. Most participants are 19–28 years of age. Other requirements: intermediate-level Russian or target language. 1–3 participant per session. Application deadline: March 1.

Costs • $3400 (includes tuition, housing, some meals, books and class materials, insurance, excursions, visa processing fee, mandatory orientation in Washington, DC). Application fee: $35. A $500 deposit is required.

Contact • Margaret Stephenson, Program Officer, ACTR/ACCELS, 1776 Massachusetts Avenue, NW, Suite 700, Washington, DC 20036; 202-833-7522; Fax: 202-833-7523; E-mail: stephens@actr.org

POLAND

APPALACHIAN STATE UNIVERSITY

POLAND

General Information • Academic study program in Poland.
Learning Focus • Courses in communications. Instruction is offered by professors from the sponsoring institution.
Program Details • Program offered once per year. Session length: 4–5 weeks. Departures are scheduled in May. Most participants are 18 years of age and older. 20 participants per session.
Costs • $3015 (includes tuition, housing, insurance, international airfare, International Student Identification card).
Contact • Dr. Frank Aycock, Professor, Appalachian State University, Department of Communications, Boone, NC 28608; 704-262-2221; Fax: 704-262-4037

FOREIGN LANGUAGE STUDY ABROAD SERVICE

INTERNATIONAL LANGUAGE STUDY HOMESTAYS IN POLAND

General Information • Language study program in Poland.
Learning Focus • Courses in Polish language. Instruction is offered by local teachers.
Accommodations • Homestays. Single rooms are available. Meals are taken with host family, in residences.
Program Details • Session length: varies. Departures are scheduled in January–December. The program is open to undergraduate students, graduate students, pre-college students, adults. Most participants are 12 years of age and older. Other requirements: students must be at least 12 years old. 1 participant per session.
Costs • Contact sponsor for information. A $300 deposit is required.
Contact • Louise Harber, Coordinator, Foreign Language Study Abroad Service, Department IH, Box 903, 5935 Southwest 64th Avenue, South Miami, FL 33143; 800-282-1090; Fax: 305-662-2907; E-mail: flsas@netpoint.net; World Wide Web: http://www.netpoint.net/~flsas

INTERHOSTEL, UNIVERSITY OF NEW HAMPSHIRE

POLAND

General Information • Cultural tour with visits to Cracow, Lublin, Warsaw, Kozlowka, Zamosc, Wieliczka Salt Mine, Zakopane, Czestochowa, Zelazowa, Warka, Auschwitz, Wola. Once at the destination country, participants travel by bus, foot, cable car. Program is affiliated with Catholic University of Lublin.
Learning Focus • Instruction in history and culture. Escorted travel to cities. Museum visits (Skansen Museum, National Museum). Attendance at performances (theater, piano recital). Other activities include visiting local people. Instruction is offered by professors, city guides. This program would appeal to people interested in history, culture.
Accommodations • Hotels. Single rooms are available for an additional $300.
Program Details • Program offered once per year. Session length: 2 weeks. Departures are scheduled in July. Program is targeted to seniors over 50. Most participants are 60–80 years of age. Participants must be 50 years or older to enroll. 35 participants per session. Reservations are recommended at least 6 months before departure.
Costs • $2675 (includes tuition, housing, all meals, excursions, international airfare, entrance fees). A $200 deposit is required.
Contact • Janice Pierson, Office Supervisor, Interhostel, University of New Hampshire, 6 Garrison Avenue, Durham, NH 03824; 800-733-9753; Fax: 603-862-1113; World Wide Web: http://www.learn.unh.edu/

LEXIA EXCHANGE INTERNATIONAL

LEXIA IN CRACOW

General Information • Academic study program in Cracow. Classes are held on the campus of Jagiellonian University Cracow. Excursions to Warsaw, Gdansk, Czech Republic (Prague), Hungary (Budapest), Tafra Mountains.
Learning Focus • Courses in civilizations, history, business, economics, political science, fine arts, Polish language, literature, cultural studies. Instruction is offered by local teachers.
Accommodations • Homestays, dormitories. Single rooms are available. Meals are taken on one's own, with host family, in central dining facility, in local restaurants.
Program Details • Program offered once per year. Session length: 8 weeks. Departures are scheduled in June. The program is open to undergraduate students, graduate students, adults. Most participants are 18–35 years of age. Other requirements: minimum 2.5 GPA. 5 participants per session. Application deadline: April 15.
Costs • $3495 (includes tuition, housing, books and class materials, excursions). Application fee: $30. A $300 deposit is required.
Contact • Justin Meilgaard, Program Coordinator, LEXIA Exchange International, 378 Cambridge Avenue, Palo Alto, CA 94306-1544; 800-775-3942; Fax: 415-327-9192; E-mail: lexia@rquarts.stanford.edu; World Wide Web: http://www.lexiaintl.org

RUSSIAN AND EAST EUROPEAN PARTNERSHIPS

POLISH LANGUAGE AND CULTURAL IMMERSION PROGRAM

General Information • Language study program in Cracow. Classes are held on the campus of University of Warsaw. Excursions to Cracow, Czestochowa.
Learning Focus • Courses in Polish language, Polish culture and art, Polish history. Instruction is offered by local teachers.
Accommodations • Homestays. Single rooms are available. Meals are taken on one's own, with host family, in local restaurants, in residences.
Program Details • Program offered 11 times per year. Session length: 4 or more weeks. Departures are scheduled in January–November. The program is open to undergraduate students, graduate students, adults. Most participants are 18 years of age and older. Other requirements: in good health and 18 or older unless chaperoned by an adult. 6 participants per session. Application deadline: 45 days prior to departure.
Costs • $3895 (includes tuition, housing, some meals, books and class materials, excursions, international airfare, local transportation, airport transfers). A $1500 deposit is required.
Contact • Kenneth Fortune, President, Russian and East European Partnerships, PO Box 227, Fineview, NY 13640; 888-873-7337; Fax: 800-910-1777; E-mail: reep@fox.nstn.ca

STATE UNIVERSITY OF NEW YORK AT BUFFALO

SUMMER PROGRAM OF POLISH LANGUAGE AND CULTURE

General Information • Language study program in Cracow. Classes are held on the campus of Jagiellonian University Cracow. Excursions to Warsaw, Tatra Mountains, Auschwitz-Birkenau, Zakopane, Peniny Mountains, Wieliczka.
Learning Focus • Courses in Polish history, Polish culture, Polish literature, art history, Polish language. Instruction is offered by professors from the sponsoring institution and local teachers.
Accommodations • Dormitories. Single rooms are available. Meals are taken as a group, on one's own, in central dining facility.
Program Details • Program offered once per year. Session length: 4-6 weeks. Departures are scheduled in July. The program is open to undergraduate students, graduate students, pre-college students, adults. Most participants are 18–75 years of age. Other requirements: minimum 2.67 GPA. 30 participants per session. Application deadline: June 1.
Costs • $700 for 4 weeks, $950 for 6 weeks (includes housing, all meals, some excursions). A $125 deposit is required.
Contact • Sandra J. Reinagel, Interim Study Abroad Coordinator, State University of New York at Buffalo, 210 Talbert Hall, Box 601604, Buffalo, NY 14260-1604; 716-645-3912; E-mail: studyabroad@acsu.buffalo.edu; World Wide Web: http://wings.buffalo.edu/academic/provost/intl/studyabroad

UNIVERSITY OF KANSAS

SUMMER LANGUAGE INSTITUTE IN CRACOW, POLAND

General Information • Language study program in Cracow. Classes are held on the campus of Jagiellonian University Cracow.
Learning Focus • Courses in Polish language, Polish civilization and culture. Instruction is offered by local teachers.
Accommodations • Dormitories. Meals are taken as a group, on one's own, in central dining facility.
Program Details • Program offered once per year. Session length: 8 weeks. Departures are scheduled in June. The program is open to undergraduate students, graduate students, adults. Most participants are 20–30 years of age. 10 participants per session. Application deadline: March 1.
Costs • $1600 (includes tuition, housing, all meals, books and class materials, excursions). Application fee: $15. A $300 deposit is required.
Contact • Susan MacNally, Coordinator of Summer Institutes, University of Kansas, Office of Study Abroad, 203 Lippincott Hall, Lawrence, KS 66045; 913-864-3742; Fax: 913-864-5040; E-mail: osa@falcon.cc.ukans.edu; World Wide Web: http://kuhub.cc.ukans.edu/~intlstdy/osa/osamain.html

UNIVERSITY OF PENNSYLVANIA

PENN-IN-WARSAW

General Information • Academic study program in Warsaw. Classes are held on the campus of Warsaw School of Economics.
Learning Focus • Courses in economics, political science. Instruction is offered by local teachers.
Accommodations • Dormitories. Single rooms are available. Meals are taken on one's own.
Program Details • Program offered once per year. Session length: 5½ weeks. Departures are scheduled in June. The program is open to undergraduate students, graduate students, adults. Most participants are 19–30 years of age. 7 participants per session. Application deadline: March 1.
Costs • $3034 (includes tuition, housing). Application fee: $35. A $300 deposit is required.
Contact • Elizabeth Sachs, Director, Penn Summer Abroad, University of Pennsylvania, 3440 Market Street, Suite 100, Philadelphia, PA 19104-3335; 215-898-5738; Fax: 215-573-2053; E-mail: esachs@mail.sas.upenn.edu

UNIVERSITY OF WISCONSIN–MILWAUKEE

SUMMER SCHOOL OF POLISH LANGUAGE AND CULTURE

General Information • Language study program in Lublin. Classes are held on the campus of Catholic University of Lublin. Excursions to Warsaw, Kazimierz, Cracow.
Learning Focus • Courses in Polish language. Instruction is offered by local teachers.
Accommodations • Dormitories. Single rooms are available. Meals are taken as a group, in central dining facility.
Program Details • Program offered once per year. Session length: 2–5 weeks. Departures are scheduled in July. The program is open to undergraduate students, graduate

students, adults. Most participants are 18–70 years of age. 14 participants per session. Application deadline: April 30.
Costs • $2259 (includes tuition, housing, all meals, books and class materials, excursions, international airfare). A $100 deposit is required.

Contact • Michael J. Mikos, Professor, University of Wisconsin-Milwaukee, Department of Slavic Languages, Milwaukee, WI 53201; 414-229-4948; Fax: 414-229-6258; E-mail: mikos@csd.uwm.edu; World Wide Web: http://www.uwm.edu/Dept/Slavic

UKRAINE

ACTR/ACCELS

CIS REGIONAL LANGUAGE TRAINING PROGRAM–UKRAINE

General Information • Language study program in Ukraine. Excursions to museums, churches, sites of historical interest.
Learning Focus • Courses in language study, Russian language, history, literature, cultural studies.
Accommodations • Homestays, dormitories. Single rooms are available. Meals are taken on one's own, with host family, in residences.
Program Details • Program offered once per year. Session length: 7 weeks. Departures are scheduled in June. The program is open to undergraduate students, graduate students, adults. Most participants are 19–28 years of age. Other requirements: intermediate-level Russian or target language. 1–3 participant per session. Application deadline: March 1.
Costs • $3400 (includes tuition, housing, some meals, books and class materials, insurance, excursions, visa processing fee, mandatory orientation in Washington, DC). Application fee: $35. A $500 deposit is required.
Contact • Margaret Stephenson, Program Officer, ACTR/ACCELS, 1776 Massachusetts Avenue, NW, Suite 700, Washington, DC 20036; 202-833-7522; Fax: 202-833-7523; E-mail: stephens@actr.org

RUSSIAN AND EAST EUROPEAN PARTNERSHIPS

UKRAINIAN LANGUAGE AND CULTURAL IMMERSION PROGRAM

General Information • Language study program in Kiev. Classes are held on the campus of Economic Information.
Learning Focus • Courses in Ukrainian language, Ukrainian culture and art, Ukrainian history. Instruction is offered by professors from the sponsoring institution and local teachers.
Accommodations • Homestays, locally-rented apartments. Single rooms are available. Meals are taken on one's own, with host family, in local restaurants, in residences.
Program Details • Program offered 11 times per year. Session length: 4 or more weeks. Departures are scheduled in January–November. The program is open to undergraduate students, graduate students, adults. Most participants are 18 years of age and older. Other requirements: good health and 18 or older unless chaperoned by an adult. 6 participants per session. Application deadline: 45 days prior to departure.
Costs • $2995 (includes tuition, housing, some meals, books and class materials, excursions, international airfare, local transportation, airport transfers). A $1500 deposit is required.
Contact • Kenneth Fortune, President, Russian and East European Partnerships, PO Box 227, Fineview, NY 13640; 888-873-7337; Fax: 800-910-1777; E-mail: reep@fox.nstn.ca

STATE UNIVERSITY OF NEW YORK COLLEGE AT BROCKPORT

KIEV, UKRAINE CULTURAL STUDY PROGRAM

General Information • Academic study program in Kiev. Classes are held on the campus of University of Kyiv-Mohyla Academy.
Learning Focus • Courses in Ukrainian culture, history, political science, geography, economics, arts and heritage, language study. Instruction is offered by professors from the sponsoring institution.
Accommodations • Dormitories. Single rooms are available. Meals are taken as a group, in central dining facility, in local restaurants.
Program Details • Program offered once per year. Session length: 3 weeks. Departures are scheduled in July. The program is open to undergraduate students, people seeking continuing education credit. Most participants are 19 years of age and older. Other requirements: minimum 2.5 GPA. 4–10 participants per session. Application deadline: May 1.
Costs • $2500 (includes tuition, housing, some meals, excursions, international airfare). A $100 deposit is required.
Contact • Dr. John J. Perry, Director, International Education, State University of New York College at Brockport, 350 New Campus Drive, Brockport, NY 14420; 716-395-2119; Fax: 716-637-3218; World Wide Web: http://www.brockport.edu/study_abroad

UNIVERSITY OF KANSAS

UKRAINIAN LANGUAGE AND AREA STUDIES

General Information • Language study program in L'Viv. Classes are held on the campus of University of L'viv. Excursions to Kiev, Carpathians.
Learning Focus • Courses in Ukrainian language and culture. Instruction is offered by local teachers.
Accommodations • Homestays. Meals are taken with host family, in residences.
Program Details • Program offered once per year. Session length: 6 weeks. Departures are scheduled in June. The program is open to graduate students. Most participants are 22–32 years of age. Other requirements: BA degree and 3 years Russian language or intermediate Ukrainian. 15 participants per session. Application deadline: March 1.
Costs • $1850 (includes tuition, housing, all meals, excursions). Application fee: $15. A $300 deposit is required.
Contact • Susan MacNally, Coordinator of Summer Institutes, University of Kansas, Office of Study Abroad, 203 Lippincott Hall, Lawrence, KS 66045; 913-864-3742; Fax: 913-864-5040; E-mail: osa@falcon.cc.ukans.edu; World Wide Web: http://kuhub.cc.ukans.edu/~intlstdy/osa/osamain.html

MIDDLE EAST

REGIONAL

Cyprus
Egypt
Israel
Jordan
United Arab Emirates
Yemen

REGIONAL

ARCHAEOLOGICAL TOURS

ISRAEL AND JORDAN

General Information • Cultural tour with visits to Israel (Haifa, Jerusalem, Sodom, Tiberias, Tel Aviv), Jordan (Amman, Petra); excursions to Massada, Arad, Bertguvem, Golan Heights, Jericho, Megiddo, Hazor, Tel Dan, La Khish, Ceasarea, Bert Shian, Jerash, Pella. Once at the destination country, participants travel by bus.
Learning Focus • Museum visits (Israel Jerusalem Museum, Amman, Tel Aviv, Haifa). Instruction is offered by professors, historians. This program would appeal to people interested in history, archaeology.
Accommodations • Hotels. Single rooms are available for an additional $950.
Program Details • Program offered once per year. Session length: 20 days. Departures are scheduled in October. Program is targeted to adults. Most participants are 30-80 years of age. 25 participants per session. Application deadline: 1 month prior to departure.
Costs • $3695 (includes housing, some meals, excursions). A $500 deposit is required.
Contact • Archaeological Tours, 271 Madison Avenue, Suite 904, New York, NY 10016; 212-986-3054; Fax: 212-370-1561

ARCHAEOLOGICAL TOURS

SYRIA AND JORDAN

General Information • Archaeological tour with visits to Jordan (Amman, Petra), Syria (Aleppo, Damascus, Der Ezzor, Latakia, Palmyra); excursions to Krak des Chevaliers, St. George's Monastery, Ugarit, Ebla, St. Simeon, Ain Dara, Resafa, Dura Europos, Mari, Basra, Jerash, Jordan (Petra), Madaba. Once at the destination country, participants travel by bus.
Learning Focus • Escorted travel to Mari and Petra. Museum visits (Damascus, Aleppo, Palmyra, Amman). Instruction is offered by professors, historians. This program would appeal to people interested in history, archaeology.
Accommodations • Hotels. Single rooms are available for an additional $660.
Program Details • Program offered 3 times per year. Session length: 17 days. Departures are scheduled in March, April, September. Program is targeted to adults. Most participants are 30-80 years of age. 28 participants per session. Application deadline: 1 month prior to departure.
Costs • $3520 (includes housing, some meals, excursions). A $500 deposit is required.
Contact • Archaeological Tours, 271 Madison Avenue, Suite 904, New York, NY 10016; 212-986-3054; Fax: 212-370-1561

CRAFT WORLD TOURS

ISRAEL AND JORDAN

General Information • Cultural tour with visits to Israel (Jerusalem, Nahsholim, Rakefet, Zfat), Jordan (Amman, Petra). Once at the destination country, participants travel by bus.
Learning Focus • Escorted travel to Dead Sea, Petra and Jerusalem. Museum visits (Folklore Museum). Instruction is offered by artists. This program would appeal to people interested in handicrafts, folk arts, village life.
Accommodations • Hotels. Single rooms are available for an additional $495.
Program Details • Program offered once per year. Session length: 18 days. Departures are scheduled in April. Most participants are 30-80 years of age. Other requirements: appreciation of handcrafts and folk arts. 18 participants per session. Application deadline: February 12. Reservations are recommended at least 6 months before departure.
Costs • $4779 (includes housing, some meals, excursions, international airfare). A $250 deposit is required.
Contact • Tom Wilson, President, Craft World Tours, 6776 Warboys Road, Byron, NY 14422; 716-548-2667; Fax: 716-548-2821

DIANE HOFF-ROME, AN ARTIST'S LIFE

ISRAEL AND PETRA ARTIST HOLIDAY

General Information • Arts program with visits to Israel (Dead Sea, Jerusalem), Jordan (Petra); excursions to Petra, Jerusalem, artist kibbutz, Gal, Dead Sea, desert, Ellat. Once at the destination country, participants travel by foot, mini-bus.
Learning Focus • Instruction in painting, drawing and composition. Attendance at performances (musical events). Nature observation (desert life). Volunteer work (working on a kibbutz). Other activities include hiking, visits with local artists. Instruction is offered by artists, historians. This program would appeal to people interested in painting, photography, history, folk arts, drawing, ancient sites, writing.
Accommodations • Homestays, hotels. Single rooms are available.
Program Details • Program offered once per year. Session length: 2 weeks. Departures are scheduled in October. Program is targeted to amateur artists and teachers. Most participants are 21-85 years of age. Participants must be 21 years or older to enroll. Other requirements: interest in visual arts. 8-16 participants per session. Application deadline: 60 days prior to departure. Reservations are recommended at least 90 days before departure.
Costs • Contact sponsor for information.
Contact • Irwin W. Rome, Co-Director, Diane Hoff-Rome, An Artist's Life, PO Box 567, Elmwood Road, Swampscott, MA 01907; 617-595-1173; Fax: 617-596-0707; E-mail: artistlf@pcix.com; World Wide Web: http://www2.pcix.com/~artistlf

FOLKWAYS INSTITUTE

MIDDLE EAST PROJECT

General Information • Cultural tour with visits to Egypt, Jordan. Once at the destination country, participants travel by train, bus.
Learning Focus • Escorted travel to historical sites. Museum visits (local museums). Instruction is offered by professors. This program would appeal to people interested in history, archaeology, culture.
Accommodations • Hotels. Single rooms are available.

Program Details • Program offered once per year. Session length: 24 days. Departures are scheduled in February. Program is targeted to seniors. Most participants are 55–80 years of age. Participants must be 55 years or older to enroll. 18 participants per session. Application deadline: October 1. Reservations are recommended at least 4 months before departure.
Costs • $4600 (includes housing, all meals, books and class materials, excursions, international airfare, instruction). A $50 deposit is required.
Contact • David Christopher, Director, Folkways Institute, 14600 Southeast Aldridge Road, Portland, OR 97236-6518; 503-658-6600; Fax: 503-658-8672

GEORGE MASON UNIVERSITY

JORDAN AND ISRAEL: THE ECONOMICS OF PEACE

General Information • Academic study program in Israel (Galilee, Golan Heights, Jerusalem), JordanAmman, Petra).
Learning Focus • Courses in business, history, government. Instruction is offered by professors from the sponsoring institution.
Accommodations • Hotels. Single rooms are available. Meals are taken as a group, on one's own.
Program Details • Program offered once per year. Session length: 2 ½ weeks. Departures are scheduled in December. The program is open to undergraduate students, graduate students, adults. Most participants are 18–65 years of age. Other requirements: minimum 2.25 GPA. 10–20 participants per session. Application deadline: October 11.
Costs • $2991 for George Mason University students, $3541 for other students (includes tuition, housing, some meals, insurance, excursions, international airfare). Application fee: $35. A $500 deposit is required.
Contact • Dr. Yehuda Lukacs, Director, Center for Global Education, George Mason University, 4400 University Drive, 235 Johnson Center, Fairfax, VA 22030; 703-993-2155; Fax: 703-993-2153; E-mail: ylukacs@gmu.edu; World Wide Web: http://www.gmu.edu/departments/oie

GOLDEN HORN TRAVEL & TOURS

SYRIA AND JORDAN TOUR

General Information • Cultural and archaeological tour with visits to Jordan (Jerash, Petra), Syria (Aleppo, Damascus, Latakia, Palmyra); excursions to Mari, Doura Europus, St. Simeon, Ugarit, Ebla, Apamaea, Krak des Chevaliers, Bosra. Once at the destination country, participants travel by bus.
Learning Focus • Escorted travel to Syrian and Jordanian archaeological sites. Museum visits (Damascus and Aleppo museums). Instruction is offered by professors, local guides. This program would appeal to people interested in archaeology, Middle East cultural studies.
Accommodations • Hotels. Single rooms are available for an additional $570.
Program Details • Program offered 6 times per year. Session length: 20 days. Departures are scheduled in March–May, September–November. Most participants are 35–75 years of age. Participants must be 16 years or older to enroll. 20 participants per session. Reservations are recommended at least 90 days before departure.
Costs • $4080 (includes housing, some meals, international airfare, admissions fees). A $250 deposit is required.
Contact • Roberta Austin, Owner and Manager, Golden Horn Travel & Tours, PO Box 207, Annapolis, MD 21404; 800-772-7009; Fax: 410-626-7696

SAGA HOLIDAYS (ROAD SCHOLAR PROGRAM)

ROAD SCHOLAR: GREEK HISTORY AND CIVILIZATION

General Information • Cultural tour with visits to Egypt (Cairo, Nile River), Israel (Jerusalem, Tel Aviv, Tiberias); excursions to Christian holy sites, Nile River. Once at the destination country, participants travel by bus. Program is affiliated with Israel Antiquities Authorities and the Egyptian Museum.
Learning Focus • Instruction in the history of civilization. Escorted travel to Nile River and Christian holy sites. Museum visits (Egyptian Museum). Instruction is offered by professors, historians. This program would appeal to people interested in history.
Accommodations • Hotels. Single rooms are available.
Program Details • Program offered 3 times per year. Session length: 16 days. Departures are scheduled in September, November, December. Program is targeted to seniors. Most participants are 50–75 years of age. Participants must be 50 years or older to enroll. Reservations are recommended at least 6 months before departure.
Costs • $3499 (includes tuition, housing, some meals, books and class materials, insurance, excursions, international airfare).
Contact • Saga Holidays (Road Scholar Program), 222 Berkeley Street, Boston, MA 02116; 800-621-2151

SANTA BARBARA MUSEUM OF ART

THE MAGNIFICENT NEAR EAST: SYRIA AND JORDAN

General Information • Cultural tour with visits to Jordan (Amman, Petra), Syria (Aleppo, Damascus, Palmyra). Once at the destination country, participants travel by bus, airplane.
Learning Focus • Instruction in art and archaeology. Field research in archaeology. Museum visits (Damascus and Amman). Instruction is offered by historians. This program would appeal to people interested in art, photography, architecture, archaeology, history.
Accommodations • Hotels. Single rooms are available.
Program Details • Program offered once per year. Session length: 13 days. Departures are scheduled in March. Most participants are 30–80 years of age. Participants must be members of the sponsoring organization (annual dues: $40). 15–20 participants per session. Application deadline: January.
Costs • $5000 (includes housing, some meals, excursions, international airfare). A $500 deposit is required.
Contact • Shelley Ruston, Director of Special Programs, Santa Barbara Museum of Art, 1130 State Street, Santa Barbara, CA 93101; 805-963-4364, ext. 336; Fax: 805-966-6840

SMITHSONIAN INSTITUTION

SMITHSONIAN STUDY TOURS AND SEMINARS IN THE MIDDLE EAST

General Information • Cultural tour with visits to Egypt, Israel, Jordan, Syria, Turkey. Once at the destination country, participants travel by bus, foot, boat, airplane.

Learning Focus • Instruction in religious history, ancient history. Escorted travel to special sites off limits to most tourists. Museum visits (major museums, important collections). Attendance at performances (traditional folk music and dance). Instruction is offered by professors, researchers, naturalists, artists, historians, scientists. This program would appeal to people interested in archaeology, religious history, photography.

Accommodations • Hotels. Single rooms are available.

Program Details • Session length: 9-17 days. Departures are scheduled throughout the year. Most participants are 25-85 years of age. Participants must be 18 years or older to enroll. Participants must be members of the sponsoring organization (annual dues: $24). 15-30 participants per session.

Costs • $1999 and up (includes tuition, housing, some meals, excursions, international airfare).

Contact • Customer Service Representative, Smithsonian Institution, Smithsonian Study Tours and Seminars, 1100 Jefferson Drive SW (MRC 702), Washington, DC 20560; 202-357-4700; Fax: 202-633-9250

CYPRUS

COLLEGE CONSORTIUM FOR INTERNATIONAL STUDIES–BROOKDALE COMMUNITY COLLEGE

CCIS SUMMER PROGRAM IN CYPRUS

General Information • Academic study program in Larnaca, Limassol, Nicosia. Classes are held on the campus of Intercollege. Excursions to Egypt, Europe, Israel, Africa.

Learning Focus • Courses in tourism, travel, international business, computer science, archaeology, marketing, hotel and restaurant management, liberal studies, business. Instruction is offered by local teachers.

Accommodations • Homestays, dormitories, program-owned apartments. Single rooms are available. Meals are taken on one's own, with host family, in local restaurants.

Program Details • Program offered once per year. Session length: 6–8 weeks. Departures are scheduled in June. The program is open to undergraduate students, graduate students. Other requirements: minimum 2.5 GPA. Application deadline: May 1.

Costs • $2000 for dorm stay, $2215 for homestay (includes tuition, housing, some meals, orientation). Application fee: $35.

Contact • Jane C. Evans, Executive Director, College Consortium for International Studies, 2000 P Street, NW, Suite 503, Washington, DC 20026; 800-453-6956; Fax: 202-223-0999; E-mail: ccis@intr.net

EGYPT

AMERICAN JEWISH CONGRESS, INTERNATIONAL TRAVEL PROGRAM

THE LAND OF EGYPT

General Information • Cultural tour with visits to Abu Simbel, Aswan, Cairo, Edfu, Esna, Luxor, Valley of the Kings, Temple of Isis, Colossi of Memnon, Temple of Horus, Aswan Dam, pyramids, Sphinx, Khan-al-Khalili Bazaar. Once at the destination country, participants travel by boat, airplane.

Learning Focus • Escorted travel to Nile River, Kon Orbo, synagogues and mosques. Museum visits (Egyptian Museum). Attendance at performances (Sound and Light Show). Instruction is offered by naturalists, historians. This program would appeal to people interested in Jewish history.

Accommodations • Hotels, boat. Single rooms are available for an additional $555.

Program Details • Program offered 18 times per year. Session length: 10 days. Departures are scheduled in January–July, October–December. Program is targeted to Jewish-American adults. Most participants are 40–75 years of age. Participants must be 15 years or older to enroll. Participants must be members of the sponsoring organization (annual dues: $50). 30 participants per session. Reservations are recommended at least 6 months before departure.

Costs • $3525–$3645 (includes housing, some meals, excursions, international airfare, business class tickets, travel bag, documents portfolio, travel journal). A $200 deposit is required.

Contact • Betty Van Dyke, Worldwide Operations Manager, American Jewish Congress, International Travel Program, 18 East 84th Street, New York, NY 10028; 212-360-1571; Fax: 212-717-1932

AMERICAN UNIVERSITY IN CAIRO

INTENSIVE ARABIC LANGUAGE PROGRAM

General Information • Language study program in Cairo. Classes are held on the campus of American University in Cairo. Excursions to city excursions, outside Cairo but within Egypt.

Learning Focus • Courses in Egyptian colloquial Arabic, Fusha language, Arabic language, Arabic of the media. Instruction is offered by professors from the sponsoring institution.

Accommodations • Dormitories, locally-rented apartments. Single rooms are available. Meals are taken on one's own, in local restaurants.

Program Details • Program offered once per year. Session length: 7½ weeks. Departures are scheduled in June. The program is open to undergraduate students, graduate students, adults. Most participants are 20–30 years of age. 60–65 participants per session. Application deadline: March 31.

Costs • $4496 (includes tuition, housing, all meals, books and class materials, insurance, required academic fees, personal expenses, visa, passport).

Contact • Mrs. Mari Davidson, Coordinator of Student Affairs, American University in Cairo, 866 United Nations Plaza, Suite 517, New York, NY 10017-1889; 212-421-6320; Fax: 212-688-5341

AMERICAN UNIVERSITY IN CAIRO

STUDY ABROAD PROGRAM

General Information • Academic study program in Cairo. Classes are held on the campus of American University in Cairo.

Learning Focus • Courses in anthropology, Egyptology, history, physics, chemistry, Arabic language, economics, political science, sociology. Instruction is offered by professors from the sponsoring institution.

Accommodations • Dormitories, locally-rented apartments. Single rooms are available. Meals are taken on one's own, in local restaurants.

Program Details • Program offered once per year. Session length: 6 weeks. Departures are scheduled in June. The program is open to undergraduate students. Most participants are 18–21 years of age. Other requirements: minimum 2.0 GPA. 1200 participants per session. Application deadline: March 31.

Costs • $4496 (includes tuition, housing, all meals, books and class materials, insurance, required academic fees, personal spending, visa, passport). Application fee: $35. A $100 deposit is required.

Contact • Mrs. Mari Davidson, Coordinator of Student Affairs, American University in Cairo, 866 United Nations Plaza, Suite 517, New York, NY 10017-1889; 212-421-6320; Fax: 212-688-5341

ARCHAEOLOGICAL TOURS

FROM SINAI TO NUBIA

General Information • Cultural tour with visits to Abu Simbel, Aswan, Cairo, Ismalia, Luxor, Sinai, St. Catherine's Monastery, Serabit el-Khadim, Lake Nasser, El Kab, Merdes. Once at the destination country, participants travel by bus, boat.

Learning Focus • Museum visits (Cairo, Luxor, St. Catherine's Monastery). Instruction is offered by professors, historians. This program would appeal to people interested in history, art, archaeology.

Accommodations • Hotels. Single rooms are available for an additional $550.

Program Details • Program offered once per year. Session length: 16 days. Departures are scheduled in October.

Program is targeted to adults. Most participants are 30–80 years of age. 22 participants per session. Application deadline: 1 month prior to departure.
Costs • $3685 (includes housing, some meals, excursions). A $500 deposit is required.
Contact • Archaeological Tours, 271 Madison Avenue, Suite 904, New York, NY 10016; 212-986-3054; Fax: 212-370-1561

ARCHAEOLOGICAL TOURS

SPLENDORS OF ANCIENT EGYPT

General Information • Cultural tour with visits to Abu Simbel, Aswan, Cairo, Ismalia, Luxor, Tanis, Fayyum Oasis, Abydos, Dendera, Esna, Edfu, Nile Cruise. Once at the destination country, participants travel by bus, boat.
Learning Focus • Museum visits (Cairo, Luxor, Aswan). Attendance at performances (Sound and Light Show in Luxor). Instruction is offered by professors, historians. This program would appeal to people interested in history, art, archaeology.
Accommodations • Hotels. Single rooms are available for an additional $680.
Program Details • Program offered 2 times per year. Session length: 20 days. Departures are scheduled in January, November. Program is targeted to adults. Most participants are 30–80 years of age. 28 participants per session. Application deadline: 1 month prior to departure.
Costs • $3770 (includes housing, some meals, excursions). A $500 deposit is required.
Contact • Archaeological Tours, 271 Madison Avenue, Suite 904, New York, NY 10016; 212-986-3054; Fax: 212-370-1561

JOURNEYS INTERNATIONAL, INC.

THE GREAT SIGHTS OF EGYPT

General Information • Cultural tour with visits to Aswan, Cairo, Edfu, Esna, Kom-Ombo, Luxor, Cairo. Once at the destination country, participants travel by boat, small vehicle.
Learning Focus • Escorted travel to temples in Egypt. Other activities include sailing down the Nile River. Instruction is offered by English-speaking Egyptologists. This program would appeal to people interested in history, culture, nature studies, photography.
Accommodations • Hotels, boat. Single rooms are available for an additional $350.
Program Details • Session length: 10 days. Departures are scheduled throughout the year. Most participants are 25–55 years of age. Participants must be 12 years or older to enroll. 2 participants per session. Application deadline: 60 days prior to departure. Reservations are recommended at least 60 days before departure.
Costs • $1550 (includes housing, some meals). A $300 deposit is required.
Contact • Michelle Gervais, Egypt Sales Director, Journeys International, Inc., 4011 Jackson Road, Ann Arbor, MI 48103; 313-665-4407; Fax: 313-665-2945; E-mail: michelle@journeys-intl.com; World Wide Web: http://www.journeys-intl.com

NORTHERN ILLINOIS UNIVERSITY

BUSINESS AND CULTURE IN EGYPT

General Information • Academic study program in Alexandria, Aswan, Cairo, Luxor.
Learning Focus • Courses in operations management, information systems. Instruction is offered by professors from the sponsoring institution.
Accommodations • Hotels. Single rooms are available. Meals are taken as a group, in local restaurants.
Program Details • Program offered once per year. Session length: 4 weeks. Departures are scheduled in December. The program is open to undergraduate students, graduate students. Most participants are 21–26 years of age. 14 participants per session. Application deadline: November 1.
Costs • $3930 (includes tuition, housing, some meals, books and class materials, insurance, excursions, international airfare). A $200 deposit is required.
Contact • Anne Seitzinger, Program Coordinator, Short-Term Study Abroad, Northern Illinois University, Study Abroad Office-WI 417, DeKalb, IL 60115; 815-752-0700; Fax: 815-753-0825; E-mail: aseitz@niu.edu; World Wide Web: http://www.niu.edu/depts/intl_prgms/intl.html

SANTA BARBARA MUSEUM OF ART

TREASURES OF CAIRO: A NILE CRUISE

General Information • Cultural tour with visits to Aswan, Cairo, Luxor, pyramids, temples, tombs. Once at the destination country, participants travel by bus, boat, airplane.
Learning Focus • Escorted travel to St. Catherine's Monastery, Abu Simbel and historical sites. Museum visits (Cairo Museum, Luxor Museum). Instruction is offered by art historians. This program would appeal to people interested in art, history, architecture, archaeology, photography.
Accommodations • Hotels. Single rooms are available.
Program Details • Program offered once per year. Session length: 12 days. Departures are scheduled in October. Most participants are 30–80 years of age. Participants must be members of the sponsoring organization (annual dues: $40). 15–20 participants per session. Application deadline: June.
Costs • $4000 (includes housing, some meals, excursions, international airfare). A $500 deposit is required.
Contact • Shelley Ruston, Director of Special Programs, Santa Barbara Museum of Art, 1130 State Street, Santa Barbara, CA 93101; 805-963-4364, ext. 336; Fax: 805-966-6840

SOUTHERN ILLINOIS UNIVERSITY AT CARBONDALE

ORIGINS: RE-THINKING THE LEGACY OF ANCIENT EGYPT

General Information • Academic study program in Aswan, Cairo, Luxor. Excursions to Abu Simbel.
Learning Focus • Courses in Egyptian studies, philosophy. Instruction is offered by professors from the sponsoring institution.
Accommodations • Single rooms are available. Meals are taken as a group, in local restaurants.

Program Details • Program offered once per year. Session length: 2 weeks. Departures are scheduled in May. The program is open to undergraduate students, graduate students, adults. Most participants are 19–60 years of age. 20–25 participants per session. Application deadline: March 1.
Costs • $2665 (includes tuition, housing, some meals, books and class materials, excursions). A $250 deposit is required.
Contact • Mr. Thomas A. Saville, Coordinator, Study Abroad Programs, Southern Illinois University at Carbondale, Mailcode 6885, Small Business Incubator, Carbondale, IL 62901-6885; 618-453-7670; Fax: 618-453-7677; E-mail: studyabr@siu.edu

 TRAVELEARN

AN EGYPTIAN ODYSSEY

General Information • Cultural tour with visits to Abu Simbel, Aswan, Cairo, Luxor, Dendera, Abydos. Once at the destination country, participants travel by bus, foot, boat, airplane. Program is affiliated with the nationwide TraveLearn network of 290 universities and colleges.
Learning Focus • Instruction in history, archaeology, art and sociology. Museum visits (Egyptian Museum, the Solar Boat, Coptic Museum). Attendance at performances (Sound and Light Show at Karnak). Instruction is offered by professors, researchers, historians, social scientists. This program would appeal to people interested in archaeology, cultural understanding, history, religion and spirituality.
Accommodations • Hotels, boat. Single rooms are available for an additional $595.
Program Details • Program offered 7 times per year. Session length: 13 days. Departures are scheduled in January, March, July, October. Program is targeted to mature adults. Most participants are 40–75 years of age. Participants must be 18 years or older to enroll. 14–20 participants per session. Application deadline: 60 days prior to departure. Reservations are recommended at least 4–8 months before departure.
Costs • $3195 (includes housing, all meals, books and class materials, excursions, international airfare). A $300 deposit is required.
Contact • Keith Williams, Director of Marketing, TraveLearn, PO Box 315, Lakeville, PA 18438; 800-235-9114; Fax: 717-226-9114; E-mail: travelearn@aol.com

 WILDLAND ADVENTURES

GREAT SIGHTS OF EGYPT

General Information • Archaeological tour with visits to Cairo, Nile River. Once at the destination country, participants travel by bus, foot, boat, airplane.
Learning Focus • Escorted travel to museums and archaeological sites. Museum visits (Cairo museums). Other activities include visiting archaeological sites. Instruction is offered by historians, Egyptologists. This program would appeal to people interested in photography, archaeology, history.
Accommodations • Hotels. Single rooms are available for an additional $290.
Program Details • Session length: 10 days. Departures are scheduled throughout the year. Most participants are 30–70 years of age. Participants must be 8 years or older to enroll. 2–8 participants per session. Application deadline: 30 days prior to departure. Reservations are recommended at least 3–6 months before departure.
Costs • $1495 (includes housing, some meals, excursions, complete pre-departure dossier). A $300 deposit is required.
Contact • Wildland Adventures, 3516 Northeast 155th Street, Seattle, WA 98155; 800-345-4453; Fax: 206-363-6615; E-mail: wildadve@aol.com; World Wide Web: http://www.wildland.com

ISRAEL

AMERICAN JEWISH CONGRESS, INTERNATIONAL TRAVEL PROGRAM

BAR MITZVAH OR BAT MITZVAH FAMILY CELEBRATION IN ISRAEL

General Information • Cultural and religious tour with visits to Dead Sea, Eilat, Galilee, Jerusalem, Tel Aviv, Jaffa, Caesarea, Sea of Galilee, Golan Heights, Belvoir Castle, Jericho, Mount Herzl, Herodian Mansions, Dead Sea, Masada, King Solomon's Pillars. Once at the destination country, participants travel by bus, foot, boat.
Learning Focus • Escorted travel to kibbutzes, synagogues, Jerusaleum Zoo, Western Wall and the Red Sea. Museum visits (Museum of the Jewish Diaspora, Yad Vashem, Israel Museum). Attendance at performances (Israeli folk dancing). Instruction is offered by naturalists, historians, rabbis. This program would appeal to people interested in Jewish history, Jewish culture.
Accommodations • Hotels, kibbutz, guest house. Single rooms are available for an additional $625–$895.
Program Details • Program offered 5 times per year. Session length: 15 days. Departures are scheduled in June–August, December. Program is targeted to Jewish-American families celebrating a Bar/Bat Mitzvah. Most participants are 10–70 years of age. Participants must be members of the sponsoring organization (annual dues: $50). 30 participants per session. Reservations are recommended at least 6 months before departure.
Costs • $3145–$4045 (minor of bar/bat mitzvah age is free) (includes housing, some meals, excursions, international airfare, rabbi for ceremony, travel bag, documents portfolio, travel journal). A $200 deposit is required.
Contact • Betty Van Dyke, Worldwide Operations Manager, American Jewish Congress, International Travel Program, 18 East 84th Street, New York, NY 10028; 212-360-1571; Fax: 212-717-1932

AMERICAN JEWISH CONGRESS, INTERNATIONAL TRAVEL PROGRAM

INSTANT ISRAEL

General Information • Cultural tour with visits to Haifa, Jerusalem, Tel Aviv, Tiberias, Herodian Mansions, Dead Sea, Herod's Palace, Mount Herzl, Mount Zion, Bahai Gardens, Atlit Camp, Independence Hall.
Learning Focus • Escorted travel to Western Wall, Knesset, Jericho, Golan, synagogues and Jaffa. Museum visits (Old Yishur Court Museum, Israel Museum, Yad Vashem, Museum of the History of Jerusalem, Tel Aviv Museum). Instruction is offered by historians. This program would appeal to people interested in Jewish history.
Accommodations • Hotels. Single rooms are available for an additional $385–$1570.
Program Details • Program offered 24 times per year. Session length: 12 days. Departures are scheduled throughout the year. Program is targeted to Jewish-American adults. Most participants are 40–75 years of age. Participants must be 15 years or older to enroll. Participants must be members of the sponsoring organization (annual dues: $50). 30 participants per session. Reservations are recommended at least 6 months before departure.
Costs • $2740–$4345 (includes housing, some meals, excursions, international airfare, travel bag, documents portfolio, travel journal). A $200 deposit is required.
Contact • Betty Van Dyke, Worldwide Operations Manager, American Jewish Congress, International Travel Program, 18 East 84th Street, New York, NY 10028; 212-360-1571; Fax: 212-717-1932

AMERICAN JEWISH CONGRESS, INTERNATIONAL TRAVEL PROGRAM

ISRAEL . . . AT A LEISURELY PACE

General Information • Cultural tour with visits to Israel (Dead Sea, Jerusalem, Netanya, Tiberias), Romania (Romania (Bucharest)); excursions to Tel Aviv, Old Jaffa, Haifa, Mount Carmel, Sea of Galilee, Golan Heights, Nazareth, Mediggo, Jericho, Mount Zion, Mount Herz, Dead Sea, Transylvania. Once at the destination country, participants travel by bus, foot, airplane.
Learning Focus • Escorted travel to hot springs, synagogues, kibbutzes and the Western Wall. Museum visits (Museum of the Diaspora, Yad Vashem, Israel Museum, Bucharest Art Museum). Attendance at performances (Israeli folklore show, Romanian folk singers). Instruction is offered by naturalists, historians, spa staff. This program would appeal to people interested in Jewish history.
Accommodations • Hotels. Single rooms are available for an additional $880–$1015.
Program Details • Program offered 6 times per year. Session length: 27 days. Departures are scheduled in May–August, October, November. Program is targeted to Jewish-American adults. Most participants are 40–75 years of age. Participants must be 15 years or older to enroll. Participants must be members of the sponsoring organization (annual dues: $50). 30 participants per session. Reservations are recommended at least 6 months before departure.
Costs • $3785–$3985 (includes housing, some meals, excursions, travel bag, documents portfolio, travel journal, business class airfare). A $200 deposit is required.
Contact • Betty Van Dyke, Worldwide Operations Manager, American Jewish Congress, International Travel Program, 18 East 84th Street, New York, NY 10028; 212-360-1571; Fax: 212-717-1932

AMERICAN JEWISH CONGRESS, INTERNATIONAL TRAVEL PROGRAM

ISRAEL SINGLES HAPPENING

General Information • Cultural tour with visits to Eilat, Jerusalem, Tel Aviv, Tiberias, Tel Maresha archaeological dig, Bell Caves, Caesarea, Atlit Camp, Sea of Galilee, Golan Heights, Jericho, Western Wall, Bethlehem, Mount Herzl, Dead Sea. Once at the destination country, participants travel by bus, foot, boat.

Learning Focus • Escorted travel to Independence Hall, Jaffa, synagogues, winery and a kibbutz. Museum visits (Museum of the Jewish Diaspora, Yad Vashem, Israel Museum). Other activities include pub tour, dancing. Instruction is offered by naturalists, historians. This program would appeal to people interested in Jewish history.

Accommodations • Hotels. Single rooms are available for an additional $540–$700.

Program Details • Program offered 5 times per year. Session length: 15 days. Departures are scheduled in May, July–September, December. Program is targeted to single Jewish-American adults. Most participants are 25–55 years of age. Participants must be 25 years or older to enroll. Participants must be members of the sponsoring organization (annual dues: $50). 30 participants per session. Reservations are recommended at least 6 months before departure.

Costs • $3465–$3665 (includes housing, some meals, excursions, international airfare, travel bag, documents portfolio, travel journal). A $200 deposit is required.

Contact • Betty Van Dyke, Reservations Manager, American Jewish Congress, International Travel Program, 18 East 84th Street, New York, NY 10028; 212-360-1571; Fax: 212-717-1932

AMERICAN JEWISH CONGRESS, INTERNATIONAL TRAVEL PROGRAM

ISRAEL THE BEAUTIFUL

General Information • Cultural tour with visits to Golan, Haifa, Jerusalem, Tel Aviv, Tiberias, Herodian Mansions, Dead Sea, Mount Herzl, Mount Zion, Mount Carmel, Bahai Gardens, Atlit Camp, Independence Hall. Once at the destination country, participants travel by bus, foot, boat.

Learning Focus • Escorted travel to Western Wall, Knesset, Jericho, synagogues and Jaffa. Museum visits (Old Yishur Court Museum, Israel Museum, Yad Vashem, Museum of the History of Jerusalem, Tel Aviv Museum, Museum of the Jewish Diaspora). Attendance at performances (Israeli folk dancing). Instruction is offered by historians. This program would appeal to people interested in Jewish history.

Accommodations • Hotels. Single rooms are available for an additional $550–$1955.

Program Details • Program offered 24 times per year. Session length: 15 days. Departures are scheduled throughout the year. Program is targeted to Jewish-American adults. Most participants are 40–75 years of age. Participants must be 15 years or older to enroll. Participants must be members of the sponsoring organization (annual dues: $50). 30 participants per session. Reservations are recommended at least 6 months before departure.

Costs • $3195–$5045 (includes housing, some meals, excursions, international airfare, travel bag, documents portfolio, travel journal). A $200 deposit is required.

Contact • Betty Van Dyke, Worldwide Operations Manager, American Jewish Congress, International Travel Program, 18 East 84th Street, New York, NY 10028; 212-360-1571; Fax: 212-717-1932

AMERICAN JEWISH CONGRESS, INTERNATIONAL TRAVEL PROGRAM

ISRAEL: THE GREAT OUTDOORS

General Information • Cultural tour with visits to Eilat, Galilee, Jerusalem, Tel Aviv, Tiberias, Mount Herzl, Mount Zion, Beersheba, Red Sea, Dead Sea, Masada, Jericho, Golan Heights, Mount Canaan, Independence Hall, Jaffa. Once at the destination country, participants travel by bus, foot, boat, jeep.

Learning Focus • Escorted travel to Western Wall, kibbutzes and synagogues. Museum visits (Yad Vashem, Museum of the History of Jerusalem, Tel Aviv museum, Museum of Jewish Diaspora). Attendance at performances (Israeli folklore show). Nature observation (waterfalls, rapids, wildflowers, pistachio trees). Other activities include hiking, camel rides, rafting. Instruction is offered by naturalists, historians. This program would appeal to people interested in Jewish history, adventure.

Accommodations • Hotels. Single rooms are available for an additional $575.

Program Details • Program offered 5 times per year. Session length: 14 days. Departures are scheduled in May, July, August, October, December. Program is targeted to Jewish–American adults. Most participants are 25–60 years of age. Participants must be 15 years or older to enroll. Participants must be members of the sponsoring organization (annual dues: $50). Other requirements: excellent physical condition. 30 participants per session. Reservations are recommended at least 6 months before departure.

Costs • $3550–$3775 (includes housing, some meals, excursions, international airfare, travel bag, documents portfolio, travel journal). A $200 deposit is required.

Contact • Betty Van Dyke, Worldwide Operations Manager, American Jewish Congress, International Travel Program, 18 East 84th Street, New York, NY 10028; 212-360-1571; Fax: 212-717-1932

DUKE UNIVERSITY

DUKE IN ISRAEL

General Information • Academic study program in Galilee, Sepphoris. Excursions to Jerusalem.

Learning Focus • Courses in religion, archaeology, cultural studies. Instruction is offered by professors from the sponsoring institution.

Accommodations • Dormitories. Meals are taken as a group, in central dining facility.

Program Details • Program offered once per year. Session length: 6 weeks. Departures are scheduled in May. The program is open to undergraduate students. Most participants are 19–23 years of age. Other requirements: minimum 2.7 GPA. 15–20 participants per session. Application deadline: February 21.

Costs • $4900 (includes tuition, housing, all meals, excursions, international airfare).
Contact • Foreign Academic Programs, Duke University, 121 Allen Building, Box 90057, Durham, NC 27708-0057; 919-684-2174; Fax: 919-684-3083; E-mail: abroad@mail01.adm.duke.edu; World Wide Web: http://www.mis.duke.edu/study_abroad/study_abroad.html

FOREIGN LANGUAGE STUDY ABROAD SERVICE

INTERNATIONAL LANGUAGE STUDY HOMESTAYS IN ISRAEL

General Information • Language study program in Israel.
Learning Focus • Courses in Hebrew language. Instruction is offered by local teachers.
Accommodations • Homestays. Single rooms are available. Meals are taken with host family, in residences.
Program Details • Session length: varies. Departures are scheduled in January–December. The program is open to undergraduate students, graduate students, pre-college students, adults. Most participants are 12 years of age and older. Other requirements: students must be at least 12 years old. 1 participant per session.
Costs • Contact sponsor for information. A $300 deposit is required.
Contact • Louise Harber, Coordinator, Foreign Language Study Abroad Service, Department IH, Box 903, 5935 Southwest 64th Avenue, South Miami, FL 33143; 800-282-1090; Fax: 305-662-2907; E-mail: flsas@netpoint.net; World Wide Web: http://www.netpoint.net/~flsas

HEBREW UNIVERSITY OF JERUSALEM

LANGUAGE COURSES IN ISRAEL

General Information • Language study program in Jerusalem. Classes are held on the campus of Hebrew University of Jerusalem. Excursions to Israel.
Learning Focus • Courses in Hebrew language, Biblical Hebrew, English language, Arabic language, Yiddish language. Instruction is offered by professors from the sponsoring institution and local teachers.
Accommodations • Dormitories. Meals are taken on one's own.
Program Details • Program offered 2 times per year. Session length: July session: 6 weeks, August session: 8 weeks. Departures are scheduled in July, August. The program is open to undergraduate students, graduate students. Most participants are 19–65 years of age. 600 participants per session. Application deadline: May 15.
Costs • $785–$1255 for July session, $1300 for August session (includes tuition, housing, insurance). Application fee: $45. A $75 deposit is required.
Contact • Renanit Levy, Admissions Officer, Office of Academic Affairs, Hebrew University of Jerusalem, 11 East 69th Street, New York, NY 10021; 212-472-2288, ext. 312; Fax: 212-517-4548; E-mail: 102232.1166@compuserve.com; World Wide Web: http://www2.huji.ac.il/www_sfos/top.html

HEBREW UNIVERSITY OF JERUSALEM

SUMMER COURSES IN JERUSALEM

General Information • Academic study program in Jerusalem. Classes are held on the campus of Hebrew University of Jerusalem. Excursions to sites in Israel, sites in Jordan.
Learning Focus • Courses in archaeology, Judaic studies, international relations, arts, Israeli studies, Middle Eastern studies, science. Instruction is offered by professors from the sponsoring institution and local teachers.
Accommodations • Dormitories. Meals are taken on one's own.
Program Details • Program offered 2 times per year. Session length: 3 weeks. Departures are scheduled in July, August. The program is open to undergraduate students, graduate students, anyone who has completed at least one year of college. Most participants are 19–60 years of age. 100 participants per session. Application deadline: May 15.
Costs • $785–$985 (includes tuition, housing, insurance). Application fee: $45. A $75 deposit is required.
Contact • Ms. Renanit Levy, Admissions Officer, Hebrew University of Jerusalem, Office of Academic Affairs, 11 East 69th Street, New York, NY 10021; 212-472-2288, ext. 312; Fax: 212-517-4548; E-mail: 102232.1166@compuserve.com; World Wide Web: http://www2.huji.ac.il/www_sfos/top.html

JAMES MADISON UNIVERSITY

SUMMER STUDY IN ISRAEL

General Information • Academic study program in Tel Miqne-Ehron. Excursions to Jerusalem, Egypt, Negev, Galilee, Massade, Judean Desert.
Learning Focus • Courses in religion, history, culture. Instruction is offered by professors from the sponsoring institution.
Accommodations • Kibbutz. Meals are taken as a group, in central dining facility, in local restaurants.
Program Details • Program offered once per year. Session length: 6 weeks. Departures are scheduled in June. The program is open to undergraduate students. Most participants are 18–22 years of age. Other requirements: 2.8 minimum GPA. 15 participants per session. Application deadline: February 1.
Costs • $2504 for Virginia residents, $2930 for non-residents (includes tuition, housing, some meals, excursions). A $400 deposit is required.
Contact • Dr. Diana Edelman, Coordinator, Tel Miqne Program, James Madison University, Office of International Education, Harrisonburg, VA 22807; 540-568-3364; Fax: 540-568-3310; E-mail: edelmadj@jmu.edu; World Wide Web: http://www.jmu.edu/intl-ed/

MICHIGAN STATE UNIVERSITY

ARCHAEOLOGY, MODERN HEBREW, AND THE HISTORY OF RELIGION

General Information • Academic study program in Galilee.

Learning Focus • Courses in archaeology, religion, Hebrew language. Instruction is offered by professors from the sponsoring institution.
Accommodations • Dormitories. Meals are taken on one's own, in central dining facility.
Program Details • Program offered once per year. Session length: 4 weeks. Departures are scheduled in June. The program is open to undergraduate students, graduate students. Most participants are 18–26 years of age. Other requirements: good academic standing and the approval of the director. 10 participants per session. Application deadline: March 14.
Costs • $2800 (includes housing, some meals, excursions). Application fee: $75. A $250 deposit is required.
Contact • Brenda S. Sprite, Educational Programs Coordinator, Michigan State University, Office of Study Abroad, 109 International Center, East Lansing, MI 48824-1035; 517-353-8920; Fax: 517-432-2082; E-mail: sprite@pilot.msu.edu; World Wide Web: http://study-abroad.msu.edu

OUACHITA BAPTIST UNIVERSITY

HEBREW STUDY PROGRAM

General Information • Academic study program in Jerusalem. Classes are held on the campus of Hebrew University of Jerusalem. Excursions to Tel Aviv.
Learning Focus • Courses in Biblical Hebrew, archaeology.
Accommodations • Dormitories. Single rooms are available. Meals are taken on one's own, in central dining facility, in local restaurants.
Program Details • Program offered once per year. Session length: 6 weeks. Departures are scheduled in July. The program is open to undergraduate students. Most participants are 19–23 years of age. Other requirements: 2.5 minimum GPA. 2 participants per session. Application deadline: April 1.
Costs • $2300 (includes tuition, housing, some meals, international airfare). A $500 deposit is required.
Contact • Dr. Trey Berry, Director of International Programs, Ouachita Baptist University, OBU Box 3777, Arkadelphia, AR 71998; 501-245-5197; Fax: 501-245-5312; E-mail: berryt@alpha.obu.edu; World Wide Web: http://www.obu.edu

RAMAPO COLLEGE OF NEW JERSEY

EXCAVATION AT TEL HADAR

General Information • Academic study program in Tel Aviv. Classes are held on the campus of Tel Aviv University. Excursions to 8-day guided tour of Israel.
Learning Focus • Courses in field archaeology, Biblical archaeology. Instruction is offered by professors from the sponsoring institution and local teachers.
Accommodations • Dormitories. Single rooms are available. Meals are taken as a group, in central dining facility.
Program Details • Program offered once per year. Session length: 5 weeks. Departures are scheduled in June. The program is open to undergraduate students, graduate students, pre-college students, adults. Most participants are 18–70 years of age. Other requirements: minimum 2.0 GPA. 15 participants per session. Application deadline: April 1.
Costs • $3000 (includes tuition, housing, all meals, excursions, international airfare). A $300 deposit is required.
Contact • Mrs. Robyn Perricelli, Coordinator, Study Abroad, Ramapo College of New Jersey, 505 Ramapo Valley Road, Mahwah, NJ 07430; 201-529-7463; Fax: 201-529-7508; E-mail: rperrice@ramapo.edu

TRAVELEARN

AN ISRAEL ODYSSEY

General Information • Cultural tour with visits to Bethlehem, Haifa, Jerusalem, Nazareth, Sea of Galilee, Tel Aviv. Once at the destination country, participants travel by bus, foot. Program is affiliated with the nationwide TraveLearn network of 290 universities and colleges.
Learning Focus • Instruction in history, archaeology and sociology. Museum visits (Holocaust Museum, Israel Museum, Vulcani Institute). Other activities include "people-to-people" experience outside of Jerusalem. Instruction is offered by professors, historians, social scientists. This program would appeal to people interested in history, religion, cultural understanding.
Accommodations • Hotels. Single rooms are available for an additional $625.
Program Details • Program offered 4 times per year. Session length: 14 days. Departures are scheduled in February, March, June, September. Program is targeted to mature adults. Most participants are 40–75 years of age. Participants must be 18 years or older to enroll. 14–20 participants per session. Application deadline: 60 days prior to departure. Reservations are recommended at least 4–8 months before departure.
Costs • $2995 (includes housing, all meals, books and class materials, excursions, international airfare). A $300 deposit is required.
Contact • Keith Williams, Director of Marketing, TraveLearn, PO Box 315, Lakeville, PA 18438; 800-235-9114; Fax: 717-226-9114; E-mail: travelearn@aol.com

UNIVERSITY OF DELAWARE

WINTER SESSION IN ISRAEL

General Information • Academic study program in Eilat, Haifa, Jerusalem, Tel Aviv.
Learning Focus • Courses in political science, political science, sociology. Instruction is offered by professors from the sponsoring institution.
Accommodations • Homestays, hotels.
Program Details • Program offered once per year. Session length: 5 weeks. Departures are scheduled in January. The program is open to undergraduate students. Other requirements: minimum 2.0 GPA. Application deadline: October.
Costs • Contact sponsor for information. A $200 deposit is required.
Contact • International Programs and Special Sessions, University of Delaware, 4 Kent Way, Newark, DE 19716-1450; 888-831-4685; Fax: 302-831-6042; E-mail: studyabroad@mvs.udel.edu

UNIVERSITY OF FLORIDA

SUMMER PROGRAM AT THE HEBREW UNIVERSITY, JERUSALEM, ISRAEL

General Information • Language study program in Jerusalem. Classes are held on the campus of Hebrew University of Jerusalem. Excursions to Jerusalem, lectures, concerts, exhibits, fairs.
Learning Focus • Courses in Hebrew language, Israeli studies, religion, legal studies, Arabic language, archaeology, science, technology. Instruction is offered by local teachers.
Accommodations • Dormitories. Meals are taken on one's own, in central dining facility, in local restaurants.
Program Details • Program offered 2 times per year. Session length: 4 or 7 weeks. Departures are scheduled in July. The program is open to undergraduate students, graduate students, adults. Most participants are 18–40 years of age. Other requirements: minimum 2.5 GPA. Application deadline: March 15.
Costs • $1500–$3000 (includes tuition, housing). Application fee: $250.
Contact • Overseas Studies, University of Florida, 123 Tigert Hall, PO Box 113225, Gainesville, FL 32611-3225; 352-392-5206; Fax: 352-392-5575; E-mail: ovrseas@nervm.nerdc.ufl.edu

UNIVERSITY OF HAIFA

SUMMER ULPAN

General Information • Language study program in Haifa. Classes are held on the campus of University of Haifa.
Learning Focus • Courses in Hebrew language. Instruction is offered by professors from the sponsoring institution.
Accommodations • Dormitories.
Program Details • Program offered once per year. Session length: 5 or 10 weeks. Departures are scheduled in July. The program is open to undergraduate students, graduate students, pre-college students, adults. Most participants are 21–50 years of age. Other requirements: minimum 2.3 GPA.
Costs • $710 for 5 weeks, $1270 for 10 weeks (includes tuition, housing). Application fee: $50.
Contact • Fran Yacoubov, North American Representative, University of Haifa, 1110 Finch Avenue, W, Suite 510, Downsview, ON M3J 2T2, Canada; 800-388-2134; Fax: 416-665-4468

VILLANOVA UNIVERSITY

SUMMER PROGRAM IN PALESTINIAN STUDIES

General Information • Academic study program in Bethlehem. Classes are held on the campus of Bethlehem University. Excursions to West Bank, Jerusalem, Israel.
Learning Focus • Courses in Arabic language, contemporary Palestinian literature, Palestinian society, political science, Palestinian culture, Palestinian history, modern Middle East history. Instruction is offered by local teachers.
Accommodations • Homestays. Single rooms are available. Meals are taken with host family, in residences.
Program Details • Program offered once per year. Session length: 6 weeks. Departures are scheduled in May. The program is open to undergraduate students. Most participants are 19–23 years of age. Other requirements: minimum 2.5 GPA and good academic standing. 10 participants per session. Application deadline: March 1.
Costs • $3000 (includes tuition, housing, all meals, books and class materials, excursions, transfers and orientation). Application fee: $100.
Contact • Dr. Thomas M. Ricks, Director of International Studies, Villanova University, St. Augustine Center, Room 415, Villanova, PA 19085; 610-519-6412; Fax: 610-519-7649; E-mail: ricks@ucis.vill.edu

JORDAN

NORTH CAROLINA STATE UNIVERSITY

ROMAN AQABA PROJECT: ANCIENT AILA ON THE RED SEA

General Information • Archaeological tour in Aqaba. Excursions to Petra.

Learning Focus • Courses in archaeology, history. Instruction is offered by local teachers.

Accommodations • Locally-rented apartments. Meals are taken on one's own, in local restaurants.

Program Details • Program offered once per year. Session length: 8 weeks. Departures are scheduled in May. The program is open to undergraduate students, graduate students. Other requirements: recommendations and approval by Director and in good health. 10 participants per session. Application deadline: February 16.

Costs • $2765 (includes tuition, housing, some meals, excursions, international airfare).

Contact • Ingrid Schmidt, Study Abroad Director, North Carolina State University, 2118 Pullen Hall, Box 7344, Raleigh, NC 27695-7344; 919-515-2087; Fax: 919-515-6021; E-mail: study_abroad@ncsu.edu; World Wide Web: http://www2.ncsu.edu/ncsu/chass/intstu/abroad.html

UNITED ARAB EMIRATES

AMERICAN UNIVERSITY OF DUBAI

THE AMERICAN UNIVERSITY IN DUBAI–MIDDLE EASTERN STUDIES

General Information • Academic study program in Dubai. Classes are held on the campus of The American University in Dubai.

Learning Focus • Courses in Arabic language, Middle Eastern history, Middle Eastern politics, Middle Eastern business, Arabic art and architecture, Arabic literature, Islam, Middle Eastern culture. Instruction is offered by professors from the sponsoring institution.

Accommodations • Locally-rented apartments. Single rooms are available. Meals are taken on one's own, in residences.

Program Details • Program offered 3 times per year. Session length: 10 weeks. Departures are scheduled in January, March, September. The program is open to undergraduate students, adults. Most participants are 20–70 years of age. Other requirements: good academic standing and permission from home institution. 10 participants per session.

Costs • $4560 (includes tuition, housing, books and class materials, fees, some activities). A $275 deposit is required.

Contact • Division of International Programs and Study Abroad, American University of Dubai, 3330 Peachtree Road, NE, Atlanta, GA 30326; 800-255-6839; Fax: 404-364-6611; E-mail: acatl@ix.netcom.com

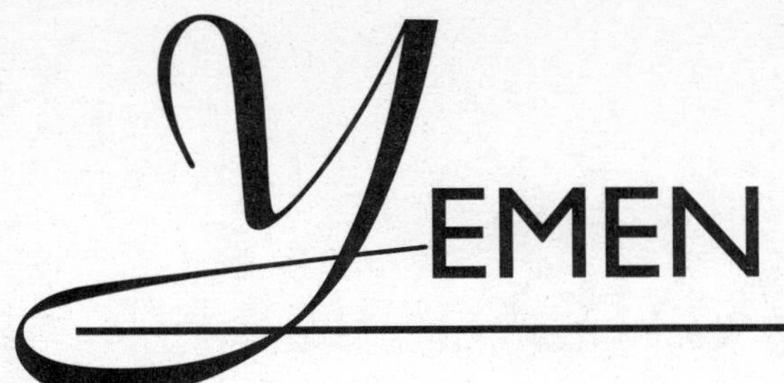

YEMEN

ARCHAEOLOGICAL TOURS

YEMEN

General Information • Archaeological tour with visits to El Mukalla, Hodeida, Marib, Sana'a, Wadi Hadhramawt, Zafar, Zu Taiz. Once at the destination country, participants travel by jeep.
Learning Focus • Museum visits (Sana'a, Zafar, Taiz). Attendance at performances (dance and music). Instruction is offered by professors, historians. This program would appeal to people interested in history, architecture, archaeology.
Accommodations • Hotels. Single rooms are available for an additional $430.
Program Details • Program offered once per year. Session length: 17 days. Departures are scheduled in February. Most participants are 30–80 years of age. Other requirements: good health. 20 participants per session. Application deadline: 1 month prior to departure.
Costs • $4710 (includes housing, all meals, excursions, international airfare). A $500 deposit is required.
Contact • Archaeological Tours, 271 Madison Avenue, Suite 904, New York, NY 10016; 212-986-3054; Fax: 212-370-1561

 LANGUAGE LIAISON

YEMEN LANGUAGE CENTER–ARABIC IN YEMEN

General Information • Language study program with visits to Sana'a.
Learning Focus • Instruction in Arabic. Instruction is offered by professors. This program would appeal to people interested in language.
Accommodations • Homestays, program-owned houses. Single rooms are available.
Program Details • Session length: unlimited. Departures are scheduled throughout the year. Program is targeted to students of any age. Most participants are 18–70 years of age. Participants must be 16 years or older to enroll. Reservations are recommended at least 35 days before departure.
Costs • Contact sponsor for information.
Contact • Nancy Forman, President, Language Liaison, 20533 Biscayne Boulevard-Station 4-162, Miami, FL 33180; 305-682-9909; Fax: 305-682-9907; E-mail: langstudy@aol.com; World Wide Web: http://languageliaison.com

RUSSIAN AND EAST EUROPEAN PARTNERSHIPS

YEMEN LANGUAGE AND CULTURAL IMMERSION PROGRAM

General Information • Language study program in Sana'a. Classes are held on the campus of Yemen Language Center. Excursions to Shibam, Kawkaban, Wadi Dhahr.
Learning Focus • Courses in Arabic language, history of the Arab Peninsula. Instruction is offered by local teachers.
Accommodations • Program-owned houses. Single rooms are available. Meals are taken on one's own, in local restaurants, in residences.
Program Details • Program offered 11 times per year. Session length: 4 or more weeks. Departures are scheduled in January–November. The program is open to undergraduate students, graduate students, adults. Most participants are 18 years of age and older. Other requirements: in good health, 18 or older unless chaperoned by an adult. 20 participants per session. Application deadline: 45 days prior to departure.
Costs • $4350 (includes tuition, housing, some meals, books and class materials, excursions, international airfare, local transportation, airport transfers). A $1500 deposit is required.
Contact • Kenneth Fortune, President, Russian and East European Partnerships, PO Box 227, Fineview, NY 13640; 888-873-7337; Fax: 800-910-1777; E-mail: reep@fox.nstn.ca

RUSSIA AND CENTRAL ASIA

REGIONAL

Armenia
Azerbaijan
Georgia
Kazakhstan
Kyrgyzstan
Mongolia
Pakistan
Russia
Tajikistan
Turkey
Turkmenistan
Uzbekistan

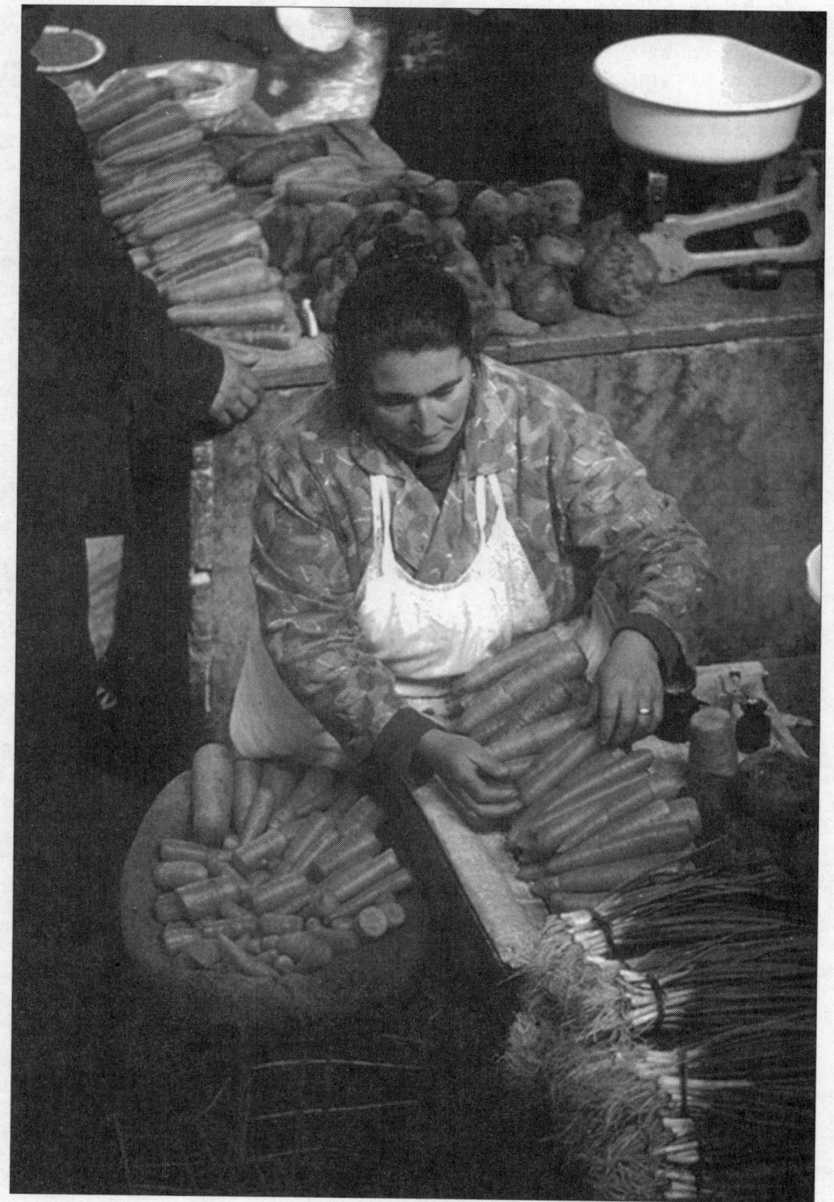

REGIONAL

ARCHAEOLOGICAL TOURS

CENTRAL ASIA: UZBEKISTAN AND TURKMENISTAN

General Information • Cultural tour with visits to Russia (St. Petersburg), Turkmenistan (Ashkhabad, Mari), Uzbekistan (Bukhara, Khiva, Samarkaut, Tashkent); excursions to Urgench, Shahr-I-Sabz, Varaksha, Old Urguch. Once at the destination country, participants travel by bus.
Learning Focus • Museum visits (Central Asian Rooms at Hermitage). Attendance at performances (dance and music shows). Instruction is offered by professors, historians. This program would appeal to people interested in history, art, archaeology, architecture.
Accommodations • Hotels. Single rooms are available for an additional $720.
Program Details • Program offered once per year. Session length: 19 days. Departures are scheduled in September. Program is targeted to adults. Most participants are 30–80 years of age. 20 participants per session. Application deadline: 1 month prior to departure.
Costs • $4665 (includes housing, some meals, excursions, internal flights). A $500 deposit is required.
Contact • Archaeological Tours, 271 Madison Avenue, Suite 904, New York, NY 10016; 212-986-3054; Fax: 212-370-1561

BOWLING GREEN STATE UNIVERSITY

SUMMER RUSSIAN LANGUAGE PROGRAM

General Information • Language study program in Russia (St. Petersburg), Ukraine (Kiev). Classes are held on the campus of St. Petersburg State University. Excursions to St. Petersburg region.
Learning Focus • Courses in Russian culture, Ukrainian culture. Instruction is offered by professors from the sponsoring institution and local teachers.
Accommodations • Homestays, hotels. Meals are taken as a group, with host family, in central dining facility.
Program Details • Program offered once per year. Session length: 5 weeks. Departures are scheduled in May. The program is open to undergraduate students, graduate students, adults. Most participants are 19–55 years of age. Other requirements: academic and personal recommendations. 12 participants per session. Application deadline: April 1.
Costs • $2680–$3280 (includes tuition, housing, all meals, books and class materials, insurance, excursions, international airfare, rail fare).
Contact • Dr. Irina Stakhanova, Bowling Green State University, Department of German, Russian and East Asian Languages, Bowling Green, OH 43403-0219; 419-372-2268; Fax: 419-372-2571; E-mail: irina@bgnet.bgsu.edu; World Wide Web: http://www.bgsu.edu/departments/greal/AYA-Salzburg.html

JOURNEYS INTERNATIONAL, INC.

CENTRAL ASIA TRAIL

General Information • Cultural tour with visits to Pakistan (Gilgit, Hunza, Islamabad), Uzbekistan (Bukhara, Peshaivar, Tashkent). Once at the destination country, participants travel by foot, small vehicle.
Learning Focus • Escorted travel to mausoleums and bazaars. Museum visits (Peshawar Muesum). Nature observation (Central Asian mountains and deserts). Other activities include hiking. Instruction is offered by local English-speaking guides. This program would appeal to people interested in culture, religion, nature studies.
Accommodations • Hotels. Single rooms are available for an additional $400.
Program Details • Program offered 4 times per year. Session length: 19 days. Departures are scheduled in May–August. Program is targeted to persons interested in culture. Most participants are 25–55 years of age. Participants must be 12 years or older to enroll. 12 participants per session. Application deadline: 60 days prior to departure. Reservations are recommended at least 60 days before departure.
Costs • $2680 (includes housing, some meals). A $300 deposit is required.
Contact • Pat Ballard, Asia Sales Director, Journeys International, Inc., 4011 Jackson Road, Ann Arbor, MI 48103; 313-665-4407; Fax: 313-665-2945; E-mail: pat@journeys-intl.com; World Wide Web: http://www.journeys-intl.com

ARMENIA

ACTR/ACCELS

CIS REGIONAL LANGUAGE TRAINING PROGRAM–ARMENIA

General Information • Language study program in Armenia. Excursions to museums, churches, sites of historical interest.

Learning Focus • Courses in language study, cultural studies, Russian language, history, literature.

Accommodations • Homestays, dormitories. Single rooms are available. Meals are taken on one's own, with host family, in residences.

Program Details • Program offered once per year. Session length: 7 weeks. Departures are scheduled in June. The program is open to undergraduate students, graduate students, adults. Most participants are 19–28 years of age. Other requirements: intermediate-level Russian or target language. 1–3 participant per session. Application deadline: March 1.

Costs • $3400 (includes tuition, housing, some meals, books and class materials, insurance, excursions, visa processing fee, mandatory orientation in Washington, DC). Application fee: $35. A $500 deposit is required.

Contact • Margaret Stephenson, Program Officer, ACTR/ACCELS, 1776 Massachusetts Avenue, NW, Suite 700, Washington, DC 20036; 202-833-7522; Fax: 202-833-7523; E-mail: stephens@actr.org

AZERBAIJAN

ACTR/ACCELS

CIS REGIONAL LANGUAGE TRAINING PROGRAM–AZERBAIJAN

General Information • Language study program in Azerbaijan. Excursions to museums, churches, historical interest.

Learning Focus • Courses in history, literature, cultural studies, Russian language, language study.

Accommodations • Homestays, dormitories. Single rooms are available. Meals are taken on one's own, with host family, in residences.

Program Details • Program offered once per year. Session length: 7 weeks. Departures are scheduled in June. The program is open to undergraduate students, graduate students, adults. Most participants are 19–28 years of age. Other requirements: intermediate-level Russian or target language. 1–3 participant per session. Application deadline: March 1.

Costs • $3400 (includes tuition, housing, some meals, books and class materials, insurance, excursions, visa processing fee, mandatory orientation in Washington, DC). Application fee: $35. A $500 deposit is required.

Contact • Margaret Stephenson, Program Officer, ACTR/ACCELS, 1776 Massachusetts Avenue, NW, Suite 700, Washington, DC 20036; 202-833-7522; Fax: 202-833-7523; E-mail: stephens@actr.org

GEORGIA

ACTR/ACCELS

CIS REGIONAL LANGUAGE TRAINING PROGRAM–GEORGIA

General Information • Language study program in Georgia. Excursions to museums, churches, sites of historical interest.

Learning Focus • Courses in language study, Russian language, history, literature, cultural studies.

Accommodations • Homestays, dormitories. Single rooms are available. Meals are taken on one's own, with host family, in residences.

Program Details • Program offered once per year. Session length: 7 weeks. Departures are scheduled in June. The program is open to undergraduate students, graduate students, adults. Most participants are 19–28 years of age. Other requirements: intermediate-level Russian or target language. 1-3 participant per session. Application deadline: March 1.

Costs • $3400 (includes tuition, housing, some meals, books and class materials, insurance, excursions, visa processing fee, mandatory orientation in Washington, DC). Application fee: $35. A $500 deposit is required.

Contact • Margaret Stephenson, Program Officer, ACTR/ACCELS, 1776 Massachusetts Avenue, NW, Suite 700, Washington, DC 20036; 202-833-7522; Fax: 202-833-7523; E-mail: stephens@actr.org

KAZAKHSTAN

 **ACTR/ACCELS**

CIS REGIONAL LANGUAGE TRAINING PROGRAM–KAZAKHSTAN

General Information • Language study program in Kazakhstan. Excursions to museums, churches, sites of historical interest.

Learning Focus • Courses in language study, Russian language, history, literature, cultural studies.

Accommodations • Homestays, dormitories. Single rooms are available. Meals are taken on one's own, with host family, in residences.

Program Details • Program offered once per year. Session length: 7 weeks. Departures are scheduled in June. The program is open to undergraduate students, graduate students, adults. Most participants are 19–28 years of age. Other requirements: intermediate-level Russian or target language. 1–3 participant per session. Application deadline: March 1.

Costs • $3400 (includes tuition, housing, some meals, books and class materials, insurance, excursions, visa processing fee, mandatory orientation in Washington, DC). Application fee: $35. A $500 deposit is required.

Contact • Margaret Stephenson, Program Officer, ACTR/ACCELS, 1776 Massachusetts Avenue, NW, Suite 700, Washington, DC 20036; 202-833-7522; Fax: 202-833-7523; E-mail: stephens@actr.org

KYRGYZSTAN

ACTR/ACCELS

CIS REGIONAL LANGUAGE TRAINING PROGRAM–KYRGYZSTAN

General Information • Language study program in Kyrgyzstan. Excursions to museums, churches, sites of historical interest.

Learning Focus • Courses in language study, Russian language, history, literature, cultural studies.

Accommodations • Homestays, dormitories. Single rooms are available. Meals are taken on one's own, with host family, in residences.

Program Details • Program offered once per year. Session length: 7 weeks. Departures are scheduled in June. The program is open to undergraduate students, graduate students, adults. Most participants are 19–28 years of age. Other requirements: intermediate-level Russian or target language. 1–3 participant per session. Application deadline: March 1.

Costs • $3400 (includes tuition, housing, some meals, books and class materials, insurance, excursions, visa processing fee, mandatory orientation in Washington, DC). Application fee: $35. A $500 deposit is required.

Contact • Margaret Stephenson, Program Officer, ACTR/ACCELS, 1776 Massachusetts Avenue, NW, Suite 700, Washington, DC 20036; 202-833-7522; Fax: 202-833-7523; E-mail: stephens@actr.org

MONGOLIA

GLOBAL EXCHANGE REALITY TOURS

MONGOLIA

General Information • Cultural tour with visits to Ulan Bator. Once at the destination country, participants travel by bus, airplane.

Learning Focus • Escorted travel to Mongolian countryside. Museum visits (National Art Museum, National History Museum). Instruction is offered by researchers, naturalists.

Accommodations • Hotels, guest houses. Single rooms are available for an additional $200–$500.

Program Details • Program offered once per year. Session length: 15 days. Departures are scheduled in July. Program is targeted to seniors, students and professionals. Participants must be 18 years or older to enroll. 8 participants per session. Application deadline: 1 month prior to departure. Reservations are recommended at least 2 months before departure.

Costs • $3000–$3300 (includes housing, some meals, books and class materials, international airfare, visa acquisition fees for China and Mongolia). A $200 deposit is required.

Contact • Reality Tours Coordinator, Global Exchange Reality Tours, 2017 Mission Street, Room 303, San Francisco, CA 94110; 415-255-7296; Fax: 415-255-7498; E-mail: globalexch@igc.apc.org

PAKISTAN

JOURNEYS EAST

PASSAGE TO PAKISTAN

General Information • Wilderness/adventure program with visits to Hindu Kush, Islamabad, Lahore. Once at the destination country, participants travel by foot, airplane, jeep.
Learning Focus • Escorted travel to off the beaten track spots. Museum visits (local museums). Attendance at performances (local shows, festivals of theater, music, dance). Other activities include camping, hiking. Instruction is offered by social anthropologists. This program would appeal to people interested in trekking, cultural adventure.
Accommodations • Hotels, campsites.
Program Details • Program offered once per year. Session length: 3 weeks. Departures are scheduled in August. Program is targeted to people with culture and adventure oriented interests. Most participants are 30–70 years of age. 13 participants per session. Reservations are recommended at least 12 months before departure.
Costs • $4685 (includes housing, some meals, excursions, international airfare, museum admissions, local tips, gifts). A $300 deposit is required.
Contact • Debra Loomis, Co-Director, Journeys East, 2443 Fillmore Street, #289, San Francisco, CA 94115; 800-527-2612; Fax: 510-601-1977

PHOTO ADVENTURE TOURS

HIDDEN VALLEYS

General Information • Photography tour with visits to Gilgit, Islamabad, Lahore, Sino-Pak Highway, Swat Valley. Once at the destination country, participants travel by bus, foot, airplane, jeep.
Learning Focus • Instruction in photography. Instruction is offered by researchers, naturalists, artists, historians, photographers. This program would appeal to people interested in hiking, adventure, photography, history, culture, ornithology, geology.
Accommodations • Hotels, campsites. Single rooms are available for an additional $675.
Program Details • Program offered once per year. Session length: 19 days. Departures are scheduled in August. Most participants are 18–80 years of age. Participants must be 18 years or older to enroll. Other requirements: good health. 12 participants per session.
Costs • $3950 (includes housing, all meals, excursions, international airfare). A $400 deposit is required.
Contact • Richard Libbey, General Partner, Photo Adventure Tours, 2035 Park Street, Atlantic Beach, NY 11509-1236; 516-371-0067; Fax: 516-371-1352

RUSSIA

ACTR/ACCELS

ADVANCED RUSSIAN LANGUAGE AND AREA STUDIES PROGRAM

General Information • Language study program in Moscow, St. Petersburg. Classes are held on the campus of Moscow State University, Moscow State Linguistic University, International University of Moscow, Russian State Pedagogical University.
Learning Focus • Courses in Russian language, Russian and Soviet culture, history, political science, literature. Instruction is offered by local teachers.
Accommodations • Homestays, dormitories. Meals are taken on one's own, with host family, in residences.
Program Details • Program offered once per year. Session length: 7 weeks. Departures are scheduled in June. The program is open to undergraduate students, graduate students, adults. Most participants are 18–28 years of age. Other requirements: two years college-level Russian language required. 45 participants per session. Application deadline: March 1.
Costs • $4450 (includes tuition, housing, some meals, books and class materials, insurance, excursions, international airfare, visa processing fee, mandatory orientation in Washington, DC). Application fee: $35. A $500 deposit is required.
Contact • Margaret Stephenson, Program Officer, ACTR/ACCELS, 1776 Massachusetts Avenue, NW, Suite 700, Washington, DC 20036; 202-833-7522; Fax: 202-833-7523; E-mail: stephens@actr.org

ALPINE ASCENTS, INTERNATIONAL

MOUNT ELBRUS EXPEDITION

General Information • Mountain climbing tour with visits to Mount Elbrus, St. Petersburg. Once at the destination country, participants travel by bus, foot, tram.
Learning Focus • Instruction in mountain climbing. Escorted travel to Baksan Valley and Priut Hut. Museum visits (Hermitage Museum). Nature observation (Caucasus Mountain Range). Other activities include camping, hiking. Instruction is offered by sports professionals. This program would appeal to people interested in mountain climbing.
Accommodations • Hotels, campsites. Single rooms are available.
Program Details • Program offered once per year. Session length: 15 days. Departures are scheduled in July. Program is targeted to mountain climbers. Other requirements: excellent physical condition. Reservations are recommended at least 6 months before departure.
Costs • $2600 (includes housing, some meals, group equipment, guides, fees). A $700 deposit is required.
Contact • Gordon Janow, Program Coordinator, Alpine Ascents, International, 16615 Saybrook Drive, Woodinville, WA 98072; 206-788-1951; Fax: 206-788-6757; E-mail: aaiclimb@accessone.com

AMERICAN INSTITUTE FOR FOREIGN STUDY (AIFS)

PROGRAM AT ST. PETERSBURG STATE TECHNICAL UNIVERSITY

General Information • Language study program in St. Petersburg. Classes are held on the campus of St. Petersburg State Insitute of Technology. Excursions to Moscow.
Learning Focus • Courses in Russian language, contemporary life in Russia.
Accommodations • Dormitories.
Program Details • Program offered once per year. Session length: 5 weeks. Departures are scheduled in June. The program is open to undergraduate students, graduate students, adults, high school graduates. Other requirements: minimum 2.0 GPA. Application deadline: March 15.
Costs • $2879 (includes tuition, housing, all meals). A $400 deposit is required.
Contact • Carmela Vigliano, Director, Summer Programs, American Institute for Foreign Study (AIFS), 102 Greenwich Avenue, Greenwich, CT 06830; 800-727-2437, ext. 6087; Fax: 203-869-9615; E-mail: info@aifs.org

APPALACHIAN STATE UNIVERSITY

RUSSIA

General Information • Academic study program in Moscow. Classes are held on the campus of Pushkin Institute of Russian Language. Excursions to St. Petersburg.
Learning Focus • Courses in Russian language. Instruction is offered by professors from the sponsoring institution.
Program Details • Program offered once per year. Session length: 4–5 weeks. Departures are scheduled in May. Most participants are 18 years of age and older. 20 participants per session.
Costs • $3000 (includes tuition, housing, insurance, international airfare, International Student Identification card).
Contact • Dr. Grigory Roytman, Professor, Appalachian State University, Department of Foreign Languages, Boone, NC 28608; 704-262-3095; Fax: 704-262-4037

BOSTON UNIVERSITY

ST. PETERSBURG INTENSIVE RUSSIAN PROGRAM

General Information • Language study program in St. Petersburg. Classes are held on the campus of Gorny Institute. Excursions to Moscow.

Learning Focus • Courses in Russian language. Instruction is offered by local teachers.

Accommodations • Dormitories. Meals are taken as a group, on one's own, in central dining facility.

Program Details • Program offered once per year. Session length: 4 weeks. Departures are scheduled in July. The program is open to undergraduate students, adults. Most participants are 19–22 years of age. Other requirements: minimum 3.0 GPA, good academic standing, 4 semesters college-level Russian language and an interview. 6 participants per session. Application deadline: March 15.

Costs • $2100 (includes tuition, housing, all meals, excursions). Application fee: $35. A $300 deposit is required.

Contact • Division of International Programs, Boston University, 232 Bay State Road, Boston, MA 02215; 617-353-9888; Fax: 617-353-5402; E-mail: abroad@bu.edu; World Wide Web: http://web.bu.edu/abroad

COLLEGE CONSORTIUM FOR INTERNATIONAL STUDIES–TRUMAN STATE UNIVERSITY

SUMMER STUDY ABROAD PROGRAM IN MOSCOW, RUSSIA

General Information • Language study program in Moscow. Classes are held on the campus of Institute of Youth.

Learning Focus • Courses in history, music, political science, Russian language. Instruction is offered by local teachers.

Accommodations • Dormitories. Single rooms are available. Meals are taken in central dining facility.

Program Details • Program offered 3 times per year. Session length: 8 weeks. Departures are scheduled in April–June. The program is open to undergraduate students, pre-college students, adults. Most participants are 20–30 years of age. Other requirements: minimum 2.5 GPA. 5 participants per session. Application deadline: March 15, April 15, May 15.

Costs • $3595 (includes tuition, housing, all meals, books and class materials, excursions, international airfare).

Live and study in Russia

Russia offers the legacy of its rich history while in the midst of the tremendous challenges of transition to a free market economy. There is no better time to experience history in the making. Study Russian at beginning to advanced levels at St. Petersburg State Technical University. A course on contemporary Russian life is offered in English. During the five weeks, you live in two-room suites with kitchenette and private bath. Three days are spent on a field trip to Moscow. The AIFS Resident Director coordinates excursions and activities to take advantage of the art collections, ballet, thriving music scene and other cultural offerings in this city of baroque splendors, palaces and riverside parks.

American Institute For Foreign Study®
Dept. PLA 102 Greenwich Ave.
Greenwich, CT 06830
Phone (800) 727-2437
E-mail info@aifs.org
http://www.aifs.org

Contact • Jane C. Evans, Executive Director, College Consortium for International Studies, 2000 P Street, NW, Suite 503, Washington, DC 20036; 800-453-6956; Fax: 202-223-0999; E-mail: ccis@intr.net

COLLEGE OF ST. SCHOLASTICA

RUSSIAN LANGUAGE CAMP

General Information • Language study program in Petrozavodsk. Classes are held on the campus of Karelian Pedagogical University. Excursions to St. Petersburg, Moscow.

Learning Focus • Courses in Russian language. Instruction is offered by local teachers.

Accommodations • Dormitories. Meals are taken as a group, in central dining facility.

Program Details • Program offered once per year. Session length: 5 weeks. Departures are scheduled in June. The program is open to undergraduate students, graduate students, pre-college students, adults, selected high school students. Most participants are 18–55 years of age. Other requirements: interview with American director. 20 participants per session. Application deadline: April 1.

Costs • $2995 (includes tuition, housing, all meals, books and class materials, insurance, excursions, international airfare). A $50 deposit is required.

Contact • Dr. Thomas Morgan, Associate Professor, College of St. Scholastica, 1200 Kenwood, Duluth, MN 55811; 218-723-6442; Fax: 218-723-6290; E-mail: tmorgan@fac1.ess.edu; World Wide Web: http://www.css.edu

COUNCIL ON INTERNATIONAL EDUCATIONAL EXCHANGE

RUSSIAN LANGUAGE FOR RESEARCH PROGRAM AT ST. PETERSBURG STATE UNIVERSITY

General Information • Language study program in St. Petersburg. Classes are held on the campus of St. Petersburg State University.

Learning Focus • Courses in Russian language, Russian studies, literature. Instruction is offered by local teachers.

Accommodations • Homestays, dormitories. Single rooms are available. Meals are taken as a group, on one's own, with host family, in central dining facility, in residences.

Program Details • Program offered once per year. Session length: 7 weeks. Departures are scheduled in June. The program is open to graduate students. Most participants are 25–35 years of age. Other requirements: graduate students with 3 years college-level Russian. 7 participants per session. Application deadline: April 1.

Costs • $4250 (includes tuition, housing, all meals, books and class materials, insurance, excursions, visa, International Student Identification Card). Application fee: $30. A $300 deposit is required.
Contact • Information Center, Council on International Educational Exchange, 205 East 42nd Street, New York, NY 10017-5706; 888-268-6245; E-mail: info@ciee.org; World Wide Web: http://www.ciee.org

COUNCIL ON INTERNATIONAL EDUCATIONAL EXCHANGE

RUSSIAN LANGUAGE PROGRAM AT ST. PETERSBURG STATE UNIVERSITY

General Information • Language study program in St. Petersburg. Classes are held on the campus of St. Petersburg State University. Excursions to Moscow.
Learning Focus • Courses in Russian language, Russian studies, literature. Instruction is offered by local teachers.
Accommodations • Homestays, dormitories. Single rooms are available. Meals are taken as a group, with host family, in central dining facility, in residences.
Program Details • Program offered once per year. Session length: 8 weeks. Departures are scheduled in June. The program is open to undergraduate students, graduate students. Most participants are 20–40 years of age. Other requirements: minimum 2.75 GPA and 2 years college-level Russian. 30 participants per session. Application deadline: April 1.
Costs • $3975 (includes tuition, housing, all meals, books and class materials, insurance, excursions, International Student Identification card, visa, orientation). Application fee: $30. A $300 deposit is required.
Contact • Information Center, Council on International Educational Exchange, 205 East 42nd Street, New York, NY 10017-5706; 888-268-6245; Fax: 212-822-2699; E-mail: info@ciee.org; World Wide Web: http://www.ciee.org

COUNCIL ON INTERNATIONAL EDUCATIONAL EXCHANGE

RUSSIAN LANGUAGE PROGRAM IN THE NATURAL AND SOCIAL SCIENCES AT NOVOSIBIRSK STATE UNIVERSITY

General Information • Language study program in Novosibirsk. Classes are held on the campus of Novosibirsk State University. Excursions to Moscow, Siberia.
Learning Focus • Courses in Russian language, Russian studies. Instruction is offered by local teachers.
Accommodations • Dormitories. Meals are taken as a group, in central dining facility.
Program Details • Program offered once per year. Session length: 8 weeks. Departures are scheduled in June. The program is open to undergraduate students, graduate students. Most participants are 20–35 years of age. Other requirements: minimum 2.75 GPA and 2 years college-level Russian. 15 participants per session. Application deadline: April 1.
Costs • $3995 (includes tuition, housing, all meals, books and class materials, insurance, excursions, visa, airfare Moscow-Novosibirsk-Moscow, International Student Identification card). Application fee: $30. A $300 deposit is required.
Contact • Information Center, Council on International Educational Exchange, 205 East 42nd Street, New York, NY 10017-5706; 888-268-6245; Fax: 212-822-2699; E-mail: info@ciee.org; World Wide Web: http://www.ciee.org

COUNCIL ON INTERNATIONAL EDUCATIONAL EXCHANGE

SUMMER RUSSIAN BUSINESS PROGRAM AT ST. PETERSBURG STATE UNIVERSITY

General Information • Academic study program in St. Petersburg. Classes are held on the campus of St. Petersburg State University. Excursions to Moscow.
Learning Focus • Courses in Russian language, economics, business. Instruction is offered by local teachers.
Accommodations • Dormitories. Meals are taken as a group, in central dining facility.
Program Details • Program offered once per year. Session length: 8 weeks. Departures are scheduled in June. The program is open to undergraduate students, graduate students, adults. Most participants are 20–35 years of age. Other requirements: minimum 2.75 GPA and a basic business background. 7 participants per session. Application deadline: April 1.
Costs • $4295 (includes tuition, housing, all meals, books and class materials, insurance, excursions, visa, orientation, International Student Identification card). Application fee: $30. A $300 deposit is required.
Contact • Information Center, Council on International Educational Exchange, 205 East 42nd Street, New York, NY 10017-5706; 888-268-6245; Fax: 212-822-2699; E-mail: info@ciee.org; World Wide Web: http://www.ciee.org

DICKINSON COLLEGE

MOSCOW SUMMER IMMERSION PROGRAM

General Information • Language study program in Moscow.
Learning Focus • Courses in Russian language, Russian culture. Instruction is offered by professors from the sponsoring institution.
Accommodations • Dormitories. Single rooms are available. Meals are taken as a group, in local restaurants.
Program Details • Program offered once per year. Session length: 6 weeks. Departures are scheduled in May. The program is open to undergraduate students. Most participants are 18–20 years of age. Other requirements: intermediate-level Russian. 18 participants per session. Application deadline: February 15.
Costs • $3600 (includes tuition, housing, all meals, books and class materials, excursions, international airfare). Application fee: $15. A $300 deposit is required.
Contact • Dr. John S. Henderson, Director of Off-Campus Studies, Dickinson College, PO Box 1773, Carlisle, PA 17013-2896; 717-245-1341; Fax: 717-245-1688; E-mail: ocs@dickinson.edu; World Wide Web: http://www.dickinson.edu

 DUKE UNIVERSITY

DUKE IN RUSSIA

General Information • Academic study program in St. Petersburg. Classes are held on the campus of St. Petersburg University. Excursions to Estonia (Thalinn), Moscow.
Learning Focus • Courses in language study, cultural studies. Instruction is offered by local teachers.
Accommodations • Locally-rented apartments. Meals are taken as a group, in residences.
Program Details • Program offered once per year. Session length: 6 weeks. Departures are scheduled in May. The program is open to undergraduate students, graduate students. Most participants are 19–25 years of age. Other requirements: minimum 2.7 GPA and 2 semesters of college-level Russian or equivalent. 15 participants per session. Application deadline: February 21.
Costs • $5141 (includes tuition, housing, all meals, excursions, international airfare, visa fee).
Contact • Foreign Academic Programs, Duke University, 121 Allen Building, Box 90057, Durham, NC 27708-0057; 919-684-2174; Fax: 919-684-3083; E-mail: abroad@mail01.adm.duke.edu; World Wide Web: http://www.mis.duke.edu/study_abroad/study_abroad.html

 EASTERN MICHIGAN UNIVERSITY

LABOR STUDIES IN MOSCOW

General Information • Academic study program in Moscow. Classes are held on the campus of Academy of Labor and Social Relations. Excursions to St. Petersburg.
Learning Focus • Courses in economics, labor history. Instruction is offered by professors from the sponsoring institution.
Accommodations • Dormitories. Meals are taken as a group, in central dining facility.
Program Details • Program offered once per year. Session length: 4 weeks. Departures are scheduled in May. The program is open to undergraduate students, graduate students. Most participants are 18–35 years of age. Other requirements: minimum 2.0 GPA and 18 years of age. 10 participants per session. Application deadline: March 1.
Costs • $2995 (includes tuition, housing, all meals, insurance, excursions, international airfare). A $150 deposit is required.
Contact • Academic Programs Abroad, Eastern Michigan University, 332 Goodison Hall, Ypsilanti, MI 48197; 800-777-3541; Fax: 313-487-2316; E-mail: programs.abroad@emich.edu; World Wide Web: http://www.emich.edu/public/cont_ed/abroad.html

THE EDUCATED TRAVELER

THE EDUCATED TRAVELER'S RUSSIA

General Information • Cultural tour with visits to Moscow, St. Petersburg. Once at the destination country, participants travel by bus, foot.
Learning Focus • Escorted travel to Moscow, Zagorsk and St. Petersburg. Museum visits (Trojan Gold Exhibit, Hermitage). Attendance at performances (Kirov [Mariinsky] and Bolshoi). Other activities include behind-the-scenes visits to artisans' workshops, music conservatories. Instruction is offered by artists, historians, curators. This program would appeal to people interested in art, history, museums, culture.
Accommodations • Hotels. Single rooms are available.
Program Details • Program offered once per year. Session length: 10 days. Departures are scheduled in March. Program is targeted to experienced adult travelers. Most participants are 40–75 years of age. 15–20 participants per session. Application deadline: 3 months prior to departure. Reservations are recommended at least 6 months before departure.
Costs • $3495 (includes housing, some meals, excursions). A $700 deposit is required.
Contact • Ann Waigand, The Educated Traveler, PO Box 220822, Chantilly, VA 22022; 800-648-5168; Fax: 703-471-4807; E-mail: edtrav@aol.com

 EUROCENTRES

LANGUAGE IMMERSION IN RUSSIA

General Information • Language study program in Moscow. Classes are held on the campus of Eurocentre Moscow Summer Centre. Excursions to Golden Ring towns, St. Petersburg.
Learning Focus • Courses in Russian language, Russian culture. Instruction is offered by professors from the sponsoring institution.
Accommodations • Homestays. Single rooms are available. Meals are taken with host family, in residences.
Program Details • Program offered 20 times per year. Session length: 2–12 weeks. Departures are scheduled in January–December. The program is open to undergraduate students, graduate students, pre-college students, adults. Most participants are 16–80 years of age. 15 participants per session.
Costs • Contact sponsor for information.
Contact • Marketing, Eurocentres, 101 North Union Street, Suite 300, Alexandria, VA 22314; 800-648-4809; Fax: 703-684-1495; E-mail: 100632.141@compuserve.com; World Wide Web: http://www.clark.net/pub/eurocent/home.htm

FINDHORN COLLEGE OF INTERNATIONAL EDUCATION

RUSSIAN ECOLOGY FIELD PROGRAM

General Information • Academic study program in Ural Mountains. Classes are held on the campus of Institute of Ecology. Excursions to Moscow, St. Petersburg.
Learning Focus • Courses in ecology, environmental studies, biology, archaeology, anthropology, paleontology. Instruction is offered by local teachers.
Accommodations • Field camp. Meals are taken as a group, in central dining facility.
Program Details • Program offered 2 times per year. Session length: 4–6 weeks. Departures are scheduled in July, August. The program is open to undergraduate students, graduate students, pre-college students, adults. Most participants are 18–30 years of age. 40 participants per session. Application deadline: rolling.
Costs • $3900–$4800 (includes tuition, housing, all meals, excursions). A $500 deposit is required.

Contact • Director of Admissions, Findhorn College of International Education, Box 1393, Boston, MA 02117; 800-932-7658; Fax: 800-932-7658; E-mail: admissions@highland-uk.org

FOREIGN LANGUAGE STUDY ABROAD SERVICE

INTERNATIONAL LANGUAGE STUDY HOMESTAYS IN RUSSIA

General Information • Language study program in Russia.
Learning Focus • Courses in Russian language. Instruction is offered by local teachers.
Accommodations • Homestays. Single rooms are available. Meals are taken with host family, in residences.
Program Details • Session length: varies. Departures are scheduled in January–December. The program is open to undergraduate students, graduate students, pre-college students, adults. Most participants are 12 years of age and older. Other requirements: students must be at least 12 years old. 1 participant per session.
Costs • Contact sponsor for information. A $300 deposit is required.
Contact • Louise Harber, Coordinator, Foreign Language Study Abroad Service, Department IH, Box 903, 5935 Southwest 64th Avenue, South Miami, FL 33143; 800-282-1090; Fax: 305-662-2907; E-mail: flsas@netpoint.net; World Wide Web: http://www.netpoint.net/~flsas

GEORGETOWN UNIVERSITY

SUMMER IN ST. PETERSBURG

General Information • Language study program in St. Petersburg. Classes are held on the campus of Gorny Institute. Excursions to Moscow.
Learning Focus • Courses in Russian language, literature, phonetics, grammar, Russian affairs. Instruction is offered by professors from the sponsoring institution and local teachers.
Accommodations • Dormitories. Single rooms are available. Meals are taken as a group, on one's own, in central dining facility, in local restaurants.
Program Details • Program offered once per year. Session length: 7 weeks. Departures are scheduled in June. The program is open to undergraduate students, graduate students, adults. Most participants are 18–25 years of age. Other requirements: minimum 3.0 GPA and Russian language study. 12 participants per session. Application deadline: March.
Costs • $3975 (includes tuition, housing, all meals, books and class materials, insurance, excursions). A $500 deposit is required.
Contact • Dr. Valentina Brougher, Director, Georgetown University, Russian Department-434ICC, Washington, DC 20057; 202-687-6147; Fax: 202-687-5712; World Wide Web: http://guweb.georgetown.edu/ssce

ILLINOIS STATE UNIVERSITY

CRIME AND CRIMINAL JUSTICE IN RUSSIA

General Information • Academic study program in Vladimir.
Learning Focus • Courses in criminal justice.
Accommodations • Hotels.
Program Details • Program offered once per year. Session length: 2 weeks. Departures are scheduled in May. The program is open to undergraduate students, graduate students, adults, teachers and professionals. Other requirements: minimum 2.5 GPA and a minimum of sophomore status. 15 participants per session. Application deadline: March 15.
Costs • $2400 (includes housing, all meals, excursions, international airfare).
Contact • Dr. Frank Morn, Illinois State University, Campus Box 5250, Normal, IL 61790-5250; 309-438-7853; Fax: 309-438-3987; E-mail: oisp@rs6000.cmp.ilstu.edu; World Wide Web: http://www.orat.ilstu.edu/

ILLINOIS STATE UNIVERSITY

RUSSIA SUMMER PROGRAM

General Information • Academic study program in Vladimir. Classes are held on the campus of Vladimir State Technical University.
Learning Focus • Courses in industrial technology.
Accommodations • Homestays.
Program Details • Program offered once per year. Session length: 3 weeks. Departures are scheduled in May. The program is open to undergraduate students, graduate students. Other requirements: minimum 2.5 GPA, industrial technology major and a minimum of sophomore status. 15 participants per session. Application deadline: March 15.
Costs • $2600 (includes tuition, housing, some meals, insurance, excursions, international airfare).
Contact • Dr. Ed Francis, Illinois State University, Campus Box 6120, Normal, IL 61790-6120; 309-438-5365; Fax: 309-438-3987; E-mail: oisp@rs6000.cmp.ilstu.edu; World Wide Web: http://www.orat.ilstu.edu/

LANGUAGE LIAISON

LIVE 'N' LEARN (LEARN IN A TEACHER'S HOME)–RUSSIA

General Information • Language study program with visits to Russia.
Learning Focus • Instruction in the Russian language. Instruction is offered by professors. This program would appeal to people interested in language.
Accommodations • Homestays. Single rooms are available.
Program Details • Session length: unlimited. Departures are scheduled throughout the year. Most participants are 18–70 years of age. Participants must be 16 years or older to enroll. Reservations are recommended at least 35 days before departure.
Costs • Contact sponsor for information.
Contact • Nancy Forman, President, Language Liaison, 20533 Biscayne Boulevard-Station 4-162, Miami, FL 33180; 305-682-9909; Fax: 305-682-9907; E-mail: langstudy@aol.com; World Wide Web: http://languageliaison.com

LOS ANGELES COMMUNITY COLLEGE DISTRICT

RUSSIAN CIVILIZATION

General Information • Academic and language study program in St. Petersburg. Classes are held on the campus of St. Petersburg State University. Excursions to Moscow.
Learning Focus • Courses in Russian language, Russian civilization. Instruction is offered by professors from the sponsoring institution and local teachers.
Accommodations • Dormitories. Single rooms are available. Meals are taken as a group, in central dining facility.
Program Details • Program offered once per year. Session length: 4 weeks. Departures are scheduled in June, July. The program is open to undergraduate students, pre-college students, adults. Most participants are 17–60 years of age. 12 participants per session. Application deadline: May 1.
Costs • $2129 (includes tuition, housing, insurance, excursions, international airfare). A $400 deposit is required.
Contact • International Education Program, Los Angeles Community College District, 770 Wilshire Boulevard, Los Angeles, CA 90017; 213-891-2282; Fax: 213-891-2150; E-mail: intered@laccd.cc.ca.us; World Wide Web: http://laccd.cc.ca.us

MARINE EXPEDITIONS

THE RUSSIAN FAR EAST

General Information • Wilderness/adventure program with visits to Russian Far East, Wrangel Island, archaeological sites, areas of high wildlife concentration. Once at the destination country, participants travel by boat.
Learning Focus • Instruction in biology and ornithology. Field research in history. Escorted travel to the Arakamchechin Archipelego, Whale Bone Alley and Wrangell Island. Nature observation (whales, polar bears, seabirds, walruses, muskoxen). Instruction is offered by naturalists, historians, scientists. This program would appeal to people interested in nature studies, photography, ornithology.
Accommodations • Boat. Single rooms are available.
Program Details • Program offered 2 times per year. Session length: 1 week. Departures are scheduled in July. Most participants are 20–90 years of age. Participants must be 10 years or older to enroll. 80 participants per session. Reservations are recommended at least 6 months before departure.
Costs • $1995 (includes tuition, housing, all meals, excursions, international airfare). A $500 deposit is required.
Contact • Anne Lex, Sales Manager, Marine Expeditions, 13 Hazelton Avenue, Toronto, ON M5R 2E1, Canada; 800-263-9147; Fax: 416-964-9069

MOSCOW INSTITUTE FOR ADVANCED STUDIES

STUDY IN RUSSIA

General Information • Academic study program in Moscow. Classes are held on the campus of International University of Moscow. Excursions to Novgorod, St. Petersburg, Tallinn, Sergeev-Posad, Ukraine (Kiev), Sochi.
Learning Focus • Courses in Russian language, political science, international affairs, arts, Russian literature, history, economics, cultural studies. Instruction is offered by professors from the sponsoring institution and local teachers.
Accommodations • Homestays, dormitories. Single rooms are available. Meals are taken as a group, in central dining facility.
Program Details • Program offered once per year. Session length: 8 weeks. Departures are scheduled in June. The program is open to undergraduate students, graduate students, pre-college students, adults. Other requirements: minimum 3.0 GPA. Application deadline: May 7.
Costs • $3900 (includes tuition, housing, all meals, books and class materials, excursions). Application fee: $20. A $250 deposit is required.
Contact • Moscow Institute for Advanced Studies, 152 West 57th Street, 49th Floor, New York, NY 10019; 212-245-0461; Fax: 212-489-4829; E-mail: mifas@panix.com

MOUNTAIN MADNESS

MOUNT ELBRUS

General Information • Wilderness/adventure program with visits to Caucasus Mountains, Moscow. Once at the destination country, participants travel by bus, foot, airplane.
Learning Focus • Escorted travel to summit of Mount Elbrus. Other activities include camping, hiking. Instruction is offered by naturalists, sports professionals, professional mountaineering guides. This program would appeal to people interested in climbing, photography.
Accommodations • Hotels, campsites, mountain huts. Single rooms are available.
Program Details • Program offered once per year. Session length: 10 days. Departures are scheduled in August. Most participants are 25–50 years of age. Participants must be 16 years or older to enroll. Other requirements: some climbing experience is recommended. 4–6 participants per session. Reservations are recommended at least 60 days before departure.
Costs • $2400 (includes housing, some meals, guides). A $1000 deposit is required.
Contact • Manomi Fernando, Program Coordinator, Mountain Madness, 4218 Southwest Alaska Street #206, Seattle, WA 98116; 206-937-8389; Fax: 206-937-1772; E-mail: mountmad@aol.com

NATIONAL REGISTRATION CENTER FOR STUDY ABROAD

EUROCENTRE: RUSSIA

General Information • Language study program in Moscow.
Learning Focus • Courses in Russian language.
Accommodations • Homestays, dormitories. Single rooms are available.
Program Details • Program offered 2 times per year. Session length: 4 weeks. Departures are scheduled in July. The program is open to undergraduate students, graduate students, adults. 7–10 participants per session. Application deadline: 2 months prior to departure.
Costs • $1230 (includes tuition, housing, some meals, insurance). Application fee: $40. A $100 deposit is required.
Contact • Reuel Zielke, Coordinator, National Registration Center for Study Abroad, 823 North Second Street,

Milwaukee, WI 53203; 414-351-6311; Fax: 414-271-8884; E-mail: inquiries@nrcsa.com; World Wide Web: http://www.nrcsa.com

NATIONAL REGISTRATION CENTER FOR STUDY ABROAD

LANGUAGE STUDIES IN RUSSIA

General Information • Language study program in Moscow, St. Petersburg.
Learning Focus • Courses in Russian language.
Accommodations • Homestays, dormitories. Single rooms are available. Meals are taken with host family.
Program Details • Program offered 2 times per year. Session length: 4 weeks. Departures are scheduled in July. The program is open to undergraduate students, graduate students, adults. 7–10 participants per session. Application deadline: 40 days prior to departure.
Costs • $965 (includes tuition, housing, some meals, insurance). Application fee: $40. A $100 deposit is required.
Contact • Reuel Zielke, Coordinator, National Registration Center for Study Abroad, 823 North Second Street, Milwaukee, WI 53203; 414-278-0631; Fax: 414-271-8884; E-mail: quest@nrcsa.com; World Wide Web: http://www.nrcsa.com

OUACHITA BAPTIST UNIVERSITY

RUSSIAN STUDY PROGRAM

General Information • Academic study program in Moscow, St. Petersburg. Classes are held on the campus of Moscow State University. Excursions to England (London).
Learning Focus • Courses in Russian language, Russian history, Russian culture, Russian economy. Instruction is offered by professors from the sponsoring institution.
Accommodations • Dormitories. Single rooms are available. Meals are taken as a group, in central dining facility.
Program Details • Program offered once per year. Session length: 4 weeks. Departures are scheduled in June. The program is open to undergraduate students. Most participants are 18–23 years of age. Other requirements: 2.5 minimum GPA. 10 participants per session. Application deadline: April 1.
Costs • $2850 (includes tuition, housing, some meals, excursions, international airfare). A $500 deposit is required.
Contact • Dr. Trey Berry, Director of International Programs, Ouachita Baptist University, OBU Box 3777, Arkadelphia, AR 71998; 501-245-5197; Fax: 501-245-5312; E-mail: berryt@alpha.obu.edu; World Wide Web: http://www.obu.edu

RUSSIAN AND EAST EUROPEAN PARTNERSHIPS

RUSSIAN LANGUAGE AND CULTURAL IMMERSION PROGRAM

General Information • Language study program in St. Petersburg. Classes are held on the campus of Economic Information. Excursions to Moscow, Novgorod.

Learning Focus • Courses in Russian language, Russian culture and art, Russian history. Instruction is offered by professors from the sponsoring institution and local teachers.

Accommodations • Homestays, locally-rented apartments. Single rooms are available. Meals are taken on one's own, with host family, in local restaurants, in residences.

Program Details • Program offered 11 times per year. Session length: 4 or more weeks. Departures are scheduled in January–November. The program is open to undergraduate students, graduate students, adults. Most participants are 18 years of age and older. Other requirements: in good health and 18 or older unless chaperoned by an adult. 6 participants per session. Application deadline: 45 days prior to departure.

Costs • $2895 (includes tuition, housing, some meals, books and class materials, excursions, international airfare, local transportation, airport transfers). A $1500 deposit is required.

Contact • Kenneth Fortune, President, Russian and East European Partnerships, PO Box 227, Fineview, NY 13640; 888-873-7337; Fax: 800-910-1777; E-mail: reep@fox.nstn.ca

RUSSIAN NATURE RESERVE EXPEDITIONS

IN THE TRACKS OF THE SIBERIAN TIGER, AMUR LEOPARD, AND USSURI BLACK BEAR

General Information • Nature study tour with visits to Kabarousk, Vladivostok, Sikhole-Alin Biosphere Reserve, Kedrovaya Pad Nature Reserve, Lazovsky Natural Reserve. Once at the destination country, participants travel by train, bus, foot, boat, airplane. Program is affiliated with Siberian Tiger Project and Siberian Forest Protection Project.

Learning Focus • Field research in nature reserves and protected areas. Nature observation (Siberian tigers, Amur leopards, Ussuri black bears, cranes). Instruction is offered by researchers. This program would appeal to people interested in zoology, botany, photography, tracking.

Accommodations • Homestays, campsites, bunkhouses.

Program Details • Program offered 3 times per year. Session length: 2 weeks. Departures are scheduled in July, August. Program is targeted to nature lovers, seniors, and students. Most participants are 22–75 years of age. Participants must be 18 years or older to enroll. Other

requirements: reasonably good health. 10–12 participants per session. Application deadline: June 10. Reservations are recommended at least 3–4 months before departure.
Costs • $3850 (includes housing, all meals, excursions, international airfare, interpreters). A $500 deposit is required.
Contact • Steven Levin, Owner, Russian Nature Reserve Expeditions, Gates Mountain Road, HC 63 Box 396, South Acworth, NH 03607-7713; 800-304-6369; Fax: 603-835-6369; E-mail: runatrvl@sover.net; World Wide Web: http://www.babushka.com

SAGA HOLIDAYS (ROAD SCHOLAR PROGRAM)

ROAD SCHOLAR: PAINTINGS AND PALACES OF ST. PETERSBURG

General Information • Cultural tour with visits to St. Petersburg, Moscow. Once at the destination country, participants travel by bus. Program is affiliated with The Hermitage, Museum of History of St. Petersburg, and the Russian Museum.
Learning Focus • Instruction in paintings. Museum visits (The Hermitage, Museum of History, The Russian Museum). Instruction is offered by historians. This program would appeal to people interested in art appreciation.
Accommodations • Hotels. Single rooms are available.
Program Details • Program offered 3 times per year. Session length: 9 days. Departures are scheduled in September–November. Program is targeted to seniors. Most participants are 50–90 years of age. Participants must be 50 years or older to enroll.
Costs • $2199 (includes tuition, housing, some meals, books and class materials, insurance, excursions, international airfare).
Contact • Saga Holidays (Road Scholar Program), 222 Berkeley Street, Boston, MA 02116; 800-621-2151

SLIPPERY ROCK UNIVERSITY OF PENNSYLVANIA

RUSSIA SUMMER PROGRAM

General Information • Academic study program in Moscow, St. Petersburg.
Learning Focus • Courses in Russian society. Instruction is offered by professors from the sponsoring institution.
Accommodations • Hotels. Single rooms are available. Meals are taken as a group, in central dining facility.
Program Details • Program offered once per year. Session length: 2 weeks. Departures are scheduled in July. The program is open to undergraduate students, adults. Most participants are 18–50 years of age. Other requirements: 2.5 minimum GPA. 8–15 participants per session. Application deadline: May 1.
Costs • $4300 (includes tuition, housing, all meals, excursions, international airfare). A $100 deposit is required.
Contact • Stan Kendziorski, Director of International Studies, Slippery Rock University of Pennsylvania, 110 Eisenberg Building, Slippery Rock, PA 16057; 412-738-2603; Fax: 412-738-2959; E-mail: sjk@sruvm.sru.edu; World Wide Web: http://www.sru.edu

STATE UNIVERSITY OF NEW YORK AT BUFFALO

TVER PROGRAM OF RUSSIAN LANGUAGE AND CULTURE

General Information • Language study program in Tver. Classes are held on the campus of Tver State University. Excursions to St. Petersburg, Moscow.
Learning Focus • Courses in cultural studies, Russian history, language study, Russian literature. Instruction is offered by professors from the sponsoring institution and local teachers.
Accommodations • Homestays. Meals are taken with host family, in residences.
Program Details • Program offered once per year. Session length: 8 weeks. Departures are scheduled in May. The program is open to undergraduate students, graduate students, pre-college students, adults. Most participants are 18–26 years of age. Other requirements: minimum 2.67 GPA and must be 18 or older. 7 participants per session. Application deadline: April 15.
Costs • $1375 (includes housing, all meals). A $125 deposit is required.
Contact • Sandra J. Reinagel, Interim Study Abroad Coordinator, State University of New York at Buffalo, 210 Talbert Hall, Box 601604, Buffalo, NY 14260-1604; 716-645-3912; Fax: 716-645-6197; E-mail: studyabroad@acsu.buffalo.edu; World Wide Web: http://wings.buffalo.edu/academic/provost/intl/studyabroad

STATE UNIVERSITY OF NEW YORK COLLEGE AT BROCKPORT

NOVGOROD, RUSSIA LANGUAGE PROGRAM

General Information • Language study program in Novgorod. Classes are held on the campus of Novgorod State University. Excursions to St. Petersburg.
Learning Focus • Courses in Russian language, cultural studies. Instruction is offered by professors from the sponsoring institution.
Accommodations • Homestays, dormitories. Meals are taken as a group, with host family, in local restaurants, in residences.
Program Details • Program offered once per year. Session length: 5 weeks. Departures are scheduled in May. The program is open to undergraduate students, people seeking continuing education credit. Most participants are 19 years of age and older. Other requirements: minimum 2.5 GPA and junior or senior status. 4–12 participants per session. Application deadline: April 15.
Costs • $3000 (includes tuition, housing, some meals, insurance, excursions, international airfare, health insurance). A $100 deposit is required.
Contact • Dr. John J. Perry, Director, International Education, State University of New York College at Brockport, Rakov Center, 350 New Campus Drive, Brockport, NY 14420; 716-395-2119; Fax: 716-637-3218; World Wide Web: http://www.brockport.edu/study_abroad

UNIVERSITY OF ARIZONA

LANGUAGE AND BUSINESS INTERNSHIP PROGRAMS IN RUSSIA

General Information • Language study program in Moscow, St. Petersburg.

Learning Focus • Courses in language study. Instruction is offered by professors from the sponsoring institution.

Accommodations • Homestays, hotels. Single rooms are available. Meals are taken on one's own, with host family, in local restaurants, in residences.

Program Details • Program offered 2 times per year. Session length: 5 weeks. Departures are scheduled in May–July. The program is open to undergraduate students, graduate students, adults. Most participants are 20–35 years of age. Other requirements: minimum 2.5 GPA and sophomore standing. 35 participants per session. Application deadline: April 1.

Costs • $5200 (includes tuition, housing, all meals, international airfare). Application fee: $35. A $300 deposit is required.

Contact • Stephanie Bleecker, Center for Global Student Programs, University of Arizona, 915 North Tyndall Avenue, Tucson, AZ 85721; 520-621-4627; Fax: 520-621-4069

UNIVERSITY OF FLORIDA

MOSCOW STATE UNIVERSITY, MOSCOW, RUSSIA (RUSSIAN LANGUAGE AND CULTURE)

General Information • Language study program in Moscow. Classes are held on the campus of Moscow State University. Excursions to theaters, concert halls, museums.

Learning Focus • Courses in Russian language, Russian culture. Instruction is offered by professors from the sponsoring institution and local teachers.

Accommodations • Dormitories. Meals are taken as a group, on one's own, in central dining facility, in local restaurants.

Program Details • Program offered once per year. Session length: 4 weeks. Departures are scheduled in June. The program is open to undergraduate students, graduate students, adults. Most participants are 19–30 years of age. Other requirements: minimum 2.5 GPA. 15 participants per session. Application deadline: March 15.

Costs • $2700 (includes tuition, housing, all meals, excursions, orientation). Application fee: $200.

Contact • Overseas Studies, University of Florida, 123 Tigert Hall, PO Box 113225, Gainesville, FL 32611-3225; 352-392-5206; Fax: 352-392-5575; E-mail: overseas@nervm.nerdc.ufl.edu

UNIVERSITY OF ILLINOIS AT URBANA-CHAMPAIGN

SUMMER PROGRAM IN ST. PETERSBURG

General Information • Language study program in St. Petersburg. Classes are held on the campus of St. Petersburg State University. Excursions to Moscow, Novgorod, Baltic Republics.

Learning Focus • Courses in language study, contemporary Russian literature. Instruction is offered by local teachers.

Accommodations • Homestays, locally-rented apartments. Single rooms are available. Meals are taken on one's own, with host family, in residences.

Program Details • Program offered once per year. Session length: 8 weeks. Departures are scheduled in June. The program is open to undergraduate students, graduate students. Most participants are 20–25 years of age. Other requirements: B average, 1 year college Russian and a recommendation by most recent Russian instructor. 15 participants per session. Application deadline: March 1.

Costs • $4200 (includes tuition, housing, books and class materials, excursions, international airfare, visa processing, International Student Identification card, access to American Medical Center, medical emergency evacuation insurance). Application fee: $35. A $500 deposit is required.

Contact • Timothy Winkler, Program Coordinator, University of Illinois at Urbana-Champaign, Study Abroad Office, 910 South Fifth Street #115, Champaign, IL 61820; 800-531-4404; Fax: 217-244-0249; E-mail: ipa@uiuc.edu

UNIVERSITY OF ROCHESTER

RUSSIAN IN RUSSIA

General Information • Language study program in St. Petersburg. Classes are held on the campus of International Education Centre.

Learning Focus • Courses in Russian language. Instruction is offered by professors from the sponsoring institution and local teachers.

Accommodations • Locally-rented apartments. Meals are taken in residences.

Program Details • Program offered once per year. Session length: 4 weeks. Departures are scheduled in May. The program is open to undergraduate students, adults. Other requirements: previous Russian language study. 10 participants per session. Application deadline: March 15.

Costs • $2350 (includes tuition, housing, all meals, excursions).

Contact • Anne Lutkus, Language Coordinator, University of Rochester, Department of Modern Languages and Cultures, Rochester, NY 14627; 716-275-4251; E-mail: adlt@db1.cc.rochester.edu; World Wide Web: http://www.rochester.edu/College/study-abroad/

UNIVERSITY OF TULSA

UNIVERSITY OF TULSA IN ZELENOGRAD, RUSSIA

General Information • Academic study program in Zelenograd. Classes are held on the campus of M.I.E.T.. Excursions to Moscow, St. Petersburg.

Learning Focus • Instruction is offered by professors from the sponsoring institution.

Accommodations • Homestays. Single rooms are available. Meals are taken with host family, in residences.

Program Details • Program offered once per year. Session length: 6 weeks. Departures are scheduled in June. The program is open to undergraduate students. Most participants are 18–21 years of age. 4 participants per session. Application deadline: April 1.

Costs • $4150 (includes tuition, housing, some meals, books and class materials, excursions, international airfare). A $500 deposit is required.

Contact • Sally Luplow, Director of Study Abroad, University of Tulsa, 600 South College Avenue, TH 102, Tulsa, OK 74104-3189; 918-631-3229; Fax: 918-631-3187; E-mail: luplowsr@centum.utulsa.edu

Following the successes of previous programs, The University of Tulsa offers its 3rd Summer Program in Zelenograd, Russia. While enjoying excursions or while in their Russian homes, students experience Russian culture for 6 weeks. Participants enroll in three 3-credit courses offered in conjunction with the Moscow Institute of Technology (MIET). A 3-credit intermediate Russian language course and a Russian cultural awareness course are taken by all participants. An elective course (in a technical area if appropriate) is arranged after participants are selected. Non-TU students are admitted to the program on the bases of academic record and letters of recommendation.

VIRTUS INSTITUTE

LEARN RUSSIAN ON THE BLACK SEA (PLUS TEN DAY CRUISE)

General Information • Language study program in Sochi. Classes are held on the campus of Pushkin Institute. Excursions to Moscow, Uglich, Petrozavodsk, St. Petersburg, Belozersk, Kizhi.
Learning Focus • Courses in Russian language, Russian folk culture, economics, political science, history. Instruction is offered by local teachers.
Accommodations • Homestays, dormitories. Single rooms are available. Meals are taken as a group, with host family, in central dining facility, in residences.
Program Details • Program offered once per year. Session length: plus 10 day cruise. Departures are scheduled in June. The program is open to undergraduate students, graduate students, adults. Most participants are 18–35 years of age. 30 participants per session. Application deadline: March 15.
Costs • $5420 (includes tuition, housing, all meals, books and class materials, excursions, international airfare). A $50 deposit is required.
Contact • Joanne Walby, Program Coordinator, Virtus Institute, 2475 Virginia Avenue, NW, #520, Washington, DC 20037; 800-274-9121; Fax: 202-337-9324; E-mail: virtus@clark.net

VIRTUS INSTITUTE

LEARN RUSSIAN ON THE BLACK SEA (PLUS THREE DAY MOSCOW TOUR)

General Information • Language study program in Sochi. Classes are held on the campus of Pushkin Institute. Excursions to Moscow.
Learning Focus • Courses in Russian language, Russian folk culture, economics, political science, history. Instruction is offered by local teachers.
Accommodations • Homestays, dormitories. Single rooms are available. Meals are taken as a group, with host family, in central dining facility, in residences.
Program Details • Program offered once per year. Session length: plus 3 day Moscow tour. Departures are scheduled in June. The program is open to undergraduate students, graduate students, adults. Most participants are 18–35 years of age. 30 participants per session. Application deadline: March 15.
Costs • $4820 (includes tuition, housing, all meals, books and class materials, excursions, international airfare). A $50 deposit is required.
Contact • Joanne Walby, Program Coordinator, Virtus Institute, 2475 Virginia Avenue, NW, #520, Washington, DC 20037; 800-274-9121; Fax: 202-337-9324; E-mail: virtus@clark.net

VIRTUS INSTITUTE

PERSONALIZED PROGRAM

General Information • Academic study program in Moscow. Classes are held on the campus of Moscow State Pedagogical University. Excursions to Zagorsk, Abrantsevo.
Learning Focus • Courses in language study, literature, business communication, art, architecture, economics, history, political science. Instruction is offered by local teachers.
Accommodations • Homestays, dormitories, locally-rented apartments. Single rooms are available. Meals are taken as a group, in central dining facility.
Program Details • Session length: 4–12 weeks. Departures are scheduled in January–December. The program is open to undergraduate students, graduate students, adults. Most participants are 18–35 years of age. 1 participant per session. Application deadline: rolling.
Costs • $2050 for a 4 week session including 80 academic hours (includes tuition, housing, all meals, books and class materials, excursions). A $50 deposit is required.
Contact • Dafna Ronn-Oxley, President, Virtus Institute, 2475 Virginia Avenue, NW, #520, Washington, DC 20037; 800-274-9121; Fax: 202-337-9324; E-mail: 73052.623@compuserve.com

VIRTUS INSTITUTE

RUSSIAN WRITERS OF THE NINETEENTH CENTURY: THEIR WORKS AND ENVIRONMENTS

General Information • Academic study program in Moscow, St. Petersburg. Excursions to Moscow, St. Petersburg.
Learning Focus • Courses in Russian literature. Instruction is offered by local teachers.
Accommodations • Homestays. Single rooms are available. Meals are taken as a group, with host family, in central dining facility, in residences.
Program Details • Program offered once per year. Session length: 6 weeks. Departures are scheduled in June. The program is open to undergraduate students, graduate students, adults. Other requirements: good knowledge of Russian and familiarity with at least one work of each: Tolstoy, Pushkin, Turgenev, Chekhov, Gogol, Lermentov and Dostoevsky. Application deadline: April 1.
Costs • $3845 (includes tuition, housing, all meals, books and class materials, excursions, international airfare). A $50 deposit is required.
Contact • Ms. Dafna Ronn-Oxley, President, Virtus Institute, 2475 Virginia Avenue, NW, #520, Washington, DC 20037; 800-274-9121; Fax: 202-337-9324; E-mail: 73052.623@compuserve.com

STUDY IN RUSSIA

—IF **you are a serious student** of Russia, her people and culture,
—IF **you are a curious, interested, hard working, exploring student**, then
OUR program ***"Russia as She Is"*** is the one to enable you to ***live your own Russian Odyssey.***

COMPARE:

"Russia As She Is"

- **YOU** study at universities in different cities, (4 to 6 weeks in each):

  Semester:
  Nizhni Novgorod on the ***Volga.***
  St. Petersburg
  Chelyabinsk in the eastern ***Urals.***
  Moscow

  Academic Year:
  Fall Semester locations as above.
  Christmas break in ***Irkutsk*** & ***Lake Baikal.***
  Continue study at universities in:
  Khabarovsk in the Russian Far East.
  Tomsk in central Siberia
  Izhevsk in the Autonomous Republic of Udmurtia.
  Moscow in-depth seminars.

- **YOU** learn the background of the differences and similarities in mentality and attitude of your hosts. You study regional and national history, politics, expressions, economics, and problems by attending lectures and participating in discussions with professors with different points of view concerning Russia's current issues.

- **YOU** live with the Russian family of a Russian student from the host university, becoming an integral part of the family: a son/daughter to the parents and a brother/sister to the student. Your Russian family takes an active part in the program: social evenings & excursions.

You return home richer in knowledge, friends, and values. You have challenged your previous ways of living, your heart, and your intellect—you have lived a RUSSIAN ODYSSEY.

Most other programs in Russia

- You live and study at only one university in one city for the duration of your stay.
- You learn only one city and attend lectures given by the same professors in one university—thereby being exposed to only one point of view during the program.
- You stay in dormitories.

COURSES OFFERED:

"Russia As She Is"—semester or academic year program

"Leaping Into Russian in Russia"— "Russia as She Is" for **absolute beginners**

"Learn Russian on the Black Sea"—summer language courses from **absolute beginners to advanced**

"Russian Writers of 19th Century: Their Works and Environments" summer 6 week seminar

"Personalized Programs in Moscow"—to suit your special requirements from **absolute beginners** to advanced

Our courses are endorsed by the Russian Federation State Committee for Higher Education.

FROM MOSCOW TO KHABAROVSK

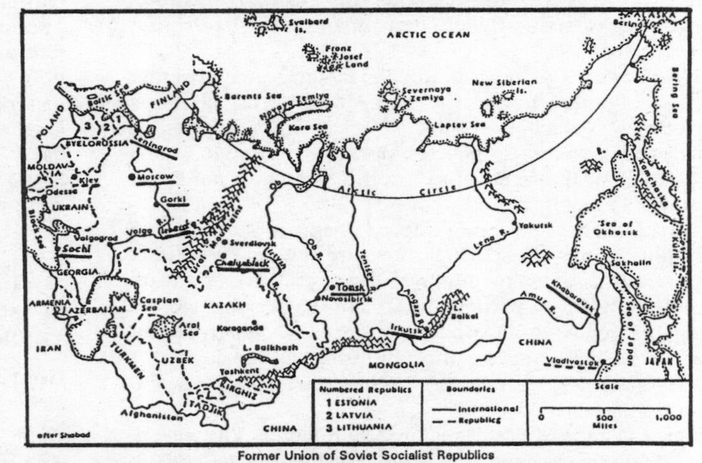

Former Union of Soviet Socialist Republics

VIRTUS INSTITUTE

Dafna Ronn-Oxley
President
2475 Virginia Ave. NW
#520
Washington, D.C. 20037

Call anytime:
1-800-274-9121
In D.C. (202)337-6279
FAX: (202)3379324

TAJIKISTAN

ACTR/ACCELS

CIS REGIONAL LANGUAGE TRAINING PROGRAM–TAJIKISTAN

General Information • Language study program in Tajikistan. Excursions to museums, churches, sites of historical interest.

Learning Focus • Courses in language study, Russian language, history, literature, cultural studies.

Accommodations • Homestays, dormitories. Single rooms are available. Meals are taken on one's own, with host family, in residences.

Program Details • Program offered once per year. Session length: 7 weeks. Departures are scheduled in June. The program is open to undergraduate students, graduate students, adults. Most participants are 19–28 years of age. Other requirements: intermediate-level Russian or target language. 1–3 participant per session. Application deadline: March 1.

Costs • $3400 (includes tuition, housing, some meals, books and class materials, insurance, excursions, visa processing fee, mandatory orientation in Washington, DC). Application fee: $35. A $500 deposit is required.

Contact • Margaret Stephenson, Program Officer, ACTR/ACCELS, 1776 Massachusetts Avenue, NW, Suite 700, Washington, DC 20036; 202-833-7522; Fax: 202-833-7523; E-mail: stephens@actr.org

TURKEY

AMERICAN JEWISH CONGRESS, INTERNATIONAL TRAVEL PROGRAM

THE WONDERS OF TURKEY

General Information • Cultural tour with visits to Ankara, Antalya, Cappadocia, Istanbul, Izmir, Pamukkale, Ataturk Mausoleum, Goreme Valley, Lake Egredir, Castle of Alexander the Great, Blue Mosque. Once at the destination country, participants travel by bus, foot, boat, airplane.

Learning Focus • Escorted travel to monasteries, Turquoise Coast, hot springs and synagogues. Museum visits (Museum of Anatolian Civilizations). Instruction is offered by historians. This program would appeal to people interested in Jewish history.

Accommodations • Hotels. Single rooms are available for an additional $500.

Program Details • Program offered 6 times per year. Session length: 15 days. Departures are scheduled in May–October. Program is targeted to Jewish-American adults. Most participants are 40–75 years of age. Participants must be 15 years or older to enroll. Participants must be members of the sponsoring organization (annual dues: $50). 30 participants per session. Reservations are recommended at least 6 months before departure.

Costs • $3150–$3395 (includes housing, some meals, excursions, international airfare, travel bag, documents portfolio, travel journal). A $200 deposit is required.

Contact • Betty Van Dyke, Worldwide Operations Manager, American Jewish Congress, International Travel Program, 18 East 84th Street, New York, NY 10028; 212-360-1571; Fax: 212-717-1932

ARCHAEOLOGICAL TOURS

EASTERN TURKEY

General Information • Archaeological tour with visits to Amasya, Ankara, Antakya, Istanbul, Nemrut Dag, Trabzon, Urfa, Van, Ani, Erzurm. Once at the destination country, participants travel by bus.

Learning Focus • Museum visits (Istanbul, Ankara, Antakya). Instruction is offered by professors, historians. This program would appeal to people interested in history, archaeology.

Accommodations • Hotels. Single rooms are available for an additional $275.

Program Details • Program offered once per year. Session length: 21 days. Departures are scheduled in June. Most participants are 30–80 years of age. 22 participants per session. Application deadline: 1 month prior to departure.

Costs • $2725 (includes housing, some meals, excursions). A $500 deposit is required.

Contact • Archaeological Tours, 271 Madison Avenue, Suite 904, New York, NY 10016; 212-986-3054; Fax: 212-370-1561

ARCHAEOLOGICAL TOURS

WESTERN TURKEY

General Information • Archaeological tour with visits to Ankara, Antalya, Bursa, Cappadocia, Istanbul, Izmir, Konya, Kusadasi, Pamukkale, Sardis, Troy Pergamon, Iznik, Bogazkoy, Termessas, Perge, Side, Aspados, Aphrodisias, Ariene, Miletus, Didyma, Ephesus. Once at the destination country, participants travel by bus.

Learning Focus • Museum visits (Ankara, Antalya, Konya, Izmir, Istanbul). Instruction is offered by professors, historians. This program would appeal to people interested in history, archaeology.

Accommodations • Hotels. Single rooms are available for an additional $535.

Program Details • Program offered 2 times per year. Session length: 21 days. Departures are scheduled in May, October. Most participants are 30–80 years of age. 25 participants per session. Application deadline: 1 month prior to departure.

Costs • $3085 (includes housing, some meals, excursions). A $500 deposit is required.

Contact • Archaeological Tours, 271 Madison Avenue, Suite 904, New York, NY 10016; 212-986-3054; Fax: 212-370-1561

CRAFT WORLD TOURS

TURKEY

General Information • Cultural tour with visits to Bursa, Istanbul, Pamukkale, Kusadasi, Urgup, Konya, Van. Once at the destination country, participants travel by bus.

Learning Focus • Escorted travel to bazaars, archeological sites, mosques and palaces. Museum visits (Museum of Turkish and Islamic Arts, Ince Minare Museum, Mevlana Museum). Instruction is offered by artists. This program would appeal to people interested in handicrafts, folk arts, village life.

Accommodations • Hotels. Single rooms are available for an additional $460.

Program Details • Program offered once per year. Session length: 21 days. Departures are scheduled in May. Most participants are 30–80 years of age. Other requirements: appreciation of handcrafts and folk arts. 18 participants per session. Application deadline: March 25. Reservations are recommended at least 6 months before departure.

Costs • $3786 (includes housing, some meals, excursions, international airfare). A $250 deposit is required.

Contact • Tom Wilson, President, Craft World Tours, 6776 Warboys Road, Byron, NY 14422; 716-548-2667; Fax: 716-548-2821

FOREIGN LANGUAGE STUDY ABROAD SERVICE

INTERNATIONAL LANGUAGE STUDY HOMESTAYS IN TURKEY

General Information • Language study program in Turkey.
Learning Focus • Courses in Turkish language. Instruction is offered by local teachers.
Accommodations • Homestays. Single rooms are available. Meals are taken with host family, in residences.
Program Details • Session length: varies. Departures are scheduled in January–December. The program is open to undergraduate students, graduate students, pre-college students, adults. Most participants are 12 years of age and older. Other requirements: students must be at least 12 years old. 1 participant per session.
Costs • Contact sponsor for information. A $300 deposit is required.
Contact • Louise Harber, Coordinator, Foreign Language Study Abroad Service, Department IH, Box 903, 5935 Southwest 64th Avenue, South Miami, FL 33143; 800-282-1090; Fax: 305-662-2907; E-mail: flsas@netpoint.net; World Wide Web: http://www.netpoint.net/~flsas

INTERHOSTEL, UNIVERSITY OF NEW HAMPSHIRE

TURKEY

General Information • Cultural tour with visits to Ankara, Istanbul, Konya, Kusadasi, Nevsehir, Pamukkale, Top Kapi Palace, Aphrodisias, Ephesus, Miletus, Dydima, Priene, Kaymakli, Soganli, Zelve. Once at the destination country, participants travel by bus, foot, boat. Program is affiliated with American University of Paris, University of Istanbul, and the Technical University of Ankara.
Learning Focus • Instruction in history and culture. Escorted travel to historical sites. Museum visits (Archaeological Museum, Museum of Anatolian Civilization). Attendance at performances (belly dancing). Instruction is offered by professors, city guides. This program would appeal to people interested in history, culture.
Accommodations • Hotels. Single rooms are available for an additional $400.
Program Details • Program offered once per year. Session length: 2½ weeks. Departures are scheduled in May. Program is targeted to seniors over 50. Most participants are 60–80 years of age. Participants must be 50 years or older to enroll. 35 participants per session. Reservations are recommended at least 6 months before departure.
Costs • $2995 (includes tuition, housing, all meals, excursions, international airfare, entrance fees). A $200 deposit is required.
Contact • Janice Pierson, Office Supervisor, Interhostel, University of New Hampshire, 6 Garrison Avenue, Durham, NH 03824; 800-733-9753; Fax: 603-862-1113; World Wide Web: http://www.learn.unh.edu/

JOURNEYS INTERNATIONAL, INC.

TURQUOISE SAIL AND TREK

General Information • Wilderness/adventure program with visits to Antalya, Cappadocia, Fethiye, Istanbul. Once at the destination country, participants travel by bus, foot, boat, airplane, small vehicle.
Learning Focus • Escorted travel to ancient ruins. Museum visits (Archaeology Museum of Termessos). Other activities include hiking, swimming, sailing, snorkeling, windsurfing. This program would appeal to people interested in history, hiking, nature studies.
Accommodations • Hotels, boat.
Program Details • Program offered 3 times per year. Session length: 17 days. Departures are scheduled in June, August, October. Program is targeted to persons interested in history and adventure. Most participants are 25–55 years of age. Participants must be 12 years or older to enroll. 12 participants per session. Application deadline: 60 days prior to departure. Reservations are recommended at least 60 days before departure.
Costs • $2895 (includes housing, some meals, boat stay). A $300 deposit is required.
Contact • Melissa Peavey, Guidebook Coordinator, Journeys International, Inc., 4011 Jackson Road, Ann Arbor, MI 48103; 313-665-4407; Fax: 313-665-2945; E-mail: melissa@journeys-intl.com; World Wide Web: http://www.journeys-intl.com

LANGUAGE LIAISON

LIVE 'N' LEARN (LEARN IN A TEACHER'S HOME)–TURKEY

General Information • Language study program with visits to Turkey.
Learning Focus • Instruction in the Turkish language. Instruction is offered by professors. This program would appeal to people interested in language.
Accommodations • Homestays. Single rooms are available.
Program Details • Session length: unlimited. Departures are scheduled throughout the year. Most participants are 18–70 years of age. Participants must be 16 years or older to enroll. Reservations are recommended at least 35 days before departure.
Costs • Contact sponsor for information.
Contact • Nancy Forman, President, Language Liaison, 20533 Biscayne Boulevard-Station 4-162, Miami, FL 33180; 305-682-9909; Fax: 305-682-9907; E-mail: langstudy@aol.com; World Wide Web: http://languageliaison.com

PHOTO EXPLORER TOURS

EXPLORE TURKEY

General Information • Photography tour with visits to Antalya, Istanbul, Kusadasi, Mediterranean Sea, Aegean Sea, ruins at Ephesus, Hieropolis, Perge, Aphrodisias. Once at the destination country, participants travel by bus, foot.
Learning Focus • Instruction in photography. Escorted travel to Cappadocci, Pamukkale, Phaselis and Aspendos. Instruction is offered by professional photographers. This program would appeal to people interested in photography.
Accommodations • Hotels. Single rooms are available for an additional $445.
Program Details • Program offered once per year. Session length: 16 days. Departures are scheduled in May. Program is targeted to amateur and professional photographers. Most participants are 35–85 years of age. Other requirements: good physical condition. 8–16 participants per session.

Application deadline: 60 days prior to departure. Reservations are recommended at least 3 months before departure.
Costs • $2990 (includes housing, all meals, excursions, international airfare). A $500 deposit is required.
Contact • Dennis Cox, Director, Photo Explorer Tours, 22111 Cleveland, #211, Dearborn, MI 48124; 800-315-4462; Fax: 313-561-1842; E-mail: decoxphoto@aol.com; World Wide Web: http://www.apogeephoto.com/photo_explorer.html

SANTA BARBARA MUSEUM OF ART

ALONG THE ANCIENT COAST OF TURKEY

General Information • Cultural tour with visits to Ankara, Antalya, Cappadocia, Istanbul, Konya. Once at the destination country, participants travel by bus, boat, airplane. Program is affiliated with San Francisco Museum of Modern Art and Smith College.
Learning Focus • Escorted travel to Cappadocia and theTurkish coast. Museum visits (Ankara and Istanbul). Instruction is offered by art historians. This program would appeal to people interested in art, photography, history, architecture.
Accommodations • Boat. Single rooms are available for an additional $1950.
Program Details • Program offered 2 times per year. Session length: 15 days. Departures are scheduled in September, October. Most participants are 30–80 years of age. Participants must be members of the sponsoring organization (annual dues: $40). 15–20 participants per session.
Costs • $5345 for September departures, $5195 for October departures (includes housing, all meals, excursions). A $1000 deposit is required.
Contact • Shelley Ruston, Director of Special Programs, Santa Barbara Museum of Art, 1130 State Street, Santa Barbara, CA 93101; 805-963-4364, ext. 336; Fax: 805-966-6840

TRAVELEARN

A TURKISH ADVENTURE

General Information • Cultural tour with visits to Ankara, Antalya, Cappadocia, Ephesus, Istanbul, Izmir, Pamukkale. Once at the destination country, participants travel by bus, foot, boat, airplane. Program is affiliated with the nationwide TraveLearn network of 290 universities and colleges.
Learning Focus • Instruction in history, art, religion and archaeology. Museum visits (St. Sophia Museum, Antalya Archaeological Museum). Other activities include "people-to-people" experience in Istanbul. Instruction is offered by professors, researchers, historians. This program would appeal to people interested in history, art, religion, cultural history and understanding.
Accommodations • Hotels. Single rooms are available for an additional $495.
Program Details • Program offered 3 times per year. Session length: 16 days. Departures are scheduled in April, July, September. Program is targeted to mature adults. Most participants are 40–75 years of age. Participants must be 18 years or older to enroll. 14–20 participants per session. Application deadline: 60 days prior to departure. Reservations are recommended at least 4–8 months before departure.
Costs • $2995 (includes housing, all meals, books and class materials, excursions, international airfare). A $300 deposit is required.
Contact • Keith Williams, Director of Marketing, TraveLearn, PO Box 315, Lakeville, PA 18438; 800-235-9114; Fax: 717-226-9114; E-mail: travelearn@aol.com

UNIVERSITY OF ILLINOIS AT URBANA-CHAMPAIGN

LIVE AND STUDY IN ISTANBUL

General Information • Academic study program in Istanbul. Classes are held on the campus of Bosphorous University. Excursions to Bursa, Gallipoli Peninsula, Troy.
Learning Focus • Courses in language study, history, literature, Middle Eastern politics. Instruction is offered by local teachers.
Accommodations • Dormitories. Meals are taken in central dining facility.
Program Details • Program offered once per year. Session length: 8 weeks. Departures are scheduled in June. The program is open to undergraduate students, graduate students. Most participants are 18–25 years of age. Other requirements: B average. 10 participants per session. Application deadline: February 15.
Costs • $2800 (includes tuition, housing, some meals, excursions, orientation, resident director, medical emergency evacuation insurance). Application fee: $35. A $300 deposit is required.
Contact • Timothy Winkler, Program Coordinator, University of Illinois at Urbana-Champaign, Study Abroad Office, 910 South Fifth Street #115, Champaign, IL 61820; 800-531-4404; Fax: 217-244-0249; E-mail: ipa@uiuc.edu

WILDLAND ADVENTURES

TURQUOISE COAST ODYSSEY

General Information • Cultural tour with visits to Antalya, Cappadocia, Istanbul, Marmaris, Aegean coast, ancient runs. Once at the destination country, participants travel by bus, foot, boat, airplane.
Learning Focus • Escorted travel to ancient ruins. Museum visits (Topkopi Palace). Other activities include hiking, private yacht charters. Instruction is offered by historians. This program would appeal to people interested in photography, history, gourmet food, cultural encounters.
Accommodations • Homestays, hotels. Single rooms are available.
Program Details • Program offered 6 times per year. Session length: 19 days. Departures are scheduled in May–October. Most participants are 40–60 years of age. Participants must be 12 years or older to enroll. Application deadline: 30 days prior to departure. Reservations are recommended at least 3–6 months before departure.
Costs • $2595 (includes housing, some meals, excursions, complete pre-departure dossier). A $300 deposit is required.
Contact • Wildland Adventures, 3516 Northeast 155th Street, Seattle, WA 98155; 800-345-4453; Fax: 206-363-6615; E-mail: wildadve@aol.com; World Wide Web: http://www.wildland.com

TURKMENISTAN

ACTR/ACCELS

CIS REGIONAL LANGUAGE TRAINING PROGRAM–TURKMENISTAN

General Information • Language study program in Turkmenistan. Excursions to churches, museums, sites of historical interest.

Learning Focus • Courses in language study, Russian language, history, literature, cultural studies.

Accommodations • Homestays, dormitories. Single rooms are available. Meals are taken on one's own, with host family, in residences.

Program Details • Program offered once per year. Session length: 7 weeks. Departures are scheduled in June. The program is open to undergraduate students, graduate students, adults. Most participants are 19–28 years of age. Other requirements: intermediate-level Russian or target language. 1–3 participant per session. Application deadline: March 1.

Costs • $3400 (includes tuition, housing, some meals, books and class materials, insurance, excursions, visa processing fee, mandatory orientation in Washington, DC). Application fee: $35. A $500 deposit is required.

Contact • Margaret Stephenson, Program Officer, ACTR/ACCELS, 1776 Massachusetts Avenue, NW, Suite 700, Washington, DC 20036; 202-833-7522; Fax: 202-833-7523; E-mail: stephens@actr.org

UZBEKISTAN

ACTR/ACCELS

CIS REGIONAL LANGUAGE TRAINING PROGRAM–UZBEKISTAN

General Information • Language study program in Uzbekistan. Excursions to museums, churches, sites of historical interest.

Learning Focus • Courses in language study, Russian language, history, literature, cultural studies.

Accommodations • Homestays, dormitories. Single rooms are available. Meals are taken on one's own, with host family, in residences.

Program Details • Program offered once per year. Session length: 7 weeks. Departures are scheduled in June. The program is open to undergraduate students, graduate students, adults. Most participants are 19–28 years of age. Other requirements: intermediate-level Russian or target language. 1–3 participant per session. Application deadline: March 1.

Costs • $3400 (includes tuition, housing, some meals, books and class materials, insurance, excursions, visa processing fee, mandatory orientation in Washington, DC). Application fee: $35. A $500 deposit is required.

Contact • Margaret Stephenson, Program Officer, ACTR/ACCELS, 1776 Massachusetts Avenue, NW, Suite 700, Washington, DC 20036; 202-833-7522; Fax: 202-833-7523; E-mail: stephens@actr.org

WESTERN EUROPE

REGIONAL

Austria
Belgium
Denmark
England
Finland
France
Germany
Greece
Iceland
Ireland
Italy
Luxembourg
Malta
Netherlands
Norway
Portugal
Scotland
Spain
Sweden
Switzerland
Wales

REGIONAL

ACCENT INTERNATIONAL CONSORTIUM FOR ACADEMIC PROGRAMS ABROAD

MUSIC, ART AND GARDENS IN LONDON AND PARIS: A TALE OF TWO CITIES

General Information • Academic study program in England (London), France (Paris). Excursions to Cotswolds, Giverny, Normandy.
Learning Focus • Courses in music, gardens, art. Instruction is offered by professors from the sponsoring institution.
Accommodations • Hotels. Single rooms are available. Meals are taken on one's own, in local restaurants.
Program Details • Program offered once per year. Session length: 16 days. Departures are scheduled in June. The program is open to undergraduate students, graduate students, pre-college students, adults. Most participants are 20–70 years of age. Other requirements: minimum of 17 years of age. 25 participants per session. Application deadline: March 5.
Costs • $3200 (includes housing, some meals, insurance, excursions, guides, in-country transportation). A $250 deposit is required.
Contact • ACCENT International Consortium for Academic Programs Abroad, 425 Market Street, 2nd Floor, San Francisco, CA 94105; 415-904-7756; Fax: 415-904-7759; E-mail: sfaccent@aol.com

AMERICAN INSTITUTE FOR FOREIGN STUDY (AIFS)

EUROPEAN ART AND ARCHITECTURE

General Information • Academic study program in Austria (Salzburg), Belgium (Bruges), England (London), France (Paris), Germany (Munich), Netherlands (Amsterdam). Classes are held on the campus of Richmond College, The American International University in London. Excursions to Italy (Florence, Rome, Sorrento).
Learning Focus • Courses in art history, European architecture. Instruction is offered by local teachers.
Accommodations • Dormitories, hotels. Single rooms are available. Meals are taken in residences.
Program Details • Program offered once per year. Session length: 4 weeks. Departures are scheduled in June. The program is open to undergraduate students, graduate students, adults, high school graduates. Most participants are 19–35 years of age. Other requirements: minimum 2.0 GPA. 45 participants per session. Application deadline: March 15.
Costs • $3379 (includes tuition, housing, some meals). A $400 deposit is required.
Contact • Carmela Vigliano, Director of Admissions, College Summer Programs, American Institute for Foreign Study (AIFS), 102 Greenwich Avenue, Greenwich, CT 06830; 800-727-2437, ext. 6087; Fax: 203-869-9615; E-mail: info@aifs.org

AMERICAN INSTITUTE FOR FOREIGN STUDY (AIFS)

RICHMOND COLLEGE INTERNATIONAL SUMMER SESSION IN LONDON, ENGLAND

General Information • Academic study program in Belgium (Brussels), England (Kensington, London), France (Paris), Netherlands (Amsterdam).
Learning Focus • Courses in art history, communications, business, history, economics, fine and studio arts, English language, performing arts, social sciences. Instruction is offered by professors from the sponsoring institution.
Accommodations • Dormitories. Single rooms are available. Meals are taken in central dining facility, in local restaurants, in residences.
Program Details • Program offered 4 times per year. Session length: 3 weeks. Departures are scheduled in May–July. The program is open to undergraduate students, graduate students, adults, high school graduates. Other requirements: minimum 2.0 GPA. Application deadline: March 15.
Costs • $2539 (includes tuition, housing, some meals, insurance). A $400 deposit is required.
Contact • Carmela Vigliano, Director of Admissions, College Summer Programs, American Institute for Foreign Study (AIFS), 102 Greenwich Avenue, Greenwich, CT 06830; 800-727-2437, ext. 6087; Fax: 203-869-9615; E-mail: info@aifs.org

AMERICAN INSTITUTE FOR FOREIGN STUDY (AIFS)

THE SINGLE EUROPEAN MARKET

General Information • Academic study program in Belgium (Brussels), England (London), France (Paris, Strasbourg), Germany (Berlin), Switzerland (Lucerne). Classes are held on the campus of Richmond College, The American International University in London.
Learning Focus • Courses in international trade and finance, marketing. Instruction is offered by local teachers.
Accommodations • Dormitories, hotels. Meals are taken in central dining facility, in residences.
Program Details • Program offered once per year. Session length: 4 weeks. Departures are scheduled in July. The program is open to undergraduate students, graduate students, adults, high school graduates. Other requirements: minimum 2.0 GPA. 35 participants per session. Application deadline: March 15.
Costs • $3439 (includes tuition, housing, some meals). A $400 deposit is required.
Contact • Carmela Vigliano, Director of Admissions, College Summer Programs, American Institute for Foreign Study (AIFS), 102 Greenwich Avenue, Greenwich, CT 06830; 800-727-2437, ext. 6087; Fax: 203-869-9615; E-mail: info@aifs.org

AMERICAN JEWISH CONGRESS, INTERNATIONAL TRAVEL PROGRAM

CATALONIA AND PROVENCE

General Information • Cultural tour with visits to France (Aix-en-Provence, Avignon, Carcassonne, Nice), Spain

(Barcelona, Costa Brava); excursions to French Riviera, Monte Carlo, Cannes, Les Milles Holocaust Museum, Fontaine Gardens, Guell Park.
Learning Focus • Escorted travel to Villa Ile de France and Fondation Maeght. Museum visits (Chagall Museum, Museum of Jewish Life, Arlatan Museum, Salvador Dali Museum, Prado). Instruction is offered by historians. This program would appeal to people interested in Jewish history.
Accommodations • Hotels. Single rooms are available for an additional $625.
Program Details • Program offered 4 times per year. Session length: 15 days. Departures are scheduled in May-July, September. Program is targeted to Jewish-American adults. Most participants are 40-75 years of age. Participants must be 15 years or older to enroll. Participants must be members of the sponsoring organization (annual dues: $50). 30 participants per session. Reservations are recommended at least 6 months before departure.
Costs • $4395-$4595 (includes housing, some meals, excursions, international airfare, travel bag, documents portfolio, travel journal). A $200 deposit is required.
Contact • Betty Van Dyke, Worldwide Operations Manager, American Jewish Congress, International Travel Program, 18 East 84th Street, New York, NY 10028; 212-360-1571; Fax: 212-717-1932

AMERICAN JEWISH CONGRESS, INTERNATIONAL TRAVEL PROGRAM

EUROPE IN BLOOM

General Information • Cultural tour with visits to Belgium (Antwerp, Brussels, Ghent), Netherlands (Amsterdam, Rotterdam, The Hague); excursions to Mint Tower, International Court of Justice, Castle of Veves, Gardens of Annevoi, Grand Palace. Once at the destination country, participants travel by bus, foot, boat.
Learning Focus • Escorted travel to synagogues, Maduradam and a spa. Museum visits (Anne Frank House, Jewish Historical Museum, Rijksmuseum). Instruction is offered by historians. This program would appeal to people interested in Jewish history.
Accommodations • Hotels. Single rooms are available for an additional $625.
Program Details • Program offered 5 times per year. Session length: 12 days. Departures are scheduled in May-September. Program is targeted to Jewish-American adults. Most participants are 40-75 years of age. Participants must be 15 years or older to enroll. Participants must be members of the sponsoring organization (annual dues: $50). 30 participants per session. Reservations are recommended at least 6 months before departure.
Costs • $3550 (includes housing, some meals, excursions, international airfare, travel bag, documents portfolio, travel journal). A $200 deposit is required.
Contact • Betty Van Dyke, Worldwide Operations Manager, American Jewish Congress, International Travel Program, 18 East 84th Street, New York, NY 10028; 212-360-1571; Fax: 212-717-1932

AMERICAN JEWISH CONGRESS, INTERNATIONAL TRAVEL PROGRAM

THE ROMANCE OF EUROPE

General Information • Cultural tour with visits to France (Paris), Greece (Athens, Crete, Mykonos), Turkey (Kusadasi); excursions to Arc de Triomphe, Eiffel Tower, Acropolis, Parthenon, Temple of Zeus, Aegean cruise, Ephesus. Once at the destination country, participants travel by boat, airplane.
Learning Focus • Escorted travel to Cathedral of Notre Dame, synogogues and the Palace of Mycenae. Museum visits (Jewish Museum of Greece). Instruction is offered by historians. This program would appeal to people interested in Jewish history.
Accommodations • Hotels, boat. Single rooms are available for an additional $700-$900.
Program Details • Program offered 4 times per year. Session length: 14 days. Departures are scheduled in June-September. Program is targeted to Jewish-American adults. Most participants are 40-75 years of age. Participants must be 15 years or older to enroll. Participants must be members of the sponsoring organization (annual dues: $50). 30 participants per session. Reservations are recommended at least 6 months before departure.
Costs • $4050-$4195 (includes housing, some meals, excursions, international airfare, travel bag, documents portfolio, travel journal). A $200 deposit is required.
Contact • Betty Van Dyke, Worldwide Operations Manager, American Jewish Congress, International Travel Program, 18 East 84th Street, New York, NY 10028; 212-360-1571; Fax: 212-717-1932

APPALACHIAN STATE UNIVERSITY

ENGLAND, WALES, AND IRELAND

General Information • Academic study program in England, Ireland, Wales.
Learning Focus • Courses in English language. Instruction is offered by professors from the sponsoring institution.
Program Details • Program offered once per year. Session length: 4 weeks. Departures are scheduled in May. Most participants are 18 years of age and older. 20 participants per session.
Costs • $2956-$3088 (includes tuition, housing, insurance, international airfare, International Student Identification card).
Contact • Dr. Georgia Rhoades, Professor, Appalachian State University, Department of English, Boone, NC 28608; 704-262-3098; Fax: 704-262-4037

APPALACHIAN STATE UNIVERSITY

SCANDINAVIA

General Information • Academic study program in Sweden (Göteborg). Classes are held on the campus of University of Göteborg. Excursions to Stockholm, Copenhagen, Oslo.
Learning Focus • Courses in management. Instruction is offered by professors from the sponsoring institution.

Program Details • Program offered once per year. Session length: 4 weeks. Departures are scheduled in May. Most participants are 18 years of age and older. 20 participants per session.
Costs • $3100 (includes tuition, housing, insurance, international airfare, International Student Identification card).
Contact • Dr. Duane Daggett, Professor, Appalachian State University, Department of Management, Boone, NC 28608; 704-262-6223; Fax: 704-262-4037

ARCHAEOLOGICAL TOURS

MALTA, SARDINIA, AND CORSICA

General Information • Archaeological tour with visits to France (Ajaccio, Bastia, Bonifacio, Propriano), Italy (Alghero, Cagliari, Oristano, St. Teresa), Malta (Gozo, Valleta); excursions to Medina, Antioch, Tharros, Sartene, Cucuruzzu, Euisa, Corte, Aleria, Rabat, Nora. Once at the destination country, participants travel by bus, boat.
Learning Focus • Escorted travel to Megalithic temples, cultural sites and ruins. Museum visits (Valleta, Gozo, Cagliari, Sassari, Aleria). Instruction is offered by professors, historians. This program would appeal to people interested in history, archaeology.
Accommodations • Hotels. Single rooms are available for an additional $475.
Program Details • Program offered once per year. Session length: 19 days. Departures are scheduled in May. Program is targeted to adults. Most participants are 30–80 years of age. 25 participants per session. Application deadline: 1 month prior to departure.
Costs • $3655 (includes housing, some meals, excursions). A $500 deposit is required.
Contact • Archaeological Tours, 271 Madison Avenue, Suite 904, New York, NY 10016; 212-986-3054; Fax: 212-370-1561

ARTS & CRAFTS TOURS

NORTHERN INDEPENDENTS

General Information • Cultural tour with visits to England (Borders, Lake District), Scotland (Argyllshire, Edinburgh, Glasgow). Once at the destination country, participants travel by bus.
Learning Focus • Escorted travel to private collections and homes. Museum visits (collections and exhibitions). Instruction is offered by professors, artists, historians, architectural historians and curators. This program would appeal to people interested in architecture, art nouveau, CR Mackintosh, decorative arts, the arts and crafts movement.
Accommodations • Hotels. Single rooms are available for an additional $500.
Program Details • Program offered once per year. Session length: 11 days. Departures are scheduled in July. Most participants are 40–80 years of age. 8–10 participants per session. Application deadline: 60 days prior to departure. Reservations are recommended at least 6 months before departure.
Costs • $5300 (includes housing, all meals, books and class materials, excursions). A $500 deposit is required.
Contact • Elaine Hirschl Ellis, President, Arts & Crafts Tours, 110 Riverside Drive, New York, NY 10024; 212-362-0761; Fax: 212-787-2823; E-mail: actours@aol.com; World Wide Web: http://www.dscweb.com/AandCTours.html

BRITISH COASTAL TRAILS SCENIC WALKING

THE PERCHED VILLAGES OF PROVENCE

General Information • Cultural tour with visits to France (Menton, Sospel), Italy (Fanghetto), Monaco (Monte Carlo); excursions to Tende, La Brigue, Piene Haute, Col de Castellar, St. Agnes, Cap Martin. Once at the destination country, participants travel by bus, foot.
Learning Focus • Escorted travel to Saorge, Breil and Fanghetto. Nature observation (forests, olive groves, wildflowers). Other activities include hiking, walking. Instruction is offered by naturalists, historians, professional guides. This program would appeal to people interested in nature studies, walking, culture, photography, history.
Accommodations • Hotels. Single rooms are available.
Program Details • Program offered 4 times per year. Session length: 8 days. Departures are scheduled in May, September, October. Most participants are 40–65 years of age. Participants must be 13 years or older to enroll. Other requirements: physician's approval, signed release form and good physical condition. 18 participants per session. Application deadline: 30 days prior to departure. Reservations are recommended at least 6 months before departure.
Costs • $1855 (includes housing, some meals, excursions, full-time guide). A $250 deposit is required.
Contact • Tour Manager, British Coastal Trails Scenic Walking, 7777 Fay Avenue, Suite 100, La Jolla, CA 92037; 800-473-1210; Fax: 619-456-2277; E-mail: lajolla@bctwalk.com; World Wide Web: http://www.bctwalk.com/lajolla

COOPERATIVE CENTER FOR STUDY ABROAD

SCOTLAND AND ENGLAND

General Information • Academic study program in England, Scotland (Edinburgh, Glasgow).
Learning Focus • Courses in economics, English language, literature, education, history, nursing. Instruction is offered by professors from the sponsoring institution.
Accommodations • Dormitories, hotels. Meals are taken as a group, on one's own, in central dining facility, in local restaurants.
Program Details • Program offered once per year. Session length: 3 weeks. Departures are scheduled in June. The program is open to undergraduate students, graduate students, adults. Most participants are 18–60 years of age. Other requirements: minimum 2.0 GPA. 30 participants per session. Application deadline: March 20.
Costs • $2195 (includes housing, some meals, insurance, excursions, international airfare). A $100 deposit is required.
Contact • Dr. Michael A. Klembara, Executive Director, Cooperative Center for Study Abroad, NKU, BEP 301, Highland Heights, KY 41099; 800-319-6015; Fax: 606-572-6650; E-mail: ccsa@nku.edu

DUKE UNIVERSITY

DUKE IN FLANDERS AND THE NETHERLANDS

General Information • Academic study program in Belgium (Ghent), Netherlands (Amsterdam, Leiden). Excursions to Utrecht, Haarlem, Delft, Rotterdam.
Learning Focus • Courses in art, art history, cultural studies. Instruction is offered by professors from the sponsoring institution.
Accommodations • Hotels. Meals are taken on one's own, in local restaurants.
Program Details • Program offered once per year. Session length: 6 weeks. Departures are scheduled in June. The program is open to undergraduate students, graduate students. Most participants are 18–21 years of age. Other requirements: minimum 2.7 GPA. 10–15 participants per session. Application deadline: February 21.
Costs • $4851 (includes tuition, housing, some meals, excursions, international airfare).
Contact • Foreign Academic Programs, Duke University, 121 Allen Building, Box 90057, Durham, NC 27708-0057; 919-684-2174; Fax: 919-684-3083; E-mail: abroad@mail01.adm.duke.edu; World Wide Web: http://www.mis.duke.edu/study_abroad/study_abroad.html

EASTERN MICHIGAN UNIVERSITY

EUROPEAN CULTURAL HISTORY TOUR

General Information • Academic study program in Western Europe.
Learning Focus • Courses in European history, art. Instruction is offered by professors from the sponsoring institution.
Accommodations • Hotels, pensiones, hostels. Meals are taken as a group, in local restaurants.
Program Details • Program offered 4 times per year. Session length: 6 or 12 weeks. Departures are scheduled in May–August. The program is open to undergraduate students, graduate students. Most participants are 18–25 years of age. Other requirements: minimum 2.0 GPA and 18 years of age. 20 participants per session. Application deadline: April 1.
Costs • $3195–$6595 (includes tuition, housing, some meals, insurance, excursions, travel in Europe). A $150 deposit is required.
Contact • Academic Programs Abroad, Eastern Michigan University, 332 Goodison Hall, Ypsilanti, MI 48197; 800-777-3541; Fax: 313-487-2316; E-mail: programs.abroad@emich.edu; World Wide Web: http://www.emich.edu/public/cont_ed/abroad.html

EASTERN MICHIGAN UNIVERSITY

GREAT ECONOMISTS IN THE UNITED KINGDOM

General Information • Academic study program in England (London, Oxford), Scotland (Edinburgh, Glasgow).
Learning Focus • Courses in economics. Instruction is offered by professors from the sponsoring institution.
Accommodations • Hotels. Meals are taken as a group, in local restaurants.
Program Details • Program offered once per year. Session length: 2 weeks. Departures are scheduled in August. The program is open to undergraduate students, graduate students. Most participants are 18–30 years of age. Other requirements: minimum 2.0 GPA and 18 years of age. 10 participants per session. Application deadline: April 1.
Costs • $2495 (includes tuition, housing, some meals, insurance, excursions, international airfare). A $150 deposit is required.
Contact • Academic Programs Abroad, Eastern Michigan University, 332 Goodison Hall, Ypsilanti, MI 48197; 800-777-3541; Fax: 313-487-2316; E-mail: programs.abroad@emich.edu; World Wide Web: http://www.emich.edu/public/cont_ed/abroad.html

EASTERN MICHIGAN UNIVERSITY

POST-IMPRESSIONIST ART TOUR

General Information • Academic study program in France (Paris), Netherlands (Amsterdam).
Learning Focus • Courses in art history. Instruction is offered by professors from the sponsoring institution.
Accommodations • Hotels. Meals are taken as a group, in local restaurants.
Program Details • Program offered once per year. Session length: 2 weeks. Departures are scheduled in June. The program is open to undergraduate students, graduate students. Most participants are 18–30 years of age. Other requirements: minimum 2.0 GPA and 18 years of age. 15 participants per session. Application deadline: March 1.
Costs • $3195 (includes tuition, housing, some meals, excursions, international airfare, travel in Europe). A $150 deposit is required.
Contact • Academic Programs Abroad, Eastern Michigan University, 332 Goodison Hall, Ypsilanti, MI 48197; 800-777-3541; Fax: 313-487-2316; E-mail: programs.abroad@emich.edu; World Wide Web: http://www.emich.edu/public/cont_ed/abroad.html

EAST STROUDSBURG UNIVERSITY OF PENNSYLVANIA

COMPARATIVE EDUCATION ABROAD

General Information • Academic study program in England (Leicester, St. Neots, Tenterden), Germany (Waldkraiburg).
Learning Focus • Courses in education. Instruction is offered by professors from the sponsoring institution.
Accommodations • Homestays. Single rooms are available. Meals are taken with host family, in residences.
Program Details • Program offered 3 times per year. Session length: 3 weeks. Departures are scheduled in January, June, July. The program is open to graduate students. Most participants are 24–55 years of age. Other requirements: graduate status, employed educator, certification and a minimum 2.5 GPA. 8–10 participants per session.

Costs • $1512 for Pennsylvania residents, $1941 for non-residents (includes tuition, housing, some meals, books and class materials). A $100 deposit is required.
Contact • Dr. Donald R. Bortz, Chair, Professional and Secondary Education, East Stroudsburg University of Pennsylvania, Stroud Hall, East Stroudsburg, PA 18301; 717-422-3680; Fax: 717-422-3777; E-mail: dbortz@po-box.esu.edu

EXPERIENCE PLUS SPECIALTY TOURS, INC.

CAMINO DE SANTIAGO: BICYCLE TOUR

General Information • Bicycle tour with visits to France (Roncesvalles), Spain (Burgos, León, Puente de la Reina, Santiago de Compostela, Santo Domingo de la Calzada). Once at the destination country, participants travel by bicycle.
Learning Focus • Museum visits (the Enolog Museum in Haro). Other activities include abbey visits, bicycling. Instruction is offered by professors, indigenous, bilingual and bi-cultural guides. This program would appeal to people interested in bicycling, history, religion, travel, Spain, culture.
Accommodations • Abbeys. Single rooms are available for an additional $300.
Program Details • Program offered 2 times per year. Session length: 13 days. Departures are scheduled in May, September. Most participants are 35–70 years of age. 16–22 participants per session. Reservations are recommended at least 6–12 months before departure.
Costs • $2400 (includes housing, some meals, excursions, a quality rental bike, 28 oz. water bottle, shirt, luggage shuttle, van support, bilingual/bi-cultural tour leaders). A $250 deposit is required.
Contact • Experience Plus Specialty Tours, Inc., 1925 Wallenberg Drive, Fort Collins, CO 80526; 800-685-4565; Fax: 800-685-4565; E-mail: tours@xplus.com

EXPERIENCE PLUS SPECIALTY TOURS, INC.

GALICIA AND THE MINHO–SPAIN TO PORTUGAL

General Information • Bicycle tour with visits to Portugal (Porto, Viana do Castelo, Vila Wova de Cerveira), Spain (Barona, Galician Coast, Santiago de Compostela); excursions to coastal Spain, Santiago de Compostela, Minho wine country. Once at the destination country, participants travel by bicycle.
Learning Focus • Escorted travel to Galicia and the Minho. Other activities include bicycling. Instruction is offered by professors, indigenous, bilingual and bi-cultural guides. This program would appeal to people interested in history, travel, culture, Spain, Portugal, bicycling.
Accommodations • Hotels. Single rooms are available for an additional $300.
Program Details • Program offered 2 times per year. Session length: 11 weeks. Departures are scheduled in June, September. Most participants are 35–70 years of age. 16–22 participants per session. Reservations are recommended at least 6–12 months before departure.
Costs • $2200 (includes housing, some meals, airport shuttle after tour, a quality bike, water bottle, shirts, luggage shuttle, van support, bilingual/bi-cultural tour leaders).
Contact • Experience Plus Specialty Tours, Inc., 1925 Wallenberg Drive, Fort Collins, CO 80526; 800-685-4565; Fax: 800-685-4565; E-mail: tours@xplus.com

FORUM TRAVEL INTERNATIONAL

PASSAU TO VIENNA

General Information • Bicycle tour with visits to Austria (Danube River, Vienna), Germany (Passau). Once at the destination country, participants travel by train, bicycle.
Learning Focus • Escorted travel to cities, towns and castles. Other activities include cycling. Instruction is offered by professional guides. This program would appeal to people interested in bicycling, culture, history.
Accommodations • Hotels. Single rooms are available for an additional $134–$225.
Program Details • Session length: 7–10 days. Departures are scheduled in April–October. Most participants are 18–60 years of age. Participants must be 16 years or older to enroll. 15 participants per session. Application deadline: 60 days prior to departure. Reservations are recommended at least 3–5 months before departure.
Costs • $555–$1016 (includes housing, some meals, luggage transport). A $200 deposit is required.
Contact • Jeannie Graves, Operations Manager, Forum Travel International, 91 Gregory Lane #21, Pleasant Hill, CA 94525; 510-671-2900; Fax: 510-671-2993; E-mail: forum@ix.netcom.com; World Wide Web: http://www.ten-io.com/forumtravel

 GEORGE MASON UNIVERSITY

UNITED STATES–EUROPEAN RELATIONS

General Information • Academic study program in Belgium (Brussels), England, France (Paris, Strasbourg).
Learning Focus • Courses in NATO, the European Community. Instruction is offered by professors from the sponsoring institution.
Accommodations • Hotels. Single rooms are available. Meals are taken as a group, on one's own, in local restaurants.
Program Details • Program offered once per year. Session length: 3 weeks. Departures are scheduled in December. The program is open to undergraduate students, graduate students, adults. Most participants are 18–65 years of age. Other requirements: minimum 2.25 GPA. 10–20 participants per session. Application deadline: October 11.
Costs • $2768 for George Mason University students, $3118 for other students (includes tuition, housing, some meals, insurance, excursions, international airfare). Application fee: $35. A $500 deposit is required.
Contact • Dr. Yehuda Lukacs, Director, Center for Global Education, George Mason University, 4400 University Drive, 235 Johnson Center, Fairfax, VA 22030; 703-993-2156; Fax: 703-993-2153; E-mail: ylukacs@gmu.edu; World Wide Web: http://www.gmu.edu/departments/oie

INSTITUTE FOR EUROPEAN BUSINESS ADMINISTRATION

DOING BUSINESS IN EUROPE

General Information • Academic study program in Belgium (Ghent), France (Strasbourg), Luxembourg. Excursions to England (London), Belgium (Brussels), France (Paris), Netherlands (Amsterdam).
Learning Focus • Courses in European business, Eastern Europe, European Community, European Monetary Union, European Market, US Commerce, multinationalism. Instruction is offered by professors from the sponsoring institution.
Accommodations • Dormitories. Single rooms are available. Meals are taken on one's own, in local restaurants.
Program Details • Program offered once per year. Session length: 4 weeks. Departures are scheduled in July. The program is open to undergraduate students, graduate students. Most participants are 19-33 years of age. Application deadline: April 15.
Costs • $2890 (includes tuition, housing, books and class materials, excursions). A $500 deposit is required.
Contact • Pierre Hendrickx, Director, Institute for European Business Administration, St. Pietersmuywstraat 202, Ghent 9000, Belgium; +32 9-3234436; Fax: +322 9-236-1221

INTERHOSTEL, UNIVERSITY OF NEW HAMPSHIRE

AUSTRIA AND ITALY

General Information • Cultural tour with visits to Austria (Innsbruck), Italy (Dorf Tirol, Verona); excursions to Ambras Castle, Hinter Horn, Stubai Glacier, Hall, Brenner Pass, Brixen, Brunnenburg Castle, Merano, Dolomite Mountains. Once at the destination country, participants travel by bus, foot, cable car. Program is affiliated with University of New Orleans and the University of Innsbruck.
Learning Focus • Instruction in history and culture. Escorted travel to castles and landmarks. Museum visits (Tirolean Museum, Medieval Museum). Attendance at performances (opera in Roman Amphitheater). Instruction is offered by professors, historians. This program would appeal to people interested in history, culture.
Accommodations • Dormitories. Single rooms are available for an additional $.
Program Details • Program offered once per year. Session length: 2 weeks. Departures are scheduled in July. Program is targeted to seniors over 50. Most participants are 60-80 years of age. Participants must be 50 years or older to enroll. 35 participants per session. Reservations are recommended at least 6 months before departure.
Costs • $3080 (includes tuition, housing, all meals, excursions, international airfare, entrance fees). A $200 deposit is required.
Contact • Janice Pierson, Office Supervisor, Interhostel, University of New Hampshire, 6 Garrison Avenue, Durham, NH 03824; 800-733-9753; Fax: 603-862-1113; World Wide Web: http://www.learn.unh.edu/

JAMES MADISON UNIVERSITY

SUMMER STUDY IN FRANCE AND ITALY

General Information • Academic study program in France (Paris), Italy (Florence, Rome, Venice). Excursions to Tours, Nice, Monte Carlo, Blois, Pisa, Cannes, Amboise.
Learning Focus • Courses in geography, history, art. Instruction is offered by professors from the sponsoring institution.
Accommodations • Hotels. Meals are taken as a group, in local restaurants.
Program Details • Program offered once per year. Session length: 20 days. Departures are scheduled in May. The program is open to undergraduate students, graduate students. Most participants are 18-22 years of age. Other requirements: minimum 2.8 GPA. 30-40 participants per session. Application deadline: February 1.
Costs • $2754 for Virginia residents, $3184 for nonresidents (includes tuition, housing, some meals, excursions, international airfare). A $400 deposit is required.
Contact • Dr. Mario Hamlet-Metz, Professor, Foreign Languages, James Madison University, Office of International Education, Harrisonburg, VA 22807; 540-568-6069; Fax: 540-568-3310; E-mail: arthurkg@jmu.edu; World Wide Web: http://www.jmu.edu/intl-ed/

LA SABRANENQUE

RESTORATION SESSIONS IN WESTERN EUROPE

General Information • Architectural tour with visits to France (St. Victor la Coste), Italy (Altamura, Gnallo, Settefonti); excursions to nearby historical, architectural or cultural sites.
Learning Focus • Volunteer work (architectural restoration). Instruction is offered by technical supervisors. This program would appeal to people interested in architectural preservation.
Accommodations • Program-owned houses.
Program Details • Program offered 3 times per year. Session length: 3 weeks. Departures are scheduled in June-August. Most participants are 18-60 years of age. Participants must be 18 years or older to enroll. Other requirements: good health. 8-10 participants per session. Reservations are recommended at least 2-3 months before departure.
Costs • $930-$990 (includes housing, all meals, excursions). A $150 deposit is required.
Contact • Jacqueline C. Simon, US Correspondent, La Sabranenque, 217 High Park Boulevard, Buffalo, NY 14226; 716-836-8698

LOUISIANA STATE UNIVERSITY

EUROPEAN FASHION FIELD STUDY

General Information • Academic study program in England (London), France (Lyon, Paris). Excursions to European cities.
Learning Focus • Courses in textiles, apparel design, merchandising. Instruction is offered by professors from the sponsoring institution.
Accommodations • Hotels. Meals are taken on one's own.
Program Details • Program offered once per year. Session length: 3 weeks. Departures are scheduled in May. The program is open to undergraduate students, graduate students, adults. Most participants are 20-25 years of age. Other requirements: minimum 2.5 GPA for 6 hours of credit and a minimum 3.0 GPA for 9 hours of credit. 15 participants per session. Application deadline: February 1.

Costs • $3000 (includes tuition, housing, some meals, excursions, international airfare, Channel crossing, some train and taxi fares). A $1000 deposit is required.
Contact • Jeannie Willamson, Study Abroad Coordinator, Louisiana State University, Academic Programs Abroad, 365 Pleasant Hall, Baton Rouge, LA 70803; 504-388-6801; Fax: 504-388-6806; E-mail: abwill@lsuvm.sncc.lsu.edu

LYNN UNIVERSITY

LYNN UNIVERSITY STUDY ABROAD

General Information • Academic study program in Germany (Paderborn), Sweden (Stockholm). Classes are held on the campus of Stockholm University, University of Paderborn.
Learning Focus • Courses in business, economics. Instruction is offered by professors from the sponsoring institution and local teachers.
Accommodations • Dormitories. Single rooms are available. Meals are taken as a group, in central dining facility.
Program Details • Program offered 3 times per year. Session length: 5 weeks. Departures are scheduled in September, January, May. The program is open to undergraduate students, graduate students. Most participants are 20–25 years of age. Other requirements: good academic standing. 5–6 participants per session. Application deadline: February 1.
Costs • $3000 (includes tuition, housing, some meals, books and class materials, international airfare). A $500 deposit is required.
Contact • Dr. Patrick Butler, Professor, Lynn University, 3601 North Military Trail, Boca Raton, FL 33431; 407-994-0770; Fax: 407-241-3552; World Wide Web: http://www.lynn.edu

MICHIGAN STATE UNIVERSITY

ENVIRONMENTAL PLANNING AND MANAGEMENT PROGRAM

General Information • Academic study program in Belgium (Brussels), France (Paris), Netherlands (Amsterdam, The Hague).
Learning Focus • Courses in environmental planning, agriculture. Instruction is offered by professors from the sponsoring institution.
Accommodations • Hotels. Meals are taken on one's own, in local restaurants.
Program Details • Program offered once per year. Session length: 4 weeks. Departures are scheduled in May. The program is open to undergraduate students, graduate students, adults. Most participants are 18–30 years of age. Other requirements: good academic standing and the approval of the director. 10–12 participants per session. Application deadline: March 14.
Costs • $2100 (includes housing, some meals, excursions). Application fee: $75. A $250 deposit is required.
Contact • Brenda S. Sprite, Educational Programs Coordinator, Michigan State University, Office of Study Abroad, 109 International Center, East Lansing, MI 48824-1035; 517-353-8920; Fax: 517-432-2082; E-mail: sprite@pilot.msu.edu; World Wide Web: http://study-abroad.msu.edu

MICHIGAN STATE UNIVERSITY

FILM IN BRITAIN

General Information • Academic study program in England (London), Scotland (Edinburgh).
Learning Focus • Courses in film studies, videography, English language. Instruction is offered by professors from the sponsoring institution.
Accommodations • Dormitories. Single rooms are available. Meals are taken on one's own, in local restaurants.
Program Details • Program offered once per year. Session length: 6 weeks. Departures are scheduled in July. The program is open to undergraduate students, graduate students, adults. Most participants are 18–26 years of age. Other requirements: good academic standing and the approval of the director. 12 participants per session. Application deadline: March 14.
Costs • $3137 (includes housing, some meals, excursions). Application fee: $75. A $250 deposit is required.
Contact • Cynthia Chalou, Educational Programs Coordinator, Michigan State University, Office of Study Abroad, 109 International Center, East Lansing, MI 48824-1035; 517-353-8920; Fax: 517-432-2082; E-mail: chalouc@pilot.msu.edu; World Wide Web: http://study-abroad.msu.edu

MICHIGAN STATE UNIVERSITY

HISTORY, ARTS, AND HUMANITIES PROGRAM

General Information • Academic study program in England (London), Scotland (Edinburgh).
Learning Focus • Courses in history, British culture, humanities. Instruction is offered by professors from the sponsoring institution.
Accommodations • Dormitories. Single rooms are available. Meals are taken on one's own, in central dining facility.
Program Details • Program offered once per year. Session length: 5 weeks. Departures are scheduled in July. The program is open to undergraduate students. Most participants are 18–22 years of age. Other requirements: good academic standing and the approval of the director. 20 participants per session. Application deadline: March 14.
Costs • $2496 (includes housing, some meals, excursions). Application fee: $75. A $250 deposit is required.
Contact • Cynthia Chalou, Educational Programs Coordinator, Michigan State University, Office of Study Abroad, 109 International Center, East Lansing, MI 48824-1035; 517-353-8920; Fax: 517-432-2082; E-mail: chalouc@pilot.msu.edu; World Wide Web: http://study-abroad.msu.edu

MICHIGAN STATE UNIVERSITY

INTERNATIONAL BUSINESS MANAGEMENT PROGRAM

General Information • Academic study program in Czech Republic (Prague), England (London), Finland (Helsinki), Sweden (Stockholm), Switzerland (Baden, Geneva, Zurich). Excursions to Germany.
Learning Focus • Courses in business, finance. Instruction is offered by professors from the sponsoring institution.
Accommodations • Hotels. Meals are taken on one's own, in local restaurants.
Program Details • Program offered once per year. Session length: 4 weeks. Departures are scheduled in May. The

program is open to undergraduate students, graduate students. Most participants are 18–26 years of age. Other requirements: good academic standing and the approval of the director. 20 participants per session. Application deadline: March 14.
Costs • $3600 (includes housing, some meals, excursions). Application fee: $75. A $250 deposit is required.
Contact • Brenda S. Sprite, Educational Programs Coordinator, Michigan State University, Office of Study Abroad, 109 International Center, East Lansing, MI 48824-1035; 517-353-8920; Fax: 517-432-2082; E-mail: sprite@pilot.msu.edu; World Wide Web: http://study-abroad.msu.edu

MICHIGAN STATE UNIVERSITY

INTERNATIONAL FOOD LAWS–EUROPE

General Information • Academic study program in Belgium (Brussels), England (London), Italy (Rome), Switzerland (Geneva).
Learning Focus • Courses in food laws, international trade, food safety. Instruction is offered by professors from the sponsoring institution.
Accommodations • Hotels. Meals are taken on one's own, in local restaurants.
Program Details • Program offered once per year. Session length: 3 weeks. Departures are scheduled in May. The program is open to undergraduate students, graduate students. Most participants are 18–30 years of age. Other requirements: good academic standing and the approval of the director. 20 participants per session. Application deadline: March 14.
Costs • $2475 (includes housing, some meals, excursions). Application fee: $75. A $250 deposit is required.
Contact • Brenda S. Sprite, Educational Programs Coordinator, Michigan State University, Office of Study Abroad, 109 International Center, East Lansing, MI 48824; 517-353-8920; Fax: 517-432-2082; E-mail: sprite@pilot.msu.edu; World Wide Web: http://study-abroad.msu.edu

MICHIGAN STATE UNIVERSITY

IS THIS A POST-MODERN WORLD?

General Information • Academic study program in Belgium (Brussels), England (London), France (Paris), Italy (Milan, Rome, Venice). Excursions to Europe via train.
Learning Focus • Courses in arts, humanities, cultural studies. Instruction is offered by professors from the sponsoring institution.
Accommodations • Hostels. Meals are taken on one's own, in local restaurants.
Program Details • Program offered once per year. Session length: 4 weeks. Departures are scheduled in May. The program is open to undergraduate students. Most participants are 18–22 years of age. Other requirements: good academic standing and the approval of the director. 16 participants per session. Application deadline: March 14.
Costs • $1838 (includes housing, some meals, excursions). Application fee: $75. A $250 deposit is required.
Contact • Cynthia Chalou, Educational Programs Coordinator, Michigan State University, Office of Study Abroad, 109 International Center, East Lansing, MI 48824; 517-353-8920; Fax: 517-432-2082; E-mail: chalouc@pilot.msu.edu; World Wide Web: http://study-abroad.msu.edu

MICHIGAN STATE UNIVERSITY

PHOTO COMMUNICATION IN ENGLAND AND SCOTLAND

General Information • Academic study program in England (Bath, Bradford, London, York), Scotland (Edinburgh).
Learning Focus • Courses in photography, communications. Instruction is offered by professors from the sponsoring institution.
Accommodations • Dormitories. Single rooms are available. Meals are taken on one's own, in central dining facility.
Program Details • Program offered once per year. Session length: 5 weeks. Departures are scheduled in July. The program is open to undergraduate students, graduate students. Most participants are 18–26 years of age. Other requirements: good academic standing and the approval of the instructor. 12 participants per session. Application deadline: March 14.
Costs • $2283 (includes housing, some meals, excursions). Application fee: $75. A $250 deposit is required.
Contact • Cynthia Chalou, Educational Programs Coordinator, Michigan State University, Office of Study Abroad, 109 International Center, East Lansing, MI 48824-1035; 517-353-8920; Fax: 517-432-2082; E-mail: chalouc@pilot.msu.edu; World Wide Web: http://study-abroad.msu.edu

MICHIGAN STATE UNIVERSITY

POLITICAL SCIENCE PROGRAM IN LONDON

General Information • Academic study program in England (London), Scotland (Edinburgh).
Learning Focus • Courses in British political system. Instruction is offered by professors from the sponsoring institution.
Accommodations • Dormitories. Single rooms are available. Meals are taken on one's own, in central dining facility.
Program Details • Program offered once per year. Session length: 5 weeks. Departures are scheduled in July. The program is open to undergraduate students, graduate students. Most participants are 18–22 years of age. Other requirements: good academic standing and the approval of the director. 20 participants per session. Application deadline: March 14.
Costs • $2422 (includes housing, some meals, excursions). Application fee: $75. A $250 deposit is required.
Contact • Cynthia Chalou, Educational Programs Coordinator, Michigan State University, Office of Study Abroad, 109 International Center, East Lansing, MI 48824-1035; 517-353-8920; Fax: 517-432-2082; E-mail: sprite@pilot.msu.edu; World Wide Web: http://study-abroad.msu.edu

MICHIGAN STATE UNIVERSITY

TELECOMMUNICATIONS PROGRAM IN EUROPE

General Information • Academic study program in Belgium (Brussels), England (London), France (Paris), Switzerland (Geneva).

Learning Focus • Courses in telecommunications. Instruction is offered by professors from the sponsoring institution.
Accommodations • Dormitories, hotels. Meals are taken on one's own, in local restaurants.
Program Details • Program offered once per year. Session length: 5 weeks. Departures are scheduled in June. The program is open to undergraduate students, graduate students, adults. Most participants are 18–30 years of age. Other requirements: good academic standing and the approval of the director. 20 participants per session. Application deadline: March 14.
Costs • $1681 (includes housing, some meals, excursions). Application fee: $75. A $250 deposit is required.
Contact • Brenda S. Sprite, Educational Programs Coordinator, Michigan State University, Office of Study Abroad, 109 International Center, East Lansing, MI 48824-1035; 517-353-8920; Fax: 517-432-2082; E-mail: sprite@pilot.msu.edu; World Wide Web: http://study-abroad.msu.edu

NATURAL HISTORY MUSEUM OF LOS ANGELES COUNTY

WALKING TOUR OF ITALY AND AUSTRIA

General Information • Walking tour with visits to Austria (Fiss), Italy (Castlerotto); excursions to Fisser Joch, Gepatsch Lake, "Hutte Walk". Once at the destination country, participants travel by bus, foot, cable car.
Learning Focus • Museum visits (Museo della Val Gardena). Other activities include hiking. Instruction is offered by naturalists. This program would appeal to people interested in hiking, natural history.
Accommodations • Hotels. Single rooms are available for an additional $110.
Program Details • Program offered once per year. Session length: 1 week. Departures are scheduled in July. Program is targeted to walkers and hikers. Most participants are 12–75 years of age. Participants must be 12 years or older to enroll. 25 participants per session. Reservations are recommended at least 6 months before departure.
Costs • $1695 (includes housing, all meals, excursions). A $400 deposit is required.
Contact • Karen Hovanitz, Travel Program Manager, Natural History Museum of Los Angeles County, 900 Exposition Boulevard, Los Angeles, CA 90007; 213-744-3350; Fax: 213-747-6718; E-mail: khovanit@mizar.usc.edu; World Wide Web: http://www.lam.mus.ca.us/lacmnh

NEW YORK UNIVERSITY

ARTS ADMINISTRATION

General Information • Academic study program in France (Paris), Germany (Berlin), Netherlands (Utrecht). Classes are held on the campus of Utrecht School for the Arts. Excursions to museums, art centers, galleries.
Learning Focus • Courses in arts administration. Instruction is offered by professors from the sponsoring institution and local teachers.
Accommodations • Hotels. Single rooms are available. Meals are taken as a group, in local restaurants.
Program Details • Program offered once per year. Session length: 3 weeks. Departures are scheduled in June. The program is open to graduate students, adults, arts administrators and qualified undergraduate seniors. Most participants are 23–40 years of age. Other requirements: minimum 3.0 GPA and a BA degree. 20 participants per session. Application deadline: April.
Costs • $5000 (includes tuition, housing, some meals, books and class materials, excursions, inter-city transportation). Application fee: $35. A $300 deposit is required.
Contact • Helen J. Kelly, Director of Special Programs, New York University, 82 Washington Square East, Room 62, New York, NY 10003; 212-998-5090; Fax: 212-995-4923; World Wide Web: http://www.nyu.edu/studyabroad

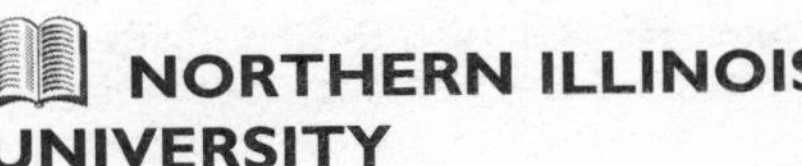

NORTHERN ILLINOIS UNIVERSITY

INTERNATIONAL BUSINESS SEMINARS

General Information • Academic study program in Austria, Belgium, England, France, Italy, Switzerland.
Learning Focus • Courses in management.
Accommodations • Hotels. Single rooms are available. Meals are taken as a group, in local restaurants.
Program Details • Program offered 2 times per year. Session length: 3 weeks. Departures are scheduled in December, May. The program is open to undergraduate students, graduate students. Most participants are 20–25 years of age. 35 participants per session. Application deadline: November 1, April 15.
Costs • $3450–$4168 (includes tuition, housing, some meals, insurance, excursions, international airfare). A $200 deposit is required.
Contact • Anne Seitzinger, Program Coordinator, Short-Term Study Abroad, Northern Illinois University, Study Abroad Office-WI 417, DeKalb, IL 60115; 815-752-0700; Fax: 815-753-0825; E-mail: aseitz@niu.edu; World Wide Web: http://www.niu.edu/depts/intl_prgms/intl.html

OUACHITA BAPTIST UNIVERSITY

EUROPEAN SUMMER STUDY AND TOUR

General Information • Academic study program in England (London, Oxford), France (Paris), Italy (Rome, Venice). Excursions to England (Bath), Italy (Florence, San Gimignano, Pisa), France (Chatres, Palace of Versailles).
Learning Focus • Courses in European history, art history. Instruction is offered by professors from the sponsoring institution.
Accommodations • Hotels. Single rooms are available. Meals are taken as a group.
Program Details • Program offered once per year. Session length: 3 weeks. Departures are scheduled in May. The program is open to undergraduate students. Most participants are 20–23 years of age. Other requirements: 2.5 minimum GPA. 20 participants per session. Application deadline: January 15.
Costs • $2995 (includes tuition, housing, some meals, insurance, excursions, international airfare). A $500 deposit is required.
Contact • Dr. Trey Berry, Director of International Programs, Ouachita Baptist University, OBU Box 3777,

Arkadelphi, AR 71998; 501-245-5197; Fax: 501-245-5312; E-mail: berryt@alpha.obu.edu; World Wide Web: http://www.obu.edu

PEOPLE TO PEOPLE INTERNATIONAL

LONDON AND DUBLIN: THE CITIES AND THEIR AUTHORS

General Information • Academic study program in England (London), Ireland (Dublin).
Learning Focus • Courses in literature, theater. Instruction is offered by professors from the sponsoring institution.
Accommodations • Dormitories, locally-rented apartments, hotels. Single rooms are available. Meals are taken as a group, on one's own, in central dining facility, in local restaurants.
Program Details • Program offered once per year. Session length: 2 weeks. Departures are scheduled in June. The program is open to undergraduate students, graduate students, pre-college students, adults. Most participants are 18–40 years of age. Other requirements: good academic standing. 15–25 participants per session. Application deadline: April 25.
Costs • $2300 (includes tuition, housing, some meals, books and class materials, insurance, excursions, some local transportation, theater events, cultural events, travel in London-Dublin). A $300 deposit is required.
Contact • Dr. Alan M. Warne, Vice President for Programs, People to People International, 501 East Armour Boulevard, Kansas City, MO 64109; 816-531-4701; Fax: 816-561-7502; E-mail: ptpi@cctr.umkc.edu

PEOPLE TO PEOPLE INTERNATIONAL

SUBSTANCE ABUSE AND HUMAN SEXUALITY: PUBLIC POLICY

General Information • Academic study program in England (London), Netherlands (Amsterdam).
Learning Focus • Courses in public policy, political science, counseling, psychology.
Accommodations • Dormitories, locally-rented apartments, hotels. Single rooms are available. Meals are taken as a group, on one's own, in central dining facility, in local restaurants.
Program Details • Program offered once per year. Session length: 2 weeks. Departures are scheduled in June. The program is open to undergraduate students, graduate students, adults, counselors, substance abuse professionals and teachers. Most participants are 20–50 years of age. Other requirements: good academic standing. 15–25 participants per session. Application deadline: April 25.
Costs • $2300 (includes tuition, housing, some meals, books and class materials, insurance, excursions, group travel in Europe). A $300 deposit is required.
Contact • Dr. Alan M. Warne, Vice President for Programs, People to People International, 501 East Armour Boulevard, Kansas City, MO 64109; 816-531-4701; Fax: 816-561-7502; E-mail: ptpi@cctr.umkc.edu

PEOPLE TO PEOPLE INTERNATIONAL

SWEDEN AND FINLAND: HEALTH CARE AND SOCIAL SERVICES

General Information • Academic study program in Finland (Helsinki), Sweden (Stockholm).
Learning Focus • Courses in health care, social policies, gender issues. Instruction is offered by professors from the sponsoring institution.
Accommodations • Homestays, hotels. Single rooms are available. Meals are taken as a group, on one's own, in local restaurants.
Program Details • Program offered once per year. Session length: 2 weeks. Departures are scheduled in June. The program is open to undergraduate students, graduate students, adults, health care professionals and social service personnel. Most participants are 20–50 years of age. Other requirements: good academic standing. 15–25 participants per session. Application deadline: April 25.
Costs • $2400 (includes tuition, housing, some meals, books and class materials, insurance, excursions, cultural events, weekend homestay, cruise to and from Stockholm and Helsinki). A $300 deposit is required.
Contact • Dr. Alan M. Warne, Vice President for Programs, People to People International, 501 East Armour Boulevard, Kansas City, MO 64109; 816-531-4701; Fax: 816-561-7502; E-mail: ptpi@cctr.umkc.edu

ST. JOHN'S UNIVERSITY

GRECO-ROMAN PROGRAM

General Information • Academic study program in Greece (Athens), Italy (Rome).
Learning Focus • Courses in art, history, literature. Instruction is offered by professors from the sponsoring institution.
Accommodations • Dormitories, hotels. Meals are taken as a group, on one's own, in local restaurants.
Program Details • Program offered once per year. Session length: 12 weeks. Departures are scheduled in September. The program is open to undergraduate students. Most participants are 20–22 years of age. Other requirements: minimum 2.5 GPA. 30 participants per session. Application deadline: March.
Costs • $9200 (includes tuition, housing, all meals, excursions). Application fee: $100.
Contact • Stephen Burmeister-May, Director, Center for International Education, St. John's University, Collegeville, MN 56321; 320-363-2082; Fax: 320-363-2013; E-mail: intleduc@csbsju.edu

SANTA BARBARA MUSEUM OF ART

GREAT PALACES OF NORTHERN EUROPE

General Information • Cultural tour with visits to Netherlands (Amsterdam), Russia (St. Petersburg), Sweden (Stockholm). Once at the destination country, participants travel by bus, airplane.
Learning Focus • Escorted travel to palaces, castles, and gardens. Instruction is offered by art historians. This program

would appeal to people interested in art, architecture, decorative arts, gardening, photography.
Accommodations • Hotels. Single rooms are available.
Program Details • Program offered once per year. Session length: 11 days. Departures are scheduled in June. Most participants are 30–80 years of age. Participants must be members of the sponsoring organization (annual dues: $40). 15–20 participants per session. Application deadline: April.
Costs • $5400 (includes housing, some meals, excursions, international airfare). A $500 deposit is required.
Contact • Shelley Ruston, Director of Special Programs, Santa Barbara Museum of Art, 1130 State Street, Santa Barbara, CA 93101; 805-963-4364, ext. 336; Fax: 805-966-6840

SMITHSONIAN INSTITUTION

SMITHSONIAN STUDY TOURS AND SEMINARS IN WESTERN EUROPE

General Information • Garden, nature study, cultural, cooking and wilderness programs with visits to Austria, England, France, Germany, Greece, Ireland, Italy, Norway, Portugal, Scotland, Spain, Switzerland, Wales. Once at the destination country, participants travel by train, bus, foot, boat, airplane.
Learning Focus • Instruction in art history, Western civilization, Italian cuisine, and other subjects. Escorted travel to special sites off limits to most tourists. Museum visits (major museums, small galleries, and private collections). Attendance at performances (opera, symphony, theater, dance, traditional folk and private recitals). Nature observation (birding, horticulture). Other activities include hiking. Instruction is offered by professors, researchers, naturalists, artists, historians, scientists. This program would appeal to people interested in archaeology, religious history, photography, natural history, trains.
Accommodations • Hotels, campsites. Single rooms are available.
Program Details • Session length: 9–17 days. Departures are scheduled throughout the year. Most participants are 25–85 years of age. Participants must be 18 years or older to enroll. Participants must be members of the sponsoring organization (annual dues: $24). 15–30 participants per session.
Costs • $1999 and up (includes tuition, housing, some meals, excursions, international airfare).
Contact • Customer Service Representative, Smithsonian Institution, Smithsonian Study Tours and Seminars, 1100 Jefferson Drive SW (MRC 702), Washington, DC 20560; 202-357-4700; Fax: 202-633-9250

SYRACUSE UNIVERSITY

COMPARATIVE CRIMINAL JUSTICE: EUROPE AND THE UNITED STATES

General Information • Academic study program in England (London), France (Strasbourg), Netherlands (Amsterdam).
Learning Focus • Courses in political science, legal studies, legal studies. Instruction is offered by professors from the sponsoring institution.
Accommodations • Hotels. Single rooms are available. Meals are taken on one's own, in local restaurants.
Program Details • Program offered once per year. Session length: 5 weeks. Departures are scheduled in June. The program is open to undergraduate students, graduate students, adults. Most participants are 19–30 years of age. Other requirements: minimum 2.7 GPA. 15 participants per session. Application deadline: March 15.
Costs • $5586 (includes tuition, housing, some meals, books and class materials, excursions). Application fee: $40. A $350 deposit is required.
Contact • Ms. Daisy Fried, Associate Director, Syracuse University, 119 Euclid Avenue, Syracuse, NY 13244-4170; 315-443-9419; Fax: 315-443-4593; E-mail: dsfried@summon3.syr.edu; World Wide Web: http://sumweb.syr.edu/dipa/dipa9.htm

UNIVERSITY OF ALABAMA AT BIRMINGHAM

UNIVERSITY OF ALABAMA AT BIRMINGHAM IN EUROPE

General Information • Academic study program in Austria (Vienna), Belgium (Brussels, Ghent), Germany (Augsburg, Frankfurt, Munich, Stuttgart), Netherlands (Amsterdam).
Learning Focus • Courses in international business. Instruction is offered by professors from the sponsoring institution and local teachers.
Accommodations • Hotels. Single rooms are available. Meals are taken on one's own, in local restaurants.
Program Details • Program offered once per year. Session length: 3 weeks. Departures are scheduled in August. The program is open to undergraduate students, graduate students. Most participants are 20–40 years of age. Other requirements: preliminary contact with program director. 24–26 participants per session. Application deadline: May 31.
Costs • $2525 (includes housing, some meals, insurance, excursions, international airfare, ground transportation). A $200 deposit is required.
Contact • Frank Romanowicz, Study Abroad Coordinator, University of Alabama at Birmingham, 1400 University Boulevard, HUC 318, Birmingham, AL 35294-1150; 205-934-5025; Fax: 205-934-8664; E-mail: ucipØ17@larry.huc.uab.edu

UNIVERSITY OF ARIZONA

ART AND ARCHITECTURE IN GREECE AND ITALY

General Information • Academic study program in Greece (Athens, Corinth), Italy (Florence, Milan, Rome).
Learning Focus • Courses in architecture, fine arts. Instruction is offered by professors from the sponsoring institution.
Accommodations • Hotels. Meals are taken on one's own, in local restaurants.
Program Details • Program offered once per year. Session length: 6 weeks. Departures are scheduled in June. The program is open to undergraduate students, graduate students, adults. Most participants are 20–30 years of age.

Other requirements: minimum 2.5 GPA and sophomore standing. 30 participants per session. Application deadline: April 1.
Costs • $4350 (includes tuition, housing, some meals, international airfare). Application fee: $35. A $300 deposit is required.
Contact • Renee Griggs, Center for Global Student Programs, University of Arizona, 915 North Tyndall Avenue, Tucson, AZ 85721; 520-621-4627; Fax: 520-621-4069

UNIVERSITY OF DELAWARE

WINTER SESSION IN ENGLAND (LONDON) AND SCOTLAND (EDINBURGH)

General Information • Academic study program in England (London), Scotland (Edinburgh). Classes are held on the campus of University of Delaware London Center, Moray House Institute of Education.
Learning Focus • Courses in education, teaching, elementary education. Instruction is offered by professors from the sponsoring institution.
Accommodations • Hotels.
Program Details • Program offered once per year. Session length: 5 weeks. Departures are scheduled in January. The program is open to undergraduate students, graduate students, adults. Most participants are 18–21 years of age. Other requirements: minimum 2.0 GPA. 20 participants per session. Application deadline: October.
Costs • Contact sponsor for information. A $200 deposit is required.
Contact • International Programs and Special Sessions, University of Delaware, 4 Kent Way, Newark, DE 19716-1450; 888-831-4685; Fax: 302-831-6042; E-mail: studyabroad@mvs.udel.edu

UNIVERSITY OF GEORGIA

DRAMA AND JOURNALISM IN ITALY AND ENGLAND

General Information • Academic study program in England (London), Italy (Parma). Classes are held on the campus of University of Parma, University of London. Excursions to Rome, Florence, Venice, Milan, Stratford.
Learning Focus • Courses in drama, journalism, art, travel writing, art criticism, history of theater, play analysis. Instruction is offered by professors from the sponsoring institution.
Accommodations • Dormitories, hotels. Single rooms are available. Meals are taken as a group, on one's own, in central dining facility, in local restaurants.
Program Details • Program offered once per year. Session length: 7 weeks. Departures are scheduled in June. The program is open to undergraduate students, graduate students, adults. Most participants are 20–22 years of age. Other requirements: minimum 2.50 GPA or permission of program leaders. 20–25 participants per session. Application deadline: April 4.
Costs • $4400 (includes tuition, housing, some meals, books and class materials, excursions, international airfare, tickets to events, ground transportation, limited insurance). A $200 deposit is required.
Contact • Dr. John English, Professor, University of Georgia, College of Journalism, Athens, GA 30602; 706-542-5028; Fax: 706-542-4785; E-mail: englishj@uga.cc.uga.edu

---

In 1988, the University of Georgia established a 6-week summer program in two different countries that combines the study of the history and criticism of drama with print journalism. The first 4 weeks are spent in Italy at the University of Parma with excursions to Rome, Florence, Milan, Sabbioneta, Mantua, Verona, Vicenza, and Venice. The group takes up residence at the University of London the last 2 weeks. In both settings, students have the chance to witness plays, concerts, exhibits, and tourist sites while they become part of a university community. The program offers an exciting and varied fare.

UNIVERSITY OF KANSAS

HUMANITIES IN GREAT BRITAIN

General Information • Academic study program in England (Cambridge, London, Oxford, York), Scotland (Edinburgh). Classes are held on the campus of University of Cambridge, University of York, University of Oxford, University of Edinburgh. Excursions to Glasgow, Durham, Exeter.
Learning Focus • Courses in history, art history, literature. Instruction is offered by professors from the sponsoring institution.
Accommodations • Dormitories, hotels. Meals are taken as a group, on one's own, in central dining facility, in local restaurants.
Program Details • Program offered once per year. Session length: 5 weeks. Departures are scheduled in June. The program is open to undergraduate students, graduate students. Most participants are 20–25 years of age. Other requirements: preference to applicants with minimum 2.5 GPA and above. 20 participants per session. Application deadline: March 1.
Costs • $3154 (includes tuition, housing, some meals, ground transportation, group cultural events). Application fee: $15. A $300 deposit is required.
Contact • Susan MacNally, Coordinator of Summer Institutes, University of Kansas, Office of Study Abroad, 203 Lippincott Hall, Lawrence, KS 66045; 913-864-3742; Fax: 913-864-5040; E-mail: osa@falcon.cc.ukans.edu; World Wide Web: http://kuhub.cc.ukans.edu/~intlstdy/osa/osamain.html

UNIVERSITY OF TENNESSEE, KNOXVILLE

GRAPHIC DESIGN IN BRITAIN

General Information • Academic study program in England (London), Scotland (Glasgow).

Learning Focus • Courses in graphic design, advertising, computer art, photography, illustration, design history. Instruction is offered by professors from the sponsoring institution.
Accommodations • Dormitories, locally-rented apartments. Single rooms are available. Meals are taken on one's own, in local restaurants.
Program Details • Program offered once per year. Session length: 4 weeks. Departures are scheduled in June. The program is open to undergraduate students, graduate students, adults. Most participants are 18–40 years of age. 15 participants per session. Application deadline: March 15.
Costs • $3000 (includes housing, some meals, excursions, international airfare, transportion passes and tickets). Application fee: $25. A $500 deposit is required.
Contact • Susan Metros, Professor of Art, University of Tennessee, Knoxville, Department of Art, 1715 Volunteer Boulevard, Knoxville, TN 37996-2410; 423-974-3208; Fax: 423-974-3198; E-mail: smetros@utk.edu; World Wide Web: http://funnelweb.utcc.utk.edu/~art

 ACTILINGUA ACADEMY

GERMAN IN VIENNA

General Information • Language study program with visits to Vienna, Salzburg, Prague, Budapest, Alpine resorts. Once at the destination country, participants travel by bus, foot.
Learning Focus • Instruction in German. Escorted travel to Budapest, Prague, Salzburg. Instruction is offered by professors. This program would appeal to people interested in language, music, art, culture.
Accommodations • Homestays, dormitories, locally-rented apartments. Single rooms are available for an additional $25.
Program Details • Session length: 2–36 weeks. Departures are scheduled throughout the year. Most participants are 16–35 years of age. Participants must be 16 years or older to enroll. 150 participants per session. Reservations are recommended at least 1 month before departure.
Costs • $1600 (includes tuition, housing, books and class materials, culture and leisure program).
Contact • Claudia Hölderl, Admissions Officer, Actilingua Academy, Gloriettegasse 8, Vienna A-1130, Austria; +43 1-877-6701; Fax: +43 1-877-6703; E-mail: actilingua@via.at

 BEAVER COLLEGE

VIENNA'S PSYCHOLOGISTS: FREUD, ADLER, AND FRANKL

General Information • Academic study program in Vienna. Classes are held on the campus of Austro-American Institute of Education. Excursions to Freud's house, former concentration camp at Mauthausen.
Learning Focus • Courses in psychology. Instruction is offered by local teachers.
Accommodations • Homestays. Single rooms are available. Meals are taken in local restaurants, in residences.
Program Details • Program offered once per year. Session length: 4 weeks. Departures are scheduled in May. The program is open to undergraduate students, graduate students, adults. Other requirements: minimum 3.0 GPA, three or four semesters of college-level course work and course prerequisites. 10 participants per session. Application deadline: March 31.
Costs • $2575 (includes tuition, housing, International Student Identification card, predeparture materials, host country support). Application fee: $35. A $500 deposit is required.
Contact • Helene Cohan, Associate Director, Beaver College, Center for Education Abroad, 450 South Easton Road, Glenside, PA 19038; 888-232-8379; Fax: 215-572-2174; E-mail: cohan@beaver.edu

BOWLING GREEN STATE UNIVERSITY

SUMMER PROGRAM IN SALZBURG

General Information • Language study program in Salzburg. Classes are held on the campus of Deutschkurse Salzburg.
Learning Focus • Courses in German language, business German, Austrian literature. Instruction is offered by local teachers.
Accommodations • Dormitories, locally-rented apartments. Single rooms are available. Meals are taken on one's own, in residences.
Program Details • Program offered 2 times per year. Session length: 3 weeks. Departures are scheduled in July, August. The program is open to undergraduate students, graduate students, adults. Most participants are 19–65 years of age. 3–10 participants per session. Application deadline: May 31.
Costs • $1255–$1355 for Ohio residents, $1697–$1797 for non-residents (includes tuition, housing, some meals, books and class materials, excursions). Application fee: $10. A $120 deposit is required.
Contact • Dr. Joseph Gray, Coordinator, Bowling Green State University, Department of German, Russian and East Asian Languages, Bowling Green, OH 43403-0219; 419-372-7140; Fax: 419-372-2571; E-mail: jgray@bgnet.bgsu.edu; World Wide Web: http://www.bgsu.edu/departments/greal/AYA-Salzburg.html

THE CENTER FOR ENGLISH STUDIES

STUDY ABROAD IN VIENNA, AUSTRIA

General Information • Language study program with visits to Vienna. Program is affiliated with International House-Vienna.
Learning Focus • Instruction in the German language. Other activities include field trips to local sites, museums, markets and churches. Instruction is offered by faculty members from host institution. This program would appeal to people interested in the German language.
Accommodations • Homestays, dormitories, locally-rented apartments, program-owned apartments, program-owned houses. Single rooms are available.
Program Details • Session length: 2 or more weeks. Departures are scheduled throughout the year. Most participants are 16–70 years of age. Participants must be 16 years or older to enroll. 6–12 participants per session. Application deadline: 2 weeks prior to departure. Reservations are recommended at least 1 month before departure.
Costs • $1000 for 2 weeks (includes tuition, housing, some meals, books and class materials, excursions). A $125 deposit is required.

Contact • Ms. Lorraine Haber, Study Abroad Coordinator, The Center for English Studies, 330 7th Avenue, 6th Floor, New York, NY 10001; 212-629-7300; Fax: 212-736-7950; E-mail: ces_newyork@cescorp.com

COUNTRY WALKERS

TYROLEAN TREASURES

General Information • Cultural, gourmet cooking, nature study and walking tour with visits to Alpbach, Inneralpbach. Once at the destination country, participants travel by foot.
Learning Focus • Escorted travel to Panoramaweg and Grosse Galtenberg. Museum visits (farm-museum). Other activities include walking. Instruction is offered by professors, researchers, naturalists, historians. This program would appeal to people interested in walking, nature studies, food and wine.
Accommodations • Hotels. Single rooms are available for an additional $300–$600.
Program Details • Program offered 4 times per year. Session length: 8 days. Departures are scheduled in June–September. Program is targeted to adults 35 to 65 years old. Most participants are 35–65 years of age. Participants must be 18 years or older to enroll. 18 participants per session. Reservations are recommended at least 5–6 months before departure.
Costs • $1995 (includes housing, all meals, excursions). A $400 deposit is required.
Contact • Heather Kellingbeck, Vice President, Country Walkers, PO Box 180, Waterbury, VT 05176; 800-464-9255; Fax: 802-244-5661; E-mail: ctrywalk@aol.com

CROSS-CULTURE

MOZART'S SALZBURG

General Information • Cultural tour with visits to Salzburg, Germany (Berchtesgaden). Once at the destination country, participants travel by bus.
Learning Focus • Escorted travel to Kaiservilla, Castle Mirabell and Hohensalzburg Fortress. Museum visits (Mozart Museum, Traditional Buildings Outdoor Museum). Attendance at performances (Vienna Philharmonic Orchestra, chamber music group, Salzburg Marionette Theater). Instruction is offered by highly educated guides. This program would appeal to people interested in culture, history, nature studies, arts, traditions, food and wine.
Accommodations • Hotels. Single rooms are available for an additional $120.
Program Details • Program offered once per year. Session length: 9 days. Departures are scheduled in July. Program is targeted to adults of all ages. Most participants are 40–70 years of age. Participants must be 12 years or older to enroll. Other requirements: good health, accompaniment of an adult if under 18. 20–25 participants per session. Application deadline: 1 month prior to departure. Reservations are recommended at least 3–12 months before departure.
Costs • $2670 (includes tuition, housing, all meals, books and class materials, excursions, international airfare). A $300 deposit is required.
Contact • Cross-Culture, 52 High Point Drive, Amherst, MA 01002-1224; 413-256-6303; Fax: 413-253-2303; E-mail: xculture@javanet.com; World Wide Web: http://www.empiremall.com/cross-culture

CROSS-CULTURE

SALZBURG CELEBRATION AND MUNICH

General Information • Cultural tour with visits to Salzburg, Germany (Munich). Once at the destination country, participants travel by bus, horse-drawn sleigh.
Learning Focus • Escorted travel to the Catacombs and St. Peter's Cemetery. Museum visits (Mozart Museum, Corolino Augusteum Museum). Attendance at performances (Vienna Philharmonic Orchestra, Salzburg Marionette Theater). Instruction is offered by highly educated guides. This program would appeal to people interested in culture, history, food and wine, arts, traditions, nature studies.
Accommodations • Hotels. Single rooms are available for an additional $175.
Program Details • Program offered once per year. Session length: 9 days. Departures are scheduled in January. Program is targeted to adults of all ages. Most participants are 40–70 years of age. Participants must be 12 years or older to enroll. Other requirements: good health, accompaniment of an adult if under 18. 20–25 participants per session. Application deadline: 1 month prior to departure. Reservations are recommended at least 3–12 months before departure.
Costs • $2420 (includes tuition, housing, all meals, books and class materials, excursions, international airfare). A $300 deposit is required.
Contact • Cross-Culture, 52 High Point Drive, Amherst, MA 01002-1224; 413-256-6303; Fax: 413-253-2303; E-mail: xculture@javanet.com; World Wide Web: http://www.empiremall.com/cross-culture

CROSS-CULTURE

VIENNA AND PRAGUE: CULTURAL CAPITALS

General Information • Cultural tour with visits to Vienna, Czech Republic (Prague). Once at the destination country, participants travel by bus.
Learning Focus • Escorted travel to St. Stephen's Cathedral, palaces and Prague. Museum visits (Belvedere Palace, Kunsthistoriches Museum). Attendance at performances (opera, Vienna Boy Choir). Instruction is offered by highly educated guides. This program would appeal to people interested in culture, history, food and wine, arts, traditions, nature studies.
Accommodations • Hotels. Single rooms are available for an additional $105.
Program Details • Program offered once per year. Session length: 9 days. Departures are scheduled in January. Program is targeted to adults of all ages. Most participants are 40–70 years of age. Participants must be 12 years or older to enroll. Other requirements: good health, accompaniment of an adult if under 18. 20–25 participants per session. Application deadline: 1 month prior to departure. Reservations are recommended at least 3–12 months before departure.
Costs • $2490 (includes tuition, housing, all meals, books and class materials, excursions, international airfare). A $300 deposit is required.
Contact • Cross-Culture, 52 High Point Drive, Amherst, MA 01002-1224; 413-256-6303; Fax: 413-253-2303; E-mail: xculture@javanet.com; World Wide Web: http://www.empiremall.com/cross-culture

CROSS-CULTURE

VIENNESE WALTZES

General Information • Cultural tour with visits to Vienna. Once at the destination country, participants travel by bus.
Learning Focus • Instruction in recent Viennese history and current Austrian national issues. Escorted travel to Schonbrunn Palace, Castle Belvedere and Haydn's home. Attendance at performances (opera, Viennese operetta music). Instruction is offered by highly educated guides. This program would appeal to people interested in culture, history, nature studies, arts, traditions, food and wine.
Accommodations • Hotels. Single rooms are available for an additional $150.
Program Details • Program offered once per year. Session length: 9 days. Departures are scheduled in July. Program is targeted to adults of all ages. Most participants are 40–70 years of age. Participants must be 12 years or older to enroll. Other requirements: good health, accompaniment of an adult if under 18. 20–25 participants per session. Application deadline: 1 month prior to departure. Reservations are recommended at least 3–12 months before departure.
Costs • $2560 (includes tuition, housing, all meals, books and class materials, excursions, international airfare). A $300 deposit is required.
Contact • Cross-Culture, 52 High Point Drive, Amherst, MA 01002-1224; 413-256-6303; Fax: 413-253-2303; E-mail: xculture@javanet.com; World Wide Web: http://www.empiremall.com/cross-culture

DEUTSCH-INSTITUT TIROL

DEUTSCH-INSTITUT TIROL

General Information • Language study program with visits to Kitzbühel, Innsbruck, Salzburg, Germany (Munich), Vienna.
Learning Focus • Instruction in the German language.
Accommodations • Dormitories. Single rooms are available.
Program Details • Session length: 1 or more weeks. Departures are scheduled throughout the year. Most participants are 16–60 years of age. Participants must be 16 years or older to enroll. 16 participants per session.
Costs • $490 per week (includes tuition, books and class materials). A $300 deposit is required.
Contact • Am Sandbühel 2, Deutsch-Institut Tirol, A-6370, Kitzbühel, Austria; +43 53-567-1274; Fax: +43 53-537-2363; E-mail: dit@kitz.netwing.at

EASTERN MICHIGAN UNIVERSITY

INTENSIVE GERMAN LANGUAGE PROGRAM

General Information • Language study program in Graz.
Learning Focus • Courses in German language. Instruction is offered by professors from the sponsoring institution.
Accommodations • Dormitories. Meals are taken on one's own, in residences.
Program Details • Program offered once per year. Session length: 6 weeks. Departures are scheduled in July. The program is open to undergraduate students, graduate students. Most participants are 18–30 years of age. Other requirements: minimum 2.0 GPA and 18 years of age. 10 participants per session. Application deadline: April 1.
Costs • $2895 (includes tuition, housing, insurance). A $150 deposit is required.
Contact • Academic Programs Abroad, Eastern Michigan University, 332 Goodison Hall, Ypsilanti, MI 48197; 800-777-3541; Fax: 313-487-2316; E-mail: programs.abroad@emich.edu; World Wide Web: http://www.emich.edu/public/cont_ed/abroad.html

EUROCENTRES

LANGUAGE IMMERSION IN AUSTRIA

General Information • Language study program in Vienna. Classes are held on the campus of Eurocentre Vienna Summer Centre. Excursions to Vienna Woods, Salzburg, Czech Republic (Prague), Hungary (Budapest).
Learning Focus • Courses in German language, Austrian culture. Instruction is offered by professors from the sponsoring institution.
Accommodations • Homestays. Single rooms are available. Meals are taken with host family, in residences.
Program Details • Program offered 20 times per year. Session length: 2–12 weeks. Departures are scheduled in January–December. The program is open to undergraduate students, graduate students, pre-college students, adults. Most participants are 16–80 years of age. 15 participants per session.
Costs • Contact sponsor for information.
Contact • Marketing, Eurocentres, 101 North Union Street, Suite 300, Alexandria, VA 22314; 800-648-4809; Fax: 703-684-1495; E-mail: 100632.141@compuserve.com; World Wide Web: http://www.clark.net/pub/eurocent/home.htm

EUROPEAN HERITAGE INSTITUTE

GERMAN LANGUAGE AND CULTURE PROGRAM IN KLAGENFURT, AUSTRIA

General Information • Language study program in Klagenfurt. Classes are held on the campus of University of Klagenfurt.
Learning Focus • Courses in German language and culture.
Accommodations • Dormitories. Meals are taken on one's own.
Program Details • Program offered 2 times per year. Session length: 3–6 weeks. Departures are scheduled in July, August. The program is open to undergraduate students, graduate students, adults. Most participants are 18–45 years of age. 10 participants per session. Application deadline: 65 days prior to departure.
Costs • $1440 (includes tuition, housing). A $350 deposit is required.
Contact • Dr. Antonio Masullo, Professor, European Heritage Institute, 2708 East Franklin Street, Richmond, VA 23223; 804-648-0826; Fax: 804-648-0826; E-mail: euritage@i2020.net

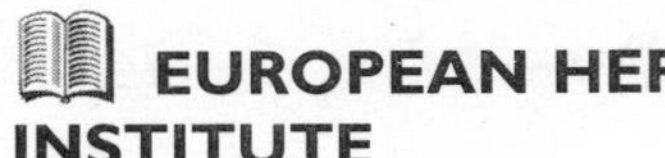

EUROPEAN HERITAGE INSTITUTE

GERMAN LANGUAGE AND CULTURE PROGRAM IN PORTSCHACH, AUSTRIA

General Information • Language study program in Portschach. Classes are held on the campus of University of Klagenfurt at Portschach.
Learning Focus • Courses in German language, German culture. Instruction is offered by local teachers.
Accommodations • Dormitories. Single rooms are available. Meals are taken on one's own.
Program Details • Program offered 5 times per year. Session length: 3–12 weeks. Departures are scheduled in May–September. The program is open to undergraduate students, graduate students, adults. Most participants are 18–45 years of age. Application deadline: 65 days prior to departure.
Costs • $1410 for 3 weeks (includes tuition, housing). A $350 deposit is required.
Contact • Dr. Antonio Masullo, Professor, European Heritage Institute, 2708 East Franklin Street, Richmond, VA 23223; 804-648-0826; Fax: 804-648-0826; E-mail: euritage@i2020.net

EUROPEAN HERITAGE INSTITUTE

MUSIC MASTERCLASS PROGRAM IN VIENNA FOR PROMISING ARTISTS

General Information • Performing arts program in Vienna. Classes are held on the campus of Wiener Meisterkurse.
Learning Focus • Courses in music.
Accommodations • Dormitories, locally-rented apartments. Single rooms are available. Meals are taken on one's own.
Program Details • Program offered 2 times per year. Session length: 2 weeks. Departures are scheduled in July, August. The program is open to gifted young artists. Most participants are 18–45 years of age. 5–8 participants per session. Application deadline: April 1.
Costs • $770–$1020 (includes tuition, administrative fees). A $350 deposit is required.
Contact • Dr. Antonio Masullo, Professor, European Heritage Institute, 2708 East Franklin Street, Richmond, VA 23223; 804-648-0826; Fax: 804-648-0826; E-mail: euritage@i2020.net

EUROPEAN HERITAGE INSTITUTE

SUMMER PROGRAM IN VIENNA

General Information • Language study program in Vienna. Classes are held on the campus of University of Vienna.
Learning Focus • Courses in German language, German literature. Instruction is offered by local teachers.
Accommodations • Dormitories, locally-rented apartments. Meals are taken on one's own, in residences.
Program Details • Program offered 3 times per year. Session length: 4, 8, and 12 weeks. Departures are scheduled in July, August, September. The program is open to undergraduate students, graduate students, adults. Most participants are 18–45 years of age. 10 participants per session. Application deadline: 65 days prior to departure.
Costs • $1315 (includes tuition, housing, administrative fees). A $350 deposit is required.
Contact • Dr. Antonio Masullo, Professor, European Heritage Institute, 2708 East Franklin Street, Richmond, VA 23223; 804-648-0826; Fax: 804-648-0826; E-mail: euritage@i2020.net

FOREIGN LANGUAGE STUDY ABROAD SERVICE

GERMAN IN VIENNA

General Information • Language study program in Vienna.
Learning Focus • Courses in language study. Instruction is offered by local teachers.
Accommodations • Homestays, dormitories, program-owned apartments, hotels. Single rooms are available. Meals are taken as a group, on one's own, with host family, in central dining facility, in local restaurants, in residences.
Program Details • Session length: varies. Departures are scheduled in January–December. The program is open to undergraduate students, graduate students, pre-college students, adults. Most participants are 18 years of age and older.
Costs • Contact sponsor for information. Application fee: $50. A $100 deposit is required.
Contact • Louise Harber, Coordinator, Foreign Language Study Abroad Service, Department IH, Box 903, 5935 Southwest 64th Avenue, South Miami, FL 33143; 800-282-1090; Fax: 305-662-2907; E-mail: flsas@netpoint.net; World Wide Web: http://www.netpoint.net/~flsas

INSTITUTE OF EUROPEAN STUDIES/INSTITUTE OF ASIAN STUDIES

VIENNA INTENSIVE GERMAN SUMMER PROGRAM

General Information • Language study program in Vienna. Excursions to Czech Republic, Hungary.
Learning Focus • Courses in German language. Instruction is offered by professors from the sponsoring institution.
Accommodations • Homestays, locally-rented apartments. Meals are taken on one's own, with host family, in central dining facility, in local restaurants, in residences.
Program Details • Program offered 2 times per year. Session length: 4 weeks. Departures are scheduled in June, July. The program is open to undergraduate students, graduate students, continuing education students. Most participants are 18–22 years of age. Other requirements: good academic standing and one semester German for July session. 10 participants per session. Application deadline: April 15.
Costs • $2150 (includes tuition, housing, excursions). Application fee: $25. A $500 deposit is required.
Contact • Department of Admissions, Institute of European Studies/Institute of Asian Studies, 223 West Ohio Street, Chicago, IL 60610-4196; 800-995-2300; Fax: 312-944-1448; E-mail: recruit@iesias.org; World Wide Web: http://www.iesias.org

INSTITUTE OF EUROPEAN STUDIES/INSTITUTE OF ASIAN STUDIES

VIENNA SUMMER PROGRAM

General Information • Academic study program in Vienna. Excursions to Czech Republic, Hungary.

Learning Focus • Courses in art history, literature, German language, economics, political science.

Accommodations • Homestays, locally-rented apartments. Meals are taken on one's own, with host family, in central dining facility, in local restaurants, in residences.

Program Details • Program offered 2 times per year. Session length: 4 weeks. Departures are scheduled in June, July. The program is open to undergraduate students, graduate students, continuing education students. Most participants are 18–25 years of age. Other requirements: good academic standing. 20 participants per session. Application deadline: April 15.

Costs • $2150 (includes tuition, housing, excursions). Application fee: $25. A $500 deposit is required.

Contact • Department of Admissions, Institute of European Studies/Institute of Asian Studies, 223 West Ohio Street, Chicago, IL 60610-4196; 800-995-2300; Fax: 312-944-1448; E-mail: recruit@iesias.org; World Wide Web: http://www.iesias.org

INTERHOSTEL, UNIVERSITY OF NEW HAMPSHIRE

CHRISTMAS IN VIENNA

General Information • Cultural tour with visits to Vienna, Schönbrun Palace, Abbey Heilingenkreuz, Baden, Abbey Melk, Luberegg Castle, Bratislava, Klosterneuburg. Once at the destination country, participants travel by bus, foot. Program is affiliated with Oekista.

Learning Focus • Instruction in history, culture and Christmas traditions. Escorted travel to palaces, castles, and villages. Museum visits (Museum of Fine Arts, Museum of Religious Folk Art). Attendance at performances (State opera, concerts). Other activities include New Year's Eve Ball. Instruction is offered by historians. This program would appeal to people interested in history, culture.

Accommodations • Hotels. Single rooms are available for an additional $375.

Program Details • Program offered once per year. Session length: 2 weeks. Departures are scheduled in December. Program is targeted to seniors over 50. Most participants are 60–80 years of age. Participants must be 50 years or older to enroll. 35 participants per session. Reservations are recommended at least 6 months before departure.

Costs • $3075 (includes tuition, housing, all meals, excursions, international airfare, entrance fees). A $200 deposit is required.

Contact • Janice Pierson, Office Supervisor, Interhostel, University of New Hampshire, 6 Garrison Avenue, Durham, NH 03824-3529; 800-733-9753; Fax: 603-862-1113; World Wide Web: http://www.learn.unh.edu/

INTERHOSTEL, UNIVERSITY OF NEW HAMPSHIRE

SALZBURG AND VIENNA, AUSTRIA

General Information • Cultural tour with visits to Salzburg, Vienna, Schönnbrun Palace, Heilingenkreuz, Baden, Rohrau, St. Florian, St. Wolfgang, Hallein. Once at the destination country, participants travel by bus, foot. Program is affiliated with Oekista.

Learning Focus • Instruction in history and culture. Escorted travel to villages. Museum visits (Imperial Treasury, Museum of Fine Arts). Attendance at performances (concerts, opera). Instruction is offered by professors, historians. This program would appeal to people interested in history, culture.

Accommodations • Hotels. Single rooms are available for an additional $250.

Program Details • Program offered once per year. Session length: 2 weeks. Departures are scheduled in June. Program is targeted to seniors over 50. Most participants are 60–80 years of age. Participants must be 50 years or older to enroll. 35 participants per session. Reservations are recommended at least 6 months before departure.

Costs • $3125 (includes tuition, housing, all meals, excursions, international airfare, entrance fees). A $200 deposit is required.

Contact • Janice Pierson, Office Supervisor, Interhostel, University of New Hampshire, 6 Garrison Avenue, Durham, NH 03824; 800-733-9753; Fax: 603-862-1113; World Wide Web: http://www.learn.unh.edu/

INTERHOSTEL, UNIVERSITY OF NEW HAMPSHIRE

VIENNA, AUSTRIA

General Information • Cultural tour with visits to Vienna, Schönnbrun Palace, Melk Abbey, Krems, Rohrau, Halbturn, Heilingen Kreuz Abbey, Mayerling, Baden. Once at the destination country, participants travel by bus, foot, boat. Program is affiliated with Oekista.

Learning Focus • Instruction in history and culture. Escorted travel to historical sites. Museum visits (Museum of Fine Arts, Museum of the History of the City of Vienna). Attendance at performances (opera, concerts). Instruction is offered by historians. This program would appeal to people interested in history, culture.

Accommodations • Hotels. Single rooms are available for an additional $350.

Program Details • Program offered once per year. Session length: 2 weeks. Departures are scheduled in May. Program is targeted to seniors over 50. Most participants are 60–80 years of age. Participants must be 50 years or older to enroll. 35 participants per session. Reservations are recommended at least 6 months before departure.

Costs • $2965 (includes tuition, housing, all meals, excursions, international airfare, entrance fees). A $200 deposit is required.

Contact • Janice Pierson, Office Supervisor, Interhostel, University of New Hampshire, 6 Garrison Avenue, Durham, NH 03824; 800-733-9753; Fax: 603-862-1113; World Wide Web: http://www.learn.unh.edu/

KENTUCKY INSTITUTE FOR INTERNATIONAL STUDIES

PROGRAM IN BREGENZ, AUSTRIA

General Information • Academic study program in Bregenz. Excursions to surrounding area.
Learning Focus • Courses in language study, cultural studies, economics, English language, political science. Instruction is offered by professors from the sponsoring institution.
Accommodations • Homestays, pensiones. Meals are taken as a group, in local restaurants.
Program Details • Program offered once per year. Session length: 5 weeks. Departures are scheduled in May. The program is open to undergraduate students, graduate students, pre-college students, adults, professionals. Most participants are 19–26 years of age. Other requirements: minimum 2.0 GPA, letter of recommendation from a faculty member, and good academic standing at home institution. 50 participants per session. Application deadline: March 1.
Costs • $2840 for students of consortia schools, $3140 for other students (includes tuition, housing, some meals, international airfare, International Student Identification card). Application fee: $50.
Contact • Dr. J. Milton Grimes, Executive Director, Kentucky Institute for International Studies, Murray State University, PO Box 9, Murray, KY 42071-0009; 502-762-3091; Fax: 502-762-3434; E-mail: kiismsu@msumusik.mursuky.edu; World Wide Web: http://www.berea.edu/KIIS/kiis.html

KENTUCKY INSTITUTE FOR INTERNATIONAL STUDIES

PROGRAM IN SALZBURG, AUSTRIA

General Information • Academic study program in Salzburg. Excursions to surrounding area.
Learning Focus • Courses in music. Instruction is offered by professors from the sponsoring institution.
Accommodations • Pensiones. Meals are taken on one's own.
Program Details • Program offered once per year. Session length: 5 weeks. Departures are scheduled in May. The program is open to undergraduate students, graduate students, pre-college students, adults, professionals. Most participants are 18–28 years of age. Other requirements: minimum 2.0 GPA, letter of recommendation from a faculty member, and good academic standing at home institution. 25 participants per session. Application deadline: March 1.
Costs • $2660 for students of consortia schools, $2960 for other students (includes tuition, housing, some meals, excursions, international airfare, International Student Identification card). Application fee: $50.
Contact • Dr. J. Milton Grimes, Executive Director, Kentucky Institute for International Studies, Murray State University, PO Box 9, Murray, KY 42071-0009; 502-762-3091; Fax: 502-762-3434; E-mail: kiismsu@msumusik.mursuky.edu; World Wide Web: http://www.berea.edu/KIIS/kiis.html

LANGUAGE LIAISON

ACTILINGUA–GERMAN IN AUSTRIA

General Information • Language study program with visits to Vienna.
Learning Focus • Instruction in the German language. Instruction is offered by professors. This program would appeal to people interested in language.
Accommodations • Homestays, dormitories, locally-rented apartments, program-owned apartments. Single rooms are available.
Program Details • Session length: unlimited. Departures are scheduled throughout the year. Most participants are 18–70 years of age. Participants must be 16 years or older to enroll. Reservations are recommended at least 35 days before departure.
Costs • Contact sponsor for information.
Contact • Nancy Forman, President, Language Liaison, 20533 Biscayne Boulevard-Station 4-162, Miami, FL 33180; 305-682-9909; Fax: 305-682-9907; E-mail: langstudy@aol.com; World Wide Web: http://languageliaison.com

NATIONAL REGISTRATION CENTER FOR STUDY ABROAD

AMADEUS ACADEMY

General Information • Language study program in Salzburg.
Learning Focus • Courses in German language.
Accommodations • Dormitories. Single rooms are available. Meals are taken as a group, in central dining facility.
Program Details • Program offered 6 times per year. Session length: 2 weeks. Departures are scheduled in June, July. The program is open to undergraduate students, graduate students, adults. 5–10 participants per session. Application deadline: 40 days prior to departure.
Costs • $1025 (includes tuition, housing, some meals, insurance). Application fee: $40. A $100 deposit is required.
Contact • Reuel Zielke, Coordinator, National Registration Center for Study Abroad, 823 North Second Street, Milwaukee, WI 53203; 417-278-0631; Fax: 417-271-8884; E-mail: inquiries@nrcsa.com; World Wide Web: http://www.nrcsa.com

NATIONAL REGISTRATION CENTER FOR STUDY ABROAD

VIENNA INTERNATIONAL UNIVERSITY COURSES

General Information • Language study program in Vienna. Classes are held on the campus of University of Vienna.
Learning Focus • Courses in German language.
Accommodations • Dormitories. Single rooms are available. Meals are taken as a group, in central dining facility.
Program Details • Program offered 3 times per year. Session length: 4 weeks. Departures are scheduled in July–September. The program is open to undergraduate students, graduate students. 20–25 participants per session. Application deadline: 40 days prior to departure.
Costs • $1300 (includes tuition, housing, insurance). Application fee: $40. A $100 deposit is required.
Contact • Reuel Zielke, Coordinator, National Registration Center for Study Abroad, 823 North Second Street, PO Box 1393, Milwaukee, WI 53203; 414-278-0631; Fax: 414-271-8884; E-mail: inquiries@nrcsa.com; World Wide Web: http://www.nrcsa.com

NORTH CAROLINA STATE UNIVERSITY

SUMMER PROGRAM IN VIENNA, AUSTRIA

General Information • Academic study program in Vienna. Excursions to Hungary (Budapest), Czech Republic (Prague), Wachau.

Learning Focus • Courses in Austrian studies, German language, international business, Central European studies, history, political science.

Accommodations • Hotels. Single rooms are available. Meals are taken on one's own, in local restaurants.

Program Details • Program offered once per year. Session length: 4 weeks. Departures are scheduled in July. The program is open to undergraduate students, graduate students, adults. Most participants are 18–50 years of age. Other requirements: approval of Director. 30 participants per session. Application deadline: March 1.

Costs • $1950 (includes tuition, housing, some meals, insurance, excursions). A $150 deposit is required.

Contact • Ingrid Schmidt, Study Abroad Director, North Carolina State University, 2118 Pullen Hall, Box 7344, Raleigh, NC 27695-7344; 919-515-2087; Fax: 919-515-6021; E-mail: study_abroad@ncsu.edu; World Wide Web: http://www2.ncsu.edu/ncsu/chass/intstu/abroad.html

NORTHERN ILLINOIS UNIVERSITY

STUDIO ART AND ART HISTORY IN SALZBURG, AUSTRIA

General Information • Academic study program in Salzburg. Classes are held on the campus of Salzburg College.

Learning Focus • Courses in studio art, art history. Instruction is offered by professors from the sponsoring institution.

Accommodations • Homestays. Single rooms are available. Meals are taken with host family.

Program Details • Program offered once per year. Session length: 5 weeks. Departures are scheduled in May. The program is open to undergraduate students, graduate students. Most participants are 21–26 years of age. 12 participants per session. Application deadline: April 15.

Costs • $3400 (includes tuition, housing, some meals, insurance, excursions). A $200 deposit is required.

Contact • Anne Seitzinger, Program Coordinator, Short-Term Study Abroad, Northern Illinois University, Study Abroad Office-WI 417, DeKalb, IL 60115; 815-752-0700; Fax: 815-753-0825; E-mail: aseitz@niu.edu; World Wide Web: http://www.niu.edu/depts/intl_prgms/intl.html

RUSSIAN AND EAST EUROPEAN PARTNERSHIPS

GERMAN LANGUAGE AND CULTURAL IMMERSION PROGRAM

General Information • Language study program in Salzburg. Classes are held on the campus of Deutschkurse Salzburg. Excursions to Germany (Munich).

Learning Focus • Courses in German language, German culture and art, German history. Instruction is offered by local teachers.

Accommodations • Homestays. Single rooms are available. Meals are taken on one's own, with host family, in local restaurants, in residences.

Program Details • Program offered 11 times per year. Session length: 4 or more weeks. Departures are scheduled in January–November. The program is open to undergraduate students, graduate students, adults. Most participants are 18 years of age and older. Other requirements: in good health and 18 or older unless chaperoned by an adult. 6 participants per session. Application deadline: 45 days prior to departure.

Costs • $3595 (includes tuition, housing, some meals, books and class materials, excursions, international airfare, local transportation, airport transfers). A $1500 deposit is required.

Contact • Kenneth Fortune, President, Russian and East European Partnerships, PO Box 227, Fineview, NY 13640; 888-USE-REEP; Fax: 800-910-1777; E-mail: reep@fox.nstn.ca

ST. JOHN'S UNIVERSITY

AUSTRIAN PROGRAM

General Information • Academic study program in Salzburg. Classes are held on the campus of University of Salzburg. Excursions to Vienna, Germany (Munich), Czech Republic (Prague).

Learning Focus • Courses in German language, political science, philosophy. Instruction is offered by professors from the sponsoring institution and local teachers.

Accommodations • Homestays, dormitories, locally-rented apartments. Single rooms are available. Meals are taken as a group, on one's own, with host family.

Program Details • Program offered once per year. Session length: 12 weeks. Departures are scheduled in September. The program is open to undergraduate students. Most participants are 20–22 years of age. Other requirements: minimum 2.5 GPA and one year college-level German. 25 participants per session. Application deadline: March.

Costs • $9200 (includes tuition, housing, all meals). Application fee: $100.

Contact • Stephen Burmeister-May, Director, Center for International Education, St. John's University, Collegeville, MN 56321; 320-363-2082; Fax: 320-363-2013; E-mail: intleduc@csbsju.edu

SLIPPERY ROCK UNIVERSITY OF PENNSYLVANIA

SALZBURG SUMMER PROGRAM

General Information • Academic study program in Salzburg. Classes are held on the campus of University of Salzburg.

Learning Focus • Courses in literature. Instruction is offered by professors from the sponsoring institution.

Accommodations • Homestays. Meals are taken in central dining facility.

Program Details • Program offered once per year. Session length: 2 weeks. Departures are scheduled in July. The program is open to undergraduate students, adults. Most

participants are 18–40 years of age. Other requirements: 2.5 minimum GPA. 10–15 participants per session. Application deadline: May 1.
Costs • $2695 (includes tuition, housing, some meals, international airfare). A $100 deposit is required.
Contact • Stan Kendziorski, Director of International Studies, Slippery Rock University of Pennsylvania, 110 Eisenberg Building, Slippery Rock, PA 16057; 412-738-2603; Fax: 412-738-2959; E-mail: sjk@sruvm.sru.edu; World Wide Web: http://www.sru.edu

SOUTHERN ILLINOIS UNIVERSITY AT CARBONDALE

SOCIAL WORK IN AUSTRIA

General Information • Academic study program in Bregenz. Excursions to Germany, Switzerland.
Learning Focus • Courses in social work, European culture. Instruction is offered by professors from the sponsoring institution.
Program Details • Program offered once per year. Session length: 2 weeks. Departures are scheduled in May. The program is open to undergraduate students. Most participants are 18–30 years of age. Other requirements: minimum 2.75 GPA. 10–15 participants per session. Application deadline: April 12.
Costs • $1560 (includes housing, insurance, excursions). Application fee: $250.
Contact • Mr. Thomas A. Saville, Coordinator, Study Abroad Programs, Southern Illinois University at Carbondale, Mailcode 6885, Small Business Incubator, Room 217, Carbondale, IL 62901; 618-453-7670; Fax: 618-453-7677; E-mail: studyabr@siu.edu

SOUTHERN METHODIST UNIVERSITY

PROGRAM IN AUSTRIA

General Information • Academic study program in Salzburg. Excursions to (Germany) Munich, Melk, Vienna.
Learning Focus • Courses in art history, German language. Instruction is offered by professors from the sponsoring institution and local teachers.
Accommodations • Homestays. Single rooms are available. Meals are taken with host family.
Program Details • Program offered once per year. Session length: 6 weeks. Departures are scheduled in May. The program is open to undergraduate students. Most participants are 19–24 years of age. Other requirements: minimum 2.5 GPA and sophomore standing. 20 participants per session. Application deadline: March 1.

Costs • $4400 (includes tuition, housing, some meals, excursions). Application fee: $35. A $400 deposit is required.
Contact • Karen Westergaard, Associate Director, Southern Methodist University, Office of International Programs, Dallas, TX 75275-0391; 214-768-2338; Fax: 214-768-1051; E-mail: intipro@mail.smu.edu; World Wide Web: http://fllcjm.clements.smu.edu

UNIVERSITY OF ILLINOIS AT URBANA-CHAMPAIGN

AUSTRIA-ILLINOIS EXCHANGE

General Information • Language study program in Vienna. Classes are held on the campus of Economics University.
Learning Focus • Courses in German language. Instruction is offered by professors from the sponsoring institution.
Accommodations • Dormitories. Meals are taken on one's own, in central dining facility.
Program Details • Program offered once per year. Session length: 4 weeks. Departures are scheduled in May. The program is open to University of Illinois students. Most participants are 19–20 years of age. Other requirements: completion of German 101 with A or B. 20 participants per session.
Costs • $2500 (includes tuition, housing, some meals, books and class materials, insurance, excursions, international airfare). A $250 deposit is required.
Contact • John Lalande, Program Coordinator, University of Illinois at Urbana-Champaign, 3072 FLB, 707 South Mathews, Urbana, IL 61801-3675; 217-244-3240

UNIVERSITY OF KENTUCKY

STUDY PROGRAM IN VIENNA, AUSTRIA

General Information • Business study and culture program in Austria (Vienna), Czech Republic (Czech Republic (Prague)). Excursions to mountains.
Learning Focus • Courses in business, economics.
Accommodations • Dormitories, hotels. Single rooms are available. Meals are taken in local restaurants.
Program Details • Program offered once per year. Session length: 3 weeks. Departures are scheduled in August. The program is open to undergraduate students, graduate students. Most participants are 20–40 years of age. Other requirements: good academic standing and must have at least junior year status. 25–30 participants per session. Application deadline: April 15.
Costs • $1250 (includes housing, some meals, excursions). A $50 deposit is required.
Contact • Curt Harvey, Professor of Economics, University of Kentucky, Lexington, KY 40506; 606-257-7634; Fax: 606-323-1920; E-mail: charv1@pop.uky.edu

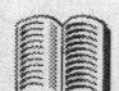

UNIVERSITY OF NEW ORLEANS

EUROPEAN CENTRE

General Information • Academic study program in Innsbruck. Classes are held on the campus of University of Innsbruck. Excursions to Munich, Vienna, Venice, Salzburg.
Learning Focus • Courses in English language, history, music, sociology. Instruction is offered by professors from the sponsoring institution.
Accommodations • Dormitories. Single rooms are available. Meals are taken as a group, in local restaurants.
Program Details • Program offered once per year. Session length: 3 weeks. Departures are scheduled in July. The program is open to adults, the general public. Most participants are 35–65 years of age. 30 participants per session. Application deadline: April 1.
Costs • $2695 (includes tuition, housing, some meals, insurance, excursions). A $200 deposit is required.
Contact • Alea Cot, Coordinator, University of New Orleans, PO Box 1097, New Orleans, LA 70148; 504-280-7318; Fax: 504-280-7317; World Wide Web: http://www.uno.edu/~inst/Welcome.html

UNIVERSITY OF NEW ORLEANS

INNSBRUCK INTERNATIONAL SUMMER SCHOOL

General Information • Academic study program in Innsbruck. Classes are held on the campus of University of Innsbruck. Excursions to Venice, Munich, Vienna.
Learning Focus • Courses in liberal arts, social sciences, science, business. Instruction is offered by professors from the sponsoring institution and local teachers.
Accommodations • Dormitories. Single rooms are available. Meals are taken as a group, in central dining facility.
Program Details • Program offered once per year. Session length: 6 weeks. Departures are scheduled in July. The program is open to undergraduate students, graduate students, adults, the general public. Most participants are 19–29 years of age. 225 participants per session. Application deadline: April 1.
Costs • $3295 (includes tuition, housing, some meals, insurance, excursions). A $200 deposit is required.
Contact • Margaret Davidson, Coordinator, University of New Orleans, PO Box 1315, New Orleans, LA 70148; 504-280-7116; Fax: 504-280-7317; World Wide Web: http://www.uno.edu/~inst/Welcome.html

---

Entering its 9th year, the European Centre records a 30% returnee rate, reflecting the successful mix of stimulating classes, lectures, excursions, and weekend field trips to experience the grandeur of Vienna, Austria, and the splendor of Italy in Venice and Verona.

The student will quickly feel at home in Innsbruck. Nestled in the Alps, Innsbruck is a perfect place to nourish body and soul with nature and culture, good food, exciting events, and breathtaking scenery. John Firestone from Marrero, Louisiana, says of the program, "The whole trip was so full of high points, it was like Innsbruck itself—surrounded by high points and peaks in every direction."

UNIVERSITY OF SOUTHERN MISSISSIPPI

AUSTRIAN STUDIES PROGRAM

General Information • Academic study program in Vienna. Excursions to Hungary (Budapest), Central Europe.
Learning Focus • Courses in music, history, international business.
Program Details • Program offered once per year. Session length: 3 weeks. Departures are scheduled in June. The program is open to undergraduate students, graduate students, teachers, professionals. Other requirements: good academic standing, 2.0 minimum GPA. 20 participants per session. Application deadline: February 1.
Costs • $3349 for undergraduates, $3649 for graduate students (includes tuition, housing, excursions, international airfare). A $200 deposit is required.
Contact • Director, Austrian Studies Program, University of Southern Mississippi, Box 10047, Hattiesburg, MS 39406-0047; 601-266-4344; Fax: 601-266-5699; E-mail: m_ravencraft@bull.cc.usm.edu

UNIVERSITY OF VIENNA INTERNATIONAL UNIVERSITY

GERMAN LANGUAGE COURSES FOR FOREIGNERS

General Information • Language study program in Vienna.
Learning Focus • Courses in German language.
Accommodations • Dormitories. Single rooms are available. Meals are taken on one's own, in central dining facility, in local restaurants, in residences.
Program Details • Program offered 3 times per year. Session length: 3–4 weeks. Departures are scheduled in July, August, September. The program is open to undergraduate students, graduate students, pre-college students, adults. Most participants are 18–25 years of age. Other requirements: minimum age of 16. 1000 participants per session.
Costs • $400 for 4 weeks (includes tuition). Application fee: $25. A $150 deposit is required.
Contact • Mag. Sigrum Inmann-Trojer, Secretary, University of Vienna International University, Dr. Karl Lueger-Ring 1, Vienna A-1010, Austria; +43 405-1254; Fax: +43 405-1210; World Wide Web: http://www.aat.telecom.at/aat/campus/campus.html

VIENNA MASTERCOURSES

VIENNA MASTERCOURSES

General Information • Performing arts program in Vienna. Classes are held on the campus of Conservatory of Music, College of Music and Dramatic Art Vienna.
Learning Focus • Courses in music.
Accommodations • Homestays, dormitories. Single rooms are available. Meals are taken on one's own, in local restaurants, in residences.
Program Details • Program offered 15 times per year. Session length: 2 weeks. Departures are scheduled in July, August. The program is open to undergraduate students, graduate students, adults. Most participants are 15–40 years of age. 15–20 participants per session. Application deadline: June 1.
Costs • $670 (includes tuition). Application fee: $150.
Contact • Elisabeth Keschmann, Vienna Mastercourses, Reisnerstrasse 3, A-1030 Vienna, Austria; +43 22-2714-8822; Fax: +43 22-27-14-88-21

BELGIUM

FOREIGN LANGUAGE STUDY ABROAD SERVICE

INTERNATIONAL LANGUAGE STUDY HOMESTAYS IN BELGIUM

General Information • Language study program in Belgium.
Learning Focus • Courses in French language. Instruction is offered by local teachers.
Accommodations • Homestays. Single rooms are available. Meals are taken with host family, in residences.
Program Details • Session length: varies. Departures are scheduled in January–December. The program is open to undergraduate students, graduate students, pre-college students, adults. Most participants are 12 years of age and older. Other requirements: students must be at least 12 years old. 1 participant per session.
Costs • Contact sponsor for information. A $300 deposit is required.
Contact • Louise Harber, Coordinator, Foreign Language Study Abroad Service, Department IH, Box 903, 5935 Southwest 64th Avenue, South Miami, FL 33143; 800-282-1090; Fax: 305-662-2907; E-mail: flsas@netpoint.net; World Wide Web: http://www.netpoint.net/~flsas

MICHIGAN STATE UNIVERSITY

INTERNATIONAL RELATIONS PROGRAM

General Information • Academic study program in Brussels.
Learning Focus • Courses in international policy, European political systems. Instruction is offered by professors from the sponsoring institution.
Accommodations • Locally-rented apartments. Meals are taken on one's own, in residences.
Program Details • Program offered once per year. Session length: 5 weeks. Departures are scheduled in July. The

program is open to undergraduate students. Most participants are 18–22 years of age. Other requirements: good academic standing and the approval of the instructor. 30 participants per session. Application deadline: March 14.
Costs • $991 (includes housing, some meals, excursions). Application fee: $75. A $250 deposit is required.
Contact • Brenda S. Sprite, Educational Programs Coordinator, Michigan State University, Office of Study Abroad, 109 International Center, East Lansing, MI 48824-1035; 517-353-8920; Fax: 517-432-2082; E-mail: sprite@pilot.msu.edu; World Wide Web: http://study-abroad.msu.edu

 RADFORD UNIVERSITY

SUMMER STUDY IN ANTWERP FOR ARTS AND SCIENCES AND BUSINESS

General Information • Academic study program in Antwerp. Classes are held on the campus of University of Antwerp. Excursions to sites within Belgium.
Learning Focus • Courses in business, economics. Instruction is offered by professors from the sponsoring institution and local teachers.
Accommodations • Hotels. Single rooms are available. Meals are taken on one's own.
Program Details • Program offered once per year. Session length: 4 weeks. Departures are scheduled in June. The program is open to undergraduate students, graduate students. Most participants are 18–25 years of age. 15 participants per session. Application deadline: March 15.
Costs • $2750 (includes tuition, housing, some meals, excursions). A $500 deposit is required.
Contact • Ms. Jane A. Wemhoener, Director, International Programs, Radford University, Box 7002, Radford, VA 24142; 703-831-6200; Fax: 703-831-6588; E-mail: jwemhoen@runet.edu; World Wide Web: http://www.runet.edu

 VESALIUS COLLEGE

SUMMER PROGRAM

General Information • Academic study program in Brussels. Classes are held on the campus of Vesalius College.
Learning Focus • Courses in French language, art history, environmental studies, economics, European politics. Instruction is offered by local teachers.
Accommodations • Homestays, locally-rented apartments. Single rooms are available. Meals are taken on one's own.
Program Details • Program offered once per year. Session length: 6 weeks. Departures are scheduled in June. The program is open to undergraduate students, pre-college students, adults. Most participants are 18–35 years of age. Other requirements: high school diploma or learning certificate. 50 participants per session. Application deadline: May 1.
Costs • $300 per credit (includes tuition). Application fee: $35. A $70 deposit is required.
Contact • Edwin D. Amrhein, Head of Admissions, Vesalius College, Pleinlaan 2, Brussels B-1050, Belgium; +32 2-629-2367; Fax: +32 2-629-3637; E-mail: vesalius@vnet3.vub.ac.be; World Wide Web: http://www.vub.ac.be/VECO/VECO-intro.html

DENMARK

DIS, DENMARK'S INTERNATIONAL STUDY PROGRAM

ARCHITECTURE AND DESIGN SUMMER PROGRAM

General Information • Academic study program in Copenhagen. Excursions to Sweden (Stockholm), Finland.
Learning Focus • Courses in interior design, landscape architecture, architectural design, visual journal, design. Instruction is offered by professors from the sponsoring institution.
Accommodations • Homestays, dormitories. Single rooms are available. Meals are taken on one's own, with host family, in residences.
Program Details • Program offered once per year. Session length: 11 weeks. Departures are scheduled in June. The program is open to undergraduate students. Most participants are 20–25 years of age. Other requirements: minimum 3.0 GPA. 40 participants per session.
Costs • $6075 (includes tuition, housing, all meals, books and class materials, excursions, local commuting, study tour). A $750 deposit is required.
Contact • Helle Gjerlufsen, Field Director, DiS, Denmark's International Study Program, North American Office, 100 Nicholson Hall, 216 Pillsbury Drive, SE, Minneapolis, MN 55455-0138; 800-247-3477; Fax: 612-626-8009; E-mail: dis@tc.umn.edu; World Wide Web: http://www.disp.dk

DIS, DENMARK'S INTERNATIONAL STUDY PROGRAM

GLOBAL STUDIES–EUROPE

General Information • Academic study program in Copenhagen. Excursions to Berlin.
Learning Focus • Courses in European conflict and security, European history, European integration. Instruction is offered by professors from the sponsoring institution.
Accommodations • Homestays, dormitories. Meals are taken on one's own, with host family, in residences.
Program Details • Program offered once per year. Session length: 3 weeks. Departures are scheduled in January. The program is open to freshmen and sophomores only. Other requirements: minimum 3.0 GPA.
Costs • $1950 (includes tuition, housing, all meals, books and class materials).
Contact • Helle Gjerlufsen, Field Director, North American Office, DiS, Denmark's International Study Program, 600 Nicholson Hall, 216 Pillsbury Drive, SE, Minneapolis, MN 55455-0138; 800-247-3477; Fax: 612-626-8009; E-mail: dis@tc.umn.edu; World Wide Web: http://www.disp.dk

EXPERIENCE PLUS SPECIALTY TOURS, INC.

CYCLING TO THE DANISH ISLES

General Information • Cultural tour with visits to Alborg, Copenhagen, Hillerod, Mariager, Tranevaer, Troense, Egeskov Castle, Copenhagen, Tivoli Gardens. Once at the destination country, participants travel by train, bicycle, ferry boat.
Learning Focus • Escorted travel to Fredericksborg Castle, Konsborg Castle and Odense. Museum visits (Louisiana Museum of Modern Art, Ship Bottle Collection, museum in Odense). Other activities include bicycling visits to famous castles. Instruction is offered by indigenous, bilingual and bi-cultural guides. This program would appeal to people interested in bicycling, history, Denmark, culture, travel.
Accommodations • Hotels. Single rooms are available for an additional $300.
Program Details • Program offered once per year. Session length: 12 days. Departures are scheduled in August. Program is targeted to bicyclists. Most participants are 35–70 years of age. 16–22 participants per session. Reservations are recommended at least 6–12 months before departure.
Costs • $2600 (includes housing, some meals, excursions, rental bike, water bottle, shirt, luggage shuttle, van support, bilingual/bicultural tour leaders). A $250 deposit is required.
Contact • Experience Plus Specialty Tours, Inc., 1925 Wallenberg Drive, Fort Collins, CO 80526; 800-685-4565; Fax: 800-685-4565; E-mail: tours@xplus.com

ENGLAND

See also Ireland, Scotland, and Wales

THE AMERICAN COLLEGE IN LONDON

ART-RELATED STUDIES AND LIBERAL ARTS

General Information • Academic study program in London. Classes are held on the campus of American College in London. Excursions to England, European countries.
Learning Focus • Courses in art history, photography, theater, fashion, interior design, architecture, communications, social sciences. Instruction is offered by professors from the sponsoring institution.
Accommodations • Hostels. Single rooms are available. Meals are taken on one's own, in local restaurants.
Program Details • Program offered 2 times per year. Session length: 4 weeks. Departures are scheduled in June, July. The program is open to undergraduate students, adults. Most participants are 18–70 years of age. Other requirements: must have good academic standing and permission from host institution. 50 participants per session.
Costs • $3085 (includes tuition, housing, books and class materials, ground transportation, some activities). A $275 deposit is required.
Contact • Division of International Programs and Study Abroad, The American College in London, 3330 Peachtree Road, NE, Atlanta, GA 30326; 800-255-6839; Fax: 404-364-6611; E-mail: acatl@ix.netcom.com

THE AMERICAN COLLEGE IN LONDON

ART AND LIBERAL ARTS-RELATED STUDIES AND INTERNSHIPS

General Information • Academic study program in London. Classes are held on the campus of American College in London. Excursions to London, United Kingdom and European capitals.
Learning Focus • Courses in studio art, art history, theater, fashion, interior design, video, communications, liberal arts, graphic design, photography. Instruction is offered by professors from the sponsoring institution.
Accommodations • Locally-rented apartments. Single rooms are available. Meals are taken on one's own, in residences.
Program Details • Program offered 5 times per year. Session length: 8–9 weeks. Departures are scheduled in October, January, March, June, August. The program is open to undergraduate students, adults. Most participants are 18–70 years of age. Other requirements: good academic standing and the approval of the home institution. 100 participants per session.
Costs • $5525 (includes tuition, housing, books and class materials, some activities). A $275 deposit is required.
Contact • Division of International Programs and Study Abroad, The American College in London, 3330 Peachtree Road, NE, Atlanta, GA 30326; 800-255-6839; Fax: 404-364-6611; E-mail: acatl@ix.netcom.com

---

At The American College in London, students choose from 300 courses in either 4- or 8-week sessions. In recent years, students from more than 350 US colleges and universities have enrolled and attended classes with full-time students from more than 100 other countries.

Centrally located and within easy walking distance to all London has to offer, The American College in London provides apartment living, travel programs, and a full student activities schedule of concerts, theater, social events, recreation, and cultural programs. All applicants are provided with a personal US-based counselor to help prepare them for their experiences in London.

THE AMERICAN COLLEGE IN LONDON

GRADUATE STUDY IN INTERNATIONAL BUSINESS

General Information • Academic study program in London. Classes are held on the campus of American College in London. Excursions to European capitals, sites in the United Kingdom.
Learning Focus • Courses in international business, the European Community, cross-cultural studies. Instruction is offered by professors from the sponsoring institution.
Accommodations • Hostels. Single rooms are available. Meals are taken on one's own, in local restaurants.
Program Details • Program offered 2 times per year. Session length: 4 weeks. Departures are scheduled in June, July. The program is open to graduate business students and business seniors. Most participants are 18–70 years of age. Other requirements: home institution approval, approval of dean, minimum 3.0 GPA for undergraduate students, institution approval, and a letter of recommendation. 50 participants per session.

Costs • $2125 (includes tuition, housing, books and class materials). A $275 deposit is required.
Contact • Division of International Programs and Study Abroad, The American College in London, 3330 Peachtree Road, NE, Atlanta, GA 30326; 800-255-6839; Fax: 404-364-6611; E-mail: acatl@ix.netcom.com

THE AMERICAN COLLEGE IN LONDON

INTERNATIONAL BUSINESS: RELATED STUDIES

General Information • Academic study program in London. Classes are held on the campus of American College in London. Excursions to London, United Kingdom and European capitals.
Learning Focus • Courses in the European Community, marketing, advertising, public relations, international business, fashion marketing, retailing, management. Instruction is offered by professors from the sponsoring institution.
Accommodations • Hostels. Single rooms are available. Meals are taken on one's own, in local restaurants.
Program Details • Program offered 2 times per year. Session length: 4 weeks. Departures are scheduled in June, July. The program is open to undergraduate students, adults. Most participants are 18–70 years of age. Other requirements: good academic standing and the approval of the home institution. 50 participants per session.
Costs • $3085 (includes tuition, housing, books and class materials, ground transportation, some activities). A $275 deposit is required.
Contact • Division of international Programs and Study Abroad, The American College in London, 3330 Peachtree Road, NE, Atlanta, GA 30326; 800-255-6839; Fax: 404-364-6611; E-mail: acatl@ix.netcom.com

THE AMERICAN COLLEGE IN LONDON

INTERNATIONAL BUSINESS: UNDERGRADUATE STUDY AND INTERNSHIPS

General Information • Academic study program in London. Classes are held on the campus of American College in London. Excursions to London, European capitals.
Learning Focus • Courses in international business, marketing, imports and exports, public relations, the European Community, management, advertising, cultural studies and business. Instruction is offered by professors from the sponsoring institution.
Accommodations • Locally-rented apartments. Single rooms are available. Meals are taken on one's own, in local restaurants, in residences.
Program Details • Program offered 5 times per year. Session length: 8–9 weeks. Departures are scheduled in October, January, March, June, August. The program is open

to undergraduate students, adults. Most participants are 18–70 years of age. Other requirements: good academic standing and the approval of the host institution. 100 participants per session.
Costs • $5525 (includes tuition, housing, books and class materials, some activities). A $275 deposit is required.
Contact • Division of International Programs and Study Abroad, The American College in London, 3330 Peachtree Road, NE, Atlanta, GA 30326; 800-255-6839; Fax: 404-364-6611; E-mail: acatl@ix.netcom.com

AMERICAN INSTITUTE FOR FOREIGN STUDY (AIFS)

LONDON SUMMER ART PROGRAM IN AFFILIATION WITH THE LONDON INSTITUTE

General Information • Academic study program in Belgium (Belgium (Brussels)), England (London), France (France (Paris)), Netherlands (Netherlands (Amsterdam)). Classes are held on the campus of Central St. Martin's College of Art and Design.
Learning Focus • Courses in studio art, drawing, jewelry, painting, photography, humanities. Instruction is offered by local teachers.
Accommodations • Dormitories. Single rooms are available. Meals are taken in central dining facility, in residences.
Program Details • Program offered 2 times per year. Session length: 3 or 6 weeks. Departures are scheduled in July. The program is open to undergraduate students, graduate students, adults, high school graduates. Other requirements: minimum 2.0 GPA. Application deadline: March 15.
Costs • $2979 for 3 weeks, $4479 for 6 weeks (includes tuition, housing, some meals, insurance). A $400 deposit is required.
Contact • Carmela Vigliano, Director of Admissions, College Summer Programs, American Institute for Foreign Study (AIFS), 102 Greenwich Avenue, Greenwich, CT 06830; 800-727-2437, ext. 6087; Fax: 203-869-9615; E-mail: info@aifs.org

APPALACHIAN STATE UNIVERSITY

ENGLAND AND SCOTLAND

General Information • Academic study program in Durham, London. Excursions to Scotland (Edinburgh), France (Paris).
Learning Focus • Courses in finance, insurance, real estate. Instruction is offered by professors from the sponsoring institution.
Program Details • Program offered once per year. Session length: 22 days. Departures are scheduled in July. Most participants are 18 years of age and older. 20 participants per session.
Costs • $2969 (includes tuition, housing, insurance, international airfare, International Student Identification card).
Contact • Dr. Robert Cherry, Professor, Appalachian State University, Department of Finance, Real Estate, and Insurance, Boone, NC 28608; 704-262-4030; Fax: 704-262-4037

ARTS & CRAFTS TOURS

CENTER OF CREATIVITY

General Information • Cultural tour with visits to Cotswolds, Home Counties, London. Once at the destination country, participants travel by bus.
Learning Focus • Escorted travel to private homes, collections and gardens. Museum visits (exhibitions and collections). Instruction is offered by artists, historians, curators and architects. This program would appeal to people interested in architecture, the arts and crafts movement, preservation, decorative arts.
Accommodations • Hotels. Single rooms are available for an additional $500.
Program Details • Program offered once per year. Session length: 1 week. Departures are scheduled in September. Most participants are 40–80 years of age. 8–10 participants per session. Application deadline: 60 days prior to departure. Reservations are recommended at least 6 months before departure.
Costs • $4000 (includes housing, all meals, books and class materials, excursions). A $500 deposit is required.
Contact • Elaine Hirschl Ellis, President, Arts & Crafts Tours, 110 Riverside Drive, New York, NY 10024; 212-362-0761; Fax: 212-787-2823; E-mail: actours@aol.com; World Wide Web: http://www.dscweb.com/AandCTours.html

ARTS & CRAFTS TOURS

EARLY UTOPIANS

General Information • Cultural tour with visits to Birmingham, Liverpool, London, Manchester, Midlands. Once at the destination country, participants travel by bus.
Learning Focus • Escorted travel to private homes, churches and planned communities. Museum visits (Liverpool, Manchester, Birmingham, Stoke-on-Treat). Instruction is offered by professors, historians, curators, architects and urban scholars. This program would appeal to people interested in architecture, history, decorative arts, urban planning.
Accommodations • Hotels. Single rooms are available.
Program Details • Program offered once per year. Session length: 9 days. Departures are scheduled in May. Most participants are 40–75 years of age. 8 participants per session. Application deadline: 60 days prior to departure. Reservations are recommended at least 6 months before departure.
Costs • $4000 (includes housing, all meals, books and class materials, excursions). A $500 deposit is required.
Contact • Elaine Hirschl Ellis, President, Arts & Crafts Tours, 110 Riverside Drive, New York, NY 10024; 212-362-0761; Fax: 212-787-2823; E-mail: actours@aol.com; World Wide Web: http://www.dscweb.com/AandCTours.html

ARTS & CRAFTS TOURS

GARDENS OF THE ARTS AND CRAFTS ERA

General Information • Garden/horticultural tour with visits to England (Burrey, Cotswolds, Hampshire, Lake District, Sussex), Scotland. Once at the destination country, participants travel by bus.
Learning Focus • Escorted travel to private gardens of the nineteenth and early twentieth century. Instruction is

offered by professors, artists, historians, landscape architects, curators and horticulturalists. This program would appeal to people interested in gardening, landscape architecture, horticulture, architecture.

Accommodations • Hotels. Single rooms are available for an additional $500.

Program Details • Program offered 2 times per year. Session length: 10 days. Departures are scheduled in June, September. Most participants are 40–75 years of age. 8–10 participants per session. Application deadline: 60 days prior to departure. Reservations are recommended at least 6 months before departure.

Costs • $4300 (includes housing, all meals, books and class materials, excursions). A $500 deposit is required.

Contact • Elaine Hirschl Ellis, President, Arts & Crafts Tours, 110 Riverside Drive, New York, NY 10024; 212-362-0761; Fax: 212-787-2823; E-mail: actours@aol.com; World Wide Web: http://www.dscweb.com/AandCTours.html

ARTS & CRAFTS TOURS

HOMAGE TO WILLIAM MORRIS

General Information • Cultural tour with visits to Cambridge, Cotswolds, Home Counties, London, Midlands. Once at the destination country, participants travel by bus.

Learning Focus • Escorted travel to private collections, churches and homes. Museum visits (collections and exhibitions). Other activities include stained glass demonstration. Instruction is offered by professors, researchers, historians, curators and preservationists. This program would appeal to people interested in William Morris, the Pre-Raphaelites, Utopians, Mehikchue, the arts and crafts movement, nineteenth century history, preservation, decorative arts.

Accommodations • Hotels. Single rooms are available for an additional $500.

Program Details • Program offered once per year. Session length: 8 days. Departures are scheduled in November. Most participants are 40–80 years of age. 8–10 participants per session. Application deadline: 60 days prior to departure. Reservations are recommended at least 6 months before departure.

Costs • $3750 (includes housing, all meals, books and class materials, excursions). A $500 deposit is required.

Contact • Elaine Hirschl Ellis, President, Arts & Crafts Tours, 110 Riverside Drive, New York, NY 10024; 212-362-0761; Fax: 212-787-2823; E-mail: actours@aol.com; World Wide Web: http://www.dscweb.com/AandCTours.html

BEAVER COLLEGE

LONDON SUMMER INTERNSHIP

General Information • Internship program in London.

Learning Focus • Courses in business, public policy, communications, social sciences. Instruction is offered by professors from the sponsoring institution.
Accommodations • Program-owned apartments. Meals are taken in residences.
Program Details • Program offered once per year. Session length: 6 weeks. Departures are scheduled in June. The program is open to undergraduate students, graduate students, adults. Other requirements: minimum 3.0 GPA and three or four semesters of college-level course work. 20 participants per session. Application deadline: March 10.
Costs • $4450 (includes tuition, housing, International Student Identification card, predeparture materials, host country support, one-way international airfare). Application fee: $35. A $500 deposit is required.
Contact • Stephanie McNerney, Program Coordinator, Beaver College, Center for Education Abroad, 450 South Easton Road, Glenside, PA 19038; 888-232-8379; Fax: 215-572-2174; E-mail: mcnerney@turret.beaver.edu

BEAVER COLLEGE

MIDDLESEX SUMMER UNIVERSITY

General Information • Academic study program in London. Classes are held on the campus of Middlesex University. Excursions to social outings, country pub crawl, London, theater.
Learning Focus • Courses in art, design, environmental studies, computer science, media, communications, criminology, British history, English language, theater, writing, publishing. Instruction is offered by local teachers.
Accommodations • Dormitories. Single rooms are available. Meals are taken in central dining facility.
Program Details • Program offered once per year. Session length: 2–5 weeks. Departures are scheduled in July. The program is open to undergraduate students, graduate students, adults. Other requirements: minimum 3.0 GPA and three or four semesters of college-level course work. Application deadline: March 31.
Costs • $3300–$3800 (includes tuition, housing, International Student Identification card, predeparture materials, host country support). Application fee: $35. A $500 deposit is required.
Contact • Audrianna Jones, Program Coordinator, Beaver College, Center for Education Abroad, 450 South Easton Road, Glenside, PA 19038; 888-232-8379; Fax: 215-572-2174; E-mail: jones@turret.beaver.edu

BERKELEY COLLEGE

LONDON STUDY ABROAD

General Information • Academic study program in London. Classes are held on the campus of Regent's College. Excursions to theater trips in London.
Learning Focus • Courses in management, international business, British theater, world cultures. Instruction is offered by local teachers.
Accommodations • Dormitories. Meals are taken on one's own, in central dining facility.
Program Details • Program offered once per year. Session length: 8 weeks. Departures are scheduled in July. The program is open to undergraduate students. Most participants are 19–26 years of age. 12 participants per session. Application deadline: March 1.
Costs • $6750 (includes tuition, housing, all meals, international airfare). Application fee: $35. A $550 deposit is required.
Contact • Cynthia Marchese, Vice President, Berkeley College, 3 East 43 Street, New York, NY 10012; 212-687-3730; Fax: 212-697-3371; E-mail: cch@berkeley.org; World Wide Web: http://www.berkeley.org/college

BOSTON UNIVERSITY

SUMMER LONDON PROGRAM

General Information • Academic study program in London.
Learning Focus • Courses in communications, drama, economics, history, art history, English language, political science, psychology. Instruction is offered by professors from the sponsoring institution.
Accommodations • Program-owned apartments. Single rooms are available. Meals are taken on one's own, in local restaurants, in residences.
Program Details • Program offered once per year. Session length: 6 weeks. Departures are scheduled in May. The program is open to undergraduate students, adults. Most participants are 18–21 years of age. Other requirements: minimum 3.0 GPA and good academic standing. 20 participants per session. Application deadline: March 15.
Costs • $4400 (includes tuition, housing). Application fee: $35. A $300 deposit is required.
Contact • Division of International Programs, Boston University, 232 Bay State Road, Boston, MA 02215; 617-353-9888; Fax: 617-353-5402; E-mail: abroad@bu.edu; World Wide Web: http://web.bu.edu/abroad

BRISTOL INTERNATIONAL CREDIT-EARNING PROGRAM

SUMMER PROGRAM

General Information • Academic study program in Bristol, Dartington, Devon. Excursions to Bath, Stonehenge, Wales, Dartmoor, Salisbury, Tintern Abbey, Cotswolds.
Learning Focus • Courses in social welfare, health care, public policy, administration.
Accommodations • Program-owned apartments. Single rooms are available. Meals are taken in residences.
Program Details • Program offered once per year. Session length: 2 weeks. Departures are scheduled in June. The program is open to seniors or graduates with relevant field experience. Most participants are 22–52 years of age. 30 participants per session. Application deadline: February, March.
Costs • $1800 (includes tuition, housing, some meals, ground transportation, some excursions). A $450 deposit is required.
Contact • Gary Lowe, Dean, Bristol International Credit-Earning Program, School of Social Work, Greenville, NC 27858-4353; 919-328-1445; Fax: 919-328-4196; E-mail: swlowe@ecuvm.cis.edu; World Wide Web: http://www.bris.ac.uk/Depts/SPS

BRISTOL INTERNATIONAL CREDIT-EARNING PROGRAM

YEAR ROUND OPPORTUNITIES

General Information • Academic study program in Bristol, Dartington, Devon. Excursions to Bath, Salisbury, Stonehenge, Tintern Abbey, Wales, Cotswolds, Dartmoor.

Learning Focus • Courses in social welfare, public policy, child welfare, health care, criminal justice, housing and urban policy, education policy.

Accommodations • Program-owned apartments. Single rooms are available. Meals are taken in residences.

Program Details • Session length: 1–4 weeks. Departures are scheduled in January, March, June, September. The program is open to undergraduate students, graduate students, adults. Most participants are 22–52 years of age. Other requirements: must have at least senior year status and relevant field experience. 15 participants per session.

Costs • Contact sponsor for information.

Contact • David Bull, Director, Bristol International Credit-Earning Program, 8 Woodland Road, Bristol BS8 1TN, England; +44 117-928-8505; Fax: +44 117-928-8578; E-mail: d.bull@bris.ac.uk; World Wide Web: http://www.bris.ac.uk/Depts/SPS

BRITISH COASTAL TRAILS SCENIC WALKING

CORNWALL AND THE LIZARD PENINSULA

General Information • Cultural tour with visits to Fowey, Mousehole, Padstow, Polrvan, Lizard Point, St. Michael's Mount, Pentire Point, Tintagel, Lanhydrock House. Once at the destination country, participants travel by bus, foot.

Learning Focus • Escorted travel to Frenchman's Creek, Mullion Cove and Penwith Moor. Nature observation (cliffs, meadows, crags, forests). Other activities include hiking, walking. Instruction is offered by naturalists, historians, professional guides. This program would appeal to people interested in nature studies, walking, culture, photography, history.

Accommodations • Hotels. Single rooms are available for an additional $170.

Program Details • Program offered 7 times per year. Session length: 8 days. Departures are scheduled in May–September. Most participants are 40–65 years of age. Participants must be 13 years or older to enroll. Other requirements: physician's approval and signed release form.

18 participants per session. Application deadline: 30 days prior to departure. Reservations are recommended at least 6 months before departure.
Costs • $1855 (includes housing, some meals, excursions, full-time guide). A $250 deposit is required.
Contact • Tour Manager, British Coastal Trails Scenic Walking, 7777 Fay Avenue, Suite 100, La Jolla, CA 92037; 800-473-1210; Fax: 619-456-2277; E-mail: lajolla@bctwalk.com; World Wide Web: http://www.bctwalk.com/lajolla

BRITISH COASTAL TRAILS SCENIC WALKING

COTSWOLD VILLAGES AND MEDIEVAL BRITAIN

General Information • Cultural tour with visits to Bristol, Chipping Campden, Rodborough, Uley, Hailes Abbey. Once at the destination country, participants travel by bus, foot.
Learning Focus • Escorted travel to Coaley Peak, Painswick and Kelmscot Manor. Other activities include hiking, walking. Instruction is offered by naturalists, historians, professional guides. This program would appeal to people interested in nature studies, walking, culture, photography, history.
Accommodations • Hotels. Single rooms are available for an additional $180.
Program Details • Program offered 9 times per year. Session length: 8 days. Departures are scheduled in April–September. Most participants are 40–65 years of age. Participants must be 13 years or older to enroll. Other requirements: physician's approval and signed release form. 18 participants per session. Application deadline: 30 days prior to departure. Reservations are recommended at least 6 months before departure.
Costs • $1895 (includes housing, some meals, excursions, full-time guide). A $250 deposit is required.
Contact • Tour Manager, British Coastal Trails Scenic Walking, 7777 Fay Avenue, Suite 100, La Jolla, CA 92037; 800-473-1210; Fax: 619-456-2277; E-mail: lajolla@bctwalk.com; World Wide Web: http://www.bctwalk.com/lajolla

BRITISH COASTAL TRAILS SCENIC WALKING

THE COTSWOLD WAY

General Information • Cultural tour with visits to Bath, Birdlip, Stroud, Tormarton, Dyrham Woods, Doddington Park, Westridge Wood, Painswick, Winchcombe. Once at the destination country, participants travel by bus, foot.
Learning Focus • Escorted travel to Dean Hill, Coaley Peak and Hailes Abbey. Other activities include hiking, walking. Instruction is offered by naturalists, historians, professional guides. This program would appeal to people interested in nature studies, walking, culture, photography, history.
Accommodations • Hotels. Single rooms are available for an additional $180.
Program Details • Program offered 3 times per year. Session length: 8 days. Departures are scheduled in May, July, August. Most participants are 40–65 years of age. Participants must be 13 years or older to enroll. Other requirements: physician's approval and signed release form.
18 participants per session. Application deadline: 30 days prior to departure. Reservations are recommended at least 6 months before departure.
Costs • $1785 (includes housing, some meals, excursions, full-time guide). A $250 deposit is required.
Contact • Tour Manager, British Coastal Trails Scenic Walking, 7777 Fay Avenue, Suite 100, La Jolla, CA 92037; 800-473-1210; Fax: 619-456-2277; E-mail: lajolla@bctwalk.com; World Wide Web: http://www.bctwalk.com/lajolla

BRITISH COASTAL TRAILS SCENIC WALKING

ENGLAND'S COAST-TO-COAST WALK

General Information • Cultural tour with visits to Ravensent, Richmond, Stonethwaite, Whitby, Grosmont, Vale of Mowbray, Pennines, Robin Hood's Grave, Lake District, Irish Sea. Once at the destination country, participants travel by bus, foot.
Learning Focus • Escorted travel to River Swale and Yorkshire Dales National Park. Nature observation (wildlife, red deer, eagles). Other activities include hiking, walking. Instruction is offered by naturalists, historians, professional guides. This program would appeal to people interested in nature studies, walking, culture, photography, history.
Accommodations • Hotels. Single rooms are available for an additional $385.
Program Details • Program offered 3 times per year. Session length: 16 days. Departures are scheduled in June, July, September. Most participants are 40–65 years of age. Participants must be 13 years or older to enroll. Other requirements: physician's approval, signed release form and good physical condition. 18 participants per session. Application deadline: 30 days prior to departure. Reservations are recommended at least 6 months before departure.
Costs • $2950 (includes housing, some meals, excursions, full-time guide). A $250 deposit is required.
Contact • Tour Manager, British Coastal Trails Scenic Walking, 7777 Fay Avenue, Suite 100, La Jolla, CA 92037; 800-473-1210; Fax: 619-456-2277; E-mail: lajolla@bctwalk.com; World Wide Web: http://www.bctwalk.com/lajolla

BRITISH COASTAL TRAILS SCENIC WALKING

THE LAKE DISTRICT AND HADRIAN'S WALL

General Information • Cultural tour with visits to Carlisle, Eskdale, Ullswater, Askham Fell, Whinlatter Pass, Hardknott Pass. Once at the destination country, participants travel by train, bus, foot.
Learning Focus • Escorted travel to Hadrian's Wall, Derwent Water and Rydal Water. Nature observation (lakes, sheep). Other activities include hiking, walking. Instruction is offered by naturalists, historians, professional guides. This program would appeal to people interested in nature studies, walking, culture, photography, history.
Accommodations • Hotels. Single rooms are available for an additional $170.
Program Details • Program offered 3 times per year. Session length: 8 days. Departures are scheduled in June, July, September. Most participants are 40–65 years of age. Participants must be 13 years or older to enroll. Other

requirements: physician's approval and signed release form. 18 participants per session. Application deadline: 30 days prior to departure. Reservations are recommended at least 6 months before departure.
Costs • $1875 (includes housing, some meals, excursions, full-time guide). A $250 deposit is required.
Contact • Tour Manager, British Coastal Trails Scenic Walking, 7777 Fay Avenue, Suite 100, La Jolla, CA 92037; 800-473-1210; Fax: 619-456-2277; E-mail: lajolla@bctwalk.com; World Wide Web: http://www.bctwalk.com/lajolla

BUTLER UNIVERSITY, INSTITUTE FOR STUDY ABROAD

INSTEP: CAMBRIDGE SUMMER SESSION

General Information • Academic study program in Cambridge.
Learning Focus • Courses in economics, political science, history.
Accommodations • Program-owned apartments, program-owned houses. Single rooms are available. Meals are taken on one's own, in residences.
Program Details • Program offered once per year. Session length: 7 weeks. Departures are scheduled in June. The program is open to undergraduate students. Most participants are 19–21 years of age. Other requirements: minimum 3.0 GPA and the approval of the students home university. 10–15 participants per session. Application deadline: April 15.
Costs • $3350 (includes tuition, housing, some meals). Application fee: $40. A $500 deposit is required.
Contact • Program Coordinator, Butler University, Institute for Study Abroad, ISA, 4600 Sunset Avenue, Indianapolis, IN 46208; 800-858-0229; Fax: 317-940-9704; E-mail: study-abroad@butler.edu; World Wide Web: http://www.butler.edu/www/isa

BUTLER UNIVERSITY, INSTITUTE FOR STUDY ABROAD

INSTEP: LONDON SUMMER SESSION

General Information • Academic study program in London.
Learning Focus • Courses in political science, social sciences, international business, legal studies.
Accommodations • Program-owned apartments, program-owned houses. Single rooms are available. Meals are taken on one's own, in residences.
Program Details • Program offered once per year. Session length: 7 weeks. Departures are scheduled in June. The program is open to undergraduate students. Most participants are 19–21 years of age. Other requirements: minimum 3.0 GPA and the approval of the students home university. 10–15 participants per session. Application deadline: April 15.
Costs • $3350 (includes tuition, housing). Application fee: $40. A $500 deposit is required.
Contact • Program Coordinator, Butler University, Institute for Study Abroad, ISA, 4600 Sunset Avenue, Indianapolis, IN 46208; 800-858-0229; Fax: 317-940-9704; E-mail: study-abroad@butler.edu; World Wide Web: http://www.butler.edu/www/isa

CANFORD SUMMER SCHOOL OF MUSIC

CANFORD SUMMER SCHOOL OF MUSIC

General Information • Performing arts program in Wimborne. Classes are held on the campus of Canford School.
Learning Focus • Courses in music, orchestras, conducting, piano, choral music, composition, jazz, voice, string and wind chamber music, opera, percussion, and brass band.
Accommodations • Dormitories. Single rooms are available. Meals are taken in central dining facility.
Program Details • Program offered once per year. Session length: 3 weeks. Departures are scheduled in August. The program is open to pre-college students, adults, professional musicians. Most participants are 16–80 years of age. 900 participants per session. Application deadline: July.
Costs • Contact sponsor for information.
Contact • Canford Summer School of Music, Canford Summer School of Music, Administrative Offices, 5 Bushey Close, Old Barn Lane, Kenley CR8 5AU, England; +44 18-16604766; Fax: +44 18-16-68-52-73

COASTAL CAROLINA UNIVERSITY

OXFORD EXPERIENCE

General Information • Academic study program in Oxford. Excursions to Bath, Winchester, Stratford-upon-Avon, London.
Learning Focus • Courses in English language, political science, history. Instruction is offered by professors from the sponsoring institution.
Accommodations • Dormitories. Single rooms are available. Meals are taken as a group, in central dining facility.
Program Details • Program offered once per year. Session length: 4 weeks. Departures are scheduled in July. The program is open to undergraduate students, graduate students. Most participants are 19–26 years of age. Other requirements: minimum 2.5 GPA. 15–20 participants per session. Application deadline: December 1.
Costs • $2750 (includes housing, some meals, excursions, international airfare). Application fee: $25. A $200 deposit is required.
Contact • Mr. Geoffrey Parsons, International Program Coordinator, Coastal Carolina University, PO Box 1954, Conway, SC 29526; 803-349-2054; Fax: 803-349-2252; E-mail: parsons@coastal.edu; World Wide Web: http://www.coastal.edu

COLLEGE CONSORTIUM FOR INTERNATIONAL STUDIES–ROCKLAND COMMUNITY COLLEGE

SUMMER SESSION IN LONDON

General Information • Academic study program in London. Classes are held on the campus of Thames Valley University. Excursions to Greenwich, Bath, Stratford-upon-Avon, Cambridge.

Learning Focus • Courses in art history, history, theater, psychology. Instruction is offered by local teachers.

Accommodations • Homestays. Single rooms are available. Meals are taken on one's own, in central dining facility, in local restaurants, in residences.

Program Details • Program offered once per year. Session length: 4 weeks. Departures are scheduled in June. The program is open to undergraduate students. Most participants are 18–50 years of age. Other requirements: minimum 2.5 GPA. 35 participants per session. Application deadline: April 30.

Costs • $1850 (includes tuition, housing, some meals, books and class materials, excursions, London Travel Card). A $100 deposit is required.

Contact • Jane C. Evans, Executive Director, College Consortium for International Studies, 2000 P Street, NW, Suite 503, Washington, DC 20036; 800-453-6956; Fax: 202-223-0999; E-mail: ccis@intr.net

COLLEGE CONSORTIUM FOR STUDY ABROAD

STUDY ABROAD IN ENGLAND

General Information • Academic study program in Bath, London. Classes are held on the campus of University of Bath. Excursions to Hampton Court Palace, Stonehenge, Avebury, Glastonbury, Wells, Chepstow Castle (Wales), Stratford-upon-Avon, Royal Shakespearean Company.

Learning Focus • Courses in English literature, Shakespeare, English history, sociology. Instruction is offered by local teachers.

Accommodations • Dormitories. Single rooms are available. Meals are taken on one's own, in central dining facility, in local restaurants.

Program Details • Program offered once per year. Session length: 6 weeks. Departures are scheduled in July. The program is open to undergraduate students, adults, graduates and teachers. Most participants are 18–72 years of age. Other requirements: minimum 2.0 GPA and sophomore standing by June. 25 participants per session. Application deadline: May 15.

Costs • $2950 (includes tuition, housing, some meals, excursions, international airfare, admissions). Application fee: $75. A $200 deposit is required.

Contact • Seymour J. Fader, Program Director, College Consortium for Study Abroad, PO Box 562, Paramus, NJ 07653-0562; 201-261-8753; Fax: 201-261-6389

The College Consortium for Study Abroad (CCSA) offers a 6-week summer session in its 15th year. Begins with 4 days in London and then moves to the University of Bath in historical Bath, Avon. Choose one or two of the four 3-credit courses taught by British faculty. Classes meet in the morning. Earned credits are transferable to any American college. Program includes all-day excursions to Wales and England, field trips, theater performance, and some meals. The Middle States evaluation report states that the program "is a wonderful opportunity...at remarkably low cost.. .Bath (75 minutes from London) is one of the most beautiful and interesting towns in Britain." Schedule includes 3-day weekends and a 5-day midsession recess for personal travel. University accommodations are in new single-room dorms, all with private bathrooms and fully equipped kitchens on each floor.

COLLEGE OF WILLIAM AND MARY

SUMMER IN CAMBRIDGE

General Information • Academic study program in Cambridge. Classes are held on the campus of University of Cambridge, Christ's College. Excursions to London.

Learning Focus • Courses in government, English literature. Instruction is offered by professors from the sponsoring institution.

Accommodations • Dormitories. Single rooms are available. Meals are taken on one's own, in local restaurants.

Program Details • Program offered once per year. Session length: 5 weeks. Departures are scheduled in July. The program is open to undergraduate students, graduate students, graduates of accredited universities. Most participants are 19–29 years of age. 30 participants per session. Application deadline: March 1.

Costs • $2800 (includes tuition, housing, some meals, books and class materials, excursions). Application fee: $40. A $500 deposit is required.

Contact • Dr. Ann M. Moore, Head of Programs Abroad, College of William and Mary, Reves Center, PO Box 8795, Williamsburg, VA 23187-8795; 757-221-3594; Fax: 757-221-3597; E-mail: ammoo2@facstaff.wm.edu

COOPERATIVE CENTER FOR STUDY ABROAD

LONDON–SUMMER

General Information • Academic study program in London. Classes are held on the campus of University of London-King's College London. Excursions to Stonehenge, Salisbury.

Learning Focus • Courses in anthropology, English language, history, literature, education, geography, journalism, marketing, mathematics, music, business, political science, philosophy, sociology. Instruction is offered by professors from the sponsoring institution.
Accommodations • Dormitories. Single rooms are available. Meals are taken as a group, on one's own, in central dining facility, in local restaurants.
Program Details • Program offered once per year. Session length: 5 weeks. Departures are scheduled in July. The program is open to undergraduate students, graduate students, adults. Most participants are 18-60 years of age. Other requirements: minimum 2.0 GPA. 150 participants per session. Application deadline: March 20.
Costs • $2995 (includes housing, some meals, insurance, excursions, international airfare). A $100 deposit is required.
Contact • Dr. Michael A. Klembara, Executive Director, Cooperative Center for Study Abroad, NKU, BEP 301, Highland Heights, KY 41099; 800-319-6015; Fax: 606-572-6650; E-mail: ccsa@nku.edu

COOPERATIVE CENTER FOR STUDY ABROAD

LONDON–WINTER

General Information • Academic study program in London. Excursions to Stratford-upon-Avon, Bath, Dover, Stonehenge, Canterbury.
Learning Focus • Courses in geography, literature, theater, psychology, economics, marketing, nursing, speech and debate, mathematics. Instruction is offered by professors from the sponsoring institution.
Accommodations • Hotels. Single rooms are available. Meals are taken as a group, on one's own, in central dining facility, in local restaurants.
Program Details • Program offered once per year. Session length: 2 weeks. Departures are scheduled in December. The program is open to undergraduate students, graduate students, adults. Most participants are 18-60 years of age. Other requirements: minimum 2.0 GPA. 120 participants per session. Application deadline: October 21.
Costs • $1995 (includes housing, some meals, insurance, excursions, international airfare). A $100 deposit is required.
Contact • Dr. Michael A. Klembara, Executive Director, Cooperative Center for Study Abroad, NKU, BEP 301, Highland Heights, KY 41099; 800-319-6015; Fax: 606-572-6650; E-mail: ccsa@nku.edu

COUNTRY WALKERS

THE COTSWOLDS PRESERVED

General Information • Cultural, gourmet cooking, nature study and walking tour with visits to Painswick, Upper Slaughter, Slad Valley, Winchcombe, Stanton, Broadway, Chipping Campden. Once at the destination country, participants travel by foot.
Learning Focus • Escorted travel to Crickley, Hailes Abbey and Northwick Park. Other activities include walking. Instruction is offered by professors, researchers, naturalists, historians. This program would appeal to people interested in walking, nature studies, food and wine.
Accommodations • Hotels. Single rooms are available for an additional $300-$600.
Program Details • Program offered 6 times per year. Session length: 7 days. Departures are scheduled in May-September. Program is targeted to adults 35 to 65 years old. Most participants are 35-65 years of age. Participants must be 18 years or older to enroll. 18 participants per session. Reservations are recommended at least 5-6 months before departure.
Costs • $1625 (includes housing, all meals, excursions). A $400 deposit is required.
Contact • Heather Kellingbeck, Vice President, Country Walkers, PO Box 180, Waterbury, VT 05176; 800-464-9255; Fax: 802-244-5661; E-mail: ctrywalk@aol.com

COUNTRY WALKERS

KING ARTHUR'S CORNWALL

General Information • Cultural, gourmet cooking, nature study and walking tour with visits to Cornwall, Land's End, Penzance, Porthcurno, Mousehole, Isle of Scilly. Once at the destination country, participants travel by foot, boat.
Learning Focus • Escorted travel to St. Michael's Mount. Attendance at performances (Greek-style open air theater, electronic theater). Other activities include walking. Instruction is offered by professors, researchers, naturalists, historians. This program would appeal to people interested in walking, nature studies, food and wine.
Accommodations • Hotels. Single rooms are available for an additional $300-$600.
Program Details • Program offered 5 times per year. Session length: 7 days. Departures are scheduled in June-September. Program is targeted to adults 35 to 65 years old. Most participants are 35-65 years of age. Participants must be 18 years or older to enroll. 18 participants per session. Reservations are recommended at least 5-6 months before departure.
Costs • $1600 (includes housing, all meals, excursions). A $400 deposit is required.
Contact • Heather Kellingbeck, Vice President, Country Walkers, PO Box 180, Waterbury, VT 05176; 800-464-9255; Fax: 802-244-5661; E-mail: ctrywalk@aol.com

COUNTRY WALKERS

POETRY IN THE LAKELANDS

General Information • Cultural, gourmet cooking, nature study and walking tour with visits to Carlisle, Duddon Valley, Hadrian's Wall, Elterwater Village, Coniston Village. Once at the destination country, participants travel by foot.
Learning Focus • Escorted travel to Aira Force Waterfall. Other activities include walking. Instruction is offered by professors, researchers, naturalists, historians. This program would appeal to people interested in walking, nature studies, food and wine.
Accommodations • Hotels. Single rooms are available for an additional $300-$600.
Program Details • Program offered 5 times per year. Session length: 7 days. Departures are scheduled in May-September. Program is targeted to adults 35 to 65 years old. Most participants are 35-65 years of age. Participants

must be 18 years or older to enroll. 18 participants per session. Reservations are recommended at least 5-6 months before departure.
Costs • $1750 (includes housing, all meals, excursions). A $400 deposit is required.
Contact • Heather Kellingbeck, Vice President, Country Walkers, PO Box 180, Waterbury, VT 05176; 800-464-9255; Fax: 802-244-5661; E-mail: ctrywalk@aol.com

CROSS-CULTURE
LAKE DISTRICT WALKS

General Information • Nature study, cultural, and hiking tour with visits to Reswick, Bassenthwaite Lake, Borrowdale, Derwent Water, Maiden Moor, Cockermouth, Windermere, Ambleside, Troutbeck. Once at the destination country, participants travel by bus, foot.
Learning Focus • Instruction in various aspects of the Lake District. Escorted travel to Ashness Bridge, Cat Bells, High Spy, Place Fell, Beda Fell and Hadrian's Wall. Attendance at performances (theater). Other activities include hiking. Instruction is offered by naturalists, historians, experienced hiking leaders. This program would appeal to people interested in nature studies, history, food and wine, culture, traditions.
Accommodations • Hotels. Single rooms are available for an additional $60.
Program Details • Program offered once per year. Session length: 9 days. Departures are scheduled in July. Program is targeted to adults of all ages. Most participants are 30-75 years of age. Participants must be 12 years or older to enroll. Other requirements: must be in good health, must be accompanied by an adult if under 18. 20 participants per session. Application deadline: 1 month prior to departure. Reservations are recommended at least 3-12 months before departure.
Costs • $1950 (includes tuition, housing, all meals, books and class materials, excursions, international airfare). A $300 deposit is required.
Contact • Cross-Culture, 52 High Point Drive, Amherst, MA 01002-1224; 413-256-6303; Fax: 413-253-2303; E-mail: xculture@javanet.com; World Wide Web: http://www.empiremall.com/cross-culture

CROSS-CULTURE
QUINTESSENTIAL ENGLAND

General Information • Cultural tour with visits to Wiltshire, Portsmouth, Bath, Oxford University, the Cotswolds. Once at the destination country, participants travel by bus, foot.
Learning Focus • Instruction in thatching a roof. Escorted travel to Roman Baths and Georgian Crescent. Museum visits (Portsmouth Naval Museum, Avebury Museum). Attendance at performances (theater, concert). Instruction is offered by highly educated guides. This program would appeal to people interested in culture, history, nature studies, arts, traditions, food and wine.
Accommodations • Hotels. Single rooms are available for an additional $60.
Program Details • Program offered once per year. Session length: 9 days. Departures are scheduled in August. Program is targeted to adults of all ages. Most participants are 40-70 years of age. Participants must be 12 years or older to enroll. Other requirements: good health, accompaniment of an adult if under 18. 20-25 participants per session. Application deadline: 1 month prior to departure. Reservations are recommended at least 3-12 months before departure.
Costs • $2100 (includes tuition, housing, all meals, books and class materials, excursions, international airfare). A $300 deposit is required.
Contact • Cross-Culture, 52 High Point Drive, Amherst, MA 01002-1224; 413-256-6303; Fax: 413-253-2303; E-mail: xculture@javanet.com; World Wide Web: http://www.empiremall.com/cross-culture

CROSS-CULTURE
SAVORING ENGLAND'S WEST COUNTRY

General Information • Cultural tour with visits to Padstow, Princetown, Plymouth, St. Ives. Once at the destination country, participants travel by bus, foot, boat.
Learning Focus • Instruction in Arthurian legends, history of The Dartmoor and clay production. Escorted travel to Tintagel, Boscastle, Bodmin Moor and The Mayflower Steps. Museum visits (Tate Gallery, Open-Air museum). Instruction is offered by highly educated guides. This program would appeal to people interested in culture, history, nature studies, arts, traditions, food and wine.
Accommodations • Hotels. Single rooms are available for an additional $115.
Program Details • Program offered once per year. Session length: 9 days. Departures are scheduled in August. Program is targeted to adults of all ages. Most participants are 40-70 years of age. Participants must be 12 years or older to enroll. Other requirements: good health, accompaniment of an adult if under 18. 20-25 participants per session. Application deadline: 1 month prior to departure. Reservations are recommended at least 3-12 months before departure.
Costs • $2370 (includes tuition, housing, all meals, books and class materials, excursions, international airfare). A $300 deposit is required.
Contact • Cross-Culture, 52 High Point Drive, Amherst, MA 01002-1224; 413-256-6303; Fax: 413-253-2303; E-mail: xculture@javanet.com; World Wide Web: http://www.empiremall.com/cross-culture

CROSS-CULTURE
WALKS IN THE YORKSHIRE DALES

General Information • Nature study, cultural, and hiking tour with visits to Hawes, Pennine Way, Gunnerside. Once at the destination country, participants travel by bus, foot.
Learning Focus • Escorted travel to Aysgarth Falls, Castle Bolton, Hardrow Force, Buttertubs, Ingleborough, Gaping Gill and Gardale Scar. Other activities include hiking. Instruction is offered by naturalists, historians, experienced hiking leaders. This program would appeal to people interested in nature studies, history, food and wine, culture, traditions.
Accommodations • Country manor house. Single rooms are available for an additional $95.
Program Details • Program offered once per year. Session length: 9 days. Departures are scheduled in June. Program is targeted to adults of all ages. Most participants are 30-75 years of age. Participants must be 12 years or older to enroll.

Other requirements: must be in good health, must be accompanied by an adult if under 18. 20 participants per session. Application deadline: 1 month prior to departure. Reservations are recommended at least 3–12 months before departure.
Costs • Contact sponsor for information. A $300 deposit is required.
Contact • Cross-Culture, 52 High Point Drive, Amherst, MA 01002-1224; 413-256-6303; Fax: 413-253-2303; E-mail: xculture@javanet.com; World Wide Web: http://www.empiremall.com/cross-culture

CROSS-CULTURE

WESSEX WALKS

General Information • Nature study, cultural, and hiking tour with visits to Devizes, Avebury, Cheddar Gorge, Painswick, Great Bedwyn, Stingford, Higher Bockhampton. Once at the destination country, participants travel by bus, foot.
Learning Focus • Instruction in regional history, flora and fauna and Wessex literature. Escorted travel to Wansdyke, Uffington White Horse, tomb of Waylands, Smithy and Glastonbury Tor. Museum visits (Hardy Museum). Other activities include hiking. Instruction is offered by naturalists, historians, experienced hiking leaders. This program would appeal to people interested in nature studies, history, food and wine, culture, traditions.
Accommodations • Manor house. Single rooms are available for an additional $60.
Program Details • Program offered once per year. Session length: 9 days. Departures are scheduled in July. Program is targeted to adults of all ages. Most participants are 30–75 years of age. Participants must be 12 years or older to enroll. Other requirements: must be in good health, must be accompanied by an adult if under 18. 20 participants per session. Application deadline: 1 month prior to departure. Reservations are recommended at least 3–12 months before departure.
Costs • $1910 (includes tuition, housing, all meals, books and class materials, excursions, international airfare). A $300 deposit is required.
Contact • Cross-Culture, 52 High Point Drive, Amherst, MA 01002-1224; 413-256-6303; Fax: 413-253-2303; E-mail: xculture@javanet.com; World Wide Web: http://www.empiremall.com/cross-culture

CUISINE INTERNATIONAL

LA PETIT BLANC COOKING SCHOOL

General Information • Gourmet cooking/wine tour with visits to Great Milton.
Learning Focus • Instruction in French cusine. Instruction is offered by chefs. This program would appeal to people interested in cooking.
Accommodations • Hotels. Single rooms are available.
Program Details • Program offered 25 times per year. Session length: 1 week. Departures are scheduled in October–April. Most participants are 18–75 years of age. Participants must be 18 years or older to enroll. 8 participants per session. Reservations are recommended at least 1 year before departure.
Costs • $2000 (includes tuition, housing, all meals, books and class materials). A $300 deposit is required.
Contact • Judy Ebrey, Owner, Cuisine International, PO Box 25228, Dallas, TX 75225; 214-373-1161; Fax: 214-373-1162; E-mail: cuisineint@aol.com; World Wide Web: http://www.iglobal.net/cuisineint

DICKINSON COLLEGE

FIELDWORK IN CLASSICAL ARCHAEOLOGY

General Information • Academic study program in Melsonby, Yorkshire.
Learning Focus • Courses in archaeology. Instruction is offered by professors from the sponsoring institution.
Accommodations • Dormitories. Meals are taken as a group, in central dining facility.
Program Details • Program offered once per year. Session length: 6 weeks. Departures are scheduled in May. The program is open to undergraduate students. Most participants are 18–20 years of age. 12 participants per session. Application deadline: February 15.
Costs • $3600 (includes tuition, housing, all meals, books and class materials, excursions, international airfare). Application fee: $15. A $300 deposit is required.
Contact • Dr. John S. Henderson, Director of Off-Campus Studies, Dickinson College, PO Box 1773, Carlisle, PA 17013-2896; 717-245-1341; Fax: 717-245-1688; E-mail: ocs@dickinson.edu; World Wide Web: http://www.dickinson.edu

DICKINSON COLLEGE

SUMMER SESSION IN ENGLAND

General Information • Academic study program in London.
Learning Focus • Courses in drama, history, music, art. Instruction is offered by professors from the sponsoring institution.
Accommodations • Dormitories. Meals are taken on one's own, in local restaurants.
Program Details • Program offered once per year. Session length: 6 weeks. Departures are scheduled in May. The program is open to undergraduate students. Most participants are 18–20 years of age. 15 participants per session. Application deadline: February 15.
Costs • $5600 (includes tuition, housing, all meals, books and class materials, excursions, international airfare). Application fee: $15. A $300 deposit is required.
Contact • Dr. John S. Henderson, Director of Off-Campus Studies, Dickinson College, PO Box 1773, Carlisle, PA 17013-2896; 717-245-1341; Fax: 717-245-1688; E-mail: ocs@dickinson.edu; World Wide Web: http://www.dickinson.edu

DUKE UNIVERSITY

DUKE IN LONDON–DRAMA

General Information • Academic study program in London. Excursions to Stratford-upon-Avon, Greenwich, Hampton Court Palace.
Learning Focus • Courses in English language, drama. Instruction is offered by professors from the sponsoring institution.

Accommodations • Dormitories. Meals are taken on one's own, in local restaurants.
Program Details • Program offered once per year. Session length: 6 weeks. Departures are scheduled in June. The program is open to undergraduate students. Most participants are 19–21 years of age. Other requirements: minimum 2.7 GPA. 20 participants per session. Application deadline: February 21.
Costs • $4141 (includes tuition, housing, some meals, excursions, international airfare).
Contact • Foreign Academic Programs, Duke University, 121 Allen Building, Box 90057, Durham, NC 27708-0057; 919-684-2174; Fax: 919-684-3083; E-mail: abroad@mail01.adm.duke.edu; World Wide Web: http://www.mis.duke.edu/study_abroad/study_abroad.html

DUKE UNIVERSITY

DUKE IN LONDON–MEDIA

General Information • Academic study program in London. Classes are held on the campus of University of London.
Learning Focus • Courses in political science. Instruction is offered by professors from the sponsoring institution and local teachers.
Accommodations • Dormitories. Single rooms are available. Meals are taken on one's own.
Program Details • Program offered once per year. Session length: 6 weeks. Departures are scheduled in July. The program is open to undergraduate students. Most participants are 19–21 years of age. Other requirements: minimum 2.7 GPA. Application deadline: February 21.
Costs • Contact sponsor for information.
Contact • Foreign Academic Programs, Duke University, 121 Allen Building, Box 90057, Durham, NC 27708-0057; 919-684-2174; Fax: 919-684-3083; E-mail: abroad@mail01.adm.duke.edu; World Wide Web: http://www.mis.duke.edu/study_abroad/study_abroad.html

DUKE UNIVERSITY

DUKE IN OXFORD

General Information • Academic study program in Oxford. Classes are held on the campus of University of Oxford. Excursions to Stratford-upon-Avon, London, Bath.
Learning Focus • Courses in English literature, history, political science. Instruction is offered by local teachers.
Accommodations • Dormitories. Meals are taken as a group, in central dining facility.
Program Details • Program offered once per year. Session length: 6 weeks. Departures are scheduled in July. The program is open to undergraduate students. Most participants are 19–21 years of age. Other requirements: minimum 3.0 GPA. 50 participants per session. Application deadline: February 21.
Costs • $5441 (includes tuition, housing, all meals, excursions, international airfare).
Contact • Foreign Academic Programs, Duke University, 121 Allen Building, Box 90057, Durham, NC 27708-0057; 919-684-2174; Fax: 919-684-3083; E-mail: abroad@mail01.adm.duke.edu; World Wide Web: http://www.mis.duke.edu/study_abroad/study_abroad.html

EASTERN MICHIGAN UNIVERSITY

SOCIAL WORK PRACTICUM IN ENGLAND

General Information • Academic study program in Brighton. Classes are held on the campus of University of Brighton.
Learning Focus • Courses in social work, health care.
Accommodations • Dormitories. Meals are taken as a group, in central dining facility.
Program Details • Program offered once per year. Session length: 6 weeks. Departures are scheduled in May. The program is open to undergraduate students, graduate students. Most participants are 18–30 years of age. Other requirements: minimum 2.0 GPA and 18 years of age. 10 participants per session. Application deadline: March 1.
Costs • $2995 (includes tuition, housing, all meals, insurance, international airfare). A $150 deposit is required.
Contact • Academic Programs Abroad, Eastern Michigan University, 332 Goodison Hall, Ypsilanti, MI 48197; 800-777-3541; Fax: 313-487-2316; E-mail: programs.abroad@emich.edu; World Wide Web: http://www.emich.edu/public/cont_ed/abroad.html

EUROCENTRES

LANGUAGE IMMERSION IN ENGLAND

General Information • Language study program in Bath, Bournemouth, Brighton, Cambridge, London, Oxford. Classes are held on the campus of Eurocentre Bournemouth, Eurocentre Cambridge, Eurocentre London Lee Green, Eurocentre London Victoria, Eurocentre Oxford Summer Centre, Eurocentre Bath Summer Centre, Eurocentre Brighton. Excursions to Dorset, Isle of Wight, York, Canterbury, Stonehenge, Salisbury.
Learning Focus • Courses in English language, English culture. Instruction is offered by professors from the sponsoring institution.
Accommodations • Homestays. Single rooms are available. Meals are taken with host family, in residences.
Program Details • Program offered 20 times per year. Session length: 2–12 weeks. Departures are scheduled in January–December. The program is open to undergraduate students, graduate students, pre-college students, adults. Most participants are 16–80 years of age. 15 participants per session.
Costs • Contact sponsor for information.
Contact • Marketing, Eurocentres, 101 North Union Street, Suite 300, Alexandria, VA 22314; 800-648-4809; Fax: 703-684-1495; E-mail: 100632.141@compuserve.com; World Wide Web: http://www.clark.net/pub/eurocent/home.htm

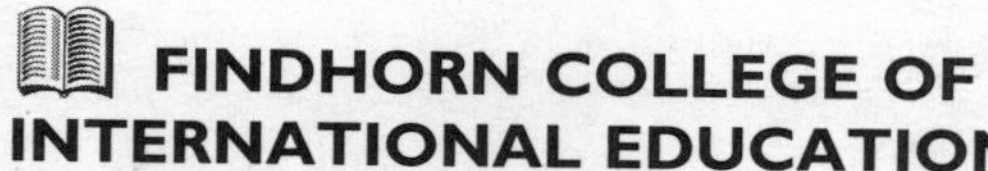

FINDHORN COLLEGE OF INTERNATIONAL EDUCATION

INSTITUTE OF DEEP ECOLOGY

General Information • Academic study program in Hailsham. Classes are held on the campus of Queen's University at Kingston–International Study Center.
Learning Focus • Courses in ecology, environmental studies. Instruction is offered by local teachers.

Accommodations • Dormitories. Single rooms are available. Meals are taken as a group, in central dining facility.
Program Details • Program offered once per year. Session length: 5 weeks. Departures are scheduled in June. The program is open to undergraduate students, graduate students, pre-college students, adults. Most participants are 18–24 years of age. 20 participants per session. Application deadline: rolling.
Costs • $3900 (includes tuition, housing, all meals, excursions). A $500 deposit is required.
Contact • Director of Admissions, Findhorn College of International Education, Box 1393, Boston, MA 02117; 800-932-7658; Fax: 800-932-7658; E-mail: admissions@highland-uk.org

FINDHORN COLLEGE OF INTERNATIONAL EDUCATION

SUMMER TERM

General Information • Academic study program in Hailsham. Classes are held on the campus of Queen's University at Kingston–International Study Center.
Learning Focus • Courses in ecology, environmental studies, liberal arts, social sciences, European studies. Instruction is offered by local teachers.
Accommodations • Dormitories. Single rooms are available. Meals are taken as a group, in central dining facility.
Program Details • Program offered once per year. Session length: 5 weeks. Departures are scheduled in June. The program is open to undergraduate students, graduate students, pre-college students, adults. Most participants are 18–24 years of age. 40 participants per session. Application deadline: rolling.
Costs • $3900 (includes tuition, housing, all meals, excursions). A $500 deposit is required.
Contact • Director of Admissions, Findhorn College of International Education, Box 1393, Boston, MA 02117; 800-932-7658; Fax: 800-932-7658; E-mail: admissions@highland-uk.org

FOREIGN LANGUAGE STUDY ABROAD SERVICE

INTERNATIONAL LANGUAGE STUDY HOMESTAYS IN ENGLAND

General Information • Language study program in England.
Learning Focus • Courses in English language. Instruction is offered by local teachers.
Accommodations • Homestays. Single rooms are available. Meals are taken with host family, in residences.
Program Details • Session length: varies. Departures are scheduled in January–December. The program is open to undergraduate students, graduate students, pre-college students, adults. Most participants are 12 years of age and older. Other requirements: students must be at least 12 years old. 1 participant per session.
Costs • Contact sponsor for information. A $300 deposit is required.
Contact • Louise Harber, Coordinator, Foreign Language Study Abroad Service, Department IH, Box 903, 5935 Southwest 64th Avenue, South Miami, FL 33143; 800-282-1090; Fax: 305-662-2907; E-mail: flsas@netpoint.net; World Wide Web: http://www.netpoint.net/~flsas

GEORGE MASON UNIVERSITY

APPLIED ECOLOGY: A STUDY OF BRITISH LANDSCAPES

General Information • Academic study program in Oxford. Classes are held on the campus of St. Peter's College, Oxford University. Excursions to Wales, north England.
Learning Focus • Courses in ecology, geography. Instruction is offered by professors from the sponsoring institution and local teachers.
Accommodations • Dormitories. Single rooms are available. Meals are taken as a group, in central dining facility.
Program Details • Program offered once per year. Session length: 4 weeks. Departures are scheduled in June. The program is open to undergraduate students, graduate students, adults. Most participants are 18–65 years of age. Other requirements: minimum 2.25 GPA. 10–15 participants per session. Application deadline: April 29.
Costs • $3527 for George Mason University students, $4077 for other students (includes tuition, all meals, insurance, excursions). Application fee: $35. A $500 deposit is required.
Contact • Dr. Yehuda Lukacs, Director, Center for Global Education, George Mason University, 4400 University Drive, 235 Johnson Center, Fairfax, VA 22030; 703-993-2156; Fax: 703-993-2153; E-mail: ylukacs@gmu.edu; World Wide Web: http://www.gmu.edu/departments/oie

GEORGE MASON UNIVERSITY

EMPLOYMENT, MONEY, AND MARKETS: EUROPEAN PRACTICES AND PERSPECTIVES

General Information • Academic study program in Oxford. Classes are held on the campus of St. Peter's College, Oxford University.
Learning Focus • Courses in economics, trade, investment. Instruction is offered by professors from the sponsoring institution and local teachers.
Accommodations • Dormitories. Meals are taken as a group, in central dining facility.
Program Details • Program offered once per year. Session length: 4 weeks. Departures are scheduled in July. The program is open to graduate students, adults. Most participants are 25–65 years of age. Other requirements: minimum 2.25 GPA. 20–25 participants per session. Application deadline: April 12.
Costs • $3515 for George Mason University students, $4065 for other students (includes tuition, housing, all meals, insurance, excursions). Application fee: $35. A $500 deposit is required.
Contact • Dr. Yehuda Lukacs, Director, Center for Global Education, George Mason University, 4400 University Drive, 235 Johnson Center, Fairfax, VA 22030; 703-993-2155; Fax: 703-993-2153; E-mail: ylukacs@gmu.edu; World Wide Web: http://www.gmu.edu/departments/oie

GEORGETOWN UNIVERSITY

GEORGETOWN GRADUATE BUSINESS PROGRAM IN INTERNATIONAL MANAGEMENT

General Information • Academic study program in Oxford. Classes are held on the campus of University of Oxford, Trinity College.

Learning Focus • Courses in international management, business and government relations, international finance, management. Instruction is offered by professors from the sponsoring institution and local teachers.

Accommodations • Dormitories. Single rooms are available. Meals are taken as a group, on one's own, in central dining facility.

Program Details • Program offered once per year. Session length: 6 weeks. Departures are scheduled in June. The program is open to graduate students. Most participants are 24–28 years of age. Other requirements: enrollment in MBA, JD, public policy, or other graduate program, or professional experience. Application deadline: March 1.

Costs • $4600 (includes tuition, housing, some meals, books and class materials, insurance, excursions). A $100 deposit is required.

Contact • Marianne T. Needham, Director, International Programs, Georgetown University, Box 571012, Washington, DC 20057; 202-687-6184; Fax: 202-687-8954; E-mail: sscefps1@gunet.georgetown.edu; World Wide Web: http://guweb.georgetown.edu/ssce

GEORGETOWN UNIVERSITY

GEORGETOWN SUMMER PROGRAM IN COMPARATIVE BUSINESS POLICY

General Information • Academic study program in Oxford. Classes are held on the campus of University of Oxford, Trinity College.

Learning Focus • Courses in comparative business, international finance. Instruction is offered by professors from the sponsoring institution and local teachers.

Accommodations • Dormitories. Single rooms are available. Meals are taken as a group.

Program Details • Program offered once per year. Session length: 6 weeks. Departures are scheduled in June. The program is open to undergraduate students. Most participants are 21 years of age. Other requirements: minimum 3.0 GPA and rising senior status only. 35 participants per session. Application deadline: March.

Costs • $4600 (includes tuition, housing, some meals, books and class materials, insurance, excursions). A $100 deposit is required.

Contact • Marianne T. Needham, Director, International Programs, Georgetown University, 306 ICC, Box 571012, Washington, DC 20057-1012; 202-687-6184; Fax: 202-687-8954; E-mail: sscefps1@gunet.georgetown.edu; World Wide Web: http://guweb.georgetown.edu/ssce

GEORGETOWN UNIVERSITY

SHAKESPEARE: TEXT AND PERFORMANCE

General Information • Academic study program in Leicester. Classes are held on the campus of DeMontfort University Leicester. Excursions to Stratford-upon-Avon, London.

Learning Focus • Courses in Shakespeare, theater. Instruction is offered by professors from the sponsoring institution and local teachers.

Accommodations • Dormitories. Single rooms are available. Meals are taken as a group, in central dining facility, in local restaurants.

Program Details • Program offered once per year. Session length: 4 weeks. Departures are scheduled in July. The program is open to undergraduate students, graduate students, pre-college students, adults. Most participants are 19–30 years of age. 16 participants per session. Application deadline: March.

Costs • $2600 (includes tuition, housing, some meals, books and class materials, insurance, excursions). A $100 deposit is required.

Contact • Marianne T. Needham, Director, International Programs, Georgetown University, 306 ICC, Box 571012, Washington, DC 20057-1012; 202-687-6184; Fax: 202-687-8954; E-mail: sscefps1@gunet.georgetown.edu; World Wide Web: http://guweb.georgetown.edu/ssce

ILLINOIS STATE UNIVERSITY

CURRICULUM AND INSTRUCTION MASTER'S PROGRAM IN EASTBOURNE, ENGLAND

General Information • Academic study program in Eastbourne. Classes are held on the campus of University of Brighton.

Accommodations • Homestays.

Program Details • Program offered once per year. Session length: 4 weeks. Departures are scheduled in July. The program is open to graduate students, adults. Other requirements: minimum 2.5 GPA, previous study in field and must be enrolled in a Master's degree program. 15 participants per session. Application deadline: March 15.

Costs • $3200 (includes tuition, housing, all meals, insurance, excursions, international airfare, fees).

Contact • Dr. Larry Kennedy, Illinois State University, Campus Box 5330, Normal, IL 61790-5330; 309-438-5365; Fax: 309-438-3987; E-mail: oisp@rs6000.cmp.ilstu.edu; World Wide Web: http://www.orat.ilstu.edu/

ILLINOIS STATE UNIVERSITY

SUMMER PROGRAM IN BRISTOL, ENGLAND

General Information • Academic study program in Bristol. Classes are held on the campus of University of the West of England at Bristol.

Learning Focus • Courses in British history, culture and civilization, business.

Accommodations • Homestays.

Program Details • Program offered once per year. Session length: 4 weeks. Departures are scheduled in May. The program is open to undergraduate students, graduate students. Other requirements: minimum 2.5 GPA and a minimum of 60 credit hours. 15 participants per session. Application deadline: March 15.

Costs • $2000 (includes tuition, housing, some meals, insurance, excursions, fees).

Summer Programs Abroad 1997

Georgetown
UNIVERSITY

BUSINESS AND ECONOMICS

☐ Undergraduate Program in International Business and Finance*
Oxford University, England

☐ Graduate Program in International Management
Oxford University, England

☐ European Economic Community
University of Antwerp, Belgium

☐ International Marketing and Business Policy*
Chinese University of Hong Kong

☐ Pacific Rim: Business Management, Politics, and Markets
Waseda University, Tokyo, Japan

LANGUAGE AND CULTURE

☐ French Language,Literature, Culture and Business
Institute de Touraine, France

☐ Spanish language, Literature, Culture and Quichua
Universidad Catolica del Ecuador, Quito

☐ German language, Literature and Business
University of Trier, Germany

☐ Portuguese Language, Literature, and Culture
Campinas, Brazil

☐ Russian Language, Literature and Culture
St. Petersburg, Russia

OTHER

☐ Life and Thought in Ancient Greece
Study-Tour, Greece

☐ Shakespeare Text and Performance
Leicester, England

☐ Reading and Writing Italy, Villa Le Balze
Florence, Italy

☐ Comparative History and Literature
University of New South Wales, Australia

**Indicates program is for rising seniors*

For further information contact:
The School for Summer and Continuing Education
Georgetown University, 306 ICC, Box 571012, Washington, D.C. 20057-1012
FAX: (202) 687-8954 PHONE: (202) 687-5942 or 687-6184
E-MAIL: sscefps1@gunet.georgetown.edu
WEB: http://guweb.georgetown.edu/ssce/

NAME ______________________________

ADDRESS ______________________________

CITY ________________ STATE ________________ ZIP ________

Georgetown University is an equal opportunity/affirmative action institution in employment and admissions.

Contact • Rodger Singley, Illinois State University, Box 5590, Normal, IL 61790-5590; 309-438-5184; Fax: 309-438-3987; E-mail: oisp@rs6000.cmp.ilstu.edu; World Wide Web: http://www.orat.ilstu.edu/

INSTITUTE OF EUROPEAN STUDIES/INSTITUTE OF ASIAN STUDIES

LONDON SUMMER PROGRAM

General Information • Academic study program in London.
Learning Focus • Courses in art history, British history, British literature, British politics.
Accommodations • Locally-rented apartments. Meals are taken on one's own, in local restaurants, in residences.
Program Details • Program offered once per year. Session length: 6 weeks. Departures are scheduled in June. The program is open to undergraduate students, graduate students, continuing education students. Most participants are 18–25 years of age. Other requirements: good academic standing. 50 participants per session. Application deadline: April 15.
Costs • $3200 (includes tuition, housing, excursions). Application fee: $25. A $500 deposit is required.
Contact • Department of Admissions, Institute of European Studies/Institute of Asian Studies, 223 West Ohio Street, Chicago, IL 60610-4196; 800-995-2300; Fax: 313-944-1448; E-mail: recruit@iesias.org; World Wide Web: http://www.iesias.org

INTERHOSTEL, UNIVERSITY OF NEW HAMPSHIRE

BRISTOL AND LONDON, ENGLAND

General Information • Cultural tour with visits to Bristol, London, Bath, Wells, Salisbury, Stonehenge, Tintern Abbey, Cotswolds, Avebury. Once at the destination country, participants travel by bus, foot. Program is affiliated with University of Bristol.
Learning Focus • Instruction in history and culture. Escorted travel to sites of interest. Museum visits (British Museum, Victoria and Albert Museum). Attendance at performances (Royal Shakespeare theater). Instruction is offered by professors. This program would appeal to people interested in history, culture, archaeology.
Accommodations • Dormitories, hotels. Single rooms are available.
Program Details • Program offered once per year. Session length: 2 weeks. Departures are scheduled in August. Program is targeted to seniors over 50. Most participants are 60–80 years of age. Participants must be 50 years or older to enroll. Other requirements: good health. 35 participants per session. Reservations are recommended at least 3 months before departure.
Costs • $2245 (includes tuition, housing, all meals, excursions, international airfare, entrance fees). A $200 deposit is required.
Contact • Janice Pierson, Office Supervisor, Interhostel, University of New Hampshire, 6 Garrison Avenue, Durham, NH 03824; 800-733-9753; Fax: 603-862-1113; World Wide Web: http://www.learn.unh.edu/

JAMES MADISON UNIVERSITY

SUMMER PROGRAM IN LONDON

General Information • Academic study program in London. Excursions to Bath, Cambridge, Wales, Lake District.
Learning Focus • Courses in art history, English literature, history, music, theater. Instruction is offered by professors from the sponsoring institution.
Accommodations • Program-owned houses. Single rooms are available. Meals are taken as a group, on one's own, in central dining facility, in local restaurants.
Program Details • Program offered once per year. Session length: 5 weeks. Departures are scheduled in May. The program is open to undergraduate students, graduate students. Most participants are 18–30 years of age. Other requirements: 2.8 minimum GPA. 20–30 participants per session. Application deadline: February 1.
Costs • $2256 for Virginia residents, $3108 for non-residents (includes tuition, housing, some meals, excursions). A $400 deposit is required.
Contact • Douglas Kehlenbrink, Director, London Programs, James Madison University, Office of International Education, Harrisonburg, VA 22807; 540-568-6419; Fax: 540-568-3310; E-mail: kehlende@jmu.edu; World Wide Web: http://www.jmu.edu/intl-ed/

LONDON COLLEGE OF FASHION

STUDY ABROAD SEMESTER PROGRAM

General Information • Academic study program in London. Classes are held on the campus of London College of Fashion. Excursions to France (Paris), Italy (Milan).
Learning Focus • Courses in fashion, design, marketing, management, theater costumes, theater makeup, journalism. Instruction is offered by professors from the sponsoring institution.
Accommodations • Dormitories, locally-rented apartments, program-owned apartments, program-owned houses. Single rooms are available. Meals are taken as a group, on one's own, in central dining facility, in local restaurants.
Program Details • Program offered 2 times per year. Session length: 12 weeks. Departures are scheduled in September, January. The program is open to undergraduate students, graduate students, pre-college students, adults. Most participants are 18–25 years of age. 30 participants per session. Application deadline: 4 weeks prior to departure.
Costs • $3000 (includes tuition, books and class materials).
Contact • Alanah Cullen, Business Manager and Director of Study Abroad, London College of Fashion, 20 John Princes Street, London W1M 0BJ, England; +44 171-514-7400; Fax: +44 171-514-7490

LOUISIANA STATE UNIVERSITY

LOUISIANA STATE UNIVERSITY IN LONDON

General Information • Academic study program in London. Excursions to Bath, Cambridge, Canterbury, Stratford-upon-Avon.

The London College of Fashion

FULL TIME DEGREE COURSES

BA(Hons)
Design Technology for the Fashion Industry.
Menswear, Womenswear, Accessories

~

BA(Hons)
Fashion Promotion

~

BA(Hons)
Costume and Make up for the Performing Arts

~

BA(Hons)
Product Development for the Fashion Industries

~

BA(Hons)
Fashion Management

New for 1997

Postgraduate Diploma/MA Fashion

For further information please call 0044 171 514 7400
or fax 0044 171 514 7484.

STUDY ABROAD PROGRAM

The London College of Fashion runs Semester Programs and Summer programs designed to complement your US course of study.

For further information please call 0044 171 514 7400
ext 7411 or fax 0044 171 514 7490.

THE LONDON INSTITUTE

Learning Focus • Courses in English language, political science, theater. Instruction is offered by professors from the sponsoring institution.
Accommodations • Dormitories. Single rooms are available. Meals are taken on one's own, in local restaurants.
Program Details • Program offered once per year. Session length: 6 weeks. Departures are scheduled in July. The program is open to undergraduate students, graduate students. Most participants are 20–25 years of age. Other requirements: minimum 2.5 GPA for 6 hours of credit and a minimum 3.0 GPA for 9 hours of credit. 40 participants per session. Application deadline: April 1.
Costs • $1950 for double room, $2100 for single room (includes tuition, housing, excursions). A $200 deposit is required.
Contact • Jeannie Willamson, Study Abroad Coordinator, Louisiana State University, Academic Programs Abroad, 365 Pleasant Hall, Baton Rouge, LA 70803; 504-388-6801; Fax: 504-388-6806; E-mail: abwill@lsuvm.sncc.lsu.edu

MICHIGAN STATE UNIVERSITY

AMERICAN THOUGHT, LANGUAGE ARTS, AND HUMANITIES PROGRAM

General Information • Academic study program in London.
Learning Focus • Courses in American literature, writing. Instruction is offered by professors from the sponsoring institution.
Accommodations • Dormitories. Single rooms are available. Meals are taken on one's own, in central dining facility.
Program Details • Program offered once per year. Session length: 5 weeks. Departures are scheduled in July. The program is open to undergraduate students. Most participants are 18–22 years of age. Other requirements: good academic standing and the approval of the director. 15–18 participants per session. Application deadline: March 14.
Costs • $2200 (includes housing, some meals, excursions). Application fee: $75. A $250 deposit is required.
Contact • Cynthia Chalou, Educational Programs Coordinator, Michigan State University, Office of Study Abroad, 109 International Center, East Lansing, MI 48824-1035; 517-353-8920; Fax: 517-432-2082; E-mail: chalouc@pilot.msu.edu; World Wide Web: http://study-abroad.msu.edu

MICHIGAN STATE UNIVERSITY

ENGLISH LITERATURE

General Information • Academic study program in London.
Learning Focus • Courses in English literature, writing, grammar. Instruction is offered by professors from the sponsoring institution.
Accommodations • Dormitories. Single rooms are available. Meals are taken on one's own, in central dining facility.
Program Details • Program offered once per year. Session length: 5 weeks. Departures are scheduled in July. The program is open to undergraduate students. Other requirements: good academic standing and the approval of the director. Application deadline: March 14.
Costs • $2587 (includes housing, some meals, excursions). Application fee: $75. A $250 deposit is required.
Contact • Cynthia Chalou, Educational Programs Coordinator, Michigan State University, Office of Study Abroad, 109 International Center, East Lansing, MI 48824-1035; 517-353-8920; Fax: 517-432-2082; E-mail: chalouc@pilot.msu.edu; World Wide Web: http://study-abroad.msu.edu

MICHIGAN STATE UNIVERSITY

INTERIOR DESIGN AND ARCHITECTURE PROGRAM IN EUROPE

General Information • Academic study program in London. Excursions to France (Paris), Italy (Milan).
Learning Focus • Courses in interior design. Instruction is offered by professors from the sponsoring institution.
Accommodations • Dormitories. Single rooms are available. Meals are taken on one's own, in central dining facility.
Program Details • Program offered once per year. Session length: 6 weeks. Departures are scheduled in June. The program is open to undergraduate students, graduate students, adults. Most participants are 18–30 years of age. Other requirements: good academic standing and the approval of the director. 15 participants per session. Application deadline: March 14.
Costs • $3018 (includes housing, some meals, excursions). Application fee: $75. A $250 deposit is required.
Contact • Brenda S. Sprite, Educational Programs Coordinator, Michigan State University, Office of Study Abroad, 109 International Center, East Lansing, MI 48824-1035; 517-353-8920; Fax: 517-432-2082; E-mail: sprite@pilot.msu.edu; World Wide Web: http://study-abroad.msu.edu

MICHIGAN STATE UNIVERSITY

MASS MEDIA PROGRAM IN BRITAIN

General Information • Academic study program in London.
Learning Focus • Courses in mass media, social effects, communications. Instruction is offered by professors from the sponsoring institution.
Accommodations • Dormitories. Single rooms are available. Meals are taken on one's own, in central dining facility.
Program Details • Program offered once per year. Session length: 5 weeks. Departures are scheduled in July. The program is open to undergraduate students. Most participants are 18–22 years of age. Other requirements: good academic standing and the approval of the instructor. 15 participants per session. Application deadline: March 14.
Costs • $2192 (includes housing, some meals, excursions). Application fee: $75. A $250 deposit is required.
Contact • Brenda S. Sprite, Educational Programs Coordinator, Michigan State University, Office of Study Abroad, 109 International Center, East Lansing, MI 48824-1035; 517-353-8920; Fax: 517-432-2082; E-mail: sprite@pilot.msu.edu; World Wide Web: http://study-abroad.msu.edu

MICHIGAN STATE UNIVERSITY

MEDICAL ETHICS AND THE HISTORY OF HEALTH CARE

General Information • Academic study program in London.
Learning Focus • Courses in British health care system, medical ethics. Instruction is offered by professors from the sponsoring institution.
Accommodations • Dormitories. Single rooms are available. Meals are taken on one's own, in residences.
Program Details • Program offered once per year. Session length: 5 weeks. Departures are scheduled in June. The program is open to undergraduate students, graduate students. Most participants are 18–26 years of age. Other requirements: good academic standing and the approval of the director. 20 participants per session. Application deadline: March 14.
Costs • $2280 (includes housing, some meals, excursions). Application fee: $75. A $250 deposit is required.
Contact • Cynthia Chalou, Educational Programs Coordinator, Michigan State University, Office of Study Abroad, 109 International Center, East Lansing, MI 48824-1035; 517-353-8920; Fax: 517-432-2082; E-mail: sprite@pilot.msu.edu; World Wide Web: http://study-abroad.msu.edu

MICHIGAN STATE UNIVERSITY

NURSING IN GREAT BRITAIN

General Information • Academic study program in London.
Learning Focus • Courses in nursing. Instruction is offered by professors from the sponsoring institution.
Accommodations • Dormitories. Single rooms are available. Meals are taken on one's own, in central dining facility.
Program Details • Program offered once per year. Session length: 5 weeks. Departures are scheduled in June. The program is open to undergraduate students, graduate students, adults. Most participants are 18–35 years of age. Other requirements: good academic standing and the approval of the director. 20 participants per session. Application deadline: March 14.
Costs • $1770 (includes housing, some meals, excursions). Application fee: $75. A $250 deposit is required.
Contact • Brenda S. Sprite, Educational Programs Coordinator, Michigan State University, Office of Study Abroad, 109 International Center, East Lansing, MI 48824-1035; 517-353-8920; Fax: 517-432-2082; E-mail: sprite@pilot.msu.edu; World Wide Web: http://study-abroad.msu.edu

MICHIGAN STATE UNIVERSITY

PACKAGING IN ENGLAND

General Information • Academic study program in London.
Learning Focus • Courses in packaging. Instruction is offered by professors from the sponsoring institution.
Accommodations • Dormitories. Single rooms are available. Meals are taken on one's own, in central dining facility.
Program Details • Program offered once per year. Session length: 4 weeks. Departures are scheduled in June. The program is open to undergraduate students, graduate students. Most participants are 18–22 years of age. Other requirements: good academic standing and the approval of the instructor. 18 participants per session. Application deadline: March 14.
Costs • $1734 (includes housing, some meals, excursions). Application fee: $75. A $250 deposit is required.
Contact • Cynthia Chalou, Educational Programs Coordinator, Michigan State University, Office of Study Abroad, 109 International Center, East Lansing, MI 48824-1035; 517-353-8920; Fax: 517-432-2082; E-mail: chalouc@pilot.msu.edu; World Wide Web: http://study-abroad.msu.edu

MICHIGAN STATE UNIVERSITY

PUBLIC AFFAIRS PROGRAM

General Information • Academic study program in Cambridge. Classes are held on the campus of University of Cambridge.
Learning Focus • Courses in British political system, economics, public policy. Instruction is offered by professors from the sponsoring institution.
Accommodations • Dormitories. Meals are taken on one's own, in central dining facility.
Program Details • Program offered once per year. Session length: 5 weeks. Departures are scheduled in June. The program is open to undergraduate students. Most participants are 18–22 years of age. Other requirements: good academic standing and the approval of the director. 30 participants per session. Application deadline: March 14.
Costs • $1692 (includes housing, some meals, excursions). Application fee: $75. A $250 deposit is required.
Contact • Cynthia Chalou, Educational Programs Director, Michigan State University, Office of Study Abroad, 109 International Center, East Lansing, MI 48824-1035; 517-353-8920; Fax: 517-432-2082; E-mail: chalouc@pilot.msu.edu; World Wide Web: http://study-abroad.msu.edu

MICHIGAN STATE UNIVERSITY

REPORTING IN LONDON

General Information • Academic study program in London.
Learning Focus • Courses in journalism, British print-media industry. Instruction is offered by professors from the sponsoring institution.
Accommodations • Dormitories. Single rooms are available. Meals are taken on one's own, in central dining facility.
Program Details • Program offered once per year. Session length: 5 weeks. Departures are scheduled in July. The program is open to undergraduate students, graduate students. Most participants are 18–26 years of age. Other requirements: good academic standing and the approval of the director. 18 participants per session. Application deadline: March 14.
Costs • $2320 (includes housing, some meals, excursions). Application fee: $75. A $250 deposit is required.
Contact • Cynthia Chalou, Educational Programs Coordinator, Michigan State University, Office of Study Abroad, 109 International Center, East Lansing, MI 48824-1035; 517-353-8920; Fax: 517-432-2082; E-mail: sprite@pilot.msu.edu; World Wide Web: http://study-abroad.msu.edu

MICHIGAN STATE UNIVERSITY

SOCIAL SCIENCE PROGRAM IN LONDON

General Information • Academic study program in London.
Learning Focus • Courses in social sciences. Instruction is offered by professors from the sponsoring institution.
Accommodations • Dormitories. Single rooms are available. Meals are taken on one's own, in central dining facility.
Program Details • Program offered once per year. Session length: 5 weeks. Departures are scheduled in July. The program is open to undergraduate students. Most participants are 18–22 years of age. Other requirements: good academic standing and the approval of the director. 15 participants per session. Application deadline: March 14.
Costs • $2338 (includes housing, some meals, excursions). Application fee: $75. A $250 deposit is required.
Contact • Cynthia Chalou, Educational Programs Coordinator, Michigan State University, Office of Study Abroad, 109 International Center, East Lansing, MI 48824-1035; 517-353-8920; Fax: 517-432-2082; E-mail: chalouc@pilot.msu.edu; World Wide Web: http://study-abroad.msu.edu

MICHIGAN STATE UNIVERSITY

SPEECH, LANGUAGE PATHOLOGY, AND AUDIOLOGY PROGRAM

General Information • Academic study program in London.
Learning Focus • Courses in speech pathology, audiology. Instruction is offered by professors from the sponsoring institution.
Accommodations • Dormitories. Single rooms are available. Meals are taken on one's own, in central dining facility.
Program Details • Program offered once per year. Session length: 5 weeks. Departures are scheduled in July. The program is open to undergraduate students, graduate students. Most participants are 18–30 years of age. Other requirements: good academic standing and the approval of the director. 20 participants per session. Application deadline: March 14.
Costs • $2088 (includes housing, some meals, excursions). Application fee: $75. A $250 deposit is required.
Contact • Cynthia Chalou, Educational Programs Coordinator, Michigan State University, Office of Study Abroad, 109 International Center, East Lansing, MI 48824-1035; 517-353-8920; Fax: 517-432-2082; E-mail: chalouc@pilot.msu.edu; World Wide Web: http://study-abroad.msu.edu

MICHIGAN STATE UNIVERSITY

THEATER IN GREAT BRITAIN

General Information • Academic study program in London.
Learning Focus • Courses in British theater, drama. Instruction is offered by professors from the sponsoring institution.
Accommodations • Dormitories. Single rooms are available. Meals are taken on one's own, in central dining facility.
Program Details • Program offered once per year. Session length: 5 weeks. Departures are scheduled in July. The program is open to undergraduate students, graduate students. Most participants are 18–26 years of age. Other requirements: good academic standing and the approval of the director. 12 participants per session. Application deadline: March 14.
Costs • $2814 (includes housing, some meals, excursions). Application fee: $75. A $250 deposit is required.
Contact • Cynthia Chalou, Educational Programs Coordinator, Michigan State University, Office of Study Abroad, 109 International Center, East Lansing, MI 48824-1035; 517-353-8920; Fax: 517-432-2082; E-mail: sprite@pilot.msu.edu; World Wide Web: http://study-abroad.msu.edu

MICHIGAN STATE UNIVERSITY

WOMEN'S STUDIES

General Information • Academic study program in London.
Learning Focus • Courses in women's studies, women's literature, feminist movement in Britain. Instruction is offered by professors from the sponsoring institution.
Accommodations • Dormitories. Single rooms are available. Meals are taken on one's own, in central dining facility.
Program Details • Program offered once per year. Session length: 5 weeks. Departures are scheduled in July. The program is open to undergraduate students, graduate students. Most participants are 18–22 years of age. Other requirements: good academic standing and the approval of the director. 15 participants per session. Application deadline: March 14.
Costs • $2397 (includes housing, some meals, excursions). Application fee: $75. A $250 deposit is required.
Contact • Cynthia Chalou, Educational Programs Coordinator, Michigan State University, Office of Study Abroad, 109 International Center, East Lansing, MI 48824; 517-353-8920; Fax: 517-432-2082; E-mail: chalouc@pilot.msu.edu; World Wide Web: http://study-abroad.msu.edu

MIDDLESEX UNIVERSITY

LONDON SUMMER SCHOOL PROGRAM

General Information • Academic study program in London. Classes are held on the campus of Middlesex University. Excursions to Stratford-upon-Avon, Blenheim Palace, Cambridge, Warwick castle, Central London, Bath.
Learning Focus • Courses in performing arts, business law, computer science, social sciences, history, political science, language study, communications, ecology. Instruction is offered by local teachers.
Accommodations • Dormitories, residence halls. Single rooms are available. Meals are taken on one's own, in central dining facility.
Program Details • Program offered once per year. Session length: 5 weeks. Departures are scheduled in July. The program is open to undergraduate students, adults. Most participants are 18–35 years of age. Other requirements: good academic standing. 15 participants per session. Application deadline: May 31.
Costs • $3000–$3500 (includes tuition, housing, some meals, insurance, excursions, social program, one-way airfare). A $70 deposit is required.

Contact • Karen Blackney, Summer School Coordinator, Middlesex University, White Hart Lane, London N14, England; +44 181-362-5782; Fax: +44 181-362-6697; E-mail: k.blackney@mdx.ac.uk

NATIONAL REGISTRATION CENTER FOR STUDY ABROAD

INTERNATIONAL SUMMER SCHOOL AT CAMBRIDGE, ENGLAND

General Information • Academic study program in Cambridge. Classes are held on the campus of University of Cambridge.

Learning Focus • Courses in art history, history, philosophy, political science, literature, economics, sociology, medieval studies.

Accommodations • Dormitories. Single rooms are available. Meals are taken as a group, in central dining facility.

Program Details • Program offered 2 times per year. Session length: 3 weeks. Departures are scheduled in July, August. The program is open to undergraduate students, graduate students, adults. Application deadline: 40 days prior to departure.

Costs • $1598 (includes tuition, housing, insurance). Application fee: $40. A $100 deposit is required.

Contact • Mary E. Croy, Information Coordinator, National Registration Center for Study Abroad, PO Box 1393, Milwaukee, WI 53203; 414-278-0631; Fax: 414-271-8884; E-mail: inquiries@nrcsa.com; World Wide Web: http://www.nrcsa.com

 NEW YORK UNIVERSITY

EARLY CHILDHOOD AND ELEMENTARY EDUCATION

General Information • Academic study program in Oxford, York. Classes are held on the campus of University College of Ripon and York St. John, University of Oxford, Trinity College.

Learning Focus • Courses in early childhood education, English education, elementary education. Instruction is offered by professors from the sponsoring institution and local teachers.

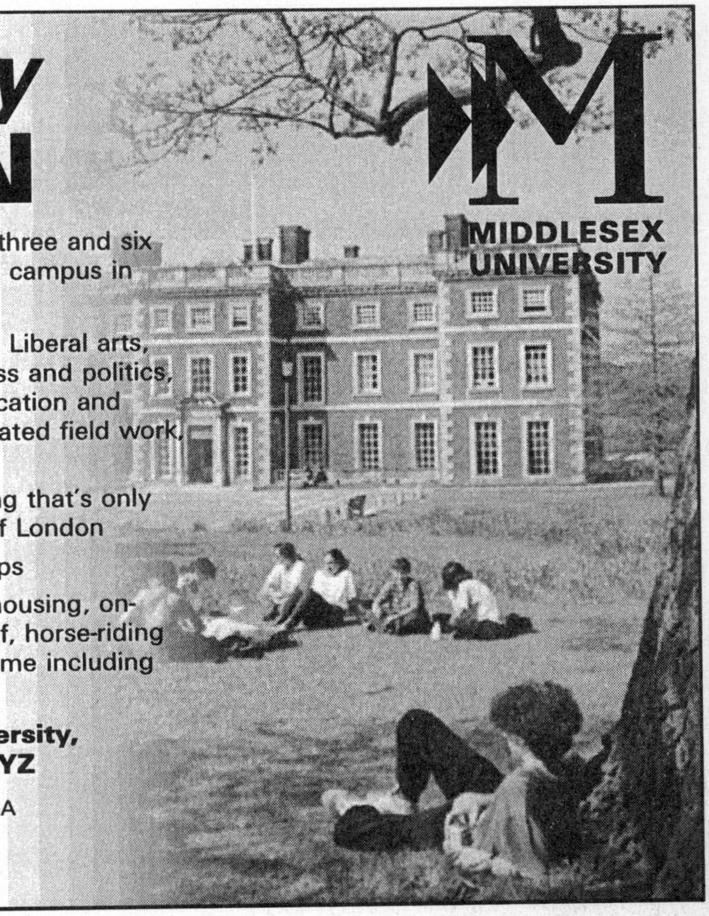

Accommodations • Homestays, dormitories. Single rooms are available. Meals are taken as a group, in central dining facility.

Program Details • Program offered once per year. Session length: 7 weeks. Departures are scheduled in July. The program is open to graduate students. Most participants are 23–45 years of age. Other requirements: BA degree. 25 participants per session. Application deadline: April 1.

Costs • $5964 (includes tuition). Application fee: $40. A $200 deposit is required.

Contact • Helen J. Kelly, Director of Special Programs, New York University, 82 Washington Square East, Room 62,

New York, NY 10003; 212-998-5090; Fax: 212-995-4923; World Wide Web: http://www.nyu.edu/studyabroad

NEW YORK UNIVERSITY

EDUCATIONAL THEATER

General Information • Academic study program in London. Classes are held on the campus of Holborne Center for The Performing Arts.
Learning Focus • Courses in educational theater. Instruction is offered by professors from the sponsoring institution and local teachers.
Accommodations • Dormitories. Single rooms are available. Meals are taken as a group, in local restaurants.
Program Details • Program offered once per year. Session length: 4 weeks. Departures are scheduled in July. The program is open to graduate students, adults, professionals in the field of educational theater. Most participants are 23–45 years of age. Other requirements: minimum 3.0 GPA and a BA degree. 32 participants per session. Application deadline: April.
Costs • $3806 (includes tuition, housing). Application fee: $35. A $400 deposit is required.
Contact • Helen J. Kelly, Director, Special Programs, New York University, 82 Washington Square East, Room 62, New York, NY 10003; 212-998-5090; Fax: 212-995-4923; World Wide Web: http://www.nyu.edu/studyabroad

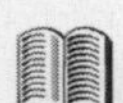

NEW YORK UNIVERSITY

ENGLISH EDUCATION

General Information • Academic study program in Oxford, York. Classes are held on the campus of University College of Ripon and York St. John, University of Oxford, Trinity College.
Learning Focus • Courses in English education, early childhood education, elementary education. Instruction is offered by professors from the sponsoring institution and local teachers.
Accommodations • Homestays, dormitories. Single rooms are available. Meals are taken as a group, in central dining facility.
Program Details • Program offered once per year. Session length: 7 weeks. Departures are scheduled in June. The program is open to graduate students, undergraduate seniors. Most participants are 23–45 years of age. Other requirements: BA degree with at least 30 points in college-level English. 25 participants per session. Application deadline: April 1.
Costs • $5964 (includes tuition). Application fee: $40. A $200 deposit is required.
Contact • Helen J. Kelly, Director of Special Programs, New York University, 82 Washington Square East, Room 62, New York, NY 10003; 212-998-5090; Fax: 212-995-4923; World Wide Web: http://www.nyu.edu/studyabroad

NEW YORK UNIVERSITY

NEW YORK UNIVERSITY IN LONDON

General Information • Academic study program in London. Classes are held on the campus of University of London–University College London. Excursions to Stratford-upon-Avon, Salisbury, Stonehenge, Selborne Village.
Learning Focus • Courses in art history, English literature, theater history. Instruction is offered by professors from the sponsoring institution and local teachers.
Accommodations • Dormitories. Meals are taken on one's own.
Program Details • Program offered once per year. Session length: 6 weeks. Departures are scheduled in July. The program is open to undergraduate students, graduate students, pre-college students, adults, foreign undergraduate and graduate students. Application deadline: April 15.
Costs • $3020 (includes tuition, housing, some meals, excursions). Application fee: $20.
Contact • Carolyn Dever, Director, NYU in London, New York University, Arts and Science Study Abroad, New York, NY 10003; 212-998-8175; Fax: 212-995-4177; E-mail: abroad@nyu.edu; World Wide Web: http://www.nyu.edu/studyabroad

NORTH CAROLINA STATE UNIVERSITY

LONDON EXPERIENCE

General Information • Academic study program in London. Excursions to France (Paris), Scotland (Edinburgh).
Learning Focus • Courses in arts, political science, British studies, history. Instruction is offered by professors from the sponsoring institution.
Accommodations • Dormitories. Single rooms are available. Meals are taken as a group, in central dining facility.
Program Details • Program offered once per year. Session length: 4 weeks. Departures are scheduled in June. The program is open to undergraduate students, graduate students. Most participants are 18–24 years of age. 15–25 participants per session. Application deadline: March 1.
Costs • $2400 (includes tuition, housing, some meals, excursions, international airfare). A $150 deposit is required.
Contact • Ingrid Schmidt, Study Abroad Director, North Carolina State University, 2118 Pullen Hall, Box 7344, Raleigh, NC 27695-7344; 919-515-2087; Fax: 919-515-6021; E-mail: study_abroad@ncsu.edu; World Wide Web: http://www2.ncsu.edu/ncsu/chass/intstu/abroad.html

NORTH CAROLINA STATE UNIVERSITY

SUMMER PROGRAM AT OXFORD, ENGLAND

General Information • Academic study program in Oxford. Classes are held on the campus of Oxford College.
Learning Focus • Courses in art, history, literature, British studies, Shakespeare, current events. Instruction is offered by local teachers.
Accommodations • Dormitories. Meals are taken as a group, in central dining facility.
Program Details • Program offered once per year. Session length: 4 weeks. Departures are scheduled in July. The program is open to undergraduate students, graduate students. Most participants are 18–24 years of age. 30 participants per session. Application deadline: March 1.

Costs • $2100 (includes tuition, housing, some meals, cultural events). Application fee: $100. A $300 deposit is required.
Contact • Ingrid Schmidt, Study Abroad Director, North Carolina State University, 2118 Pullen Hall, Box 7344, Raleigh, NC 27695-7344; 919-515-2087; Fax: 919-515-6021; E-mail: study_abroad@ncsu.edu; World Wide Web: http://www2.ncsu.edu/ncsu/chass/intstu/abroad.html

NORTHERN ILLINOIS UNIVERSITY

BRITISH LITERATURE AND STUDIES IN OXFORD

General Information • Academic study program in Oxford. Classes are held on the campus of Oriel College, Oxford University. Excursions to Stratford-upon-Avon.
Learning Focus • Courses in English language, history. Instruction is offered by professors from the sponsoring institution.
Accommodations • Dormitories. Single rooms are available. Meals are taken on one's own, in central dining facility.
Program Details • Program offered once per year. Session length: 6 weeks. Departures are scheduled in July. The program is open to undergraduate students, graduate students. Most participants are 21–26 years of age. 25 participants per session. Application deadline: May 1.
Costs • $3800 (includes tuition, housing, some meals, insurance, excursions). A $200 deposit is required.
Contact • Anne Seitzinger, Program Coordinator, Short-Term Study Abroad, Northern Illinois University, Study Abroad Office-WI 417, DeKalb, IL 60115; 815-752-0700; Fax: 815-753-0825; E-mail: aseitz@niu.edu; World Wide Web: http://www.niu.edu/depts/intl_prgms/intl.html

NORTHERN ILLINOIS UNIVERSITY

CHILDREN'S LITERATURE IN ENGLAND

General Information • Academic study program in Keswick, London, York.
Learning Focus • Courses in children's literature. Instruction is offered by professors from the sponsoring institution.
Accommodations • Dormitories, hotels. Single rooms are available. Meals are taken as a group, in local restaurants.
Program Details • Program offered once per year. Session length: 3 weeks. Departures are scheduled in June. The program is open to undergraduate students, graduate students, adults. Most participants are 22–50 years of age. 12 participants per session. Application deadline: May 1.
Costs • $2575 (includes tuition, housing, some meals, insurance, excursions). A $200 deposit is required.
Contact • Anne Seitzinger, Program Coordinator, Short-Term Study Abroad, Northern Illinois University, Study Abroad Office-WI 417, DeKalb, IL 60115; 815-752-0700; Fax: 815-753-0825; E-mail: aseitz@niu.edu; World Wide Web: http://www.niu.edu/depts/intl_prgms/intl.html

OXFORD ADVANCED STUDIES PROGRAM

OXFORD ADVANCED STUDIES PROGRAM

General Information • Academic study program in Oxford. Classes are held on the campus of Oxford Advanced Study Program, Oxford Tutorial College.
Learning Focus • Courses in creative writing, English literature, anthropology, history, mathematics.
Accommodations • Homestays, locally-rented apartments. Meals are taken with host family, in residences.
Program Details • Program offered 2 times per year. Session length: 11–12 weeks. Departures are scheduled in April, September. The program is open to undergraduate students, pre-college students. Other requirements: minimum age of 17. 7 participants per session. Application deadline: rolling.
Costs • $4350–$5900 (includes tuition, excursions). Application fee: $150. A $100 deposit is required.
Contact • Ruth Crawford, Registrar, Oxford Advanced Studies Program, 12 King Edward Street, Oxford OX1 4HT, England; +44 1865-793-333; Fax: +44 1865-793-233; E-mail: oxtutor@msn.com

OXFORD ASSOCIATE STUDENT PROGRAMME

OXFORD ASSOCIATE STUDENT PROGRAM WITH LADY MARGARET HALL

General Information • Academic study program in Oxford. Excursions to Stonehenge, Wales, Cambridge.
Learning Focus • Courses in liberal arts, theoretical sciences.
Accommodations • Homestays, dormitories, locally-rented apartments, program-owned apartments, program-owned houses. Single rooms are available. Meals are taken as a group, in central dining facility.
Program Details • Session length: 3–9 weeks. Departures are scheduled in January–December. The program is open to undergraduate students, graduate students, adults. Most participants are 19–22 years of age. Other requirements: minimum 3.0 GPA. 10 participants per session. Application deadline: rolling.
Costs • $2550 for 3 weeks, $4200 for 6 weeks (includes tuition, housing, some meals, excursions). A $150 deposit is required.
Contact • Program Director, Oxford Associate Student Programme, Cherry Tree Court, Dunstan Road, Heddington, Oxford OX3 9BY, England; +44 1865-62-495; Fax: +44 1865-62-495; E-mail: 100645.3460@compuserve.com

The Oxford Associate Student Programme (OASP), in cooperation with Lady Margaret Hall, is an academically challenging summer study-abroad session. Oxford works with the students and their home advisers to set up individually taught courses based on either a home university syllabus or the students' special interests and/or requirements. Weekly excursions to such places as Stratford-upon-Avon, Windsor, Wales, and Cambridge are included in the fee. Excursions to Scotland, Paris, and Dublin are planned for an extra fee. The 14-acre grounds of the college form a lovely backdrop for studying on the lawn, croquet, and punting on the adjacent river. A Shakespeare performance course is also available. Housing is usually in individual college rooms and 2 meals a day are served in Hall. Students become associate members of the Middle Common Room (MCR), one of the two largest student-run organizations in the college.

THE PARTNERSHIP FOR SERVICE-LEARNING

ENGLAND

General Information • Academic study and volunteer service program in London. Classes are held on the campus of Roehampton Institute.
Learning Focus • Courses in institutions in British society. Instruction is offered by local teachers.
Accommodations • Dormitories. Single rooms are available. Meals are taken on one's own, in central dining facility.
Program Details • Program offered once per year. Session length: 10 weeks. Departures are scheduled in June. The program is open to undergraduate students, graduate students, pre-college students, adults. Most participants are 19–24 years of age. 7 participants per session. Application deadline: 2 months prior to departure.
Costs • $4300 (includes tuition, housing, some meals, service placement and supervision, pre-departure and orientation materials). A $250 deposit is required.
Contact • Maureen Lowney, Coordinator of Student Programs, The Partnership for Service-Learning, 815 Second Avenue, Suite 315, New York, NY 10960; 212-986-0989; Fax: 212-986-5039; E-mail: pslny@aol.com

PEOPLE TO PEOPLE INTERNATIONAL

FOUNDATIONS OF WORLD DRAMA–LONDON THEATER

General Information • Academic study program in London. Excursions to Stratford-upon-Avon.
Learning Focus • Courses in drama, theater. Instruction is offered by professors from the sponsoring institution.

Accommodations • Dormitories, locally-rented apartments. Single rooms are available. Meals are taken as a group, on one's own, in central dining facility, in local restaurants.
Program Details • Program offered once per year. Session length: 2 weeks. Departures are scheduled in December. The program is open to undergraduate students, graduate students, pre-college students, adults, all interested individuals. Most participants are 18–65 years of age. Other requirements: good academic standing. 15–25 participants per session. Application deadline: November 15.
Costs • $2200 (includes tuition, housing, some meals, books and class materials, insurance, excursions, theatre tickets, cultural events). A $300 deposit is required.
Contact • Dr. Alan M. Warne, Vice President for Programs, People to People International, 501 East Armour Boulevard, Kansas City, MO 64109; 816-531-4701; Fax: 816-561-7502; E-mail: pepi@cctr.umkc.edu

PEOPLE TO PEOPLE INTERNATIONAL

LONDON ART: CONTEMPORARY AND VISUAL ARTS

General Information • Academic study program in London.
Learning Focus • Courses in visual and contemporary art issues. Instruction is offered by professors from the sponsoring institution.
Accommodations • Dormitories, locally-rented apartments. Single rooms are available. Meals are taken as a group, on one's own, in central dining facility, in local restaurants.
Program Details • Program offered once per year. Session length: 2 or more weeks. Departures are scheduled in May. The program is open to undergraduate students, graduate students, pre-college students, adults, artists and other interested individuals. Most participants are 20–50 years of age. Other requirements: good academic standing. 15–25 participants per session. Application deadline: March 31.
Costs • $2300 (includes tuition, housing, some meals, books and class materials, insurance, excursions, gallery visits, theater and cultural events). A $300 deposit is required.
Contact • Dr. Alan M. Warne, Vice President for Programs, People to People International, 501 East Armour Boulevard, Kansas City, MO 64109; 816-531-4701; Fax: 816-561-7502; E-mail: pepi@cctr.umkc.edu

QUEEN'S UNIVERSITY AT KINGSTON

HERSTMONCEUX CASTLE

General Information • Academic study program in Hailsham. Classes are held on the campus of Queen's

University at Kingston–International Study Center at Herstmonceux Castle. Excursions to France, Brussels, Amsterdam, England.

Learning Focus • Courses in English language, geography, commerce, political science, history, economics, language study, film studies. Instruction is offered by professors from the sponsoring institution and local teachers.

Accommodations • Dormitories. Single rooms are available. Meals are taken as a group, in central dining facility.

Program Details • Program offered 3 times per year. Session length: 12 weeks. Departures are scheduled in September, January, May. The program is open to undergraduate students, graduate students, adults. Most participants are 20–30 years of age. 200 participants per session.

Costs • $6000 (includes tuition, housing, all meals, books and class materials, excursions). Application fee: $30. A $300 deposit is required.

Contact • Ms. Heather Ball, Executive Assistant, Queen's University at Kingston, B206 MacKintosh-Corry Hall, Kingston, ON K7L 3N6, Canada; 800-733-0390; Fax: 613-545-6453; E-mail: heather@qucis.queensu.ca; World Wide Web: http://castle.isc.queensu.ca/isc/welcome.html

QUEEN'S UNIVERSITY AT KINGSTON

QUEEN'S UNIVERSITY INTERNATIONAL STUDY CENTRE

General Information • Academic study program in Hailsham. Classes are held on the campus of Queen's University at Kingston–International Study Center. Excursions to Netherlands (Amsterdam), Belgium (Brussels), France (Paris), London.

Learning Focus • Courses in arts and humanities, economics, social sciences, business, legal studies, political science, education. Instruction is offered by professors from the sponsoring institution and local teachers.

Accommodations • Dormitories. Single rooms are available. Meals are taken as a group, in central dining facility.

Program Details • Session length: 8 weeks. Departures are scheduled in May. The program is open to undergraduate students, graduate students, adults. Most participants are 20–24 years of age. Other requirements: one year of university or college. 180 participants per session. Application deadline: April.

Costs • $6500 (Canadian dollars) (includes tuition, housing, all meals, books and class materials, excursions). Application fee: $40. A $300 deposit is required.

Contact • Ms. Heather Ball, Executive Assistant, Queen's University at Kingston, B206 Mackintosh-Corry Hall, Kingston, ON K7L 3N6, Canada; 613-545-6000, ext. 5301; Fax: 613-545-6453; E-mail: heather@qucis.queensu.ca; World Wide Web: http://castle.isc.queensu.ca/isc/welcome.html

RADFORD UNIVERSITY

LONDON FINE ARTS AND ARTS AND SCIENCES PROGRAM

General Information • Academic study program in London. Classes are held on the campus of Institute for European Studies.

Learning Focus • Courses in theater, literature, history, fine arts. Instruction is offered by professors from the sponsoring institution and local teachers.

Accommodations • Locally-rented apartments. Meals are taken on one's own.

Program Details • Program offered once per year. Session length: 4 weeks. Departures are scheduled in May, June. The program is open to undergraduate students, graduate students. Most participants are 18–25 years of age. 10–15 participants per session. Application deadline: March 15.

Costs • $2875 (includes tuition, housing, excursions, theatre tickets). A $500 deposit is required.

Contact • Ms. Jane A. Wemhoener, Director of International Programs, Radford University, PO Box 7002, 130 Young Hall, Radford, VA 24142; 540-831-6200; Fax: 540-831-6588; E-mail: jwemhoen@runet.edu; World Wide Web: http://www.runet.edu

RAMAPO COLLEGE OF NEW JERSEY

WINTER STUDY IN ENGLAND

General Information • Academic study program in London. Classes are held on the campus of Regent's College. Excursions to Winter Castle, British businesses, EEC offices.

Learning Focus • Courses in international business, European film, English literature. Instruction is offered by professors from the sponsoring institution and local teachers.

Accommodations • Dormitories. Single rooms are available. Meals are taken as a group, in central dining facility.

Program Details • Program offered once per year. Session length: 3 weeks. Departures are scheduled in January. The program is open to undergraduate students, graduate students, pre-college students, adults. Most participants are 18–30 years of age. Other requirements: minimum 2.0 GPA. 40 participants per session. Application deadline: November 15.

Costs • $1550 (includes tuition, housing, all meals, excursions, international airfare). A $300 deposit is required.

Contact • Dr. Ronald J. Kase, Director, Study Abroad, Ramapo College of New Jersey, 505 Ramapo Valley Road, Mahwah, NJ 07430; 201-529-7533; Fax: 201-529-7651; E-mail: rperrice@ramapo.edu

RHODES COLLEGE

BRITISH STUDIES AT OXFORD

General Information • Academic study program in Oxford. Classes are held on the campus of St. John's College, Oxford.

Learning Focus • Courses in British history, British literature, British art, British architecture, British politics, British music, British science. Instruction is offered by professors from the sponsoring institution and local teachers.

Accommodations • Dormitories. Single rooms are available. Meals are taken as a group, in central dining facility.

Program Details • Program offered once per year. Session length: 6 weeks. Departures are scheduled in July. The program is open to undergraduate students, graduate students, adults, non-US college students. Most participants

are 18–45 years of age. Other requirements: minimum 2.0 GPA. 80 participants per session.
Costs • $4750 (includes tuition, housing, all meals, excursions). A $150 deposit is required.
Contact • Mary Allie Baldwin, Assistant to the Dean, British Studies at Oxford, Rhodes College, 2000 North Parkway, Memphis, TN 38112; 901-726-3715; Fax: 901-726-3717; E-mail: bsao@rhodes.edu

ROCKLAND COMMUNITY COLLEGE

WINTER SESSION IN LONDON

General Information • Academic study program in London. Excursions to Greenwich, Bath, Cambridge, Stratford-upon-Avon.
Learning Focus • Courses in art history, business, communications, nursing, psychology, criminal justice, literature, theater. Instruction is offered by professors from the sponsoring institution.
Accommodations • Hotels. Single rooms are available. Meals are taken on one's own, in local restaurants.
Program Details • Program offered once per year. Session length: 2 weeks. Departures are scheduled in January. The program is open to undergraduate students, adults. Most participants are 18–80 years of age. 200 participants per session. Application deadline: November 1.
Costs • $1475 (includes tuition, housing, some meals, excursions, international airfare). A $200 deposit is required.
Contact • Jody Dudderar, Coordinator, Study Abroad, Rockland Community College, Suffern, NY 10907; 914-574-4205; Fax: 914-574-4423; E-mail: jdudderar@sunyrockland.edu

ST. JOHN'S UNIVERSITY

BRITISH STUDY PROGRAM

General Information • Academic study program in London. Excursions to Canterbury, Cambridge, Oxford, Bath.
Learning Focus • Courses in art history, drama, sociology. Instruction is offered by professors from the sponsoring institution.
Accommodations • Locally-rented apartments. Meals are taken on one's own.
Program Details • Program offered once per year. Session length: 12 weeks. Departures are scheduled in January. The program is open to undergraduate students. Most participants are 20–22 years of age. Other requirements: minimum 2.5 GPA. 30 participants per session. Application deadline: November 1.
Costs • $9200 (includes tuition, housing, all meals, excursions). Application fee: $100.
Contact • Stephen Burmeister-May, Director, Center for International Education, St. John's University, Collegeville, MN 56321; 320-363-2082; Fax: 320-363-2013; E-mail: intleduc@csbsju.edu

SLIPPERY ROCK UNIVERSITY OF PENNSYLVANIA

LONDON SUMMER PROGRAM

General Information • Academic study program in London.
Learning Focus • Courses in science, literature. Instruction is offered by professors from the sponsoring institution.
Accommodations • Hotels. Meals are taken in central dining facility, in local restaurants.
Program Details • Program offered 2 times per year. Session length: 2 weeks. Departures are scheduled in August. The program is open to undergraduate students, adults. Most participants are 18–40 years of age. Other requirements: 2.5 minimum GPA. 10–25 participants per session. Application deadline: May 1.
Costs • $2695 (includes tuition, housing, some meals, excursions, international airfare, London tube pass). A $100 deposit is required.
Contact • Stan Kendziorski, Director of International Studies, Slippery Rock University of Pennsylvania, 110 Eisenberg Building, Slippery Rock, PA 16057; 412-738-2603; Fax: 412-738-2959; E-mail: sjk@sruvm.sru.edu; World Wide Web: http://www.sru.edu

SOUTHERN ILLINOIS UNIVERSITY AT CARBONDALE

GLOBAL BROADCASTING IN LONDON

General Information • Academic study program in London, Manchester, Plymouth.
Learning Focus • Courses in broadcasting, mass communication. Instruction is offered by professors from the sponsoring institution.
Accommodations • Locally-rented apartments.
Program Details • Program offered once per year. Session length: 2 weeks. Departures are scheduled in May. The program is open to undergraduate students, graduate students. Most participants are 18–30 years of age. Other requirements: minimum 2.5 GPA. 20 participants per session. Application deadline: April 19.
Costs • $2275 (includes housing, insurance). A $250 deposit is required.
Contact • Mr. Thomas A. Saville, Coordinator, Study Abroad Programs, Southern Illinois University at Carbondale, Mailcode 6885, Small Business Incubator, Room 217, Carbondale, IL 62901-6885; 618-453-7670; Fax: 618-453-7677; E-mail: studyabr@siu.edu

SOUTHERN METHODIST UNIVERSITY

PROGRAM IN LONDON: COMMUNICATIONS

General Information • Academic study program in London. Excursions to Bath, Cambridge, Brighton, Stratford-upon-Avon.
Learning Focus • Courses in communications. Instruction is offered by professors from the sponsoring institution.
Accommodations • Dormitories. Meals are taken as a group, in central dining facility.

Program Details • Program offered once per year. Session length: 6 weeks. Departures are scheduled in July. The program is open to undergraduate students. Most participants are 19–23 years of age. Other requirements: minimum 2.5 GPA and sophomore standing. 30 participants per session. Application deadline: March 1.
Costs • $3850 (includes tuition, housing, some meals, excursions). A $400 deposit is required.
Contact • Karen Westergaard, Associate Director, Southern Methodist University, Office of International Programs, Dallas, TX 75275-0391; 214-768-2338; Fax: 214-768-1051; E-mail: intipro@mail.smu.edu; World Wide Web: http://fllcjm.clements.smu.edu

SOUTHERN METHODIST UNIVERSITY

PROGRAM IN OXFORD

General Information • Academic study program in Oxford. Classes are held on the campus of University College. Excursions to London, Bath, Stratford-upon-Avon, Stonehenge.
Learning Focus • Courses in English language, history. Instruction is offered by professors from the sponsoring institution and local teachers.
Accommodations • Dormitories. Meals are taken as a group, in central dining facility.
Program Details • Program offered once per year. Session length: 6 weeks. Departures are scheduled in July. The program is open to undergraduate students. Most participants are 19–23 years of age. Other requirements: minimum 2.7 GPA and sophomore standing. 60 participants per session. Application deadline: March 1.
Costs • $4950 (includes tuition, housing, some meals, excursions). A $400 deposit is required.
Contact • Karen Westergaard, Associate Director, Southern Methodist University, Office of International Programs, Dallas, TX 75275-0391; 214-768-2338; Fax: 214-768-1051; E-mail: intipro@mail.smu.edu; World Wide Web: http://fllcjm.clements.smu.edu

STATE UNIVERSITY OF NEW YORK AT NEW PALTZ

THE LONDON ART SEMINAR

General Information • Academic study program in London.
Learning Focus • Courses in studio art, art history, art education. Instruction is offered by professors from the sponsoring institution.
Accommodations • Hotels. Single rooms are available. Meals are taken on one's own.
Program Details • Program offered once per year. Session length: 2 weeks. Departures are scheduled in January. The program is open to undergraduate students, graduate students, pre-college students, adults. Most participants are 18–50 years of age. Other requirements: good academic standing. 20 participants per session. Application deadline: October 31.
Costs • $1400 (includes tuition, housing, insurance, international airfare). Application fee: $25. A $100 deposit is required.
Contact • Office of International Education, State University of New York at New Paltz, HAB 33, New Paltz, NY 12561; 914-257-3125; Fax: 914-257-3129; E-mail: sillnerb@npvm.newpaltz.edu; World Wide Web: http://www.newpaltz.edu/oie/

STATE UNIVERSITY OF NEW YORK AT NEW PALTZ

LONDON THEATER SEMINAR

General Information • Academic study program in London. Excursions to Oxford, Camden Lock, Stratford-upon-Avon, Bath.
Learning Focus • Courses in British theater. Instruction is offered by professors from the sponsoring institution.
Accommodations • Hotels. Meals are taken on one's own.
Program Details • Program offered once per year. Session length: 2 weeks. Departures are scheduled in January. The program is open to undergraduate students, graduate students, pre-college students, adults. Most participants are 18 years of age and older. Other requirements: good academic standing. 15 participants per session. Application deadline: October 31.
Costs • $1400 (includes housing, international airfare). Application fee: $25. A $100 deposit is required.
Contact • Office of International Education, State University of New York at New Paltz, HAB 33, New Paltz, NY 12561; 914-257-3125; Fax: 914-257-3129; E-mail: sillnerb@npvm.newpaltz.edu; World Wide Web: http://www.newpaltz.edu/oie/

STATE UNIVERSITY OF NEW YORK AT NEW PALTZ

MUSIC FESTIVAL SUMMER PROGRAM

General Information • Academic study program in London. Classes are held on the campus of Middlesex University. Excursions to Stratford-upon-Avon, Stonehedge.
Learning Focus • Courses in piano, applied music, music literature.
Accommodations • Dormitories. Single rooms are available. Meals are taken as a group, in central dining facility.
Program Details • Program offered once per year. Session length: 4 weeks. Departures are scheduled in July. The program is open to undergraduate students, graduate students, pre-college students, adults. Most participants are 17–25 years of age. Other requirements: music training. 35 participants per session. Application deadline: March 15.
Costs • $3015 (includes tuition, housing, some meals, insurance, excursions). Application fee: $165.
Contact • Office of International Education, State University of New York at New Paltz, HAB 33, New Paltz, NY 12561; 914-257-3125; Fax: 914-257-3129; E-mail: sillnerb@npvm.newpaltz.edu; World Wide Web: http://www.newpaltz.edu/oie/

STATE UNIVERSITY OF NEW YORK AT NEW PALTZ

SUMMER STUDIES IN LONDON

General Information • Academic study program in London. Classes are held on the campus of Middlesex University. Excursions to Stratford-upon-Avon, Oxford.
Learning Focus • Courses in English language, media and communication, cultural studies, social sciences, humanities, computing, information technology. Instruction is offered by local teachers.
Accommodations • Dormitories. Single rooms are available. Meals are taken as a group, in central dining facility.
Program Details • Program offered once per year. Session length: 5 weeks. Departures are scheduled in July. The program is open to undergraduate students, graduate students. Most participants are 18 years of age and older. Other requirements: good academic standing. 15 participants per session. Application deadline: March 1.
Costs • $3690 (includes tuition, housing, some meals, insurance, excursions, international airfare). Application fee: $25. A $100 deposit is required.
Contact • Office of International Education, State University of New York at New Paltz, HAB 33, New Paltz, NY 12561; 914-257-3125; Fax: 914-257-3129; E-mail: sillnerb@npvm.newpaltz.edu; World Wide Web: http://www.newpaltz.edu/oie/

STATE UNIVERSITY OF NEW YORK COLLEGE AT BROCKPORT

OXFORD SUMMER STUDY TOUR

General Information • Academic study program in Oxford.
Learning Focus • Courses in English literature. Instruction is offered by professors from the sponsoring institution.
Accommodations • Dormitories. Single rooms are available. Meals are taken as a group, in central dining facility.
Program Details • Program offered once per year. Session length: 3 weeks. Departures are scheduled in July. The program is open to undergraduate students. Most participants are 19–45 years of age. Other requirements: minimum 2.75 GPA. 15 participants per session. Application deadline: May 15.
Costs • $4100 (includes tuition, housing, all meals, books and class materials, excursions, international airfare). A $100 deposit is required.
Contact • Dr. John J. Perry, Director, Office of International Education, State University of New York College at Brockport, 350 New Campus Drive, Brockport, NY 14420; 716-395-2119; Fax: 716-637-3218; E-mail: jperry@acspr1.acs.brockport.e; World Wide Web: http://www.brockport.edu/study_abroad

STATE UNIVERSITY OF NEW YORK COLLEGE AT BROCKPORT

RECREATION AND LEISURE SERVICES IN ENGLAND PROGRAM

General Information • Academic study program in London. Classes are held on the campus of Brunel University.
Learning Focus • Courses in recreation, leisure.
Accommodations • Dormitories. Single rooms are available. Meals are taken as a group, in central dining facility.
Program Details • Program offered once per year. Session length: 12 weeks. Departures are scheduled in June. The program is open to undergraduate students, graduate students. Most participants are 20 years of age and older. Other requirements: minimum 2.0 GPA, must have a recreation and leisure degree or professional experience for graduate credit. 4–15 participants per session. Application deadline: January 1.
Costs • $3660 (includes tuition, housing, some meals, excursions, international airfare). A $200 deposit is required.
Contact • Dr. John J. Perry, Director, International Education, State University of New York College at Brockport, 350 New Campus Drive, Brockport, NY 14420; 716-395-2119; Fax: 716-637-3218; World Wide Web: http://www.brockport.edu/study_abroad

STATE UNIVERSITY OF NEW YORK COLLEGE AT BROCKPORT

UNITED KINGDOM CULTURAL TOUR

General Information • Academic study program in England. Excursions to Penrith, London, Oxford, Chester, Stratford, Yorkshire.
Learning Focus • Courses in English literature. Instruction is offered by professors from the sponsoring institution.
Accommodations • Dormitories. Single rooms are available. Meals are taken as a group, in central dining facility, in local restaurants.
Program Details • Program offered once per year. Session length: 3 weeks. Departures are scheduled in July. The program is open to undergraduate students, graduate students. Most participants are 20 years of age and older. 15–25 participants per session. Application deadline: April 15.
Costs • $2200 (includes tuition, housing, some meals, excursions, international airfare). A $200 deposit is required.
Contact • Dr. John J. Perry, Director, International Education, State University of New York College at Brockport, Rakov Center, 350 New Campus Drive, Brockport, NY 14420; 716-395-2119; Fax: 716-637-3218; World Wide Web: http://www.brockport.edu/study_abroad

STATE UNIVERSITY OF WEST GEORGIA

INTERNATIONAL BANKING AND FINANCE

General Information • Academic study program in London.
Learning Focus • Courses in finance, international business, economics, business. Instruction is offered by professors from the sponsoring institution.
Accommodations • Dormitories. Single rooms are available. Meals are taken as a group, in central dining facility.
Program Details • Program offered once per year. Session length: 37 days. Departures are scheduled in July. The program is open to undergraduate students, graduate students. Most participants are 20–26 years of age. Other requirements: minimum 2.0 GPA and previous study of

microeconomics and macroeconomics. 12–18 participants per session. Application deadline: March 31.
Costs • $3995 (includes tuition, housing, some meals, books and class materials, excursions, international airfare, admission fees, transcript fees). A $500 deposit is required.
Contact • Dr. Ara G. Volkan, Chair, Department of Finance, State University of West Georgia, School of Business, Department of Finance, Carrollton, GA 30118; 770-836-6469; Fax: 770-836-6774; E-mail: avolkan@sbf.bus.westga.edu; World Wide Web: http://www.westga.edu/

STATE UNIVERSITY OF WEST GEORGIA

INTERNATIONAL ECONOMICS AND BUSINESS

General Information • Academic study program in London.
Learning Focus • Courses in finance, international business, economics, business. Instruction is offered by professors from the sponsoring institution.
Accommodations • Dormitories. Single rooms are available. Meals are taken as a group, in central dining facility.
Program Details • Program offered once per year. Session length: 37 days. Departures are scheduled in July. The program is open to undergraduate students, graduate students. Most participants are 20–26 years of age. Other requirements: minimum 2.0 GPA and previous study of microeconomics and macroeconomics. 12–18 participants per session. Application deadline: March 31.
Costs • $3995 (includes tuition, housing, some meals, books and class materials, admission fees, transcript fees). A $500 deposit is required.
Contact • Dr. Ara G. Volkan, Chair, Department of Finance, State University of West Georgia, School of Business, Department of Finance, Carrollton, GA 30118; 770-836-6469; Fax: 770-836-6774; E-mail: avolkan@sbf.bus.westga.edu; World Wide Web: http://www.westga.edu/

SYRACUSE UNIVERSITY

LAW IN LONDON: CLINICAL INTERNSHIPS

General Information • Internship program in London.
Learning Focus • Courses in legal studies. Instruction is offered by professors from the sponsoring institution.
Accommodations • Locally-rented apartments. Meals are taken on one's own, in residences.
Program Details • Program offered once per year. Session length: 8 weeks. Departures are scheduled in May. The program is open to graduate students. Most participants are 22–30 years of age. Other requirements: must have completed one year of law school. 30 participants per session. Application deadline: February 15.
Costs • $3850 (includes tuition, some meals, books and class materials, excursions). Application fee: $40. A $350 deposit is required.
Contact • Ms. Daisy Fried, Associate Director, Syracuse University, 119 Euclid Avenue, Syracuse, NY 13244; 315-443-9419; Fax: 315-443-4593; E-mail: dsfried@summon3.syr.edu; World Wide Web: http://sumweb.syr.edu/dipa/dipa9.htm

SYRACUSE UNIVERSITY

MANAGEMENT INTERNSHIPS IN LONDON

General Information • Internship program in London.
Learning Focus • Courses in management. Instruction is offered by professors from the sponsoring institution.
Accommodations • Locally-rented apartments. Single rooms are available. Meals are taken on one's own, in residences.
Program Details • Program offered once per year. Session length: 7 weeks. Departures are scheduled in May. The program is open to undergraduate students, graduate students. Most participants are 21–30 years of age. Other requirements: must have completed junior year with a 2.7 cumulative GPA. 25 participants per session. Application deadline: March 15.
Costs • $3770 (includes tuition, some meals). Application fee: $40. A $350 deposit is required.
Contact • Ms. Daisy Fried, Associate Director, Syracuse University, 119 Euclid Avenue, Syracuse, NY 13244-4170; 315-443-9419; Fax: 315-443-4593; E-mail: dsfried@summon3.syr.edu; World Wide Web: http://sumweb.syr.edu/dipa/dipa9.htm

SYRACUSE UNIVERSITY

POLITICS AND MEDIA PROGRAM IN ENGLAND

General Information • Academic study program in London.
Learning Focus • Courses in political science, media. Instruction is offered by professors from the sponsoring institution.
Accommodations • Locally-rented apartments. Single rooms are available. Meals are taken on one's own, in residences.
Program Details • Program offered once per year. Session length: 5 weeks. Departures are scheduled in June. The program is open to undergraduate students. Most participants are 19–23 years of age. 18 participants per session. Application deadline: March 15.
Costs • $3441 (includes tuition, some meals, books and class materials, excursions). Application fee: $40. A $350 deposit is required.
Contact • Ms. Daisy Fried, Associate Director, Syracuse University, 119 Euclid Avenue, Syracuse, NY 13244-4170; 315-443-9419; Fax: 315-443-4593; E-mail: dsfried@summon3.syr.edu; World Wide Web: http://sumweb.syr.edu/dipa/dipa9.htm

TEMPLE UNIVERSITY

LONDON SEMINAR IN BRITISH MASS MEDIA

General Information • Academic study program in London.
Learning Focus • Courses in communications, mass media. Instruction is offered by professors from the sponsoring institution.
Accommodations • Locally-rented apartments. Meals are taken on one's own.
Program Details • Program offered once per year. Session length: 6 weeks. Departures are scheduled in July. The

program is open to undergraduate students. 25 participants per session. Application deadline: May 1.
Costs • $2450–$3050 (includes tuition, housing, international airfare). Application fee: $50. A $150 deposit is required.
Contact • Robert M. Greenberg, Associate Dean, Temple University, Office of Dean, School of Communications and Theater, Philadelphia, PA 19122; 215-204-1902; Fax: 215-204-6641; World Wide Web: http://www.temple.edu/intlprog/

UNIVERSITY OF BATH

INTRODUCTION TO BRITISH LIFE AND CULTURE

General Information • Academic study and recreational program in Bath. Classes are held on the campus of University of Bath. Excursions to London, Dorset, Stratford-upon- Avon, Longleat, Stonehenge, Glastonbury.
Learning Focus • Courses in English literature, economics, history, political science. Instruction is offered by professors from the sponsoring institution and local teachers.
Accommodations • Dormitories. Meals are taken in central dining facility, in residences.
Program Details • Program offered once per year. Session length: 3 weeks. Departures are scheduled in September. The program is open to undergraduate students, graduate students, adults. Most participants are 19–35 years of age. 20 participants per session. Application deadline: August 15.
Costs • $1000 (includes tuition, housing, some meals, excursions). A $150 deposit is required.
Contact • Judith Rogers, Assistant International Officer, University of Bath, Claverton Down, Bath BA2 7AY, England; +44 12-25-826900; Fax: +44 12-25-826-366; E-mail: j.a.rogers@bath.ac.uk

UNIVERSITY OF COLORADO AT BOULDER

SEMINAR IN INTERNATIONAL FINANCE AND BUSINESS

General Information • Academic study program in London.
Learning Focus • Courses in international finance. Instruction is offered by professors from the sponsoring institution.
Accommodations • Dormitories. Single rooms are available. Meals are taken on one's own, in local restaurants.
Program Details • Program offered once per year. Session length: 4 weeks. Departures are scheduled in July. The program is open to undergraduate students, graduate students. Most participants are 21–26 years of age. Other requirements: minimum 2.75 GPA and 1 course in international business or international economics. 25 participants per session. Application deadline: March 1.
Costs • $3600 for Colorado residents, $4350 for non-residents (includes tuition, housing, some meals, insurance, excursions). A $300 deposit is required.
Contact • Study Abroad Program, University of Colorado at Boulder, International Education, Campus Box 123, Boulder, CO 80309-0123; 303-492-7741; Fax: 303-492-5185; E-mail: studyabr@colorado.edu; World Wide Web: http://www.colorado.edu/OIE/StudyAbroad

UNIVERSITY OF DAYTON

ISSAP '97–LONDON COMMUNICATIONS

General Information • Academic study program in London.
Learning Focus • Courses in communications. Instruction is offered by professors from the sponsoring institution.
Accommodations • Dormitories, locally-rented apartments. Meals are taken as a group, in local restaurants, in residences.
Program Details • Program offered once per year. Session length: 4 weeks. Departures are scheduled in May. The program is open to undergraduate students. Most participants are 18–21 years of age. Other requirements: minimum 2.4 GPA. 25 participants per session. Application deadline: April 15.
Costs • $3100 (includes tuition, housing, some meals, excursions, International Student Identification card). A $75 deposit is required.
Contact • DeVonda Vanderpool, Coordinator, International Education Programs, University of Dayton, Dayton, OH 45469-1481; 513-229-3728; Fax: 513-229-2766; E-mail: vanderpo@trinity.udayton.edu; World Wide Web: http://www.udayton.edu/~cip

UNIVERSITY OF DELAWARE

SUMMER SESSION IN LONDON

General Information • Academic study program in London. Classes are held on the campus of University of Delaware London Center. Excursions to Scotland, Ireland.
Learning Focus • Courses in political science, English language, art history. Instruction is offered by professors from the sponsoring institution.
Accommodations • Apartments. Single rooms are available. Meals are taken on one's own, in residences.
Program Details • Program offered once per year. Session length: 5 weeks. Departures are scheduled in June. The program is open to undergraduate students, graduate students, adults. Most participants are 18–21 years of age. Other requirements: minimum 2.0 GPA. 20 participants per session. Application deadline: April.
Costs • $3800 (includes tuition, housing, excursions, international airfare). A $200 deposit is required.
Contact • International Programs and Special Sessions, University of Delaware, 4 Kent Way, Newark, DE 19716-1450; 888-831-4685; Fax: 302-831-6042; E-mail: studyabroad@mvs.udel.edu

UNIVERSITY OF DELAWARE

WINTER SESSION ECONOMICS PROGRAM IN LONDON

General Information • Academic study program in London. Classes are held on the campus of University of Delaware London Center. Excursions to Ireland (Dublin, Galway), Scotland (Edinburgh), York, France (Paris).
Learning Focus • Courses in economics. Instruction is offered by professors from the sponsoring institution.
Accommodations • Hotels. Meals are taken as a group, in local restaurants.
Program Details • Program offered once per year. Session length: 5 weeks. Departures are scheduled in January. The

program is open to undergraduate students. Most participants are 18–21 years of age. Other requirements: minimum 2.0 GPA. 25 participants per session. Application deadline: October.
Costs • $4780 (includes tuition, housing, all meals, excursions, international airfare). A $200 deposit is required.
Contact • International Programs and Special Sessions, University of Delaware, 4 Kent Way, Newark, DE 19716-1450; 888-831-4685; Fax: 302-831-6042; E-mail: studyabroad@mvs.udel.edu

UNIVERSITY OF DELAWARE

WINTER SESSION IN LONDON

General Information • Academic study program in London. Classes are held on the campus of University of Delaware London Center.
Learning Focus • Courses in theater, drama. Instruction is offered by professors from the sponsoring institution.
Accommodations • Hotels.
Program Details • Program offered once per year. Session length: 5 weeks. Departures are scheduled in January. The program is open to undergraduate students. Most participants are 18–21 years of age. Other requirements: minimum 2.0 GPA. 25 participants per session. Application deadline: October.
Costs • $3407 (includes tuition, housing, some meals, excursions, international airfare). A $200 deposit is required.
Contact • International Programs and Special Sessions, University of Delaware, 4 Kent Way, Newark, DE 19716-1450; 888-831-4685; Fax: 302-831-6042; E-mail: studyabroad@mvs.udel.edu

UNIVERSITY OF DELAWARE

WINTER SESSION IN LONDON: SHAKESPEARE AND MODERN BRITISH THEATER

General Information • Academic study program in London. Classes are held on the campus of University of Delaware London Center. Excursions to Stratford-upon-Avon.
Learning Focus • Courses in drama, theater, English literature, Shakespeare. Instruction is offered by professors from the sponsoring institution.
Accommodations • Homestays, hotels.
Program Details • Program offered once per year. Session length: 5 weeks. Departures are scheduled in January. The program is open to undergraduate students. Most participants are 18–21 years of age. Other requirements: minimum 2.0 GPA. 20 participants per session. Application deadline: October.
Costs • $3357 (includes tuition, housing, some meals, excursions, international airfare). A $200 deposit is required.
Contact • International Programs and Special Sessions, University of Delaware, 4 Kent Way, Newark, DE 19716-1450; 888-831-4685; Fax: 302-831-6042; E-mail: studyabroad@mvs.udel.edu

UNIVERSITY OF DETROIT MERCY

BRITISH STUDIES AT OXFORD

General Information • Academic study program in Oxford. Classes are held on the campus of University of Oxford. Excursions to Stratford-upon-Avon, London, Bath, Cambridge, Canterbury.
Learning Focus • Courses in art history, business, communications, education, history, literature, drama, political science. Instruction is offered by local teachers.
Accommodations • Dormitories. Single rooms are available. Meals are taken as a group, in central dining facility.
Program Details • Program offered 2 times per year. Session length: 3 weeks. Departures are scheduled in July. The program is open to undergraduate students, graduate students, adults. Most participants are 18–70 years of age. Other requirements: minimum 2.5 GPA. 50 participants per session. Application deadline: April 20.
Costs • $2950 (includes tuition, housing, some meals, excursions, theater tickets, museum fees). A $250 deposit is required.
Contact • Dr. Margaret Pigott, Director of Study Abroad, University of Detroit Mercy, 322 Wilson Hall, Rochester, MI 48309-4401; 810-652-3405; Fax: 810-650-9107; E-mail: pigott@oakland.edu

UNIVERSITY OF FLORIDA

UNIVERSITY OF CAMBRIDGE–CAMBRIDGE, ENGLAND

General Information • Academic study program in Cambridge. Classes are held on the campus of University of Cambridge. Excursions to cultural events, churches.
Learning Focus • Courses in history, literature. Instruction is offered by local teachers.
Accommodations • Program-owned apartments. Single rooms are available. Meals are taken as a group, on one's own, in central dining facility, in local restaurants, in residences.
Program Details • Program offered once per year. Session length: 5–6 weeks. Departures are scheduled in June. The program is open to undergraduate students, graduate students, adults. Other requirements: minimum 2.5 GPA and a minimum age of 18. Application deadline: March 15.
Costs • $3400 (includes tuition, housing, some meals, administration fee). Application fee: $250.
Contact • Overseas Studies, University of Florida, 123 Tigert Hall, PO Box 113225, Gainesville, FL 32611-3225; 352-392-5206; Fax: 352-392-5575; E-mail: overseas@nervm.nerdc.ufl.edu

UNIVERSITY OF GEORGIA

UNIVERSITY OF GEORGIA AT OXFORD

General Information • Academic study program in Oxford. Classes are held on the campus of University of Oxford. Excursions to London, York, Bath.
Learning Focus • Courses in English literature, political science, anthropology, religion, English history, ecology, Irish literature. Instruction is offered by professors from the sponsoring institution and local teachers.

Accommodations • Dormitories. Single rooms are available. Meals are taken as a group, in central dining facility.
Program Details • Program offered 2 times per year. Session length: summer session 6 weeks, spring session 8 weeks. Departures are scheduled in April, July. The program is open to undergraduate students, graduate students. Most participants are 19–27 years of age. Other requirements: must get transient admission to University of Georgia and a 2.50 minimum GPA. 30–70 participants per session. Application deadline: January 20.
Costs • $4000 for summer, $5000 for spring (includes tuition, housing, some meals, excursions). A $150 deposit is required.
Contact • Kasee Clifton Laster, Assistant Director, University of Georgia, Park Hall 325, Athens, GA 30602; 706-542-2244; Fax: 706-542-2181; E-mail: klaster@uga.cc.uga.edu

UNIVERSITY OF HARTFORD

DISCOVERING BRITAIN

General Information • Academic study program in Oxford. Excursions to London, Stonehenge.
Learning Focus • Courses in literature, history. Instruction is offered by professors from the sponsoring institution.
Accommodations • Dormitories. Single rooms are available. Meals are taken as a group, in central dining facility.
Program Details • Program offered once per year. Session length: 4 weeks. Departures are scheduled in June, July. The program is open to undergraduate students, graduate students, adults. Most participants are 18–60 years of age. Other requirements: minimum 2.5 GPA. 15–20 participants per session. Application deadline: April 1.
Costs • $3500 (includes tuition, housing, some meals, excursions, international airfare). A $400 deposit is required.
Contact • Ms. Domenica DiMatteo, Study Abroad Coordinator, University of Hartford, International Center, West Hartford, CT 06117; 860-768-5100; Fax: 860-768-4726; E-mail: ddimatteo@uhavax.hartford.edu

UNIVERSITY OF KANSAS

BRITISH ORIENTATION PROGRAM

General Information • Academic study program in London. Excursions to London, Bloomsbury, West End theater district.
Learning Focus • Courses in British studies. Instruction is offered by local teachers.
Accommodations • Program-owned apartments, hotels. Meals are taken on one's own, in local restaurants.
Program Details • Program offered once per year. Session length: 1 week. Departures are scheduled in September. The program is open to undergraduate students, graduate students. Most participants are 21–26 years of age. Other

requirements: must be admitted to a British study abroad program for fall or academic year. 15 participants per session. Application deadline: August 1.
Costs • $775 for Kansas University students, $925 for other students (includes tuition, housing, some meals, excursions, tube and bus pass). A $300 deposit is required.
Contact • Program Coordinator, British Orientation Program, University of Kansas, Office of Study Abroad, 203 Lippincott Hall, Lawrence, KS 66045; 913-864-3742; Fax: 913-864-5040; E-mail: osa@falcon.cc.ukans.edu; World Wide Web: http://kuhub.cc.ukans.edu/~intlstdy/osa/osamain.html

UNIVERSITY OF KANSAS

LEGAL HISTORY IN CAMBRIDGE, ENGLAND

General Information • Academic study program in Cambridge. Classes are held on the campus of St. John's College, Cambridge University. Excursions to Ely Cathedral, London.
Learning Focus • Courses in legal history. Instruction is offered by professors from the sponsoring institution.
Accommodations • Dormitories. Meals are taken on one's own, in central dining facility, in local restaurants, in residences.
Program Details • Program offered once per year. Session length: 4 weeks. Departures are scheduled in July. The program is open to undergraduate students, graduate students. Most participants are 21–29 years of age. 20 participants per session. Application deadline: March 1.
Costs • $2755 (includes tuition, housing, some meals, excursions, group cultural activities). Application fee: $15. A $300 deposit is required.
Contact • Susan MacNally, Coordinator of Summer Institutes, University of Kansas, Office of Study Abroad, 203 Lippincott Hall, Lawrence, KS 66045; 913-864-3742; Fax: 913-864-5040; E-mail: osa@falcon.cc.ukans.edu; World Wide Web: http://kuhub.cc.ukans.edu/~intlstdy/osa/osamain.html

UNIVERSITY OF KANSAS

SUMMER INSTITUTE AT THE LONDON SCHOOL OF ECONOMICS

General Information • Academic study program in London. Classes are held on the campus of University of London–London School of Economics.
Learning Focus • Courses in economics, business management, international business. Instruction is offered by local teachers.
Accommodations • Dormitories, locally-rented apartments. Meals are taken on one's own, in central dining facility, in local restaurants, in residences.
Program Details • Program offered 2 times per year. Session length: 3–6 weeks. Departures are scheduled in June, July. The program is open to undergraduate students, graduate students, adults. Most participants are 20–30 years of age. Other requirements: minimum 3.3 GPA and prerequisites for some courses. 20 participants per session. Application deadline: March 1.
Costs • $2143–$3653 (includes tuition, housing). Application fee: $15. A $300 deposit is required.
Contact • Susan MacNally, Coordinator of Summer Institutes, University of Kansas, Office of Study Abroad, 203 Lippincott Hall, Lawrence, KS 66045; 913-864-3742; Fax: 913-864-5040; E-mail: osa@falcon.cc.ukans.edu; World Wide Web: http://kuhub.cc.ukans.edu/~intlstdy/osa/osamain.html

UNIVERSITY OF LANCASTER

LANCASTER SUMMER UNIVERSITY

General Information • Academic study program in Lancaster. Classes are held on the campus of University of Lancaster.
Learning Focus • Courses in religion, English literature, theater studies, philosophy, European history. Instruction is offered by local teachers.
Accommodations • Dormitories. Single rooms are available.
Program Details • Program offered once per year. Session length: 4 weeks. Departures are scheduled in July. The program is open to undergraduate students, pre-college students, adults. Most participants are 18–65 years of age. 300 participants per session. Application deadline: May 23.
Costs • $1350 (includes tuition, housing, some meals). Application fee: $80.
Contact • Ethel Sussman, North American Officer, University of Lancaster, 111 East 10th Street, New York, NY 10003; 212-228-0321; E-mail: 7544.1273@compuserve.com

---

Lancaster's Summer University is one of the most prestigious academic summer schools in the U.K. Students from North America, the U.K., and around the world will gather to study high-quality, upper-division courses (each worth 4 credits) between July 23 and August 22, 1997.

The historic city of Lancaster and the University's picturesque campus are a perfect setting for a summer of learning. However, Summer University students are also able to discover something of British social and cultural life, with trips to theatres, football matches (that's soccer to you!), and pubs, forming an important part of the summer experience.

UNIVERSITY OF LANCASTER

THIS SCEPTER'D ISLE: ASPECTS OF BRITISH HISTORY AND CULTURE

General Information • Academic study program in Ambleside, Lancaster. Classes are held on the campus of Lancaster University. Excursions to northwest England.
Learning Focus • Courses in Tudor England, social history, William Wordsworth, British politics. Instruction is offered by local teachers.
Accommodations • Program-owned houses. Single rooms are available. Meals are taken as a group, in residences.
Program Details • Program offered once per year. Session length: 4 weeks. Departures are scheduled in August. The

program is open to undergraduate students. Most participants are 19–25 years of age. 15 participants per session. Application deadline: June 27.
Costs • $1100 (includes tuition, housing, excursions). Application fee: $80.
Contact • Ethel Sussman, North American Officer, University of Lancaster, 111 East 10th Street, New York, NY 10003; 212-228-0321; E-mail: 74544.1273@compuserve.com

UNIVERSITY OF MASSACHUSETTS AMHERST

OXFORD SUMMER SEMINAR

General Information • Academic study program in Oxford. Classes are held on the campus of University of Oxford, Trinity College. Excursions to Royal Shakespearean Company, London.
Learning Focus • Courses in English literature, history, art history, legal studies. Instruction is offered by local teachers.
Accommodations • Dormitories. Single rooms are available. Meals are taken as a group, in central dining facility.
Program Details • Program offered once per year. Session length: 6 weeks. Departures are scheduled in June. The program is open to undergraduate students, graduate students, adults. Most participants are 20–25 years of age. Other requirements: minimum 3.0 GPA. 50–60 participants per session. Application deadline: April 1.
Costs • $3650–$3850 (includes tuition, housing, some meals, tickets and transport to tour plays). A $150 deposit is required.
Contact • Dr. David Paroissien, Director, University of Massachusetts Amherst, Box 30515, Amherst, MA 01003; 413-545-1914; Fax: 413-545-3880; E-mail: paroissien@english.umass.edu; World Wide Web: http://www.umass.edu/ipo/

UNIVERSITY OF MICHIGAN

SUMMER PROGRAM AT OXFORD

General Information • Academic study program in Oxford. Classes are held on the campus of St. Peter's College, Oxford University.
Learning Focus • Courses in urban and environmental studies, medieval studies. Instruction is offered by local teachers.
Accommodations • Dormitories. Single rooms are available. Meals are taken as a group, in central dining facility.
Program Details • Program offered once per year. Session length: 6 weeks. Departures are scheduled in June. The program is open to undergraduate students. Most participants are 19–22 years of age. Other requirements: minimum 3.0 GPA. 20 participants per session. Application deadline: February 28.
Costs • $4300–$4600 (includes tuition, housing, all meals, excursions). Application fee: $50. A $250 deposit is required.
Contact • Office of International Programs, University of Michigan, G-513 Michigan Union, 530 South State Street, Ann Arbor, MI 48109-1349; 313-764-4311; Fax: 313-764-3229; E-mail: oip@umich.edu; World Wide Web: http://www.umich.edu/~iinet/oip/

UNIVERSITY OF MICHIGAN

SUMMER PROGRAM IN LONDON

General Information • Academic study program in London.
Learning Focus • Courses in British studies. Instruction is offered by professors from the sponsoring institution.
Accommodations • Locally-rented apartments. Meals are taken on one's own, in local restaurants.
Program Details • Program offered once per year. Session length: 6 weeks. Departures are scheduled in June. The program is open to undergraduate students. Most participants are 19–22 years of age. Other requirements: minimum 3.0 GPA. 25 participants per session. Application deadline: February 28.
Costs • $4200–$4500 (includes tuition, housing, some meals, excursions). Application fee: $50. A $250 deposit is required.
Contact • Office of International Programs, University of Michigan, G-513 Michigan Union, 530 South State Street, Ann Arbor, MI 48109-1349; 313-764-4311; Fax: 313-764-3229; E-mail: oip@umich.edu; World Wide Web: http://www.umich.edu/~iinet/oip/

UNIVERSITY OF MINNESOTA, THE GLOBAL CAMPUS

LIBERAL EDUCATION IN ENGLAND

General Information • Academic study program in London, Nottingham. Classes are held on the campus of Nottingham Trent University, Imperial College.
Learning Focus • Courses in English culture, England, English history. Instruction is offered by professors from the sponsoring institution and local teachers.
Accommodations • Homestays, dormitories. Single rooms are available. Meals are taken as a group, on one's own, with host family, in local restaurants, in residences.
Program Details • Program offered once per year. Session length: 6 weeks. Departures are scheduled in June. The program is open to undergraduate students, graduate students, pre-college students, adults. Most participants are 18–23 years of age. Other requirements: minimum 2.0 GPA and academic recommendation. 15–20 participants per session. Application deadline: April 1.
Costs • $2750–$3000 (includes tuition, housing, some meals, books and class materials, pre-departure and on-site orientation). Application fee: $40. A $400 deposit is required.
Contact • Liberal Education in England, University of Minnesota, The Global Campus, 106 P2 Nicholson Hall, 216 Pillsbury Drive, SE, Minneapolis, MN 55455-0138; 612-625-3379; Fax: 612-626-8009; E-mail: globalc@maroon.tc.umn.edu; World Wide Web: http://www.isp.umn.edu/tgchome/tgchome.html

UNIVERSITY OF NEW HAMPSHIRE

CAMBRIDGE SUMMER PROGRAM

General Information • Academic study program in Cambridge. Classes are held on the campus of University of

Cambridge. Excursions to London, Canterbury, Dover, Stratford-upon-Avon, Coventry, Wales, Scotland.
Learning Focus • Courses in English language, history, humanities. Instruction is offered by professors from the sponsoring institution and local teachers.
Accommodations • Dormitories. Single rooms are available. Meals are taken as a group, in central dining facility.
Program Details • Program offered once per year. Session length: 6 weeks. Departures are scheduled in July. The program is open to undergraduate students, graduate students, those who have completed their formal education. Most participants are 20–26 years of age. Other requirements: good academic standing. 50 participants per session. Application deadline: March 15.
Costs • $4475 (includes tuition, housing, some meals, excursions). Application fee: $35. A $300 deposit is required.
Contact • Dr. Romana Huk, Director, University of New Hampshire, Hamilton Smith Hall, 95 Main Street, Durham, NH 03824-3574; 603-862-3962; Fax: 603-862-3962; E-mail: cambridge.program@unh.edu

UNIVERSITY OF NORTH CAROLINA AT CHARLOTTE

SHAKESPEARE IN PERFORMANCE

General Information • Academic study program in London, Stratford-upon-Avon.
Learning Focus • Courses in literature, Shakespeare, theater. Instruction is offered by professors from the sponsoring institution.
Accommodations • Dormitories, bed and breakfasts. Single rooms are available. Meals are taken as a group, in central dining facility.
Program Details • Program offered once per year. Session length: 3 weeks. Departures are scheduled in July. The program is open to undergraduate students, graduate students, pre-college students, adults. Most participants are 18–35 years of age. 20 participants per session. Application deadline: April 15.
Costs • $2995 (includes tuition, housing, some meals, insurance, excursions, international airfare, ground transportation, tickets to plays). Application fee: $10. A $200 deposit is required.
Contact • Elizabeth A. Adams, Director of Education Abroad Programs, University of North Carolina at Charlotte, Office of International Programs, 9201 University City Boulevard, Charlotte, NC 28223-0001; 704-547-2464; Fax: 704-547-3168; E-mail: eaadams@email.uncc.edu; World Wide Web: http://unccvm.uncc.edu

UNIVERSITY OF PENNSYLVANIA

PENN-IN-LONDON

General Information • Academic study program in London.

Learning Focus • Courses in literature, theater. Instruction is offered by professors from the sponsoring institution.
Accommodations • Dormitories. Meals are taken on one's own.
Program Details • Program offered once per year. Session length: 5 weeks. Departures are scheduled in June. The program is open to undergraduate students, graduate students. Most participants are 18–30 years of age. 29 participants per session. Application deadline: April 1.
Costs • $3859 (includes tuition, housing, excursions). Application fee: $35. A $300 deposit is required.
Contact • Elizabeth Sachs, Director, Penn Summer Abroad, University of Pennsylvania, 3440 Market Street, Suite 100, Philadelphia, PA 19104-3335; 215-898-5738; Fax: 215-573-2053; E-mail: esachs@mail.sas.upenn.edu

UNIVERSITY OF ROCHESTER

INTERNSHIPS IN EUROPE

General Information • Internship program in London.
Learning Focus • Courses in political science, health sciences, media, legal studies, arts, business, psychology. Instruction is offered by professors from the sponsoring institution.
Accommodations • Homestays, locally-rented apartments. Single rooms are available. Meals are taken on one's own, with host family, in local restaurants, in residences.
Program Details • Program offered 2 times per year. Session length: 10 weeks. Departures are scheduled in May, June. The program is open to undergraduate students, recent graduates. Most participants are 20–25 years of age. Other requirements: minimum 3.0 GPA. 15 participants per session. Application deadline: April 1.
Costs • $4750 (includes tuition, some meals, fees, some or all housing, depending on type of accomodation). Application fee: $30. A $300 deposit is required.
Contact • Ms. Jacqueline Levine, Study Abroad Director, University of Rochester, Lattimore 206, Rochester, NY 14627-0408; 716-275-7532; Fax: 716-461-5131; E-mail: jlle@troi.cc.rochester.edu; World Wide Web: http://www.rochester.edu/College/study-abroad/

UNIVERSITY OF SOUTHERN MISSISSIPPI

BRITISH STUDIES PROGRAM

General Information • Academic study program in London. Classes are held on the campus of King's College. Excursions to Scotland, France.
Learning Focus • Courses in anthropology, art, business, management, computer science, criminal justice, political science, English literature, theater and drama, fashion, finance, geography, library science, marketing, speech pathology, insurance. Instruction is offered by professors from the sponsoring institution and local teachers.
Accommodations • Dormitories. Single rooms are available. Meals are taken as a group, on one's own, in local restaurants.
Program Details • Program offered once per year. Session length: 6 weeks. Departures are scheduled in July. The program is open to undergraduate students, graduate students, teachers, professionals. Most participants are 18–65 years of age. Other requirements: good academic standing. 250 participants per session. Application deadline: May 31.
Costs • $3399 for undergraduates, $3649 for graduate students (includes tuition, housing, some meals, books and class materials, international airfare). A $200 deposit is required.
Contact • Dr. Tim W. Hudson, Dean, College of International and Continuing Education, University of Southern Mississippi, Box 10047, Hattiesburg, MS 39406-0047; 601-266-4344; Fax: 601-266-5699; E-mail: m_ravencraft@bull.cc.usm.edu

UNIVERSITY OF WISCONSIN–MILWAUKEE

THE CANTERBURY COURSE

General Information • Academic study program in Canterbury. Classes are held on the campus of Duke University Divinity School.
Learning Focus • Courses in religion, Anglicanism, liturgy, theology, history.
Accommodations • Dormitories. Single rooms are available. Meals are taken in central dining facility.
Program Details • Program offered once per year. Session length: 3 weeks. Departures are scheduled in July. The program is open to lay and ordained future leaders in the church. Most participants are 30–50 years of age. Other requirements: working knowledge of theology. 25 participants per session.
Costs • $2275 (includes tuition, housing, all meals). A $200 deposit is required.
Contact • Executive Director, University of Wisconsin–Milwaukee, Canterbury Cathedral Trust in America, 2300 Cathedral Avenue, NW, Washington, DC 20008; 202-328-8788; Fax: 202-328-8485; E-mail: ccta@aol.com; World Wide Web: http://www.uwm.edu/Dept/Slavic

UNIVERSITY OF WISCONSIN–PLATTEVILLE

SUMMER SESSION IN LONDON

General Information • Academic study program in London. Classes are held on the campus of Thames Valley University. Excursions to London, Oxford, Bath, Brighton, Stonehenge, Blenheim Palace.
Learning Focus • Courses in history, art, theater, psychology. Instruction is offered by local teachers.
Accommodations • Homestays. Single rooms are available. Meals are taken on one's own, with host family, in local restaurants, in residences.
Program Details • Program offered once per year. Session length: 4 weeks. Departures are scheduled in June. The program is open to undergraduate students, adults. Most participants are 18–23 years of age. Other requirements: minimum 2.0 GPA, good academic standing, and 2 recommendations. 40 participants per session. Application deadline: April 1.
Costs • $1950 for Wisconsin residents, $2200 for non-residents (includes tuition, some meals, books and class

materials, excursions, International Student Identification card). Application fee: $25. A $200 deposit is required.
Contact • Dr. William K. Spofford, Director, Study Aborad Programs, University of Wisconsin–Platteville, Institute for Study Abroad Programs, 308 Warner Hall, 1 University Plaza, Platteville, WI 53818-3099; 800-342-1725; Fax: 608-342-1736; E-mail: spofford@uwplatt.edu

UNIVERSITY STUDIES ABROAD CONSORTIUM

GRADUATE TEACHER EDUCATION: BRIGHTON, ENGLAND

General Information • Academic study program in Brighton. Classes are held on the campus of University of Brighton. Excursions to London, Cambridge, France (Paris), Oxford.
Learning Focus • Courses in education. Instruction is offered by local teachers.
Accommodations • Homestays, dormitories. Single rooms are available. Meals are taken on one's own, in central dining facility.
Program Details • Program offered once per year. Session length: 5 weeks. Departures are scheduled in June. The program is open to graduate students, adults, educators. Most participants are 21–30 years of age. Other requirements: graduate-level standing. Application deadline: April 15.
Costs • $1250 (includes tuition, insurance, International Student Identification card). Application fee: $50. A $150 deposit is required.
Contact • Dr. Carmelo Urza, Coordinator, University Studies Abroad Consortium, University of Nevada Library/ 323, Reno, NV 89557-0093; 702-784-6569; Fax: 702-784-6010; E-mail: usac@equinox.unr.edu; World Wide Web: http://www.scs.unr.edu/~usac

YALE UNIVERSITY

YALE-IN-LONDON SUMMER PROGRAM

General Information • Academic study program in London. Classes are held on the campus of Paul Mellon Centre for Studies in British Art. Excursions to country houses, theaters, literary sites, museums, art galleries.
Learning Focus • Courses in British art, British history, English literature, British architecture. Instruction is offered by professors from the sponsoring institution and local teachers.
Accommodations • Dormitories. Single rooms are available.
Program Details • Program offered once per year. Session length: 6 weeks. Departures are scheduled in June. The program is open to undergraduate students. Most participants are 19–23 years of age. 12 participants per session. Application deadline: March 1.
Costs • $4000 (includes tuition, housing). Application fee: $200.
Contact • Shelia Best, Administrative Assistant, Yale University, Yale Center for British Art, 1080 Chapel Street, PO Box 208280, New Haven, CT 06520-8280; 203-432-2824; Fax: 203-432-4538; E-mail: shelia.best@yale.edu

FINLAND

FOREIGN LANGUAGE STUDY ABROAD SERVICE

INTERNATIONAL LANGUAGE STUDY HOMESTAYS IN FINLAND

General Information • Language study program in Finland.
Learning Focus • Courses in Finnish language. Instruction is offered by local teachers.
Accommodations • Homestays. Single rooms are available. Meals are taken with host family, in residences.
Program Details • Session length: varies. Departures are scheduled in January–December. The program is open to undergraduate students, graduate students, pre-college students, adults. Most participants are 12 years of age and older. Other requirements: students must be at least 12 years old. 1 participant per session.
Costs • Contact sponsor for information. A $300 deposit is required.
Contact • Louise Harber, Coordinator, Foreign Language Study Abroad Service, Department IH, Box 903, 5935 Southwest 64th Avenue, South Miami, FL 33143; 800-282-1090; Fax: 305-662-2907; E-mail: flsas@netpoint.net; World Wide Web: http://www.netpoint.net/~flsas

ACCENT INTERNATIONAL CONSORTIUM FOR ACADEMIC PROGRAMS ABROAD

PARIS SUMMER STUDY

General Information • Language study program in Paris. Excursions to Normandy, Chartres, Versailles, Brittany, Loire Valley, Giverny.
Learning Focus • Courses in French language, French civilization, art history. Instruction is offered by professors from the sponsoring institution.
Accommodations • Homestays, dormitories. Single rooms are available. Meals are taken on one's own, in central dining facility, in local restaurants.
Program Details • Program offered once per year. Session length: 4 weeks. Departures are scheduled in July. The program is open to undergraduate students, graduate students, pre-college students, adults. Most participants are 18–60 years of age. 100 participants per session. Application deadline: May 1.
Costs • $2500 (includes tuition, housing, some meals, books and class materials, insurance, excursions). Application fee: $250. A $150 deposit is required.
Contact • Director, Paris Program, ACCENT International Consortium for Academic Programs Abroad, 425 Market Street, 2nd Floor, San Francisco, CA 94105; 415-904-7756; Fax: 415-904-7759; E-mail: sfaccent@aol.com

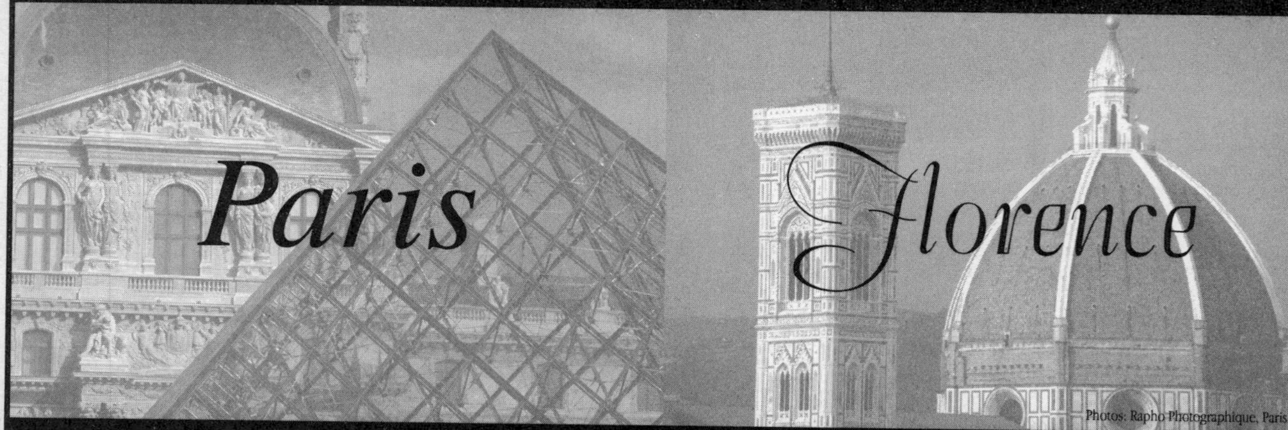

ALMA COLLEGE

SUMMER PROGRAM OF STUDIES IN FRANCE

General Information • Language study program in Paris. Classes are held on the campus of Alliance Française. Excursions to Loire Valley, Mont St. Michel.

Learning Focus • Courses in French language. Instruction is offered by local teachers.
Accommodations • Homestays, locally-rented apartments. Single rooms are available. Meals are taken with host family, in residences.
Program Details • Program offered 3 times per year. Session length: 4–12 weeks. Departures are scheduled in May, June. The program is open to undergraduate students, graduate students, adults. Most participants are 20–24 years of age. Other requirements: minimum 2.5 GPA. 10 participants per session. Application deadline: March 15.
Costs • $3010–$7445 (includes tuition, housing, some meals, excursions). Application fee: $35. A $200 deposit is required.
Contact • Patricia Landis, Director of International Education, Alma College, 614 West Superior Street, Alma, MI 48801; 517-463-7247; Fax: 517-463-7126; E-mail: landis@alma.edu; World Wide Web: http://www.alma.edu

AMERICAN INSTITUTE FOR FOREIGN STUDY (AIFS)

COLLÈGE INTERNATIONAL DE CANNES

General Information • Language study program in Cannes. Classes are held on the campus of Collége International de Cannes. Excursions to Paris.
Learning Focus • Courses in French language, civilizations.
Accommodations • Dormitories. Single rooms are available.
Program Details • Program offered 2 times per year. Session length: 4 weeks. Departures are scheduled in June, July. The program is open to undergraduate students, graduate students, adults, high school graduates. Other requirements: minimum 2.0 GPA. Application deadline: March 15.
Costs • $3539 (includes tuition, housing, all meals). A $400 deposit is required.
Contact • Carmela Vigliano, Director, Summer Programs, American Institute for Foreign Study (AIFS), 102 Greenwich Avenue, Greenwich, CT 06830; 800-727-2437, ext. 6087; Fax: 203-869-9615; E-mail: info@aifs.org

AMERICAN INSTITUTE FOR FOREIGN STUDY (AIFS)

PROGRAM AT THE UNIVERSITY OF PARIS

General Information • Language study program in Paris. Classes are held on the campus of University of Paris.
Learning Focus • Courses in French language, civilizations, architecture, history.
Accommodations • Homestays, dormitories. Single rooms are available.
Program Details • Program offered once per year. Session length: 4, 6, or 8 weeks. Departures are scheduled in June. The program is open to undergraduate students, graduate students, adults, high school graduates. Other requirements: minimum 2.0 GPA. Application deadline: March 15.
Costs • $2979 for 4 weeks, $3779 for 6 weeks, $4679 for 8 weeks (includes tuition, housing, some meals). A $400 deposit is required.
Contact • Carmela Vigliano, Director, Summer Programs, American Institute for Foreign Study (AIFS), 102 Greenwich Avenue, Greenwich, CT 06830; 800-727-2437, ext. 6087; Fax: 203-869-9615; E-mail: info@aifs.org

AMERICAN UNIVERSITY OF PARIS

FRENCH IMMERSION PROGRAM

General Information • Language study program in Paris.
Learning Focus • Courses in language study. Instruction is offered by professors from the sponsoring institution.
Accommodations • Homestays, locally-rented apartments, program-owned apartments. Single rooms are available. Meals are taken on one's own, in residences.
Program Details • Program offered once per year. Session length: 3 weeks. Departures are scheduled in June. The program is open to undergraduate students, graduate students, pre-college students, adults. Application deadline: May 24.
Costs • $1865 (includes tuition, some meals).
Contact • Candace McLaughlin, Admissions Counselor and Assistant Director, American University of Paris, 60 East 42nd Street, Suite 1463, New York, NY 10017; 212-983-1414; Fax: 212-983-0444; E-mail: summer@aup.fr; World Wide Web: http://www.aup.fr

APPALACHIAN STATE UNIVERSITY

FRANCE: LANGUAGE

General Information • Academic study program in Angers. Classes are held on the campus of Angers University.
Learning Focus • Courses in French language. Instruction is offered by professors from the sponsoring institution.
Program Details • Program offered once per year. Session length: 4 weeks. Departures are scheduled in June. Most participants are 18 years of age and older. 20 participants per session.
Costs • $1850 (includes tuition, housing, insurance, international airfare, International Student Identification card).
Contact • Dr. Max Feghali, Professor, Appalachian State University, Department of Foreign Languages, Boone, NC 28608; 704-262-2304; Fax: 704-262-4037

APPALACHIAN STATE UNIVERSITY

FRANCE: MARKETING

General Information • Academic study program in England (England (London)), France (Angers, Nice, Paris). Excursions to Versailles, Louvre, Normandy.
Learning Focus • Courses in marketing. Instruction is offered by professors from the sponsoring institution.
Program Details • Program offered once per year. Session length: 4–5 weeks. Departures are scheduled in May. Most participants are 18 years of age and older. 20 participants per session.

Live and study in Paris

Four, six or eight-week programs at the *Cours de Civilisation Française de la Sorbonne* offer elementary (no previous study required) to advanced French courses as well as French civilization and art history. A seminar for University-level French professors examines recent advances in the teaching of French. Earn up to 12 credits. Noncredit electives offer enrichment in fashion, cuisine and drawing. You live in a student residence or Parisian home. Enjoy all Paris has to offer with trips and excursions organized by the on-site AIFS staff.

American Institute For Foreign Study®
Dept. PLA 102 Greenwich Ave.
Greenwich, CT 06830
Phone (800) 727-2437
E-mail info@aifs.org
http://www.aifs.org

Costs • $3050 (includes tuition, housing, insurance, international airfare, International Student Identification card).
Contact • Dr. Mike Dotson, Professor, Appalachian State University, Department of Marketing, Boone, NC 28608; 704-262-6195; Fax: 704-262-4037

ARCHETOURS, INC.

PROVENCE: LOVE AMONG THE RUINS

General Information • Architectural and archaeology tour with visits to Arles/Provence, Vaison-La-Romaine, Orange, St. Rémy, Nimes, Pont du Gard. Once at the destination country, participants travel by bus, foot. Program is affiliated with American Institute of Architects Continuing Education System.
Learning Focus • Instruction in Roman city planning and the history of Romans in Provence. Escorted travel to Roman ruins throughout Provence. Museum visits (Arles Archaeology Museum). Instruction is offered by professors, artists, historians. This program would appeal to people interested in archaeology, history, design, architecture, art.
Accommodations • Hotels. Single rooms are available for an additional $275.
Program Details • Program offered 4 times per year. Session length: 1 week. Departures are scheduled in June, September. Most participants are 30–70 years of age. Participants must be 21 years or older to enroll. Other requirements: good health, capability of walking, standing and climbing to visit sites. 8–16 participants per session. Application deadline: 60 days prior to departure. Reservations are recommended at least 4–6 months before departure.
Costs • $1995 (includes housing, some meals, books and class materials, excursions, museum and site fees, airport transfers, lecturer fees, tips). A $250 deposit is required.
Contact • Ms. Gail Cornell, President, Archetours, Inc., 235 East 22nd Street, Suite 14F, New York, NY 10010; 800-770-3051; Fax: 212-779-7130; E-mail: archetours.@aol.com

ART TREK

A PAINTER'S FRANCE

General Information • Arts program with visits to Antibes, Luberon, Paris, "en plein air" painting locations in Aix-en-Provence, St. Remy, and Nice. Once at the destination country, participants travel by train, bus, foot, airplane.
Learning Focus • Instruction in watercolor painting and printmaking. Escorted travel to Paris, Provence and Cote d'Azur. Museum visits (Orsay, Picasso, Giverny, Maeght, Matisse). Instruction is offered by professors, artists. This program would appeal to people interested in fine arts, education, art therapy.
Accommodations • Hotels. Single rooms are available for an additional $550.
Program Details • Program offered once per year. Session length: 16 days. Departures are scheduled in June. Most participants are 35–55 years of age. Participants must be 14 years or older to enroll. 16 participants per session. Application deadline: April 20. Reservations are recommended at least 4–6 months before departure.
Costs • $4450 (includes housing, some meals, excursions, international airfare, instruction and leadership). A $450 deposit is required.
Contact • Carol Duchamp, Director, Art Trek, PO Box 807, Bolinas, CA 94924; 415-868-9558; Fax: 415-868-9033

ART TREK

STUDIO ANTIBES

General Information • Arts program with visits to Antibes, St. Paul-de-Vencei, Biot. Once at the destination country, participants travel by foot, jeep or van.
Learning Focus • Instruction in drawing, painting and printmaking. Museum visits (Picasso Museum Antibes). Instruction is offered by professors, artists. This program would appeal to people interested in art.
Accommodations • Homestays, hotels. Single rooms are available for an additional $100–$160.
Program Details • Program offered 14 times per year. Session length: 1–2 weeks. Departures are scheduled in January–August, October–December. Most participants are 18–60 years of age. Participants must be 14 years or older to enroll. 8 participants per session. Application deadline: 1 month prior to departure. Reservations are recommended at least 2–4 months before departure.
Costs • $450 (includes tuition).
Contact • Carol Duchamp, Director, Art Trek, PO Box 807, Bolinas, CA 94924; 415-868-9558; Fax: 415-868-9033

ART TREK

WATERCOLOR PAINTING AND SAILING ON THE MEDITERRANEAN

General Information • Arts program with visits to Antibes, Cannes, Lérins Islands, Porquerolles Islands, St. Tropez, Cote d'Azur. Once at the destination country, participants travel by foot, boat, bicycle.
Learning Focus • Instruction in watercolor painting. Escorted travel to Cote d'Azur, France. Museum visits (Picasso Museum Antibes). Instruction is offered by professors, artists, sports professionals. This program would appeal to people interested in art, sailing.
Accommodations • Boat.
Program Details • Program offered once per year. Session length: 7 days. Departures are scheduled in July. Most participants are 35–55 years of age. Participants must be 14 years or older to enroll. 8 participants per session. Application deadline: May 1. Reservations are recommended at least 4–6 months before departure.
Costs • $2000 (includes housing, all meals, excursions, instruction and leadership). A $450 deposit is required.
Contact • Carol Duchamp, Director, Art Trek, PO Box 807, Bolinas, CA 94924; 415-868-9558; Fax: 415-868-9033

AVALON WINE TOURS

WINE VACATIONS

General Information • Gourmet cooking/wine tour with visits to Bordeaux, Burgundy, Dordogne, castles. Once at the destination country, participants travel by mini-bus.
Learning Focus • Escorted travel to vineyards. Other activities include golfing, cooking demonstrations. Instruc-

tion is offered by wine expert. This program would appeal to people interested in wine, cooking, golf.
Accommodations • Hotels, châteaux. Single rooms are available for an additional $400.
Program Details • Program offered 12 times per year. Session length: 1–2 weeks. Departures are scheduled in April, July, September, November. Most participants are 30–65 years of age. 8 participants per session. Application deadline: 45 days prior to departure. Reservations are recommended at least 4–6 months before departure.
Costs • $3500 for 1 week (includes all meals, excursions, vineyard visits, travel insurance). A $300 deposit is required.
Contact • Peter Smith, Owner, Avalon Wine Tours, PO Box 8911, Newport Beach, CA 92658; 714-673-7376; Fax: 714-673-6533; E-mail: winetours@earthlink.net

BOSTON UNIVERSITY

HISTORY AND CULTURE IN PARIS

General Information • Academic study program in Paris.
Learning Focus • Courses in history. Instruction is offered by professors from the sponsoring institution.
Accommodations • Dormitories. Single rooms are available. Meals are taken on one's own, in central dining facility, in local restaurants.
Program Details • Program offered once per year. Session length: 6 weeks. Departures are scheduled in June, July. The program is open to undergraduate students, adults. Most participants are 19–23 years of age. Other requirements: minimum 3.0 GPA and good academic standing. 15 participants per session. Application deadline: March 15.
Costs • $4400 (includes tuition, housing, some meals, excursions). Application fee: $35. A $300 deposit is required.
Contact • Division of International Programs, Boston University, 232 Bay State Road, Boston, MA 02215; 617-353-9888; Fax: 617-353-5402; E-mail: abroad@bu.edu; World Wide Web: http://web.bu.edu/abroad

BOSTON UNIVERSITY

SUMMER GRENOBLE PROGRAM

General Information • Language study program in Grenoble. Classes are held on the campus of University of Grenoble. Excursions to Avignon, Vallorune (Mont Blanc region of the Alps).
Learning Focus • Courses in French language, French civilization. Instruction is offered by local teachers.
Accommodations • Homestays. Single rooms are available. Meals are taken on one's own, with host family, in local restaurants, in residences.
Program Details • Program offered once per year. Session length: 6 weeks. Departures are scheduled in June. The program is open to undergraduate students, adults. Most participants are 19–21 years of age. Other requirements:

minimum 3.0 GPA, good academic standing and 2 or more semesters of college-level French. 15 participants per session. Application deadline: March 15.
Costs • $3950 (includes tuition, housing, some meals, excursions). Application fee: $35. A $300 deposit is required.
Contact • Division of International Programs, Boston University, 232 Bay State Road, Boston, MA 02215; 617-353-9888; Fax: 617-353-5402; E-mail: abroad@bu.edu; World Wide Web: http://web.bu.edu/abroad

BRITISH COASTAL TRAILS SCENIC WALKING

CHÂTEAUX OF THE LOIRE

General Information • Cultural tour with visits to Chenonceau, Cheverny, Chouzé-sur-Loire, Samur, Fontevraud Forest, Candes St. Martin, Gardens of Villandry, Chambord. Once at the destination country, participants travel by bus, foot.
Learning Focus • Escorted travel to Loire Valley and a châteaux. Nature observation (forests, vineyards). Other activities include hiking, walking. Instruction is offered by naturalists, historians, professional guides. This program would appeal to people interested in nature studies, walking, culture, photography, history.
Accommodations • Hotels, châteaux. Single rooms are available.
Program Details • Program offered 4 times per year. Session length: 7 days. Departures are scheduled in May, June, August, October. Most participants are 40–65 years of age. Participants must be 13 years or older to enroll. Other requirements: physician's approval and signed release form. 18 participants per session. Application deadline: 30 days prior to departure. Reservations are recommended at least 6 months before departure.
Costs • $1895 (includes housing, some meals, excursions, full-time guide). A $250 deposit is required.
Contact • Tour Manager, British Coastal Trails Scenic Walking, 7777 Fay Avenue, Suite 100, La Jolla, CA 92037; 800-473-1210; Fax: 619-456-2277; E-mail: lajolla@bctwalk.com; World Wide Web: http://www.bctwalk.com/lajolla

BRITISH COASTAL TRAILS SCENIC WALKING

THE ENCHANTING VALLEY OF DORDOGNE

General Information • Cultural tour with visits to Les-Eyzies, Rocamadour, Sarlat, St. Leon, Sergeac, Château de Castelnaud, Château de Beynac, Loubressac, Autoire. Once at the destination country, participants travel by train, bus, foot.
Learning Focus • Escorted travel to Domme and Souillac. Nature observation (caves, rivers). Other activities include hiking, walking. Instruction is offered by naturalists, historians, professional guides. This program would appeal to people interested in nature studies, walking, culture, photography, history.
Accommodations • Hotels, châteaux. Single rooms are available.
Program Details • Program offered 4 times per year. Session length: 7 days. Departures are scheduled in May, July, September, October. Most participants are 40–65 years of age. Participants must be 13 years or older to enroll. Other requirements: physician's approval and signed release form. 18 participants per session. Application deadline: 30 days prior to departure. Reservations are recommended at least 6 months before departure.
Costs • $1895 (includes housing, some meals, excursions, full-time guide). A $250 deposit is required.
Contact • Tour Manager, British Coastal Trails Scenic Walking, 7777 Fay Avenue, Suite 100, La Jolla, CA 92037; 800-473-1210; Fax: 619-456-2277; E-mail: lajolla@bctwalk.com; World Wide Web: http://www.bctwalk.com/lajolla

BRITISH COASTAL TRAILS SCENIC WALKING

NORMANDY AND BRITTANY

General Information • Cultural tour with visits to Bayeux, Caen, Dinard, River Orne, St. Malo, Charentais Marshlands, Hambye Abbey, Mont-St.-Michel, Maison de Marais. Once at the destination country, participants travel by train, bus, foot, boat.
Learning Focus • Escorted travel to Omaha Beach and the American Cemetery. Nature observation (wildlife, flowers, birds, orchards, cliffs). Other activities include hiking, walking. Instruction is offered by naturalists, historians, professional guides. This program would appeal to people interested in nature studies, walking, culture, photography, history.
Accommodations • Châteaux. Single rooms are available.
Program Details • Program offered 3 times per year. Session length: 7 days. Departures are scheduled in May, June, September. Most participants are 40–65 years of age. Participants must be 13 years or older to enroll. Other requirements: physician's approval and signed release form. 18 participants per session. Application deadline: 30 days prior to departure. Reservations are recommended at least 6 months before departure.
Costs • $1835 (includes housing, some meals, excursions, full-time guide). A $250 deposit is required.
Contact • Tour Manager, British Coastal Trails Scenic Walking, 7777 Fay Avenue, Suite 100, La Jolla, CA 92037; 800-473-1210; Fax: 619-456-2277; E-mail: lajolla@bctwalk.com; World Wide Web: http://www.bctwalk.com/lajolla

BRITISH COASTAL TRAILS SCENIC WALKING

A WEEK IN PROVENCE

General Information • Cultural tour with visits to Aix-en-Provence, Pays d'Aigues, Vaison la Romaine, Montagne Saint Victoire, Buoux, "Old Salt Routes", Sénangue Abbey, Avignon. Once at the destination country, participants travel by bus, foot.
Learning Focus • Escorted travel to Luberon, vineyards, olive groves and an olive mill. Nature observation (wildflowers). Other activities include hiking, walking. Instruction is offered by naturalists, historians, professional guides. This program would appeal to people interested in nature studies, walking, culture, photography, history.
Accommodations • Hotels. Single rooms are available.
Program Details • Program offered 4 times per year. Session length: 7 days. Departures are scheduled in April,

May, June, September. Most participants are 40–65 years of age. Participants must be 13 years or older to enroll. Other requirements: physician's approval, signed release form. 18 participants per session. Application deadline: 30 days prior to departure. Reservations are recommended at least 6 months before departure.
Costs • $1895 (includes housing, some meals, excursions, full-time guide). A $250 deposit is required.
Contact • Tour Manager, British Coastal Trails Scenic Walking, 7777 Fay Avenue, Suite 100, La Jolla, CA 92037; 800-473-1210; Fax: 619-456-2277; E-mail: lajolla@bctwalk.com; World Wide Web: http://www.bctwalk.com/lajolla

CAMPUS INTERNATIONAL CÔTE D'AZUR

PROGRAM IN TOULON, FRANCE

General Information • Language study program in Toulon. Classes are held on the campus of University of Toulon. Excursions to French Riviera, Southern France, Marseille, Nice, Cannes.
Learning Focus • Courses in French language, civilizations. Instruction is offered by local teachers.
Accommodations • Dormitories. Single rooms are available. Meals are taken as a group.
Program Details • Program offered 4 times per year. Session length: 7 weeks. Departures are scheduled in July, August. The program is open to undergraduate students, graduate students, pre-college students. Most participants are 18–26 years of age. 110 participants per session. Application deadline: 1 month prior to departure.
Costs • $1700 (includes tuition, housing, all meals). Application fee: $150. A $500 deposit is required.
Contact • Dr. Janice E. Ovadiah, US Representative, Campus International Côte d'Azur, 303 West 66th Street, #4HE, New York, NY 10023-6305; 212-724-5823; Fax: 212-496-2264

Dr. Janice E. Ovadiah offers a varied menu of French study programs for many needs, budgets, and durations. Accommodations include homestays, hotels, college campuses, or apartments. Participants may choose to study in accredited schools in Paris, on the French Riviera, in Bordeaux, or in other attractive French cities. French language programs and 1-week French cuisine courses are available during the summer and throughout the year. Programs cater to general students, teachers, adults, and business professionals for either leisure or intensive study.

THE CENTER FOR ENGLISH STUDIES

STUDY ABROAD IN NICE, FRANCE

General Information • Language study program with visits to Nice. Program is affiliated with International House Centre de Langues Riviera.
Learning Focus • Instruction in the French language. Other activities include field trips to local sites, museums, markets and churches. Instruction is offered by faculty members from host institution. This program would appeal to people interested in the French language.
Accommodations • Homestays, dormitories, locally-rented apartments, program-owned apartments, program-owned houses, hotels. Single rooms are available.
Program Details • Session length: 2 or more weeks. Departures are scheduled throughout the year. Most participants are 12–70 years of age. Participants must be 12 years or older to enroll. 6–12 participants per session. Application deadline: 2 weeks prior to departure. Reservations are recommended at least 1 month before departure.
Costs • $1000 for 2 weeks (includes tuition, housing, some meals, books and class materials). A $125 deposit is required.
Contact • Ms. Lorraine Haber, Study Abroad Coordinator, The Center for English Studies, 330 7th Avenue, 6th Floor, New York, NY 10001; 212-629-7300; Fax: 212-736-7950; E-mail: ces_newyork@cescorp.com

THE CENTER FOR ENGLISH STUDIES

STUDY ABROAD IN TOURS, FRANCE

General Information • Language study program with visits to Tours. Program is affiliated with CLE-Centre Linguistique Pour Étrangers.
Learning Focus • Instruction in the French language. Other activities include field trips to local sites, museums, markets and churches. Instruction is offered by faculty members from host institution. This program would appeal to people interested in the French language, French for tourism, business and legal French.
Accommodations • Homestays, locally-rented apartments, program-owned apartments, hotels. Single rooms are available.
Program Details • Session length: 2 or more weeks. Departures are scheduled throughout the year. Most participants are 16–70 years of age. Participants must be 16 years or older to enroll. 6–12 participants per session. Application deadline: 2 weeks prior to departure. Reservations are recommended at least 1 month before departure.
Costs • $1300 for 2 weeks (includes tuition, housing, some meals, excursions). A $125 deposit is required.
Contact • Ms. Lorraine Haber, Study Abroad Coordinator, The Center for English Studies, 330 7th Avenue, 6th Floor, New York, NY 10001; 212-629-7300; Fax: 212-736-7950; E-mail: ces_newyork@cescorp.com

COAST COMMUNITY COLLEGE DISTRICT

SUMMER IN PARIS

General Information • Language study program in Paris. Classes are held on the campus of University of Paris–Sorbonne (Paris IV). Excursions to Normandy, Brittany.
Learning Focus • Instruction is offered by professors from the sponsoring institution and local teachers.
Accommodations • Homestays, dormitories. Single rooms are available. Meals are taken on one's own, in central dining facility.

Program Details • Program offered once per year. Session length: 4 weeks. Departures are scheduled in July. The program is open to undergraduate students, graduate students, pre-college students, adults, high school students with principal's recommendation. Most participants are 16–80 years of age. Other requirements: minimum 2.0 GPA. 25 participants per session. Application deadline: April 15.
Costs • $3500 (includes housing, some meals, insurance, excursions, international airfare). A $250 deposit is required.
Contact • Christine Russell, Study Abroad Advisor, Coast Community College District, 1370 Adams Avenue, Costa Mesa, CA 92626; 714-432-5963; Fax: 714-432-5964; E-mail: crussell@cccd.edu

COLLEGE CONSORTIUM FOR INTERNATIONAL STUDIES–MIAMI-DADE COMMUNITY COLLEGE

AVIGNON SUMMER PROGRAM

General Information • Academic study program in Avignon. Classes are held on the campus of Institute for American Universities (IAU)–Avignon.
Learning Focus • Courses in French language, French literature, French civilization. Instruction is offered by local teachers.
Accommodations • Homestays. Single rooms are available. Meals are taken with host family.
Program Details • Program offered once per year. Session length: 6 weeks. Departures are scheduled in June. The program is open to undergraduate students, adults. Most participants are 18–65 years of age. Other requirements: minimum 2.5 GPA. 30 participants per session. Application deadline: April 20.
Costs • $3160 (includes tuition, housing, some meals, insurance). Application fee: $25. A $350 deposit is required.
Contact • Jane C. Evans, Executive Director, College Consortium for International Studies, 2000 P Street, NW, Suite 503, Washington, DC 20036; 800-453-6956; Fax: 202-223-0999; E-mail: ccis@intr.net

COLLEGE CONSORTIUM FOR INTERNATIONAL STUDIES–MIAMI-DADE COMMUNITY COLLEGE

SUMMER IN FRANCE

General Information • Academic study program in Aix-en-Provence, Paris. Classes are held on the campus of Institute for American Universities (IAU)–Aix-en-Provence.
Learning Focus • Courses in French language, international relations, international business, art history. Instruction is offered by local teachers.
Accommodations • Homestays. Single rooms are available. Meals are taken with host family.
Program Details • Program offered once per year. Session length: 6 weeks. Departures are scheduled in June. The program is open to undergraduate students, adults. Most participants are 18–65 years of age. Other requirements: minimum 2.5 GPA. 90 participants per session. Application deadline: April 20.
Costs • $3095 (includes tuition, housing, some meals, books and class materials, insurance). Application fee: $25. A $350 deposit is required.
Contact • Jane C. Evans, Executive Director, College Consortium for International Studies, 2000 P Street, NW, Suite 503, Washington, DC 20036; 800-453-6956; Fax: 202-223-0999; E-mail: ccis@intr.net

COLLEGE CONSORTIUM FOR INTERNATIONAL STUDIES–MIAMI-DADE COMMUNITY COLLEGE

SUMMER STUDIO ART

General Information • Academic study program in Aix-en-Provence. Classes are held on the campus of Institute for American Universities (IAU)–Aix-en-Provence.
Learning Focus • Courses in drawing, painting, art criticism. Instruction is offered by local teachers.
Accommodations • Homestays, student residences. Single rooms are available. Meals are taken with host family.
Program Details • Program offered once per year. Session length: 6 weeks. Departures are scheduled in June. The program is open to undergraduate students, professionals. Most participants are 18–60 years of age. Other requirements: minimum 2.5 GPA. 15 participants per session. Application deadline: April 20.
Costs • $3160 (includes tuition, housing, some meals, insurance). Application fee: $25. A $350 deposit is required.
Contact • Jane C. Evans, Executive Director, College Consortium for International Studies, 2000 P Street, NW, Suite 503, Washington, DC 20036; 800-453-6956; Fax: 202-223-0999; E-mail: ccis@intr.net

COLLEGE OF WILLIAM AND MARY

SUMMER IN MONTPELLIER

General Information • Language study program in Montpellier, Paris, Versailles. Classes are held on the campus of University Paul Valéry (Montpellier III). Excursions to Nîmes, Arles, Roquefort.
Learning Focus • Courses in French language. Instruction is offered by professors from the sponsoring institution and local teachers.
Accommodations • Dormitories. Single rooms are available. Meals are taken as a group, in central dining facility.
Program Details • Program offered once per year. Session length: 4 weeks. Departures are scheduled in July. The program is open to undergraduate students, graduate students, people in good academic standing, including graduates. Most participants are 19–30 years of age. Other requirements: 2 years of French and good academic standing. 17 participants per session. Application deadline: February 15.
Costs • $3790 (includes tuition, housing, some meals, books and class materials, excursions, international airfare, tours of Paris and Versailles, transportation to Montpellier). Application fee: $40. A $500 deposit is required.
Contact • Dr. Ann M. Moore, Head of Programs Abroad, College of William and Mary, Reves Center, PO Box 8795,

Williamsburg, VA 23187-8795; 757-221-3594; Fax: 757-221-3597; E-mail: ammoo2@facstaff.wm.edu

COLUMBIA UNIVERSITY

REID HALL SUMMER PROGRAMS

General Information • Language study program in Paris.
Learning Focus • Courses in French language, art history, French literature. Instruction is offered by professors from the sponsoring institution.
Accommodations • Homestays, dormitories, locally-rented apartments. Single rooms are available. Meals are taken on one's own, in residences.
Program Details • Program offered 2 times per year. Session length: 4, 6, or 8 weeks. Departures are scheduled in June, July. The program is open to undergraduate students, graduate students, adults. Most participants are 18–30 years of age. Other requirements: good academic standing. 40 participants per session. Application deadline: May 1.
Costs • $3914 for 2 courses (includes tuition, housing, excursions). Application fee: $25.
Contact • Dr. Frank Wolf, Director, Columbia University, 303 Lewisohn Hall, 2970 Broadway MC 4115, New York, NY 10027-6902; 212-854-2559; Fax: 212-854-5861; E-mail: reidhall@columbia.edu; World Wide Web: http://www.columbia.edu/cu/ssp/

COUNTRY WALKERS

BOUNTIFUL BURGUNDY

General Information • Cultural, gourmet cooking, nature study and walking tour with visits to Beaune, Dijon, Nuit St. George, Fixin, Pernand–Vergelesses, Echevronne. Once at the destination country, participants travel by foot.
Learning Focus • Escorted travel to Clos du Vougeot and Abbaye de Ste. Marguerite. Museum visits (Musée du Vin). Other activities include walking. Instruction is offered by professors, researchers, naturalists, historians. This program would appeal to people interested in walking, nature studies, food and wine.
Accommodations • Hotels. Single rooms are available for an additional $300–$600.
Program Details • Program offered 5 times per year. Session length: 7 days. Departures are scheduled in June–September. Program is targeted to adults 35 to 65 years old. Most participants are 35-65 years of age. Participants must be 18 years or older to enroll. 18 participants per session. Reservations are recommended at least 5–6 months before departure.
Costs • $2095 (includes housing, all meals, excursions). A $400 deposit is required.
Contact • Heather Kellingbeck, Vice President, Country Walkers, PO Box 180, Waterbury, VT 05176; 800-464-9255; Fax: 802-244-5661; E-mail: ctrywalk@aol.com

COUNTRY WALKERS

THE DELICACIES OF DORDOGNE

General Information • Cultural, gourmet cooking, nature study and walking tour with visits to Montignac, Sarlat, Vitrac, Tamnies, Montfort, Domme, Beynac. Once at the destination country, participants travel by foot.
Learning Focus • Escorted travel to Lascaux II and Le Thot. Other activities include walking. Instruction is offered by professors, researchers, naturalists, historians. This program would appeal to people interested in walking, nature studies, food and wine.
Accommodations • Hotels. Single rooms are available for an additional $300–$600.
Program Details • Program offered 5 times per year. Session length: 7 days. Departures are scheduled in May, September, October. Program is targeted to adults 35 to 65 years old. Most participants are 35-65 years of age. Participants must be 18 years or older to enroll. 18 participants per session. Reservations are recommended at least 5–6 months before departure.
Costs • $2090 (includes housing, all meals, excursions). A $400 deposit is required.
Contact • Heather Kellingbeck, Vice President, Country Walkers, PO Box 180, Waterbury, VT 05176; 800-464-9255; Fax: 802-244-5661; E-mail: ctrywalk@aol.com

CROSS-CULTURE

AUTUMN IN THE SOUTH OF FRANCE III: THE GASCOGNE

General Information • Cultural tour with visits to Condom, Larresingle, Fources Lectoure, Seviac, Bassoues, Toulouse. Once at the destination country, participants travel by bus, foot.
Learning Focus • Escorted travel to the Abbey of Flaran, the Chateau de Cassaigne and the Cathedral of Ste. Marie. Museum visits (Museum of Armagnac). Attendance at performances (town band). Instruction is offered by highly educated guides. This program would appeal to people interested in culture, history, nature studies, arts, traditions, food and wine.
Accommodations • Hotels. Single rooms are available for an additional $190.
Program Details • Program offered once per year. Session length: 9 days. Departures are scheduled in September. Program is targeted to adults of all ages. Most participants are 40–70 years of age. Participants must be 12 years or older to enroll. Other requirements: good health, accompaniment of an adult if under 18. 20–25 participants per session. Application deadline: 1 month prior to departure. Reservations are recommended at least 3–12 months before departure.
Costs • $2400 (includes tuition, housing, all meals, books and class materials, excursions, international airfare). A $300 deposit is required.
Contact • Cross-Culture, 52 High Point Drive, Amherst, MA 01002-1224; 413-256-6303; Fax: 413-253-2303; E-mail: xculture@javanet.com; World Wide Web: http://www.empiremall.com/cross-culture

CROSS-CULTURE

AUTUMN IN THE SOUTH OF FRANCE II: THE ALBIGEOIS

General Information • Cultural tour with visits to Albi, Cordes, Castres, Ville France-de-Rouergue, Conques, Penne, Bruniquel, St. Antonin-Noble-Val, Toulouse. Once at the destination country, participants travel by foot.

Learning Focus • Instruction in agriculture and culinary specialties of the Tarn/Albigeois region. Escorted travel to Cathedral of St. Cecile, Chateau Mauriac and Le Sidobre Plateau. Museum visits (Palais de la Berbie, Goya Museum). Instruction is offered by highly educated guides. This program would appeal to people interested in culture, history, nature studies, arts, traditions, food and wine.
Accommodations • Hotels. Single rooms are available.
Program Details • Program offered once per year. Session length: 9 days. Departures are scheduled in September. Program is targeted to adults of all ages. Most participants are 40–70 years of age. Participants must be 12 years or older to enroll. Other requirements: good health, accompaniment of an adult if under 18. 20–25 participants per session. Application deadline: 1 month prior to departure. Reservations are recommended at least 3–12 months before departure.
Costs • $2440 (includes tuition, housing, all meals, books and class materials, excursions, international airfare). A $300 deposit is required.
Contact • Cross-Culture, 52 High Point Drive, Amherst, MA 01002-1224; 413-256-6303; Fax: 413-253-2303; E-mail: xculture@javanet.com; World Wide Web: http://www.empiremall.com/cross-culture

CROSS-CULTURE

AUTUMN IN THE SOUTH OF FRANCE I: THE DORDOGNE

General Information • Cultural tour with visits to Sarlat-la-Caneda, Beynac, La Roque Gageac, Domme, Les Gyzies-de-Tayac, Rocamadour, Bergerac, Toulouse. Once at the destination country, participants travel by bus, foot.
Learning Focus • Instruction in the history of Bergerac. Escorted travel to Font de Gaume Cave, Cap Blanc, Lascaux II and the Grotto of Pech-Merle. Museum visits (The National Museum of Prehistory). Instruction is offered by highly educated guides. This program would appeal to people interested in culture, history, nature studies, arts, traditions, food and wine.
Accommodations • Hotels. Single rooms are available for an additional $215.
Program Details • Program offered once per year. Session length: 9 days. Departures are scheduled in September. Program is targeted to adults of all ages. Most participants are 40–70 years of age. Participants must be 12 years or older to enroll. Other requirements: good health, accompaniment of an adult if under 18. 20–25 participants per session. Application deadline: 1 month prior to departure. Reservations are recommended at least 3–12 months before departure.
Costs • $2670 (includes tuition, housing, all meals, books and class materials, excursions, international airfare). A $300 deposit is required.
Contact • Cross-Culture, 52 High Point Drive, Amherst, MA 01002-1224; 413-256-6303; Fax: 413-253-2303; E-mail: xculture@javanet.com; World Wide Web: http://www.empiremall.com/cross-culture

CROSS-CULTURE

AUTUMN IN THE SOUTH OF FRANCE IV: THE LANGUEDOC

General Information • Cultural tour with visits to Carcassonne, Tautavel, Narbonne, Mirepoix, Toulouse.
Learning Focus • Instruction in the Cathares in Languedoc-Roussillon. Escorted travel to Fontfroide Abbey and the Church of Rieux-Minervois. Museum visits (Prehistoric Museum). Instruction is offered by highly educated guides. This program would appeal to people interested in French culture.
Accommodations • Hotels. Single rooms are available for an additional $215.
Program Details • Program offered once per year. Session length: 9 days. Departures are scheduled in September. Program is targeted to adults of all ages. Most participants are 40–70 years of age. Participants must be 12 years or older to enroll. Other requirements: good health, accompaniment of an adult if under 18. 20–25 participants per session. Application deadline: 1 month prior to departure. Reservations are recommended at least 3–12 months before departure.
Costs • $2500 (includes tuition, housing, all meals, books and class materials, excursions, international airfare). A $300 deposit is required.
Contact • Cross-Culture, 52 High Point Drive, Amherst, MA 01002-1224; 413-256-6303; Fax: 413-253-2303; E-mail: xculture@javanet.com; World Wide Web: http://www.empiremall.com/cross-culture

CROSS-CULTURE

BIKING FRANCE'S BORDEAUX COAST

General Information • Nature study, cultural, and bicycling tour with visits to Arcachon, Dax, Hossegor, Lit-et-Mixe, San Sebastian, Biscarrosse, Carcans, Medoc Peninsula. Once at the destination country, participants travel by bus, boat, bicycle.
Learning Focus • Escorted travel to Dune du Pyla, Chateau La Fite and Chateau Margaux. Other activities include bicycling. Instruction is offered by naturalists, historians, bicycle leaders. This program would appeal to people interested in nature studies, history, food and wine, traditions, culture.
Accommodations • Hotels. Single rooms are available for an additional $310.
Program Details • Program offered once per year. Session length: 10 days. Departures are scheduled in July. Program is targeted to adults of all ages. Most participants are 30–75 years of age. Participants must be 12 years or older to enroll. Other requirements: must be in good health and have some biking experience, must be accompanied by an adult if under 18. 20 participants per session. Application deadline: 1 month prior to departure. Reservations are recommended at least 3–12 months before departure.
Costs • $2890 (includes tuition, housing, all meals, books and class materials, excursions, international airfare). A $300 deposit is required.
Contact • Cross-Culture, 52 High Point Drive, Amherst, MA 01002-1224; 413-256-6303; Fax: 413-253-2303; E-mail: xculture@javanet.com; World Wide Web: http://www.empiremall.com/cross-culture

CROSS-CULTURE

THE BRITTANY COAST AND ITS ANCIENT CULTURES

General Information • Cultural tour with visits to Quimper. Once at the destination country, participants travel by foot.

Learning Focus • Instruction in megalithic monument stone formations. Escorted travel to Pleyben and St. Thegonec Guimiliau. Museum visits (Museum of Breton Folk Art, Museum of Fine Arts). Instruction is offered by highly educated guides.
Accommodations • Hotels. Single rooms are available for an additional $250.
Program Details • Program offered once per year. Session length: 9 days. Departures are scheduled in May. Program is targeted to adults of all ages. Most participants are 40–70 years of age. Participants must be 12 years or older to enroll. Other requirements: good health, accompaniment of an adult if under 18. 20–25 participants per session. Application deadline: 1 month prior to departure. Reservations are recommended at least 3–12 months before departure.
Costs • $2550 (includes tuition, housing, all meals, books and class materials, excursions, international airfare). A $300 deposit is required.
Contact • Cross-Culture, 52 High Point Drive, Amherst, MA 01002-1224; 413-256-6303; Fax: 413-253-2303; E-mail: xculture@javanet.com; World Wide Web: http://www.empiremall.com/cross-culture

CROSS-CULTURE

PARIS PLUS

General Information • Cultural tour with visits to Paris, Giverny, Normandy, Loire Valley. Once at the destination country, participants travel by bus, foot.
Learning Focus • Instruction in French and Parisian history and culture and French fine arts. Escorted travel to Meridon area and the rose garden of the Bagatelle. Museum visits (Marmottan Museum, the Louvre, Orsay Museum). Attendance at performances (concerts). Instruction is offered by highly educated guides. This program would appeal to people interested in culture, history, nature studies, arts, traditions, food and wine.
Accommodations • Hotels. Single rooms are available.
Program Details • Program offered 2 times per year. Session length: 12 days. Departures are scheduled in May, June. Program is targeted to adults of all ages. Most participants are 40–70 years of age. Participants must be 12 years or older to enroll. Other requirements: good health, accompaniment of an adult if under 18. 20–25 participants per session. Application deadline: 1 month prior to departure. Reservations are recommended at least 3–12 months before departure.
Costs • $2690 (includes tuition, housing, all meals, books and class materials, excursions, international airfare). A $300 deposit is required.
Contact • Cross-Culture, 52 High Point Drive, Amherst, MA 01002-1224; 413-256-6303; Fax: 413-253-2303; E-mail: xculture@javanet.com; World Wide Web: http://www.empiremall.com/cross-culture

CROSS-CULTURE

WALKS IN THE SOUTH OF FRANCE

General Information • Nature study, cultural, and hiking tour with visits to Carcassonne, Bages, Narbonne, Minerve. Once at the destination country, participants travel by bus, foot.
Learning Focus • Escorted travel to the Gorges of Galamus, Hermitage of St. Antoine and Fadesdolmen. Other activities include hiking. Instruction is offered by naturalists, historians, experienced hiking leaders. This program would appeal to people interested in nature studies, history, food and wine, culture, traditions.
Accommodations • Hotels. Single rooms are available.
Program Details • Program offered once per year. Session length: 9 days. Departures are scheduled in October. Program is targeted to adults of all ages. Most participants are 30–75 years of age. Participants must be 12 years or older to enroll. Other requirements: must be in good health, must be accompanied by an adult if under 18. 20 participants per session. Application deadline: 1 month prior to departure. Reservations are recommended at least 3–12 months before departure.
Costs • Contact sponsor for information. A $300 deposit is required.
Contact • Cross-Culture, 52 High Point Drive, Amherst, MA 01002-1224; 413-256-6303; Fax: 413-253-2303; E-mail: xculture@javanet.com; World Wide Web: http://www.empiremall.com/cross-culture

CSA–CENTER FOR STUDY ABROAD

ELFCA–FRENCH LANGUAGE (RIVIERA)

General Information • Language study program in Hyères. Excursions to Cannes, Nice.
Learning Focus • Courses in French language. Instruction is offered by professors from the sponsoring institution.
Accommodations • Homestays. Single rooms are available. Meals are taken with host family.
Program Details • Program offered 52 times per year. Session length: 2–8 weeks. Departures are scheduled in January–December. The program is open to undergraduate students, graduate students, pre-college students, adults. Most participants are 17–45 years of age. Other requirements: minimum age of 17. 6–8 participants per session.
Costs • $1395 for 2 weeks (includes tuition, housing, some meals, books and class materials, insurance, registration, orientation). Application fee: $45. A $50 deposit is required.
Contact • Philip Virtue, Program Director, CSA–Center for Study Abroad, 2802 East Madison Street MS #160, Seattle, WA 98112; 206-726-1498; Fax: 206-285-9197; E-mail: virtuecsa@aol.com

CSA–CENTER FOR STUDY ABROAD

FRENCH AMERICAN STUDY CENTER

General Information • Language study program in Lisieux. Excursions to Paris.
Learning Focus • Instruction is offered by professors from the sponsoring institution.
Accommodations • Homestays, program-owned houses. Single rooms are available. Meals are taken with host family, in residences.
Program Details • Program offered 36 times per year. Session length: 2–10 weeks. Departures are scheduled in March–November. The program is open to undergraduate

students, graduate students, pre-college students, adults. Most participants are 17–38 years of age. Other requirements: minimum age of 17. 6–8 participants per session.
Costs • $1895 for 2 weeks (includes tuition, housing, some meals, books and class materials, insurance, registration, orientation). Application fee: $45. A $50 deposit is required.
Contact • Philip Virtue, Program Director, CSA-Center for Study Abroad, 2802 East Madison Street MS #160, Seattle, WA 98112; 206-726-1498; Fax: 206-285-9197; E-mail: virtuecsa@aol.com

CSA–CENTER FOR STUDY ABROAD

UNIVERSITY OF PARIS–SORBONNE (FRENCH STUDIES)

General Information • Language study program in Paris.
Learning Focus • Courses in French language, French literature, French history, political science. Instruction is offered by professors from the sponsoring institution.
Accommodations • Locally-rented apartments. Single rooms are available. Meals are taken on one's own, in residences.
Program Details • Program offered 6 times per year. Session length: 4-8 weeks. Departures are scheduled in June-September. The program is open to undergraduate students, graduate students, pre-college students, adults. Most participants are 17–32 years of age. Other requirements: minimum age of 17. 10–15 participants per session.
Costs • $995 for 4 weeks (includes tuition, books and class materials, insurance, registration, orientation). Application fee: $45. A $50 deposit is required.
Contact • Philip Virtue, Program Director, CSA–Center for Study Abroad, 2802 East Madison Street MS #160, Seattle, WA 98112; 206-726-1498; Fax: 206-285-9197; E-mail: virtuecsa@aol.com

CUISINE INTERNATIONAL

LE MAS DES OLIVIER'S COOKING SCHOOL

General Information • Gourmet cooking/wine tour with visits to Theoule Sur Mer, markets, glass blowers, Escoffier' Museum. Once at the destination country, participants travel by private coach.
Learning Focus • Instruction in regional cuisine. Instruction is offered by chefs. This program would appeal to people interested in cooking.
Accommodations • Program-owned houses. Single rooms are available for an additional $300.
Program Details • Program offered 10 times per year. Session length: 1 week. Departures are scheduled in June–August. Most participants are 18–75 years of age. 6 participants per session. Reservations are recommended at least 6 months before departure.
Costs • $2000 (includes tuition, housing, all meals, books and class materials, excursions). A $1000 deposit is required.
Contact • Judy Ebrey, Owner, Cuisine International, PO Box 25228, Dallas, TX 75225; 214-373-1161; Fax: 214-373-1162; E-mail: cuisineint@aol.com; World Wide Web: http://www.iglobal.net/cuisineint

CUISINE INTERNATIONAL

MAS DE CORNUN COOKING SCHOOL

General Information • Gourmet cooking/wine tour with visits to St. Remy de Provence, markets. Once at the destination country, participants travel by private coach.
Learning Focus • Instruction in regional cuisine. Instruction is offered by cooking teachers and chefs. This program would appeal to people interested in cooking.
Accommodations • Homestays. Single rooms are available for an additional $500.
Program Details • Session length: 1 week. Departures are scheduled throughout the year. Most participants are 18–75 years of age. 6 participants per session. Reservations are recommended at least 6 months before departure.
Costs • $2000 (includes tuition, housing, all meals, books and class materials, excursions). A $1000 deposit is required.
Contact • Judy Ebrey, Owner, Cuisine International, PO Box 25228, Dallas, TX 75225; 214-373-1161; Fax: 214-373-1162; E-mail: cuisineint@aol.com; World Wide Web: http://www.iglobal.net/cuisineint

CULTURAL EXPERIENCES ABROAD

FRENCH LANGUAGE AND CULTURE IN DIJON

General Information • Language study program in Dijon. Excursions to Burgundy region, Provence, Loire Valley.
Learning Focus • Courses in French language, French culture, European studies, international studies, translation.
Accommodations • Homestays, dormitories. Single rooms are available. Meals are taken in central dining facility.
Program Details • Program offered 3 times per year. Session length: 4, 6 or 8 weeks. Departures are scheduled in July, August. The program is open to undergraduate students, pre-college students. Most participants are 16–27 years of age. 15 participants per session. Application deadline: May 1.
Costs • $2995 (includes tuition, housing, books and class materials, insurance, excursions, resident director, International Student Identification card). A $350 deposit is required.
Contact • Sharon Dahlen, Coordinator, Cultural Experiences Abroad, 5319 West Patterson Avenue, Chicago, IL 60641-3347; 800-266-4441; Fax: 773-725-9256; E-mail: ceabroad@aol.com

DIANE HOFF-ROME, AN ARTIST'S LIFE

PROVENCE: FRANCE ARTIST HOLIDAY

General Information • Arts program with visits to Provence, Les Baux, Cassis, Nice, Aix-en-Provence, artists' studios, markets. Once at the destination country, participants travel by bus, foot, boat, mini-bus.
Learning Focus • Instruction in painting, drawing and composition. Museum visits (Nice, Aix-en-Provence). Attendance at performances (musical events). Nature observation (wildflowers, herbal plants). Other activities include hiking, visits with local artists. Instruction is offered by artists, historians. This program would appeal to people interested

in painting, nature studies, drawing, history, photography, art, writing, the French language.
Accommodations • Famliy run "logis". Single rooms are available for an additional $.
Program Details • Program offered 2 times per year. Session length: 1-2 weeks. Departures are scheduled in June, September. Program is targeted to amateur artists and teachers. Most participants are 25-85 years of age. Participants must be 21 years or older to enroll. Other requirements: interest in art, nature, cultural experience. 8 participants per session. Application deadline: 45 days prior to departure. Reservations are recommended at least 60-90 days before departure.
Costs • $1195 (includes tuition, housing, some meals, excursions). A $650 deposit is required.
Contact • Irwin W. Rome, Co-Director, Diane Hoff-Rome, An Artist's Life, PO Box 567, Elmwood Road, Swampscott, MA 01907; 617-595-1173; Fax: 617-596-0707; E-mail: artistlf@pcix.com; World Wide Web: http://www2.pcix.com/~artistlf

DICKINSON COLLEGE

TOULOUSE SUMMER IMMERSION PROGRAM

General Information • Language study program in Toulouse.
Learning Focus • Courses in French language, French culture. Instruction is offered by professors from the sponsoring institution.
Accommodations • Homestays. Single rooms are available. Meals are taken with host family, in residences.
Program Details • Program offered once per year. Session length: 6 weeks. Departures are scheduled in May. The program is open to undergraduate students. Most participants are 18-20 years of age. Other requirements: intermediate-level French. 15 participants per session. Application deadline: February 15.
Costs • $3600 (includes tuition, housing, all meals, books and class materials, excursions, international airfare). Application fee: $15. A $300 deposit is required.
Contact • Dr. John S. Henderson, Director of Off-Campus Studies, Dickinson College, PO Box 1773, Carlisle, PA 17013-2896; 717-245-1341; Fax: 717-245-1688; E-mail: ocs@dickinson.edu; World Wide Web: http://www.dickinson.edu

DUKE UNIVERSITY

DUKE IN PARIS

General Information • Academic study program in Paris.
Learning Focus • Courses in language study, literature, cultural studies. Instruction is offered by professors from the sponsoring institution.
Accommodations • Dormitories. Meals are taken on one's own, in local restaurants.
Program Details • Program offered once per year. Session length: 6 weeks. Departures are scheduled in June. The program is open to undergraduate students. Most participants are 19-21 years of age. Other requirements: minimum 2.7 GPA. 12-15 participants per session. Application deadline: February 21.
Costs • $5241 (includes tuition, housing, some meals, international airfare).
Contact • Foreign Academic Programs, Duke University, 121 Allen Building, Box 90057, Durham, NC 27708-0057; 919-684-2174; Fax: 919-684-3083; E-mail: abroad@mail01.adm.duke.edu; World Wide Web: http://www.mis.duke.edu/study_abroad/study_abroad.html

ECKERD COLLEGE

SUMMER STUDY ABROAD IN AIX-EN-PROVENCE

General Information • Academic study program in Aix-en-Provence. Classes are held on the campus of Institute for American Universities (IAU)-Aix-en-Provence.
Learning Focus • Courses in art history, cultural studies, economics, European studies, French language, literature, political science, liberal arts. Instruction is offered by local teachers.
Accommodations • Homestays, dormitories, program-owned apartments. Meals are taken on one's own, in central dining facility.
Program Details • Program offered 2 times per year. Session length: 6 weeks. Departures are scheduled in June, July. The program is open to undergraduate students. Most participants are 18-24 years of age. Other requirements: minimum 2.5 GPA and good academic standing. 20 participants per session. Application deadline: May 1.
Costs • $3400 (includes tuition, housing, some meals, insurance, excursions, books). Application fee: $30. A $200 deposit is required.
Contact • Susan Heitmann, Study Abroad Coordinator, Eckerd College, International Education, 4200 54th Avenue, S, St. Petersburg, FL 33711; 813-864-8381; Fax: 813-864-7995; E-mail: heitmas@eckerd.edu; World Wide Web: http://www.eckerd.edu

ECKERD COLLEGE

SUMMER STUDY ABROAD IN AVIGNON

General Information • Academic study program in Avignon. Classes are held on the campus of Institute for American Universities (IAU)-Avignon.
Learning Focus • Courses in art history, French studies, literature, French language, history. Instruction is offered by local teachers.
Accommodations • Homestays. Meals are taken on one's own, in central dining facility.
Program Details • Program offered 2 times per year. Session length: 6 weeks. Departures are scheduled in June, July. The program is open to undergraduate students. Most participants are 18-24 years of age. Other requirements: minimum 2.5 GPA and good academic standing. 20 participants per session. Application deadline: May 1.
Costs • $3400 (includes tuition, housing, some meals, insurance, excursions, books). Application fee: $30. A $200 deposit is required.
Contact • Susan Heitmann, Study Abroad Coordinator, Eckerd College, International Education, 4200 54th Avenue, S, St. Petersburg, FL 33711; 813-864-8381; Fax: 813-864-7995; E-mail: heitmas@eckerd.edu; World Wide Web: http://www.eckerd.edu

ECOLE DE LANGUE FRANÇAISE POUR ETRANGERS

ACCORD

General Information • Language study program in Paris.
Learning Focus • Courses in French language, civilizations.
Accommodations • Homestays, dormitories, hotels. Single rooms are available. Meals are taken with host family, in local restaurants.
Program Details • Program offered 21 times per year. Session length: 2 weeks. Departures are scheduled in January–December. The program is open to undergraduate students, graduate students, pre-college students, adults. Most participants are 18–40 years of age. 40 participants per session. Application deadline: 1 month prior to departure.
Costs • $1025 for 2 weeks, $2000 for 1 month (includes tuition, housing, some meals). Application fee: $250. A $500 deposit is required.
Contact • Dr. Janice E. Ovadiah, US Representative, Ecole de Langue Française pour Etrangers, 303 West 66th Street, New York, NY 10023; 212-724-5823; Fax: 212-496-2264

ECOLE DE LANGUE FRANÇAISE POUR ETRANGERS

AZURLINGUA

General Information • Language study program in Nice.
Learning Focus • Courses in French language.
Accommodations • Homestays, program-owned apartments, program-owned houses, hotels. Single rooms are available. Meals are taken on one's own, with host family, in local restaurants, in residences.
Program Details • Program offered 21 times per year. Session length: 2 weeks. Departures are scheduled in January–December. The program is open to undergraduate students, graduate students, pre-college students, adults. Most participants are 18–55 years of age. 30 participants per session. Application deadline: 1 month prior to departure.
Costs • $1250 (includes tuition, housing, some meals). Application fee: $150. A $500 deposit is required.
Contact • Dr. Janice E. Ovadiah, US Representative, Ecole de Langue Française pour Etrangers, 303 West 66th Street, New York, NY 10023; 212-724-5823; Fax: 212-496-2264

ECOLE DE LANGUE FRANÇAISE POUR ETRANGERS

BORDEAUX LANGUAGE SCHOOL

General Information • Language study program in Bordeaux.
Learning Focus • Courses in French language, French cooking, wine, civilizations.
Accommodations • Homestays, hotels. Single rooms are available. Meals are taken with host family, in local restaurants.
Program Details • Program offered 21 times per year. Session length: 2 weeks. Departures are scheduled in January–December. The program is open to undergraduate students, graduate students, pre-college students, adults. Most participants are 18–55 years of age. 40 participants per session. Application deadline: 1 month prior to departure.
Costs • $1300 (includes tuition, housing, some meals). Application fee: $150. A $500 deposit is required.
Contact • Dr. Janice E. Ovadiah, US Representative, Ecole de Langue Française pour Etrangers, 303 West 66th Street, New York, NY 10023; 212-724-5823; Fax: 212-496-2264

ECOLE DE LANGUE FRANÇAISE POUR ETRANGERS

CAVILAM

General Information • Language study program in Vichy.
Learning Focus • Courses in French language, civilizations.
Accommodations • Homestays, locally-rented apartments, hotels. Single rooms are available. Meals are taken on one's own, with host family, in local restaurants.
Program Details • Program offered 52 times per year. Session length: 1 week. Departures are scheduled in January–December. The program is open to undergraduate students, graduate students, pre-college students, adults. Most participants are 16–60 years of age. 125 participants per session. Application deadline: 1 month prior to departure.
Costs • $1200 (includes tuition, housing, some meals). Application fee: $150. A $500 deposit is required.
Contact • Dr. Janice E. Ovadiah, US Representative, Ecole de Langue Française pour Etrangers, 303 West 66th Street, New York, NY 10023; 212-724-5823; Fax: 212-496-2264

ECOLE DE LANGUE FRANÇAISE POUR ETRANGERS

FRENCH LANGUAGE STUDY

General Information • Language study program in Paris. Excursions to Loire Valley, sites near Paris.
Learning Focus • Courses in French language.
Accommodations • Homestays, hotels. Single rooms are available. Meals are taken on one's own, with host family, in local restaurants.
Program Details • Program offered 21 times per year. Session length: 2 or more weeks. Departures are scheduled in January–December. The program is open to undergraduate students, graduate students, pre-college students, adults. Most participants are 18–65 years of age. 75 participants per session. Application deadline: 1 month prior to departure.
Costs • $1990 (includes tuition, housing, some meals). Application fee: $150. A $500 deposit is required.
Contact • Dr. Janice E. Ovadiah, US Representative, Ecole de Langue Française pour Etrangers, 303 West 66th Street, New York, NY 10023; 212-724-5823; Fax: 212-496-2264

ECOLE DE LANGUE FRANÇAISE POUR ETRANGERS

INSTITUT PARISIEN

General Information • Language study program in Paris.
Learning Focus • Courses in French language, French literature, French civilization, French fashion.

Accommodations • Homestays, dormitories, hotels. Single rooms are available. Meals are taken with host family, in local restaurants.
Program Details • Program offered 21 times per year. Session length: 2 weeks. Departures are scheduled in January–December. The program is open to undergraduate students, graduate students, pre-college students, adults. Most participants are 18–60 years of age. 75 participants per session. Application deadline: 1 month prior to departure.
Costs • $1200 (includes tuition, housing, some meals). Application fee: $250. A $500 deposit is required.
Contact • Dr. Janice E. Ovadiah, US Representative, Ecole de Langue Française pour Etrangers, 303 West 66th Street, New York, NY 10023; 212-724-5823; Fax: 212-496-2264

ECOLE DE LANGUE FRANÇAISE POUR ETRANGERS

LA CUISINE DE MARIE–BLANCHE

General Information • Gourmet cooking/wine tour in Paris.
Learning Focus • Courses in French cooking.
Accommodations • Hotels. Single rooms are available. Meals are taken on one's own.
Program Details • Program offered 52 times per year. Session length: 1 week. Departures are scheduled in January–December. The program is open to undergraduate students, graduate students, pre-college students, adults. Most participants are 18–55 years of age. 8 participants per session. Application deadline: 1 month prior to departure.
Costs • $1200 (includes tuition, some meals). Application fee: $150. A $500 deposit is required.
Contact • Dr. Janice E. Ovadiah, US Representative, Ecole de Langue Française pour Etrangers, 303 West 66th Street, New York, NY 10023; 212-724-5823; Fax: 212-496-2264

EF INTERNATIONAL LANGUAGE SCHOOLS

FRENCH IN NICE

General Information • Language study program in Nice. Classes are held on the campus of EF Ecole Internationale de Français. Excursions to Monaco, Paris, Alps, Musée Chagall.
Learning Focus • Courses in French language. Instruction is offered by professors from the sponsoring institution and local teachers.
Accommodations • Homestays, dormitories. Single rooms are available. Meals are taken as a group, with host family, in central dining facility, in residences.
Program Details • Program offered 26 times per year. Session length: 2–12 weeks. Departures are scheduled in January–December. The program is open to undergraduate students, graduate students, pre-college students, adults. Most participants are 16–25 years of age. 40 participants per session. Application deadline: 60 days prior to departure.
Costs • Principal: $990 per 2 weeks, intensive: $1130 per 2 weeks (includes tuition, housing, some meals, books and class materials). Application fee: $90. A $350 deposit is required.
Contact • Kari Larson, Admissions Manager, EF International Language Schools, 204 Lake Street, Boston, MA 02135; 800-992-1892; Fax: 617-746-1800; E-mail: ils@ef.com

EF INTERNATIONAL LANGUAGE SCHOOLS

FRENCH IN REIMS

General Information • Language study program in Reims. Classes are held on the campus of EF Ecole Internationale de Français. Excursions to Paris, Versailles, Fontainebleau, England (London), Netherlands (Amsterdam), Alps.
Learning Focus • Courses in French language. Instruction is offered by professors from the sponsoring institution and local teachers.
Accommodations • Homestays, dormitories. Single rooms are available. Meals are taken as a group, with host family, in central dining facility, in residences.
Program Details • Program offered 26 times per year. Session length: 2–12 weeks. Departures are scheduled in January–December. The program is open to undergraduate students, graduate students, pre-college students, adults. Most participants are 16–25 years of age. Other requirements: minimum age of 16. 40 participants per session. Application deadline: 60 days prior to departure.
Costs • Principal: $990 per 2 weeks, intensive: $1130 per 2 weeks (includes tuition, housing, some meals, books and class materials). Application fee: $90. A $350 deposit is required.
Contact • Kari Larson, Admissions Manager, EF International Language Schools, 204 Lake Street, Boston, MA 02135; 800-992-1892; Fax: 617-746-1800; E-mail: ils@ef.com

EF International Language Schools is a division of EF Education and subscribes to the philosophy that one can best learn a language in the country where it is spoken. EF International Language Schools offers foreign language immersion programs in Spain, Ecuador, France, Germany, and Italy. Language classes are taught in up to 8 proficiency levels and are suitable for beginners as well as people with advanced linguistic skills. All courses include accommodations and meals in a host family or student residence. A wide variety of cultural, athletic, and social activities are offered for students during afternoons and weekends. Round-trip international flights can be arranged upon request.

ELFCA (INSTITUT INTERNATIONAL DE LANGUE FRANCAISE DE LA COTE D'AZUR)

FRENCH LANGUAGE PROGRAM

General Information • Language study program in Toulon.
Learning Focus • Courses in French language, civilizations.
Accommodations • Homestays, locally-rented apartments, hotels. Single rooms are available. Meals are taken with host family, in central dining facility, in local restaurants.

Program Details • Program offered 21 times per year. Session length: 2 or more weeks. Departures are scheduled in January–December. The program is open to undergraduate students, graduate students, pre-college students, adults. Most participants are 18–70 years of age. 80 participants per session. Application deadline: 1 month prior to departure.
Costs • $1050 for 2 weeks (includes tuition, housing, some meals). Application fee: $150. A $500 deposit is required.
Contact • Dr. Janice E. Ovadiah, US Representative, ELFCA (Institut International de Langue Francaise de la Cote d'Azur), 303 West 66th Street, #4HE, New York, NY 10023; 212-724-5823; Fax: 212-496-2264

EUROCENTRES

LANGUAGE IMMERSION IN FRANCE

General Information • Language study program in France (Amboise, La Rochelle, Paris), Switzerland (Switzerland (Lausanne, Neuchâtel)). Classes are held on the campus of Eurocentre Paris, Eurocentre Amboise, Eurocentre La Rochelle, Eurocentre Lausanne/Neuchâtel Summer Centre. Excursions to Rheims, Chambord, Switzerland (Geneva, Berne).
Learning Focus • Courses in French language, French culture. Instruction is offered by professors from the sponsoring institution.
Accommodations • Homestays, hotels. Single rooms are available. Meals are taken with host family, in residences.
Program Details • Program offered 20 times per year. Session length: 2–12 weeks. Departures are scheduled in January–December. The program is open to undergraduate students, graduate students, pre-college students, adults. Most participants are 16–80 years of age. 15 participants per session.
Costs • Contact sponsor for information.
Contact • Marketing, Eurocentres, 101 North Union Street, Suite 300, Alexandria, VA 22314; 800-648-4809; Fax: 703-684-1495; E-mail: 100632.141@compuserve.com; World Wide Web: http://www.clark.net/pub/eurocent/home.htm

EUROPEAN HERITAGE INSTITUTE

ART IN PARIS

General Information • Academic study program in Paris. Classes are held on the campus of Paris American Academy.
Learning Focus • Courses in painting, drawing, fashion, interior design, studio art, French language. Instruction is offered by local teachers.
Accommodations • Locally-rented apartments. Meals are taken on one's own.
Program Details • Program offered 2 times per year. Session length: 4 weeks. Departures are scheduled in June, July. The program is open to undergraduate students, graduate students, adults. Application deadline: 65 days prior to departure.
Costs • $3300 (includes tuition, housing). A $350 deposit is required.
Contact • Dr. Antonio Masullo, Professor, European Heritage Institute, 2708 East Franklin Street, Richmond, VA 23223; 804-648-0826; Fax: 804-648-0826; E-mail: euritage@i2020.net

EUROPEAN HERITAGE INSTITUTE

SUMMER PROGRAM IN PARIS

General Information • Academic study program in Paris. Classes are held on the campus of University of Paris-Sorbonne (Paris IV). Excursions to Mont St. Michel, Avignon.
Learning Focus • Courses in French language, literature, civilizations, grammar, contemporary France.
Accommodations • Homestays, locally-rented apartments. Meals are taken on one's own.
Program Details • Program offered 4 times per year. Session length: 4–8 weeks. Departures are scheduled in June, July, August, September. The program is open to undergraduate students, graduate students, adults. Application deadline: March 1, April 1, May 15, June 1.
Costs • $990–$2375 (includes tuition).
Contact • Dr. Antonio Masullo, Professor, European Heritage Institute, 2708 East Franklin Street, Richmond, VA 23223; 804-648-0826; Fax: 804-648-0826; E-mail: euritage@i2020.net

EXPERIENCE PLUS SPECIALTY TOURS, INC.

CYCLING THE DORDOGNE–FRANCE

General Information • Bicycle tour with visits to Brike La Gaillarde, Rocamadour, Sarlat, St. Emilion, Lascaux Caves, Sarlat, Rocamadour, Monbazillac, Côtes de Bergerac, St. Emilion. Once at the destination country, participants travel by bicycle.
Learning Focus • Escorted travel to the Dorgogne River Valley. Other activities include bicycling, castle visits, wine tastings. Instruction is offered by professors, indigenous, bilingual and bi-cultural guides. This program would appeal to people interested in bicycling, gourmet food, wine, culture, travel, France.
Accommodations • Hotels. Single rooms are available for an additional $300.
Program Details • Program offered 3 times per year. Session length: 11 days. Departures are scheduled in June–August. Most participants are 35–70 years of age. 16–22 participants per session. Reservations are recommended at least 6–12 months before departure.
Costs • $2095 (includes housing, some meals, excursions, wine tastings, gourmet dinners, quality rental bike, luggage shuttle, van support, bilingual/bi-cultural tour leaders). A $250 deposit is required.
Contact • Experience Plus Specialty Tours, Inc., 1925 Wallenberg Drive, Fort Collins, CO 80526; 800-685-4565; Fax: 800-685-4565; E-mail: tours@xplus.com

EXPERIENCE PLUS SPECIALTY TOURS, INC.

PROVENCE AND THE SOUTH OF FRANCE

General Information • Bicycle tour with visits to Aix-en-Provence, Arles, Luberon Regional Park, Sete, Mont Ste. Victoire, St. Rémy, Pont-du-Gard, The Cevennes. Once at the destination country, participants travel by bicycle.
Learning Focus • Escorted travel to Provence and the South of France. Other activities include bicycling visit to the

ancient ruins of Bories. Instruction is offered by professors, indigenous, bilingual and bi-cultural guides. This program would appeal to people interested in bicycling, gourmet food, wine, culture, travel, France, history.
Accommodations • Hotels. Single rooms are available for an additional $300.
Program Details • Program offered 4 times per year. Session length: 11 days. Departures are scheduled in May–October. Most participants are 35–70 years of age. 16–22 participants per session. Reservations are recommended at least 6–12 months before departure.
Costs • $2095 (includes housing, some meals, quality rental bike, water bottle, shirt, luggage shuttle, van support, bilingual/bi-cultural tour leaders). A $250 deposit is required.
Contact • Experience Plus Specialty Tours, Inc., 1925 Wallenberg Drive, Fort Collins, CO 80526; 800-685-4565; Fax: 800-685-4565; E-mail: tours@xplus.com

FOREIGN LANGUAGE STUDY ABROAD SERVICE

FRENCH IN FRANCE

General Information • Language study program in Aix-en-Provence, Avignon, Bordeaux, Brest, Nice, Paris, St. Malo, Tours, Vichy.
Learning Focus • Courses in language study. Instruction is offered by local teachers.
Accommodations • Homestays, hotels. Single rooms are available. Meals are taken on one's own, with host family, in local restaurants, in residences.
Program Details • Session length: varies. Departures are scheduled in January–December. The program is open to undergraduate students, graduate students, pre-college students, adults. Most participants are 16 years of age and older.
Costs • Contact sponsor for information. Application fee: $50. A $100 deposit is required.
Contact • Louise Harber, Coordinator, Foreign Language Study Abroad Service, Department IH, Box 903, 5935 Southwest 64th Avenue, South Miami, FL 33143; 800-282-1090; Fax: 305-662-2907; E-mail: flsas@netpoint.net; World Wide Web: http://www.netpoint.net/~flsas

FOREIGN LANGUAGE STUDY ABROAD SERVICE

INTERNATIONAL LANGUAGE STUDY HOMESTAYS IN FRANCE

General Information • Language study program in France.
Learning Focus • Courses in French language. Instruction is offered by local teachers.
Accommodations • Homestays. Single rooms are available. Meals are taken with host family, in residences.
Program Details • Session length: varies. Departures are scheduled in January–December. The program is open to undergraduate students, graduate students, pre-college students, adults. Most participants are 12 years of age and older. Other requirements: students must be at least 12 years old. 1 participant per session.
Costs • Contact sponsor for information. A $300 deposit is required.
Contact • Louise Harber, Coordinator, Foreign Language Study Abroad Service, Department IH, Box 903, 5935 Southwest 64th Avenue, South Miami, FL 33143; 800-282-1090; Fax: 305-662-2907; E-mail: flsas@netpoint.net; World Wide Web: http://www.netpoint.net/~flsas

FORUM TRAVEL INTERNATIONAL

CASTLES, WINES, AND EPICUREAN DELIGHTS IN TOURAINE

General Information • Bicycle tour with visits to Joue-les-Tours, Loire Valley. Once at the destination country, participants travel by bicycle.
Learning Focus • Instruction in art history. Escorted travel to castles. Other activities include cycling. Instruction is offered by artists, historians, architects. This program would appeal to people interested in history, wine, the outdoors, culture.
Accommodations • Hotels. Single rooms are available for an additional $230.
Program Details • Session length: 8 days. Departures are scheduled in May–October. Most participants are 16–60 years of age. Participants must be 16 years or older to enroll. 2 participants per session. Application deadline: 60 days prior to departure. Reservations are recommended at least 3–5 months before departure.
Costs • $863 (includes housing, some meals, luggage transport). A $200 deposit is required.
Contact • Jeannie Graves, Operations Manager, Forum Travel International, 91 Gregory Lane #21, Pleasant Hill, CA 94525; 510-671-2900; Fax: 510-671-2993; E-mail: forum@ix.netcom.com; World Wide Web: http://www.ten-io.com/forumtravel

FOURTH WORLD MOVEMENT

INTERNATIONAL WORKCAMPS

General Information • Volunteer service program with visits to Méry Sur Oise. Program is affiliated with ATD Quart Monde.
Learning Focus • Instruction in manual work. Volunteer work (assist extremely poor families in everyday needs). Other activities include manual work to discover a possible commitment with very poor families. Instruction is offered by full-time Fourth World volunteers. This program would appeal to people interested in social interests.
Accommodations • Campsites.
Program Details • Program offered 3 times per year. Session length: 2 weeks. Departures are scheduled in July, August, September. Most participants are 18–35 years of age. Participants must be 18 years or older to enroll. Other requirements: willingness to work in a team and to learn about families living in extreme poverty and their movement. 30 participants per session. Reservations are recommended at least 3 months before departure.
Costs • $100 (includes housing, all meals).
Contact • ATD-Fourth World-Summer Activities, Fourth World Movement, BP 7726, Cergy Pontaise Cedex 45046, France; +33 1-3421-6969; Fax: +33 1-34-21-69-70

FRANCE IN YOUR GLASS

ECOLE DU BORDEAUX

General Information • Gourmet cooking/wine tour with visits to Bordeaux, wine chateaux. Once at the destination country, participants travel by mini-van.
Learning Focus • Instruction in wine tasting. Field research in enology and viticulture. Escorted travel to wine chateaux. Instruction is offered by professors, scientists, wine makers. This program would appeal to people interested in wine.
Accommodations • Hotels. Single rooms are available.
Program Details • Session length: 2–5 days. Departures are scheduled in March–November. Program is targeted to wine lovers. Most participants are 25–65 years of age. 2–6 participants per session. Reservations are recommended at least 2 months before departure.
Costs • $2995 (includes tuition, housing, all meals, excursions). A $1000 deposit is required.
Contact • Andrea Mielke, Director of Marketing, France in Your Glass, 814 35th Avenue, Seattle, WA 98122; 800-578-0903; Fax: 800-578-7069; E-mail: ronald@inyourglass.com; World Wide Web: http://www.inyourglass.com

FRENCH-AMERICAN EXCHANGE

INTENSIVE LANGUAGE PROGRAM IN SOUTHERN FRANCE

General Information • Language study program in Montpellier. Classes are held on the campus of Institute Linguistique du Peyrou. Excursions to Paris, Avignon, La Camargue, Aigue Mortes, Nîmes, Mediterranean beaches.
Learning Focus • Courses in French language, French culture, French literature. Instruction is offered by local teachers.
Accommodations • Homestays, dormitories, locally-rented apartments, hotels. Single rooms are available. Meals are taken in local restaurants, in residences.
Program Details • Program offered 9 times per year. Session length: 2–8 weeks. Departures are scheduled in January–December. The program is open to undergraduate students, adults, independent travelers and seniors. Most participants are 20–70 years of age. Other requirements: minimum age of 19. 4 participants per session. Application deadline: 2 months prior to departure.
Costs • $2455 (includes tuition, housing, all meals, international airfare). A $500 deposit is required.
Contact • Jim Pondolfino, Executive Director, French-American Exchange, 111 Roberts Court, Box 7, Alexandria, VA 22314; 703-549-5087; Fax: 703-683-8444

Montpellier, just 8 km from the Mediterranean Sea and long sandy beaches, has been a reputable university and cultural center since the Middle Ages. Today, Montpellier is also well-known for its warm climate and the beauty of its natural sites. The region is host to national music, dance, and theater festivals during the summer and offers numerous attractions throughout the year, including bullfights.

"Staying with a French host family was the greatest aspect of my stay in France. I would definitely recommend it!" — a former student.

"The visit to Paris was a great beginning to my program. Everyone should see Paris!" — a former student.

GEORGE MASON UNIVERSITY

TOULON INTENSIVE FRENCH LANGUAGE AND CULTURE

General Information • Language study program in Toulon. Classes are held on the campus of University of Toulon. Excursions to Les Villages medievaux, Marseille, Hoedic, St. Tropez, Nice-Monaco.
Learning Focus • Courses in language study, cultural studies. Instruction is offered by professors from the sponsoring institution.
Accommodations • Dormitories. Meals are taken as a group, in residences.
Program Details • Program offered once per year. Session length: 4 weeks. Departures are scheduled in July, August. The program is open to undergraduate students, adults. Most participants are 18–65 years of age. Other requirements: minimum 2.25 GPA. 10–15 participants per session. Application deadline: April.
Costs • $3120 for George Mason University students, $3670 for other students (includes tuition, housing, insurance, excursions). Application fee: $35. A $500 deposit is required.
Contact • Dr. Yehuda Lukacs, Director, Center for Global Education, George Mason University, 4400 University Drive, 235 Johnson Center, Fairfax, VA 22030; 703-993-2155; Fax: 703-993-2153; E-mail: ylukacs@gmu.edu; World Wide Web: http://www.gmu.edu/departments/oie

GEORGETOWN UNIVERSITY

SUMMER IN TOURS, FRANCE

General Information • Language study program in Tours. Classes are held on the campus of Institut de Touraine. Excursions to chateaux in Loire Valley, Mont St. Michel.
Learning Focus • Courses in language study, business French, civilizations, cultural studies, literature. Instruction is offered by professors from the sponsoring institution and local teachers.
Accommodations • Homestays, dormitories. Single rooms are available. Meals are taken as a group, with host family, in central dining facility, in residences.
Program Details • Program offered once per year. Session length: 6 weeks. Departures are scheduled in June, July. The program is open to undergraduate students, graduate students, pre-college students, adults, high school students, teachers and professionals. Most participants are 18–22 years of age. 38 participants per session. Application deadline: March.
Costs • $3200 (includes housing, some meals, books and class materials, insurance, excursions). A $100 deposit is required.
Contact • Marianne T. Needham, Director, International Programs, Georgetown University, 306 ICC, Box 571012,

Washington, DC 20057-1012; 202-687-6184; Fax: 202-687-8954; E-mail: sscefps1@gunet.georgetown.edu; World Wide Web: http://guweb.georgetown.edu/ssce

HOFSTRA UNIVERSITY

HOFSTRA IN NICE

General Information • Language study program in Nice. Classes are held on the campus of Université de Nice.
Learning Focus • Courses in French language. Instruction is offered by professors from the sponsoring institution and local teachers.
Accommodations • Homestays. Meals are taken with host family.
Program Details • Program offered once per year. Session length: 5 weeks. Departures are scheduled in June or July. The program is open to undergraduate students, graduate students, pre-college students, adults. Most participants are 18 years of age and older. Other requirements: 1 year of college French or equivalent. 20 participants per session. Application deadline: May 15.
Costs • $3800 (includes tuition, housing, all meals, excursions). A $200 deposit is required.
Contact • Hofstra University, Department of French, Hofstra University, Hempstead, NY 11550; 516-463-5484; Fax: 516-463-4848; E-mail: frerma@hofstra.edu

HOOD COLLEGE

MAY TERM IN STRASBOURG–EUROPEAN ECONOMY

General Information • Academic study program in Strasbourg. Excursions to Alsace, Paris, Germany.
Learning Focus • Courses in economics. Instruction is offered by professors from the sponsoring institution.
Accommodations • Hostels, hotels. Single rooms are available. Meals are taken as a group.
Program Details • Program offered once per year. Session length: 3 weeks. Departures are scheduled in May. The program is open to undergraduate students. Most participants are 18–60 years of age. Other requirements: introductory economics course. 8 participants per session. Application deadline: February 1.
Costs • $2600 (includes tuition, housing, some meals, excursions, international airfare, tour of European parliament, museum fees). A $400 deposit is required.
Contact • Loretta M. Bassler, Associate Dean of Academic Affairs, Hood College, 401 Rosemont Avenue, Frederick, MD 21701; 301-698-3599; Fax: 301-894-7653; E-mail: bassler@nimue.hood.edu

ILLINOIS STATE UNIVERSITY

SUMMER INSTITUTE IN FRENCH

General Information • Language study program in Grenoble. Classes are held on the campus of University of Grenoble.
Learning Focus • Courses in civilizations, cultural studies, French language, literature.
Accommodations • Dormitories.
Program Details • Program offered once per year. Session length: 8 weeks. Departures are scheduled in June. The program is open to undergraduate students, graduate students. Other requirements: minimum 2.5 GPA and a minimum of sophomore status. 15 participants per session. Application deadline: March 15.
Costs • $3100 (includes tuition, housing, some meals, excursions).
Contact • Dr. George Petrossian, Illinois State University, Mail Code 4300, Normal, IL 61790-4300; 309-438-3604; Fax: 309-438-3987; World Wide Web: http://www.orat.ilstu.edu/

INSTITUTE FOR AMERICAN UNIVERSITIES (IAU)

ART IN PROVENCE–THE MARCHUTZ SCHOOL

General Information • Academic study program in Aix-en-Provence. Excursions to Arles, The Vaucluse, St. Remy, Aix countryside.
Learning Focus • Courses in painting, aesthetics, drawing, art history. Instruction is offered by professors from the sponsoring institution.
Accommodations • Homestays, locally-rented apartments. Meals are taken on one's own, with host family.
Program Details • Program offered once per year. Session length: 6 weeks. Departures are scheduled in June. The program is open to undergraduate students, graduate students, pre-college students, adults, students and adults with an interest in and a commitment to art. Most participants are 18–25 years of age. 15–20 participants per session. Application deadline: rolling.
Costs • $2910 (includes tuition, housing, books and class materials, insurance, excursions). Application fee: $45. A $500 deposit is required.
Contact • Linda Proctor, Coordinator, IAU United States Office, Institute for American Universities (IAU), PO Box 592, 1830 Sherman Avenue at University Place, Evanston, IL 60204; 800-221-2051; Fax: 847-864-6897; E-mail: iauadm@univ-aix.fr; World Wide Web: http://www.univ-aix.fr/iau/iau.html

INSTITUTE FOR AMERICAN UNIVERSITIES (IAU)

INTENSIVE FRENCH

General Information • Academic study program in Aix-en-Provence.
Learning Focus • Courses in French language. Instruction is offered by professors from the sponsoring institution.
Accommodations • Homestays, locally-rented apartments. Meals are taken on one's own, with host family.
Program Details • Program offered once per year. Session length: 6 weeks. Departures are scheduled in June. The program is open to undergraduate students, adults, people at least 18 years old. Most participants are 18–22 years of age. Other requirements: intermediate-level French proficiency. 6–8 participants per session. Application deadline: rolling.
Costs • $2910 (includes tuition, housing, some meals, books and class materials, insurance, excursions). Application fee: $45. A $500 deposit is required.
Contact • Linda Proctor, Coordinator, IAU United States Office, Institute for American Universities (IAU), PO Box 592, 1830 Sherman Avenue at University Place, Evanston, IL 60204; 800-221-2051; Fax: 847-864-6897; E-mail: iauadm@univ-aix.fr; World Wide Web: http://www.univ-aix.fr/iau/iau.html

INSTITUTE FOR AMERICAN UNIVERSITIES (IAU)

LE CENTRE D'AIX

General Information • Academic study program in Aix-en-Provence. Excursions to The Vaucluse, Arles, St. Remy, Nîmes, Les Baux, St. Paul de Vence, Antibes.
Learning Focus • Courses in art history, international business, French language and literature, economics, government. Instruction is offered by professors from the sponsoring institution.
Accommodations • Homestays, locally-rented apartments. Meals are taken on one's own, with host family.
Program Details • Program offered once per year. Session length: 6 weeks. Departures are scheduled in June. The program is open to undergraduate students, adults, people at least 18 years old. Most participants are 18–22 years of age. Other requirements: minimum 3.0 GPA. 90 participants per session. Application deadline: rolling.
Costs • $2910 (includes tuition, housing, some meals, books and class materials, insurance, excursions). Application fee: $45. A $500 deposit is required.
Contact • Linda Proctor, Coordinator, IAU United States Office, Institute for American Universities (IAU), PO Box 592, 1830 Sherman Avenue at University Place, Evanston, IL 60204; 800-221-2051; Fax: 847-864-6897; E-mail: iauadm@univ-aix.fr; World Wide Web: http://www.univ-aix.fr/iau/iau.html

INSTITUTE FOR AMERICAN UNIVERSITIES (IAU)

LE CENTRE D'AVIGNON

General Information • Academic study program in Avignon. Excursions to Arles, Marseille, Luberon Valley.
Learning Focus • Courses in French language, French literature, art history. Instruction is offered by professors from the sponsoring institution.
Accommodations • Homestays, locally-rented apartments. Meals are taken on one's own, with host family.
Program Details • Program offered once per year. Session length: 6 weeks. Departures are scheduled in June. The program is open to undergraduate students, adults, people at least 18 years old. Other requirements: minimum 3.0 GPA and 2 years college French. Application deadline: rolling.
Costs • $2910 (includes tuition, housing, some meals, books and class materials, insurance, excursions). Application fee: $45. A $500 deposit is required.
Contact • Linda Proctor, Coordinator, IAU United States Office, Institute for American Universities (IAU), PO Box 592, 1830 Sherman Avenue at University Place, Evanston, IL 60204; 800-221-2051; Fax: 847-864-6897; E-mail: iauadm@univ-aix.fr; World Wide Web: http://www.univ-aix.fr/iau/iau.html

INSTITUTE OF EUROPEAN STUDIES/INSTITUTE OF ASIAN STUDIES

PARIS SUMMER PROGRAM

General Information • Academic study program in Paris. Classes are held on the campus of Institut d'Etudes Européeunes. Excursions to Loire Valley, sites in Paris.
Learning Focus • Courses in language study, literature, art history, history. Instruction is offered by professors from the sponsoring institution.
Accommodations • Homestays. Single rooms are available. Meals are taken on one's own, in local restaurants.
Program Details • Program offered once per year. Session length: 6 weeks. Departures are scheduled in June. The program is open to undergraduate students, graduate students, continuing education students. Most participants are 20–50 years of age. 52 participants per session. Application deadline: April 15.
Costs • $2900 (includes tuition, housing, some meals, excursions). Application fee: $25.
Contact • Department of Admissions, Institute of European Studies/Institute of Asian Studies, 223 West Ohio Street, Chicago, IL 60610-4196; 800-995-2300; Fax: 312-944-1448; E-mail: recruit@iesias.org; World Wide Web: http://www.iesias.org

INSTITUT FRANCAIS DES ALPES ET DE MÉDITERRANÉE

LANGUAGE PROGRAM

General Information • Language study program in Megeve.
Learning Focus • Courses in French language, skiing.
Accommodations • Hotels. Single rooms are available. Meals are taken as a group, in central dining facility.
Program Details • Program offered 12 times per year. Session length: 12 weeks. Departures are scheduled in January–March. The program is open to undergraduate students, graduate students, pre-college students, adults. Most participants are 18–60 years of age. 60 participants per session. Application deadline: 1 month prior to departure.
Costs • $2500 (includes tuition, housing, all meals). Application fee: $150. A $500 deposit is required.
Contact • Dr. Janice E. Ovadiah, US Representative, Institut Francais des Alpes et de Méditerranée, 303 West 66th Street, #4HE, New York, NY 10023-6305; 212-724-5823; Fax: 212-496-2264

INTERHOSTEL, UNIVERSITY OF NEW HAMPSHIRE

ALSACE AND LORRAINE, FRANCE

General Information • Cultural tour with visits to Klingenthal, Nancy, Paris, Domremy, Metz, Vosges Mountains, Mont Sainte Odile, Obernai, Colmar, Riquewhir, Kaysersberg, Strasbourg. Once at the destination country, participants travel by bus, foot, boat. Program is affiliated with American University of Paris.
Learning Focus • Instruction in history and culture. Escorted travel to villages and landmarks. Museum visits (Historical Museum of Lorraine, Unterlinden Museum). Instruction is offered by professors. This program would appeal to people interested in history, culture.
Accommodations • Hotels. Single rooms are available for an additional $400.
Program Details • Program offered once per year. Session length: 2 weeks. Departures are scheduled in August. Program is targeted to seniors over 50. Most participants are 60–80 years of age. Participants must be 50 years or older to

enroll. 35 participants per session. Reservations are recommended at least 6 months before departure.
Costs • $2975 (includes tuition, housing, all meals, excursions, international airfare, entrance fees). A $200 deposit is required.
Contact • Janice Pierson, Office Supervisor, Interhostel, University of New Hampshire, 6 Garrison Avenue, Durham, NH 03824; 800-733-9753; Fax: 603-862-1113; World Wide Web: http://www.learn.unh.edu/

INTERHOSTEL, UNIVERSITY OF NEW HAMPSHIRE

APRIL IN PARIS, FRANCE

General Information • Cultural tour with visits to Paris, Notre Dame, Sainte Chapelle, Marais District, Giverny, Versailles. Once at the destination country, participants travel by bus, foot, boat. Program is affiliated with American University of Paris.
Learning Focus • Instruction in history and culture. Escorted travel to cities and landmarks. Museum visits (Louvre, d'Orsay, Carnavalet). Instruction is offered by professors. This program would appeal to people interested in history, culture.
Accommodations • Hotels. Single rooms are available for an additional $275.
Program Details • Program offered 2 times per year. Session length: 9 days. Departures are scheduled in April. Program is targeted to seniors over 50. Most participants are 60–80 years of age. Participants must be 50 years or older to enroll. 35 participants per session. Reservations are recommended at least 6 months before departure.
Costs • $1995 (includes tuition, housing, all meals, excursions, international airfare, entrance fees). A $200 deposit is required.
Contact • Janice Pierson, Office Supervisor, Interhostel, University of New Hampshire, 6 Garrison Avenue, Durham, NH 03824; 800-733-9753; Fax: 603-862-1113; World Wide Web: http://www.learn.unh.edu/

INTERHOSTEL, UNIVERSITY OF NEW HAMPSHIRE

CHRISTMAS IN FRANCE

General Information • Cultural tour with visits to Alsace, Paris, Strasbourg, Riquewihr, Colmar, Fontainebleau, Chartres, Versailles. Once at the destination country, participants travel by train, bus, foot. Program is affiliated with American University of Paris.
Learning Focus • Instruction in history, culture and Christmas traditions. Escorted travel to cities and landmarks. Museum visits (Louvre, d'Orsay, Unterlinden). Attendance at performances (organ concert, opera or ballet). Instruction is

offered by professors. This program would appeal to people interested in history, culture, Christmas traditions.
Accommodations • Hotels. Single rooms are available for an additional $550.
Program Details • Program offered once per year. Session length: 2 weeks. Departures are scheduled in December. Program is targeted to seniors over 50. Most participants are 60–80 years of age. Participants must be 50 years or older to enroll. 35 participants per session. Reservations are recommended at least 6 months before departure.
Costs • $2995 (includes tuition, housing, all meals, excursions, international airfare, entrance fees).
Contact • Janice Pierson, Office Supervisor, Interhostel, University of New Hampshire, 6 Garrison Avenue, Durham, NH 03824-3529; 800-733-9753; Fax: 603-862-1113; World Wide Web: http://www.learn.unh.edu/

INTERHOSTEL, UNIVERSITY OF NEW HAMPSHIRE

PARIS AND THE BASQUE COUNTRY, FRANCE

General Information • Cultural tour with visits to Biarritz, Paris, Giverny, Versailles, St. Jean de Luz, Cambo, St. Jean Pied-de-Port, Ascain, Bayonne Pau, Lourdes, Fuentarrabia, Ainhoa. Once at the destination country, participants travel by train, bus, foot. Program is affiliated with American University of Paris.
Learning Focus • Instruction in history and culture. Escorted travel to historical sites. Museum visits (Louvre, d'Orsay, Bonnat). Instruction is offered by professors. This program would appeal to people interested in history, culture.
Accommodations • Hotels. Single rooms are available for an additional $375.
Program Details • Program offered 2 times per year. Session length: 2 weeks. Departures are scheduled in May. Program is targeted to seniors over 50. Most participants are 60–80 years of age. Participants must be 50 years or older to enroll. 35 participants per session. Reservations are recommended at least 6 months before departure.
Costs • $2775 (includes tuition, housing, all meals, excursions, international airfare, entrance fees). A $200 deposit is required.
Contact • Janice Pierson, Office Supervisor, Interhostel, University of New Hampshire, 6 Garrison Avenue, Durham, NH 03824; 800-733-9753; Fax: 603-862-1113; World Wide Web: http://www.learn.unh.edu/

INTERHOSTEL, UNIVERSITY OF NEW HAMPSHIRE

PARIS, NORMANDY AND THE LOIRE VALLEY, FRANCE

General Information • Cultural tour with visits to Bayeux, Blois, Mont St. Michel, Paris, Arromanches, Caen, Amboise, Chaumont Chateau, Beauregard Chateau, Chambord, Chenonceau, Chartres, Giverny, Versailles, Fontainebleau. Once at the destination country, participants travel by bus, foot.
Learning Focus • Instruction in history and culture. Escorted travel to chateaus. Museum visits (Louvre, Museum of Normandy). Instruction is offered by professors, historians. This program would appeal to people interested in history, culture.
Accommodations • Hotels. Single rooms are available for an additional $425.
Program Details • Program offered once per year. Session length: 2 weeks. Departures are scheduled in July. Program is targeted to seniors over 50. Most participants are 60–80 years of age. Participants must be 50 years or older to enroll. 35 participants per session. Reservations are recommended at least 6 months before departure.
Costs • $3075 (includes tuition, housing, all meals, excursions, international airfare, entrance fees). A $200 deposit is required.
Contact • Janice Pierson, Office Supervisor, Interhostel, University of New Hampshire, 6 Garrison Avenue, Durham, NH 03824; 800-733-9753; Fax: 603-862-1113; World Wide Web: http://www.learn.unh.edu/

INTERHOSTEL, UNIVERSITY OF NEW HAMPSHIRE

PROVENCE AND THE RIVIERA, FRANCE

General Information • Cultural tour with visits to Nice, Tarascon, Pont Du Gard, Nimes, Aigues Mortes, Avlgnon, Orange, Les Baux de Provence, Aix-en-Provence, Marseille, St. Tropez, Cannes. Once at the destination country, participants travel by bus, foot. Program is affiliated with American University of Paris.
Learning Focus • Instruction in history and culture. Escorted travel to historical sites. Museum visits (Fine Arts Museum of Marseille, Archaeological Museum of Nice). Instruction is offered by professors, historians. This program would appeal to people interested in history, culture.
Accommodations • Hotels. Single rooms are available for an additional $400.
Program Details • Program offered 2 times per year. Session length: 2 weeks. Departures are scheduled in June. Program is targeted to seniors over 50. Most participants are 60–80 years of age. Participants must be 50 years or older to enroll. 35 participants per session. Reservations are recommended at least 6 months before departure.
Costs • $3055 (includes tuition, housing, all meals, excursions, international airfare, entrance fees). A $200 deposit is required.
Contact • Janice Pierson, Office Supervisor, Interhostel, University of New Hampshire, 6 Garrison Avenue, Durham, NH 03824; 800-733-9753; Fax: 603-862-1113; World Wide Web: http://www.learn.unh.edu/

INTERHOSTEL, UNIVERSITY OF NEW HAMPSHIRE

TOULOUSE AND THE DORDOGNE VALLEY, FRANCE

General Information • Cultural tour with visits to Paris, Rocamadour, Sarlat, Toulouse, Albi, Ste. Cecile, Carcasonne, Cahors, Gouffre de Padirac, St. Ciro-Lapopie, Pech Merle, Lascaux II. Once at the destination country, participants travel by bus, foot, boat. Program is affiliated with American University of Paris.
Learning Focus • Instruction in history, culture and archaeology. Escorted travel to cities and landmarks.

Museum visits (National Museum of Prehistory, Louvre, D'Orsay). Instruction is offered by professors, site guides. This program would appeal to people interested in history, culture, archaeology.
Accommodations • Hotels. Single rooms are available for an additional $450.
Program Details • Program offered once per year. Session length: 2 weeks. Departures are scheduled in June. Program is targeted to seniors over 50. Most participants are 60–80 years of age. Participants must be 50 years or older to enroll. 35 participants per session. Reservations are recommended at least 6 months before departure.
Costs • $3065 (includes tuition, housing, all meals, excursions, international airfare, entrance fees). A $200 deposit is required.
Contact • Janice Pierson, Office Supervisor, Interhostel, University of New Hampshire, 6 Garrison Avenue, Durham, NH 03824; 800-733-9753; Fax: 603-862-1113; World Wide Web: http://www.learn.unh.edu/

INTERHOSTEL, UNIVERSITY OF NEW HAMPSHIRE

WALKING IN FRANCE: BORDEAUX AND THE DORDOGNE VALLEY

General Information • Cultural tour with visits to Bordeaux, Paris, Rocamadour, Sarlat, Villan Drault, Cadillac, Gouffre de Padirac, Peche Merle, Lascaux II, La Roque St. Christophe, St. Emilion. Once at the destination country, participants travel by bus, foot. Program is affiliated with The American University of Paris.
Learning Focus • Instruction in history, prehistory and culture. Escorted travel to villages and landmarks. Museum visits (Musée d'Orsay, Louvre, Museum of Aquitaine). Nature observation (walk through pine forest). Other activities include hiking. Instruction is offered by professors, naturalists, historians. This program would appeal to people interested in walking, history, pre-history, culture.
Accommodations • Hotels. Single rooms are available for an additional $425.
Program Details • Program offered once per year. Session length: 2 weeks. Departures are scheduled in September. Program is targeted to senior walkers. Most participants are 60–75 years of age. Participants must be 50 years or older to enroll. 25 participants per session. Reservations are recommended at least 3 months before departure.
Costs • $3065 (includes tuition, housing, all meals, excursions, international airfare, entrance fees). A $200 deposit is required.
Contact • Janice Pierson, Office Supervisor, Interhostel, University of New Hampshire, 6 Garrison Avenue, Durham, NH 03824-3529; 800-733-9753; Fax: 603-862-1113; World Wide Web: http://www.learn.unh.edu/

INTERNATIONAL STUDIES ABROAD

INSTITUT DE TOURAINE

General Information • Language study program in Tours. Classes are held on the campus of Institut de Touraine. Excursions to Paris, Mont St. Michel, Versailles, Angers.
Learning Focus • Courses in grammar, cultural studies, history, literature, business. Instruction is offered by local teachers.
Accommodations • Homestays. Single rooms are available. Meals are taken with host family.
Program Details • Program offered 2 times per year. Session length: 4 weeks. Departures are scheduled in June, July. The program is open to undergraduate students, graduate students, pre-college students, adults. Most participants are 18–24 years of age. Other requirements: minimum 2.5 GPA and a letter of recommendation. 10 participants per session. Application deadline: April 5.
Costs • $3300 (includes tuition, housing, all meals, insurance, excursions, resident director, tutoring, entrance fees, ground transportation). A $200 deposit is required.
Contact • Gustavo Artaza, Director, International Studies Abroad, 817 West 24th Street, Austin, TX 78705; 800-580-8826; Fax: 512-480-8866; E-mail: 76331.336@compuserve.com

INTERNATIONAL STUDIES ABROAD

UNIVERSITÉ CATHOLIQUE DE L'OUEST

General Information • Language study program in Angers. Excursions to Paris, Mont San Michel, Versailles, Tours.
Learning Focus • Courses in grammar, cultural studies, history, literature, business. Instruction is offered by local teachers.
Accommodations • Homestays. Single rooms are available. Meals are taken in central dining facility.
Program Details • Program offered 2 times per year. Session length: 4 weeks. Departures are scheduled in June, July. The program is open to undergraduate students, graduate students, pre-college students, adults. Most participants are 18–24 years of age. Other requirements: minimum 2.5 GPA and a letter of recommendation. 10 participants per session. Application deadline: April 5.
Costs • $3300 (includes tuition, housing, some meals, insurance, excursions, ground transportation, entrance fees, tutoring, resident director). A $200 deposit is required.
Contact • Gustavo Artaza, Director, International Studies Abroad, 817 West 24th Street, Austin, TX 78705; 800-580-8826; Fax: 512-480-8866; E-mail: 76331.336@compuserve.com

IONA COLLEGE

IONA IN PARIS

General Information • Academic and language study program in Paris. Classes are held on the campus of Catholic Institute of Paris. Excursions to La Rochelle.
Learning Focus • Courses in French language, history and culture. Instruction is offered by professors from the sponsoring institution and local teachers.
Accommodations • Dormitories. Single rooms are available. Meals are taken as a group, in central dining facility.
Program Details • Program offered once per year. Session length: 4 weeks. Departures are scheduled in July. The program is open to undergraduate students. Most partici-

pants are 19–22 years of age. Other requirements: minimum 2.3 GPA. 20 participants per session. Application deadline: May 1.
Costs • $2200 (includes tuition, housing, some meals, insurance, excursions, international airfare). A $200 deposit is required.
Contact • Madame van den Bossche, Director of International Studies, Iona College, 715 North Avenue, New Rochelle, NY 10801-1890; 914-633-2695

KENTUCKY INSTITUTE FOR INTERNATIONAL STUDIES

PROGRAM IN AUTUN AND PARIS, FRANCE

General Information • Academic study program in Autun, Paris. Excursions to surrounding area.
Learning Focus • Courses in language study, humanities, English language. Instruction is offered by professors from the sponsoring institution.
Accommodations • Dormitories, pensiones. Meals are taken as a group.
Program Details • Program offered once per year. Session length: 5 weeks. Departures are scheduled in May. The program is open to undergraduate students, graduate students, pre-college students, adults, professionals. Most participants are 18–28 years of age. Other requirements: minimum 2.0 GPA, letter of recommendation from faculty member, good academic standing at home institution. 30 participants per session. Application deadline: March 1.
Costs • $2940 for students of consortia schools, $3240 for other students (includes tuition, housing, some meals, international airfare). Application fee: $50.
Contact • Dr. J. Milton Grimes, Executive Director, Kentucky Institute for International Studies, Murray State University, PO Box 9, Murray, KY 42071-0009; 502-762-3091; Fax: 502-762-3434; E-mail: kiismsu@msumusik.mursuky.edu; World Wide Web: http://www.berea.edu/KIIS/kiis.html

LANGUAGE IMMERSION INSTITUTE

FRANCE

General Information • Language study program with visits to Hyères. Once at the destination country, participants travel by train, bus, foot, airplane. Program is affiliated with ELFCA.
Learning Focus • Instruction in the French language. Instruction is offered by professors. This program would appeal to people interested in the French language.
Accommodations • Homestays, locally-rented apartments, hotels. Single rooms are available.
Program Details • Session length: 2 or more weeks. Departures are scheduled throughout the year. Program is targeted to adult professionals. Most participants are 20–70 years of age. Participants must be 18 years or older to enroll. Other requirements: students must be at least advanced beginners.
Costs • Contact sponsor for information.
Contact • Henry Urbanski, Director, Language Immersion Institute, Language Immersion Institute, 75 South Manheim Boulevard, New Paltz, NY 12561; 914-257-3500; Fax: 914-257-3569; E-mail: lii@newpaltz.edu

LANGUAGE LIAISON

CENTRE D'ETUDES LINGUISTIQUES D'AVIGNON (CELA)–LEARN FRENCH IN AVIGNON

General Information • Language study program with visits to France.
Learning Focus • Instruction in the French language. Instruction is offered by professors. This program would appeal to people interested in language.
Accommodations • Homestays, locally-rented apartments, hotels. Single rooms are available.
Program Details • Session length: unlimited. Departures are scheduled throughout the year. Program is targeted to students of any age. Most participants are 18–70 years of age. Participants must be 16 years or older to enroll. Reservations are recommended at least 35 days before departure.
Costs • Contact sponsor for information.
Contact • Nancy Forman, President, Language Liaison, 20533 Biscayne Boulevard-Station 4-162, Miami, FL 33180; 305-682-9909; Fax: 305-682-9907; E-mail: langstudy@aol.com; World Wide Web: http://languageliaison.com

LANGUAGE LIAISON

CENTRE INTERNATIONAL D'ANTIBES (CIA)–LEARN FRENCH IN ANTIBES

General Information • Language study program with visits to France.
Learning Focus • Instruction in the French language. Instruction is offered by professors. This program would appeal to people interested in language.
Accommodations • Homestays, dormitories, locally-rented apartments, hotels. Single rooms are available.
Program Details • Session length: unlimited. Departures are scheduled throughout the year. Program is targeted to students of any age. Most participants are 18–70 years of age. Participants must be 16 years or older to enroll. Reservations are recommended at least 35 days before departure.
Costs • Contact sponsor for information.
Contact • Nancy Forman, President, Language Liaison, 20533 Biscayne Boulevard-Station 4-162, Miami, FL 33180; 305-682-9909; Fax: 305-682-9907; E-mail: langstudy@aol.com; World Wide Web: http://languageliaison.com

LANGUAGE LIAISON

ECOLE DES TROIS PONTS–LEARN FRENCH IN A CHATEAU

General Information • Language study program with visits to France.
Learning Focus • Instruction in the French language and cooking. Instruction is offered by professors. This program would appeal to people interested in language.
Accommodations • Homestays. Single rooms are available.
Program Details • Session length: unlimited. Departures are scheduled throughout the year. Program is targeted to students of any age. Most participants are 18–70 years of age.

Participants must be 16 years or older to enroll. Reservations are recommended at least 35 days before departure.
Costs • Contact sponsor for information.
Contact • Nancy Forman, President, Language Liaison, 20533 Biscayne Boulevard-Station 4-162, Miami, FL 33180; 305-682-9909; Fax: 305-682-9907; E-mail: langstudy@aol.com; World Wide Web: http://languageliaison.com

LANGUAGE LIAISON

ELFI–LEARN FRENCH IN PARIS

General Information • Language study program with visits to France.
Learning Focus • Instruction in the French language. Instruction is offered by professors. This program would appeal to people interested in language.
Accommodations • Homestays, locally-rented apartments, hotels. Single rooms are available.
Program Details • Session length: unlimited. Departures are scheduled throughout the year. Program is targeted to students of any age. Most participants are 18–70 years of age. Participants must be 16 years or older to enroll. Reservations are recommended at least 35 days before departure.
Costs • Contact sponsor for information.
Contact • Nancy Forman, President, Language Liaison, 20533 Biscayne Boulevard-Station 4-162, Miami, FL 33180; 305-682-9909; Fax: 305-682-9907; E-mail: langstudy@aol.com; World Wide Web: http://languageliaison.com

LANGUAGE LIAISON

FRENCH IN VICHY–CAVILAM

General Information • Language study program with visits to Vichy.
Learning Focus • Instruction in the French language. Instruction is offered by professors. This program would appeal to people interested in language.
Accommodations • Homestays, locally-rented apartments, flats. Single rooms are available.
Program Details • Session length: unlimited. Departures are scheduled throughout the year. Program is targeted to students of any age. Most participants are 18–70 years of age. Participants must be 16 years or older to enroll. Reservations are recommended at least 35 days before departure.
Costs • Contact sponsor for information.
Contact • Nancy Forman, President, Language Liaison, 20533 Biscayne Boulevard-Station 4-162, Miami, FL 33180; 305-682-9909; Fax: 305-682-9907; E-mail: langstudy@aol.com; World Wide Web: http://languageliaison.com

LANGUAGE LIAISON

INSTITUT FRANCO–SCANDINAVE–LEARN FRENCH IN AIX-EN-PROVENCE

General Information • Language study program with visits to France.
Learning Focus • Instruction in the French language. Instruction is offered by professors. This program would appeal to people interested in language.
Accommodations • Homestays, locally-rented apartments, hotels. Single rooms are available.
Program Details • Session length: unlimited. Departures are scheduled throughout the year. Program is targeted to students of any age. Most participants are 18–70 years of age. Participants must be 16 years or older to enroll. Reservations are recommended at least 35 days before departure.
Costs • Contact sponsor for information.
Contact • Nancy Forman, President, Language Liaison, 20533 Biscayne Boulevard-Station 4-162, Miami, FL 33180; 305-682-9909; Fax: 305-682-9907; E-mail: langstudy@aol.com; World Wide Web: http://languageliaison.com

LANGUAGE LIAISON

LIVE 'N' LEARN (LEARN IN A TEACHER'S HOME)–FRANCE

General Information • Language study program with visits to France.
Learning Focus • Instruction in the French language. Instruction is offered by professors. This program would appeal to people interested in language.
Accommodations • Homestays. Single rooms are available.
Program Details • Session length: unlimited. Departures are scheduled throughout the year. Most participants are 18–70 years of age. Participants must be 16 years or older to enroll. Reservations are recommended at least 35 days before departure.
Costs • Contact sponsor for information.
Contact • Nancy Forman, President, Language Liaison, 20533 Biscayne Boulevard-Station 4-162, Miami, FL 33180; 305-682-9909; Fax: 305-682-9907; E-mail: langstudy@aol.com; World Wide Web: http://languageliaison.com

LANGUAGE STUDIES ABROAD

ECOLE DE LANGUE FRANÇAISE POUR ETRANGERS

General Information • Language study program with visits to Paris. Once at the destination country, participants travel by train, bus, foot.
Learning Focus • Instruction in the French language. Instruction is offered by trained teachers with bachelor's degrees. This program would appeal to people interested in the French language.
Accommodations • Homestays. Single rooms are available for an additional $250 per week.
Program Details • Session length: 2 or more weeks. Departures are scheduled throughout the year. Most participants are 16–80 years of age. Participants must be 16 years or older to enroll. 4–6 participants per session. Application deadline: 3 weeks prior to departure. Reservations are recommended at least 2 months before departure.
Costs • $3000–$3500 (includes tuition, housing, some meals, books and class materials). A $100 deposit is required.
Contact • Charlene Biddulph, Director, Language Studies Abroad, 249 South Highway 101, Suite 226, Solana Beach, CA 92075; 800-424-5522; Fax: 619-943-1201; E-mail: cbiddulph@aol.com; World Wide Web: http://www.dnai.com/~bid/language/

 LANGUAGE STUDIES ABROAD

INSTITUT D'ENSEIGNEMENT DE LA LANGUE FRANÇAISE SUR LA CÔTE D'AZUR

General Information • Language study program with visits to Hyères. Once at the destination country, participants travel by train, bus, foot, bicycle.

Learning Focus • Instruction in the French language. Instruction is offered by trained teachers with bachelor's degrees. This program would appeal to people interested in the French language.

Accommodations • Homestays. Single rooms are available for an additional $275 per week.

Program Details • Session length: 2 or more weeks. Departures are scheduled throughout the year. Most participants are 16–80 years of age. Participants must be 16 years or older to enroll. Other requirements: a minimum amount of French study. 12 participants per session. Application deadline: 3 weeks prior to departure. Reservations are recommended at least 2 months before departure.

Costs • $2700 for 4 weeks (includes tuition, housing, some meals, books and class materials). A $100 deposit is required.

Contact • Charlene Biddulph, Director, Language Studies Abroad, 249 South Highway 101, Suite 226, Solana Beach, CA 92075; 800-424-5522; Fax: 619-943-1201; E-mail: cbiddulph@aol.com; World Wide Web: http://www.dnai.com/~bid/language/

 LA SABRANENQUE

FRENCH LANGUAGE SESSIONS: 12-WEEK PROGRAM

General Information • Language study program with visits to St. Victor la Coste, Camargue region, Préalpes region, Marseilles.

Learning Focus • Instruction in French history and Mediterranean culture. Instruction is offered by professors. This program would appeal to people interested in France, civilization.

Accommodations • Program-owned houses.

Program Details • Program offered 2 times per year. Session length: 12 weeks. Departures are scheduled in September, February. Most participants are 18–30 years of age. Participants must be 18 years or older to enroll. Other requirements: intermediate-level knowledge of French. 12 participants per session.

Costs • $5100 (includes tuition, housing, all meals, books and class materials, international airfare). A $600 deposit is required.

Contact • Jacqueline C. Simon, US Correspondent, La Sabranenque, 217 High Park Boulevard, Buffalo, NY 14226; 716-836-8698

LA SABRANENQUE

FRENCH LANGUAGE SESSIONS: FOUR-WEEK PROGRAM

General Information • Language study program with visits to St. Victor la Coste.

Learning Focus • Instruction in the French language. Museum visits (local museums). Instruction is offered by professors. This program would appeal to people interested in the French language, civilization, France.

Accommodations • Program-owned houses.

Program Details • Program offered once per year. Session length: 4 weeks. Departures are scheduled in September. Most participants are 18–50 years of age. Other requirements: intermediate-level knowledge of French. 4 participants per session.

Costs • $1960 (includes tuition, housing, all meals, books and class materials, international airfare). A $600 deposit is required.

Contact • Jacqueline C. Simon, US Correspondent, La Sabranenque, 217 High Park Boulevard, Buffalo, NY 14226; 716-836-8698

LA SABRANENQUE

RESTORATION SESSIONS IN FRANCE

General Information • Architectural tour with visits to St. Victor la Coste, day visits to nearby historical or architectural sites.

Learning Focus • Instruction in restoration techniques. Volunteer work (architectural restoration of medieval buildings). Instruction is offered by technical supervisors. This program would appeal to people interested in architectural preservation.

Accommodations • Program-owned houses.

Program Details • Program offered 6 times per year. Session length: 2 weeks. Departures are scheduled in June–August. Most participants are 18–60 years of age. Participants must be 18 years or older to enroll. Other requirements: good health. 30 participants per session. Reservations are recommended at least 3–4 months before departure.

Costs • $535 (includes housing, all meals, excursions). A $150 deposit is required.

Contact • Jacqueline C. Simon, US Correspondent, La Sabranenque, 217 High Park Boulevard, Buffalo, NY 14226; 716-836-8698

LEARNING PROGRAMS INTERNATIONAL

TOUR DE FRANCE

General Information • Cultural tour with visits to Angers, Bayeux, Paris. Once at the destination country, participants travel by bus, foot.

Learning Focus • Escorted travel to Tour Eiffel, Champs Elysées, Versailles, Louvre, Cathédral de Notre-Dame de Paris, D-Day beaches, Omaha Beach. Museum visits (Musée d'Orsay). This program would appeal to people interested in culture and language.

Accommodations • Hotels. Single rooms are available.

Program Details • Program offered 2 times per year. Session length: 10 days. Departures are scheduled in June, spring break, and custom dates. Program is targeted to high school students. Most participants are 14–18 years of age. 15–20 participants per session. Application deadline: April 1 for summer session, December 15 for spring session.

Costs • $2380 (includes housing, some meals, insurance, excursions, international airfare, on site supervisor, full-time director). A $200 deposit is required.

Contact • Natalie Nation, Director, Learning Programs International, 816 West 23rd Street, Austin, TX 78705;

800-259-4439; Fax: 512-474-1021; E-mail: 76331.336@compuserve.com; World Wide Web: http://www.studiesabroad.com

LEARNING PROGRAMS INTERNATIONAL

UNIVERSITÉ CATHOLIQUE DE L'OUEST: ANGERS, FRANCE

General Information • Language study program with visits to Angers, Paris, Versailles, Mont St. Michel, St. Malo, Le Golfe du Morbihan, Carnac, Vannes. Once at the destination country, participants travel by train, bus, foot.

Learning Focus • Instruction in French. Museum visits (Musée du Louvre, Museé d'Orsay). Instruction is offered by professors. This program would appeal to people interested in language and culture.

Accommodations • Homestays. Single rooms are available for an additional $150 per month.

Program Details • Program offered once per year. Session length: 31 days. Departures are scheduled in June. Program is targeted to high school students. Most participants are 15–18 years of age. Participants must be 14 years or older to enroll. 10–20 participants per session. Application deadline: April 1.

Costs • $4175 (includes tuition, housing, all meals, books and class materials, insurance, excursions, international airfare, medical insurance, entrance fees, on site directors, tutorial assistance). A $200 deposit is required.

Contact • Natalie Nation, Director, Learning Programs International, 816 West 23rd Street, Austin, TX 78705; 800-259-4439; Fax: 512-474-1021; E-mail: 76331.336@compuserve.com; World Wide Web: http://www.studiesabroad.com

LOS ANGELES COMMUNITY COLLEGE DISTRICT

SUMMER SESSION IN PARIS

General Information • Language study program in Paris. Classes are held on the campus of University of Paris-Sorbonne (Paris IV). Excursions to Chartres, Loire Valley.

Learning Focus • Courses in French language. Instruction is offered by professors from the sponsoring institution and local teachers.

Accommodations • Homestays, dormitories, locally-rented apartments. Single rooms are available. Meals are taken on one's own, in central dining facility, in residences.

Program Details • Program offered once per year. Session length: 4 weeks. Departures are scheduled in July. The program is open to undergraduate students, graduate students, pre-college students, adults. Most participants are 17–65 years of age. 25 participants per session. Application deadline: May 1.

Costs • $2490 (includes tuition, housing, some meals, books and class materials, insurance, excursions). A $200 deposit is required.

Contact • International Education Program, Los Angeles Community College District, 770 Wilshire Boulevard, Los Angeles, CA 90017; 213-891-2282; Fax: 213-891-2150; E-mail: intered@laccd.cc.ca.us; World Wide Web: http://laccd.cc.ca.us

LOUISIANA STATE UNIVERSITY

LOUISIANA STATE UNIVERSITY IN PARIS

General Information • Academic study program in Paris. Excursions to Mont St. Michel, Giverny, Chartres, Strasbourg, Versailles.

Learning Focus • Courses in French language, art, English literature. Instruction is offered by professors from the sponsoring institution.

Accommodations • Dormitories. Meals are taken as a group, in central dining facility.

Program Details • Program offered once per year. Session length: 6 weeks. Departures are scheduled in June. The program is open to undergraduate students, graduate students. Most participants are 20–25 years of age. Other requirements: minimum 2.5 GPA for 6 hours of credit and a minimum 3.0 GPA for 9 hours of credit. 45 participants per session. Application deadline: April 1.

Costs • $2795 (includes tuition, housing, some meals, excursions). A $200 deposit is required.

Contact • Jeannie Willamson, Study Abroad Coordinator, Louisiana State University, Academic Programs Abroad, 365 Pleasant Hall, Baton Rouge, LA 70803; 504-388-6801; Fax: 504-388-6806; E-mail: abwill@lsuvm.sncc.lsu.edu

MANKATO STATE UNIVERSITY

SUMMER STUDY PROGRAM IN FRANCE

General Information • Language study program in La Rochelle, Normandy, Paris. Classes are held on the campus of Institut International d'Etudes Françaises. Excursions to Vendée, Epernay, Fontainebleau, Loire Valley, Chartres.

Learning Focus • Courses in French language, French civilization. Instruction is offered by professors from the sponsoring institution and local teachers.

Accommodations • Homestays, hostels. Single rooms are available. Meals are taken on one's own, with host family.

Program Details • Program offered once per year. Session length: 6 weeks. Departures are scheduled in June. The program is open to undergraduate students, graduate students, pre-college students, adults. Most participants are 18–25 years of age. Other requirements: must have studied French. 15 participants per session. Application deadline: April 1.

Costs • $3700 (includes tuition, housing, some meals, excursions). A $50 deposit is required.

Contact • Dr. John J. Janc, Director, Summer Study in France Program, Mankato State University, AH87, Mankato, MN 56002-8400; 507-387-1817; Fax: 507-389-5887; E-mail: janc@vax1.mankato.msus.edu

MICHIGAN STATE UNIVERSITY

FRENCH LANGUAGE, LITERATURE, AND CULTURE PROGRAM

General Information • Language study program in Tours.

Learning Focus • Courses in French literature, French culture, French language. Instruction is offered by professors from the sponsoring institution.
Accommodations • Homestays. Meals are taken with host family, in residences.
Program Details • Program offered once per year. Session length: 6 weeks. Departures are scheduled in June. The program is open to undergraduate students, graduate students. Most participants are 18–26 years of age. Other requirements: good academic standing and the approval of the director. 20 participants per session. Application deadline: March 14.
Costs • $2200 (includes housing, some meals, excursions). Application fee: $75. A $250 deposit is required.
Contact • Brenda S. Sprite, Educational Programs Coordinator, Michigan State University, Office of Study Abroad, 109 International Center, East Lansing, MI 48824-1035; 517-353-8920; Fax: 517-432-2082; E-mail: sprite@pilot.msu.edu; World Wide Web: http://study-abroad.msu.edu

NATIONAL REGISTRATION CENTER FOR STUDY ABROAD

CENTRE D'ETUDES LINGUISTIQUES

General Information • Language study program in Avignon.
Learning Focus • Courses in French language.
Accommodations • Homestays.
Program Details • Program offered 50 times per year. Session length: 2 weeks. Departures are scheduled in January–December. The program is open to undergraduate students, graduate students, adults. 8–10 participants per session. Application deadline: 40 days prior to departure.
Costs • $804 (includes tuition, insurance). Application fee: $40. A $100 deposit is required.
Contact • Reuel Zielke, Coordinator, National Registration Center for Study Abroad, 823 North Second Street, PO Box 1393, Milwaukee, WI 53203; 414-278-0631; Fax: 414-271-8884; E-mail: quest@nrcsa.com; World Wide Web: http://www.nrcsa.com

NATIONAL REGISTRATION CENTER FOR STUDY ABROAD

ELFCA

General Information • Language study program in Hyères.
Learning Focus • Courses in French language.
Accommodations • Homestays. Single rooms are available. Meals are taken with host family.
Program Details • Program offered 23 times per year. Session length: 2 weeks. Departures are scheduled in January–December. The program is open to undergraduate students, graduate students, adults. 10–12 participants per session. Application deadline: 40 days prior to departure.
Costs • Contact sponsor for information. Application fee: $40. A $100 deposit is required.
Contact • Reuel Zielke, Coordinator, National Registration Center for Study Abroad, 823 North Second Street, Milwaukee, WI 53203; 414-278-0631; Fax: 414-276-8884; E-mail: quest@nrcsa.com; World Wide Web: http://www.nrcsa.com

NATIONAL REGISTRATION CENTER FOR STUDY ABROAD

ELFE

General Information • Language study program in Paris.
Learning Focus • Courses in French language.
Accommodations • Homestays. Single rooms are available. Meals are taken on one's own.
Program Details • Program offered 50 times per year. Session length: 2 weeks. Departures are scheduled in January–December. The program is open to undergraduate students, graduate students, adults. 4–7 participants per session. Application deadline: 40 days prior to departure.
Costs • $1600 (includes tuition, housing, some meals, insurance). Application fee: $40. A $100 deposit is required.
Contact • Reuel Zielke, Coordinator, National Registration Center for Study Abroad, 823 North Second Street, Milwaukee, WI 53203; 414-278-0631; Fax: 414-271-8884; E-mail: quest@nrcsa.com; World Wide Web: http://www.nrcsa.com

NATIONAL REGISTRATION CENTER FOR STUDY ABROAD

EUROCENTRE: AMBOISE

General Information • Language study program in Amboise.
Learning Focus • Courses in French language.
Accommodations • Homestays. Single rooms are available. Meals are taken with host family.
Program Details • Program offered 15 times per year. Session length: 3 weeks. Departures are scheduled in January–December. The program is open to undergraduate students, graduate students, adults. 10–15 participants per session.
Costs • $1672 (includes tuition, housing, some meals, insurance). Application fee: $40. A $100 deposit is required.
Contact • Reuel Zielke, Coordinator, National Registration Center for Study Abroad, PO Box 1393, Milwaukee, WI 53201; 414-278-0631; Fax: 414-271-8884; E-mail: inquiries@nrcsa.com; World Wide Web: http://www.nrcsa.com

NATIONAL REGISTRATION CENTER FOR STUDY ABROAD

INTERNATIONAL HOUSE

General Information • Language study program in Nice.
Learning Focus • Courses in French language.
Accommodations • Homestays, hotels. Single rooms are available. Meals are taken with host family, in residences.
Program Details • Program offered 24 times per year. Session length: 2 weeks. Departures are scheduled in January–December. The program is open to undergraduate students, graduate students, adults. 8–10 participants per session. Application deadline: 40 days prior to departure.
Costs • $1017 (includes tuition, housing, some meals, insurance). Application fee: $40. A $100 deposit is required.
Contact • June Domoe, Educational Consultant, National Registration Center for Study Abroad, Box 1393, Milwaukee, WI 53201; 414-351-6311; Fax: 414-271-8884; E-mail: ask@nrcsa.com; World Wide Web: http://www.nrcsa.com

NATIONAL REGISTRATION CENTER FOR STUDY ABROAD

PROVENCE LANGUES

General Information • Language study program in Avignon.
Learning Focus • Courses in French language.
Accommodations • Homestays, hotels. Single rooms are available. Meals are taken on one's own, in local restaurants.
Program Details • Program offered 50 times per year. Session length: 4 weeks. Departures are scheduled in January–December. The program is open to undergraduate students, graduate students, adults. 6–8 participants per session. Application deadline: 40 days prior to departure.
Costs • $1548 (includes tuition, housing, insurance). Application fee: $40. A $100 deposit is required.
Contact • June Domoe, Educational Consultant, National Registration Center for Study Abroad, Box 1393, Milwaukee, WI 53201; 414-351-6311; Fax: 414-271-8884; E-mail: ask@nrcsa.com; World Wide Web: http://www.nrcsa.com

NEW YORK UNIVERSITY

EDUCATIONAL COMMUNICATION AND TECHNOLOGY

General Information • Academic study program in Paris. Classes are held on the campus of University of Paris.
Learning Focus • Courses in communications, multimedia specialist, educational communications. Instruction is offered by professors from the sponsoring institution and local teachers.
Accommodations • Hotels. Single rooms are available. Meals are taken as a group, in local restaurants.
Program Details • Program offered once per year. Session length: 3 weeks. Departures are scheduled in July. The program is open to graduate students, professionals in the area of multimedia. Most participants are 25–47 years of age. Other requirements: BA degree. 15 participants per session. Application deadline: April 1.
Costs • $3000 (includes tuition). Application fee: $40. A $200 deposit is required.
Contact • Helen J. Kelly, Director of Special Programs, New York University, 82 Washington Square East, Room 62, New York, NY 10003; 212-998-5090; Fax: 212-995-4923; World Wide Web: http://www.nyu.edu/studyabroad

NEW YORK UNIVERSITY

NEW YORK UNIVERSITY IN FRANCE

General Information • Academic study program in Paris. Classes are held on the campus of University of Paris. Excursions to Loire Valley, Brussels, Strasbourg.
Learning Focus • Courses in cinema studies, political science, French language, international relations, French literature, art history. Instruction is offered by professors from the sponsoring institution and local teachers.
Accommodations • Homestays, dormitories, locally-rented apartments. Single rooms are available. Meals are taken on one's own, with host family, in local restaurants, in residences.
Program Details • Program offered 3 times per year. Session length: 6–14 weeks. Departures are scheduled in January, July, August. The program is open to undergraduate students. Most participants are 19–23 years of age. Other requirements: minimum 3.0 GPA. 50–80 participants per session. Application deadline: rolling.
Costs • $6500 (includes tuition, housing, some meals, excursions). Application fee: $25. A $200 deposit is required.
Contact • New York University in France, New York University, 19 University Place, New York, NY 10003-4556; 212-998-8720; Fax: 212-473-4498; E-mail: international.study@nyu.edu; World Wide Web: http://www.nyu.edu/studyabroad

NICHOLLS STATE UNIVERSITY

STUDY PROGRAM ABROAD IN NICE, FRANCE

General Information • Academic and language study program in Nice. Classes are held on the campus of Nicholls State University–Nice. Excursions to museums, theater, markets, monuments.
Learning Focus • Courses in language study, literature, linguistics, cultural studies, civilizations. Instruction is offered by professors from the sponsoring institution.
Accommodations • Homestays, dormitories, locally-rented apartments, pensiones. Single rooms are available. Meals are taken on one's own, with host family, in local restaurants, in residences.
Program Details • Program offered 15 times per year. Session length: 3 weeks–one year. Departures are scheduled in January–December. The program is open to undergraduate students, graduate students, pre-college students, adults. Most participants are 18–55 years of age. Other requirements: high school seniors or graduates. 15 participants per session. Application deadline: 30 days prior to departure.
Costs • $1494 for 3 weeks non-credit, $1789 for 6 hours of college credit (includes tuition, housing, some meals, books and class materials). A $170 deposit is required.
Contact • Dr. Gary McCann, Director of Study Programs Abroad, Nicholls State University, PO Box 2080, Thibodaux, LA 70310; 504-448-4440; Fax: 504-449-7028; E-mail: fl-caw@nich-nsunet.nich.edu

NICHOLLS STATE UNIVERSITY

STUDY PROGRAM ABROAD IN PARIS, FRANCE

General Information • Academic and language study program in Paris. Classes are held on the campus of Nicholls State University–Paris. Excursions to museums, theater, markets, monuments.
Learning Focus • Courses in language study, literature, linguistics, cultural studies, civilizations. Instruction is offered by professors from the sponsoring institution.
Accommodations • Homestays, dormitories, locally-rented apartments, pensiones. Single rooms are available. Meals are taken on one's own, with host family, in local restaurants, in residences.
Program Details • Program offered 15 times per year. Session length: 3 weeks–one year. Departures are scheduled in January–December. The program is open to undergraduate students, graduate students, pre-college students, adults. Most participants are 18–55 years of age. Other requirements: high school seniors or graduates. 25 participants per session. Application deadline: 30 days prior to departure.

Costs • $1545 for non-credit program, $1840 for 6 hours of college credit (includes tuition, housing, some meals, books and class materials). A $170 deposit is required.
Contact • Dr. Gary McCann, Director of Study Programs Abroad, Nicholls State University, PO Box 2080, Thibodaux, LA 70310; 504-448-4440; Fax: 504-449-7028; E-mail: fl-caw@nich.nsunet.nich.edu

NORTHERN ILLINOIS UNIVERSITY

COMPARATIVE AND INTERNATIONAL LAW IN AGEN, FRANCE

General Information • Academic study program in Agen. Classes are held on the campus of University of Bordeaux III.
Learning Focus • Courses in international law, comparative law. Instruction is offered by professors from the sponsoring institution and local teachers.
Accommodations • Dormitories. Single rooms are available. Meals are taken on one's own, in central dining facility.
Program Details • Program offered once per year. Session length: 4 weeks. Departures are scheduled in June. The program is open to graduate students, adults. Most participants are 22–35 years of age. Other requirements: good standing in a law program or J.D. degree. 12 participants per session. Application deadline: May 1.
Costs • $2500 (includes tuition, housing, some meals, insurance, excursions). A $200 deposit is required.
Contact • Anne Seitzinger, Program Coordinator, Short-Term Study Abroad, Northern Illinois University, Study Abroad Office-WI 417, DeKalb, IL 60115; 815-752-0700; Fax: 815-753-0825; E-mail: aseitz@niu.edu; World Wide Web: http://www.niu.edu/depts/intl_prgms/intl.html

NORTHERN ILLINOIS UNIVERSITY

FRENCH LANGUAGE AND LITERATURE IN AVIGNON

General Information • Language study program in Avignon. Classes are held on the campus of Institute for American Universities (IAU)–Avignon.
Learning Focus • Courses in French language, French literature. Instruction is offered by professors from the sponsoring institution.
Accommodations • Homestays. Single rooms are available. Meals are taken with host family.
Program Details • Program offered once per year. Session length: 6 weeks. Departures are scheduled in June, July. The program is open to undergraduate students, graduate students. Most participants are 20–30 years of age. Other requirements: 2 years of college-level French. 12 participants per session. Application deadline: April 15.
Costs • $3290 (includes tuition, housing, some meals, insurance, excursions). A $200 deposit is required.
Contact • Anne Seitzinger, Program Coordinator, Short-Term Study Abroad, Northern Illinois University, Study Abroad Office-WI 417, DeKalb, IL 60115; 815-752-0700; Fax: 815-753-0825; E-mail: aseitz@niu.edu; World Wide Web: http://www.niu.edu/depts/intl_prgms/intl.html

THE PARTNERSHIP FOR SERVICE-LEARNING

FRANCE

General Information • Academic study and volunteer service program in Montpellier. Classes are held on the campus of University of Montpellier I.
Learning Focus • Courses in French language. Instruction is offered by local teachers.
Accommodations • Homestays. Single rooms are available. Meals are taken with host family.
Program Details • Program offered once per year. Session length: 8 weeks. Departures are scheduled in June. The program is open to undergraduate students, graduate students, pre-college students, adults. Most participants are 19–24 years of age. Other requirements: 1 year of college or 2 years of high school-level of French language. 10 participants per session. Application deadline: 2 months prior to departure.
Costs • $4700 (includes tuition, housing, some meals, service placement and supervision, pre-departure and orientation materials). A $250 deposit is required.
Contact • Maureen Lowney, Coordinator of Student Programs, The Partnership for Service-Learning, 815 Second Avenue, Suite 315, New York, NY 10960; 212-986-0989; Fax: 212-986-5039; E-mail: pslny@aol.com

PONT-AVEN SCHOOL OF ART

ARTISTS WITHOUT BORDERS

General Information • Academic study program in Pont-Aven. Excursions to Carnac, Concarneau, Quimper.
Learning Focus • Courses in art history, French literature, sculpture, drawing, French language, painting, works on paper. Instruction is offered by professors from the sponsoring institution.
Accommodations • Homestays. Single rooms are available. Meals are taken as a group, in central dining facility.
Program Details • Program offered 2 times per year. Session length: 4 and 6 weeks. Departures are scheduled in June, July. The program is open to undergraduate students, graduate students, adults, art teachers and practicing artists. Most participants are 18–24 years of age. Other requirements: equivalent of basic first year art. 30–40 participants per session. Application deadline: April 10.
Costs • $2000–$5000 (includes tuition, housing, some meals, insurance, excursions, credits transferable from Rhode Island School of Design). Application fee: $50.
Contact • Dr. Caroline Boyce-Turner, Director, Pont-Aven School of Art, 4 Duggan Road, Acton, MA 01720; 508-263-1684; Fax: 508-263-1654; E-mail: pontavensa@aol.com; World Wide Web: http://www.pontavensa.org

ROCKLAND COMMUNITY COLLEGE

ARTIST SALONS IN 20TH CENTURY PARIS

General Information • Academic study program in Paris.
Learning Focus • Courses in literature, art history, humanities. Instruction is offered by professors from the sponsoring institution.

Accommodations • Hotels. Single rooms are available. Meals are taken on one's own, in local restaurants.
Program Details • Program offered once per year. Session length: 2 weeks. Departures are scheduled in June. The program is open to undergraduate students, adults. Most participants are 18–65 years of age. 15–20 participants per session. Application deadline: April 15.
Costs • $2200 (includes tuition, housing, some meals, excursions, international airfare). A $200 deposit is required.
Contact • Jody Dudderar, Coordinator, Study Abroad, Rockland Community College, Suffern, NY 10907; 914-574-4205; Fax: 914-574-4423; E-mail: jdudderar@sunyrockland.edu

RUSSIAN AND EAST EUROPEAN PARTNERSHIPS

FRENCH LANGUAGE AND CULTURAL IMMERSION PROGRAM

General Information • Language study program in Strasbourg. Classes are held on the campus of University of Strasbourg. Excursions to Paris, Verdun.
Learning Focus • Courses in French language, French history, French culture and art. Instruction is offered by local teachers.
Accommodations • Homestays. Single rooms are available. Meals are taken on one's own, with host family, in local restaurants, in residences.
Program Details • Program offered 11 times per year. Session length: 4 or more weeks. Departures are scheduled in January–November. The program is open to undergraduate students, graduate students, adults. Most participants are 18 years of age and older. Other requirements: in good health and 18 or older unless chaperoned by an adult. 6 participants per session. Application deadline: 45 days prior to departure.
Costs • $3595 (includes tuition, housing, some meals, books and class materials, excursions, international airfare, local transportation, airport transfers). A $1500 deposit is required.
Contact • Kenneth Fortune, President, Russian and East European Partnerships, PO Box 227, Fineview, NY 13640; 888-873-7337; Fax: 800-910-1777; E-mail: reep@fox.nstn.ca

RUTGERS, THE STATE UNIVERSITY OF NEW JERSEY, NEW BRUNSWICK

SUMMER ART HISTORY IN PARIS

General Information • Academic study program in Paris.

Learning Focus • Courses in art history. Instruction is offered by professors from the sponsoring institution.
Accommodations • Locally-rented apartments. Meals are taken on one's own, in residences.
Program Details • Program offered once per year. Session length: 6 weeks. Departures are scheduled in June. The program is open to undergraduate students. Most participants are 19–25 years of age. Other requirements: minimum 3.0 GPA. 15 participants per session. Application deadline: April 1.
Costs • Contact sponsor for information. Application fee: $20.
Contact • Dr. Seth A. Gopin, Director, Study Abroad, Rutgers, The State University of New Jersey, New Brunswick, Milledoler Hall, Room 205, New Brunswick, NJ 08903; 908-932-7787; Fax: 908-932-8659; E-mail: gopin@rci.rutgers.edu; World Wide Web: http://www.rutgers.edu/Academics/Study_Abroad

RUTGERS, THE STATE UNIVERSITY OF NEW JERSEY, NEW BRUNSWICK

SUMMER INSTITUTE IN EUROPEAN STUDIES

General Information • Academic study program in Tours. Classes are held on the campus of University of Tours.
Learning Focus • Courses in political science. Instruction is offered by local teachers.
Accommodations • Homestays. Meals are taken on one's own, in residences.
Program Details • Program offered once per year. Session length: 6 weeks. Departures are scheduled in June. The program is open to undergraduate students. Most participants are 18–25 years of age. Other requirements: minimum 3.0 GPA. 20 participants per session. Application deadline: April 1.
Costs • $1900 for New Jersey residents, $2150 for non-residents (includes tuition, housing). Application fee: $20.
Contact • Dr. Seth A. Gopin, Director, Rutgers Study Aboard, Rutgers, The State University of New Jersey, New Brunswick, Milledoler Hall, Room 205, New Brunswick, NJ 08903; 908-932-7787; Fax: 908-932-8659; E-mail: gopin@rci.rutgers.edu; World Wide Web: http://www.rutgers.edu/Academics/Study_Abroad

ST. JOHN'S UNIVERSITY

FRENCH PROGRAM

General Information • Academic study program in Cannes. Classes are held on the campus of Collége International de Cannes.

Learning Focus • Courses in French language, art, management. Instruction is offered by local teachers.
Accommodations • Homestays, dormitories. Meals are taken as a group, in central dining facility.
Program Details • Program offered once per year. Session length: 12 weeks. Departures are scheduled in September. The program is open to undergraduate students. Most participants are 20–22 years of age. Other requirements: minimum 2.5 GPA and one year college-level French. 25 participants per session. Application deadline: March.
Costs • $9200 (includes tuition, housing, all meals, excursions). Application fee: $100.
Contact • Stephen Burmeister-May, Director, Center for International Education, St. John's University, Collegeville, MN 56321; 320-363-2082; Fax: 320-363-2013; E-mail: intleduc@csbsju.edu

SANTA BARBARA MUSEUM OF ART

ART AND GARDENS IN PROVENCE AND THE COTE D'AZUR

General Information • Cultural tour with visits to Aix-en-Provence, Nice, villas, palaces, gardens. Once at the destination country, participants travel by bus, airplane.
Learning Focus • Escorted travel to Arles and Nice. Museum visits (local museums). Instruction is offered by art historians. This program would appeal to people interested in art, cuisine, decorative arts, photography, architecture, gardening.
Accommodations • Hotels. Single rooms are available.
Program Details • Program offered once per year. Session length: 12 days. Departures are scheduled in April. Most participants are 30–80 years of age. Participants must be members of the sponsoring organization (annual dues: $40). 15–20 participants per session. Application deadline: January.
Costs • $4500 (includes housing, some meals, excursions, international airfare). A $500 deposit is required.
Contact • Shelley Ruston, Director of Special Programs, Santa Barbara Museum of Art, 1130 State Street, Santa Barbara, CA 93101; 805-963-4364, ext. 336; Fax: 805-966-6840

SOUTHERN METHODIST UNIVERSITY

PROGRAM IN THE SOUTH OF FRANCE

General Information • Language study program in Antibes. Excursions to Cannes, Grasse, Monaco, Saint Tropez, Nice.
Learning Focus • Courses in French language, French culture. Instruction is offered by professors from the sponsoring institution.
Accommodations • Homestays, program-owned apartments. Meals are taken as a group, in central dining facility.
Program Details • Program offered once per year. Session length: 6 weeks. Departures are scheduled in May. The program is open to undergraduate students. Most participants are 19–23 years of age. Other requirements: minimum 2.5 GPA, one year college-level French and sophomore standing. 20 participants per session. Application deadline: March 1.
Costs • $4400 (includes tuition, housing, some meals, excursions). A $400 deposit is required.
Contact • Karen Westergaard, Associate Director, Southern Methodist University, Office of International Programs, Dallas, TX 75275-0391; 214-768-2338; Fax: 214-768-1051; E-mail: intipro@mail.smu.edu; World Wide Web: http://fllcjm.clements.smu.edu

SPÉOS PARIS PHOTOGRAPHIC INSTITUTE

SUMMER PROGRAM

General Information • Academic study program in Paris. Classes are held on the campus of Spéos Paris Photographic Institute.
Learning Focus • Courses in photography. Instruction is offered by professors from the sponsoring institution.
Accommodations • Homestays, locally-rented apartments. Single rooms are available. Meals are taken on one's own.
Program Details • Program offered once per year. Session length: 10 weeks. Departures are scheduled in June. The program is open to undergraduate students, graduate students, pre-college students, adults, professionals in photography or related fields. Most participants are 18–35 years of age. 25 participants per session. Application deadline: May.
Costs • $550 per week (includes tuition).
Contact • Karen Archer, Administrative Director, Spéos Paris Photographic Institute, 8 Rue Jules Vallés (Bat Cour), Paris 75011, France; +33 40-09-18-58; Fax: +33 40-09-84-97; World Wide Web: http://www.speos.fr

STATE UNIVERSITY OF NEW YORK AT BUFFALO

CULTURE OF PROVENCE

General Information • Language study program in Aix-en-Provence. Excursions to Avignon, Vaison-la-Romaine, Les Baux, Glanum, Arles, Pont du Gard.
Learning Focus • Courses in the history of Provence, culture of Provence, French language, medieval studies, architecture, culinary arts. Instruction is offered by professors from the sponsoring institution.
Accommodations • Houses. Meals are taken as a group, in local restaurants, in residences.
Program Details • Program offered once per year. Session length: 4 weeks. Departures are scheduled in June. The program is open to undergraduate students, graduate students, French teachers of any level. Most participants are 18–35 years of age. Other requirements: minimum 2.67 GPA. 10 participants per session. Application deadline: April 15.
Costs • $2345 (includes housing, all meals). A $125 deposit is required.
Contact • Sandra J. Reinagel, Interim Study Abroad Coordinator, State University of New York at Buffalo, 210 Talbert Hall, Box 601604, Buffalo, NY 14260-1604; 716-645-3912; Fax: 716-645-6197; E-mail: studyabroad@acsu.buffalo.edu; World Wide Web: http://wings.buffalo.edu/academic/provost/intl/studyabroad

STATE UNIVERSITY OF NEW YORK AT NEW PALTZ

SUMMER STUDY IN FRANCE

General Information • Language study program in Paris. Excursions to "Châteaux de la Loire", Monet's Giverny, Chartres, La Malmaison, Versailles.

Learning Focus • Courses in French literature, French culture, civilizations. Instruction is offered by professors from the sponsoring institution.

Accommodations • Dormitories. Single rooms are available. Meals are taken as a group, in central dining facility.

Program Details • Program offered once per year. Session length: 5 weeks. Departures are scheduled in July. The program is open to undergraduate students, graduate students, pre-college students, adults. Most participants are 18-60 years of age. Other requirements: 2 years of high school or 2 semesters of college-level French. 13 participants per session. Application deadline: March 15.

Costs • $3491 (includes tuition, housing, all meals, insurance, excursions, international airfare). Application fee: $25. A $100 deposit is required.

Contact • Office of International Education, State University of New York at New Paltz, HAB 33, New Paltz, NY 12561; 914-257-3125; Fax: 914-257-3129; E-mail: sillnerb@npvm.newpaltz.edu; World Wide Web: http://www.newpaltz.edu/oie/

STATE UNIVERSITY OF WEST GEORGIA

STUDY ABROAD PROGRAM IN PARIS, TOURS, AND NICE

General Information • Language study program in Nice, Paris, Tours. Excursions to Loire castle, Mont St. Michel, Versailles, Monaco, Locke opera.

Learning Focus • Courses in photography, hiking, art, cycling, French language.

Accommodations • Homestays, hotels. Single rooms are available. Meals are taken with host family, in local restaurants, in residences.

Program Details • Program offered once per year. Session length: 6 weeks. Departures are scheduled in June. The program is open to undergraduate students, graduate students. Most participants are 20-35 years of age. Other requirements: minimum 2.0 GPA and 2 quarters of French language if enrolling for credit. 45 participants per session. Application deadline: April 1.

Costs • $3900 (includes tuition, housing, some meals, books and class materials, excursions, international airfare, museum pass, Metro pass in Paris). A $300 deposit is required.

Contact • Dr. Purritte Frickey, State University of West Georgia, Department of Foreign Languages and Literatures,

Carrollton, GA 30118; 770-830-2211; Fax: 770-854-8068; E-mail: pfrickey@westga.edu; World Wide Web: http://www.westga.edu/

The State University of West Georgia has a study-abroad program in France that allows students to study in Tours, explore Paris, and visit Provence. Excursions to the castles of the Loire Valley, Mont St. Michel, Versailles, and others. Ten to 15 credit hours. Courses in intensive language training, culture and civilization, a seminar on Balzac, and business French (upon request). The cost is $3900, which includes flight (RT), lodging, food, tuition, books, excursions, and transportation.

SYRACUSE UNIVERSITY

A FRENCH EXPERIENCE IN STRASBOURG

General Information • Language study program in Strasbourg. Excursions to Paris, Belgium (Brussels).
Learning Focus • Courses in European politics. Instruction is offered by professors from the sponsoring institution.
Accommodations • Homestays. Single rooms are available. Meals are taken with host family, in residences.
Program Details • Program offered once per year. Session length: 6 weeks. Departures are scheduled in May. The program is open to undergraduate students. Most participants are 18–22 years of age. 15 participants per session. Application deadline: March 15.
Costs • $4986 (includes tuition, housing, some meals, books and class materials, excursions). Application fee: $40. A $350 deposit is required.
Contact • Darlene Grome, Admissions Counselor, Summer Programs, Syracuse University, 119 Euclid Avenue, Syracuse, NY 13244-4170; 315-443-9420; Fax: 315-443-4593; World Wide Web: http://sumweb.syr.edu/dipa/dipa9.htm

TEMPLE UNIVERSITY

SORBONNE STUDY PROGRAM

General Information • Language study program in Paris. Classes are held on the campus of University of Paris–Sorbonne (Paris IV).
Learning Focus • Courses in French language. Instruction is offered by professors from the sponsoring institution and local teachers.
Accommodations • Homestays, pensiones. Single rooms are available. Meals are taken with host family, in central dining facility, in residences.
Program Details • Program offered once per year. Session length: 4–6 weeks. Departures are scheduled in July. The program is open to undergraduate students, graduate students. 20–25 participants per session. Application deadline: May 1.
Costs • $2265–$4264 (includes tuition, housing, some meals, excursions). Application fee: $30. A $200 deposit is required.
Contact • Ruth Thomas, Co-Director, Temple University, Department of French and Italian, Philadelphia, PA 19122; 215-204-8266; Fax: 215-204-7752; World Wide Web: http://www.temple.edu/intlprog/

TUFTS UNIVERSITY

FRANCE BEFORE FRANCE: HISTORY AND ARCHAEOLOGY OF CELTIC AND ROMAN GAUL

General Information • Academic study program in Talloires. Classes are held on the campus of Tufts University Talloires Campus. Excursions to Lyons, Geneva, Vienne.
Learning Focus • Courses in archaeology, ancient civilization. Instruction is offered by professors from the sponsoring institution and local teachers.
Accommodations • Dormitories. Meals are taken as a group, in central dining facility.
Program Details • Program offered once per year. Session length: 6 weeks. Departures are scheduled in May. The program is open to undergraduate students. Most participants are 18–25 years of age. Other requirements: completion of one college semester. 15 participants per session. Application deadline: March 1.
Costs • $2990 (includes tuition, housing, some meals). Application fee: $40. A $500 deposit is required.
Contact • Sally Pym, Director, Tufts University, Tufts European Center, 108 Packard Avenue, Medford, MA 02155; 617-627-3290; Fax: 617-627-3856; E-mail: france@infonet.tufts.edu; World Wide Web: http://www.tufts.edu/as/tuec/tuec.html

TUFTS UNIVERSITY

FRENCH IN ANNECY

General Information • Language study program in Annecy. Classes are held on the campus of Institut Savoisien d'Etudes Françaises, University de Savoie. Excursions to Avignon.
Learning Focus • Courses in French language. Instruction is offered by local teachers.
Accommodations • Homestays, dormitories. Single rooms are available. Meals are taken with host family, in residences.
Program Details • Program offered once per year. Session length: 4 weeks. Departures are scheduled in July. The program is open to undergraduate students, graduate students, adults. Most participants are 18–30 years of age. Other requirements: one semester of college-level French or previous French study. 15 participants per session. Application deadline: April 1.
Costs • $2590 (includes tuition, housing, all meals). Application fee: $40. A $500 deposit is required.
Contact • Sally Pym, Director, Tufts University, Tufts European Center, 108 Packard Avenue, Medford, MA 02155; 617-627-3290; Fax: 617-627-3856; E-mail: france@infonet.tufts.edu; World Wide Web: http://www.tufts.edu/as/tuec/tuec.html

TUFTS UNIVERSITY

LANDSCAPE PAINTING AND DRAWING

General Information • Arts program in Talloires. Classes are held on the campus of Tufts University Talloires Campus. Excursions to Annecy.

Learning Focus • Courses in painting, drawing. Instruction is offered by professors from the sponsoring institution.

Accommodations • Dormitories. Single rooms are available. Meals are taken as a group, in central dining facility.

Program Details • Program offered once per year. Session length: 10 days. Departures are scheduled in August. The program is open to undergraduate students, graduate students, adults. Most participants are 18–70 years of age. 15 participants per session. Application deadline: June 1.

Costs • $2590 (includes tuition, housing, all meals, excursions). A $500 deposit is required.

Contact • Sally Pym, Director, Tufts University, Tufts European Center, 108 Packard Avenue, Medford, MA 02155; 617-627-3290; Fax: 617-627-3856; E-mail: france@infonet.tufts.edu; World Wide Web: http://www.tufts.edu/as/tuec/tuec.html

TUFTS UNIVERSITY

TUFTS IN TALLOIRES

General Information • Academic study program in Talloires. Classes are held on the campus of Tufts University Talloires Campus. Excursions to Paris, Geneva, Chamonix.

Learning Focus • Courses in European studies, French language, art history, international relations, French culture. Instruction is offered by local teachers.

Accommodations • Homestays. Single rooms are available. Meals are taken with host family, in residences.

Program Details • Program offered once per year. Session length: 6 weeks. Departures are scheduled in May. The program is open to undergraduate students. Most participants are 18–23 years of age. Other requirements: minimum 2.0 GPA. 40 participants per session. Application deadline: March 1.

Costs • $3950 (includes tuition, housing, all meals). Application fee: $40. A $500 deposit is required.

Contact • Sally Pym, Director, Tufts University, Tufts European Center, 108 Packard Avenue, Medford, MA 02155; 617-627-3290; Fax: 617-627-3856; E-mail: france@infonet.tufts.edu; World Wide Web: http://www.tufts.edu/as/tuec/tuec.html

Tufts in Talloires is one of Tufts Summer Programs in the French Alps open to college students and adult learners interested in improving their French and exploring the fields of archaeology, international relations, European studies, or painting. Course work combines high-quality Tufts instruction with the discovery of alpine lakes and mountains. Extracurricular activities include visits to local sites as well as hiking and swimming. Located on Lake Annecy, Tufts in Talloires is just an hour from Geneva, headquarters to numerous international organizations. Excursions to Lyon and Paris enable students to develop a better understanding of today's Europe.

UNIVERSITÉ DE REIMS CHAMPAGNE-ARDENNE

SUMMER PROGRAM IN REIMS, FRANCE

General Information • Language study program in Reims. Classes are held on the campus of Université de Reims Champagne-Ardenne. Excursions to Paris, Champagne area.

Learning Focus • Courses in civilizations, culinary arts, French language, literature, drama. Instruction is offered by professors from the sponsoring institution and local teachers.

Accommodations • Homestays, program-owned apartments. Single rooms are available. Meals are taken as a group, in central dining facility.

Program Details • Program offered once per year. Session length: 4 weeks. Departures are scheduled in July. The program is open to undergraduate students, graduate students, adults. Most participants are 18 years of age and older. Other requirements: level of the French baccalauréat. 40 participants per session. Application deadline: 1 week prior to departure.

Costs • $580 (includes tuition, books and class materials, excursions). A $100 deposit is required.

Contact • Secretary for Mr. Dargaud, Université de Reims Champagne-Ardenne, 17 Rue du Jard, 51100 Reims, France; +33 26-470411; Fax: +33 26-47-05-40

UNIVERSITY OF ALABAMA AT BIRMINGHAM

UNIVERSITY OF ALABAMA AT BIRMINGHAM IN FRANCE

General Information • Language study and cultural program in Dijon. Classes are held on the campus of University of Burgundy, Dijon. Excursions to Paris.

Learning Focus • Courses in French language, French culture. Instruction is offered by professors from the sponsoring institution and local teachers.

Accommodations • University housing. Single rooms are available. Meals are taken on one's own, in local restaurants.

Program Details • Program offered once per year. Session length: 4 weeks. Departures are scheduled in August. The program is open to undergraduate students, graduate students. Most participants are 20–40 years of age. Other requirements: completion of French 101 and 102. 15–20 participants per session. Application deadline: May 31.

Costs • $2875 (includes tuition, housing, some meals, insurance, excursions, international airfare). A $200 deposit is required.

Contact • Frank Romanowicz, Study Abroad Coordinator, University of Alabama at Birmingham, 1400 University Boulevard, HUC 318, Birmingham, AL 35294-1150; 205-934-5025; Fax: 205-934-8664; E-mail: ucipØ17@larry.huc.uab.edu

UNIVERSITY OF ARIZONA

ARIZONA IN PARIS

General Information • Language study program in Paris. Excursions to Loire Valley, Chartres, Versailles.
Learning Focus • Courses in French language, French culture. Instruction is offered by professors from the sponsoring institution.
Accommodations • Homestays. Single rooms are available. Meals are taken with host family, in residences.
Program Details • Program offered once per year. Session length: 6 weeks. Departures are scheduled in June. The program is open to undergraduate students. Most participants are 20–30 years of age. Other requirements: minimum 2.5 GPA and 1 year college-level French. 25 participants per session. Application deadline: April 1.
Costs • $3400 (includes tuition, housing, some meals, excursions). Application fee: $35. A $300 deposit is required.
Contact • Renee Griggs, Center for Global Student Programs, University of Arizona, 915 North Tyndall Avenue, Tucson, AZ 85721; 520-621-4627; Fax: 520-621-4069

UNIVERSITY OF COLORADO AT BOULDER

SUMMER INTENSIVE FRENCH PROGRAM

General Information • Language study program in Annecy. Classes are held on the campus of Institut Français Des Alpes (IFALDES).
Learning Focus • Courses in French language, French culture. Instruction is offered by local teachers.
Accommodations • Homestays, dormitories. Single rooms are available. Meals are taken on one's own, with host family.
Program Details • Program offered 3 times per year. Session length: 4 weeks. Departures are scheduled in June–August. The program is open to undergraduate students. Most participants are 19–23 years of age. Other requirements: minimum 2.75 GPA and some French recommended. 15–20 participants per session. Application deadline: March 1.
Costs • $1779 for Colorado residents, $2529 for non-residents (includes tuition, housing, some meals, insurance). A $300 deposit is required.
Contact • Study Abroad Program, University of Colorado at Boulder, International Education, Campus Box 123, Boulder, CO 80309-0123; 303-492-7741; Fax: 303-492-5185; E-mail: studyabr@colorado.edu; World Wide Web: http://www.colorado.edu/OIE/StudyAbroad

UNIVERSITY OF DELAWARE

SUMMER SESSION IN PARIS

General Information • Academic study program in Paris. Classes are held on the campus of University of the New Sorbonne (Paris III). Excursions to Versailles, Giverny.
Learning Focus • Courses in French language, music, art history. Instruction is offered by professors from the sponsoring institution and local teachers.
Accommodations • Homestays. Meals are taken on one's own, with host family, in local restaurants, in residences.
Program Details • Program offered once per year. Session length: 5 weeks. Departures are scheduled in June. The program is open to undergraduate students, graduate students, adults. Most participants are 18–21 years of age. Other requirements: minimum 2.0 GPA. 20 participants per session. Application deadline: April 15.
Costs • $4261 (includes tuition, housing, some meals, excursions, international airfare). A $200 deposit is required.
Contact • International Programs and Special Sessions, University of Delaware, 4 Kent Way, Newark, DE 19716-1450; 888-831-4685; Fax: 302-831-6042; E-mail: studyabroad@mvs.udel.edu

UNIVERSITY OF DELAWARE

WINTER SESSION IN FRANCE

General Information • Language study program in Caen. Classes are held on the campus of University of Caen. Excursions to Paris, Versailles, Normandy beaches.
Learning Focus • Courses in civilizations, cultural studies, French studies, French language. Instruction is offered by professors from the sponsoring institution.
Accommodations • Homestays. Single rooms are available.
Program Details • Program offered once per year. Session length: 5 weeks. Departures are scheduled in January. The program is open to undergraduate students. Most participants are 18–21 years of age. Other requirements: minimum 2.0 GPA and 2 semesters of college-level French. 25 participants per session. Application deadline: October.
Costs • $4110 (includes tuition, housing, some meals, excursions, international airfare). A $200 deposit is required.
Contact • International Programs and Special Sessions, University of Delaware, 4 Kent Way, Newark, DE 19716-1450; 888-831-4685; Fax: 302-831-6042; E-mail: studyabroad@mvs.udel.edu

UNIVERSITY OF DELAWARE

WINTER SESSION IN PARIS, FRANCE

General Information • Academic study program in Paris.
Learning Focus • Courses in fashion, fashion house management, fashion merchandising. Instruction is offered by professors from the sponsoring institution.
Accommodations • Locally-rented apartments.
Program Details • Program offered once per year. Session length: 5 weeks. Departures are scheduled in January. The program is open to undergraduate students. Most participants are 18–21 years of age. Other requirements: minimum 2.0 GPA. 20 participants per session. Application deadline: October.
Costs • $4110 (includes tuition, housing, some meals, excursions, international airfare). A $200 deposit is required.
Contact • International Programs and Special Sessions, University of Delaware, 4 Kent Way, Newark, DE 19716-1450; 888-831-4685; Fax: 302-831-6042; E-mail: studyabroad@mvs.udel.edu

UNIVERSITY OF FLORIDA

UNIVERSITY OF MONTPELLIER, COLLEGE OF LAW

General Information • Academic study program in Montpellier. Classes are held on the campus of University of Montpellier I. Excursions to Camargue National Park.

Learning Focus • Courses in legal studies. Instruction is offered by local teachers.
Accommodations • Hostels. Meals are taken on one's own.
Program Details • Program offered once per year. Session length: 4 weeks. Departures are scheduled in July. The program is open to graduate students. Most participants are 23–40 years of age. Other requirements: law students that have completed first year. Application deadline: April 15.
Costs • $5000–$7500 (includes tuition, housing, some meals, insurance, international airfare, administration fees, some living expenses). Application fee: $250.
Contact • Overseas Studies, University of Florida, 123 Tigert Hall, PO Box 113225, Gainesville, FL 32611-3225; 352-392-5206; Fax: 352-392-5575; E-mail: ovrseas@nervm.nerdc.ufl.edu

UNIVERSITY OF KANSAS

ARCHITECTURAL STUDIES IN PARIS, FRANCE

General Information • Academic study program in Paris. Classes are held on the campus of Ecole Camando. Excursions to Barcelona, Nîmes, Lyons, Chartres.
Learning Focus • Courses in architecture. Instruction is offered by professors from the sponsoring institution.
Accommodations • Dormitories, hotels. Meals are taken as a group, on one's own, in central dining facility, in local restaurants.
Program Details • Program offered once per year. Session length: 6 weeks. Departures are scheduled in June. The program is open to undergraduate students, graduate students. Most participants are 22–25 years of age. Other requirements: preparation for fifth-year Architecture Studio. 20 participants per session. Application deadline: March 1.
Costs • $3904 (includes tuition, housing, studio facilities). Application fee: $15. A $300 deposit is required.
Contact • Susan MacNally, Coordinator of Summer Institutes, University of Kansas, Office of Study Abroad, 203 Lippincott Hall, Lawrence, KS 66045; 913-864-3742; Fax: 913-864-5040; E-mail: osa@falcon.cc.ukans.edu; World Wide Web: http://kuhub.cc.ukans.edu/~intlstdy/osa/osamain.html

UNIVERSITY OF KANSAS

FRENCH LANGUAGE AND CULTURE IN PARIS

General Information • Language study program in Paris. Classes are held on the campus of Étoile Coutre de Langues et Vie. Excursions to Normandy, Touraine, Brittany.
Learning Focus • Courses in French language, French culture, French literature. Instruction is offered by professors from the sponsoring institution and local teachers.
Accommodations • Dormitories, hotels. Meals are taken as a group, on one's own, in central dining facility, in local restaurants, in residences.
Program Details • Program offered once per year. Session length: 6 weeks. Departures are scheduled in June. The program is open to undergraduate students, graduate students. Most participants are 18–28 years of age. Other requirements: 2 semesters of college-level French or equivalent. 25 participants per session. Application deadline: March 1.
Costs • $3300 (includes tuition, housing, some meals, 10-day tour of northern France, entry to group cultural events). Application fee: $15. A $300 deposit is required.
Contact • Susan MacNally, Coordinator of Summer Institutes, University of Kansas, Office of Study Abroad, 203 Lippincott Hall, Lawrence, KS 66045; 913-864-3742; Fax: 913-864-5040; E-mail: osa@falcon.cc.ukans.edu; World Wide Web: http://kuhub.cc.ukans.edu/~intlstdy/osa/osamain.html

UNIVERSITY OF KANSAS

PARIS ORIENTATION PROGRAM

General Information • Academic study program in Paris. Classes are held on the campus of Cité Universitaire Internationale de Paris. Excursions to châteaux and cathedrals outside Paris, Chartres, Ste. Chappelle, Fontainebleau.
Learning Focus • Courses in French language, French culture. Instruction is offered by local teachers.
Accommodations • Dormitories. Meals are taken on one's own, in central dining facility, in local restaurants, in residences.
Program Details • Program offered once per year. Session length: 3 weeks. Departures are scheduled in September. The program is open to undergraduate students, graduate students. Most participants are 20–28 years of age. Other requirements: 4 semesters college-level French or equivalent, minimum overall GPA of 2.8, minimum 3.0 GPA or above in French. 18 participants per session. Application deadline: July 15.
Costs • $1720 (includes tuition, housing, some meals, excursions, cultural activities, transportation pass, museum pass). A $300 deposit is required.
Contact • Laura Leonard, Program Coordinator, Paris Orientation Program, University of Kansas, Office of Study Abroad, 203 Lippincott Hall, Lawrence, KS 66045; 913-864-3742; Fax: 913-864-5040; E-mail: osa@falcon.cc.ukans.edu; World Wide Web: http://kuhub.cc.ukans.edu/~intlstdy/osa/osamain.html

UNIVERSITY OF LOUISVILLE

MONTPELLIER WORK EXCHANGE PROGRAM

General Information • Work abroad program in Montpellier. Classes are held on the campus of University Paul Valéry (Montpellier III).
Learning Focus • Courses in French language, French culture. Instruction is offered by professors from the sponsoring institution and local teachers.
Accommodations • Dormitories. Single rooms are available. Meals are taken on one's own, in local restaurants.
Program Details • Program offered once per year. Session length: 4 weeks. Departures are scheduled in July. The program is open to undergraduate students, graduate students, adults. Most participants are 20–30 years of age. Other requirements: 2 years of French. 30 participants per session. Application deadline: February 1.
Costs • Students are paid a stipend of about $600 per month to cover room and board. Application fee: $250.
Contact • Luis A. Canales, Associate Director, University of Louisville, International Center, Louisville, KY 40292; 502-852-6602; Fax: 502-852-7216; E-mail: lacana01@ulkyvm.louisville.edu

 UNIVERSITY OF MIAMI

SUMMER PROGRAM IN INTENSIVE FRENCH AT UNIVERSITÉ D'ORLÉANS

General Information • Language study program in Orléans. Classes are held on the campus of University of Orléans.
Learning Focus • Instruction is offered by local teachers.
Accommodations • Dormitories. Single rooms are available. Meals are taken on one's own, in central dining facility.
Program Details • Program offered once per year. Session length: 4 weeks. Departures are scheduled in July. The program is open to undergraduate students, graduate students. Most participants are 19–25 years of age. Other requirements: minimum 3.0 GPA. Application deadline: April 1.
Costs • $2500 (includes tuition). Application fee: $30. A $500 deposit is required.
Contact • Peggy Ting, Study Abroad Program, University of Miami, PO Box 248005, Coral Gables, FL 33124-1610; 305-557-5421; Fax: 305-284-6629; E-mail: ieep@cstudies.msmail.miami.edu; World Wide Web: http://www.miami.edu/cstudies/ieep.html

 UNIVERSITY OF MICHIGAN

SUMMER LANGUAGE PROGRAM IN SAINT MALO, FRANCE

General Information • Language study program in St. Malo. Excursions to Paris, Tours.
Learning Focus • Courses in French language. Instruction is offered by professors from the sponsoring institution.
Accommodations • Homestays. Single rooms are available. Meals are taken with host family, in residences.
Program Details • Program offered once per year. Session length: 6 weeks. Departures are scheduled in June. The program is open to undergraduate students. Most participants are 19–22 years of age. Other requirements: three semesters college-level French or equivalent and a minimum 3.0 GPA. 30 participants per session. Application deadline: February 28.
Costs • $4000–$4300 (includes tuition, housing, some meals, excursions). Application fee: $50. A $250 deposit is required.
Contact • Office of International Programs, University of Michigan, G-513 Michigan Union, 530 South State Street, Ann Arbor, MI 48109-1349; 313-764-4311; Fax: 313-764-3229; E-mail: oip@umich.edu; World Wide Web: http://www.umich.edu/~iinet/oip/

 UNIVERSITY OF MINNESOTA, THE GLOBAL CAMPUS

BEGINNING FRENCH IN NANTES

General Information • Language study program in Nantes. Classes are held on the campus of Institute for European Studies. Excursions to local areas around Nantes.
Learning Focus • Courses in French language. Instruction is offered by professors from the sponsoring institution and local teachers.
Accommodations • Homestays. Single rooms are available. Meals are taken as a group, on one's own, with host family, in local restaurants, in residences.
Program Details • Program offered once per year. Session length: 8 weeks. Departures are scheduled in June. The program is open to undergraduate students, graduate students, pre-college students, adults. Most participants are 18–25 years of age. Other requirements: minimum 2.5 GPA and a B average for recent high school graduates. 15 participants per session. Application deadline: March 15.
Costs • $2550–$2800 (includes tuition, housing, some meals, books and class materials, excursions, pre-departure and on-site orientation). Application fee: $40. A $400 deposit is required.
Contact • Beginning French in Nantes, University of Minnesota, The Global Campus, 106 P2 Nicholson Hall, 216 Pillsbury Drive, SE, Minneapolis, MN 55455; 612-625-3379; Fax: 612-626-8009; E-mail: globalc@maroon.tc.umn.edu; World Wide Web: http://www.isp.umn.edu/tgchome/tgchome.html

 UNIVERSITY OF NEW ORLEANS

GLORIES OF FRANCE

General Information • Language study program in Montpellier. Classes are held on the campus of Cours Intensiu de Française. Excursions to Southern France.
Learning Focus • Courses in French language. Instruction is offered by local teachers.
Accommodations • Dormitories. Single rooms are available. Meals are taken as a group, in central dining facility.
Program Details • Program offered once per year. Session length: 4 weeks. Departures are scheduled in July. The program is open to undergraduate students, pre-college students. Most participants are 17–25 years of age. 30 participants per session. Application deadline: April 1.
Costs • $2495 (includes tuition, housing, some meals, books and class materials, insurance, excursions). A $200 deposit is required.
Contact • Marie Kaposchyn, Coordinator, University of New Orleans, PO Box 569, New Orleans, LA 70148; 504-280-7455; Fax: 504-280-7317; World Wide Web: http://www.uno.edu/~inst/Welcome.html

UNIVERSITY OF NORTH CAROLINA AT CHARLOTTE

ARCHITECTURAL FIELD STUDY IN PARIS

General Information • Academic study program in Paris.
Learning Focus • Courses in architecture. Instruction is offered by professors from the sponsoring institution.
Accommodations • Hostels. Meals are taken as a group, in local restaurants.
Program Details • Program offered once per year. Session length: 3 weeks. Departures are scheduled in May. The program is open to undergraduate students, graduate students. Most participants are 18–30 years of age. 6 participants per session. Application deadline: January.
Costs • $2000 (includes tuition, housing, books and class materials, insurance, excursions). Application fee: $10. A $500 deposit is required.

Contact • Elizabeth A. Adams, Director, Education Abroad Programs, University of North Carolina at Charlotte, Office of International Programs, 9201 University City Boulevard, Charlotte, NC 28223-0001; 704-547-2464; Fax: 704-547-3168; E-mail: eaadams@email.uncc.edu; World Wide Web: http://unccvm.uncc.edu

 UNIVERSITY OF PENNSYLVANIA

PENN-IN-BORDEAUX

General Information • Academic study program in Bordeaux. Classes are held on the campus of University of Bordeaux III.

Learning Focus • Courses in anthropology. Instruction is offered by professors from the sponsoring institution and local teachers.

Accommodations • Dormitories. Single rooms are available. Meals are taken on one's own, in local restaurants.

Program Details • Program offered once per year. Session length: 2½ weeks. Departures are scheduled in June. The program is open to undergraduate students, graduate students. Most participants are 19–50 years of age. 16 participants per session. Application deadline: April 1.

Costs • $1742 (includes tuition, housing, excursions). Application fee: $35. A $300 deposit is required.

Contact • Elizabeth Sachs, Director, Penn Summer Abroad, University of Pennsylvania, 3440 Market Street, Suite 100, Philadelphia, PA 19104-3335; 215-898-5738; Fax: 215-573-2053; E-mail: esachs@mail.sas.upenn.edu

 UNIVERSITY OF PENNSYLVANIA

PENN-IN-CANNES

General Information • Academic study program in Cannes.

Learning Focus • Courses in film studies. Instruction is offered by professors from the sponsoring institution.

Accommodations • Hostels. Meals are taken on one's own, in local restaurants.

Program Details • Program offered once per year. Session length: 2 weeks. Departures are scheduled in May. The program is open to undergraduate students, graduate students, adults. Most participants are 18–35 years of age. 29 participants per session. Application deadline: February 1.

Costs • $1700 (includes tuition, housing). Application fee: $35. A $300 deposit is required.

Contact • Elizabeth Sachs, Director, Penn Summer Abroad, University of Pennsylvania, 3440 Market Street, Suite 100, Philadelphia, PA 19104-3335; 215-898-5738; Fax: 215-573-2053; E-mail: esachs@mail.sas.upenn.edu

 UNIVERSITY OF PENNSYLVANIA

PENN-IN-COMPIÈGNE

General Information • Academic study program in Compiègne. Classes are held on the campus of L'Université de Technologie de Compiègne.

Learning Focus • Courses in French language, economics. Instruction is offered by local teachers.

Accommodations • Homestays. Single rooms are available. Meals are taken with host family.

Program Details • Program offered once per year. Session length: 7½ weeks. Departures are scheduled in May. The program is open to undergraduate students, graduate students. Most participants are 20–24 years of age. Other requirements: proficiency in French. 10 participants per session. Application deadline: March 15.

Costs • $3884 (includes tuition, housing). Application fee: $35. A $300 deposit is required.

Contact • Elizabeth Sachs, Director, Penn Summer Abroad, University of Pennsylvania, 3440 Market Street, Suite 100, Philadelphia, PA 19104-3335; 215-898-5738; Fax: 215-573-2053; E-mail: esachs@mail.sas.upenn.edu

 UNIVERSITY OF PENNSYLVANIA

PENN-IN-TOURS

General Information • Academic study program in Tours. Classes are held on the campus of University of Tours.

Learning Focus • Courses in French language, art history, European culture. Instruction is offered by professors from the sponsoring institution.

Accommodations • Homestays. Meals are taken with host family, in residences.

Program Details • Program offered once per year. Session length: 6 weeks. Departures are scheduled in May. The program is open to undergraduate students, graduate students. Most participants are 19–35 years of age. 26 participants per session. Application deadline: February 15.

Costs • $4184 (includes tuition, housing, some meals, excursions). Application fee: $35. A $300 deposit is required.

Contact • Elizabeth Sachs, Director, Penn Summer Abroad, University of Pennsylvania, 3440 Market Street, Suite 100, Philadelphia, PA 19104-3335; 215-898-5738; Fax: 215-573-2053; E-mail: esachs@mail.sas.upenn.edu

UNIVERSITY OF ROCHESTER

FRENCH IN FRANCE

General Information • Language study program in Rennes. Classes are held on the campus of Institut Franco-Americain.

Learning Focus • Courses in language study. Instruction is offered by professors from the sponsoring institution and local teachers.

Accommodations • Homestays. Meals are taken with host family, in residences.

Program Details • Program offered once per year. Session length: 4 weeks. Departures are scheduled in May. The program is open to undergraduate students, adults. Most participants are 18–25 years of age. Other requirements: previous French language study, either 3 years high school or 1 year college. 8–10 participants per session. Application deadline: March 15.

Costs • $2750 (includes tuition, housing, some meals, excursions).

Contact • Anne Lutkus, Language Coordinator, University of Rochester, Department of Modern Languages and Cultures, Rochester, NY 14627; 716-275-4251; E-mail: adlt@db1.cc.rochester.edu; World Wide Web: http://www.rochester.edu/College/study-abroad/

UNIVERSITY OF SOUTHERN MISSISSIPPI

CONTEMPORARY FRENCH HISTORY

General Information • Academic study program in Paris. Excursions to Normandy, Fontainebleau.
Learning Focus • Courses in history.
Accommodations • Hotels, hostels.
Program Details • Program offered once per year. Session length: 3 weeks. Departures are scheduled in May. The program is open to undergraduate students, graduate students. Other requirements: minimum 2.0 GPA and good academic standing. Application deadline: March 3.
Costs • $2499 for undergraduates, $2799 for graduate students (includes tuition, international airfare). A $100 deposit is required.
Contact • Director, Contemporary French History, University of Southern Mississippi, Box 10047, Hattiesburg, MS 39406-0047; 601-266-4344; Fax: 601-266-5699

UNIVERSITY OF TOLEDO

SUMMER STUDY IN PARIS AND MONTPELLIER, FRANCE

General Information • Language study program in Montpellier, Paris. Excursions to Nîmes, Avignon, Pezenes.
Learning Focus • Courses in French language, cultural studies. Instruction is offered by professors from the sponsoring institution.
Accommodations • Homestays, hotels. Single rooms are available. Meals are taken with host family, in residences.
Program Details • Program offered once per year. Session length: 5 weeks. Departures are scheduled in June. The program is open to undergraduate students, graduate students. Most participants are 20–25 years of age. Other requirements: must have completed intermediate French. 10–15 participants per session. Application deadline: February 28.
Costs • $3800 (includes tuition, housing, some meals, books and class materials, excursions, international airfare). Application fee: $25. A $100 deposit is required.
Contact • Joel A. Gallegos, Study Abroad Coordinator, University of Toledo, C.I.S.P. SWAC 2357, Toledo, OH 43606; 419-530-1240; Fax: 419-537-1245; E-mail: jgalleg@utnet.utoledo.edu; World Wide Web: http://www.utoledo.edu/www/cisp/study-abroad/

UNIVERSITY STUDIES ABROAD CONSORTIUM

FRENCH AND BASQUE STUDIES IN PAU, FRANCE

General Information • Academic study program in Pau. Classes are held on the campus of University of Pau. Excursions to Paris, St. Jean Pied-de-Port, Pyrénées, French Basque coast.
Learning Focus • Courses in French language, history, French culture, French government and politics, contemporary French society. Instruction is offered by local teachers.
Accommodations • Homestays, dormitories, locally-rented apartments. Single rooms are available. Meals are taken on one's own, with host family, in central dining facility, in residences.
Program Details • Program offered 2 times per year. Session length: 4 weeks. Departures are scheduled in June, July. The program is open to undergraduate students, graduate students, pre-college students, adults. Most participants are 18–50 years of age. Other requirements: minimum 2.5 GPA. 20 participants per session. Application deadline: April 15.
Costs • $1770 (includes tuition, housing, insurance, International Student Identification card). Application fee: $50. A $150 deposit is required.
Contact • Dr. Carmelo Urza, Director, University Studies Abroad Consortium, University of Nevada Library/323, Reno, NV 89557-0009; 702-784-6569; Fax: 702-784-6010; E-mail: usac@equinox.unr.edu; World Wide Web: http://www.scs.unr.edu/~usac

VANDERBILT UNIVERSITY

VANDERBILT IN FRANCE

General Information • Academic study program in Aix-en-Provence. Excursions to Paris.
Learning Focus • Courses in French language, French literature, cultural studies, civilizations, art history. Instruction is offered by professors from the sponsoring institution.
Accommodations • Homestays. Single rooms are available. Meals are taken on one's own, with host family, in local restaurants, in residences.
Program Details • Program offered once per year. Session length: 6 weeks. Departures are scheduled in June. The program is open to undergraduate students. Most participants are 19–21 years of age. Other requirements: minimum 2.7 GPA, 2 years college French and a faculty recommendation. 16–20 participants per session. Application deadline: March 1.
Costs • $5175 (includes tuition, housing, some meals, excursions). A $300 deposit is required.
Contact • Dr. Luigi Monga, Director of Overseas Study, Vanderbilt University, Office of Overseas Study, Box 1573-Station B, Nashville, TN 37235; 615-343-3139; Fax: 615-322-2305

VILLANOVA UNIVERSITY

SUMMER FRENCH LANGUAGE PROGRAM

General Information • Language study program in Dijon, Paris. Classes are held on the campus of University of Burgundy, Dijon. Excursions to Normandy, chateaux in Loire Valley, St. Malo, Paris.
Learning Focus • Courses in French language, explication de textes, French culture. Instruction is offered by local teachers.
Accommodations • Homestays, dormitories. Meals are taken as a group, with host family, in central dining facility.
Program Details • Program offered once per year. Session length: 6 weeks. Departures are scheduled in July. The program is open to undergraduate students. Most participants are 19–23 years of age. Other requirements: minimum

2.5 GPA, good academic standing, and 2 semesters college-level French. 15 participants per session. Application deadline: March 1.

Costs • $3150 (includes tuition, housing, some meals, books and class materials, excursions, transfers and orientation). Application fee: $100.

Contact • Dr. Thomas M. Ricks, Director, International Studies, Villanova University, St. Augustine Center, Room 415, Villanova, PA 19085; 610-519-6412; Fax: 610-519-7649; E-mail: ricks@ucis.vill.edu

GERMANY

 ALMA COLLEGE

SUMMER PROGRAM OF STUDIES IN GERMANY

General Information • Language study program in Kassel. Classes are held on the campus of Europa-Kolleg. Excursions to Buchenwald, palaces.
Learning Focus • Courses in German language. Instruction is offered by local teachers.
Accommodations • Homestays. Single rooms are available. Meals are taken with host family, in residences.
Program Details • Program offered 5 times per year. Session length: 3–11 weeks. Departures are scheduled in June–August. The program is open to undergraduate students, graduate students, adults. Most participants are 20–23 years of age. Other requirements: minimum 2.5 GPA. 2 participants per session. Application deadline: March 15.
Costs • $2495–$6950 (includes tuition, housing, all meals, excursions). Application fee: $35. A $200 deposit is required.
Contact • Patricia Landis, Director of International Education, Alma College, 614 West Superior Street, Alma, MI 48801; 517-463-7247; Fax: 517-463-7126; E-mail: landis@alma.edu; World Wide Web: http://www.alma.edu

APPALACHIAN STATE UNIVERSITY

GERMANY

General Information • Academic study program in Würzburg. Excursions to Munich, Austria.
Learning Focus • Courses in foreign languages. Instruction is offered by professors from the sponsoring institution.
Program Details • Program offered once per year. Session length: 4 weeks. Departures are scheduled in July. Most participants are 18 years of age and older. 20 participants per session.
Costs • $1850 (includes tuition, housing, insurance, international airfare, International Student Identification card).
Contact • Dr. Uli Froelich, Professor, Appalachian State University, Department of Foreign Languages, Boone, NC 28608; 704-262-3095; Fax: 704-262-4037

THE CENTER FOR ENGLISH STUDIES

STUDY ABROAD IN FREIBURG, GERMANY

General Information • Language study program with visits to Freiburg. Program is affiliated with International House LGS Sprachkurse.
Learning Focus • Instruction in the German language. Other activities include field trips to local sites, museums, markets and churches. Instruction is offered by faculty members from host institution. This program would appeal to people interested in the German language, the German language.
Accommodations • Homestays, dormitories, locally-rented apartments, program-owned apartments, program-owned houses. Single rooms are available.
Program Details • Session length: 2 or more weeks. Departures are scheduled throughout the year. Most participants are 12–70 years of age. Participants must be 12 years or older to enroll. 6–12 participants per session. Application deadline: 2 weeks prior to departure. Reservations are recommended at least 1 month before departure.
Costs • $1000 for 2 weeks (includes tuition, housing, some meals, books and class materials, excursions). A $125 deposit is required.
Contact • Ms. Lorraine Haber, Study Abroad Coordinator, The Center for English Studies, 330 7th Avenue, 6th Floor, New York, NY 10001; 212-629-7300; Fax: 212-736-7950; E-mail: ces_newyork@cescorp.com

COLLEGE CONSORTIUM FOR INTERNATIONAL STUDIES–OCEAN COUNTY COLLEGE

INTENSIVE GERMAN LANGUAGE

General Information • Language study program in Heidelberg. Excursions to Berlin.
Learning Focus • Courses in European area studies.
Accommodations • Homestays, dormitories, locally-rented apartments, program-owned houses. Single rooms are available. Meals are taken on one's own, with host family, in central dining facility, in residences.
Program Details • Program offered 6 times per year. Departures are scheduled in January, March, May, July, September, October. The program is open to undergraduate students, graduate students, adults. Most participants are 20–25 years of age. Other requirements: minimum 3.0 GPA. 6–10 participants per session. Application deadline: 90 days prior to departure.
Costs • $3565 (includes tuition, housing, excursions). Application fee: $15.
Contact • Jane C. Evans, Executive Director, College Consortium for International Studies, 2000 P Street, NW, Suite 503, Washington, DC 20036; 800-453-6956; Fax: 202-223-0999; E-mail: ccis@intr.net

CROSS-CULTURE

WALKS IN GERMANY'S HUNSRUCK

General Information • Nature study, cultural, and hiking tour with visits to Dhaun, Idar-Oberstein, Kirn, Oberhausen, Kallenfels, Kirschroth, Disibodenberg, Bad Munster, Cochem, Bingen, St. Goar, Wappenroth, Altburg, Herrenberg,

Schmidtburg, Herrstein. Once at the destination country, participants travel by bus, foot, boat.
Learning Focus • Instruction in flora and fauna and historical and contemporary topics of interest. Escorted travel to Church of St. Johannsberg, Eltz Castle and Lorelei Rock. Other activities include hiking. Instruction is offered by naturalists, historians, experienced hiking leaders. This program would appeal to people interested in nature studies, history, food and wine, culture, traditions.
Accommodations • Hotels. Single rooms are available for an additional $65.
Program Details • Program offered once per year. Session length: 9 days. Departures are scheduled in August. Program is targeted to adults of all ages. Most participants are 30–75 years of age. Participants must be 12 years or older to enroll. Other requirements: must be in good health, must be accompanied by an adult if under 18. 20 participants per session. Application deadline: 1 month prior to departure. Reservations are recommended at least 3–12 months before departure.
Costs • $2230 (includes tuition, housing, all meals, books and class materials, excursions, international airfare). A $300 deposit is required.
Contact • Cross-Culture, 52 High Point Drive, Amherst, MA 01002-1224; 413-256-6303; Fax: 413-253-2303; E-mail: xculture@javanet.com; World Wide Web: http://www.empiremall.com/cross-culture

CSA–CENTER FOR STUDY ABROAD

AGI–STUTTGART: GERMAN LANGUAGE

General Information • Language study program in Stuttgart.
Learning Focus • Courses in German language. Instruction is offered by professors from the sponsoring institution.
Accommodations • Homestays, locally-rented apartments. Single rooms are available. Meals are taken on one's own, with host family.
Program Details • Program offered 52 times per year. Session length: 1–8 weeks. Departures are scheduled in January–November. The program is open to undergraduate students, graduate students, pre-college students, adults. Most participants are 20–38 years of age. Other requirements: minimum age of 17. 6–8 participants per session.
Costs • $1595 for 2 weeks (includes tuition, housing, some meals, books and class materials, insurance, registration and orientation). Application fee: $45. A $50 deposit is required.
Contact • Philip Virtue, Program Director, CSA–Center for Study Abroad, 2802 East Madison Street MS #160, Seattle, WA 98112; 206-726-1498; Fax: 206-285-9197; E-mail: virtuecsa@aol.com

CSA–CENTER FOR STUDY ABROAD

GLS–BERLIN

General Information • Language study program in Berlin.
Learning Focus • Courses in German language. Instruction is offered by professors from the sponsoring institution.
Accommodations • Homestays, locally-rented apartments. Single rooms are available. Meals are taken on one's own, with host family.
Program Details • Program offered 52 times per year. Session length: 1–12 weeks. Departures are scheduled in January–December. The program is open to undergraduate students, graduate students, pre-college students, adults. Most participants are 21–42 years of age. Other requirements: minimum age of 17. 5–10 participants per session.
Costs • $1595 for 2 weeks (includes tuition, housing, some meals, books and class materials, insurance, registration, orientation). Application fee: $45. A $50 deposit is required.
Contact • Philip Virtue, Program Director, CSA–Center for Study Abroad, 2802 East Madison Street MS #160, Seattle, WA 98112; 206-726-1498; Fax: 206-285-9197; E-mail: virtuecsa@aol.com

DICKINSON COLLEGE

BREMEN PRACTICUM

General Information • Language study program in Bremen.
Learning Focus • Courses in German language, German culture. Instruction is offered by professors from the sponsoring institution.
Accommodations • Homestays. Single rooms are available. Meals are taken with host family, in residences.
Program Details • Program offered once per year. Session length: 6 weeks. Departures are scheduled in May. The program is open to undergraduate students. Most participants are 18–20 years of age. Other requirements: intermediate-level German. 15 participants per session. Application deadline: February 15.
Costs • Contact sponsor for information. Application fee: $15. A $300 deposit is required.
Contact • Dr. John S. Henderson, Director of Off-Campus Studies, Dickinson College, PO Box 1773, Carlisle, PA 17013-2896; 717-245-1341; Fax: 717-245-1688; E-mail: ocs@dickinson.edu; World Wide Web: http://www.dickinson.edu

DUKE UNIVERSITY

DUKE IN ERLANGEN

General Information • Academic study program in Erlangen. Classes are held on the campus of Friedrich Alexander University of Erlangen-Nüremberg. Excursions to Berlin, Czech Republic (Prague), Nuremburg, Bamberg.
Learning Focus • Courses in language study, German culture.
Accommodations • Homestays. Meals are taken on one's own, in local restaurants.
Program Details • Program offered once per year. Session length: 6 weeks. Departures are scheduled in May. The program is open to undergraduate students. Most participants are 19–21 years of age. Other requirements: minimum 2.7 GPA and 2 semesters college-level German or equivalent. 15 participants per session. Application deadline: February 21.
Costs • $3891 (includes tuition, housing, some meals, excursions, international airfare).
Contact • Foreign Academic Programs, Duke University, 121 Allen Building, Box 90057, Durham, NC 27708-0057;

919-684-2174; Fax: 919-684-3083; E-mail: abroad@mail01.adm.duke.edu; World Wide Web: http://www.mis.duke.edu/study_abroad/study_abroad.html

EF INTERNATIONAL LANGUAGE SCHOOLS

GERMAN IN MUNICH

General Information • Language study program in Munich. Classes are held on the campus of EF Internationale Sprachschule. Excursions to Nuremberg, Czech Republic (Prague), Neuschwanzstein, Austria (Vienna, Innsbruck, Salzburg).
Learning Focus • Courses in German language. Instruction is offered by local teachers.
Accommodations • Homestays. Single rooms are available. Meals are taken as a group, with host family, in central dining facility, in residences.
Program Details • Program offered 26 times per year. Session length: 2–12 weeks. Departures are scheduled in January–December. The program is open to undergraduate students, graduate students, pre-college students, adults. Most participants are 16–25 years of age. Other requirements: minimum age of 16. 40 participants per session. Application deadline: 60 days prior to departure.
Costs • Principal: $990 per 2 weeks, intensive: $1110 per 2 weeks (includes tuition, housing, some meals, books and class materials). Application fee: $90. A $350 deposit is required.
Contact • Kari Larson, Admissions Manager, EF International Language Schools, 204 Lake Street, Boston, MA 02135; 800-992-1892; Fax: 617-746-1800

EUROCENTRES

LANGUAGE IMMERSION IN GERMANY

General Information • Language study program in Cologne. Classes are held on the campus of Eurocentre-Cologne. Excursions to Moselle Valley, Heidelberg, Berlin, Aachen, Maastricht, Düsseldorf.
Learning Focus • Courses in German language, German culture. Instruction is offered by professors from the sponsoring institution.
Accommodations • Homestays. Single rooms are available. Meals are taken with host family, in residences.
Program Details • Program offered 20 times per year. Session length: 2–12 weeks. Departures are scheduled in January–December. The program is open to undergraduate students, graduate students, pre-college students, adults. Most participants are 16–80 years of age. 15 participants per session.
Costs • Contact sponsor for information.
Contact • Marketing, Eurocentres, 101 North Union Street, Suite 300, Alexandria, VA 22314; 800-648-4809; Fax: 703-684-1495; E-mail: 100632.141@compuserve.com; World Wide Web: http://www.clark.net/pub/eurocent/home.htm

FOREIGN LANGUAGE STUDY ABROAD SERVICE

GERMAN IN GERMANY

General Information • Language study program in Berlin, Munich, Quedlinburg, Stuttgart.
Learning Focus • Courses in language study. Instruction is offered by local teachers.
Accommodations • Homestays, program-owned apartments, hotels. Single rooms are available. Meals are taken on one's own, with host family, in local restaurants, in residences.
Program Details • Session length: varies. Departures are scheduled in January–December. The program is open to undergraduate students, graduate students, pre-college students, adults. Most participants are 18 years of age and older.
Costs • Contact sponsor for information. Application fee: $50. A $100 deposit is required.
Contact • Louise Harber, Coordinator, Foreign Language Study Abroad Service, Department IH, Box 903, 5935 Southwest 64th Avenue, South Miami, FL 33143; 800-282-1090; Fax: 305-662-2907; E-mail: flsas@netpoint.net; World Wide Web: http://www.netpoint.net/~flsas

FOREIGN LANGUAGE STUDY ABROAD SERVICE

INTERNATIONAL LANGUAGE STUDY HOMESTAYS IN GERMANY

General Information • Language study program in Germany.
Learning Focus • Courses in German language. Instruction is offered by local teachers.
Accommodations • Homestays. Single rooms are available. Meals are taken with host family, in residences.
Program Details • Session length: varies. Departures are scheduled in January–December. The program is open to undergraduate students, graduate students, pre-college students, adults. Most participants are 12 years of age and older. Other requirements: students must be at least 12 years old. 1 participant per session.
Costs • Contact sponsor for information. A $300 deposit is required.
Contact • Louise Harber, Coordinator, Foreign Language Study Abroad Service, Department IH, Box 903, 5935 Southwest 64th Avenue, South Miami, FL 33143; 800-282-1090; Fax: 305-662-2907; E-mail: flsas@netpoint.net; World Wide Web: http://www.netpoint.net/~flsas

FORUM TRAVEL INTERNATIONAL

WUNDERHIKING IN THE BLACK FOREST

General Information • Sports program with visits to Black Forest, Triberg. Once at the destination country, participants travel by foot.
Learning Focus • Museum visits (Museum of Natural History, Clock Museum). Nature observation (wildlife and plantlife in the Black Forest). Other activities include hiking. Instruction is offered by professors, researchers, naturalists, artists, sports professionals. This program would appeal to people interested in hiking.

Accommodations • Hotels. Single rooms are available for an additional $150.
Program Details • Session length: 9 days. Departures are scheduled in January–November. Most participants are 20–60 years of age. Participants must be 16 years or older to enroll. 3 participants per session. Application deadline: 60 days prior to departure. Reservations are recommended at least 3–5 months before departure.
Costs • $885 (includes housing, some meals, luggage transport). A $200 deposit is required.
Contact • Jeannie Graves, Operations Manager, Forum Travel International, 91 Gregory Lane #21, Pleasant Hill, CA 94525; 510-671-2900; Fax: 510-671-2993; E-mail: forum@ix.netcom.com; World Wide Web: http://www.ten-io.com/forumtravel

GEORGETOWN UNIVERSITY

SUMMER IN TRIER

General Information • Language study program in Trier. Classes are held on the campus of University of Trier.
Learning Focus • Courses in business, German language, literature, business German. Instruction is offered by professors from the sponsoring institution and local teachers.
Accommodations • Homestays. Single rooms are available. Meals are taken with host family, in residences.
Program Details • Program offered once per year. Session length: 5 weeks. Departures are scheduled in June, July. The program is open to undergraduate students, graduate students, pre-college students, adults. Most participants are 18–22 years of age. Other requirements: minimum 3.0 GPA. 35 participants per session. Application deadline: March.
Costs • $3000 (includes tuition, housing, all meals, books and class materials, insurance, excursions). A $100 deposit is required.
Contact • Marianne T. Needham, Director, International Programs, Georgetown University, 306 ICC, Box 571012, Washington, DC 20057-1012; 202-687-6184; Fax: 202-687-8954; E-mail: sscefps1@gunet.georgetown.edu; World Wide Web: http://guweb.georgetown.edu/ssce

GERMAN WINE INFORMATION BUREAU

GERMAN WINE ACADEMY

General Information • Gourmet cooking/wine tour with visits to Frankfurt, Rhine River, Mosel River. Once at the destination country, participants travel by bus.
Learning Focus • Escorted travel to the German wine country. Other activities include wine tasting, lectures. Instruction is offered by educators. This program would appeal to people interested in wine.
Accommodations • Hotels. Single rooms are available for an additional $250.
Program Details • Program offered once per year. Session length: 7 days. Departures are scheduled in October. Most participants are 20–60 years of age. Participants must be 21 years or older to enroll. 20 participants per session. Application deadline: 6–8 weeks prior to departure. Reservations are recommended at least 6–8 weeks before departure.
Costs • $1500 (includes housing, all meals, books and class materials, excursions). A $35 deposit is required.
Contact • German Wine Information Bureau, 79 Madison Avenue, New York, NY 10016; 212-213-7028; Fax: 212-213-7042; E-mail: sullassocl@aol.com

GLS-SPRACHENZENTRUM BERLIN

GERMAN AS A FOREIGN LANGUAGE

General Information • Language study program in Berlin. Excursions to Dresden, Prague, Hamburg.
Learning Focus • Courses in cultural studies, history, literature, German language. Instruction is offered by professors from the sponsoring institution.
Accommodations • Homestays, locally-rented apartments, flats, bed and breakfasts, hostels, hotels. Single rooms are available. Meals are taken on one's own, with host family, in local restaurants, in residences.
Program Details • Program offered 50 times per year. Session length: 2–12 weeks. Departures are scheduled in January–December. The program is open to undergraduate students, graduate students, pre-college students, adults. Most participants are 18–35 years of age. 12 participants per session. Application deadline: 1 week prior to departure.
Costs • $1000 for 2 weeks (includes tuition, housing, some meals, books and class materials, excursions). A $200 deposit is required.
Contact • Beate Guertler, Marketing Assistant, GLS-Sprachenzentrum Berlin, Kolonnenstrasse 26, D-10829 Berlin-Schoeneberg, Germany; +49 30-787-4152; Fax: +49 30-787-4192

Located in the heart of the German capital, GLS SPRACHENZENTRUM offers American students from high schools, colleges, and universities a unique opportunity to improve their German skills while getting a deeper insight into German culture, history, and society.

Founded in 1983, GLS SPRACHENZENTRUM has successfully established itself as an internationally known institution for language training and intercultural education. Academic programs include language courses, university preparation (entrance exams and audit permission), a semester or academic year at German schools, language training combined with internship, and an international study year in Berlin.

GOETHE-INSTITUT

GERMAN LANGUAGE COURSES

General Information • Language study program with visits to Berlin, Bonn, Boppard, Bremen, Constance, Dresden, Düsseldorf, Frankfurt, Göttingen, Iserlohn, Mannheim, Munich, Murnau, Prien, Rothenburg, Schwäbisch Hall, Staufen. Once at the destination country, participants travel by train, bus.

Learning Focus • Instruction in German language. Instruction is offered by professors.
Accommodations • Homestays, dormitories, program-owned houses. Single rooms are available.
Program Details • Session length: 4–8 weeks. Departures are scheduled throughout the year. Most participants are 18 years of age and older.
Costs • Contact sponsor for information.
Contact • Elly Epstein, Goethe-Institut, 1014 Fifth Avenue, New York, NY 10028; 212-439-8700; Fax: 212-439-8705

Each year, approximately 23,000 students attend the Goethe Institute in Germany. All teachers at the Goethe Institute have completed the postgraduate state exams as language teachers and received special training for teaching German as a foreign language. The intensive courses comprise 20 to 30 units (45 minutes each) of German instruction per week. Courses are taught Monday through Friday. Students learn everything they need to communicate in German, including correct speech, accurate pronunciation, reading, writing, and grammar. The textbook, a folder with information about the course location, and additional course materials are included in the course fee, as are a number of excursions.

INTERHOSTEL, UNIVERSITY OF NEW HAMPSHIRE

BAMBERG AND MUNICH, GERMANY

General Information • Cultural tour with visits to Bamberg, Munich, Pommersfelden, Altenburg, Würzburg, Bayreuth, Nürnberg, Rothenburg Ober Der Tauber, Nymphenburg. Once at the destination country, participants travel by bus, foot. Program is affiliated with Sprachen Institut.
Learning Focus • Instruction in history and culture. Escorted travel to historical sites. Museum visits (Neue Pinakothek, Wagner Museum). Attendance at performances (concerts, choir, organ). Other activities include Bavarian evening. Instruction is offered by historians. This program would appeal to people interested in history, culture.
Accommodations • Hotels. Single rooms are available for an additional $375.
Program Details • Program offered once per year. Session length: 2 weeks. Departures are scheduled in June. Program is targeted to seniors over 50. Most participants are 60–80 years of age. Participants must be 50 years or older to enroll. 35 participants per session. Reservations are recommended at least 6 months before departure.
Costs • $2795 (includes tuition, housing, all meals, excursions, international airfare, entrance fees). A $200 deposit is required.
Contact • Janice Pierson, Office Supervisor, Interhostel, University of New Hampshire, 6 Garrison Avenue, Durham, NH 03824; 800-733-9753; Fax: 603-862-1113; World Wide Web: http://www.learn.unh.edu/

INTERHOSTEL, UNIVERSITY OF NEW HAMPSHIRE

BAVARIA AND KARLSBAD AT CHRISTMASTIME

General Information • Cultural tour with visits to Czech Republic (Czech Republic (Karlsbad)), Germany (Bamberg, Garmisch-Partenkirchen, Munich); excursions to Neuschwanstein Castle, Oberammegau, Kloster Ettal, Weiskirche, Nürnberg. Once at the destination country, participants travel by bus, foot. Program is affiliated with Sprachen Institut.
Learning Focus • Instruction in history and culture. Escorted travel to castles and cities. Museum visits (Deutsche Museum, Neue Pinakothek). Attendance at performances (four musical events). Instruction is offered by historians. This program would appeal to people interested in history, culture.
Accommodations • Hotels. Single rooms are available for an additional $395.
Program Details • Program offered once per year. Session length: 2 weeks. Departures are scheduled in December. Program is targeted to seniors over 50. Most participants are 60–80 years of age. Participants must be 50 years or older to enroll. 30 participants per session. Reservations are recommended at least 6 months before departure.
Costs • $2535 (includes tuition, housing, all meals, excursions, international airfare, entrance fees). A $200 deposit is required.
Contact • Janice Pierson, Office Supervisor, Interhostel, University of New Hampshire, 6 Garrison Avenue, Durham, NH 03824-3529; 800-733-9753; Fax: 603-862-1113; World Wide Web: http://www.learn.unh.edu/

INTERHOSTEL, UNIVERSITY OF NEW HAMPSHIRE

HAMBURG, BERLIN, AND DRESDEN, GERMANY

General Information • Cultural tour with visits to Berlin, Dresden, Hamburg, Lubeck, Schwerin, Potsdam, Leipzig, Meissen, Switzerland (Saxon). Once at the destination country, participants travel by bus, foot. Program is affiliated with Sprachen Institut.
Learning Focus • Instruction in history and culture. Escorted travel to villages. Museum visits (Kuntshalle, Pergamon Museum, Dahlem). Attendance at performances (concerts). Instruction is offered by historians. This program would appeal to people interested in history, culture.
Accommodations • Hotels. Single rooms are available for an additional $395.
Program Details • Program offered once per year. Session length: 2 weeks. Departures are scheduled in October. Program is targeted to seniors over 50. Most participants are 60–80 years of age. Participants must be 50 years or older to enroll. 30 participants per session. Reservations are recommended at least 3 months before departure.
Costs • $3025 (includes tuition, housing, all meals, excursions, international airfare, entrance fees). A $200 deposit is required.

Contact • Janice Pierson, Office Supervisor, Interhostel, University of New Hampshire, 6 Garrison Avenue, Durham, NH 03824-3529; 800-733-9753; Fax: 603-862-1113; World Wide Web: http://www.learn.unh.edu/

INTERHOSTEL, UNIVERSITY OF NEW HAMPSHIRE

TRIER, GERMANY

General Information • Cultural tour with visits to Trier, Bernkastel, Burgeltz, St. Paulin, Luxembourg, Mainz, Rhine River, Bonn, Cologne, Metz. Once at the destination country, participants travel by boat. Program is affiliated with University of Trier.
Learning Focus • Instruction in history and culture. Escorted travel to cities and landmarks. Museum visits (Bishops Museum, Gutenberg Museum). Other activities include meeting with local families. Instruction is offered by professors, historians. This program would appeal to people interested in history, culture.
Accommodations • Hotels. Single rooms are available for an additional $450.
Program Details • Program offered once per year. Session length: 2 weeks. Departures are scheduled in September. Program is targeted to seniors over 50. Most participants are 60–80 years of age. Participants must be 50 years or older to enroll. 35 participants per session. Reservations are recommended at least 6 months before departure.
Costs • $3175 (includes tuition, housing, all meals, excursions, international airfare, entrance fees). A $200 deposit is required.
Contact • Janice Pierson, Office Supervisor, Interhostel, University of New Hampshire, 6 Garrison Avenue, Durham, NH 03824; 800-733-9753; Fax: 603-862-1113; World Wide Web: http://www.learn.unh.edu/

KENTUCKY INSTITUTE FOR INTERNATIONAL STUDIES

PROGRAM IN GERMANY

General Information • Language study program in Munich. Excursions to Berlin.
Learning Focus • Courses in German language. Instruction is offered by professors from the sponsoring institution.
Accommodations • Homestays. Single rooms are available. Meals are taken on one's own.
Program Details • Program offered once per year. Session length: 6 weeks. Departures are scheduled in June. The program is open to undergraduate students, graduate students, pre-college students, adults, professionals. Most participants are 19–26 years of age. Other requirements: minimum 2.0 GPA, letter of recommendation from a faculty member, good academic standing at home institution, and one year college-level German or equivalent. 20 participants per session. Application deadline: March 1.
Costs • $2950 for students of consortia schools, $3250 for other students (includes tuition, housing, some meals, excursions, international airfare, International Student Identification card). Application fee: $50.
Contact • Dr. J. Milton Grimes, Executive Director, Kentucky Institute for International Studies, Murray State University, PO Box 9, Murray, KY 42071-0009; 502-762-3091; Fax: 502-762-3434; E-mail: kiismsu@msumusik.mursuky.edu; World Wide Web: http://www.berea.edu/KIIS/kiis.html

LANGUAGE LIAISON

ANGLO-GERMAN INSTITUTE–LEARN GERMAN IN GERMANY

General Information • Language study program with visits to Germany.
Learning Focus • Instruction in the German language. Instruction is offered by professors. This program would appeal to people interested in language.
Accommodations • Homestays, locally-rented apartments, hotels. Single rooms are available.
Program Details • Session length: unlimited. Departures are scheduled throughout the year. Program is targeted to students of any age. Most participants are 18–70 years of age. Participants must be 16 years or older to enroll. Reservations are recommended at least 35 days before departure.
Costs • Contact sponsor for information.
Contact • Nancy Forman, President, Language Liaison, 20533 Biscayne Boulevard-Station 4-162, Miami, FL 33180; 305-682-9909; Fax: 305-682-9907; E-mail: langstudy@aol.com; World Wide Web: http://languageliaison.com

LANGUAGE LIAISON

BERLIN–LEARN GERMAN IN GERMANY

General Information • Language study program with visits to Germany.
Learning Focus • Instruction in the German language. Instruction is offered by professors. This program would appeal to people interested in language.
Accommodations • Homestays, locally-rented apartments, hotels. Single rooms are available.
Program Details • Session length: unlimited. Departures are scheduled throughout the year. Program is targeted to students of any age. Most participants are 18–70 years of age. Participants must be 16 years or older to enroll. Reservations are recommended at least 35 days before departure.
Costs • Contact sponsor for information.
Contact • Nancy Forman, President, Language Liaison, 20533 Biscayne Boulevard-Station 4-162, Miami, FL 33180; 305-682-9909; Fax: 305-682-9907; E-mail: langstudy@aol.com; World Wide Web: http://languageliaison.com

LANGUAGE LIAISON

FREMDSPRACHEN INSTITUT COLON–LEARN GERMAN IN GERMANY

General Information • Language study program with visits to Germany.
Learning Focus • Instruction in the German language. Instruction is offered by professors. This program would appeal to people interested in language.
Accommodations • Homestays, locally-rented apartments, hotels. Single rooms are available.
Program Details • Session length: unlimited. Departures are scheduled throughout the year. Program is targeted to students of any age. Most participants are 18–70 years of age.

Participants must be 16 years or older to enroll. Reservations are recommended at least 35 days before departure.
Costs • Contact sponsor for information.
Contact • Nancy Forman, President, Language Liaison, 20533 Biscayne Boulevard-Station 4-162, Miami, FL 33180; 305-682-9909; Fax: 305-682-9907; E-mail: langstudy@aol.com; World Wide Web: http://languageliaison.com

LANGUAGE LIAISON

UNTERRICHT BEI BAVIERA–LEARN GERMAN IN GERMANY

General Information • Language study program with visits to Germany.
Learning Focus • Instruction in the German language. Instruction is offered by professors. This program would appeal to people interested in language.
Accommodations • Homestays, locally-rented apartments, hotels. Single rooms are available.
Program Details • Session length: unlimited. Departures are scheduled throughout the year. Program is targeted to students of any age. Most participants are 18–70 years of age. Participants must be 16 years or older to enroll. Reservations are recommended at least 35 days before departure.
Costs • Contact sponsor for information.
Contact • Nancy Forman, President, Language Liaison, 20533 Biscayne Boulevard-Station 4-162, Miami, FL 33180; 305-682-9909; Fax: 305-682-9907; E-mail: langstudy@aol.com; World Wide Web: http://languageliaison.com

LANGUAGE STUDIES ABROAD

GLS–SPRACHENZENTRUM

General Information • Language study program with visits to Berlin. Once at the destination country, participants travel by bus, foot.
Learning Focus • Instruction in the German language. Instruction is offered by trained teachers with bachelor's degrees. This program would appeal to people interested in the German language.
Accommodations • Homestays, apartments. Single rooms are available for an additional $270–$360 per week.
Program Details • Session length: 2 or more weeks. Departures are scheduled throughout the year. Most participants are 16–80 years of age. Participants must be 16 years or older to enroll. 12 participants per session. Application deadline: 3 weeks prior to departure. Reservations are recommended at least 2 months before departure.
Costs • $2000–$2400 (includes tuition, housing, some meals, books and class materials). A $100 deposit is required.
Contact • Charlene Biddulph, Director, Language Studies Abroad, 249 South Highway 101, Suite 226, Solana Beach, CA 92075; 800-424-5522; Fax: 619-943-1201; E-mail: cbiddulph@aol.com; World Wide Web: http://www.dnai.com/~bid/language/

LEXIA EXCHANGE INTERNATIONAL

LEXIA IN BERLIN

General Information • Academic study program in Berlin. Classes are held on the campus of Free University of Berlin. Excursions to Czech Republic (Prague), Poland (Cracow), Munich, Hamburg, Switzerland (Zurich), Hungary (Budapest).
Learning Focus • Courses in history, economics, architecture, fine arts, theater, German language, political science, business. Instruction is offered by local teachers.
Accommodations • Homestays. Single rooms are available. Meals are taken on one's own, with host family.
Program Details • Program offered once per year. Session length: 8 weeks. Departures are scheduled in June. The program is open to undergraduate students, graduate students, adults. Most participants are 18–35 years of age. Other requirements: minimum 2.5 GPA. 5–7 participants per session. Application deadline: April 15.
Costs • $4495 (includes tuition, housing, books and class materials, excursions). Application fee: $30. A $300 deposit is required.
Contact • Justin Meilgaard, Program Coordinator, LEXIA Exchange International, 378 Cambridge Avenue, Palo Alto, CA 94306-1544; 800-775-3942; Fax: 415-327-9192; E-mail: lexia@rquartz.stanford.edu; World Wide Web: http://www.lexiaintl.org

MICHIGAN STATE UNIVERSITY

GERMAN LANGUAGE AND CULTURE PROGRAM

General Information • Language study program in Mayen.
Learning Focus • Courses in German literature, German culture, German language. Instruction is offered by professors from the sponsoring institution.
Accommodations • Homestays. Meals are taken with host family, in residences.
Program Details • Program offered once per year. Session length: 6 weeks. Departures are scheduled in May. The program is open to undergraduate students, graduate students. Most participants are 18–26 years of age. Other requirements: good academic standing and the approval of the director. 20 participants per session. Application deadline: March 14.
Costs • $1420 (includes housing, some meals, excursions). Application fee: $75. A $250 deposit is required.
Contact • Brenda S. Sprite, Educational Programs Coordinator, Michigan State University, Office of Study Abroad, 109 International Center, East Lansing, MI 48824-1035; 517-353-8920; Fax: 517-432-2082; E-mail: sprite@pilot.msu.edu; World Wide Web: http://study-abroad.msu.edu

NATIONAL REGISTRATION CENTER FOR STUDY ABROAD

AGI LANGUAGE INSTITUTE

General Information • Language study program in Stuttgart.
Learning Focus • Courses in German language.
Accommodations • Homestays.
Program Details • Program offered 25 times per year. Session length: 2 weeks. Departures are scheduled in

January–December. The program is open to undergraduate students, graduate students, adults. 8–10 participants per session. Application deadline: 40 days prior to departure.
Costs • $921 (includes tuition, housing, some meals, insurance, excursions). Application fee: $40. A $100 deposit is required.
Contact • Reuel Zielke, Coordinator, National Registration Center for Study Abroad, Box 1393, Milwaukee, WI 53201; 414-278-0631; Fax: 414-271-8884; E-mail: ask@nrcsa.com; World Wide Web: http://www.nrcsa.com

NATIONAL REGISTRATION CENTER FOR STUDY ABROAD

COLON LANGUAGE CENTER

General Information • Language study program in Hamburg.
Learning Focus • Courses in German language.
Accommodations • Homestays. Single rooms are available. Meals are taken on one's own, in local restaurants.
Program Details • Program offered 50 times per year. Session length: 2 weeks. Departures are scheduled in January–December. The program is open to undergraduate students, graduate students, adults. 10–12 participants per session. Application deadline: 40 days prior to departure.
Costs • $977 (includes tuition, housing, some meals, insurance). Application fee: $40. A $100 deposit is required.
Contact • Reuel Zielke, Coordinator, National Registration Center for Study Abroad, Box 1393, Milwaukee, WI 53201; 414-278-0631; Fax: 414-271-8884; E-mail: ask@nrcsa.com; World Wide Web: http://www.nrcsa.com

NATIONAL REGISTRATION CENTER FOR STUDY ABROAD

EUROCENTRE: GERMANY

General Information • Language study program in Weimar.
Learning Focus • Courses in German language.
Accommodations • Homestays. Single rooms are available. Meals are taken with host family.
Program Details • Program offered 2 times per year. Session length: 3 weeks. Departures are scheduled in July. The program is open to undergraduate students, graduate students, adults. Application deadline: 40 days prior to departure.
Costs • $1585 (includes tuition, housing, some meals, insurance). Application fee: $40. A $100 deposit is required.
Contact • Reuel Zielke, Coordinator, National Registration Center for Study Abroad, PO Box 1393, Milwaukee, WI 53201; 414-278-0631; Fax: 414-271-8884; E-mail: inquiries@nrcsa.com; World Wide Web: http://www.nrcsa.com

NATIONAL REGISTRATION CENTER FOR STUDY ABROAD

GLS–SPRACHENZENTRUM

General Information • Language study program in Berlin.
Learning Focus • Courses in German language.
Accommodations • Homestays. Single rooms are available. Meals are taken on one's own.
Program Details • Program offered 25 times per year. Session length: 2 weeks. Departures are scheduled in January–December. The program is open to undergraduate students, graduate students, adults. 8–10 participants per session. Application deadline: 40 days prior to departure.
Costs • $1006 (includes tuition, housing, some meals, insurance). Application fee: $40. A $100 deposit is required.
Contact • Reuel Zielke, Coordinator, National Registration Center for Study Abroad, PO Box 1393, Milwaukee, WI 53201; 414-278-0631; Fax: 414-271-8884; E-mail: inquiries@nrcsa.com; World Wide Web: http://www.nrcsa.com

 NEW YORK UNIVERSITY

MEDIA ECOLOGY

General Information • Academic study program in Mainz. Classes are held on the campus of Stiftung Lesen–The Reading Institute of Germany.
Learning Focus • Courses in media ecology, communications. Instruction is offered by professors from the sponsoring institution and local teachers.
Accommodations • Hotels, guest houses. Meals are taken as a group, in local restaurants.
Program Details • Program offered once per year. Session length: 1 week. Departures are scheduled in July. The program is open to graduate students. Most participants are 23–45 years of age. Other requirements: BA degree. 25 participants per session. Application deadline: April 1.
Costs • $1527 (includes tuition). Application fee: $40. A $200 deposit is required.
Contact • Dr. Terence Moran, Director, Media Ecology: Studies in Communications Program, New York University, 239 Greene Street, Room 735, New York, NY 10003; 212-998-5254; Fax: 212-995-4046; World Wide Web: http://www.nyu.edu/studyabroad

 NICHOLLS STATE UNIVERSITY

STUDY PROGRAM ABROAD IN BERLIN, GERMANY

General Information • Academic and language study program in Berlin. Classes are held on the campus of Nicholls State University in Germany. Excursions to museums, theater, markets.
Learning Focus • Courses in language study, literature, cultural studies, civilizations. Instruction is offered by professors from the sponsoring institution.
Accommodations • Homestays, locally-rented apartments. Single rooms are available. Meals are taken on one's own, with host family, in local restaurants, in residences.
Program Details • Program offered 15 times per year. Session length: 3 weeks–one year. Departures are scheduled in January–December. The program is open to undergraduate students, graduate students, pre-college students, adults. Most participants are 18–55 years of age. Other requirements: high school seniors or graduates. 20 participants per session. Application deadline: 30 days prior to departure.
Costs • $1580 for 3 weeks non-credit, $1875 for 6 hours of college credit (includes tuition, housing, some meals, books and class materials). A $215 deposit is required.

Contact • Dr. Gary McCann, Director of Study Programs Abroad, Nicholls State University, PO Box 2080, Thibodaux, LA 70310; 504-448-4440; Fax: 504-449-7028; E-mail: fl-caw@nich-nsunet.nich.edu

RUTGERS, THE STATE UNIVERSITY OF NEW JERSEY, NEW BRUNSWICK

SUMMER PROGRAM IN GERMANY

General Information • Language study program in Constance. Excursions to France (Strasbourg, Colmar), Munich, Switzerland (Zurich, St. Gallen).
Learning Focus • Courses in German language, landscape architecture, art history. Instruction is offered by professors from the sponsoring institution.
Accommodations • Dormitories. Single rooms are available. Meals are taken on one's own, in residences.
Program Details • Program offered once per year. Session length: 6 weeks. Departures are scheduled in July. The program is open to undergraduate students, graduate students, pre-college students, adults. Most participants are 19–65 years of age. 40 participants per session. Application deadline: April 1.
Costs • $2450 (includes tuition, housing, some meals, insurance, excursions). Application fee: $25. A $1000 deposit is required.
Contact • Sonya Ristau, Co-Director, Summer Program in Constance, Rutgers, The State University of New Jersey, New Brunswick, German Department, Konstanz Program, 64 College Avenue, New Brunswick, NJ 08903; 908-932-7201; Fax: 908-932-1111; E-mail: sristau@rci.rutgers.edu; World Wide Web: http://www.rutgers.edu/Academics/Study_Abroad

SLIPPERY ROCK UNIVERSITY OF PENNSYLVANIA

BERLIN SUMMER PROGRAM

General Information • Language study program in Berlin. Classes are held on the campus of Humboldt University of Berlin. Excursions to Potsdam.
Learning Focus • Courses in German language. Instruction is offered by professors from the sponsoring institution and local teachers.
Accommodations • Homestays. Single rooms are available. Meals are taken on one's own.
Program Details • Program offered once per year. Session length: 4 weeks. Departures are scheduled in June. The program is open to undergraduate students, adults. Most participants are 18–26 years of age. Other requirements: minimum 2.5 GPA. 6–10 participants per session. Application deadline: May 1.
Costs • $2900 (includes tuition, housing, books and class materials, excursions, international airfare). A $100 deposit is required.
Contact • Stan Kendziorski, Director of International Studies, Slippery Rock University of Pennsylvania, 110 Eisenberg Building, Slippery Rock, PA 16057; 412-738-2603; Fax: 412-738-2959; E-mail: sjk@sruvm.sru.edu; World Wide Web: http://www.sru.edu

SPRACHINSTITUT DIALOGE

MAIN COURSE

General Information • Language study program in Lindau. Excursions to Munich, Austria, Switzerland, Alps.
Learning Focus • Courses in German language. Instruction is offered by professors from the sponsoring institution.
Accommodations • Homestays, locally-rented apartments, program-owned apartments. Single rooms are available. Meals are taken on one's own, with host family.
Program Details • Program offered 26 times per year. Session length: 2–12 weeks (12 week limit). Departures are scheduled in January–December. The program is open to undergraduate students, graduate students, pre-college students, adults. Most participants are 18–28 years of age. Other requirements: health insurance. 25–40 participants per session. Application deadline: 2–3 weeks prior to departure.
Costs • $800 for 4 weeks (includes tuition, books and class materials). A $300 deposit is required.
Contact • Frank Gebhard, Managing Director, Sprachinstitut Dialoge, Bürsteigane 5, Lindau 88131, Germany; +49 83-829-44600; Fax: +49 838-294-4602; E-mail: dialoge.lindau@t-online.de

SPRACHINSTITUT DIALOGE

TRIMESTER COURSE

General Information • Language study program in Lindau. Excursions to Munich, Austria, Switzerland, Alps, Island of Mainau.
Learning Focus • Courses in German language. Instruction is offered by professors from the sponsoring institution.
Accommodations • Homestays, locally-rented apartments, program-owned apartments. Single rooms are available. Meals are taken on one's own, with host family.
Program Details • Program offered 4 times per year. Session length: 10–12 weeks. Departures are scheduled in January, March, June, September. The program is open to undergraduate students, graduate students, pre-college students, adults. Most participants are 18–25 years of age. Other requirements: health insurance. 25–40 participants per session. Application deadline: 2–3 weeks prior to departure.
Costs • $2000–$4000 (includes tuition, books and class materials, leisure program). A $300 deposit is required.
Contact • Sprachinstitut Dialoge, Bürsteigane 5, 88131 Lindau, Germany; +49 83-829-44600; Fax: +49 838-294-4602; E-mail: dialoge.lindau@t-online.de

SPRACHINSTITUT DIALOGE

YOUTH COURSE

General Information • Language study program in Lindau. Excursions to Munich, Island of Mainau, Meersburg, Austria.
Learning Focus • Courses in German language. Instruction is offered by professors from the sponsoring institution.
Accommodations • Homestays. Single rooms are available. Meals are taken with host family.
Program Details • Program offered 8 times per year. Session length: 2–4 weeks. Departures are scheduled in June–August. The program is open to students between 14 and 17 years of age. Most participants are 14–17 years of age.

Other requirements: health insurance. 10-60 participants per session. Application deadline: 2-3 weeks prior to departure.
Costs • $1400 (includes tuition, housing, all meals, books and class materials, excursions). A $300 deposit is required.
Contact • Frank Gebhard, Managing Director, Sprachinstitut Dialoge, Bürsteigane 5, Lindau 88131, Germany; +49 83-829-44600; Fax: +49 838-294-4602; E-mail: dialoge.lindau@t-online.de

STATE UNIVERSITY OF NEW YORK AT NEW PALTZ

SUMMER STUDY IN GERMANY

General Information • Language study program in Hamburg, Stade. Classes are held on the campus of University of Hamburg. Excursions to Harz Mountains, Lübeck, Potsdam, Bremen, Berlin.
Learning Focus • Courses in German language. Instruction is offered by professors from the sponsoring institution.
Accommodations • Homestays. Meals are taken with host family.
Program Details • Program offered once per year. Session length: 7 weeks. Departures are scheduled in June. The program is open to undergraduate students, graduate students, pre-college students, adults. Most participants are 18-30 years of age. Other requirements: 2 years of high school German or 2 semesters of college-level German. 10 participants per session. Application deadline: March 15.
Costs • $3998 (includes tuition, housing, all meals, insurance, excursions, international airfare). Application fee: $25. A $100 deposit is required.
Contact • Office of International Education, State University of New York at New Paltz, HAB 33, New Paltz, NY 12561; 914-257-3125; Fax: 914-257-3129; E-mail: sillnerb@npvm.newpaltz.edu; World Wide Web: http://www.newpaltz.edu/oie/

TEXAS CHRISTIAN UNIVERSITY

SUMMER IN GERMANY

General Information • Academic study program in Cologne. Excursions to Dresden, Freiburg.
Learning Focus • Courses in business. Instruction is offered by professors from the sponsoring institution.
Accommodations • Homestays. Meals are taken on one's own, in local restaurants.
Program Details • Program offered once per year. Session length: 30 days. Departures are scheduled in June. The program is open to undergraduate students, graduate students. Most participants are 20-30 years of age. Other requirements: junior, senior or graduate standing and a minimum GPA of 2.75 for undergraduates or 3.0 for graduates. 20 participants per session. Application deadline: January.
Costs • $1825 (includes housing, some meals, books and class materials, insurance, excursions, Eurail pass). A $500 deposit is required.
Contact • Janice Titsworth, Assistant Dean, Texas Christian University, TCU Box 298530, Fort Worth, TX 76137; 817-921-7527; Fax: 817-921-7227; E-mail: j.titsworth@tcu.edu; World Wide Web: http://www.neeley.edu

UNIVERSITÄT GESAMTHOCHSCHULE KASSEL

FIFTH INTERNATIONAL SUMMER UNIVERSITY 1997

General Information • Language study program in Kassel. Classes are held on the campus of Universität Gesamthochschule Kassel. Excursions to Eisenach, Marburg, Cologne, Weimar, Bad Hersfeld.
Learning Focus • Courses in contemporary art, sociocultural studies, history, political science, literature, German philology, phonetics. Instruction is offered by professors from the sponsoring institution and local teachers.
Accommodations • Homestays, dormitories, locally-rented apartments. Single rooms are available. Meals are taken on one's own, with host family, in central dining facility.
Program Details • Program offered once per year. Session length: 5 weeks. Departures are scheduled in July. The program is open to undergraduate students, graduate students, other interested persons. Most participants are 20-35 years of age. Other requirements: 2 years of German. 50 participants per session. Application deadline: June 15.
Costs • Contact sponsor for information.
Contact • Ulrike Mengedoht, Managing Director, Universität Gesamthochschule Kassel, Sprachenzentrum, Mönchebergstrasse 7, D-34125 Kassel, Germany; +49 561-804-2020; Fax: +49 561-804-3815; E-mail: sz@hrz.uni-kassel.de

UNIVERSITY AT ALBANY, STATE UNIVERSITY OF NEW YORK

SUMMER PROGRAM IN BRAUNSCHWEIG

General Information • Language study program in Braunschweig. Classes are held on the campus of Technische Universität Carolo-Wilhelmina. Excursions to Harz Mountians, Hannover, Berlin.
Learning Focus • Courses in German language, German culture. Instruction is offered by local teachers.
Accommodations • Homestays, dormitories, locally-rented apartments. Single rooms are available. Meals are taken on one's own, in central dining facility, in local restaurants, in residences.
Program Details • Program offered once per year. Session length: 6 weeks. Departures are scheduled in July. The program is open to undergraduate students, graduate students, pre-college students, adults. Most participants are 18 years of age and older. Other requirements: 1 year college-level German or equivalent. 60 participants per session. Application deadline: April 1.
Costs • $2307 (includes housing, all meals, books and class materials, insurance, excursions, in-state tuition and fees). A $125 deposit is required.
Contact • Dr. Alex M. Shane, Director, University at Albany, State University of New York, Office of International Programs, LI 85, Albany, NY 12222; 518-442-3525; Fax: 518-442-3338; E-mail: oipua@csc.albany.edu; World Wide Web: http://www.albany.edu/~oipwebua

UNIVERSITY AT ALBANY, STATE UNIVERSITY OF NEW YORK

SUMMER PROGRAM IN WÜRZBURG

General Information • Academic study program in Würzburg. Classes are held on the campus of University of Würzburg. Excursions to Munich, Berlin.
Learning Focus • Courses in German language, economics, German history, literature. Instruction is offered by local teachers.
Accommodations • Homestays, locally-rented apartments. Single rooms are available. Meals are taken on one's own, in central dining facility, in local restaurants, in residences.
Program Details • Program offered once per year. Session length: 10 weeks. Departures are scheduled in May. The program is open to undergraduate students. Most participants are 19–23 years of age. 20 participants per session. Application deadline: March 15.
Costs • $4586 (includes housing, all meals, books and class materials, insurance, excursions, in-state tuition and fees). A $125 deposit is required.
Contact • Dr. Alex M. Shane, Director, University at Albany, State University of New York, Office of International Programs, LI 85, Albany, NY 12222; 518-442-3525; Fax: 518-442-3338; E-mail: oipua@csc.albany.edu; World Wide Web: http://www.albany.edu/~oipwebua

UNIVERSITY OF COLORADO AT BOULDER

SUMMER INTENSIVE GERMAN PROGRAM

General Information • Language study program in Kassel. Classes are held on the campus of Europa-Kolleg.
Learning Focus • Courses in German language, German culture. Instruction is offered by local teachers.
Accommodations • Homestays. Meals are taken with host family.
Program Details • Program offered 2 times per year. Session length: 4 weeks. Departures are scheduled in July, August. The program is open to undergraduate students. Most participants are 19–24 years of age. Other requirements: minimum 2.75 GPA and second semester freshman standing. 15–20 participants per session. Application deadline: March 1.
Costs • $2392 for Colorado residents, $3142 for non-residents (includes tuition, housing, all meals, insurance, excursions). A $300 deposit is required.
Contact • Study Abroad Program, University of Colorado at Boulder, International Education, Campus Box 123, Boulder, CO 80309-0123; 303-492-7741; Fax: 303-492-5185; E-mail: studyabr@colorado.edu; World Wide Web: http://www.colorado.edu/OIE/StudyAbroad

UNIVERSITY OF DAYTON

ISSAP '97–MUNICH

General Information • Academic study program in Munich.
Learning Focus • Courses in history, philosophy. Instruction is offered by professors from the sponsoring institution.
Accommodations • Pensiones. Meals are taken as a group.
Program Details • Program offered once per year. Session length: 4 weeks. Departures are scheduled in May. The program is open to undergraduate students. Most participants are 18–21 years of age. Other requirements: minimum 2.0 GPA. 25 participants per session. Application deadline: April 15.
Costs • $3100 (includes tuition, housing, some meals, excursions, International Student Identification card). A $75 deposit is required.
Contact • DeVonda Vanderpool, Coordinator, International Education Programs, University of Dayton, Dayton, OH 45469-1481; 513-229-3728; Fax: 513-229-2766; E-mail: vanderpo@trinity.udayton.edu; World Wide Web: http://www.udayton.edu/~cip

UNIVERSITY OF DAYTON

SCHOOL OF BUSINESS AUGSBURG PROGRAM

General Information • Academic study program in Augsburg. Excursions to Czech Republic (Prague), Munich.
Learning Focus • Courses in business. Instruction is offered by professors from the sponsoring institution.
Accommodations • Homestays, dormitories, locally-rented apartments. Meals are taken as a group, with host family, in central dining facility, in local restaurants, in residences.
Program Details • Program offered once per year. Session length: 11 weeks. Departures are scheduled in May. The program is open to undergraduate students. Most participants are 18–24 years of age. Other requirements: 1 semester of German and good academic standing. 35 participants per session. Application deadline: February.
Costs • $6500 (includes tuition, housing, excursions). A $200 deposit is required.
Contact • DeVonda Vanderpool, Coordinator, International Education Programs, University of Dayton, Dayton, OH 45469-1481; 515-229-3728; Fax: 515-229-2766; E-mail: vanderpo@trinity.udayton.edu; World Wide Web: http://www.udayton.edu/~cip

UNIVERSITY OF DELAWARE

WINTER SESSION IN GERMANY

General Information • Language study program in Bayreuth. Classes are held on the campus of University of Bayreuth. Excursions to Berlin, Weimar.
Learning Focus • Courses in civilizations, cultural studies, German language. Instruction is offered by professors from the sponsoring institution.
Accommodations • Homestays. Meals are taken on one's own, in central dining facility.
Program Details • Program offered once per year. Session length: 5 weeks. Departures are scheduled in January. The program is open to undergraduate students. Most participants are 18–21 years of age. Other requirements: minimum 2.0 GPA and 1 year college German. 25 participants per session. Application deadline: October.
Costs • $4110 (includes tuition, housing, some meals, excursions, international airfare). A $200 deposit is required.
Contact • International Programs and Special Sessions, University of Delaware, 4 Kent Way, Newark, DE 19716-1450; 888-831-4685; Fax: 302-831-6042; E-mail: studyabroad@mvs.udel.edu

UNIVERSITY OF FLORIDA

UNIVERSITY OF MANNHEIM

General Information • Language study program in Mannheim. Classes are held on the campus of University of Mannheim. Excursions to scenic sites, historic sites.
Learning Focus • Courses in German language. Instruction is offered by local teachers.
Accommodations • Dormitories. Meals are taken as a group, on one's own, in central dining facility, in local restaurants.
Program Details • Program offered once per year. Session length: 6 weeks. Departures are scheduled in June. The program is open to undergraduate students, graduate students, adults. Other requirements: minimum 2.5 GPA and at least 18 years old. 15 participants per session. Application deadline: March 15.
Costs • $3500 (includes tuition, housing, some meals, excursions, on site orientation). Application fee: $250.
Contact • Overseas Studies, University of Florida, 123 Tigert Hall, PO Box 113225, Gainesville, FL 32611-3225; 352-392-5206; Fax: 352-392-5575; E-mail: ovrseas@nervm.nerdc.ufl.edu

UNIVERSITY OF KANSAS

ADVANCED SUMMER LANGUAGE INSTITUTE IN HOLZKIRCHEN–MUNICH, GERMANY

General Information • Language study program in Holzkirchen. Classes are held on the campus of Volkshochschule Holzkirchen. Excursions to Cologne, Nuremberg, Würzburg, Rothenburg ob der Tauber.
Learning Focus • Courses in German language, German culture, German literature. Instruction is offered by professors from the sponsoring institution and local teachers.
Accommodations • Homestays, hotels. Meals are taken as a group, with host family, in local restaurants, in residences.
Program Details • Program offered once per year. Session length: 8 weeks. Departures are scheduled in June. The program is open to undergraduate students, graduate students. Most participants are 20–30 years of age. Other requirements: 4 semesters college-level German or equivalent. 25 participants per session. Application deadline: February 16.
Costs • $2955 (includes tuition, housing, all meals, study tour of Germany, group cultural events and activities). Application fee: $15. A $300 deposit is required.
Contact • Susan MacNally, Coordinator of Summer Institutes, University of Kansas, Office of Study Abroad, 203 Lippincott Hall, Lawrence, KS 66045; 913-864-3742; Fax: 913-864-5040; E-mail: osa@falcon.cc.ukans.edu; World Wide Web: http://kuhub.cc.ukans.edu/~intlstdy/osa/osamain.html

UNIVERSITY OF KANSAS

SUMMER LANGUAGE INSTITUTE IN EUTIN, GERMANY

General Information • Language study program in Eutin. Excursions to Lübeck, Kiel, Mainz, Hamburg, Berlin, Munich.
Learning Focus • Courses in German language and culture. Instruction is offered by professors from the sponsoring institution.
Accommodations • Homestays, hotels. Meals are taken as a group, with host family, in local restaurants, in residences.
Program Details • Program offered once per year. Session length: 8 weeks. Departures are scheduled in May. The program is open to undergraduate students, graduate students. Most participants are 19–26 years of age. Other requirements: 2 semesters of college-level German or equivalent. 15 participants per session. Application deadline: February 16.
Costs • $3055 (includes tuition, housing, all meals, 12-day study tour throughout Germany, group cultural events and activities). Application fee: $15. A $300 deposit is required.
Contact • Susan MacNally, Coordinator of Summer Institutes, University of Kansas, Office of Study Abroad, 203 Lippincott Hall, Lawrence, KS 66045; 913-864-3742; Fax: 913-864-5040; E-mail: osa@falcon.cc.ukans.edu; World Wide Web: http://kuhub.cc.ukans.edu/~intlstdy/osa/osamain.html

UNIVERSITY OF MIAMI

STUDY ABROAD UNIVERSITÄT TÜBINGEN–SUMMER SPACH INSTITUT

General Information • Language study program in Tübingen. Classes are held on the campus of University of Tübingen.
Learning Focus • Courses in language study. Instruction is offered by local teachers.
Accommodations • Dormitories. Single rooms are available. Meals are taken on one's own, in central dining facility.
Program Details • Program offered once per year. Session length: 4 weeks. Departures are scheduled in June. The program is open to undergraduate students, graduate students. Most participants are 19–35 years of age. Other requirements: minimum 3.0 GPA. Application deadline: April 1.
Costs • $2400 (includes tuition). Application fee: $30. A $500 deposit is required.
Contact • Peggy Ting, Study Abroad Program, University of Miami, PO Box 248005, Coral Gables, FL 33124-1610; 800-557-5421; Fax: 305-284-6629; E-mail: ieep@cstudies.msmail.miami.edu; World Wide Web: http://www.miami.edu/cstudies/ieep.html

UNIVERSITY OF PENNSYLVANIA

PENN-IN-FREIBURG

General Information • Language study program in Freiburg.
Learning Focus • Courses in German language. Instruction is offered by professors from the sponsoring institution.
Accommodations • Dormitories. Single rooms are available. Meals are taken on one's own, in local restaurants, in residences.
Program Details • Program offered once per year. Session length: 5½ weeks. Departures are scheduled in July. The program is open to undergraduate students, graduate students. Most participants are 18–30 years of age. Other requirements: one year of college-level German or equivalent. 15 participants per session. Application deadline: April 1.
Costs • $3284 (includes tuition, housing, excursions). Application fee: $35. A $300 deposit is required.

Contact • Elizabeth Sachs, Director, Penn Summer Abroad, University of Pennsylvania, 3440 Market Street, Suite 100, Philadelphia, PA 19104-3335; 215-898-5738; Fax: 215-573-2053; E-mail: esachs@mail.sas.upenn.edu

UNIVERSITY OF ROCHESTER

GERMAN IN GERMANY

General Information • Language study program in Marburg.
Learning Focus • Courses in language study. Instruction is offered by professors from the sponsoring institution and local teachers.
Accommodations • Homestays. Meals are taken with host family, in residences.
Program Details • Program offered once per year. Session length: 4 weeks. Departures are scheduled in June. The program is open to undergraduate students, adults. Other requirements: previous German language study, either 3 years high school or 1 year college. 8-10 participants per session. Application deadline: March 15.
Costs • $2700 (includes tuition, housing, some meals, excursions). A $250 deposit is required.
Contact • Anne Lutkus, Language Coordinator, University of Rochester, Department of Modern Languages and Cultures, Rochester, NY 14627; 716-275-4251; E-mail: adlt@db1.cc.rochester.edu; World Wide Web: http://www.rochester.edu/College/study-abroad/

UNIVERSITY OF SOUTHERN MISSISSIPPI

DAS TREFFEN–MUSIC AND PERFORMING ARTS FESTIVAL

General Information • Academic study program in Bayreuth.
Learning Focus • Courses in music.
Program Details • Program offered once per year. Session length: 3 weeks. Departures are scheduled in August. The program is open to undergraduate students, graduate students. Other requirements: minimum 2.0 GPA and good academic standing.
Costs • $1295 for undergraduates, $1395 for graduate students (includes tuition, housing, insurance, admission to most events). A $200 deposit is required.
Contact • Das Treffen, University of Southern Mississippi, Box 5081, Hattiesburg, MS 39406; 601-266-4361; Fax: 601-266-5699

UNIVERSITY STUDIES ABROAD CONSORTIUM

GERMAN STUDIES: LÜNEBURG, GERMANY

General Information • Academic study program in Lüneburg. Classes are held on the campus of Lüneburg University. Excursions to Hamburg, Lübeck, Schwerin, Berlin.
Learning Focus • Courses in German language, German culture, German government and politics, German literature. Instruction is offered by local teachers.
Accommodations • Homestays, locally-rented apartments. Single rooms are available. Meals are taken on one's own, with host family, in central dining facility, in residences.
Program Details • Program offered 2 times per year. Session length: 4 weeks. Departures are scheduled in June, July. The program is open to undergraduate students, graduate students, pre-college students, adults. Most participants are 18–50 years of age. Other requirements: minimum 2.5 GPA. 15 participants per session. Application deadline: April 15.
Costs • $1385 (includes tuition, insurance, excursions, International Student Identification card). Application fee: $50. A $150 deposit is required.
Contact • Dr. Carmelo Urza, Director, University Studies Abroad Consortium, University of Nevada Library/323, Reno, NV 89557-0093; 702-784-6569; Fax: 702-784-6010; E-mail: usac@equinox.unr.edu; World Wide Web: http://www.scs.unr.edu/~usac

WITTENBERG UNIVERSITY

WITTENBERG, GERMANY: CITY OF REFORMATION AND REFORM

General Information • Language study program in Wittenberg. Classes are held on the campus of Martin Luther Universität Halls-Wittenberg. Excursions to Berlin, Potsdam, Dresden, Halle.
Learning Focus • Courses in German language, German culture and development. Instruction is offered by professors from the sponsoring institution and local teachers.
Accommodations • Homestays. Meals are taken with host family.
Program Details • Program offered once per year. Session length: 6 weeks. Departures are scheduled in May. The program is open to undergraduate students, graduate students, pre-college students, adults. Most participants are 19–22 years of age. Other requirements: 1 year of college German or equivalent; minimum 2.50 GPA. 12 participants per session. Application deadline: February 1.
Costs • $3365 (includes tuition, housing, all meals, books and class materials, excursions, international airfare). A $100 deposit is required.
Contact • Mrs. JoAnn Bennett, Director, International Education, Wittenberg University, PO Box 720, Springfield, OH 45501; 937-327-6185; Fax: 937-327-6340; E-mail: vagabond@wittenberg.edu

GREECE

ARCHAEOLOGICAL TOURS

MINOAN GREECE

General Information • Archaeological tour with visits to Athens, Ayios Nikolas, Delphi, Heraklion, Nauplia, Olympia, Santorini, Sparta, Mistra, Mycenae, Epidaurus, Tiryns, Corinth, Gortyn, Phautos, Knossos, Mallia, Kato Zakro, Akrotiri, Thera. Once at the destination country, participants travel by bus, boat, airplane.

Learning Focus • Escorted travel to Crete, the Peloponnese and Byzantine churches. Museum visits (Athens, Olympia, Delphi, Heraklion, Santorini). Instruction is offered by professors, historians. This program would appeal to people interested in history, archaeology.

Accommodations • Hotels. Single rooms are available for an additional $925.

Program Details • Program offered once per year. Session length: 19 days. Departures are scheduled in June. Program is targeted to adults. Most participants are 30–80 years of age. 22 participants per session. Application deadline: 1 month prior to departure.

Costs • $3390 (includes housing, some meals, excursions, internal flights, ferry). A $500 deposit is required.

Contact • Archaeological Tours, 271 Madison Avenue, Suite 904, New York, NY 10016; 212-986-3054; Fax: 212-370-1561

 BEAVER COLLEGE

HISTORY AND ARCHAEOLOGY OF GREECE

General Information • Academic study program in Athens. Classes are held on the campus of Beaver College Athens Center. Excursions to Delphi, Nestor's Palace above Pylos, Corinth, Mycenae, Sparta, Thermopylae.

Learning Focus • Courses in history, archaeology, ancient Greece. Instruction is offered by professors from the sponsoring institution.

Accommodations • Locally-rented apartments, hotels. Single rooms are available. Meals are taken as a group, on one's own, in residences.

Program Details • Program offered once per year. Session length: 4 weeks. Departures are scheduled in June. The program is open to undergraduate students, graduate students, adults. Most participants are 19–24 years of age. Other requirements: sophomore standing and a minimum GPA of 3.0. 6–8 participants per session. Application deadline: March 31.

Costs • $3300 (includes tuition, housing, some meals, excursions, international airfare, International Student Identification card, host country support). Application fee: $35. A $500 deposit is required.

Contact • Audrianna Jones, Program Coordinator, Beaver College, Center for Education Abroad, 450 South Easton Road, Glenside, PA 19038; 888-232-8379; Fax: 215-572-2174; E-mail: jones@beaver.edu

 BEAVER COLLEGE

SANCTUARIES, CITIES, AND WAR

General Information • Academic study program in Athens. Classes are held on the campus of Beaver College Athens Center. Excursions to Mycenae, Pylos, Sparta, Corinth, Thermopylae, Delphi.

Learning Focus • Courses in history, archaeology. Instruction is offered by professors from the sponsoring institution and local teachers.

Accommodations • Locally-rented apartments, hotels. Meals are taken in local restaurants, in residences.

Program Details • Program offered once per year. Session length: 4 weeks. Departures are scheduled in June. The program is open to undergraduate students, graduate students, adults. Other requirements: minimum 3.0 GPA and three or four semesters of college-level course work. Application deadline: March 31.

Costs • $3300 (includes tuition, housing, some meals, excursions, international airfare, International Student Identification card, predeparture materials, host country support, some ground transportation). Application fee: $35. A $500 deposit is required.

Contact • Audrianna Jones, Program Coordinator, Beaver College, Center for Education Abroad, 450 South Easton Road, Glenside, PA 19038; 888-232-8379; Fax: 215-572-2174; E-mail: jones@turret.beaver.edu

COUNTRY WALKERS

REMOTE FOOTHILLS OF TAYGETUS

General Information • Cultural, gourmet cooking, nature study and walking tour with visits to Athens, Kardamili, Mystras, Petrovouni, Agia Sofia, Vathia, Porto Cayio Bay. Once at the destination country, participants travel by foot, boat.

Learning Focus • Escorted travel to the Acropolis, Viros Gorge and Pirgos Dirou. Other activities include walking. Instruction is offered by professors, researchers, naturalists, historians. This program would appeal to people interested in nature studies, walking, food and wine.

Accommodations • Hotels. Single rooms are available for an additional $300–$600.

Program Details • Program offered 4 times per year. Session length: 10 days. Departures are scheduled in April, May, September, October. Program is targeted to adults 35 to 65 years old. Most participants are 35–65 years of age. Participants must be 18 years or older to enroll. 18

participants per session. Reservations are recommended at least 5–6 months before departure.
Costs • $1950 (includes housing, all meals, excursions). A $400 deposit is required.
Contact • Heather Kellingbeck, Vice President, Country Walkers, PO Box 180, Waterbury, VT 05176; 800-464-9255; Fax: 802-244-5661; E-mail: ctrywalk@aol.com

CROSS-CULTURE

CRETE, MYKONOS, AND DELOS

General Information • Cultural tour with visits to Crete, Delos, Mykonos, Knossos, Malia, Phaestos, Ayia Triada, Gortyn. Once at the destination country, participants travel by foot, boat, airplane.
Learning Focus • Escorted travel to Matala and the Church of Panayia Kera. Museum visits (Heraklion Archaeological Museum). Instruction is offered by highly educated guides. This program would appeal to people interested in culture, history.
Accommodations • Hotels. Single rooms are available for an additional $210.
Program Details • Program offered once per year. Session length: 9 days. Departures are scheduled in May. Program is targeted to adults of all ages. Most participants are 40–70 years of age. Participants must be 12 years or older to enroll. Other requirements: good health, accompaniment of an adult if under 18. 20–25 participants per session. Application deadline: 1 month prior to departure. Reservations are recommended at least 3–12 months before departure.
Costs • $2500 (includes tuition, housing, all meals, books and class materials, excursions, international airfare). A $300 deposit is required.
Contact • Cross-Culture, 52 High Point Drive, Amherst, MA 01002-1224; 413-256-6303; Fax: 413-253-2303; E-mail: xculture@javanet.com; World Wide Web: http://www.empiremall.com/cross-culture

CROSS-CULTURE

GRECIAN SPRING

General Information • Cultural tour with visits to Athens, Peloponnese, Tolo, Sparta, Mystra Nauplia, Mycenae, Olympia, Delphi. Once at the destination country, participants travel by bus, boat, airplane.
Learning Focus • Instruction in Greek history. Escorted travel to Agamemnon's Tomb, the Parthenon and the Acropolis. Museum visits (Folklore Museum, National Archaeological Museum). Attendance at performances (costumed folk dancing). Nature observation (still-active volcano). Instruction is offered by highly educated guides. This program would appeal to people interested in culture, history, nature studies, arts, traditions, food and wine.
Accommodations • Hotels. Single rooms are available for an additional $210.

Program Details • Program offered once per year. Session length: 15 days. Departures are scheduled in April. Program is targeted to adults of all ages. Most participants are 40–70 years of age. Participants must be 12 years or older to enroll. Other requirements: good health, accompaniment of an adult if under 18. 20–25 participants per session. Application deadline: 1 month prior to departure. Reservations are recommended at least 3–12 months before departure.
Costs • $3200 (includes tuition, housing, all meals, books and class materials, excursions, international airfare). A $300 deposit is required.
Contact • Cross-Culture, 52 High Point Drive, Amherst, MA 01002-1224; 413-256-6303; Fax: 413-253-2303; E-mail: xculture@javanet.com; World Wide Web: http://www.empiremall.com/cross-culture

DUKE UNIVERSITY

DUKE IN ANCIENT GREECE

General Information • Academic study program in Athens, Delphi, Thera. Excursions to historic sites.
Learning Focus • Courses in classical studies, art. Instruction is offered by professors from the sponsoring institution.
Accommodations • Hotels. Meals are taken as a group, in local restaurants.
Program Details • Program offered once per year. Session length: 4 weeks. Departures are scheduled in May. The program is open to undergraduate students. Most participants are 19–21 years of age. Other requirements: minimum 2.7 GPA. 15–20 participants per session. Application deadline: February 21.
Costs • $4378 (includes tuition, housing, some meals, excursions, international airfare).
Contact • Foreign Academic Programs, Duke University, 121 Allen Building, Box 90057, Durham, NC 27708-0057; 919-684-2174; Fax: 919-684-3083; E-mail: abroad@mail01.adm.duke.edu; World Wide Web: http://www.mis.duke.edu/study_abroad/study_abroad.html

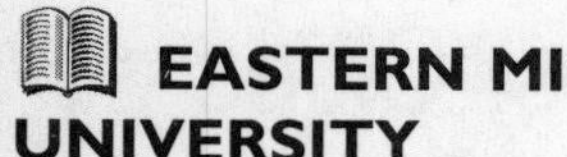

EASTERN MICHIGAN UNIVERSITY

ART HISTORY AND DRAWING IN GREECE

General Information • Academic study program in Athens.
Learning Focus • Courses in art history, drawing. Instruction is offered by professors from the sponsoring institution.
Accommodations • Hotels. Meals are taken as a group, in local restaurants.
Program Details • Program offered once per year. Session length: 3 weeks. Departures are scheduled in May. The program is open to undergraduate students, graduate students. Most participants are 18–30 years of age. Other requirements: minimum 2.0 GPA and 18 years of age. 25 participants per session. Application deadline: January 15.
Costs • $2995 (includes tuition, housing, some meals, insurance, excursions, international airfare, travel in Greece). A $200 deposit is required.
Contact • Academic Programs Abroad, Eastern Michigan University, 332 Goodison Hall, Ypsilanti, MI 48197; 800-777-3541; Fax: 313-487-2316; E-mail: programs.abroad@emich.edu; World Wide Web: http://www.emich.edu/public/cont_ed/abroad.html

FOREIGN LANGUAGE STUDY ABROAD SERVICE

GREEK IN GREECE

General Information • Language study program in Athens, Crete.
Learning Focus • Courses in language study. Instruction is offered by local teachers.
Accommodations • Homestays, hotels. Single rooms are available. Meals are taken on one's own, with host family, in local restaurants, in residences.
Program Details • Session length: varies. Departures are scheduled in January–December. The program is open to undergraduate students, graduate students, pre-college students, adults. Most participants are 16 years of age and older.
Costs • Contact sponsor for information. Application fee: $50. A $100 deposit is required.
Contact • Louise Harber, Coordinator, Foreign Language Study Abroad Service, Department IH, Box 903, 5935 Southwest 64th Avenue, South Miami, FL 33143; 800-282-1090; Fax: 305-662-2907; E-mail: flsas@netpoint.net; World Wide Web: http://www.netpoint.net/~flsas

GEORGETOWN UNIVERSITY

GREECE: A STUDY-TRAVEL COURSE

General Information • Academic study program in Greece. Excursions to Aegina, Delphi, Mycenae, Athens, Epidaurus, Satorini.
Learning Focus • Courses in archaeology, drama, theater, philosophy, art, history. Instruction is offered by professors from the sponsoring institution.
Accommodations • Hotels. Single rooms are available. Meals are taken as a group, in local restaurants.
Program Details • Program offered once per year. Session length: 3 weeks. Departures are scheduled in May, June. The program is open to undergraduate students, graduate students, pre-college students, adults. Most participants are 18–22 years of age. Other requirements: minimum 3.0 GPA. 18 participants per session. Application deadline: March.
Costs • $3800 (includes tuition, housing, some meals, books and class materials, insurance, excursions, international airfare). A $200 deposit is required.
Contact • Marianne T. Needham, Director, International Programs, Georgetown University, 306 ICC, Box 571012, Washington, DC 20057-1012; 202-687-6184; Fax: 202-687-8954; E-mail: sscefps1@gunet.georgetown.edu; World Wide Web: http://guweb.georgetown.edu/ssce

HELLENIC AMERICAN UNION

MODERN AND SPOKEN GREEK LANGUAGE AND CULTURE

General Information • Language study program in Athens, Poros. Excursions to Delphi, Mycenae, Delos, Olympia, Sounion.

Learning Focus • Courses in Greek language, history, Byzantine studies, art, philosophy, archaeology, political science. Instruction is offered by professors from the sponsoring institution.
Accommodations • Hotels. Single rooms are available. Meals are taken as a group, on one's own, in local restaurants.
Program Details • Program offered 26 times per year. Session length: 2–4 weeks. Departures are scheduled in January–December. The program is open to undergraduate students, graduate students, pre-college students, adults. Most participants are 17 years of age and older. 15–20 participants per session.
Costs • $313 (includes tuition).
Contact • Dimitrios Tolias, Academic Assistant, Hellenic American Union, 22 Massalias Street, Athens 10680, Greece; +30 1-360-7305; Fax: +30 1-363-3174

INTERHOSTEL, UNIVERSITY OF NEW HAMPSHIRE

ATHENS AND THE GREEK ISLANDS

General Information • Cultural tour with visits to Athens, Mykonos, Arahova, Delphi, Cape Sounion, Corinth, Epidaurus, Nauplia, Mycenae, Delos. Once at the destination country, participants travel by bus, foot, boat. Program is affiliated with American College of Greece, Deree Campus.
Learning Focus • Instruction in history and culture. Escorted travel to historical sites. Museum visits (National Archaeological Museum, Vorres Museum). Instruction is offered by professors. This program would appeal to people interested in history, culture.
Accommodations • Dormitories. Single rooms are available for an additional $475.
Program Details • Program offered once per year. Session length: 2 weeks. Departures are scheduled in April. Program is targeted to seniors over 50. Most participants are 60–80 years of age. Participants must be 50 years or older to enroll. 35 participants per session. Reservations are recommended at least 6 months before departure.
Costs • $3525 (includes tuition, housing, all meals, excursions, international airfare, entrance fees). A $200 deposit is required.
Contact • Janice Pierson, Office Supervisor, Interhostel, University of New Hampshire, 6 Garrison Avenue, Durham, NH 03824; 800-733-9753; Fax: 603-862-1113; World Wide Web: http://www.learn.unh.edu/

LANGUAGE LIAISON

HELLENIC LANGUAGE ALEXANDER THE GREAT–LEARN GREEK IN GREECE

General Information • Language study program with visits to Greece.
Learning Focus • Instruction in the Greek language. Instruction is offered by professors. This program would appeal to people interested in language.
Accommodations • Homestays, locally-rented apartments, hotels. Single rooms are available.
Program Details • Session length: unlimited. Departures are scheduled throughout the year. Program is targeted to students of any age. Most participants are 18–70 years of age. Participants must be 16 years or older to enroll. Reservations are recommended at least 35 days before departure.
Costs • Contact sponsor for information.
Contact • Nancy Forman, President, Language Liaison, 20533 Biscayne Boulevard-Station 4-162, Miami, FL 33180; 305-682-9909; Fax: 305-682-9907; E-mail: langstudy@aol.com; World Wide Web: http://languageliaison.com

NATIONAL REGISTRATION CENTER FOR STUDY ABROAD

HELLENIC LANGUAGE SCHOOL ALEXANDER THE GREAT

General Information • Language study program in Athens, Crete.
Learning Focus • Courses in Greek language.
Accommodations • Homestays, hotels. Single rooms are available. Meals are taken on one's own.
Program Details • Program offered 22 times per year. Session length: 2 weeks. Departures are scheduled in January–December. The program is open to undergraduate students, graduate students, adults. 8–10 participants per session. Application deadline: 40 days prior to departure.
Costs • $1245 (includes tuition, housing, some meals, insurance). Application fee: $40. A $100 deposit is required.
Contact • Reuel Zielke, Coordinator, National Registration Center for Study Abroad, PO Box 1393, Milwaukee, WI 53201; 414-278-0631; Fax: 414-271-8884; E-mail: inquiries@nrcsa.com; World Wide Web: http://www.nrcsa.com

NORTHERN ILLINOIS UNIVERSITY

ART HISTORY, ARCHITECTURE, AND ARCHAEOLOGY IN GREECE

General Information • Academic study program in Athens, Delphi, Nauplia, Olympia.
Learning Focus • Courses in art, archaeology, art history. Instruction is offered by professors from the sponsoring institution.
Accommodations • Hotels. Single rooms are available. Meals are taken as a group, in local restaurants.
Program Details • Program offered once per year. Session length: 3 weeks. Departures are scheduled in June. The program is open to undergraduate students, graduate students. Most participants are 21–55 years of age. 20 participants per session. Application deadline: May 1.
Costs • $3200 (includes tuition, housing, some meals, insurance, excursions). A $200 deposit is required.
Contact • Anne Seitzinger, Program Coordinator, Short-Term Study Abroad, Northern Illinois University, Study Abroad Office-WI 417, DeKalb, IL 60115; 815-752-0700; Fax: 815-753-0825; E-mail: aseitz@niu.edu; World Wide Web: http://www.niu.edu/depts/intl_prgms/intl.html

RAMAPO COLLEGE OF NEW JERSEY

SUMMER STUDY IN GREECE

General Information • Academic study program in Athens. Excursions to Delphi, Armenistice, Island of Lesvos, Ikaria, Ikarian hot springs, Athens, Roman Baths at Therma, Samos, Fanari Tower, Nas, Ayios Kirikos.
Learning Focus • Courses in social ecology, philosophy. Instruction is offered by professors from the sponsoring institution.
Accommodations • Hotels. Single rooms are available. Meals are taken as a group.
Program Details • Program offered once per year. Session length: 3 weeks. Departures are scheduled in June. The program is open to undergraduate students, graduate students, pre-college students, adults. Most participants are 18–45 years of age. 18 participants per session.
Costs • $2850 (includes housing, some meals, excursions, international airfare). A $300 deposit is required.
Contact • Mrs. Robyn Perricelli, Coordinator, Study Abroad, Ramapo College of New Jersey, 505 Ramapo Valley Road, Mahwah, NJ 07430; 201-529-7463; Fax: 201-529-7508; E-mail: rperrice@ramapo.edu

SOUTHERN ILLINOIS UNIVERSITY AT CARBONDALE

ORIGINS: RE-THINKING THE LEGACY OF ANCIENT GREECE

General Information • Academic study program in Greece (Delphi, Kos Island, Samos Island), Turkey.
Learning Focus • Courses in philosophy. Instruction is offered by professors from the sponsoring institution.
Accommodations • Hotels. Meals are taken in local restaurants.
Program Details • Program offered once per year. Session length: 2 weeks. Departures are scheduled in May. The program is open to undergraduate students, adults. Most participants are 18–50 years of age. Other requirements: minimum 2.75 GPA. 20 participants per session. Application deadline: April 1.
Costs • $2500 (includes tuition, housing, some meals, excursions). A $250 deposit is required.
Contact • Thomas Saville, Coordinator, Study Abroad Programs, Southern Illinois University at Carbondale, Mailcode 6885, Small Business Incubator, Room 217, Carbondale, IL 62901; 618-453-7670; Fax: 618-453-7677; E-mail: studyabr@siu.edu

---

The program ORIGINS: Re-Thinking the Legacy of Ancient Greece is designed as an interdisciplinary and team-taught activity that offers hands-on experience in an effort to help participants understand more deeply both other cultures and their own. Faculty from many disciplines join together to conduct activities that illuminate early chapters in Western heritage. The program is not merely lectures and tours; instead, it encourages participation in diverse activities such as model-making reconstructions of ancient buildings, recreating ancient debates in the law courts, designing and painting terra-cotta vessels, reenacting selections from the writings of early philosophers in historical settings, and performing a classical Greek play in an ancient theater.

STATE UNIVERSITY OF NEW YORK COLLEGE AT BROCKPORT

SUMMER STUDY TOUR OF GREECE

General Information • Academic study program in Athens.
Learning Focus • Courses in mythology, literature. Instruction is offered by professors from the sponsoring institution.
Accommodations • Hotels. Single rooms are available.
Program Details • Program offered once per year. Session length: 3 weeks. Departures are scheduled in June. The program is open to undergraduate students, adults. Most participants are 19–65 years of age. 15 participants per session. Application deadline: May 15.
Costs • $3000 (includes tuition, housing, all meals, excursions, international airfare). A $100 deposit is required.
Contact • Dr. John J. Perry, Director, Office of International Education, State University of New York College at Brockport, 350 New Campus Drive, Brockport, NY 14420; 716-395-2119; Fax: 716-637-3218; E-mail: jperry@acspr1.acs.brockport.e; World Wide Web: http://www.brockport.edu/study_abroad

TRAVELEARN

A GREEK ODYSSEY

General Information • Cultural tour with visits to Athens, Delphi, Kalambaka, Mauplia, Olympia, Sparta, Santorini, Herklion, Rhodes, Kusadasi, Patmos. Once at the destination country, participants travel by bus, foot. Program is affiliated with the nationwide TraveLearn network of 290 universities and colleges.
Learning Focus • Instruction in history, literature, art and archaeology. Museum visits (National Archaeological Museum, Acropolis Museum). Other activities include "people-to-people" experience in Nauplia. Instruction is offered by professors, historians, social scientists. This program would appeal to people interested in literature, history, archaeology, cultural understanding, religion.
Accommodations • Hotels. Single rooms are available for an additional $450.
Program Details • Program offered 3 times per year. Session length: 12–16 days. Departures are scheduled in May, June, October. Program is targeted to mature adults. Most participants are 40–75 years of age. Participants must be 18 years or older to enroll. 14–20 participants per session. Application deadline: 60 days prior to departure. Reservations are recommended at least 4–8 months before departure.

Costs • $2995 (includes housing, all meals, books and class materials, excursions, international airfare). A $300 deposit is required.
Contact • Keith Williams, Director of Marketing, TraveLearn, PO Box 315, Lakeville, PA 18438; 800-235-9114; Fax: 717-226-9114; E-mail: travelearn@aol.com

UNIVERSITY OF DETROIT MERCY

CLASSICAL THEATRE PROGRAM IN GREECE

General Information • Performing arts program in Spetses Island. Excursions to Delphi, Athens, Epidaurus, Mycenae.
Learning Focus • Courses in classical Greek drama. Instruction is offered by professors from the sponsoring institution.
Accommodations • Dormitories. Single rooms are available. Meals are taken as a group, in central dining facility.
Program Details • Program offered once per year. Session length: 4 weeks. Departures are scheduled in June. The program is open to undergraduate students, graduate students, adults. Most participants are 16–70 years of age. 25–40 participants per session. Application deadline: May 15.
Costs • $2700 (includes tuition, housing, some meals, excursions). Application fee: $200.
Contact • Dr. Arthur Beer, Theatre Program Director, University of Detroit Mercy, 4001 West McNichols Road, PO Box 19900, Detroit, MI 48219-0900; 313-993-1287; Fax: 313-993-1166

UNIVERSITY OF DETROIT MERCY

MODERN GREEK LANGUAGE

General Information • Language study program in Athens, Spetses Island.
Learning Focus • Courses in Greek language. Instruction is offered by professors from the sponsoring institution.
Accommodations • Program-owned apartments. Single rooms are available. Meals are taken on one's own.
Program Details • Program offered 35 times per year. Session length: 3, 4, 7, or 10 weeks. Departures are scheduled in January–December. The program is open to undergraduate students, graduate students, pre-college students, adults. Most participants are 17–70 years of age. 10–14 participants per session. Application deadline: 2 weeks prior to departure.
Costs • $475 (includes tuition). Application fee: $10. A $50 deposit is required.
Contact • Rosemary Donnelly, Program Director, University of Detroit Mercy, 48 Archimidous Street, Athens 11636, Greece; +30 1-701-2268; Fax: +30 1-701-8603; E-mail: athenscr@compulink.gr

UNIVERSITY OF KANSAS

THE SECOND SUMMER THEATRE IN GREECE

General Information • Academic study program in Katohi. Excursions to Lafkada, Sounion, Athens.
Learning Focus • Courses in Greek language, classical Greek culture, Greek song and dance, history of ancient Greek theater and architecture, theater production. Instruction is offered by professors from the sponsoring institution.
Accommodations • Dormitories. Meals are taken as a group, in residences.
Program Details • Program offered once per year. Session length: 6 weeks. Departures are scheduled in June. The program is open to undergraduate students, graduate students, adults with theater background. Application deadline: March 1.
Costs • $2100 (includes tuition, housing, some meals, excursions, land transportation from Athens to Katohi). Application fee: $15. A $300 deposit is required.
Contact • Susan MacNally, Coordinator of Summer Institutes, University of Kansas, Office of Study Abroad, 203 Lippincott Hall, Lawrence, KS 66045; 913-864-3742; Fax: 913-864-5040; E-mail: osa@falcon.cc.ukans.edu; World Wide Web: http://kuhub.cc.ukans.edu/~intlstdy/osa/osamain.html

UNIVERSITY OF LA VERNE

STUDY ABROAD IN ATHENS, GREECE

General Information • Academic study program in Athens. Classes are held on the campus of University of LaVerne, Athens Campus. Excursions to Egypt, Turkey, Europe.
Learning Focus • Courses in liberal arts, computer science, accounting, art, behavioral science, business, economics, English language, marketing, counseling. Instruction is offered by professors from the sponsoring institution.
Accommodations • Dormitories, locally-rented apartments, program-owned apartments. Meals are taken on one's own, in central dining facility, in local restaurants, in residences.
Program Details • Program offered 4 times per year. Session length: 6–12 weeks. Departures are scheduled in March, June, September, December. The program is open to undergraduate students, graduate students, adults. Most participants are 22–28 years of age. Other requirements: minimum 2.5 GPA. 900 participants per session. Application deadline: rolling.
Costs • $2500 (includes tuition, fees). Application fee: $30. A $100 deposit is required.
Contact • Office of Admissions, University of La Verne, 18 Panagi Psaldari Street, Kifissia, Athens 14561, Greece; +30 1-620-6188; Fax: +30 1-620-5929

UNIVERSITY OF MINNESOTA, THE GLOBAL CAMPUS

ARCHAEOLOGICAL FIELDWORK IN GREECE

General Information • Academic study program in Pylos.
Learning Focus • Courses in archaeology, art history, classical studies, anthropology. Instruction is offered by professors from the sponsoring institution.
Accommodations • Dormitories, campsites. Meals are taken as a group, on one's own, in local restaurants, in residences.
Program Details • Program offered 3 times per year. Session length: 3–4 weeks. Departures are scheduled in June–August. The program is open to undergraduate

students, graduate students. Most participants are 18–30 years of age. Other requirements: previous course or field work in topic. 25–30 participants per session. Application deadline: March 1.

Costs • $800 (includes tuition, housing, some meals). A $100 deposit is required.

Contact • Dr. F. Cooper, University of Minnesota, The Global Campus, 331 Folwell Hall, 9 Pleasant Street, SE, Minneapolis, MN 55455-0138; 612-625-5353; Fax: 612-626-8009; World Wide Web: http://www.isp.umn.edu/tgchome/tgchome.html

ICELAND

DIS, DENMARK'S INTERNATIONAL STUDY PROGRAM

ARCTIC BIOLOGY IN ICELAND

General Information • Academic study program in Reykjavik. Classes are held on the campus of University of Iceland. Excursions to Vestmanna Islands, Skaftafell National Park.
Learning Focus • Courses in geology, marine biology, ecology, biology, humans in the arctic. Instruction is offered by professors from the sponsoring institution and local teachers.
Accommodations • Rented rooms. Meals are taken as a group, on one's own, in residences.
Program Details • Program offered once per year. Session length: 6 weeks. Departures are scheduled in June. The program is open to undergraduate students. Most participants are 20–25 years of age. Other requirements: minimum 3.0 GPA. 15–25 participants per session.
Costs • $3625 (includes tuition, housing, some meals, books and class materials, excursions). A $750 deposit is required.
Contact • Helle Gjerlufsen, Field Director, DiS, Denmark's International Study Program, North American Office, 50 Nicholson Hall, 216 Pillsbury Drive, SE, Minneapolis, MN 55455-0138; 800-247-3477; Fax: 612-626-8009; World Wide Web: http://www.disp.dk

PHOTO ADVENTURE TOURS

ICELAND: NORTH AND SOUTH

General Information • Photography tour with visits to Akureyri, Blue Lagoon, Geysir, Gullfoss, Hekla, Keflavik, Myvatn, Olafsfjordur, Reykjavik, Skaga Fjord. Once at the destination country, participants travel by bus, foot.
Learning Focus • Instruction in photography. Escorted travel to Iceland. Museum visits (folk museum in Glaumbaer). Nature observation (waterfalls, geysers, hot springs, birds and wildlife, glaciers, volcanic formations). Other activities include hiking. Instruction is offered by naturalists, artists, historians, photographers. This program would appeal to people interested in photography, geology, adventure, hiking, ornithology.
Accommodations • Homestays, hotels, guest houses. Single rooms are available for an additional $545.
Program Details • Program offered once per year. Session length: 9 days. Departures are scheduled in July. Most participants are 18–80 years of age. Other requirements: a positive attitude and an open mind. 12 participants per session. Application deadline: 60 days prior to departure. Reservations are recommended at least 60 days before departure.
Costs • $3333 (includes housing, all meals, excursions, international airfare, entry fees). A $400 deposit is required.
Contact • Richard Libbey, General Partner, Photo Adventure Tours, 2035 Park Street, Atlantic Beach, NY 11509-1236; 516-371-0067; Fax: 516-371-1352

PHOTO ADVENTURE TOURS

ICELAND: SOUTHERN PHOTO TOUR

General Information • Photography tour with visits to Blue Lagoon, Geysir, Gullfoss, Jokulsarlon, Keflavik, Landmannalaugar, Reykjavik, Skaftafell, Vik. Once at the destination country, participants travel by bus, foot, boat, bicycle.
Learning Focus • Instruction in photography. Escorted travel to Iceland. Museum visits (folk museum in Skogar). Nature observation (waterfalls, geysers, birds, animals, hot springs, glaciers). Other activities include hiking. Instruction is offered by naturalists, artists, historians, photographers. This program would appeal to people interested in photography, geology, adventure, culture, ornithology.
Accommodations • Hotels, guest houses. Single rooms are available for an additional $485.
Program Details • Program offered once per year. Session length: 8 days. Departures are scheduled in July. Most participants are 18–80 years of age. Other requirements: a positive attitude and an open mind. 12 participants per session. Application deadline: 60 days prior to departure. Reservations are recommended at least 60 days before departure.
Costs • $2890 (includes housing, all meals, excursions, international airfare, entry fees). A $400 deposit is required.
Contact • Richard Libbey, General Partner, Photo Adventure Tours, 2035 Park Street, Atlantic Beach, NY 11509-1236; 516-371-0067; Fax: 516-371-1352

IRELAND

See also England, Scotland, and Wales

BEAVER COLLEGE

BURREN COLLEGE OF ART SUMMER PROGRAMS

General Information • Arts program in Ballyvaughan. Classes are held on the campus of Burren College of Art. Excursions to Galway, Aran Islands.
Learning Focus • Courses in painting, drawing, photography, sculpture, three dimensional studies, scientific illustration, ecology. Instruction is offered by local teachers.
Accommodations • Program-owned houses. Meals are taken in central dining facility, in local restaurants.
Program Details • Program offered 2 times per year. Session length: 3 or 8 weeks. Departures are scheduled in May, June. The program is open to undergraduate students, graduate students, adults. Other requirements: minimum 3.0 GPA and three or four semesters of college-level course work. Application deadline: March 15.
Costs • $2650 for 3 weeks, $4750 for 8 weeks (includes tuition, housing, excursions, International Student Identification card, predeparture materials, host country support). Application fee: $35. A $500 deposit is required.
Contact • Meghan Mazick, Program Coordinator, Beaver College, Center for Education Abroad, 450 South Easton Road, Glenside, PA 19038; 888-232-8379; Fax: 215-572-2174; E-mail: mazick@turret.beaver.edu

BEAVER COLLEGE

SUMMER IN DUBLIN: IRISH HISTORY, LITERATURE, AND POLITICS

General Information • Academic study program in Dublin. Classes are held on the campus of Institute of Public Administration. Excursions to Irish Parliament, theater visits in Dublin.
Learning Focus • Courses in history, literature, political science. Instruction is offered by local teachers.
Accommodations • Locally-rented apartments. Meals are taken in residences.
Program Details • Program offered once per year. Session length: 6 weeks. Departures are scheduled in July. The program is open to undergraduate students, graduate students, adults. Other requirements: minimum 3.0 GPA and three or four semesters of college-level course work. Application deadline: March 31.
Costs • $3400 (includes tuition, housing, International Student Identification card, predeparture materials, host country support). Application fee: $35. A $500 deposit is required.
Contact • Meghan Mazick, Program Coordinator, Beaver College, Center for Education Abroad, 450 South Easton Road, Glenside, PA 19038; 888-232-8379; Fax: 215-572-2174; E-mail: mazick@turret.beaver.edu

BRITISH COASTAL TRAILS SCENIC WALKING

CONNEMARA AND ANCIENT IRELAND

General Information • Cultural tour with visits to Clifden, Lahinch, Renvyl Peninsula, Burren, Ardbear Bay, Omey Island, Inishbofin Island, Mweellrea Mountain. Once at the destination country, participants travel by bus, foot, boat.
Learning Focus • Escorted travel to Cliffs of Moher and Cloch na Ron. Nature observation (fjord, seabirds, wildlife, mountains, ocean). Other activities include hiking, walking. Instruction is offered by naturalists, historians, professional guides. This program would appeal to people interested in nature studies, walking, culture, photography, history.
Accommodations • Hotels, inns. Single rooms are available.
Program Details • Program offered 3 times per year. Session length: 8 days. Departures are scheduled in June, July, September. Most participants are 40-65 years of age. Participants must be 13 years or older to enroll. Other requirements: physician's approval and signed release form. 18 participants per session. Application deadline: 30 days prior to departure. Reservations are recommended at least 6 months before departure.
Costs • $1875 (includes housing, some meals, excursions, full-time guide). A $250 deposit is required.
Contact • Tour Manager, British Coastal Trails Scenic Walking, 7777 Fay Avenue, Suite 100, La Jolla, CA 92037; 800-473-1210; Fax: 619-456-2277; E-mail: lajolla@bctwalk.com; World Wide Web: http://www.bctwalk.com/lajolla

BRITISH COASTAL TRAILS SCENIC WALKING

COUNTY KERRY AND THE DINGLE PENINSULA

General Information • Cultural tour with visits to Dingle, Killarney, Waterville, Gap of Dunloe, MacGillicuddy's Reeks, Ballinskelligs Bay, Great Blasket Island. Once at the destination country, participants travel by bus, foot, boat.
Learning Focus • Escorted travel to Valencia Island, Derrynane National Park and Abbey Island. Other activities include hiking, walking. Instruction is offered by naturalists, historians, professional guides. This program would appeal to people interested in nature studies, walking, culture, photography, history.
Accommodations • Hotels. Single rooms are available for an additional $180.
Program Details • Program offered 3 times per year. Session length: 8 days. Departures are scheduled in June, July, September. Most participants are 40-65 years of age. Participants must be 13 years or older to enroll. Other requirements: physician's approval and signed release form.

18 participants per session. Application deadline: 30 days prior to departure. Reservations are recommended at least 6 months before departure.
Costs • $1895 (includes housing, some meals, excursions, full-time guide). A $250 deposit is required.
Contact • Tour Manager, British Coastal Trails Scenic Walking, 7777 Fay Avenue, Suite 100, La Jolla, CA 92037; 800-473-1210; Fax: 619-456-2277; E-mail: lajolla@bctwalk.com; World Wide Web: http://www.bctwalk.com/lajolla

COOPERATIVE CENTER FOR STUDY ABROAD

IRELAND PROGRAM

General Information • Academic study program in Dublin, Galway.
Learning Focus • Courses in English language, health issues, history, literature, marketing. Instruction is offered by professors from the sponsoring institution.
Accommodations • Homestays, dormitories, budget accommodations. Meals are taken as a group, on one's own, in central dining facility, in local restaurants.
Program Details • Program offered 2 times per year. Session length: 2 weeks. Departures are scheduled in May, August. The program is open to undergraduate students, graduate students, adults. Most participants are 18–60 years of age. Other requirements: 2.0 minimum GPA. 60 participants per session. Application deadline: March 1, March 20.
Costs • $1950 (includes housing, some meals, insurance, excursions, international airfare). A $100 deposit is required.
Contact • Dr. Michael A. Klembara, Executive Director, Cooperative Center for Study Abroad, BEP 301, Highland Heights, KY 41099; 800-319-6015; Fax: 606-572-6650; E-mail: ccsa@nku.edu

COUNTRY WALKERS

THE EMERALD ISLE: CAPTURE THE IRISH SPIRIT

General Information • Cultural, gourmet cooking, nature study and walking tour with visits to Inishbofin, Shannon, The Burren, Clifden, Rantstone Bog, Sheeauns, Cleggan. Once at the destination country, participants travel by foot, boat.
Learning Focus • Escorted travel to cliffs of Moher and Glenisheen. Nature observation (active seabird colonies). Other activities include walking. Instruction is offered by professors, researchers, naturalists, historians. This program would appeal to people interested in walking, nature studies, food and wine.
Accommodations • Hotels. Single rooms are available for an additional $300–$600.

Program Details • Program offered 5 times per year. Session length: 8 days. Departures are scheduled in May–August. Program is targeted to adults 35 to 65 years old. Most participants are 35–65 years of age. Participants must be 18 years or older to enroll. 18 participants per session. Reservations are recommended at least 5–6 months before departure.
Costs • $1950 (includes housing, all meals, excursions). A $400 deposit is required.
Contact • Heather Kellingbeck, Vice President, Country Walkers, PO Box 180, Waterbury, VT 05176; 800-464-9255; Fax: 802-244-5661; E-mail: ctrywalk@aol.com

COUNTRY WALKERS

THE MAGICAL SOUTHWEST

General Information • Cultural, gourmet cooking, nature study and walking tour with visits to Ballingeary, Dingle, Killarney, Slea Head, Bantry. Once at the destination country, participants travel by foot, boat.
Learning Focus • Escorted travel to the Gap of Dunloe. Museum visits (Victorian Muckross House). Attendance at performances (traditional Irish music). Other activities include walking. Instruction is offered by professors, researchers, naturalists, historians. This program would appeal to people interested in walking, nature studies, food and wine.
Accommodations • Hotels. Single rooms are available for an additional $300–$600.
Program Details • Program offered 5 times per year. Session length: 8 days. Departures are scheduled in May–September. Program is targeted to adults 35 to 65 years old. Most participants are 35–65 years of age. Participants must be 18 years or older to enroll. 18 participants per session. Reservations are recommended at least 5–6 months before departure.
Costs • $1950 (includes housing, all meals, excursions). A $400 deposit is required.
Contact • Heather Kellingbeck, Vice President, Country Walkers, PO Box 180, Waterbury, VT 05176; 800-464-9255; Fax: 802-244-5661; E-mail: ctrywalk@aol.com

CROSS-CULTURE

IRISH WALKS

General Information • Nature study, cultural, and hiking tour with visits to Killarney, Kenmare, Derrycunnihy, Inch Strand, Dingle Peninsula, Inishmore. Once at the destination country, participants travel by bus, foot.
Learning Focus • Escorted travel to the Gap of Dunloe, Torc Waterfall, Gallarus Oratory, The Burren and Dun Aenghus. Attendance at performances (traditional Irish music). Nature observation (native flora and fauna). Other activities include hiking. Instruction is offered by naturalists, historians, experienced hiking leaders. This program would appeal to people interested in nature studies, history, food and wine, culture, traditions.
Accommodations • Hotels. Single rooms are available for an additional $200.
Program Details • Program offered once per year. Session length: 9 days. Departures are scheduled in July. Program is targeted to adults of all ages. Most participants are 30–75 years of age. Participants must be 12 years or older to enroll. Other requirements: must be in good health, must be accompanied by an adult if under 18. 20 participants per session. Application deadline: 1 month prior to departure. Reservations are recommended at least 3–12 months before departure.
Costs • $2350 (includes tuition, housing, all meals, books and class materials, excursions, international airfare). A $300 deposit is required.
Contact • Cross-Culture, 52 High Point Drive, Amherst, MA 01002-1224; 413-256-6303; Fax: 413-253-2303; E-mail: xculture@javanet.com; World Wide Web: http://www.empiremall.com/cross-culture

CROSS-CULTURE

A TASTE OF IRELAND

General Information • Cultural tour with visits to Dublin, Killarney, Dingle peninsula, Glendalough. Once at the destination country, participants travel by bus, foot.
Learning Focus • Instruction in native Irish language and culture and whiskey production. Escorted travel to Torc Waterfall, Rock of Cashel and St. Patrick's Cathedral. Museum visits (Museum of Kerry Folk Life, Rock of Cashel Museum). Attendance at performances (Irish National Theater). Instruction is offered by highly educated guides. This program would appeal to people interested in culture, history, nature studies, arts, traditions, food and wine.
Accommodations • Hotels. Single rooms are available for an additional $260.
Program Details • Program offered once per year. Session length: 9 days. Departures are scheduled in August. Program is targeted to adults of all ages. Most participants are 40–70 years of age. Participants must be 12 years or older to enroll. Other requirements: good health, accompaniment of an adult if under 18. 20–25 participants per session. Application deadline: 1 month prior to departure. Reservations are recommended at least 3–12 months before departure.
Costs • $2480 (includes tuition, housing, all meals, books and class materials, excursions, international airfare). A $300 deposit is required.
Contact • Cross-Culture, 52 High Point Drive, Amherst, MA 01002-1224; 413-256-6303; Fax: 413-253-2303; E-mail: xculture@javanet.com; World Wide Web: http://www.empiremall.com/cross-culture

 EUROCENTRES

LANGUAGE IMMERSION IN IRELAND

General Information • Language study program in Dublin. Classes are held on the campus of Eurocentre Dublin Summer Centre. Excursions to Galway, Aran Islands, Wicklaw Mountains, Connemara, Ring of Kerry.
Learning Focus • Courses in English language, Irish culture. Instruction is offered by professors from the sponsoring institution.
Accommodations • Homestays. Single rooms are available. Meals are taken with host family, in residences.
Program Details • Program offered 20 times per year. Session length: 2–12 weeks. Departures are scheduled in January–December. The program is open to undergraduate students, graduate students, pre-college students, adults. Most participants are 16–80 years of age. 15 participants per session.

Costs • Contact sponsor for information.
Contact • Marketing, Eurocentres, 101 North Union Street, Suite 300, Alexandria, VA 22314; 800-648-4809; Fax: 703-684-1495; E-mail: 100632.141@compuserve.com; World Wide Web: http://www.clark.net/pub/eurocent/home.htm

FOREIGN LANGUAGE STUDY ABROAD SERVICE

INTERNATIONAL LANGUAGE STUDY HOMESTAYS IN IRELAND

General Information • Language study program in Ireland.
Learning Focus • Courses in English language. Instruction is offered by local teachers.
Accommodations • Homestays. Single rooms are available. Meals are taken with host family, in residences.
Program Details • Session length: varies. Departures are scheduled in January–December. The program is open to undergraduate students, graduate students, pre-college students, adults. Most participants are 12 years of age and older. Other requirements: students must be at least 12 years old. 1 participant per session.
Costs • Contact sponsor for information. A $300 deposit is required.
Contact • Louise Harber, Coordinator, Foreign Language Study Abroad Service, Department IH, Box 903, 5935 Southwest 64th Avenue, South Miami, FL 33143; 800-282-1090; Fax: 305-662-2907; E-mail: flsas@netpoint.net; World Wide Web: http://www.netpoint.net/~flsas

FORUM TRAVEL INTERNATIONAL

WEST CORK AND KERRY CYCLING SAFARI

General Information • Bicycle tour with visits to Bantry Bay, Killarney. Once at the destination country, participants travel by bicycle.
Learning Focus • Instruction in nature, culture, and social interaction in Ireland. Escorted travel to pubs. Other activities include cycling. Instruction is offered by professional guides. This program would appeal to people interested in bicycling, the outdoors.
Accommodations • Hotels.
Program Details • Program offered 13 times per year. Session length: 8 days. Departures are scheduled in May–September. Most participants are 20–60 years of age. Participants must be 16 years or older to enroll. 15 participants per session. Application deadline: 60 days prior to departure. Reservations are recommended at least 3–5 months before departure.
Costs • $625 (includes housing, some meals). A $200 deposit is required.
Contact • Jeannie Graves, Operations Manager, Forum Travel International, 91 Gregory Lane #21, Pleasant Hill, CA 94525; 510-671-2900; Fax: 510-671-2993; E-mail: forum@ix.netcom.com; World Wide Web: http://www.ten-io.com/forumtravel

GLOBAL EXCHANGE REALITY TOURS

IRELAND

General Information • Academic study program with visits to Ireland (Cullyhanna, Dublin), Northern Ireland (Belfast, Derry). Once at the destination country, participants travel by bus, airplane.
Learning Focus • Instruction in the political and economic conflict in Northern Ireland. Instruction is offered by researchers, naturalists. This program would appeal to people interested in grassroots organizations, women's issues, Irish politics.
Accommodations • Hotels, guest houses. Single rooms are available for an additional $200–$500.
Program Details • Program offered 2 times per year. Session length: 14 days. Departures are scheduled in June, November. Program is targeted to seniors, students and professionals. Participants must be 18 years or older to enroll. 10 participants per session. Application deadline: 1 month prior to departure. Reservations are recommended at least 2 months before departure.
Costs • $2250 from San Francisco or Los Angeles, 2150 from New York (includes housing, some meals, books and class materials, international airfare). A $200 deposit is required.
Contact • Reality Tours Coordinator, Global Exchange Reality Tours, 2017 Mission Street, Room 303, San Francisco, CA 94110; 415-255-7296; Fax: 415-255-7498; E-mail: globalexch@igc.apc.org

ILLINOIS STATE UNIVERSITY

STROKESTOWN, COUNTY ROSCOMMON, IRELAND SUMMER

General Information • Academic study program in Strokestown.
Learning Focus • Courses in archaeology.
Accommodations • Bed and breakfasts.
Program Details • Program offered once per year. Session length: 4 weeks. Departures are scheduled in July. The program is open to undergraduate students, graduate students, professionals. Other requirements: minimum 2.5 GPA and a minimum of sophomore status. 15 participants per session. Application deadline: March 15.
Costs • $1950 (includes housing, all meals, excursions, fees).
Contact • Dr. Charles Orser, Illinois State University, Campus Box 4640, Normal, IL 61790-4640; 309-438-2271; Fax: 309-438-3987; E-mail: oisp@rs6000.cmp.ilstu.edu; World Wide Web: http://www.orat.ilstu.edu/

INTERHOSTEL, UNIVERSITY OF NEW HAMPSHIRE

DUBLIN, IRELAND

General Information • Cultural tour with visits to Dublin, Ennis, Trinity College, County Wicklow, Powerscourt, Glendalough, The Burren, Cliffs of Mohr, Cragge Nowen, Newgrange. Once at the destination country, participants travel by bus, foot. Program is affiliated with Trinity College, Dublin.

Learning Focus • Instruction in history and culture. Escorted travel to the countryside. Museum visits (National Museum of Ireland, National Gallery). Attendance at performances (theater). Instruction is offered by historians. This program would appeal to people interested in history, culture.
Accommodations • Dormitories. Single rooms are available for an additional $30.
Program Details • Program offered once per year. Session length: 2 weeks. Departures are scheduled in August. Program is targeted to seniors over 50. Most participants are 60–80 years of age. Participants must be 50 years or older to enroll. 35 participants per session. Reservations are recommended at least 6 months before departure.
Costs • $2575 (includes tuition, housing, all meals, excursions, international airfare, entrance fees). A $200 deposit is required.
Contact • Janice Pierson, Office Supervisor, Interhostel, University of New Hampshire, 6 Garrison Avenue, Durham, NH 03824; 800-733-9753; Fax: 603-862-1113; World Wide Web: http://www.learn.unh.edu/

INTERHOSTEL, UNIVERSITY OF NEW HAMPSHIRE

GALWAY, IRELAND

General Information • Cultural tour with visits to Galway, Aran Islands, Rathbaun Farm, Thoor Bally Lee, Kylemore Abbey, Coole Park, Cliffs of Mohr, Ballintubber, Westport House, Clonmac Noise, Clonfert. Once at the destination country, participants travel by bus, foot.
Learning Focus • Instruction in history and culture. Escorted travel to the countryside and villages. Instruction is offered by professors, historians. This program would appeal to people interested in history, culture.
Accommodations • Hotels. Single rooms are available for an additional $300.
Program Details • Program offered once per year. Session length: 2 weeks. Departures are scheduled in September. Program is targeted to seniors over 50. Most participants are 60–80 years of age. Participants must be 50 years or older to enroll. 35 participants per session. Reservations are recommended at least 6 months before departure.
Costs • $2395 (includes tuition, housing, all meals, excursions, international airfare, entrance fees). A $200 deposit is required.
Contact • Janice Pierson, Office Supervisor, Interhostel, University of New Hampshire, 6 Garrison Avenue, Durham, NH 03824; 800-733-9753; Fax: 603-862-1113; World Wide Web: http://www.learn.unh.edu/

INTERHOSTEL, UNIVERSITY OF NEW HAMPSHIRE

WALKING IN GALWAY, IRELAND

General Information • Cultural tour with visits to Galway, Killarney, Dublin, Bunratty Castle, Adare, Muckross, Aran Islands, Athenry, Clifden, Streamstown, Moher, Kylemore Abbey. Once at the destination country, participants travel by bus, foot, boat. Program is affiliated with University College, Galway.
Learning Focus • Instruction in history and culture. Escorted travel to historical sites. Museum visits (National Gallery in Dublin). Attendance at performances (Irish music). Other activities include walking. Instruction is offered by professors, naturalists. This program would appeal to people interested in history, culture, walking.
Accommodations • Hotels. Single rooms are available for an additional $250.
Program Details • Program offered once per year. Session length: 2 weeks. Departures are scheduled in June. Program is targeted to seniors over 50. Most participants are 60–80 years of age. Participants must be 50 years or older to enroll. 35 participants per session. Reservations are recommended at least 6 months before departure.
Costs • $2495 (includes tuition, housing, all meals, excursions, international airfare, entrance fees). A $200 deposit is required.
Contact • Janice Pierson, Office Supervisor, Interhostel, University of New Hampshire, 6 Garrison Avenue, Durham, NH 03824; 800-733-9753; Fax: 603-862-1113; World Wide Web: http://www.learn.unh.edu/

 IONA COLLEGE

IONA PEACE INSTITUTE IN IRELAND

General Information • Academic study program in Dublin. Classes are held on the campus of Marino Institute of Education.
Learning Focus • Courses in justice studies, peace studies. Instruction is offered by professors from the sponsoring institution.
Accommodations • Homestays, dormitories. Single rooms are available. Meals are taken as a group, with host family, in central dining facility, in residences.
Program Details • Program offered once per year. Session length: 4 weeks. Departures are scheduled in June. The program is open to undergraduate students. Most participants are 19–22 years of age. Other requirements: minimum 2.3 GPA. 12 participants per session. Application deadline: May 1.
Costs • $2100 (includes tuition, housing, some meals, insurance, excursions, international airfare). A $200 deposit is required.
Contact • Prof. Michael Hovey, Director, Iona Peace Institute in Ireland, Iona College, 715 North Avenue, New Rochelle, NY 10801-1890; 914-633-2630; E-mail: kpd1@iona.bitnet

AN IRISH SOJOURN

LITERATURE, PEOPLE, AND PLACE

General Information • Cultural tour with visits to Burren, County Clare. Once at the destination country, participants travel by bus, foot, boat.
Learning Focus • Instruction in Irish history and literature. Attendance at performances (Irish traditional music). Instruction is offered by professors, naturalists, historians, scientists. This program would appeal to people interested in history, literature, botany, geology, archaeology, music, folklore.
Accommodations • Locally-rented apartments, houses.
Program Details • Program offered 3 times per year. Session length: 10 days. Departures are scheduled in June–August. Most participants are 45–75 years of age. 8–12

participants per session. Reservations are recommended at least 3 months before departure.
Costs • $2150 (includes tuition, housing, some meals, books and class materials, excursions). A $500 deposit is required.
Contact • Dermot Dix, Director, An Irish Sojourn, 227 Columbus Avenue, #55, New York, NY 10023; 212-501-0457; E-mail: dsdix@aol.com

LYNN UNIVERSITY

STUDY ABROAD IN IRELAND

General Information • Academic study program in Dublin. Classes are held on the campus of American College Dublin. Excursions to France, other areas of Ireland, Belgium.
Learning Focus • Courses in international business, liberal studies, behavioral science, hospitality services, tourism and travel. Instruction is offered by local teachers.
Accommodations • Homestays, locally-rented apartments. Meals are taken on one's own, with host family, in local restaurants, in residences.
Program Details • Program offered once per year. Session length: 6 weeks. Departures are scheduled in June. The program is open to undergraduate students. Most participants are 19–23 years of age. Other requirements: minimum 2.5 GPA and must be entering sophomore, junior, or senior year. 15 participants per session. Application deadline: May 1.
Costs • $3825 (includes tuition, housing). Application fee: $20. A $150 deposit is required.
Contact • Kathleen Sullivan, Director, Study Abroad Programs, Lynn University, 3601 North Military Trail, Boca Raton, FL 33431; 800-453-8306; Fax: 561-241-3552; World Wide Web: http://www.lynn.edu

METROPOLITAN OPERA GUILD

METROPOLITAN OPERA GUILD MEMBERS TRAVEL PROGRAM

General Information • Cultural tour with visits to Adave, Dublin, Wexford, Moher, Rock of Cashel, Waterford. Once at the destination country, participants travel by bus, foot, airplane. Program is affiliated with Metropolitan Opera Guild.
Learning Focus • Escorted travel to Glin Castle, St. Patrick's Cathedral and estate gardens. Museum visits (Russborough House, National Art Gallery). Attendance at performances (opera, concerts, theater). Instruction is offered by researchers, journalists. This program would appeal to people interested in opera, music, art, architecture.
Accommodations • Hotels. Single rooms are available for an additional $150.
Program Details • Departures are scheduled throughout the year. Program is targeted to opera lovers. Most participants are 35–80 years of age. Participants must be members of the sponsoring organization (annual dues: $50). Reservations are recommended at least 4–5 months before departure.
Costs • $3195 (includes housing, some meals, excursions, international airfare, performance tickets, museum admission, transfers). A $950 deposit is required.
Contact • Amy Caplan, Coordinator of Members Travel Program, Metropolitan Opera Guild, 70 Lincoln Center Plaza, New York, NY 10023; 212-769-7062; Fax: 212-769-7002; World Wide Web: http://www.metguild.org

NATIONAL REGISTRATION CENTER FOR STUDY ABROAD

INSTITUTE OF IRISH STUDIES–DUBLIN

General Information • Language study program in Dublin.
Learning Focus • Courses in history, political science, literature.
Accommodations • Dormitories. Single rooms are available. Meals are taken on one's own.
Program Details • Program offered 14 times per year. Session length: 2 weeks. Departures are scheduled in June–August. The program is open to undergraduate students, graduate students, adults. Application deadline: 40 days prior to departure.
Costs • $1598 (includes tuition, housing, some meals, insurance, excursions). Application fee: $40. A $100 deposit is required.
Contact • Reuel Zielke, Coordinator, National Registration Center for Study Abroad, PO Box 1393, Milwaukee, WI 53201; 414-278-0631; Fax: 414-271-8884; E-mail: inquiries@nrcsa.com; World Wide Web: http://www.nrcsa.com

NORTHERN ILLINOIS UNIVERSITY

MEDIA AND CULTURE IN IRELAND

General Information • Academic study program in Dublin. Classes are held on the campus of Dublin City University.
Learning Focus • Courses in communications, English literature. Instruction is offered by professors from the sponsoring institution.
Accommodations • Homestays. Single rooms are available. Meals are taken with host family.
Program Details • Program offered once per year. Session length: 4 weeks. Departures are scheduled in June, July. The program is open to undergraduate students, graduate students. Most participants are 21–26 years of age. 18 participants per session. Application deadline: May 1.
Costs • $2050 (includes tuition, housing, some meals, insurance). A $200 deposit is required.
Contact • Anne Seitzinger, Program Coordinator, Short-Term Study Abroad, Northern Illinois University, Study Abroad Office-WI 417, DeKalb, IL 60115; 815-752-0700; Fax: 815-753-0825; E-mail: aseitz@niu.edu; World Wide Web: http://www.niu.edu/depts/intl_prgms/intl.html

OIDEAS GAEL, FORAS CULTUIR ULADH

ARCHAEOLOGY SUMMER SCHOOL

General Information • Academic study program in Glencolmcille, Donegal. Excursions to Island Hermitage.
Learning Focus • Courses in archaeology. Instruction is offered by professors from the sponsoring institution.

Accommodations • Homestays, locally-rented apartments, program-owned apartments. Single rooms are available. Meals are taken with host family, in local restaurants, in residences.
Program Details • Program offered once per year. Session length: 1 week. Departures are scheduled in August. The program is open to undergraduate students, graduate students, pre-college students, adults. Most participants are 18–80 years of age. 30 participants per session. Application deadline: 4 weeks prior to departure.
Costs • $180 (includes tuition, housing). A $130 deposit is required.
Contact • Liam Ó. Cuinneagáin, Director, Oideas Gael, Foras Cultuir Uladh, Oideas Gael, Glencolmcille, Donegal, Ireland; +353 73-30-248; Fax: +73 30-348; E-mail: oidsgael@iol.ie; World Wide Web: http://www.xs4all.nl/~conaill/Oideas_Gael/iodeas.html

OIDEAS GAEL, FORAS CULTUIR ULADH

CULTURAL HILLWALKING

General Information • Academic study program in Glencolmcille, Donegal.
Learning Focus • Courses in cultural studies, folklore. Instruction is offered by professors from the sponsoring institution.
Accommodations • Homestays, locally-rented apartments, program-owned apartments. Single rooms are available. Meals are taken with host family, in local restaurants.
Program Details • Program offered 6 times per year. Session length: 1 week. Departures are scheduled in April, June, July, August. The program is open to undergraduate students, graduate students, pre-college students, adults. Most participants are 18–50 years of age. 40 participants per session. Application deadline: 4 weeks prior to departure.
Costs • $170 (includes tuition, housing). A $120 deposit is required.
Contact • Liam Ó. Cuinneagáin, Director, Oideas Gael, Foras Cultuir Uladh, Oideas Gael, Glencolmcille, Donegal, Ireland; +353 73-30-248; Fax: +73 30-348; E-mail: oidsgael@iol.ie; World Wide Web: http://www.xs4all.nl/~conaill/Oideas_Gael/iodeas.html

OIDEAS GAEL, FORAS CULTUIR ULADH

IRISH LANGUAGE AND CULTURE PROGRAM

General Information • Language study program in Glencolmcille, Donegal.
Learning Focus • Courses in Irish language, Irish culture. Instruction is offered by professors from the sponsoring institution.
Accommodations • Homestays, locally-rented apartments, program-owned apartments. Single rooms are available. Meals are taken with host family, in local restaurants, in residences.
Program Details • Program offered once per year. Session length: 1 week. Departures are scheduled in July. The program is open to undergraduate students, graduate students, pre-college students, adults. Most participants are 18–80 years of age. 100 participants per session. Application deadline: 1 month prior to departure.
Costs • $180 (includes tuition, housing). A $130 deposit is required.
Contact • Liam Ó. Cuinneagáin, Director, Oideas Gael, Foras Cultuir Uladh, Donegal, Ireland; +353 73-30-248; Fax: +73 30-348; E-mail: oidsgael@iol.ie; World Wide Web: http://www.xs4all.nl/~conaill/Oideas_Gael/iodeas.html

OIDEAS GAEL, FORAS CULTUIR ULADH

IRISH LANGUAGE FOR ADULTS

General Information • Language study program in Glencolmcille, Donegal.
Learning Focus • Courses in Irish language. Instruction is offered by professors from the sponsoring institution.
Accommodations • Homestays, locally-rented apartments, program-owned apartments. Single rooms are available. Meals are taken with host family, in local restaurants, in residences.
Program Details • Program offered 12 times per year. Session length: 1 week. Departures are scheduled in April, June, July, August. The program is open to undergraduate students, graduate students, pre-college students, adults. Most participants are 18–80 years of age. 60 participants per session. Application deadline: 1 month prior to departure.
Costs • $180 (includes tuition, housing). A $130 deposit is required.
Contact • Liam Ó. Cuinneagáin, Director, Oideas Gael, Foras Cultuir Uladh, Oideas Gael, Glencolmcille, Donegal, Ireland; +353 73-30-248; Fax: +73 30-348; E-mail: oidsgael@iol.ie; World Wide Web: http://www.xs4all.nl/~conaill/Oideas_Gael/iodeas.html

OIDEAS GAEL, FORAS CULTUIR ULADH

NATURAL DYEING AND TAPESTRY WEAVING

General Information • Arts program in Glencolmcille, Donegal.
Learning Focus • Courses in crafts. Instruction is offered by professors from the sponsoring institution.
Accommodations • Homestays, locally-rented apartments, program-owned houses. Single rooms are available. Meals are taken with host family, in local restaurants, in residences.
Program Details • Program offered 2 times per year. Session length: 1 week. Departures are scheduled in July, August. The program is open to undergraduate students, graduate students, pre-college students, adults. Most participants are 18–70 years of age. 30 participants per session. Application deadline: 4 weeks prior to departure.
Costs • $180 (includes tuition, housing). A $130 deposit is required.
Contact • Liam Ó. Cuinneagáin, Director, Oideas Gael, Foras Cultuir Uladh, Oideas Gael, Glencolmcille, Donegal, Ireland; +353 73-30-248; Fax: +73 30-348; E-mail: oidsgael@iol.ie; World Wide Web: http://www.xs4all.nl/~conaill/Oideas_Gael/iodeas.html

OIDEAS GAEL, FORAS CULTUIR ULADH

PAINTING IN IRELAND

General Information • Arts program in Glencolmcille, Donegal.
Learning Focus • Courses in painting, sketching. Instruction is offered by professors from the sponsoring institution.
Accommodations • Homestays, locally-rented apartments, program-owned apartments. Single rooms are available. Meals are taken with host family, in local restaurants, in residences.
Program Details • Program offered 2 times per year. Session length: 1 week. Departures are scheduled in July, September. The program is open to undergraduate students, graduate students, pre-college students, adults. Most participants are 18–70 years of age. 30 participants per session. Application deadline: 4 weeks prior to departure.
Costs • $180 (includes tuition, housing). A $130 deposit is required.
Contact • Liam Ó. Cuinneagáin, Director, Oideas Gael, Foras Cultuir Uladh, Oideas Gael, Glenclmcille, Donegal, Ireland; +353 73-30-248; Fax: +73 30-348; E-mail: oidsgael@iol.ie; World Wide Web: http://www.xs4all.nl/~conaill/Oideas_Gael/iodeas.html

OIDEAS GAEL, FORAS CULTUIR ULADH

TRADITIONAL DANCES OF IRELAND

General Information • Academic study program in Glencolmcille, Donegal.
Learning Focus • Courses in dance, music. Instruction is offered by professors from the sponsoring institution.
Accommodations • Homestays, locally-rented apartments, program-owned apartments. Single rooms are available. Meals are taken with host family, in local restaurants, in residences.
Program Details • Program offered once per year. Session length: 1 week. Departures are scheduled in July. The program is open to undergraduate students, graduate students, pre-college students, adults. Most participants are 18–60 years of age. 30 participants per session. Application deadline: 4 weeks prior to departure.
Costs • $180 (includes tuition, housing). A $130 deposit is required.
Contact • Liam Ó. Cuinneagáin, Director, Oideas Gael, Foras Cultuir Uladh, Oideas Gael, Glencolmcille, Donegal, Ireland; +353 73-30-248; Fax: +73 30-348; E-mail: oidsgael@iol.ie; World Wide Web: http://www.xs4all.nl/~conaill/Oideas_Gael/iodeas.html

PHOTO ADVENTURE TOURS

EMERALD ISLE

General Information • Photography tour with visits to Aran Islands, Cork County, Dublin, Kesey, Shannon. Once at the destination country, participants travel by bus, foot, boat, airplane.
Learning Focus • Instruction in photography. Instruction is offered by researchers, naturalists, artists, historians, photographers. This program would appeal to people interested in photography, culture, ornithology, adventure.
Accommodations • Hotels. Single rooms are available for an additional $825.
Program Details • Program offered 3 times per year. Session length: 10 days. Departures are scheduled in July, August. Most participants are 18–80 years of age. Participants must be 18 years or older to enroll. 12 participants per session. Application deadline: 2 months prior to departure. Reservations are recommended at least 6 months before departure.
Costs • $2875 (includes housing, some meals, excursions, international airfare). A $400 deposit is required.
Contact • Richard Libbey, General Partner, Photo Adventure Tours, 2035 Park Street, Atlantic Beach, NY 11509-1236; 516-371-0067; Fax: 516-371-1352

ROCKLAND COMMUNITY COLLEGE

YOUTH ISSUES IN IRELAND

General Information • Academic study program in Dublin.
Learning Focus • Courses in criminal justice, sociology. Instruction is offered by professors from the sponsoring institution.
Accommodations • Dormitories. Single rooms are available. Meals are taken as a group, in central dining facility.
Program Details • Program offered once per year. Session length: 2 weeks. Departures are scheduled in June. The program is open to undergraduate students, adults, professionals and teachers. Most participants are 18–65 years of age. 15–20 participants per session. Application deadline: April 15.
Costs • $2000 (includes tuition, housing, some meals, excursions, international airfare). A $200 deposit is required.
Contact • Jody Dudderar, Coordinator, Study Abroad, Rockland Community College, Suffern, NY 10907; 914-574-4205; Fax: 914-574-4423; E-mail: jdudderar@sunyrockland.edu

ST. JOHN'S UNIVERSITY

IRELAND PROGRAM

General Information • Academic study program in Spiddal.
Learning Focus • Courses in Irish history, Gaelic literature, sociology. Instruction is offered by professors from the sponsoring institution.
Accommodations • Cottages. Meals are taken on one's own, in residences.
Program Details • Program offered once per year. Session length: 12 weeks. Departures are scheduled in September. The program is open to undergraduate students. Most participants are 20–22 years of age. Other requirements: minimum 2.5 GPA. 30 participants per session. Application deadline: March.
Costs • $9200 (includes tuition, housing, all meals, excursions). Application fee: $100.
Contact • Stephen Burmeister-May, Director, Center for International Education, St. John's University, Collegeville, MN 56321; 320-363-2082; Fax: 320-363-2013; E-mail: intleduc@csbsju.edu

SLIPPERY ROCK UNIVERSITY OF PENNSYLVANIA

IRELAND PROGRAM

General Information • Academic study program in Dublin. Classes are held on the campus of University of Dublin–Trinity College.
Learning Focus • Courses in health issues, geography. Instruction is offered by professors from the sponsoring institution.
Accommodations • Dormitories. Single rooms are available. Meals are taken in central dining facility, in local restaurants.
Program Details • Program offered 2 times per year. Session length: 2 weeks. Departures are scheduled in June. The program is open to undergraduate students, adults. Most participants are 18–40 years of age. Other requirements: 2.5 minimum GPA. 12–25 participants per session. Application deadline: May 1.
Costs • $2995 (includes tuition, housing, some meals, books and class materials, international airfare). A $100 deposit is required.
Contact • Stan Kendziorski, Director of International Studies, Slippery Rock University of Pennsylvania, 110 Eisenberg Building, Slippery Rock, PA 16057; 412-738-2603; Fax: 412-728-2959; E-mail: sjk@sruvm.sru.edu; World Wide Web: http://www.sru.edu

STATE UNIVERSITY OF NEW YORK COLLEGE AT BROCKPORT

IRELAND AND ENGLAND: SPECIAL EDUCATION PROGRAM

General Information • Academic study program in Dublin.
Learning Focus • Courses in special education. Instruction is offered by professors from the sponsoring institution.
Accommodations • Dormitories. Single rooms are available. Meals are taken as a group, in central dining facility.
Program Details • Program offered once per year. Session length: 3 weeks. Departures are scheduled in June. The program is open to graduate students. Most participants are 22 years of age and older. Other requirements: 2.5 minimum GPA, graduate students in Education, present teachers. 4–10 participants per session. Application deadline: April 15.
Costs • $2280 (includes tuition, housing, some meals, excursions, international airfare). A $200 deposit is required.
Contact • Dr. John J. Perry, Director, International Education, State University of New York College at Brockport, Rakov Center, 350 New Campus Drive, Brockport, NY 14420; 716-395-2119; Fax: 716-637-3218; World Wide Web: http://www.brockport.edu/study_abroad

SYRACUSE UNIVERSITY

IRISH DRAMA: POLITICS AND WAR

General Information • Academic study program in Dublin, Galway.
Learning Focus • Courses in drama, literature. Instruction is offered by professors from the sponsoring institution.
Accommodations • Dormitories. Meals are taken on one's own, in local restaurants.
Program Details • Program offered once per year. Session length: 4 weeks. Departures are scheduled in June. The program is open to undergraduate students, graduate students, adults. Most participants are 19–50 years of age. Other requirements: minimum 2.5 GPA. 12 participants per session. Application deadline: March 15.
Costs • $4741 (includes tuition, housing, some meals, books and class materials, excursions). Application fee: $40. A $350 deposit is required.
Contact • Ms. Daisy Fried, Associate Director, Syracuse University, 119 Euclid Avenue, Syracuse, NY 13244; 315-443-9419; Fax: 315-443-4593; E-mail: dsfried@summon3.syr.edu; World Wide Web: http://sumweb.syr.edu/dipa/dipa9.htm

TRAVELEARN

AN IRELAND ODYSSEY

General Information • Cultural tour with visits to Donegal, Dublin, Galway, Killarney, Nire Valley, Ring of Kerry. Once at the destination country, participants travel by bus, foot, boat. Program is affiliated with the nationwide TraveLearn network of 290 universities and colleges.
Learning Focus • Instruction in history, literature and archaeology. Museum visits (National Museum, New Grange, Trinity College). Attendance at performances (Abbey theater). Other activities include "people-to-people" experience in rural Nire Valley. Instruction is offered by professors, artists, historians. This program would appeal to people interested in history, cultural understanding, literature.
Accommodations • Hotels. Single rooms are available for an additional $595.
Program Details • Program offered 3 times per year. Session length: 15 days. Departures are scheduled in April, July, September. Program is targeted to mature adults. Most participants are 40–75 years of age. Participants must be 18 years or older to enroll. 14–20 participants per session. Application deadline: 60 days prior to departure. Reservations are recommended at least 4–8 months before departure.
Costs • $3395 (includes housing, all meals, books and class materials, excursions, international airfare). A $300 deposit is required.
Contact • Keith Williams, Director of Marketing, TraveLearn, PO Box 315, Lakeville, PA 18438; 800-235-9114; Fax: 717-226-9114; E-mail: travelearn@aol.com

UNIVERSITY OF DAYTON

ISSAP '97–DUBLIN

General Information • Academic study program in Dublin. Classes are held on the campus of University of Dublin–Trinity College.
Learning Focus • Courses in sociology, English literature, visual arts. Instruction is offered by professors from the sponsoring institution.
Accommodations • Dormitories. Meals are taken as a group, in residences.
Program Details • Program offered once per year. Session length: 4 weeks. Departures are scheduled in June. The program is open to undergraduate students. Most partici-

pants are 18–21 years of age. Other requirements: minimum 2.0 GPA. 20–25 participants per session. Application deadline: May 15.
Costs • $3100 (includes tuition, housing, some meals, excursions, International Student Identification card). A $75 deposit is required.
Contact • DeVonda Vanderpool, Coordinator, International Education Programs, University of Dayton, 300 College Park, Dayton, OH 45469-1481; 513-229-3728; Fax: 513-229-2766; E-mail: vanderpo@trinity.udayton.edu; World Wide Web: http://www.udayton.edu/~cip

UNIVERSITY OF ILLINOIS AT URBANA-CHAMPAIGN

ART AND DESIGN IN IRELAND

General Information • Arts program in Ballyvaughan. Classes are held on the campus of Burren College of Art. Excursions to Galway, Aran Islands.
Learning Focus • Courses in painting, drawing, sculpture, art history, photography, Irish studies. Instruction is offered by local teachers.
Accommodations • Cottages, houses, hotels. Single rooms are available. Meals are taken on one's own, in residences.
Program Details • Program offered once per year. Session length: 4–8 weeks. Departures are scheduled in June. The program is open to undergraduate students, graduate students, pre-college students, adults. Most participants are 17–30 years of age. Other requirements: B average. 10 participants per session. Application deadline: March 1.
Costs • $2200 for 4 weeks, $4000 for 8 weeks (includes tuition, housing, excursions, medical emergency evacuation insurance, orientation). Application fee: $35. A $500 deposit is required.
Contact • Timothy Winkler, Program Coordinator, University of Illinois at Urbana-Champaign, Study Abroad Office, 910 South Fifth Street #115, Champaign, IL 61820; 800-531-4404; Fax: 217-244-0249; E-mail: ipa@uiuc.edu

UNIVERSITY OF SOUTHERN MISSISSIPPI

IRISH STUDIES PROGRAM

General Information • Academic study program in Dublin.
Learning Focus • Courses in anthropology, English language.
Accommodations • Bed and breakfasts.
Program Details • Program offered once per year. Session length: 3 weeks. Departures are scheduled in June. The program is open to undergraduate students, graduate students, students in good academic standing with a 2.0 minimum GPA. Application deadline: May 5.
Costs • $2349 for undergraduates, $2649 for graduate students (includes tuition, housing, international airfare). A $100 deposit is required.
Contact • Director, Irish Studies Program, University of Southern Mississippi, Box 10047, Hattiesburg, MS 39406-0047; 601-266-4344; Fax: 601-266-5699

UNIVERSITY OF TOLEDO

COMPARATIVE EDUCATION IN CORK, IRELAND

General Information • Academic study program in Cork. Classes are held on the campus of National University of Ireland–University College, Cork. Excursions to Ring of Kerry, Blarney, Kilarney.
Learning Focus • Courses in education. Instruction is offered by professors from the sponsoring institution and local teachers.
Accommodations • Apartments. Meals are taken on one's own, in residences.
Program Details • Program offered once per year. Session length: 2 weeks. Departures are scheduled in June. The program is open to undergraduate students, graduate students. Most participants are 20–45 years of age. 20 participants per session. Application deadline: March 17.
Costs • $3000 (includes tuition, housing, some meals, books and class materials, international airfare). Application fee: $25. A $100 deposit is required.
Contact • Joel A. Gallegos, Study Abroad Coordinator, University of Toledo, C.I.S.P. SWAC Suite 2357, Toledo, OH 43606; 419-530-1240; Fax: 419-537-1245; E-mail: jgalleg@utnet.utoledo.edu; World Wide Web: http://www.utoledo.edu/www/cisp/study-abroad/

VILLANOVA UNIVERSITY

SUMMER IRISH STUDIES PROGRAM

General Information • Academic study program in Galway. Classes are held on the campus of National University of Ireland–University College, Galway. Excursions to Dublin, Aran Islands.
Learning Focus • Courses in Irish literature, Irish history, Irish society, archaeology, Gaelic culture, Gaelic literature. Instruction is offered by local teachers.
Accommodations • Homestays, bed and breakfasts, lodges. Meals are taken on one's own, with host family, in local restaurants, in residences.
Program Details • Program offered once per year. Session length: 7 weeks. Departures are scheduled in June. The program is open to undergraduate students. Most participants are 19–23 years of age. Other requirements: minimum 2.50 GPA and good academic standing. 15–20 participants per session. Application deadline: March 1.
Costs • $3250 (includes tuition, housing, some meals, books and class materials, excursions, transfers, Dublin orientation, tour of Aran Islands). Application fee: $100.
Contact • Dr. Thomas M. Ricks, Director, International Studies, Villanova University, St. Augustine Center, Room 415, Villanova, PA 19085; 610-519-6412; Fax: 610-519-7649; E-mail: ricks@ucis.vill.edu

VOYAGERS INTERNATIONAL

PHOTOGRAPHIC TOUR AND WORKSHOP IN IRELAND

General Information • Photography tour with visits to Ireland. Once at the destination country, participants travel by foot, small vehicle.
Learning Focus • Instruction in photography. Escorted travel to Ballintubber Abbey, Cong, Ceide Fields and Thoor Ballylee. Museum visits (W.B. Yeats Museum). Nature observation (wildlife and scenery). Instruction is offered by

photographers. This program would appeal to people interested in photography, culture, nature studies.

Accommodations • Hotels, lodges. Single rooms are available for an additional $350.

Program Details • Program offered 8 times per year. Session length: 12 days. Departures are scheduled in April–October. Program is targeted to photography enthusiasts. Most participants are 30–70 years of age. 8–10 participants per session. Reservations are recommended at least 8–10 months before departure.

Costs • $1990 (includes tuition, housing, some meals, excursions). A $400 deposit is required.

Contact • David Blanton, Managing Director, Voyagers International, PO Box 915, Ithaca, NY 14851; 800-633-0299; Fax: 607-273-3873; E-mail: voyint@aol.com

ITALY

ACCENT INTERNATIONAL CONSORTIUM FOR ACADEMIC PROGRAMS ABROAD

FLORENCE: ART, MUSIC, AND CULTURE

General Information • Academic study program in Florence. Excursions to Venice, Pisa, Verona, Siena, Lucca, San Gimignano, Torre del Lago.

Learning Focus • Courses in art history, Italian culture, music. Instruction is offered by professors from the sponsoring institution.

Accommodations • Homestays, locally-rented apartments. Single rooms are available. Meals are taken on one's own, in local restaurants, in residences.

Program Details • Program offered once per year. Session length: 4 weeks. Departures are scheduled in July. The program is open to undergraduate students, graduate students, pre-college students, adults. Most participants are 18–60 years of age. 30 participants per session. Application deadline: May 1.

Costs • $2400 (includes tuition, housing, books and class materials, excursions). Application fee: $250. A $150 deposit is required.

Contact • Director, Florence Art and Music Program, ACCENT International Consortium for Academic Programs Abroad, 425 Market Street, 2nd Floor, San Francisco, CA 94105; 415-904-7756; Fax: 415-904-7759; E-mail: sfaccent@aol.com

ACCENT INTERNATIONAL CONSORTIUM FOR ACADEMIC PROGRAMS ABROAD

FLORENCE: SUMMER STUDY

General Information • Language study program in Florence. Excursions to Venice, Pisa, Verona, Siena, Lucca, San Gimignano.

Learning Focus • Courses in Italian language, art history, Italian culture. Instruction is offered by professors from the sponsoring institution.

Accommodations • Homestays, locally-rented apartments. Single rooms are available. Meals are taken on one's own, in local restaurants, in residences.

Program Details • Program offered once per year. Session length: 4 weeks. Departures are scheduled in July. The program is open to undergraduate students, graduate students, pre-college students, adults. Most participants are 18–60 years of age. 30 participants per session. Application deadline: May 1.

Costs • $2550 (includes tuition, housing, some meals, books and class materials, insurance, excursions). Application fee: $250. A $150 deposit is required.

Contact • Director, Florence Program, ACCENT International Consortium for Academic Programs Abroad, 425 Market Street, 2nd Floor, San Francisco, CA 94105; 415-904-7756; Fax: 415-904-7759; E-mail: sfaccent@aol.com

---

Spend a summer in Florence, one of the world's centers of art and culture. Students are immersed in the language and culture of the Renaissance in a city that houses the sculpture, architecture, and paintings of Brunelleschi, Michelangelo, Leonardo, Botticelli, and Cellini. Florence is a classroom where a student can learn Italian or music and study art history and Italian culture with on-site lectures at the many galleries, museums, and cultural sites throughout the city. Students take day excursions to towns outside Florence and a 3-day, 2-night excursion to Venice. Both programs offer a unique opportunity to expand a student's educational experience while earning transferable college credit.

AMERICAN INSTITUTE FOR FOREIGN STUDY (AIFS)

RICHMOND COLLEGE IN FLORENCE

General Information • Academic and language study program in Florence. Excursions to Rome, Venice.

Learning Focus • Courses in Italian language, art history, studio art.

Accommodations • Homestays, locally-rented apartments.

Program Details • Program offered once per year. Session length: 5 weeks. Departures are scheduled in June. The program is open to undergraduate students, graduate students, adults, high school graduates. Other requirements: minimum 2.0 GPA. Application deadline: March 15.

Costs • $3359 (includes tuition, housing, some meals). A $400 deposit is required.

Contact • Carmela Vigliano, Director, Summer Programs, American Institute for Foreign Study (AIFS), 102 Greenwich Avenue, Greenwich, CT 06830; 800-727-2437, ext. 6087; Fax: 203-869-9615; E-mail: info@aifs.org

AMERICAN JEWISH CONGRESS, INTERNATIONAL TRAVEL PROGRAM

ITALIAN HIGHLIGHTS

General Information • Cultural tour with visits to Florence, Rome, Siena, Venice, Trevi Fountain, Basilica of St. Peter, Sistine Chapel, Colosseum, Ponte Vecchio Bridge.

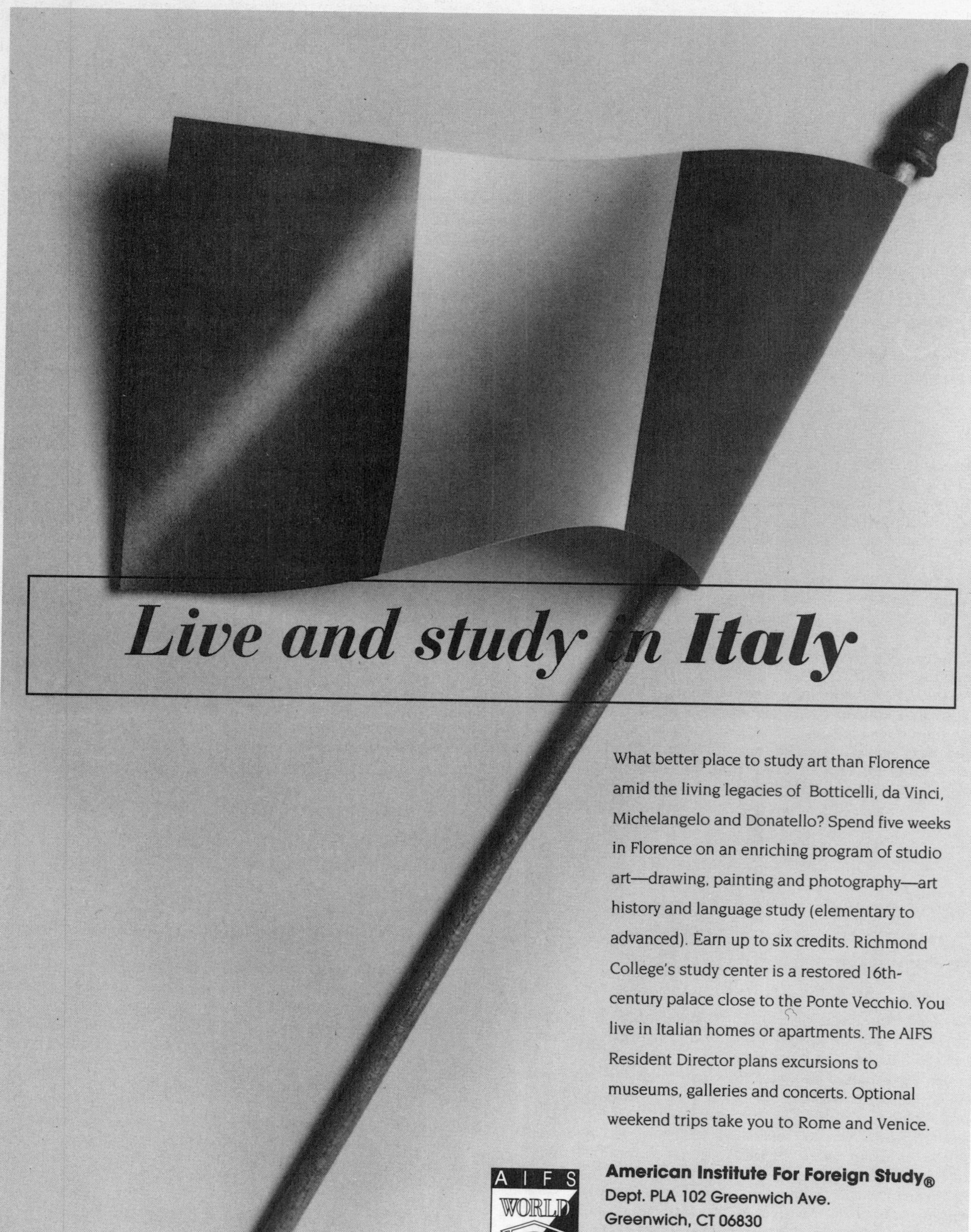

Live and study in Italy
What better place to study art than Florence amid the living legacies of Botticelli, da Vinci, Michelangelo and Donatello? Spend five weeks in Florence on an enriching program of studio art—drawing, painting and photography—art history and language study (elementary to advanced). Earn up to six credits. Richmond College's study center is a restored 16th-century palace close to the Ponte Vecchio. You live in Italian homes or apartments. The AIFS Resident Director plans excursions to museums, galleries and concerts. Optional weekend trips take you to Rome and Venice.
AIFS
WORLD
CLASS
American Institute For Foreign Study®
Dept. PLA 102 Greenwich Ave.
Greenwich, CT 06830
Phone (800) 727-2437
E-mail info@aifs.org
http://www.aifs.org

Learning Focus • Escorted travel to synagogues, Palazzo Venezia and the Grand Canal. Museum visits (Pitti Palace, Uffizi Gallery, Guggenheim Museum). Instruction is offered by historians. This program would appeal to people interested in Jewish history.
Accommodations • Hotels. Single rooms are available for an additional $400.
Program Details • Program offered 6 times per year. Session length: 11 days. Departures are scheduled in May–September. Program is targeted to Jewish-American adults. Most participants are 40–75 years of age. Participants must be 15 years or older to enroll. Participants must be members of the sponsoring organization (annual dues: $50). 30 participants per session. Reservations are recommended at least 6 months before departure.
Costs • $3495 (includes housing, some meals, excursions, international airfare, travel bag, documents portfolio, travel journal). A $200 deposit is required.
Contact • Betty Van Dyke, Worldwide Operations Manager, American Jewish Congress, International Travel Program, 18 East 84th Street, New York, NY 10028; 212-360-1571; Fax: 212-717-1932

APPALACHIAN STATE UNIVERSITY

ITALY

General Information • Academic study program in Italy.
Learning Focus • Courses in geology. Instruction is offered by professors from the sponsoring institution.
Program Details • Program offered once per year. Session length: 5–6 weeks. Departures are scheduled in May. Most participants are 18 years of age and older. 20 participants per session.
Costs • $3100 (includes tuition, housing, insurance, international airfare, International Student Identification card).
Contact • Dr. Fred Webb, Professor, Appalachian State University, Department of Geology, Boone, NC 28608; 704-262-3049; Fax: 704-262-4037

ARCHAEOLOGICAL TOURS

ETRUSCAN

General Information • Cultural tour with visits to Florence, Orvieto, Perugia, Rome, Siena, Targunia, Corveteri, Norchia, Tuscania, Vulci, Grosseto, Mulo, Volterra, Fiesole, Bologna, Marzabotto, Chiusi, Sovana, Veii. Once at the destination country, participants travel by bus.
Learning Focus • Escorted travel to cities and countryside. Museum visits (local museums). Instruction is offered by professors, historians. This program would appeal to people interested in history, art, archaeology.
Accommodations • Hotels. Single rooms are available for an additional $545.
Program Details • Program offered once per year. Session length: 17 days. Departures are scheduled in June. Program is targeted to adults. Most participants are 30–80 years of age. 22 participants per session. Application deadline: 1½ months prior to departure.
Costs • $3990 (includes housing, some meals, excursions). A $500 deposit is required.
Contact • Archaeological Tours, 271 Madison Avenue, Suite 904, New York, NY 10016; 212-986-3054; Fax: 212-370-1561

ARCHAEOLOGICAL TOURS

SICILY AND SOUTHERN ITALY

General Information • Archaeological tour with visits to Agrigento, Naples, Paetum, Palermo, Siracusa, Taormina, Segesta, Moyta, Mon Reale, Selinute, Morgantina, Villa Casale, Reggio Calabria, Pompeii, Herculaneum. Once at the destination country, participants travel by bus.
Learning Focus • Escorted travel to the island of Sicily. Museum visits (Palermo, Moyta, Agrigento, Siracusa, Reggio, Pompeii, Naples). Instruction is offered by professors, historians. This program would appeal to people interested in history, archaeology.
Accommodations • Hotels. Single rooms are available for an additional $465.
Program Details • Program offered 2 times per year. Session length: 17 days. Departures are scheduled in May, October. Program is targeted to adults. Most participants are 30–80 years of age. 25 participants per session. Application deadline: 1 month prior to departure.
Costs • $3565 (includes housing, some meals, excursions). A $500 deposit is required.
Contact • Archaeological Tours, 271 Madison Avenue, Suite 904, New York, NY 10016; 212-986-3054; Fax: 212-370-1561

ARCHETOURS, INC.

ROME: UNRAVELING URBAN ARCHAEOLOGY

General Information • Architectural and archaeology tour with visits to Rome, Palestrina, Appian Way, Capannelle Aqueducts, Tivoli, Ostia Antica. Once at the destination country, participants travel by bus, foot. Program is affiliated with American Institute of Architects Continuing Education System.
Learning Focus • Instruction in Roman history and classical architecture. Escorted travel to Roman Forum, Pantheon, Trajan's Forum and Palatine. Museum visits (Archaeological Museum at Palestrina, Campodogico Museum). Instruction is offered by professors, artists, historians. This program would appeal to people interested in archaeology, history, design, architecture, art.
Accommodations • Hotels. Single rooms are available for an additional $275.
Program Details • Program offered 4 times per year. Session length: 1 week. Departures are scheduled in June, September. Most participants are 30–70 years of age. Participants must be 21 years or older to enroll. Other requirements: good health, capability of walking, standing and climbing to visit sites. 8–16 participants per session. Application deadline: 60 days prior to departure. Reservations are recommended at least 4–6 months before departure.
Costs • $1995 (includes housing, some meals, books and class materials, excursions, museum and site fees, airport transfers, lecturer fees, tips). A $250 deposit is required.

Contact • Ms. Gail Cornell, President, Archetours, Inc., 235 East 22nd Street, Suite 14F, New York, NY 10010; 800-770-3051; Fax: 212-779-7130; E-mail: archetours.@aol.com

ARCHETOURS, INC.

TUSCANY: HIDDEN ARCHITECTURAL JEWELS

General Information • Architectural tour with visits to Tuscany, Montepulciano, Orvietto, Siena, Montechiello, Pienza, Montalcino. Once at the destination country, participants travel by bus, foot. Program is affiliated with American Institute of Architects Continuing Education System.
Learning Focus • Instruction in history. Escorted travel to cathedrals, palaces and gardens. Instruction is offered by professors, artists, historians. This program would appeal to people interested in architecture, history, archaeology, art, design.
Accommodations • Hotels. Single rooms are available for an additional $275.
Program Details • Program offered 4 times per year. Session length: 1 week. Departures are scheduled in May, September. Most participants are 30–70 years of age. Participants must be 21 years or older to enroll. Other requirements: good health, capability of walking, standing and climbing to visit sites. 8–16 participants per session. Application deadline: 60 days prior to departure. Reservations are recommended at least 4–6 months before departure.
Costs • $1995 (includes housing, some meals, books and class materials, excursions, museum and site fees, airport transfers, lecturer fees, tips). A $250 deposit is required.
Contact • Ms. Gail Cornell, President, Archetours, Inc., 235 East 22nd Street, Suite 14F, New York, NY 10010; 800-770-3051; Fax: 212-779-7130; E-mail: archetours.@aol.com

ARCHETOURS, INC.

VILLAS OF VENETO: LIFE ON A GRAND SCALE

General Information • Architectural tour with visits to Veneto, Vicenza, Mira, Treviso, Verona, Venice. Once at the destination country, participants travel by bus, foot. Program is affiliated with American Institute of Architects Continuing Education System.
Learning Focus • Instruction in Renaissance architecture and Palladian architecture. Escorted travel to sixteenth-century villas and Renaissance Gardens. Museum visits (Vicenza Art Museum). Instruction is offered by professors, artists, historians. This program would appeal to people interested in architecture, art, archaeology, interior design, history.
Accommodations • Hotels. Single rooms are available for an additional $275.
Program Details • Program offered 2 times per year. Session length: 1 week. Departures are scheduled in May, June. Most participants are 30–70 years of age. Participants must be 21 years or older to enroll. Other requirements: good health, capability of walking, standing and climbing to visit sites. 8–16 participants per session. Application deadline: 60 days prior to departure. Reservations are recommended at least 4–6 months before departure.
Costs • $1995 (includes housing, some meals, books and class materials, excursions, museum and site fees, airport transfers, lecture fees, tips). A $250 deposit is required.
Contact • Ms. Gail Cornell, President, Archetours, Inc., 235 East 22nd Street, Suite 14F, New York, NY 10010; 800-770-3051; Fax: 212-779-7130; E-mail: archetours.@aol.com

 BENTLEY COLLEGE

LANGUAGE AND CULTURE IN FLORENCE

General Information • Academic study program in Florence. Classes are held on the campus of Lorenzo de' Medici School. Excursions to Siena, Rome, Venice.
Learning Focus • Courses in language study, cultural studies. Instruction is offered by local teachers.
Accommodations • Dormitories, locally-rented apartments. Single rooms are available. Meals are taken on one's own, in local restaurants.
Program Details • Program offered 2 times per year. Session length: 4 weeks. Departures are scheduled in June, July. The program is open to undergraduate students, adults. Most participants are 19–22 years of age. Other requirements: minimum 2.7 GPA. 5–10 participants per session. Application deadline: April 1.
Costs • $2500 (includes tuition, housing, International Student Identification card). Application fee: $35. A $500 deposit is required.
Contact • Jennifer L. Scully, Director of Study Abroad, Bentley College, 175 Forest Street, Waltham, MA 02154; 617-891-3474; Fax: 617-891-2819; E-mail: inprinfo@bentley.edu

 BOSTON UNIVERSITY

SUMMER PADUA PROGRAM

General Information • Language study program in Padua. Excursions to Venice, Veneto region.
Learning Focus • Courses in Italian language, Italian culture, art. Instruction is offered by professors from the sponsoring institution.
Accommodations • Homestays. Single rooms are available. Meals are taken on one's own, with host family, in local restaurants, in residences.
Program Details • Program offered once per year. Session length: 6 weeks. Departures are scheduled in May. The program is open to undergraduate students, adults. Most participants are 19–21 years of age. Other requirements: minimum 3.0 GPA and good academic standing. 15 participants per session. Application deadline: March 15.
Costs • $4400 (includes tuition, housing, some meals, excursions). Application fee: $35. A $300 deposit is required.
Contact • Division of International Programs, Boston University, 232 Bay State Road, Boston, MA 02215; 617-353-9888; Fax: 617-353-5402; E-mail: abroad@bu.edu; World Wide Web: http://web.bu.edu/abroad

BRITISH COASTAL TRAILS SCENIC WALKING

THE CINQUE TERRE

General Information • Cultural tour with visits to Monterosso, Nervi, Santa Margherita Ligure, Sestri Levante, Vernazza, Riomaggiore, Manarola, Corniglia, Levanto, Portofino, Genoa. Once at the destination country, participants travel by train, bus, foot, boat.
Learning Focus • Escorted travel to Bay of San Fruttuogo, vinyards and olive groves. Other activities include hiking, walking. Instruction is offered by naturalists, historians, professional guides. This program would appeal to people interested in nature studies, walking, culture, photography, history.
Accommodations • Hotels. Single rooms are available.
Program Details • Program offered 3 times per year. Session length: 8 days. Most participants are 40–65 years of age. Participants must be 13 years or older to enroll. Other requirements: physician's approval and signed release form. 18 participants per session. Application deadline: 30 days prior to departure. Reservations are recommended at least 6 months before departure.
Costs • $2085 (includes housing, some meals, excursions, full-time guide). A $250 deposit is required.
Contact • Tour Manager, British Coastal Trails Scenic Walking, 7777 Fay Avenue, Suite 100, La Jolla, CA 92037; 800-473-1210; Fax: 619-456-2277; E-mail: lajolla@bctwalk.com; World Wide Web: http://www.bctwalk.com/lajolla

BRITISH COASTAL TRAILS SCENIC WALKING

HILLTOWNS OF TUSCANY

General Information • Cultural tour with visits to Florence, Radda in Chianti, Trequanda, Badia a Passignano Monastery, San Gimignano, Monteriggioni, Castelvecchio, Brolio Castle, Abbey of Monte Oliveto Maggiore. Once at the destination country, participants travel by bus, foot.
Learning Focus • Escorted travel to vinyards and olive groves. Nature observation (forest, mountains). Other activities include hiking, walking. Instruction is offered by naturalists, historians, professional guides. This program would appeal to people interested in nature studies, walking, culture, photography, history.
Accommodations • Hotels. Single rooms are available for an additional $325.
Program Details • Program offered 5 times per year. Session length: 8 days. Departures are scheduled in April, May, September, October. Most participants are 40–65 years of age. Participants must be 13 years or older to enroll. Other requirements: physician's approval and signed release form.

18 participants per session. Application deadline: 30 days prior to departure. Reservations are recommended at least 6 months before departure.
Costs • $2185 (includes housing, some meals, excursions, full-time guide). A $250 deposit is required.
Contact • Tour Manager, British Coastal Trails Scenic Walking, 7777 Fay Avenue, Suite 100, La Jolla, CA 92037; 800-473-1210; Fax: 619-456-2277; E-mail: lajolla@bctwalk.com; World Wide Web: http://www.bctwalk.com/lajolla

BRITISH COASTAL TRAILS SCENIC WALKING

ITALIAN LAKES AND DOLOMITES

General Information • Cultural tour with visits to Cortina, Daiano, Torri del Benaco, Venice, Passo Falzarego, Lake District, Verona. Once at the destination country, participants travel by bus, foot, boat, cable car.
Learning Focus • Escorted travel to Dolomites. Nature observation (glaciers, mountains, wildlife). Other activities include hiking, walking. Instruction is offered by naturalists, historians, professional guides. This program would appeal to people interested in nature studies, walking, culture, photography, history.
Accommodations • Hotels, pensiones. Single rooms are available for an additional $225.
Program Details • Program offered 2 times per year. Session length: 7 days. Departures are scheduled in June, September. Most participants are 40–65 years of age. Participants must be 13 years or older to enroll. Other requirements: physician's approval and signed release form. 18 participants per session. Application deadline: 30 days prior to departure. Reservations are recommended at least 6 months before departure.
Costs • $1975 (includes housing, some meals, excursions, full-time guide). A $250 deposit is required.
Contact • Tour Manager, British Coastal Trails Scenic Walking, 7777 Fay Avenue, Suite 100, La Jolla, CA 92037; 800-473-1210; Fax: 619-456-2277; E-mail: lajolla@bctwalk.com; World Wide Web: http://www.bctwalk.com/lajolla

THE CENTER FOR ENGLISH STUDIES

STUDY ABROAD IN BOLOGNA, ITALY

General Information • Language study program with visits to Bologna. Program is affiliated with Centro di Cultura Italiana Bologna.
Learning Focus • Instruction in the Italian language. Other activities include field trips to local sites, museums, markets and churches. Instruction is offered by faculty members from host institution. This program would appeal to people interested in Italian language, literature.
Accommodations • Homestays, dormitories, locally-rented apartments, program-owned apartments. Single rooms are available.
Program Details • Session length: 2 or more weeks. Departures are scheduled throughout the year. Most participants are 18–70 years of age. Participants must be 18 years or older to enroll. 6–12 participants per session. Application deadline: 2 weeks prior to departure. Reservations are recommended at least 1 month before departure.
Costs • $1100 for 4 weeks (includes tuition, housing, some meals). A $125 deposit is required.
Contact • Ms. Lorraine Haber, Study Abroad Coordinator, The Center for English Studies, 330 7th Avenue, 6th Floor, New York, NY 10001; 212-629-7300; Fax: 212-736-7950; E-mail: ces_newyork@cescorp.com

THE CENTER FOR ENGLISH STUDIES

STUDY ABROAD IN FLORENCE, ITALY

General Information • Language study program with visits to Florence. Program is affiliated with Europass Centro Studi Europeo.
Learning Focus • Instruction in the Italian language. Other activities include field trips to local sites, museums, markets and churches. Instruction is offered by faculty members from host institution. This program would appeal to people interested in Italian language, Italian studies, economics, history, art history, drawing, painting.
Accommodations • Homestays, locally-rented apartments, program-owned apartments, hotels, pensiones. Single rooms are available.
Program Details • Session length: 2 or more weeks. Departures are scheduled throughout the year. Most participants are 16–70 years of age. Participants must be 16 years or older to enroll. 6–12 participants per session. Application deadline: 2 weeks prior to departure. Reservations are recommended at least 1 month before departure.
Costs • $1000 for 4 weeks (includes tuition, housing, books and class materials). A $125 deposit is required.
Contact • Ms. Lorraine Haber, Study Abroad Coordinator, The Center for English Studies, 330 7th Avenue, 6th Floor, New York, NY 10001; 212-629-7300; Fax: 212-736-7950; E-mail: ces_newyork@cescorp.com

THE CENTER FOR ENGLISH STUDIES

STUDY ABROAD IN RIMINI, ITALY

General Information • Language study program with visits to Rimini. Program is affiliated with Centro Culturale Tiberius.
Learning Focus • Instruction in the Italian language. Other activities include field trips to local sites, museums, markets and churches. Instruction is offered by faculty members from host institution. This program would appeal to people interested in Italian language, culture, commerce, law.
Accommodations • Homestays, locally-rented apartments, program-owned apartments, hotels. Single rooms are available.
Program Details • Session length: 1 or more weeks. Departures are scheduled throughout the year. Most participants are 16–70 years of age. Participants must be 16 years or older to enroll. 6–12 participants per session. Application deadline: 2 weeks prior to departure. Reservations are recommended at least 1 month before departure.
Costs • $1000 for 2 weeks (includes tuition, housing, some meals, books and class materials, excursions). A $125 deposit is required.
Contact • Ms. Lorraine Haber, Study Abroad Coordinator, The Center for English Studies, 330 7th Avenue, 6th Floor, New York, NY 10001; 212-629-7300; Fax: 212-736-7950; E-mail: ces_newyork@cescorp.com

THE CENTER FOR ENGLISH STUDIES

STUDY ABROAD IN ROME, ITALY

General Information • Language study program with visits to Rome. Program is affiliated with International House Dilit.
Learning Focus • Instruction in the Italian language. Other activities include field trips to local sites, museums, markets and churches. Instruction is offered by faculty members from host institution. This program would appeal to people interested in Italian language.
Accommodations • Homestays, dormitories, locally-rented apartments, program-owned apartments, program-owned houses. Single rooms are available.
Program Details • Session length: 2 or more weeks. Departures are scheduled throughout the year. Most participants are 14–70 years of age. Participants must be 14 years or older to enroll. 6–12 participants per session. Application deadline: 2 weeks prior to departure. Reservations are recommended at least 1 month before departure.
Costs • $1000 for 2 weeks (includes tuition, housing, some meals, books and class materials, excursions). A $125 deposit is required.
Contact • Ms. Lorraine Haber, Study Abroad Coordinator, The Center for English Studies, 330 7th Avenue, 6th Floor, New York, NY 10001; 212-629-7300; Fax: 212-736-7950; E-mail: ces_newyork@cescorp.com

THE CENTER FOR ENGLISH STUDIES

STUDY ABROAD IN SIENA, ITALY

General Information • Language study program with visits to Siena. Program is affiliated with Scuola Leonardo da Vinci.
Learning Focus • Instruction in the Italian language. Other activities include field trips to local sites, museums, markets and churches. Instruction is offered by faculty members from host institution. This program would appeal to people interested in Italian language, civilization, culture.
Accommodations • Homestays, dormitories, locally-rented apartments, program-owned apartments, hotels. Single rooms are available.
Program Details • Session length: 2 or more weeks. Departures are scheduled throughout the year. Most participants are 16–70 years of age. Participants must be 16 years or older to enroll. 6–12 participants per session. Application deadline: 2 weeks prior to departure. Reservations are recommended at least 1 month before departure.
Costs • $1300 for 4 weeks (includes tuition, housing, some meals, excursions). A $125 deposit is required.
Contact • Ms. Lorraine Haber, Study Abroad Coordinator, The Center for English Studies, 330 7th Avenue, 6th Floor, New York, NY 10001; 212-629-7300; Fax: 212-736-7950; E-mail: ces_newyork@cescorp.com

CENTRO DI CULTURA ITALIANA IN CASENTINO

ITALIAN LANGUAGE SCHOOL FOR FOREIGNERS

General Information • Language study program in Poppi. Classes are held on the campus of Centro di Cultura Italiana in Casentino.
Learning Focus • Courses in Italian language, history, cultural studies. Instruction is offered by local teachers.
Accommodations • Locally-rented apartments. Single rooms are available. Meals are taken as a group, in local restaurants.
Program Details • Program offered 12 times per year. Session length: 2 weeks. Departures are scheduled in April–October. The program is open to undergraduate students, graduate students, pre-college students, adults. Most participants are 18–80 years of age. 10–20 participants per session. Application deadline: 1 month prior to departure.
Costs • $1000 (includes tuition, housing, some meals, books and class materials, excursions). Application fee: $50. A $200 deposit is required.
Contact • Stephen Casale, US Agent, Centro di Cultura Italiana in Casentino, One University Place, Apartment 17R, New York, NY 10003-4522; 212-228-9273; Fax: 212-353-1942; World Wide Web: http://www.teta.it/lynx/

Centro di Cultura Italiana in Casentino (CCIC), "Piero della Francesca," located in the Tuscan hill town of Poppi, Italy, offers 2- or 4-week sessions of intensive, low-pressure Italian language instruction in an ambience of tranquil natural beauty. All instruction, including beginner classes, is conducted in Italian. Outside the classroom, students find themselves in a region of Italy where only pure Italian is spoken. Even buying a loaf of bread becomes an Italian lesson. The programs have no tests (beyond an initial diagnostic test for placement), grades, or diplomas; they do, however, offer plenty of grammar, conversation, reinforcement, and satisfaction.

COLLEGE CONSORTIUM FOR INTERNATIONAL STUDIES–COLLEGE OF STATEN ISLAND, CUNY

CCIS FLORENCE, ITALY PROGRAM

General Information • Academic study program in Florence. Classes are held on the campus of Lorenzo de' Medici School.
Learning Focus • Courses in Italian language, art history, studio art, Italian civilization, cultural studies. Instruction is offered by local teachers.
Accommodations • Locally-rented apartments, hotels. Single rooms are available. Meals are taken on one's own, in local restaurants, in residences.
Program Details • Program offered 3 times per year. Session length: 4 weeks. Departures are scheduled in May–July. The program is open to undergraduate students, graduate students, adults. Most participants are 19–25 years of age. Other requirements: minimum 2.5 GPA. 4–25 participants per session. Application deadline: March 15, April 15.
Costs • $1310 for language only, $1710 for all-inclusive program (includes tuition, fees). A $100 deposit is required.

Contact • Jane C. Evans, Executive Director, College Consortium for International Studies, 2000 P Street, NW, Suite 503, Washington, DC 20036; 800-453-6956; Fax: 202-233-0999; E-mail: ccis@intr.net

COLLEGE CONSORTIUM FOR INTERNATIONAL STUDIES–COLLEGE OF STATEN ISLAND, CUNY

CCIS ROME, ITALY PROGRAM

General Information • Academic study program in Rome. Classes are held on the campus of American University of Rome.
Learning Focus • Courses in international business. Instruction is offered by local teachers.
Accommodations • Studio apartments. Single rooms are available. Meals are taken on one's own, in local restaurants, in residences.
Program Details • Program offered 2 times per year. Session length: 4 weeks. Departures are scheduled in May, June. The program is open to undergraduate students. Most participants are 19–20 years of age. Other requirements: minimum 2.5 GPA. 2 participants per session. Application deadline: March 15.
Costs • $1640 (includes tuition, fees). A $100 deposit is required.
Contact • Jane C. Evans, Executive Director, College Consortium for International Studies, 2000 P Street, NW, Suite 503, Washington, DC 20036; 800-453-6956; Fax: 202-223-0999; E-mail: ccis@intr.net

COLLEGE OF WILLIAM AND MARY

ART IN URBINO

General Information • Academic study program in Urbino. Classes are held on the campus of University of Urbino. Excursions to Rome, Florence, Venice.
Learning Focus • Courses in ceramics, sculpture. Instruction is offered by professors from the sponsoring institution and local teachers.
Accommodations • Dormitories. Single rooms are available. Meals are taken as a group, in central dining facility.
Program Details • Program offered once per year. Session length: 5–6 weeks. Departures are scheduled in July. The program is open to undergraduate students, graduate students, adults with college degrees. Most participants are 18–29 years of age. Other requirements: good academic standing. 30–40 participants per session. Application deadline: March 1.
Costs • $3750 (includes tuition, housing, all meals, books and class materials, excursions, international airfare). Application fee: $40. A $500 deposit is required.
Contact • Ann M. Moore, Head of Programs Abroad, College of William and Mary, PO Box 8795, Williamsburg, VA 23187-8795; 757-221-3594; Fax: 757-221-3597; E-mail: ammoo2@facstaff.wm.edu

COLLEGE OF WILLIAM AND MARY

SUMMER IN FLORENCE

General Information • Academic study program in Florence. Classes are held on the campus of Linguaviva Italian School. Excursions to Pisa, Rome, Siena, Bologna, Venice.
Learning Focus • Courses in Italian language, art history. Instruction is offered by professors from the sponsoring institution and local teachers.
Accommodations • Pensiones. Meals are taken as a group, in central dining facility.
Program Details • Program offered once per year. Session length: 4 weeks. Departures are scheduled in May. The program is open to undergraduate students, graduate students, graduates of accredited universities. Most participants are 18–29 years of age. Other requirements: good academic standing. 17 participants per session. Application deadline: February 15.
Costs • $3790 (includes tuition, housing, some meals, books and class materials, excursions). Application fee: $40. A $500 deposit is required.
Contact • Dr. Ann M. Moore, Head of Programs Abroad, College of William and Mary, Reves Center, PO Box 8795, Williamsburg, VA 23187-8795; 757-221-3594; Fax: 757-221-3597; E-mail: ammoo2@facstaff.wm.edu

COLUMBIA UNIVERSITY

SUMMER PROGRAM IN ITALY

General Information • Language study program in Scandiano.
Learning Focus • Courses in Italian language.
Accommodations • Homestays, locally-rented apartments. Single rooms are available. Meals are taken as a group, on one's own, with host family, in local restaurants, in residences.
Program Details • Program offered once per year. Session length: 6 weeks. Departures are scheduled in June. The program is open to undergraduate students, graduate students, adults. Most participants are 18–25 years of age. Other requirements: one year of Italian and a grade of B or better. 20–25 participants per session. Application deadline: April 1.
Costs • $4218 (includes tuition, housing, some meals, excursions). Application fee: $35.
Contact • Jo Ann Cavallo, Professor, Columbia University, Italian Department, 502 Hamilton MC 2835, 1130 Amsterdam Avenue, New York, NY 10027; 212-854-2308; Fax: 212-854-5306; E-mail: jac3@columbia.edu; World Wide Web: http://www.columbia.edu/cu/ssp/

CONNECT

ISTITUTO EUROPEO DI DESIGN

General Information • Arts program in Milan.
Learning Focus • Courses in fashion design, interior design.
Accommodations • Locally-rented apartments, hotels. Single rooms are available. Meals are taken on one's own, in central dining facility, in local restaurants, in residences.
Program Details • Program offered once per year. Session length: 4 weeks. Departures are scheduled in July. The

program is open to undergraduate students, graduate students, adults, professionals. Most participants are 20–35 years of age. Other requirements: 2nd year college students or above. 25 participants per session. Application deadline: May 15.
Costs • $2000 (includes tuition, housing, books and class materials). A $300 deposit is required.
Contact • Mrs. Vera Dickson Frumkes, US Representative, CONNECT, 28 Garey Drive, Chappaqua, NY 10514; 914-242-8223; Fax: 914-666-8160

CONNECT

PERCORSI ITALIANI

General Information • Language study program in Elba, Florence, Milan, Rome, Siena.
Learning Focus • Courses in Italian language, Italian culture.
Accommodations • Homestays, locally-rented apartments. Single rooms are available. Meals are taken on one's own, with host family, in local restaurants.
Program Details • Program offered 12 times per year. Session length: 4 or more weeks. Departures are scheduled in January–December. The program is open to undergraduate students, graduate students, pre-college students, adults. Most participants are 18–22 years of age. Other requirements: entrance exam for placement. 8–15 participants per session. Application deadline: 6 weeks prior to departure.
Costs • $560–$620 (includes tuition, books and class materials, social and some cultural activities). A $175 deposit is required.
Contact • Mrs. Vera Dickson Frumkes, US Representative, CONNECT, 28 Garey Drive, Chappaqua, NY 10514; 914-242-8223; Fax: 914-666-8160

COUNTRY WALKERS

CINQUE TERRE: POETIC ODYSSEY

General Information • Cultural, gourmet cooking, nature study and walking tour with visits to Santa Margherita Ligure, Portofino, Camogli, Monterosso, Vernazza, Corniglia, Manarda, Riomaggiore. Once at the destination country, participants travel by foot.
Learning Focus • Escorted travel to Poet's Gulf, Riviera di Levante and San Fruttuoso. Other activities include walking. Instruction is offered by professors, researchers, naturalists, historians. This program would appeal to people interested in walking, nature studies, food and wine.
Accommodations • Hotels. Single rooms are available for an additional $300–$600.
Program Details • Program offered 4 times per year. Session length: 7 days. Departures are scheduled in May, June, September, October. Program is targeted to adults 35 to 65 years old. Most participants are 35–65 years of age. Participants must be 18 years or older to enroll. 18 participants per session. Reservations are recommended at least 5–6 months before departure.
Costs • $1800 (includes housing, all meals, excursions). A $400 deposit is required.
Contact • Heather Kellingbeck, Vice President, Country Walkers, PO Box 180, Waterbury, VT 05176; 800-464-9255; Fax: 802-244-5661; E-mail: ctrywalk@aol.com

COUNTRY WALKERS

PEAKS AND VALLEYS OF THE DOLOMITES

General Information • Cultural, gourmet cooking, nature study and walking tour with visits to Bressanone, Carezza al Iago, Sella, Trent, Val Pusteria, Valle del Rio, Val Fiscalina, San Cipriano. Once at the destination country, participants travel by foot.
Learning Focus • Escorted travel to Passo Nigra, Tre Cime and Lake Braies. Nature observation (Fanes-Sennes-Braies Nature Reserve). Other activities include walking. Instruction is offered by professors, researchers, naturalists, historians. This program would appeal to people interested in nature studies, walking, food and wine.
Accommodations • Hotels. Single rooms are available for an additional $300–$600.
Program Details • Program offered 4 times per year. Session length: 8 days. Departures are scheduled in June, July, September. Program is targeted to adults 35 to 65 years old. Most participants are 35–65 years of age. Participants must be 18 years or older to enroll. 18 participants per session. Reservations are recommended at least 5–6 months before departure.
Costs • $1950 (includes housing, all meals, excursions). A $400 deposit is required.
Contact • Heather Kellingbeck, Vice President, Country Walkers, PO Box 180, Waterbury, VT 05176; 800-464-9255; Fax: 802-244-5661; E-mail: ctrywalk@aol.com

COUNTRY WALKERS

THE TUSCAN MIRACLE

General Information • Cultural, gourmet cooking, nature study and walking tour with visits to Pisa, San Gimignano, Siena, Volterra, Monteriggioni. Once at the destination country, participants travel by foot, coach.
Learning Focus • Escorted travel to Etruscan tombs, Roman baths and Piazza del Duomo. Nature observation (vineyards, oak forest). Other activities include walking. Instruction is offered by professors, researchers, naturalists, historians. This program would appeal to people interested in walking, nature studies, food and wine.
Accommodations • Hotels. Single rooms are available for an additional $300–$600.
Program Details • Program offered 10 times per year. Session length: 8 days. Departures are scheduled in May, June, August–November. Program is targeted to adults 35 to 65 years old. Most participants are 35–65 years of age. Participants must be 18 years or older to enroll. 18 participants per session. Reservations are recommended at least 5–6 months before departure.
Costs • $1950 (includes housing, all meals, excursions). A $400 deposit is required.
Contact • Heather Kellingbeck, Vice President, Country Walkers, PO Box 180, Waterbury, VT 05176; 800-464-9255; Fax: 802-244-5661; E-mail: ctrywalk@aol.com

CROSS-CULTURE

BIKING ITALY'S PO VALLEY

General Information • Nature study, cultural, and bicycling tour with visits to Cervesina, Cremona, Miradolo,

Pavia, Vigevano, Certosa di Pavia, Po River. Once at the destination country, participants travel by bus, bicycle.
Learning Focus • Escorted travel to Piazza Ducale, Piazza del Comune and Torrazzo. Museum visits (Museo Stradivariano). Attendance at performances (Stradivarius violins). Other activities include bicycling. Instruction is offered by naturalists, historians, bicycle leaders. This program would appeal to people interested in nature studies, history, traditions, culture, food and wine.
Accommodations • Hotels. Single rooms are available for an additional $270.
Program Details • Program offered once per year. Session length: 9 days. Departures are scheduled in August. Program is targeted to adults of all ages. Most participants are 30–75 years of age. Participants must be 12 years or older to enroll. Other requirements: must be in good health and have some biking experience, must be accompanied by an adult if under 18. 20 participants per session. Application deadline: 1 month prior to departure. Reservations are recommended at least 3–12 months before departure.
Costs • $2790 (includes tuition, housing, all meals, books and class materials, excursions, international airfare). A $300 deposit is required.
Contact • Cross-Culture, 52 High Point Drive, Amherst, MA 01002-1224; 413-256-6303; Fax: 413-253-2303; E-mail: xculture@javanet.com; World Wide Web: http://www.empiremall.com/cross-culture

CROSS-CULTURE

FLORENCE AND THE TUSCAN HILLTOWNS

General Information • Cultural tour with visits to Florence. Once at the destination country, participants travel by foot.
Learning Focus • Escorted travel to Piazzadella Signoria, Santa Crocé Church and Siena. Museum visits (Academia Museum, Archaeological Museum). Attendance at performances (concerts, theater). Instruction is offered by highly educated guides. This program would appeal to people interested in culture, history, nature studies, arts, traditions, food and wine.
Accommodations • Hotels. Single rooms are available for an additional $220.
Program Details • Program offered 2 times per year. Session length: 9 days. Departures are scheduled in May, September. Program is targeted to adults of all ages. Most participants are 40–70 years of age. Participants must be 12 years or older to enroll. Other requirements: good health, accompaniment of an adult if under 18. 20–25 participants per session. Application deadline: 1 month prior to departure. Reservations are recommended at least 3–12 months before departure.
Costs • $2470 (includes tuition, housing, all meals, books and class materials, excursions, international airfare). A $300 deposit is required.
Contact • Cross-Culture, 52 High Point Drive, Amherst, MA 01002-1224; 413-256-6303; Fax: 413-253-2303; E-mail: xculture@javanet.com; World Wide Web: http://www.empiremall.com/cross-culture

CROSS-CULTURE

ROMAN HOLIDAY

General Information • Cultural tour with visits to Rome. Once at the destination country, participants travel by bus, foot.
Learning Focus • Escorted travel to Colosseum, St. Peter's Basilica, Sistine Chapel and Hadrian's Villa. Museum visits (Vatican Museums). Attendance at performances (music, theater). Instruction is offered by highly educated guides. This program would appeal to people interested in culture, history, nature studies, arts, traditions, food and wine.
Accommodations • Hotels. Single rooms are available for an additional $160.
Program Details • Program offered 2 times per year. Session length: 8 days. Departures are scheduled in May, September. Program is targeted to adults of all ages. Most participants are 40–70 years of age. Participants must be 12 years or older to enroll. Other requirements: good health, accompaniment of an adult if under 18. 20–25 participants per session. Application deadline: 1 month prior to departure. Reservations are recommended at least 3–12 months before departure.
Costs • $2210 (includes tuition, housing, all meals, books and class materials, excursions, international airfare). A $300 deposit is required.
Contact • Cross-Culture, 52 High Point Drive, Amherst, MA 01002-1224; 413-256-6303; Fax: 413-253-2303; E-mail: xculture@javanet.com; World Wide Web: http://www.empiremall.com/cross-culture

CROSS-CULTURE

SOJOURN IN SOUTHERN ITALY

General Information • Cultural tour with visits to Vico Equense, Naples, Amalfi, Duomo, Isle of Capri. Once at the destination country, participants travel by bus, boat.
Learning Focus • Escorted travel to ruins of Herculaneum and Pompeii and Palazzo Rufolo. Museum visits (National Archaeological Museum). Attendance at performances (traditional dance). Instruction is offered by highly educated guides. This program would appeal to people interested in culture, history, nature studies, arts, traditions, food and wine.
Accommodations • Hotels. Single rooms are available for an additional $160.
Program Details • Program offered 2 times per year. Session length: 9 days. Departures are scheduled in May, October. Program is targeted to adults of all ages. Most participants are 40–70 years of age. Participants must be 12 years or older to enroll. Other requirements: good health, accompaniment of an adult if under 18. 20–25 participants per session. Application deadline: 1 month prior to departure. Reservations are recommended at least 3–12 months before departure.
Costs • $2250 (includes tuition, housing, all meals, books and class materials, excursions, international airfare). A $300 deposit is required.
Contact • Cross-Culture, 52 High Point Drive, Amherst, MA 01002-1224; 413-256-6303; Fax: 413-253-2303; E-mail: xculture@javanet.com; World Wide Web: http://www.empiremall.com/cross-culture

CROSS-CULTURE

VENICE AND VENETIA

General Information • Cultural tour with visits to Venetia, Venice. Once at the destination country, participants travel by foot, boat.
Learning Focus • Escorted travel to Vicenza, the Basilica, Grand Canal and Doge's Palace. Museum visits (Accademia). Attendance at performances (music, theater). Instruction is offered by highly educated guides. This program would appeal to people interested in culture, history, nature studies, arts, traditions, food and wine.
Accommodations • Hotels. Single rooms are available for an additional $235.
Program Details • Program offered 2 times per year. Session length: 9 days. Departures are scheduled in June, September. Program is targeted to adults of all ages. Most participants are 40–70 years of age. Participants must be 12 years or older to enroll. Other requirements: good health, accompaniment of an adult if under 18. 20–25 participants per session. Application deadline: 1 month prior to departure. Reservations are recommended at least 3–12 months before departure.
Costs • $2450 (includes tuition, housing, all meals, books and class materials, excursions, international airfare). A $300 deposit is required.
Contact • Cross-Culture, 52 High Point Drive, Amherst, MA 01002-1224; 413-256-6303; Fax: 413-253-2303; E-mail: xculture@javanet.com; World Wide Web: http://www.empiremall.com/cross-culture

CSA–CENTER FOR STUDY ABROAD

ITALIAN LANGUAGE CENTER–ROME

General Information • Language study program in Rome.
Learning Focus • Courses in Italian language. Instruction is offered by professors from the sponsoring institution.
Accommodations • Homestays. Single rooms are available. Meals are taken on one's own, with host family.
Program Details • Program offered 52 times per year. Session length: 2–12 weeks. Departures are scheduled in January–December. The program is open to undergraduate students, graduate students, pre-college students, adults. Most participants are 22–45 years of age. Other requirements: minimum age of 17. 6–12 participants per session.
Costs • $895 for 2 weeks (includes tuition, housing, some meals, books and class materials, insurance, registration, orientation). Application fee: $45. A $50 deposit is required.
Contact • Philip Virtue, Program Director, CSA–Center for Study Abroad, 2802 East Madison Street MS #160, Seattle, WA 98112; 206-726-1498; Fax: 206-285-9197; E-mail: virtuecsa@aol.com

CSA–CENTER FOR STUDY ABROAD

ITALIAN UNIVERSITY FOR FOREIGNERS (PERUGIA)

General Information • Language study program in Perugia.
Learning Focus • Courses in Italian language. Instruction is offered by professors from the sponsoring institution.
Accommodations • Homestays, locally-rented apartments. Single rooms are available. Meals are taken on one's own, with host family.
Program Details • Program offered 12 times per year. Session length: 4–12 weeks. Departures are scheduled in January–December. The program is open to undergraduate students, graduate students, pre-college students, adults. Most participants are 19–35 years of age. Other requirements: minimum age of 17. 8–15 participants per session.
Costs • $1495 for 4 weeks (includes tuition, housing, some meals, insurance, registration, orientation). Application fee: $45. A $50 deposit is required.
Contact • Philip Virtue, Program Director, CSA–Center for Study Abroad, 2802 East Madison Street MS #160, Seattle, WA 98112; 206-726-1498; Fax: 206-285-9197; E-mail: virtuecsa@aol.com

CUISINE INTERNATIONAL

COOKING SCHOOL AT LE SIRENUSE IN POSITANO

General Information • Gourmet cooking/wine tour with visits to Positano, Amalfi, Ravello, wineries, Le Moncello Factory, St. Agata. Once at the destination country, participants travel by private coach.
Learning Focus • Instruction in cooking regional cuisine. Instruction is offered by chefs. This program would appeal to people interested in cooking, wine.
Accommodations • Hotels. Single rooms are available for an additional $400.
Program Details • Program offered 4 times per year. Session length: 5 days. Departures are scheduled in April, October. Most participants are 20–75 years of age. Participants must be 20 years or older to enroll. 12 participants per session. Reservations are recommended at least 6 months before departure.
Costs • $3000 (includes tuition, housing, all meals, books and class materials, excursions). A $300 deposit is required.
Contact • Judy Ebrey, Owner, Cuisine International, PO Box 25228, Dallas, TX 75225; 214-373-1161; Fax: 214-373-1162; E-mail: cuisineint@aol.com; World Wide Web: http://www.iglobal.net/cuisineint

CUISINE INTERNATIONAL

ITALIAN COOKERY WEEKS IN UMBRIA WITH SUSANNA GELMETTI

General Information • Gourmet cooking/wine tour with visits to Mondello, Orvieto, Umbria, Assisi, Orvieto. Once at the destination country, participants travel by private coach.
Learning Focus • Instruction in cooking regional cuisine. Instruction is offered by chefs. This program would appeal to people interested in cooking.
Accommodations • Program-owned houses. Single rooms are available for an additional $200.
Program Details • Program offered 20 times per year. Session length: 1 week. Departures are scheduled in May–September. Most participants are 18–65 years of age. Participants must be 18 years or older to enroll. 18 participants per session. Reservations are recommended at least 6 months before departure.

Costs • $1400 (includes tuition, housing, all meals, books and class materials, excursions). A $300 deposit is required.
Contact • Judy Ebrey, Owner, Cuisine International, PO Box 25228, Dallas, TX 75225; 214-373-1161; Fax: 214-373-1162; E-mail: cuisineint@aol.com; World Wide Web: http://www.iglobal.net/cuisineint

CUISINE INTERNATIONAL

LUNA CONVENTO COOKING SCHOOL WITH ENRICO FRANZESE

General Information • Gourmet cooking/wine tour with visits to Amalfi, Sorrento, Pompeii, St. Agata, Ravello, markets, paper mill. Once at the destination country, participants travel by private coach.
Learning Focus • Instruction in regional cuisine. Instruction is offered by chefs. This program would appeal to people interested in cooking.
Accommodations • Hotels. Single rooms are available for an additional $300.
Program Details • Program offered 4 times per year. Session length: 1 week. Departures are scheduled in May, October. Most participants are 20–75 years of age. Participants must be 18 years or older to enroll. 15–18 participants per session. Reservations are recommended at least 6 months before departure.
Costs • $2000 (includes tuition, housing, all meals, books and class materials, excursions). A $300 deposit is required.
Contact • Judy Ebrey, Owner, Cuisine International, PO Box 25228, Dallas, TX 75225; 214-373-1161; Fax: 214-373-1162; E-mail: cuisineint@aol.com; World Wide Web: http://www.iglobal.net/cuisineint

CUISINE INTERNATIONAL

MEDITERRANEAN COOKING AT ILMELOGRANO WITH DIANE SEED

General Information • Gourmet cooking/wine tour with visits to Monopoli, Pugua, Alberobello, Lecce, wineries, Contadina. Once at the destination country, participants travel by private coach.
Learning Focus • Instruction in regional cuisine. Instruction is offered by cooking teachers and chefs. This program would appeal to people interested in cooking, wine.
Accommodations • Hotels. Single rooms are available for an additional $300.
Program Details • Program offered 4 times per year. Session length: 1 week. Departures are scheduled in May, October. Most participants are 20–75 years of age. Participants must be 20 years or older to enroll. 15 participants per session. Reservations are recommended at least 6 months before departure.
Costs • $2500 (includes tuition, housing, all meals, books and class materials, excursions). A $300 deposit is required.
Contact • Judy Ebrey, Owner, Cuisine International, PO Box 25228, Dallas, TX 75225; 214-373-1161; Fax: 214-373-1162; E-mail: cuisineint@aol.com; World Wide Web: http://www.iglobal.net/cuisineint

CUISINE INTERNATIONAL

VENETIAN COOKING WITH FULUIA SESANI

General Information • Gourmet cooking/wine tour with visits to Venice, Doge's Palace, Basilica of St. Mark, Rialto Market, private homes. Once at the destination country, participants travel by foot.
Learning Focus • Instruction in regional cuisine. Instruction is offered by chefs. This program would appeal to people interested in cooking, wine.
Accommodations • Hotels. Single rooms are available for an additional $600.
Program Details • Program offered 6 times per year. Session length: 1 week. Departures are scheduled in May, September. Most participants are 20–75 years of age. Participants must be 18 years or older to enroll. 10–12 participants per session. Reservations are recommended at least 6 months before departure.
Costs • $3250 (includes tuition, housing, all meals, books and class materials, excursions). A $500 deposit is required.
Contact • Judy Ebrey, Owner, Cuisine International, PO Box 25228, Dallas, TX 75225; 214-373-1161; Fax: 214-373-1162; E-mail: cuisineint@aol.com; World Wide Web: http://www.iglobal.net/cuisineint

CUISINE INTERNATIONAL

VILLA MICHAELA COOKING SCHOOL

General Information • Gourmet cooking/wine tour with visits to Lucca, Vorno, wineries, markets, Lucca. Once at the destination country, participants travel by private coach.
Learning Focus • Instruction in regional cuisine. Instruction is offered by chefs. This program would appeal to people interested in cooking, wine.
Accommodations • Program-owned houses. Single rooms are available for an additional $300.
Program Details • Program offered 6 times per year. Session length: 1 week. Departures are scheduled in September, October. Most participants are 18–75 years of age. Participants must be 18 years or older to enroll. 12 participants per session. Reservations are recommended at least 6 months before departure.
Costs • $2000 (includes tuition, housing, all meals, books and class materials, excursions). A $1000 deposit is required.
Contact • Judy Ebrey, Owner, Cuisine International, PO Box 25228, Dallas, TX 75225; 214-373-1161; Fax: 214-373-1162; E-mail: cuisineint@aol.com; World Wide Web: http://www.iglobal.net/cuisineint

CUISINE INTERNATIONAL

THE VILLA TABLE AT BADIA A COLTIBUONO

General Information • Gourmet cooking/wine tour with visits to Gaiole in Chianti, Siena, private homes, wineries. Once at the destination country, participants travel by private coach.
Learning Focus • Instruction in cooking regional cuisine. Escorted travel to Siena and wineries. Instruction is offered by cooking teacher. This program would appeal to people interested in cooking, wine.
Accommodations • Private residence. Single rooms are available for an additional $500.

Program Details • Program offered 8 times per year. Session length: 6 days. Departures are scheduled in May, June, September, October. Most participants are 25–75 years of age. 15 participants per session. Reservations are recommended at least 6–9 months before departure.
Costs • $3900 (includes tuition, housing, all meals, books and class materials, excursions). A $400 deposit is required.
Contact • Judy Ebrey, Owner, Cuisine International, PO Box 25228, Dallas, TX 75225; 214-373-1161; Fax: 214-373-1162; E-mail: cuisineint@aol.com; World Wide Web: http://www.iglobal.net/cuisineint

CUISINE INTERNATIONAL

WORLD OF REGALEALI COOKING SCHOOL WITH ANNATASCA LANZA

General Information • Gourmet cooking/wine tour with visits to Sicily, wineries, markets. Once at the destination country, participants travel by private coach.
Learning Focus • Instruction in cooking. Escorted travel to vineyards and Greek temples of Agrigento. Instruction is offered by cooking teachers. This program would appeal to people interested in cooking, wine.
Accommodations • Program-owned houses. Single rooms are available.
Program Details • Program offered 6 times per year. Session length: 1 week. Departures are scheduled in May, October, November. Most participants are 18–75 years of age. Participants must be 18 years or older to enroll. 12 participants per session. Reservations are recommended at least 6 months before departure.
Costs • $2200 (includes tuition, housing, all meals, books and class materials, excursions). A $500 deposit is required.
Contact • Judy Ebrey, Owner, Cuisine International, PO Box 25228, Dallas, TX 75225; 214-373-1161; Fax: 214-373-1162; E-mail: cuisineint@aol.com; World Wide Web: http://www.iglobal.net/cuisineint

DIANE HOFF-ROME, AN ARTIST'S LIFE

ITALY AND GREEK ISLES ARTIST CRUISE HOLIDAY

General Information • Arts program with visits to Adriatic Coast, Venice, Greek Isles of Mykonos, Santorini, Rhodes, Kithera, Katakolon. Once at the destination country, participants travel by bus, foot, boat, mini-bus.
Learning Focus • Instruction in painting, drawing and composition. Museum visits (Venice, ancient sites). Other activities include visits to local artisans. Instruction is offered by artists, historians. This program would appeal to people interested in painting, nature studies, writing, ancient history, photography, art, folk arts.
Accommodations • Hotels, boat. Single rooms are available for an additional $875.
Program Details • Program offered once per year. Session length: 11 days. Departures are scheduled in October. Program is targeted to amateur artists and teachers. Most participants are 25–85 years of age. Participants must be 21 years or older to enroll. Other requirements: interest in art, nature, cultural experience. 8 participants per session. Application deadline: 90 days prior to departure. Reservations are recommended at least 120 days before departure.
Costs • $2995 (includes tuition, housing, some meals, some excursions). A $750 deposit is required.
Contact • Irwin W. Rome, Co-Director, Diane Hoff-Rome, An Artist's Life, PO Box 567, Elmwood Road, Swampscott, MA 01907; 617-595-1173; Fax: 617-596-0707; E-mail: artistlf@pcix.com; World Wide Web: http://www2.pcix.com/~artistlf

DICKINSON COLLEGE

BOLOGNA SUMMER IMMERSION PROGRAM

General Information • Language study program in Bologna.
Learning Focus • Courses in Italian language, Italian culture. Instruction is offered by professors from the sponsoring institution.
Accommodations • Homestays, program-owned apartments. Meals are taken on one's own, with host family, in local restaurants, in residences.
Program Details • Program offered once per year. Session length: 6 weeks. Departures are scheduled in May. The program is open to undergraduate students. Most participants are 18–20 years of age. Other requirements: intermediate-level Italian. 15 participants per session. Application deadline: February 15.
Costs • $3600 (includes tuition, housing, all meals, books and class materials, excursions, international airfare). Application fee: $15. A $300 deposit is required.
Contact • Dr. John S. Henderson, Director of Off-Campus Studies, Dickinson College, PO Box 1773, Carlisle, PA 17013-2896; 717-245-1341; Fax: 717-245-1688; E-mail: ocs@dickinson.edu; World Wide Web: http://www.dickinson.edu

DICKINSON COLLEGE

CLASSICS IMMERSION PROGRAM

General Information • Academic study program in Rome.
Learning Focus • Courses in classical studies, Latin language. Instruction is offered by professors from the sponsoring institution.
Accommodations • Locally-rented apartments. Meals are taken as a group, in local restaurants.
Program Details • Program offered once per year. Session length: 6 weeks. Departures are scheduled in May. The program is open to undergraduate students. Most participants are 18–20 years of age. Other requirements: 2 years of college-level Latin. 12 participants per session. Application deadline: February 15.
Costs • $3600 (includes tuition, housing, all meals, excursions, international airfare). Application fee: $15. A $300 deposit is required.
Contact • Dr. John S. Henderson, Director of Off-Campus Studies, Dickinson College, PO Box 1773, Carlisle, PA 17013-2896; 717-245-1341; Fax: 717-245-1688; E-mail: ocs@dickinson.edu; World Wide Web: http://www.dickinson.edu

DRAKE UNIVERSITY, INSTITUTE OF ITALIAN STUDIES

FLORENCE SUMMER PROGRAM

General Information • Academic study program in Florence. Classes are held on the campus of Institute of Italian Studies–Florence. Excursions to Tuscany.
Learning Focus • Courses in studio art, art history, language study, photography. Instruction is offered by local teachers.
Accommodations • Homestays, locally-rented apartments. Single rooms are available. Meals are taken in central dining facility, in local restaurants.
Program Details • Program offered 3 times per year. Session length: 4–8 weeks. Departures are scheduled in May–July. The program is open to undergraduate students, graduate students, adults. Most participants are 19 years of age and older. Other requirements: minimum 2.5 GPA. 40–50 participants per session. Application deadline: April 15.
Costs • $3000 (includes tuition, housing, some meals, international airfare). Application fee: $25. A $500 deposit is required.
Contact • Dr. Mario T. Soria, US Program Director, Drake University, Institute of Italian Studies, PO Box 23007, Des Moines, IA 50325-9406; 800-443-7253, ext. 3984; Fax: 515-225-0196; World Wide Web: http://www.drake.edu

DUKE UNIVERSITY

DUKE IN FLORENCE

General Information • Academic study program in Florence.
Learning Focus • Courses in history, art, art history. Instruction is offered by professors from the sponsoring institution.
Accommodations • Hotels. Meals are taken on one's own, in local restaurants.
Program Details • Program offered once per year. Session length: 6 weeks. Departures are scheduled in May. The program is open to undergraduate students. Most participants are 19–21 years of age. Other requirements: minimum 2.7 GPA. 25 participants per session. Application deadline: February 21.
Costs • $4741 (includes tuition, housing, some meals, excursions, international airfare).
Contact • Foreign Academic Programs, Duke University, 121 Allen Building, Box 90057, Durham, NC 27708-0057; 919-684-2174; Fax: 919-684-3083; E-mail: abroad@mail01.adm.duke.edu; World Wide Web: http://www.mis.duke.edu/study_abroad/study_abroad.html

DUKE UNIVERSITY

DUKE IN ROME

General Information • Academic study program in Rome. Excursions to Pompeii, Monte Cassino, Palestrina, Tivoli, Alban Hills.
Learning Focus • Courses in art history, classical studies, history. Instruction is offered by professors from the sponsoring institution.
Accommodations • Dormitories, hotels. Meals are taken on one's own, in local restaurants.
Program Details • Program offered once per year. Session length: 4 weeks. Departures are scheduled in June. The program is open to undergraduate students. Most participants are 19–21 years of age. Other requirements: minimum 2.7 GPA. 20 participants per session. Application deadline: February 21.
Costs • $4012 (includes tuition, housing, some meals, excursions, international airfare).
Contact • Foreign Academic Programs, Duke University, 121 Allen Building, Box 90057, Durham, NC 27708-0057; 919-684-2174; Fax: 919-684-3083; E-mail: abroad@mail01.adm.duke.edu; World Wide Web: http://www.mis.duke.edu/study_abroad/study_abroad.html

EF INTERNATIONAL LANGUAGE SCHOOLS

ITALIAN IN FLORENCE

General Information • Language study program in Florence. Classes are held on the campus of Centro Linguistico Italiano Dante Alighieri. Excursions to Pisa, Siena, San Gimignano, Perugia, Rome.
Learning Focus • Courses in Italian language. Instruction is offered by professors from the sponsoring institution and local teachers.
Accommodations • Homestays, program-owned apartments. Single rooms are available. Meals are taken as a group, with host family, in central dining facility, in residences.
Program Details • Program offered 11 times per year. Session length: 2–12 weeks. Departures are scheduled in January–July, September–November. The program is open to undergraduate students, graduate students, pre-college students, adults. Most participants are 16–25 years of age. Other requirements: minimum age of 16. 40 participants per session. Application deadline: 60 days prior to departure.
Costs • Principal: $1090 for 2 weeks, $1580 for 4 weeks, intensive: $1230 for 2 weeks, $1840 for 4 weeks (includes tuition, housing, some meals, books and class materials). Application fee: $90. A $350 deposit is required.
Contact • Kari Larson, Admissions Manager, EF International Language Schools, 204 Lake Street, Boston, MA 02135; 800-992-1892; Fax: 617-746-1800

EUROCENTRES

LANGUAGE IMMERSION IN ITALY

General Information • Language study program in Florence. Classes are held on the campus of Eurocentre Florence. Excursions to Pisa, San Gimignano, Siena, Venice, Rome.
Learning Focus • Courses in Italian language, Italian culture. Instruction is offered by professors from the sponsoring institution.
Accommodations • Homestays. Single rooms are available. Meals are taken with host family, in residences.
Program Details • Program offered 20 times per year. Session length: 2–12 weeks. Departures are scheduled in January–December. The program is open to undergraduate

students, graduate students, pre-college students, adults. Most participants are 16–80 years of age. 15 participants per session.
Costs • Contact sponsor for information.
Contact • Marketing, Eurocentres, 101 North Union Street, Suite 300, Alexandria, VA 22314; 800-648-4809; Fax: 703-684-1495; E-mail: 100632.141@compuserve.com; World Wide Web: http://www.clark.net/pub/eurocent/home.htm

EUROPEAN HERITAGE INSTITUTE

ART PROGRAM IN FLORENCE

General Information • Academic study program in Florence. Classes are held on the campus of Lorenzo de' Medici–Art Institute.
Learning Focus • Courses in art. Instruction is offered by local teachers.
Accommodations • Dormitories, locally-rented apartments. Single rooms are available. Meals are taken on one's own.
Program Details • Session length: 1 or more months. Departures are scheduled in May–September. The program is open to undergraduate students, graduate students, adults, high school graduates. Other requirements: must be at least 18. Application deadline: 60 days prior to departure.
Costs • $1390 (includes tuition, administrative fees). A $350 deposit is required.
Contact • Dr. Antonio Masullo, Professor, European Heritage Institute, 2708 East Franklin Street, Richmond, VA 23223; 804-648-0826; Fax: 804-648-0826; E-mail: euritage@i2020.net

EUROPEAN HERITAGE INSTITUTE

SUMMER PROGRAM IN ASSISI

General Information • Language study program in Assisi. Classes are held on the campus of Academy of Italian Language.
Learning Focus • Courses in Italian language. Instruction is offered by local teachers.
Program Details • Session length: 1 or more months. Departures are scheduled in May–September. The program is open to undergraduate students, adults, high school graduates. Other requirements: must be at least 18. Application deadline: 60 days prior to departure.
Costs • $1150 (includes tuition, housing). A $350 deposit is required.

Contact • Dr. Antonio Masullo, Professor, European Heritage Institute, 2708 East Franklin Street, Richmond, VA 23223; 804-648-0826; Fax: 804-648-0826; E-mail: euritage@i2020.net

EUROPEAN HERITAGE INSTITUTE

SUMMER PROGRAM IN PERUGIA

General Information • Academic study program in Perugia. Classes are held on the campus of University of Italian Studies for Foreigners Perugia.
Learning Focus • Courses in Italian language, Italian literature, Italian culture, philosophy, history. Instruction is offered by local teachers.
Accommodations • Homestays, locally-rented apartments. Meals are taken on one's own.
Program Details • Program offered 5 times per year. Session length: 4–12 weeks. Departures are scheduled in May–September. The program is open to undergraduate students, graduate students, adults. Application deadline: 65 days prior to departure.
Costs • $990 (includes tuition, housing). A $350 deposit is required.
Contact • Dr. Antonio Masullo, Professor, European Heritage Institute, 2708 East Franklin Street, Richmond, VA 23223; 804-648-0826; Fax: 804-648-0826; E-mail: euritage@i2020.net

EXPERIENCE PLUS SPECIALTY TOURS, INC.

A CULINARY CYCLING CIRCUS–ITALY

General Information • Food, wine and bicycle tour with visits to Apennine Mountains, Bertinoro, Cervia, Dozza, Faenza, Parma. Once at the destination country, participants travel by bicycle.
Learning Focus • Escorted travel to Italy. Museum visits (Emilia Romagna Wine Museum). Other activities include bicycling, wine tasting, culinary events, pasta-making. Instruction is offered by professors, indigenous, bilingual and bi-cultural guides. This program would appeal to people interested in bicycling, food, wine, culture, travel, Italy.
Accommodations • Hotels. Single rooms are available for an additional $300.
Program Details • Program offered 2 times per year. Session length: 9 days. Departures are scheduled in June, August. Most participants are 35–70 years of age. 16–22 participants per session. Reservations are recommended at least 6–12 months before departure.
Costs • $1995 (includes all meals, culinary events, rental bike, water bottle, luggage shuttle, van support, tour leaders, shirt). A $250 deposit is required.
Contact • Experience Plus Specialty Tours, Inc., 1925 Wallenberg Drive, Fort Collins, CO 80526; 800-685-4565; Fax: 800-685-4565; E-mail: tours@xplus.com

EXPERIENCE PLUS SPECIALTY TOURS, INC.

ITALY'S CINQUE TERRE: A WALKING TOUR

General Information • Cultural tour with visits to Cinque Terre, Lucca, Monterosso, Lucca's Guinigi Tower, olive orchards, vineyards, Monterosso, Cinque Terre. Once at the destination country, participants travel by foot.
Learning Focus • Escorted travel to Italy's Cinque Terre. Other activities include walking, a visit to an olive oil press. Instruction is offered by professors, indigenous, bilingual and bi-cultural guides. This program would appeal to people interested in walking, Italy, gourmet food, wine, culture, travel.
Accommodations • Hotels. Single rooms are available for an additional $300.
Program Details • Program offered once per year. Session length: 8 days. Departures are scheduled in May. Most participants are 35–70 years of age. 16–22 participants per session. Reservations are recommended at least 6–12 months before departure.
Costs • $1495 (includes housing, some meals, excursions, 1 wine tasting, Cinque Terre train pass, luggage shuttle, van support, bilingual/bi-cultural tour leaders). A $250 deposit is required.
Contact • Experience Plus Specialty Tours, Inc., 1925 Wallenberg Drive, Fort Collins, CO 80526; 800-685-4565; Fax: 800-685-4565; E-mail: tours@xplus.com

EXPERIENCE PLUS SPECIALTY TOURS, INC.

VENICE TO FLORENCE

General Information • Bicycle tour with visits to Faenza, Florence, Forli, Ravenna, Venice, Venice, Mausoleum of Galla Placida, Faenza's ceramic studios, Florence art museums. Once at the destination country, participants travel by bicycle.
Learning Focus • Escorted travel to Venice and Florence. Museum visits (Venice and Florence). Other activities include bicycling through the Apennines, swimming in the Adriatic Sea, visiting the mosaics of San Vitale. Instruction is offered by professors, indigenous, bilingual and bi-cultural guides. This program would appeal to people interested in bicycling, gourmet food, wine, culture, travel, Italy.
Accommodations • Hotels. Single rooms are available for an additional $300.
Program Details • Session length: 8 days. Departures are scheduled in May–September. Most participants are 35–70 years of age. 16–22 participants per session. Reservations are recommended at least 6–12 months before departure.
Costs • $1395 (includes housing, some meals, quality rental bike, water bottle, shirt, luggage shuttle, van support, bilingual/bi-cultural tour leaders). A $250 deposit is required.
Contact • Experience Plus Specialty Tours, Inc., 1925 Wallenberg Drive, Fort Collins, CO 80526; 800-685-4565; Fax: 800-685-4565; E-mail: tours@xplus.com

FOREIGN LANGUAGE STUDY ABROAD SERVICE

INTERNATIONAL LANGUAGE STUDY HOMESTAYS IN ITALY

General Information • Language study program in Italy.
Learning Focus • Courses in Italian language. Instruction is offered by local teachers.
Accommodations • Homestays. Single rooms are available. Meals are taken with host family, in residences.
Program Details • Session length: varies. Departures are scheduled in January–December. The program is open to undergraduate students, graduate students, pre-college students, adults. Most participants are 12 years of age and older. Other requirements: students must be at least 12 years old. 1 participant per session.
Costs • Contact sponsor for information. A $300 deposit is required.
Contact • Louise Harber, Coordinator, Foreign Language Study Abroad Service, Department IH, Box 903, 5935 Southwest 64th Avenue, South Miami, FL 33143; 800-282-1090; Fax: 305-662-2907; E-mail: flsas@netpoint.net; World Wide Web: http://www.netpoint.net/~flsas

FOREIGN LANGUAGE STUDY ABROAD SERVICE

ITALIAN IN ITALY

General Information • Language study program in Bologna, Florence, Manciano, Rimini, Rome, Siena.
Learning Focus • Courses in language study. Instruction is offered by local teachers.
Accommodations • Homestays, program-owned apartments, hotels. Single rooms are available. Meals are taken as a group, on one's own, in local restaurants, in residences.
Program Details • Session length: varies. Departures are scheduled in January–December. The program is open to undergraduate students, graduate students, pre-college students, adults. Most participants are 16 years of age and older.
Costs • Contact sponsor for information. Application fee: $50. A $100 deposit is required.
Contact • Louise Harber, Coordinator, Foreign Language Study Abroad Service, Department IH, Box 903, 5935 Southwest 64th Avenue, South Miami, FL 33143; 800-282-1090; Fax: 305-662-2907; E-mail: flsas@netpoint.net; World Wide Web: http://www.netpoint.net/~flsas

GONZAGA UNIVERSITY

GONZAGA-IN-FLORENCE

General Information • Academic study program in Florence. Excursions to Rome, Pompeii, Capri, Naples, Amalfi, Assisi.
Learning Focus • Courses in Italian language, history, business, art, art history, philosophy, religion, political science. Instruction is offered by professors from the sponsoring institution.
Accommodations • Hotels. Single rooms are available. Meals are taken as a group.
Program Details • Program offered once per year. Session length: 7 weeks. Departures are scheduled in May. The program is open to undergraduate students, graduate students, adults. Most participants are 18 years of age and older. Other requirements: minimum 2.5 GPA. 30 participants per session. Application deadline: March 1.
Costs • $4000 (includes tuition, housing, some meals, excursions). A $100 deposit is required.
Contact • Wanda Reynolds, Director, Studies Abroad, Gonzaga University, 502 Boone, Spokane, WA 99258; 509-328-4220; Fax: 509-324-5987; E-mail: reynolds@ga.gonzaga.edu

ILLINOIS STATE UNIVERSITY

SUMMER PROGRAM IN FLORENCE

General Information • Academic study program in Florence. Excursions to Rome, Siena, Pisa, Chianti.
Learning Focus • Courses in Renaissance, art history. Instruction is offered by professors from the sponsoring institution.
Accommodations • Homestays. Meals are taken with host family.
Program Details • Program offered once per year. Session length: 4 weeks. Departures are scheduled in May. The program is open to undergraduate students, graduate students. Most participants are 19–25 years of age. Other requirements: sophomore standing. 12–15 participants per session. Application deadline: March 1.
Costs • $3000 (includes tuition, housing, all meals, books and class materials, excursions, international airfare). Application fee: $100. A $200 deposit is required.
Contact • Dr. Ron Mottram, Chair, Department of Art, Illinois State University, 5020 Art Department, Normal, IL 61790-5020; 309-438-5621; Fax: 309-438-8318; E-mail: oisp@ilstu.edu; World Wide Web: http://www.orat.ilstu.edu/

INSTITUTO DELLA LINGUA ITALIANA "GALILEO GALILEI"

ONE TO ONE COURSES IN ITALIAN LANGUAGE

General Information • Language study program in Florence, Island of Elba. Excursions to Chianti countryside.
Learning Focus • Courses in art history, Italian language. Instruction is offered by professors from the sponsoring institution.
Accommodations • Homestays, locally-rented apartments, pensiones, hotels. Single rooms are available. Meals are taken with host family, in local restaurants.
Program Details • Session length: 1 or more weeks. Departures are scheduled in January–December. The program is open to undergraduate students, graduate students, pre-college students, adults. Most participants are 17–40 years of age. 1–4 participant per session. Application deadline: 15 days prior to departure.
Costs • $699 per week (includes tuition, some meals, books and class materials, non-specialized medical assistance).
Contact • Ms. Alexandra Schmitz, Secretary, Instituto Della Lingua Italiana "Galileo Galilei", Via degli Alfani 68, Florence 50121, Italy; +39 55-294-680; Fax: +39 55-283-481; E-mail: institute.galilei@agora.stm.it

INTERHOSTEL, UNIVERSITY OF NEW HAMPSHIRE

CHRISTMAS IN ROME AND FLORENCE, ITALY

General Information • Cultural tour with visits to Florence, Rome, Sant' Andrea al Quirinal, San Carlino, Certosa di Galluzzo. Once at the destination country, participants travel by bus, foot. Program is affiliated with Art Institute of Florence and Lorenzo De' Medici.

Learning Focus • Instruction in history, culture and art history. Escorted travel to villages and landmarks. Museum visits (Vatican Museum, Uffizi, Academia). Attendance at performances (concerts and Gregorian chants). Other activities include New Year's Day Renaissance Banquet. Instruction is offered by professors. This program would appeal to people interested in history, culture, art.

Accommodations • Hotels. Single rooms are available for an additional $600.

Program Details • Program offered once per year. Session length: 2 weeks. Departures are scheduled in December. Program is targeted to seniors over 50. Most participants are 60–80 years of age. Participants must be 50 years or older to enroll. 35 participants per session. Reservations are recommended at least 6 months before departure.

Costs • $3045 (includes tuition, housing, all meals, excursions, international airfare, entrance fees). A $200 deposit is required.

Contact • Janice Pierson, Office Supervisor, Interhostel, University of New Hampshire, 6 Garrison Avenue, Durham, NH 03824-3529; 800-733-9753; Fax: 603-862-1113; World Wide Web: http://www.learn.unh.edu/

INTERHOSTEL, UNIVERSITY OF NEW HAMPSHIRE

FLORENCE AND SIENA, ITALY

General Information • Cultural tour with visits to Florence, Siena, San Galgano, Pienza, Monte Pulciano, San Gimignano. Once at the destination country, participants travel by bus, foot. Program is affiliated with The Art Institute of Florence and Lorenzo De' Medici.

Learning Focus • Instruction in history and culture. Escorted travel to cities and landmarks. Museum visits (Uffizi, Academy Gallery). Instruction is offered by professors, historians. This program would appeal to people interested in history, culture, art.

Accommodations • Hotels. Single rooms are available for an additional $550.

Program Details • Program offered once per year. Session length: 2 weeks. Departures are scheduled in May. Program is targeted to seniors over 50. Most participants are 60–80 years of age. Participants must be 50 years or older to enroll. 35 participants per session. Reservations are recommended at least 6 months before departure.

Costs • $3075 (includes tuition, housing, all meals, excursions, international airfare, entrance fees). A $200 deposit is required.

Contact • Janice Pierson, Office Supervisor, Interhostel, University of New Hampshire, 6 Garrison Avenue, Durham, NH 03824; 800-733-9753; Fax: 603-862-1113; World Wide Web: http://www.learn.unh.edu/

INTERHOSTEL, UNIVERSITY OF NEW HAMPSHIRE

FLORENCE, ITALY

General Information • Cultural tour with visits to Assisi, Florence, Pisa, Tuscan countryside, Siena, San Gimignano. Once at the destination country, participants travel by bus, foot. Program is affiliated with Lorenzo De' Medici Institute.

Learning Focus • Instruction in history, culture and art. Escorted travel to cities and villages. Museum visits (Opera del Duomo Museum, Uffizi). Other activities include Tuscan cooking class. Instruction is offered by professors. This program would appeal to people interested in history, culture, art.

Accommodations • Hotels. Single rooms are available for an additional $500.

Program Details • Program offered 2 times per year. Session length: 2 weeks. Departures are scheduled in March. Program is targeted to seniors over 50. Most participants are 60–80 years of age. Participants must be 50 years or older to enroll. 35 participants per session. Reservations are recommended at least 6 months before departure.

Costs • $2740 (includes tuition, housing, all meals, excursions, international airfare, entrance fees). A $200 deposit is required.

Contact • Janice Pierson, Office Supervisor, Interhostel, University of New Hampshire, 6 Garrison Avenue, Durham, NH 03824; 800-733-9753; Fax: 603-862-1113; World Wide Web: http://www.learn.unh.edu/

INTERHOSTEL, UNIVERSITY OF NEW HAMPSHIRE

ROME, ITALY

General Information • Cultural tour with visits to Rome. Program is affiliated with The Art Institute of Florence and Lorenzo De' Medici.

Learning Focus • Instruction in history and culture. Museum visits (Vatican Museum, Etruscan Museum, Capitoline Museums). Other activities include Papal audience. Instruction is offered by professors, historians, city guides. This program would appeal to people interested in history, culture.

Accommodations • Hotels. Single rooms are available for an additional $600.

Program Details • Program offered once per year. Session length: 2 weeks. Departures are scheduled in August. Program is targeted to seniors over 50. Most participants are 60–80 years of age. Participants must be 50 years or older to enroll. 35 participants per session. Reservations are recommended at least 6 months before departure.

Costs • $3125 (includes tuition, housing, all meals, excursions, international airfare, entrance fees). A $200 deposit is required.

Contact • Janice Pierson, Office Supervisor, Interhostel, University of New Hampshire, 6 Garrison Avenue, Durham, NH 03824; 800-733-9753; Fax: 603-862-1113; World Wide Web: http://www.learn.unh.edu/

INTERHOSTEL, UNIVERSITY OF NEW HAMPSHIRE

VENICE, ITALY

General Information • Cultural tour with visits to Venice, Murano, Burano, Torcello Island, Verona, San Giorgio Island, Padua. Once at the destination country, participants travel by bus, foot. Program is affiliated with Lorenzo De' Medici Institute and Instituto Zambler.

Learning Focus • Instruction in history and culture. Escorted travel to cities and landmarks. Museum visits (Academy Gallery, Scuola Grande). Instruction is offered by professors, city guides. This program would appeal to people interested in history, culture.

Accommodations • Hotels. Single rooms are available for an additional $600.

Program Details • Program offered once per year. Session length: 2 weeks. Departures are scheduled in October. Program is targeted to seniors over 50. Most participants are 60–80 years of age. Participants must be 50 years or older to enroll. 35 participants per session. Reservations are recommended at least 6 months before departure.

Costs • $3250 (includes tuition, housing, all meals, excursions, international airfare, entrance fees). A $200 deposit is required.

Contact • Janice Pierson, Office Supervisor, Interhostel, University of New Hampshire, 6 Garrison Avenue, Durham, NH 03824-3529; 800-733-9753; Fax: 603-862-1113; World Wide Web: http://www.learn.unh.edu/

INTERHOSTEL, UNIVERSITY OF NEW HAMPSHIRE

WALKING IN TUSCANY

General Information • Cultural tour with visits to Assisi, Florence, Gaiole in Chianti, Montepulciano, Greve, Vertine, Radda, Pienza, Bagno Vignoni, Gnoni, San Quirico D'Orcia, Montichiello, Todi, Orvieto, Perugia. Once at the destination country, participants travel by bus, foot. Program is affiliated with Art Institute of Florence and Lorenzo De' Medici.

Learning Focus • Instruction in history and culture. Escorted travel to villages and landmarks. Museum visits (Uffizi, Accademia, Etruscan Museum). Other activities include walking. Instruction is offered by professors, naturalists, historians. This program would appeal to people interested in history, walking, culture.

Accommodations • Hotels. Single rooms are available for an additional $600.

Program Details • Program offered once per year. Session length: 2 weeks. Departures are scheduled in October. Program is targeted to walkers over 50. Most participants are 60–75 years of age. Participants must be 50 years or older to enroll. 25 participants per session. Reservations are recommended at least 4 months before departure.

Costs • $2995 (includes tuition, housing, all meals, excursions, international airfare, entrance fees). A $200 deposit is required.

Contact • Janice Pierson, Office Supervisor, Interhostel, University of New Hampshire, 6 Garrison Avenue, Durham, NH 03824-3529; 800-733-9753; Fax: 603-862-1113; World Wide Web: http://www.learn.unh.edu/

IONA COLLEGE

IONA IN ITALY

General Information • Academic study program in Rome. Excursions to Florence, Naples, Pisa.

Learning Focus • Courses in history and culture, international business, art, religion. Instruction is offered by professors from the sponsoring institution.

Accommodations • Dormitories. Single rooms are available. Meals are taken as a group, in central dining facility.

Program Details • Program offered once per year. Session length: 4 weeks. Departures are scheduled in May. The program is open to undergraduate students. Most participants are 19–22 years of age. Other requirements: minimum 2.3 GPA. 35 participants per session. Application deadline: May 1.

Costs • $2200 (includes tuition, housing, some meals, insurance, international airfare). A $200 deposit is required.

Contact • Mary R. Veith, Assistant Dean, Iona College, Hagan School of Business, 715 North Avenue, New Rochelle, NY 10801-1890; 914-633-2256; Fax: 914-633-2012

JAMES MADISON UNIVERSITY

SUMMER PROGRAM IN FLORENCE

General Information • Academic study program in Florence. Excursions to Rome, Siena, San Gimignano, Venice, Pisa.

Learning Focus • Courses in Italian language, Italian literature, music, art history, political science, Italian cinema. Instruction is offered by professors from the sponsoring institution.

Accommodations • Homestays. Single rooms are available. Meals are taken as a group, with host family, in local restaurants, in residences.

Program Details • Program offered once per year. Session length: 6 weeks. Departures are scheduled in May. The program is open to undergraduate students. Most participants are 18–22 years of age. Other requirements: minimum 2.8 GPA. 15 participants per session. Application deadline: February 1.

Costs • $3648 for Virginia residents, $5736 for nonresidents (includes tuition, housing, some meals, books and class materials, excursions). A $400 deposit is required.

Contact • Dr. Kay Arthur, Director, Florence Program, James Madison University, Office of International Education, Harrisonburg, VA 22801; 540-568-6642; Fax: 540-568-3310; E-mail: arthurkg@jmu.edu; World Wide Web: http://www.jmu.edu/intl-ed/

JAMES MADISON UNIVERSITY

SUMMER STUDY IN ROME

General Information • Academic study program in Rome. Classes are held on the campus of Marymount International School. Excursions to Venice, Florence.

Learning Focus • Courses in education. Instruction is offered by professors from the sponsoring institution.

Accommodations • Dormitories. Meals are taken as a group, in central dining facility.

Program Details • Program offered once per year. Session length: 3 weeks. Departures are scheduled in May. The

program is open to undergraduate students. Most participants are 18–22 years of age. Other requirements: students must be enrolled in a teacher education program, 2.8 minimum GPA. 10–20 participants per session. Application deadline: February 1.
Costs • $1915 for Virginia residents, $2053 for nonresidents (includes tuition, housing, some meals, excursions). A $400 deposit is required.
Contact • Dr. Violet Allain, Professor, Department of Secondary Education, James Madison University, Office of International Education, Harrisonburg, VA 22807; 540-568-6708; Fax: 540-568-2829; E-mail: allainl@jmu,edu; World Wide Web: http://www.jmu.edu/intl-ed/

JOHN CABOT UNIVERSITY

SUMMER SESSION–STUDY ABROAD IN ROME

General Information • Academic study program in Rome. Classes are held on the campus of John Cabot University. Excursions to historic sites near Rome, Venice, Sicily, Naples, Florence.
Learning Focus • Courses in art history, Italian studies, political science, studio art, English literature, classical studies, international business, computer science. Instruction is offered by professors from the sponsoring institution and local teachers.
Accommodations • Homestays, locally-rented apartments, pensiones, hotels. Single rooms are available. Meals are taken on one's own, with host family, in local restaurants, in residences.
Program Details • Program offered once per year. Session length: 5 weeks. Departures are scheduled in June. The program is open to undergraduate students, graduate students, adults, high school students. Most participants are 18–25 years of age. Other requirements: good academic standing at home institution. 15 participants per session. Application deadline: May 15.
Costs • $2900 (includes tuition, books and class materials, excursions). Application fee: $40. A $165 deposit is required.
Contact • Dr. Francesca R. Gleason, Director of Admissions, John Cabot University, Via della Lungara, 233, Rome 00165, Italy; +39 6-687-8881; Fax: +39 6-683-2088; E-mail: jcu@nexus.it

KENTUCKY INSTITUTE FOR INTERNATIONAL STUDIES

PROGRAM IN ITALY

General Information • Academic study program in Florence. Excursions to Rome.
Learning Focus • Courses in studio art, art history, photography, Italian language. Instruction is offered by professors from the sponsoring institution.
Accommodations • Pensiones. Meals are taken as a group, in central dining facility.
Program Details • Program offered once per year. Session length: 5 weeks. Departures are scheduled in June. The program is open to undergraduate students, graduate students, pre-college students, adults, professionals. Most participants are 19–26 years of age. Other requirements: minimum 2.0 GPA, letter of recommendation from a faculty member, and good academic standing at home institution. 35 participants per session. Application deadline: March 1.
Costs • $3060 for students of consortia schools, $3360 for other students (includes tuition, housing, some meals, excursions, international airfare, International Student Identification card). Application fee: $50.
Contact • Dr. J. Milton Grimes, Executive Director, Kentucky Institute for International Studies, Murray State University, PO Box 9, Murray, KY 42071-0009; 502-762-3091; Fax: 502-762-3434; E-mail: kiismsu@msumusik.mursuky.edu; World Wide Web: http://www.berea.edu/KIIS/kiis.html

LANGUAGE LIAISON

THE ART INSTITUTE OF FLORENCE–ART STUDIES IN FLORENCE

General Information • Arts program with visits to Florence.
Learning Focus • Instruction in the English language. Instruction is offered by professors. This program would appeal to people interested in arts.
Accommodations • Homestays, apartments, pensiones. Single rooms are available.
Program Details • Session length: unlimited. Departures are scheduled throughout the year. Most participants are 18–70 years of age. Participants must be 16 years or older to enroll. Reservations are recommended at least 35 days before departure.
Costs • Contact sponsor for information.
Contact • Nancy Forman, President, Language Liaison, 20533 Biscayne Boulevard-Station 4-162, Miami, FL 33180; 305-682-9909; Fax: 305-682-9907; E-mail: langstudy@aol.com; World Wide Web: http://languageliaison.com

LANGUAGE LIAISON

CENTRO DI LINGUA E CULTURA ITALIANA I MALATESTA–ITALIAN IN ITALY

General Information • Language study program with visits to Rimini, Venice, Florence, Pisa, Ravenna, Verona, San Marino.
Learning Focus • Instruction in the Italian language. Instruction is offered by professors. This program would appeal to people interested in language.
Accommodations • Homestays, locally-rented apartments, hotels, flats, pensiones. Single rooms are available.
Program Details • Session length: unlimited. Departures are scheduled throughout the year. Most participants are 18–70 years of age. Participants must be 16 years or older to enroll. Reservations are recommended at least 35 days before departure.
Costs • Contact sponsor for information.
Contact • Nancy Forman, President, Language Liaison, 20533 Biscayne Boulevard-Station 4-162, Miami, FL 33180; 305-682-9909; Fax: 305-682-9907; E-mail: langstudy@aol.com; World Wide Web: http://languageliaison.com

LANGUAGE LIAISON

CENTRO INTERNAZIONALE DANTE ALIGHERI–LEARN ITALIAN IN SIENA

General Information • Language study program with visits to Siena.
Learning Focus • Instruction in the Italian language. Instruction is offered by professors. This program would appeal to people interested in language.
Accommodations • Homestays, hotels, flats, pensiones. Single rooms are available.
Program Details • Session length: unlimited. Departures are scheduled throughout the year. Most participants are 18–70 years of age. Participants must be 16 years or older to enroll. Reservations are recommended at least 35 days before departure.
Costs • Contact sponsor for information.
Contact • Nancy Forman, President, Language Liaison, 20533 Biscayne Boulevard-Station 4-162, Miami, FL 33180; 305-682-9909; Fax: 305-682-9907; E-mail: langstudy@aol.com; World Wide Web: http://languageliaison.com

LANGUAGE LIAISON

CENTRO LINGUISTICO ITALIANO DANTE ALIGHIERI–LEARN ITALIAN IN FLORENCE

General Information • Language study program with visits to Florence, Florence, Chianti, city visits.
Learning Focus • Instruction in the Italian language. Instruction is offered by professors. This program would appeal to people interested in language.
Accommodations • Homestays, locally-rented apartments, hotels, flats, pensiones. Single rooms are available.
Program Details • Session length: unlimited. Departures are scheduled throughout the year. Program is targeted to students of any age. Most participants are 18–70 years of age. Participants must be 16 years or older to enroll. Reservations are recommended at least 35 days before departure.
Costs • Contact sponsor for information.
Contact • Nancy Forman, President, Language Liaison, 20533 Biscayne Boulevard-Station 4-162, Miami, FL 33180; 305-682-9909; Fax: 305-682-9907; E-mail: langstudy@aol.com; World Wide Web: http://languageliaison.com

LANGUAGE LIAISON

DILIT–LEARN ITALIAN IN ROME

General Information • Language study program with visits to Rome.
Learning Focus • Instruction in the Italian language. Instruction is offered by professors. This program would appeal to people interested in language.
Accommodations • Homestays, locally-rented apartments, hotels. Single rooms are available.
Program Details • Session length: unlimited. Departures are scheduled throughout the year. Most participants are 18–70 years of age. Participants must be 16 years or older to enroll. Reservations are recommended at least 35 days before departure.
Costs • Contact sponsor for information.
Contact • Nancy Forman, President, Language Liaison, 20533 Biscayne Boulevard-Station 4-162, Miami, FL 33180; 305-682-9909; Fax: 305-682-9907; E-mail: langstudy@aol.com; World Wide Web: http://languageliaison.com

LANGUAGE LIAISON

KOINE–LEARN ITALIAN IN FLORENCE, LUCCA, CORTONA, ORBETELLO AND BOLOGNA

General Information • Language study program with visits to Bologna, Cortina, Florence, Lucca, Orbetello.
Learning Focus • Instruction in the Italian language. Instruction is offered by professors. This program would appeal to people interested in language.
Accommodations • Homestays, locally-rented apartments, hotels, flats, pensiones. Single rooms are available.
Program Details • Session length: unlimited. Departures are scheduled throughout the year. Most participants are 18–70 years of age. Participants must be 16 years or older to enroll. Reservations are recommended at least 35 days before departure.
Costs • Contact sponsor for information.
Contact • Nancy Forman, President, Language Liaison, 20533 Biscayne Boulevard-Station 4-162, Miami, FL 33180; 305-682-9909; Fax: 305-682-9907; E-mail: langstudy@aol.com; World Wide Web: http://languageliaison.com

LANGUAGE LIAISON

LINGUADUE–ITALIAN IN MILAN, ITALY

General Information • Language study program with visits to Milan.
Learning Focus • Instruction in the Italian language. Instruction is offered by professors. This program would appeal to people interested in language.
Accommodations • Homestays, locally-rented apartments. Single rooms are available.
Program Details • Session length: unlimited. Departures are scheduled throughout the year. Most participants are 18–70 years of age. Participants must be 16 years or older to enroll. Reservations are recommended at least 35 days before departure.
Costs • Contact sponsor for information.
Contact • Nancy Forman, President, Language Liaison, 20533 Biscayne Boulevard-Station 4-162, Miami, FL 33180; 305-682-9909; Fax: 305-682-9907; E-mail: langstudy@aol.com; World Wide Web: http://languageliaison.com

LANGUAGE LIAISON

LINGUAVIVA–ITALIAN IN FLORENCE

General Information • Language study program with visits to Florence.
Learning Focus • Instruction in the Italian language. Instruction is offered by professors. This program would appeal to people interested in language.
Accommodations • Homestays, locally-rented apartments. Single rooms are available.
Program Details • Session length: unlimited. Departures are scheduled throughout the year. Most participants are 18–70 years of age. Participants must be 16 years or older to enroll. Reservations are recommended at least 35 days before departure.

Costs • Contact sponsor for information.
Contact • Nancy Forman, President, Language Liaison, 20533 Biscayne Boulevard-Station 4-162, Miami, FL 33180; 305-682-9909; Fax: 305-682-9907; E-mail: langstudy@aol.com; World Wide Web: http://languageliaison.com

LANGUAGE LIAISON

LIVE 'N' LEARN (LEARN IN A TEACHER'S HOME)–ITALY

General Information • Language study program with visits to Italy.
Learning Focus • Instruction in the Italian language. Instruction is offered by professors. This program would appeal to people interested in language.
Accommodations • Homestays. Single rooms are available.
Program Details • Session length: unlimited. Departures are scheduled throughout the year. Most participants are 18–70 years of age. Participants must be 16 years or older to enroll. Reservations are recommended at least 35 days before departure.
Costs • Contact sponsor for information.
Contact • Nancy Forman, President, Language Liaison, 20533 Biscayne Boulevard-Station 4-162, Miami, FL 33180; 305-682-9909; Fax: 305-682-9907; E-mail: langstudy@aol.com; World Wide Web: http://languageliaison.com

LANGUAGE LIAISON

LORENZO DE MEDICI–LEARN ITALIAN IN FLORENCE

General Information • Language study program with visits to Florence, Pisa, Venice, Siena, Assisi, San Gimignano.
Learning Focus • Instruction in the Italian language. Instruction is offered by professors. This program would appeal to people interested in language.
Accommodations • Homestays, apartments, pensiones. Single rooms are available.
Program Details • Session length: unlimited. Departures are scheduled throughout the year. Most participants are 18–70 years of age. Participants must be 16 years or older to enroll. Reservations are recommended at least 35 days before departure.
Costs • Contact sponsor for information.
Contact • Nancy Forman, President, Language Liaison, 20533 Biscayne Boulevard-Station 4-162, Miami, FL 33180; 305-682-9909; Fax: 305-682-9907; E-mail: langstudy@aol.com; World Wide Web: http://languageliaison.com

LANGUAGE LIAISON

MICHELANGELO–LEARN ITALIAN IN FLORENCE

General Information • Language study program with visits to Florence, Center of Tuscan agriculture (wine emphasis), Chianti Classico.
Learning Focus • Instruction in the Italian language. Instruction is offered by professors. This program would appeal to people interested in language, cooking.
Accommodations • Homestays, locally-rented apartments, pensiones. Single rooms are available.
Program Details • Session length: unlimited. Departures are scheduled throughout the year. Program is targeted to students of any age. Most participants are 18–70 years of age. Participants must be 16 years or older to enroll. Reservations are recommended at least 35 days before departure.
Costs • Contact sponsor for information.
Contact • Nancy Forman, President, Language Liaison, 20533 Biscayne Boulevard-Station 4-162, Miami, FL 33180; 305-682-9909; Fax: 305-682-9907; E-mail: langstudy@aol.com; World Wide Web: http://languageliaison.com

LANGUAGE STUDIES ABROAD

CENTRO INTERNAZIONALE DANTE ALIGHIERI

General Information • Language study program with visits to Siena. Once at the destination country, participants travel by bus, foot.
Learning Focus • Instruction in the Italian language and art. Museum visits (Siena). Instruction is offered by trained teachers with bachelor's degrees. This program would appeal to people interested in Italian language, art.
Accommodations • Homestays, flats. Single rooms are available for an additional $500–$720 for 4 weeks.
Program Details • Session length: 2 or more weeks. Departures are scheduled throughout the year. Most participants are 16–80 years of age. Participants must be 16 years or older to enroll. 10 participants per session. Application deadline: 3 weeks prior to departure. Reservations are recommended at least 2 months before departure.
Costs • $1000–$1300 (includes tuition, housing, some meals, books and class materials). A $100 deposit is required.
Contact • Charlene Biddulph, Director, Language Studies Abroad, 249 South Highway 101, Suite 226, Solana Beach, CA 92075; 800-424-5522; Fax: 619-943-1201; E-mail: cbiddulph@aol.com; World Wide Web: http://www.dnai.com/~bid/language/

LANGUAGE STUDIES ABROAD

I MALATESTA

General Information • Language study program with visits to Rimini. Once at the destination country, participants travel by bus, foot.
Learning Focus • Instruction in the Italian language. Instruction is offered by trained teachers with bachelor's degrees. This program would appeal to people interested in Italian language.
Accommodations • Homestays. Single rooms are available for an additional $260 for two weeks.
Program Details • Session length: 2 or more weeks. Departures are scheduled throughout the year. Most participants are 16–80 years of age. Participants must be 16 years or older to enroll. 10 participants per session. Application deadline: 3 weeks prior to departure. Reservations are recommended at least 2 months before departure.
Costs • $1035–$2000 for 4 weeks (includes tuition, housing, some meals). A $100 deposit is required.
Contact • Charlene Biddulph, Director, Language Studies Abroad, 249 South Highway 101, Suite 226, Solana Beach, CA 92075; 800-424-5522; Fax: 619-943-1201; E-mail: cbiddulph@aol.com; World Wide Web: http://www.dnai.com/~bid/language/

LANGUAGE STUDIES ABROAD

ISTITUTO MICHELANGELO

General Information • Language study program with visits to Florence. Once at the destination country, participants travel by train, foot.
Learning Focus • Instruction in the Italian language. Museum visits (Florence). Instruction is offered by trained teachers with bachelor's degrees. This program would appeal to people interested in Italian language, art.
Accommodations • Homestays, apartments. Single rooms are available for an additional $430–$760 for 4 weeks.
Program Details • Session length: 2 or more weeks. Departures are scheduled throughout the year. Most participants are 16–80 years of age. Participants must be 16 years or older to enroll. 9 participants per session. Application deadline: 3 weeks prior to departure. Reservations are recommended at least 2 months before departure.
Costs • $1000–$1400 (includes tuition, housing, some meals, books and class materials, excursions). A $100 deposit is required.
Contact • Charlene Biddulph, Director, Language Studies Abroad, 249 South Highway 101, Suite 226, Solana Beach, CA 92075; 800-424-5522; Fax: 619-943-1201; E-mail: cbiddulph@aol.com; World Wide Web: http://www.dnai.com/~bid/language/

LA SABRANENQUE

RESTORATION SESSIONS IN ITALY

General Information • Architectural tour with visits to Gnallo, historical and architectural sites.
Learning Focus • Instruction in architectural restoration. Volunteer work (restoration of village buildings). Instruction is offered by technical supervisors. This program would appeal to people interested in architectural preservation.
Accommodations • Program-owned houses.
Program Details • Program offered once per year. Session length: 2 weeks. Departures are scheduled in August. Most participants are 18–60 years of age. Participants must be 18 years or older to enroll. Other requirements: good health. 4 participants per session. Reservations are recommended at least 3–4 months before departure.
Costs • $490 (includes housing, all meals, excursions). A $150 deposit is required.
Contact • Jacqueline C. Simon, US Correspondent, La Sabranenque, 217 High Park Boulevard, Buffalo, NY 14226; 716-836-8698

LEXIA EXCHANGE INTERNATIONAL

LEXIA IN VENICE

General Information • Academic study program in Venice. Classes are held on the campus of Zambler Institute, University of Venice. Excursions to Florence, Padua, Verona, Rome, Vicenza, Trieste.
Learning Focus • Courses in art history, literature, philosophy, business, Italian language, political science, environmental studies. Instruction is offered by local teachers.
Accommodations • Homestays, locally-rented apartments. Single rooms are available. Meals are taken on one's own, in residences.
Program Details • Program offered 2 times per year. Session length: 4 and 8 weeks. Departures are scheduled in June, July. The program is open to undergraduate students, graduate students, adults. Most participants are 18–70 years of age. Other requirements: minimum 2.5 GPA. Application deadline: April 15.
Costs • $4495 (includes tuition, housing, books and class materials, excursions). Application fee: $30. A $300 deposit is required.
Contact • Justin Meilgaard, Program Coordinator, LEXIA Exchange International, 378 Cambridge Avenue, Palo Alto, CA 94306-1544; 800-775-3942; Fax: 415-327-9192; E-mail: lexia@rquartz.stanford.edu; World Wide Web: http://www.lexiaintl.org

LORENZO DE MEDICI–THE ART INSTITUTE OF FLORENCE

LORENZO DE MEDICI SCHOOL–THE ART INSTITUTE OF FLORENCE

General Information • Arts program in Florence. Classes are held on the campus of Lorenzo de' Medici–Art Institute.
Learning Focus • Courses in studio art, art history, European studies, Italian language. Instruction is offered by professors from the sponsoring institution.
Accommodations • Homestays, locally-rented apartments, apartments. Single rooms are available. Meals are taken on one's own, with host family, in local restaurants, in residences.
Program Details • Program offered 4 times per year. Session length: 4 weeks. Departures are scheduled in May–August. The program is open to undergraduate students, graduate students, pre-college students, adults, high school graduates. Most participants are 18–25 years of age. Other requirements: minimum 2.0 GPA. 300 participants per session. Application deadline: 30 days prior to departure.
Costs • $1000 (includes tuition, books and class materials). A $500 deposit is required.
Contact • Michael Cruciano, US Representative, Lorenzo de Medici–The Art Institute of Florence, 7560 Bodega Avenue, Sebastopol, CA 95472; 707-824-8965; Fax: 707-824-9165; E-mail: cruc@metro.net

LOS ANGELES COMMUNITY COLLEGE DISTRICT

SUMMER SESSION IN FLORENCE

General Information • Language study program in Florence. Classes are held on the campus of Scuola Leonardo da Vinci. Excursions to Venice.
Learning Focus • Courses in Italian language. Instruction is offered by professors from the sponsoring institution and local teachers.
Accommodations • Homestays. Single rooms are available. Meals are taken in local restaurants.
Program Details • Program offered once per year. Session length: 4 weeks. Departures are scheduled in July. The

program is open to undergraduate students, graduate students, pre-college students, adults. Most participants are 17–65 years of age. 20 participants per session. Application deadline: May 1.
Costs • $2650 (includes tuition, housing, some meals, insurance, excursions). A $200 deposit is required.
Contact • International Education Program, Los Angeles Community College District, 770 Wilshire Boulevard, Los Angeles, CA 90017; 213-891-2282; Fax: 213-891-2150; E-mail: intered@laccd.cc.ca.us; World Wide Web: http://laccd.cc.ca.us

LOUISIANA STATE UNIVERSITY

LOUISIANA STATE UNIVERSITY IN FLORENCE

General Information • Academic study program in Florence. Excursions to Siena, Pisa, Vareggio, Rome, Venice.
Learning Focus • Courses in Italian language, art history. Instruction is offered by professors from the sponsoring institution.
Accommodations • Pensiones. Meals are taken as a group, in central dining facility.
Program Details • Program offered once per year. Session length: 6 weeks. Departures are scheduled in May. The program is open to undergraduate students, graduate students. Most participants are 20–25 years of age. Other requirements: minimum 2.5 GPA for 6 hours of credit and a minimum 3.0 GPA for 9 hours of credit. 40 participants per session. Application deadline: March 15.
Costs • $2895 (includes tuition, housing, some meals, excursions). A $200 deposit is required.
Contact • Jeannie Willamson, Study Abroad Coordinator, Louisiana State University, Academic Programs Abroad, 365 Pleasant Hall, Baton Rouge, LA 70803; 504-388-6801; Fax: 504-388-6806; E-mail: abwill@lsuvm.sncc.lsu.edu

LOUISIANA TECH UNIVERSITY

TECH ROME

General Information • Academic study program in Rome. Excursions to Greece, Switzerland, Venice, France, Naples, Tivoli, Ostia.
Learning Focus • Courses in business, art, history, Italian language, archaeology, architecture, speech. Instruction is offered by professors from the sponsoring institution.
Accommodations • Hotels. Meals are taken as a group, in central dining facility.
Program Details • Program offered once per year. Session length: 6 weeks. Departures are scheduled in May. The program is open to undergraduate students, graduate students, adults. Most participants are 18–25 years of age. 130 participants per session. Application deadline: April 1.
Costs • $4328 (includes tuition, housing, all meals, excursions). A $200 deposit is required.
Contact • S. D. Rodakis, Director, Special Programs, Louisiana Tech University, PO Box 3172, Ruston, LA 71272; 800-346-8324; Fax: 318-257-4938; E-mail: techrome@latech.edu

MICHIGAN STATE UNIVERSITY

HISTORY IN ROME

General Information • Academic study program in Rome.
Learning Focus • Courses in history, arts, Italian language, Italian culture, humanities. Instruction is offered by professors from the sponsoring institution.
Accommodations • Locally-rented apartments. Meals are taken on one's own, in residences.
Program Details • Program offered once per year. Session length: 5 weeks. Departures are scheduled in June. The program is open to undergraduate students, graduate students. Most participants are 18–26 years of age. Other requirements: good academic standing and the approval of the instructor. 15 participants per session. Application deadline: March 14.
Costs • $2500 (includes housing, some meals, excursions). Application fee: $75. A $250 deposit is required.
Contact • Brenda S. Sprite, Educational Programs Coordinator, Michigan State University, Office of Study Abroad, 109 International Center, East Lansing, MI 48824-1035; 517-353-8920; Fax: 517-432-2082; E-mail: sprite@pilot.msu.edu; World Wide Web: http://study-abroad.msu.edu

MICHIGAN STATE UNIVERSITY

ITALIAN LANGUAGE, LITERATURE, AND CULTURE PROGRAM

General Information • Language study program in Florence.
Learning Focus • Courses in Italian language, Italian culture, Italian literature. Instruction is offered by professors from the sponsoring institution.
Accommodations • Homestays. Meals are taken with host family, in residences.
Program Details • Program offered once per year. Session length: 6 weeks. Departures are scheduled in May. The program is open to undergraduate students. Most participants are 18–22 years of age. Other requirements: good academic standing and the approval of the instructor. 20 participants per session. Application deadline: March 14.
Costs • $2924 (includes housing, some meals, excursions). Application fee: $75. A $250 deposit is required.
Contact • Brenda S. Sprite, Educational Programs Coordinator, Michigan State University, Office of Study Abroad, 109 International Center, East Lansing, MI 48824-1035; 517-353-8920; Fax: 517-432-2082; E-mail: sprite@pilot.msu.edu; World Wide Web: http://study-abroad.msu.edu

MICHIGAN STATE UNIVERSITY

SOCIAL SCIENCE PROGRAM IN ROME

General Information • Academic study program in Rome.
Learning Focus • Courses in social sciences, anthropology. Instruction is offered by professors from the sponsoring institution.
Accommodations • Hotels. Single rooms are available. Meals are taken on one's own, in local restaurants.
Program Details • Program offered once per year. Session length: 4 weeks. Departures are scheduled in June. The program is open to undergraduate students. Most participants are 18–22 years of age. Other requirements: good

academic standing and the approval of the director. 12 participants per session. Application deadline: March 14.
Costs • $2760 (includes housing, some meals, excursions). Application fee: $75. A $250 deposit is required.
Contact • Brenda S. Sprite, Educational Programs Coordinator, Michigan State University, Office of Study Abroad, 109 International Center, East Lansing, MI 48824-1035; 517-353-8920; Fax: 517-432-2082; E-mail: sprite@pilot.msu.edu; World Wide Web: http://study-abroad.msu.edu

NATIONAL REGISTRATION CENTER FOR STUDY ABROAD

CENTRO CULTURALE GIACOMO PUCCINI

General Information • Language study program in Viareggio.
Learning Focus • Courses in Italian language.
Accommodations • Program-owned apartments. Single rooms are available. Meals are taken on one's own.
Program Details • Program offered 8 times per year. Session length: 2 weeks. Departures are scheduled in June–September. The program is open to undergraduate students, graduate students, adults. 10–12 participants per session. Application deadline: 40 days prior to departure.
Costs • $966 (includes tuition, housing, insurance). Application fee: $40. A $100 deposit is required.
Contact • Reuel Zielke, Coordinator, National Registration Center for Study Abroad, 823 North Second Street, Milwaukee, WI 53203; 414-278-0631; Fax: 414-271-8884; E-mail: inquiries@nrcsa.com; World Wide Web: http://www.nrcsa.com

NATIONAL REGISTRATION CENTER FOR STUDY ABROAD

CENTRO CULTURALE L'OLMO

General Information • Language study program in Portico di Romayna.
Learning Focus • Courses in Italian language.
Accommodations • Program-owned apartments. Single rooms are available. Meals are taken on one's own.
Program Details • Program offered 10 times per year. Session length: 2 weeks. Departures are scheduled in June–October. The program is open to undergraduate students, graduate students, adults. 10–12 participants per session. Application deadline: 40 days prior to departure.
Costs • $813 (includes tuition, housing, insurance). Application fee: $40. A $100 deposit is required.
Contact • Reuel Zielke, Coordinator, National Registration Center for Study Abroad, 823 North Second Street, Milwaukee, WI 53203; 414-278-0631; Fax: 414-271-8884; E-mail: inquiries@nrcsa.com; World Wide Web: http://www.nrcsa.com

NATIONAL REGISTRATION CENTER FOR STUDY ABROAD

CENTRO INTERNAZIONALE DANTE ALIGHERI–SIENA

General Information • Language study program in Siena.
Learning Focus • Courses in Italian language.
Accommodations • Homestays, locally-rented apartments. Single rooms are available. Meals are taken on one's own.
Program Details • Program offered 12 times per year. Session length: 4 weeks. Departures are scheduled in January–December. The program is open to undergraduate students, graduate students, adults. 8–10 participants per session. Application deadline: 40 days prior to departure.
Costs • $695 (includes tuition, insurance). Application fee: $40. A $140 deposit is required.
Contact • Reuel Zielke, Coordinator, National Registration Center for Study Abroad, PO Box 1393, Milwaukee, WI 53201; 414-278-0631; Fax: 414-271-8884; E-mail: quest@nrcsa.com; World Wide Web: http://www.nrcsa.com

NATIONAL REGISTRATION CENTER FOR STUDY ABROAD

LANGUAGE AND CULTURE IN ITALY

General Information • Language study program in Livorno, Pisa.
Learning Focus • Courses in Italian language.
Accommodations • Homestays. Single rooms are available. Meals are taken on one's own.
Program Details • Program offered 15 times per year. Session length: 3 weeks. Departures are scheduled in January–December. The program is open to undergraduate students, graduate students, adults. Application deadline: 40 days prior to departure.
Costs • $935 (includes tuition, housing, some meals, insurance). Application fee: $40. A $100 deposit is required.
Contact • Reuel Zielke, Coordinator, National Registration Center for Study Abroad, PO Box 1393, Milwaukee, WI 53201; 414-278-0631; Fax: 414-271-8884; E-mail: inquiries@nrcsa.com; World Wide Web: http://www.nrcsa.com

NATIONAL REGISTRATION CENTER FOR STUDY ABROAD

SCUOLA LEONARDO DA VINCI

General Information • Language study program in Florence, Rome, Siena.
Learning Focus • Courses in Italian language.
Accommodations • Homestays, program-owned apartments. Single rooms are available. Meals are taken on one's own.
Program Details • Program offered 23 times per year. Session length: 4 weeks. Departures are scheduled in January–December. The program is open to undergraduate students, graduate students, adults. Application deadline: 40 days prior to departure.
Costs • $1270 (includes tuition, housing, some meals, insurance). Application fee: $40. A $100 deposit is required.
Contact • Reuel Zielke, Coordinator, National Registration Center for Study Abroad, PO Box 1393, Milwaukee, WI 53201; 414-278-0631; Fax: 414-271-8884; E-mail: inquiries@nrcsa.com; World Wide Web: http://www.nrcsa.com

NATIONAL REGISTRATION CENTER FOR STUDY ABROAD

TORRE DI BABELE–PISCIOTTA

General Information • Language study program in Pisciotta.
Learning Focus • Courses in Italian language.
Accommodations • Program-owned apartments. Single rooms are available. Meals are taken on one's own, in local restaurants.
Program Details • Program offered 6 times per year. Session length: 2 weeks. Departures are scheduled in July–September. The program is open to undergraduate students, graduate students, adults. 10–12 participants per session. Application deadline: 40 days prior to departure.
Costs • $788 (includes tuition, housing, insurance). Application fee: $40. A $100 deposit is required.
Contact • Reuel Zielke, Coordinator, National Registration Center for Study Abroad, 823 North Second Street, Milwaukee, WI 53203; 414-278-0631; Fax: 414-271-8884; E-mail: inquiries@nrcsa.com; World Wide Web: http://www.nrcsa.com

NATIONAL REGISTRATION CENTER FOR STUDY ABROAD

TORRE DI BABELE–ROME

General Information • Language study program in Rome.
Learning Focus • Courses in Italian language.
Accommodations • Homestays. Single rooms are available.
Program Details • Program offered 23 times per year. Session length: 4 weeks. Departures are scheduled in January–December. The program is open to undergraduate students, graduate students, adults. 10–12 participants per session. Application deadline: 40 days prior to departure.
Costs • Contact sponsor for information. Application fee: $40. A $100 deposit is required.
Contact • Reuel Zielke, Coordinator, National Registration Center for Study Abroad, 823 North Second Street, Milwaukee, WI 53203; 414-278-0631; Fax: 414-271-8884; E-mail: inquiries@nrcsa.com; World Wide Web: http://www.nrcsa.com

NEW YORK UNIVERSITY

GRAPHIC COMMUNICATION MANAGEMENT AND TECHNOLOGY

General Information • Academic study program in Florence.
Learning Focus • Courses in graphic arts, communications. Instruction is offered by professors from the sponsoring institution.
Accommodations • Hotels. Meals are taken as a group, in local restaurants.
Program Details • Program offered once per year. Session length: 1 week. Departures are scheduled in May. The program is open to graduate students. Most participants are 23–45 years of age. Other requirements: BA degree. 13 participants per session. Application deadline: April 1.
Costs • $3000 (includes tuition, housing, some meals). Application fee: $40. A $200 deposit is required.
Contact • Helen J. Kelly, Director of Special Programs, New York University, 82 Washington Square East, Room 62, New York, NY 10003; 212-998-5090; Fax: 212-995-4923; World Wide Web: http://www.nyu.edu/studyabroad

NEW YORK UNIVERSITY

MUSIC

General Information • Academic study program in Pisa. Classes are held on the campus of National Center for Research.
Learning Focus • Courses in music performance, music composition. Instruction is offered by professors from the sponsoring institution and local teachers.
Accommodations • Hotels. Single rooms are available. Meals are taken as a group, in local restaurants.
Program Details • Program offered once per year. Session length: 6 weeks. Departures are scheduled in July. The program is open to graduate students, undergraduate seniors. Most participants are 20–45 years of age. Other requirements: BA degree and an audition. 20 participants per session. Application deadline: April 1.
Costs • $5964 (includes tuition). Application fee: $40. A $200 deposit is required.
Contact • Helen J. Kelly, Director of Special Programs, New York University, 82 Washington Square East, Room 62, New York, NY 10003; 212-998-5090; Fax: 212-995-4923; World Wide Web: http://www.nyu.edu/studyabroad

NEW YORK UNIVERSITY

NEW YORK UNIVERSITY IN FLORENCE: STUDIES IN THE RENAISSANCE

General Information • Academic study program in Florence. Excursions to Pisa, Tuscany.
Learning Focus • Courses in art history, Renaissance studies, Italian language. Instruction is offered by professors from the sponsoring institution.
Accommodations • Hotels. Single rooms are available. Meals are taken as a group.
Program Details • Program offered once per year. Session length: 5 weeks. Departures are scheduled in July. The program is open to undergraduate students, pre-college students. Most participants are 18–21 years of age. Other requirements: minimum 2.75 GPA. 32 participants per session. Application deadline: May 15.
Costs • $3020 (includes tuition, housing, all meals, excursions). Application fee: $20.
Contact • Jenny M. Gibbs, Director, New York University, Arts and Science Summer Programs, 285 Mercer Street, 2nd Floor, New York, NY 10003; 212-998-8175; Fax: 212-995-4177; E-mail: gibbs@is.nyu.edu; World Wide Web: http://www.nyu.edu/studyabroad

NEW YORK UNIVERSITY

STUDIO ART

General Information • Academic study program in Venice. Classes are held on the campus of Venice Institute of Architecture.

Learning Focus • Courses in studio art, ceramics, sculpture. Instruction is offered by professors from the sponsoring institution and local teachers.
Accommodations • Locally-rented apartments. Meals are taken as a group, in local restaurants.
Program Details • Program offered once per year. Session length: 8 weeks. Departures are scheduled in June. The program is open to graduate students. Most participants are 25–45 years of age. Other requirements: BA degree and 20 slides of recent work. 30 participants per session. Application deadline: March 15.
Costs • $5964 (includes tuition). Application fee: $40. A $200 deposit is required.
Contact • Helen J. Kelly, Director of Special Programs, New York University, 82 Washington Square East, Room 62, New York, NY 10003; 212-998-5090; Fax: 212-995-4923; World Wide Web: http://www.nyu.edu/studyabroad

NICHOLLS STATE UNIVERSITY

STUDY PROGRAM ABROAD IN FLORENCE, ITALY

General Information • Academic and language study program in Florence. Classes are held on the campus of Nicholls State University–Florence. Excursions to museums, theater, markets, festivals, sporting events.
Learning Focus • Courses in language study, literature, linguistics, cultural studies, civilizations. Instruction is offered by professors from the sponsoring institution.
Accommodations • Homestays. Single rooms are available. Meals are taken on one's own, with host family, in local restaurants, in residences.
Program Details • Program offered 15 times per year. Session length: 3 weeks–one year. Departures are scheduled in January–December. The program is open to undergraduate students, graduate students, pre-college students, adults. Most participants are 18–55 years of age. 20 participants per session. Application deadline: 30 days prior to departure.
Costs • $1049 for non-credit program, $1344 for 6 hours of college credit (includes tuition, housing, some meals, books and class materials). A $110 deposit is required.
Contact • Dr. Gary McCann, Director of Study Programs Abroad, Nicholls State University, PO Box 2080, Thibodaux, LA 70310; 504-448-4440; Fax: 504-449-7028; E-mail: fl-caw@nich-nsunet.nich.edu

NORTH CAROLINA STATE UNIVERSITY

LANDSCAPE ARCHITECTURE AND URBAN PLANNING IN ITALY–SUMMER

General Information • Academic study program in Gubbio. Excursions to Rome, Pompeii, Assisi, Urbino, Florence, Perugia, Siena.
Learning Focus • Courses in architecture, fine arts, landscape architecture. Instruction is offered by local teachers.
Accommodations • Hotels. Meals are taken as a group, in central dining facility.
Program Details • Program offered once per year. Session length: 6 weeks. Departures are scheduled in June. The program is open to undergraduate students, graduate students, adults. Most participants are 18–50 years of age. 15–20 participants per session. Application deadline: March 1.
Costs • $3650 (includes tuition, housing, some meals, insurance, excursions, international airfare). A $150 deposit is required.
Contact • Ingrid Schmidt, Study Abroad Director, North Carolina State University, 2118 Pullen Hall, Box 7344, Raleigh, NC 27695-7344; 919-515-2087; Fax: 919-515-6021; E-mail: ingrid_schmidt@ncsu.edu; World Wide Web: http://www2.ncsu.edu/ncsu/chass/intstu/abroad.html

NORTHERN ILLINOIS UNIVERSITY

ART AND ARCHITECTURE IN ROME: FROM THE CAESARS TO MUSSOLINI

General Information • Academic study program in Rome. Classes are held on the campus of American University of Rome.
Learning Focus • Courses in art, architecture. Instruction is offered by professors from the sponsoring institution.
Accommodations • Locally-rented apartments. Single rooms are available. Meals are taken on one's own, in local restaurants, in residences.
Program Details • Program offered once per year. Session length: 4 weeks. Departures are scheduled in June. The program is open to undergraduate students, graduate students. Most participants are 21–50 years of age. 15 participants per session. Application deadline: April 15.
Costs • $1600 (includes tuition, housing, insurance, excursions). A $200 deposit is required.
Contact • Anne Seitzinger, Program Coordinator, Short-Term Study Abroad, Northern Illinois University, Study Abroad Office-WI 417, DeKalb, IL 60115; 815-752-0700; Fax: 815-753-0825; E-mail: aseitz@niu.edu; World Wide Web: http://www.niu.edu/depts/intl_prgms/intl.html

PEOPLE TO PEOPLE INTERNATIONAL

ITALY: ITS PEOPLE, CULTURE, AND MUSIC

General Information • Academic study program in Florence, Milan, Rome, Siena, Venice.
Learning Focus • Courses in cultural studies, music.
Accommodations • Hotels. Single rooms are available. Meals are taken as a group, on one's own, in local restaurants.
Program Details • Program offered once per year. Session length: 2 weeks. Departures are scheduled in December. The program is open to undergraduate students, graduate students, pre-college students, adults, all interested students and adults. Most participants are 18–65 years of age. Other requirements: good academic standing. 15–25 participants per session. Application deadline: November 15.
Costs • $2300 (includes tuition, housing, some meals, books and class materials, insurance, excursions, all group travel, cultural programs). A $300 deposit is required.

Contact • Dr. Alan M. Warne, Vice President for Programs, People to People International, 501 East Armour Boulevard, Kansas City, MO 64109; 816-531-4701; Fax: 816-561-7502; E-mail: pepi@cctr.umkc.edu

RAMAPO COLLEGE OF NEW JERSEY

SUMMER STUDY IN ITALY

General Information • Academic study program in Urbino. Classes are held on the campus of University of Urbino. Excursions to Assisi, Gradara, San Leo, Florence, Perugia, San Marino, Siena, Venice.
Learning Focus • Courses in Italian language, Italian Renaissance studies, modern Italy. Instruction is offered by professors from the sponsoring institution.
Accommodations • Dormitories. Meals are taken as a group, in central dining facility.
Program Details • Program offered once per year. Session length: 6 weeks. Departures are scheduled in July. The program is open to undergraduate students, graduate students, pre-college students, adults. Most participants are 17 years of age and older. Other requirements: minimum 2.0 GPA. 46 participants per session. Application deadline: April 29.
Costs • $2800 (includes tuition, housing, all meals, excursions, international airfare). A $300 deposit is required.
Contact • Mrs. Robyn Perricelli, Coordinator, Study Abroad, Ramapo College of New Jersey, 505 Ramapo Valley Road, Mahwah, NJ 07430; 201-529-7463; Fax: 201-529-7508; E-mail: rperrice@ramapo.edu

ROCKLAND COMMUNITY COLLEGE

ITALIAN RENAISSANCE: PRESENCE OF THE PAST

General Information • Academic study program in Florence, Rome.
Learning Focus • Courses in art history, literature. Instruction is offered by professors from the sponsoring institution.
Accommodations • Hotels. Single rooms are available. Meals are taken on one's own, in local restaurants.
Program Details • Program offered once per year. Session length: 2 weeks. Departures are scheduled in June. The program is open to undergraduate students, adults. Most participants are 18–65 years of age. 15–20 participants per session. Application deadline: April 15.
Costs • $2300 (includes tuition, housing, some meals, excursions, international airfare). A $200 deposit is required.
Contact • Jody Dudderar, Coordinator, Study Abroad, Rockland Community College, Suffern, NY 10907; 914-574-4205; Fax: 914-574-4423; E-mail: jdudderar@sunyrockland.edu

ROSARY COLLEGE

SUMMER PROGRAM IN FLORENCE

General Information • Language study program in Florence. Excursions to Siena, Lucca, San Gimignano.
Learning Focus • Courses in art history, drawing, painting, Italian language, political science, Italian history.
Accommodations • Hotels. Meals are taken in local restaurants.
Program Details • Program offered once per year. Session length: 6 weeks. Departures are scheduled in June. The program is open to undergraduate students. Most participants are 18–26 years of age. 40 participants per session. Application deadline: March 1.
Costs • $2650 (includes tuition, housing, some meals, museum fees). A $50 deposit is required.
Contact • Pat Klbecka, Adjunct Director of Study Abroad, Rosary College, 7900 West Division Street, River Forest, IL 60305; 800-828-8475; Fax: 708-366-5360; E-mail: intstudy@email.rosary.edu

---

Rosary College/ASU Summer Program in Florence is an academically oriented, 6-week program of immersion into Italian culture. No prior study of Italian is required since classes in the Italian language are offered at elementary, intermediate, or advanced levels. Additional courses in studio art, art history, politics, and Italian history are taught in English. Florence, the home of Dante, Leonardo da Vinci, and Machiavelli, offers students the very best of Italy. Three-star hotel accommodations are located in the city's center. Art professor Jeffery Cote de Luna invites students to join him for this summer's unforgettable learning experience.

SKIDMORE COLLEGE

SUMMER SCHOOL IN FLORENCE

General Information • Arts program in Florence. Classes are held on the campus of Studio Art Center International (SACI). Excursions to area surrounding Florence.
Learning Focus • Courses in studio art, Italian language, art history. Instruction is offered by professors from the sponsoring institution and local teachers.
Accommodations • Locally-rented apartments. Single rooms are available. Meals are taken on one's own, in local restaurants, in residences.
Program Details • Program offered once per year. Session length: 4–5 weeks. Departures are scheduled in May. The program is open to undergraduate students. Most participants are 19–21 years of age. 15 participants per session. Application deadline: April 1.
Costs • $4400 (includes tuition, housing, excursions, international airfare). Application fee: $80. A $300 deposit is required.
Contact • James Chansky, Director, Summer Special Programs and Summer School, Skidmore College, Office of the Dean of Special Programs, Saratoga Springs, NY 12866; 518-584-5000, ext. 2264; Fax: 518-584-7963; E-mail: jchansky@skidmore.edu; World Wide Web: http://don.skidmore.edu

Skidmore College, in conjunction with Studio Art Centers International (SACI), well established in Florence and enjoying an international reputation as a premier art facility, offers this concentrated, fully accredited, 2 course, 4-week program of study. Students enjoy an educational experience that couples intense studio, classroom, and art historical fieldwork with the rich past of Florence, its artistic resources, and its cultural offerings. Students study various subjects, including studio art, art history, and Italian in the heart of Florence, 100 meters from Michelangelo's Medici Chapel, the Laurentian Library, Fra Angelico's masterpieces in San Marco, and the bustling activity of Florence's colorful central market.

SLIPPERY ROCK UNIVERSITY OF PENNSYLVANIA

ROME SUMMER PROGRAM

General Information • Academic study program in Rome.
Learning Focus • Courses in health issues. Instruction is offered by professors from the sponsoring institution.
Accommodations • Hotels. Single rooms are available. Meals are taken in local restaurants.
Program Details • Program offered once per year. Session length: 2 weeks. Departures are scheduled in June. The program is open to undergraduate students, graduate students, adults. Most participants are 18–30 years of age. Other requirements: 2.5 minimum GPA. 6–12 participants per session. Application deadline: May 1.
Costs • $2695 (includes tuition, housing, some meals, books and class materials, international airfare). A $100 deposit is required.
Contact • Stan Kendziorski, Director of International Studies, Slippery Rock University of Pennsylvania, 110 Eisenberg Building, Slippery Rock, PA 16057; 412-738-2603; Fax: 412-738-2959; E-mail: sjk@sruvm.sru.edu; World Wide Web: http://www.sru.edu

SOUTHERN CONNECTICUT STATE UNIVERSITY

SOUTHERN CONNECTICUT STATE UNIVERSITY IN URBINO, ITALY

General Information • Academic study program in Urbino. Classes are held on the campus of University of Urbino. Excursions to Venice, Rome, Sorrento, Florence, Ravenna.
Learning Focus • Courses in Italian language, art history, studio art, ceramics. Instruction is offered by professors from the sponsoring institution and local teachers.
Accommodations • Homestays, dormitories. Single rooms are available. Meals are taken in central dining facility.
Program Details • Program offered once per year. Session length: 5 or 10 weeks. Departures are scheduled in July. The program is open to undergraduate students, graduate students. Most participants are 18–70 years of age. Other requirements: minimum 2.5 GPA. 30–60 participants per session. Application deadline: March 1.
Costs • $3500 (includes tuition, housing, all meals, excursions, international airfare). Application fee: $150. A $150 deposit is required.
Contact • Dr. Michael Vena, Professor of Foreign Language, Southern Connecticut State University, 501 Crescent Street, New Haven, CT 06515; 203-392-6766; Fax: 203-392-6805

SOUTHERN ILLINOIS UNIVERSITY AT CARBONDALE

THE ANCIENT ROMANS IN ITALY

General Information • Academic study program in Etruria, Florence, Herculaneum, Pompeii, Rome.
Learning Focus • Courses in classics, Roman civilization. Instruction is offered by professors from the sponsoring institution.
Accommodations • Hotels.
Program Details • Program offered once per year. Session length: 3 weeks. Departures are scheduled in May. The program is open to undergraduate students. Most participants are 18–30 years of age. Other requirements: minimum 2.75 GPA. 15–20 participants per session. Application deadline: April 12.
Costs • $2325 (includes housing, books and class materials, insurance, excursions, international airfare). A $100 deposit is required.
Contact • Mr. Thomas A. Saville, Coordinator, Study Abroad Programs, Southern Illinois University at Carbondale, Mailcode 6885, Small Business Incubator, Room 217, Carbondale, IL 62901; 618-453-7670; Fax: 618-453-7677; E-mail: studyabr@siu.edu

SOUTHERN METHODIST UNIVERSITY

ARCHAEOLOGY IN ITALY

General Information • Archaeological tour in Florence. Excursions to Etruria.
Learning Focus • Courses in art history, field methods. Instruction is offered by professors from the sponsoring institution.
Accommodations • Dormitories. Meals are taken as a group.
Program Details • Program offered once per year. Session length: 5 weeks. Departures are scheduled in June. The program is open to undergraduate students. Most participants are 20–23 years of age. Other requirements: minimum 2.5 GPA and sophomore standing. Application deadline: March 15.
Costs • $2600 (includes tuition, housing). A $400 deposit is required.
Contact • Karen Westergaard, Associate Director, Southern Methodist University, Office of International Programs,

Dallas, TX 75275-0391; 214-768-2338; Fax: 214-768-1051; E-mail: intipro@mail.smu.edu; World Wide Web: http://fllcjm.clements.smu.edu

SOUTHERN METHODIST UNIVERSITY

PROGRAM IN ROME

General Information • Academic study program in Rome. Excursions to Switzerland, Orvieto, Tuscany, Florence, Milan, Rome.

Learning Focus • Courses in art history, political science. Instruction is offered by professors from the sponsoring institution.

Accommodations • Dormitories, locally-rented apartments. Meals are taken as a group, in local restaurants.

Program Details • Program offered once per year. Session length: 6 weeks. Departures are scheduled in June. The program is open to undergraduate students. Most participants are 19–23 years of age. Other requirements: minimum 2.5 GPA and sophomore standing. 60 participants per session. Application deadline: March 1.

Costs • $3400 (includes tuition, housing, some meals, excursions). A $400 deposit is required.

Contact • Karen Westergaard, Associate Director, Southern Methodist University, Office of International Programs, Dallas, TX 75275-0391; 214-768-2338; Fax: 214-768-1051; E-mail: intipro@mail.smu.edu; World Wide Web: http://fllcjm.clements.smu.edu

STATE UNIVERSITY OF NEW YORK AT NEW PALTZ

ON-SITE ART HISTORY SUMMER ABROAD PROGRAM

General Information • Academic study program in Rome, Sorrento.

Learning Focus • Courses in art history. Instruction is offered by professors from the sponsoring institution.

Accommodations • Convents, hostels. Meals are taken as a group, in local restaurants.

Program Details • Program offered once per year. Session length: 3 weeks. Departures are scheduled in June. The program is open to undergraduate students, graduate students. Most participants are 18–40 years of age. Other requirements: previous study in art history. 15 participants per session. Application deadline: March 15.

Costs • $1599 for New York residents, $2199 for non-residents (includes tuition, housing, some meals, insurance, excursions). Application fee: $25. A $100 deposit is required.

Contact • Office of International Education, State University of New York at New Paltz, HAB 33, New Paltz, NY 12561; 914-257-3125; Fax: 914-257-3129; E-mail: sillnerb@npvm.newpaltz.edu; World Wide Web: http://www.newpaltz.edu/oie/

STATE UNIVERSITY OF NEW YORK AT NEW PALTZ

SUMMER DANCE PROGRAM

General Information • Academic study program in Urbino. Classes are held on the campus of University of Urbino. Excursions to Rimini, Venice, Florence.

Learning Focus • Courses in dance. Instruction is offered by professors from the sponsoring institution.

Accommodations • Dormitories. Meals are taken as a group, in central dining facility.

Program Details • Program offered once per year. Session length: 4 weeks. Departures are scheduled in July. The program is open to undergraduate students, graduate students, pre-college students, adults. Most participants are 18–35 years of age. Other requirements: prior dance training. 15 participants per session. Application deadline: March 1.

Costs • $2311 (includes tuition, housing, all meals, insurance, excursions, international airfare). Application fee: $25. A $100 deposit is required.

Contact • Office of International Education, State University of New York at New Paltz, HAB 33, New Paltz, NY 12561; 914-257-3125; Fax: 914-257-3129; E-mail: sillnerb@npvm.newpaltz.edu; World Wide Web: http://www.newpaltz.edu/oie/

STATE UNIVERSITY OF NEW YORK AT NEW PALTZ

SUMMER STUDY IN ITALY

General Information • Language study program in Urbino. Classes are held on the campus of University of Urbino. Excursions to Sorrento, Assisi, Florence, Capri, Venice, Rome, Gubbio.

Learning Focus • Courses in Italian language, literature. Instruction is offered by professors from the sponsoring institution and local teachers.

Accommodations • Dormitories. Meals are taken as a group, in central dining facility.

Program Details • Program offered once per year. Session length: 5 weeks. Departures are scheduled in June. The program is open to undergraduate students, graduate students, pre-college students, adults, teachers. Most participants are 18–40 years of age. Other requirements: 1 year of Italian. 15 participants per session. Application deadline: March 15.

Costs • $4060 (includes tuition, housing, all meals, insurance, international airfare). Application fee: $25. A $100 deposit is required.

Contact • Office of International Education, State University of New York at New Paltz, HAB 33, New Paltz, NY 12561; 914-257-3125; Fax: 914-257-3129; E-mail: sillnerb@npvm.newpaltz.edu; World Wide Web: http://www.newpaltz.edu/oie/

STATE UNIVERSITY OF NEW YORK COLLEGE AT BROCKPORT

ART HISTORY IN FAENZA, ITALY

General Information • Academic study program in Faenza.

Learning Focus • Courses in ceramics, art history. Instruction is offered by professors from the sponsoring institution.
Accommodations • Locally-rented apartments. Single rooms are available. Meals are taken on one's own.
Program Details • Program offered once per year. Session length: 3 weeks. Departures are scheduled in July. The program is open to undergraduate students. Most participants are 19–35 years of age. Other requirements: minimum 2.75 GPA. 12 participants per session. Application deadline: May 15.
Costs • $4100 (includes tuition, housing, all meals, international airfare). A $100 deposit is required.
Contact • Dr. John J. Perry, Director, Office of International Education, State University of New York College at Brockport, 350 New Campus Drive, Brockport, NY 14420; 716-395-2119; Fax: 716-637-3218; E-mail: jperry@acspr1.acs.brockport.e; World Wide Web: http://www.brockport.edu/study_abroad

STUDIO ART CENTERS INTERNATIONAL

INTERNATIONAL FLORENCE PROGRAM

General Information • Arts program in Florence. Excursions to Siena, Pisa, Ravenna, San Gimignano, Lucca, Arezzo.
Learning Focus • Courses in studio art, Italian language, photography, printmaking, art history, art conservation, design workshop, ceramics. Instruction is offered by professors from the sponsoring institution.
Accommodations • Locally-rented apartments. Single rooms are available. Meals are taken on one's own, in residences.
Program Details • Program offered 2 times per year. Session length: 4 weeks. Departures are scheduled in May, July. The program is open to undergraduate students, graduate students, pre-college students, adults. Most participants are 18–50 years of age. Other requirements: minimum 2.5 GPA. 75 participants per session. Application deadline: May 15, June 15.
Costs • $3475 (includes tuition, housing, excursions, guest lectures). Application fee: $40.
Contact • Laura Moore, SACI Coordinator, Studio Art Centers International, Institute of International Education U.S. Student Programs, 809 United Nations Plaza, New York, NY 10017; 212-984-5548; Fax: 212-984-5325; E-mail: lmoore@iie.org

SYRACUSE UNIVERSITY

ARCHITECTURE IN FLORENCE

General Information • Academic study program in Florence. Excursions to Rome, Urbino, Verona, Venice, Assisi, Pompeii.

Learning Focus • Courses in architecture, architectural history. Instruction is offered by professors from the sponsoring institution.
Accommodations • Locally-rented apartments. Single rooms are available. Meals are taken on one's own.
Program Details • Program offered once per year. Session length: 9 weeks. Departures are scheduled in June. The program is open to undergraduate students, graduate students. Most participants are 20–28 years of age. Other requirements: minimum 2.7 GPA and three years of architectural design. 10 participants per session. Application deadline: March 15.
Costs • $7169 (includes tuition, housing, some meals, books and class materials, excursions). Application fee: $40. A $350 deposit is required.
Contact • Ms. Daisy Fried, Associate Director, Syracuse University, 119 Euclid Avenue, Syracuse, NY 13244-4170; 315-443-9419; Fax: 315-443-4593; E-mail: dsfried@summon3.syr.edu; World Wide Web: http://sumweb.syr.edu/dipa/dipa9.htm

SYRACUSE UNIVERSITY

EDUCATION IN ITALY: AN INCLUSIVE APPROACH

General Information • Academic study program in Florence, Parma, Rome, Venice.
Learning Focus • Courses in special education. Instruction is offered by professors from the sponsoring institution.
Accommodations • Hotels. Single rooms are available. Meals are taken on one's own, in local restaurants.
Program Details • Program offered once per year. Session length: 4 weeks. Departures are scheduled in May. The program is open to undergraduate students, graduate students, adults. Most participants are 19–50 years of age. Other requirements: minimum 2.8 GPA. 18 participants per session. Application deadline: March 15.
Costs • $4661 (includes tuition, housing, some meals, books and class materials, excursions). Application fee: $40. A $350 deposit is required.
Contact • Ms. Daisy Fried, Associate Director, Syracuse University, 119 Euclid Avenue, Syracuse, NY 13244-4170; 315-443-9419; Fax: 315-443-4593; E-mail: dsfried@summon3.syr.edu; World Wide Web: http://sumweb.syr.edu/dipa/dipa9.htm

SYRACUSE UNIVERSITY

ENVIRONMENTAL DESIGN IN FLORENCE

General Information • Academic study program in Florence.
Learning Focus • Courses in environmental design. Instruction is offered by professors from the sponsoring institution.
Accommodations • Locally-rented apartments. Single rooms are available. Meals are taken on one's own, in residences.
Program Details • Program offered once per year. Session length: 6 weeks. Departures are scheduled in June. Most participants are 19–25 years of age. Other requirements: drawing ability. 20 participants per session. Application deadline: March 15.
Costs • $5616 (includes tuition, housing, some meals, books and class materials, excursions). Application fee: $40. A $350 deposit is required.
Contact • Ms. Daisy Fried, Associate Director, Syracuse University, 119 Euclid Avenue, Syracuse, NY 13244-4170; 315-443-9419; Fax: 315-443-4593; E-mail: dsfried@summon3.syr.edu; World Wide Web: http://sumweb.syr.edu/dipa/dipa9.htm

SYRACUSE UNIVERSITY

HUMANISM AND THE ARTS IN RENAISSANCE ITALY

General Information • Academic study program in Arezzo, Florence, Naples, Pisa, Ravenna, Rome, Urbino, Venice, Vicenza.
Learning Focus • Courses in art history, humanism. Instruction is offered by professors from the sponsoring institution.
Accommodations • Hotels. Single rooms are available. Meals are taken on one's own, in local restaurants.
Program Details • Program offered once per year. Session length: 5 weeks. Departures are scheduled in June. The program is open to undergraduate students, graduate students, adults. Most participants are 19–65 years of age. Other requirements: minimum 2.7 GPA. 25 participants per session. Application deadline: March 15.
Costs • $5900 (includes tuition, housing, some meals, books and class materials, excursions, field trips, museums). A $350 deposit is required.
Contact • Ms. Daisy Fried, Associate Director, Syracuse University, 119 Euclid Avenue, Syracuse, NY 13244-4170; 315-443-9419; Fax: 315-443-4593; E-mail: dsfried@summon3.syr.edu; World Wide Web: http://sumweb.syr.edu/dipa/dipa9.htm

SYRACUSE UNIVERSITY

ITALIAN LANGUAGE AND CULTURE

General Information • Language study program in Florence, Rome, San Gimignano, Siena, Venice.
Learning Focus • Courses in Italian language, art history. Instruction is offered by professors from the sponsoring institution.
Accommodations • Homestays. Single rooms are available. Meals are taken with host family.
Program Details • Program offered once per year. Session length: 6 weeks. Departures are scheduled in June. The program is open to undergraduate students. Most participants are 18–25 years of age. Other requirements: minimum 2.5 GPA. 15 participants per session. Application deadline: March 15.
Costs • $5406 (includes tuition, housing, some meals, excursions). Application fee: $40. A $350 deposit is required.
Contact • Ms. Daisy Fried, Associate Director, Syracuse University, 119 Euclid Avenue, Syracuse, NY 13244-4170; 315-443-9419; Fax: 315-443-4593; E-mail: dsfried@summon3.syr.edu; World Wide Web: http://sumweb.syr.edu/dipa/dipa9.htm

SYRACUSE UNIVERSITY

PRE-ARCHITECTURE IN FLORENCE

General Information • Academic study program in Florence, Lucca, Rome, San Gimignano, Siena, Venice.
Learning Focus • Courses in architecture. Instruction is offered by professors from the sponsoring institution.
Accommodations • Locally-rented apartments. Single rooms are available. Meals are taken on one's own, in residences.
Program Details • Program offered once per year. Session length: 6 weeks. Departures are scheduled in June. The program is open to undergraduate students. Most participants are 19–28 years of age. Other requirements: minimum 2.7 GPA. 18 participants per session. Application deadline: March 15.
Costs • $5321 (includes tuition, housing, some meals, books and class materials, excursions). Application fee: $40. A $350 deposit is required.
Contact • Ms. Daisy Fried, Associate Director, Syracuse University, 119 Euclid Avenue, Syracuse, NY 13244-4170; 315-443-9419; Fax: 315-443-4593; E-mail: dsfried@summon3.syr.edu; World Wide Web: http://sumweb.syr.edu/dipa/dipa9.htm

SYRACUSE UNIVERSITY

VISUAL ARTS IN FLORENCE

General Information • Academic study program in Florence, Rome, Venice.
Learning Focus • Courses in painting, art history, fibers, photography, metalsmithing, restoration. Instruction is offered by professors from the sponsoring institution.
Accommodations • Locally-rented apartments. Single rooms are available. Meals are taken on one's own, in residences.
Program Details • Program offered once per year. Session length: 6 weeks. Departures are scheduled in June. The program is open to undergraduate students. Most participants are 18–55 years of age. Other requirements: minimum 2.5 GPA. 25 participants per session. Application deadline: March 15.
Costs • $5321 (includes tuition). Application fee: $40. A $350 deposit is required.
Contact • Ms. Daisy Fried, Associate Director, Syracuse University, 119 Euclid Avenue, Syracuse, NY 13244-4170; 315-443-9419; Fax: 315-443-4593; E-mail: dsfried@summon3.syr.edu; World Wide Web: http://sumweb.syr.edu/dipa/dipa9.htm

TEMPLE UNIVERSITY

ARCHITECTURE WORKSHOP IN ROME

General Information • Academic study program in Rome.
Learning Focus • Courses in architecture. Instruction is offered by professors from the sponsoring institution.
Accommodations • Locally-rented apartments. Meals are taken on one's own, in residences.
Program Details • Program offered once per year. Session length: 6 weeks. Departures are scheduled in June. The program is open to undergraduate students, graduate students. Other requirements: minimum 2.5 GPA. 10 participants per session. Application deadline: March 1.
Costs • $3110–$3716 (includes tuition, housing, excursions, international airfare). Application fee: $30. A $100 deposit is required.
Contact • Denise A. Connerty, Interim Director of International Programs, Temple University, Conwell Hall, 5th Floor, Suite 501, Philadelphia, PA 19122; 215-204-4684; Fax: 215-204-5735; E-mail: intlprog@vm.temple.edu; World Wide Web: http://www.temple.edu/intlprog/

TEMPLE UNIVERSITY

ART AND CULTURE SEMINAR

General Information • Academic study program in Rome.
Learning Focus • Courses in cultural criticism, literary criticism. Instruction is offered by professors from the sponsoring institution.
Accommodations • Locally-rented apartments. Meals are taken on one's own, in residences.
Program Details • Program offered once per year. Session length: 4 weeks. Departures are scheduled in June. The program is open to undergraduate students, graduate students. Other requirements: must be advanced undergraduate students. 15–20 participants per session. Application deadline: March 15.
Costs • $2564–$3242 (includes tuition, housing, excursions). Application fee: $30. A $100 deposit is required.
Contact • Denise A. Connerty, Interim Director of International Programs, Temple University, Conwell Hall, 5th Floor, Suite 501, Philadelphia, PA 19122; 215-204-4684; Fax: 215-204-5735; E-mail: intlprog@vm.temple.edu; World Wide Web: http://www.temple.edu/intlprog/

TEMPLE UNIVERSITY

INTERNATIONAL BUSINESS SEMINAR IN ROME

General Information • Academic study program in Rome.
Learning Focus • Courses in international business, marketing. Instruction is offered by professors from the sponsoring institution.
Accommodations • Locally-rented apartments. Meals are taken on one's own, in residences.
Program Details • Program offered once per year. Session length: 5 weeks. Departures are scheduled in May. The program is open to undergraduate students. Other requirements: minimum 2.5 GPA. 10–20 participants per session. Application deadline: March 1.
Costs • $2000–$2600 (includes tuition, housing). Application fee: $30. A $100 deposit is required.
Contact • Denise A. Connerty, Interim Director of International Programs, Temple University, Conwell Hall, 5th Floor, Suite 501, Philadelphia, PA 19122; 215-204-4684; Fax: 215-204-5735; E-mail: intlprog@vm.temple.edu; World Wide Web: http://www.temple.edu/intlprog/

TEMPLE UNIVERSITY

ROME SUMMER SESSION

General Information • Academic study program in Rome.

Learning Focus • Courses in art history, Italian language, Italian history, classics. Instruction is offered by professors from the sponsoring institution.
Accommodations • Locally-rented apartments. Meals are taken on one's own, in residences.
Program Details • Program offered once per year. Session length: 6 weeks. Departures are scheduled in June. The program is open to undergraduate students. Other requirements: minimum 2.5 GPA. 20 participants per session. Application deadline: March 15.
Costs • $2500–$3200 (includes tuition, housing). Application fee: $30. A $150 deposit is required.
Contact • Denise A. Connerty, Interim Director of International Programs, Temple University, Conwell Hall, 5th Floor, Suite 501, Philadelphia, PA 19122; 215-204-4684; Fax: 215-204-5735; E-mail: intlprog@vm.temple.edu; World Wide Web: http://www.temple.edu/intlprog/

 TRAVELEARN

AN ITALIAN ODYSSEY

General Information • Cultural tour with visits to Assisi, Florence, Milan/Lake Maggorio, Pisa, Rome, Venice. Once at the destination country, participants travel by bus, foot. Program is affiliated with the nationwide TraveLearn network of 290 universities and colleges.
Learning Focus • Instruction in history, art and religion. Museum visits (Vatican Museum, The Accademia, Uffizi Gallery). Instruction is offered by professors, historians. This program would appeal to people interested in history, religion, art, culture.
Accommodations • Hotels. Single rooms are available for an additional $895.
Program Details • Program offered 4 times per year. Session length: 15 days. Departures are scheduled in February, April, July, November. Program is targeted to mature adults. Most participants are 40–75 years of age. Participants must be 18 years or older to enroll. 14–20 participants per session. Application deadline: 60 days prior to departure. Reservations are recommended at least 4–8 months before departure.
Costs • $4395 (includes housing, all meals, books and class materials, excursions, international airfare). A $300 deposit is required.
Contact • Keith Williams, Director of Marketing, TraveLearn, PO Box 315, Lakeville, PA 18438; 800-235-9114; Fax: 717-226-9114; E-mail: travelearn@aol.com

 TRINITY COLLEGE

SUMMER PROGRAM

General Information • Academic study program in Rome. Classes are held on the campus of Trinity College.
Learning Focus • Courses in art history, Italian language, Roman civilization, Italian history. Instruction is offered by professors from the sponsoring institution.
Accommodations • Dormitories. Meals are taken as a group, in central dining facility.
Program Details • Program offered once per year. Session length: 6 weeks. Departures are scheduled in June. The program is open to undergraduate students. Most participants are 18–22 years of age. Other requirements: good academic standing. 20 participants per session. Application deadline: rolling.
Costs • $3695 (includes tuition, housing, some meals, books and class materials, excursions). Application fee: $50. A $450 deposit is required.
Contact • Sandy Andrews, Administrative Assistant, Italian Programs, Trinity College, Box 702533, 300 Summit Street, Hartford, CT 06106-3100; 203-297-2562; Fax: 203-297-2257; E-mail: sandra.andrews@mail.trincoll.edu; World Wide Web: http://www.trincoll.edu/

 UNIVERSITY OF COLORADO AT BOULDER

ART HISTORY IN ITALY

General Information • Academic study program in Florence, Rome, Venice.
Learning Focus • Courses in art history. Instruction is offered by professors from the sponsoring institution.
Accommodations • Hotels, pensiones. Meals are taken on one's own, in local restaurants.
Program Details • Program offered once per year. Session length: 5 weeks. Departures are scheduled in June. The program is open to undergraduate students. Most participants are 19–26 years of age. Other requirements: minimum 2.75 GPA and an art history background. 20–30 participants per session. Application deadline: March 1.
Costs • $3350 for Colorado residents, $4100 for nonresidents (includes tuition, housing, some meals, insurance, excursions). A $300 deposit is required.
Contact • Study Abroad Program, University of Colorado at Boulder, International Education, Campus Box 123, Boulder, CO 80309-0123; 303-492-7741; Fax: 303-492-5185; E-mail: studyabr@colorado.edu; World Wide Web: http://www.colorado.edu/OIE/StudyAbroad

UNIVERSITY OF DAYTON

ISSAP '97–FLORENCE

General Information • Academic study program in Florence.
Learning Focus • Courses in visual arts, music. Instruction is offered by professors from the sponsoring institution.
Accommodations • Locally-rented apartments. Meals are taken as a group, in residences.
Program Details • Program offered once per year. Session length: 4 weeks. Departures are scheduled in May. The program is open to undergraduate students. Most participants are 18–21 years of age. Other requirements: minimum 2.0 GPA. 25 participants per session. Application deadline: April 15.
Costs • $3100 (includes tuition, housing, some meals, excursions, International Student Identification card). A $75 deposit is required.
Contact • DeVonda Vanderpool, Coordinator, International Education Programs, University of Dayton, Dayton, OH 45469-1481; 513-229-3728; Fax: 513-229-2766; E-mail: vanderpo@trinity.udayton.edu; World Wide Web: http://www.udayton.edu/~cip

UNIVERSITY OF DELAWARE

WINTER SESSION IN ITALY

General Information • Academic study program in Rome, Venice. Excursions to Bologna, Naples, Florence, Rome, Milan, Siena, Trente, Venice.
Learning Focus • Courses in political science, political science. Instruction is offered by professors from the sponsoring institution.
Accommodations • Hotels.
Program Details • Program offered once per year. Session length: 5 weeks. Departures are scheduled in January. The program is open to undergraduate students. Other requirements: minimum 2.0 GPA. Application deadline: October.
Costs • Contact sponsor for information. A $200 deposit is required.
Contact • International Programs and Special Sessions, University of Delaware, 4 Kent Way, Newark, DE 19716-1450; 888-831-4685; Fax: 302-831-6042; E-mail: studyabroad@mvs.udel.edu

UNIVERSITY OF DELAWARE

WINTER SESSION IN SIENA, ITALY

General Information • Academic study program in Siena. Classes are held on the campus of University of Italian Studies for Foreigners Siena.
Learning Focus • Courses in civilizations, cultural studies, Italian language. Instruction is offered by professors from the sponsoring institution.
Accommodations • Pensiones.
Program Details • Program offered once per year. Session length: 5 weeks. Departures are scheduled in January. The program is open to undergraduate students. Other requirements: minimum 2.0 GPA and 1 semester of college-level Italian. Application deadline: October.
Costs • $4050 (includes tuition, housing, all meals, excursions, international airfare). A $200 deposit is required.
Contact • International Programs and Special Sessions, University of Delaware, 4 Kent Way, Newark, DE 19716-1450; 888-831-4685; Fax: 302-831-6042; E-mail: studyabroad@mvs.udel.edu

UNIVERSITY OF FLORIDA

CONSERVATORIO DI MUSICA, CASTELFRANCO-VENETO, ITALY

General Information • Performing arts program in Castelfranco, Veneto. Classes are held on the campus of University of Florida, College of Fine Arts. Excursions to Cittadella, Mount Grappa, Aslo.
Learning Focus • Courses in voice, music history, Italian language, opera, literature. Instruction is offered by professors from the sponsoring institution and local teachers.
Accommodations • Dormitories. Meals are taken as a group, on one's own, in local restaurants, in residences.
Program Details • Program offered once per year. Session length: 5 weeks. Departures are scheduled in July. The program is open to undergraduate students, graduate students, adults. Most participants are 18–25 years of age. Other requirements: minimum 2.5 GPA. 15 participants per session. Application deadline: March 15.
Costs • $3500 (includes tuition, housing, some meals, excursions, orientation). Application fee: $250.
Contact • Overseas Studies, University of Florida, 123 Tigert Hall, PO Box 113225, Gainesville, FL 32611-3225; 352-392-5206; Fax: 352-392-5575; E-mail: ovrseas@nervm.nerdc.ufl.edu

UNIVERSITY OF FLORIDA

ROME ITALIAN CULTURE AND LANGUAGE PROGRAM, ROME, ITALY

General Information • Culture and language study program in Rome. Excursions to Naples, Florence.
Learning Focus • Courses in art, anthropology, Italian language. Instruction is offered by professors from the sponsoring institution.
Accommodations • Dormitories, program-owned apartments. Meals are taken on one's own, in central dining facility, in local restaurants, in residences.
Program Details • Program offered once per year. Session length: 6 weeks. Departures are scheduled in May. The program is open to undergraduate students, graduate students, adults. Other requirements: minimum 2.5 GPA and must have completed freshman year. 35 participants per session. Application deadline: March 15.
Costs • $3300 (includes tuition, housing, some meals, excursions). Application fee: $250.
Contact • Overseas Studies, University of Florida, 123 Tigert Hall, PO Box 113225, Gainesville, FL 32611-3225; 352-392-5206; Fax: 352-392-5575; E-mail: ovrseas@nervm.nerdc.ufl.edu

UNIVERSITY OF GEORGIA

STUDY ABROAD PROGRAM IN CORTONA, ITALY

General Information • Academic study program in Cortona. Excursions to Rome, Venice, Florence, Brussels, Naples, Siena, Perugia, Urbino.
Learning Focus • Courses in art history, painting, photography, ceramics, sculpture, book arts, jewelry, Italian language, drawing, papermaking. Instruction is offered by professors from the sponsoring institution.
Accommodations • Dormitory-style rentals, hotels. Meals are taken as a group, in central dining facility.
Program Details • Program offered 3 times per year. Session length: 10 weeks. Departures are scheduled in March, June, September. The program is open to undergraduate students, graduate students, adults with college degrees. Most participants are 19–65 years of age. Other requirements: minimum 2.5 GPA. 40–90 participants per session. Application deadline: January 10, April 10, June 10.
Costs • $5880 (includes tuition, housing, some meals, excursions, international airfare). A $100 deposit is required.
Contact • Laura Patrick, Secretary for Admissions, University of Georgia, School of Art, Visual Arts Building, Athens, GA 30602-4102; 706-542-7011; Fax: 706-542-2467; E-mail: cortona@uga.cc.uga.edu

UNIVERSITY OF KANSAS

ARCHITECTURAL STUDIES IN SPANNOCCHIA

General Information • Academic study program in Spannocchia. Classes are held on the campus of Etruscan Foundation. Excursions to Siena, Florence, Venice, small towns in countryside.

Learning Focus • Courses in architectural field studies, architectural history. Instruction is offered by professors from the sponsoring institution.

Accommodations • Castello di Spannocchia. Meals are taken as a group, in residences.

Program Details • Program offered once per year. Session length: 4 weeks. Departures are scheduled in May. The program is open to undergraduate students. Most participants are 20–26 years of age. Other requirements: architecture major. 12 participants per session. Application deadline: March 1.

Costs • $1850 (includes tuition, housing, some meals, excursions, admissions to group cultural activities). Application fee: $15. A $300 deposit is required.

Contact • Susan MacNally, Coordinator of Summer Institutes, University of Kansas, Office of Study Abroad, 203 Lippincott Hall, Lawrence, KS 66045; 913-864-3742; Fax: 913-864-5040; E-mail: osa@falcon.cc.ukans.edu; World Wide Web: http://kuhub.cc.ukans.edu/~intlstdy/osa/osamain.html

UNIVERSITY OF KANSAS

DESIGN STUDIES IN ITALY

General Information • Academic study program in Milan, Rome. Classes are held on the campus of Instituto Europeo di Design. Excursions to Venice, east coast of Italy, Florence.

Learning Focus • Courses in design, design history. Instruction is offered by professors from the sponsoring institution and local teachers.

Accommodations • Dormitories, hotels, student residences. Meals are taken as a group, on one's own, in local restaurants.

Program Details • Program offered once per year. Session length: 4 weeks. Departures are scheduled in May. The program is open to undergraduate students. Most participants are 21–25 years of age. Other requirements: open to students of visual, interior, industrial design, or fine arts programs. 15 participants per session. Application deadline: March 1.

Costs • $4002 (includes tuition, housing, all meals, group cultural admissions and activities, transportation during tour). Application fee: $15. A $300 deposit is required.

Contact • Susan MacNally, Coordinator of Summer Institutes, University of Kansas, Office of Study Abroad, 203 Lippincott Hall, Lawrence, KS 66045; 913-864-3742; Fax: 913-864-5040; E-mail: osa@falcon.cc.ukans.edu; World Wide Web: http://kuhub.cc.ukans.edu/~intlstdy/osa/osamain.html

UNIVERSITY OF KANSAS

ITALIAN LANGUAGE AND CULTURE IN FLORENCE, ITALY

General Information • Language study program in Florence. Classes are held on the campus of Centro Linguistico Italiano Dante Alighieri.

Learning Focus • Courses in Italian language, Italian culture, civilizations, Italian literature. Instruction is offered by professors from the sponsoring institution and local teachers.

Accommodations • Homestays. Meals are taken on one's own, with host family, in local restaurants, in residences.

Program Details • Program offered 2 times per year. Session length: 4–8 weeks. Departures are scheduled in June, July. The program is open to undergraduate students, graduate students, adults. Most participants are 19–33 years of age. Other requirements: one year of college-level Italian recommended. 20 participants per session. Application deadline: March 1.

Costs • $2364 (includes tuition, housing, some meals). Application fee: $15. A $300 deposit is required.

Contact • Susan MacNally, Coordinator of Summer Institutes, University of Kansas, Office of Study Abroad, 203 Lippincott Hall, Lawrence, KS 66045; 913-864-3742; Fax: 913-864-5040; E-mail: osa@falcon.cc.ukans.edu; World Wide Web: http://kuhub.cc.ukans.edu/~intlstdy/osa/osamain.html

UNIVERSITY OF KANSAS

MUSIC, ART, AND HISTORY OF ROME

General Information • Academic study program in Rome. Excursions to Naples, Palestrina, Ostia-Antigua, Pompeii.

Learning Focus • Courses in music history, ancient history, art history. Instruction is offered by professors from the sponsoring institution.

Accommodations • Pensiones. Meals are taken as a group, in central dining facility.

Program Details • Program offered once per year. Session length: 3 weeks. Departures are scheduled in June. The program is open to undergraduate students, graduate students, adults. Most participants are 18–35 years of age. 30 participants per session. Application deadline: March 1.

Costs • $2450 (includes tuition, housing, all meals, excursions, cultural events). Application fee: $15. A $300 deposit is required.

Contact • Susan MacNally, Coordinator of Summer Institutes, University of Kansas, Office of Study Abroad, 203 Lippincott Hall, Lawrence, KS 66045; 913-864-3742; Fax: 913-864-5040; E-mail: osa@falcon.cc.ukans.edu; World Wide Web: http://kuhub.cc.ukans.edu/~intlstdy/osa/osamain.html

UNIVERSITY OF MICHIGAN

SUMMER PROGRAM IN FLORENCE, ITALY

General Information • Academic study program in Florence.

Learning Focus • Courses in art history, studio art, architectural history, Italian language. Instruction is offered by professors from the sponsoring institution.

Accommodations • Villa. Single rooms are available. Meals are taken as a group, in central dining facility.

Program Details • Program offered once per year. Session length: 6 weeks. Departures are scheduled in June. The program is open to undergraduate students. Most participants are 19–22 years of age. Other requirements: minimum 3.0 GPA. 45 participants per session. Application deadline: February 28.

Costs • $4700–$4900 (includes tuition, housing, all meals, excursions). Application fee: $50. A $250 deposit is required.
Contact • Office of International Programs, University of Michigan, G-513 Michigan Union, 530 South State Street, Ann Arbor, MI 48109-1349; 313-764-4311; Fax: 313-764-3229; E-mail: oip@umich.edu; World Wide Web: http://www.umich.edu/~iinet/oip/

UNIVERSITY OF NEW ORLEANS

BRUNNENBURG ANTHROPOLOGY FIELD STUDY

General Information • Academic study program in Merano. Excursions to South Tyrol.
Learning Focus • Courses in anthropology. Instruction is offered by professors from the sponsoring institution.
Accommodations • Castle. Single rooms are available. Meals are taken as a group, in central dining facility.
Program Details • Program offered once per year. Session length: 4 weeks. Departures are scheduled in June. The program is open to undergraduate students, graduate students, adults. Most participants are 20–30 years of age. 15 participants per session. Application deadline: April 1.
Costs • $1895 (includes tuition, housing, some meals, insurance, excursions). A $100 deposit is required.
Contact • Margaret Davidson, Coordinator, University of New Orleans, PO Box 1315, New Orleans, LA 70148; 504-280-7116; Fax: 504-280-7317; World Wide Web: http://www.uno.edu/~inst/Welcome.html

UNIVERSITY OF NORTH CAROLINA AT CHARLOTTE

ARCHITECTURAL DESIGN STUDIO AND FIELD STUDY IN ITALY

General Information • Academic study program in Tuscany. Excursions to Venice, Rome, Vicenza, Florence, Milan.
Learning Focus • Courses in architecture. Instruction is offered by professors from the sponsoring institution.
Accommodations • Locally-rented apartments. Meals are taken as a group.
Program Details • Program offered once per year. Session length: 6 weeks. Departures are scheduled in May. The program is open to undergraduate students, graduate students. Other requirements: previous architectural studies. Application deadline: October.
Costs • $3600 (includes tuition, housing, books and class materials, insurance, excursions).
Contact • Elizabeth A. Adams, Director of Education Abroad Programs, University of North Carolina at Charlotte, Office of International Programs, 9201 University City Boulevard, Charlotte, NC 28223-0001; 704-547-2464; Fax: 704-547-3168; E-mail: eaadams@email.uncc.edu; World Wide Web: http://unccvm.uncc.edu

UNIVERSITY OF PENNSYLVANIA

BRYN MAWR–UNIVERSITY OF PENNSYLVANIA ITALIAN STUDIES SUMMER INSTITUTE IN FLORENCE

General Information • Academic study program in Florence.
Learning Focus • Courses in Italian language, Italian literature, Italian culture, art history. Instruction is offered by professors from the sponsoring institution.
Accommodations • Hotels. Meals are taken on one's own, in local restaurants, in residences.
Program Details • Program offered once per year. Session length: 5½ weeks. Departures are scheduled in June. The program is open to undergraduate students, graduate students. Most participants are 18–35 years of age. 52 participants per session. Application deadline: March 15.
Costs • $5000 (includes tuition, housing, some meals, insurance, excursions, international airfare). Application fee: $50. A $400 deposit is required.
Contact • Elizabeth Sachs, Director, Penn Summer Abroad, University of Pennsylvania, 3440 Market Street, Suite 100, Philadelphia, PA 19104-3335; 215-898-5738; Fax: 215-573-2053; E-mail: esachs@mail.sas.upenn.edu

UNIVERSITY OF ROCHESTER

ITALIAN IN ITALY

General Information • Language study program in Padua.
Learning Focus • Courses in language study. Instruction is offered by professors from the sponsoring institution.
Accommodations • Homestays. Meals are taken with host family, in residences.
Program Details • Program offered once per year. Session length: 4 weeks. Departures are scheduled in May. The program is open to undergraduate students, adults. Most participants are 18–25 years of age. Other requirements: previous Italian language study, either 3 years high school or 1 year college. 8–10 participants per session. Application deadline: March 15.
Costs • $2650 (includes tuition, housing, some meals, excursions).
Contact • Anne Lutkus, Language Coordinator, University of Rochester, Department of Modern Languages and Cultures, Rochester, NY 14627; 716-275-4251; E-mail: adlt@db1.cc.rochester.edu; World Wide Web: http://www.rochester.edu/College/study-abroad/

UNIVERSITY OF TULSA

SUMMER ART IN ITALY

General Information • Academic study program in Montone. Excursions to Rome, Florence.
Learning Focus • Courses in studio art. Instruction is offered by professors from the sponsoring institution.
Accommodations • Convent, monastery. Single rooms are available. Meals are taken as a group, in local restaurants.
Program Details • Program offered once per year. Session length: 4 weeks. Departures are scheduled in May. The program is open to undergraduate students, graduate students, adults. Most participants are 18–70 years of age. Other requirements: motivated studio artists. 15 participants per session. Application deadline: March 15.

Costs • $3850 (includes tuition, housing, some meals, books and class materials, excursions, international airfare). A $500 deposit is required.

Contact • Sally Luplow, Director of Study Abroad, University of Tulsa, 600 South College Avenue, TH 102, Tulsa, OK 74104-3189; 918-631-3229; Fax: 918-631-3187; E-mail: luplowsr@centum.utulsa.edu

The University of Tulsa School of Art again offers its art program in Montone, Italy, in the summer of 1997. This is an opportunity to study art in an area of great artistic traditions. Located in central Umbria, the medieval hill town of Montone serves as the residence and base of operations for a 4-week workshop on painting and drawing from the landscape. Montone's central location makes it ideal for field trips to nearby art centers and museums that exhibit some of Italy's best-known monuments and masters. The program includes excursions to Rome and Florence.

UNIVERSITY OF WISCONSIN–MADISON

PROGRAM IN ITALY

General Information • Language study program in Perugia. Classes are held on the campus of University of Italian Studies for Foreigners Perugia. Excursions to Assisi, Spoleto, Florence, Todi, Siena.

Learning Focus • Courses in Italian language, Renaissance civilization. Instruction is offered by local teachers.

Accommodations • Locally-rented apartments. Single rooms are available. Meals are taken on one's own, in central dining facility.

Program Details • Program offered once per year. Session length: 8 weeks. Departures are scheduled in May. The program is open to undergraduate students. Other requirements: sophomore standing. 17–25 participants per session. Application deadline: first Friday in March.

Costs • $4230–$4680 (includes tuition, housing, all meals, international airfare, local transportation, personal and miscellaneous expenses). A $100 deposit is required.

Contact • Peer Advisors, Office of International Studies and Programs, University of Wisconsin–Madison, 261 Bascom Hall, 500 Lincoln Drive, Madison, WI 53706; 608-265-6329; Fax: 608-262-6998; E-mail: abroad@macc.wisc.edu; World Wide Web: http://www.wisc.edu/uw-oisp/

UNIVERSITY STUDIES ABROAD CONSORTIUM

BUSINESS, ECONOMICS, AND ITALIAN STUDIES IN TURIN, ITALY

General Information • Academic study program in Turin. Classes are held on the campus of University of Turin. Excursions to Milan, Italian Riviera, Florence.

Learning Focus • Courses in Italian language, corporate finance, government and politics, management, international marketing, art history, economics, history. Instruction is offered by local teachers.

Accommodations • Locally-rented apartments. Single rooms are available. Meals are taken on one's own, in central dining facility.

Program Details • Program offered 2 times per year. Session length: 3 weeks. Departures are scheduled in June. The program is open to undergraduate students, graduate students, pre-college students, adults. Most participants are 18–50 years of age. Other requirements: minimum 2.5 GPA. 25 participants per session. Application deadline: April 15.

Costs • $1570 (includes tuition, housing, insurance, excursions, International Student Identification card). Application fee: $50. A $150 deposit is required.

Contact • Dr. Carmelo Urza, Director, University Studies Abroad Consortium, University of Nevada Library/323, Reno, NV 89557-0093; 702-784-6569; Fax: 702-784-6010; E-mail: usac@equinox.unr.edu; World Wide Web: http://www.scs.unr.edu/~usac

VILLANOVA UNIVERSITY

SUMMER ITALIAN LANGUAGE AND LITERATURE PROGRAM

General Information • Language study program in Florence, Urbino. Classes are held on the campus of University of Urbino, Lorenzo de' Medici School. Excursions to Ravenna, Venice, Perugia, Florence, Rome.

Learning Focus • Courses in Italian civilization, Italian literature. Instruction is offered by local teachers.

Accommodations • Dormitories, locally-rented apartments. Meals are taken as a group, in central dining facility, in local restaurants.

Program Details • Program offered once per year. Session length: 6 weeks. Departures are scheduled in July. The program is open to undergraduate students. Most participants are 19–23 years of age. Other requirements: minimum 2.5 GPA, university or college student status and good academic standing. 15 participants per session. Application deadline: March 1.

Costs • $3150 (includes tuition, housing, all meals, books and class materials, excursions, transfers and orientation). Application fee: $100.

Contact • Dr. Thomas M. Ricks, Director, International Studies, Villanova University, St. Augustine Center, Room 415, Villanova, PA 19085; 610-519-6412; Fax: 610-519-7649; E-mail: ricks@ucis.vill.edu

VILLANOVA UNIVERSITY AND ROSEMONT COLLEGE

SUMMER PROGRAM IN ITALY

General Information • Academic study program in Florence, Rome, Siena, Venice, Vicenza. Classes are held on the campus of University of Siena. Excursions to Viterbo.

Learning Focus • Courses in Italian language, history, art history. Instruction is offered by professors from the sponsoring institution.

Accommodations • Hotels. Single rooms are available. Meals are taken as a group, in central dining facility.
Program Details • Program offered once per year. Session length: 30 days. Departures are scheduled in June. The program is open to undergraduate students, adults, pre-college seniors. Most participants are 18–68 years of age. Other requirements: minimum 2.5 GPA. 65 participants per session. Application deadline: April 1.
Costs • $2780 (includes tuition, all meals, excursions, instruction in museums, galleries, churches). Application fee: $100. A $100 deposit is required.
Contact • George Radan, Professor, Villanova University and Rosemont College, 42 Haverford Road, Wynnewood, PA 19096; 610-519-4610; Fax: 610-519-7749

VOYAGERS INTERNATIONAL

PHOTOGRAPHIC TOUR AND WORKSHOP IN ITALY

General Information • Photography tour with visits to Tuscany, Venice. Once at the destination country, participants travel by foot, small vehicle.
Learning Focus • Instruction in photography. Nature observation (wildlife and scenery). Instruction is offered by photographers. This program would appeal to people interested in photography, culture, nature studies.
Accommodations • Hotels, lodges. Single rooms are available.
Program Details • Program offered 3 times per year. Session length: 10–12 days. Departures are scheduled in May, June, September. Program is targeted to photography enthusiasts. Most participants are 30–70 years of age. 8–10 participants per session. Reservations are recommended at least 6–12 months before departure.
Costs • $2000 (includes tuition, housing, some meals, excursions). A $400 deposit is required.
Contact • David Blanton, Managing Director, Voyagers International, PO Box 915, Ithaca, NY 14851; 800-633-0299; Fax: 607-273-3873; E-mail: voyint@aol.com

VOYAGERS INTERNATIONAL

SKETCHING IN VENICE

General Information • Arts program with visits to Venice. Once at the destination country, participants travel by foot, boat.
Learning Focus • Instruction in sketching. Instruction is offered by professors, artists, historians. This program would appeal to people interested in art, sketching, painting, visual arts.
Accommodations • Hotels. Single rooms are available.
Program Details • Program offered once per year. Session length: 10–12 days. Departures are scheduled in September. Most participants are 30–70 years of age. 10–12 participants per session. Reservations are recommended at least 6–12 months before departure.
Costs • $2000–$2500 (includes tuition, housing, some meals). A $400 deposit is required.
Contact • David Blanton, Managing Director, Voyagers International, PO Box 915, Ithaca, NY 14851; 800-633-0299; Fax: 607-257-3699; E-mail: voyint@aol.com

WALKING THE WORLD

WALKING IN TUSCANY

General Information • Cultural tour with visits to Abruzzo National Park, Barbarano Romano, Bracciano, Montepulciano, Pienza, Rome, Brunello, Fattoria di Naro, Bracciano Castle. Once at the destination country, participants travel by foot, van.
Learning Focus • Escorted travel to Italy. Museum visits (major museums). Other activities include walking. Instruction is offered by professors, naturalists. This program would appeal to people interested in walking, photography, history, culture.
Accommodations • Homestays, hotels.
Program Details • Program offered 2 times per year. Session length: 12 days. Departures are scheduled in May, September. Program is targeted to walkers 50 and over. Most participants are 50 years of age and older. Participants must be 50 years or older to enroll. 16 participants per session. Reservations are recommended at least 6 months before departure.
Costs • $2495 (includes housing, some meals, excursions). A $400 deposit is required.
Contact • Walking The World, PO Box 1186, Ft. Collins, CO 80522; 970-225-0500; Fax: 970-225-9100; E-mail: cougar@frii.com

LUXEMBOURG

LANGUAGE LIAISON

PROLINGUA INTERNATIONAL LANGUAGE CENTER–LEARN FRENCH AND/OR GERMAN IN LUXEMBOURG

General Information • Language study program with visits to Luxembourg.

Learning Focus • Instruction in the French and German languages. Instruction is offered by professors. This program would appeal to people interested in language.

Accommodations • Homestays. Single rooms are available.

Program Details • Departures are scheduled throughout the year. Most participants are 18–70 years of age. Participants must be 16 years or older to enroll. Reservations are recommended at least 35 days before departure.

Costs • Contact sponsor for information.

Contact • Nancy Forman, President, Language Liaison, 20533 Biscayne Boulevard-Station 4-162, Miami, FL 33180; 305-682-9909; Fax: 305-682-9907; E-mail: langstudy@aol.com; World Wide Web: http://languageliaison.com

GEORGE MASON UNIVERSITY

CONTEMPORARY SOCIETIES AND POLITICS IN THE MEDITERRANEAN

General Information • Academic study program in Malta. Classes are held on the campus of University of Malta. Excursions to Sicily, Tunisia.

Learning Focus • Courses in anthropology, sociology, geography, history. Instruction is offered by professors from the sponsoring institution.

Accommodations • Apartments. Meals are taken as a group, in central dining facility.

Program Details • Program offered once per year. Session length: 4 weeks. Departures are scheduled in July. The program is open to undergraduate students, graduate students, adults. Most participants are 18–65 years of age. Other requirements: minimum 2.25 GPA. 10–15 participants per session. Application deadline: April 12.

Costs • $2765 for George Mason University students, $3315 for other students (includes tuition, housing, all meals, insurance). Application fee: $35. A $500 deposit is required.

Contact • Dr. Yehuda Lukacs, Director, Center for Global Education, George Mason University, 4400 University Drive, 235 Johnson Center, Fairfax, VA 22030; 703-993-2155; Fax: 703-993-2153; E-mail: ylukacs@gmu.edu; World Wide Web: http://www.gmu.edu/departments/oie

NETHERLANDS

AMSTERDAM SUMMER UNIVERSITY

THE AMSTERDAM SUMMER SCHOOL

General Information • Academic study program in Amsterdam.
Learning Focus • Courses in arts and sciences.
Accommodations • Homestays, locally-rented apartments, hotels. Single rooms are available. Meals are taken on one's own.
Program Details • Program offered once per year. Session length: 7 weeks. Departures are scheduled in July. The program is open to undergraduate students, graduate students, adults. Most participants are 20–70 years of age. 500 participants per session. Application deadline: June 30.
Costs • Contact sponsor for information.
Contact • Niels Gladdines, Office Manager, Amsterdam Summer University, PO Box 53066, Amsterdam 1007RB, Netherlands; +31 20-620-0225; Fax: +31 20-624-9368; E-mail: niels@felix.meritis.nl

 BENTLEY COLLEGE

BUSINESS STUDY TOUR TO MAASTRICHT

General Information • Academic study program in Maastricht. Classes are held on the campus of University of Limburg. Excursions to Amsterdam, Belgium (Brussels).
Learning Focus • Courses in business. Instruction is offered by professors from the sponsoring institution and local teachers.
Accommodations • Hotels. Single rooms are available. Meals are taken as a group, in local restaurants.
Program Details • Program offered once per year. Session length: 2 weeks. Departures are scheduled in May. The program is open to undergraduate students, graduate students. Most participants are 19–35 years of age. Other requirements: minimum 3.0 GPA. 15 participants per session. Application deadline: March 15.
Costs • $3800 (includes tuition, housing, excursions, international airfare, International Student Identification card). Application fee: $35. A $1500 deposit is required.
Contact • Jennifer L. Scully, Director of Study Abroad, Bentley College, International Center, 175 Forest Street, Waltham, MA 02154; 617-891-3474; Fax: 617-891-2819; E-mail: inprinfo@bentley.edu

CROSS-CULTURE

BIKING HOLLAND IN TULIP TIME

General Information • Nature study, cultural, and bicycling tour with visits to Amsterdam, North Holland, West Friesland, Friesland, Gaasterland, Overijssel, Gelderland. Once at the destination country, participants travel by bus, bicycle.
Learning Focus • Instruction in land reclamation and Friesian language and customs. Escorted travel to Radboud Castle and a bird sanctuary. Nature observation (flowers, rabbits, birds). Other activities include bicycling. Instruction is offered by naturalists, historians, bicycle leaders. This program would appeal to people interested in nature studies, history, traditions, culture.
Accommodations • Hotels. Single rooms are available for an additional $230.
Program Details • Program offered once per year. Session length: 9 days. Departures are scheduled in April. Program is targeted to adults of all ages. Most participants are 30–75 years of age. Participants must be 12 years or older to enroll. Other requirements: must be in good health and have some biking experience, must be accompanied by an adult if under 18. 20 participants per session. Application deadline: 1 month prior to departure. Reservations are recommended at least 3–12 months before departure.
Costs • $2480 (includes tuition, housing, all meals, books and class materials, excursions, international airfare). A $300 deposit is required.
Contact • Cross-Culture, 52 High Point Drive, Amherst, MA 01002-1224; 413-256-6303; Fax: 413-253-2303; E-mail: xculture@javanet.com; World Wide Web: http://www.empiremall.com/cross-culture

EASTERN MICHIGAN UNIVERSITY

GRAPHIC DESIGN IN THE NETHERLANDS

General Information • Academic study program in Rotterdam. Excursions to Belgium (Antwerp), France (Paris).
Learning Focus • Courses in graphic design. Instruction is offered by professors from the sponsoring institution.
Accommodations • Hotels. Single rooms are available. Meals are taken as a group, in local restaurants.
Program Details • Program offered once per year. Session length: 3 weeks. Departures are scheduled in July. The program is open to undergraduate students, graduate students. Most participants are 18–35 years of age. Other requirements: minimum 2.0 GPA, 18 years of age, and portfolio review. 10 participants per session. Application deadline: April 1.
Costs • $3000 (includes tuition, housing, some meals, insurance, excursions, travel in Europe). A $150 deposit is required.
Contact • Doug Kisor, Director, Visual Communications Area, Eastern Michigan University, 114 Ford Hall, Ypsilanti, MI 48197; 313-487-3388; Fax: 313-480-1927; E-mail: fa_kisor@emuvax.emich.edu; World Wide Web: http://www.emich.edu/public/cont_ed/abroad.html

 FOREIGN LANGUAGE STUDY ABROAD SERVICE

INTERNATIONAL LANGUAGE STUDY HOMESTAYS IN THE NETHERLANDS

General Information • Language study program in Netherlands.

Learning Focus • Courses in Dutch language. Instruction is offered by local teachers.
Accommodations • Homestays. Single rooms are available. Meals are taken with host family, in residences.
Program Details • Session length: varies. Departures are scheduled in January–December. The program is open to undergraduate students, graduate students, pre-college students, adults. Most participants are 12 years of age and older. Other requirements: students must be at least 12 years old. 1 participant per session.
Costs • Contact sponsor for information. A $300 deposit is required.
Contact • Louise Harber, Coordinator, Foreign Language Study Abroad Service, Department IH, Box 903, 5935 Southwest 64th Avenue, South Miami, FL 33143; 800-282-1090; Fax: 305-662-2907; E-mail: flsas@netpoint.net; World Wide Web: http://www.netpoint.net/~flsas

INTERHOSTEL, UNIVERSITY OF NEW HAMPSHIRE

THE NETHERLANDS

General Information • Cultural tour with visits to Leiden, Amsterdam, Delft, Antwerpen, Beemster Polder, Het Loo, The Hague, Delfshaven. Once at the destination country, participants travel by bus, foot. Program is affiliated with Stichting Educatieve Projekten.
Learning Focus • Instruction in history, culture and art history. Escorted travel to villages and cities. Museum visits (Rijksmuseum, Boymans, Frans Hals). Attendance at performances (Baroque concert). Instruction is offered by historians. This program would appeal to people interested in history, culture.
Accommodations • Hotels. Single rooms are available for an additional $400.
Program Details • Program offered 2 times per year. Session length: 2 weeks. Departures are scheduled in April, September. Program is targeted to seniors over 50. Most participants are 60–80 years of age. Participants must be 50 years or older to enroll. 40 participants per session. Reservations are recommended at least 3 months before departure.
Costs • $2750 (includes tuition, housing, all meals, excursions, international airfare, entrance fees). A $200 deposit is required.
Contact • Janice Pierson, Office Supervisor, Interhostel, University of New Hampshire, 6 Garrison Avenue, Durham, NH 03824-3529; 800-733-9753; Fax: 603-862-1113; World Wide Web: http://www.learn.unh.edu/

LANGUAGE LIAISON

LIVE 'N' LEARN (LEARN IN A TEACHER'S HOME)–NETHERLANDS

General Information • Language study program with visits to Netherlands.
Learning Focus • Instruction in the Dutch language. Instruction is offered by professors. This program would appeal to people interested in language.
Accommodations • Homestays. Single rooms are available.
Program Details • Session length: unlimited. Departures are scheduled throughout the year. Most participants are 18–70 years of age. Participants must be 16 years or older to enroll. Reservations are recommended at least 35 days before departure.
Costs • Contact sponsor for information.
Contact • Nancy Forman, President, Language Liaison, 20533 Biscayne Boulevard-Station 4-162, Miami, FL 33180; 305-682-9909; Fax: 305-682-9907; E-mail: langstudy@aol.com; World Wide Web: http://languageliaison.com

RAMAPO COLLEGE OF NEW JERSEY

NETHERLANDS

General Information • Academic study program in Maastricht. Classes are held on the campus of European Orientation Center.
Learning Focus • Courses in international business, journalism, telecommunications. Instruction is offered by local teachers.
Accommodations • Dormitories. Single rooms are available. Meals are taken as a group, in central dining facility.
Program Details • Program offered once per year. Session length: 3 weeks. Departures are scheduled in June. The program is open to undergraduate students, graduate students, pre-college students, adults, teachers. Other requirements: must have at least sophomore standing. Application deadline: April.
Costs • $2500 (includes tuition, housing, all meals, excursions, international airfare). Application fee: $300. A $300 deposit is required.
Contact • Mrs. Robyn Perricelli, Director, Study Abroad, Ramapo College of New Jersey, 505 Ramapo Valley Road, Mahwah, NJ 07430; 201-529-7463; Fax: 201-529-7508; E-mail: rperrice@ramapo.edu

UNIVERSITY OF FLORIDA

UNIVERSITY OF UTRECHT, THE NETHERLANDS–DUTCH LANGUAGE AND CULTURE

General Information • Academic study program in Utrecht. Classes are held on the campus of Utrecht University. Excursions to local cultural sites.
Learning Focus • Courses in political science, geography, Dutch language, Dutch culture, history, fine arts. Instruction is offered by professors from the sponsoring institution and local teachers.
Accommodations • Flats. Meals are taken on one's own, in local restaurants, in residences.
Program Details • Program offered once per year. Session length: 6 weeks. Departures are scheduled in June. The program is open to undergraduate students, graduate students, adults. Other requirements: minimum 2.5 GPA and at least 18 years old. 25 participants per session. Application deadline: March 15.
Costs • $1750 for University of Florida students, $2500 for other students (includes tuition, housing, excursions, administration fee, orientation). Application fee: $200.
Contact • Overseas Studies, University of Florida, 123 Tigert Hall, PO Box 113225, Gainesville, FL 32611-3225; 352-392-5206; Fax: 352-392-5575; E-mail: ovrseas@nervm.nerdc.ufl.edu

NORWAY

INTERHOSTEL, UNIVERSITY OF NEW HAMPSHIRE

BERGEN AND OSLO, NORWAY

General Information • Cultural tour with visits to Bergen, Oslo, Bryggen, Torgalmenningen, Troldhaugen, Songnefjord, Flam, Mount Floien, Lysoen, Hardanderfjord, Akershus Castle, Myrdal. Once at the destination country, participants travel by train, bus, foot, boat, funicular. Program is affiliated with Asane Folkehog Skole.
Learning Focus • Instruction in history and culture. Escorted travel to villages and castles. Museum visits (National Gallery, Munch Museum, Fram Museum). Attendance at performances (concerts, folk music). Other activities include meeting local people. Instruction is offered by professors, historians. This program would appeal to people interested in history, culture.
Accommodations • Dormitories. Single rooms are available for an additional $300.
Program Details • Program offered once per year. Session length: 2 weeks. Departures are scheduled in July. Program is targeted to seniors over 50. Most participants are 60–80 years of age. Participants must be 50 years or older to enroll. 35 participants per session. Reservations are recommended at least 6 months before departure.
Costs • $2825 (includes tuition, housing, all meals, excursions, international airfare, entrance fees). A $200 deposit is required.
Contact • Janice Pierson, Office Supervisor, Interhostel, University of New Hampshire, 6 Garrison Avenue, Durham, NH 03824; 800-733-9753; Fax: 603-862-1113; World Wide Web: http://www.learn.unh.edu/

MICHIGAN STATE UNIVERSITY

HOSPITALITY MANAGEMENT

General Information • Academic study program in Stavanger. Classes are held on the campus of Norwegian College of Hotel Management.
Learning Focus • Courses in hotel and restaurant management, business. Instruction is offered by professors from the sponsoring institution.
Accommodations • Dormitories. Meals are taken on one's own, in local restaurants.
Program Details • Program offered once per year. Session length: 5 weeks. Departures are scheduled in June. The program is open to undergraduate students, graduate students. Most participants are 18–26 years of age. Other requirements: good academic standing and the approval of the director. 12 participants per session. Application deadline: March 14.
Costs • $2500 (includes housing, some meals, excursions). Application fee: $75. A $250 deposit is required.
Contact • Brenda S. Sprite, Educational Programs Coordinator, Michigan State University, Office of Study Abroad, 109 International Center, East Lansing, MI 48824-1035; 517-353-8920; Fax: 517-432-2082; E-mail: sprite@pilot.msu.edu; World Wide Web: http://study-abroad.msu.edu

ST. OLAF COLLEGE

UNIVERSITY OF OSLO–ISS PROGRAM

General Information • Academic study program in Oslo. Classes are held on the campus of University of Oslo.
Learning Focus • Courses in Norwegian language, economics, cultural studies, political science, international health problems, peace research, Norwegian history, art history, international relations, environmental studies, communications, special education. Instruction is offered by local teachers.
Accommodations • Dormitories. Single rooms are available. Meals are taken as a group, on one's own, in central dining facility, in local restaurants.
Program Details • Program offered once per year. Session length: 6 weeks. Departures are scheduled in June. The program is open to undergraduate students, graduate students, adults. Most participants are 18–67 years of age. Other requirements: minimum of one year of college and a BA required for graduate students. 500 participants per session. Application deadline: March 1.
Costs • $2340 (includes tuition, housing, all meals, one weekend excursion). Application fee: $7. A $200 deposit is required.
Contact • Torild Homstad, Administrator of North American Office, St. Olaf College, Northfield, MN 55057-1098; 800-639-0058; Fax: 507-646-3549; E-mail: iss@stolaf.edu

A former summer school student from Africa said that to attend the ISS is "to be welded together with students from Africa, the Middle East, Asia, Europe, and the Americas into a peaceful community in which all share the same notions of peace, excitement, and knowledge." During the day, ISS students attend classes, but in the evening they talk, travel, and make the world a little bit smaller. The unofficial motto of the ISS is "Friendliness, Frankness and Tolerance," and the 6-week program is designed to get students to mix, whether in the classroom, on the soccer field, or on excursions.

UNIVERSITY OF OSLO

PROGRAM IN OSLO, NORWAY: OSLO INTERNATIONAL SUMMER SCHOOL

General Information • Academic study program in Oslo. Classes are held on the campus of University of Oslo.

Learning Focus • Courses in Norwegian language, literature, political science, economics, art history, Nordic history, international relations, public administration. Instruction is offered by professors from the sponsoring institution.

Accommodations • Dormitories. Single rooms are available. Meals are taken as a group, in central dining facility.

Program Details • Program offered once per year. Session length: 6 weeks. Departures are scheduled in June. The program is open to undergraduate students, graduate students, adults. Most participants are 20–70 years of age. 500 participants per session. Application deadline: March 1.

Costs • $2340 (includes tuition, housing, all meals). A $200 deposit is required.

Contact • Jo Ann Kleber, Director, University of Oslo, 1520 St. Olaf Avenue, Northfield, MN 55057-1098; 800-639-0058; Fax: 507-646-3549; E-mail: iss@stolaf.edu; World Wide Web: http://www.uio.no/iss/iss.html

PORTUGAL

THE CENTER FOR ENGLISH STUDIES

STUDY ABROAD IN LISBON, PORTUGAL

General Information • Language study program with visits to Lisbon. Program is affiliated with International House-Lisbon.

Learning Focus • Instruction in the Portuguese language. Other activities include field trips to local sites, museums, markets and churches. Instruction is offered by faculty members from host institution. This program would appeal to people interested in the Portuguese language.

Accommodations • Homestays, locally-rented apartments, program-owned apartments, hotels, pensiones. Single rooms are available.

Program Details • Session length: 3 or more weeks. Departures are scheduled throughout the year. Most participants are 16–70 years of age. Participants must be 16 years or older to enroll. 6-12 participants per session. Application deadline: 2 weeks prior to departure. Reservations are recommended at least 1 month before departure.

Costs • $650 for 4 weeks (includes tuition). A $125 deposit is required.

Contact • Ms. Lorraine Haber, Study Abroad Coordinator, The Center for English Studies, 330 7th Avenue, 6th Floor, New York, NY 10021; 212-629-7300; Fax: 212-736-7950; E-mail: ces_newyork@cescorp.com

COLLEGE CONSORTIUM FOR INTERNATIONAL STUDIES–CAPE COD COMMUNITY COLLEGE

SUMMER PROGRAM IN PORTUGAL

General Information • Language study program in Faro, Lisbon, Oporto.

Learning Focus • Courses in language study.

Accommodations • Homestays, locally-rented apartments. Single rooms are available. Meals are taken with host family, in residences.

Program Details • Program offered 12 times per year. Session length: 4 weeks. Departures are scheduled in January–December. The program is open to undergraduate students, graduate students, adults. Most participants are 18–65 years of age. Other requirements: minimum 2.5 GPA. 1 participant per session. Application deadline: 45 days prior to departure.

Costs • $1550 (includes tuition, housing, some meals, books and class materials, excursions, fees, International Student Identification card).

Contact • Jane C. Evans, Executive Director, College Consortium for International Studies, 2000 P Street, NW, Suite 503, Washington, DC 20036; 800-453-6956; Fax: 202-223-0999; E-mail: ccis@intr.net

CRAFT WORLD TOURS

PORTUGAL

General Information • Cultural tour with visits to Bussaco, Evora, Lamego, Lisbon, Vila do Conde. Once at the destination country, participants travel by bus.

Learning Focus • Escorted travel to St. George's Castle and Roman Gothic Cathedral. Museum visits (Coach Museum, Tile Museum). Instruction is offered by artists. This program would appeal to people interested in handicrafts, folk arts, village life.

Accommodations • Hotels. Single rooms are available for an additional $695.

Program Details • Program offered once per year. Session length: 15 days. Departures are scheduled in April. Most participants are 30–80 years of age. Other requirements: appreciation of handcrafts and folk arts. 18 participants per session. Application deadline: March 11. Reservations are recommended at least 6 months before departure.

Costs • $3996 (includes housing, some meals, excursions, international airfare). A $250 deposit is required.

Contact • Tom Wilson, President, Craft World Tours, 6776 Warboys Road, Byron, NY 14422; 716-548-2667; Fax: 716-548-2821

CROSS-CULTURE

PORTAL TO PORTUGAL

General Information • Cultural tour with visits to Coimbra, Lisbon, Azeitao, Sintra, Estoril, Cascais, Obidos, Caldas, Nazare. Once at the destination country, participants travel by bus, foot, boat.

Learning Focus • Escorted travel to Barrio Alto, San Roque Church and the University of Coimbra. Museum visits (Maritime Musuem, National Coach Museum, Madrede Deuschurch and Tile Museum, Gulbenkian Museum). Attendance at performances (fado musicians). Instruction is offered by highly educated guides.

Accommodations • Hotels. Single rooms are available for an additional $415.

Program Details • Program offered once per year. Session length: 9 days. Departures are scheduled in September. Program is targeted to adults of all ages. Most participants are 40–70 years of age. Participants must be 12 years or older to enroll. Other requirements: good health, accompaniment of an adult if under 18. 20–25 participants per session. Application deadline: 1 month prior to departure. Reservations are recommended at least 3–12 months before departure.

Costs • $2690 (includes tuition, housing, all meals, books and class materials, excursions, international airfare). A $300 deposit is required.

Contact • Cross-Culture, 52 High Point Drive, Amherst, MA 01002-1224; 413-256-6303; Fax: 413-253-2303; E-mail: xculture@javanet.com; World Wide Web: http://www.empiremall.com/cross-culture

CSA–CENTER FOR STUDY ABROAD

CIAL–PORTUGAL

General Information • Language study program in Lisbon.
Learning Focus • Courses in Portuguese language. Instruction is offered by professors from the sponsoring institution.
Accommodations • Homestays, locally-rented apartments. Single rooms are available. Meals are taken on one's own, with host family.
Program Details • Program offered 50 times per year. Session length: 1 or more weeks. Departures are scheduled in January–December. The program is open to undergraduate students, graduate students, pre-college students, adults. Most participants are 21–32 years of age. Other requirements: minimum age of 17. 5–8 participants per session.
Costs • $1295 for 2 weeks (includes tuition, housing, some meals, books and class materials, insurance, registration, orientation). Application fee: $45. A $50 deposit is required.
Contact • Philip Virtue, Program Director, CSA–Center for Study Abroad, 2802 East Madison Street MS #160, Seattle, WA 98112; 206-726-1498; Fax: 206-285-9197; E-mail: virtuecsa@aol.com

EXPERIENCE PLUS SPECIALTY TOURS, INC.

CASTLES AND CORKTREES (THE ALENTEJO)

General Information • Bicycle tour with visits to Cascais, Elvas, Evora, Marvão, Monsaraz, Portalegre, castles, medieval walled towns, Spanish border. Once at the destination country, participants travel by bicycle.
Learning Focus • Escorted travel to the Alentejo region. Other activities include bicycling. Instruction is offered by professors, indigenous, bilingual and bi-cultural guides. This program would appeal to people interested in architecture, history, culture, Portugal, wine, bicycling, travel.
Accommodations • Hotels. Single rooms are available for an additional $300.
Program Details • Program offered once per year. Session length: 11 days. Departures are scheduled in May. Most participants are 35–70 years of age. 16–22 participants per session. Reservations are recommended at least 6–12 months before departure.
Costs • Contact sponsor for information. A $250 deposit is required.
Contact • Experience Plus Specialty Tours, Inc., 1925 Wallenberg Drive, Fort Collins, CO 80526; 800-685-4565; Fax: 800-685-4565; E-mail: tours@xplus.com

FOREIGN LANGUAGE STUDY ABROAD SERVICE

INTERNATIONAL LANGUAGE STUDY HOMESTAYS IN PORTUGAL

General Information • Language study program in Portugal.
Learning Focus • Courses in Portuguese language. Instruction is offered by local teachers.
Accommodations • Homestays. Single rooms are available. Meals are taken with host family, in residences.
Program Details • Session length: varies. Departures are scheduled in January–December. The program is open to undergraduate students, graduate students, pre-college students, adults. Most participants are 12 years of age and older. Other requirements: students must be at least 12 years old. 1 participant per session.
Costs • Contact sponsor for information. A $300 deposit is required.
Contact • Louise Harber, Coordinator, Foreign Language Study Abroad Service, Department IH, Box 903, 5935 Southwest 64th Avenue, South Miami, FL 33143; 800-282-1090; Fax: 305-662-2907; E-mail: flsas@netpoint.net; World Wide Web: http://www.netpoint.net/~flsas

FOREIGN LANGUAGE STUDY ABROAD SERVICE

PORTUGESE IN PORTUGAL

General Information • Language study program in Faro, Lisbon, Oporto.
Learning Focus • Courses in language study. Instruction is offered by local teachers.
Accommodations • Homestays, program-owned apartments, hotels. Single rooms are available. Meals are taken as a group, on one's own, in central dining facility, in local restaurants.
Program Details • Session length: varies. Departures are scheduled in January–December. The program is open to undergraduate students, graduate students, pre-college students, adults. Most participants are 16 years of age and older.
Costs • Contact sponsor for information. Application fee: $50. A $100 deposit is required.
Contact • Louise Harber, Coordinator, Foreign Language Study Abroad Service, Department IH, Box 903, 5935 Southwest 64th Avenue, South Miami, FL 33143; 800-282-1090; Fax: 305-662-2907; E-mail: flsas@netpoint.net; World Wide Web: http://www.netpoint.net/~flsas

INTERHOSTEL, UNIVERSITY OF NEW HAMPSHIRE

LISBON AND OPORTO, PORTUGAL

General Information • Cultural tour with visits to Lisbon, Porto, Tomar, Quinta do Morgado, Queluz, Sintra, Éuora, Arriolos, Sesimbaa, Setubal, Arrabida, Obidos, Nazare Batalha, Fatima, Coimbra. Once at the destination country, participants travel by bus, foot. Program is affiliated with CIAL–Lingua Service International.
Learning Focus • Instruction in history and culture. Escorted travel to villages and landmarks. Museum visits

(Gulbenkian museum, Romantic Museum). Instruction is offered by professors. This program would appeal to people interested in history, culture.

Accommodations • Hotels. Single rooms are available for an additional $450.

Program Details • Program offered once per year. Session length: 2 weeks. Departures are scheduled in March. Program is targeted to seniors over 50. Most participants are 60–80 years of age. Participants must be 50 years or older to enroll. 35 participants per session. Reservations are recommended at least 6 months before departure.

Costs • $3210 (includes tuition, housing, all meals, excursions, international airfare, entrance fees). A $200 deposit is required.

Contact • Janice Pierson, Office Supervisor, Interhostel, University of New Hampshire, 6 Garrison Avenue, Durham, NH 03824; 800-733-9753; Fax: 603-862-1113; World Wide Web: http://www.learn.unh.edu/

LANGUAGE LIAISON

CIAL CENTRO DE LINGUAS–STUDY PORTUGESE IN PORTUGAL

General Information • Language study program with visits to Faro, Lisbon, Porto.

Learning Focus • Instruction in the Portuguese language. Instruction is offered by professors. This program would appeal to people interested in language.

Accommodations • Homestays, hotels. Single rooms are available.

Program Details • Session length: unlimited. Departures are scheduled throughout the year. Program is targeted to students of any age. Most participants are 18–70 years of age. Participants must be 16 years or older to enroll. Reservations are recommended at least 35 days before departure.

Costs • Contact sponsor for information.

Contact • Nancy Forman, President, Language Liaison, 20533 Biscayne Boulevard-Station 4-162, Miami, FL 33180; 305-682-9909; Fax: 305-682-9907; E-mail: langstudy@aol.com; World Wide Web: http://languageliaison.com

NATIONAL REGISTRATION CENTER FOR STUDY ABROAD

CIAL CENTRO DE LINGUAS–LANGUAGE STUDIES IN PORTUGAL

General Information • Language study program in Faro, Lisbon, Oporto.

Learning Focus • Courses in Portuguese language.

Accommodations • Homestays. Single rooms are available. Meals are taken on one's own.

Program Details • Program offered 11 times per year. Session length: 1 week. Departures are scheduled in January–November. The program is open to undergraduate students, graduate students, adults. 4–6 participants per session. Application deadline: 40 days prior to departure.

Costs • $743 (includes tuition, housing, some meals, insurance). Application fee: $40. A $100 deposit is required.

Contact • June Domoe, Educational Consultant, National Registration Center for Study Abroad, 823 North Second Street, Milwaukee, WI 53203; 414-278-0631; Fax: 414-271-8884; E-mail: inquiries@nrcsa.com; World Wide Web: http://www.nrcsa.com

NATURAL HABITAT ADVENTURES

AZORES WHALE WATCH

General Information • Nature study tour with visits to Azores Islands. Once at the destination country, participants travel by bus, boat. Program is affiliated with International Fund for Animal Welfare.

Learning Focus • Instruction in field observation of whales. Field research in whale behavior and population. Escorted travel to the Azores archipelago. Nature observation (whales and other marine life). Instruction is offered by professors, researchers, naturalists, scientists. This program would appeal to people interested in wildlife, photography, nature travel.

Accommodations • Boat.

Program Details • Program offered 2 times per year. Session length: 8–10 days. Departures are scheduled in June, August. Most participants are 27–80 years of age. 8 participants per session. Reservations are recommended at least 10–12 months before departure.

Costs • $2195 (includes housing, all meals, excursions). A $500 deposit is required.

Contact • Natural Habitat Adventures, 2945 Center Green Court, Suite H, Boulder, CO 80301; 800-543-8917; Fax: 303-449-3712

SCOTLAND

See also England, Ireland, and Wales

BEAVER COLLEGE

SCOTTISH UNIVERSITIES' INTERNATIONAL SUMMER SCHOOL

General Information • Academic study program in Edinburgh. Classes are held on the campus of University of Edinburgh.

Learning Focus • Courses in British literature, history, cultural studies. Instruction is offered by local teachers.

Accommodations • Dormitories. Single rooms are available. Meals are taken in central dining facility.

Program Details • Program offered 2 times per year. Session length: 3–6 weeks. Departures are scheduled in July. The program is open to undergraduate students, graduate students, adults. Other requirements: minimum 3.0 GPA and three or four semesters of college-level course work. 30 participants per session. Application deadline: March 31.

Costs • $2675 for 3 weeks, $4300 for 6 weeks (includes tuition, housing, some meals, International Student Identification card, predeparture materials, host country support). Application fee: $35. A $500 deposit is required.

Contact • Audrianna Jones, Program Coordinator, Beaver College, Center for Education Abroad, 450 South Easton Road, Glenside, PA 19038; 888-232-8379; Fax: 215-572-2174; E-mail: jones@turret.beaver.edu

BRITISH COASTAL TRAILS SCENIC WALKING

SCOTTISH BORDERS, KEEPS, AND CASTLES

General Information • Cultural tour with visits to England (Bamburgh), Scotland (Edinburgh, Melrose, Moffat); excur-

sions to Neidpath Castle, Devil's Beef Tub, Wanlockhead, Abbottsford (home of Sir Walter Scott), Pennine Way, Lindisfarne Abbey, St. Abbs Head Nature Reserve. Once at the destination country, participants travel by bus, foot.
Learning Focus • Escorted travel to Royal Mile, River Tweed and Holy Island. Nature observation (lochs, seabirds, wildlife). Other activities include hiking, walking. Instruction is offered by naturalists, historians, professional guides. This program would appeal to people interested in nature studies, walking, culture, photography, history.
Accommodations • Hotels. Single rooms are available.
Program Details • Program offered 3 times per year. Session length: 8 days. Departures are scheduled in June, July, September. Most participants are 40-65 years of age. Participants must be 13 years or older to enroll. Other requirements: physician's approval and signed release form. 18 participants per session. Application deadline: 30 days prior to departure. Reservations are recommended at least 6 months before departure.
Costs • $1855 (includes housing, some meals, excursions, full-time guide). A $250 deposit is required.
Contact • Tour Manager, British Coastal Trails Scenic Walking, 7777 Fay Avenue, Suite 100, La Jolla, CA 92037; 800-473-1210; Fax: 619-456-2277; E-mail: lajolla@bctwalk.com; World Wide Web: http://www.bctwalk.com/lajolla

BRITISH COASTAL TRAILS SCENIC WALKING

SCOTTISH HIGHLANDS, LOCHS, AND GLENS

General Information • Cultural tour with visits to Boat of Garten, Callander, Edinburgh, Kenmore, Bracklinn Falls, River Tay, Glen Ogle Gorge. Once at the destination country, participants travel by bus, foot.
Learning Focus • Escorted travel to Royal Mile and the Pass of Ryvoan Abernathy Forest. Nature observation (lochs, osprey, red deer). Other activities include hiking, walking. Instruction is offered by naturalists, historians, professional guides. This program would appeal to people interested in nature studies, walking, culture, photography, history.
Accommodations • Hotels. Single rooms are available for an additional $180.
Program Details • Program offered 4 times per year. Session length: 8 days. Departures are scheduled in June-September. Most participants are 40-65 years of age. Participants must be 13 years or older to enroll. Other requirements: physician's approval and signed release form. 18 participants per session. Application deadline: 30 days prior to departure. Reservations are recommended at least 6 months before departure.
Costs • $1875 (includes housing, some meals, excursions, full-time guide). A $250 deposit is required.
Contact • Tour Manager, British Coastal Trails Scenic Walking, 7777 Fay Avenue, Suite 100, La Jolla, CA 92037; 800-473-1210; Fax: 619-456-2277; E-mail: lajolla@bctwalk.com; World Wide Web: http://www.bctwalk.com/lajolla

COUNTRY WALKERS

FROM EDINBURGH TO THE HISTORIC BORDERS

General Information • Cultural, gourmet cooking, nature study and walking tour with visits to Edinburgh, Peebles, St. Mary's Loch. Once at the destination country, participants travel by foot.
Learning Focus • Escorted travel to Salsburg Crags, Neidpath Castle and Venlaw Castle. Museum visits (Bow Hill Estate). Other activities include walking. Instruction is offered by professors, researchers, naturalists, historians. This program would appeal to people interested in walking, nature studies, food and wine.
Accommodations • Hotels. Single rooms are available for an additional $300-$600.
Program Details • Program offered 5 times per year. Session length: 8 days. Departures are scheduled in May-September. Program is targeted to adults 35 to 65 years old. Most participants are 35-65 years of age. Participants must be 18 years or older to enroll. 18 participants per session. Reservations are recommended at least 5-6 months before departure.
Costs • $1950 (includes housing, all meals, excursions). A $400 deposit is required.
Contact • Heather Kellingbeck, Vice President, Country Walkers, PO Box 180, Waterbury, VT 05176; 802-464-9255; Fax: 802-244-5661; E-mail: ctrywalk@aol.com

CROSS-CULTURE

SCOTTISH FLING

General Information • Cultural tour with visits to Edinburgh, The New Town, St. Andrew's Crail, Anstruther, Glasgow. Once at the destination country, participants travel by bus, foot, boat.
Learning Focus • Instruction in Scottish history. Escorted travel to Edinburgh Castle and Gladstone's Land. Museum visits (Golf Museum, Scottish Fisheries Museum, Burrell Collection, Hunterian Art Gallery). Attendance at performances (Edinburgh Tattoo, Edinburgh International Festival). Instruction is offered by highly educated guides. This program would appeal to people interested in culture, history, nature studies, arts, traditions, food and wine.
Accommodations • Hotels. Single rooms are available for an additional $200.
Program Details • Program offered once per year. Session length: 9 days. Departures are scheduled in August. Program is targeted to adults of all ages. Most participants are 40-70 years of age. Participants must be 12 years or older to enroll. Other requirements: good health, accompaniment of an adult if under 18. 20-25 participants per session. Application deadline: 1 month prior to departure. Reservations are recommended at least 3-12 months before departure.
Costs • $2280 (includes tuition, housing, all meals, books and class materials, excursions, international airfare). A $300 deposit is required.
Contact • Cross-Culture, 52 High Point Drive, Amherst, MA 01002-1224; 413-256-6303; Fax: 413-253-2303; E-mail: xculture@javanet.com; World Wide Web: http://www.empiremall.com/cross-culture

CROSS-CULTURE

WALKS ON THE ISLE OF SKYE

General Information • Nature study, cultural, and hiking tour with visits to Isle of Skye, The Ounvegas Area, Trotternish, Glendale, The Cuillins Sleat. Once at the destination country, participants travel by bus, foot.
Learning Focus • Instruction in local history. Escorted travel to Cuillin Hills, Quiraing and Talisker distillery.

Museum visits (folk museum). Nature observation (otters and seals, geological formations). Other activities include hiking. Instruction is offered by naturalists, historians, experienced hiking leaders. This program would appeal to people interested in nature studies, history, food and wine, culture, traditions.
Accommodations • Hotels. Single rooms are available.
Program Details • Program offered 2 times per year. Session length: 9 days. Departures are scheduled in June, July. Program is targeted to adults of all ages. Most participants are 30–75 years of age. Participants must be 12 years or older to enroll. Other requirements: must be in good health, must be accompanied by an adult if under 18. 20 participants per session. Application deadline: 1 month prior to departure. Reservations are recommended at least 3–12 months before departure.
Costs • $2160 (includes tuition, housing, all meals, books and class materials, excursions, international airfare). A $300 deposit is required.
Contact • Cross-Culture, 52 High Point Drive, Amherst, MA 01002-1224; 413-256-6303; Fax: 413-253-2303; E-mail: xculture@javanet.com; World Wide Web: http://www.empiremall.com/cross-culture

DIANE HOFF-ROME, AN ARTIST'S LIFE

ISLE OF SKYE SCOTLAND ARTIST HOLIDAY

General Information • Arts program with visits to Isle of Skye, Glasgow museums, castle, artists' studios, crafts studio, heritage center distillery. Once at the destination country, participants travel by train, bus, foot, boat.
Learning Focus • Instruction in painting, drawing and composition. Museum visits (heritage center on Skye). Attendance at performances (musical events). Nature observation (seals, birds, red deer). Other activities include hiking, visits with local artists and native inhabitants. Instruction is offered by artists, historians. This program would appeal to people interested in painting, nature studies, drawing, crafts, photography, ancient sites, writing, golf and fishing.
Accommodations • Homestays, hotels. Single rooms are available.
Program Details • Program offered 6 times per year. Session length: 1–2 weeks. Departures are scheduled in May–September. Program is targeted to amateur artists and teachers. Most participants are 25–85 years of age. Participants must be 21 years or older to enroll. Other requirements: interest in visual arts, nature, cultural experience. 8 participants per session. Application deadline: 45–60 days prior to departure. Reservations are recommended at least 90–120 days before departure.
Costs • $945 (includes tuition, housing, some meals, excursions). A $500 deposit is required.
Contact • Irwin W. Rome, Co-Director, Diane Hoff-Rome, An Artist's Life, PO Box 567, Elmwood Road, Swampscott, MA 01907-3567; 617-595-1173; Fax: 617-596-0707; E-mail: artistlf@pcix.com; World Wide Web: http://www2.pcix.com/~artistlf

 EUROCENTRES

LANGUAGE IMMERSION IN SCOTLAND

General Information • Language study program in Edinburgh. Classes are held on the campus of Eurocentre Edinburgh Summer Centre. Excursions to highlands, east coast castles.
Learning Focus • Courses in English language, Scottish culture. Instruction is offered by professors from the sponsoring institution.
Accommodations • Homestays. Single rooms are available. Meals are taken with host family, in residences.
Program Details • Program offered 20 times per year. Session length: 2–12 weeks. Departures are scheduled in January–December. The program is open to undergraduate students, graduate students, pre-college students, adults. Most participants are 16–80 years of age. 15 participants per session.
Costs • Contact sponsor for information.
Contact • Marketing, Eurocentres, 101 North Union Street, Suite 300, Alexandria, VA 22314; 800-648-4809; Fax: 703-684-1495; E-mail: 100632.141@compuserve.com; World Wide Web: http://www.clark.net/pub/eurocent/home.htm

 FOREIGN LANGUAGE STUDY ABROAD SERVICE

INTERNATIONAL LANGUAGE STUDY HOMESTAYS IN SCOTLAND

General Information • Language study program in Scotland.
Learning Focus • Courses in English language. Instruction is offered by local teachers.
Accommodations • Homestays. Single rooms are available. Meals are taken with host family, in residences.
Program Details • Session length: varies. Departures are scheduled in January–December. The program is open to undergraduate students, graduate students, pre-college students, adults. Most participants are 12 years of age and older. Other requirements: students must be at least 12 years old. 1 participant per session.
Costs • Contact sponsor for information. A $300 deposit is required.
Contact • Louise Harber, Coordinator, Foreign Language Study Abroad Service, Department IH, Box 903, 5935 Southwest 64th Avenue, South Miami, FL 33143; 800-282-1090; Fax: 305-662-2907; E-mail: flsas@netpoint.net; World Wide Web: http://www.netpoint.net/~flsas

 ILLINOIS STATE UNIVERSITY

STIRLING, SCOTLAND SUMMER PROGRAM

General Information • Academic study program in Stirling. Classes are held on the campus of University of Stirling.
Learning Focus • Courses in Scottish history, literature, society and environment, media in Scotland, adult learning, political science, business management.
Accommodations • Dormitories.
Program Details • Program offered once per year. Session length: 6 weeks. Departures are scheduled in July. The program is open to undergraduate students, graduate

students. Other requirements: minimum 3.0 GPA and a minimum of sophomore status. 15 participants per session. Application deadline: March 15.
Costs • $2100 (includes tuition, housing, fees).
Contact • International Studies, Illinois State University, Campus Box 6120, Normal, IL 61790-6120; 309-438-5365; Fax: 309-438-3987; E-mail: oisp@rs6000.cmp.ilstu.edu; World Wide Web: http://www.orat.ilstu.edu/

INTERHOSTEL, UNIVERSITY OF NEW HAMPSHIRE

SCOTLAND

General Information • Cultural tour with visits to Stirling, Airthrey Castle, Glasgow, St. Andrews, Falkland Palace, Endinburgh, Loch Lomond, Trossachs. Once at the destination country, participants travel by bus, foot. Program is affiliated with University of Stirling.
Learning Focus • Instruction in history and culture. Escorted travel to castles and villages. Museum visits (Burrell Collection). Attendance at performances (Edinburgh Festival). Other activities include evening with local residents, Edinburgh Military Tattoo. Instruction is offered by professors. This program would appeal to people interested in history, culture.
Accommodations • Conference center.
Program Details • Program offered 2 times per year. Session length: 2 weeks. Departures are scheduled in August. Program is targeted to seniors over 50. Most participants are 60–80 years of age. Participants must be 50 years or older to enroll. 35 participants per session. Reservations are recommended at least 6 months before departure.
Costs • $2925 (includes tuition, housing, all meals, excursions, international airfare, entrance fees). A $200 deposit is required.
Contact • Janice Pierson, Office Supervisor, Interhostel, University of New Hampshire, 6 Garrison Avenue, Durham, NH 03824; 800-733-9753; Fax: 603-862-1113; World Wide Web: http://www.learn.unh.edu/

INTERHOSTEL, UNIVERSITY OF NEW HAMPSHIRE

WALKING IN SCOTLAND

General Information • Cultural tour with visits to Stirling, Edinburgh, St. Andrews, Fife Region, Queen Elizabeth Forest Park, Trossachs, Culross. Once at the destination country, participants travel by foot. Program is affiliated with University of Stirling.
Learning Focus • Instruction in history and culture. Museum visits (Burrell Collection). Attendance at performances (Scottish music and dance). Instruction is offered by professors, naturalists. This program would appeal to people interested in history, culture, walking.
Accommodations • Conference center.
Program Details • Program offered once per year. Session length: 2 weeks. Departures are scheduled in April. Program is targeted to seniors over 50. Most participants are 60–80 years of age. Participants must be 50 years or older to enroll. 35 participants per session. Reservations are recommended at least 6 months before departure.
Costs • $2725 (includes tuition, housing, all meals, excursions, international airfare, entrance fees). A $200 deposit is required.
Contact • Janice Pierson, Office Supervisor, Interhostel, University of New Hampshire, 6 Garrison Avenue, Durham, NH 03824; 800-733-9753; Fax: 603-862-1113; World Wide Web: http://www.learn.unh.edu/

JOURNEYS EAST

HIGHLAND HIKING

General Information • Cultural tour with visits to Glasgow, Isle of Skye, Outer Hebrides, Ullapool. Once at the destination country, participants travel by train, foot, horse-drawn caravan.
Learning Focus • Escorted travel to off the beaten track spots. Museum visits (local museums). Attendance at performances (local shows, festivals of dance, music, theater). Other activities include camping, hiking, horse-drawn caravan. Instruction is offered by social anthropologists. This program would appeal to people interested in Celtic culture, horse caravanning, hiking.
Accommodations • Hotels, inns, lodges, caravans.
Program Details • Program offered 2 times per year. Session length: 2 weeks. Departures are scheduled in June, July. Program is targeted to people with culture and adventure oriented interests. Most participants are 30–70 years of age. 16 participants per session. Reservations are recommended at least 12 months before departure.
Costs • $3500 (includes housing, some meals, excursions, museum admissions). A $300 deposit is required.
Contact • Debra Loomis, Co-Director, Journeys East, 2443 Fillmore Street, #289, San Francisco, CA 94115; 800-527-2612; Fax: 510-601-1977

JOURNEYS THRU SCOTLAND

CASTLES AND GARDENS

General Information • Cultural tour with visits to Deeside, Edinburgh, Fife, Glasgow, Loch Linnke, Greywalls Garden, Hopetown House, Earlshall Castle, Perthshire, Glamis Castle, Pitmedden Gardens, Kildrummy Castle. Once at the destination country, participants travel by bus, foot, car.
Learning Focus • Nature observation (lochs, mountains, countryside). Other activities include sightseeing. This program would appeal to people interested in history, photography, heritage.
Accommodations • Hotels. Single rooms are available.
Program Details • Session length: 12 days. Departures are scheduled in May–October. Other requirements: at least one licensed driver per trip. 2–20 participants per session. Application deadline: 60 days prior to departure. Reservations are recommended at least 90 days–6 months before departure.
Costs • $1450–$2390 (includes housing, some meals, rental car, guidebook). A $500 deposit is required.
Contact • Harry Wallace, Co-Owner, Journeys Thru Scotland, PO Box 116, Sheridan, OR 97378; 800-828-7583; Fax: 503-843-4557

JOURNEYS THRU SCOTLAND

SCOTTISH GOLF

General Information • Sports program with visits to Ayrshire, St. Andrews, Troon, Culzean Castle, Ayr, Isle of Arran, Brodick Castle and Gardens, Edinburgh, Glamis Castle, Scone Palace. Once at the destination country, participants travel by bus, foot, boat, car.
Learning Focus • Museum visits (major museums). Other activities include golf, sightseeing. This program would appeal to people interested in golf, photography, history.
Accommodations • Locally-rented apartments, hotels. Single rooms are available.
Program Details • Session length: 8 days. Program is targeted to golfers. Most participants are 30–60 years of age. Other requirements: at least one licensed driver per trip. 4–20 participants per session. Application deadline: 60 days prior to departure. Reservations are recommended at least 90 days–6 months before departure.
Costs • $1510–$1960 (includes housing, some meals, British Heritage Pass, some greens fees, guidebook, rental car). A $500 deposit is required.
Contact • Harry Wallace, Co-Owner, Journeys Thru Scotland, PO Box 116, Sheridan, OR 97378; 800-828-7583; Fax: 503-843-4557

NATURAL HABITAT ADVENTURES

SHETLAND ISLANDS AND PUFFIN WATCH

General Information • Nature study tour with visits to Shetland Islands. Once at the destination country, participants travel by foot, boat, airplane.
Learning Focus • Instruction in field observation. Field research in puffins, whales and seals. Escorted travel to research and cultural areas. Nature observation (local flora and fauna). Instruction is offered by professors, researchers, naturalists, scientists. This program would appeal to people interested in photography, nature travel, wildlife.
Accommodations • Dormitories, hotels. Single rooms are available for an additional $295.
Program Details • Program offered once per year. Session length: 13 days. Departures are scheduled in June. Most participants are 30–68 years of age. 12 participants per session. Reservations are recommended at least 8–10 months before departure.
Costs • $2695 (includes housing, all meals, excursions). A $500 deposit is required.
Contact • Natural Habitat Adventures, 2945 Center Green Court, Suite H, Boulder, CO 80301; 800-543-8917; Fax: 303-449-3711

SOUTHERN ILLINOIS UNIVERSITY AT CARBONDALE

ART AND CULTURE IN THE SCOTTISH LANDSCAPE

General Information • Academic study program in Arbroath, Edinburgh, Glasgow.
Learning Focus • Courses in studio art, art history. Instruction is offered by professors from the sponsoring institution.
Accommodations • Castle.
Program Details • Program offered once per year. Session length: 3 weeks. Departures are scheduled in May. The program is open to undergraduate students. Most participants are 18–30 years of age. Other requirements: minimum 2.5 GPA. 10 participants per session. Application deadline: April 12.
Costs • $3015 (includes tuition, housing, all meals, books and class materials, excursions, international airfare, laundry, passport). A $1150 deposit is required.
Contact • Mr. Thomas A. Saville, Coordinator, Study Abroad Programs, Southern Illinois University at Carbondale, Mailcode 6885, Small Business Incubator, Room 217, Cardondale, IL 62901-6885; 618-453-7670; Fax: 618-453-7677; E-mail: studyabr@siu.edu

STATE UNIVERSITY OF NEW YORK COLLEGE AT BROCKPORT

DUNDEE, SCOTLAND HEALTH SCIENCE GRADUATE PROGRAM

General Information • Academic study program in Dundee. Classes are held on the campus of University of Dundee.
Learning Focus • Courses in health sciences. Instruction is offered by professors from the sponsoring institution.
Accommodations • Dormitories. Single rooms are available. Meals are taken as a group, on one's own, in central dining facility, in local restaurants.
Program Details • Program offered once per year. Session length: 10 days. Departures are scheduled in June. The program is open to graduate students. Most participants are 22 years of age and older. Other requirements: health science graduate majors. 10–20 participants per session. Application deadline: April 1.
Costs • $2500 (includes tuition, housing, some meals, books and class materials, excursions, international airfare). A $100 deposit is required.
Contact • Dr. John J. Perry, Director, International Education, State University of New York College at Brockport, Rakov Center, 350 New Campus Drive, Brockport, NY 14420; 716-395-2119; Fax: 716-637-3218; World Wide Web: http://www.brockport.edu/study_abroad

STATE UNIVERSITY OF NEW YORK COLLEGE AT BROCKPORT

EDINBURGH, SCOTLAND THEATRE FESTIVAL PROGRAM

General Information • Academic study program in Edinburgh. Classes are held on the campus of Queen Margaret College.
Learning Focus • Courses in theater. Instruction is offered by professors from the sponsoring institution.
Accommodations • Dormitories. Single rooms are available. Meals are taken on one's own, in central dining facility, in local restaurants.
Program Details • Program offered once per year. Session length: 3 weeks. Departures are scheduled in August. The program is open to undergraduate students, graduate students. Most participants are 19 years of age and older. 5–15 participants per session. Application deadline: May 1.

Costs • $3000 (includes tuition, housing, some meals, international airfare, theatre tickets). A $100 deposit is required.
Contact • Dr. John J. Perry, Director, International Education, State University of New York College at Brockport, Rakov Center, 350 New Campus Drive, Brockport, NY 14420; 716-395-2119; Fax: 716-637-3218; World Wide Web: http://www.brockport.edu/study_abroad

TEMPLE UNIVERSITY

TYLER ART WORKSHOP IN SCOTLAND

General Information • Academic study program in Glasgow. Excursions to England (London), Scottish Highlands.
Learning Focus • Courses in visual arts. Instruction is offered by professors from the sponsoring institution.
Accommodations • Dormitories, bed and breakfasts. Meals are taken as a group.
Program Details • Program offered once per year. Session length: 5 weeks. Departures are scheduled in June. The program is open to undergraduate students. Other requirements: minimum 2.5 GPA. 20 participants per session. Application deadline: March 1.
Costs • $4000 (includes tuition, housing, some meals, books and class materials, excursions, international airfare). Application fee: $30. A $150 deposit is required.
Contact • Denise A. Connerty, Interim Director of International Programs, Temple University, Conwell Hall, 5th Floor, Suite 501, Philadelphia, PA 19122; 215-204-4684; Fax: 215-204-5735; E-mail: intlprog@vm.temple.edu; World Wide Web: http://www.temple.edu/intlprog/

UNIVERSITY OF ALABAMA AT BIRMINGHAM

UNIVERSITY OF ALABAMA AT BIRMINGHAM IN SCOTLAND

General Information • Academic study program in Edinburgh. Classes are held on the campus of University of Edinburgh. Excursions to Isle of Skye.
Learning Focus • Courses in Scottish literature, Scottish history. Instruction is offered by professors from the sponsoring institution and local teachers.
Accommodations • Dormitories. Single rooms are available. Meals are taken on one's own, in local restaurants.
Program Details • Program offered once per year. Session length: 4 weeks. Departures are scheduled in July. The program is open to undergraduate students. Most participants are 19–39 years of age. Other requirements: must have completed English composition 101 and 102. 20–25 participants per session. Application deadline: May 31.
Costs • Contact sponsor for information. A $200 deposit is required.
Contact • Frank Romanowicz, Study Abroad Coordinator, University of Alabama at Birmingham, 1400 University Boulevard, HUC 318, Birmingham, AL 35294-1150; 205-934-5025; Fax: 205-934-8664; E-mail: ucipØ17@larry.huc.uab.edu

UNIVERSITY OF EDINBURGH

ARCHAEOLOGY IN SCOTLAND

General Information • Academic study program in Edinburgh. Classes are held on the campus of University of Edinburgh. Excursions to Argyll.
Learning Focus • Courses in archaeology. Instruction is offered by professors from the sponsoring institution.
Accommodations • Homestays, dormitories, program-owned apartments. Single rooms are available. Meals are taken on one's own, in local restaurants.
Program Details • Program offered once per year. Session length: 2 weeks. Departures are scheduled in July. The program is open to undergraduate students, graduate students, adults. Most participants are 18–50 years of age. Other requirements: fluency in English and a minimum age 18. 15 participants per session. Application deadline: June.
Costs • $550 (includes tuition, excursions, class materials). A $50 deposit is required.
Contact • Elaine Mowat, International Summer Courses Secretary, University of Edinburgh, CCE, 11 Buccleuch Place, Edinburgh EH8 9LW, Scotland; +44 131-650-4400; Fax: +44 131-667-6097; E-mail: cce@ed.ac.uk; World Wide Web: http://www.ed.ac.uk/~cce

UNIVERSITY OF EDINBURGH

EDINBURGH FESTIVAL ARTS

General Information • Academic study program in Edinburgh. Classes are held on the campus of University of Edinburgh.
Learning Focus • Courses in drama, music. Instruction is offered by professors from the sponsoring institution.
Accommodations • Homestays, dormitories, program-owned houses. Single rooms are available. Meals are taken on one's own, in local restaurants.
Program Details • Program offered once per year. Session length: 3 weeks. Departures are scheduled in August. The program is open to undergraduate students, graduate students, adults. Most participants are 18–80 years of age. Other requirements: fluency in English and a minimum age 18. 50 participants per session. Application deadline: July 15.
Costs • $795 (includes tuition, theatre and concert tickets, class materials). A $50 deposit is required.
Contact • Elaine Mowat, International Summer Courses Secretary, University of Edinburgh, CCE, 11 Buccleuch Place, Edinburgh EH8 9LW, Scotland; +44 131-650-4400; Fax: +44 131-667-6097; E-mail: cce@ed.ac.uk; World Wide Web: http://www.ed.ac.uk/~cce

UNIVERSITY OF EDINBURGH

FILM STUDIES

General Information • Academic study program in Edinburgh. Classes are held on the campus of University of Edinburgh.
Learning Focus • Courses in film studies. Instruction is offered by professors from the sponsoring institution.
Accommodations • Homestays, dormitories, program-owned apartments. Single rooms are available. Meals are taken on one's own, in local restaurants.

Program Details • Program offered once per year. Session length: 2 weeks. Departures are scheduled in August. The program is open to undergraduate students, graduate students, adults. Most participants are 18–65 years of age. Other requirements: fluency in English and a minimum age 18. 25 participants per session. Application deadline: July 15.
Costs • $315 (includes tuition, class materials). A $75 deposit is required.
Contact • Elaine Mowat, International Summer Courses Secretary, University of Edinburgh, CCE, 11 Buccleuch Place, Edinburgh EH8 9LW, Scotland; +44 131-650-4400; Fax: +44 131-667-6097; E-mail: cce@ed.ac.uk; World Wide Web: http://www.ed.ac.uk/~cce

UNIVERSITY OF EDINBURGH

NATURE CONSERVATION

General Information • Academic study program in Edinburgh. Classes are held on the campus of University of Edinburgh.
Learning Focus • Courses in nature conservation. Instruction is offered by professors from the sponsoring institution.
Accommodations • Homestays, dormitories, program-owned apartments. Single rooms are available. Meals are taken on one's own, in local restaurants.
Program Details • Program offered once per year. Session length: 1 week. Departures are scheduled in July. The program is open to undergraduate students, graduate students, adults. Most participants are 18–60 years of age. Other requirements: fluency in English and a minimum age 18. 12 participants per session. Application deadline: June 15.
Costs • $270 (includes tuition, excursions, class materials). A $50 deposit is required.
Contact • Elaine Mowat, International Summer Courses Secretary, University of Edinburgh, CCE, 11 Buccleuch Place, Edinburgh EH8 9LW, Scotland; +44 131-650-4400; Fax: +44 131-667-6097; E-mail: cce@ed.ac.uk; World Wide Web: http://www.ed.ac.uk/~cce

UNIVERSITY OF EDINBURGH

NEW WRITING IN ENGLISH

General Information • Academic study program in Edinburgh. Classes are held on the campus of University of Edinburgh.
Learning Focus • Courses in 20th century literature. Instruction is offered by professors from the sponsoring institution.
Accommodations • Homestays, dormitories, program-owned apartments. Single rooms are available. Meals are taken on one's own, in local restaurants.
Program Details • Program offered once per year. Session length: 3 weeks. Departures are scheduled in July, August. The program is open to undergraduate students, graduate students, adults. Most participants are 18–65 years of age. Other requirements: fluency in English and a minimum age 18. 70 participants per session. Application deadline: June 15.
Costs • $500 (includes tuition, cinema tickets, class materials). A $50 deposit is required.
Contact • Elaine Mowat, International Summer Courses Secretary, University of Edinburgh, CCE, 11 Buccleuch Place, Edinburgh EH8 9LW, Scotland; +44 131-650-4400; Fax: +44 131-667-6097; E-mail: cce@ed.ac.uk; World Wide Web: http://www.ed.ac.uk/~cce

UNIVERSITY OF EDINBURGH

SCOTLAND THROUGH THE AGES

General Information • Academic study program in Edinburgh. Classes are held on the campus of University of Edinburgh.
Learning Focus • Courses in Scottish culture. Instruction is offered by professors from the sponsoring institution.
Accommodations • Homestays, dormitories, program-owned apartments. Single rooms are available. Meals are taken on one's own, in local restaurants.
Program Details • Program offered once per year. Session length: 4 weeks. Departures are scheduled in July. The program is open to undergraduate students, graduate students, adults. Most participants are 18–65 years of age. Other requirements: fluency in English and a minimum age 18. 25 participants per session. Application deadline: June 15.
Costs • $840 (includes tuition, excursions, class materials). A $75 deposit is required.
Contact • Elaine Mowat, International Summer Courses Secretary, University of Edinburgh, CCE, 11 Buccleuch Place, Edinburgh EH8 9LW, Scotland; +44 131-650-4400; Fax: +44 131-667-6097; E-mail: cce@ed.ac.uk; World Wide Web: http://www.ed.ac.uk/~cce

UNIVERSITY OF EDINBURGH

SCOTTISH ARCHITECTURE

General Information • Academic study program in Edinburgh. Classes are held on the campus of University of Edinburgh.
Learning Focus • Courses in architectural history. Instruction is offered by professors from the sponsoring institution.
Accommodations • Homestays, dormitories, program-owned apartments. Single rooms are available. Meals are taken on one's own, in local restaurants.
Program Details • Program offered once per year. Session length: 2 weeks. Departures are scheduled in July, August. The program is open to undergraduate students, graduate students, adults. Most participants are 18–65 years of age. Other requirements: fluency in English and a minimum age 18. 20 participants per session. Application deadline: June.
Costs • $480 (includes tuition, excursions). A $50 deposit is required.
Contact • Elaine Mowat, International Summer Courses Secretary, University of Edinburgh, CCE, 11 Buccleuch Place, Edinburgh EH8 9LW, Scotland; +44 131-650-4400; Fax: +44 131-667-6097; E-mail: cce@ed.ac.uk; World Wide Web: http://www.ed.ac.uk/~cce

UNIVERSITY OF EDINBURGH

SCOTTISH GAELIC LANGUAGE AND LITERATURE

General Information • Academic study program in Edinburgh. Classes are held on the campus of University of Edinburgh.

Learning Focus • Courses in Gaelic language. Instruction is offered by professors from the sponsoring institution.

Accommodations • Homestays, dormitories, program-owned apartments. Single rooms are available. Meals are taken on one's own, in local restaurants.

Program Details • Program offered once per year. Session length: 3 weeks. Departures are scheduled in July. The program is open to undergraduate students, graduate students, adults. Most participants are 18–65 years of age. Other requirements: fluency in English and a minimum age 18. 35 participants per session. Application deadline: May 31.

Costs • $345 (includes tuition, class materials). A $75 deposit is required.

Contact • Elaine Mowat, Summer Courses Secretary, University of Edinburgh, CCE, 11 Buccleuch Place, Edinburgh EH8 9LW, Scotland; +44 131-650-4400; Fax: +44 131-667-6097; E-mail: cce@ed.ac.uk; World Wide Web: http://www.ed.ac.uk/~cce

UNIVERSITY OF MIAMI

PRINCES, POETS, AND CASTLES

General Information • Academic study program in Edinburgh. Classes are held on the campus of University of Edinburgh.

Learning Focus • Courses in history. Instruction is offered by local teachers.

Accommodations • Dormitories. Single rooms are available. Meals are taken as a group, in central dining facility.

Program Details • Program offered once per year. Session length: 3 weeks. Departures are scheduled in June. The program is open to undergraduate students. Most participants are 19–25 years of age. Other requirements: minimum 3.3 GPA. 20 participants per session. Application deadline: April 1.

Costs • $3200 (includes tuition, housing, some meals, books and class materials). Application fee: $30. A $500 deposit is required.

Contact • Betsy Nyhart, Advisor, International Education and Exchange Programs, University of Miami, PO Box 248005, Coral Gables, FL 33124; 800-557-5421; Fax: 305-284-6629; E-mail: ieep@cstudies.msmail.miami.edu; World Wide Web: http://www.miami.edu/cstudies/ieep.html

UNIVERSITY OF NORTH CAROLINA AT CHARLOTTE

COMMUNITY SERVICE AND ENRICHMENT IN SCOTLAND

General Information • Academic study program in England (London), Scotland (Stirling).

Learning Focus • Courses in community service, psychology. Instruction is offered by professors from the sponsoring institution.

Accommodations • Hostels. Meals are taken as a group, in central dining facility.

Program Details • Program offered once per year. Session length: 3 weeks. Departures are scheduled in June. The program is open to undergraduate students, graduate students. Most participants are 18–25 years of age. 10 participants per session. Application deadline: March.

Costs • $1995 (includes tuition, housing, some meals, insurance, international airfare). Application fee: $10. A $900 deposit is required.

Contact • Elizabeth A. Adams, Director, Education Abroad Programs, University of North Carolina at Charlotte, Office of International Programs, 9201 University City Boulevard, Charlotte, NC 28223-0001; 704-547-2464; Fax: 704-547-3168; E-mail: eaadams@email.uncc.edu; World Wide Web: http://unccvm.uncc.edu

UNIVERSITY OF SOUTHERN MISSISSIPPI

PROTESTANTISM AND POLITICS IN GREAT BRITAIN

General Information • Academic study program in Edinburgh.

Learning Focus • Courses in political science, history, religion and theology, philosophy.

Accommodations • Locally-rented apartments.

Program Details • Program offered once per year. Session length: 2 weeks. Departures are scheduled in August. The program is open to undergraduate students, graduate students. Other requirements: minimum 2.0 GPA and good academic standing. Application deadline: May 20.

Costs • $2149 for undergraduates, $2499 for graduate students (includes tuition, housing, excursions, international airfare). A $200 deposit is required.

Contact • Director, Protestantism and Politics in Great Britain, University of Southern Mississippi, Box 10047, Hattiesburg, MS 39406-0047; 601-266-4344; Fax: 601-266-5699; E-mail: m_ravencraft@bull.cc.usm.edu

PAIN

ALMA COLLEGE

SUMMER PROGRAM OF STUDIES IN MADRID, SPAIN

General Information • Language study program in Madrid. Classes are held on the campus of Tandem Escuela Internacional. Excursions to Prado, Segovia, Toledo.
Learning Focus • Courses in Spanish language. Instruction is offered by local teachers.
Accommodations • Homestays, locally-rented apartments. Single rooms are available. Meals are taken with host family, in residences.
Program Details • Program offered 6 times per year. Session length: 2–12 weeks. Departures are scheduled in May–August. The program is open to undergraduate students, graduate students, adults. Most participants are 19–24 years of age. Other requirements: minimum 2.5 GPA. 10 participants per session. Application deadline: March 15.
Costs • $2090–$9360 (includes tuition, housing, all meals, excursions). Application fee: $35. A $200 deposit is required.
Contact • Patricia Landis, Director of International Education, Alma College, 614 West Superior Street, Alma, MI 48801; 517-463-7247; Fax: 517-463-7126; E-mail: landis@alma.edu; World Wide Web: http://www.alma.edu

ALMA COLLEGE

SUMMER PROGRAM OF STUDIES IN SEGOVIA, SPAIN

General Information • Language study program in Segovia. Classes are held on the campus of Cursos Americanos e Internacionales. Excursions to Route of Castles, El Escorial Monastery, Prado.
Learning Focus • Courses in Spanish language. Instruction is offered by local teachers.
Accommodations • Homestays. Single rooms are available. Meals are taken with host family, in residences.
Program Details • Program offered once per year. Session length: 6 weeks. Departures are scheduled in June. The program is open to undergraduate students, graduate students, adults. Most participants are 19–24 years of age. Other requirements: minimum 2.5 GPA and 2 years college-level Spanish. 12 participants per session. Application deadline: March 15.
Costs • $4150 (includes tuition, housing, all meals, excursions). Application fee: $35. A $200 deposit is required.
Contact • Patricia Landis, Director of International Education, Alma College, 614 West Superior Street, Alma, MI 48801; 517-463-7247; Fax: 517-463-7126; E-mail: landis@alma.edu; World Wide Web: http://www.alma.edu

AMERICAN INSTITUTE FOR FOREIGN STUDY (AIFS)

UNIVERSITY OF SALAMANCA

General Information • Language study program in Salamanca. Classes are held on the campus of University of Salamanca. Excursions to Madrid, Granada, Seville.
Learning Focus • Courses in Spanish language.
Accommodations • Homestays, dormitories.
Program Details • Program offered once per year. Session length: 4 or 6 weeks. Departures are scheduled in June. The program is open to undergraduate students, graduate students, adults, high school graduates. Other requirements: minimum 2.0 GPA. Application deadline: March 15.
Costs • $2639 for 4 weeks, $3339 for 6 weeks (includes tuition, housing, all meals). A $400 deposit is required.
Contact • Carmela Vigliano, Director, Summer Programs, American Institute for Foreign Study (AIFS), 102 Greenwich Avenue, Greenwich, CT 06830; 800-727-2437, ext. 6087; Fax: 203-869-9615; E-mail: info@aifs.org

AMERICAN JEWISH CONGRESS, INTERNATIONAL TRAVEL PROGRAM

THE GRAND TOUR OF SPAIN

General Information • Cultural tour with visits to Almagro, Barcelona, Granada, Madrid, Marbella, Seville, Toledo Cathedral, Montjuich, Arco del Triunfo, Carral de las Comedias, Costa del Sol, Gibraltar. Once at the destination country, participants travel by bus, foot, airplane.
Learning Focus • Escorted travel to synagogues, La Mancha and St. Michael's Cave. Museum visits (Prado Museum, Museum of Sephardic Culture). Attendance at performances (flamenco dancing show). Instruction is offered by historians. This program would appeal to people interested in Jewish history.
Accommodations • Hotels. Single rooms are available for an additional $600.
Program Details • Program offered 6 times per year. Session length: 15 days. Departures are scheduled in May–October. Program is targeted to Jewish-American adults. Most participants are 40–75 years of age. Participants must be 15 years or older to enroll. Participants must be members of the sponsoring organization (annual dues: $50). 30 participants per session. Reservations are recommended at least 6 months before departure.
Costs • $3695–$3795 (includes housing, some meals, excursions, international airfare, travel bag, documents portfolio, travel journal). A $200 deposit is required.
Contact • Betty Van Dyke, Worldwide Operations Manager, American Jewish Congress, International Travel Program, 18 East 84th Street, New York, NY 10028; 212-360-1571; Fax: 212-717-1932

APPALACHIAN STATE UNIVERSITY

SPAIN: LANGUAGE

General Information • Academic study program in Madrid. Excursions to Barcelona.
Learning Focus • Courses in Spanish language. Instruction is offered by professors from the sponsoring institution.
Program Details • Program offered once per year. Session length: 4–5 weeks. Departures are scheduled in May. Most participants are 18 years of age and older. 20 participants per session.
Costs • $2535 (includes tuition, housing, insurance, international airfare, International Student Identification card).
Contact • Dr. Ramon Solis, Professor, Appalachian State University, Department of Foreign Languages, Boone, NC 28608; 704-262-3095; Fax: 704-262-4037

APPALACHIAN STATE UNIVERSITY

SPAIN: LIBRARY SCIENCE, LEADERSHIP, AND EDUCATIONAL STUDIES

General Information • Academic study program in Spain.
Learning Focus • Courses in library science, leadership and educational studies. Instruction is offered by professors from the sponsoring institution.
Program Details • Program offered once per year. Session length: 15 days. Departures are scheduled in June. Most participants are 18 years of age and older. 20 participants per session.
Costs • $2877 (includes tuition, housing, insurance, international airfare, International Student Identification card).
Contact • Loles Solis, Professor, Appalachian State University, Department of Library Science, Boone, NC 28608; 704-262-2824; Fax: 704-262-4037

ARCHETOURS, INC.

BARCELONA: CONTEMPORARY ARCHITECTURE AND ART

General Information • Architectural tour with visits to Barcelona. Once at the destination country, participants travel by bus, foot. Program is affiliated with American Institute of Architects Continuing Education System.
Learning Focus • Instruction in contemporary architecture and art. Escorted travel to the Olympic Village, the waterfront area, the National Theatre, Montjuic and the Barcelona Pavilion. Museum visits (Miro Museum, Picasso Museum, Dali Museum). Instruction is offered by professors, artists, historians. This program would appeal to people interested in architecture, archaeology, art, design.
Accommodations • Hotels. Single rooms are available for an additional $275.
Program Details • Program offered 2 times per year. Session length: 1 week. Departures are scheduled in May–October. Most participants are 30–70 years of age. Participants must be 21 years or older to enroll. Other requirements: good health, capability of walking, standing and climbing to visit sites. 8–16 participants per session. Application deadline: 60 days prior to departure. Reservations are recommended at least 4–6 months before departure.
Costs • $1995 (includes housing, some meals, books and class materials, excursions, museum and site fees, airport transfers, lecturer fees, tips). A $250 deposit is required.
Contact • Ms. Gail Cornell, President, Archetours, Inc., 235 East 22nd Street, Suite 14F, New York, NY 10010; 800-770-3051; Fax: 212-779-7130; E-mail: archetours.@aol.com

ARCHETOURS, INC.

BARCELONA: HOWDY, GAUDI!

General Information • Architectural tour with visits to Barcelona, Sitges. Once at the destination country, participants travel by bus, foot. Program is affiliated with American Institute of Architects Continuing Education System.
Learning Focus • Instruction in Art Nouveau and the Moderniste architecture of the turn of the century. Escorted travel to residences, parks and commercial buildings designed by Gaudi and contemporaries. Museum visits (Gaudi Museum and Residence). Instruction is offered by professors, artists, historians. This program would appeal to people interested in architecture, art, archaeology, interior design, textile design.
Accommodations • Hotels. Single rooms are available for an additional $275.
Program Details • Program offered 2 times per year. Session length: 1 week. Departures are scheduled in May, October. Most participants are 30–70 years of age. Participants must be 21 years or older to enroll. Other requirements: good health, capability of walking, standing and climbing to visit sites. 8–16 participants per session. Application deadline: 60 days prior to departure. Reservations are recommended at least 4–6 months before departure.
Costs • $1995 (includes housing, some meals, books and class materials, excursions, museum and site fees, airport transfers, lecturer fees, tips). A $250 deposit is required.
Contact • Ms. Gail Cornell, President, Archetours, Inc., 235 East 22nd Street, Suite 14F, New York, NY 10010; 800-770-3051; Fax: 212-779-7130; E-mail: archetours.@aol.com

AUGUSTA STATE UNIVERSITY

SALAMANCA PROGRAM

General Information • Academic study program in Salamanca. Classes are held on the campus of University of Salamanca. Excursions to Madrid, Segovia, Toledo, Barcelona, Palma de Mallorca.
Learning Focus • Courses in translation, literature, Spanish language, culture, composition, art history, economics. Instruction is offered by local teachers.
Accommodations • Homestays.
Program Details • Program offered once per year. Session length: 5 weeks. Departures are scheduled in June. The program is open to undergraduate students, graduate students. Other requirements: 3 college-level Spanish courses, 3.00 GPA in Spanish courses, 2.50 GPA overall, two recommendations.. Application deadline: March 15.

Costs • $3400–$4050 (includes tuition, housing, all meals, books and class materials, excursions, international airfare, laundry).
Contact • Dr. Jana Sandarg, Program Director, Augusta State University, Department of Languages, Literature, and Culture, Augusta, GA 30904-2200; 706-737-1500; Fax: 706-737-1773

Former participants in the program say, "Salamanca is the greatest possible college town. Don't go anywhere else!" and, "I am so happy I chose the ASU program because after talking to students on other Salamanca programs, I realize what a great deal ASU offers. So many excursions, a great educational program, great experiences—for much less than what other students paid."

The director provides a predeparture orientation and meets regularly with students in Spain for tutoring, excursions, and parties. The price of this program includes excursions that many programs offer as optional. Other return dates are available for students wishing to travel in Europe after the program.

BENTLEY COLLEGE

LANGUAGE AND CULTURE IN MADRID

General Information • Academic study program in Madrid. Classes are held on the campus of College for International Studies. Excursions to Barcelona, Segovia, Toledo.
Learning Focus • Courses in language study, cultural studies. Instruction is offered by local teachers.
Accommodations • Homestays. Single rooms are available. Meals are taken with host family, in local restaurants.
Program Details • Program offered once per year. Session length: 4 weeks. Departures are scheduled in May. The program is open to undergraduate students, adults. Most participants are 19–22 years of age. Other requirements: minimum 2.7 GPA. 8–10 participants per session. Application deadline: April 1.
Costs • $3000 (includes tuition, housing, some meals, International Student Identification card). Application fee: $35. A $500 deposit is required.
Contact • Jennifer L. Scully, Director of Study Abroad, Bentley College, 175 Forest Street, Waltham, MA 02154; 617-891-3474; Fax: 617-891-2819; E-mail: inprinfo@bentley.edu

BOSTON UNIVERSITY

MADRID INTERNSHIP PROGRAM

General Information • Internship program in Madrid. Classes are held on the campus of Instituto Internacional en España. Excursions to Segovia, Granada, Toledo, Córdoba.
Learning Focus • Courses in Spanish culture, political science, broadcasting and film, international organization, arts and architecture, public relations. Instruction is offered by professors from the sponsoring institution.
Accommodations • Homestays. Single rooms are available. Meals are taken with host family, in residences.
Program Details • Program offered once per year. Session length: 7 weeks. Departures are scheduled in May. The program is open to undergraduate students, adults. Most participants are 19–22 years of age. Other requirements: minimum 3.0 GPA, good academic standing, minimum 5 semesters college-level Spanish and an interview. 10 participants per session. Application deadline: March 15.
Costs • $4400 (includes tuition, housing, all meals). Application fee: $35. A $300 deposit is required.
Contact • Division of International Programs, Boston University, 232 Bay State Road, Boston, MA 02215; 617-353-9888; Fax: 617-353-5402; E-mail: abroad@bu.edu; World Wide Web: http://web.bu.edu/abroad

BOSTON UNIVERSITY

SUMMER PROGRAM IN MADRID

General Information • Language study program in Madrid. Classes are held on the campus of Instituto Internacional en España. Excursions to Segovia, Granada, Toledo, Córdoba.
Learning Focus • Courses in Spanish language, Spanish literature, Spanish art, Spanish culture. Instruction is offered by professors from the sponsoring institution and local teachers.
Accommodations • Homestays. Single rooms are available. Meals are taken with host family, in residences.
Program Details • Program offered once per year. Session length: 6 weeks. Departures are scheduled in May. The program is open to undergraduate students, adults. Most participants are 19–21 years of age. Other requirements: minimum 3.0 GPA, good academic standing and a minimum 2 semesters of college-level Spanish. 20 participants per session. Application deadline: March 15.
Costs • $3950 (includes tuition, housing, all meals, excursions). Application fee: $35. A $300 deposit is required.
Contact • Division of International Programs, Boston University, 232 Bay State Road, Boston, MA 02215; 617-353-9888; Fax: 617-353-5402; E-mail: abroad@bu.edu; World Wide Web: http://web.bu.edu/abroad

BRYN MAWR COLLEGE

CENTRO DE ESTUDIOS HISPÁNICOS EN MADRID

General Information • Language study program in Madrid. Excursions to Salamanca, Toledo, Segovia, Soto del Real.
Learning Focus • Courses in art history, economics. Instruction is offered by professors from the sponsoring institution.
Accommodations • Homestays. Single rooms are available. Meals are taken with host family.
Program Details • Program offered once per year. Session length: 6 weeks. Departures are scheduled in June. The program is open to undergraduate students, graduate students, adults. Most participants are 19–26 years of age. Other requirements: 2 years of Spanish. 20–30 participants per session. Application deadline: rolling.

Costs • $4150 (includes tuition, housing, all meals, insurance, excursions, 1 month transportation pass for Madrid). Application fee: $25. A $400 deposit is required.
Contact • Enrique Sacerio-Garí, Director, Centro de Estudios Hispánicos, Bryn Mawr College, 101 North Merion Avenue, Bryn Mawr, PA 19010-2899; 610-526-5198; Fax: 610-526-7479; E-mail: esacerio@brynmawr.edu; World Wide Web: http://www.brynmawr.edu/Adm/academic/special/study.html

CENTER FOR CROSS-CULTURAL STUDY

JANUARY TERM IN SEVILLE, SPAIN

General Information • Academic study program in Seville. Excursions to Mérida, Cáceres, Córdoba, Alcázar Palace, Itálka, Seville cathedral, Trujillo ruins.
Learning Focus • Courses in language study, Spanish poetry. Instruction is offered by professors from the sponsoring institution.
Accommodations • Homestays, student residencias. Single rooms are available. Meals are taken with host family, in residences.
Program Details • Program offered once per year. Session length: 3½ weeks. Departures are scheduled in January. The program is open to undergraduate students, pre-college students, adults. Most participants are 15–22 years of age. Other requirements: minimum 3.0 GPA in Spanish and a minimum of 2.5 GPA overall. 35 participants per session. Application deadline: October 15.
Costs • $1910 (includes tuition, housing, all meals, excursions, laundry, International Student Identification card, orientation, reception). Application fee: $30. A $300 deposit is required.
Contact • Dr. Judith M. Ortiz, Associate Director, Center for Cross-Cultural Study, Department PS, 446 Main Street, Amherst, MA 01002; 800-ESPAÑA-1; Fax: 413-256-1968; E-mail: cccs@crocker.com; World Wide Web: http://www.cccs.com

CENTER FOR CROSS-CULTURAL STUDY

SUMMER BUSINESS PROGRAM IN SEVILLE, SPAIN

General Information • Academic study program in Seville. Excursions to local industry, multinationals, agricultural regions.
Learning Focus • Courses in Spanish business. Instruction is offered by professors from the sponsoring institution.
Accommodations • Homestays, student residencias. Single rooms are available. Meals are taken with host family, in residences.
Program Details • Program offered once per year. Session length: 3½ weeks. Departures are scheduled in July. The

program is open to undergraduate students, adults. Most participants are 18–23 years of age. Other requirements: previous study of business or economics. 25 participants per session. Application deadline: April 15.
Costs • Contact sponsor for information. Application fee: $30. A $300 deposit is required.
Contact • Dr. Judith M. Ortiz, Associate Director, Center for Cross-Cultural Study, Department PS, 446 Main Street, Amherst, MA 01002; 800-ESPANA-1; Fax: 413-256-1968; E-mail: cccs@crocker.com; World Wide Web: http://www.cccs.com

CENTER FOR CROSS-CULTURAL STUDY

SUMMER PROGRAM IN SEVILLE, SPAIN

General Information • Academic study program in Seville. Excursions to La Bábida Monastery, Córdoba, beaches, Alcázar Palace, Fine Arts Museum, Guadalquivir River cruise.
Learning Focus • Courses in language study, literature, history, Spanish theater, civilizations, business. Instruction is offered by professors from the sponsoring institution.
Accommodations • Homestays, student residencias. Single rooms are available. Meals are taken with host family, in residences.
Program Details • Program offered 2 times per year. Session length: 3½ weeks. Departures are scheduled in June, July. The program is open to undergraduate students, graduate students, pre-college students, adults. Most participants are 18–22 years of age. 50 participants per session. Application deadline: April 15.
Costs • $1755 (includes tuition, housing, all meals, excursions, laundry, International Student Identification card, orientation, reception). Application fee: $30. A $300 deposit is required.
Contact • Dr. Judith M. Ortiz, Associate Director, Center for Cross-Cultural Study, Department PS, 446 Main Street, Amherst, MA 01002-2314; 800-ESPAÑA-1; Fax: 413-256-1968; E-mail: cccs@crocker.com; World Wide Web: http://www.cccs.com

THE CENTER FOR ENGLISH STUDIES

STUDY ABROAD IN BARCELONA, SPAIN

General Information • Language study program with visits to Barcelona. Program is affiliated with International House–Barcelona.
Learning Focus • Instruction in the Spanish language. Other activities include field trips to local sites, museums, markets and churches. Instruction is offered by faculty members from host institution. This program would appeal to people interested in Spanish language.
Accommodations • Homestays, dormitories, locally-rented apartments, program-owned apartments, program-owned houses. Single rooms are available.
Program Details • Session length: 2 or more weeks. Departures are scheduled throughout the year. Most participants are 16–70 years of age. 6–12 participants per session. Application deadline: 2 weeks prior to departure. Reservations are recommended at least 1 month before departure.
Costs • $1000 for 2 weeks (includes tuition, housing, some meals, books and class materials, excursions). A $125 deposit is required.
Contact • Ms. Lorraine Haber, Study Abroad Coordinator, The Center for English Studies, 330 7th Avenue, 6th Floor, New York, NY 10001; 212-629-7300; Fax: 212-736-7950; E-mail: ces_newyork@cescorp.com

THE CENTER FOR ENGLISH STUDIES

STUDY ABROAD IN GRANADA, SPAIN

General Information • Language study program with visits to Granada. Program is affiliated with CEGRI–Centro Granadi de Espanol.
Learning Focus • Instruction in the Spanish language. Other activities include field trips to local sites, museums, markets and churches. Instruction is offered by faculty members from host institution. This program would appeal to people interested in Spanish language, culture, commerical Spanish.
Accommodations • Homestays, locally-rented apartments, program-owned apartments, hotels, hostels. Single rooms are available.
Program Details • Session length: 2 or more weeks. Departures are scheduled throughout the year. Most participants are 16–70 years of age. Participants must be 16 years or older to enroll. 6–12 participants per session. Application deadline: 2 weeks prior to departure. Reservations are recommended at least 1 month before departure.
Costs • $1000 for 4 weeks (includes tuition, housing, some meals, books and class materials, excursions). A $125 deposit is required.
Contact • Ms. Lorraine Haber, Study Abroad Coordinator, The Center for English Studies, 330 7th Avenue, 6th Floor, New York, NY 10021; 212-629-7300; Fax: 212-736-7950; E-mail: ces_newyork@cescorp.com

THE CENTER FOR ENGLISH STUDIES

STUDY ABROAD IN MADRID, SPAIN

General Information • Language study program with visits to Madrid. Program is affiliated with International House–Madrid.
Learning Focus • Instruction in the Spanish language. Other activities include field trips to local sites, museums, markets and churches. Instruction is offered by faculty members from host institution. This program would appeal to people interested in Spanish language.
Accommodations • Homestays, dormitories, locally-rented apartments, program-owned apartments, program-owned houses. Single rooms are available.
Program Details • Session length: 2 or more weeks. Departures are scheduled throughout the year. Most participants are 16–70 years of age. Participants must be 16 years or older to enroll. 6–12 participants per session. Application deadline: 2 weeks prior to departure. Reservations are recommended at least 1 month before departure.
Costs • $1000 for 2 weeks (includes tuition, housing, some meals, books and class materials, excursions). A $125 deposit is required.
Contact • Ms. Lorraine Haber, Study Abroad Coordinator, The Center for English Studies, 330 7th Avenue, 6th Floor,

New York, NY 10001; 212-629-7300; Fax: 212-736-7950; E-mail: ces_newyork@cescorp.com

THE CENTER FOR ENGLISH STUDIES

STUDY ABROAD IN SAN SEBASTIAN, SPAIN

General Information • Language study program with visits to San Sebastian. Program is affiliated with International House-Academy Lacunza.

Learning Focus • Instruction in the Spanish language. Other activities include field trips to local sites, museums, markets and churches. Instruction is offered by faculty members from host institution. This program would appeal to people interested in Spanish language.

Accommodations • Homestays, locally-rented apartments, program-owned apartments, program-owned houses. Single rooms are available.

Program Details • Session length: 2 or more weeks. Departures are scheduled throughout the year. Most participants are 17–70 years of age. Participants must be 17 years or older to enroll. 6–12 participants per session. Application deadline: 2 weeks prior to departure. Reservations are recommended at least 1 month before departure.

Costs • $1000 for 2 weeks (includes tuition, housing, some meals, books and class materials, excursions). A $125 deposit is required.

Contact • Ms. Lorraine Haber, Study Abroad Coordinator, The Center for English Studies, 330 7th Avenue, 6th Floor, New York, NY 10001; 212-629-7300; Fax: 212-736-7950; E-mail: ces_newyork@cescorp.com

CENTRO DE ESTUDIOS DE CASTELLANO

SPANISH COURSES

General Information • Language study program in Málaga. Excursions to Granada, Seville, Marruecos, Gibraltar, Ronda, Nerja.

Learning Focus • Courses in Spanish language.

Accommodations • Homestays, dormitories, locally-rented apartments, program-owned apartments, program-owned houses. Single rooms are available. Meals are taken on one's own, with host family, in central dining facility, in local restaurants, in residences.

Program Details • Session length: 2–16 weeks. Departures are scheduled in January–December. The program is open to undergraduate students, graduate students, pre-college students, adults. Most participants are 16 years of age and older. Application deadline: contact sponsor.

Costs • Contact sponsor for information.

Contact • F. Marin Fernández, Director, Centro de Estudios de Castellano, Avda. Juan Sebastian Elcano. 120, Málaga 29017, Spain; +34 52-290-551; Fax: +34 52-290-551

COLLEGE CONSORTIUM FOR INTERNATIONAL STUDIES–BROWARD COMMUNITY COLLEGE AND ST. BONAVENTURE UNIVERSITY

CCIS SUMMER IN SPAIN

General Information • Academic study program in Seville. Classes are held on the campus of Institute of International Studies. Excursions to Córdoba, La Rabida/Mazagon, Granada.
Learning Focus • Courses in Spanish language, Spanish culture. Instruction is offered by local teachers.
Accommodations • Homestays, locally-rented apartments. Single rooms are available. Meals are taken on one's own, with host family, in local restaurants, in residences.
Program Details • Program offered once per year. Session length: 4 weeks. Departures are scheduled in June. The program is open to undergraduate students, graduate students, adults. Most participants are 18–65 years of age. Other requirements: minimum 2.5 GPA. 20 participants per session. Application deadline: May 10.
Costs • $1850 (includes tuition, housing, all meals, insurance, excursions). Application fee: $25.
Contact • Jane C. Evans, Executive Director, College Consortium for International Studies, 2000 P Street, NW, Suite 503, Washington, DC 20036; 800-453-6956; Fax: 202-233-0999; E-mail: ccis@intr.net

COUNCIL ON INTERNATIONAL EDUCATIONAL EXCHANGE

COUNCIL STUDY CENTER ART RESTORATION AND ART HISTORY PROGRAM IN SEVILLE

General Information • Academic study program in Seville. Classes are held on the campus of Escucla de Artes Aplicadas. Excursions to Córdoba, Carmona.
Learning Focus • Courses in art restoration, Spanish language, art history. Instruction is offered by local teachers.
Accommodations • Homestays. Meals are taken with host family, in residences.
Program Details • Program offered once per year. Session length: 6 weeks. Departures are scheduled in June. The program is open to undergraduate students, adults. Most participants are 20–25 years of age. Other requirements: minimum 2.75 GPA. 10–20 participants per session. Application deadline: April 1.
Costs • Contact sponsor for information. Application fee: $30. A $300 deposit is required.
Contact • Council on International Educational Exchange, College and University Division, 205 East 42nd Street, New York, NY 10017; 888-368-6245; Fax: 212-822-2699; World Wide Web: http://www.ciee.org

COUNCIL ON INTERNATIONAL EDUCATIONAL EXCHANGE

SPANISH MEDITERRANEAN: LANGUAGE AND AREA STUDIES AT THE UNIVERSITY OF ALICANTE

General Information • Language study program in Alicante. Classes are held on the campus of University of Alicante. Excursions to Valencia, Santiago de Compostela, Granada.
Learning Focus • Courses in civilizations, cultural studies, Mediterrean studies, art history, Spanish language. Instruction is offered by local teachers.
Accommodations • Homestays. Meals are taken with host family, in residences.
Program Details • Program offered once per year. Session length: 6 weeks. Departures are scheduled in June. The program is open to undergraduate students, adults. Most participants are 20 years of age and older. Other requirements: minimum 2.75 GPA and completion of 1 college semester. Application deadline: April 1.
Costs • $3100 (includes tuition, housing, all meals, insurance, excursions, International Student Identification card). Application fee: $30. A $300 deposit is required.
Contact • Council on International Educational Exchange, College and University Division, 205 East 42nd Street, New York, NY 10017; 888-268-6245; Fax: 212-822-2699; E-mail: weuropereg@ciee.org; World Wide Web: http://www.ciee.org

COUNTRY WALKERS

WILD AND ROMANTIC ALPUJARRAS

General Information • Cultural, gourmet cooking, nature study and walking tour with visits to Bérchules, Granada, Trevélez. Once at the destination country, participants travel by foot.
Learning Focus • Escorted travel to Bubión, Poqueira Gorge and Arroyo de Prado Largo. Other activities include walking. Instruction is offered by professors, researchers, naturalists, historians. This program would appeal to people interested in walking, nature studies, food and wine.
Accommodations • Hotels. Single rooms are available for an additional $300–$600.
Program Details • Program offered 7 times per year. Session length: 8 days. Departures are scheduled in March–May, September–November. Program is targeted to adults 35 to 65 years old. Most participants are 35–65 years of age. Participants must be 18 years or older to enroll. 18

participants per session. Reservations are recommended at least 5-6 months before departure.
Costs • $1895 (includes housing, all meals, excursions). A $400 deposit is required.
Contact • Heather Kellingbeck, Vice President, Country Walkers, PO Box 180, Waterbury, VT 05176; 800-464-9255; Fax: 802-244-5661; E-mail: ctrywalk@aol.com

CROSS-CULTURE

SPANISH DISCOVERY I

General Information • Cultural tour with visits to Madrid, Toledo, Segovia, Guadarrama mountains. Once at the destination country, participants travel by bus, foot.
Learning Focus • Instruction in the art of bull fighting. Escorted travel to Plaza Mayor, Puerto del Sol, Toledo Cathedral and El Greco's house. Museum visits (Prado, Thyssen-Bornemisza Museum). Attendance at performances (Spanish music, bullfight, northern flamenco dancing). Instruction is offered by highly educated guides. This program would appeal to people interested in culture, history, nature studies, arts, traditions, food and wine.
Accommodations • Hotels. Single rooms are available for an additional $230.
Program Details • Program offered once per year. Session length: 8 days. Departures are scheduled in September. Program is targeted to adults of all ages. Most participants are 40–70 years of age. Participants must be 12 years or older to enroll. Other requirements: good health, accompaniment of an adult if under 18. 20–25 participants per session. Application deadline: 1 month prior to departure. Reservations are recommended at least 3–12 months before departure.
Costs • $2110 (includes tuition, housing, all meals, books and class materials, excursions, international airfare). A $300 deposit is required.
Contact • Cross-Culture, 52 High Point Drive, Amherst, MA 01002-1224; 413-256-6303; Fax: 413-253-2303; E-mail: xculture@javanet.com; World Wide Web: http://www.empiremall.com/cross-culture

CROSS-CULTURE

SPANISH DISCOVERY II

General Information • Cultural tour with visits to Granada, Seville, Jerez, Cordoba. Once at the destination country, participants travel by bus, foot.
Learning Focus • Escorted travel to Cathedral, Great Mosque, Jewish Quarter and Alhambra. Museum visits (Seville). Attendance at performances (Lipizzan horses, flamenco show). Instruction is offered by highly educated guides. This program would appeal to people interested in culture, history, nature studies, arts, traditions, food and wine.
Accommodations • Hotels. Single rooms are available for an additional $295.
Program Details • Program offered once per year. Session length: 9 days. Departures are scheduled in September. Program is targeted to adults of all ages. Most participants are 40–70 years of age. Participants must be 12 years or older to enroll. Other requirements: good health, accompaniment of an adult if under 18. 20–25 participants per session. Application deadline: 1 month prior to departure. Reservations are recommended at least 3–12 months before departure.
Costs • $2490 (includes tuition, housing, all meals, books and class materials, excursions, international airfare). A $300 deposit is required.
Contact • Cross-Culture, 52 High Point Drive, Amherst, MA 01002-1224; 413-256-6303; Fax: 413-253-2303; E-mail: xculture@javanet.com; World Wide Web: http://www.empiremall.com/cross-culture

CSA–CENTER FOR STUDY ABROAD

CATHEDRALS AND CASTLES OF SPAIN

General Information • Cultural tour in Granada, Madrid, Salamanca, Seville, Toledo.
Learning Focus • Courses in cultural studies.
Accommodations • Hotels. Single rooms are available. Meals are taken as a group, in local restaurants.
Program Details • Program offered 3 times per year. Session length: 15 days. Departures are scheduled in May, July, September. The program is open to undergraduate students, graduate students, pre-college students, adults. Most participants are 35–60 years of age. Other requirements: minimum age of 17. 10 participants per session.
Costs • $2795 (includes tuition, housing, all meals, books and class materials, insurance, excursions, international airfare, registration, orientation). Application fee: $45. A $50 deposit is required.
Contact • Philip Virtue, Program Director, CSA–Center for Study Abroad, 2802 East Madison Street MS #160, Seattle, WA 98112; 206-726-1498; Fax: 206-285-9197; E-mail: virtuecsa@aol.com

CSA–CENTER FOR STUDY ABROAD

DON QUIJOTE SPANISH LANGUAGE SCHOOL

General Information • Language study program in Barcelona, Granada, Málaga, Salamanca.
Learning Focus • Courses in Spanish language. Instruction is offered by professors from the sponsoring institution.
Accommodations • Homestays. Single rooms are available. Meals are taken with host family.
Program Details • Program offered 52 times per year. Session length: 2–10 weeks. Departures are scheduled in January–December. The program is open to undergraduate students, graduate students, pre-college students, adults. Other requirements: minimum age of 17.
Costs • $1095 for 2 weeks (includes tuition, housing, all meals, books and class materials, insurance, registration, orientation). Application fee: $45. A $50 deposit is required.
Contact • Philip Virtue, Program Director, CSA–Center for Study Abroad, 2802 East Madison Street MS #160, Seattle, WA 98112; 206-726-1498; Fax: 206-285-9197; E-mail: virtuecsa@aol.com

CSA–CENTER FOR STUDY ABROAD

LENGUAVIVA–SEVILLE

General Information • Language study program in Seville. Excursions to Granada, Malaga.
Learning Focus • Courses in Spanish language. Instruction is offered by professors from the sponsoring institution.
Accommodations • Homestays. Single rooms are available. Meals are taken with host family.
Program Details • Program offered 26 times per year. Session length: 2–6 weeks. Departures are scheduled in January–December. The program is open to undergraduate students, graduate students, pre-college students, adults. Most participants are 17–35 years of age. Other requirements: minimum age of 17. 5–8 participants per session.
Costs • $995 for 2 weeks (includes tuition, housing, all meals, books and class materials, insurance, registration, orientation). Application fee: $45. A $50 deposit is required.
Contact • Philip Virtue, Program Director, CSA–Center for Study Abroad, 2802 East Madison Street MS #160, Seattle, WA 98112; 206-726-1498; Fax: 206-285-9197; E-mail: virtuecsa@aol.com

DICKINSON COLLEGE

MÁLAGA SUMMER IMMERSION PROGRAM

General Information • Language study program in Málaga.
Learning Focus • Courses in Spanish language, Spanish culture. Instruction is offered by professors from the sponsoring institution.
Accommodations • Homestays. Single rooms are available. Meals are taken with host family, in residences.
Program Details • Program offered once per year. Session length: 6 weeks. Departures are scheduled in May. The program is open to undergraduate students. Most participants are 18–20 years of age. Other requirements: intermediate-level Spanish. 15 participants per session. Application deadline: February 15.
Costs • $3600 (includes tuition, housing, all meals, books and class materials, excursions, international airfare). Application fee: $15. A $300 deposit is required.
Contact • Dr. John S. Henderson, Director of Off-Campus Studies, Dickinson College, PO Box 1773, Carlisle, PA 17013-2896; 717-245-1341; Fax: 717-245-1688; E-mail: ocs@dickinson.edu; World Wide Web: http://www.dickinson.edu

DON QUIJOTE

D.E.L.E. PREPARATION COURSE IN BARCELONA, SPAIN

General Information • Language study program in Barcelona. Excursions to Girona, building of Gaudí, Figueras, Montserrat.
Learning Focus • Instruction is offered by professors from the sponsoring institution.
Accommodations • Homestays, locally-rented apartments, hotels, hostels. Single rooms are available. Meals are taken on one's own, with host family, in local restaurants.
Program Details • Program offered 2 times per year. Session length: 8, 13, or 18 days. Departures are scheduled in May, November. The program is open to undergraduate students, graduate students, adults. Most participants are 18 years of age and older. Other requirements: minimum age of 18. 10 participants per session.
Costs • $1070 for 3 weeks (includes tuition, housing, some meals, books and class materials, activities, welcome dinner, pick-up service at bus or train station, certificate). Application fee: $23. A $120 deposit is required.
Contact • Elvira Zingone, Central Promotion Office, Don Quijote, Apdo. de Correos 333, 37080 Salamanca, Spain; +34 23-268-860; Fax: +34 23-268-815; E-mail: donquijote@offcampus.es

DON QUIJOTE

D.E.L.E. PREPARATION COURSE IN GRANADA, SPAIN

General Information • Language study program in Granada. Excursions to Seville, Córdoba, Sierra Nevada, Alpujarra, Nerja, The Caves of Guadix.
Learning Focus • Instruction is offered by professors from the sponsoring institution.
Accommodations • Homestays, locally-rented apartments, hotels, hostels. Single rooms are available. Meals are taken on one's own, with host family, in local restaurants.
Program Details • Program offered 2 times per year. Session length: 8, 13 or 18 days. Departures are scheduled in May, November. The program is open to undergraduate students, graduate students, adults. Most participants are 18 years of age and older. Other requirements: minimum age of 18. 10 participants per session.
Costs • $1070 for 18 days (includes tuition, housing, some meals, books and class materials, activities, welcome dinner, pick-up service at Granada airport, certificate). Application fee: $23. A $120 deposit is required.
Contact • Elvira Zingone, Central Promotion Office, Don Quijote, Apdo. de Carreos 333, Salamanca 37080, Spain; +34 23-268-860; Fax: +34 23-268-815; E-mail: donquijote@offcampus.es

DON QUIJOTE

INTENSIVE BUSINESS

General Information • Language study program in Barcelona.
Learning Focus • Courses in finance, international commerce. Instruction is offered by professors from the sponsoring institution.
Accommodations • Homestays, locally-rented apartments, hotels, hostels. Single rooms are available. Meals are taken on one's own, with host family, in local restaurants.
Program Details • Program offered 4 times per year. Session length: 2–4 weeks. Departures are scheduled in July, August, September. The program is open to undergraduate students, graduate students, adults, business people. Most participants are 18 years of age and older. Other requirements: minimum age of 18. 6 participants per session.
Costs • $597 for 2 weeks (includes tuition, housing, some meals, books and class materials). Application fee: $23. A $120 deposit is required.
Contact • Elvira Zingone, Central Promotion Office, Don Quijote, USPE97, Apdo. de Correos 333, 37080 Salamanca, Spain; +34 23-268-860; Fax: +34 23-268-815; E-mail: donquijote@offcampus.es

DON QUIJOTE

REFRESHER COURSES FOR TEACHERS OF SPANISH IN BARCELONA, SPAIN

General Information • Language study program in Barcelona. Excursions to Gerona, Mont Serrat, building of Gaudi, Figueras.
Learning Focus • Courses in Spanish grammar. Instruction is offered by professors from the sponsoring institution.
Accommodations • Homestays. Single rooms are available. Meals are taken with host family.
Program Details • Program offered 2 times per year. Session length: 2 weeks. Departures are scheduled in April, August. The program is open to Spanish teachers. Most participants are 18 years of age and older. 9 participants per session.
Costs • $1242 (includes tuition, housing, some meals, books and class materials, excursions, activities, pick-up service at bus and train stations, welcome dinner). Application fee: $23. A $120 deposit is required.
Contact • Elvira Zingone, Central Promotion Office, Don Quijote, Apdo. de Correos 333, Salamanca 37080, Spain; +34 23-268-860; Fax: +34 23-268-815; E-mail: donquijote@offcampus.es

DON QUIJOTE

REFRESHER COURSES FOR TEACHERS OF SPANISH IN GRANADA, SPAIN

General Information • Language study program in Granada. Excursions to Sierra Nevada, Córdoba, The Caves of Guadix, Seville, Nerja.
Learning Focus • Courses in Spanish grammar. Instruction is offered by professors from the sponsoring institution.
Accommodations • Homestays. Single rooms are available. Meals are taken with host family.
Program Details • Program offered 2 times per year. Session length: 2 weeks. Departures are scheduled in April, July. The program is open to Spanish teachers. Most participants are 18 years of age and older. 9 participants per session.
Costs • $1242 (includes tuition, housing, some meals, books and class materials, excursions, visits, Spanish dancing-singing lessons, pick up service at Granada airport). Application fee: $23. A $120 deposit is required.
Contact • Elvira Zingone, Central Promotion Office, Don Quijote, Apdo. de Correos 333, Salamanca 37080, Spain; +34 23-268-860; Fax: +34 23-268-815; E-mail: donquijote@offcampus.es

DON QUIJOTE

REFRESHER COURSES FOR TEACHERS OF SPANISH IN SALAMANCA, SPAIN

General Information • Language study program in Salamanca. Excursions to Avila, Madrid, Sierra de Francia, Segovia, Escorial.
Learning Focus • Courses in Spanish grammar. Instruction is offered by professors from the sponsoring institution.
Accommodations • Homestays. Single rooms are available. Meals are taken with host family.
Program Details • Program offered 2 times per year. Session length: 2 weeks. Departures are scheduled in March, October. The program is open to Spanish teachers. Most participants are 18 years of age and older. 9 participants per session.
Costs • $1242 (includes tuition, housing, some meals, books and class materials, excursions, all visits, dancing and singing lessons, pick up service at bus and train stations). Application fee: $23. A $120 deposit is required.
Contact • Elvira Zingone, Central Promotion Office, Don Quijote, Apdo. de Correos 333, Salamanca 37080, Spain; +34 23-268-860; Fax: +34 23-268-815; E-mail: donquijote@offcampus.es

 DON QUIJOTE

SPANISH IN SPAIN–STANDARD COURSE IN BARCELONA, SPAIN

General Information • Language study program in Barcelona. Excursions to Figueras, Montserrat, Girona, building of Gaudi.
Learning Focus • Courses in grammar, conservation. Instruction is offered by professors from the sponsoring institution.
Accommodations • Homestays, locally-rented apartments, hotels, hostels. Meals are taken on one's own, with host family, in local restaurants.
Program Details • Program offered 52 times per year. Session length: 2–12 weeks. Departures are scheduled in January–December. The program is open to undergraduate students, graduate students, adults. Most participants are 18 years of age and older. Other requirements: minimum age of 18. 5–6 participants per session.
Costs • $1200 for 4 weeks (includes tuition, housing, some meals, books and class materials, excursions, pick up service at the bus or train station, welcome dinner, certificate). Application fee: $23. A $120 deposit is required.
Contact • Elvira Zingone, Central Promotion Office, Don Quijote, Apdo. de Correos 333, 37080 Salamanca, Spain; +34 23-268-860; Fax: +34 23-268-815; E-mail: donquijote@offcampus.es

 DON QUIJOTE

SPANISH IN SPAIN–STANDARD COURSE IN GRANADA, SPAIN

General Information • Language study program in Granada. Excursions to Costa Granadina, Alpujarra, caves of Guadix, Seville, Córdoba, Sierra Nevada.
Learning Focus • Courses in grammar. Instruction is offered by professors from the sponsoring institution.
Accommodations • Homestays, locally-rented apartments, hotels, hostels. Single rooms are available. Meals are taken on one's own, with host family, in local restaurants.
Program Details • Program offered 52 times per year. Session length: 2–12 weeks. Departures are scheduled in January–December. The program is open to undergraduate students, graduate students, adults. Most participants are 18 years of age and older. Other requirements: minimum age of 18. 5–6 participants per session.
Costs • $1200 for 4 weeks (includes tuition, housing, some meals, books and class materials, excursions, pick up service

at Granada airport, welcome dinner, Spanish singing and dancing lessons, certificate). Application fee: $23. A $120 deposit is required.
Contact • Elvira Zingone, Central Promotion Office, Don Quijote, USPE97, Apdo. de Correos 333, 37080 Salamanca, Spain; +34 23-268-860; Fax: +34 23-268-815; E-mail: donquijote@offcampus.es

DON QUIJOTE

SPANISH IN SPAIN–STANDARD COURSE IN SALAMANCA, SPAIN

General Information • Language study program in Salamanca. Excursions to Madrid, Avila, Sierra de Francia, Escorial, Segovia.
Learning Focus • Courses in grammar. Instruction is offered by professors from the sponsoring institution.
Accommodations • Homestays, locally-rented apartments, hotels, hostels. Meals are taken on one's own, with host family, in local restaurants.
Program Details • Program offered 52 times per year. Session length: 2–12 weeks. Departures are scheduled in January–December. The program is open to undergraduate students, graduate students, adults. Most participants are 18 years of age and older. Other requirements: minimum age of 18. 5–6 participants per session.
Costs • $1200 for 4 weeks (includes tuition, housing, some meals, books and class materials, pick up service at the bus or train station, welcome dinner, Spanish singing and dancing lessons, certificate). Application fee: $23. A $120 deposit is required.
Contact • Elvira Zingone, Central Promotion Office, Don Quijote, USPE97, Apdo. de Correos 333, 37080 Salamanca, Spain; +34 23-268-860; Fax: +34 23-268-815; E-mail: donquijote@offcampus.es

DON QUIJOTE

SUMMER SCHOOL SALAMANCA

General Information • Language study program in Salamanca. Excursions to Madrid, Avila, Sierra de Francia, Escorial, Segovia.
Learning Focus • Courses in grammar. Instruction is offered by professors from the sponsoring institution.
Accommodations • Homestays, locally-rented apartments, hotels, hostels. Meals are taken on one's own, with host family, in local restaurants.
Program Details • Program offered 12 times per year. Session length: 2–12 weeks. Departures are scheduled in July, August, September. The program is open to undergraduate students, graduate students, pre-college students, adults. Most participants are 16–60 years of age. Other requirements: minimum age of 16. 10–11 participants per session.
Costs • $800 for 4 weeks (includes tuition, housing, some meals, welcome dinner, International Student Identification card, certificate, reduction on activities cost). Application fee: $23. A $120 deposit is required.
Contact • Elvira Zingone, Central Promotion Office, Don Quijote, USPE97, Apdo. de Correos 333, 37080 Salamanca, Spain; +34 23-268-860; Fax: +34 23-268-815; E-mail: donquijote@offcampus.es

DUKE UNIVERSITY

DUKE IN SPAIN

General Information • Academic study program in Costa Del Sol, Madrid. Classes are held on the campus of College for International Studies, University of Málaga. Excursions to Seville, Granada, Córdoba, Ronda, Salamanca, Segovia, Toledo.
Learning Focus • Courses in literature, art and civilization, language study. Instruction is offered by professors from the sponsoring institution and local teachers.
Accommodations • Homestays. Meals are taken on one's own, with host family.
Program Details • Program offered once per year. Session length: 6 weeks. Departures are scheduled in May. The program is open to undergraduate students. Most participants are 19–21 years of age. Other requirements: minimum 2.7 GPA. Application deadline: February 21.
Costs • $3915 (includes tuition, housing, excursions, international airfare).
Contact • Foreign Academic Programs, Duke University, 121 Allen Building, Box 90057, Durham, NC 27708-0057; 919-684-2174; Fax: 919-684-3083; E-mail: abroad@mail01.adm.duke.edu; World Wide Web: http://www.mis.duke.edu/study_abroad/study_abroad.html

EASTERN CONNECTICUT STATE UNIVERSITY

SUMMER STUDY PROGRAM IN SPAIN

General Information • Language study program in Alicante. Classes are held on the campus of Colegio de España, Alicante. Excursions to Valencia, Barcelona, Granada, Córdoba, Sevilla, Madrid.
Learning Focus • Courses in Spanish language, Spanish literature, Spanish culture.
Accommodations • Dormitories, locally-rented apartments. Single rooms are available. Meals are taken in central dining facility, in residences.
Program Details • Program offered once per year. Session length: 5 weeks. Departures are scheduled in May. The program is open to undergraduate students, graduate students. Most participants are 19–27 years of age. 15 participants per session. Application deadline: April 15.
Costs • $2900 (includes tuition, housing, all meals, books and class materials, insurance, excursions, international airfare, ground transportation, transcripts). A $250 deposit is required.
Contact • Agustin S. Bernal, Assistant Professor of Spanish, Eastern Connecticut State University, Department of Modern Languages, Willimantic, CT 06226-2295; 860-465-5273; Fax: 860-465-4575; E-mail: bernala@ecsu.ctstateu.edu

THE EDUCATED TRAVELER

THE EDUCATED TRAVELER'S SPAIN

General Information • Cultural tour with visits to Barcelona. Once at the destination country, participants travel by bus, foot.
Learning Focus • Escorted travel to Barcelona and surrounding regions. Other activities include behind-the-scenes visits to artisans' workshops and private collections.

Instruction is offered by artists, historians, curators. This program would appeal to people interested in art, museums, history, culture.
Accommodations • Hotels. Single rooms are available.
Program Details • Program offered once per year. Session length: 8 days. Departures are scheduled in May. Program is targeted to experienced adult travelers. Most participants are 40–75 years of age. 15–20 participants per session. Application deadline: 3 months prior to departure. Reservations are recommended at least 6 months before departure.
Costs • Contact sponsor for information. A $700 deposit is required.
Contact • Ann Waigand, The Educated Traveler, PO Box 220822, Chantilly, VA 22022; 800-648-5168; Fax: 703-471-4807; E-mail: edtrav@aol.com

EF INTERNATIONAL LANGUAGE SCHOOLS

SPANISH IN BARCELONA

General Information • Language study program in Barcelona. Classes are held on the campus of EF Escuela Internacional de Español. Excursions to Costa Brava, Madrid, Seville, Pyrénées.
Learning Focus • Courses in Spanish language. Instruction is offered by professors from the sponsoring institution and local teachers.
Accommodations • Homestays, dormitories. Single rooms are available. Meals are taken as a group, with host family, in central dining facility, in residences.
Program Details • Program offered 26 times per year. Session length: 2–12 weeks. Departures are scheduled in January–December. The program is open to undergraduate students, graduate students, pre-college students, adults. Most participants are 16–25 years of age. Other requirements: minimum age of 16. 40 participants per session. Application deadline: 60 days prior to departure.
Costs • Principal: $840 per 2 weeks, intensive: $960 per 2 weeks (includes tuition, housing, some meals, books and class materials). Application fee: $90. A $350 deposit is required.
Contact • Kari Larson, Admissions Manager, EF International Language Schools, 204 Lake Street, Boston, MA 02135; 800-992-1892; Fax: 617-746-1800; E-mail: ils@ef.com

EUROCENTRES

LANGUAGE IMMERSION IN SPAIN

General Information • Language study program in Barcelona, Madrid, Salamanca. Classes are held on the campus of Eurocentre, Institutos Mangold S.A. Barcelona, Eurocentre Salamanca. Excursions to Avila, Montserrat, Toledo.
Learning Focus • Courses in Spanish language, Spanish culture. Instruction is offered by professors from the sponsoring institution.
Accommodations • Homestays. Single rooms are available. Meals are taken with host family, in residences.
Program Details • Program offered 20 times per year. Session length: 2–12 weeks. Departures are scheduled in January–December. The program is open to undergraduate students, graduate students, pre-college students, adults. Most participants are 16–80 years of age. 15 participants per session.
Costs • Contact sponsor for information.
Contact • Marketing, Eurocentres, 101 North Union Street, Suite 300, Alexandria, VA 22314; 800-648-4809; Fax: 703-684-1495; E-mail: 100632.141@compuserve.com; World Wide Web: http://www.clark.net/pub/eurocent/home.htm

EUROPEAN HERITAGE INSTITUTE

SUMMER PROGRAM IN BARCELONA

General Information • Language study program in Barcelona. Classes are held on the campus of Don Quijote Institute.
Learning Focus • Courses in Spanish language. Instruction is offered by local teachers.
Accommodations • Homestays, locally-rented apartments. Meals are taken on one's own.
Program Details • Session length: 4–12 weeks. Departures are scheduled in May–September. The program is open to undergraduate students, adults. 6 participants per session. Application deadline: 65 days prior to departure.
Costs • $560–$1350 (includes tuition, housing, some meals). A $350 deposit is required.
Contact • Dr. Antonio Masullo, Professor, European Heritage Institute, 2708 East Franklin Street, Richmond, VA 23223; 804-648-0826; Fax: 804-648-0826; E-mail: euritage@i2020.net

EUROPEAN HERITAGE INSTITUTE

SUMMER PROGRAM IN GRANADA

General Information • Language study program in Granada. Classes are held on the campus of Don Quijote Institute.
Learning Focus • Courses in Spanish language. Instruction is offered by local teachers.
Accommodations • Homestays, locally-rented apartments. Meals are taken on one's own, with host family.
Program Details • Program offered 5 times per year. Session length: 4–12 weeks. Departures are scheduled in May–September. The program is open to undergraduate students, adults. Application deadline: 65 days prior to departure.
Costs • $560–$1350 (includes tuition, housing, some meals). A $350 deposit is required.
Contact • Dr. Antonio Masullo, Professor, European Heritage Institute, 2708 East Franklin Street, Richmond, VA 23223; 804-648-0826; Fax: 804-648-0826; E-mail: euritage@i2020.net

EUROPEAN HERITAGE INSTITUTE

SUMMER PROGRAM IN SALAMANCA

General Information • Language study program in Salamanca. Classes are held on the campus of Don Quijote Institute.

Learning Focus • Courses in Spanish language. Instruction is offered by local teachers.
Accommodations • Homestays, locally-rented apartments. Meals are taken on one's own.
Program Details • Program offered 5 times per year. Session length: 4–12 weeks. Departures are scheduled in May–September. The program is open to undergraduate students, adults. Most participants are 18–45 years of age. Application deadline: 65 days prior to departure.
Costs • $560–$1350 (includes tuition, housing, some meals). A $350 deposit is required.
Contact • Dr. Antonio Masullo, Professor, European Heritage Institute, 2708 East Franklin Street, Richmond, VA 23223; 804-648-0826; Fax: 804-648-0826; E-mail: euritage@i2020.net

EUROSTUDY, INC.

SUMMER STUDY AT THE UNIVERSITY OF CÁDIZ, SPAIN

General Information • Language study program in Cádiz. Classes are held on the campus of University of Cádiz. Excursions to Andalucia, Sevilla, Jerez de la Frontera, Malaga, Puerto Santa Maria, San Fernando, San Lucar.
Learning Focus • Courses in Spanish language, Spanish literature, Spanish culture, business, methodology. Instruction is offered by local teachers.
Accommodations • Homestays. Single rooms are available. Meals are taken with host family, in residences.
Program Details • Program offered once per year. Session length: 5 weeks. Departures are scheduled in June. The program is open to undergraduate students, graduate students, adults, high school seniors with 3 years of Spanish language study. Application deadline: March 7.
Costs • $3300 (includes tuition, housing, all meals, books and class materials, insurance). A $250 deposit is required.
Contact • Carol McCloskey, President, Eurostudy, Inc., PO Box 1023, Blue Bell, PA 19422; 215-646-2492

Summer study at the University of Cadiz, Spain, offers programs in Spanish culture, conversation, Spanish literature, methodology, and business. The student is immersed in the Spanish language by living with a Spanish family. Each student will increase his/her proficiency in understanding, speaking, reading, and writing Spanish while integrating these skills with a better understanding of Spanish culture. Professors are native instructors. Class sizes are small. Students may earn up to 6 credits. Many weekly excursions and activities are included.

EXPERIENCE PLUS SPECIALTY TOURS, INC.

ANDALUSIA: SEVILLE TO GRANADA

General Information • Bicycle tour with visits to Córdoba, Granada, Loja, Montilla, Seville, Guadalquiver River. Once at the destination country, participants travel by bicycle.
Learning Focus • Escorted travel to Seville and Granada. Attendance at performances (flamenco dancing). Other activities include bicycling. Instruction is offered by professors, indigenous, bilingual and bi-cultural guides. This program would appeal to people interested in architecture, history, bicycling, travel, Spain, wine.
Accommodations • Hotels. Single rooms are available for an additional $300.
Program Details • Program offered 2 times per year. Session length: 10 days. Departures are scheduled in March, October. Most participants are 35–70 years of age. 16–22 participants per session. Reservations are recommended at least 6–12 months before departure.
Costs • $1995 (includes housing, some meals, quality rental bike, 28 oz. water bottle, shirt, luggage shuttle, van support, bilingual/bi-cultural tour leaders). A $250 deposit is required.
Contact • Experience Plus Specialty Tours, Inc., 1925 Wallenberg Drive, Fort Collins, CO 80526; 800-685-4565; Fax: 800-685-4565; E-mail: tours@xplus.com

FOREIGN LANGUAGE STUDY ABROAD SERVICE

INTERNATIONAL LANGUAGE STUDY HOMESTAYS IN SPAIN

General Information • Language study program in Spain.
Learning Focus • Courses in Spanish language. Instruction is offered by local teachers.
Accommodations • Homestays. Single rooms are available. Meals are taken with host family, in residences.
Program Details • Session length: varies. Departures are scheduled in January–December. The program is open to undergraduate students, graduate students, pre-college students, adults. Most participants are 12 years of age and older. Other requirements: students must be at least 12 years old. 1 participant per session.
Costs • Contact sponsor for information. A $300 deposit is required.
Contact • Louise Harber, Coordinator, Foreign Language Study Abroad Service, Department IH, Box 903, 5935 Southwest 64th Avenue, South Miami, FL 33143; 800-282-1090; Fax: 305-662-2907; E-mail: flsas@netpoint.net; World Wide Web: http://www.netpoint.net/~flsas

FOREIGN LANGUAGE STUDY ABROAD SERVICE

SPANISH IN SPAIN

General Information • Language study program in Avila, Barcelona, Granada, Isla Cristina, Madrid, Málaga, Nerja, Salamanca, Santander, Seville, Valencia.
Learning Focus • Courses in language study. Instruction is offered by local teachers.
Accommodations • Homestays, hotels. Single rooms are available. Meals are taken on one's own, with host family, in local restaurants, in residences.
Program Details • Session length: varies. Departures are scheduled in January–December. The program is open to undergraduate students, graduate students, pre-college students, adults. Most participants are 16 years of age and older.

Costs • Contact sponsor for information. Application fee: $50. A $100 deposit is required.
Contact • Louise Harber, Coordinator, Foreign Language Study Abroad Service, Department IH, Box 903, 5935 Southwest 64th Avenue, South Miami, FL 33143; 800-282-1090; Fax: 305-662-2907; E-mail: flsas@netpoint.net; World Wide Web: http://www.netpoint.net/~flsas

GEORGE MASON UNIVERSITY

MADRID AND SEVILLE: SPANISH LANGUAGE AND CULTURE

General Information • Language study program in Madrid, Seville. Classes are held on the campus of Complutense University of Madrid. Excursions to Segovia, Toledo, Pamplona.
Learning Focus • Courses in Spanish language, Spanish culture. Instruction is offered by professors from the sponsoring institution.
Accommodations • Dormitories. Meals are taken as a group, in central dining facility.
Program Details • Program offered once per year. Session length: 6 weeks. Departures are scheduled in June. The program is open to undergraduate students, adults. Most participants are 18–65 years of age. Other requirements: minimum 2.25 GPA. 10 participants per session. Application deadline: April 12.
Costs • $4441 for George Mason University students, $5541 for other students (includes tuition, housing, all meals, insurance, excursions). Application fee: $35. A $500 deposit is required.
Contact • Dr. Yehuda Lukacs, Director, Center for Global Education, George Mason University, 4400 University Drive, 235 Johnson Center, Fairfax, VA 22030; 703-993-2156; Fax: 703-993-2153; E-mail: ylukacs@gmu.edu; World Wide Web: http://www.gmu.edu/departments/oie

GEORGE MASON UNIVERSITY

MADRID: SPANISH LANGUAGE AND CULTURE

General Information • Language study program in Madrid. Classes are held on the campus of Complutense University of Madrid. Excursions to Segovia, Ruta del Quijote, Toledo.
Learning Focus • Courses in language study, cultural studies. Instruction is offered by professors from the sponsoring institution.
Accommodations • Dormitories. Meals are taken as a group, in residences.
Program Details • Program offered once per year. Session length: 4 weeks. Departures are scheduled in June. The program is open to undergraduate students, graduate students, adults. Most participants are 18–65 years of age. Other requirements: minimum 2.25 GPA. 35–40 participants per session. Application deadline: April 12.
Costs • $2788 for George Mason University students, $3338 for other students (includes tuition, housing, all meals, insurance, excursions). Application fee: $35. A $500 deposit is required.
Contact • Dr. Yehuda Lukacs, Director, Center for Global Education, George Mason University, 4400 University Drive, 235 Johnson Center, Fairfax, VA 22030; 703-993-2156; Fax: 703-993-2153; E-mail: ylukacs@gmu.edu; World Wide Web: http://www.gmu.edu/departments/oie

INSTITUTE FOR SOCIAL AND INTERNATIONAL STUDIES (ISIS)

BARCELONA

General Information • Academic study program in Barcelona. Excursions to Girona, Figueras.
Learning Focus • Courses in Spanish language, art, architecture, Spanish history, Spanish society. Instruction is offered by professors from the sponsoring institution.
Accommodations • Homestays, residencias. Single rooms are available. Meals are taken with host family.
Program Details • Program offered once per year. Session length: 4 weeks. Departures are scheduled in June. The program is open to undergraduate students, graduate students. Most participants are 21–38 years of age. Other requirements: minimum 3.0 GPA. 20 participants per session. Application deadline: May 15.
Costs • $2875 (includes tuition, housing, some meals, books and class materials, insurance, excursions). Application fee: $50. A $300 deposit is required.
Contact • Julie Resnick, Dean of Admissions, Institute for Social and International Studies (ISIS), ISIS at Portland State University, International Education Services, PO Box 751, Portland, OR 97207; 800-547-8887, ext. 4029; Fax: 503-725-5320; E-mail: isis@pdx.edu

INSTITUTE FOR SOCIAL AND INTERNATIONAL STUDIES (ISIS)

PROFESSIONAL DEVELOPMENT PROGRAM FOR TEACHERS OF SPANISH

General Information • Academic study program in Barcelona. Excursions to Figueras, Cap Creus, Cadaqués, Montserrat.
Learning Focus • Courses in teaching, Spanish language, Spanish culture. Instruction is offered by professors from the sponsoring institution.
Accommodations • Homestays, pensiones, residencias. Single rooms are available. Meals are taken with host family.
Program Details • Program offered once per year. Session length: 3 weeks. Departures are scheduled in July. The program is open to Spanish teachers. Most participants are 25–50 years of age. Other requirements: graduate-level and teaching experience. 5–18 participants per session. Application deadline: May 31.
Costs • $2500 (includes tuition, housing, some meals, books and class materials, insurance, excursions). Application fee: $50. A $300 deposit is required.
Contact • Teresa Taylor, Academic Dean, Institute for Social and International Studies (ISIS), ISIS at Portland State University, International Education Services, PO Box 751, Portland, OR 97207; 800-547-8887, ext. 4029; Fax: 503-725-5320; E-mail: isis@pdx.edu

INSTITUTE OF EUROPEAN STUDIES/INSTITUTE OF ASIAN STUDIES

MADRID SUMMER PROGRAM

General Information • Academic study program in Madrid. Classes are held on the campus of Complutense University of Madrid. Excursions to Segovia, Pedraza.

Learning Focus • Courses in literature, history, language study, art history. Instruction is offered by professors from the sponsoring institution.

Accommodations • Homestays. Single rooms are available. Meals are taken with host family, in residences.

Program Details • Program offered once per year. Session length: 6 weeks. Departures are scheduled in June. The program is open to undergraduate students, graduate students, continuing education students. Most participants are 20–23 years of age. 25 participants per session. Application deadline: April 15.

Costs • $2900 (includes tuition, housing, some meals, excursions). Application fee: $25.

Contact • Department of Admissions, Institute of European Studies/Institute of Asian Studies, 223 West Ohio Street, Chicago, IL 60610-4196; 800-995-2300; Fax: 312-944-1448; E-mail: recruit@iesias.org; World Wide Web: http://www.iesias.org

INSTITUTE OF SPANISH STUDIES

SUMMER SESSIONS ABROAD IN VALENCIA, SPAIN

General Information • Academic study program in Valencia. Classes are held on the campus of Institute of Spanish Studies. Excursions to Madrid, Córdoba, Seville, Torremolinos, Benalmadena, Granada.

Learning Focus • Courses in Spanish language, Spanish literature, Spanish-American culture, Spanish drama, Spanish civilization, France era, Arabs in Spain, Jews in Spain, modern Spain, art, geography of Spain. Instruction is offered by professors from the sponsoring institution and local teachers.

Accommodations • Homestays, dormitories. Single rooms are available. Meals are taken as a group, with host family, in central dining facility, in residences.

Program Details • Program offered 2 times per year. Session length: 4 weeks. Departures are scheduled in May, June. The program is open to undergraduate students, graduate students, pre-college students, adults, teachers. Most participants are 18–30 years of age. Other requirements: recommendation of home institution. 50 participants per session.

Costs • $2200 (includes tuition, housing, all meals, excursions). A $300 deposit is required.

Contact • Dr. Francisca Sanchez, Director, Institute of Spanish Studies, 1315 Monterey Boulevard, San Francisco, CA 94127; 415-586-0180; Fax: 415-334-3928

INTERNATIONAL STUDIES ABROAD

UNIVERSITY OF GRANADA

General Information • Language study program in Granada. Classes are held on the campus of University of Granada. Excursions to Madrid, Córdoba, El Escorial, Toledo, Seville.

Learning Focus • Courses in grammar, cultural studies. Instruction is offered by local teachers.

Accommodations • Homestays. Single rooms are available. Meals are taken with host family.

Program Details • Program offered 2 times per year. Session length: 5 weeks. Departures are scheduled in June, July. The program is open to undergraduate students, graduate students, pre-college students, adults. Most participants are 18–24 years of age. Other requirements: minimum 2.5 GPA and a letter of recommendation. 20–25 participants per session. Application deadline: April 5.

Costs • $3000 (includes tuition, housing, all meals, excursions, entrance fees, tutoring, resident director, ground transportation, laundry). A $200 deposit is required.

Contact • Gustavo Artaza, Director, International Studies Abroad, 817 West 24th Street, Austin, TX 78705; 800-580-8826; Fax: 512-480-8866; E-mail: 76331.336@compuserve.com

INTERNATIONAL STUDIES ABROAD

UNIVERSITY OF SALAMANCA

General Information • Language study program in Salamanca. Classes are held on the campus of University of Salamanca. Excursions to Madrid, Segovia, El Escorial, Toledo, Portugal, Avila.

Learning Focus • Courses in grammar, cultural studies, business, conservation, literature. Instruction is offered by local teachers.

Accommodations • Homestays. Single rooms are available. Meals are taken with host family.

Program Details • Program offered 2 times per year. Session length: 5 weeks. Departures are scheduled in June, July. The program is open to undergraduate students, graduate students, pre-college students, adults. Most participants are 18–24 years of age. Other requirements: minimum 2.5 GPA and a letter of recommendation. 30–60 participants per session. Application deadline: April 5.

Costs • $3050 (includes tuition, housing, all meals, insurance, excursions, ground transportation, tutoring, resident director, entrance fees, laundry). A $200 deposit is required.

Contact • Gustavo Artaza, Director, International Studies Abroad, 817 West 24th Street, Austin, TX 78705; 800-580-8826; Fax: 512-480-8866; E-mail: 76331.336@compuserve.com

JAMES MADISON UNIVERSITY

SUMMER PROGRAM IN SALAMANCA

General Information • Academic study program in Salamanca. Classes are held on the campus of University of Salamanca. Excursions to Madrid, Toledo, Cuenca, Segovia, Santander, Granada.

Learning Focus • Courses in Spanish language, political science, art history, international business, economics. Instruction is offered by professors from the sponsoring institution and local teachers.
Accommodations • Homestays. Single rooms are available. Meals are taken as a group, on one's own, with host family, in local restaurants, in residences.
Program Details • Program offered once per year. Session length: 8 weeks. Departures are scheduled in May, June. The program is open to undergraduate students. Most participants are 18–22 years of age. Other requirements: minimum 2.8 GPA and intermediate-level Spanish. 25 participants per session. Application deadline: February 1.
Costs • $4500 for Virginia residents, $5778 for non-residents (includes tuition, housing, some meals, excursions). A $400 deposit is required.
Contact • Dr. Carmenza Kline, Professor, Foreign Languages, James Madison University, Office of International Education, Harrisonburg, VA 22807; 540-568-6946; Fax: 540-568-6946; E-mail: klineca@jmu.edu; World Wide Web: http://www.jmu.edu/intl-ed/

KENTUCKY INSTITUTE FOR INTERNATIONAL STUDIES

PROGRAM IN SPAIN

General Information • Academic study program in Madrid, Segovia. Excursions to surrounding area.
Learning Focus • Courses in Spanish language. Instruction is offered by professors from the sponsoring institution.
Accommodations • Homestays, residencias. Meals are taken with host family, in central dining facility.
Program Details • Program offered once per year. Session length: 5 weeks. Departures are scheduled in June. The program is open to undergraduate students, graduate students, pre-college students, adults, professionals. Most participants are 19–28 years of age. Other requirements: minimum 2.0 GPA, 2 years college-level Spanish or equivalent, letter of recommendation from a faculty member, good standing at home institution. 40 participants per session. Application deadline: March 1.
Costs • $2770 for students of consortia schools, $3070 for other students (includes tuition, housing, all meals, excursions, international airfare, International Student Identification card). Application fee: $50.
Contact • Dr. J. Milton Grimes, Executive Director, Kentucky Institute for International Studies, Murray State University, PO Box 9, Murray, KY 42071-0009; 502-762-3091; Fax: 502-762-3434; E-mail: kiismsu@msumusik.mursuky.edu; World Wide Web: http://www.berea.edu/KIIS/kiis.html

LANGUAGE IMMERSION INSTITUTE

SPAIN

General Information • Language study program with visits to Barcelona, Granada, Malaga, Salamanca. Once at the destination country, participants travel by train, bus, foot. Program is affiliated with Don Quijote Schools.
Learning Focus • Instruction in the Spanish language. Instruction is offered by professors. This program would appeal to people interested in Spanish language.
Accommodations • Homestays, dormitories, locally-rented apartments, hotels. Single rooms are available.
Program Details • Session length: 2 or more weeks. Departures are scheduled throughout the year. Program is targeted to adult professionals. Most participants are 18–70 years of age. Participants must be 18 years or older to enroll.
Costs • Contact sponsor for information.
Contact • Henry Urbanski, Director, Language Immersion Institute, Language Immersion Institute, 75 South Manheim Boulevard, New Paltz, NY 12561; 914-257-3500; Fax: 914-257-3569; E-mail: lii@newpaltz.edu

LANGUAGE LIAISON

CENTRO DE ESTUDIOS DE ESPAÑOL–SPANISH IN SPAIN

General Information • Language study program with visits to Malaga.
Learning Focus • Instruction in the Spanish language. Instruction is offered by professors. This program would appeal to people interested in language.
Accommodations • Homestays, locally-rented apartments. Single rooms are available.
Program Details • Session length: unlimited. Departures are scheduled throughout the year. Program is targeted to students of any age. Most participants are 18–70 years of age. Participants must be 16 years or older to enroll. Reservations are recommended at least 35 days before departure.
Costs • Contact sponsor for information.
Contact • Nancy Forman, President, Language Liaison, 20533 Biscayne Boulevard-Station 4-162, Miami, FL 33180; 305-682-9909; Fax: 305-682-9907; E-mail: langstudy@aol.com; World Wide Web: http://languageliaison.com

LANGUAGE LIAISON

CENTRO DE LENGUAS E INTERCAMBIO CULTURAL–SPANISH IN SPAIN

General Information • Language study program with visits to Seville, neighboring cities.
Learning Focus • Instruction in the Spanish language. Instruction is offered by professors. This program would appeal to people interested in language.
Accommodations • Homestays, locally-rented apartments, hotels, residence halls, student flats. Single rooms are available.
Program Details • Session length: unlimited. Departures are scheduled throughout the year. Program is targeted to students of any age. Most participants are 18–70 years of age. Participants must be 16 years or older to enroll. Reservations are recommended at least 35 days before departure.
Costs • Contact sponsor for information.
Contact • Nancy Forman, President, Language Liaison, 20533 Biscayne Boulevard-Station 4-162, Miami, FL 33180; 305-682-9909; Fax: 305-682-9907; E-mail: langstudy@aol.com; World Wide Web: http://languageliaison.com

LANGUAGE LIAISON

CENTRO INTERNACIONAL DE LENGUA Y CULTURA ESPAÑOLA–SPANISH IN SPAIN

General Information • Language study program with visits to Valencia.
Learning Focus • Instruction in the Spanish language. Instruction is offered by professors. This program would appeal to people interested in language.
Accommodations • Homestays, hotels, flats. Single rooms are available.
Program Details • Session length: unlimited. Departures are scheduled throughout the year. Program is targeted to students of any age. Most participants are 18–70 years of age. Participants must be 16 years or older to enroll. Reservations are recommended at least 35 days before departure.
Costs • Contact sponsor for information.
Contact • Nancy Forman, President, Language Liaison, 20533 Biscayne Boulevard-Station 4-162, Miami, FL 33180; 305-682-9909; Fax: 305-682-9907; E-mail: langstudy@aol.com; World Wide Web: http://languageliaison.com

LANGUAGE LIAISON

COLEGIO MARAVILLAS–SPANISH IN MALAGA, SPAIN

General Information • Language study program with visits to Benalmadena-Malaga.
Learning Focus • Instruction in the Spanish language. Instruction is offered by professors. This program would appeal to people interested in language.
Accommodations • Homestays, locally-rented apartments, flats. Single rooms are available.
Program Details • Session length: unlimited. Departures are scheduled throughout the year. Program is targeted to students of any age. Most participants are 18–70 years of age. Participants must be 16 years or older to enroll. Reservations are recommended at least 35 days before departure.
Costs • Contact sponsor for information.
Contact • Nancy Forman, President, Language Liaison, 20533 Biscayne Boulevard-Station 4-162, Miami, FL 33180; 305-682-9909; Fax: 305-682-9907; E-mail: langstudy@aol.com; World Wide Web: http://languageliaison.com

LANGUAGE LIAISON

DON QUIJOTE–LEARN SPANISH IN SPAIN

General Information • Language study program with visits to Barcelona, Granada, Malaga, Salamanca.
Learning Focus • Instruction in the Spanish language. Instruction is offered by professors. This program would appeal to people interested in language.
Accommodations • Homestays, dormitories, locally-rented apartments, hotels, flats. Single rooms are available.
Program Details • Session length: unlimited. Departures are scheduled throughout the year. Program is targeted to students of any age. Most participants are 18–70 years of age. Participants must be 16 years or older to enroll. Reservations are recommended at least 35 days before departure.
Costs • Contact sponsor for information.
Contact • Nancy Forman, President, Language Liaison, 20533 Biscayne Boulevard-Station 4-162, Miami, FL 33180; 305-682-9909; Fax: 305-682-9907; E-mail: langstudy@aol.com; World Wide Web: http://languageliaison.com

LANGUAGE LIAISON gives its 5-star rating to ¿? don Quijote Schools in Spain. Exciting programs in Salamanca, Barcelona, and Granada from 2–36 weeks year round. For people of all ages and any level. Special programs available for business, tourism, and teachers. Experience life in Spain by living with a native family and participate in exciting activities and excursions. One participant says of the program, "More than I could have ever expected. My host family went beyond the call of duty. I was exposed to more of their culture, foods, and traditions than if I had traveled any other way. More than a host family, I found friends for life!"

LANGUAGE LIAISON

ESCUELA DE IDIOMAS "NERJA"–SPANISH IN SPAIN

General Information • Language study program with visits to Nerja, caves, villages, Granada, Seville, Cordoba.
Learning Focus • Instruction in the Spanish language. Instruction is offered by professors. This program would appeal to people interested in language.
Accommodations • Homestays, locally-rented apartments, hotels, flats. Single rooms are available.
Program Details • Session length: unlimited. Departures are scheduled throughout the year. Program is targeted to students of any age. Most participants are 18–70 years of age. Participants must be 16 years or older to enroll. Reservations are recommended at least 35 days before departure.
Costs • Contact sponsor for information.
Contact • Nancy Forman, President, Language Liaison, 20533 Biscayne Boulevard-Station 4-162, Miami, FL 33180; 305-682-9909; Fax: 305-682-9907; E-mail: langstudy@aol.com; World Wide Web: http://languageliaison.com

LANGUAGE LIAISON

ESTUDIO INTERNACIONAL SAMPERE–SPANISH IN SPAIN

General Information • Language study program with visits to El Puerto, Madrid, neighboring towns and villages, museums, monuments.
Learning Focus • Instruction in the Spanish language. Instruction is offered by professors. This program would appeal to people interested in language.
Accommodations • Homestays, locally-rented apartments, hotels, flats. Single rooms are available.
Program Details • Session length: unlimited. Departures are scheduled throughout the year. Program is targeted to students of any age. Most participants are 18–70 years of age. Participants must be 16 years or older to enroll. Reservations are recommended at least 35 days before departure.
Costs • Contact sponsor for information.

Contact • Nancy Forman, President, Language Liaison, 20533 Biscayne Boulevard-Station 4-162, Miami, FL 33180; 305-682-9909; Fax: 305-682-9907; E-mail: langstudy@aol.com; World Wide Web: http://languageliaison.com

LANGUAGE LIAISON

GRAN CANARIA SCHOOL OF LANGUAGES–SPANISH IN SPAIN

General Information • Language study program with visits to Las Palmas.
Learning Focus • Instruction in the Spanish language. Instruction is offered by professors. This program would appeal to people interested in language.
Accommodations • Homestays, hotels. Single rooms are available.
Program Details • Session length: unlimited. Departures are scheduled throughout the year. Program is targeted to students of any age. Most participants are 18–70 years of age. Participants must be 16 years or older to enroll. Reservations are recommended at least 35 days before departure.
Costs • Contact sponsor for information.
Contact • Nancy Forman, President, Language Liaison, 20533 Biscayne Boulevard-Station 4-162, Miami, FL 33180; 305-682-9909; Fax: 305-682-9907; E-mail: langstudy@aol.com; World Wide Web: http://languageliaison.com

LANGUAGE LIAISON

LIVE 'N' LEARN (LEARN IN A TEACHER'S HOME)–SPAIN

General Information • Language study program with visits to Spain.
Learning Focus • Instruction in the Spanish language. Instruction is offered by professors. This program would appeal to people interested in language.
Accommodations • Homestays. Single rooms are available.
Program Details • Session length: unlimited. Departures are scheduled throughout the year. Most participants are 18–70 years of age. Participants must be 16 years or older to enroll. Reservations are recommended at least 35 days before departure.
Costs • Contact sponsor for information.
Contact • Nancy Forman, President, Language Liaison, 20533 Biscayne Boulevard-Station 4-162, Miami, FL 33180; 305-682-9909; Fax: 305-682-9907; E-mail: langstudy@aol.com; World Wide Web: http://languageliaison.com

LANGUAGE STUDIES ABROAD

CENTRO INTERNACIONAL DE LENGUA Y CULTURA ESPAÑOLES

General Information • Language study program with visits to Valencia. Once at the destination country, participants travel by bus, foot.
Learning Focus • Instruction in the Spanish language. Instruction is offered by trained teachers with bachelor's degrees. This program would appeal to people interested in Spanish language.
Accommodations • Homestays. Single rooms are available for an additional $185 per week.
Program Details • Session length: 2 or more weeks. Departures are scheduled throughout the year. Most participants are 16–80 years of age. Participants must be 16 years or older to enroll. 6–7 participants per session. Application deadline: 3 weeks prior to departure. Reservations are recommended at least 2 months before departure.
Costs • $1500 for 4 weeks (includes tuition, housing, some meals, books and class materials). A $100 deposit is required.
Contact • Charlene Biddulph, Director, Language Studies Abroad, 249 South Highway 101, Suite 226, Solana Beach, CA 92075; 800-424-5522; Fax: 619-943-1201; E-mail: cbiddulph@aol.com; World Wide Web: http://www.dnai.com/~bid/language/

LANGUAGE STUDIES ABROAD

ESCUELA DE IDIOMAS NERJA

General Information • Language study program with visits to Nerja. Once at the destination country, participants travel by bus, foot.
Learning Focus • Instruction in the Spanish language. Instruction is offered by trained teachers with bachelor's degrees. This program would appeal to people interested in Spanish language.
Accommodations • Homestays, flats. Single rooms are available for an additional $530–$820 for 4 weeks.
Program Details • Session length: 2 or more weeks. Departures are scheduled throughout the year. Most participants are 16–80 years of age. Participants must be 16 years or older to enroll. 9 participants per session. Application deadline: 3 weeks prior to departure. Reservations are recommended at least 2 months before departure.
Costs • $1000–$1450 for 4 weeks (includes tuition, housing, some meals, books and class materials). A $100 deposit is required.
Contact • Charlene Biddulph, Director, Language Studies Abroad, 249 South Highway 101, Suite 226, Solana Beach, CA 92075; 800-424-5522; Fax: 619-943-1201; E-mail: cbiddulph@aol.com; World Wide Web: http://www.dnai.com/~bid/language/

LANGUAGE STUDIES ABROAD

ESTUDIO INTERNACIONAL SAMPERE

General Information • Language study program with visits to Madrid. Once at the destination country, participants travel by bus, foot.
Learning Focus • Instruction in the Spanish language. Instruction is offered by trained teachers with bachelor's degrees. This program would appeal to people interested in Spanish language.
Accommodations • Homestays. Single rooms are available for an additional $220 per week.
Program Details • Session length: 2 or more weeks. Departures are scheduled throughout the year. Most participants are 16–80 years of age. Participants must be 16 years or older to enroll. 9 participants per session. Application deadline: 3 weeks prior to departure. Reservations are recommended at least 2 months before departure.

Costs • $1500–$1700 for 4 weeks (includes tuition, housing, some meals, books and class materials, insurance). A $100 deposit is required.
Contact • Charlene Biddulph, Director, Language Studies Abroad, 249 South Highway 101, Suite 226, Solana Beach, CA 92075; 800-424-5522; Fax: 619-943-1201; E-mail: cbiddulph@aol.com; World Wide Web: http://www.dnai.com/~bid/language/

LEARNING PROGRAMS INTERNATIONAL

SIGHTS OF SPAIN

General Information • Cultural tour with visits to Cadiz, Córdoba, Granada, Madrid, Seville. Once at the destination country, participants travel by bus, foot.
Learning Focus • Escorted travel to Palacio Real, Parque de Betiro, Segovia, Alhambra, Mezquita. Museum visits (Museo del Prado, Museo Reina Sofia). Attendance at performances (flamenco show). This program would appeal to people interested in culture and language.
Accommodations • Hotels. Single rooms are available.
Program Details • Program offered 2 times per year. Session length: 10 days. Departures are scheduled in May, spring break, and custom dates. Program is targeted to high school students. Most participants are 14–18 years of age. 15–20 participants per session. Application deadline: April 1 for summer session, December 15 for spring session.
Costs • $2325 (includes housing, some meals, insurance, excursions, international airfare, on-site supervisor, full-time director). A $200 deposit is required.
Contact • Natalie Nation, Director, Learning Programs International, 816 West 23rd Street, Austin, TX 78705; 800-259-4439; Fax: 512-474-1021; E-mail: 76331.336@compuserve.com; World Wide Web: http://www.studiesabroad.com

LEARNING PROGRAMS INTERNATIONAL

UNIVERSIDAD DE SALAMANCA: SALAMANCA, SPAIN

General Information • Language study program with visits to Salamanca, Madrid, El Escorial, El Valle de Los Caidos, Avila, La Granja, Segovia, Toledo, Santander. Once at the destination country, participants travel by bus, foot.
Learning Focus • Instruction in Spanish language. Museum visits (Museo del Prado, Museo Reina Sofia). Instruction is offered by professors. This program would appeal to people interested in language and culture.
Accommodations • Homestays. Single rooms are available for an additional $150 per month.
Program Details • Program offered 2 times per year. Session length: 28 days. Departures are scheduled in June, July. Program is targeted to high school students. Most participants are 14–18 years of age. Participants must be 14 years or older to enroll. 20–40 participants per session. Application deadline: April 1.
Costs • $3350–$3450 (includes tuition, housing, all meals, books and class materials, insurance, excursions, international airfare, medical insurance, entrance fees, on site directors, tutorial assistance). A $200 deposit is required.
Contact • Natalie Nation, Director, Learning Programs International, 816 West 23rd Street, Austin, TX 78705; 800-259-4439; Fax: 512-474-1021; E-mail: 76331.336@compuserve.com; World Wide Web: http://www.studiesabroad.com

LOS ANGELES COMMUNITY COLLEGE DISTRICT

SUMMER SESSION IN SPAIN

General Information • Language study program in Salamanca. Classes are held on the campus of Colegio Miguel de Unamuno.
Learning Focus • Courses in Spanish language. Instruction is offered by professors from the sponsoring institution and local teachers.
Accommodations • Homestays, dormitories. Single rooms are available. Meals are taken with host family, in residences.
Program Details • Program offered once per year. Session length: 4 weeks. Departures are scheduled in July. The program is open to undergraduate students, graduate students, pre-college students, adults. Most participants are 17–65 years of age. 20 participants per session. Application deadline: May 1.
Costs • $2680 (includes tuition, housing, all meals, insurance, excursions, international airfare). A $400 deposit is required.
Contact • International Education Program, Los Angeles Community College District, 770 Wilshire Boulevard, Los Angeles, CA 90017; 213-891-2282; Fax: 213-891-2150; E-mail: intered@laccd.cc.ca.us; World Wide Web: http://laccd.cc.ca.us

The International Education Program of the Los Angeles Community Colleges provides a wide range of low-cost, high-quality learning experiences around the globe. The first classes were offered 20 years ago. Several thousand students of all ages and backgrounds have learned a foreign language, earned transferable college credit, and added a significant plus to their résumés as a result of enrolling with the program. The most popular programs continue to be language study in Salamanca, Spain; Paris, France; Cuernavaca, Mexico; and Florence, Italy; as well as a semester in Cambridge, England. New programs are planned for Bali, Thailand, Costa Rica, St. Petersburg, and London.

MCM EXCHANGE STUDENTS, S.C.

HOMESTAY EXPLORER

General Information • Cultural tour with visits to Barcelona, Costa Brava. Once at the destination country, participants travel by bus, foot.

Learning Focus • Nature observation (Spanish countryside). Instruction is offered by host family. This program would appeal to people interested in Spanish people, travel, culture.
Accommodations • Homestays. Single rooms are available.
Program Details • Session length: 2 weeks. Departures are scheduled throughout the year. Program is targeted to students enrolled in universities and recent college graduates. Most participants are 22–33 years of age. Participants must be 18 years or older to enroll. Other requirements: minimal knowledge of Spanish. Application deadline: one month. Reservations are recommended at least one month before departure.
Costs • $1200 for 4 weeks (includes housing, some meals, some excursions, airport pickup, on-site coordinator). A $250 deposit is required.
Contact • Alex Ferrer, Director, MCM Exchange Students, S.C., Au. Pau Casals, Barcelona 08021, Spain; +34 3-414-4422; Fax: +34 34-141-211; E-mail: 100776.546@compuserve.com; World Wide Web: http://www.muskoka.com:80/adventures

MCM EXCHANGE STUDENTS, S.C.

LANGUAGE PROGRAM AT ESADE

General Information • Language study program with visits to Barcelona, city sightseeing, Costa Brava. Once at the destination country, participants travel by bus, foot. Program is affiliated with ESADE.
Learning Focus • Instruction in the Spanish language. Museum visits (Picasso Museum, Dali Museum, Art Museum). Other activities include cultural activities. Instruction is offered by professors. This program would appeal to people interested in language, Spanish culture, tourism.
Accommodations • Homestays, dormitories, locally-rented apartments. Single rooms are available.
Program Details • Session length: 4 weeks. Departures are scheduled throughout the year. Program is targeted to university students, teachers and adults in general. Most participants are 20–35 years of age. Participants must be 18 years or older to enroll. 75–100 participants per session. Reservations are recommended at least 1 month before departure.
Costs • $2100 (includes tuition, housing, some meals, books and class materials, excursions, airport pick-up, on-site coordinator). A $250 deposit is required.
Contact • Alex Ferrer, Director, MCM Exchange Students, S.C., Au Pau Casals 11012, Barcelona 08021, Spain; +34 34-144-422; Fax: +34 34-141-211; E-mail: 100776.546@compuserve.com; World Wide Web: http://www.muskoka.com:80/adventures

MICHIGAN STATE UNIVERSITY

SPANISH LANGUAGE, LITERATURE, AND CULTURE PROGRAM

General Information • Language study program in Alcalá.
Learning Focus • Courses in Spanish language, Spanish culture, Spanish literature. Instruction is offered by professors from the sponsoring institution.
Accommodations • Homestays. Meals are taken with host family, in residences.
Program Details • Program offered once per year. Session length: 6 weeks. Departures are scheduled in June. The program is open to undergraduate students. Most participants are 18–22 years of age. Other requirements: good academic standing and the approval of the director. 40 participants per session. Application deadline: March 14.
Costs • $2222 (includes housing, some meals, excursions). Application fee: $75. A $250 deposit is required.
Contact • Brenda S. Sprite, Educational Programs Coordinator, Michigan State University, Office of Study Abroad, 109 International Center, East Lansing, MI 48824-1035; 517-353-8920; Fax: 517-432-2082; E-mail: sprite@pilot.msu.edu; World Wide Web: http://study-abroad.msu.edu

MODERN LANGUAGE STUDIES ABROAD

SUMMER STUDY AT UNIVERSITY OF MADRID

General Information • Academic study program in Madrid. Classes are held on the campus of Complutense University of Madrid. Excursions to Segovia, Pamplona, Sur de España, Escorial, Ruta del Quijote, Barcelona, Toledo.
Learning Focus • Courses in language study, literature, cultural studies. Instruction is offered by local teachers.
Accommodations • Dormitories. Single rooms are available. Meals are taken in central dining facility.
Program Details • Program offered 3 times per year. Session length: 2–4 weeks. Departures are scheduled in June, July. The program is open to undergraduate students, graduate students, adults. Most participants are 17–80 years of age. 100 participants per session. Application deadline: April 1.
Costs • $1985 for 2 weeks, $2575 for 3 weeks, $2785 for 4 weeks (includes tuition, housing, all meals, international airfare). Application fee: $85.
Contact • Dr. Celestino Ruiz, Professor of Spanish, Modern Language Studies Abroad, PO Box 623, Griffith, IN 46319; 219-838-9460; Fax: 219-838-9460

NATIONAL REGISTRATION CENTER FOR STUDY ABROAD

COLEGIO MARAVILLAS SPANISH LANGUAGE STUDIES

General Information • Language study program in Benalmadena.
Learning Focus • Courses in Spanish language.
Accommodations • Homestays, program-owned apartments. Single rooms are available. Meals are taken on one's own, in local restaurants.
Program Details • Program offered 50 times per year. Session length: 2 weeks. Departures are scheduled in January–December. The program is open to undergraduate students, graduate students, adults. Application deadline: 40 days prior to departure.
Costs • $783 (includes tuition, housing, some meals, insurance). Application fee: $40. A $100 deposit is required.
Contact • June Domoe, Educational Consultant, National Registration Center for Study Abroad, 823 North Second Street, Milwaukee, WI 53203; 414-278-0631; Fax: 414-271-8884; E-mail: inquiries@nrcsa.com; World Wide Web: http://www.nrcsa.com

NATIONAL REGISTRATION CENTER FOR STUDY ABROAD

DON QUIJOTE

General Information • Language study program in Barcelona, Granada, Salamanca.
Learning Focus • Courses in Spanish language.
Accommodations • Homestays. Meals are taken on one's own.
Program Details • Program offered 40 times per year. Session length: 2 weeks. Departures are scheduled in January–December. The program is open to undergraduate students, graduate students, adults. 8 participants per session. Application deadline: 40 days prior to departure.
Costs • $881 (includes tuition, housing, some meals, insurance). Application fee: $40. A $100 deposit is required.
Contact • June Domoe, Educational Consultant, National Registration Center for Study Abroad, Box 1393, Milwaukee, WI 53201; 414-278-0631; Fax: 414-271-8884; E-mail: ask@nrcsa.com; World Wide Web: http://www.nrcsa.com

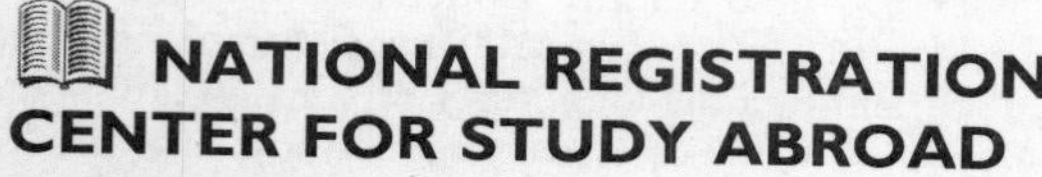

NATIONAL REGISTRATION CENTER FOR STUDY ABROAD

EUROCENTRE: SPAIN

General Information • Language study program in Barcelona, Madrid, Salamanca.
Learning Focus • Courses in Spanish language.
Accommodations • Homestays. Single rooms are available. Meals are taken with host family.
Program Details • Program offered 12 times per year. Session length: 4 weeks. Departures are scheduled in January–December. The program is open to undergraduate students, graduate students, adults. 10–15 participants per session. Application deadline: 40 days prior to departure.
Costs • $1668 (includes tuition, housing, some meals, insurance). Application fee: $40. A $100 deposit is required.
Contact • June Domoe, Educational Consultant, National Registration Center for Study Abroad, PO Box 1393, Milwaukee, WI 53201; 414-278-0631; Fax: 414-271-8884; E-mail: inquiries@nrcsa.com; World Wide Web: http://www.nrcsa.com

NATIONAL REGISTRATION CENTER FOR STUDY ABROAD

MALACA INSTITUTO

General Information • Language study program in Málaga.
Learning Focus • Courses in Spanish language.
Accommodations • Homestays, dormitories. Single rooms are available. Meals are taken on one's own.
Program Details • Program offered 22 times per year. Session length: 2 weeks. Departures are scheduled in January–December. The program is open to undergraduate

students, graduate students, adults. 5–10 participants per session. Application deadline: 40 days prior to departure.
Costs • $1061 (includes tuition, housing, insurance). Application fee: $40. A $100 deposit is required.
Contact • Reuel Zielke, Coordinator, National Registration Center for Study Abroad, 823 North Second Street, Milwaukee, WI 53203; 414-278-0631; Fax: 414-271-8884; E-mail: quest@nrcsa.com; World Wide Web: http://www.nrcsa.com

NATIONAL REGISTRATION CENTER FOR STUDY ABROAD

SEC SANTANDER

General Information • Language study program in Santander.
Learning Focus • Courses in Spanish language.
Accommodations • Homestays. Single rooms are available. Meals are taken with host family, in residences.
Program Details • Program offered 50 times per year. Session length: 2 weeks. Departures are scheduled in January–December. The program is open to undergraduate students, graduate students, adults. 6–8 participants per session. Application deadline: 40 days prior to departure.
Costs • $855 (includes tuition, housing, some meals, insurance). Application fee: $40. A $100 deposit is required.
Contact • June Domoe, Educational Consultant, National Registration Center for Study Abroad, Box 1393, Milwaukee, WI 53201; 414-278-0631; Fax: 414-271-8884; E-mail: ask@nrcsa.com; World Wide Web: http://www.nrcsa.com

NEW YORK UNIVERSITY

PROGRAM IN SPAIN

General Information • Academic study program in Salamanca. Classes are held on the campus of University of Salamanca. Excursions to Toledo, El Escorial, Segovia.
Learning Focus • Courses in Spanish language, European history, Spanish theater, European literature. Instruction is offered by professors from the sponsoring institution and local teachers.
Accommodations • Homestays, dormitories. Meals are taken as a group.
Program Details • Program offered once per year. Session length: 4 weeks. Departures are scheduled in July. The program is open to undergraduate students, graduate students, pre-college students, adults, foreign graduate and undergraduate students.
Costs • $3020 (includes tuition, housing, all meals, excursions). Application fee: $20.
Contact • Jenny M. Gibbs, Director, New York University, Arts and Science Summer Programs, 285 Mercer Street, 2nd Floor, New York, NY 10003; 212-998-8175; Fax: 212-995-4177; E-mail: abroad@nyu.edu; World Wide Web: http://www.nyu.edu/studyabroad

NICHOLLS STATE UNIVERSITY

STUDY PROGRAM ABROAD IN SEVILLE, SPAIN

General Information • Academic and language study program in Seville. Classes are held on the campus of Nicholls State University–Seville. Excursions to bullfights, Isla Cristina, beaches, film sessions, sporting events.
Learning Focus • Courses in language study, literature, linguistics, cultural studies, civilizations. Instruction is offered by professors from the sponsoring institution.
Accommodations • Homestays. Single rooms are available. Meals are taken on one's own, with host family, in local restaurants, in residences.
Program Details • Program offered 15 times per year. Session length: 3 weeks–one year. Departures are scheduled in January–December. The program is open to undergraduate students, graduate students, pre-college students, adults. Most participants are 18–55 years of age. Other requirements: high school seniors or graduates. 25 participants per session. Application deadline: 30 days prior to departure.
Costs • $1031 for non-credit program, $1326 for 6 hours of college credit (includes tuition, housing, some meals, books and class materials). A $180 deposit is required.
Contact • Dr. Gary McCann, Director of Study Programs Abroad, Nicholls State University, PO Box 2080, Thibodaux, LA 70310; 504-448-4440; Fax: 504-449-7028; E-mail: fl-caw@nich-nsunet.nich.edu

NORTHERN ILLINOIS UNIVERSITY

SPANISH LANGUAGE AND CULTURE IN SEGOVIA

General Information • Language study program in Segovia.
Learning Focus • Courses in Spanish language, Spanish literature. Instruction is offered by professors from the sponsoring institution.
Accommodations • Homestays. Meals are taken with host family.
Program Details • Program offered once per year. Session length: 6 weeks. Departures are scheduled in June. The program is open to undergraduate students. Most participants are 20–26 years of age. Other requirements: 2 years of college-level Spanish. 25 participants per session. Application deadline: May 1.
Costs • $3800 (includes tuition, housing, some meals, insurance, excursions). A $200 deposit is required.
Contact • Anne Seitzinger, Program Coordinator, Short-Term Study Abroad, Northern Illinois University, Study Abroad Office-WI 417, DeKalb, IL 60115; 815-752-0700; Fax: 815-753-0825; E-mail: aseitz@niu.edu; World Wide Web: http://www.niu.edu/depts/intl_prgms/intl.html

RICE UNIVERSITY

SUMMER PROGRAM IN SPAIN

General Information • Language study program in Santiago de Compostela, Seville. Excursions to Madrid, Toledo, Córdoba, Granada, Osuna, Mérida, Cáceres, Salamanca, Portugal, Itálica.
Learning Focus • Courses in Spanish art, Spanish language. Instruction is offered by professors from the sponsoring institution.
Accommodations • Homestays, dormitory-like residences. Single rooms are available. Meals are taken with host family, in central dining facility.

Program Details • Program offered once per year. Session length: 6 weeks. Departures are scheduled in June. The program is open to undergraduate students, graduate students, pre-college students, adults. Most participants are 20–22 years of age. Other requirements: one year of Spanish or equivalent and a minimum GPA of 3.0. 40–45 participants per session. Application deadline: March.
Costs • $2650 (includes tuition, housing, some meals, excursions, bus transportation [Madrid to Seville/Seville to Santiago de Compostela and back]). Application fee: $50. A $50 deposit is required.
Contact • Beverly Konzem, Program and Department Coordinator, Rice University, Department of Hispanic and Classical Studies-MS34, 6100 Main Street, Houston, TX 77005-1892; 713-285-5451; Fax: 713-527-4863; E-mail: span@rice.edu; World Wide Web: http://www.ruf.rice.edu/~span/spain_96/

 ROLLINS COLLEGE

VERANO ESPAÑOL

General Information • Language study program in Madrid. Classes are held on the campus of College for International Studies. Excursions to Toledo, Pamplona, Segovia, Salamanca.
Learning Focus • Courses in Spanish language, Spanish culture, Spanish art, Spanish literature. Instruction is offered by professors from the sponsoring institution and local teachers.
Accommodations • Homestays. Meals are taken with host family, in residences.
Program Details • Program offered once per year. Session length: 6 weeks. Departures are scheduled in June. The program is open to undergraduate students, graduate students, adults, qualified high school seniors. Most participants are 18–24 years of age. Other requirements: some proficiency in Spanish, normally 3 semesters of college Spanish. 18 participants per session. Application deadline: April 15.
Costs • $2895 (includes tuition, housing, all meals, excursions). A $50 deposit is required.
Contact • Dr. Edward E. Borsoi, Coordinator, Verano Español, Rollins College, Box 2702, Winter Park, FL 32789-4499; 407-646-2135; Fax: 407-646-2265; E-mail: eborsoi@rollins.edu; World Wide Web: http://www.rollins.edu

 RUSSIAN AND EAST EUROPEAN PARTNERSHIPS

SPAIN LANGUAGE AND CULTURAL IMMERSION PROGRAM

General Information • Language study program in Madrid. Classes are held on the campus of Alba Institute.
Learning Focus • Courses in Spanish language, Spanish culture and art, Spanish history. Instruction is offered by local teachers.
Accommodations • Homestays. Single rooms are available. Meals are taken on one's own, with host family, in local restaurants, in residences.
Program Details • Program offered 11 times per year. Session length: 4 or more weeks. Departures are scheduled in January–November. The program is open to undergraduate students, graduate students, adults. Most participants are 18 years of age and older. Other requirements: in good health and 18 or older unless chaperoned by an adult. 6 participants per session. Application deadline: 45 days prior to departure.
Costs • $2950 (includes tuition, housing, some meals, books and class materials, excursions, international airfare, local transportation, airport transfers). A $1500 deposit is required.
Contact • Kenneth Fortune, President, Russian and East European Partnerships, PO Box 227, Fineview, NY 13640; 888-873-7337; Fax: 800-910-1777; E-mail: reep@fox.nstn.ca

RUTGERS, THE STATE UNIVERSITY OF NEW JERSEY, NEW BRUNSWICK

SUMMER PROGRAM IN SPAIN

General Information • Language study program in Salamanca. Classes are held on the campus of University of Salamanca. Excursions to Palacio Real, Segovia, Peña de Francia, Museo del Prado el Rastro, El Escorial, Toledo, Ciudad Rodrigo, Avila.
Learning Focus • Courses in Spanish culture, Spanish language, Spanish civilization. Instruction is offered by professors from the sponsoring institution and local teachers.
Accommodations • Dormitories, hotels. Single rooms are available. Meals are taken as a group, in central dining facility, in local restaurants.
Program Details • Program offered once per year. Session length: 5 weeks. Departures are scheduled in June. The program is open to undergraduate students, graduate students, adults. Most participants are 18–66 years of age. Other requirements: 1 year college-level Spanish and must be 18 or older. 30 participants per session. Application deadline: March 1.
Costs • $4095 (includes tuition, housing, all meals, books and class materials, insurance, excursions, international airfare). Application fee: $25. A $2000 deposit is required.
Contact • Flora Feldman, Administrative Assistant, Rutgers, The State University of New Jersey, New Brunswick, Department of Spanish and Portuguese, New Brunswick, NJ 08903; 908-932-9323; Fax: 908-932-9837; E-mail: ffeldman@rci.rut.edu; World Wide Web: http://www.rutgers.edu/Academics/Study_Abroad

SAGA HOLIDAYS (ROAD SCHOLAR PROGRAM)

ROAD SCHOLAR: MASTERPIECES OF SPAIN

General Information • Cultural tour with visits to Aranjuez, Córdoba, Granada, Madrid, Seville, Toledo. Once at the destination country, participants travel by bus.
Learning Focus • Field research in the heritage of ancient Spain. Escorted travel to Madrid, Seville and Granada. Museum visits (Reina Sofia Arts Center). Instruction is offered by professors, researchers. This program would appeal to people interested in history.
Accommodations • Hotels. Single rooms are available.

Program Details • Program offered 4 times per year. Session length: 11 days. Departures are scheduled in September, October. Program is targeted to seniors. Most participants are 50–75 years of age. Participants must be 50 years or older to enroll.
Costs • $2099 (includes tuition, housing, some meals, books and class materials, insurance, excursions, international airfare, tour director and lecture).
Contact • Saga Holidays (Road Scholar Program), 222 Berkeley Street, Boston, MA 02116; 800-621-2151

ST. JOHN'S UNIVERSITY

SPAIN PROGRAM

General Information • Academic study program in Segovia.
Learning Focus • Courses in Spanish language, art history, political science. Instruction is offered by professors from the sponsoring institution.
Accommodations • Homestays. Meals are taken with host family, in residences.
Program Details • Program offered once per year. Session length: 12 weeks. Departures are scheduled in January. The program is open to undergraduate students. Most participants are 20–22 years of age. Other requirements: minimum 2.5 GPA and at least one year of college-level Spanish. 30 participants per session. Application deadline: March.
Costs • $9200 (includes tuition, housing, all meals, excursions, International Student Identification card, Youth Hostel card). Application fee: $100.
Contact • Stephen Burmeister-May, Director, Center for International Education, St. John's University, Collegeville, MN 56321; 320-363-2082; Fax: 320-363-2013; E-mail: intleduc@csbsju.edu

SAINT LOUIS UNIVERSITY

SPAIN PROGRAM

General Information • Academic study program in Madrid. Excursions to Segovia, Toledo, San Sebastian, Granada.
Learning Focus • Courses in business, Spanish language, communications, humanities. Instruction is offered by professors from the sponsoring institution.
Accommodations • Homestays, dormitories, locally-rented apartments. Meals are taken as a group, with host family, in central dining facility.
Program Details • Program offered once per year. Session length: 8 weeks. Departures are scheduled in June. The program is open to undergraduate students, graduate students, pre-college students, adults. Most participants are 18–23 years of age. Other requirements: minimum 2.50 GPA. 50 participants per session. Application deadline: first week of May.
Costs • Contact sponsor for information. Application fee: $25. A $100 deposit is required.
Contact • Maria Bravo, US Coordinator, Spain Program, Saint Louis University, 221 North Grand Boulevard, Room 155, St. Louis, MO 63103; 800-758-3678; Fax: 314-977-3413; E-mail: spain@sluvca.slu.edu

SAN DIEGO STATE UNIVERSITY

SPANISH IMMERSION IN ALCALÁ DE HENARES, SPAIN

General Information • Language study program in Alcalá de Henares.
Learning Focus • Courses in language study, cultural studies. Instruction is offered by professors from the sponsoring institution.
Accommodations • Homestays, dormitories. Single rooms are available. Meals are taken with host family, in residences.
Program Details • Program offered once per year. Session length: 4 weeks. Departures are scheduled in July. The program is open to undergraduate students, graduate students, pre-college students, adults. Most participants are 18–80 years of age. 25 participants per session. Application deadline: 60 days prior to departure.
Costs • $1200 (includes tuition, housing, some meals). A $400 deposit is required.
Contact • Patrick Lathrop, Travel Coordinator, San Diego State University, 5250 Campanile Drive, San Diego, CA 92115-1919; 619-594-5154; Fax: 619-594-7080

SANTA BARBARA MUSEUM OF ART

BARCELONA AND MALLORCA

General Information • Cultural tour with visits to Barcelona, Mallorca. Once at the destination country, participants travel by bus, airplane.
Learning Focus • Escorted travel to Barcelona, Mallorca, Menorca and the Spanish countryside. Museum visits (private collections and small, local museums). Instruction is offered by art historians. This program would appeal to people interested in art, decorative arts, architecture, gardening, photography.
Accommodations • Hotels. Single rooms are available.
Program Details • Program offered once per year. Session length: 2 weeks. Departures are scheduled in November. Most participants are 30–80 years of age. Participants must be members of the sponsoring organization (annual dues: $40). 15–20 participants per session. Application deadline: September.
Costs • $5000 (includes housing, some meals, excursions, international airfare). A $500 deposit is required.
Contact • Shelley Ruston, Director of Special Programs, Santa Barbara Museum of Art, 1130 State Street, Santa Barbara, CA 93101; 805-963-4364, ext. 336; Fax: 805-966-6840

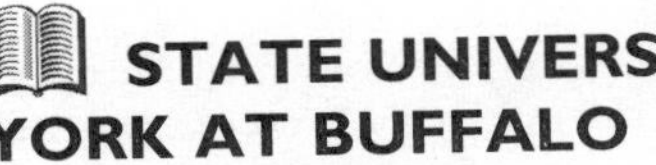

STATE UNIVERSITY OF NEW YORK AT BUFFALO

SALAMANCA PROGRAM

General Information • Language study program in Salamanca. Classes are held on the campus of University of Salamanca. Excursions to Toledo, Leon, Avila, Madrid, Zamora, El Escorial.
Learning Focus • Courses in Spanish language, Spanish democracy, Spanish culture.
Accommodations • Homestays. Single rooms are available. Meals are taken with host family, in residences.
Program Details • Program offered once per year. Session length: 5 weeks. Departures are scheduled in June. The

program is open to undergraduate students, graduate students, adults, Spanish teachers. Most participants are 18–45 years of age. Other requirements: mimimum GPA 2.67 and one year of college-level Spanish. 28 participants per session. Application deadline: April 1.
Costs • $2500 (includes tuition, housing, excursions). Application fee: $10. A $200 deposit is required.
Contact • Sandra J. Reinagel, Interim Study Abroad Coordinator, State University of New York at Buffalo, 210 Talbert Hall, Box 601604, Buffalo, NY 14260-1604; 716-645-3912; Fax: 716-645-6197; E-mail: studyabroad@acsu.buffalo.edu; World Wide Web: http://wings.buffalo.edu/academic/provost/intl/studyabroad

STATE UNIVERSITY OF NEW YORK AT NEW PALTZ

SUMMER STUDY IN SPAIN

General Information • Language study program in Oviedo, Seville. Classes are held on the campus of University of Oviedo. Excursions to Madrid, Segovia, Covadonga (Asturias), Toledo, Córdoba.
Learning Focus • Courses in Spanish language. Instruction is offered by professors from the sponsoring institution and local teachers.
Accommodations • Locally-rented apartments. Meals are taken as a group, in central dining facility.
Program Details • Program offered once per year. Session length: 5 weeks. Departures are scheduled in June. The program is open to undergraduate students, graduate students, pre-college students, adults. Most participants are 18–40 years of age. Other requirements: good academic standing. 15 participants per session. Application deadline: March 15.
Costs • $3352 (includes tuition, housing, all meals, insurance, excursions, international airfare). Application fee: $25. A $100 deposit is required.
Contact • Office of International Education, State University of New York at New Paltz, HAB 33, New Paltz, NY 12561; 914-357-3125; Fax: 914-257-3129; E-mail: sillnerb@npvm.newpaltz.edu; World Wide Web: http://www.newpaltz.edu/oie/

SYRACUSE UNIVERSITY

ECOLOGY OF SPAIN

General Information • Academic study program in Asturias, Guadalajara, Madrid.
Learning Focus • Courses in ecology, art history, photography. Instruction is offered by professors from the sponsoring institution.
Accommodations • Homestays. Single rooms are available. Meals are taken with host family, in residences.
Program Details • Program offered once per year. Session length: 5 weeks. Departures are scheduled in June. The program is open to undergraduate students, graduate students, adults. Most participants are 18–25 years of age. Other requirements: minimum 2.5 GPA. 15 participants per session. Application deadline: March 15.
Costs • $5306 (includes tuition, housing, some meals, books and class materials, excursions). Application fee: $40. A $350 deposit is required.
Contact • Ms. Daisy Fried, Associate Director, Syracuse University, 119 Euclid Avenue, Syracuse, NY 13244-4170; 315-443-9419; Fax: 315-443-4593; E-mail: dsfried@summon3.syr.edu; World Wide Web: http://sumweb.syr.edu/dipa/dipa9.htm

SYRACUSE UNIVERSITY

SPANISH LANGUAGE AND CULTURE

General Information • Academic study program in Barcelona, Cáceres, Madrid, Mérida, Toledo.
Learning Focus • Courses in Spanish language, anthropology. Instruction is offered by professors from the sponsoring institution.
Accommodations • Homestays. Single rooms are available. Meals are taken with host family, in residences.
Program Details • Program offered once per year. Session length: 5 weeks. Departures are scheduled in June. The program is open to undergraduate students. Most participants are 18–25 years of age. Other requirements: minimum 2.5 GPA. 25 participants per session. Application deadline: March 15.
Costs • $4881 (includes tuition, housing, some meals, books and class materials, excursions). Application fee: $40. A $350 deposit is required.
Contact • Ms. Daisy Fried, Associate Director, Syracuse University, 119 Euclid Avenue, Syracuse, NY 13244-4170; 315-443-9419; Fax: 315-443-4593; E-mail: dsfried@summon3.syr.edu; World Wide Web: http://sumweb.syr.edu/dipa/dipa9.htm

TRINITY CHRISTIAN COLLEGE

STUDY IN SEVILLE

General Information • Language study program in Seville. Classes are held on the campus of Windsor School. Excursions to Granada, Córdoba, Toledo.
Learning Focus • Instruction is offered by local teachers.
Accommodations • Homestays. Single rooms are available. Meals are taken with host family, in residences.
Program Details • Program offered 3 times per year. Session length: 4 weeks. Departures are scheduled in January, June, July. The program is open to undergraduate students, graduate students, adults. Most participants are 18–30 years of age. Other requirements: minimum 2.0 GPA. 10 participants per session. Application deadline: December 1, May 1, June 1.
Costs • $2000 (includes tuition, housing, all meals, books and class materials, excursions, orientation). Application fee: $25. A $100 deposit is required.
Contact • Ms. Debra Veenstra, US Coordinator-Study in Seville, Trinity Christian College, 6601 West College Drive, Palos Heights, IL 60463; 800-748-0087; Fax: 708-385-5665; E-mail: spain@trnty.edu; World Wide Web: http://www.trnty.edu/spain

---

Students spend a January or summer term in Seville, Spain, one of the most beautiful and exciting cities in Europe. Trinity Christian College has 17 years of experience in

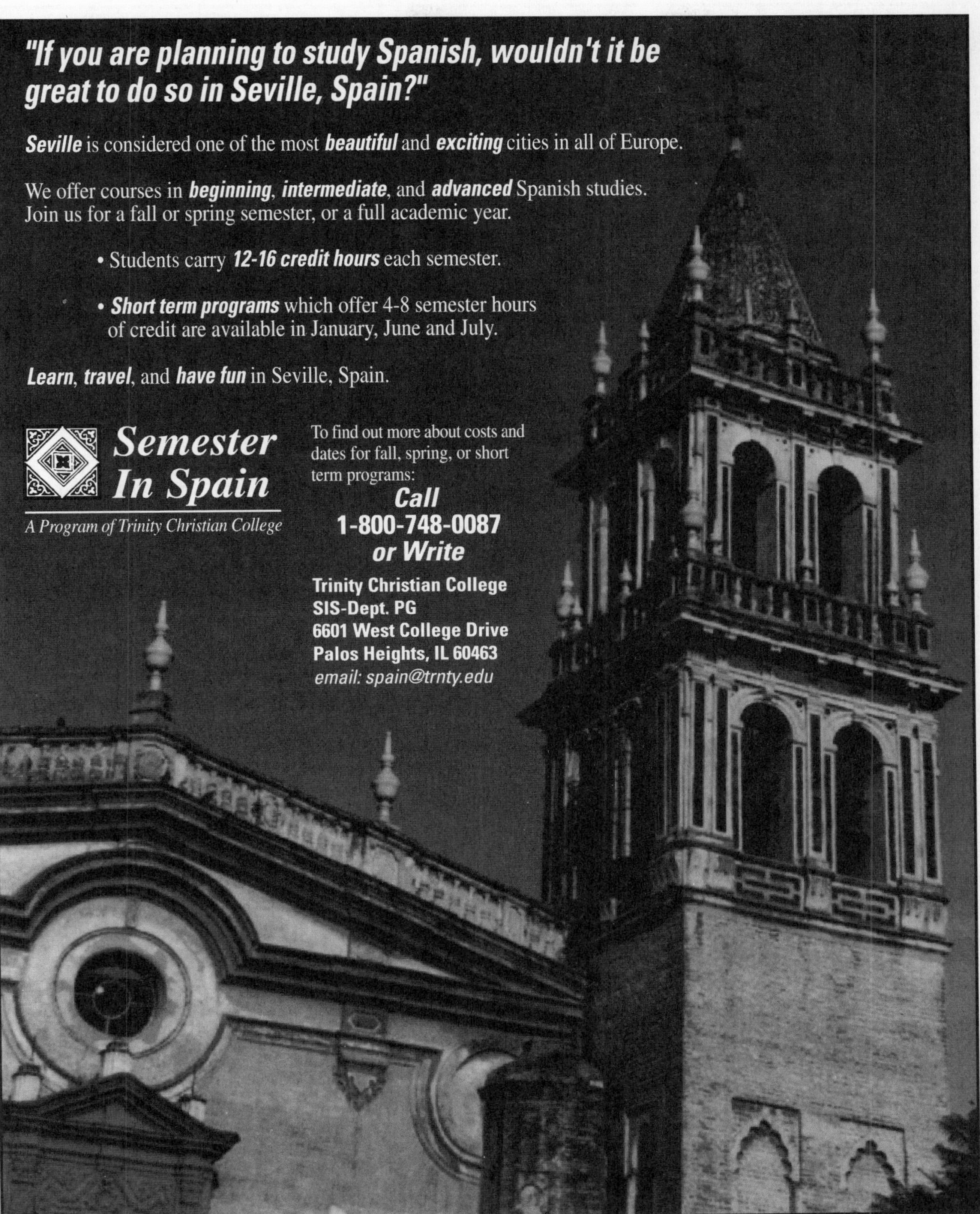
"If you are planning to study Spanish, wouldn't it be great to do so in Seville, Spain?"
Seville is considered one of the most beautiful and exciting cities in all of Europe.
We offer courses in beginning, intermediate, and advanced Spanish studies. Join us for a fall or spring semester, or a full academic year.
• Students carry 12-16 credit hours each semester.
• Short term programs which offer 4-8 semester hours of credit are available in January, June and July.
Learn, travel, and have fun in Seville, Spain.
Semester In Spain
A Program of Trinity Christian College
To find out more about costs and dates for fall, spring, or short term programs:
Call
1-800-748-0087
or Write
Trinity Christian College
SIS-Dept. PG
6601 West College Drive
Palos Heights, IL 60463
email: spain@trnty.edu

Spanish language instruction. The College's professors are highly qualified native Spaniard teachers. The program offers all levels of Spanish instruction from beginning to advanced. The terms are arranged to provide some 3-day weekends for short trips. Popular places to visit are Portugal, Morocco, Madrid, Cadiz, Barcelona, and the beaches of Spain. While in Seville, students can experience ancient ruins, palm and orange trees, fiestas, cathedrals, night life, palaces, fantastic foods, museums, and beautiful people.

UNIVERSITY OF ARIZONA

SUMMER IN SPAIN

General Information • Language study program in Madrid, Puerto de Santa Marie, Salamanca.
Learning Focus • Courses in language study, cultural studies. Instruction is offered by professors from the sponsoring institution.
Accommodations • Homestays. Single rooms are available. Meals are taken with host family, in residences.
Program Details • Program offered 2 times per year. Session length: 5 weeks. Departures are scheduled in June, July. The program is open to undergraduate students. Most participants are 20-25 years of age. Other requirements: minimum 2.5 GPA and one semester college-level Spanish. 25 participants per session. Application deadline: April 1.
Costs • $2400 (includes tuition, housing, all meals, books and class materials, insurance, excursions). Application fee: $35. A $300 deposit is required.
Contact • Renee Griggs, Center for Global Student Programs, University of Arizona, 915 North Tyndall Avenue, Tucson, AZ 85721; 520-621-4627; Fax: 520-621-4069

UNIVERSITY OF DELAWARE

SUMMER SESSION IN GRANADA

General Information • Academic study program in Granada. Classes are held on the campus of University of Granada. Excursions to Madrid, Segovia, Toledo, Córdoba, Seville.
Learning Focus • Courses in Spanish language, art history, music. Instruction is offered by professors from the sponsoring institution and local teachers.
Accommodations • Homestays. Meals are taken with host family, in residences.
Program Details • Program offered once per year. Session length: 5 weeks. Departures are scheduled in June. The program is open to undergraduate students, adults. Most participants are 18-21 years of age. Other requirements: minimum 2.0 GPA. 20 participants per session. Application deadline: April.
Costs • $4336 (includes tuition, housing, all meals, excursions, international airfare). A $200 deposit is required.
Contact • International Programs and Special Sessions, University of Delaware, 4 Kent Way, Newark, DE 19716-1450; 888-831-4685; Fax: 302-831-6042; E-mail: studyabroad@mvs.udel.edu

UNIVERSITY OF DELAWARE

WINTER SESSION IN SPAIN

General Information • Language study program in Granada. Classes are held on the campus of University of Granada. Excursions to Madrid, Segovia, Toledo, Córdoba, Seville.
Learning Focus • Courses in civilizations, cultural studies, Spanish language. Instruction is offered by professors from the sponsoring institution.
Accommodations • Homestays. Meals are taken with host family.
Program Details • Program offered once per year. Session length: 5 weeks. Departures are scheduled in January. The program is open to undergraduate students. Most participants are 18-21 years of age. Other requirements: minimum 2.0 GPA and 2 semesters college Spanish. Application deadline: October.
Costs • $4210 (includes tuition, housing, all meals, excursions, international airfare). A $200 deposit is required.
Contact • International Programs and Special Sessions, University of Delaware, 4 Kent Way, Newark, DE 19716-1450; 888-831-4685; Fax: 302-831-6042; E-mail: studyabroad@mvs.udel.edu

UNIVERSITY OF KANSAS

SPANISH LANGUAGE AND CULTURE IN BARCELONA, SPAIN

General Information • Language study program in Barcelona. Excursions to Salamanca, Peñiscola, Granada, Córdoba, Madrid, Alicante.
Learning Focus • Courses in Spanish language, Spanish history and culture, Spanish literature. Instruction is offered by professors from the sponsoring institution.
Accommodations • Dormitories, hotels. Meals are taken as a group, on one's own, in central dining facility, in local restaurants.
Program Details • Program offered once per year. Session length: 6 weeks. Departures are scheduled in June. The program is open to undergraduate students, graduate students. Most participants are 19-25 years of age. Other requirements: 2 semesters of college-level Spanish or equivalent. 30 participants per session. Application deadline: March 1.
Costs • $3100 (includes tuition, housing, all meals, excursions, 10-day excursion throughout Spain, weekend excursion while in Barcelona, group cultural events). Application fee: $15. A $300 deposit is required.
Contact • Ellen Strubert, Program Coordinator, Office of Study Abroad, University of Kansas, 203 Lippincott Hall, Lawrence, KS 66045; 913-864-3742; Fax: 913-864-5040; E-mail: osa@falcon.cc.ukans.edu; World Wide Web: http://kuhub.cc.ukans.edu/~intlstdy/osa/osamain.html

UNIVERSITY OF MASSACHUSETTS AMHERST

SUMMER PROGRAM IN SPAIN

General Information • Language study program in Salamanca. Classes are held on the campus of Colegio de España.
Learning Focus • Courses in Spanish language, literature, Spanish culture, linguistics. Instruction is offered by local teachers.
Accommodations • Homestays, dormitories. Single rooms are available.
Program Details • Program offered once per year. Session length: 4 weeks. Departures are scheduled in July. The program is open to undergraduate students, graduate students. 72 participants per session. Application deadline: May 20.
Costs • Contact sponsor for information. Application fee: $150.
Contact • Director, University of Massachusetts Amherst, Department of Spanish Portuguese, 418 Herter Hall, Box 33945, Amherst, MA 01003; 413-545-4920; Fax: 413-545-3178; E-mail: salamanca@spanport.umass.edu; World Wide Web: http://www.umass.edu/ipo/

UNIVERSITY OF MIAMI

SUMMER LANGUAGE PROGRAM IN GRANADA

General Information • Language study program in Granada. Classes are held on the campus of University of Granada.
Learning Focus • Courses in Spanish language. Instruction is offered by local teachers.
Accommodations • Homestays. Single rooms are available. Meals are taken on one's own, with host family, in local restaurants, in residences.
Program Details • Program offered 3 times per year. Session length: 4 weeks. Departures are scheduled in June–August. The program is open to undergraduate students, adults. Other requirements: minimum 2.5 GPA. Application deadline: April 1.
Costs • $2900 (includes tuition, housing, some meals). Application fee: $30. A $500 deposit is required.
Contact • Study Abroad Program, University of Miami, PO Box 248005, Coral Gables, FL 33124-1610; 800-557-5421; Fax: 305-284-6629; E-mail: ieep@cstudies.msmail.miami.edu; World Wide Web: http://www.miami.edu/cstudies/ieep.html

UNIVERSITY OF MIAMI

SUMMER LANGUAGE PROGRAM IN SANTANDER

General Information • Language study program in Santander. Classes are held on the campus of University of Cantabria.
Learning Focus • Courses in Spanish language. Instruction is offered by local teachers.
Accommodations • Dormitories. Single rooms are available. Meals are taken as a group, in central dining facility, in residences.
Program Details • Program offered 2 times per year. Session length: 4 weeks. Departures are scheduled in July, August. The program is open to undergraduate students, adults. Other requirements: minimum 2.5 GPA. Application deadline: April 1.
Costs • $2900 (includes tuition, all meals). Application fee: $30. A $500 deposit is required.
Contact • Study Abroad Program, University of Miami, PO Box 248005, Coral Gables, FL 33124-1610; 800-557-5421; Fax: 305-284-6629; E-mail: ieep@cstudies.msmail.miami.edu; World Wide Web: http://www.miami.edu/cstudies/ieep.html

UNIVERSITY OF MICHIGAN

SUMMER LANGUAGE PROGRAM IN BARCELONA, SPAIN

General Information • Language study program in Barcelona. Excursions to Madrid.
Learning Focus • Courses in Spanish language, Spanish history, Spanish culture. Instruction is offered by professors from the sponsoring institution.
Accommodations • Homestays. Meals are taken with host family, in residences.
Program Details • Program offered once per year. Session length: 6 weeks. Departures are scheduled in June. The program is open to undergraduate students. Most participants are 19–22 years of age. Other requirements: three semesters of college-level Spanish or equivalent and a minimum 3.0 GPA. 35 participants per session. Application deadline: February 28.
Costs • $3000–$3500 (includes tuition, housing, all meals, excursions). Application fee: $50. A $250 deposit is required.
Contact • Office of International Programs, University of Michigan, G-513 Michigan Union, 530 South State Street, Ann Arbor, MI 48109-1349; 313-764-4311; Fax: 313-764-3229; E-mail: oip@umich.edu; World Wide Web: http://www.umich.edu/~iinet/oip/

UNIVERSITY OF MINNESOTA, THE GLOBAL CAMPUS

INTERNATIONAL PROGRAM OF SPANISH LANGUAGE, LATIN AMERICAN, AND EUROPEAN STUDIES IN TOLEDO, SPAIN

General Information • Academic study program in Toledo. Excursions to Madrid, Route of Don Quixote, Segovia, Cuenca, Andalucia, El Escorial.
Learning Focus • Courses in Spanish language, art history, archaeology, anthropology, literature, political science, economics, history.
Accommodations • Homestays, San Juan de la Penitencia Residence. Single rooms are available. Meals are taken as a group, with host family, in central dining facility.
Program Details • Program offered 4 times per year. Session length: 6 weeks. Departures are scheduled in January, June, September. The program is open to undergraduate students, graduate students, pre-college students, adults. Most participants are 18–28 years of age. Other requirements: minimum of 1 year of University level Spanish for the June session, minimum of 2 years of University level Spanish for the January and September sessions. 60–75 participants per session. Application deadline: Apr 15.

Costs • $3280 (includes tuition, housing, all meals, insurance, excursions). Application fee: $40. A $400 deposit is required.

Contact • University of Minnesota, The Global Campus, International Program in Toledo, Spain, 106 P2 Nicholson Hall, 216 Pillsbury Drive, SE, Minneapolis, MN 55455-0138; 612-625-3379; Fax: 612-626-8009; E-mail: globalc@maroon.tc.umn.edu; World Wide Web: http://www.isp.umn.edu/tgchome/tgchome.html

UNIVERSITY OF MINNESOTA, THE GLOBAL CAMPUS

SUMMER PROGRAM FOR TEACHERS OF SPANISH

General Information • Graduate-level professional development program in Madrid. Excursions to Toledo, Segovia, Chinchón.

Learning Focus • Courses in Spanish culture, classroom applications, literature, teaching through literature, Spanish language.

Accommodations • Homestays, dormitories. Single rooms are available. Meals are taken as a group, with host family, in residences.

Program Details • Program offered once per year. Session length: 4 weeks. Departures are scheduled in July. The program is open to undergraduate students, graduate students, adults, administrators and teachers. Most participants are 25–60 years of age. Other requirements: intermediate-level Spanish proficiency. 40–60 participants per session. Application deadline: May 15.

Costs • $2400 (includes tuition, housing, all meals, insurance, excursions). Application fee: $50. A $400 deposit is required.

Contact • Summer Program for Teachers of Spanish, University of Minnesota, The Global Campus, 106 P2 Nicholson Hall, 216 Pillsbury Drive, SE, Minneapolis, MN 55455-0138; 612-625-3379; Fax: 612-626-8009; E-mail: globalc@maroon.tc.umn.edu; World Wide Web: http://www.isp.umn.edu/tgchome/tgchome.html

UNIVERSITY OF NORTH CAROLINA AT CHARLOTTE

ARCHITECTURAL DESIGN STUDIO AND FIELD STUDY IN SPAIN

General Information • Academic study program in Cabezón de la Sal. Excursions to Toledo, Córdoba, Seville, Granada.

Learning Focus • Courses in architecture. Instruction is offered by professors from the sponsoring institution.

Accommodations • Dormitories. Meals are taken as a group.

Program Details • Program offered once per year. Session length: 6 weeks. Departures are scheduled in May, June. The program is open to undergraduate students, graduate students. Most participants are 18–30 years of age. Other requirements: completion of architecture courses. 12 participants per session. Application deadline: October.

Costs • $3600 (includes tuition, housing, books and class materials, insurance, excursions). Application fee: $10. A $500 deposit is required.

Contact • Elizabeth A. Adams, Director of Education Abroad Programs, University of North Carolina at Charlotte, Office of International Programs, 9201 University City Boulevard, Charlotte, NC 28223-0001; 704-547-2464; Fax: 704-547-3168; E-mail: eaadams@email.uncc.edu; World Wide Web: http://unccvm.uncc.edu

UNIVERSITY OF PENNSYLVANIA

PENN-IN-ALICANTE

General Information • Academic study program in Alicante. Classes are held on the campus of University of Alicante. Excursions to Madrid, Toledo.

Learning Focus • Courses in Spanish language, Spanish literature, Spanish civilization. Instruction is offered by professors from the sponsoring institution.

Accommodations • Homestays. Meals are taken with host family, in residences.

Program Details • Program offered once per year. Session length: 4½ weeks. Departures are scheduled in June. The program is open to undergraduate students, graduate students, adults. Most participants are 18–35 years of age. 36 participants per session. Application deadline: April 1.

Costs • $5074 (includes tuition, housing, all meals, international airfare). Application fee: $35. A $300 deposit is required.

Contact • Elizabeth Sachs, Director, Penn Summer Abroad, University of Pennsylvania, 3440 Market Street, Suite 100, Philadelphia, PA 19104-3335; 215-898-5738; Fax: 215-573-2053; E-mail: esachs@mail.sas.upenn.edu

UNIVERSITY OF RHODE ISLAND

SUMMER STUDY PROGRAM IN SALAMANCA, SPAIN

General Information • Academic study program in Salamanca. Classes are held on the campus of Colegio de España. Excursions to Segovia, Avila, Burgos, Valladolid.

Learning Focus • Courses in language study, literature. Instruction is offered by professors from the sponsoring institution and local teachers.

Accommodations • Homestays, dormitories. Single rooms are available. Meals are taken as a group, with host family, in central dining facility, in residences.

Program Details • Program offered once per year. Session length: 30 days. Departures are scheduled in July. The program is open to undergraduate students, graduate students, pre-college students, adults, business people. Most participants are 17–74 years of age. 65–90 participants per session. Application deadline: May 10.

Costs • $1725–$1925 (includes tuition, housing, all meals, insurance, excursions). A $100 deposit is required.

Contact • Dr. Mario F. Trubiano, Director, URI Summer Study Program in Spain, University of Rhode Island, Department of Modern and Classical Languages and Literature, Kingston, RI 02881; 401-874-4717; Fax: 401-874-4694

UNIVERSITY OF TULSA

SUMMER IMMERSION PROGRAM IN SPAIN

General Information • Academic study program in Málaga. Classes are held on the campus of University of Málaga. Excursions to Madrid, Toledo, Córdoba, Seville, Granada, El Rocio, Morocco.
Learning Focus • Courses in Spanish language, Spanish culture. Instruction is offered by professors from the sponsoring institution.
Accommodations • Homestays. Single rooms are available. Meals are taken with host family, in residences.
Program Details • Program offered once per year. Session length: 6 weeks. Departures are scheduled in May. The program is open to undergraduate students. Most participants are 18–40 years of age. Other requirements: minimum 3.0 GPA in Spanish and a minimum 2.5 GPA overall. 30 participants per session. Application deadline: March 1.
Costs • $4300 (includes tuition, housing, all meals, books and class materials, excursions, international airfare). A $500 deposit is required.
Contact • Sally Luplow, Director of Study Abroad, University of Tulsa, 600 South College Avenue, TH 102, Tulsa, OK 74104-3189; 918-631-3229; Fax: 918-631-3187; E-mail: luplowsr@centum.utulsa.edu

The University of Tulsa celebrates its 6th Summer Immersion Program in Màlaga, Spain. The program accommodates students who have completed the equivalent of 1 year of college-level Spanish. Students range from intermediate-level students who wish to fulfill their language proficiency requirement while abroad to Spanish majors and minors. Whether they are in class, on excursions, or at their Màlaga residences, participants extend their cultural and linguistic horizons. In addition to serving students from all colleges at The University of Tulsa, the Office of Study Abroad welcomes applications from students at other colleges and universities.

UNIVERSITY OF WISCONSIN–PLATTEVILLE

SUMMER SESSION IN SEVILLE

General Information • Academic study program in Seville. Classes are held on the campus of Spanish-American Institute of International Education. Excursions to Itálica, Gibraltar, Jerez, Portugal, Sanlucar.
Learning Focus • Courses in history, Spanish language. Instruction is offered by local teachers.
Accommodations • Homestays. Single rooms are available. Meals are taken on one's own, with host family, in local restaurants, in residences.
Program Details • Program offered once per year. Session length: 4 weeks. Departures are scheduled in June. The program is open to undergraduate students, adults. Most participants are 18–23 years of age. Other requirements: minimum 2.0 GPA, good academic standing, 2 recommendations, and 1 year of college-level Spanish. 40 participants per session. Application deadline: April 1.
Costs • $2450 for Wisconsin residents, $2700 for non-residents (includes tuition, housing, some meals, books and class materials, excursions, International Student Identification card). Application fee: $25. A $200 deposit is required.
Contact • Dr. William K. Spofford, Director, Study Abroad Programs, University of Wisconsin–Platteville, Institute for Study Abroad Programs, 308 Warner Hall, 1 University Plaza, Platteville, WI 53818-3099; 800-342-1725; Fax: 608-342-1736; E-mail: spofford@uwplatt.edu

UNIVERSITY STUDIES ABROAD CONSORTIUM

SPANISH AND BASQUE STUDIES: SAN SEBASTIAN

General Information • Academic study program in San Sebastian. Classes are held on the campus of University of the Basque Country. Excursions to La Guardia, France-Iparralde, Province of Biz Kaia, Madrid, Toledo, Segovia.
Learning Focus • Courses in Spanish language, Basque language, Basque culture, Iberian culture, Spanish government and politics, international relations, history. Instruction is offered by local teachers.
Accommodations • Homestays, dormitories, locally-rented apartments. Single rooms are available. Meals are taken on one's own, with host family, in central dining facility, in residences.
Program Details • Program offered 2 times per year. Session length: 4 weeks. Departures are scheduled in June–July. The program is open to undergraduate students, graduate students, pre-college students, adults. Most participants are 18–50 years of age. Other requirements: minimum 2.5 GPA. 60 participants per session. Application deadline: April 15.
Costs • $1770 (includes tuition, housing, insurance, excursions, International Student Identification card). Application fee: $50. A $150 deposit is required.
Contact • Dr. Carmelo Urza, Director, University Studies Abroad Consortium, University of Nevada Library/323, Reno, NV 89557-0093; 702-784-6569; Fax: 702-784-6010; E-mail: usac@equinox.unr.edu; World Wide Web: http://www.scs.unr.edu/~usac

VANDERBILT UNIVERSITY

VANDERBILT IN SPAIN

General Information • Academic study program in Madrid.
Learning Focus • Courses in Spanish language, art history, Spanish literature, cultural studies, civilizations. Instruction is offered by professors from the sponsoring institution.
Accommodations • Homestays. Single rooms are available. Meals are taken with host family, in residences.
Program Details • Program offered once per year. Session length: 6 weeks. Departures are scheduled in May. The program is open to undergraduate students. Most participants are 19–21 years of age. Other requirements: minimum

2.7 GPA, 2 years college Spanish and a teacher recommendations. 15–20 participants per session. Application deadline: March 1.
Costs • $5300 (includes tuition, housing, all meals, excursions). A $300 deposit is required.
Contact • Dr. Luigi Monga, Director of Overseas Study, Vanderbilt University, Office of Overseas Study, Box 1573-Station B, Nashville, TN 37235; 615-343-3139; Fax: 615-322-2305

 VILLANOVA UNIVERSITY

LITERATURE AND CIVILIZATION PROGRAM

General Information • Language study program in Cádiz. Classes are held on the campus of University of Cádiz. Excursions to Madrid, Granada, Córdoba, Seville.
Learning Focus • Courses in Spanish language, Spanish culture, Peninsular literature, Spanish civilization. Instruction is offered by local teachers.
Accommodations • Homestays, dormitories. Single rooms are available. Meals are taken as a group, with host family, in central dining facility.
Program Details • Program offered once per year. Session length: 6 weeks. Departures are scheduled in July. The program is open to undergraduate students. Most participants are 19–23 years of age. Other requirements: minimum 2.5 GPA and good academic standing. 25 participants per session. Application deadline: March 1.
Costs • $3250 (includes tuition, housing, all meals, books and class materials, excursions, transfers and orientation). Application fee: $100.
Contact • Dr. Thomas M. Ricks, Director, International Studies, Villanova University, St. Augustine Center, Room 415, Villanova, PA 19085; 610-519-6412; Fax: 610-519-7649; E-mail: ricks@ucis.vill.edu

 WILDLAND ADVENTURES

PYRENEES MOUNTAIN ADVENTURE

General Information • Wilderness/adventure program with visits to Madrid, Pyrenees. Once at the destination country, participants travel by bus, foot, boat, airplane, bicycle.
Learning Focus • Instruction in canyoneering. Other activities include hiking, mountain biking, horseback riding. Instruction is offered by naturalists, historians, sports professionals. This program would appeal to people interested in bicycling, horseback riding.
Accommodations • Hotels, campsites. Single rooms are available.
Program Details • Program offered 2 times per year. Session length: 12 days. Departures are scheduled in May, September. Most participants are 30–60 years of age. Participants must be 15 years or older to enroll. 6–12 participants per session. Application deadline: 30 days prior to departure. Reservations are recommended at least 3–6 months before departure.
Costs • $2295 (includes housing, some meals, excursions, complete pre-departure dossier). A $300 deposit is required.
Contact • Wildland Adventures, 3516 Northeast 155th Street, Seattle, WA 98155; 800-345-4453; Fax: 206-363-6615; E-mail: wildadve@aol.com; World Wide Web: http://www.wildland.com

FOREIGN LANGUAGE STUDY ABROAD SERVICE

INTERNATIONAL LANGUAGE STUDY HOMESTAYS IN SWEDEN

General Information • Language study program in Sweden.

Learning Focus • Courses in Swedish language. Instruction is offered by local teachers.

Accommodations • Homestays. Single rooms are available. Meals are taken with host family, in residences.

Program Details • Session length: varies. Departures are scheduled in January–December. The program is open to undergraduate students, graduate students, pre-college students, adults. Most participants are 12 years of age and older. Other requirements: students must be at least 12 years old. 1 participant per session.

Costs • Contact sponsor for information. A $300 deposit is required.

Contact • Louise Harber, Coordinator, Foreign Language Study Abroad Service, Department IH, Box 903, 5935 Southwest 64th Avenue, South Miami, FL 33143; 800-282-1090; Fax: 305-662-2907; E-mail: flsas@netpoint.net; World Wide Web: http://www.netpoint.net/~flsas

INTERHOSTEL, UNIVERSITY OF NEW HAMPSHIRE

JÖNKÖPING AND STOCKHOLM, SWEDEN

General Information • Cultural tour with visits to Jönköping, Stockholm, Huskvarna, Väx Jö, Gränna, Visingsö, Göteborg, Drottningholm. Once at the destination country, participants travel by bus, foot. Program is affiliated with Södra Vätterbygdens and Folhhogskola of Jönköping.

Learning Focus • Instruction in history and culture. Escorted travel to historical sites. Museum visits (Wasa Museum, Skansen, Museum of Fine Arts). Other activities include visiting local people. Instruction is offered by professors, historians. This program would appeal to people interested in history, culture.

Accommodations • Residential facility. Single rooms are available for an additional $395.

Program Details • Program offered once per year. Session length: 2 weeks. Departures are scheduled in June. Program is targeted to seniors over 50. Most participants are 60–80 years of age. Participants must be 50 years or older to enroll. 35 participants per session. Reservations are recommended at least 6 months before departure.

Costs • $2695 (includes tuition, housing, all meals, excursions, international airfare, entrance fees). A $200 deposit is required.

Contact • Janice Pierson, Office Supervisor, Interhostel, University of New Hampshire, 6 Garrison Avenue, Durham, NH 03824; 800-733-9753; Fax: 603-862-1113; World Wide Web: http://www.learn.unh.edu/

LANGUAGE LIAISON

LIVE 'N' LEARN (LEARN IN A TEACHER'S HOME)–SWEDEN

General Information • Language study program with visits to Sweden.

Learning Focus • Instruction in the Swedish language. Instruction is offered by professors. This program would appeal to people interested in language.

Accommodations • Homestays. Single rooms are available.

Program Details • Session length: unlimited. Departures are scheduled throughout the year. Most participants are 18–70 years of age. Participants must be 16 years or older to enroll. Reservations are recommended at least 35 days before departure.

Costs • Contact sponsor for information.

Contact • Nancy Forman, President, Language Liaison, 20533 Biscayne Boulevard-Station 4-162, Miami, FL 33180; 305-682-9909; Fax: 305-682-9907; E-mail: langstudy@aol.com; World Wide Web: http://languageliaison.com

MICHIGAN STATE UNIVERSITY

PACKAGING IN SWEDEN

General Information • Academic study program in Lund.

Learning Focus • Courses in packaging. Instruction is offered by professors from the sponsoring institution.

Accommodations • Dormitories, hotels. Meals are taken on one's own, in local restaurants.

Program Details • Program offered once per year. Session length: 3½ weeks. Departures are scheduled in July. The program is open to undergraduate students, graduate students. Most participants are 18–22 years of age. Other requirements: good academic standing and the approval of the director. 12 participants per session. Application deadline: March 14.

Costs • $1665 (1995 cost) (includes housing, some meals, excursions). Application fee: $75. A $250 deposit is required.

Contact • Brenda S. Sprite, Educational Programs Coordinator, Michigan State University, Office of Study Abroad, 108 International Center, East Lansing, MI 48824-1035; 517-353-8920; Fax: 517-432-2082; E-mail: sprite@pilot.msu.edu; World Wide Web: http://study-abroad.msu.edu

NATIONAL REGISTRATION CENTER FOR STUDY ABROAD

FOLKUNIVERSITETET

General Information • Language study program in Lund, Uppsala.
Learning Focus • Courses in Swedish language.
Accommodations • Dormitories. Single rooms are available. Meals are taken on one's own.
Program Details • Program offered 5 times per year. Session length: 2 weeks. Departures are scheduled in July–October. The program is open to undergraduate students, graduate students, adults. 8 participants per session. Application deadline: 40 days prior to departure.
Costs • $965–$2585 (includes tuition, housing, insurance). Application fee: $40. A $100 deposit is required.
Contact • Reuel Zielke, Coordinator, National Registration Center for Study Abroad, Box 1393, Milwaukee, WI 53201; 414-278-0631; Fax: 414-271-8884; E-mail: ask@nrcsa.com; World Wide Web: http://www.nrcsa.com

UNIVERSITY OF MIAMI

SUMMER PROGRAM IN SWEDEN

General Information • Language study program in Uppsala.
Learning Focus • Courses in language study.
Accommodations • Dormitories. Single rooms are available. Meals are taken on one's own, in central dining facility.
Program Details • Program offered once per year. Session length: 4 weeks. Departures are scheduled in June. The program is open to undergraduate students, graduate students. Most participants are 19–25 years of age. Other requirements: minimum 3.0 GPA. Application deadline: April 1.
Costs • $3150 (includes tuition). Application fee: $30. A $500 deposit is required.
Contact • Peggy Ting, Study Abroad Program, University of Miami, PO Box 248005, Coral Gables, FL 33124-1610; 305-557-5421; Fax: 305-284-6629; E-mail: ieep@cstudies.msmail.miami.edu; World Wide Web: http://www.miami.edu/cstudies/ieep.html

UPPSALA UNIVERSITY

UPPSALA UNIVERSITY INTERNATIONAL SUMMER SESSION

General Information • Language study program in Uppsala. Classes are held on the campus of Uppsala University. Excursions to Stockholm, Finland (Helsinki), Varmland, Dalarna.
Learning Focus • Courses in Swedish language, history, Swedish films, Swedish arts, social institutions, literature. Instruction is offered by local teachers.
Accommodations • Dormitories, locally-rented apartments. Single rooms are available. Meals are taken as a group.
Program Details • Program offered 3 times per year. Session length: 2, 4, or 8 weeks. Departures are scheduled in June–August. The program is open to undergraduate students, graduate students, adults. Most participants are 18–60 years of age. Other requirements: university eligibility. 260 participants per session. Application deadline: May 15.
Costs • $1700 for 4 weeks (includes tuition, housing, some meals, excursions, free time activity program). Application fee: $25. A $450 deposit is required.
Contact • Dellehe Dorrestyn, Uppsala University, UISS, Box 513, Uppsala 75120, Sweden; +46 18-50-66-80; Fax: +46 18-50-66-80; E-mail: nduiss@worldaccess.nl

SWITZERLAND

BRITISH COASTAL TRAILS SCENIC WALKING

SWITZERLAND'S BERNESE OVERLAND

General Information • Cultural tour with visits to Château-d'Oex, Lauterbrunnen, Lenk, Pays d'Enhaut, Corniche Walk, Simme River, Leiterli, Simme Valley, Grindelwald Glacier. Once at the destination country, participants travel by train, bus, foot, boat, tram.
Learning Focus • Escorted travel to La Braye Peak and blue ice cave. Nature observation (massifs, meadows, glaciers). Other activities include hiking, walking. Instruction is offered by naturalists, historians, professional guides. This program would appeal to people interested in nature studies, walking, culture, photography, history.
Accommodations • Hotels, chalets. Single rooms are available for an additional $200.
Program Details • Program offered 3 times per year. Session length: 7 days. Departures are scheduled in June, August. Most participants are 40–65 years of age. Participants must be 13 years or older to enroll. Other requirements: physician's approval and signed release form. 18 participants per session. Application deadline: 30 days prior to departure. Reservations are recommended at least 6 months before departure.
Costs • $1895 (includes housing, some meals, excursions, full-time guide). A $250 deposit is required.
Contact • Tour Manager, British Coastal Trails Scenic Walking, 7777 Fay Avenue, Suite 100, La Jolla, CA 92037; 800-473-1210; Fax: 619-456-2277; E-mail: lajolla@bctwalk.com; World Wide Web: http://www.bctwalk.com/lajolla

C. G. JUNG INSTITUTE

INTENSIVE STUDY PROGRAM

General Information • Academic study program in Küsnacht. Classes are held on the campus of C. G. Jung Institute Zurich.
Learning Focus • Courses in analytical psychology. Instruction is offered by professors from the sponsoring institution.
Accommodations • Students make own arrangements. Single rooms are available. Meals are taken on one's own, in local restaurants.
Program Details • Program offered once per year. Session length: 2 weeks. Departures are scheduled in July. The program is open to graduate students, adults. Most participants are 28–65 years of age. 60 participants per session. Application deadline: April 15.
Costs • $1350 (includes tuition, some meals).
Contact • Ms. Frances Kaufmann, C. G. Jung Institute, C. G. Jung Institute Zurich, Hornweg 28, 8700 Küsnacht, Switzerland; +41 19-10-53-23; Fax: +41 19-10-54-51

COLLEGE CONSORTIUM FOR INTERNATIONAL STUDIES–EMPIRE STATE COLLEGE, SUNY

SWITZERLAND SUMMER PROGRAM

General Information • Academic study program in Lugano. Classes are held on the campus of Franklin College.
Learning Focus • Courses in international business, foreign languages, international politics, history, European arts. Instruction is offered by local teachers.
Accommodations • Locally-rented apartments, program-owned apartments. Single rooms are available. Meals are taken on one's own, in central dining facility, in local restaurants, in residences.
Program Details • Program offered 2 times per year. Session length: 4 weeks. Departures are scheduled in May, June. The program is open to undergraduate students. Most participants are 21–24 years of age. Other requirements: 2.5 minimum GPA. 2 participants per session. Application deadline: April 15.
Costs • $3273 (includes tuition, housing, insurance). A $200 deposit is required.
Contact • Kenneth T. Abrams, Dean for International Programs, College Consortium for International Studies–Empire State College, 320 Broadway, Saratoga Springs, NY 12866; 518-587-2100, ext. 231; Fax: 518-587-4382; E-mail: kabrams@sescva.esc.edu

COUNTRY WALKERS

UPPER ENGADINE AND BEYOND

General Information • Cultural, gourmet cooking, nature study and walking tour with visits to Pontresina, Thun, Hilterflingen, Bergell Valley, Roseg Valley. Once at the destination country, participants travel by foot, boat.
Learning Focus • Escorted travel to Lake Thun, Oberhofen and the Engadine Valley. Museum visits (Bernese Historical Museum). Nature observation (Swiss National Park). Other activities include walking. Instruction is offered by professors, researchers, naturalists, historians. This program would appeal to people interested in walking, nature studies, food and wine.
Accommodations • Hotels. Single rooms are available for an additional $300–$600.
Program Details • Program offered 5 times per year. Session length: 9 days. Departures are scheduled in June–September. Program is targeted to adults 35 to 65 years old. Most participants are 35–65 years of age. Participants must be 18 years or older to enroll. 18 participants per session. Reservations are recommended at least 5–6 months before departure.
Costs • $2550 (includes housing, all meals, excursions). A $400 deposit is required.

Contact • Heather Kellingbeck, Vice President, Country Walkers, PO Box 180, Waterbury, VT 05176; 802-464-9255; Fax: 802-244-5661; E-mail: ctrywalk@aol.com

EUROCENTRES

LANGUAGE IMMERSION IN SWITZERLAND

General Information • Language study program in Lucerne. Classes are held on the campus of Eurocentre Lucerne Summer Centre. Excursions to Stanserhorn, Brunnen, Zurich.
Learning Focus • Courses in German language, Swiss culture. Instruction is offered by professors from the sponsoring institution.
Accommodations • Homestays. Single rooms are available. Meals are taken with host family, in residences.
Program Details • Program offered 20 times per year. Session length: 2-12 weeks. Departures are scheduled in January-December. The program is open to undergraduate students, graduate students, pre-college students, adults. Most participants are 16-80 years of age. 15 participants per session.
Costs • Contact sponsor for information.
Contact • Marketing, Eurocentres, 101 North Union Street, Suite 300, Alexandria, VA 22314; 800-648-4809; Fax: 703-684-1495; E-mail: 100632.141@compuserve.com; World Wide Web: http://www.clark.net/pub/eurocent/home.htm

FOLKWAYS INSTITUTE

SWISS ALPS PROJECT

General Information • Hiking tour with visits to Switzerland. Once at the destination country, participants travel by train, bus, foot.
Learning Focus • Museum visits (local museums). Nature observation (wildlife, scenery). Instruction is offered by naturalists. This program would appeal to people interested in nature studies, hiking, culture, botany.
Accommodations • Hotels. Single rooms are available.
Program Details • Program offered once per year. Session length: 12 days. Departures are scheduled in August. Program is targeted to seniors. Participants must be 55 years or older to enroll. 12 participants per session. Application deadline: February 1. Reservations are recommended at least 6 months before departure.
Costs • $2900 (includes housing, some meals, excursions, international airfare). A $50 deposit is required.
Contact • David Christopher, Director, Folkways Institute, 14600 Southeast Aldridge Road, Portland, OR 97236-6518; 503-658-6600; Fax: 503-658-8672

GEORGE MASON UNIVERSITY

EUROPEAN BUSINESS ENVIRONMENT

General Information • Academic study program in Lausanne. Classes are held on the campus of University of Lausanne.
Learning Focus • Courses in business, trade, finance, marketing, international business. Instruction is offered by professors from the sponsoring institution and local teachers.
Accommodations • Dormitories, hotels. Single rooms are available. Meals are taken as a group, on one's own.
Program Details • Program offered once per year. Session length: 3 weeks. Departures are scheduled in December. The program is open to undergraduate students, graduate students, adults. Most participants are 18-65 years of age. Other requirements: minimum 2.25 GPA. 10-20 participants per session. Application deadline: October 11.
Costs • $2795 for George Mason University students, $3345 for other students (includes tuition, housing, some meals, insurance, excursions, international airfare). Application fee: $35. A $500 deposit is required.
Contact • Dr. Yehuda Lukacs, Director, Center for Global Education, George Mason University, 4400 University Drive, 235 Johnson Center, Fairfax, VA 22030; 703-993-2156; Fax: 703-993-2153; E-mail: ylukacs@gmu.edu; World Wide Web: http://www.gmu.edu/departments/oie

INTERHOSTEL, UNIVERSITY OF NEW HAMPSHIRE

LUGANO, SWITZERLAND

General Information • Cultural tour with visits to Lugano, St. Moritz, Milan, Luino, Valle Verzasca, Lake Maggiore, Gothard Pass, Andermatt, Gemsstock, Luzern. Once at the destination country, participants travel by bus, foot, boat, cable car. Program is affiliated with Franklin College.
Learning Focus • Instruction in history and culture. Escorted travel to lakes and villages. Museum visits (Brera in Milan, Smuggler's Museum). Attendance at performances (outdoor concerts). Other activities include visiting local people. Instruction is offered by professors, historians. This program would appeal to people interested in history, culture.
Accommodations • Hotels. Single rooms are available for an additional $.
Program Details • Program offered once per year. Session length: 2 weeks. Departures are scheduled in July. Program is targeted to seniors over 50. Most participants are 60-80 years of age. Participants must be 50 years or older to enroll. 35 participants per session. Reservations are recommended at least 6 months before departure.
Costs • $3225 (includes tuition, housing, all meals, excursions, international airfare, entrance fees). A $200 deposit is required.
Contact • Janice Pierson, Office Supervisor, Interhostel, University of New Hampshire, 6 Garrison Avenue, Durham, NH 03824; 800-733-9753; Fax: 603-862-1113; World Wide Web: http://www.learn.unh.edu/

LANGUAGE LIAISON

DIAVOX–LEARN FRENCH OR GERMAN IN SWITZERLAND

General Information • Language study program with visits to Lausanne.
Learning Focus • Instruction in the French and German languages. Instruction is offered by professors. This program would appeal to people interested in language.
Accommodations • Homestays, locally-rented apartments, hotels, studios, pensiones. Single rooms are available.

Program Details • Session length: unlimited. Departures are scheduled throughout the year. Program is targeted to students of any age. Most participants are 18–70 years of age. Participants must be 16 years or older to enroll. Reservations are recommended at least 35 days before departure.
Costs • Contact sponsor for information.
Contact • Nancy Forman, President, Language Liaison, 20533 Biscayne Boulevard-Station 4-162, Miami, FL 33180; 305-682-9909; Fax: 305-682-9907; E-mail: langstudy@aol.com; World Wide Web: http://languageliaison.com

NATIONAL REGISTRATION CENTER FOR STUDY ABROAD

EUROCENTRE: SWITZERLAND

General Information • Language study program in Lucerne.
Learning Focus • Courses in German language.
Accommodations • Homestays. Single rooms are available. Meals are taken with host family.
Program Details • Program offered 2 times per year. Session length: 2 weeks. Departures are scheduled in July. The program is open to undergraduate students, graduate students, adults. Application deadline: 40 days prior to departure.
Costs • $1744 (includes tuition, housing, some meals, insurance). Application fee: $40. A $100 deposit is required.
Contact • Reuel Zielke, Coordinator, National Registration Center for Study Abroad, 823 North Second Street, Milwaukee, WI 53203; 414-278-0631; Fax: 414-271-8884; E-mail: inquiries@nrcsa.com; World Wide Web: http://www.nrcsa.com

NATIONAL REGISTRATION CENTER FOR STUDY ABROAD

EUROCENTRE: SWITZERLAND (LAUSANNE)

General Information • Language study program in Lausanne.
Learning Focus • Courses in French language.
Accommodations • Homestays. Single rooms are available. Meals are taken with host family.
Program Details • Program offered 12 times per year. Session length: 4 weeks. Departures are scheduled in January–December. The program is open to undergraduate students, graduate students, adults.
Costs • $2416 (includes tuition, housing, some meals, insurance). Application fee: $40. A $100 deposit is required.
Contact • Reuel Zielke, Coordinator, National Registration Center for Study Abroad, PO Box 1393, Milwaukee, WI 53201; 414-278-0631; Fax: 414-271-8884; E-mail: inquiries@nrcsa.com; World Wide Web: http://www.nrcsa.com

NATIONAL REGISTRATION CENTER FOR STUDY ABROAD

EUROCENTRE: SWITZERLAND (NEUCHÂTEL)

General Information • Language study program in Neuchâtel.
Learning Focus • Courses in French language.
Accommodations • Homestays. Single rooms are available. Meals are taken with host family.
Program Details • Program offered 2 times per year. Session length: 3 weeks. Departures are scheduled in July. The program is open to undergraduate students, graduate students, adults. 10–12 participants per session. Application deadline: 2 months prior to departure.
Costs • $1744 (includes tuition, housing, some meals, insurance). Application fee: $40. A $100 deposit is required.
Contact • Reuel Zielke, Coordinator, National Registration Center for Study Abroad, PO Box 1393, Milwaukee, WI 53201; 414-278-0631; Fax: 414-271-8884; E-mail: inquiries@nrcsa.com; World Wide Web: http://www.nrcsa.com

 SYRACUSE UNIVERSITY

GRADUATE INTERNSHIPS IN INTERNATIONAL ORGANIZATIONS IN GENEVA

General Information • Internship program in Geneva.
Learning Focus • Courses in international relations. Instruction is offered by professors from the sponsoring institution.
Accommodations • Dormitories. Single rooms are available. Meals are taken on one's own, in local restaurants.
Program Details • Program offered once per year. Session length: 7 weeks. Departures are scheduled in June. The program is open to graduate students. Most participants are 21–30 years of age. Other requirements: minimum 2.8 GPA. 18 participants per session. Application deadline: February 15.
Costs • $4395 (includes tuition, housing, books and class materials, excursions). Application fee: $40. A $350 deposit is required.
Contact • Ms. Daisy Fried, Associate Director, Syracuse University, 119 Euclid Avenue, Syracuse, NY 13244; 315-443-9419; Fax: 315-443-4593; E-mail: dsfried@summon3.syr.edu; World Wide Web: http://sumweb.syr.edu/dipa/dipa9.htm

 UNIVERSITY OF DELAWARE

SWISS HOSPITALITY SUMMER SESSION

General Information • Academic study program in Chur. Classes are held on the campus of Swiss School of Hotel and Tourism Management. Excursions to Lake Constance, Vaduz, Liechtenstein, Lucerne.
Learning Focus • Courses in hotel management, German language, restaurant management. Instruction is offered by professors from the sponsoring institution and local teachers.
Accommodations • Dormitories. Single rooms are available. Meals are taken in central dining facility.
Program Details • Program offered once per year. Session length: 5 weeks. Departures are scheduled in June. The program is open to undergraduate students. Most participants are 18–21 years of age. Other requirements: minimum 2.0 GPA. 15 participants per session. Application deadline: April.
Costs • $4061 (includes tuition, housing, some meals, excursions, international airfare). A $200 deposit is required.
Contact • Paul Olchvary, Program Coordinator, University of Delaware, International Programs and Special Sessions, 4

Kent Way, Newark, DE 19716-1450; 302-831-4408; Fax: 302-831-6042; E-mail: paul.olchvary@mvs.udel.edu

UNIVERSITY OF DELAWARE

WINTER SESSION IN GENEVA, SWITZERLAND

General Information • Academic study program in Geneva.
Learning Focus • Courses in economics, international relations, French language, international business, political science. Instruction is offered by professors from the sponsoring institution.
Accommodations • Hotels.
Program Details • Program offered once per year. Session length: 5 weeks. Departures are scheduled in January. The program is open to undergraduate students. Other requirements: minimum 2.0 GPA. Application deadline: October.
Costs • Contact sponsor for information. A $200 deposit is required.
Contact • International Programs and Special Sessions, University of Delaware, 4 Kent Way, Newark, DE 19716-1450; 888-831-4685; Fax: 302-831-6042; E-mail: studyabroad@mvs.udel.edu

UNIVERSITY OF MIAMI

PROGRAM AT UNIVERSITÉ DE LAUSANNE–ÉCOLE DE FRANÇAIS MODERNE

General Information • Language study program in Lausanne. Classes are held on the campus of University of Lausanne.
Learning Focus • Courses in French language. Instruction is offered by local teachers.
Accommodations • Dormitories, program-owned apartments. Single rooms are available. Meals are taken on one's own, in central dining facility.
Program Details • Program offered once per year. Session length: 3 weeks. Departures are scheduled in July. The program is open to undergraduate students, graduate students. Most participants are 19–25 years of age. Other requirements: minimum 3.0 GPA. Application deadline: April 1.
Costs • $1612 (includes tuition). Application fee: $30. A $500 deposit is required.
Contact • Peggy Ting, Study Abroad Program, University of Miami, PO Box 248005, Coral Gables, FL 33124-1610; 800-557-5241; Fax: 305-284-6629; E-mail: ieep@cstudies.msmail.miami.edu; World Wide Web: http://www.miami.edu/cstudies/ieep.html

WALKING THE WORLD

WALKING IN SWITZERLAND

General Information • Cultural tour with visits to Eggen, Grutschalp, Lauterbrunnen, Tuftern, Zermatt, Zurich, Mannlichen Mountain, Ritzengrat Ridge. Once at the destination country, participants travel by train, foot, van.
Learning Focus • Escorted travel to Switzerland. Museum visits (major museums). Attendance at performances (folk festival). Other activities include walking. Instruction is offered by professors, naturalists. This program would appeal to people interested in walking, photography, culture, history.
Accommodations • Hotels.
Program Details • Program offered 2 times per year. Session length: 11 days. Departures are scheduled in June, September. Program is targeted to walkers 50 and over. Most participants are 50 years of age and older. Participants must be 50 years or older to enroll. 16 participants per session. Reservations are recommended at least 6 months before departure.
Costs • $2495 (includes housing, some meals, excursions). A $400 deposit is required.
Contact • Walking The World, PO Box 1186, Ft. Collins, CO 80522; 970-225-0500; Fax: 970-225-9100; E-mail: cougar@frii.com

WALES

See also England, Ireland, Northern Ireland, and Scotland

ARTS & CRAFTS TOURS

AN ARTS AND CRAFTS SAMPLER IN WALES

General Information • Cultural tour with visits to England (Chester), Wales (Southern-Cardiff). Once at the destination country, participants travel by bus.
Learning Focus • Escorted travel to private homes and churches. Museum visits (collections and exhibits). Instruction is offered by professors, artists, historians, architectural historians and curators. This program would appeal to people interested in Wales, the arts and crafts movement, architecture, the Pre-Raphaelites.
Accommodations • Hotels. Single rooms are available for an additional $500.
Program Details • Program offered once per year. Session length: 8 days. Departures are scheduled in May. Most participants are 40–80 years of age. 8–10 participants per session. Application deadline: 60 days prior to departure. Reservations are recommended at least 6 months before departure.
Costs • $3800 (includes housing, all meals, books and class materials, excursions). A $500 deposit is required.
Contact • Elaine Hirschl Ellis, President, Arts & Crafts Tours, 110 Riverside Drive, New York, NY 10024; 212-362-0761; Fax: 212-787-2823; E-mail: actours@aol.com; World Wide Web: http://www.dscweb.com/AandCTours.html

BRITISH COASTAL TRAILS SCENIC WALKING

THE MYSTICAL LAND OF WALES

General Information • Cultural tour with visits to Dolgellau, Llanarmon Dyffryn Ceiriog, Shrewsbury, River Severn, Shropshire Canal, Vale of Llangollen, Eglwyseg Rocks. Once at the destination country, participants travel by train, bus, foot.
Learning Focus • Escorted travel to Offa's Dyke and the Berwyn Mountains. Nature observation (birds, sheep). Other activities include hiking, walking. Instruction is offered by naturalists, historians, professional guides. This program would appeal to people interested in nature studies, walking, culture, photography, history.
Accommodations • Hotels, inns. Single rooms are available.
Program Details • Program offered 3 times per year. Session length: 8 days. Departures are scheduled in June, July, September. Most participants are 40–65 years of age. Participants must be 13 years or older to enroll. Other requirements: physician's approval and signed release form. 18 participants per session. Application deadline: 30 days prior to departure. Reservations are recommended at least 6 months before departure.
Costs • $1855 (includes housing, some meals, excursions, full-time guide). A $250 deposit is required.
Contact • Tour Manager, British Coastal Trails Scenic Walking, 7777 Fay Avenue, Suite 100, La Jolla, CA 92037; 800-473-1210; Fax: 619-456-2277; E-mail: lajolla@bctwalk.com; World Wide Web: http://www.bctwalk.com/lajolla

CROSS-CULTURE

WELSH WALKS

General Information • Nature study, cultural, and hiking tour with visits to Abergavenny, The Sugar Loaf, Chepstow, Offa's Dyke, Wye Valley, Black Mountains, The Great Forest, Penderyn. Once at the destination country, participants travel by bus, foot.
Learning Focus • Escorted travel to the Abergavenny Castle, the Sugar Loaf Winery, the Devil's Pulpit, the Tintern Abbey and Sgwd yr Eira. Nature observation (indigenous plant and animal life). Other activities include hiking. Instruction is offered by naturalists, historians, experienced hiking leaders. This program would appeal to people interested in nature studies, history, food and wine, culture, traditions.
Accommodations • Manor house. Single rooms are available.
Program Details • Program offered once per year. Session length: 9 days. Departures are scheduled in July. Program is targeted to adults of all ages. Most participants are 30–75 years of age. Participants must be 12 years or older to enroll. Other requirements: must be in good health, must be accompanied by an adult if under 18. 20 participants per session. Application deadline: 1 month prior to departure. Reservations are recommended at least 3–12 months before departure.
Costs • $1910 (includes tuition, housing, all meals, books and class materials, excursions, international airfare). A $300 deposit is required.
Contact • Cross-Culture, 52 High Point Drive, Amherst, MA 01002-1224; 413-256-6303; Fax: 413-253-2303; E-mail: xculture@javanet.com; World Wide Web: http://www.empiremall.com/cross-culture

CROSS-CULTURE

WONDERFUL WALES

General Information • Cultural tour with visits to Gwynedd. Once at the destination country, participants travel by bus, foot.
Learning Focus • Escorted travel to Dolwyddelan Castle, Hereford Cathedral and Brecon. Museum visits (world's largest chained library). Attendance at performances (traditional male choir). Instruction is offered by highly educated

guides. This program would appeal to people interested in culture, history, nature studies, arts, traditions, food and wine.
Accommodations • Hotels. Single rooms are available.
Program Details • Program offered once per year. Session length: 9 days. Departures are scheduled in August. Program is targeted to adults of all ages. Most participants are 40–70 years of age. Participants must be 12 years or older to enroll. Other requirements: good health, accompaniment of an adult if under 18. 20–25 participants per session. Application deadline: 1 month prior to departure. Reservations are recommended at least 3–12 months before departure.
Costs • $1990 (includes tuition, housing, all meals, books and class materials, excursions, international airfare). A $300 deposit is required.
Contact • Cross-Culture, 52 High Point Drive, Amherst, MA 01002-1224; 413-256-6303; Fax: 413-253-2303; E-mail: xculture@javanet.com; World Wide Web: http://www.empiremall.com/cross-culture

FOREIGN LANGUAGE STUDY ABROAD SERVICE

INTERNATIONAL LANGUAGE STUDY HOMESTAYS IN WALES

General Information • Language study program in Wales.
Learning Focus • Courses in English language. Instruction is offered by local teachers.
Accommodations • Homestays. Single rooms are available. Meals are taken with host family, in residences.
Program Details • Session length: varies. Departures are scheduled in January–December. The program is open to undergraduate students, graduate students, pre-college students, adults. Most participants are 12 years of age and older. Other requirements: students must be at least 12 years old. 1 participant per session.
Costs • Contact sponsor for information. A $300 deposit is required.
Contact • Louise Harber, Coordinator, Foreign Language Study Abroad Service, Department IH, Box 903, 5935 Southwest 64th Avenue, South Miami, FL 33143; 800-282-1090; Fax: 305-662-2907; E-mail: flsas@netpoint.net; World Wide Web: http://www.netpoint.net/~flsas

INTERHOSTEL, UNIVERSITY OF NEW HAMPSHIRE

WALES

General Information • Cultural tour with visits to Abergavenny, Betws-Y-Coed, Brecon Beacons National Park, Gower Peninsula, Cardiff, Caerleon, Raglan Castle, Chepstow Castle, Wye Valley, Tintern Abbey. Once at the destination country, participants travel by bus, foot. Program is affiliated with The Hill Residential College.
Learning Focus • Instruction in history and culture. Escorted travel to castles and towns. Museum visits (Welsh Folk Museum, Living History Museum). Attendance at performances (Welsh Male Choir, folk music). Other activities include sheepdog demonstration. Instruction is offered by historians. This program would appeal to people interested in history, culture.
Accommodations • Dormitories. Single rooms are available for an additional $150.
Program Details • Program offered once per year. Session length: 2 weeks. Departures are scheduled in August. Program is targeted to seniors over 50. Most participants are 60–80 years of age. Participants must be 50 years or older to enroll. 35 participants per session. Reservations are recommended at least 6 months before departure.
Costs • $2535 (includes tuition, housing, all meals, excursions, international airfare, entrance fees). A $200 deposit is required.
Contact • Janice Pierson, Office Supervisor, Interhostel, University of New Hampshire, 6 Garrison Avenue, Durham, NH 03824; 800-733-9753; Fax: 603-862-1113; World Wide Web: http://www.learn.unh.edu/

UNIVERSITY OF WALES, SWANSEA

SUMMER INTERNSHIP PROGRAM

General Information • Internship program in Swansea. Classes are held on the campus of University of Wales, University College of Swansea. Excursions to Gower Peninsula N.P..
Learning Focus • Courses in business, education, Welsh history, legal studies, journalism, social work, leisure, media. Instruction is offered by professors from the sponsoring institution.
Accommodations • Dormitories. Single rooms are available. Meals are taken as a group, in central dining facility.
Program Details • Program offered once per year. Session length: 6 weeks. Departures are scheduled in May. The program is open to undergraduate students, graduate students, adults. Most participants are 20 years of age and older. 6 participants per session. Application deadline: April 1.
Costs • $1200 (includes tuition, housing, some meals).
Contact • Emma Frearson, Administrative Assistant, University of Wales, Swansea, Singleton Park, Swansea, SA28PP, Wales; +44 179-229-5135; Fax: +44 179-229-5719; E-mail: e.frearson@swan.ac.uic

WESTERN HEMISPHERE

REGIONAL

Argentina
Bahamas
Belize
Bermuda
Bolivia
Brazil
Canada
Chile
Costa Rica
Cuba
Dominican Republic
Ecuador
El Salvador
Guatemala
Haiti
Honduras
Jamaica
Martinique
Mexico
Nicaragua
Panama
Paraguay
Peru
Puerto Rico
Suriname
Trinidad and Tobago
U.S. Virgin Islands
Uruguay
Venezuela

REGIONAL

AMERICAN JEWISH CONGRESS, INTERNATIONAL TRAVEL PROGRAM

THE TREASURES OF SOUTH AMERICA

General Information • Cultural tour with visits to Ecuador (Quito), Peru (Lima); excursions to Plaza de la Independencia, Equatorial Monument, Cotopaxi Volcano National Park, Sacsayhuamán. Once at the destination country, participants travel by bus, foot, boat, airplane.

Learning Focus • Escorted travel to the Galapagos Islands, Machu Picchu and synagogues. Nature observation (sea birds, sea lions, dolphins, octopi, starfish, fur seals, iguanas, tortoises). Instruction is offered by naturalists, historians. This program would appeal to people interested in Jewish history.

Accommodations • Hotels, boat. Single rooms are available for an additional $825.

Program Details • Program offered 9 times per year. Session length: 15 days. Departures are scheduled in January-February, May-December. Program is targeted to Jewish-American adults. Most participants are 40-75 years of age. Participants must be 15 years or older to enroll. Participants must be members of the sponsoring organization (annual dues: $50). 30 participants per session. Reservations are recommended at least 6 months before departure.

Costs • $4495 (includes housing, some meals, excursions, international airfare, travel bag, travel journal, documents portfolio). A $200 deposit is required.

Contact • Betty Van Dyke, Worldwide Operations Manager, American Jewish Congress, International Travel Program, 18 East 84th Street, New York, NY 10028; 212-360-1571; Fax: 212-717-1932

APPALACHIAN STATE UNIVERSITY

GUATEMALA AND HONDURAS

General Information • Academic study program in Guatemala, Honduras.

Learning Focus • Courses in anthropology. Instruction is offered by professors from the sponsoring institution.

Program Details • Program offered once per year. Session length: 4-5 weeks. Departures are scheduled in July. Most participants are 18 years of age and older. 20 participants per session.

Costs • $2309-$2177 (includes tuition, housing, insurance, international airfare, International Student Identification card).

Contact • Dr. Jeff Boyer, Professor, Appalachian State University, Department of Anthropology, Boone, NC 28608; 704-262-2295; Fax: 704-262-4037

ARCHAEOLOGICAL TOURS

MAYA KINGDOMS: HONDURAS, GUATEMALA, AND BELIZE

General Information • Archaeological tour with visits to Belize (Belize City, Corozal, San Ignacio), Guatemala (Guatemala City, Tikal), Honduras (Copan, San Pedro, Sula, Tegucigalpa); excursions to Aguateca, Mixco Viejo, Caracol, Lamanai, Atun Ha. Once at the destination country, participants travel by bus.

Learning Focus • Escorted travel to Maya Tenampua, Mixco Viejo and Lamanai. Museum visits (San Pedro Sula, Copan, Tikal, Guatemala City). Instruction is offered by professors, historians. This program would appeal to people interested in history, archaeology.

Accommodations • Hotels. Single rooms are available for an additional $560.

Program Details • Program offered once per year. Session length: 16 days. Departures are scheduled in November. Program is targeted to adults. Most participants are 30-80 years of age. 20 participants per session. Application deadline: 1 month prior to departure.

Costs • $3280 (includes housing, some meals, excursions, internal airfare). A $500 deposit is required.

Contact • Archaeological Tours, 271 Madison Avenue, Suite 904, New York, NY 10016; 212-986-3054; Fax: 212-370-1561

ARCHAEOLOGICAL TOURS

PERU AND BOLIVIA

General Information • Archaeological tour with visits to Bolivia (La Paz), Peru (Chiclayo, Cuzco, Ica, Lima, Machu Picchu, Puno, Trujillo); excursions to Sipán, Chan-Chan, Nazca Lines, Sacred Valley, Tiahuanaco, Lake Titicaca. Once at the destination country, participants travel by bus, boat, airplane.

Learning Focus • Escorted travel to Incan ruins and the Sacred Valley. Museum visits (Lima). Attendance at performances (music). Instruction is offered by professors, historians. This program would appeal to people interested in archaeology, history.

Accommodations • Hotels. Single rooms are available for an additional $810.

Program Details • Program offered once per year. Session length: 20 days. Departures are scheduled in September. Program is targeted to adults. Most participants are 30-80 years of age. 20 participants per session. Application deadline: 1½ months prior to departure.

Costs • $4155 (includes housing, some meals, excursions). A $500 deposit is required.

Contact • Archaeological Tours, 271 Madison Avenue, Suite 904, New York, NY 10016; 212-986-3054; Fax: 212-370-1561

EXPLORATIONS, INC.

AMAZON JUNGLE CRUISE

General Information • Nature study tour with visits to Brazil (Tabatinga), Colombia (Leticia), Peru (Iquitos); excursions to Amazon rivers, rain forests. Once at the destination country, participants travel by boat.

Learning Focus • Instruction in neotropical natural history. Field research in neotropical natural history. Escorted travel to rainforest and local villages. Nature observation (bird watching, wildlife). Instruction is offered by professors, researchers, naturalists, scientists. This program would appeal to people interested in nature studies, rain forest studies, culture.

Accommodations • Boat. Single rooms are available for an additional $300.
Program Details • Program offered 12 times per year. Session length: 8 days. Departures are scheduled throughout the year. Most participants are 30–70 years of age. Participants must be 10 years or older to enroll. 20 participants per session. Application deadline: 30 days prior to departure. Reservations are recommended at least 60 days before departure.
Costs • $1895 (includes housing, all meals, books and class materials, excursions, international airfare). A $300 deposit is required.
Contact • Charlie Strader, President, Explorations, Inc., 27655 Kent Road, Bonita Springs, FL 34135; 800-446-9660; Fax: 941-992-7666; E-mail: cesxplor@aol.com

EXPLORATIONS, INC.

MUNDO MAYA EXPLORATIONS

General Information • Cultural tour with visits to Guatemala (Antigua, Peten), Honduras (Copan), Mexico (Chiapas, Quintana Roo, Yucatán); excursions to Mayan archaeology, local villages, Spanish colonial sites. Once at the destination country, participants travel by bus.
Learning Focus • Instruction in Mayan cultures. Field research in Mayan archaeology. Escorted travel to sites and towns. Museum visits (local and regional museums). Nature observation (bird watching, wildlife). Instruction is offered by naturalists, historians. This program would appeal to people interested in archaeology, history.
Accommodations • Hotels. Single rooms are available for an additional $200.
Program Details • Program offered 4 times per year. Session length: 9 days. Most participants are 30–60 years of age. Participants must be 12 years or older to enroll. 8 participants per session. Application deadline: 60 days prior to departure. Reservations are recommended at least 90 days before departure.
Costs • $1895 (includes housing, some meals, books and class materials, excursions, international airfare). A $300 deposit is required.
Contact • Charlie Strader, President, Explorations, Inc., 27655 Kent Road, Bonita Springs, FL 34135; 800-446-9660; Fax: 941-992-7666; E-mail: cesxplor@aol.com

FOLKWAYS INSTITUTE

INCA PROJECT

General Information • Cultural tour with visits to Bolivia, Peru. Once at the destination country, participants travel by train, bus, foot.
Learning Focus • Museum visits (local museums). Nature observation (wildlife). Instruction is offered by naturalists, historians. This program would appeal to people interested in Inca culture, history.
Accommodations • Hotels. Single rooms are available.
Program Details • Program offered once per year. Session length: 20 days. Departures are scheduled in July. 16 participants per session. Application deadline: February 1. Reservations are recommended at least 5 months before departure.
Costs • $3200 (includes housing, all meals, books and class materials, excursions, international airfare, instruction). A $50 deposit is required.
Contact • David Christopher, Director, Folkways Institute, 14600 Southeast Aldridge Road, Portland, OR 97236-6518; 503-658-6600; Fax: 503-658-8672

FORUM TRAVEL INTERNATIONAL

REALM OF THE INCA

General Information • Nature study and cultural tour with visits to Bolivia (Copacabana, Tiahuanaco), Peru (Cuzco, Lake Titicaca, Machu Picchu, Pisac, Puno, Taquile Island, Urubamba Valley); excursions to major archaeological, anthropological and cultural history sites. Once at the destination country, participants travel by train, bus, foot, boat, airplane. Program is affiliated with International Ecosystems University.
Learning Focus • Escorted travel to major archeological, anthropological, and cultural sites. Nature observation (Andean and high Puna ecosystems). Instruction is offered by naturalists, cultural specialists. This program would appeal to people interested in culture, nature studies, people.
Accommodations • Hotels, pensiones.
Program Details • Program offered 12 times per year. Session length: 10–17 days. Departures are scheduled throughout the year. Program is targeted to students of all ages interested in nature and cultures.
Costs • $1815 (includes tuition, housing, some meals, excursions). A $300 deposit is required.
Contact • Jeannie Graves, Operations Manager, Forum Travel International, 91 Gregory Lane #21, Pleasant Hill, CA 94525; 510-671-2900; Fax: 510-671-2993; E-mail: forum@ix.netcom.com; World Wide Web: http://www.ten-io.com/forumtravel

GLOBAL AWARENESS THROUGH EXPERIENCE (GATE)

GLOBAL AWARENESS THROUGH EXPERIENCE

General Information • Cultural tour with visits to El Salvador, Guatemala, Mexico. Once at the destination country, participants travel by bus, foot. Program is affiliated with The Franciscan Sisters of Perpetual Adoration.
Learning Focus • Instruction in history, social, economic and religious topics. Escorted travel to villages, historical and religious sites. Museum visits (pertinent exhibits). Attendance at performances (folklorico, celebrations). Instruction is offered by professors, researchers. This program would appeal to people interested in cross-cultural study, social justice, consciousness-raising, alternative tourism, people-to-people contact.
Accommodations • Dormitories, hotels.
Program Details • Program offered 8 times per year. Session length: 10 days. Departures are scheduled throughout the year. Program is targeted to able adults. Most participants are 16–80 years of age. Other requirements: a sensitivity to people of other cultures. 12 participants per

session. Application deadline: determined by number applying. Reservations are recommended at least 6 months before departure.
Costs • $650 (includes housing, all meals, books and class materials). A $50 deposit is required.
Contact • Beverly Budelier FSPA, North American Gate Coordinator, Global Awareness Through Experience (GATE), 912 Market Street, La Crosse, WI 54601; 608-791-5283; Fax: 608-782-6301; E-mail: fspa_gate@viterbo.edu

INTERHOSTEL, UNIVERSITY OF NEW HAMPSHIRE

BELIZE AND TIKAL

General Information • Cultural tour with visits to Belize (Belize City, San Ignacio), Guatemala (Tikal); excursions to New River, Dangriga, Blue Hole National Park, Caracol, Xunantunich, Fuanacaste, Goff Caye, Flores. Once at the destination country, participants travel by bus, foot, boat. Program is affiliated with Cemanahuac Educational Community.
Learning Focus • Instruction in history, archaeology and culture. Escorted travel to villages and parks. Museum visits (Tikal Archaeological Museum). Attendance at performances (Garifuna dancers). Instruction is offered by historians. This program would appeal to people interested in history, culture, archaeology.
Accommodations • Hotels. Single rooms are available for an additional $425.
Program Details • Program offered 2 times per year. Session length: 2 weeks. Departures are scheduled in December, February. Program is targeted to seniors over 50. Most participants are 60–80 years of age. Participants must be 50 years or older to enroll. 35 participants per session. Reservations are recommended at least 4 months before departure.
Costs • $2720 (includes tuition, housing, all meals, excursions, international airfare, entrance fees). A $200 deposit is required.
Contact • Janice Pierson, Office Supervisor, Interhostel, University of New Hampshire, 6 Garrison Avenue, Durham, NH 03824-3529; 800-733-9753; Fax: 603-862-1113; World Wide Web: http://www.learn.unh.edu/

JOURNEYS INTERNATIONAL, INC.

PATAGONIAN EXPLORER

General Information • Wilderness/adventure program with visits to Argentina (Chalten, Patagonian Steppe, Rio Gallegos, Tierra del Fuego Park), Chile (Puerto Natales, Torres del Paine National Park); excursions to Iguazu Falls, Lake District. Once at the destination country, participants travel by foot, airplane, small vehicle.
Learning Focus • Escorted travel to areas of interest related to nature. Nature observation (flora, fauna, scenic landscapes). Other activities include hiking. Instruction is offered by naturalists, local English-speaking guides. This program would appeal to people interested in photography, wildlife, bird watching, nature studies.
Accommodations • Hotels, lodges. Single rooms are available for an additional $455.
Program Details • Program offered 6 times per year. Session length: 16 days. Departures are scheduled in November–March. Program is targeted to active persons with an interest in nature. Most participants are 25–55 years of age. Participants must be 12 years or older to enroll. 2–14 participants per session. Reservations are recommended at least 60 days before departure.
Costs • $2695 (includes housing, some meals, excursions, porters and naturalist guide). A $300 deposit is required.
Contact • Michelle Gervais, Latin America Sales Director, Journeys International, Inc., 4011 Jackson Road, Ann Arbor, MI 48103; 313-665-4407; Fax: 313-662-2945; E-mail: michelle@journeys-intl.com; World Wide Web: http://www.journeys-intl.com

MICHIGAN STATE UNIVERSITY

SUMMER SCHOOL IN THE CARIBBEAN

General Information • Academic study program in Barbados (Bridgetown), Guyana (Georgetown), Suriname, Trinidad and Tobago.
Learning Focus • Courses in comparative political systems. Instruction is offered by professors from the sponsoring institution.
Accommodations • Dormitories. Meals are taken on one's own, in local restaurants.
Program Details • Program offered once per year. Session length: 4 weeks. Departures are scheduled in June. The program is open to undergraduate students. Most participants are 18–22 years of age. Other requirements: good academic standing and the approval of the instructor. 20 participants per session. Application deadline: March 14.
Costs • $1730 (includes housing, some meals, excursions). Application fee: $75. A $250 deposit is required.
Contact • Brenda S. Sprite, Educational Programs Coordinator, Michigan State University, Office of Study Abroad, 109 International Center, East Lansing, MI 48824-1035; 517-353-8920; Fax: 517-432-2082; E-mail: sprite@pilot.msu.edu; World Wide Web: http://study-abroad.msu.edu

NATURAL HISTORY MUSEUM OF LOS ANGELES COUNTY

THE AMAZON'S FULL NAVIGABLE LENGTH

General Information • Nature study tour with visits to Brazil (Belém, Manaus), Colombia (Leticia), Peru (Iquitos, Lima); excursions to Peru (Lima), Opera House-Manaus. Once at the destination country, participants travel by boat, airplane.
Learning Focus • Instruction in natural history. Museum visits (Goeldi Museum-Belem). Nature observation (birds, botany). Other activities include hiking. Instruction is offered by professors, researchers, naturalists, scientists. This program would appeal to people interested in natural history, adventure.
Accommodations • Hotels, boat. Single rooms are available for an additional $500.
Program Details • Program offered once per year. Session length: 2 weeks. Departures are scheduled in April. Most participants are 15–75 years of age. Participants must be 12 years or older to enroll. 98 participants per session. Reservations are recommended at least 3 months before departure.

Costs • $4695–$8995 (includes housing, all meals, excursions). A $1000 deposit is required.
Contact • Karen Hovanitz, Travel Program Manager, Natural History Museum of Los Angeles County, 900 Exposition Boulevard, Los Angeles, CA 90007; 213-744-3350; Fax: 213-747-6718; E-mail: khovanit@mizar.usc.edu; World Wide Web: http://www.lam.mus.ca.us/lacmnh

NATURE EXPEDITIONS INTERNATIONAL

MUNDO MAYA EXPEDITION: GUATEMALA, BELIZE, AND HONDURAS

General Information • Cultural tour with visits to Belize (Caracol ruins, Caves Branch Estate, Xuanantunich), Guatemala (Chichicastenango, Tikal), Honduras (Copan ruins). Once at the destination country, participants travel by airplane, mini-van.
Learning Focus • Escorted travel to Maya ruins in Guatemala, Belize and Honduras. Instruction is offered by professors, naturalists, anthropologists. This program would appeal to people interested in archaeology, anthropology, ancient and native cultures, ancient art.
Accommodations • Hotels. Single rooms are available for an additional $500.
Program Details • Program offered once per year. Session length: 15 days. Departures are scheduled in December. Most participants are 25–75 years of age. Other requirements: doctor's permission for participants 70 years and older. Reservations are recommended at least 6 months before departure.
Costs • $299 (includes housing, some meals, excursions, all guiding). A $400 deposit is required.
Contact • Christopher Kyle, President, Nature Expeditions International, 6400 East El Dorado Circle, Suite 210, Tucson, AZ 85715; 800-869-0639; Fax: 520-721-6719

NATURE EXPEDITIONS INTERNATIONAL

SPANNING THE CONTINENT: AMAZON EXPEDITION

General Information • Nature study tour with visits to Brazil (Belém, Manaus, Santarem), Colombia (Leticia), Peru (Explornapo Camp); excursions to Ariau Jungle Tower, canopy walkway, Monkey Island, Amazon (riverboat cruise). Once at the destination country, participants travel by foot, boat, airplane.
Learning Focus • Escorted travel to the Amazon region. Instruction is offered by naturalists. This program would appeal to people interested in nature studies, rain forest studies, bird watching, wildlife, native cultures, ecology.
Accommodations • Hotels, campsites. Single rooms are available for an additional $400.
Program Details • Program offered 4 times per year. Session length: 18 days. Departures are scheduled in March, June, August, October. Most participants are 25–75 years of age. Other requirements: doctor's permission for participants 70 years and older. Reservations are recommended at least 6 months before departure.
Costs • $2990 (includes housing, some meals, excursions, all guiding). A $400 deposit is required.
Contact • Christopher Kyle, President, Nature Expeditions International, 6400 East El Dorado Circle, Suite 210, Tucson, AZ 85715; 800-869-0639; Fax: 520-721-6719

SAGA HOLIDAYS (ROAD SCHOLAR PROGRAM)

ROAD SCHOLAR: PERU AND BOLIVIA

General Information • Cultural tour with visits to Bolivia (La Paz, Tiwanaku), Peru (Lima, Machu Picchu, Puno); excursions to Valley of the Incas, Cuzco, Pisac, Indian Market, Machu Picchu. Once at the destination country, participants travel by bus. Program is affiliated with National Institute of Archaeology–Bolivia, University of Lima, and the University of San Antonio de Abad.
Learning Focus • Instruction in history. Escorted travel to Valley of the Incas and Machu Picchu. Museum visits (National Institute of Archaeology of Bolivia). Instruction is offered by professors. This program would appeal to people interested in history.
Accommodations • Hotels. Single rooms are available for an additional $449.
Program Details • Program offered 6 times per year. Session length: 13 days. Departures are scheduled throughout the year. Program is targeted to seniors. Most participants are 50–75 years of age. Participants must be 50 years or older to enroll. Reservations are recommended at least 3–12 months before departure.
Costs • $2999–$3299 (includes tuition, housing, some meals, books and class materials, insurance, excursions, international airfare).
Contact • Customer Service Representative, Saga Holidays (Road Scholar Program), 222 Berkeley Street, Boston, MA 02116; 800-621-2151

SANTA BARBARA MUSEUM OF ART

SOUTH AMERICA: BUENOS AIRES, RIO, SANTIAGO, AND LIMA

General Information • Cultural tour with visits to Argentina (Buenos Aires), Brazil (Rio de Janeiro), Chile (Santiago), Peru (Lima); excursions to Iguassu Falls, Machu Picchu. Once at the destination country, participants travel by train, bus, airplane. Program is affiliated with San Francisco Museum of Modern Art.
Learning Focus • Escorted travel to see world-renowned artwork. Museum visits (major museums). Instruction is offered by art historians. This program would appeal to people interested in art, gardening, architecture, archaeology, photography, decorative arts.
Accommodations • Hotels. Single rooms are available.
Program Details • Program offered once per year. Session length: 13 days. Departures are scheduled in March. Most participants are 30–80 years of age. Participants must be members of the sponsoring organization (annual dues: $40). 15–20 participants per session. Application deadline: January.
Costs • $3995 (includes housing, some meals, excursions, international airfare). A $500 deposit is required.
Contact • Shelley Ruston, Director of Special Programs, Santa Barbara Museum of Art, 1130 State Street, Santa Barbara, CA 93101; 805-963-4364, ext. 336; Fax: 805-966-6840

SMITHSONIAN INSTITUTION

SMITHSONIAN STUDY TOURS AND SEMINARS IN THE AMERICAS

General Information • Nature study, cultural, and wilderness programs with visits to Belize, Bermuda, Brazil, Canada, Chile, Costa Rica, Guatemala, Honduras, Mexico, Peru. Once at the destination country, participants travel by train, bus, foot, boat, airplane.

Learning Focus • Instruction in archaeology, history, culture, natural history. Escorted travel to special sites off limits to most tourists. Museum visits (major museums, private collections). Attendance at performances (traditional folk music and dance). Nature observation (plant and wildlife of the Amazon, reef ecosystems). Instruction is offered by professors, researchers, naturalists, artists, historians, scientists. This program would appeal to people interested in bird watching, archaeology, snorkeling, religious history, natural history, trains, photography.

Accommodations • Hotels. Single rooms are available.

Program Details • Session length: 9–17 days. Departures are scheduled throughout the year. Most participants are 25–85 years of age. Participants must be 18 years or older to enroll. Participants must be members of the sponsoring organization (annual dues: $24). 15–30 participants per session.

Costs • $1999 and up (includes tuition, housing, some meals, excursions, international airfare).

Contact • Customer Service Representative, Smithsonian Institution, Smithsonian Study Tours and Seminars, 1100 Jefferson Drive SW (MRC 702), Washington, DC 20560; 202-357-4700; Fax: 202-633-9250

ARGENTINA

ALPINE ASCENTS, INTERNATIONAL

ACONCAGUA EXPEDITIONS

General Information • Mountain climbing tour with visits to Plaza Argentina, Puente del Inca, Chile (Santiago). Once at the destination country, participants travel by bus.
Learning Focus • Instruction in mountain climbing. Escorted travel to Vacas Valley and Polish Glacier. Nature observation (Andes Mountains, desert valleys, Pacific Ocean). Other activities include camping, hiking. Instruction is offered by sports professionals. This program would appeal to people interested in mountain climbing.
Accommodations • Hotels, campsites. Single rooms are available.
Program Details • Program offered 2 times per year. Session length: 24 days. Departures are scheduled in January, February. Program is targeted to mountain climbers. Other requirements: excellent physical condition, intermediate ice climbing skills for Polish Glacier. Reservations are recommended at least 6 months before departure.
Costs • $3000–$3200 (includes housing, some meals, group equipment, porters, mules, guides, permits). A $500 deposit is required.
Contact • Gordon Janow, Program Coordinator, Alpine Ascents, International, 16615 Saybrook Drive, Woodinville, WA 98072; 206-788-1951; Fax: 206-788-6757; E-mail: aaiclimb@accessone.com

 AMERISPAN UNLIMITED

SPANISH CLASSES AND HOMESTAYS IN ARGENTINA

General Information • Language study program with visits to Buenos Aires.
Learning Focus • Instruction in the Spanish language. Instruction is offered by trained Spanish teachers. This program would appeal to people interested in Spanish language, Latin America.
Accommodations • Homestays. Single rooms are available.
Program Details • Session length: 2–12 weeks. Departures are scheduled throughout the year. Most participants are 16–70 years of age. Participants must be 16 years or older to enroll. 2-3 participants per session. Reservations are recommended at least 4 weeks before departure.
Costs • $995 for 2 weeks, $1875 for 4 weeks, $440 for each additional week (includes tuition, housing, some meals, books and class materials, insurance). A $100 deposit is required.
Contact • AmeriSpan Unlimited, PO Box 40513, Philadelphia, PA 19106; 800-879-6640; Fax: 215-985-4524; E-mail: info@amerispan.com; World Wide Web: http://www.amerispan.com

FOREIGN LANGUAGE STUDY ABROAD SERVICE

INTERNATIONAL LANGUAGE STUDY HOMESTAYS IN ARGENTINA

General Information • Language study program in Argentina.
Learning Focus • Courses in Spanish language. Instruction is offered by local teachers.
Accommodations • Homestays. Single rooms are available. Meals are taken with host family, in residences.
Program Details • Session length: varies. Departures are scheduled in January–December. The program is open to undergraduate students, graduate students, pre-college students, adults. Most participants are 12 years of age and older. Other requirements: students must be at least 12 years old. 1 participant per session.
Costs • Contact sponsor for information. A $300 deposit is required.
Contact • Louise Harber, Coordinator, Foreign Language Study Abroad Service, Department IH, Box 903, 5935 Southwest 64th Avenue, South Miami, FL 33143; 800-282-1090; Fax: 305-662-2907; E-mail: flsas@netpoint.net; World Wide Web: http://www.netpoint.net/~flsas

FOREIGN LANGUAGE STUDY ABROAD SERVICE

SPANISH IN BUENOS AIRES

General Information • Language study program in Buenos Aires.
Learning Focus • Courses in language study. Instruction is offered by local teachers.
Accommodations • Homestays, program-owned apartments, hotels. Single rooms are available. Meals are taken on one's own, with host family, in local restaurants, in residences.
Program Details • Session length: varies. Departures are scheduled in January–December. The program is open to undergraduate students, graduate students, pre-college students, adults. Most participants are 18 years of age and older.
Costs • Contact sponsor for information. Application fee: $50. A $100 deposit is required.
Contact • Louise Harber, Coordinator, Foreign Language Study Abroad Service, Department IH, Box 903, 5935 Southwest 64th Avenue, South Miami, FL 33143; 800-282-1090; Fax: 305-662-2907; E-mail: flsas@netpoint.net; World Wide Web: http://www.netpoint.net/~flsas

INSTITUTO DE LENGUA ESPAÑOLA PARA EXTRANJEROS (ILEE)

SPANISH LANGUAGE SCHOOL FOR FOREIGNERS

General Information • Language study program in Buenos Aires. Excursions to Patagonia, Iguazú Falls, Salta, Ushuaia.
Learning Focus • Courses in Spanish language, South American history, political science, economics, literature. Instruction is offered by professors from the sponsoring institution.
Accommodations • Homestays, locally-rented apartments, program-owned apartments. Single rooms are available. Meals are taken on one's own, with host family, in residences.
Program Details • Program offered 52 times per year. Session length: 2 or more weeks, average is 4-8 weeks. Departures are scheduled in January–December. The program is open to undergraduate students, graduate students, adults. Most participants are 18–35 years of age. 1-5 participant per session. Application deadline: 5 weeks prior to departure.
Costs • $500–$700 (includes tuition, housing, some meals, books and class materials). Application fee: $100.
Contact • Daniel Alberto Korman, Director, Instituto de Lengua Española para Extranjeros (ILEE), Lavalle 1619, 7th C and Lavalle 1616. 4th A, Buenos Aires 1048, Argentina; +54 1-375-073; Fax: +54 1-864-4942

JOURNEYS INTERNATIONAL, INC.

PATAGONIA WILDLIFE SAFARI

General Information • Wilderness/adventure program with visits to Perito Moreno Glacier, Punta Tombo, Rio Gallegos, Tierra del Fuego, Ushuaia, Valdes Peninsula, Iguazu. Once at the destination country, participants travel by foot, airplane, small vehicle.
Learning Focus • Escorted travel to areas of interest relating to flora and fauna. Nature observation (flora and fauna). Other activities include hiking. Instruction is offered by naturalists, local English-speaking guides. This program would appeal to people interested in photography, wildlife, bird watching, nature studies.
Accommodations • Hotels, lodges. Single rooms are available for an additional $350.
Program Details • Program offered 13 times per year. Session length: 10 days. Departures are scheduled in October–March. Program is targeted to active persons with an interest in nature. Most participants are 25–55 years of age. Participants must be 12 years or older to enroll. 2–12 participants per session. Reservations are recommended at least 60 days before departure.
Costs • $1750 (includes housing, some meals, excursions, porters and naturalist guide). A $300 deposit is required.
Contact • Michelle Gervais, Latin America Sales Director, Journeys International, Inc., 4011 Jackson Road, Ann Arbor, MI 48103; 313-665-4407; Fax: 313-665-2945; E-mail: michelle@journeys-intl.com; World Wide Web: http://www.journeys-intl.com

 LANGUAGE LIAISON

INSTITUTO DE LENGUA ESPAÑOLA PARA EXTRANJEROS–LEARN SPANISH IN ARGENTINA

General Information • Language study program with visits to Buenos Aires.
Learning Focus • Instruction in the Spanish language. Instruction is offered by professors. This program would appeal to people interested in language.
Accommodations • Homestays. Single rooms are available.
Program Details • Session length: unlimited. Departures are scheduled throughout the year. Most participants are 18–70 years of age. Participants must be 16 years or older to enroll. Reservations are recommended at least 35 days before departure.
Costs • Contact sponsor for information.
Contact • Nancy Forman, President, Language Liaison, 20533 Biscayne Boulevard-Station 4-162, Miami, FL 33180; 305-682-9909; Fax: 305-682-9907; E-mail: langstudy@aol.com; World Wide Web: http://languageliaison.com

 LANGUAGE LIAISON

LIVE 'N' LEARN (LEARN IN A TEACHER'S HOME)–ARGENTINA

General Information • Language study program with visits to Argentina.
Learning Focus • Instruction in the Spanish language. Instruction is offered by professors. This program would appeal to people interested in language.
Accommodations • Homestays. Single rooms are available.
Program Details • Session length: unlimited. Departures are scheduled throughout the year. Most participants are 18–70 years of age. Participants must be 16 years or older to enroll. Reservations are recommended at least 35 days before departure.
Costs • Contact sponsor for information.
Contact • Nancy Forman, President, Language Liaison, 20533 Biscayne Boulevard-Station 4-162, Miami, FL 33180; 305-682-9909; Fax: 305-682-9907; E-mail: langstudy@aol.com; World Wide Web: http://languageliaison.com

 LEXIA EXCHANGE INTERNATIONAL

LEXIA IN BUENOS AIRES

General Information • Academic study program in Buenos Aires. Classes are held on the campus of University of Buenos Aires. Excursions to Paraguay, La Plata, Brazil (Rio De Janiero), Patagonia.
Learning Focus • Courses in civilizations, political science, business, Spanish language, economics, fine arts, cultural studies. Instruction is offered by local teachers.
Accommodations • Homestays, dormitories. Meals are taken on one's own, with host family, in central dining facility, in local restaurants.
Program Details • Program offered once per year. Session length: 8 weeks. Departures are scheduled in June. The program is open to undergraduate students, graduate students, adults. Most participants are 18–35 years of age.

Other requirements: minimum 2.5 GPA. 10–15 participants per session. Application deadline: April 15.
Costs • $4495 (includes tuition, housing, some meals, books and class materials, excursions). Application fee: $30. A $300 deposit is required.
Contact • Justin Meilgaard, Program Coordinator, LEXIA Exchange International, 378 Cambridge Avenue, Palo Alto, CA 94306-1544; 800-775-3942; Fax: 415-327-9192; E-mail: lexia@rquartz.stanford.edu; World Wide Web: http://www.lexiaintl.org

NATIONAL REGISTRATION CENTER FOR STUDY ABROAD

INSTITUTE DE LINGUA ESPAÑOLA

General Information • Language study program in Buenos Aires.
Learning Focus • Courses in Spanish language.
Accommodations • Homestays. Single rooms are available. Meals are taken on one's own.
Program Details • Program offered 24 times per year. Session length: 2 weeks. Departures are scheduled in January–December. The program is open to undergraduate students, graduate students, adults. Application deadline: 40 days prior to departure.
Costs • $897 (includes tuition, housing, insurance). Application fee: $40. A $100 deposit is required.
Contact • June Domoe, Educational Consultant, National Registration Center for Study Abroad, PO Box 1393, Milwaukee, WI 53201; 414-278-0631; Fax: 414-271-8884; E-mail: inquiries@nrcsa.com; World Wide Web: http://www.nrcsa.com

UNIVERSITY BLAS PASCAL CÓDOBA

ARGENTUM

General Information • Language study program in Córdoba. Classes are held on the campus of University Blas Pascal.
Learning Focus • Courses in language study, cultural studies. Instruction is offered by local teachers.
Accommodations • Homestays. Single rooms are available. Meals are taken with host family, in residences.
Program Details • Program offered once per year. Session length: 5 weeks. Departures are scheduled in June. The program is open to undergraduate students, graduate students, pre-college students, adults. Most participants are 19–30 years of age. Other requirements: minimum 2.8 GPA, 1 semester of college Spanish. 10 participants per session. Application deadline: March 15.
Costs • $2200 (includes tuition, housing, all meals, excursions, transportation from the airport to the home). Application fee: $50. A $180 deposit is required.
Contact • Marta Rosso-O'Laughlin, US Coordinator, University Blas Pascal Códoba, PO Box 99, Medford, MA 02153-0099; 617-488-3552; Fax: 617-488-3552; E-mail: mrosso@aol.com

UNIVERSITY OF ILLINOIS AT URBANA-CHAMPAIGN

SUMMER SPANISH LANGUAGE PROGRAM IN ARGENTINA

General Information • Language study program in Buenos Aires. Classes are held on the campus of University of Buenos Aires. Excursions to Uruguay (Colonia), El Tigre, Estancia.
Learning Focus • Courses in Spanish language, Argentine state and society, contemporary Argentine literature. Instruction is offered by professors from the sponsoring institution and local teachers.
Accommodations • Homestays. Meals are taken with host family.
Program Details • Program offered once per year. Session length: 6 weeks. Departures are scheduled in June. The program is open to undergraduate students, graduate students. Most participants are 18–25 years of age. Other requirements: 4 semesters college-level Spanish or equivalent and a B average. 20 participants per session. Application deadline: March 1.
Costs • $3000 (includes tuition, housing, some meals, excursions, Argentina health insurance, resident director, medical emergency evacuation insurance). Application fee: $35. A $500 deposit is required.
Contact • Timothy Winkler, Program Coordinator, University of Illinois at Urbana-Champaign, Study Abroad Office, 910 South Fifth Street #115, Champaign, IL 61820; 800-531-4404; Fax: 217-244-0249; E-mail: ipa@uiuc.edu

WILDLAND ADVENTURES

BEST OF PATAGONIA

General Information • Nature study tour with visits to Buenos Aires, Calafate, Moreno Glacier, Peninsula Valdez, Punta Tombo, Tierra del Fuego, galciers, wildlife reserves. Once at the destination country, participants travel by bus, foot, airplane.
Learning Focus • Escorted travel to national parks. Nature observation (Patagonian wildlife). Other activities include hiking. Instruction is offered by naturalists. This program would appeal to people interested in photography, wildlife, hiking, bird watching.
Accommodations • Hotels. Single rooms are available.
Program Details • Program offered 8 times per year. Session length: 10 days. Departures are scheduled in October–March. Most participants are 30–60 years of age. 2–12 participants per session. Application deadline: 30 days prior to departure. Reservations are recommended at least 3–6 months before departure.
Costs • $2180 (includes housing, some meals, excursions, complete pre-departure dossier). A $300 deposit is required.
Contact • Wildland Adventures, 3516 Northeast 155th Street, Seattle, WA 98155; 800-345-4453; Fax: 206-363-6615; E-mail: wildadve@aol.com; World Wide Web: http://www.wildland.com

BAHAMAS

APPALACHIAN STATE UNIVERSITY

BAHAMAS

General Information • Academic study program in San Salvador Island.
Learning Focus • Courses in anthropology. Instruction is offered by professors from the sponsoring institution.
Program Details • Program offered once per year. Session length: 3 weeks. Departures are scheduled in May. Most participants are 18 years of age and older. 20 participants per session.
Costs • $1453 (includes tuition, housing, insurance, international airfare, International Student Identification card).
Contact • Dr. Thomas Whyte, Professor of Anthropology, Appalachian State University, Department of Anthropology, Boone, NC 28608; 704-262-2295; Fax: 704-262-4037

MICHIGAN STATE UNIVERSITY

TROPICAL FISHERIES AND WILDLIFE MANAGEMENT PROGRAM

General Information • Academic study program in San Salvador Island.
Learning Focus • Courses in tropical ecology, fisheries, wildlife. Instruction is offered by professors from the sponsoring institution.
Accommodations • Dormitories. Meals are taken on one's own, in local restaurants.
Program Details • Program offered once per year. Session length: 3 weeks. Departures are scheduled in May. The program is open to undergraduate students, graduate students. Most participants are 18–26 years of age. Other requirements: good academic standing and the approval of the instructor. 13 participants per session. Application deadline: March 14.
Costs • $1418 (includes housing, some meals, excursions). Application fee: $75. A $250 deposit is required.
Contact • Brenda S. Sprite, Educational Programs Coordinator, Michigan State University, Office of Study Abroad, 109 International Center, East Lansing, MI 48824-1035; 517-353-8920; Fax: 517-432-2082; E-mail: sprite@pilot.msu.edu; World Wide Web: http://study-abroad.msu.edu

NATURAL HABITAT ADVENTURES

DOLPHIN WATCH

General Information • Nature study tour with visits to Grand Bahama Island. Once at the destination country, participants travel by boat.
Learning Focus • Nature observation (swim with dolphins and tropical fish). Other activities include snorkeling. Instruction is offered by naturalists. This program would appeal to people interested in nature studies, photography, wildlife.
Accommodations • Boat.
Program Details • Program offered 5 times per year. Session length: 8 days. Departures are scheduled in June, July, August. Participants must be 14 years or older to enroll. 8 participants per session. Reservations are recommended at least 6–12 months before departure.
Costs • $1795–$1995 (includes housing, all meals). A $500 deposit is required.
Contact • Natural Habitat Adventures, 2945 Center Green Court, Suite H, Boulder, CO 80301; 800-543-8917; Fax: 303-449-3712; E-mail: nathab@worldnet.att.net

NORTHERN ILLINOIS UNIVERSITY

ETHNIC AND RACIAL INTERGROUP RELATIONS

General Information • Academic study program in Nassau.
Learning Focus • Courses in sociology. Instruction is offered by professors from the sponsoring institution.
Accommodations • Hotels. Single rooms are available. Meals are taken on one's own, in local restaurants.
Program Details • Program offered once per year. Session length: 3 weeks. Departures are scheduled in December. The program is open to undergraduate students, graduate students. Most participants are 20–30 years of age. 14 participants per session. Application deadline: November 1.
Costs • $1260 (includes tuition, housing, insurance, excursions). A $200 deposit is required.
Contact • Anne Seitzinger, Program Coordinator, Short-Term Study Abroad, Northern Illinois University, Study Abroad Office-WI 417, DeKalb, IL 60115; 815-752-0700; Fax: 815-753-0825; E-mail: aseitz@niu.edu; World Wide Web: http://www.niu.edu/depts/intl_prgms/intl.html

OCEANIC SOCIETY EXPEDITIONS

BAHAMAS DOLPHINS FOR HIGH SCHOOL STUDENTS

General Information • Research expedition with visits to Little Bahamas Banks, West End, Little Bahamas Banks. Once at the destination country, participants travel by boat.
Learning Focus • Instruction in field research methods and marine science careers. Field research in wild spotted dolphin ecology. Volunteer work (baseline data collection). Instruction is offered by researchers, naturalists. This program would appeal to people interested in dolphin ecology, dolphin communication, dolphin behavior, marine sciences.
Accommodations • Boat.

Program Details • Program offered once per year. Session length: 8 days. Departures are scheduled in July. Program is targeted to high school students, 16–18 years old. Most participants are 16–18 years of age. Participants must be 16 years or older to enroll. Other requirements: swimming and snorkeling experience. 8 participants per session. Application deadline: 60 days prior to departure. Reservations are recommended at least 6 months before departure.
Costs • $1475 (includes all meals, boat accommodations, research leadership). A $300 deposit is required.
Contact • Silke Schroeder, Expedition Manager, Oceanic Society Expeditions, Fort Mason Center, Building E, #230, San Francisco, CA 94123; 415-441-1106; Fax: 415-474-3395

OCEANIC SOCIETY EXPEDITIONS

BAHAMAS PROJECT DOLPHIN

General Information • Research expedition with visits to Freeport-Lucaya, Little Bahamas Banks, Little Bahamas Banks. Once at the destination country, participants travel by boat.
Learning Focus • Instruction in field research methods. Field research in wild spotted dolphin ecology and conservation. Volunteer work (data collection). Instruction is offered by researchers, naturalists. This program would appeal to people interested in dolphin ecology, dolphin communication, dolphin behavior, photography.
Accommodations • Boat.
Program Details • Program offered 12 times per year. Session length: 8 days. Departures are scheduled in May–September. Most participants are 16–80 years of age. Participants must be 16 years or older to enroll. Other requirements: swimming and snorkeling experience. 8 participants per session. Application deadline: 60 days prior to departure. Reservations are recommended at least 6 months before departure.
Costs • $1495 (includes excursions, most meals, accommodations aboard boat, research leadership, excursions by Zodiac). A $300 deposit is required.
Contact • Silke Schroeder, Expedition Manager, Oceanic Society Expeditions, Fort Mason Center, Building E, #230, San Francisco, CA 94123; 415-441-1106; Fax: 415-474-3395

UNIVERSITY OF ALABAMA AT BIRMINGHAM

UNIVERSITY OF ALABAMA AT BIRMINGHAM IN THE BAHAMAS

General Information • Academic study program in San Salvador Island. Classes are held on the campus of Bahamian Field Station.
Learning Focus • Courses in tropical ecology. Instruction is offered by professors from the sponsoring institution.
Accommodations • Dormitories. Single rooms are available. Meals are taken as a group, in central dining facility.
Program Details • Program offered once per year. Session length: 1 week. Departures are scheduled in June. The program is open to undergraduate students, graduate students. Most participants are 19 years of age and older. Other requirements: biology major or minor and the approval of the program director. 16–18 participants per session. Application deadline: May 1.
Costs • $1235–$1541 (includes tuition, housing, all meals, books and class materials, insurance, excursions, international airfare). A $100 deposit is required.
Contact • Frank Romanowicz, Study Abroad Coordinator, University of Alabama at Birmingham, 1400 University Boulevard, HUC 318, Birmingham, AL 35294-1150; 205-934-5025; Fax: 205-934-8664; E-mail: ucipØ17@larry.huc.uab.edu

BELIZE

APPALACHIAN STATE UNIVERSITY

BELIZE

General Information • Academic study program in Barrier Reef.
Learning Focus • Courses in biology. Instruction is offered by professors from the sponsoring institution.
Program Details • Program offered once per year. Session length: 2 weeks. Departures are scheduled in June. Most participants are 18 years of age and older. 20 participants per session.
Costs • $1790 (includes tuition, housing, insurance, international airfare, International Student Identification card).
Contact • Dr. Richard Henson, Professor of Biology, Appalachian State University, Department of Biology, Boone, NC 28608; 704-262-3025; Fax: 704-262-4037

FORUM TRAVEL INTERNATIONAL

BELIZE EXPERIENCE

General Information • Wilderness/adventure program with visits to Blackbird Caye, Blue Hole, Mayan Ruins, Turneffe Atoll, natural and cultural (archaeological) sites. Once at the destination country, participants travel by bus, foot, boat, airplane. Program is affiliated with International Ecosystems University.
Learning Focus • Instruction in marine biology, archeology and natural history. Field research in dolphins. Other activities include hiking. Instruction is offered by professors, researchers, naturalists. This program would appeal to people interested in nature studies, culture.
Accommodations • Program-owned houses, hotels. Single rooms are available.
Program Details • Program offered 8 times per year. Departures are scheduled throughout the year. Program is targeted to adventurous and inquisitive people of any age. Most participants are 16–80 years of age. 8–16 participants per session.
Costs • $999 (includes tuition, housing, all meals, excursions, international airfare). A $200 deposit is required.
Contact • Jeannie Graves, Operations Manager, Forum Travel International, 91 Gregory Lane #21, Pleasant Hill, CA 94525; 510-671-2900; Fax: 510-671-2993; E-mail: forum@ix.netcom.com; World Wide Web: http://www.ten-io.com/forumtravel

INTERNATIONAL ZOOLOGICAL EXPEDITIONS

DISCOVER SCUBA

General Information • Scuba diving program with visits to Glovers Reef Atoll, Long Caye, South Water Caye, Walls, Black Crack, Spurr and Grooves, Turtle Cliffs. Once at the destination country, participants travel by boat, airplane. Program is affiliated with Professional Association of Diving Instructors.
Learning Focus • Instruction in scuba diving. Field research in marine research. Escorted travel to coral reefs. Nature observation (sea turtles, whales, sharks). Instruction is offered by naturalists, sports professionals, dive instructors. This program would appeal to people interested in marine sciences, snorkeling, coral reefs, scuba diving, fish watching.
Accommodations • Program-owned houses, campsites, biological field stations. Single rooms are available.
Program Details • Session length: 1 or more weeks. Departures are scheduled throughout the year. Most participants are 14–60 years of age. Participants must be 14 years or older to enroll. Other requirements: good swimming ability. 6 participants per session. Reservations are recommended at least 3 months before departure.
Costs • $895 (includes tuition, housing, all meals, excursions, diving equipment). A $250 deposit is required.
Contact • Sandra Pembroke, Administrative Assistant, International Zoological Expeditions, IZE, 210 Wash Street, Sherborn, MA 01770; 508-655-1461; Fax: 508-655-4445; E-mail: ize2belize@aol.com; World Wide Web: http://www.ize2belize.com

INTERNATIONAL ZOOLOGICAL EXPEDITIONS

TROPICAL ECOLOGY WORKSHOPS

General Information • Wilderness adventure program and research expedition with visits to Blue Creek Rainforest, South Water Caye, rain forests, caves, coral reefs. Once at the destination country, participants travel by bus, foot, boat.
Learning Focus • Instruction in rainforest ecology and marine biology. Field research in rainforest ecology and marine biology. Escorted travel to coral reefs and caves. Nature observation (from canopy skywalk observation decks). Instruction is offered by professors, researchers, naturalists, scientists. This program would appeal to people interested in botany, rain forest studies, scuba diving, marine biology, coral reefs, nature studies, snorkeling, bird watching.
Accommodations • Campsites, biological field stations. Single rooms are available.

Program Details • Session length: 2 weeks. Departures are scheduled throughout the year. Program is targeted to naturalists, teachers, students and professionals. Most participants are 14–50 years of age. 20 participants per session. Reservations are recommended at least 6 months–1 year before departure.
Costs • $789 (includes tuition, housing, all meals, excursions, guides and instructors). A $250 deposit is required.
Contact • Sandra Pembroke, Administrative Assistant, International Zoological Expeditions, IZE, 210 Wash Street, Sherborn, MA 01770; 508-655-1461; Fax: 508-655-4445; E-mail: ize2belize@aol.com; World Wide Web: http://www.ize2belize.com

JOURNEYS INTERNATIONAL, INC.

BELIZE EXPLORER WEEK

General Information • Cultural tour with visits to Belize (Cahal Pech, Maya Mountain Lodge, Rio Frio Caves, South Water Caye), Guatemala (Guatemala (Che Chem Ha Cave, Tikal)). Once at the destination country, participants travel by foot, boat, small vehicle.
Learning Focus • Escorted travel to barrier reef and ruins. Nature observation (wildlife). Other activities include snorkeling, swimming. Instruction is offered by naturalists, native English-speaking naturalists. This program would appeal to people interested in snorkeling, culture, wildlife, nature studies, photography, bird watching.
Accommodations • Hotels, lodges. Single rooms are available for an additional $225.
Program Details • Program offered 4 times per year. Session length: 8 days. Departures are scheduled in January, February, March, April. Most participants are 25–55 years of age. Participants must be 12 years or older to enroll. 15 participants per session. Application deadline: 60 days prior to departure. Reservations are recommended at least 60 days before departure.
Costs • $1695 (includes housing, some meals, excursions). A $300 deposit is required.
Contact • Michelle Gervais, Latin America Sales Director, Journeys International, Inc., 4011 Jackson Road, Ann Arbor, MI 48103; 313-665-4407; Fax: 313-665-2945; E-mail: michelle@journeys-intl.com; World Wide Web: http://www.journeys-intl.com

JOURNEYS INTERNATIONAL, INC.

BELIZE FAMILY EXPLORER WEEK

General Information • Family tour with visits to Belize City, Che Chemtla Pottery Caves, Garifona Village, Jaguar Reserve, Maya Mountain Lodge, Pelican Beach, Tikal extensions. Once at the destination country, participants travel by foot.
Learning Focus • Instruction in the myths of Mayan culture. Escorted travel to Mayan caves. Nature observation (wildlife, Barrier Reef). Other activities include snorkeling, swimming, horseback riding, scuba diving. This program would appeal to people interested in bird watching, snorkeling, culture, wildlife, nature studies, photography.
Accommodations • Hotels, lodges.
Program Details • Session length: 8 days. Departures are scheduled throughout the year. Program is targeted to active families. Most participants are 4–70 years of age. Participants must be 4 years or older to enroll. 2–14 participants per session. Application deadline: 60 days prior to departure. Reservations are recommended at least 60 days before departure.
Costs • $1350 for adults, $890 for children under 12 (includes housing, some meals). A $300 deposit is required.
Contact • Joan Weber, Family Trips Director and Owner, Journeys International, Inc., 4011 Jackson Road, Ann Arbor, MI 48103; 313-665-4407; Fax: 313-665-2945; E-mail: joan@journeys-intl.com; World Wide Web: http://www.journeys-intl.com

JOURNEYS INTERNATIONAL, INC.

BELIZE, MAYAS, AND THE JUNGLE EDUCATOR'S WORKSHOP

General Information • Educator/student workshop with visits to Belize (Belizo Zoo, Pottery Caves, Ruins at Cahal Pech, San Ignacio), Guatemala (Guatemala (Tikal)). Once at the destination country, participants travel by bus, foot.
Learning Focus • Instruction in Mayan history. Escorted travel to rain forests, Caracol and Tikal. Nature observation (reefs). Other activities include hiking, pottery, canoeing, horseback riding. Instruction is offered by expert guides. This program would appeal to people interested in ancient civilization, archaeology, indigenous cultures, rain forest studies.
Accommodations • Hotels. Single rooms are available for an additional $175.
Program Details • Session length: 8 days. Departures are scheduled throughout the year. Program is targeted to educators and students. Application deadline: 60 days prior to departure. Reservations are recommended at least 60 days before departure.
Costs • $1395 for adults, $890 for children under 12 (includes housing, some meals, excursions). A $300 deposit is required.
Contact • Joan Weber, Educator's Trips Director and Owner, Journeys International, Inc., 4011 Jackson Road, Ann Arbor, MI 48103; 313-665-4407; Fax: 313-665-2945; E-mail: joan@journeys-intl.com; World Wide Web: http://www.journeys-intl.com

NATURAL HABITAT ADVENTURES

BELIZE EXPLORER

General Information • Nature study tour with visits to Baboon Sanctuary, Barrier Reef, Cockscomb Jaguar Reserve, Crooked Tree Lagoon, Lamanai, Xuanantunich. Once at the destination country, participants travel by private van.
Learning Focus • Nature observation (rain forests, barrier reef). Instruction is offered by naturalists. This program would appeal to people interested in nature studies, photography, wildlife.
Accommodations • Jungle lodges. Single rooms are available for an additional $395.
Program Details • Program offered 5 times per year. Session length: 12 days. Departures are scheduled in January–May. Participants must be 13 years or older to enroll. 10 participants per session. Reservations are recommended at least 6 months before departure.

Costs • $2695 (includes housing, all meals, park entrance fees). A $500 deposit is required.
Contact • Natural Habitat Adventures, 2945 Center Green Court, Suite H, Boulder, CO 80301; 800-543-8917; Fax: 303-449-3712; E-mail: nathab@worldnet.att.net

NATURE EXPEDITIONS INTERNATIONAL

FROM REEF TO RUINS: BELIZE EXPEDITION

General Information • Nature study tour with visits to Belize City, Blackbird Caye, Chaa Creek, Chan Chich. Once at the destination country, participants travel by bus, boat, airplane, mini-van.
Learning Focus • Nature observation (rain forest, jungle walks). Other activities include marine observation. Instruction is offered by naturalists. This program would appeal to people interested in nature studies, marine biology, rain forest habitats, wildlife, archaeology, ecology.
Accommodations • Hotels, lodges. Single rooms are available for an additional $400.
Program Details • Program offered 3 times per year. Session length: 10 days. Departures are scheduled in February, April, December. Most participants are 25–75 years of age. Other requirements: doctor's permission for participants 70 years and older. Reservations are recommended at least 6 months before departure.
Costs • $2390 (includes housing, some meals, excursions, all guiding). A $400 deposit is required.
Contact • Christopher Kyle, President, Nature Expeditions International, 6400 East El Dorado Circle, Suite 210, Tucson, AZ 85715; 800-869-0639; Fax: 520-721-6719; E-mail: naturexp@aol.com

OCEANIC SOCIETY EXPEDITIONS

BELIZE ARCHAEOLOGY PROJECT

General Information • Archaeological tour with visits to Lamanai, Indian Church Village, river cruise. Once at the destination country, participants travel by foot, boat, airplane, van.
Learning Focus • Instruction in archaeology and Mayan history. Field research in archaeology. Escorted travel to an Indian Church village. Museum visits (Lamanai Mayan ruins). Nature observation (birds, plants, animals). Volunteer work (archaeological excavation, cataloging). Instruction is offered by archaeologists. This program would appeal to people interested in archaeology.
Accommodations • Cabanas.
Program Details • Program offered 28 times per year. Session length: 8–10 days. Departures are scheduled throughout the year. Program is targeted to adults. Most participants are 16–80 years of age. Participants must be 16 years or older to enroll. 4–16 participants per session. Application deadline: 60 days prior to departure. Reservations are recommended at least 6 months before departure.
Costs • $1233–$1497 (includes housing, all meals, books and class materials, excursions, international airfare). A $300 deposit is required.
Contact • Randi Reiremo, Expedition Manager, Oceanic Society Expeditions, Fort Mason Center, Building E, #230, San Francisco, CA 94123; 415-441-1106; Fax: 415-474-3395

OCEANIC SOCIETY EXPEDITIONS

BELIZE DOLPHIN PROJECT: SURFACE AND UNDERWATER RESEARCH

General Information • Research expedition with visits to Belize, barrier reef. Once at the destination country, participants travel by boat.
Learning Focus • Field research in dolphin behavior, ecology and social organization. Nature observation (dolphins, coral reef). Volunteer work (data collection). Other activities include evening lectures and discussions on dolphin communication, other marine mammal research, coral reefs. Instruction is offered by researchers, naturalists. This program would appeal to people interested in dolphin ecology, research methods, reef ecology.
Accommodations • Cabanas.
Program Details • Program offered 20 times per year. Session length: 8 days. Departures are scheduled throughout the year. Most participants are 16–80 years of age. Participants must be 16 years or older to enroll. Other requirements: swimming and snorkeling experience, general good health. 8 participants per session. Application deadline: 60 days prior to departure. Reservations are recommended at least 6 months before departure.
Costs • $1663 from Miami, $1669 from Houston, $1932 from Los Angeles (includes housing, all meals, excursions, international airfare, boat transfers, research leadership, snorkeling excursions). A $300 deposit is required.
Contact • Jennifer Austin, Expedition Manager, Oceanic Society Expeditions, Fort Mason Center, Building E, #230, San Francisco, CA 94123; 415-441-1106; Fax: 415-474-3395

OCEANIC SOCIETY EXPEDITIONS

BELIZE GALES POINT: SEA TURTLE AND MANATEE PROJECT

General Information • Research expedition with visits to Gales Point, beaches, southern lagoon. Once at the destination country, participants travel by foot, boat.
Learning Focus • Instruction in field research methods and sustainable development. Field research in Hawksbill sea turtle restoration and manatee distribution. Volunteer work (maintaining turtle nests, building protective cages). Instruction is offered by researchers, naturalists. This program would appeal to people interested in sea turtles, cultural exchange, manatees.
Accommodations • Homestays.
Program Details • Program offered 2 times per year. Session length: 8 days. Departures are scheduled in August. Most participants are 16–80 years of age. Participants must be 16 years or older to enroll. Other requirements: travel experience in remote environment, general good health, and be able to walk up to 5 miles every other day. 8 participants per session. Application deadline: 60 days prior to departure. Reservations are recommended at least 6 months before departure.

Costs • $1188 from Miami, $1460 from Houston, $1597 from Los Angeles (includes housing, all meals, excursions, international airfare, boat transfers, research leadership). A $300 deposit is required.
Contact • Silke Schroeder, Expedition Manager, Oceanic Society Expeditions, Fort Mason Center, Building E, #230, San Francisco, CA 94123; 415-441-1106; Fax: 415-474-3395

OCEANIC SOCIETY EXPEDITIONS

BELIZE HOWLER MONKEY RESEARCH PROJECT

General Information • Research expedition with visits to Lamanai, Indian Church Village, river cruise. Once at the destination country, participants travel by boat, van.
Learning Focus • Instruction in biology, ecology and conservation. Field research in howler monkey biology. Escorted travel to an Indian Church village. Museum visits (Lamanai Mayan ruins). Nature observation (birds, plants, animals). Volunteer work (howler monkey research). Instruction is offered by researchers. This program would appeal to people interested in biology, ecology, conservation.
Accommodations • Cabanas.
Program Details • Program offered 22 times per year. Session length: 8 days. Departures are scheduled throughout the year. Program is targeted to adults. Most participants are 16–80 years of age. Participants must be 16 years or older to enroll. 2–14 participants per session. Application deadline: 60 days prior to departure. Reservations are recommended at least 6 months before departure.
Costs • $1626–$1895 (includes housing, all meals, books and class materials, excursions, international airfare). A $300 deposit is required.
Contact • Randi Reiremo, Expedition Manager, Oceanic Society Expeditions, Fort Mason Center, Building E, #230, San Francisco, CA 94123; 415-441-1106; Fax: 415-474-3395

OCEANIC SOCIETY EXPEDITIONS

BELIZE MANATEES

General Information • Research expedition with visits to Caye Caulker/coastal cayes, manatee aggregation areas from Ambergris Caye to Bluefield Range. Once at the destination country, participants travel by boat, airplane.
Learning Focus • Instruction in field research methods. Field research in manatee distribution and behavior. Volunteer work (assisting with data collection). Instruction is offered by researchers, naturalists. This program would appeal to people interested in manatee conservation.
Accommodations • Hotels. Single rooms are available.
Program Details • Program offered 6 times per year. Session length: 8 days. Departures are scheduled in February, March, July, October, November. Most participants are 16–80 years of age. Participants must be 16 years or older to enroll. Other requirements: swimming and snorkeling experience, general good health. 8 participants per session. Application deadline: 60 days prior to departure. Reservations are recommended at least 6 months before departure.
Costs • $1428 from Miami, $1460 from Houston, $1597 from Los Angeles (includes housing, all meals, international airfare, boat excursions, research leadership). A $300 deposit is required.
Contact • Silke Schroeder, Expedition Manager, Oceanic Society Expeditions, Fort Mason Center, Building E, #230, San Francisco, CA 94123; 415-441-1106; Fax: 415-474-3395

OCEANIC SOCIETY EXPEDITIONS

BELIZE TEACHERS' WORKSHOP–MARINE BIOLOGY, CORAL REEFS, AND DOLPHINS

General Information • Teachers' workshop with visits to Spanish Caye. Once at the destination country, participants travel by boat. Program is affiliated with MARE (Marine Activities, Resources and Education) and the University of California at Berkeley.
Learning Focus • Instruction in research techniques. Field research in bottlenose dolphin ecology. Nature observation (dolphins, coral reef). Volunteer work (assisting with data collection). Other activities include evening discussions, journal writing, lesson planning. Instruction is offered by professors, researchers, naturalists. This program would appeal to people interested in marine biology, coral reefs, dolphin ecology.
Accommodations • Cabanas.
Program Details • Program offered once per year. Session length: 7 days. Departures are scheduled in June. Program is targeted to kindergarten through 12th grade teachers. Most participants are 16–80 years of age. 18 participants per session. Application deadline: 60 days prior to departure. Reservations are recommended at least 6 months before departure.
Costs • $1345 from Miami or Houston, $1575 from Los Angeles (includes housing, all meals, books and class materials, excursions, international airfare). A $300 deposit is required.
Contact • Jennifer Austin, Expedition Manager, Oceanic Society Expeditions, Fort Mason Center, Building E, #230, San Francisco, CA 94123; 415-441-1106; Fax: 415-474-3395

TRAVELEARN

A BELIZE ADVENTURE

General Information • Nature study and cultural tour with visits to Altun Ha, Caracol, Dangriga, Lamanai, Maya Mountains, Xuanantunich, Guatemala (Tikal). Once at the destination country, participants travel by bus, foot. Program is affiliated with the nationwide TraveLearn network of 290 universities and colleges.
Learning Focus • Instruction in natural and cultural history and archaeology. Nature observation (national parks and reserves). Instruction is offered by researchers, naturalists, scientists. This program would appeal to people interested in natural history, archaeology, cultural history and understanding.
Accommodations • Hotels. Single rooms are available for an additional $695.
Program Details • Program offered 4 times per year. Session length: 9 days. Departures are scheduled in January, February, March, July. Program is targeted to mature adults. Most participants are 40–75 years of age. Participants must be 18 years or older to enroll. 14–20 participants per session.

Application deadline: 60 days prior to departure. Reservations are recommended at least 4–8 months before departure.
Costs • $3195 (includes housing, all meals, books and class materials, excursions, international airfare). A $300 deposit is required.
Contact • Keith Williams, Director of Marketing, TraveLearn, PO Box 315, Lakeville, PA 18438; 800-235-9114; Fax: 717-226-9114; E-mail: travelearn@aol.com

UNIVERSITY RESEARCH EXPEDITIONS PROGRAM

RAINFORESTS OF THE MAYAN MOUNTAINS

General Information • Research expedition with visits to Bladen Nature Reserve. Once at the destination country, participants travel by foot. Program is affiliated with University of California.
Learning Focus • Instruction in field techniques in forest ecology. Field research in plant and mammal interaction and rain forest regeneration. Other activities include hiking. Instruction is offered by professors, researchers, scientists. This program would appeal to people interested in ecology.
Accommodations • Campsites.
Program Details • Session length: 2–3 weeks. Most participants are 16–80 years of age. Participants must be 16 years or older to enroll. 8–10 participants per session. Reservations are recommended at least 3 months before departure.
Costs • Contact sponsor for information. A $200 deposit is required.
Contact • Anne Forrest, Project Coordinator, University Research Expeditions Program, 2223 Fulton Street, 4th Floor, Berkeley, CA 94720-7050; 510-642-6586; Fax: 510-642-6791; E-mail: urep@uclink.berkeley.edu; World Wide Web: http://www.mip.berkeley.edu/urep

UNIVERSITY RESEARCH EXPEDITIONS PROGRAM

WETLANDS OF BELIZE

General Information • Research expedition with visits to Orange Walk. Program is affiliated with University of California.
Learning Focus • Field research in wetlands ecology and collecting water, air, soil, and plant samples. Instruction is offered by professors, researchers, scientists. This program would appeal to people interested in ecology, conservation.
Accommodations • Houses.
Program Details • Session length: 2–3 weeks. Most participants are 16–80 years of age. Participants must be 16 years or older to enroll. 8–10 participants per session. Reservations are recommended at least 3 months before departure.
Costs • Contact sponsor for information. A $200 deposit is required.
Contact • Anne Forrest, Project Coordinator, University Research Expeditions Program, 2223 Fulton Street, 4th Floor, Berkeley, CA 94720-7050; 510-642-6586; Fax: 510-642-6791; E-mail: urep@uclink.berkeley.edu; World Wide Web: http://www.mip.berkeley.edu/urep

WILDLAND ADVENTURES

RUINS, REEFS AND RAINFORESTS

General Information • Wilderness/adventure program with visits to Belize City, Chan Chich, Dangriga, rain forests, barrier reef. Once at the destination country, participants travel by foot, boat, airplane.
Learning Focus • Nature observation (wildlife). Other activities include hiking. Instruction is offered by naturalists, local Maya indians. This program would appeal to people interested in photography, snorkeling, hiking, natural history, scuba diving.
Accommodations • Single rooms are available.
Program Details • Program offered 8 times per year. Session length: 9 days. Departures are scheduled in December–July. Most participants are 30–60 years of age. Participants must be 5 years or older to enroll. 2–8 participants per session. Application deadline: 30 days prior to departure. Reservations are recommended at least 3–6 months before departure.
Costs • $1645 (includes housing, some meals, excursions, complete pre-departure dossier). A $300 deposit is required.
Contact • Wildland Adventures, 3516 Northeast 155th Street, Seattle, WA 98155; 800-345-4453; Fax: 206-363-6615; E-mail: wildadve@aol.com; World Wide Web: http://www.wildland.com

ERMUDA

TRAVELEARN

A BERMUDA ODYSSEY

General Information • Nature study and cultural tour with visits to Hamilton, Somerset, St. George, Stonington Beach. Once at the destination country, participants travel by bus, foot, boat. Program is affiliated with the nationwide TraveLearn network of 290 universities and colleges.

Learning Focus • Instruction in cultural and natural history. Museum visits (Royal Naval Dockyard, Maritime Museum). Nature observation (Spittal Pond and Bermuda Biological Station). Other activities include "people-to-people" experience in Paget Parish. Instruction is offered by professors, naturalists, historians. This program would appeal to people interested in cultural history, natural history, ecology.

Accommodations • Hotels. Single rooms are available for an additional $595.

Program Details • Program offered 2 times per year. Session length: 10 days. Departures are scheduled in March, November. Program is targeted to mature adults. Most participants are 40–75 years of age. Participants must be 18 years or older to enroll. 14–20 participants per session. Application deadline: 60 days prior to departure. Reservations are recommended at least 4–8 months before departure.

Costs • $2195 (includes housing, all meals, books and class materials, excursions). A $300 deposit is required.

Contact • Keith Williams, Director of Marketing, TraveLearn, PO Box 315, Lakeville, PA 18438; 800-235-9114; Fax: 717-226-9114; E-mail: travelearn@aol.com

BOLIVIA

ALPINE ASCENTS, INTERNATIONAL

ANCOHUMA

General Information • Mountain climbing tour with visits to Ancohuma, La Paz, Yankho Hayo, Tiwanku.
Learning Focus • Instruction in mountain climbing. Escorted travel to the Chachacomani region. Nature observation (Lake Titicaca, Amazon Basin, Apolamba Mountains). Other activities include camping, hiking. Instruction is offered by sports professionals. This program would appeal to people interested in mountain climbing.
Accommodations • Hotels, campsites. Single rooms are available.
Program Details • Program offered once per year. Session length: 21 days. Departures are scheduled in August. Program is targeted to intermediate mountain climbers. Reservations are recommended at least 6 months before departure.
Costs • $3380 (includes housing, some meals, group equipment).
Contact • Gordon Janow, Program Coordinator, Alpine Ascents, International, 16615 Saybrook Drive, Woodinville, WA 98072; 206-788-1951; Fax: 206-788-6757; E-mail: aaiclimb@accessone.com

AMERICAN ALPINE INSTITUTE, LTD.

MOUNTAINEERING AND TREKKING IN BOLIVIA

General Information • Wilderness/adventure program with visits to La Paz. Once at the destination country, participants travel by foot, van.
Learning Focus • Instruction in mountaineering. Museum visits (National Museum of Art). Other activities include camping, hiking, climbing. Instruction is offered by sports professionals. This program would appeal to people interested in climbing.
Accommodations • Hotels, campsites. Single rooms are available.
Program Details • Program offered 5 times per year. Session length: 21–28 days. Departures are scheduled in May–September. Program is targeted to people over 18, with previous backpacking experience. Most participants are 20–60 years of age. Participants must be 18 years or older to enroll. Other requirements: very good physical condition. Application deadline: 6 weeks prior to departure. Reservations are recommended at least 3 months before departure.
Costs • $2990 (includes tuition, housing, some meals, excursions, group camping and cooking gear, group climbing gear). A $250 deposit is required.
Contact • Sheilagh Brown, Assistant Director, American Alpine Institute, Ltd., 1515 12th Street, Bellingham, WA 98225; 360-671-1505; Fax: 360-734-8890; E-mail: aai@a2.com; World Wide Web: http://www.mtnguide.com/~aai

AMERISPAN UNLIMITED

SPANISH CLASSES AND HOMESTAYS IN BOLIVIA

General Information • Language study program with visits to La Paz. Once at the destination country, participants travel by bus.
Learning Focus • Instruction in the Spanish language. Instruction is offered by trained Spanish teachers. This program would appeal to people interested in Spanish language, Latin America.
Accommodations • Homestays. Single rooms are available.
Program Details • Session length: 2–12 weeks. Departures are scheduled throughout the year. Most participants are 16–70 years of age. Participants must be 16 years or older to enroll. Reservations are recommended at least 4 weeks before departure.
Costs • Contact sponsor for information. A $100 deposit is required.
Contact • AmeriSpan Unlimited, PO Box 40513, Philadelphia, PA 19106; 800-879-6640; Fax: 215-985-4524; E-mail: info@amerispan.com; World Wide Web: http://www.amerispan.com

CRAFT WORLD TOURS

BOLIVIA

General Information • Cultural tour with visits to Cochambamba, La Paz, Sucre. Once at the destination country, participants travel by bus.
Learning Focus • Escorted travel to La Cancha market, regional villages and a knitting cooperative. Museum visits (Archeological Museum, Popular Art Museum, Musical Instrument Museum). Instruction is offered by artists. This program would appeal to people interested in handicrafts, folk arts, village life.
Accommodations • Hotels. Single rooms are available for an additional $269.
Program Details • Program offered once per year. Session length: 14 days. Departures are scheduled in July. Most participants are 30–80 years of age. Other requirements: appreciation of handcrafts and folk arts. 18 participants per session. Application deadline: June. Reservations are recommended at least 6 months before departure.
Costs • $2976 (includes housing, some meals, excursions, international airfare). A $250 deposit is required.
Contact • Tom Wilson, President, Craft World Tours, 6776 Warboys Road, Byron, NY 14422; 716-548-2667; Fax: 716-548-2821

FOREIGN LANGUAGE STUDY ABROAD SERVICE

SPANISH IN COCHABAMBA

General Information • Language study program in Cochabamba.

Learning Focus • Courses in language study. Instruction is offered by local teachers.
Accommodations • Homestays, hotels. Single rooms are available. Meals are taken on one's own, with host family, in local restaurants, in residences.
Program Details • Session length: varies. Departures are scheduled in January–December. The program is open to undergraduate students, graduate students, pre-college students, adults. Most participants are 17 years of age and older.
Costs • Contact sponsor for information. Application fee: $50. A $100 deposit is required.
Contact • Louise Harber, Coordinator, Foreign Language Study Abroad Service, Department IH, Box 903, 5935 Southwest 64th Avenue, South Miami, FL 33143; 800-282-1090; Fax: 305-662-2907; E-mail: flsas@netpoint.net; World Wide Web: http://www.netpoint.net/~flsas

JOURNEYS INTERNATIONAL, INC.

ISLANDS OF THE SUN

General Information • Wilderness/adventure program with visits to Copacabana, Coroico, Island of the Sun, La Paz, Valley of the Moon. Once at the destination country, participants travel by foot, boat, hiking or car.
Learning Focus • Escorted travel to Valley of the Moon and Copacabana. Nature observation (wildlife, sunsets). Other activities include hiking. Instruction is offered by local English-speaking guides. This program would appeal to people interested in photography, culture, hiking, nature studies.
Accommodations • Hotels, lodges, inns. Single rooms are available.
Program Details • Session length: 8 days. Departures are scheduled throughout the year. Most participants are 25–55 years of age. Participants must be 12 years or older to enroll. 2–12 participants per session. Reservations are recommended at least 60 days before departure.
Costs • $1095 (includes housing, some meals, admission fees and airport transfers). A $300 deposit is required.
Contact • Michelle Gervais, Latin America Director, Journeys International, Inc., 4011 Jackson Road, Ann Arbor, MI 48103; 313-665-4407; Fax: 313-665-2945; E-mail: michelle@journeys-intl.com; World Wide Web: http://www.journeys-intl.com

THE CENTER FOR ENGLISH STUDIES

STUDY ABROAD IN SALVADOR DA BAHIA, BRAZIL

General Information • Language study program with visits to Salvador da Bahia. Program is affiliated with Dialogo Institute-Brazil Workshop.
Learning Focus • Instruction in the Portuguese language. Other activities include field trips to local sites, museums, markets and churches. Instruction is offered by faculty members from host institution. This program would appeal to people interested in the Portuguese language.
Accommodations • Homestays, hotels, guest houses. Single rooms are available.
Program Details • Session length: 2 or more weeks. Departures are scheduled throughout the year. Most participants are 17–70 years of age. Participants must be 17 years or older to enroll. 4–8 participants per session. Application deadline: 2 weeks prior to departure. Reservations are recommended at least 1 month before departure.
Costs • $1100 for 3 weeks (includes tuition, housing, some meals). A $125 deposit is required.
Contact • Ms. Lorraine Haber, Study Abroad Coordinator, The Center for English Studies, 330 7th Avenue, 6th Floor, New York, NY 10001; 212-629-7300; Fax: 212-736-7950; E-mail: ces_newyork@cescorp.com

ECOTOUR EXPEDITIONS, INC.

NATURAL HISTORY PROGRAMS IN CENTRAL AND SOUTH AMERICA

General Information • Nature study tour with visits to Amazon Region, Pantanal, Amazon. Once at the destination country, participants travel by foot, boat.
Learning Focus • Nature observation (bird watching). Other activities include camping, hiking, walk in forest, exploration in canoes. Instruction is offered by researchers, naturalists, scientists. This program would appeal to people interested in nature studies.
Accommodations • Hotels, campsites. Single rooms are available.
Program Details • Session length: 12 days. Departures are scheduled throughout the year. Most participants are 20–70 years of age. Participants must be 8 years or older to enroll. Other requirements: curiosity about nature. 12 participants per session. Reservations are recommended at least 6–8 months before departure.
Costs • $2500 (includes housing, some meals, excursions, international airfare). A $300 deposit is required.
Contact • Elisabeth Kneib, Treasurer, Ecotour Expeditions, Inc., PO Box 381066, Cambridge, MA 02238; 617-876-5817; Fax: 617-876-3638; E-mail: nature@tiac.com

FOREIGN LANGUAGE STUDY ABROAD SERVICE

INTERNATIONAL LANGUAGE STUDY HOMESTAYS IN BRAZIL

General Information • Language study program in Brazil.
Learning Focus • Courses in Portuguese language. Instruction is offered by local teachers.
Accommodations • Homestays. Single rooms are available. Meals are taken with host family, in residences.
Program Details • Session length: varies. Departures are scheduled in January–December. The program is open to undergraduate students, graduate students, pre-college students, adults. Most participants are 12 years of age and older. Other requirements: students must be at least 12 years old. 1 participant per session.
Costs • Contact sponsor for information. A $300 deposit is required.
Contact • Louise Harber, Coordinator, Foreign Language Study Abroad Service, Department IH, Box 903, 5935 Southwest 64th Avenue, South Miami, FL 33143; 800-282-1090; Fax: 305-662-2907; E-mail: flsas@netpoint.net; World Wide Web: http://www.netpoint.net/~flsas

FOREIGN LANGUAGE STUDY ABROAD SERVICE

PORTUGESE IN BRAZIL

General Information • Language study program in Rio de Janeiro, Sao Paulo.
Learning Focus • Courses in language study. Instruction is offered by local teachers.
Accommodations • Homestays, hotels. Single rooms are available. Meals are taken on one's own, in local restaurants.
Program Details • Session length: varies. Departures are scheduled in January–December. The program is open to undergraduate students, graduate students, pre-college students, adults. Most participants are 18 years of age and older.
Costs • Contact sponsor for information. Application fee: $50. A $100 deposit is required.
Contact • Louise Harber, Coordinator, Foreign Language Study Abroad Service, Department IH, Box 903, 5935 Southwest 64th Avenue, South Miami, FL 33143; 800-282-1090; Fax: 305-662-2907; E-mail: flsas@netpoint.net; World Wide Web: http://www.netpoint.net/~flsas

GEORGETOWN UNIVERSITY

GEORGETOWN UNIVERSITY IN CAMPINAS, BRAZIL

General Information • Language study program in Campinas. Classes are held on the campus of State University of Campinas. Excursions to Ouro Preto.

Learning Focus • Courses in Portuguese language, Brazilian culture, literature. Instruction is offered by professors from the sponsoring institution and local teachers.
Accommodations • Homestays. Single rooms are available. Meals are taken with host family, in residences.
Program Details • Program offered once per year. Session length: 6 weeks. Departures are scheduled in June, July. The program is open to undergraduate students, graduate students, pre-college students, adults. Most participants are 18–25 years of age. Other requirements: minimum 3.0 GPA. 15 participants per session. Application deadline: March.
Costs • $2725 (includes tuition, housing, some meals, books and class materials, insurance, excursions). A $100 deposit is required.
Contact • Marianne T. Needham, Director, International Programs, Georgetown University, 306 ICC, Box 571012, Washington, DC 20057-1012; 202-687-6184; Fax: 202-687-8954; E-mail: sscefps1@gunet.georgetown.edu; World Wide Web: http://guweb.georgetown.edu/ssce

JOURNEYS INTERNATIONAL, INC.

BRAZIL AMAZON EXPLORER

General Information • Wilderness/adventure program with visits to Ahavilhanas, Manaus, Rio Negro, Rio Solimoes. Once at the destination country, participants travel by foot, boat, canoe.
Learning Focus • Nature observation (Amazon River, giant water lilies). Other activities include hiking, swimming, canoeing. Instruction is offered by local English-speaking guides. This program would appeal to people interested in bird watching, culture, wildlife, nature studies.
Accommodations • Hotels, boat. Single rooms are available for an additional $100.
Program Details • Program offered 6 times per year. Session length: 12 days. Departures are scheduled in December–July. Program is targeted to active persons interested in nature and culture observation. Most participants are 25–55 years of age. Participants must be 12 years or older to enroll. 6 participants per session. Reservations are recommended at least 60 days before departure.
Costs • $1995 (includes housing, some meals, excursions, local captain and cook). A $300 deposit is required.
Contact • Michelle Gervais, Latin America Sales Director, Journeys International, Inc., 4011 Jackson Road, Ann Arbor, MI 48103; 313-665-4407; Fax: 313-665-2945; E-mail: michelle@journeys-intl.com; World Wide Web: http://www.journeys-intl.com

LANGUAGE LIAISON

SALVADOR DE BAHIA–PORTUGUESE IN BRAZIL

General Information • Language study program with visits to Salvador da Bahia.
Learning Focus • Instruction in the Portuguese language. Instruction is offered by professors. This program would appeal to people interested in language.
Accommodations • Homestays, hotels, guest houses. Single rooms are available.
Program Details • Session length: unlimited. Departures are scheduled throughout the year. Most participants are 18–70 years of age. Participants must be 16 years or older to enroll. Reservations are recommended at least 35 days before departure.
Costs • Contact sponsor for information.
Contact • Nancy Forman, President, Language Liaison, 20533 Biscayne Boulevard-Station 4-162, Miami, FL 33180; 305-682-9909; Fax: 305-682-9907; E-mail: langstudy@aol.com; World Wide Web: http://languageliaison.com

MICHIGAN STATE UNIVERSITY

BIODIVERSITY AND ECOSYSTEM MANAGEMENT

General Information • Academic study program in Curitiba, Sao Paulo.
Learning Focus • Courses in forestry, ecology. Instruction is offered by professors from the sponsoring institution.
Accommodations • Dormitories. Meals are taken on one's own, in local restaurants.
Program Details • Program offered once per year. Session length: 4 weeks. Departures are scheduled in May. The program is open to undergraduate students, graduate students. Most participants are 18–26 years of age. Other requirements: good academic standing and the approval of the director. 20 participants per session. Application deadline: March 14.
Costs • $1895 (includes housing, some meals, excursions). Application fee: $75. A $250 deposit is required.
Contact • Brenda S. Sprite, Educational Programs Coordinator, Michigan State University, Office of Study Abroad, 109 International Center, East Lansing, MI 48824; 517-353-8920; Fax: 517-432-2082; E-mail: sprite@pilot.msu.edu; World Wide Web: http://study-abroad.msu.edu

MICHIGAN STATE UNIVERSITY

BRAZILIAN SOCIETY AND ENVIRONMENT: PAST AND PRESENT

General Information • Academic study program in Bahia, Belo Horizonte, Ouro Preto, Rio de Janeiro, Salvador. Excursions to rain forests, Pantanal wetland.
Learning Focus • Courses in social sciences, arts and humanities, history, geography. Instruction is offered by professors from the sponsoring institution.
Accommodations • Hotels. Meals are taken on one's own, in local restaurants.
Program Details • Program offered once per year. Session length: 5 weeks. Departures are scheduled in June. The program is open to undergraduate students, graduate students. Most participants are 18–22 years of age. Other requirements: good academic standing and the approval of the instructor. 12 participants per session. Application deadline: March 14.
Costs • $2210 (includes housing, some meals, excursions). Application fee: $75. A $250 deposit is required.
Contact • Brenda S. Sprite, Educational Programs Coordinator, Michigan State University, Office of Study Abroad, 109 International Center, East Lansing, MI 48824-1035; 517-353-8920; Fax: 517-432-2082; E-mail: sprite@pilot.msu.edu; World Wide Web: http://study-abroad.msu.edu

RUSSIAN AND EAST EUROPEAN PARTNERSHIPS

BRAZIL LANGUAGE AND CULTURAL IMMERSION PROGRAM

General Information • Language study program in Salvador de Bahia. Classes are held on the campus of Dialogo Language Institute.
Learning Focus • Courses in Portuguese language, South American culture and art, South American history. Instruction is offered by local teachers.
Accommodations • Homestays, locally-rented apartments. Single rooms are available. Meals are taken on one's own, with host family, in local restaurants, in residences.
Program Details • Program offered 11 times per year. Session length: 4 or more weeks. Departures are scheduled in January–November. The program is open to undergraduate students, graduate students, adults. Most participants are 18 years of age and older. Other requirements: in good health and 18 or older unless chaperoned by an adult. 6 participants per session. Application deadline: 45 days prior to departure.
Costs • $2900 (includes tuition, housing, some meals, books and class materials, excursions, international airfare, local transportation, airport transfers). A $1500 deposit is required.
Contact • Kenneth Fortune, President, Russian and East European Partnerships, PO Box 227, Fineview, NY 13640; 888-USE-REEP; Fax: 800-910-1777; E-mail: reep@fox.nstn.ca

UNIVERSITY OF ARIZONA

UNIVERSIDADE FEDERAL DO CEARÁ

General Information • Language study program in Fortaleza. Classes are held on the campus of Federal University of Ceará.
Learning Focus • Courses in language study. Instruction is offered by local teachers.
Accommodations • Homestays. Single rooms are available. Meals are taken with host family, in residences.
Program Details • Program offered once per year. Session length: 6 weeks. Departures are scheduled in June. The program is open to undergraduate students, graduate students. Most participants are 20–30 years of age. Other requirements: minimum 2.5 GPA, 1 or more years of Portuguese and sophomore standing. 12–16 participants per session. Application deadline: April 1.
Costs • $1800 (includes tuition, housing, some meals, books and class materials, excursions). Application fee: $35. A $300 deposit is required.
Contact • Stephanie Bleecker, Study Abroad Advisor, University of Arizona, Center for Global Student Programs, 915 North Tyndall, Tucson, AZ 85721; 520-621-4627; Fax: 520-621-4069

UNIVERSITY OF FLORIDA

INSTITUTO BRASIL ESTADOS UNIDOS, RIO DE JANEIRO, BRAZIL (PORTUGUESE AND BRAZILIAN CULTURE)

General Information • Language study program in Rio de Janeiro. Classes are held on the campus of Instituto Brasil Estados Unìdos. Excursions to Parti, Sugar Loaf, Petropolis, Corcovado.
Learning Focus • Courses in Portuguese language, Portuguese culture. Instruction is offered by local teachers.
Accommodations • Homestays. Meals are taken with host family.
Program Details • Program offered once per year. Session length: 4 weeks. Departures are scheduled in June. The program is open to undergraduate students, graduate students, adults. Other requirements: minimum 2.5 GPA, 18 years old and one semester of Portugeuse or two years of Spanish. 15–30 participants per session. Application deadline: March 15.
Costs • $2700 (includes tuition, housing, some meals, excursions, on site orientation). Application fee: $250.
Contact • Overseas Studies, University of Florida, 123 Tigert Hall, PO Box 113225, Gainesville, FL 32611-3225; 352-392-5206; Fax: 352-392-5575; E-mail: overseas@nervm.nerdc.ufl.edu

UNIVERSITY OF ILLINOIS AT URBANA-CHAMPAIGN

BRAZIL'S ECONOMY AND BUSINESS ENVIRONMENT

General Information • Business and language study program in Sao Paulo. Classes are held on the campus of University of Sao Paulo.
Learning Focus • Courses in business, Portuguese language, economics. Instruction is offered by local teachers.
Accommodations • Homestays, locally-rented apartments. Single rooms are available. Meals are taken on one's own, with host family.
Program Details • Program offered once per year. Session length: 6 weeks. Departures are scheduled in May. The program is open to undergraduate students, graduate students. Most participants are 20–25 years of age. Other requirements: B average and an advanced undergraduate or graduate status. 10 participants per session. Application deadline: March 1.
Costs • $3100 (includes tuition, housing, some meals, medical emergency evacuation insurance). Application fee: $35. A $500 deposit is required.
Contact • Timothy Winkler, Program Coordinator, University of Illinois at Urbana-Champaign, Study Abroad Office, 910 South Fifth Street #115, Champaign, IL 61820; 800-531-4404; Fax: 217-244-0249; E-mail: ipa@uiuc.edu

UNIVERSITY OF KANSAS

PORTUGUESE LANGUAGE AND CULTURE IN FLORIANÓPOLIS, BRAZIL

General Information • Language study program in Florianópolis. Classes are held on the campus of University of South Santa Catarina. Excursions to Iguazú Falls, Rio de Janeiro, Manaus, Salvador.
Learning Focus • Courses in Brazilian-Portuguese language, Brazilian culture. Instruction is offered by professors from the sponsoring institution and local teachers.
Accommodations • Homestays, hotels. Meals are taken on one's own, with host family, in central dining facility, in local restaurants, in residences.
Program Details • Program offered once per year. Session length: 7 weeks with tour, 5 weeks without tour. Departures are scheduled in June. The program is open to undergraduate students, graduate students. Most participants are 19–28 years of age. Other requirements: 2 semesters Portuguese. 15 participants per session.

Costs • $1900 without tour, $3300 with optional tour (includes tuition, housing, some meals, optional study tour to four of Brazil's five main regions). Application fee: $15. A $300 deposit is required.

Contact • Susan MacNally, Coordinator of Summer Institutes, University of Kansas, Office of Study Abroad, 203 Lippincott Hall, Lawrence, KS 66045; 913-864-3742; Fax: 913-864-5040; E-mail: osa@falcon.cc.ukans.edu; World Wide Web: http://kuhub.cc.ukans.edu/~intlstdy/osa/osamain.html

UNIVERSITY RESEARCH EXPEDITIONS PROGRAM

ISLANDS IN THE SKY

General Information • Research expedition with visits to Parque Nacional de Itotiaia. Once at the destination country, participants travel by foot. Program is affiliated with University of California.

Learning Focus • Field research in vegetation surveying, taking soil samples and mapping using global positioning systems. Instruction is offered by professors, researchers, scientists. This program would appeal to people interested in ecology, Brazilian culture, conservation.

Accommodations • Cabins.

Program Details • Session length: 2-3 weeks. Most participants are 16-80 years of age. Participants must be 16 years or older to enroll. 8-10 participants per session. Reservations are recommended at least 3 months before departure.

Costs • Contact sponsor for information. A $200 deposit is required.

Contact • Anne Forrest, Project Coordinator, University Research Expeditions Program, 2223 Fulton Street, 4th Floor, Berkeley, CA 94720-7050; 510-642-6586; Fax: 510-642-6791; E-mail: urep@uclink.berkeley.edu; World Wide Web: http://www.mip.berkeley.edu/urep

CANADA

BALL STATE UNIVERSITY

ENGLISH DRAMATIC LITERATURE: FIELD STUDY

General Information • Academic study program in Niagara-on-the-Lake, Stratford.
Learning Focus • Courses in drama. Instruction is offered by professors from the sponsoring institution.
Accommodations • Dormitories. Single rooms are available. Meals are taken on one's own, in local restaurants.
Program Details • Program offered once per year. Session length: 2 weeks. Departures are scheduled in June. The program is open to undergraduate students, graduate students, adults. Most participants are 19–80 years of age. 6–12 participants per session. Application deadline: April 1.
Costs • $760 (includes tuition, housing, some meals, insurance, transportation by van). A $100 deposit is required.
Contact • William T. Liston, Professor of English, Ball State University, Department of English, Muncie, IN 47306; 317-285-8573; Fax: 317-285-3765; E-mail: 00wtliston@bsu.edu

COLLEGE CONSORTIUM FOR INTERNATIONAL STUDIES–BROOKDALE COMMUNITY COLLEGE

CCIS SUMMER PROGRAM IN QUÉBEC

General Information • Language study program in Chicoutimi. Classes are held on the campus of University of Quebec at Chicoutimi. Excursions to Quebec City, Saguenay-Lac-St. Jean.
Learning Focus • Courses in French language, business French. Instruction is offered by local teachers.
Accommodations • Homestays. Single rooms are available. Meals are taken with host family, in residences.
Program Details • Program offered 4 times per year. Session length: 3–5 weeks. Departures are scheduled in May, June. The program is open to undergraduate students, graduate students. Other requirements: minimum 2.5 GPA. 1 participant per session. Application deadline: April 1 for May session, June 1 for June session.
Costs • $1225 for 3 weeks, $1550 for 5 weeks (includes tuition, housing, some meals). Application fee: $35.
Contact • Jane C. Evans, Executive Director, College Consortium for International Studies, 2000 P Street, NW, Suite 503, Washington, DC 20036; 800-453-6956; Fax: 202-223-0999; E-mail: ccis@intr.net

COUNTRY WALKERS

ISLAND PLEASURES

General Information • Cultural, gourmet cooking, nature study and walking tour with visits to Cheticamp, Cheticamp Island, Glasgow Lake Hills. Once at the destination country, participants travel by foot, boat.
Learning Focus • Escorted travel to a lighthouse, Burnt Mountain and Beulach Ban Falls. Nature observation (wildflowers, moose, orchids, carnivorous plants). Other activities include walking. Instruction is offered by professors, researchers, naturalists, historians. This program would appeal to people interested in walking, nature studies, food and wine.
Accommodations • Hotels. Single rooms are available for an additional $300–$600.
Program Details • Program offered 7 times per year. Session length: 7 days. Departures are scheduled in June, July, August, September. Program is targeted to adults 35 to 65 years old. Most participants are 35–65 years of age. Participants must be 18 years or older to enroll. 18 participants per session. Reservations are recommended at least 5–6 months before departure.
Costs • $1500 (includes housing, all meals, excursions). A $400 deposit is required.
Contact • Heather Kellingbeck, Vice President, Country Walkers, PO Box 180, Waterbury, VT 05176; 800-464-9255; Fax: 802-244-5661; E-mail: ctrywalk@aol.com

EASTERN MICHIGAN UNIVERSITY

INTENSIVE FRENCH LANGUAGE PROGRAM IN CANADA

General Information • Language study program in Chicoutimi. Classes are held on the campus of University of Quebec at Chicoutimi.
Learning Focus • Courses in French language. Instruction is offered by professors from the sponsoring institution.
Accommodations • Dormitories. Meals are taken as a group, in central dining facility.
Program Details • Program offered once per year. Session length: 6 weeks. Departures are scheduled in July. The program is open to undergraduate students, graduate students. Most participants are 18–30 years of age. Other requirements: minimum 2.0 GPA and 18 years of age. 10 participants per session. Application deadline: April 1.
Costs • $2595 (includes tuition, housing, all meals, insurance). A $150 deposit is required.
Contact • Academic Programs Abroad, Eastern Michigan University, 332 Goodison Hall, Ypsilanti, MI 48197; 800-777-3541; Fax: 313-487-2316; E-mail: programs.abroad@emich.edu; World Wide Web: http://www.emich.edu/public/cont_ed/abroad.html

FEDERATION OF ONTARIO NATURALISTS

ADULT NATURALIST CAMP

General Information • Nature study tour with visits to Bruce Peninsula, provincial parks, national parks. Once at the destination country, participants travel by bus, foot, boat, carpool or van.

Learning Focus • Instruction in flora and fauna identification. Escorted travel to nature reserves, parks and trails. Nature observation (bird watching, botany, geology, fauna). Other activities include hiking, natural history. Instruction is offered by researchers, naturalists, artists, outdoor educators. This program would appeal to people interested in botany, geology, fauna, natural history, bird watching, herpetofauna, canoeing, photography, art.

Accommodations • Camp lodges, cabins.

Program Details • Program offered once per year. Session length: 7–9 days. Departures are scheduled in June, July. Most participants are 30–70 years of age. Participants must be 20 years or older to enroll. Participants must be members of the sponsoring organization (annual dues: $22). Other requirements: must be comfortable following moderate hiking trails. 10 participants per session. Reservations are recommended at least 2 months before departure.

Costs • $510 (includes housing, all meals, insurance, excursions, leadership and some text materials). A $65 deposit is required.

Contact • Lisa Nevar, Nature Excursions Coordinator, Federation of Ontario Naturalists, 355 Lesmill Road, Don Mills, ON M3B 2W8, Canada; 416-444-8419; Fax: 416-444-9866; E-mail: fon@web.apc.org; World Wide Web: http://www.web.net/fon

FEDERATION OF ONTARIO NATURALISTS

CONSERVATION EXPEDITION

General Information • Environmental conservation field work program with visits to Bruce Peninsula. Once at the destination country, participants travel by van. Program is affiliated with British Trust for Conservation Volunteers.

Learning Focus • Field research in botany and human impacts. Escorted travel to natural areas and national parks. Nature observation (volunteer work within nature reserves, excursions to see flora and fauna of Bruce Peninsula). Volunteer work (nature trail building, biological monitoring). Other activities include hiking. Instruction is offered by naturalists, scientists. This program would appeal to people interested in nature studies, environmental issues, botany, the outdoors.

Accommodations • Cabins.

Program Details • Program offered once per year. Session length: 11 days. Departures are scheduled in Spring, Fall. Most participants are 19–44 years of age. Participants must be 17 years or older to enroll. Participants must be members of the sponsoring organization (annual dues: $22). Other requirements: must be able to perform some carrying and lifting. 10 participants per session. Reservations are recommended at least 3 weeks before departure.

Costs • $160 (includes housing, all meals, insurance, excursions).

Contact • Graham Bryan, Natural Areas Projects Coordinator, Federation of Ontario Naturalists, Federation of Ontario Naturalists, 355 Lesmill Road, Don Mills, ON M3B 2W8, Canada; 416-444-8419; Fax: 416-444-9866; E-mail: fon@web.apc.org; World Wide Web: http://www.web.net/fon

FEDERATION OF ONTARIO NATURALISTS

FURTHER AFIELD NATURE EXCURSIONS

General Information • Wilderness/adventure program with visits to Alberta, Northern Ontario, Yukon Territory. Once at the destination country, participants travel by canoe, kayak, or horse. Program is affiliated with Quest Nature Tours.

Learning Focus • Instruction in paddling and riding. Nature observation (flora, fauna). Other activities include camping, hiking, natural history. Instruction is offered by naturalists, outdoor educators. This program would appeal to people interested in wilderness adventure, natural history, canoeing, wildlife, botany, photography, camping.

Accommodations • Hotels, campsites.

Program Details • Program offered 3 times per year. Session length: 6–14 days. Departures are scheduled in July–September. Program is targeted to adults with some experience in wilderness travel. Most participants are 30–55 years of age. Participants must be 20 years or older to enroll. Participants must be members of the sponsoring organization (annual dues: $22). Other requirements: preferably have some previous experience camping, paddling or riding. 10 participants per session. Reservations are recommended at least 2 months before departure.

Costs • $500–$1130 (includes housing, all meals, insurance, excursions). A $130 deposit is required.

Contact • Lisa Nevar, Nature Excursions Coordinator, Federation of Ontario Naturalists, 355 Lesmill Road, Don Mills, ON M3B 2W8, Canada; 416-444-8419; Fax: 416-444-9866; E-mail: fon@web.apc.org; World Wide Web: http://www.web.net/fon

FEDERATION OF ONTARIO NATURALISTS

WILDERNESS CANOE TRIPS

General Information • Wilderness/adventure program with visits to Northern Ontario, Yukon Territory, rivers of Ontario. Once at the destination country, participants travel by canoe.

Learning Focus • Instruction in improving paddling skills. Escorted travel to northern Ontario. Nature observation (bird watching, botany). Other activities include camping, hiking, flatwater or white water paddling, portaging, natural history. Instruction is offered by naturalists, outdoor educators. This program would appeal to people interested in canoeing, botany, natural history, camping, bird watching, photography.

Accommodations • Hotels, campsites.

Program Details • Program offered 10 times per year. Session length: 7–12 days. Departures are scheduled in June–August. Program is targeted to anyone physically fit. Most participants are 18–65 years of age. Participants must be 18 years or older to enroll. Participants must be members

of the sponsoring organization (annual dues: $22). Other requirements: ability to canoe comfortably and participate in short portages. 10 participants per session. Reservations are recommended at least 1 month before departure.
Costs • $450–$850 (includes housing, all meals, insurance, excursions, use of campsite facilities, leadership, equipment). A $100 deposit is required.
Contact • Lisa Nevar, Nature Excursions Coordinator, Federation of Ontario Naturalists, 355 Lesmill Road, Don Mills, ON M3B 2W8, Canada; 416-444-8419; Fax: 416-444-9866; E-mail: fon@web.apc.org; World Wide Web: http://www.web.net/fon

FEDERATION OF ONTARIO NATURALISTS

YOUNG NATURALIST CAMP

General Information • Nature study tour with visits to Algonquin Park, Bruce Peninsula, provincial parks, nature reserves. Once at the destination country, participants travel by bus, foot, canoe.
Learning Focus • Instruction in camping and canoeing skills. Escorted travel to nature reserves. Nature observation (flora, fauna). Other activities include camping, hiking, natural history, camp craft, paddling. Instruction is offered by naturalists, outdoor educators and teachers. This program would appeal to people interested in camping, camp craft, botany, canoeing, nature studies, wildlife.
Accommodations • Dormitories, campsites.
Program Details • Program offered 2 times per year. Session length: 7–9 days. Departures are scheduled in August. Most participants are 11–15 years of age. Participants must be 11 years or older to enroll. Participants must be members of the sponsoring organization (annual dues: $26). 14–24 participants per session. Reservations are recommended at least 2 months before departure.
Costs • $240–$250 (includes housing, all meals, insurance, excursions, leadership, camping equipment, some text materials). A $33 deposit is required.
Contact • Lisa Nevar, Nature Excursions Coordinator, Federation of Ontario Naturalists, 355 Lesmill Road, Don Mills, ON M3B 2W8, Canada; 416-444-8419; Fax: 416-444-9866; E-mail: fon@web.apc.org; World Wide Web: http://www.web.net/fon

FOREIGN LANGUAGE STUDY ABROAD SERVICE

FRENCH IN CANADA

General Information • Language study program in Montréal, Quebec City.
Learning Focus • Courses in language study. Instruction is offered by local teachers.
Accommodations • Homestays, hotels. Single rooms are available. Meals are taken on one's own, with host family, in local restaurants, in residences.
Program Details • Session length: varies. Departures are scheduled in January–December. The program is open to undergraduate students, graduate students, pre-college students, adults. Most participants are 16 years of age and older.
Costs • Contact sponsor for information. Application fee: $50. A $100 deposit is required.
Contact • Louise Harber, Coordinator, Foreign Language Study Abroad Service, Department IH, Box 903, 5935 Southwest 64th Avenue, South Miami, FL 33143; 800-282-1090; Fax: 305-662-2907; E-mail: flsas@netpoint.net; World Wide Web: http://www.netpoint.net/~flsas

FOREIGN LANGUAGE STUDY ABROAD SERVICE

INTERNATIONAL LANGUAGE STUDY HOMESTAYS IN CANADA

General Information • Language study program in Canada.
Learning Focus • Courses in English language. Instruction is offered by local teachers.
Accommodations • Homestays. Single rooms are available. Meals are taken with host family, in residences.
Program Details • Session length: varies. Departures are scheduled in January–December. The program is open to undergraduate students, graduate students, pre-college students, adults. Most participants are 12 years of age and older. Other requirements: students must be at least 12 years old. 1 participant per session.
Costs • Contact sponsor for information. A $300 deposit is required.
Contact • Louise Harber, Coordinator, Foreign Language Study Abroad Service, Department IH, Box 903, 5935 Southwest 64th Avenue, South Miami, FL 33143; 800-282-1090; Fax: 305-662-2907; E-mail: flsas@netpoint.net; World Wide Web: http://www.netpoint.net/~flsas

GEORGE MASON UNIVERSITY

INTENSIVE FRENCH LANGUAGE

General Information • Language study program in Quebec City. Classes are held on the campus of Université Laval.
Learning Focus • Courses in language study, cultural studies. Instruction is offered by local teachers.
Accommodations • Dormitories. Meals are taken as a group, in central dining facility.
Program Details • Program offered once per year. Session length: 4 weeks. Departures are scheduled in July. The program is open to undergraduate students, adults. Most participants are 18–65 years of age. Other requirements: minimum 2.25 GPA. 10–12 participants per session. Application deadline: April 12.
Costs • $2075 for George Mason University students, $2625 for other students (includes tuition, housing, all meals, insurance, excursions). Application fee: $35. A $500 deposit is required.
Contact • Dr. Yehuda Lukacs, Director, Center for Global Education, George Mason University, 4400 University Drive, 235 Johnson Center, Fairfax, VA 22030; 703-993-2155; Fax: 703-993-2153; E-mail: ylukacs@gmu.edu; World Wide Web: http://www.gmu.edu/departments/oie

LANGUAGE LIAISON

FRENCH IN MONTREAL–LSC

General Information • Language study program with visits to Montreal.

Learning Focus • Instruction in the French language. Instruction is offered by professors. This program would appeal to people interested in language.
Accommodations • Homestays, locally-rented apartments, hotels. Single rooms are available.
Program Details • Session length: unlimited. Departures are scheduled throughout the year. Most participants are 18–70 years of age. Participants must be 16 years or older to enroll. Reservations are recommended at least 35 days before departure.
Costs • Contact sponsor for information.
Contact • Nancy Forman, President, Language Liaison, 20533 Biscayne Boulevard-Station 4-162, Miami, FL 33180; 305-682-9909; Fax: 305-682-9907; E-mail: langstudy@aol.com; World Wide Web: http://languageliaison.com

LANGUAGE STUDIES ABROAD

LANGUAGE STUDIES–CANADA

General Information • Language study program with visits to Montreal. Once at the destination country, participants travel by bus, foot.
Learning Focus • Instruction in the French language. Instruction is offered by trained teachers with bachelor's degrees. This program would appeal to people interested in the French language.
Accommodations • Homestays, YMCA. Single rooms are available for an additional $500–$600 for 4 weeks.
Program Details • Session length: 2 or more weeks. Departures are scheduled throughout the year. Most participants are 16–80 years of age. Participants must be 16 years or older to enroll. 12 participants per session. Application deadline: 3 weeks prior to departure. Reservations are recommended at least 2 months before departure.
Costs • $1225–$1325 for 4 weeks (includes tuition, housing, some meals, books and class materials). A $100 deposit is required.
Contact • Charlene Biddulph, Director, Language Studies Abroad, 249 South Highway 101, Suite 226, Solana Beach, CA 92075; 800-424-5522; Fax: 619-943-1201; E-mail: cbiddulph@aol.com; World Wide Web: http://www.dnai.com/~bid/language/

LANGUAGE STUDIES CANADA

INTENSIVE FRENCH: GROUP LESSONS

General Information • Language study program in Montréal. Excursions to Quebec City, Ottawa.
Learning Focus • Courses in French language. Instruction is offered by professors from the sponsoring institution.
Accommodations • Homestays, locally-rented apartments, student residences. Single rooms are available. Meals are taken on one's own, with host family.
Program Details • Session length: 2 or more weeks. Departures are scheduled in January–December. The program is open to undergraduate students, graduate students, adults. Most participants are 18–50 years of age. 75–100 participants per session.
Costs • $390 for 2 weeks (includes tuition, books and class materials).
Contact • Paula Eileen Pereira, Registrar, Language Studies Canada, 1450 City Councillors, Suite 300, Montréal H3H 1P2, Canada; 514-499-9911; Fax: 514-499-0332

LANGUAGE STUDIES CANADA

SUMMER LANGUAGE ADVENTURE

General Information • Language study program in Montréal. Excursions to Quebec City, Ottawa.
Learning Focus • Courses in French language. Instruction is offered by professors from the sponsoring institution.
Accommodations • Homestays, dormitories, locally-rented apartments, hotels, YWCA. Single rooms are available. Meals are taken on one's own, with host family.
Program Details • Program offered 8 times per year. Session length: 2 or more weeks. Departures are scheduled in July, August. The program is open to pre-college students. Most participants are 13–17 years of age.
Costs • $955 for 2 weeks (includes tuition, housing, all meals, books and class materials, insurance, 3 hours of supervised activities daily, bus tickets or pass).
Contact • Paula Eileen Pereira, Registrar, Language Studies Canada, 1450 City Councillors, Suite 300, Montréal H3H 1P2, Canada; 514-499-9911; Fax: 514-499-0332

MARINE EXPEDITIONS

CIRCUMNAVIGATION OF NEWFOUNDLAND

General Information • Wilderness/adventure program with visits to Gros Morne, Harbour Deep, Lanseaux Meadows, Red Bay, St. John's, bird cliffs, archaeological sites, areas of high wildlife concentration. Once at the destination country, participants travel by boat.
Learning Focus • Instruction in history, ornithology and biology. Field research in history, ornithology and biology. Nature observation (wildlife). Other activities include hiking. Instruction is offered by naturalists, historians, scientists. This program would appeal to people interested in nature studies, photography, ornithology.
Accommodations • Boat. Single rooms are available.
Program Details • Program offered 2 times per year. Session length: 1 week. Departures are scheduled in July, August. Most participants are 20–90 years of age. Participants must be 10 years or older to enroll. 80 participants per session.
Costs • $1995 (includes tuition, housing, all meals, excursions, international airfare). A $500 deposit is required.
Contact • Anne Lex, Sales Manager, Marine Expeditions, 13 Hazelton Avenue, Toronto, ON M5R 2E1, Canada; 800-263-9147; Fax: 416-964-9069

MICHIGAN STATE UNIVERSITY

NATURAL SCIENCE PROGRAM IN CANADIAN ROCKIES

General Information • Academic study program in Alberta, Banff, Jasper.
Learning Focus • Courses in natural science, environmental studies. Instruction is offered by professors from the sponsoring institution.
Accommodations • Campsites, lodges. Meals are taken as a group, on one's own, in residences.
Program Details • Program offered 2 times per year. Session length: 4 weeks. Departures are scheduled in July. The program is open to undergraduate students. Most participants are 18–22 years of age. Other requirements: good academic standing and the approval of the director. 14 participants per session. Application deadline: March 14.

Costs • $838 (includes housing, some meals, excursions). Application fee: $75. A $250 deposit is required.
Contact • Brenda S. Sprite, Educational Programs Coordinator, Michigan State University, Office of Study Abroad, 109 International Center, East Lansing, MI 48824-1035; 517-353-8920; Fax: 517-432-2082; E-mail: sprite@pilot.msu.edu; World Wide Web: http://study-abroad.msu.edu

NATIONAL REGISTRATION CENTER FOR STUDY ABROAD

LANGUAGE AND CULTURE IN FRENCH CANADA

General Information • Language study program in Montréal.
Learning Focus • Courses in French language.
Accommodations • Homestays. Single rooms are available. Meals are taken with host family.
Program Details • Program offered 12 times per year. Session length: 4 weeks. Departures are scheduled in January–December. The program is open to undergraduate students, graduate students, adults. 8–12 participants per session.
Costs • $1386 (includes tuition, housing, some meals, insurance).
Contact • Reuel Zielke, Coordinator, National Registration Center for Study Abroad, PO Box 1393, Milwaukee, WI 53201; 414-278-0631; Fax: 414-271-8884; E-mail: inquiries@nrcsa.com; World Wide Web: http://www.nrcsa.com

NATURAL HABITAT ADVENTURES

CHURCHILL SUMMER

General Information • Nature study tour with visits to Churchill, Winnipeg. Once at the destination country, participants travel by train, bus, foot, boat, airplane, tundra buggy.
Learning Focus • Museum visits (Eskimo Museum, Museum of Man and Nature). Nature observation (polar bears, beluga whales, arctic fox, ringed seals, caribou, ptarmigan, gyrfalcon). Instruction is offered by naturalists. This program would appeal to people interested in nature studies, photography, wildlife.
Accommodations • Hotels, sleeper train. Single rooms are available for an additional $395.
Program Details • Program offered 2 times per year. Session length: 9 days. Departures are scheduled in June, July. Participants must be 14 years or older to enroll. 12 participants per session. Reservations are recommended at least 6–12 months before departure.
Costs • Contact sponsor for information. A $500 deposit is required.
Contact • Natural Habitat Adventures, 2945 Center Green Court, Suite H, Boulder, CO 80301; 800-543-8917; Fax: 303-449-3712; E-mail: nathab@worldnet.att.net

NATURAL HABITAT ADVENTURES

POLAR BEAR WATCH

General Information • Nature study tour with visits to Churchill, Northern Studies Centre of Churchill. Once at the destination country, participants travel by bus, airplane.
Learning Focus • Instruction in field observation and bear behavior. Field research in bear behavior and population. Escorted travel to a research center and field sites. Nature observation (polar bears). Instruction is offered by professors, researchers, naturalists, scientists, photographers. This program would appeal to people interested in photography, nature travel, wildlife.
Accommodations • Dormitories, hotels. Single rooms are available for an additional $175.
Program Details • Program offered 2 times per year. Session length: 7–9 days. Departures are scheduled in October, November. Most participants are 32–68 years of age. 12 participants per session. Reservations are recommended at least 8–10 months before departure.
Costs • $2795 (includes housing, all meals, excursions). A $300 deposit is required.
Contact • Natural Habitat Adventures, 2945 Center Green Court, Suite H, Boulder, CO 80301; 800-543-8917; Fax: 303-449-3712

NATURAL HABITAT ADVENTURES

SEAL WATCH

General Information • Nature study tour with visits to Halifax, Magdalen Islands. Once at the destination country, participants travel by airplane, helicopter. Program is affiliated with International Fund for Animal Welfare.
Learning Focus • Instruction in helicopter safety, photography, seal life. Escorted travel to ice floes. Nature observation (whitecoats, baby harp seals). Instruction is offered by naturalists, photographers. This program would appeal to people interested in nature studies, photography, wildlife.
Accommodations • Hotels. Single rooms are available for an additional $255–$285.
Program Details • Program offered 5 times per year. Session length: 5–6 days. Departures are scheduled in February–March. 35 participants per session. Reservations are recommended at least 6–12 months before departure.
Costs • $1695–$3095 (includes housing, some meals, excursions, helicopter transportation, outdoor equipment, guided outdoor activities). A $300 deposit is required.
Contact • Natural Habitat Adventures, 2945 Center Green Court, Suite H, Boulder, CO 80301; 800-543-8917; Fax: 303-449-3712; E-mail: nathab@worldnet.att.net

NATURAL HABITAT ADVENTURES

WOLF QUEST

General Information • Nature study tour with visits to Jack Cartier Park, Quebec City, research station in Jack Cartier Park. Once at the destination country, participants travel by bus, snowmobile and helicopter.
Learning Focus • Instruction in field observation. Field research in wolf and other forest ecology. Escorted travel to wildlife sites. Nature observation (wolves). Instruction is offered by professors, researchers, naturalists, scientists. This program would appeal to people interested in photography, nature travel, wildlife.
Accommodations • Program-owned houses, hotels. Single rooms are available for an additional $100.
Program Details • Program offered 2 times per year. Session length: 8 days. Departures are scheduled in February,

March. Most participants are 30–70 years of age. 8 participants per session. Reservations are recommended at least 10–12 months before departure.
Costs • $1995 (includes housing, all meals, excursions). A $500 deposit is required.
Contact • Natural Habitat Adventures, 2945 Center Green Court, Suite H, Boulder, CO 80301; 800-543-8917; Fax: 303-449-3711

PHOTO ADVENTURE TOURS

CANADIAN ROCKIES

General Information • Photography tour and archaeological tour with visits to Banff, Calgary, Jasper, Lake Louise, Waterton Lake. Once at the destination country, participants travel by bus, foot. Program is affiliated with Sierra Club-Atlantic Division.
Learning Focus • Instruction in photography. Volunteer work (dinosaur dig). Instruction is offered by researchers, naturalists, artists, scientists, photographers. This program would appeal to people interested in photography, archaeology, adventure, geology, hiking.
Accommodations • Hotels. Single rooms are available for an additional $755.
Program Details • Program offered 2 times per year. Session length: 14 days. Departures are scheduled in October. Program is targeted to Sierra Club members. Participants must be members of the sponsoring organization. Application deadline: 2 months prior to departure. Reservations are recommended at least 6 months before departure.
Costs • $2995 (includes housing, all meals, international airfare, membership in Sierra Club). A $400 deposit is required.
Contact • Richard Libbey, General Partner, Photo Adventure Tours, 2035 Park Street, Atlantic Beach, NY 11509-1236; 516-371-0067; Fax: 516-371-1352

SLIPPERY ROCK UNIVERSITY OF PENNSYLVANIA

CANADA SUMMER PROGRAM

General Information • Academic study program in Stratford.
Learning Focus • Courses in Shakespeare. Instruction is offered by professors from the sponsoring institution.
Accommodations • Hotels. Single rooms are available. Meals are taken on one's own, in local restaurants.
Program Details • Program offered once per year. Session length: 2 weeks. Departures are scheduled in June. The program is open to undergraduate students, graduate students, adults. Most participants are 18–60 years of age. Other requirements: minimum 2.5 GPA. 15–30 participants per session. Application deadline: May 1.
Costs • $895 (includes tuition, housing, transportation from Slippery Rock University, theater tickets). A $100 deposit is required.
Contact • Stan Kendziorski, Director of International Studies, Slippery Rock University of Pennsylvania, 110 Eisenberg Building, Slippery Rock, PA 16057; 412-738-2603; Fax: 412-738-2959; E-mail: sjk@sruvm.sru.edu; World Wide Web: http://www.sru.edu

STATE UNIVERSITY OF NEW YORK AT BUFFALO

FRENCH IMMERSION PROGRAM

General Information • Language study program in Trois-Pistoles. Classes are held on the campus of Trois-Pistoles French Immersion School. Excursions to Quebec City.
Learning Focus • Courses in French language, Quebecois culture. Instruction is offered by professors from the sponsoring institution and local teachers.
Accommodations • Homestays. Single rooms are available. Meals are taken with host family, in residences.
Program Details • Program offered once per year. Session length: 3 weeks. Departures are scheduled in June. The program is open to undergraduate students, graduate students, adults. Most participants are 22–53 years of age. Other requirements: minimum 2.5 GPA. 10 participants per session. Application deadline: April 1.
Costs • $1911 for New York residents, $3165 for non-residents (includes tuition, housing, all meals, insurance, excursions, transportation by train from Niagara Falls, Ontario). Application fee: $10. A $200 deposit is required.
Contact • Dr. Lee Ann Grace, Director, International Education, State University of New York at Buffalo, 1300 Elmwood Avenue, Buffalo, NY 14222-1095; 716-878-4620; Fax: 716-878-3054; E-mail: gracela@snybufaa.cs.snybuf.edu; World Wide Web: http://www.snybuf.edu/

STATE UNIVERSITY OF NEW YORK COLLEGE AT BROCKPORT

TORONTO, CANADA HEALTH SCIENCE GRADUATE PROGRAM

General Information • Academic study program in Toronto. Classes are held on the campus of Ryerson Polytechnic Institute.
Learning Focus • Courses in health sciences. Instruction is offered by professors from the sponsoring institution.
Accommodations • Dormitories. Single rooms are available. Meals are taken as a group, in central dining facility, in local restaurants.
Program Details • Program offered once per year. Session length: 1 week. Departures are scheduled in July. The program is open to graduate students. Most participants are 22 years of age and older. Other requirements: health science major. 10–20 participants per session. Application deadline: April 1.
Costs • $1030 (includes tuition, housing, all meals, excursions, transportation). A $75 deposit is required.
Contact • Dr. John J. Perry, Director, International Education, State University of New York College at Brockport, Rakov Center, 350 New Campus Drive, Brockport, NY 14420; 716-395-2119; Fax: 716-637-3218; World Wide Web: http://www.brockport.edu/study_abroad

STATE UNIVERSITY OF NEW YORK COLLEGE AT PLATTSBURGH

SUMMER FRENCH IMMERSION IN MONTREAL AT UNIVERSITÉ DE MONTREAL

General Information • Language study program in Montréal. Classes are held on the campus of Université de Montreal.
Learning Focus • Courses in French language. Instruction is offered by local teachers.
Accommodations • Homestays, dormitories, locally-rented apartments. Single rooms are available. Meals are taken on one's own, with host family, in local restaurants.
Program Details • Program offered 3 times per year. Session length: 3 weeks. Departures are scheduled in May, June, July. The program is open to undergraduate students, graduate students, adults. Most participants are 18–35 years of age. Other requirements: must be 18 years or older and have good academic standing. 15 participants per session. Application deadline: March 15 for May departure or April 1 for July departure.
Costs • $875 (includes tuition, housing, insurance). Application fee: $15. A $100 deposit is required.
Contact • Dodie Giltz, Assistant Director, State University of New York College at Plattsburgh, International Programs, Plattsburgh, NY 12901; 518-564-2086; Fax: 518-564-2112; E-mail: international@plattsburgh.edu; World Wide Web: http://www.plattsburgh.edu

STATE UNIVERSITY OF NEW YORK COLLEGE AT PLATTSBURGH

SUMMER FRENCH IMMERSION IN QUÉBEC CITY AT UNIVERSITÉ LAVAL

General Information • Language study program in Quebec City. Classes are held on the campus of Université Laval.
Learning Focus • Courses in French language. Instruction is offered by local teachers.
Accommodations • Homestays, dormitories, locally-rented apartments. Single rooms are available. Meals are taken on one's own, in local restaurants.
Program Details • Program offered 2 times per year. Session length: 5 weeks. Departures are scheduled in May, July. The program is open to undergraduate students, graduate students, adults. Most participants are 18–25 years of age. Other requirements: must be 18 years or older and have good academic standing. 20 participants per session. Application deadline: March 15 for May departure or April 1 for July departure.
Costs • $1430 (includes tuition, housing, insurance). Application fee: $15. A $100 deposit is required.
Contact • Dodie Giltz, Assistant Director, State University of New York College at Plattsburgh, International Programs, Plattsburgh, NY 12901; 518-564-2086; Fax: 518-564-2112; E-mail: international@plattsburgh.edu; World Wide Web: http://www.plattsburgh.edu

STATE UNIVERSITY OF NEW YORK COLLEGE AT PLATTSBURGH

SUMMER FRENCH IMMERSION PROGRAM IN CHICOUTIMI AT UNIVERSITÉ DU QUÉBEC À CHICOUTIMI

General Information • Language study program in Chicoutimi. Classes are held on the campus of University of Quebec at Chicoutimi. Excursions to Quebec City.
Learning Focus • Courses in French language. Instruction is offered by local teachers.
Accommodations • Homestays. Single rooms are available. Meals are taken with host family.
Program Details • Program offered 4 times per year. Session length: 3–5 weeks. Departures are scheduled in May, June. The program is open to undergraduate students, graduate students, adults. Most participants are 18–55 years of age. Other requirements: must be 18 years or older and have good academic standing. 15 participants per session. Application deadline: March 15 for May departure or April 1 for July departure.
Costs • $1465–$1906 (includes tuition, housing, all meals, insurance). Application fee: $15. A $100 deposit is required.
Contact • Dodie Giltz, Assistant Director, State University of New York College at Plattsburgh, International Programs, Plattsburgh, NY 12901; 518-564-2086; Fax: 518-564-2112; E-mail: international@plattsburgh.edu; World Wide Web: http://www.plattsburgh.edu

TRAVELEARN

A NOVA SCOTIA ADVENTURE: BAY OF FUNDY

General Information • Nature study and cultural tour with visits to Brier Island, Cape Breton, Grand Manan Island, Halifax, Parrsboro, St. John. Once at the destination country, participants travel by bus, foot, boat. Program is affiliated with the nationwide TraveLearn network of 290 universities and colleges.
Learning Focus • Instruction in natural history, ecology and cultural history. Museum visits (The Citadel, Fortress of Louisberg). Attendance at performances (Ship's Company theater). Nature observation (Bay of Fundy). Instruction is offered by professors, researchers, naturalists, historians. This program would appeal to people interested in natural history, ecology, cultural history.
Accommodations • Hotels. Single rooms are available for an additional $695.
Program Details • Program offered 3 times per year. Session length: 15 days. Departures are scheduled in July, August, September. Program is targeted to mature adults. Most participants are 40–75 years of age. Participants must be 18 years or older to enroll. 14–20 participants per session. Application deadline: 60 days prior to departure. Reservations are recommended at least 4–8 months before departure.
Costs • $1995 (includes housing, all meals, books and class materials, excursions). A $300 deposit is required.
Contact • Keith Williams, Director of Marketing, TraveLearn, PO Box 315, Lakeville, PA 18438; 800-235-9114; Fax: 717-226-9114; E-mail: travelearn@aol.com

WILLARDS ADVENTURE CLUB

BACKPACKING EXPEDITION: CANADIAN ROCKIES

General Information • Wilderness/adventure program with visits to Kananaskis, Mount Bourgeous, Ribbon Creek, Buller Pass, Banff National Park, Wonder Pass, Og Lake, Valley of the Rocks, Citadel Pass. Once at the destination country, participants travel by foot.

Learning Focus • Escorted travel to Spray Lake and Assiniboine. Nature observation (mountain scenery, lakes, vistas). Other activities include camping, hiking. Instruction is offered by naturalists, wilderness guides. This program would appeal to people interested in hiking, camping, backpacking.

Accommodations • Campsites. Single rooms are available.

Program Details • Program offered once per year. Session length: 8 days. Departures are scheduled in July. Program is targeted to experienced backpackers. Most participants are 16–60 years of age. Participants must be members of the sponsoring organization (annual dues: $5). Other requirements: excellent physical condition. 20 participants per session. Reservations are recommended at least 3 months before departure.

Costs • $725 (includes housing, some meals). A $50 deposit is required.

Contact • Willard Kinzie, President, Willards Adventure Club, Box 10, Barrie, ON L4M 4S9, Canada; 705-737-1881; Fax: 705-737-5123

WILLARDS ADVENTURE CLUB

BASE CAMP: CANADIAN ROCKIES

General Information • Wilderness/adventure program with visits to Kananaskis, Takakkaw Falls. Once at the destination country, participants travel by foot.

Learning Focus • Escorted travel to the Canadian Rockies. Nature observation (mountain scenery, wildlife). Other activities include camping, hiking. Instruction is offered by naturalists, wilderness guides. This program would appeal to people interested in hiking, camping, backpacking.

Accommodations • Campsites, hostels. Single rooms are available.

Program Details • Program offered once per year. Session length: 7 days. Departures are scheduled in July. Most participants are 9–80 years of age. Participants must be members of the sponsoring organization (annual dues: $5). 20 participants per session. Reservations are recommended at least 3 months before departure.

Costs • $830 (includes housing, some meals). A $50 deposit is required.

Contact • Willard Kinzie, President, Willards Adventure Club, Box 10, Barrie, ON L4M 4S9, Canada; 705-737-1881; Fax: 705-737-5123

CHILE

AMERISPAN UNLIMITED

SPANISH CLASSES AND HOMESTAYS IN CHILE

General Information • Language study program with visits to Santiago.
Learning Focus • Instruction in the Spanish language. Instruction is offered by trained Spanish teachers. This program would appeal to people interested in Spanish language, Latin America.
Accommodations • Homestays. Single rooms are available.
Program Details • Session length: 2–12 weeks. Departures are scheduled throughout the year. Most participants are 16–70 years of age. Participants must be 16 years or older to enroll. 2-3 participants per session. Reservations are recommended at least 4 weeks before departure.
Costs • $995 for 2 weeks, $1795 for 4 weeks, $420 for each additional week (includes tuition, housing, some meals, insurance). A $100 deposit is required.
Contact • AmeriSpan Unlimited, PO Box 40513, Philadelphia, PA 19106; 800-879-6640; Fax: 215-985-4524; E-mail: info@amerispan.com; World Wide Web: http://www.amerispan.com

ARCHAEOLOGICAL TOURS

CHILE AND EASTER ISLAND

General Information • Archaeological tour with visits to Arica, Easter Island, Iquique, San Pedro de Atacama, Santiago. Once at the destination country, participants travel by bus, airplane.
Learning Focus • Escorted travel to Incan fortresses and ruins. Museum visits (historical landmarks). Attendance at performances (dance and music shows). Instruction is offered by professors, historians. This program would appeal to people interested in history, archaeology.
Accommodations • Hotels. Single rooms are available for an additional $470.
Program Details • Program offered once per year. Session length: 14 days. Departures are scheduled in November. Program is targeted to adults. Most participants are 30–80 years of age. 20 participants per session. Application deadline: 1 month prior to departure.
Costs • $3095 (includes housing, some meals, excursions). A $500 deposit is required.
Contact • Archaeological Tours, 271 Madison Avenue, Suite 904, New York, NY 10016; 212-986-3054; Fax: 212-370-1561

COSTA RICA RAINFOREST OUTWARD BOUND SCHOOL

SCHOOL OF ADVENTURE AND CONSERVATION–SURF AND SNOWBOARD

General Information • Sports program with visits to Santiago. Once at the destination country, participants travel by bus, snowboard.
Learning Focus • Instruction in surfing and snow boarding. Instruction is offered by sports professionals.
Accommodations • Homestays, dormitories, hotels.
Program Details • Program offered 2 times per year. Session length: 15 days. Departures are scheduled in June, August. Most participants are 14–22 years of age. Participants must be 14 years or older to enroll. 15 participants per session.
Costs • $6800 (includes tuition, housing, all meals, international airfare). A $500 deposit is required.
Contact • School of Adventure and Conservation, Costa Rica Rainforest Outward Bound School, Student Services, PO Box 243, Quepos, Costa Rica; +506 777-1222; E-mail: crrobs@sol.racsa.co.cr

COUNCIL ON INTERNATIONAL EDUCATIONAL EXCHANGE

COUNCIL STUDY CENTER IN SANTIAGO, CHILE

General Information • Academic study program in Santiago. Classes are held on the campus of Facultad Latinoamencara de Ciencias Sociales (FLACSO-Chile), Catholic University of Chile.
Learning Focus • Courses in Spanish language, social services, gender studies, political science. Instruction is offered by local teachers.
Accommodations • Homestays. Single rooms are available. Meals are taken with host family.
Program Details • Program offered once per year. Session length: 8 weeks. Departures are scheduled in June. The program is open to undergraduate students, graduate students. Other requirements: minimum 2.75 GPA and 4 semesters college-level Spanish. 18 participants per session. Application deadline: April 1.
Costs • $3660 (includes tuition, housing, books and class materials, insurance, excursions, International Student Identification card). Application fee: $30. A $300 deposit is required.
Contact • Lisa Feder, Program Registrar, Council on International Educational Exchange, 205 East 42nd Street, New York, NY 10017-5706; 212-822-2771; E-mail: latinamreg@ciee.org; World Wide Web: http://www.ciee.org

COUNTRY WALKERS

LAKES REGION AND LOFTY PATAGONIA

General Information • Cultural, gourmet cooking, nature study and walking tour with visits to Puerto Montt, Torres del Paine National Park, Peulla, Pontarenas. Once at the destination country, participants travel by foot, boat.
Learning Focus • Escorted travel to Osorno Volclano and Petrohue Waterfalls. Nature observation (long-tailed meadowlarks and Chilean flickers). Other activities include walking. Instruction is offered by professors, researchers, naturalists, historians. This program would appeal to people interested in walking, nature studies, food and wine.
Accommodations • Hotels. Single rooms are available for an additional $300–$600.
Program Details • Program offered 4 times per year. Session length: 12 days. Departures are scheduled in December, January, February, March. Program is targeted to adults 35 to 65 years old. Most participants are 35–65 years of age. Participants must be 18 years or older to enroll. 18 participants per session. Reservations are recommended at least 5–6 months before departure.
Costs • $3200 (includes housing, all meals, excursions).
Contact • Heather Kellingbeck, Vice President, Country Walkers, PO Box 180, Waterbury, VT 05176; 800-464-9255; Fax: 802-244-5661; E-mail: ctrywalk@aol.com

FOREIGN LANGUAGE STUDY ABROAD SERVICE

INTERNATIONAL LANGUAGE STUDY HOMESTAYS IN CHILE

General Information • Language study program in Chile.
Learning Focus • Courses in Spanish language. Instruction is offered by local teachers.
Accommodations • Homestays. Single rooms are available. Meals are taken with host family, in residences.
Program Details • Session length: varies. Departures are scheduled in January–December. The program is open to undergraduate students, graduate students, pre-college students, adults. Most participants are 12 years of age and older. Other requirements: students must be at least 12 years old. 1 participant per session.
Costs • Contact sponsor for information. A $300 deposit is required.
Contact • Louise Harber, Coordinator, Foreign Language Study Abroad Service, Department IH, Box 903, 5935 Southwest 64th Avenue, South Miami, FL 33143; 800-282-1090; Fax: 305-662-2907; E-mail: flsas@netpoint.net; World Wide Web: http://www.netpoint.net/~flsas

FOREIGN LANGUAGE STUDY ABROAD SERVICE

SPANISH IN SANTIAGO

General Information • Language study program in Santiago.
Learning Focus • Courses in language study. Instruction is offered by local teachers.
Accommodations • Homestays, hotels. Single rooms are available. Meals are taken on one's own, with host family, in local restaurants, in residences.
Program Details • Session length: varies. Departures are scheduled in January–December. The program is open to undergraduate students, graduate students, pre-college students, adults. Most participants are 18 years of age and older.
Costs • Contact sponsor for information. Application fee: $50. A $100 deposit is required.
Contact • Louise Harber, Coordinator, Foreign Language Study Abroad Service, Department IH, Box 903, 5935 Southwest 64th Avenue, South Miami, FL 33143; 800-282-1090; Fax: 305-662-2907; E-mail: flsas@netpoint.net; World Wide Web: http://www.netpoint.net/~flsas

FORUM TRAVEL INTERNATIONAL

PATAGONIA AND ATACAMA: GODS, GRAVES, AND GRUMBLING GIANTS

General Information • Wilderness/adventure program with visits to Atacama, Easter Island, Patagonia, Chile's 3 major ecosystems. Once at the destination country, participants travel by train, bus, foot, airplane. Program is affiliated with International Ecosystems University.
Learning Focus • Nature observation (deserts, volcanoes, islands, forests). Other activities include camping, hiking. Instruction is offered by naturalists, mountain guides and anthropologists. This program would appeal to people interested in nature studies, photography.
Accommodations • Program-owned houses, hotels, lodges.
Program Details • Program offered 8 times per year. Session length: 2 weeks. Departures are scheduled throughout the year. Program is targeted to people interested in nature and adventure. Most participants are 18–84 years of age. Participants must be 18 years or older to enroll. 2–20 participants per session.
Costs • $1984 (includes tuition, housing, all meals, excursions). A $300 deposit is required.
Contact • Jeannie Graves, Operations Manager, Forum Travel International, 91 Gregory Lane #21, Pleasant Hill, CA 94525; 510-671-2900; Fax: 510-671-2993; E-mail: forum@ix.netcom.com; World Wide Web: http://www.ten-io.com/forumtravel

GEORGETOWN UNIVERSITY

GEORGETOWN GRADUATE PROGRAM IN SANTIAGO

General Information • Academic study program in Santiago.
Learning Focus • Courses in Latin American studies, comparative politics.
Accommodations • Students make own arrangements. Meals are taken on one's own, in local restaurants.
Program Details • Program offered once per year. Session length: 9 weeks. Departures are scheduled in June. The program is open to graduate students. Most participants are 23–30 years of age. Other requirements: proficiency in Spanish and knowledgable in Latin American studies. Application deadline: March.
Costs • Contact sponsor for information.
Contact • Diana Bartholomew, Center for Latin American Studies, Georgetown University, ICC 484, Washington, DC

20057; 202-687-0144; Fax: 202-687-0141; E-mail: barthold@gunet.georgetown.edu; World Wide Web: http://guweb.georgetown.edu/ssce

GLOBAL EXCHANGE REALITY TOURS

CHILE

General Information • Environment and indigenous peoples study program with visits to Chiloe, Colina, Isla Negra, Santiago, Temuco. Once at the destination country, participants travel by train, bus, airplane.
Learning Focus • Instruction in sustainable development. Museum visits (Pablo Neruda's house in Isla Negra). Other activities include meeting with Mapuche leaders to discuss the future of indigenous groups in Chile. Instruction is offered by researchers, naturalists. This program would appeal to people interested in environmental issues, indigenous cultures.
Accommodations • Hotels, guest houses. Single rooms are available for an additional $200–$500.
Program Details • Program offered 2 times per year. Session length: 17 days. Departures are scheduled in August. Program is targeted to seniors, students and professionals. Participants must be 18 years or older to enroll. 10–15 participants per session. Application deadline: 1 month prior to departure. Reservations are recommended at least 2 months before departure.
Costs • $2000 from Miami, 2200 from San Francisco (includes housing, some meals, books and class materials, international airfare). A $200 deposit is required.
Contact • Reality Tours Coordinator, Global Exchange Reality Tours, 2017 Mission Street, Room 303, San Francisco, CA 94110; 415-255-7296; Fax: 415-255-7498; E-mail: globalexch@igc.apc.org

LANGUAGE LIAISON

LIVE 'N' LEARN (LEARN IN A TEACHER'S HOME)–CHILE

General Information • Language study program with visits to Chile.
Learning Focus • Instruction in the Spanish language. Instruction is offered by professors. This program would appeal to people interested in language.
Accommodations • Homestays. Single rooms are available.
Program Details • Session length: unlimited. Departures are scheduled throughout the year. Most participants are 18–70 years of age. Participants must be 16 years or older to enroll. Reservations are recommended at least 35 days before departure.
Costs • Contact sponsor for information.
Contact • Nancy Forman, President, Language Liaison, 20533 Biscayne Boulevard-Station 4-162, Miami, FL 33180; 305-682-9909; Fax: 305-682-9907; E-mail: langstudy@aol.com; World Wide Web: http://languageliaison.com

LANGUAGE LIAISON

SPANISH IN CHILE

General Information • Language study program with visits to Chile.
Learning Focus • Instruction in the Spanish language. Instruction is offered by professors. This program would appeal to people interested in language.
Accommodations • Homestays, locally-rented apartments, hotels. Single rooms are available.
Program Details • Session length: unlimited. Departures are scheduled throughout the year. Program is targeted to students of any age. Most participants are 18–70 years of age. Participants must be 16 years or older to enroll. Reservations are recommended at least 35 days before departure.
Costs • Contact sponsor for information.
Contact • Nancy Forman, President, Language Liaison, 20533 Biscayne Boulevard-Station 4-162, Miami, FL 33180; 305-682-9909; Fax: 305-682-9907; E-mail: langstudy@aol.com; World Wide Web: http://languageliaison.com

NATIONAL REGISTRATION CENTER FOR STUDY ABROAD

LANGUAGE AND CULTURE IN CHILE

General Information • Language study program in Santiago.
Learning Focus • Courses in Spanish language.
Accommodations • Homestays. Single rooms are available. Meals are taken with host family.
Program Details • Program offered 24 times per year. Session length: 4 weeks. Departures are scheduled in January–December. The program is open to undergraduate students, graduate students, adults. 6–8 participants per session. Application deadline: 40 days prior to departure.
Costs • Contact sponsor for information. Application fee: $40. A $100 deposit is required.
Contact • June Domoe, Educational Consultant, National Registration Center for Study Abroad, PO Box 1393, Milwaukee, WI 53201; 414-278-0631; Fax: 414-271-8884; E-mail: inquiries@nrcsa.com; World Wide Web: http://www.nrcsa.com

NATURE EXPEDITIONS INTERNATIONAL

CHILE AND EASTER ISLAND EXPEDITION

General Information • Cultural tour with visits to Easter Island, Lake District, Puerto Montt, Santiago. Once at the destination country, participants travel by airplane, mini-van.
Learning Focus • Escorted travel to Santiago, Lake District, Puerto Montt and Easter Island. Instruction is offered by naturalists, historians, archaeologists and anthropologists. This program would appeal to people interested in ancient cultures, archaeology, natural history, anthropology.
Accommodations • Hotels. Single rooms are available for an additional $500.
Program Details • Program offered once per year. Session length: 17 days. Departures are scheduled in January. Most participants are 25–75 years of age. Other requirements:

doctor's permission for participants 70 years and older. Reservations are recommended at least 6 months before departure.

Costs • $2890 (includes housing, some meals, excursions, all guiding). A $400 deposit is required.

Contact • Christopher Kyle, President, Nature Expeditions International, 6400 East El Dorado Circle, Suite 210, Tucson, AZ 85715; 800-869-0639; Fax: 520-721-6719; E-mail: naturexp@aol.com

UNIVERSITY OF ILLINOIS AT URBANA-CHAMPAIGN

SUMMER SPANISH LANGUAGE PROGRAM IN CHILE

General Information • Language study program in Valparaíso. Classes are held on the campus of Catholic University of Valparaíso. Excursions to Santiago, Isla Negra, Pomaire, La Serena.

Learning Focus • Courses in Spanish language, social and political issues, contemporary Chilean literature. Instruction is offered by local teachers.

Accommodations • Homestays. Meals are taken with host family, in residences.

Program Details • Program offered once per year. Session length: 6 weeks. Departures are scheduled in June. The program is open to undergraduate students, graduate students. Most participants are 18–25 years of age. Other requirements: 4 semesters college-level Spanish or equivalent and a B average. 15 participants per session. Application deadline: March 1.

Costs • $3000 (includes tuition, housing, some meals, excursions, medical emergency evacuation insurance, resident director). Application fee: $35. A $500 deposit is required.

Contact • Timothy Winkler, Program Coordinator, University of Illinois at Urbana-Champaign, Study Abroad Office, 910 South Fifth Street #115, Champaign, IL 61820; 800-531-4404; Fax: 217-244-0249; E-mail: ipa@uiuc.edu

VILLANOVA UNIVERSITY

SUMMER LATIN AMERICAN STUDIES PROGRAM

General Information • Academic study program in Valparaíso. Classes are held on the campus of Universidad de Playa Ancha. Excursions to Santiago, Valle Nevado, Vina del Mar.

Learning Focus • Courses in Spanish language, Spanish-American literature, Spanish-American history, Spanish-American people, Spanish-American culture. Instruction is offered by local teachers.

Accommodations • Homestays. Single rooms are available. Meals are taken with host family, in local restaurants.

Program Details • Program offered once per year. Session length: 6 weeks. Departures are scheduled in July. The program is open to undergraduate students. Most participants are 19–23 years of age. Other requirements: minimum 2.5 GPA and good academic standing. 12 participants per session. Application deadline: March 1.

Costs • $2750 (includes tuition, housing, all meals, books and class materials, excursions, transfers and orientation). Application fee: $100.

Contact • Dr. Thomas M. Ricks, Director, International Studies, Villanova University, St. Augustine Center, Room 415, Villanova, PA 19085; 610-519-6412; Fax: 610-519-7649; E-mail: ricks@ucis.vill.edu

COSTA RICA

AMERICAN JEWISH CONGRESS, INTERNATIONAL TRAVEL PROGRAM

COSTA RICA

General Information • Cultural tour with visits to San José, Orosi Valley, Ujarras, Lankester Botanical Gardens, butterfly farm, Carrara Biological Reserve, Poas Volcano. Once at the destination country, participants travel by bus, foot.
Learning Focus • Escorted travel to synagogues, National Theatre and coffee factory. Nature observation (fauna, flora, birds, craters). Instruction is offered by naturalists, historians. This program would appeal to people interested in Jewish history.
Accommodations • Hotels. Single rooms are available for an additional $460.
Program Details • Program offered 8 times per year. Session length: 8 days. Departures are scheduled in January–May, September–November. Program is targeted to Jewish-American adults. Most participants are 40–75 years of age. Participants must be 15 years or older to enroll. Participants must be members of the sponsoring organization (annual dues: $50). 30 participants per session. Reservations are recommended at least 6 months before departure.
Costs • $1995 (includes housing, some meals, excursions, international airfare, travel bag, documents portfolio, travel journal). A $200 deposit is required.
Contact • Betty Van Dyke, Worldwide Operations Manager, American Jewish Congress, International Travel Program, 18 East 84th Street, New York, NY 10028; 212-360-1571; Fax: 212-717-1932

AMERICAN JEWISH CONGRESS, INTERNATIONAL TRAVEL PROGRAM

COSTA RICA HOLIDAY CELEBRATION

General Information • Cultural tour with visits to Puntarenas, San José, Moravia, Gulf of Nicoya, Tortuga, Orosi Valley, Carrara Biological Reserve. Once at the destination country, participants travel by bus, foot, boat.
Learning Focus • Escorted travel to synagogues, National Theatre and Póas Volcano. Other activities include whitewater rafting, New Year's Eve Dinner. Instruction is offered by naturalists. This program would appeal to people interested in Jewish history.
Accommodations • Hotels. Single rooms are available for an additional $525.
Program Details • Program offered once per year. Session length: 8 days. Departures are scheduled in December. Program is targeted to Jewish-American adults. Most participants are 20–45 years of age. Participants must be 15 years or older to enroll. Participants must be members of the sponsoring organization (annual dues: $50). Reservations are recommended at least 6 months before departure.
Costs • $2295 (includes housing, some meals, excursions, international airfare, travel bag, documents portfolio, travel journal). A $200 deposit is required.
Contact • Betty Van Dyke, Worldwide Operations Manager, American Jewish Congress, International Travel Program, 18 East 84th Street, New York, NY 10028; 212-360-1571; Fax: 212-717-1932

 AMERISPAN UNLIMITED

SPANISH CLASSES AND HOMESTAYS IN COSTA RICA

General Information • Language study program with visits to Alajuela, Escazu, Heredia, Manuel Antonio, San José, beaches, volcanoes, rain forests. Once at the destination country, participants travel by bus.
Learning Focus • Instruction in the Spanish language. Instruction is offered by trained Spanish teachers. This program would appeal to people interested in Spanish language, Latin America.
Accommodations • Homestays. Single rooms are available.
Program Details • Session length: 2–12 weeks. Departures are scheduled throughout the year. Most participants are 16–70 years of age. Participants must be 16 years or older to enroll. 4–6 participants per session. Reservations are recommended at least 4 weeks before departure.
Costs • Contact sponsor for information. A $100 deposit is required.
Contact • AmeriSpan Unlimited, PO Box 40513, Philadelphia, PA 19106; 800-879-6640; Fax: 215-985-4524; E-mail: info@amerispan.com; World Wide Web: http://www.amerispan.com

CENTRAL AMERICAN INSTITUTE FOR INTERNATIONAL AFFAIRS (ICAI)

SPANISH LANGUAGE IN COSTA RICA

General Information • Language study program with visits to San José, Tortuguero, Monteverde Cloud Forest, Arenal Volcano, Cahuita National Park. Once at the destination country, participants travel by bus, foot, boat, airplane.
Learning Focus • Instruction in the Spanish language. Other activities include hiking. Instruction is offered by professors. This program would appeal to people interested in photography, marine biology, zoology, bird watching, hiking, botany, fishing, scuba diving and snorkeling.
Accommodations • Homestays, locally-rented apartments, hotels. Single rooms are available for an additional $20 per day.

Program Details • Session length: 4 weeks. Departures are scheduled throughout the year. Most participants are 16–85 years of age. Participants must be 16 years or older to enroll. Other requirements: must be over 16 years old. 6 participants per session. Application deadline: 15 days prior to departure. Reservations are recommended at least 30 days before departure.
Costs • $1298 (includes tuition, housing, all meals, books and class materials, excursions). A $100 deposit is required.
Contact • Bill Fagan, Director, Central American Institute for International Affairs (ICAI), 13948 Hemlock Drive, Penn Valley, CA 95946; 916-432-7690; Fax: 916-432-7615; E-mail: bfaglsec@nccn.net; World Wide Web: http://www.expreso.co.cr/icai/index.htm

COLLEGE CONSORTIUM FOR INTERNATIONAL STUDIES–MIAMI-DADE COMMUNITY COLLEGE

INTENSIVE SPANISH IN COSTA RICA

General Information • Language study program in Santa Ana. Classes are held on the campus of Centra Linguístico CONVERSA.
Learning Focus • Courses in Spanish language. Instruction is offered by local teachers.
Accommodations • Homestays, lodges. Single rooms are available. Meals are taken with host family, in central dining facility.
Program Details • Program offered 13 times per year. Session length: 4 weeks. Departures are scheduled in January–December. The program is open to undergraduate students, adults. Most participants are 18–75 years of age. Other requirements: minimum 2.5 GPA. Application deadline: rolling.
Costs • $2240 (includes tuition, housing, all meals, books and class materials). Application fee: $25. A $350 deposit is required.
Contact • Jane C. Evans, Executive Director, College Consortium for International Studies, 2000 P Street, NW, Suite 503, Washington, DC 20036; 800-453-6956; Fax: 202-223-0999; E-mail: ccis@intr.net

COSTA RICA RAINFOREST OUTWARD BOUND SCHOOL

KAYAK AND WHITE WATER COURSES

General Information • Sports program with visits to Costa Rica. Once at the destination country, participants travel by boat.
Learning Focus • Instruction in rafting and kayaking. Instruction is offered by naturalists.
Accommodations • Homestays, dormitories, hotels.
Program Details • Program offered 7 times per year. Session length: 2 weeks. Departures are scheduled in December–August. Most participants are 14–22 years of age. Participants must be 14 years or older to enroll. 4–8 participants per session.
Costs • $1795 (includes tuition, housing, all meals, excursions). A $200 deposit is required.
Contact • Student Services, Costa Rica Rainforest Outward Bound School, PO Box 243, Quepos, Costa Rica; +506 777-1222; E-mail: crrobs@sol.racsa.co.cr

COSTA RICA RAINFOREST OUTWARD BOUND SCHOOL

MULTI-ELEMENT COURSES

General Information • Wilderness/adventure program with visits to Costa Rica.
Learning Focus • Instruction in climbing, rafting and hiking. Other activities include camping, hiking, village homestays, community service, beach activities, kayaking. Instruction is offered by naturalists, sports professionals. This program would appeal to people interested in adventure, anthropology, travel, Spanish language.
Accommodations • Homestays, campsites.
Program Details • Session length: 2–4 weeks. Departures are scheduled throughout the year. Program is targeted to teens and university students. Most participants are 15–22 years of age. Participants must be 6 years or older to enroll. 8–12 participants per session. Reservations are recommended at least 30 days before departure.
Costs • $1695 for 2 weeks, $2895 for 4 weeks (includes tuition, housing, all meals, excursions). A $200 deposit is required.
Contact • Student Services, Costa Rica Rainforest Outward Bound School, PO Box 247, Quepos, Costa Rica; +506 777-1222; E-mail: crrobs@sol.racsa.co.cr

COSTA RICA RAINFOREST OUTWARD BOUND SCHOOL

SURF CAMP

General Information • Sports program with visits to Dominica, Manuel Antonio, Roca Biva. Once at the destination country, participants travel by jeep.
Learning Focus • Instruction in surfing. Other activities include kayaking, river rafting. Instruction is offered by sports professionals. This program would appeal to people interested in surfing, boogie boarding.
Accommodations • Homestays, dormitories, locally-rented apartments.
Program Details • Program offered 7 times per year. Session length: 15–30 days. Departures are scheduled in December–August. Program is targeted to people in their teens to early 20's. Participants must be 14 years or older to enroll. 4–6 participants per session.
Costs • $1795 for 15 days, $2815 for 30 days (includes tuition, housing, all meals, surf instruction). A $200 deposit is required.
Contact • Student Services, Costa Rica Rainforest Outward Bound School, PO Box 243, Quepos, Costa Rica; +506 777-1222

COUNCIL ON INTERNATIONAL EDUCATIONAL EXCHANGE

COUNCIL STUDY CENTER FOR ECOLOGY OF THE RAINFOREST: TROPICAL BIOLOGY AND CONSERVATION AT THE MONTEVERDE INSTITUTE

General Information • Academic study program in Monteverde. Classes are held on the campus of Monteverde Institute. Excursions to Santa Rosa, Pacific coast, Carcovado, Penas Blancas.

Learning Focus • Courses in tropical biology, agroecology, Spanish language. Instruction is offered by professors from the sponsoring institution and local teachers.

Accommodations • Homestays, dormitories, biological field stations. Meals are taken as a group, with host family, in central dining facility.

Program Details • Program offered once per year. Session length: 8 weeks. Departures are scheduled in June. The program is open to undergraduate students, graduate students. Most participants are 19–22 years of age. Other requirements: 2 sequential courses in biology and a minimum 2.75 GPA. 25 participants per session. Application deadline: April 1.

Costs • $3995 (includes tuition, housing, all meals, books and class materials, insurance, excursions, International Student Identification card). Application fee: $30. A $300 deposit is required.

Contact • Lisa Feder, Program Registrar, Council on International Educational Exchange, College and University Division, 205 East 42nd Street, New York, NY 10017-5706; 212-822-2771; E-mail: latinamreg@ciee.org; World Wide Web: http://www.ciee.org

COUNTRY WALKERS

RAINFOREST ADVENTURE

General Information • Cultural, gourmet cooking, nature study and walking tour with visits to Central Valley, Arenal Observatory Lodge, Monte Verde Cloud Forest, Nicoya peninsula. Once at the destination country, participants travel by foot, boat.

Learning Focus • Escorted travel to primary rain forest and Tabacon Springs. Nature observation (bird watching, various ecological zones). Other activities include walking. Instruction is offered by professors, researchers, naturalists, historians. This program would appeal to people interested in walking, food and wine, nature studies.

Accommodations • Hotels. Single rooms are available for an additional $300–$600.

Program Details • Program offered 8 times per year. Session length: 8 days. Departures are scheduled in January, February, March, April. Program is targeted to adults 35 to 65 years old. Most participants are 35–65 years of age. Participants must be 18 years or older to enroll. 18 participants per session. Reservations are recommended at least 5–6 months before departure.

Costs • $1800 (includes housing, all meals, excursions). A $400 deposit is required.

Contact • Heather Kellingbeck, Vice President, Country Walkers, PO Box 180, Waterbury, VT 05176; 800-464-9255; Fax: 802-244-5661; E-mail: ctrywalk@aol.com

CULTURAL EXPERIENCES ABROAD

SPANISH LANGUAGE AND LATIN AMERICAN STUDIES IN COSTA RICA

General Information • Academic study program in San José. Classes are held on the campus of Forester Institute. Excursions to Poás volcano, Irazú volcano, Bravilio Carrilo rain forest, Orosi Valley.

Learning Focus • Courses in Spanish language, Latin American studies, tropical field research, education. Instruction is offered by local teachers.

Accommodations • Homestays, hotels. Single rooms are available. Meals are taken in local restaurants, in residences.

Program Details • Session length: 2–4 weeks. Departures are scheduled in January–December. The program is open to undergraduate students, graduate students, pre-college students, adults. Most participants are 18–55 years of age. Other requirements: minimum 2.75 GPA, recommendation, minimum age 18. 5–10 participants per session. Application deadline: 3 months prior to departure.

Costs • $1895 for 4 weeks (includes tuition, housing, all meals, books and class materials, insurance, excursions, International Student Identification card, orientation). A $200 deposit is required.

Contact • Sharon Dahlen, Program Coordinator, Cultural Experiences Abroad, 5319 West Patterson Avenue, Chicago, IL 60641; 800-266-4441; Fax: 773-725-9256; E-mail: ceabroad@aol.com

ESCUELA LATINA DE LENGUAS

ESCUELA LATINA DE LENGUAS

General Information • Language study program in Barva de Heredia. Excursions to Volcán Arenal, Monte Verde, Manuel Antonio beach, Tortuguero.

Learning Focus • Courses in Spanish language, Latin music, Latin dance, Costa Rican cooking, cultural studies. Instruction is offered by professors from the sponsoring institution.

Accommodations • Homestays, hotels, aparthotels. Single rooms are available. Meals are taken with host family.

Program Details • Program offered 52 times per year. Session length: unlimited, typically 1–4 weeks. Departures are scheduled in January–December. The program is open to undergraduate students, graduate students, pre-college students, adults, people of all ages. Most participants are 16–50 years of age. 15–30 participants per session. Application deadline: 2 weeks prior to departure.

Costs • $255 per week, $875 per month (includes tuition, housing, some meals, books and class materials, some excursions). A $100 deposit is required.

Contact • Roger Dewey, Program Coordinator, Escuela Latina de Lenguas, 720 Pebble Hill Lane, Prescott, AZ 86303; 520-776-7189; Fax: 520-445-2546

EXPERIENCE PLUS SPECIALTY TOURS, INC.

COSTA RICA: BUTTERFLIES, BICYCLES, AND BEACHES

General Information • Bicycle tour with visits to Alajuela, La Fortuna, Nicoya, Sámara, Sarchí, rain forests, Arenal

Volcano, hot springs, Palo Verde National Park. Once at the destination country, participants travel by bicycle.
Learning Focus • Escorted travel to Costa Rica. Nature observation (wildlife cruise and escorted rainforest walk). Other activities include bicycling, bird watching, wildlife viewing. Instruction is offered by indigenous, bilingual and bi-cultural guides. This program would appeal to people interested in wildlife, geography, bicycling, travel, culture, Costa Rica.
Accommodations • Hotels. Single rooms are available for an additional $300.
Program Details • Program offered 5 times per year. Session length: 9 days. Departures are scheduled in January, February, March, November, December. Most participants are 35–70 years of age. 16–22 participants per session. Reservations are recommended at least 6–12 months before departure.
Costs • $1595 (includes housing, some meals, excursions, shuttle at end of tour, rental bike, 28 oz. water bottle, luggage shuttle, van support, bilingual/bi-cultural tour leaders). A $250 deposit is required.
Contact • Experience Plus Specialty Tours, Inc., 1925 Wallenberg Drive, Fort Collins, CO 80526; 800-685-4565; Fax: 800-685-4565; E-mail: tours@xplus.com

FOREIGN LANGUAGE STUDY ABROAD SERVICE

INTERNATIONAL LANGUAGE STUDY HOMESTAYS IN COSTA RICA

General Information • Language study program in Costa Rica.
Learning Focus • Courses in Spanish language. Instruction is offered by local teachers.
Accommodations • Homestays. Single rooms are available. Meals are taken with host family, in residences.
Program Details • Session length: varies. Departures are scheduled in January–December. The program is open to undergraduate students, graduate students, pre-college students, adults. Most participants are 12 years of age and older. Other requirements: students must be at least 12 years old. 1 participant per session.
Costs • Contact sponsor for information. A $300 deposit is required.
Contact • Louise Harber, Coordinator, Foreign Language Study Abroad Service, Department IH, Box 903, 5935 Southwest 64th Avenue, South Miami, FL 33143; 800-282-1090; Fax: 305-662-2907; E-mail: flsas@netpoint.net; World Wide Web: http://www.netpoint.net/~flsas

FOREIGN LANGUAGE STUDY ABROAD SERVICE

SPANISH IN SAN JOSÉ

General Information • Language study program in San José.
Learning Focus • Courses in language study. Instruction is offered by local teachers.
Accommodations • Homestays, hotels. Single rooms are available. Meals are taken on one's own, with host family, in local restaurants, in residences.
Program Details • Session length: varies. Departures are scheduled in January–December. The program is open to undergraduate students, graduate students, pre-college students, adults. Most participants are 16 years of age and older.
Costs • Contact sponsor for information. Application fee: $50. A $100 deposit is required.
Contact • Louise Harber, Coordinator, Foreign Language Study Abroad Service, Department IH, Box 903, 5935 Southwest 64th Avenue, South Miami, FL 33143; 800-282-1090; Fax: 305-662-2907; E-mail: flsas@netpoint.net; World Wide Web: http://www.netpoint.net/~flsas

FORESTER INSTITUTO INTERNACIONAL

FORESTER INSTITUTO INTERNACIONAL

General Information • Language study program with visits to San José. Once at the destination country, participants travel by bus, foot.
Learning Focus • Instruction in Spanish language. Escorted travel to rainforests, volcanoes. Instruction is offered by professors. This program would appeal to people interested in language.
Accommodations • Homestays, locally-rented apartments, hotels. Single rooms are available for an additional $130 per week.
Program Details • Session length: 2–12 weeks. Departures are scheduled throughout the year. Program is targeted to students, teachers, professionals, seniors. Most participants are 20–60 years of age. Participants must be 16 years or older to enroll. 6 participants per session. Reservations are recommended at least 1–2 months before departure.
Costs • $675–$815 for 2 weeks (includes tuition, housing, some meals, books and class materials). A $200 deposit is required.
Contact • Horacio Loprete, Director, Forester Instituto Internacional, Los Yoses, Del Automercado, 75 Sur, San Jose, Costa Rica; +506 225-3155; Fax: +506 225-9236; E-mail: forester@sol.racsa.co.cr

FORUM TRAVEL INTERNATIONAL

EXOTIC COSTA RICA

General Information • Nature study tour with visits to Cahuita Marine Reserve, Corcavado, Guanacaste, Monteverde, Osa Peninsula, Tortuguero. Once at the destination country, participants travel by bus, foot, boat, airplane. Program is affiliated with International Ecosystems University.
Learning Focus • Escorted travel to main sites in Costa Rica. Nature observation (ecosystems and exotic sites). Instruction is offered by professors, naturalists. This program would appeal to people interested in nature studies, wildlife.
Accommodations • Program-owned houses, hotels, campsites.
Program Details • Program offered 12 times per year. Session length: 10 days. Departures are scheduled throughout the year. Most participants are 16–84 years of age. 20 participants per session.
Costs • $1495 (includes tuition, housing, some meals, excursions, international airfare). A $200 deposit is required.

Contact • Jeannie Graves, Operations Manager, Forum Travel International, 91 Gregory Lane #21, Pleasant Hill, CA 94525; 510-671-2900; Fax: 510-671-2993; E-mail: forum@ix.netcom.com; World Wide Web: http://www.ten-io.com/forumtravel

GEO EXPEDITIONS

THE BEST OF COSTA RICA

General Information • Nature study tour with visits to Arenal Volcano, Corcavado National Park, Monteverde Reserve, San José. Once at the destination country, participants travel by bus, foot, airplane.
Learning Focus • Nature observation (naturalist-guided jungle walks). Instruction is offered by naturalists. This program would appeal to people interested in rain forest studies, wildlife, ecology.
Accommodations • Hotels, jungle lodges. Single rooms are available for an additional $320.
Program Details • Session length: 9 days. Departures are scheduled throughout the year. Most participants are 30–70 years of age. Participants must be 10 years or older to enroll. 8 participants per session. Reservations are recommended at least 6 months before departure.
Costs • $1545 (includes housing, some meals, excursions). A $300 deposit is required.
Contact • David Risard, President, GEO Expeditions, PO Box 3656, Sonora, CA 95370; 800-351-5041; Fax: 209-532-1979; E-mail: geoexped@mlode.com

GEO EXPEDITIONS

COSTA RICA EXPLORER

General Information • Nature study tour with visits to Arenal Volcano, Monteverde Reserve, San José, Tortuguero National Park. Once at the destination country, participants travel by bus, foot, airplane.
Learning Focus • Nature observation (naturalist-guided tours). Instruction is offered by naturalists. This program would appeal to people interested in rain forest studies, wildlife, ecology.
Accommodations • Hotels, jungle lodges. Single rooms are available for an additional $342.
Program Details • Session length: 10 days. Departures are scheduled throughout the year. Most participants are 30–70 years of age. Participants must be 10 years or older to enroll. 12 participants per session.
Costs • $1498–$1698 (includes housing, some meals, excursions). A $300 deposit is required.
Contact • David Risard, President, GEO Expeditions, PO Box 3656, Sonora, CA 95370; 800-351-5041; Fax: 209-532-1979; E-mail: geoexped@mlode.com

INSTITUTO PROFESIONAL DE ESPAÑOL PARA EXTRANJEROS

PROFESSIONAL COURSES IN LATIN AMERICA

General Information • Academic study program in San José.
Learning Focus • Courses in imports and exports, medical, international relations, finance, telecommunications, Latin American marketing, political science, ecotourism. Instruction is offered by professors from the sponsoring institution.
Accommodations • Homestays, locally-rented apartments, hotels. Single rooms are available. Meals are taken on one's own, with host family, in local restaurants, in residences.
Program Details • Session length: 2–4 weeks. Departures are scheduled in January–December. The program is open to undergraduate students, graduate students, pre-college students, adults. Most participants are 21–65 years of age. Application deadline: 3 weeks prior to departure.
Costs • $855–$1620 1–4 weeks (includes tuition, housing, some meals, books and class materials, excursions). A $200 deposit is required.
Contact • Robert Levy, Director, Instituto Profesional de Español para Extranjeros, 16057 Tampa Palms Boulevard, Suite 158, Tampa, FL 33647; 813-988-3916; Fax: 813-988-3916; E-mail: ipee@gate.net; World Wide Web: http://www.gate.net/~ipee/

The principal objective of IPEE is the teaching of Spanish as a second language, along with introducing the student to the cultural values and natural wealth that our country offers. IPEE was created as a response to the need that Costa Rica has for a serious and professional language school that offers, in addition to the customary language courses that are taught in this country, a more specialized and personalized program. IPEE's teaching methods emphasize communication, and to this end, the most modern techniques are used, with didactic materials, audiovisuals, and books written by the Institute's professors as well as field trips and excursions.

INSTITUTO PROFESIONAL DE ESPAÑOL PARA EXTRANJEROS

SPANISH LANGUAGE IMMERSION SCHOOL

General Information • Language study program in San José.
Learning Focus • Courses in Spanish language, Latin American cultures. Instruction is offered by professors from the sponsoring institution.
Accommodations • Homestays, aparthotels, hotels. Single rooms are available. Meals are taken with host family, in residences.
Program Details • Program offered 50 times per year. Session length: 2 weeks–2 months. Departures are scheduled in January–December. The program is open to undergraduate students, graduate students, pre-college students, adults. Most participants are 16–70 years of age. 6 participants per session. Application deadline: 2 weeks prior to departure.
Costs • $560–$1020 2–4 weeks (includes tuition, housing, some meals, books and class materials). A $200 deposit is required.

Contact • Mr. Robert Levy, Director, Instituto Profesional de Español para Extranjeros, 16057 Tampa Palms Boulevard, Suite 158, Tampa, FL 33647; 813-988-3916; Fax: 813-988-3916; E-mail: ipee@gate.net; World Wide Web: http://www.gate.net/~ipee/

INSTITUTO PROFESIONAL DE ESPAÑOL PARA EXTRANJEROS

SPANISH TEACHERS COURSES

General Information • Language study program in San José.
Learning Focus • Courses in methodology, motivation. Instruction is offered by professors from the sponsoring institution.
Accommodations • Homestays, locally-rented apartments. Single rooms are available. Meals are taken with host family, in residences.
Program Details • Program offered 25 times per year. Session length: 2 weeks. Departures are scheduled in January–December. The program is open to undergraduate students, graduate students, adults, Spanish teachers. Most participants are 25–45 years of age. 3–4 participants per session. Application deadline: 3 weeks prior to departure.
Costs • $800 (includes tuition, housing, some meals, books and class materials). A $200 deposit is required.
Contact • Robert Levy, Director, Instituto Profesional de Español para Extranjeros, 16057 Tampa Palms Boulevard, Suite 158, Tampa, FL 33647; 813-988-3916; Fax: 813-988-3916; E-mail: ipee@gate.net; World Wide Web: http://www.gate.net/~ipee/

INTERCULTURA COSTA RICA

INTENSIVE SPANISH WITH CULTURAL ACTIVITIES

General Information • Language study program in Heredia. Excursions to Arenal volcano, Monteverde Cloud Forest, Tortuguero Jungle Canals, Manuel Antonio National Park, Pacuare River, Tortuga Island.
Learning Focus • Courses in Spanish language, Latin dance, literature. Instruction is offered by professors from the sponsoring institution.
Accommodations • Homestays, locally-rented apartments, hotels. Single rooms are available. Meals are taken with host family.
Program Details • Program offered 20 times per year. Session length: 1 week–2 months. Departures are scheduled in January–December. The program is open to undergraduate students, graduate students, pre-college students, adults. Most participants are 18–60 years of age. Other requirements: minimum age of 15. 30 participants per session. Application deadline: 3 weeks prior to departure.
Costs • $960 per month (includes tuition, housing, some meals, class materials).
Contact • Laura Ellington, Co-Director, Intercultura Costa Rica, Apartado 1952-3000, Heredia, Costa Rica; +506 260-8480; Fax: +506 260-9243; E-mail: intercul@sol.racsa.co.cr

INTERHOSTEL, UNIVERSITY OF NEW HAMPSHIRE

COSTA RICA

General Information • Cultural tour with visits to Monteverde, Puerto Viejo, San José, Orosi River Valley, Cartago, Guayabo, Poas Volcano, Lankester Botanical Gardens, Cahuita, Limon. Once at the destination country, participants travel by bus, foot. Program is affiliated with Cemanahuac Educational Community.
Learning Focus • Instruction in history and culture. Escorted travel to villages and landmarks. Museum visits (Gold Museum, Jade Museum, Art Museum). Attendance at performances (Costa Rican music). Instruction is offered by naturalists, historians. This program would appeal to people interested in history, culture.
Accommodations • Hotels. Single rooms are available for an additional $450.
Program Details • Program offered 2 times per year. Session length: 2 weeks. Departures are scheduled in January, March. Program is targeted to seniors over 50. Most participants are 60–80 years of age. Participants must be 50 years or older to enroll. 35 participants per session. Reservations are recommended at least 6 months before departure.
Costs • $2650 (includes tuition, housing, all meals, excursions, international airfare, entrance fees). A $200 deposit is required.
Contact • Janice Pierson, Office Supervisor, Interhostel, University of New Hampshire, 6 Garrison Avenue, Durham, NH 03824; 800-733-9753; Fax: 603-862-1113; World Wide Web: http://www.learn.unh.edu/

JOURNEYS INTERNATIONAL, INC.

ATLANTIC ADVENTURE WEEK

General Information • Wilderness/adventure program with visits to Poas Region, Rara Avis, San José, Selva Verde, Tortuguero. Once at the destination country, participants travel by bus, hiking.
Learning Focus • Escorted travel to Tortuguero canals and Poas Volcano. Nature observation (sea turtles). Other activities include hiking. Instruction is offered by naturalists, native English-speaking guides. This program would appeal to people interested in photography, nature studies, bird watching, wildlife.
Accommodations • Hotels. Single rooms are available for an additional $175.
Program Details • Program offered 12 times per year. Session length: 8 days. Departures are scheduled throughout the year. Most participants are 6–60 years of age. Participants must be 6 years or older to enroll. 2–12 participants per session. Application deadline: 60 days prior to departure. Reservations are recommended at least 60 days before departure.
Costs • $1350 (includes housing, some meals, excursions). A $300 deposit is required.
Contact • Michelle Gervais, Latin American Program Director, Journeys International, Inc., 4011 Jackson Road, Ann Arbor, MI 48103; 313-665-4407; Fax: 313-665-2945; E-mail: michelle@journeys-intl.com; World Wide Web: http://www.journeys-intl.com

JOURNEYS INTERNATIONAL, INC.

CLOUD FOREST TO COAST

General Information • Wilderness/adventure program with visits to Arenal Observatory, La Pacifica, Monteverde, Palo Verde National Park, San José, Tamarindo. Once at the destination country, participants travel by foot, boat, hiking.
Learning Focus • Escorted travel to national parks. Nature observation (wildlife). Other activities include hiking. Instruction is offered by naturalists, native English-speaking guides. This program would appeal to people interested in bird watching, nature studies, wildlife, photography.
Accommodations • Hotels, lodges. Single rooms are available for an additional $175.
Program Details • Program offered 24 times per year. Session length: 8 days. Departures are scheduled throughout the year. Most participants are 6–60 years of age. Participants must be 6 years or older to enroll. 2–12 participants per session. Application deadline: 60 days prior to departure. Reservations are recommended at least 60 days before departure.
Costs • $1395 (includes housing, some meals, excursions, airfare within Costa Rica). A $300 deposit is required.
Contact • Michelle Gervais, Latin American Program Director, Journeys International, Inc., 4011 Jackson Road, Ann Arbor, MI 48103; 313-665-4407; Fax: 313-665-2945; E-mail: michelle@journeys-intl.com; World Wide Web: http://www.journeys-intl.com

JOURNEYS INTERNATIONAL, INC.

FAMILY RAINFOREST DISCOVERY

General Information • Family tour with visits to Carara, Orotina, Poas, San José, Sarapiqui River, Sarchí. Once at the destination country, participants travel by foot, boat, hiking.
Learning Focus • Escorted travel to areas within Costa Rica. Other activities include hiking, horseback riding, swimming, rafting. Instruction is offered by naturalists, native English-speaking guides. This program would appeal to people interested in nature studies, bird watching, wildlife.
Accommodations • Hotels, lodges.
Program Details • Program offered 2 times per year. Departures are scheduled in December. Program is targeted to active families. Most participants are 4–70 years of age. Participants must be 4 years or older to enroll. 2–14 participants per session. Application deadline: 60 days prior to departure. Reservations are recommended at least 60 days before departure.
Costs • Contact sponsor for information. A $300 deposit is required.
Contact • Joan Weber, Family Trips Director and Owner, Journeys International, Inc., 4011 Jackson Road, Ann Arbor, MI 48103; 313-665-4407; Fax: 313-665-2945; E-mail: joan@journeys-intl.com; World Wide Web: http://www.journeys-intl.com

JOURNEYS INTERNATIONAL, INC.

HOLIDAY TROPICAL ODYSSEY

General Information • Wilderness/adventure program with visits to Cloud Forest Reserve, Monteverde, Palo Verde National Park, San José, Tamarindo. Once at the destination country, participants travel by foot, hiking.
Learning Focus • Escorted travel to national parks. Nature observation (wildlife). Other activities include hiking, horseback riding, boat ride. Instruction is offered by naturalists, native English-speaking guides. This program would appeal to people interested in nature studies, wildlife.
Accommodations • Hotels, lodges. Single rooms are available for an additional $250.
Program Details • Program offered 2 times per year. Session length: 11 days. Departures are scheduled in December. Most participants are 25–55 years of age. Participants must be 12 years or older to enroll. 2–14 participants per session. Application deadline: 60 days prior to departure. Reservations are recommended at least 60 days before departure.
Costs • $1895 (includes housing, some meals, excursions, flights in country). A $300 deposit is required.
Contact • Michelle Gervais, Latin America Director, Journeys International, Inc., 4011 Jackson Road, Ann Arbor, MI 48103; 313-665-4407; Fax: 313-665-2945; E-mail: michelle@journeys-intl.com; World Wide Web: http://www.journeys-intl.com

JOURNEYS INTERNATIONAL, INC.

REMOTE RAINFOREST WEEK

General Information • Wilderness/adventure program with visits to La Amistad, Los Cusingos, San Isidro de General, San José, Tiskita. Once at the destination country, participants travel by bus, foot, airplane, hiking.
Learning Focus • Escorted travel to national parks. Nature observation (wildlife). Other activities include hiking. Instruction is offered by naturalists, native English-speaking guides. This program would appeal to people interested in nature studies, photography, wildlife, culture, bird watching.
Accommodations • Hotels, lodges. Single rooms are available for an additional $175.
Program Details • Program offered 24 times per year. Session length: 8 days. Departures are scheduled throughout the year. Most participants are 6–60 years of age. Participants must be 6 years or older to enroll. 2–12 participants per session. Application deadline: 60 days prior to departure. Reservations are recommended at least 60 days before departure.
Costs • $1290 (includes housing, some meals, excursions, all flights in country). A $300 deposit is required.
Contact • Michelle Gervais, Latin American Program Director, Journeys International, Inc., 4011 Jackson Road, Ann Arbor, MI 48103; 313-665-4407; Fax: 313-665-2945; E-mail: michelle@journeys-intl.com; World Wide Web: http://www.journeys-intl.com

JOURNEYS INTERNATIONAL, INC.

TROPICAL WILDERNESS EXPLORER

General Information • Wilderness/adventure program with visits to Arenal, Monteverde, San José, Tiskita Jungle Lodge. Once at the destination country, participants travel by foot, boat, airplane.
Learning Focus • Escorted travel to national parks. Nature observation (wildlife). Other activities include horseback riding, swimming. Instruction is offered by naturalists, native

English-speaking guides. This program would appeal to people interested in botany, photography, hiking, wildlife, bird watching.
Accommodations • Hotels, lodges. Single rooms are available for an additional $175.
Program Details • Program offered 3 times per year. Session length: 10 days. Departures are scheduled in January, February, March. Most participants are 25–55 years of age. 2 participants per session. Application deadline: 60 days prior to departure. Reservations are recommended at least 60 days before departure.
Costs • $1375 (includes housing, some meals, excursions, flights in country). A $300 deposit is required.
Contact • Michelle Gervais, Latin America Director, Journeys International, Inc., 4011 Jackson Road, Ann Arbor, MI 48103; 313-665-4407; Fax: 313-665-2945; E-mail: michelle@journeys-intl.com; World Wide Web: http://www.journeys-intl.com

LANGUAGE IMMERSION INSTITUTE

COSTA RICA

General Information • Language study program with visits to San José, San Jose. Once at the destination country, participants travel by bus, foot. Program is affiliated with Forester Instituto Internacional.
Learning Focus • Instruction in the Spanish language. Instruction is offered by professors. This program would appeal to people interested in Spanish language.
Accommodations • Homestays, locally-rented apartments, hotels. Single rooms are available.
Program Details • Session length: 2 or more weeks. Departures are scheduled throughout the year. Program is targeted to adult professionals. Most participants are 20–60 years of age. Participants must be 16 years or older to enroll.
Costs • Contact sponsor for information.
Contact • Henry Urbanski, Director, Language Immersion Institute, Language Immersion Institute, 75 South Manheim Boulevard, New Paltz, NY 12561; 914-257-3500; Fax: 914-257-3569; E-mail: lii@newpaltz.edu

LANGUAGE LIAISON

CENTRO LINGUISTICO CONVERSA–LEARN SPANISH IN COSTA RICA

General Information • Language study program with visits to San José.
Learning Focus • Instruction in the Spanish language. Instruction is offered by professors. This program would appeal to people interested in language.
Accommodations • Homestays, dormitories, locally-rented apartments. Single rooms are available.
Program Details • Session length: unlimited. Departures are scheduled throughout the year. Most participants are 18–70 years of age. Participants must be 16 years or older to enroll. Reservations are recommended at least 35 days before departure.
Costs • Contact sponsor for information.
Contact • Nancy Forman, President, Language Liaison, 20533 Biscayne Boulevard-Station 4-162, Miami, FL 33180; 305-682-9909; Fax: 305-682-9907; E-mail: langstudy@aol.com; World Wide Web: http://languageliaison.com

LANGUAGE LIAISON

FORRESTER INSTITUTO INTERNACIONAL–SPANISH IN COSTA RICA

General Information • Language study program with visits to San José.
Learning Focus • Instruction in the Spanish language. Nature observation (rain forests). Instruction is offered by professors. This program would appeal to people interested in language.
Accommodations • Homestays, locally-rented apartments. Single rooms are available.
Program Details • Session length: unlimited. Departures are scheduled throughout the year. Most participants are 18–70 years of age. Participants must be 16 years or older to enroll. Reservations are recommended at least 35 days before departure.
Costs • Contact sponsor for information.
Contact • Nancy Forman, President, Language Liaison, 20533 Biscayne Boulevard-Station 4-162, Miami, FL 33180; 305-682-9909; Fax: 305-682-9907; E-mail: langstudy@aol.com; World Wide Web: http://languageliaison.com

LANGUAGE LIAISON

IPEE–LEARN SPANISH IN COSTA RICA

General Information • Language study program with visits to San José.
Learning Focus • Instruction in the Spanish language. Instruction is offered by professors. This program would appeal to people interested in language.
Accommodations • Homestays, locally-rented apartments. Single rooms are available.
Program Details • Session length: unlimited. Departures are scheduled throughout the year. Most participants are 18–70 years of age. Participants must be 16 years or older to enroll. Reservations are recommended at least 35 days before departure.
Costs • Contact sponsor for information.
Contact • Nancy Forman, President, Language Liaison, 20533 Biscayne Boulevard-Station 4-162, Miami, FL 33180; 305-682-9909; Fax: 305-682-9907; E-mail: langstudy@aol.com; World Wide Web: http://languageliaison.com

LANGUAGE LINK

ILISA

General Information • Language study program in San José. Excursions to rainforests, volcanoes.
Learning Focus • Courses in Spanish language.
Accommodations • Homestays. Single rooms are available. Meals are taken with host family.
Program Details • Session length: 1–12 weeks. Departures are scheduled in January–December. The program is open to undergraduate students, graduate students, pre-college students, adults. Most participants are 18–75 years of age. 50 participants per session.

Costs • $715 for 2 weeks (includes tuition, housing, some meals, insurance). A $143 deposit is required.
Contact • Kay Rafool, Director, US Office, Language Link, PO Box 3006, Peoria, IL 61612-3006; 800-552-2051; Fax: 309-692-2926; E-mail: info@langlink.com; World Wide Web: http://www.langlink.com

LANGUAGE LINK

INTERCULTURA

General Information • Language study program in Heredia. Excursions to Jaco Beach, volcanoes, rain forests.
Learning Focus • Courses in Spanish language.
Accommodations • Homestays. Single rooms are available. Meals are taken with host family.
Program Details • Session length: 1–12 weeks. Departures are scheduled in January–December. The program is open to undergraduate students, graduate students, pre-college students, adults. Most participants are 16–75 years of age. 50 participants per session.
Costs • $495 for 2 weeks (includes tuition, housing, some meals, insurance). A $99 deposit is required.
Contact • Kay Rafool, Director, US Office, Language Link, PO Box 3006, Peoria, IL 61612-3006; 800-552-2051; Fax: 309-692-2926; E-mail: info@langlink.com; World Wide Web: http://www.langlink.com

LANGUAGE STUDIES ABROAD

FORESTER INSTITUTO INTERNACIONAL

General Information • Language study program with visits to San José, rain forests, volcanoes, coffee plantation. Once at the destination country, participants travel by bus, foot.
Learning Focus • Instruction in the Spanish language. Escorted travel to rain forests, coffee plantations and areas outlying San Jose. Nature observation (volcanoes). Instruction is offered by naturalists, language teachers with bachelor degrees. This program would appeal to people interested in Spanish language, nature studies.
Accommodations • Homestays. Single rooms are available for an additional $130 per week.
Program Details • Session length: 2 or more weeks. Departures are scheduled throughout the year. Most participants are 16–80 years of age. Participants must be 16 years or older to enroll. 6–7 participants per session. Application deadline: 3 weeks prior to departure. Reservations are recommended at least 2 months before departure.
Costs • $1020–$1300 for 4 weeks (includes tuition, housing, some meals, books and class materials, excursions). A $100 deposit is required.
Contact • Charlene Biddulph, Director, Language Studies Abroad, 249 South Highway 101, Suite 226, Solana Beach, CA 92075; 800-424-5522; Fax: 619-943-1201; E-mail: cbiddulph@aol.com; World Wide Web: http://www.dnai.com/~bid/language/

MODERN LANGUAGE STUDIES ABROAD

SUMMER STUDY AT THE UNIVERSIDAD DE COSTA RICA

General Information • Academic study program in San José. Classes are held on the campus of University of Costa Rica. Excursions to Isla Tortuga, Ciudad de San Jose, Cartago, Volcán Poas.
Learning Focus • Courses in language study, civilizations, composition, cultural studies, literature. Instruction is offered by local teachers.
Accommodations • Homestays. Single rooms are available. Meals are taken with host family.
Program Details • Program offered 2 times per year. Session length: 4 weeks. Departures are scheduled in May, June. The program is open to undergraduate students, graduate students, adults. Most participants are 18–56 years of age. 100 participants per session. Application deadline: April 1.
Costs • $1885 (includes tuition, housing, some meals, books and class materials, international airfare). Application fee: $85.
Contact • Dr. Celestino Ruiz, Modern Language Studies Abroad, PO Box 623, Griffith, IN 46319; 219-838-9460; Fax: 219-838-9460

NATIONAL REGISTRATION CENTER FOR STUDY ABROAD

ESCUELA DE IDIOMAS D'AMORE

General Information • Language study program in Quepos.
Learning Focus • Courses in Spanish language.
Accommodations • Homestays, hotels. Single rooms are available. Meals are taken with host family, in residences.
Program Details • Program offered 50 times per year. Session length: 3 weeks. Departures are scheduled in January–December. The program is open to undergraduate students, graduate students, adults. 10 participants per session. Application deadline: 40 days prior to departure.
Costs • $1053 (includes tuition, housing, some meals, insurance). Application fee: $40. A $100 deposit is required.
Contact • Reuel Zielke, National Registration Center for Study Abroad, 823 North Second Street, Milwaukee, WI 53203; 414-278-0631; Fax: 414-271-8884; E-mail: quest@nrcsa.com; World Wide Web: http://www.nrcsa.com

NATIONAL REGISTRATION CENTER FOR STUDY ABROAD

FORESTER INSTITUTO INTERNACIONAL

General Information • Language study program in San José.
Learning Focus • Courses in Spanish language.
Accommodations • Homestays. Single rooms are available. Meals are taken with host family.
Program Details • Program offered 48 times per year. Session length: 3 weeks. Departures are scheduled in January–December. The program is open to undergraduate students, graduate students, adults. Application deadline: 40 days prior to departure.

Costs • $1109 (includes tuition, housing, some meals, insurance). Application fee: $40. A $100 deposit is required.
Contact • June Domoe, Coordinator, National Registration Center for Study Abroad, 823 North Second Street, Milwaukee, WI 53203; 414-278-0631; Fax: 414-271-8884; E-mail: inquiries@nrcsa.com; World Wide Web: http://www.nrcsa.com

NATIONAL REGISTRATION CENTER FOR STUDY ABROAD

INSTITUTO DE INTERAMERICANO DE IDIOMAS INTENSA

General Information • Language study program in San José.
Learning Focus • Courses in Spanish language.
Accommodations • Homestays. Single rooms are available. Meals are taken with host family.
Program Details • Program offered 50 times per year. Session length: 3 weeks. Departures are scheduled in January–December. The program is open to undergraduate students, graduate students, adults. 3–5 participants per session. Application deadline: 40 days prior to departure.
Costs • $885 (includes tuition, housing, some meals, insurance). Application fee: $40. A $100 deposit is required.
Contact • Mike Wittig, Director, National Registration Center for Study Abroad, 823 North Second Street, Milwaukee, WI 53203; 414-278-0631; Fax: 414-271-8884; E-mail: ask@nrcsa.com; World Wide Web: http://www.nrcsa.com

NATIONAL REGISTRATION CENTER FOR STUDY ABROAD

INTENSIVE SPANISH PROGRAM IN COSTA RICA

General Information • Language study program in San José.
Learning Focus • Courses in Spanish language.
Accommodations • Homestays. Single rooms are available. Meals are taken with host family, in residences.
Program Details • Program offered 50 times per year. Session length: 3 weeks. Departures are scheduled in January–December. The program is open to undergraduate students, graduate students, adults. 5–9 participants per session.
Costs • $890 (includes tuition, housing, some meals, insurance). Application fee: $40. A $100 deposit is required.
Contact • June Domoe, Educational Consultant, National Registration Center for Study Abroad, PO Box 1393, 823 North Second Street, Milwaukee, WI 53203; 414-278-0631; Fax: 414-271-8884; E-mail: inquiries@nrcsa.com; World Wide Web: http://www.nrcsa.com

NATIONAL REGISTRATION CENTER FOR STUDY ABROAD

LANGUAGE AND CULTURE IN COSTA RICA

General Information • Language study program in Santa Ana.
Learning Focus • Courses in Spanish language.
Accommodations • Homestays. Single rooms are available. Meals are taken with host family.
Program Details • Program offered 40 times per year. Session length: 2 weeks. Departures are scheduled in January–December. The program is open to undergraduate students, graduate students, adults. Application deadline: 40 days prior to departure.
Costs • $969 (includes tuition, housing, all meals, books and class materials, insurance). Application fee: $40. A $100 deposit is required.
Contact • June Domoe, Educational Consultant, National Registration Center for Study Abroad, PO Box 1393, Milwaukee, WI 53201; 414-278-0631; Fax: 414-271-8884; E-mail: inquiries@nrcsa.com; World Wide Web: http://www.nrcsa.com

NATURAL HABITAT ADVENTURES

COSTA RICA

General Information • Nature study tour with visits to Arenal Volcano, Monteverde Cloud Forest, San José, Tiskita Rainforest Lodge, Tortuguero Canals. Once at the destination country, participants travel by private van.
Learning Focus • Nature observation (rain forests). Instruction is offered by naturalists. This program would appeal to people interested in nature studies, photography, wildlife.
Accommodations • Jungle lodges. Single rooms are available for an additional $395.
Program Details • Program offered 12 times per year. Session length: 12 days. Departures are scheduled in November–April. Participants must be 13 years or older to enroll. 10 participants per session. Reservations are recommended at least 6–12 months before departure.
Costs • $2395 (includes housing, all meals, park entrance fees). A $500 deposit is required.
Contact • Natural Habitat Adventures, 2945 Center Green Court, Suite H, Boulder, CO 80301; 800-543-8917; Fax: 303-449-3712; E-mail: nathab@worldnet.att.net

NATURE EXPEDITIONS INTERNATIONAL

COSTA RICA WILDLIFE EXPEDITION

General Information • Wilderness/adventure program with visits to Lake Arenal, Monteverde, Palo Verde, San José, Tiskita, Tortuguero. Once at the destination country, participants travel by airplane, mini-van.
Learning Focus • Escorted travel to Costa Rica's natural parks. Instruction is offered by professors, naturalists. This program would appeal to people interested in natural history, ecology, wildlife, rain forest studies.
Accommodations • Hotels. Single rooms are available for an additional $500.
Program Details • Program offered 3 times per year. Session length: 15 days. Departures are scheduled in January, March, December. Most participants are 25–75 years of age. Other requirements: doctor's permission for participants 70 years and older. Reservations are recommended at least 6 months before departure.
Costs • $2590 (includes housing, some meals, excursions, all guiding). A $400 deposit is required.
Contact • Christopher Kyle, President, Nature Expeditions International, 6400 East El Dorado Circle, Suite 210, Tucson, AZ 85715; 800-869-0639; Fax: 520-721-6719; E-mail: naturexp@aol.com

NICHOLLS STATE UNIVERSITY

STUDY PROGRAM ABROAD IN SAN JOSÉ, COSTA RICA

General Information • Academic and language study program in San José. Classes are held on the campus of Nicholls State University–San José. Excursions to museums, markets, theater, rain forests, Manuel Antonio Beach, white water rafting.
Learning Focus • Courses in Spanish language, literature, linguistics, Costa Rican culture, civilizations. Instruction is offered by professors from the sponsoring institution.
Accommodations • Homestays. Single rooms are available. Meals are taken on one's own, with host family, in local restaurants, in residences.
Program Details • Program offered 15 times per year. Session length: 3 weeks–one year. Departures are scheduled in January–December. The program is open to undergraduate students, graduate students, pre-college students, adults. Most participants are 18–55 years of age. Other requirements: high school seniors or graduates. 250 participants per session. Application deadline: 30 days prior to departure.
Costs • $834 for non-credit program, $1129 with 6 hours of college credit for 3 week session (includes tuition, housing, some meals, books and class materials). A $170 deposit is required.
Contact • Dr. Gary McCann, Director of Study Programs Abroad, Nicholls State University, PO Box 2080, Thibodaux, LA 70310; 504-448-4440; Fax: 504-449-7028; E-mail: fl-caw@nich-nsunet.nich.edu

NORTH CAROLINA STATE UNIVERSITY

ANTHROPOLOGY AND SOCIOLOGY OF TOURISM–SUMMER

General Information • Academic study program in San José. Excursions to Heredia, San José, Manuel Antonio, Quepos region.
Learning Focus • Courses in anthropology, field research.
Accommodations • Homestays. Meals are taken with host family, in residences.
Program Details • Program offered once per year. Session length: 5 weeks. Departures are scheduled in May. The program is open to undergraduate students, graduate students, adults. Most participants are 18–50 years of age. Other requirements: approval of Director. 10 participants per session. Application deadline: March 1.

Costs • $2350 (includes tuition, housing, all meals, insurance, excursions, international airfare). A $200 deposit is required.
Contact • Ingrid Schmidt, Study Abroad Director, North Carolina State University, 2118 Pullen Hall, Box 7344, Raleigh, NC 27695-7344; 919-515-2087; Fax: 919-515-6021; E-mail: ingrid_schmidt@ncsu.edu; World Wide Web: http://www2.ncsu.edu/ncsu/chass/intstu/abroad.html

NORTHERN ILLINOIS UNIVERSITY

TROPICAL BIOLOGY IN COSTA RICA

General Information • Academic study program in Monteverde. Classes are held on the campus of Monteverde Institute.
Learning Focus • Courses in biology, Spanish language, agroecology. Instruction is offered by local teachers.
Accommodations • Dormitories. Meals are taken as a group, in central dining facility.
Program Details • Program offered once per year. Session length: 4½ weeks. Departures are scheduled in July. The program is open to undergraduate students. Most participants are 20–30 years of age. Other requirements: 1 semester of college biology and an additional semester of biology, ecology, or environmental science, a minimum 2.75 GPA, and Spanish is recommended. 35 participants per session. Application deadline: March 15.
Costs • $4230 (includes tuition, housing, some meals, insurance, excursions). A $200 deposit is required.
Contact • Anne Seitzinger, Program Coordinator, Short-Term Study Abroad, Northern Illinois University, Study Abroad Office-WI 417, DeKalb, IL 60115; 815-752-0700; Fax: 815-753-0825; E-mail: aseitz@niu.edu; World Wide Web: http://www.niu.edu/depts/intl_prgms/intl.html

OVERSEAS ADVENTURE TRAVEL

REAL, AFFORDABLE COSTA RICA

General Information • Wilderness/adventure program with visits to Arenal Volcano, Buena Vista, Chachagua, Punta Coral, Punta Leona, San José. Once at the destination country, participants travel by bus, foot, boat.
Learning Focus • Escorted travel to all areas of Costa Rica. Nature observation (Chachagua rain forest, Caño Negro wildlife refuge, La Selva biological station). Other activities include nature hikes, whitewater rafting, horseback riding. Instruction is offered by naturalists. This program would appeal to people interested in bird watching, photography, nature study, botany.
Accommodations • Hotels, lodges. Single rooms are available for an additional $390.
Program Details • Program offered 60 times per year. Session length: 10 days. Departures are scheduled throughout the year. Most participants are 40–70 years of age. Participants must be 10 years or older to enroll. 16 participants per session. Application deadline: 30 days prior to departure.
Costs • $1990 (includes housing, all meals, excursions, international airfare). A $300 deposit is required.
Contact • Sales Department, Overseas Adventure Travel, Sales Department, 625 Mount Auburn Street, Cambridge, MA 02138; 800-221-0814

RAMAPO COLLEGE OF NEW JERSEY

COSTA RICA–INTENSA

General Information • Language study program in San José. Classes are held on the campus of Intensa.
Learning Focus • Courses in Spanish language. Instruction is offered by local teachers.
Accommodations • Homestays. Single rooms are available. Meals are taken with host family.
Program Details • Program offered 26 times per year. Session length: 2 weeks. Departures are scheduled in January–December. The program is open to undergraduate students, graduate students, pre-college students, adults. Most participants are 18–70 years of age. Other requirements: minimum 2.0 GPA. Application deadline: rolling.
Costs • $800 (includes tuition, housing, some meals, books and class materials). A $300 deposit is required.
Contact • Mrs. Robyn Perricelli, Coordinator, Study Abroad, Ramapo College of New Jersey, 505 Ramapo Valley Road, Mahwah, NJ 07430; 201-529-7463; Fax: 201-529-7508; E-mail: rperrice@ramapo.edu

RAMAPO COLLEGE OF NEW JERSEY

COSTA RICA PROGRAM

General Information • Academic study program in San José. Excursions to Monteverde Cloud Forest Preserve, Palo Verde National Park, Manuel Antonio National Park, La Selva.
Learning Focus • Courses in tropical ecosystems. Instruction is offered by professors from the sponsoring institution.
Accommodations • Dormitories, hotels. Single rooms are available. Meals are taken as a group, in central dining facility.
Program Details • Program offered once per year. Session length: 2 weeks. Departures are scheduled in May. The program is open to undergraduate students, graduate students, pre-college students, adults. Most participants are 19–70 years of age. Other requirements: minimum age of 19, course work in biology, environmental studies and a minimum 2.0 GPA. 18 participants per session. Application deadline: April 15.
Costs • $2200 (includes tuition, housing, all meals, excursions, international airfare). A $300 deposit is required.
Contact • Mrs. Robyn Perricelli, Coordinator, Study Abroad, Ramapo College of New Jersey, 505 Ramapo Valley Road, Mahwah, NJ 07430; 201-529-7463; Fax: 201-529-7508; E-mail: rperrice@ramapo.edu

RUSSIAN AND EAST EUROPEAN PARTNERSHIPS

COSTA RICAN LANGUAGE AND CULTURAL IMMERSION PROGRAM

General Information • Language study program in San José. Classes are held on the campus of Forester Institute.

Learning Focus • Courses in Spanish language, Central American culture and art, Central American history. Instruction is offered by local teachers.
Accommodations • Homestays. Single rooms are available. Meals are taken on one's own, with host family, in local restaurants, in residences.
Program Details • Program offered 11 times per year. Session length: 4 or more weeks. Departures are scheduled in January–November. The program is open to undergraduate students, graduate students, adults. Most participants are 18 years of age and older. Other requirements: in good health and 18 or older unless chaperoned by an adult. 6 participants per session. Application deadline: 45 days prior to departure.
Costs • $2595 (includes tuition, housing, some meals, books and class materials, excursions, international airfare, local transportation, airport transfers). A $1500 deposit is required.
Contact • Kenneth Fortune, President, Russian and East European Partnerships, PO Box 227, Fineview, NY 13640; 888-USE-REEP; Fax: 800-910-1777; E-mail: reep@fox.nstn.ca

SAN DIEGO STATE UNIVERSITY

SPANISH LANGUAGE IMMERSION IN COSTA RICA

General Information • Language study program in Alajuela.
Learning Focus • Courses in language study, cultural studies. Instruction is offered by professors from the sponsoring institution.
Accommodations • Homestays. Single rooms are available. Meals are taken with host family, in residences.
Program Details • Program offered once per year. Session length: 3 weeks. Departures are scheduled in January. The program is open to undergraduate students, graduate students, pre-college students, adults. Most participants are 18–80 years of age. 25 participants per session. Application deadline: 60 days prior to departure.
Costs • $1200 (includes tuition, housing, some meals). A $400 deposit is required.
Contact • Patrick Lathrop, Travel Coordinator, San Diego State University, College of Extended Studies, San Deigo, CA 92182; 619-594-5154; Fax: 619-594-7080

SPECIAL INTEREST TOURS

COSTA RICAN NATURE ODYSSEY

General Information • Nature study tour with visits to Arenal Volcano, Monteverde Cloud Forest, San José, Tortuguero Reserve, Poas Volcano. Once at the destination country, participants travel by bus, foot, boat, airplane.
Learning Focus • Instruction in botany and wildlife. Nature observation (tropical wildlife and birds). Other activities include hiking. Instruction is offered by naturalists. This program would appeal to people interested in wildlife, botany, photography, natural history.
Accommodations • Hotels. Single rooms are available for an additional $250.
Program Details • Session length: 10 days. Departures are scheduled throughout the year. Most participants are 20–60 years of age. Participants must be 10 years or older to enroll. 12 participants per session. Application deadline: 2 months prior to departure. Reservations are recommended at least 6 months before departure.
Costs • $1395 (includes housing, some meals, excursions). A $350 deposit is required.
Contact • Nancy Koch, Vice President, Special Interest Tours, 10220 North 27 Street, Phoenix, AZ 85028; 800-525-6772; Fax: 602-493-3630; E-mail: GoSafari@usa.net

SPECIAL INTEREST TOURS

THE FOREST AND THE SEA

General Information • Nature study tour with visits to Corcavado National Park, Curu Reserve, Manuel Antonio, Monteverde Cloud Forest, Poas Volcano, San José. Once at the destination country, participants travel by bus, boat.
Learning Focus • Nature observation (tropical wildlife and flora). Other activities include hiking. Instruction is offered by naturalists. This program would appeal to people interested in nature studies, oceanography, photography, wildlife.
Accommodations • Hotels, boat. Single rooms are available for an additional $275.
Program Details • Session length: 10 days. Departures are scheduled throughout the year. Program is targeted to seniors. Most participants are 40–70 years of age. 12 participants per session. Application deadline: 2 months prior to departure. Reservations are recommended at least 6 months before departure.
Costs • $1450 (includes housing, all meals, excursions). A $300 deposit is required.
Contact • Nancy Koch, Vice President, Special Interest Tours, 10220 North 27 Street, Phoenix, AZ 85028; 800-525-6772; Fax: 602-493-3630; E-mail: GoSafari@usa.net

STATE UNIVERSITY OF NEW YORK COLLEGE AT BROCKPORT

SUMMER COSTA RICAN INTERNSHIP PROGRAM

General Information • Internship program in San José.
Learning Focus • Courses in political science, business, international business. Instruction is offered by professors from the sponsoring institution.
Accommodations • Homestays. Single rooms are available. Meals are taken on one's own, with host family.
Program Details • Program offered once per year. Session length: 6 weeks. Departures are scheduled in June. The program is open to undergraduate students. Most participants are 19–26 years of age. Other requirements: minimum 2.75 GPA. 10 participants per session. Application deadline: May 15.
Costs • $3600 (includes tuition, housing, all meals, international airfare). A $100 deposit is required.
Contact • Dr. John J. Perry, Director, Office of International Education, State University of New York College at Brockport, 350 New Campus Drive, Brockport, NY 14420; 716-395-2119; Fax: 716-637-3218; E-mail: jperry@acspr1.acs.brockport.e; World Wide Web: http://www.brockport.edu/study_abroad

TRAVELEARN

A COSTA RICA ADVENTURE

General Information • Nature study and cultural tour with visits to Arenal, Guanacaste, Monteverde, San José, Tamarindo, Pacific Coast-Tamarindo. Once at the destination country, participants travel by bus, foot, boat. Program is affiliated with the nationwide TraveLearn network of 290 universities and colleges.
Learning Focus • Instruction in natural history, ecology and cultural history. Museum visits (National Museum, Arenal Volcano Observatory). Nature observation (national parks, reserves). Other activities include "people-to-people" experience in San Jose. Instruction is offered by professors, researchers, naturalists, social scientists. This program would appeal to people interested in natural history, botany, ecology, cultural history and understanding.
Accommodations • Hotels. Single rooms are available for an additional $495.
Program Details • Program offered 4 times per year. Session length: 11–14 days. Departures are scheduled in January, February, March, May. Program is targeted to mature adults. Most participants are 40–75 years of age. Participants must be 18 years or older to enroll. 14–20 participants per session. Application deadline: 60 days prior to departure. Reservations are recommended at least 4–8 months before departure.
Costs • $2595 (includes housing, all meals, books and class materials, excursions, international airfare). A $300 deposit is required.
Contact • Keith Williams, Director of Marketing, TraveLearn, PO Box 315, Lakeville, PA 18438; 800-235-9114; Fax: 717-226-9114; E-mail: travelearn@aol.com

UNIVERSITY OF ALABAMA AT BIRMINGHAM

UNIVERSITY OF ALABAMA AT BIRMINGHAM IN COSTA RICA

General Information • Academic study program in San José. Excursions to volcanoes, tropical rainforests, seacoast.
Learning Focus • Courses in tropical ecology, rainforest ecology. Instruction is offered by professors from the sponsoring institution.
Accommodations • Program-owned houses. Meals are taken as a group, in central dining facility.
Program Details • Program offered once per year. Session length: 1 week. Departures are scheduled in December. The program is open to undergraduate students, graduate students. Most participants are 20–40 years of age. Other requirements: biology major or minor. 18–20 participants per session. Application deadline: October 31.
Costs • $2105–$2411 (includes tuition, housing, all meals, excursions, international airfare). A $200 deposit is required.
Contact • Frank Romanowicz, Study Abroad Coordinator, University of Alabama at Birmingham, 1400 University Boulevard, HUC 318, Birmingham, AL 35294-1150; 205-934-5025; Fax: 205-934-8664; E-mail: ucipØ17@larry.huc.uab.edu

UNIVERSITY OF CONNECTICUT

FORESTER INSTITUTE SPANISH LANGUAGE STUDY

General Information • Language study program in San José.
Learning Focus • Courses in Spanish language. Instruction is offered by local teachers.
Accommodations • Homestays. Single rooms are available. Meals are taken with host family, in local restaurants.
Program Details • Program offered 12 times per year. Session length: 2–4 weeks. Departures are scheduled in January–December. The program is open to undergraduate students, graduate students. Application deadline: 8 weeks prior to departure.
Costs • $675 for 2 weeks, $1300 for 4 weeks (includes tuition, housing, some meals).
Contact • Study Abroad Program, University of Connecticut, 843 Bolton Road, U-207, Storrs, CT 06269-1207; 203-486-5022; Fax: 203-486-2976; World Wide Web: http://www.ucc.uconn.edu/~wwwsab

UNIVERSITY OF DELAWARE

WINTER SESSION IN COSTA RICA

General Information • Language study program in San José. Classes are held on the campus of University of Costa Rica. Excursions to Caribbean coast, Irazú, Sarchí, Póas, Arenal, Orosi Valley.
Learning Focus • Courses in Spanish language. Instruction is offered by professors from the sponsoring institution.
Accommodations • Homestays. Meals are taken with host family, in residences.
Program Details • Program offered once per year. Session length: 5 weeks. Departures are scheduled in January. The program is open to undergraduate students, graduate students, adults. Most participants are 18–21 years of age. Other requirements: minimum 2.0 GPA. 25 participants per session. Application deadline: October.
Costs • $3810 (includes tuition, housing, all meals, international airfare). A $200 deposit is required.
Contact • International Programs and Special Sessions, University of Delaware, 4 Kent Way, Newark, DE 19716-1450; 888-831-4685; Fax: 302-831-6042; E-mail: studyabroad@mvs.udel.edu

UNIVERSITY OF KANSAS

ENVIRONMENTAL STUDIES IN GOLFITO

General Information • Academic study program in Golfito. Excursions to San José, Corcovado National Park, Cartago.
Learning Focus • Courses in anthropology, Spanish language, biology. Instruction is offered by professors from the sponsoring institution and local teachers.
Accommodations • Homestays. Meals are taken with host family, in residences.
Program Details • Program offered once per year. Session length: 6 weeks. Departures are scheduled in May. The program is open to undergraduate students, adults. Most participants are 20–27 years of age. Other requirements: minimum 2.5 GPA. 20 participants per session. Application deadline: March 1.

Costs • $2254 for Kansas University students, $2775 for other students (includes tuition, housing, all meals, excursions, orientation in San Jose, field work transportation and laboratories). Application fee: $15. A $300 deposit is required.
Contact • Ellen Strubert, Program Coordinator, University of Kansas, Office of Study Abroad, 203 Lippincott Hall, Lawrence, KS 66045; 913-864-3742; Fax: 913-864-5040; E-mail: osa@falcon.cc.ukans.edu; World Wide Web: http://kuhub.cc.ukans.edu/~intlstdy/osa/osamain.html

UNIVERSITY OF NEW ORLEANS

COSTA RICA

General Information • Academic study program in San Ramon. Classes are held on the campus of University of Costa Rica-San Ramon. Excursions to Monteverde, San José, Quepos, Póas.
Learning Focus • Courses in Spanish language, biology, anthropology, geography, political science, English language. Instruction is offered by professors from the sponsoring institution and local teachers.
Accommodations • Homestays. Single rooms are available. Meals are taken with host family.
Program Details • Program offered once per year. Session length: 5 weeks. Departures are scheduled in May. The program is open to undergraduate students, graduate students, adults. Most participants are 20–45 years of age. 30 participants per session. Application deadline: April 1.
Costs • $1695 (includes tuition, housing, some meals, insurance, excursions). A $100 deposit is required.
Contact • Marie Kaposchyn, Coordinator, University of New Orleans, PO Box 569, New Orleans, LA 70148; 504-280-7455; Fax: 504-280-7317; World Wide Web: http://www.uno.edu/~inst/Welcome.html

UNIVERSITY OF NORTH CAROLINA AT CHARLOTTE

SPANISH LANGUAGE AND CULTURE IN COSTA RICA

General Information • Academic study program in San José. Classes are held on the campus of Forester Institute. Excursions to Arenal.
Learning Focus • Courses in Spanish language, Spanish culture. Instruction is offered by professors from the sponsoring institution and local teachers.
Accommodations • Homestays. Single rooms are available. Meals are taken with host family, in residences.
Program Details • Program offered once per year. Session length: 4 weeks. Departures are scheduled in June. The program is open to undergraduate students, graduate students, adults. Most participants are 18–28 years of age. 20 participants per session. Application deadline: March 15.
Costs • $2040 (includes tuition, housing, some meals, books and class materials, insurance, excursions). Application fee: $10. A $300 deposit is required.
Contact • Elizabeth A. Adams, Director of Education Abroad Programs, University of North Carolina at Charlotte, Office of International Programs, 9201 University City Boulevard, Charlotte, NC 28223-0001; 704-547-2464; Fax: 704-547-3168; E-mail: eaadams@email.uncc.edu; World Wide Web: http://unccvm.uncc.edu

UNIVERSITY STUDIES ABROAD CONSORTIUM

COSTA RICA PROGRAM

General Information • Academic study program in Heredia. Classes are held on the campus of National University of Costa Rica. Excursions to Poás, Manuel Antonio National Park, Braulio Carrillo National Park, Cahuita National Park, northern Costa Rica, Southern Costa Rica.
Learning Focus • Courses in Spanish language, ecology, Latin American history, political economy, Spanish-American poetry, Latin American cultures. Instruction is offered by local teachers.
Accommodations • Homestays. Single rooms are available. Meals are taken with host family, in residences.
Program Details • Program offered 2 times per year. Session length: 4 weeks. Departures are scheduled in June, July. The program is open to undergraduate students, graduate students, pre-college students, adults. Most participants are 18–50 years of age. Other requirements: minimum 2.5 GPA. 35 participants per session. Application deadline: April 15.
Costs • $1360 (includes tuition, insurance, excursions, International Student Identification card). Application fee: $50. A $150 deposit is required.
Contact • Dr. Carmelo Urza, Director, University Studies Abroad Consortium, University of Nevada Library/323, Reno, NV 89557-0093; 702-784-6569; Fax: 702-784-6010; E-mail: usac@equinox.unr.edu; World Wide Web: http://www.scs.unr.edu/~usac

WILDLAND ADVENTURES

COSTA RICA FAMILY ADVENTURE

General Information • Wilderness/adventure program with visits to San José, rain forests, beaches. Once at the destination country, participants travel by bus, foot, airplane.
Learning Focus • Escorted travel to jungle and beaches. Instruction is offered by naturalists. This program would appeal to people interested in hiking.
Accommodations • Hotels. Single rooms are available.
Program Details • Program offered 4 times per year. Session length: 10 days. Departures are scheduled in December, April, July, August. Program is targeted to families with young children. Most participants are 5–70 years of age. 4–14 participants per session. Application deadline: 30 days prior to departure. Reservations are recommended at least 3–6 months before departure.
Costs • $1095 (includes housing, some meals, excursions, complete pre-departure dossier). A $300 deposit is required.
Contact • Wildland Adventures, 3516 Northeast 155th Street, Seattle, WA 98155; 800-343-4453; Fax: 206-363-6615; E-mail: wildadve@aol.com; World Wide Web: http://www.wildland.com

WILDLAND ADVENTURES

NOSARA YOGA RETREAT

General Information • Yoga program with visits to Nosara, San José. Once at the destination country, participants travel by foot, airplane.

Learning Focus • Instruction in yoga. Nature observation (turtle nesting). Instruction is offered by yoga instructor. This program would appeal to people interested in yoga.
Accommodations • Program-owned houses.
Program Details • Program offered 24 times per year. Session length: 6 days. Departures are scheduled in January–July, November, December. Most participants are 30–60 years of age. 2–12 participants per session. Application deadline: 30 days prior to departure. Reservations are recommended at least 3–6 months before departure.
Costs • $1125 (includes housing, some meals, excursions, complete pre-departure dossier). A $300 deposit is required.
Contact • Wildland Adventures, 3516 Northeast 155th Street, Seattle, WA 98155; 800-345-4453; Fax: 206-363-6615; E-mail: wildadve@aol.com; World Wide Web: http://www.wildland.com

WILDLAND ADVENTURES

RAIN FOREST WORKSHOP

General Information • Nature study tour with visits to San José, Monteverde Cloud Forest, Corcorado National Park. Once at the destination country, participants travel by bus, foot, airplane. Program is affiliated with Organization for Tropical Studies.
Learning Focus • Instruction in tropical ecology. Instruction is offered by researchers, naturalists, scientists. This program would appeal to people interested in tropical ecology.
Accommodations • Program-owned houses. Single rooms are available.
Program Details • Program offered 4 times per year. Session length: 9 days. Departures are scheduled in January–April. Program is targeted to adults. Most participants are 30–60 years of age. 2–12 participants per session. Application deadline: 30 days prior to departure. Reservations are recommended at least 3–6 months before departure.
Costs • $1890 (includes housing, some meals, excursions, complete pre-departure dossier). A $300 deposit is required.
Contact • Wildland Adventures, 3516 Northeast 155th Street, Seattle, WA 98155; 800-345-4453; Fax: 206-363-6615; E-mail: wildadve@aol.com; World Wide Web: http://www.wildland.com

WILDLAND ADVENTURES

TEMPTRESS ADVENTURE VOYAGE

General Information • Nature study tour with visits to San José. Once at the destination country, participants travel by boat, airplane.
Learning Focus • Escorted travel to national parks. Nature observation (rain forest wildlife). Other activities include hiking, snorkeling. Instruction is offered by naturalists. This program would appeal to people interested in family travel, nature studies, photography.
Accommodations • Boat. Single rooms are available.
Program Details • Session length: 4 days. Departures are scheduled throughout the year. Most participants are 5–70 years of age. 2–8 participants per session. Application deadline: 30 days prior to departure. Reservations are recommended at least 3–6 months before departure.
Costs • $895 (includes housing, some meals, excursions, complete pre-departure dossier). A $300 deposit is required.
Contact • Wildland Adventures, 3516 Northeast 155th Street, Seattle, WA 98155; 800-345-4453; Fax: 206-363-6615; E-mail: wildadve@aol.com; World Wide Web: http://www.wildland.com

WILDLAND ADVENTURES

TROPICAL TRAILS ODYSSEY

General Information • Nature study tour with visits to Monteverde, Osa Peninsula, San José, rain forests of the Osa Penninsula, cloud forests of Monteverde. Once at the destination country, participants travel by bus, foot, boat, airplane.
Learning Focus • Escorted travel to rain forests. Nature observation (birdwatching, mammals). Other activities include hiking. Instruction is offered by naturalists. This program would appeal to people interested in natural history, hiking, ecology, photography.
Accommodations • Hotels, lodges. Single rooms are available for an additional $175.
Program Details • Program offered 24 times per year. Session length: 8 days. Departures are scheduled throughout the year. Most participants are 35–60 years of age. Participants must be 8 years or older to enroll. Application deadline: 30 days prior to departure. Reservations are recommended at least 3–6 months before departure.
Costs • $1735 (includes housing, some meals, excursions, complete pre-departure dossier). A $300 deposit is required.
Contact • Wildland Adventures, 3516 Northeast 155th Street, Seattle, WA 98155; 800-345-4453; Fax: 206-363-6615; E-mail: wildadve@aol.com; World Wide Web: http://www.wildland.com

CUBA

CENTER FOR CROSS-CULTURAL STUDY

INTRODUCTION TO CONTEMPORARY CUBA

General Information • Academic study program in Havana. Classes are held on the campus of University of Havana. Excursions to Pinar del Rio, Matanzas Provinces.
Learning Focus • Courses in Spanish language, history, political science, Latin American studies. Instruction is offered by local teachers.
Accommodations • Hotels. Meals are taken in central dining facility.
Program Details • Program offered 2 times per year. Session length: 3 weeks. Departures are scheduled in January, June. The program is open to undergraduate students, graduate students. Most participants are 18–22 years of age. 20 participants per session. Application deadline: November 1, April 1.
Costs • $2175 (includes tuition, housing, some meals, insurance, ground transportation, airfare from Cancún to Havana). A $500 deposit is required.
Contact • Dr. Judith M. Ortiz, Associate Director, Center for Cross-Cultural Study, 446 Main Street, Amherst, MA 01002; 800-377-2621; Fax: 413-256-1968; E-mail: cccs@crocker.com; World Wide Web: http://www.cccs.com

GLOBAL EXCHANGE REALITY TOURS

CUBA LANGUAGE SCHOOL

General Information • Language study program with visits to Havana, small town in nearby province. Once at the destination country, participants travel by bus, airplane, bicycle.
Learning Focus • Instruction in the Spanish language and Cuban culture. Instruction is offered by researchers, naturalists. This program would appeal to people interested in Spanish language, film, ecotourism, agriculture, Cuban culture, public health, women's issues.
Accommodations • Hotels, guest houses. Single rooms are available for an additional $200–$500.
Program Details • Session length: 15 days. Departures are scheduled throughout the year. Program is targeted to seniors, students and professionals. Participants must be 18 years or older to enroll. 10 participants per session. Application deadline: 1 month prior to departure. Reservations are recommended at least 2 months before departure.
Costs • $1200 for 2 weeks, $1700 for 1 month (includes tuition, housing, some meals, visa acquisition fees, airfare from Cancun, Mexico). A $200 deposit is required.
Contact • Cuba Language School Coordinator, Global Exchange Reality Tours, 2017 Mission Street, Room 303, San Francisco, CA 94110; 415-255-7296; Fax: 415-255-7498; E-mail: globalexch@igc.apc.org

GLOBAL EXCHANGE REALITY TOURS

CUBA STUDY SEMINARS

General Information • Academic study program with visits to Havana, Pinar del Rio, countryside. Once at the destination country, participants travel by bus, airplane.
Learning Focus • Escorted travel to provinces. Museum visits (Museum of the Revolution). Instruction is offered by researchers, naturalists. This program would appeal to people interested in agriculture, alternative medicine, film, arts, public health, women's issues, Santeria.
Accommodations • Hotels, guest houses. Single rooms are available for an additional $200–$500.
Program Details • Session length: 10 days. Departures are scheduled throughout the year. Program is targeted to seniors, students and professionals. Participants must be 18 years or older to enroll. 15 participants per session. Application deadline: 1 month prior to departure. Reservations are recommended at least 2 months before departure.
Costs • $1350 (includes housing, some meals, books and class materials, airfare from Cancun to Havana, visa). A $200 deposit is required.
Contact • Cuba Coordinator, Global Exchange Reality Tours, 2017 Mission Street, Room 303, San Francisco, CA 94110; 415-255-7296; Fax: 415-255-7498; E-mail: globalexch@igc.apc.org

DOMINICAN REPUBLIC

AMERISPAN UNLIMITED

SPANISH CLASSES AND HOMESTAYS IN THE DOMINICAN REPUBLIC

General Information • Language study program with visits to Santo Domingo. Once at the destination country, participants travel by bus.
Learning Focus • Instruction in the Spanish language. Instruction is offered by trained Spanish teachers. This program would appeal to people interested in Spanish language, Latin America.
Accommodations • Homestays, hotels. Single rooms are available.
Program Details • Session length: 2–12 weeks. Departures are scheduled throughout the year. Most participants are 16–70 years of age. Reservations are recommended at least 4 weeks before departure.
Costs • Contact sponsor for information. A $100 deposit is required.
Contact • AmeriSpan Unlimited, PO Box 40513, Philadelphia, PA 19106; 800-879-6640; Fax: 215-985-4524; E-mail: info@amerispan.com; World Wide Web: http://www.amerispan.com

COUNCIL ON INTERNATIONAL EDUCATIONAL EXCHANGE

COUNCIL STUDY CENTER IN SANTIAGO, DOMINICAN REPUBLIC

General Information • Academic study program in Santiago. Classes are held on the campus of Catholic University 'Madre y Maestra' Santiago. Excursions to Santo Domingo.
Learning Focus • Courses in health issues, Spanish language. Instruction is offered by local teachers.
Accommodations • Homestays. Single rooms are available. Meals are taken with host family, in residences.
Program Details • Program offered once per year. Session length: 8 weeks. Departures are scheduled in June. The program is open to undergraduate students, graduate students. Other requirements: minimum 2.75 GPA. Application deadline: April 1.
Costs • $2995 (includes tuition, housing, all meals, books and class materials, insurance, excursions, International Student Identification card). Application fee: $30. A $300 deposit is required.
Contact • Lisa Feder, Program Registrar, Council on International Educational Exchange, College and University Division, 205 East 42nd Street, New York, NY 10017-5706; 212-822-2771; E-mail: latinamreg@ciee.org; World Wide Web: http://www.ciee.org

NATURAL HABITAT ADVENTURES

CARIBBEAN HUMPBACKS

General Information • Nature study tour with visits to Puerto Plata, Silver Bank. Once at the destination country, participants travel by boat.
Learning Focus • Escorted travel to visit whales (in boats and in water). Nature observation (humpback whales, bottlenose and spotted dolphins, tropical fish, and seabirds). Instruction is offered by researchers, naturalists. This program would appeal to people interested in nature studies, photography, wildlife.
Accommodations • Boat. Single rooms are available for an additional $595.
Program Details • Program offered once per year. Session length: 8 days. Departures are scheduled in March. Participants must be 14 years or older to enroll. 18 participants per session. Reservations are recommended at least 6–12 months before departure.
Costs • $2995 (includes housing, all meals). A $500 deposit is required.
Contact • Natural Habitat Adventures, 2945 Center Green Court, Suite H, Boulder, CO 80301; 800-543-8917; Fax: 303-449-3712; E-mail: nathab@worldnet.att.net

UNIVERSITY AT ALBANY, STATE UNIVERSITY OF NEW YORK

SUMMER PROGRAM IN THE DOMINICAN REPUBLIC

General Information • Academic study program in Santo Domingo. Classes are held on the campus of National University 'Pedro Henriquez Ureña' Santo Domingo.
Learning Focus • Courses in Caribbean studies, Latin American studies, African studies, Spanish language. Instruction is offered by professors from the sponsoring institution and local teachers.
Accommodations • Homestays. Meals are taken with host family.
Program Details • Program offered once per year. Session length: 6 weeks. Departures are scheduled in summer. The program is open to undergraduate students.
Costs • $952 (includes in-state tuition and fees).
Contact • Joan Savitt, Associate Director, University at Albany, State University of New York, Albany, NY 12208; 518-442-3525; Fax: 518-442-3338; E-mail: oipua@csc.albany.edu; World Wide Web: http://www.albany.edu/~oipwebua

ECUADOR

ALPINE ASCENTS, INTERNATIONAL

VOLCANOES OF ECUADOR

General Information • Mountain climbing tour with visits to Cayambe, Chimborazo, Cotopaxi, Pichincha, Quito. Once at the destination country, participants travel by bus, foot.
Learning Focus • Instruction in glacier travel, rope techniques, snow climbing and ice axe techniques. Escorted travel to Cotopaxi National Park. Nature observation (Cordillera ranges, Andes Mountains, Amazon basin, hot springs). Other activities include camping, hiking. Instruction is offered by sports professionals. This program would appeal to people interested in mountain climbing.
Accommodations • Hotels, campsites. Single rooms are available.
Program Details • Program offered 2 times per year. Session length: 14 days. Departures are scheduled in November, December. Program is targeted to mountain climbers. Other requirements: mountaineering skills, ice axe, crampon, and snow/ice experience. 8 participants per session. Reservations are recommended at least 6 months before departure.
Costs • $2100 (includes housing, some meals, group equipment, fees). A $500 deposit is required.
Contact • Gordon Janow, Program Coordinator, Alpine Ascents, International, 16615 Saybrook Drive, Woodinville, WA 98072; 206-788-1951; Fax: 206-788-6757; E-mail: aaiclimb@accessone.com

 AMERISPAN UNLIMITED

SPANISH CLASSES AND HOMESTAYS IN ECUADOR

General Information • Language study program with visits to Quito, markets, Galapagos Islands.
Learning Focus • Instruction in the Spanish language. Instruction is offered by trained Spanish teachers. This program would appeal to people interested in Spanish language, Latin America.
Accommodations • Homestays. Single rooms are available.
Program Details • Session length: 2–12 weeks. Departures are scheduled throughout the year. Participants must be 16 years or older to enroll. Participants must be members of the sponsoring organization. Reservations are recommended at least 4 weeks before departure.
Costs • Contact sponsor for information. A $100 deposit is required.
Contact • AmeriSpan Unlimited, PO Box 40513, Philadelphia, PA 19106; 800-879-6640; Fax: 215-985-4524; E-mail: info@amerispan.com; World Wide Web: http://www.amerispan.com

APPALACHIAN STATE UNIVERSITY

ECUADOR

General Information • Academic study program in Quito. Excursions to Andes mountains, Pacific Coast.
Learning Focus • Courses in history. Instruction is offered by professors from the sponsoring institution.
Program Details • Program offered once per year. Session length: 5 weeks. Departures are scheduled in May. Most participants are 18 years of age and older. 20 participants per session.
Costs • $2496 (includes tuition, housing, insurance, international airfare, International Student Identification card).
Contact • Dr. Nick Biddle, Professor, Appalachian State University, Department of History, Boone, NC 28608; 704-262-2046; Fax: 704-262-4037

CALIFORNIA ACADEMY OF SCIENCES

THE GALAPAGOS ISLANDS

General Information • Wilderness/adventure program with visits to Galapagos Islands, Quito, Otavalo, Cotopaxi National Park, North Seymour Island, Española (Hood) Island, Santa Cruz Island, Floreana Island, Genovesa (Tower) Island, Isabela and Ferdinand Islands, Santiago and Bartolomé Islands, Baltra. Once at the destination country, participants travel by foot, boat.
Learning Focus • Instruction in research and fieldwork to conserve the Galápagos ecology. Escorted travel to Devil's Crown, Punta Cormorant, Pinnacle Rock and the Charles Darwin Research Station. Nature observation (active volcano, flora and fauna unique to Galápagos and Ecuador). Other activities include snorkeling. Instruction is offered by researchers, naturalists, scientists. This program would appeal to people interested in natural history, geology, bird watching, wildlife, seventeenth century architecture.
Accommodations • Hotels, boat. Single rooms are available for an additional $350–$1260.
Program Details • Program offered once per year. Session length: 13 days. Departures are scheduled in February. Most participants are 35–80 years of age. Participants must be 12 years or older to enroll. Participants must be members of the sponsoring organization. 15–20 participants per session.
Costs • $5190 (includes housing, some meals, excursions, international airfare, guides, lecturer, airport and park fees). A $500 deposit is required.
Contact • Nancy Fuller, Travel Assistant, California Academy of Sciences, San Francisco, CA 94118; 415-750-7348; Fax: 415-750-7346

COLLEGE CONSORTIUM FOR INTERNATIONAL STUDIES–BROOKDALE COMMUNITY COLLEGE AND COLLEGE OF STATEN ISLAND, CUNY

CCIS SUMMER PROGRAM IN GUAYAQUIL, ECUADOR

General Information • Language study program in Guayaquil. Classes are held on the campus of Laica University. Excursions to Quito, Chanduy, Cuenca.

Learning Focus • Courses in Spanish language, history, sociology, Latin American studies, Ecuadorian studies, international business, bilingual education. Instruction is offered by local teachers.

Accommodations • Homestays. Single rooms are available. Meals are taken with host family.

Program Details • Program offered 6 times per year. Session length: 4 weeks. Departures are scheduled in January, June, July, August. The program is open to undergraduate students, graduate students, adults. Most participants are 19–50 years of age. Other requirements: minimum 2.5 GPA, letter of recommendation, and essay. 30 participants per session. Application deadline: November 1, April 15, May 15, August 15.

Costs • $1475 (includes tuition, housing, some meals, excursions, orientation). Application fee: $35. A $100 deposit is required.

Contact • Jane C. Evans, Executive Director, College Consortium for International Studies, 2000 P Street, NW, Suite 503, Washington, DC 20036; 800-453-6956; Fax: 202-223-0999; E-mail: ccis@intr.net

COLLEGE CONSORTIUM FOR INTERNATIONAL STUDIES–BROOKDALE COMMUNITY COLLEGE AND COLLEGE OF STATEN ISLAND, CUNY

CCIS SUMMER PROGRAM IN QUITO

General Information • Academic study program in Quito. Classes are held on the campus of Universidad San Francisco de Quito. Excursions to Guayaquil, Cotopaxi, Otavalo.

Learning Focus • Courses in Spanish literature, Andean studies, tropical ecology, Latin American studies, Ecuadorian studies, anthropology, literature. Instruction is offered by local teachers.

Accommodations • Homestays. Single rooms are available. Meals are taken with host family, in residences.

Program Details • Program offered once per year. Session length: 5 weeks. Departures are scheduled in July. The program is open to undergraduate students, graduate

students, adults. Most participants are 19–35 years of age. Other requirements: minimum 2.5 GPA, letter of recommendation, and essay. 10 participants per session. Application deadline: May 15.
Costs • $1975 (includes tuition, housing, some meals, excursions, orientation). Application fee: $35. A $100 deposit is required.
Contact • Jane C. Evans, Executive Director, College Consortium for International Studies, 2000 P Street, NW, Suite 503, Washington, DC 20036; 800-438-6956; Fax: 202-223-0999; E-mail: ccis@intr.net

CRAFT WORLD TOURS

ECUADOR

General Information • Cultural tour with visits to Cuenca, Otavalo, Quito. Once at the destination country, participants travel by bus.
Learning Focus • Escorted travel to Otavalo Market, Calderon and a Panama hat factory. Museum visits (Guyasamin Gallery, Olga Fisch Gallery, Equator Monument). Instruction is offered by artists. This program would appeal to people interested in handicrafts, folk arts, village life.
Accommodations • Hotels. Single rooms are available for an additional $300.
Program Details • Program offered once per year. Session length: 11 days. Departures are scheduled in March. Most participants are 30–80 years of age. Other requirements: appreciation of handcrafts and folk arts. 18 participants per session. Application deadline: January 18. Reservations are recommended at least 6 months before departure.
Costs • $2866 (includes housing, some meals, excursions, international airfare). A $250 deposit is required.
Contact • Tom Wilson, President, Craft World Tours, 6776 Warboys Road, Byron, NY 14422; 716-548-2667; Fax: 716-548-2821

FOREIGN LANGUAGE STUDY ABROAD SERVICE

SPANISH IN QUITO

General Information • Language study program in Quito.
Learning Focus • Courses in language study. Instruction is offered by local teachers.
Accommodations • Homestays, hotels. Single rooms are available. Meals are taken with host family, in residences.
Program Details • Session length: varies. Departures are scheduled in January–December. The program is open to undergraduate students, graduate students, pre-college students, adults. Most participants are 16 years of age and older.
Costs • Contact sponsor for information. Application fee: $50. A $100 deposit is required.
Contact • Louise Harber, Coordinator, Foreign Language Study Abroad Service, Department IH, Box 903, 5935 Southwest 64th Avenue, South Miami, FL 33143; 800-282-1090; Fax: 305-662-2907; E-mail: flsas@netpoint.net; World Wide Web: http://www.netpoint.net/~flsas

FORUM TRAVEL INTERNATIONAL

ISLANDS AND RAINFORESTS: GO WILD IN GALAPAGOS AND AMAZON

General Information • Nature study tour with visits to Amazon Rainforest, Galapagos Islands, main islands in Galapagos Archipelago, Ecuadoran Highlands, Oriente Province rainforests, cloud forests. Once at the destination country, participants travel by bus, foot, boat, airplane. Program is affiliated with International Ecosystems University.
Learning Focus • Instruction in natural history, ecology and biology. Nature observation (marine ecosystem, wildlife). Instruction is offered by naturalists. This program would appeal to people interested in nature studies, culture.
Accommodations • Hotels. Single rooms are available.
Program Details • Program offered 12 times per year. Session length: 2 weeks. Departures are scheduled throughout the year. Most participants are 23–80 years of age. 12–20 participants per session.
Costs • $2145 (includes tuition, some meals, excursions, international airfare). A $300 deposit is required.
Contact • Jeannie Graves, Operations Manager, Forum Travel International, 91 Gregory Lane #21, Pleasant Hill, CA 94525; 510-671-2900; Fax: 510-671-2993; E-mail: forum@ix.netcom.com; World Wide Web: http://www.ten-io.com/forumtravel

GEO EXPEDITIONS

GALAPAGOS NATURAL HISTORY

General Information • Nature study tour with visits to Galapagos Islands, Quito, Ecuadoran highlands, headwaters of the Amazon River, Peru (Machu Picchu). Once at the destination country, participants travel by bus, foot, boat.
Learning Focus • Escorted travel to Galapagos Islands. Nature observation (hiking island nature trails with a naturalist). Instruction is offered by naturalists. This program would appeal to people interested in wildlife, conservation.
Accommodations • Hotels, boat. Single rooms are available.
Program Details • Session length: 11 days. Departures are scheduled throughout the year. Most participants are 30–70 years of age. Participants must be 10 years or older to enroll. 10 participants per session. Reservations are recommended at least 6 months before departure.
Costs • Contact sponsor for information. A $300 deposit is required.
Contact • David Risard, President, GEO Expeditions, PO Box 3656, Sonora, CA 95370; 800-351-5041; Fax: 209-532-1979; E-mail: geoexped@mlode.com

GEORGE MASON UNIVERSITY

ECOLOGY AND CULTURE

General Information • Academic study program in Galapagos Islands, Mainland.
Learning Focus • Courses in biology, ecology, anthropology. Instruction is offered by professors from the sponsoring institution.

Accommodations • Dormitories, boat. Single rooms are available. Meals are taken as a group, in central dining facility, in local restaurants.
Program Details • Program offered once per year. Session length: 3 weeks. Departures are scheduled in December. The program is open to undergraduate students, graduate students, adults. Most participants are 18–65 years of age. Other requirements: minimum 2.25 GPA. 15–20 participants per session. Application deadline: October.
Costs • $3400 for George Mason University students, $3900 for other students (includes tuition, housing, some meals, insurance, excursions, international airfare). Application fee: $35. A $500 deposit is required.
Contact • Dr. Yehuda Lukacs, Director, Center for Global Education, George Mason University, 4400 University Drive, 235 Johnson Center, Fairfax, VA 22030; 703-993-2156; Fax: 703-993-2153; E-mail: ylukacs@gmu.edu; World Wide Web: http://www.gmu.edu/departments/oie

 GEORGETOWN UNIVERSITY

GEORGETOWN IN QUITO

General Information • Language study program in Quito. Classes are held on the campus of Pontifical Catholic University of Ecuador Quito.
Learning Focus • Courses in Spanish language, cultural studies, civilizations, literature, linguistics. Instruction is offered by professors from the sponsoring institution and local teachers.
Accommodations • Homestays. Single rooms are available. Meals are taken with host family, in residences.
Program Details • Program offered once per year. Session length: 6 or 7 weeks. Departures are scheduled in June, July. The program is open to undergraduate students, graduate students, pre-college students, adults, teachers. Most participants are 18–30 years of age. Other requirements: minimum 3.0 GPA. 60 participants per session. Application deadline: March.
Costs • $2900 (includes tuition, housing, all meals, books and class materials, insurance, excursions). A $100 deposit is required.
Contact • Marianne T. Needham, Director, International Programs, Georgetown University, 306 ICC, Box 571012, Washington, DC 20057-1012; 202-687-6184; Fax: 202-687-8954; E-mail: sscefps1@gunet.georgetown.edu; World Wide Web: http://guweb.georgetown.edu/ssce

 GLOBAL EXCHANGE REALITY TOURS

ECUADOR

General Information • Academic study program with visits to Imbabura, Quito, indigenous communities south of Quito, Ecuador. Once at the destination country, participants travel by bus, airplane.
Learning Focus • Instruction in current issues and alternative health projects. Escorted travel to the Mindo Protected Area. Museum visits ("Ciudad Mitad del Mundo", Museum of the Incas). Nature observation (Ecuadorian Amazon). Instruction is offered by researchers, naturalists. This program would appeal to people interested in environmental issues, indigenous cultures.
Accommodations • Hotels, guest houses. Single rooms are available for an additional $200–$500.
Program Details • Program offered 2 times per year. Session length: 12 days. Departures are scheduled in November, July. Program is targeted to seniors, students and professionals. Most participants are 22–70 years of age. Participants must be 18 years or older to enroll. 10–15 participants per session. Application deadline: 1 month prior to departure. Reservations are recommended at least 2 months before departure.
Costs • $1600 from Miami, $1900 from San Francisco or New York (includes housing, some meals, books and class materials, international airfare). A $200 deposit is required.
Contact • Reality Tours Coordinator, Global Exchange Reality Tours, 2017 Mission Street, Room 303, San Francisco, CA 94110; 415-255-7296; Fax: 415-255-7498; E-mail: globalexch@igc.apc.org

 JAMES MADISON UNIVERSITY

SUMMER STUDY IN GALAPAGOS

General Information • Academic study program in Galapagos Islands. Excursions to Quito, Amazon, Cotopaxi, Galapagos Islands.
Learning Focus • Courses in natural history. Instruction is offered by professors from the sponsoring institution.
Accommodations • Hotels, boat, jungle huts. Meals are taken as a group, in local restaurants.
Program Details • Program offered once per year. Session length: 17 days. Departures are scheduled in May, June. The program is open to undergraduate students. Most participants are 18–22 years of age. 10 participants per session. Application deadline: February 1.
Costs • $3000 (includes tuition, housing, all meals, excursions, international airfare). A $200 deposit is required.
Contact • Dr. James Grimm, Director, Life Science Museum, James Madison University, Office of International Education, Harrisonburg, VA 22807; 540-568-6378; Fax: 540-568-3310; E-mail: grimmjk@jmu.edu; World Wide Web: http://www.jmu.edu/intl-ed/

JOURNEYS INTERNATIONAL, INC.

ECUADOR OVERVIEW

General Information • Cultural tour with visits to Cotopaxi, Cuenca, Ingapirca, Otavalo, Quito, Saquisilli. Once at the destination country, participants travel by bus, foot.
Learning Focus • Nature observation (Cotopaxi National Park). Other activities include camping, hiking. Instruction is offered by local English-speaking guides. This program would appeal to people interested in photography, culture, nature studies, wildlife.
Accommodations • Hotels. Single rooms are available.
Program Details • Session length: 9 days. Departures are scheduled throughout the year. Most participants are 25–55 years of age. Participants must be 12 years or older to enroll. Other requirements: must be in good health and physical condition. 2–12 participants per session. Application deadline: 60 days prior to departure. Reservations are recommended at least 60 days before departure.
Costs • $1195 (includes housing, some meals). A $300 deposit is required.

Contact • Michelle Gervais, Latin America Sales Director, Journeys International, Inc., 4011 Jackson Road, Ann Arbor, MI 48103; 313-665-4407; Fax: 313-665-2945; E-mail: michelle@journeys-intl.com; World Wide Web: http://www.journeys-intl.com

JOURNEYS INTERNATIONAL, INC.

GALAPAGOS WILDLIFE ODYSSEY

General Information • Wilderness/adventure program with visits to Baltra, Española, Floreana, North Seymour/Bartolome, Rabida, Santa Cruz, Ecuador. Once at the destination country, participants travel by foot, boat.

Learning Focus • Nature observation (wildlife). Other activities include hiking, swimming, snorkeling, kayaking. Instruction is offered by naturalists. This program would appeal to people interested in photography, wildlife, nature studies.

Accommodations • Hotels, boat. Single rooms are available.

Program Details • Program offered 40 times per year. Session length: 11 days. Departures are scheduled throughout the year. Most participants are 25–55 years of age. Participants must be 12 years or older to enroll. 8–12 participants per session. Application deadline: 60 days prior to departure. Reservations are recommended at least 60 days before departure.

Costs • $2195 (includes housing, some meals). A $500 deposit is required.

Contact • Michelle Gervais, Latin America Sales Director, Journeys International, Inc., 4011 Jackson Road, Ann Arbor, MI 48103; 313-665-4407; Fax: 313-665-2945; E-mail: michelle@journeys-intl.com; World Wide Web: http://www.journeys-intl.com

JOURNEYS INTERNATIONAL, INC.

HIGHLIGHTS OF ECUADOR

General Information • Wilderness/adventure program with visits to Lasso, Otavalo, Quito, San Pablo, Santo Domingo, Valle Hermoso. Once at the destination country, participants travel by hiking.

Learning Focus • Escorted travel to Otavalo. Other activities include hiking, rafting, swimming. Instruction is offered by native English-speaking guides. This program would appeal to people interested in photography, culture, rafting, nature studies, hiking.

Accommodations • Hotels. Single rooms are available.

Program Details • Session length: 9 days. Departures are scheduled throughout the year. Most participants are 25–55 years of age. Participants must be 12 years or older to enroll. 2–14 participants per session. Application deadline: 60 days prior to departure. Reservations are recommended at least 60 days before departure.

Costs • $1195 (includes housing, some meals, excursions). A $300 deposit is required.

Contact • Michelle Gervais, Latin America Sales Director, Journeys International, Inc., 4011 Jackson Road, Ann Arbor, MI 48103; 313-665-4407; Fax: 313-665-2945; E-mail: michelle@journeys-intl.com; World Wide Web: http://www.journeys-intl.com

JOURNEYS INTERNATIONAL, INC.

SNOW-CAPPED VOLCANOES

General Information • Wilderness/adventure program with visits to Cotocchoa, Cotopaxi, Huagrahasi, Pitatambo River, Quito, Sincholagua. Once at the destination country, participants travel by bus, foot.

Learning Focus • Escorted travel to volcanoes. Other activities include camping, hiking. Instruction is offered by local English-speaking guides. This program would appeal to people interested in nature studies, hiking, wildlife, culture, photography, botany.

Accommodations • Hotels, campsites. Single rooms are available.

Program Details • Session length: 8 days. Departures are scheduled throughout the year. Most participants are 25–55 years of age. Participants must be 12 years or older to enroll. Other requirements: must be in good health and physical condition. 2–15 participants per session. Application deadline: 60 days prior to departure. Reservations are recommended at least 60 days before departure.

Costs • $1195 (includes housing, some meals, excursions, porters and cooks). A $300 deposit is required.

Contact • Michelle Gervais, Latin America Sales Director, Journeys International, Inc., 4011 Jackson Road, Ann Arbor, MI 48103; 313-665-4407; Fax: 313-665-2945; E-mail: michelle@journeys-intl.com; World Wide Web: http://www.journeys-intl.com

KENTUCKY INSTITUTE FOR INTERNATIONAL STUDIES

PROGRAM IN ECUADOR

General Information • Academic study program in Quito. Excursions to Amazon Rainforest, Mount Chimborazo, Guayaquil.

Learning Focus • Courses in biology, geoscience, political science. Instruction is offered by professors from the sponsoring institution.

Accommodations • Homestays. Meals are taken with host family.

Program Details • Program offered once per year. Session length: 5 weeks. Departures are scheduled in July. The program is open to undergraduate students, graduate students, adults, professionals. Most participants are 18–28 years of age. Other requirements: minimum 2.0 GPA, letter of recommendation from a faculty member, and good academic standing at home institution. 25 participants per session. Application deadline: March 1.

Costs • $2960 for students of consortia schools; $3260 for other students (includes tuition, housing, all meals, excursions, international airfare, International Student Identification card). Application fee: $50.

Contact • Dr. J. Milton Grimes, Executive Director, Kentucky Institute for International Studies, Murray State University, PO Box 9, Murray, KY 42071-0009; 502-762-3091; Fax: 502-762-3434; E-mail: kiismsu@msumusik.mursuky.edu; World Wide Web: http://www.berea.edu/KIIS/kiis.html

LANGUAGE LIAISON

ACADEMIA DE ESPANO–SPANISH IN ECUADOR

General Information • Language study program with visits to Quito.
Learning Focus • Instruction in the Spanish language. Instruction is offered by professors. This program would appeal to people interested in language.
Accommodations • Homestays, locally-rented apartments. Single rooms are available.
Program Details • Session length: unlimited. Departures are scheduled throughout the year. Most participants are 18–70 years of age. Participants must be 16 years or older to enroll. Reservations are recommended at least 35 days before departure.
Costs • Contact sponsor for information.
Contact • Nancy Forman, President, Language Liaison, 20533 Biscayne Boulevard-Station 4-162, Miami, FL 33180; 305-682-9909; Fax: 305-682-9907; E-mail: langstudy@aol.com; World Wide Web: http://languageliaison.com

LANGUAGE LIAISON

SPANISH IN ECUADOR

General Information • Language study program with visits to Cuenca.
Learning Focus • Instruction in the Spanish language. Instruction is offered by professors. This program would appeal to people interested in language.
Accommodations • Homestays. Single rooms are available.
Program Details • Session length: unlimited. Departures are scheduled throughout the year. Most participants are 18–70 years of age. Participants must be 16 years or older to enroll. Reservations are recommended at least 35 days before departure.
Costs • Contact sponsor for information.
Contact • Nancy Forman, President, Language Liaison, 20533 Biscayne Boulevard-Station 4-162, Miami, FL 33180; 305-682-9909; Fax: 305-682-9907; E-mail: langstudy@aol.com; World Wide Web: http://languageliaison.com

LANGUAGE LINK

ACADEMIA DE ESPAÑOL–QUITO

General Information • Language study program in Quito. Excursions to Amazon Jungle, Galapagos Islands.
Learning Focus • Courses in Spanish language.
Accommodations • Homestays. Single rooms are available. Meals are taken with host family.
Program Details • Session length: 1–12 weeks. Departures are scheduled in January–December. The program is open to undergraduate students, graduate students, pre-college students, adults. Most participants are 18–70 years of age. 40 participants per session.
Costs • $260 per week (includes tuition, housing, all meals, insurance). Application fee: $30.
Contact • Kay Rafool, Director, US Office, Language Link, PO Box 3006, Peoria, IL 61612-3006; 800-552-2051; Fax: 309-692-2926; E-mail: info@langlink.com; World Wide Web: http://www.langlink.com

MICHIGAN STATE UNIVERSITY

PRIMARY HEALTH CARE

General Information • Academic study program in Guayaquil, Quito.
Learning Focus • Courses in rural health, public health. Instruction is offered by professors from the sponsoring institution.
Accommodations • Hotels. Meals are taken on one's own, in local restaurants.
Program Details • Program offered once per year. Session length: 4 weeks. Departures are scheduled in July. The program is open to graduate students, pre-clinical medical students. Most participants are 20–30 years of age. Other requirements: good academic standing and the approval of the director. 16 participants per session. Application deadline: March 14.
Costs • $1800 (includes housing, some meals, excursions). Application fee: $75. A $250 deposit is required.
Contact • Brenda S. Sprite, Educational Programs Coordinator, Michigan State University, Office of Study Abroad, 109 International Center, East Lansing, MI 48824; 517-353-8920; Fax: 517-432-2082; E-mail: sprite@pilot.msu.edu; World Wide Web: http://study-abroad.msu.edu

MOUNTAIN MADNESS

ECUADOR VOLCANOES

General Information • Wilderness/adventure program with visits to Mount Chimbarazo, Mount Cotopaxi, Quito. Once at the destination country, participants travel by bus, foot.
Learning Focus • Escorted travel to mountain summits. Other activities include camping, hiking. Instruction is offered by historians, sports professionals, professional mountaineering guides. This program would appeal to people interested in climbing, photography.
Accommodations • Hotels, campsites. Single rooms are available.
Program Details • Program offered once per year. Session length: 2 weeks. Departures are scheduled in June. Most participants are 20–50 years of age. Participants must be 16 years or older to enroll. Other requirements: some climbing experience is recommended. 4 participants per session. Reservations are recommended at least 60 days before departure.
Costs • $1920 (includes housing, some meals, guides, porters, camp equipment). A $1000 deposit is required.
Contact • Manomi Fernando, Program Coordinator, Mountain Madness, 4218 Southwest Alaska Street #206, Seattle, WA 98116; 206-937-8389; Fax: 206-937-1772; E-mail: mountmad@aol.com

MYTHS AND MOUNTAINS

ECUADOR: INDIGENOUS PEOPLE OF THE ANDES

General Information • Language study program with visits to Andean Highlands, Central Valley, Cuenca, Misahualli, Quito. Once at the destination country, participants travel by train, bus, foot, boat. Program is affiliated with Centro de Estudios Interamericanos.
Learning Focus • Instruction in Ecuadorian history, culture, indigenous people and the Spanish language. Field

research in local villages. Escorted travel to local villages. Nature observation (jungle, mountains). Other activities include camping, hiking. Instruction is offered by professors, naturalists, historians, indigenous teachers. This program would appeal to people interested in Spanish teachers, culture, history.
Accommodations • Homestays, hotels, lodges. Single rooms are available.
Program Details • Program offered once per year. Session length: 31 days. Departures are scheduled in June. Most participants are 20–50 years of age. Participants must be 18 years or older to enroll. Other requirements: fluency in Spanish. 7–10 participants per session. Application deadline: 1 month prior to departure. Reservations are recommended at least 6 months before departure.
Costs • $2495 (includes tuition, housing, some meals, books and class materials, excursions). A $350 deposit is required.
Contact • Debra Moye, Manager of Operations, Myths and Mountains, 976 Tee Court, Incline Village, NV 89451; 800-670-6984; Fax: 702-832-4454; E-mail: edutrav@sierra.net; World Wide Web: http://mythsandmountains.com

NATIONAL REGISTRATION CENTER FOR STUDY ABROAD

ACADEMIA LATINOAMERICANA

General Information • Language study program in Quito.
Learning Focus • Courses in Spanish language.
Accommodations • Homestays, hotels. Single rooms are available. Meals are taken with host family, in residences.
Program Details • Program offered 50 times per year. Session length: 2 weeks. Departures are scheduled in January–December. The program is open to undergraduate students, graduate students, adults. 1 participant per session. Application deadline: 40 days prior to departure.
Costs • $675 (includes tuition, housing, some meals, insurance). Application fee: $40. A $100 deposit is required.
Contact • June Domoe, Educational Consultant, National Registration Center for Study Abroad, Box 1393, Milwaukee, WI 53201; 414-278-0631; Fax: 414-271-8884; E-mail: ask@nrcsa.com; World Wide Web: http://www.nrcsa.com

NATIONAL REGISTRATION CENTER FOR STUDY ABROAD

EJS CUENCA

General Information • Language study program in Cuenca.
Learning Focus • Courses in Spanish language.
Accommodations • Homestays. Single rooms are available. Meals are taken with host family, in residences.
Program Details • Program offered 24 times per year. Session length: 2 weeks. Departures are scheduled in January–December. The program is open to undergraduate students, graduate students, adults. 1 participant per session. Application deadline: 40 days prior to departure.
Costs • $830 (includes tuition, housing, all meals, insurance). Application fee: $40. A $100 deposit is required.
Contact • June Domoe, Educational Consultant, National Registration Center for Study Abroad, Box 1393, Milwaukee, WI 53201; 414-278-0631; Fax: 414-271-8884; E-mail: ask@nrcsa.com; World Wide Web: http://www.nrcsa.com

NATIONAL REGISTRATION CENTER FOR STUDY ABROAD

SOUTH AMERICAN SPANISH INSTITUTE

General Information • Language study program in Quito.
Learning Focus • Courses in Spanish language.
Accommodations • Homestays. Single rooms are available. Meals are taken with host family.
Program Details • Program offered 50 times per year. Session length: 8 weeks. Departures are scheduled in January–December. The program is open to undergraduate students, graduate students, adults. 1 participant per session.
Costs • $2450 (includes tuition, housing, all meals, insurance). Application fee: $40. A $100 deposit is required.
Contact • June Domoe, Educational Consultant, National Registration Center for Study Abroad, PO Box 1393, Milwaukee, WI 53201; 414-278-0631; Fax: 414-271-8884; E-mail: inquiries@nrcsa.com; World Wide Web: http://www.nrcsa.com

NATURAL HABITAT ADVENTURES

GALAPAGOS ISLANDS

General Information • Nature study tour with visits to Española, Floreana, Genovesa, Quito, Santiago/Bartolome, South Plaza, Charles Darwin Research Station. Once at the destination country, participants travel by boat, airplane.
Learning Focus • Nature observation (sea lions, seals, iguanas, giant tortoises, blue-footed, red and masked boobies, frigatebirds, penguins and flamingoes). Instruction is offered by researchers, naturalists. This program would appeal to people interested in nature studies, photography, wildlife.
Accommodations • Boat. Single rooms are available for an additional $180–$500.
Program Details • Program offered 5 times per year. Session length: 11 days. Departures are scheduled in December, January. Participants must be 14 years or older to enroll. 19 participants per session. Reservations are recommended at least 6–12 months before departure.
Costs • $2895 (includes housing, some meals, round-trip airfare between Quito and Galapagos). A $500 deposit is required.
Contact • Natural Habitat Adventures, 2945 Center Green Court, Suite H, Boulder, CO 80301; 800-543-8917; Fax: 303-449-3712; E-mail: nathab@worldnet.att.net

NATURAL HABITAT ADVENTURES

UNTOUCHED GALAPAGOS

General Information • Nature study tour with visits to Galapagos Islands, Quito, Otavalo market. Once at the destination country, participants travel by bus, boat, airplane.
Learning Focus • Nature observation (sea lions, giant tortoises, iguanas, lava lizards, blue-footed, red and masked boobies, frigatebirds, flamingoes and penguins). Other activities include hiking, snorkeling. Instruction is offered by

naturalists, photographers. This program would appeal to people interested in nature studies, photography, wildlife.
Accommodations • Hotels, boat. Single rooms are available for an additional $180–$1000.
Program Details • Program offered 2 times per year. Session length: 18 days. Departures are scheduled in May, July. Participants must be 14 years or older to enroll. 17 participants per session. Reservations are recommended at least 6–12 months before departure.
Costs • $4695 (includes housing, some meals, excursions, round-trip airfare between Quito and Galapagos, all transfers and park fees).
Contact • Natural Habitat Adventures, 2945 Center Green Court, Suite H, Boulder, CO 80301; 800-543-8917; Fax: 303-449-3712; E-mail: nathab@worldnet.att.net

NATURE EXPEDITIONS INTERNATIONAL

IN THE WAKE OF DARWIN: GALAPAGOS ISLANDS

General Information • Nature study tour with visits to Galapagos Islands, Quito. Once at the destination country, participants travel by boat, airplane.
Learning Focus • Escorted travel to the Galapagos Islands. Instruction is offered by naturalists. This program would appeal to people interested in wildlife, bird watching, nature studies.
Accommodations • Hotels, boat. Single rooms are available for an additional $450.
Program Details • Program offered 7 times per year. Session length: 11 days. Departures are scheduled in January, March, May, July, August, November, December. Most participants are 25–75 years of age. Other requirements: doctor's permission for participants 70 years and older. Reservations are recommended at least 6 months before departure.
Costs • $2490 (includes housing, some meals, excursions, all guiding). A $400 deposit is required.
Contact • Christopher Kyle, President, Nature Expeditions International, 6400 East El Dorado Circle, Suite 210, Tucson, AZ 85715; 800-869-0639; Fax: 520-721-6719; E-mail: naturexp@aol.com

NICHOLLS STATE UNIVERSITY

STUDY PROGRAM ABROAD IN QUITO, ECUADOR

General Information • Academic and language study program in Quito. Classes are held on the campus of Nicholls State University–Quito. Excursions to museums, theater, markets, Merida marketplace, volcanoes, Amazon region, Galapagos Islands.
Learning Focus • Courses in language study, literature, linguistics, cultural studies, civilizations. Instruction is offered by professors from the sponsoring institution.
Accommodations • Homestays. Single rooms are available. Meals are taken on one's own, with host family, in local restaurants, in residences.
Program Details • Program offered 15 times per year. Session length: 3 weeks–one year. Departures are scheduled in January–December. The program is open to undergraduate students, graduate students, pre-college students, adults. Most participants are 18–55 years of age. Other requirements: high school seniors or graduates. 20 participants per session. Application deadline: 30 days prior to departure.
Costs • $889 for non-credit program, $1189 for 6 hours of college credit (includes tuition, housing, some meals, books and class materials). A $235 deposit is required.
Contact • Dr. Gary McCann, Director of Study Programs Abroad, Nicholls State University, PO Box 2080, Thibodaux, LA 70310; 504-448-4440; Fax: 504-440-7028; E-mail: fl-caw@nich-nsunet.nich.edu

THE PARTNERSHIP FOR SERVICE-LEARNING

ECUADOR

General Information • Academic study and volunteer service program in Guayaquil. Classes are held on the campus of Laica University. Excursions to Quito, Cuenca.
Learning Focus • Courses in Spanish language, contemporary Ecuador, institutions in society. Instruction is offered by local teachers.
Accommodations • Homestays. Single rooms are available. Meals are taken with host family.
Program Details • Program offered 3 times per year. Session length: 11½ weeks. Departures are scheduled in January, June, September. The program is open to undergraduate students, graduate students, pre-college students, adults. Most participants are 19–24 years of age. Other requirements: 2 years of high school or 1 year of college-level Spanish. 12 participants per session. Application deadline: 2 months prior to departure.
Costs • $5200 (includes tuition, housing, some meals, excursions, service placement and supervision, pre-departure and orientation materials). A $250 deposit is required.
Contact • Maureen Lowney, Coordinator of Student Programs, The Partnership for Service-Learning, 815 Second Avenue, Suite 315, New York, NY 10960; 212-986-0989; Fax: 212-986-5039; E-mail: pslny@aol.com

RUSSIAN AND EAST EUROPEAN PARTNERSHIPS

ECUADOR LANGUAGE AND CULTURAL IMMERSION PROGRAM

General Information • Language study program in Quito. Classes are held on the campus of Academia de Español Quito.
Learning Focus • Courses in Spanish language, culture and art of Ecuador, the history of Ecuador. Instruction is offered by professors from the sponsoring institution and local teachers.
Accommodations • Homestays. Single rooms are available. Meals are taken on one's own, with host family, in local restaurants, in residences.
Program Details • Program offered 11 times per year. Session length: 4 or more weeks. Departures are scheduled in January–November. The program is open to undergraduate students, graduate students, adults. Most participants are 18 years of age and older. Other requirements: in good

health and 18 or older unless chaperoned by an adult. 6 participants per session. Application deadline: 45 days prior to departure.

Costs • $2695 (includes tuition, housing, some meals, books and class materials, excursions, international airfare, local transportation, airport transfers). A $1500 deposit is required.

Contact • Kenneth Fortune, President, Russian and East European Partnerships, PO Box 227, Fineview, NY 13640; 888-USE-REEP; Fax: 800-910-1777; E-mail: reep@fox.nstn.ca

SPECIAL INTEREST TOURS

GALAPAGOS YACHTING ADVENTURES

General Information • Nature study tour with visits to Galapagos Islands, Quito, Amazon Rain Forest, Indian markets, Machu Picchu. Once at the destination country, participants travel by boat.

Learning Focus • Escorted travel to volcanoes, caves and reserves. Nature observation (owls, albatross, herons, lizards, iguanas, boobies, sea lions, tortoises, penguins). Other activities include hiking. Instruction is offered by naturalists. This program would appeal to people interested in natural history, biology, photography, botany.

Accommodations • Hotels, boat.

Program Details • Session length: 11 days. Departures are scheduled throughout the year. Most participants are 25–70 years of age. Participants must be 12 years or older to enroll. 10–12 participants per session. Application deadline: 60 days prior to departure. Reservations are recommended at least 6 months before departure.

Costs • $1595–$2075 (includes housing, all meals, excursions). A $350 deposit is required.

Contact • Nancy Koch, Vice President, Special Interest Tours, 10220 North 27 Street, Phoenix, AZ 85028; 800-525-6772; Fax: 602-493-3630; E-mail: GoSafari@usa.net

TRAVELEARN

GALAPAGOS ISLANDS AND ECUADOR

General Information • Nature study and cultural tour with visits to Galapagos Islands, Otavalo, Quito, upper Amazon, Peru (Machu Picchu). Once at the destination country, participants travel by bus, foot, boat, airplane. Program is affiliated with the nationwide TraveLearn network of 290 universities and colleges.

Learning Focus • Instruction in natural history, ecology and cultural history. Attendance at performances (Ballet Folklorico). Nature observation (Galapagos Islands). Other activities include "people-to-people" experience in Quito. Instruction is offered by professors, naturalists, historians, social scientists. This program would appeal to people interested in natural history, cultural history and understanding, ecology.

Accommodations • Hotels, boat. Single rooms are available for an additional $795.

Program Details • Program offered 6 times per year. Session length: 14–18 days. Departures are scheduled in January, March, June–September. Program is targeted to mature adults. Most participants are 40–75 years of age. Participants must be 18 years or older to enroll. 14–20 participants per session. Application deadline: 60 days prior to departure. Reservations are recommended at least 4–8 months before departure.

Costs • $3895 (includes housing, all meals, books and class materials, excursions, international airfare). A $300 deposit is required.

Contact • Keith Williams, Director of Marketing, TraveLearn, PO Box 315, Lakeville, PA 18438; 800-235-9114; Fax: 717-226-9114; E-mail: travelearn@aol.com

VOYAGERS INTERNATIONAL

PHOTOGRAPHIC TOUR AND WORKSHOP IN ECUADOR

General Information • Photography tour with visits to Galapagos Islands. Once at the destination country, participants travel by foot, small vehicle.

Learning Focus • Instruction in photography. Nature observation (wildlife and scenery). Instruction is offered by photographers. This program would appeal to people interested in photography, culture, nature studies.

Accommodations • Hotels, lodges. Single rooms are available.

Program Details • Session length: 10–14 days. Departures are scheduled throughout the year. Program is targeted to photography enthusiasts. Most participants are 30–70 years of age. 8–10 participants per session. Reservations are recommended at least 6–12 months before departure.

Costs • $2800–$3400 (includes tuition, housing, all meals, excursions, international airfare, cruise). A $400 deposit is required.

Contact • David Blanton, Managing Director, Voyagers International, PO Box 915, Ithaca, NY 14851; 800-633-0299; Fax: 607-273-3873; E-mail: voyint@aol.com

WILDLAND ADVENTURES

GALAPAGOS WILDLIFE ODYSSEY

General Information • Nature study tour with visits to Galapagos Islands. Once at the destination country, participants travel by foot, boat, airplane. Program is affiliated with Charles Darwin Foundation.

Learning Focus • Nature observation (unusual wildlife and evoultion). Other activities include hiking, snorkeling, yacht excursion. Instruction is offered by naturalists. This program would appeal to people interested in photography, geology, snorkeling.

Accommodations • Boat. Single rooms are available for an additional $175.

Program Details • Program offered 52 times per year. Session length: 12 days. Departures are scheduled throughout the year. Most participants are 30–70 years of age. Participants must be 5 years or older to enroll. 10–20 participants per session. Application deadline: 30 days prior to departure. Reservations are recommended at least 3–6 months before departure.

Costs • $1895 (includes housing, some meals, excursions, complete pre-departure dossier). A $300 deposit is required.

Contact • Wildland Adventures, 3516 Northeast 155th Street, Seattle, WA 98155; 800-345-4453; Fax: 206-363-6615; E-mail: wildadve@aol.com; World Wide Web: http://www.wildland.com

WILDLAND ADVENTURES

LA SELVA AMAZON TREK

General Information • Wilderness/adventure program with visits to Amazon, Quito. Once at the destination country, participants travel by foot, boat, airplane.

Learning Focus • Escorted travel to the Amazon jungle. Nature observation (rain forest wildlife). Other activities include camping, hiking, contact with Amazon Indians. Instruction is offered by naturalists, Native Indians. This program would appeal to people interested in photography, bird watching, botany, culture.

Accommodations • Hotels, campsites. Single rooms are available.

Program Details • Program offered 52 times per year. Session length: 7 days. Departures are scheduled throughout the year. Most participants are 30-50 years of age. Participants must be 12 years or older to enroll. 2-10 participants per session. Application deadline: 30 days prior to departure. Reservations are recommended at least 3-6 months before departure.

Costs • $1895 (includes housing, some meals, excursions, complete pre-departure dossier). A $300 deposit is required.

Contact • Wildland Adventures, 3516 Northeast 155th Street, Seattle, WA 98155; 800-345-4453; Fax: 206-363-6615; E-mail: wildadve@aol.com; World Wide Web: http://www.wildland.com

WILLARDS ADVENTURE CLUB

GALAPAGOS ISLES EXPEDITION CRUISE

General Information • Nature study tour with visits to Quito, Playa Ochoa, Española Island, Gardner Bay, Punta Suarez, Punta Cormorant, Peru (Lima). Once at the destination country, participants travel by foot, boat, airplane.

Learning Focus • Escorted travel to Darwin Research Station and San Cristobol Island. Nature observation (sea lions, marine iguanas, albatrosses, flamingoes, wildlife). Instruction is offered by naturalists, wilderness guides. This program would appeal to people interested in wildlife, nature studies.

Accommodations • Hotels, boat. Single rooms are available.

Program Details • Program offered once per year. Session length: 9 days. Departures are scheduled in October. Most participants are 9-80 years of age. Participants must be members of the sponsoring organization (annual dues: $5). 15 participants per session. Reservations are recommended at least 6 months before departure.

Costs • $2360 (includes housing, some meals). A $300 deposit is required.

Contact • Willard Kinzie, President, Willards Adventure Club, Box 10, Barrie, ON L4M 4S9, Canada; 705-737-1881; Fax: 705-737-5123

El Salvador

AMERISPAN UNLIMITED

SPANISH CLASSES AND HOMESTAYS IN EL SALVADOR

General Information • Language study program with visits to San Salvador. Once at the destination country, participants travel by bus.
Learning Focus • Instruction in the Spanish language. Instruction is offered by trained Spanish teachers. This program would appeal to people interested in Spanish language, Latin America.
Accommodations • Homestays. Single rooms are available.
Program Details • Session length: 2–12 weeks. Departures are scheduled throughout the year. Most participants are 16–70 years of age. Reservations are recommended at least 4 weeks before departure.
Costs • $345 for 2 weeks, $695 for 4 weeks, $150 for each additional week (includes tuition, housing, all meals, insurance). A $100 deposit is required.
Contact • AmeriSpan Unlimited, PO Box 40513, Philadelphia, PA 19106; 800-879-6640; Fax: 215-985-4524; E-mail: info@amerispan.com; World Wide Web: http://www.amerispan.com

CENTER FOR GLOBAL EDUCATION AT AUGSBURG COLLEGE

EL SALVADOR ELECTIONS

General Information • Academic study program with visits to San Salvador, countryside. Once at the destination country, participants travel by bus, foot, van.
Learning Focus • Instruction in current issues facing El Salvador. Volunteer work (elections observer). Other activities include meetings with community leaders and political candidates. Instruction is offered by in-country coordinators. This program would appeal to people interested in social justice, peace studies, El Salvador, democracy, politics.
Accommodations • Guest houses.
Program Details • Program offered once per year. Session length: 8 days. Departures are scheduled in March. Most participants are 20–70 years of age. Participants must be 18 years or older to enroll. Other requirements: accompanied by an adult if under 18 years of age. 15 participants per session. Application deadline: February 23. Reservations are recommended at least 6 weeks before departure.
Costs • $1450 (includes housing, all meals, books and class materials, excursions, international airfare, translation). A $100 deposit is required.
Contact • International Travel Seminars, Center for Global Education at Augsburg College, Center for Global Education, 2211 Riverside Avenue, Minneapolis, MN 55454; 800-299-8889; Fax: 612-330-1695; E-mail: globaled@augsburg.edu; World Wide Web: http://www.augsburg.edu/global

GUATEMALA

AMERISPAN UNLIMITED

SPANISH CLASSES AND HOMESTAYS IN GUATEMALA

General Information • Language study program with visits to Antigua, Quetzaltenango, Tikal Ruins, Lake Atitlan, markets, villages. Once at the destination country, participants travel by bus.
Learning Focus • Instruction in the Spanish language. Instruction is offered by trained Spanish teachers. This program would appeal to people interested in Spanish language, Latin America.
Accommodations • Homestays. Single rooms are available.
Program Details • Session length: 2–12 weeks. Departures are scheduled throughout the year. Most participants are 16–70 years of age. Participants must be 16 years or older to enroll. Reservations are recommended at least 4 weeks before departure.
Costs • In Antigua $325–$375 for 2 weeks, $625–$725 for 4 weeks, $150–$175 each additional week; in Quetzaltenango: $345 for 2 weeks, $645 for 4 weeks, $150 each additional week (includes tuition, housing, all meals, insurance). A $100 deposit is required.
Contact • AmeriSpan Unlimited, PO Box 40513, Philadelphia, PA 19106; 800-879-6640; Fax: 215-985-4524; E-mail: info@amerispan.com; World Wide Web: http://www.amerispan.com

ARCHAEOLOGICAL TOURS

GUATEMALA

General Information • Cultural tour with visits to Antigua and Barbuda, Guatemala (Chichicastenango, Guatemala City, Lake Atitlan, Tikal), Honduras (Honduras (Copan)); excursions to Quirigua, Uaxactum, Aguateca. Once at the destination country, participants travel by bus.
Learning Focus • Museum visits (Guatemala City, Copan, Tikal). Instruction is offered by professors, historians. This program would appeal to people interested in history, archaeology.
Accommodations • Hotels. Single rooms are available for an additional $585.
Program Details • Program offered once per year. Session length: 15 days. Departures are scheduled in February. Program is targeted to adults. Most participants are 30–80 years of age. 18 participants per session. Application deadline: 1 month prior to departure.
Costs • $3050 (includes housing, some meals, excursions, internal flights). A $500 deposit is required.
Contact • Archaeological Tours, 271 Madison Avenue, Suite 904, New York, NY 10016; 212-986-3054; Fax: 212-370-1561

CASA DE ESPANOL XELAJU

COMPREHENSIVE SPANISH AND CULTURAL STUDIES

General Information • Language study program in Quetzaltenango.
Learning Focus • Courses in Spanish language, culture, Mayan language. Instruction is offered by professors from the sponsoring institution.
Accommodations • Homestays. Single rooms are available. Meals are taken with host family, in residences.
Program Details • Session length: varies. Departures are scheduled in January–December. The program is open to undergraduate students, graduate students, pre-college students, adults. Most participants are 25–60 years of age. Application deadline: 2 weeks before classes begin.
Costs • $145–$170 per week (includes tuition, housing, all meals, excursions, daily social and cultural activities).
Contact • Julio E. Batres, Director, Casa De Espanol Xelaju, 2206 Falcon Hill Drive, Austin, TX 78745; 512-416-6991; Fax: 512-416-8968; E-mail: cexspanish@aol.com

CENTER FOR GLOBAL EDUCATION AT AUGSBURG COLLEGE

CULTURAL AND POLITICAL REALITIES IN GUATEMALA

General Information • Academic study program with visits to Guatemala City, Guatemalan highlands. Once at the destination country, participants travel by bus, foot.
Learning Focus • Instruction in current issues facing Guatemala. Escorted travel to local communities. Other activities include meetings with community leaders, political representatives, human rights workers. Instruction is offered by in-country coordinators. This program would appeal to people interested in social justice, development, Guatemala, third world studies.
Accommodations • Guest houses.
Program Details • Program offered 2 times per year. Session length: 8 days. Departures are scheduled in March, May. Most participants are 20–70 years of age. Participants must be 18 years or older to enroll. 15 participants per session. Reservations are recommended at least 6 weeks before departure.
Costs • $1550 (includes housing, all meals, books and class materials, excursions, international airfare, translation). A $100 deposit is required.
Contact • International Travel Seminars, Center for Global Education at Augsburg College, Center for Global Education, 2211 Riverside Avenue, Minneapolis, MN 55454; 800-299-8889; Fax: 612-330-1695; E-mail: globaled@augsburg.edu; World Wide Web: http://www.augsburg.edu/global

CENTER FOR GLOBAL EDUCATION AT AUGSBURG COLLEGE

SPIRITUAL TRANSFORMATION: CULTURE AND POLITICS IN GUATEMALA

General Information • Academic study program with visits to Guatemala City, Guatemalan highlands. Once at the destination country, participants travel by bus, foot. Program is affiliated with Center for Social Justice of the Society of Mary.

Learning Focus • Instruction in current issues facing Guatemala. Escorted travel to local communities. Other activities include meetings with community leaders, indigenous peoples, political representatives. Instruction is offered by in-country coordinators. This program would appeal to people interested in social justice, third world development, human rights, peace studies.

Accommodations • Guest houses.

Program Details • Program offered once per year. Session length: 9 days. Departures are scheduled in June. Most participants are 20–70 years of age. Participants must be 18 years or older to enroll. Other requirements: accompaniment by an adult if under 18 years of age. 15 participants per session. Application deadline: May 23. Reservations are recommended at least 6 weeks before departure.

Costs • $1550 (includes housing, all meals, books and class materials, excursions, international airfare, translation). A $100 deposit is required.

Contact • International Travel Seminars, Center for Global Education at Augsburg College, Center for Global Education, 2211 Riverside Avenue, Minneapolis, MN 55454; 800-299-8889; Fax: 612-330-1695; E-mail: globaled@augsburg.edu; World Wide Web: http://www.augsburg.edu/global

FOREIGN LANGUAGE STUDY ABROAD SERVICE

SPANISH IN ANTIGUA

General Information • Language study program in Antigua.

Learning Focus • Courses in language study. Instruction is offered by local teachers.

Accommodations • Homestays, hotels. Single rooms are available. Meals are taken with host family, in residences.

Program Details • Session length: varies. Departures are scheduled in January–December. The program is open to undergraduate students, graduate students, pre-college students, adults. Most participants are 16 years of age and older.

Costs • Contact sponsor for information. Application fee: $50. A $100 deposit is required.

Contact • Louise Harber, Coordinator, Foreign Language Study Abroad Service, Department IH, Box 903, 5935 Southwest 64th Avenue, South Miami, FL 33143; 800-282-1090; Fax: 305-662-2907; E-mail: flsas@netpoint.net; World Wide Web: http://www.netpoint.net/~flsas

GEORGE MASON UNIVERSITY

GUATEMALA

General Information • Language study program in Quetzaltenango. Classes are held on the campus of Casa de Espanol Xelaju.

Learning Focus • Courses in Spanish language, cultural studies. Instruction is offered by professors from the sponsoring institution and local teachers.

Accommodations • Homestays. Single rooms are available. Meals are taken as a group, in central dining facility, in local restaurants.

Program Details • Program offered once per year. Session length: 2 ½ weeks. Departures are scheduled in January. The program is open to undergraduate students, graduate students, adults. Most participants are 18–65 years of age. Other requirements: minimum 2.25 GPA. 10–20 participants per session. Application deadline: October 11.

Costs • $1800 for George Mason University students, $2300 for other students (includes tuition, housing, all meals, insurance, excursions, international airfare). Application fee: $35. A $500 deposit is required.

Contact • Dr. Yehuda Lukacs, Director, International Exchange and Study Abroad, George Mason University, 4400 University Drive, 235 Johnson Center, Fairfax, VA 22030; 703-993-2155; Fax: 703-993-2153; E-mail: ylukacs@gmu.edu; World Wide Web: http://www.gmu.edu/departments/oie

GLOBAL EXCHANGE REALITY TOURS

GUATEMALA

General Information • Human rights, indigenous issues study program with visits to Chimaltenango, Cobán, Guatemala City. Once at the destination country, participants travel by bus, airplane.

Learning Focus • Instruction in human rights issues and grassroots, indigenous groups. Escorted travel to Mayan ruins. Instruction is offered by researchers, naturalists. This program would appeal to people interested in human rights, indigenous issues, grassroots development.

Accommodations • Hotels, guest houses. Single rooms are available.

Program Details • Program offered 3 times per year. Session length: 13 days. Departures are scheduled in April, August. Program is targeted to seniors, students and professionals. Participants must be 18 years or older to enroll. 10–15 participants per session. Application deadline: 1 month prior to departure. Reservations are recommended at least 2 months before departure.

Costs • $800 from Guatemala City (includes housing, some meals). A $200 deposit is required.

Contact • Loreto Curti, Reality Tours Coordinator, Global Exchange Reality Tours, 2017 Mission Street, Room 303, San Francisco, CA 94110; 415-255-7296; Fax: 415-255-7498; E-mail: globalexch@igc.apc.org

LANGUAGE LIAISON

SPANISH IN GUATEMALA

General Information • Language study program with visits to Guatemala.

Learning Focus • Instruction in the Spanish language. Instruction is offered by professors. This program would appeal to people interested in language.

Accommodations • Homestays, locally-rented apartments, hotels. Single rooms are available.

Program Details • Session length: unlimited. Departures are scheduled throughout the year. Program is targeted to students of any age. Most participants are 18–70 years of age. Participants must be 16 years or older to enroll. Reservations are recommended at least 35 days before departure.
Costs • Contact sponsor for information.
Contact • Nancy Forman, President, Language Liaison, 20533 Biscayne Boulevard-Station 4-162, Miami, FL 33180; 305-682-9909; Fax: 305-682-9907; E-mail: langstudy@aol.com; World Wide Web: http://languageliaison.com

LANGUAGE LINK

ONE ON ONE SPANISH IN ANTIGUA–PROYECTO LINGUISTICO FRANCISCO MARROQUIN

General Information • Language study program in Antigua.
Learning Focus • Courses in Spanish language, Mayan language.
Accommodations • Homestays. Single rooms are available. Meals are taken with host family.
Program Details • Session length: 1–12 weeks. Departures are scheduled in January–December. The program is open to undergraduate students, graduate students, pre-college students, adults. Most participants are 14–80 years of age. 125 participants per session.
Costs • $200 per week (includes tuition, housing, all meals). Application fee: $35.
Contact • Kay Rafool, Director, Language Link, PO Box 3006, Peoria, IL 61612; 800-552-2051; Fax: 309-692-2926; E-mail: info@langlink.com; World Wide Web: http://www.langlink.com

NATIONAL REGISTRATION CENTER FOR STUDY ABROAD

SAB SPANISH SCHOOL

General Information • Language study program in Quetzaltenango.
Learning Focus • Courses in Spanish language.
Accommodations • Homestays. Single rooms are available. Meals are taken with host family.
Program Details • Program offered 12 times per year. Session length: 4 weeks. Departures are scheduled in January–December. The program is open to undergraduate students, graduate students, adults. Application deadline: 40 days prior to departure.
Costs • $665 (includes tuition, housing, all meals, insurance). Application fee: $40. A $100 deposit is required.
Contact • June Domoe, Educational Consultant, National Registration Center for Study Abroad, PO Box 1393, Milwaukee, WI 53201; 414-278-0631; Fax: 414-271-8884; E-mail: inquiries@nrcsa.com; World Wide Web: http://www.nrcsa.com

 WILDLAND ADVENTURES

SCARLET MACAW TIKAL TREK

General Information • Cultural tour with visits to Flores, Guatemala City, Tikal, Maya Biosphere Reserve, ancient ruins. Once at the destination country, participants travel by foot, airplane, four-wheel drive vehicle. Program is affiliated with Conservation International.
Learning Focus • Nature observation (scarlet macaws and monkeys). Other activities include camping, hiking. Instruction is offered by naturalists, Mayan natives. This program would appeal to people interested in photography, archaeology, trekking.
Accommodations • Hotels, campsites. Single rooms are available.
Program Details • Program offered 2 times per year. Session length: 12 days. Departures are scheduled in May. Most participants are 30–60 years of age. Participants must be 12 years or older to enroll. 4–12 participants per session. Application deadline: 30 days prior to departure. Reservations are recommended at least 3-6 months before departure.
Costs • $1495 (includes housing, some meals, excursions, complete pre-departure dossier). A $300 deposit is required.
Contact • Wildland Adventures, 3516 Northeast 155th Street, Seattle, WA 98155; 800-345-4453; Fax: 206-363-6615; E-mail: wildadve@aol.com; World Wide Web: http://www.wildland.com

HAITI

GLOBAL EXCHANGE REALITY TOURS

HAITI: ART, CULTURE, AND VODOU

General Information • Cultural tour with visits to Cap Haiten/Milot, Port-au-Prince, Tacmel. Once at the destination country, participants travel by bus.

Learning Focus • Museum visits (Mupanah, Musee, St. Pierre). Instruction is offered by researchers, naturalists. This program would appeal to people interested in history, voodoo religion, arts, crafts.

Accommodations • Hotels, guest houses. Single rooms are available for an additional $200–$500.

Program Details • Program offered 3 times per year. Session length: 11 days. Departures are scheduled in December, July, April. Program is targeted to seniors, students and professionals. Participants must be 18 years or older to enroll. 10–15 participants per session. Application deadline: 1 month prior to departure. Reservations are recommended at least 2 months before departure.

Costs • $1050 (includes housing, some meals, books and class materials, international airfare). A $200 deposit is required.

Contact • Sonia Lee, Reality Tours Coordinator, Global Exchange Reality Tours, 2017 Mission Street, Room 303, San Francisco, CA 94110; 415-255-7296; Fax: 415-255-7498; E-mail: globalexch@igc.apc.org

AMERISPAN UNLIMITED

SPANISH CLASSES AND HOMESTAYS IN HONDURAS

General Information • Language study program with visits to Copan, La Ceiba, Trujillo. Once at the destination country, participants travel by bus.
Learning Focus • Instruction in the Spanish language. Instruction is offered by trained Spanish teachers. This program would appeal to people interested in Spanish language, Latin America.
Accommodations • Homestays. Single rooms are available.
Program Details • Session length: 2–12 weeks. Departures are scheduled throughout the year. Most participants are 16–70 years of age. Participants must be 16 years or older to enroll. 1 participant per session. Reservations are recommended at least 4 weeks before departure.
Costs • $325 for 2 weeks, $625 for 4 weeks, $150 for each additional week (includes tuition, housing, all meals, insurance). A $100 deposit is required.
Contact • AmeriSpan Unlimited, PO Box 40513, Philadelphia, PA 19106; 800-879-6640; Fax: 215-985-4524; E-mail: info@amerispan.com; World Wide Web: http://www.amerispan.com

JAMES MADISON UNIVERSITY

SUMMER HEALTH SCIENCES STUDY IN HONDURAS

General Information • Academic study program in Pinalejo, Roatan. Excursions to villages throughout Honduras.
Learning Focus • Courses in health sciences. Instruction is offered by professors from the sponsoring institution.
Accommodations • Homestays, hotels. Meals are taken as a group, on one's own, with host family, in local restaurants.
Program Details • Program offered once per year. Session length: 4 weeks. Departures are scheduled in May, June. The program is open to undergraduate students, graduate students. Most participants are 18–25 years of age. Other requirements: health science majors. 10 participants per session. Application deadline: February 1.
Costs • $5747 for Virginia residents, $7887 for nonresidents (includes tuition, housing, some meals, excursions). A $400 deposit is required.
Contact • Marcia Ball, Professor, College of Education, James Madison University, Office of International Education, Harrisonburg, VA 22807; 540-568-3951; Fax: 540-568-2829; E-mail: ballml@jmu.edu; World Wide Web: http://www.jmu.edu/intl-ed/

LOUISIANA STATE UNIVERSITY

AGRICULTURAL FIELD STUDY IN HONDURAS

General Information • Academic study program in Honduras. Classes are held on the campus of Zamorano. Excursions to Lancetilla Botanical Gardens, Copan Ruins.
Learning Focus • Courses in agriculture. Instruction is offered by professors from the sponsoring institution.
Accommodations • Dormitories. Meals are taken as a group, in central dining facility.
Program Details • Program offered once per year. Session length: 2 weeks. Departures are scheduled in March. The program is open to undergraduate students, graduate students. Most participants are 20–25 years of age. Other requirements: minimum 2.5 GPA for 6 hours of credit and a minimum 3.0 GPA for 9 hours of credit. 15–20 participants per session. Application deadline: January 31.
Costs • $864 (includes tuition, housing, some meals, excursions). A $200 deposit is required.
Contact • Jeannie Willamson, Study Abroad Coordinator, Louisiana State University, Academic Programs Abroad, 365 Pleasant Hall, Baton Rouge, LA 70803; 504-388-6801; Fax: 504-388-6806; E-mail: abwill@lsuvm.sncc.lsu.edu

NATIONAL REGISTRATION CENTER FOR STUDY ABROAD

CENTRO INTERNACIONAL DE IDIOMAS

General Information • Language study program in Trujillo.
Learning Focus • Courses in Spanish language, Garifuna language.
Accommodations • Homestays, program-owned apartments. Single rooms are available. Meals are taken with host family, in residences.
Program Details • Program offered 50 times per year. Session length: 4 weeks. Departures are scheduled in January–December. The program is open to undergraduate students, graduate students, adults. 1 participant per session. Application deadline: 40 days prior to departure.
Costs • $786 (includes tuition, housing, all meals, insurance). Application fee: $40. A $100 deposit is required.
Contact • June Domoe, Educational Consultant, National Registration Center for Study Abroad, Box 1393, Milwaukee, WI 53201; 414-278-0631; Fax: 414-271-8884; E-mail: ask@nrcsa.com; World Wide Web: http://www.nrcsa.com

UNIVERSITY OF FLORIDA

HONDURAS, AGRICULTURE AND NATURAL RESOURCES PROGRAM

General Information • Academic study program in Zamorano. Classes are held on the campus of Escuela Agrícola Panamericana. Excursions to ruins at Capan, forests, Garifuna villages, mountains, beaches.
Learning Focus • Courses in agriculture, cultural studies, ecology, Spanish language. Instruction is offered by professors from the sponsoring institution and local teachers.

Accommodations • Dormitories. Meals are taken as a group, on one's own, in central dining facility, in local restaurants, in residences.

Program Details • Program offered once per year. Session length: 5 weeks. Departures are scheduled in June. The program is open to undergraduate students, graduate students, adults. Most participants are 18–40 years of age. Other requirements: minimum 2.5 GPA. Application deadline: March 15.

Costs • $4200–$5700 depending on residency and school (includes tuition, housing, some meals, books and class materials, insurance, excursions, international airfare, administration/development costs, estimated living expenses). Application fee: $250.

Contact • Overseas Studies, University of Florida, 123 Tigert Hall, PO Box 113225, Gainesville, FL 32611-3225; 352-392-5206; Fax: 352-392-5575; E-mail: ovrseas@nervm.nerdc.ufl.edu

JAMAICA

BALDWIN-WALLACE COLLEGE

STUDY ABROAD IN THE CARIBBEAN

General Information • Academic study program in Kingston.
Learning Focus • Courses in political science. Instruction is offered by professors from the sponsoring institution.
Accommodations • Hotels.
Program Details • Program offered once per year. Session length: 3 weeks. Departures are scheduled in August. Most participants are 18–25 years of age. Other requirements: minimum 2.3 GPA. 15 participants per session. Application deadline: January 20.
Costs • Contact sponsor for information. A $100 deposit is required.
Contact • Mrs. Dorothy Hunter, Coordinator, Baldwin-Wallace College, Study Abroad Center, 275 Eastland Road, Berea, OH 44017-2088; 216-826-2231; Fax: 216-826-3021; E-mail: dhunter@rs6000.baldwin.edu; World Wide Web: http://www.baldwinw.edu

THE PARTNERSHIP FOR SERVICE-LEARNING

JAMAICA

General Information • Academic study and volunteer service program in Kingston. Classes are held on the campus of University of Technology.
Learning Focus • Courses in literature, sociology, Caribbean studies. Instruction is offered by local teachers.
Accommodations • Homestays. Single rooms are available. Meals are taken with host family, in residences.
Program Details • Program offered once per year. Session length: 8½ weeks. Departures are scheduled in June. The program is open to undergraduate students, graduate students, pre-college students, adults. Most participants are 19–24 years of age. 7 participants per session. Application deadline: 2 months prior to departure.
Costs • $4200 (includes tuition, housing, some meals, excursions, service placement and supervision, pre-departure and orientation materials). A $250 deposit is required.
Contact • Maureen Lowney, Coordinator of Student Programs, The Partnership for Service-Learning, 815 Second Avenue, Suite 315, New York, NY 10960; 212-986-0989; Fax: 212-986-5039; E-mail: pslny@aol.com

UNIVERSITY OF MICHIGAN

SUMMER PROGRAM IN JAMAICA

General Information • Academic study program in Kingston. Classes are held on the campus of University of the West Indies.
Learning Focus • Courses in Caribbean studies. Instruction is offered by professors from the sponsoring institution and local teachers.
Accommodations • Dormitories. Meals are taken on one's own, in local restaurants.
Program Details • Program offered once per year. Session length: 6 weeks. Departures are scheduled in June. The program is open to undergraduate students. Most participants are 19–24 years of age. Other requirements: minimum 3.0 GPA. 15 participants per session. Application deadline: February 28.
Costs • $4700–$4900 (includes tuition, housing, some meals, excursions). Application fee: $50. A $250 deposit is required.
Contact • Office of International Programs, University of Michigan, G-513 Michigan Union, 530 South State Street, Ann Arbor, MI 48109-1349; 313-764-4311; Fax: 313-764-3229; E-mail: oip@umich.edu; World Wide Web: http://www.umich.edu/~iinet/oip/

UNIVERSITY OF SOUTHERN MISSISSIPPI

CARIBBEAN STUDIES PROGRAM

General Information • Academic study program in Ocho Rios.
Learning Focus • Courses in anthropology, criminal justice, international business, literature, Caribbean studies, geography, international marketing, nursing, sociology.
Accommodations • Hotels, condominiums.
Program Details • Program offered once per year. Session length: 3 weeks. Departures are scheduled in June. The program is open to undergraduate students, graduate students. Other requirements: minimum 2.0 GPA and good academic standing. Application deadline: April 5.
Costs • $1999 for undergraduates, $2299 for graduate students (includes tuition, housing, excursions, international airfare). Application fee: $100.
Contact • Dr. Mark Miller, Assistant Dean and Director, Caribbean Studies Program, University of Southern Mississippi, College of International and Continuing Education, Box 10047, Hattiesburg, MS 39406-0047; 601-266-4736; Fax: 601-266-5699; E-mail: m_ravencraft@bull.cc.usm.edu

MARTINIQUE

INTERHOSTEL, UNIVERSITY OF NEW HAMPSHIRE

FRENCH WEST INDIES

General Information • Cultural tour with visits to Gosier, Plantation Leyritz, Trois Ilets, Fort-De-France, La Pagerie, La Trace, Balata Botanical Gardens, St. Pierre, Basse-Terre, Pointe-a-Pitre, Cousteau Reservation, Les Saintes. Once at the destination country, participants travel by bus, foot, boat, airplane. Program is affiliated with American University of Paris and Université des Antilles-Guyane.

Learning Focus • Instruction in history, culture and ecology. Escorted travel to villages, parks and gardens. Museum visits (pre-Columbian Archaeological Museum, Schoelcher Museum, Museum of Volcanology). Attendance at performances (folk dancing). Instruction is offered by professors, historians. This program would appeal to people interested in history, culture.

Accommodations • Hotels. Single rooms are available for an additional $525.

Program Details • Program offered 2 times per year. Session length: 2 weeks. Departures are scheduled in December, January. Program is targeted to seniors over 50. Most participants are 60–80 years of age. Participants must be 50 years or older to enroll. 35 participants per session. Reservations are recommended at least 6 months before departure.

Costs • $2855 (includes tuition, housing, all meals, excursions, international airfare, entrance fees). A $200 deposit is required.

Contact • Janice Pierson, Office Supervisor, Interhostel, University of New Hampshire, 6 Garrison Avenue, Durham, NH 03824-3529; 800-733-9753; Fax: 603-862-1113; World Wide Web: http://www.learn.unh.edu/

RUSSIAN AND EAST EUROPEAN PARTNERSHIPS

MARTINIQUE LANGUAGE AND CULTURAL IMMERSION PROGRAM

General Information • Language study program in Martinique.

Learning Focus • Courses in French language, local culture and art, local history. Instruction is offered by professors from the sponsoring institution.

Accommodations • Homestays. Single rooms are available. Meals are taken on one's own, with host family, in local restaurants, in residences.

Program Details • Program offered 11 times per year. Session length: 4 or more weeks. Departures are scheduled in January–November. The program is open to undergraduate students, graduate students, adults. Most participants are 18 years of age and older. Other requirements: in good health and 18 or older unless chaperoned by an adult. 6 participants per session. Application deadline: 45 days prior to departure.

Costs • $2950 (includes tuition, housing, some meals, books and class materials, excursions, international airfare, local transportation, airport transfers). A $1500 deposit is required.

Contact • Kenneth Fortune, President, Russian and East European Partnerships, PO Box 227, Fineview, NY 13640; 888-873-7337; Fax: 800-910-1777; E-mail: reep@fox.nstn.ca

UNIVERSITY OF DELAWARE

WINTER SESSION IN MARTINIQUE

General Information • Language study program in Fort de France. Classes are held on the campus of University of the Antilles and Guyane.

Learning Focus • Courses in Caribbean studies, French language, literature. Instruction is offered by professors from the sponsoring institution.

Accommodations • Homestays. Meals are taken with host family.

Program Details • Program offered once per year. Session length: 5 weeks. Departures are scheduled in January. The program is open to undergraduate students. Most participants are 18–21 years of age. Other requirements: minimum 2.0 GPA. 25 participants per session. Application deadline: October.

Costs • $4310 (includes tuition, housing, some meals, excursions, international airfare). A $200 deposit is required.

Contact • International Programs and Special Sessions, University of Delaware, 4 Kent Way, Newark, DE 19716-1450; 888-831-4685; Fax: 302-831-6042; E-mail: studyabroad@mvs.udel.edu

MEXICO

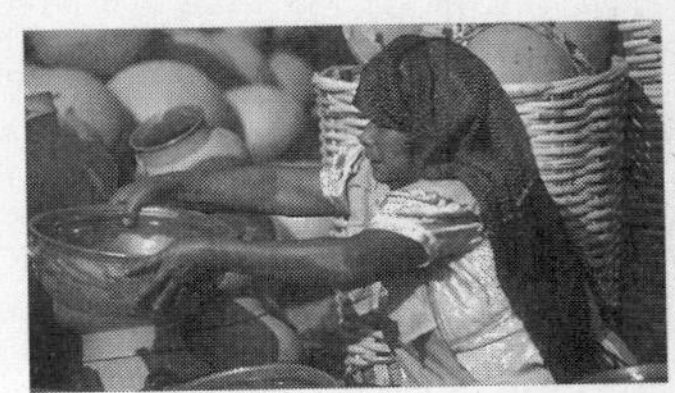

ACADEMIA HISPANO AMERICANA

ACADEMIA HISPANO AMERICANA

General Information • Language study program in San Miguel de Allende.

Learning Focus • Courses in Spanish language. Instruction is offered by professors from the sponsoring institution.

Accommodations • Homestays, locally-rented apartments, hotels. Single rooms are available. Meals are taken with host family, in residences.

Program Details • Program offered 12 times per year. Session length: 4 weeks. Departures are scheduled in January–December. The program is open to undergraduate students, graduate students, pre-college students. Most participants are 16–70 years of age. 50–100 participants per session.

Costs • $820 (includes tuition, housing, all meals). Application fee: $70. A $50 deposit is required.

Contact • Carmen Araiza, Registrar, Academia Hispano Americana, Mesones 4, San Miguel de Allende 37700, Mexico; +52 415-20-349; Fax: +52 415-22-333; E-mail: academia@mail.intermex.com.mx

ALMA COLLEGE

SUMMER PROGRAM OF STUDIES IN MEXICO

General Information • Language study program in Mexico City. Classes are held on the campus of Iberian-American University Mexico. Excursions to Teotihuacán, Taxco, Tula, Tepoztlan.

Learning Focus • Courses in Spanish language, Latin American studies. Instruction is offered by local teachers.

Accommodations • Homestays. Single rooms are available. Meals are taken with host family, in residences.

Program Details • Program offered 2 times per year. Session length: 6 weeks. Departures are scheduled in June. The program is open to undergraduate students, graduate students, adults. Most participants are 20–23 years of age. Other requirements: minimum 2.5 GPA. 6 participants per session. Application deadline: March 15.

Costs • $3260 (includes tuition, housing, all meals, excursions). Application fee: $35. A $200 deposit is required.

Contact • Patricia Landis, Director of International Education, Alma College, 614 West Superior Street, Alma, MI 48801; 517-463-7247; Fax: 517-463-7126; E-mail: landis@alma.edu; World Wide Web: http://www.alma.edu

ALPINE ASCENTS, INTERNATIONAL

VOLCANOES OF MEXICO

General Information • Mountain climbing tour with visits to El Pico de Orizaba, Popocatepetl, Mexico City. Once at the destination country, participants travel by foot, van.

Learning Focus • Instruction in mountain climbing. Escorted travel to Amecameca. Museum visits (National Museum of Anthropology). Nature observation (Gulf of Mexico, craters). Other activities include camping, hiking. Instruction is offered by sports professionals. This program would appeal to people interested in mountain climbing.

Accommodations • Hotels, campsites. Single rooms are available.

Program Details • Program offered 2 times per year. Session length: 9 days. Departures are scheduled in October, November. Program is targeted to mountain climbers. Other requirements: mountaineering skills, ice axe, crampon, and snow/ice experience. 8 participants per session. Reservations are recommended at least 6 months before departure.

Costs • $1400 (includes housing, some meals, group equipment, fees). A $300 deposit is required.

Contact • Gordon Janow, Program Coordinator, Alpine Ascents, International, 16615 Saybrook Drive, Woodinville, WA 98072; 206-788-1951; Fax: 206-788-6757

AMERICAN INSTITUTE FOR FOREIGN STUDY (AIFS)

UNIVERSITY OF MAYAB

General Information • Academic and language study program in Mérida. Classes are held on the campus of University of the Mayab. Excursions to Mexico City.

Learning Focus • Courses in Spanish language, Mexican history, Latin American literature, Mayan culture.

Accommodations • Homestays.

Program Details • Program offered once per year. Session length: 5 weeks. Departures are scheduled in July. The program is open to undergraduate students, graduate students, adults, high school graduates. Other requirements: minimum 2.0 GPA. Application deadline: March 15.

Costs • $2559 (includes tuition, housing, all meals). A $400 deposit is required.

Contact • Carmela Vigliano, Director, Summer Programs, American Institute for Foreign Study (AIFS), 102 Greenwich Avenue, Greenwich, CT 06830; 800-727-2437, ext. 6087; Fax: 203-869-9615; E-mail: info@aifs.org

AMERICAN INTERNATIONAL COLLEGE OF MEXICO

STUDY IN MEXICO

General Information • Academic study program in Mexico City, Oberetaro, San Miguel de Allende. Classes are held on the campus of Universidad del Valle de Mexico.

Live and study in Mexico

The University of Mayab in Mérida offers the perfect starting point for exploring the Yucatán. Courses in English delve into the history of Mayan culture and survey Mexican history. Latin American literature is offered in Spanish. Language study placement may be elementary (no previous study required), intermediate or advanced. Earn up to six credits. Students live and take meals in Mexican households. The AIFS Resident Director organizes excursions to Chichén Itzá, Uxmal, Kabah and Mexico City as well as other local cultural activities.

American Institute For Foreign Study®
Dept. PLA 102 Greenwich Avenue
Greenwich, CT 06830
Phone (800) 727-2437
E-mail info@aifs.org
http://www.aifs.org

Learning Focus • Courses in history, language study, art. Instruction is offered by professors from the sponsoring institution.
Accommodations • Homestays. Single rooms are available. Meals are taken on one's own, with host family, in central dining facility, in local restaurants, in residences.
Program Details • Program offered 3 times per year. Session length: 12 weeks. Departures are scheduled in January, May, August. The program is open to undergraduate students, graduate students, pre-college students, adults. Most participants are 18–45 years of age. 15–20 participants per session.
Costs • $750 (includes tuition, insurance, excursions). A $100 deposit is required.
Contact • Dr. David Bates, Dean, American International College of Mexico, Paseo de las Aves No. 1, Lomas Verdes 53220, Mexico; +52 238-73-56; Fax: +52 238-73-61

AMERISPAN UNLIMITED

SPANISH CLASSES AND HOMESTAYS IN MEXICO

General Information • Language study program with visits to Cuernavaca, Guanajuato, Mazatlán, Merida, Morelia, Oaxaca, San Miguel de Allende. Once at the destination country, participants travel by bus.
Learning Focus • Instruction in the Spanish language. Instruction is offered by trained Spanish teachers. This program would appeal to people interested in Spanish language, Latin America.
Accommodations • Homestays, hotels. Single rooms are available.
Program Details • Session length: 2–12 weeks. Departures are scheduled throughout the year. Most participants are 16–70 years of age. Participants must be 16 years or older to enroll. Reservations are recommended at least 4 weeks before departure.
Costs • Contact sponsor for information. A $100 deposit is required.
Contact • AmeriSpan Unlimited, PO Box 40513, Philadelphia, PA 19106; 800-879-6640; Fax: 215-985-4524; E-mail: info@amerispan.com; World Wide Web: http://www.amerispan.com

APPALACHIAN STATE UNIVERSITY

MEXICO

General Information • Academic study program in Mexico City, Oaxaca, Puebla, Taxco.
Learning Focus • Courses in art, anthropology. Instruction is offered by professors from the sponsoring institution.
Program Details • Program offered once per year. Session length: 16 days. Departures are scheduled in July. Most participants are 18 years of age and older. 20 participants per session.
Costs • $1796 (includes tuition, housing, insurance, international airfare, International Student Identification card).
Contact • Dr. Marilyn Smith, Professor, Appalachian State University, Art Department, Boone, NC 28608; 704-262-2220; Fax: 704-262-4037

AUSTIN PEAY STATE UNIVERSITY

STUDY ABROAD PROGRAM IN MEXICO

General Information • Academic study program in Cuernavaca. Excursions to Acapulco, Tepeypo, Basilica, haciendas, Teotihuacán, Xochicalco, Puebla, Oaxaca.
Learning Focus • Courses in history, language study, literature, business, art, cultural studies, political science, social work. Instruction is offered by professors from the sponsoring institution.
Accommodations • Homestays. Single rooms are available. Meals are taken with host family, in residences.
Program Details • Program offered 4 times per year. Session length: 4–16 weeks. Departures are scheduled in January, May, August, December. The program is open to undergraduate students, graduate students, pre-college students, adults. Most participants are 18–60 years of age. Other requirements: minimum 2.0 GPA. 25–35 participants per session.
Costs • $1795 (includes tuition, housing, all meals, books and class materials, insurance, excursions, transfer). Application fee: $200. A $200 deposit is required.
Contact • Dr. Ramón Majnóns, Professor, Austin Peay State University, Box 4487, Clarksville, TN 37044; 615-648-7848; Fax: 615-647-0387; E-mail: magnons@apsdoi.apsu.edu

BEAVER COLLEGE

SUMMER IN GUADALAJARA

General Information • Language study program in Guadalajara. Classes are held on the campus of Autonomous University of Guadalajara.
Learning Focus • Courses in Spanish language. Instruction is offered by local teachers.
Accommodations • Homestays. Single rooms are available. Meals are taken in residences.
Program Details • Program offered 2 times per year. Session length: 4 weeks. Departures are scheduled in June, July. The program is open to undergraduate students, graduate students. Other requirements: minimum 3.0 GPA and three or four semesters of college-level course work. Application deadline: March 31.
Costs • $1350 (includes tuition, housing, International Student Identification card, predeparture materials, host country support). Application fee: $35. A $500 deposit is required.
Contact • Meredith Chamorro, Program Coordinator, Beaver College, Center for Education Abroad, 450 South Easton Road, Glenside, PA 19038; 888-232-8379; Fax: 215-572-2174; E-mail: chamorro@turret.beaver.edu

BENTLEY COLLEGE

SUMMER PROGRAM IN PUEBLA, MEXICO

General Information • Language study program in Puebla. Classes are held on the campus of University of the Americas–Puebla. Excursions to Mexico City.
Learning Focus • Courses in language study, cultural studies. Instruction is offered by local teachers.

Accommodations • Homestays, dormitories. Single rooms are available. Meals are taken on one's own, in central dining facility, in local restaurants.
Program Details • Program offered once per year. Session length: 5 weeks. Departures are scheduled in May. The program is open to undergraduate students, adults. Most participants are 18–25 years of age. 15 participants per session. Application deadline: April 1.
Costs • $2500 (includes tuition, housing, International Student Identification card). Application fee: $35. A $500 deposit is required.
Contact • Jennifer L. Scully, Director of Study Abroad, Bentley College, International Center, 175 Forest Street, Waltham, MA 02154; 617-891-3474; Fax: 617-891-2819; E-mail: inprinfo@bentley.edu

CEMANAHUAC EDUCATIONAL COMMUNITY

SPANISH LANGUAGE PROGRAM AND LATIN AMERICAN STUDIES

General Information • Language study program in Cuernavaca. Excursions to Mexico, Guatemala, Costa Rica, Belize.
Learning Focus • Courses in language study, history, archaeology, art, anthropology. Instruction is offered by professors from the sponsoring institution.
Accommodations • Homestays, locally-rented apartments. Single rooms are available. Meals are taken with host family.
Program Details • Program offered 52 times per year. Session length: 1 or more weeks. Departures are scheduled in January–December. The program is open to undergraduate students, graduate students, pre-college students, adults. Most participants are 16–70 years of age. 100 participants per session.
Costs • $309 (includes tuition, housing, all meals). Application fee: $90.
Contact • Vivian B. Harvey, Educational Programs Coordinator, Cemanahuac Educational Community, Apartado 5-21, Cuernavaca, Morales, Mexico; +52 73-18-64-07; Fax: +52 73-12-54-18; E-mail: 74052.2570@compuserve.com; World Wide Web: http://www.cemanahuac.com

Cemanahuac offers a total language immersion program with an emphasis on oral communication in Spanish using ACTFL guidelines. Additional classes, at no extra fee, focus on grammar, composition, and comprehension. Class size is very small. Classes and programs include professional vocabulary, "Spanish for Business," Latin American studies courses, an extensive field study program, and a rural studies program. There is an extensive library and a conference center.

Academic credit, graduate and undergraduate, is available. Intensive programs are offered for professionals (teachers, medical personnel, social workers, business, clergy) who need to improve their Spanish. Individualized group programs and tutoring are also available.

Colonial Cuernavaca offers an almost perfect climate, with proximity (60 kilometers) to the historic, cultural, and business heart of the country, Mexico City. There are weekend and afternoon field study trips to archaeological sites, led by anthropologists. Housing includes stays with carefully selected families, and apartments and hotel housing is available at reasonable prices, most within easy walking distance. The rural studies program gives opportunity to experience life in a small Mexican village. Volunteer programs are available in many areas of Mexican life.

CENTER FOR BILINGUAL MULTICULTURAL STUDIES

CENTER FOR BILINGUAL MULTICULTURAL STUDIES

General Information • Language study program with visits to Mexico. Once at the destination country, participants travel by bus.
Learning Focus • Instruction in the Spanish language. Instruction is offered by professors, historians. This program would appeal to people interested in Spanish language.
Accommodations • Homestays. Single rooms are available.
Program Details • Session length: 1–2 weeks. Departures are scheduled throughout the year. Program is targeted to students and seniors. Most participants are 16–85 years of age. 3–5 participants per session. Reservations are recommended at least 1 month before departure.
Costs • $175 per week (includes tuition). A $100 deposit is required.
Contact • Maria Elena Young, Coordinator, Center for Bilingual Multicultural Studies, Center for Bilingual Studies, PO Box 1860, Los Angeles, CA 90078; 800-426-4660; Fax: 213-851-3684

CENTER FOR GLOBAL EDUCATION AT AUGSBURG COLLEGE

HUMAN RIGHTS TRAVEL AND STUDY SEMINAR TO MEXICO

General Information • Academic study program with visits to Mexico City, rural areas. Once at the destination country, participants travel by bus, foot. Program is affiliated with St. Mary's University School of Law.
Learning Focus • Instruction in international human rights. Escorted travel to local communities. Other activities include meetings with human rights workers, community representatives, political leaders. Instruction is offered by professors. This program would appeal to people interested in Mexico, social justice, human rights.
Accommodations • Guest houses.

Program Details • Program offered once per year. Session length: 8 days. Departures are scheduled in June. Most participants are 20–70 years of age. Participants must be 18 years or older to enroll. 15 participants per session. Application deadline: May 7. Reservations are recommended at least 6 weeks before departure.
Costs • $1800 (includes tuition, housing, all meals, books and class materials, excursions, international airfare, translation). A $100 deposit is required.
Contact • International Travel Seminars, Center for Global Education at Augsburg College, Center for Global Education, 2211 Riverside Avenue, Minneapolis, MN 55454; 800-299-8889; Fax: 612-330-1695; E-mail: globaled@augsburg.edu; World Wide Web: http://www.augsburg.edu/global

CENTER FOR GLOBAL EDUCATION AT AUGSBURG COLLEGE

MEXICO: CROSSING BORDERS, BUILDING COMMUNITY

General Information • Academic study program with visits to Cuernavaca, local communities, ruins. Once at the destination country, participants travel by bus, foot. Program is affiliated with Interfaith Hunger Appeal.
Learning Focus • Instruction in curriculum development. Other activities include meetings with local leaders and educators. Instruction is offered by professors, in-country coordinators. This program would appeal to people interested in education, Mexico, experiential education, social justice, development.
Accommodations • Program-owned houses.
Program Details • Program offered once per year. Session length: 9 days. Departures are scheduled in July. Program is targeted to university or seminary faculty. Most participants are 20–70 years of age. Participants must be 18 years or older to enroll. 15 participants per session. Application deadline: June 19. Reservations are recommended at least 6 weeks before departure.
Costs • $850 (includes housing, all meals, books and class materials, excursions, translation). A $100 deposit is required.
Contact • Church and Educators Team, Center for Global Education at Augsburg College, Center for Global Education, 2211 Riverside Avenue, Minneapolis, MN 55454; 800-299-8889; Fax: 612-330-1695; E-mail: globaled@augsburg.edu; World Wide Web: http://www.augsburg.edu/global

CENTER FOR GLOBAL EDUCATION AT AUGSBURG COLLEGE

MEXICO: EXPERIENTIAL EDUCATION IN THE DEVELOPING WORLD

General Information • Academic study program with visits to Cuernavaca, local communities, ruins. Once at the destination country, participants travel by bus, foot. Program is affiliated with Field Study for Social Change.
Learning Focus • Instruction in experiential education. Escorted travel to local communities. Museum visits (Diego Rivera murals). Other activities include meetings with educators, students, women's groups. Instruction is offered by professors, local community hosts. This program would appeal to people interested in Mexico, alternative education, experiential education, social justice, international education.
Accommodations • Program-owned houses.
Program Details • Program offered once per year. Session length: 8 days. Departures are scheduled in January. Program is targeted to study abroad professionals and others involved in international education. Most participants are 20–70 years of age. Participants must be 18 years or older to enroll. 15 participants per session. Application deadline: December 20. Reservations are recommended at least 6 weeks before departure.
Costs • $885 (includes housing, all meals, books and class materials, excursions, translation, trip leadership). A $100 deposit is required.
Contact • Church and Educators Team, Center for Global Education at Augsburg College, Center for Global Education, 2211 Riverside Avenue, Minneapolis, MN 55454; 612-330-1159; Fax: 612-330-1695; E-mail: globaled@augsburg.edu; World Wide Web: http://www.augsburg.edu/global

CENTER FOR GLOBAL EDUCATION AT AUGSBURG COLLEGE

MUSIC AMIDST THE STRUGGLE: NOURISHMENT AND HOPE IN MEXICO

General Information • Academic study program with visits to Cuernavaca, Mexico City, Tepoztlán.
Learning Focus • Instruction in the role of music in the struggle for justice and human dignity. Attendance at performances (National Folk Ballet). Instruction is offered by in-country coordinators. This program would appeal to people interested in music, social justice, Mexico.
Accommodations • Program-owned houses, guest houses.
Program Details • Program offered once per year. Session length: 8 days. Departures are scheduled in July. Most participants are 20–70 years of age. Participants must be 18 years or older to enroll. 15 participants per session. Reservations are recommended at least 6 weeks before departure.
Costs • $1400 (includes housing, all meals, books and class materials, international airfare, translation). A $100 deposit is required.
Contact • International Travel Seminars, Center for Global Education at Augsburg College, Center for Global Education, 2211 Riverside Avenue, Minneapolis, MN 55454; 800-299-8889; Fax: 612-330-1695; E-mail: globaled@augsburg.edu; World Wide Web: http://www.augsburg.edu/global

CENTER FOR GLOBAL EDUCATION AT AUGSBURG COLLEGE

SEMINAR ON INTERNATIONAL BUSINESS AND DEVELOPMENT ETHICS

General Information • Academic study program with visits to Cuernavaca, Mexico City, local communities, ruins. Once at the destination country, participants travel by foot. Program is affiliated with University of Wisconsin–River Falls.

Learning Focus • Instruction in ethical issues in international business and development. Other activities include meetings with local community leaders. Instruction is offered by professors, in-country coordinators. This program would appeal to people interested in business, ethics, development, economics, social justice.
Accommodations • Program-owned houses.
Program Details • Program offered once per year. Session length: 10 days. Departures are scheduled in July. Program is targeted to undergraduate students. Most participants are 18–30 years of age. Participants must be 18 years or older to enroll. 15 participants per session. Application deadline: June 28. Reservations are recommended at least 6 weeks before departure.
Costs • $1445 (includes housing, all meals, books and class materials, excursions, international airfare, translation). A $100 deposit is required.
Contact • Church and Educators Team, Center for Global Education at Augsburg College, Center for Global Education, 2211 Riverside Avenue, Minneapolis, MN 55454; 800-299-8889; Fax: 612-330-1695; E-mail: globaled@augsburg.edu; World Wide Web: http://www.augsburg.edu/global

CENTER FOR GLOBAL EDUCATION AT AUGSBURG COLLEGE

SUMMER INSTITUTE FOR GLOBAL EDUCATION

General Information • Academic study program with visits to Cuernavaca, ruins, local communities. Once at the destination country, participants travel by bus, foot, van.
Learning Focus • Instruction in multiculturalism and diversity issues. Escorted travel to local communities. Other activities include meetings with local community leaders, visits to schools. Instruction is offered by professors, in-country coordinators. This program would appeal to people interested in education, diversity, multiculturalism, social justice, Mexico.
Accommodations • Program-owned houses.
Program Details • Program offered once per year. Session length: 2 weeks. Departures are scheduled in June. Most participants are 20–70 years of age. Participants must be 18 years or older to enroll. Other requirements: accompaniment by an adult if under 18 years of age. 15 participants per session. Application deadline: May 23. Reservations are recommended at least 6 weeks before departure.
Costs • $1575 (includes housing, all meals, books and class materials, excursions, international airfare, translation). A $100 deposit is required.
Contact • Church and Educators Team, Center for Global Education at Augsburg College, Center for Global Education, 2211 Riverside Avenue, Minneapolis, MN 55454; 800-299-8889; Fax: 612-330-1685; E-mail: globaled@augsburg.edu; World Wide Web: http://www.augsburg.edu/global

CENTRO DE IDIOMAS, S.A.

SPANISH LANGUAGE PROGRAM

General Information • Language study program in Mazatlán.
Learning Focus • Courses in Spanish language. Instruction is offered by professors from the sponsoring institution.
Accommodations • Homestays, locally-rented apartments, hotels. Single rooms are available. Meals are taken with host family, in residences.
Program Details • Program offered 50 times per year. Session length: 2 or more weeks. Departures are scheduled in January–December. The program is open to undergraduate students, graduate students, pre-college students, adults. Most participants are 17–60 years of age. Other requirements: minimum age of 16. 25 participants per session. Application deadline: 30 days prior to departure.
Costs • $1020 per month (includes housing, all meals, books and class materials, excursions, orientation, counseling). Application fee: $105. A $235 deposit is required.
Contact • Dixie Davis, Director, Centro de Idiomas, S.A., Belisario Dominguez 1908, Mazatian, Sinaloa, Mexico; +52 69-82-20-53; Fax: +52 69-82-20-53; E-mail: 74174.1340@compuserve.com

In the words of former participants, "The teachers are not only professional, but helpful, enthusiastic, and very patient. I had no idea I could learn so much Spanish in such a short period of time." Constant evaluation and program improvement have contributed toward ranking the institute among the top language schools in Mexico. References from former participants are available upon request. Excellent beaches, semitropical climate, and convenient air connections have made Mazatlán one of Mexico's most popular vacation spots. It offers all the amenities of an international resort while still retaining the charm and hospitality of a typical Mexican town.

CENTRO MEXICANO INTERNACIONAL

SPANISH LANGUAGE STUDY–INTENSIVE PROGRAM

General Information • Language study program in Morelia. Classes are held on the campus of Centro Mexicano Internacional. Excursions to Santa Clara del Cobre, Pátzcuaro.
Learning Focus • Courses in Spanish language, Mexican culture, history. Instruction is offered by professors from the sponsoring institution and local teachers.
Accommodations • Homestays, locally-rented apartments, hotels. Single rooms are available. Meals are taken on one's own, with host family, in local restaurants, in residences.
Program Details • Program offered 52 times per year. Session length: 1 or more weeks. Departures are scheduled in January–December. The program is open to undergraduate students, graduate students, pre-college students, adults. Most participants are 16–85 years of age.
Costs • $325–$395 per week (includes tuition, excursions, campus siestas, doctor's office fees). A $150 deposit is required.

Contact • Centro Mexicano Internacional, Fray Antonio de San Miguel #173, Morelia, Michoacan 58000, Mexico; +52 43-12-45-96; Fax: +52 43-13-98-98; E-mail: cmi@giga.com

Participants are immersed in the Spanish language while living in Morelia, the capital of the state of Michoacan. Students stay with carefully screened Mexican families. Classes are conducted at the beautiful campus in the heart of colonial Morelia. Classes are small, offering individual attention by the bilingual staff. The core Spanish courses are taught by native speakers. Visiting U.S. and Mexican faculty members teach a wide range of subjects in various programs. Program offerings include university, intensive, high school, tutorials, Master of Arts in the teaching of languages, executive, and many internship opportunities.

CENTRO MEXICANO INTERNACIONAL

SPANISH LANGUAGE STUDY–UNIVERSITY PROGRAM

General Information • Language study program in Morelia. Classes are held on the campus of Centro Mexicano Internacional. Excursions to Santa Clara del Cobre, Pátzcuaro.
Learning Focus • Courses in Spanish language, Mexican culture, history. Instruction is offered by professors from the sponsoring institution and local teachers.
Accommodations • Homestays, locally-rented apartments, hotels. Single rooms are available. Meals are taken on one's own, with host family, in local restaurants, in residences.
Program Details • Program offered 12 times per year. Session length: 4 or 9 weeks. Departures are scheduled in January–December. The program is open to undergraduate students, graduate students, pre-college students, adults. Most participants are 16–85 years of age. Other requirements: minimum 2.50 GPA, minimum age of 16. 45 participants per session.
Costs • $955 for 4 weeks, $1890 for 9 weeks (includes tuition, excursions, campus siestas, on-campus doctor's fees). A $150 deposit is required.
Contact • Centro Mexicano Internacional, Fray Antonio de San Miguel #173, Morelia, Michoacan 58000, Mexico; +52 43-12-45-96; Fax: +52 43-13-98-98; E-mail: cmi@giga.com

CITY COLLEGE OF SAN FRANCISCO

SUMMER IN OAXACA

General Information • Language study program in Oaxaca. Classes are held on the campus of Instituto Cultural de Oaxaca. Excursions to Teotitlan del Valle, Mitla, Yagul, Monte Alban, other indiginous, artisan and pre-colonial villages.
Learning Focus • Courses in Spanish language. Instruction is offered by professors from the sponsoring institution and local teachers.
Accommodations • Homestays, locally-rented apartments. Single rooms are available. Meals are taken on one's own, with host family.
Program Details • Program offered once per year. Session length: 3 weeks. Departures are scheduled in June, July. The program is open to undergraduate students, adults. Most participants are 18–56 years of age. 20 participants per session. Application deadline: April 17.
Costs • $1700 for California residents, non-residents contact sponsor (includes tuition, housing, some meals, insurance, international airfare, transportation to and from homestay, workshops, Guelaguetza, intercambio). A $200 deposit is required.
Contact • Ms. Jill Heffron, Study Abroad Coordinator, City College of San Francisco, 50 Phelan Avenue, Box A71, San Francisco, CA 94112; 415-239-3778; Fax: 415-239-3804; E-mail: stdyabrd@ccsf.cc.ca.us

COLLEGE CONSORTIUM FOR INTERNATIONAL STUDIES–MIAMI-DADE COMMUNITY COLLEGE

CCIS PROGRAM IN MEXICO

General Information • Academic study program in Querétaro. Classes are held on the campus of Universidad del Valle de Mexico and American International College of Mexico. Excursions to Guanajuato, San Miguel.
Learning Focus • Courses in history, studio art, Spanish language, international relations. Instruction is offered by local teachers.
Accommodations • Homestays. Single rooms are available. Meals are taken with host family.
Program Details • Program offered once per year. Session length: 4 ½ weeks. Departures are scheduled in July. The program is open to undergraduate students. Most participants are 18 years of age and older. Other requirements: minimum 2.5 GPA. Application deadline: April 15.
Costs • $1350 (includes tuition, insurance). Application fee: $25. A $350 deposit is required.
Contact • Jane C. Evans, Executive Director, College Consortium for International Studies–Miami-Dade Community College, 2000 P Street, NW, Suite 503, Washington, DC 20036; 800-453-6956; Fax: 202-223-0999; E-mail: ccis@intr.net

COUNCIL ON INTERNATIONAL EDUCATIONAL EXCHANGE

COUNCIL STUDY CENTER IN GUADALAJARA

General Information • Academic study program in Guadalajara. Classes are held on the campus of University of Guadalajara.
Learning Focus • Courses in Spanish language, business. Instruction is offered by local teachers.
Accommodations • Homestays. Single rooms are available. Meals are taken with host family.
Program Details • Program offered once per year. Session length: 3 weeks. Departures are scheduled in January. The

program is open to undergraduate students, graduate students, adults. Other requirements: minimum 2.75 GPA. Application deadline: November 1.
Costs • $995 (includes tuition, housing, some meals, insurance, excursions, International Student Identification card). Application fee: $30. A $300 deposit is required.
Contact • Lisa Feder, Program Registrar, Council on International Educational Exchange, 205 East 42nd Street, New York, NY 10017; 212-822-2771; E-mail: lfeder@ciee.org; World Wide Web: http://www.ciee.org

COUNTRY WALKERS

YUCATAN DISCOVERY

General Information • Cultural, gourmet cooking, nature study and walking tour with visits to Cancun, El Cuyo, Izamal, Sayil, Xlaapak, Labna. Once at the destination country, participants travel by foot, boat.
Learning Focus • Instruction in Mayan history. Escorted travel to Uxmal archeological park and Chichen Itza. Nature observation (sea turtles, flamingoes, waterfowl). Other activities include walking. Instruction is offered by professors, researchers, naturalists, historians. This program would appeal to people interested in walking, nature studies, food and wine.
Accommodations • Hotels. Single rooms are available for an additional $300–$600.
Program Details • Program offered 3 times per year. Session length: 6 days. Departures are scheduled in January, February, March. Program is targeted to adults 35 to 65 years old. Most participants are 35–65 years of age. Participants must be 18 years or older to enroll. 18 participants per session. Reservations are recommended at least 5–6 months before departure.
Costs • $1450 (includes housing, all meals, excursions). A $400 deposit is required.
Contact • Heather Kellingbeck, Vice President, Country Walkers, PO Box 180, Waterbury, VT 05176; 800-464-9255; Fax: 802-244-5661; E-mail: ctrywalk@aol.com

CULTURAL EXPERIENCES ABROAD

SPANISH LANGUAGE AND CULTURE IN MAZATLÁN

General Information • Language study program in Mazatlán. Classes are held on the campus of Instituto Tecnológico y de Estudios Superiores de Monterrey: Mazatlán Campus. Excursions to Guadalajara, Copper Canyon, Isla de la Piedra.
Learning Focus • Courses in language study, business, hotel and tourism, environmental engineering, Mexican culture. Instruction is offered by local teachers.

Accommodations • Homestays, dormitories, locally-rented apartments. Single rooms are available. Meals are taken with host family, in central dining facility.
Program Details • Program offered once per year. Session length: 6 weeks. Departures are scheduled in June. The program is open to undergraduate students, graduate students, pre-college students, adults. Most participants are 18–35 years of age. Other requirements: minimum 2.75 GPA and a letter of recommendation. 15–20 participants per session. Application deadline: May 1.
Costs • $1995 (includes tuition, housing, all meals, insurance, excursions, email account, International Student Identification card, orientation). A $100 deposit is required.
Contact • Sharon Dahlen, Program Coordinator, Cultural Experiences Abroad, 5319 West Patterson Avenue, Chicago, IL 60641-3347; 800-266-4441; Fax: 773-725-9256; E-mail: ceabroad@aol.com

CULTURAL EXPERIENCES ABROAD

SPANISH LANGUAGE AND LATIN AMERICAN STUDIES IN MEXICO

General Information • Academic study program in Guadalajara. Classes are held on the campus of University of Guadalajara. Excursions to Lake Chapala, Mexico City, Puerto Vallarta, Guanajuato, Oaxaca.
Learning Focus • Courses in Spanish language, international business, literature, history, Latin American studies, education, Mexican studies. Instruction is offered by local teachers.
Accommodations • Homestays. Single rooms are available. Meals are taken in local restaurants, in residences.
Program Details • Session length: 5 weeks. Departures are scheduled in January–December. The program is open to undergraduate students, pre-college students, adults. Most participants are 18–35 years of age. Other requirements: minimum 2.75 GPA, recommendation. 5–10 participants per session. Application deadline: 3 months prior to departure.
Costs • $1700–$2000 (includes tuition, housing, all meals, books and class materials, insurance, excursions, e-mail, International Student Identification card, orientation). A $100 deposit is required.
Contact • Brian Boubek, Director, Cultural Experiences Abroad, 5319 West Patterson Avenue, Chicago, IL 60641; 773-725-8151; Fax: 773-725-9256; E-mail: ceabroad@aol.com

DIANE HOFF-ROME, AN ARTIST'S LIFE

MEXICO ARTIST HOLIDAY

General Information • Arts program with visits to Guanajuato, Guanajuato City, Sierra Madre Mountains, San Miguel de Allende, Dolores Hidalgo. Once at the destination country, participants travel by foot, mini-van or car.
Learning Focus • Instruction in painting, drawing and composition. Museum visits (Cervantes and Diego Rivera). Attendance at performances (musical events). Instruction is offered by artists. This program would appeal to people interested in painting, nature studies, drawing, crafts, photography, ancient sites, writing, folk arts.
Accommodations • Hacienda. Single rooms are available for an additional $210 per week.
Program Details • Program offered 2 times per year. Session length: 1–2 weeks. Departures are scheduled in March. Program is targeted to amateur artists and teachers. Most participants are 25–85 years of age. Participants must be 21 years or older to enroll. Other requirements: interest in visual arts, nature, cultural experience. 8 participants per session. Application deadline: 45 days prior to departure. Reservations are recommended at least 60–90 days before departure.
Costs • $995 (includes tuition, housing, some meals, excursions). A $500 deposit is required.
Contact • Irwin W. Rome, Co-Director, Diane Hoff-Rome, An Artist's Life, PO Box 567, Elmwood Road, Swampscott, MA 01907; 617-595-1173; Fax: 617-596-0707; E-mail: artistlf@pcix.com; World Wide Web: http://www2.pcix.com/~artistlf

EASTERN MICHIGAN UNIVERSITY

INTENSIVE SPANISH LANGUAGE PROGRAM

General Information • Language study program in Querétaro. Classes are held on the campus of Autonomous University of Querétaro. Excursions to Mexico City, Teotihuacán, Guadalajara, Puerto Vallarta.
Learning Focus • Courses in Spanish language. Instruction is offered by professors from the sponsoring institution.
Accommodations • Homestays, hotels. Meals are taken on one's own, with host family, in local restaurants, in residences.
Program Details • Program offered once per year. Session length: 6 weeks. Departures are scheduled in July. The program is open to undergraduate students, graduate students. Most participants are 18–30 years of age. Other requirements: minimum 2.0 GPA and 18 years of age. 25 participants per session. Application deadline: April 1.
Costs • $2585 (includes tuition, housing, some meals, insurance, excursions, travel in Mexico). A $150 deposit is required.
Contact • Academic Programs Abroad, Eastern Michigan University, 332 Goodison Hall, Ypsilanti, MI 48197; 800-777-3541; Fax: 313-487-2316; E-mail: programs.abroad@emich.edu; World Wide Web: http://www.emich.edu/public/cont_ed/abroad.html

EASTERN MICHIGAN UNIVERSITY

SOCIAL WORK PRACTICUM IN MEXICO

General Information • Academic study program in Mexico City.
Learning Focus • Courses in social work, health care and hospitals. Instruction is offered by professors from the sponsoring institution.
Accommodations • Dormitories. Meals are taken on one's own, in central dining facility.
Program Details • Program offered once per year. Session length: 6 weeks. Departures are scheduled in May. The program is open to undergraduate students, graduate

students. Most participants are 18–30 years of age. Other requirements: minimum 2.0 GPA and 18 years of age. 10 participants per session. Application deadline: March 1.
Costs • $2795 (includes tuition, housing, all meals, insurance, excursions, international airfare). A $150 deposit is required.
Contact • Academic Programs Abroad, Eastern Michigan University, 332 Goodison Hall, Ypsilanti, MI 48197; 800-777-3541; Fax: 313-487-2316; E-mail: programs.abroad@emich.edu; World Wide Web: http://www.emich.edu/public/cont_ed/abroad.html

ENROLLMENT CENTER INTERNATIONAL, INC.

ACADEMIA DE LA LENGUA ESPAÑOLA DE MAZATLÁN

General Information • Language study program in Mazatlán. Excursions to colonial villages of Copala and Concordia, nearby fishing village, neighboring ranch for horseback riding.
Learning Focus • Courses in Spanish for medical professionals, Spanish for flight attendants, language immersion. Instruction is offered by professors from the sponsoring institution.
Accommodations • Homestays, locally-rented apartments. Single rooms are available. Meals are taken with host family, in residences.
Program Details • Session length: 2–16 weeks. Departures are scheduled in January–December. The program is open to undergraduate students, graduate students, pre-college students, adults. Most participants are 18–70 years of age. 30 participants per session. Application deadline: 45 days prior to departure.
Costs • $1200 (includes tuition, housing, all meals, books and class materials, pickup at airport upon arrival, special on-site activities). Application fee: $50. A $100 deposit is required.
Contact • Carolyn Gillis, Director, Enrollment Center International, Inc., PO Box 191, Revere, MA 02151-0002; 617-284-6973

FOREIGN LANGUAGE STUDY ABROAD SERVICE

INTERNATIONAL LANGUAGE STUDY HOMESTAYS IN MEXICO

General Information • Language study program in Mexico.
Learning Focus • Courses in Spanish language. Instruction is offered by local teachers.
Accommodations • Homestays. Single rooms are available. Meals are taken with host family, in residences.
Program Details • Session length: varies. Departures are scheduled in January–December. The program is open to undergraduate students, graduate students, pre-college students, adults. Most participants are 12 years of age and older. Other requirements: students must be at least 12 years old. 1 participant per session.
Costs • Contact sponsor for information. A $300 deposit is required.
Contact • Louise Harber, Coordinator, Foreign Language Study Abroad Service, Department IH, Box 903, 5935 Southwest 64th Avenue, South Miami, FL 33143; 800-282-1090; Fax: 305-662-2907; E-mail: flsas@netpoint.net; World Wide Web: http://www.netpoint.net/~flsas

FOREIGN LANGUAGE STUDY ABROAD SERVICE

SPANISH IN MEXICO

General Information • Language study program in Cuernavaca, Ensenada, Mazatlán, Mérida, Morelia, Oaxaca, Puebla, San Miguel de Allende.
Learning Focus • Courses in language study. Instruction is offered by local teachers.
Accommodations • Homestays, hotels. Single rooms are available. Meals are taken with host family, in residences.
Program Details • Session length: varies. Departures are scheduled in January–December. The program is open to undergraduate students, graduate students, pre-college students, adults. Most participants are 16 years of age and older.
Costs • Contact sponsor for information. Application fee: $50. A $100 deposit is required.
Contact • Louise Harber, Coordinator, Foreign Language Study Abroad Service, Department IH, Box 903, 5935 Southwest 64th Avenue, South Miami, FL 33143; 800-282-1090; Fax: 305-662-2907; E-mail: flsas@netpoint.net; World Wide Web: http://www.netpoint.net/~flsas

GEORGE MASON UNIVERSITY

MEXICO STUDY TOUR

General Information • Language study program in Cuernavaca. Classes are held on the campus of Cemanahuac Educational Community. Excursions to Xochicalco, Teotihuacán, Templo Mayor, Mexico City.
Learning Focus • Courses in Spanish language, Mexican culture. Instruction is offered by professors from the sponsoring institution.
Accommodations • Homestays. Meals are taken with host family.
Program Details • Program offered once per year. Session length: 4 weeks. Departures are scheduled in July. The program is open to undergraduate students, adults. Most participants are 18–65 years of age. Other requirements: minimum 2.25 GPA. 10–15 participants per session. Application deadline: April 12.
Costs • $1990 for George Mason University students, $2540 for other students (includes tuition, housing, all meals, insurance). Application fee: $35. A $500 deposit is required.
Contact • Dr. Yehuda Lukacs, Director, Center for Global Education, George Mason University, 4400 University Drive, 235 Johnson Center, Fairfax, VA 22030; 703-993-2156; Fax: 703-993-2153; E-mail: ylukacs@gmu.edu; World Wide Web: http://www.gmu.edu/departments/oie

GEORGE MASON UNIVERSITY

US–MEXICO RELATIONS AND NAFTA

General Information • Academic study program in Puebla. Classes are held on the campus of University of the Americas–Puebla. Excursions to Taxco, Guerrero, Xochicalco, Tepoztlan, Cuernavaca.

Learning Focus • Courses in Mexican economy, international business and trade, Mexican society, Mexican culture. Instruction is offered by professors from the sponsoring institution and local teachers.
Accommodations • Dormitories, hotels. Single rooms are available. Meals are taken as a group, in central dining facility.
Program Details • Program offered once per year. Session length: 3 weeks. Departures are scheduled in December. The program is open to graduate students, adults. Most participants are 22–65 years of age. Other requirements: minimum 2.25 GPA. 10–20 participants per session. Application deadline: October 11.
Costs • $2260 for George Mason University students, $2810 for other students (includes tuition, housing, some meals, insurance, excursions, international airfare). Application fee: $35. A $500 deposit is required.
Contact • Dr. Yehuda Lukacs, Director, Center for Global Education, George Mason University, 4400 University Drive, 235 Johnson Center, Fairfax, VA 22030; 703-993-2156; Fax: 703-993-2153; E-mail: ylukacs@gmu.edu; World Wide Web: http://www.gmu.edu/departments/oie

GLOBAL EXCHANGE REALITY TOURS

MEXICO

General Information • Academic study program with visits to Chiapas, Guerrero, Oaxaca, Tabasco. Once at the destination country, participants travel by bus, airplane.
Learning Focus • Instruction in human rights and education projects. Instruction is offered by researchers, naturalists. This program would appeal to people interested in human rights, education, agriculture, indigenous cultures.
Accommodations • Hotels, guest houses. Single rooms are available for an additional $200–$500.
Program Details • Session length: 7–14 days. Departures are scheduled throughout the year. Program is targeted to seniors, students and professionals. Participants must be 18 years or older to enroll. 10 participants per session. Application deadline: 1 month prior to departure. Reservations are recommended at least 2 months before departure.
Costs • $650–$900 (includes housing, some meals, books and class materials, international airfare). A $200 deposit is required.
Contact • Loreto Curti, Reality Tours Coordinator, Global Exchange Reality Tours, 2017 Mission Street, Room 303, San Francisco, CA 94110; 415-255-7296; Fax: 415-255-7498; E-mail: globalexch@igc.apc.org

IBERIAN-AMERICAN UNIVERSITY MEXICO

INTENSIVE SPANISH SUMMER: FOUR-WEEK SESSION

General Information • Language study program in Mexico City. Classes are held on the campus of Iberian-American University Mexico. Excursions to Teotihuacán pyramids, Taxco.
Learning Focus • Courses in Spanish language. Instruction is offered by professors from the sponsoring institution.
Accommodations • Homestays. Single rooms are available. Meals are taken on one's own, in local restaurants, in residences.
Program Details • Program offered once per year. Session length: 4 weeks. Departures are scheduled in June. The program is open to undergraduate students, adults, anyone interested in learning Spanish. Most participants are 18–25 years of age. Other requirements: minimum 2.5 GPA and a minimum age 16. 15 participants per session. Application deadline: May 2.
Costs • $1690 (includes tuition, housing, all meals, Mexico City tour, student services). Application fee: $75. A $55 deposit is required.
Contact • Maria Eugenia Castro-Septién, Director, International Division, Iberian-American University Mexico, Prol. Paseo de la Reforma #880, Col. Lomas de Santa Fe DF 01210, Mexico; +52 5-292-1883; Fax: +52 5-292-1266; E-mail: ecastro@uibero.uia.mx; World Wide Web: http://www.uia.mx/Home/Dirs/ESTEXT/InfoIngles.html

IBERIAN-AMERICAN UNIVERSITY MEXICO

INTENSIVE SPANISH SUMMER: SIX-WEEK SESSION

General Information • Language study program in Mexico City. Classes are held on the campus of Iberian-American University Mexico. Excursions to Teotihuacán pyramids, Taxco.
Learning Focus • Courses in Spanish language. Instruction is offered by professors from the sponsoring institution.
Accommodations • Homestays. Single rooms are available. Meals are taken on one's own, in local restaurants, in residences.
Program Details • Program offered once per year. Session length: 6 weeks. Departures are scheduled in June. The program is open to undergraduate students, adults, anyone interested in learning Spanish. Most participants are 18–25 years of age. Other requirements: minimum 2.5 GPA and a minimum age 16. 15 participants per session. Application deadline: May 2.
Costs • $2030 (includes tuition, housing, all meals, Mexico City tour, student services). Application fee: $75. A $55 deposit is required.
Contact • Maria Eugenia Castro-Septién, Director, Iberian-American University Mexico, Prol. Paseo de la Reforma #880, Col. Lomas de Santa Fe DF 01210, Mexico; +52 5-292-1883; Fax: +52 5-292-1266; E-mail: ecastro@uibero.uia.mx; World Wide Web: http://www.uia.mx/Home/Dirs/ESTEXT/InfoIngles.html

IBERIAN-AMERICAN UNIVERSITY MEXICO

SIX-WEEK SUMMER SESSION

General Information • Academic, language study and culture program in Mexico City. Classes are held on the campus of Iberian-American University Mexico. Excursions to Mexico City, Taxco, Teotihuacán pyramids.
Learning Focus • Courses in history, literature, political science, sociology, Spanish language, anthropology, cultural

studies, archaeology. Instruction is offered by professors from the sponsoring institution.
Accommodations • Homestays. Single rooms are available. Meals are taken on one's own, in local restaurants, in residences.
Program Details • Program offered once per year. Session length: 6 weeks. Departures are scheduled in May. The program is open to undergraduate students, adults, anyone interested in learning Spanish. Most participants are 18–25 years of age. Other requirements: minimum 2.5 GPA and a minimum age of 16. 80 participants per session. Application deadline: April 30.
Costs • $1890 (includes tuition, housing, all meals, excursions, student services). Application fee: $75. A $55 deposit is required.
Contact • Maria Eugenia Castro-Septién, Director, International Division, Iberian-American University Mexico, Prol. Paseo de la Reforma #880, Col. Lomas de Santa Fe DF 01210, Mexico; +52 5-292-1883; Fax: +52 5-292-1266; E-mail: ecastro@uibero.uia.mx; World Wide Web: http://www.uia.mx/Home/Dirs/ESTEXT/InfoIngles.html

ILLINOIS STATE UNIVERSITY

SUMMER PROGRAM IN MEXICO CITY, MEXICO

General Information • Language study program in Mexico City. Classes are held on the campus of National Autonomous University of Mexico (UNAM).
Learning Focus • Courses in civilizations, cultural studies, Latin American studies, literature, Spanish language, Mexican studies.
Accommodations • Homestays.
Program Details • Program offered once per year. Session length: 7 weeks. Departures are scheduled in June. The program is open to undergraduate students, graduate students. Other requirements: minimum 2.5 GPA and at least sophomore status. 15 participants per session. Application deadline: March 15.
Costs • $2000 (includes tuition, housing, some meals, excursions, international airfare).
Contact • James J. Alstrum, Illinois State University, 4300 Foreign Language, Normal, IL 61790-4300; 309-438-7620; Fax: 309-438-3987; E-mail: oisp@rs6000.cmp.ilstu.edu; World Wide Web: http://www.orat.ilstu.edu/

ILLINOIS STATE UNIVERSITY

SUMMER STUDY IN QUERÉTARO, MEXICO

General Information • Academic study program in Querétaro. Classes are held on the campus of Instituto Tecnológico y de Estudios Superiores de Monterrey.
Learning Focus • Courses in international business, Mexican history, culture and civilization.
Accommodations • Homestays.
Program Details • Program offered once per year. Session length: 6 weeks. Departures are scheduled in June. The program is open to graduate students. Other requirements: minimum 2.5 GPA and a minimum of 60 credit hours completed. 15 participants per session. Application deadline: March 15.
Costs • $2501 (includes tuition, housing, some meals, insurance, excursions, fees).
Contact • Rodger Singley, Illinois State University, Campus Box 5590, Normal, IL 61790-5590; 309-438-5184; Fax: 309-438-3987; E-mail: oisp@rs6000.cmp.ilstu.edu; World Wide Web: http://www.orat.ilstu.edu/

INSTITUTO TECNOLÓGICO Y DE ESTUDIOS SUPERIORES DE MONTERREY, QUERETARO CAMPUS

SUMMER IN MEXICO

General Information • Language study program in Querétaro. Classes are held on the campus of Instituto Tecnológico y de Estudios Superiores de Monterrey. Excursions to Teotihuacán, Mexico City, Michoacan, Tula, Hidalgo, Guanajuato, San Miguel de Allende.
Learning Focus • Courses in Spanish language, international business, Spanish literature, social sciences.
Accommodations • Homestays, locally-rented apartments. Meals are taken with host family.
Program Details • Program offered once per year. Session length: 6 weeks. Departures are scheduled in June. The program is open to undergraduate students, graduate students, adults. Other requirements: minimum age of 17 and a minimum 2.5 GPA. Application deadline: May 30.
Costs • $2000 (includes tuition, housing, all meals, books and class materials, insurance). Application fee: $100. A $100 deposit is required.
Contact • Jennifer J. Chambers, Director, International Programs, Instituto Tecnológico y de Estudios Superiores de Monterrey, Queretaro Campus, Jesus Oviedo Avendaño #10, Parques Industriales, Queretaro 76130, Mexico; +52 42-11-82-88; Fax: +52 42-11-82-88

INTERHOSTEL, UNIVERSITY OF NEW HAMPSHIRE

CHRISTMAS IN MEXICO

General Information • Cultural tour with visits to Cuernavaca, Mexico City, Taxco, Cuicuilco, Chalma, San Angel. Once at the destination country, participants travel by bus, foot. Program is affiliated with Cemanahuac Educational Community.
Learning Focus • Instruction in history and culture. Escorted travel to villages and landmarks. Museum visits (Museum of Anthropology, Brady Museum). Attendance at performances (Ballet Folklorico). Other activities include Christmas Dinner Party, New Year's Eve Dinner. Instruction is offered by historians. This program would appeal to people interested in history, culture.
Accommodations • Hotels. Single rooms are available for an additional $375.
Program Details • Program offered once per year. Session length: 2 weeks. Departures are scheduled in December. Program is targeted to seniors over 50. Most participants are 60–80 years of age. Participants must be 50 years or older to enroll. 35 participants per session. Reservations are recommended at least 6 months before departure.
Costs • $2325 (includes tuition, housing, all meals, excursions, international airfare, entrance fees). A $200 deposit is required.

Contact • Janice Pierson, Office Supervisor, Interhostel, University of New Hampshire, 6 Garrison Avenue, Durham, NH 03824-3529; 800-733-9753; Fax: 603-862-1113; World Wide Web: http://www.learn.unh.edu/

INTERHOSTEL, UNIVERSITY OF NEW HAMPSHIRE

COLONIAL MEXICO

General Information • Cultural tour with visits to Guanajuato, Morelia, Patzcuaro, Tula, San Miguel de Allende, Dolores Hidalgo, Santa Clara de Cobre, Tzintzuantzan, Michoacan, Eduardo Ruiz National Park. Once at the destination country, participants travel by bus, foot. Program is affiliated with Cemanahuac Educational Community.
Learning Focus • Instruction in history and culture. Escorted travel to ruins and villages. Museum visits (Folk Art Museum at Tula). Attendance at performances (regional folk dance). Other activities include visiting a primary school. Instruction is offered by historians. This program would appeal to people interested in history, culture.
Accommodations • Hotels. Single rooms are available for an additional $375.
Program Details • Program offered once per year. Session length: 2 weeks. Departures are scheduled in February. Program is targeted to seniors over 50. Most participants are 60–80 years of age. Participants must be 50 years or older to enroll. 35 participants per session. Reservations are recommended at least 6 months before departure.
Costs • $2195 (includes tuition, housing, all meals, excursions, international airfare, entrance fees). A $200 deposit is required.
Contact • Janice Pierson, Office Supervisor, Interhostel, University of New Hampshire, 6 Garrison Avenue, Durham, NH 03824; 800-733-9753; Fax: 603-862-1113; World Wide Web: http://www.learn.unh.edu/

INTERHOSTEL, UNIVERSITY OF NEW HAMPSHIRE

PUEBLA AND OAXACA "DAYS OF THE DEAD", MEXICO

General Information • Cultural tour with visits to Oaxaca, Puebla, Teotihuacan, Chapingo, Cholvla, Cacaxtla, Tlaxacala, Monte Alban, Mitla, San Bartolo Coyotopec, Ocotlán, Atzompa. Once at the destination country, participants travel by bus, foot. Program is affiliated with Cemanahuac Educational Community.
Learning Focus • Instruction in history, culture and religion. Escorted travel to villages and ruins. Museum visits (Frissel, Regional Museum of Oaxaca). Attendance at performances (Ballet Folklorico). Other activities include trying Mexican cuisine. Instruction is offered by professors, historians. This program would appeal to people interested in history, culture.
Accommodations • Hotels. Single rooms are available for an additional $375.
Program Details • Program offered once per year. Session length: 2 weeks. Departures are scheduled in October. Program is targeted to seniors over 50. Most participants are 60–80 years of age. Participants must be 50 years or older to enroll. 35 participants per session. Reservations are recommended at least 4 months before departure.
Costs • $2215 (includes tuition, housing, all meals, excursions, international airfare, entrance fees). A $200 deposit is required.
Contact • Janice Pierson, Office Supervisor, Interhostel, University of New Hampshire, 6 Garrison Avenue, Durham, NH 03824-3529; 800-733-9753; Fax: 603-862-1113; World Wide Web: http://www.learn.unh.edu/

INTERNATIONAL STUDIES ABROAD

UNIVERSITY OF GUANAJUATO

General Information • Language study program in Guanajuato. Classes are held on the campus of University of Guanájuato. Excursions to Mexico City, Barra de Navidad, San Miguel de Allende, Leon.
Learning Focus • Courses in grammar, cultural studies, literature. Instruction is offered by professors from the sponsoring institution and local teachers.
Accommodations • Homestays. Single rooms are available. Meals are taken with host family.
Program Details • Program offered 2 times per year. Session length: 5 weeks. Departures are scheduled in June, July. The program is open to undergraduate students, graduate students, pre-college students, adults. Most participants are 18–24 years of age. Other requirements: minimum 2.5 GPA and a letter of recommendation. 30–40 participants per session. Application deadline: April 5.
Costs • $2175 (includes tuition, housing, insurance, excursions, ground transportation, laundry, tutoring, resident director, entrance fees). A $200 deposit is required.
Contact • Gustavo Artaza, Director, International Studies Abroad, 817 West 24th Street, Austin, TX 78705; 800-580-8826; Fax: 512-480-8866; E-mail: 76331.336@compuserve.com

IVORY ISLE TRAVEL

INTENSIVE SPANISH AT CUAUHNAHUAC

General Information • Language study program with visits to Cuernavaca, Mexico City, Taxco, Acapulco, Puebla, pyramids of Teotihuacan. Once at the destination country, participants travel by bus.
Learning Focus • Instruction in Spanish language. Escorted travel to Mexico City, Taxco, Acapulco, Puebla, pyramids of Teotihuacan. Museum visits (Mexico City and Cuernavaca). Attendance at performances (Baile Folklorico). Volunteer work (teaching English to Mexican children). Instruction is offered by professors. This program would appeal to people interested in Spanish language.
Accommodations • Homestays, locally-rented apartments, hotels. Single rooms are available for an additional $25 per day.
Program Details • Session length: 1 week to 1 semester. Departures are scheduled throughout the year. Most participants are 15–85 years of age. Participants must be 15 years or older to enroll. Reservations are recommended at least 6 weeks before departure.
Costs • $650 for 4 weeks (includes tuition).

Contact • Marcia Snell, US Representative, Ivory Isle Travel, 519 Park Drive, Kenilworth, IL 60043; 847-256-7570; Fax: 847-256-9475

Cuauhnáhuac, a Spanish language school founded in 1972, is located in Cuernavaca, Mexico. The school is dedicated to providing a variety of intensive programs for those interested in acquiring functional fluency in Spanish in the shortest possible time. New classes begin every week, and students may study for any length of time. There are never more than 4 students to a class, and classes meet for 6 hours a day. There are special classes for people in different professions, and college credit is available. Cuauhnáhuac is unique in its personal attention and flexibility in order to meet each student's individual needs. Students normally live with carefully selected Mexican families who really care about them and involve the student in their everyday lives. Many extra activities and excursions are offered each week to enhance the program.

JOURNEYS INTERNATIONAL, INC.

COPPER CANYON

General Information • Wilderness/adventure program with visits to Batopilas, Chihuahua, Creel. Once at the destination country, participants travel by train, foot, hiking.
Learning Focus • Escorted travel to Copper Canyon. Nature observation (wildlife, scenery). Other activities include hiking, interaction with Tarahumara Indians. Instruction is offered by naturalists, local guides. This program would appeal to people interested in nature studies, photography, culture.
Accommodations • Hotels, lodges. Single rooms are available.
Program Details • Session length: 9 days. Departures are scheduled throughout the year. Application deadline: 60 days prior to departure. Reservations are recommended at least 60 days before departure.
Costs • $1045 (includes housing, some meals). A $300 deposit is required.
Contact • Pat Ballard, Sales Director, Journeys International, Inc., 4011 Jackson Road, Ann Arbor, MI 48103; 313-665-4407; Fax: 313-665-2945; E-mail: pat@journeys-intl.com; World Wide Web: http://www.journeys-intl.com

KENTUCKY INSTITUTE FOR INTERNATIONAL STUDIES

PROGRAM IN MEXICO

General Information • Academic study program in Morelia. Excursions to Pátzcuaro, Guanajuato, Santa Clara del Cobre, Janitzio.
Learning Focus • Courses in Spanish language, humanities. Instruction is offered by professors from the sponsoring institution.
Accommodations • Homestays. Meals are taken with host family.
Program Details • Program offered once per year. Session length: 5 weeks. Departures are scheduled in May. The program is open to undergraduate students, graduate students, adults, professionals. Most participants are 19–26 years of age. Other requirements: minimum 2.0 GPA, letter of recommendation from a faculty member, and good academic standing at home institution. 30 participants per session. Application deadline: March 1.
Costs • $1790 for students of consortia schools, $2090 for other students (includes tuition, housing, all meals, excursions, international airfare, International Student Identification card). Application fee: $50.
Contact • Dr. J. Milton Grimes, Executive Director, Kentucky Institute for International Studies, Murray State University, PO Box 9, Murray, KY 42071-0009; 502-762-3091; Fax: 502-762-3434; E-mail: kiismsu@msumusik.mursuky.edu; World Wide Web: http://www.berea.edu/KIIS/kiis.html

LANGUAGE LIAISON

ACADEMIA HISPANO AMERICANA–SPANISH IN MEXICO

General Information • Language study program with visits to San Miguel de Allende.
Learning Focus • Instruction in the Spanish language. Instruction is offered by professors. This program would appeal to people interested in language.
Accommodations • Homestays, hotels. Single rooms are available.
Program Details • Session length: unlimited. Departures are scheduled throughout the year. Program is targeted to students of any age. Most participants are 18–70 years of age. Participants must be 16 years or older to enroll. Reservations are recommended at least 35 days before departure.
Costs • Contact sponsor for information.
Contact • Nancy Forman, President, Language Liaison, 20533 Biscayne Boulevard-Station 4-162, Miami, FL 33180; 305-682-9909; Fax: 305-682-9907; E-mail: langstudy@aol.com; World Wide Web: http://languageliaison.com

LANGUAGE LIAISON

CEMANAHUAC–LEARN SPANISH IN MEXICO

General Information • Language study program with visits to Cuernavaca.
Learning Focus • Instruction in the Spanish language. Instruction is offered by professors. This program would appeal to people interested in language.
Accommodations • Homestays, hotels. Single rooms are available.
Program Details • Session length: unlimited. Departures are scheduled throughout the year. Program is targeted to students of any age. Most participants are 18–70 years of age. Participants must be 16 years or older to enroll. Reservations are recommended at least 35 days before departure.
Costs • Contact sponsor for information.

Contact • Nancy Forman, President, Language Liaison, 20533 Biscayne Boulevard-Station 4-162, Miami, FL 33180; 305-682-9909; Fax: 305-682-9907; E-mail: langstudy@aol.com; World Wide Web: http://languageliaison.com

 LANGUAGE LIAISON

CENTER FOR BILINGUAL MULTICULTURAL STUDIES–SPANISH IN MEXICO

General Information • Language study program with visits to Cuernavaca, Mexico City, Taxco, Teotihuacán, Acapulco.
Learning Focus • Instruction in the Spanish language. Instruction is offered by professors. This program would appeal to people interested in language.
Accommodations • Homestays, locally-rented apartments, hotels. Single rooms are available.
Program Details • Session length: unlimited. Departures are scheduled throughout the year. Most participants are 18–70 years of age. Participants must be 16 years or older to enroll. Reservations are recommended at least 35 days before departure.
Costs • Contact sponsor for information.
Contact • Nancy Forman, President, Language Liaison, 20533 Biscayne Boulevard-Station 4-162, Miami, FL 33180; 305-682-9909; Fax: 305-682-9907; E-mail: langstudy@aol.com; World Wide Web: http://languageliaison.com

 LANGUAGE LIAISON

LIVE 'N' LEARN (LEARN IN A TEACHER'S HOME)–MEXICO

General Information • Language study program with visits to Mexico.
Learning Focus • Instruction in the Spanish language. Instruction is offered by professors. This program would appeal to people interested in language.
Accommodations • Homestays. Single rooms are available.
Program Details • Session length: unlimited. Departures are scheduled throughout the year. Most participants are 18–70 years of age. Participants must be 16 years or older to enroll. Reservations are recommended at least 35 days before departure.
Costs • Contact sponsor for information.
Contact • Nancy Forman, President, Language Liaison, 20533 Biscayne Boulevard-Station 4-162, Miami, FL 33180; 305-682-9909; Fax: 305-682-9907; E-mail: langstudy@aol.com; World Wide Web: http://languageliaison.com

 LANGUAGE LINK

SPANISH LANGUAGE INSTITUTE

General Information • Language study program in Cuernavaca. Excursions to Taxco, Mexico City, Acapulco.

Learning Focus • Courses in Spanish language, Latin American cultures.
Accommodations • Homestays. Single rooms are available. Meals are taken with host family.
Program Details • Session length: 1–12 weeks. Departures are scheduled in January–December. The program is open to undergraduate students, graduate students, pre-college students, adults. Most participants are 18–80 years of age. 125 participants per session.
Costs • $255 per week (includes tuition, housing, all meals, insurance). Application fee: $100.
Contact • Kay Rafool, Director, US Office, Language Link, PO Box 3006, Peoria, IL 61612-3006; 800-552-2051; Fax: 309-692-2926; E-mail: info@langlink.com; World Wide Web: http://www.langlink.com

LANGUAGE STUDIES ABROAD

CENTRO DE IDIOMAS DEL SURESTE, AC

General Information • Language study program with visits to Merida. Once at the destination country, participants travel by bus, foot.
Learning Focus • Instruction in the Spanish language. Instruction is offered by teachers with bachelor's degrees. This program would appeal to people interested in Spanish language.
Accommodations • Homestays. Single rooms are available.
Program Details • Session length: 2 or more weeks. Departures are scheduled throughout the year. Most participants are 15–80 years of age. Participants must be 15 years or older to enroll. 7–8 participants per session. Application deadline: 3 weeks prior to departure. Reservations are recommended at least 2 months before departure.
Costs • $1000–$1500 for 4 weeks (includes tuition, housing, all meals). A $100 deposit is required.
Contact • Charlene Biddulph, Director, Language Studies Abroad, 249 South Highway 101, Suite 226, Solana Beach, CA 92075; 800-424-5522; Fax: 619-943-1201; E-mail: cbiddulph@aol.com; World Wide Web: http://www.dnai.com/~bid/language/

LANGUAGE STUDIES ABROAD

CENTRO MEXICANO INTERNACIONAL

General Information • Language study program with visits to Morelia. Once at the destination country, participants travel by bus, foot.
Learning Focus • Instruction in the Spanish language. Instruction is offered by teachers with bachelor's degrees. This program would appeal to people interested in Spanish language.
Accommodations • Homestays. Single rooms are available for an additional $15 per day.
Program Details • Session length: 2 or more weeks. Departures are scheduled throughout the year. Most participants are 15–80 years of age. Participants must be 15 years or older to enroll. 5 participants per session. Application deadline: 3 weeks prior to departure. Reservations are recommended at least 2 months before departure.
Costs • $1100–$1250 (includes tuition, housing, all meals). A $100 deposit is required.
Contact • Charlene Biddulph, Director, Language Studies Abroad, 249 South Highway 101, Suite 226, Solana Beach, CA 92075; 800-424-5522; Fax: 619-943-1201; E-mail: cbiddulph@aol.com; World Wide Web: http://www.dnai.com/~bid/language/

LANGUAGE STUDIES ABROAD

CUAUHNAHUAC

General Information • Language study program with visits to Cuernavaca. Once at the destination country, participants travel by bus, foot.
Learning Focus • Instruction in the Spanish language. Instruction is offered by teachers with bachelor's degrees. This program would appeal to people interested in Spanish language.
Accommodations • Homestays. Single rooms are available for an additional $25 per day.
Program Details • Session length: 2 or more weeks. Departures are scheduled throughout the year. Most participants are 15–80 years of age. Participants must be 15 years or older to enroll. 4 participants per session. Application deadline: 3 weeks prior to departure. Reservations are recommended at least 2 months before departure.
Costs • $1100–$1300 for 4 weeks (includes tuition, housing, all meals). A $100 deposit is required.
Contact • Charlene Biddulph, Director, Language Studies Abroad, 249 South Highway 101, Suite 226, Solana Beach, CA 92075; 800-424-5522; Fax: 619-943-1201; E-mail: cbiddulph@aol.com; World Wide Web: http://www.dnai.com/~bid/language/

LEARNING PROGRAMS INTERNATIONAL

COLONIAL MEXICO

General Information • Cultural tour with visits to Guanajuato, Mexico City, San Miguel de Allende. Once at the destination country, participants travel by bus, foot.
Learning Focus • Escorted travel to Palacio Nacional de Mexico, Catedral Metropolitana, Templo Mayor, pyramids of Teotihuacan, El Jardin de la Union. Museum visits (Museo Nacional de Antropología, Museo de las Momias, El Museo de la Alhondiga). This program would appeal to people interested in culture and language.
Accommodations • Hotels. Single rooms are available.
Program Details • Program offered 2 times per year. Session length: 8 days. Departures are scheduled in June, spring break, and custom dates. Program is targeted to high school students. Most participants are 14–18 years of age. 15–20 participants per session. Application deadline: April 1 for summer session, December 15 for spring session.
Costs • $1060 (includes housing, some meals, insurance, excursions, international airfare, on-site supervisor, full-time director). A $200 deposit is required.
Contact • Natalie Nation, Director, Learning Programs International, 816 West 23rd Street, Austin, TX 78705; 800-259-4439; Fax: 512-474-1021; E-mail: 76331.336@compuserve.com; World Wide Web: http://www.studiesabroad.com

LEARNING PROGRAMS INTERNATIONAL

UNIVERSIDAD DE GUANAJUATO: GUANAJUATO, MEXICO

General Information • Language study program with visits to Guanajuato, Mexico City, Teotihuacan, San Miguel de Allende, Dolores Hidalgo, Barra de Navidad. Once at the destination country, participants travel by bus, foot.
Learning Focus • Instruction in Spanish language. Museum visits (Museo Nacional de Catedral Metropolitana). Instruction is offered by professors. This program would appeal to people interested in language and culture.
Accommodations • Homestays. Single rooms are available for an additional $150 per month.
Program Details • Program offered 2 times per year. Session length: 27 days. Departures are scheduled in June, July. Program is targeted to high school students. Most participants are 14–18 years of age. Participants must be 14 years or older to enroll. 20–40 participants per session. Application deadline: April 1.
Costs • Contact sponsor for information. A $200 deposit is required.
Contact • Natalie Nation, Director, Learning Programs International, 816 West 23rd Street, Austin, TX 78705; 800-259-4439; Fax: 512-474-1021; E-mail: 76331.336@compuserve.com; World Wide Web: http://www.studiesabroad.com

LOS ANGELES COMMUNITY COLLEGE DISTRICT

BIOLOGY OF THE SEA OF CORTEZ

General Information • Academic study program in Bahia de Los Angeles.
Learning Focus • Courses in marine biology. Instruction is offered by professors from the sponsoring institution.
Accommodations • Dormitories. Meals are taken as a group, in central dining facility.
Program Details • Program offered once per year. Session length: 2 weeks. Departures are scheduled in July. The program is open to undergraduate students, pre-college students, adults. Most participants are 17–35 years of age. 22 participants per session. Application deadline: May 1.
Costs • $695 (includes tuition, housing, all meals, insurance, excursions). A $400 deposit is required.
Contact • International Education Program, Los Angeles Community College District, 770 Wilshire Boulevard, Los Angeles, CA 90017; 213-891-2282; Fax: 213-891-2150; E-mail: intered@laccd.cc.ca.us; World Wide Web: http://laccd.cc.ca.us

LOS ANGELES COMMUNITY COLLEGE DISTRICT

SUMMER SESSION IN MEXICO

General Information • Language study program in Cuernavaca. Classes are held on the campus of Instituto IDEAL.
Learning Focus • Courses in Spanish language. Instruction is offered by professors from the sponsoring institution and local teachers.
Accommodations • Homestays. Single rooms are available. Meals are taken with host family.
Program Details • Program offered once per year. Session length: 4 weeks. Departures are scheduled in July. The program is open to undergraduate students, graduate students, pre-college students, adults. Most participants are 17–65 years of age. 25 participants per session. Application deadline: May 1.
Costs • $1820 (includes tuition, housing, all meals, books and class materials, insurance, excursions, international airfare). A $400 deposit is required.
Contact • International Education Program, Los Angeles Community College District, 770 Wilshire Boulevard, Los Angeles, CA 90017; 213-891-2282; Fax: 213-891-2150; E-mail: intered@laccd.cc.ca.us; World Wide Web: http://laccd.cc.ca.us

LOYOLA UNIVERSITY, NEW ORLEANS

SUMMER SESSIONS IN MEXICO CITY

General Information • Academic study program in Mexico City. Classes are held on the campus of Iberian-American University Mexico. Excursions to Teotihuacán, Puebla, Cuernavaca, Tasco, Tula.
Learning Focus • Courses in Latin American studies, history, art, political science, Spanish language, economics, sociology, communications. Instruction is offered by professors from the sponsoring institution and local teachers.
Accommodations • Homestays. Single rooms are available. Meals are taken on one's own, with host family.
Program Details • Program offered 3 times per year. Session length: 4 and 6 weeks. Departures are scheduled in May, June. The program is open to undergraduate students, graduate students, adults. Most participants are 18–40 years of age. Other requirements: official transcript and interview. Application deadline: April 15.
Costs • $2500 (includes tuition, housing, some meals, excursions). Application fee: $25.
Contact • Dr. Maurice Brungardt, Director, Mexico Program, Loyola University, New Orleans, 6363 Saint Charles Avenue, New Orleans, LA 70118; 504-865-3539; Fax: 504-865-2010; E-mail: brungard@beta.loyno.edu

MARQUETTE UNIVERSITY

MARQUETTE SUMMER PROGRAM AT THE UNIVERSITY OF VERACRUZ

General Information • Academic study program in Xalapa. Classes are held on the campus of University of Veracruz. Excursions to Veracruz, Puebla, Teotihuacán, Tajin.
Learning Focus • Courses in language study, literature, anthropology, history, social studies, art. Instruction is offered by local teachers.
Accommodations • Homestays. Single rooms are available. Meals are taken with host family, in residences.
Program Details • Program offered once per year. Session length: 6 weeks. Departures are scheduled in June, July. The

program is open to undergraduate students, graduate students. Most participants are 20–23 years of age. Other requirements: minimum 2.5 GPA. 15–25 participants per session. Application deadline: March 15.
Costs • Contact sponsor for information. A $250 deposit is required.
Contact • Dr. Armando Gonzalez-Perez, Director, Marquette University, Department of Foreign Languages, PO Box 1881, Milwaukee, WI 53202-1881; 414-288-7063; Fax: 414-288-7665

MICHIGAN STATE UNIVERSITY

FILM IN MEXICO

General Information • Academic study program in Acapulco, Cocotitlán, Mexico City, Puebla.
Learning Focus • Courses in film studies, videography. Instruction is offered by professors from the sponsoring institution.
Accommodations • Hotels. Meals are taken on one's own, in local restaurants.
Program Details • Program offered once per year. Session length: 2 weeks. Departures are scheduled in December. The program is open to undergraduate students, graduate students. Most participants are 18–26 years of age. Other requirements: good academic standing and the approval of the director. 15 participants per session. Application deadline: November 8.
Costs • $870 (includes housing, some meals, excursions). Application fee: $75. A $250 deposit is required.
Contact • Brenda S. Sprite, Educational Programs Coordinator, Michigan State University, Office of Study Abroad, 109 International Center, East Lansing, MI 48824; 517-353-8920; Fax: 517-432-2082; E-mail: sprite@pilot.msu.edu; World Wide Web: http://study-abroad.msu.edu

MICHIGAN STATE UNIVERSITY

TOURISM MANAGEMENT

General Information • Academic study program in Acapulco, Guadalajara, Mexico City, Oaxaca, Veracruz. Excursions to Pacific coast, other points on the Gulf.
Learning Focus • Courses in tourism industry in Mexico. Instruction is offered by professors from the sponsoring institution.
Accommodations • Hotels. Meals are taken on one's own, in local restaurants.
Program Details • Program offered once per year. Session length: 4 weeks. Departures are scheduled in May. The program is open to undergraduate students, graduate students. Most participants are 18–26 years of age. Other requirements: good academic standing and the approval of the director. 15 participants per session. Application deadline: March 14.
Costs • $1947 (includes housing, some meals, excursions). Application fee: $75. A $250 deposit is required.
Contact • Brenda S. Sprite, Educational Programs Coordinator, Michigan State University, Office of Study Abroad, 109 Center for International Programs, East Lansing, MI 48824-1035; 517-353-8920; Fax: 517-432-2082; E-mail: sprite@pilot.msu.edu; World Wide Web: http://study-abroad.msu.edu

MIRAMAR ADVENTURES

WHALE WATCHING AND SEA KAYAKING IN BAJA, MEXICO

General Information • Wilderness/adventure program with visits to Bahia de Los Angeles, Baja Peninsula. Once at the destination country, participants travel by bus, airplane, kayak.
Learning Focus • Instruction in sea kayaking. Nature observation (whales, seabirds). Volunteer work (sea turtles). Other activities include camping, hiking. Instruction is offered by naturalists, experienced wilderness professionals. This program would appeal to people interested in marine biology.
Accommodations • Beach cabins. Single rooms are available.
Program Details • Program offered 10 times per year. Session length: 1 week. Departures are scheduled in March–June. Most participants are 16–50 years of age. Other requirements: children under 16 must be accompanied by an adult. 6–8 participants per session. Application deadline: 60 days prior to departure.
Costs • $800 (includes housing, all meals, equipment, guides). A $300 deposit is required.
Contact • Florin Botezatu, Owner, Miramar Adventures, 2802 East Madison, Suite 126, Seattle, WA 98112; 206-322-6559; Fax: 206-320-0717

NATIONAL REGISTRATION CENTER FOR STUDY ABROAD

CEMANAHUAC

General Information • Language study program in Buena Vista, Cuernavaca.
Learning Focus • Courses in Spanish language.
Accommodations • Homestays. Single rooms are available. Meals are taken with host family.
Program Details • Program offered 50 times per year. Session length: 8 weeks. Departures are scheduled in January–December. The program is open to undergraduate students, graduate students, adults. Application deadline: 40 days prior to departure.
Costs • $2450 (includes tuition, housing, all meals, insurance). Application fee: $40. A $100 deposit is required.
Contact • June Domoe, Coordinator, National Registration Center for Study Abroad, 823 North Second Street, Milwaukee, WI 53203; 414-278-0631; Fax: 414-271-8884; E-mail: quest@nrcsa.com; World Wide Web: http://www.nrcsa.com

NATIONAL REGISTRATION CENTER FOR STUDY ABROAD

CENTER FOR BILINGUAL MULTICULTURAL STUDIES

General Information • Language study program in Cuernavaca.
Learning Focus • Courses in Spanish language.
Accommodations • Homestays. Single rooms are available. Meals are taken with host family, in residences.
Program Details • Program offered 50 times per year. Session length: 4 weeks. Departures are scheduled in

January–December. The program is open to undergraduate students, graduate students, adults. Application deadline: 40 days prior to departure.
Costs • $1225 (includes tuition, housing, all meals, insurance). Application fee: $40. A $100 deposit is required.
Contact • June Domoe, Educational Consultant, National Registration Center for Study Abroad, PO Box 1393, 823 North Second Street, Milwaukee, WI 53203; 414-278-0631; Fax: 414-271-8884; E-mail: quest@nrcsa.com; World Wide Web: http://www.nrcsa.com

NATIONAL REGISTRATION CENTER FOR STUDY ABROAD

CONCEPTO UNIVERSAL

General Information • Language study program in Cuernavaca.
Learning Focus • Courses in Spanish language.
Accommodations • Homestays. Single rooms are available. Meals are taken with host family.
Program Details • Program offered 50 times per year. Session length: 4 weeks. Departures are scheduled in January–December. The program is open to undergraduate students, graduate students, pre-college students, adults. Application deadline: 40 days prior to departure.
Costs • $1098 (includes tuition, housing, all meals, insurance). Application fee: $40. A $100 deposit is required.
Contact • Mike Wittig, Director, National Registration Center for Study Abroad, 823 North Second Street, Milwaukee, WI 53203; 414-278-0631; Fax: 414-271-8884; E-mail: quest@nrcsa.com; World Wide Web: http://www.nrcsa.com

NATIONAL REGISTRATION CENTER FOR STUDY ABROAD

LANGUAGE AND CRAFTS IN MEXICO

General Information • Language study program in Oaxaca.
Learning Focus • Courses in Spanish language.
Accommodations • Homestays. Single rooms are available. Meals are taken on one's own.
Program Details • Program offered 12 times per year. Session length: 4 weeks. Departures are scheduled in January–December. The program is open to undergraduate students, graduate students, adults. Application deadline: 40 days prior to departure.
Costs • $815 (includes tuition, housing, some meals, insurance). Application fee: $40. A $100 deposit is required.
Contact • June Domoe, Educational Consultant, National Registration Center for Study Abroad, PO Box 1393, Milwaukee, WI 53201; 414-278-0631; Fax: 414-271-8884; E-mail: inquiries@nrcsa.com; World Wide Web: http://www.nrcsa.com

NATURAL HABITAT ADVENTURES

ULTIMATE BAJA ADVENTURE

General Information • Nature study tour with visits to Baja Peninsula, Isla Catalina, Isla Espiritu Santo, Isla San Francisco, Isla San Jose, Magdelara Bay. Once at the destination country, participants travel by bus, boat.

Learning Focus • Nature observation (gray, blue, humpback, sperm, Bryde's, orca, and fin whales, sea lions, dolphins, herons, egrets, brown and blue-footed boobies and manta rays). Other activities include snorkeling. Instruction is offered by naturalists, photographers. This program would appeal to people interested in nature studies, photography, wildlife.

Accommodations • Boat. Single rooms are available for an additional $500.

Program Details • Program offered 2 times per year. Session length: 10 days. Departures are scheduled in February. Participants must be 14 years or older to enroll. 22 participants per session. Reservations are recommended at least 6–12 months before departure.

Costs • $2895 (includes housing, all meals, all transfers). A $500 deposit is required.

Contact • Natural Habitat Adventures, 2945 Center Green Court, Suite H, Boulder, CO 80301; 800-543-8917; Fax: 303-449-3712; E-mail: nathab@worldnet.att.net

NATURAL HISTORY MUSEUM OF LOS ANGELES COUNTY

COPPER CANYON: MEXICO'S SIERRA MADRES

General Information • Cultural tour with visits to Chihuahua, Creel, Divisadero, El Fuerte, Los Mochis, Chihuahua al Pacifico Railroad. Once at the destination country, participants travel by train, bus, foot, boat, airplane.

Learning Focus • Museum visits (Pancho Villa's Home, Chihuahua Museum). Nature observation (birds, geology). Other activities include hiking, observing Tarahumara Indian culture. Instruction is offered by naturalists. This program would appeal to people interested in history, anthropology, geology.

Accommodations • Hotels. Single rooms are available for an additional $290.

Program Details • Program offered once per year. Session length: 1 week. Departures are scheduled in April. Most participants are 40–75 years of age. Participants must be 12 years or older to enroll. 25 participants per session. Reservations are recommended at least 3 months before departure.

Costs • $2470 (includes housing, some meals, excursions, international airfare). A $400 deposit is required.

Contact • Karen Hovanitz, Travel Program Manager, Natural History Museum of Los Angeles County, 900 Exposition Boulevard, Los Angeles, CA 90007; 213-744-3350; Fax: 213-747-6718; E-mail: khovanit@mizar.usc.edu; World Wide Web: http://www.lam.mus.ca.us/lacmnh

NATURAL HISTORY MUSEUM OF LOS ANGELES COUNTY

MESOAMERICAN ARCHAEOLOGY

General Information • Archaeological tour with visits to Yucatán, Maya archaeological sites in the Yucatan. Once at the destination country, participants travel by bus, foot.

Learning Focus • Instruction in archaeology. Escorted travel to Yucatan. Other activities include hiking. Instruction is offered by researchers, scientists. This program would appeal to people interested in archaeology.

Accommodations • Hotels. Single rooms are available.

Program Details • Program offered once per year. Session length: 2 weeks. Departures are scheduled in November. Most participants are 30–75 years of age. Participants must be 12 years or older to enroll. 20 participants per session. Reservations are recommended at least 3 months before departure.

Costs • Contact sponsor for information. A $500 deposit is required.

Contact • Karen Hovanitz, Travel Program Manager, Natural History Museum of Los Angeles County, 900 Exposition Boulevard, Los Angeles, CA 90007; 213-744-3350; Fax: 213-747-6718; E-mail: khovanit@mizar.usc.edu; World Wide Web: http://www.lam.mus.ca.us/lacmnh

NATURAL HISTORY MUSEUM OF LOS ANGELES COUNTY

MONARCH BUTTERFLIES, COLONIAL CITIES, AND PRE-COLUMBIAN RUINS

General Information • Nature study tour with visits to Mexico City, Morelia, San Jose de Purua, San Juan del Rio, Teotihuacán, Querétaro, Pátzcuaro, Santa Clara, Angangueo, Butterfly Sanctuary. Once at the destination country, participants travel by bus, foot, boat.

Learning Focus • Museum visits (Mexico City, Pátzcuaro). Attendance at performances (Ballet Folklorico). Nature observation (Monarch butterfly sanctuary). Other activities include hiking. Instruction is offered by naturalists. This program would appeal to people interested in entomology, archaeology, anthropology.

Accommodations • Hotels. Single rooms are available for an additional $380.

Program Details • Program offered once per year. Session length: 9 days. Departures are scheduled in January. Most participants are 40–75 years of age. Participants must be 10 years or older to enroll. 20 participants per session. Application deadline: December 18. Reservations are recommended at least 3 months before departure.

Costs • $1695 (includes housing, some meals, excursions, guides, museum donation, predeparture information). A $300 deposit is required.

Contact • Karen Hovanitz, Travel Program Manager, Natural History Museum of Los Angeles County, 900 Exposition Boulevard, Los Angeles, CA 90007; 213-744-3350; Fax: 213-747-6718; E-mail: khovanit@mizar.usc.edu; World Wide Web: http://www.lam.mus.ca.us/lacmnh

NATURAL HISTORY MUSEUM OF LOS ANGELES COUNTY

THE VALLEY OF OAXACA

General Information • Cultural tour with visits to Oaxaca, Monte Alban, Mitla, Teotitlán del Valle, Arrazola, Tlacolula, Ocotlán, Abastos. Once at the destination country, participants travel by bus, foot.

Learning Focus • Instruction in Oaxacan cooking. Museum visits (Rutino Tamayo Museum). Attendance at performances

(Guelaguetza [regional dance]). Other activities include lectures on Nacimientos-Nativity Scenes. Instruction is offered by professors, artists. This program would appeal to people interested in folk arts, archaeology, anthropology.
Accommodations • Hotels. Single rooms are available for an additional $280.
Program Details • Program offered once per year. Session length: 1 week. Departures are scheduled in December. Most participants are 40–75 years of age. Participants must be 10 years or older to enroll. 20 participants per session. Reservations are recommended at least 3 months before departure.
Costs • $1645 (includes housing, some meals, excursions). A $300 deposit is required.
Contact • Karen Hovanitz, Travel Program Manager, Natural History Museum of Los Angeles County, 900 Exposition Boulevard, Los Angeles, CA 90007; 213-744-3350; Fax: 213-747-6718; E-mail: khovanit@mizar.usc.edu; World Wide Web: http://www.lam.mus.ca.us/lacmnh

 NICHOLLS STATE UNIVERSITY

STUDY PROGRAM ABROAD IN CUERNAVACA, MEXICO

General Information • Academic and language study program in Cuernavaca. Classes are held on the campus of Nicholls State University–Cuernavaca. Excursions to mountain wool market, Museum of Anthropology, Teotihuacán pyramids, Xochicalco Archaeological zone.
Learning Focus • Courses in language study, literature, linguistics, cultural studies, civilizations. Instruction is offered by professors from the sponsoring institution.
Accommodations • Homestays. Single rooms are available. Meals are taken on one's own, with host family, in local restaurants, in residences.
Program Details • Program offered 15 times per year. Session length: 3 weeks–one year. Departures are scheduled in January–December. The program is open to undergraduate students, graduate students, pre-college students, adults. Most participants are 18–55 years of age. Other requirements: high school seniors or graduates. 125 participants per session. Application deadline: 30 days prior to departure.
Costs • $1057 for non-credit program, $1352 for 6 hours of college credits (includes tuition, housing, some meals, books and class materials). A $235 deposit is required.
Contact • Dr. Gary McCann, Director of Study Programs Abroad, Nicholls State University, PO Box 2080, Thibodaux, LA 70310; 504-448-4440; Fax: 504-449-7028; E-mail: fl-caw@nich-nsunet.nich.edu

 NORTH CAROLINA STATE UNIVERSITY

LANGUAGE AND CULTURE MEXICO SUMMER PROGRAM

General Information • Language study program in Cuernavaca. Classes are held on the campus of Center for Bilingual and Multicultural Studies. Excursions to Acapulco, Teotihuacán, Taxco, Xochicalco.
Learning Focus • Courses in Spanish language, Mexican history, Spanish literature, Mexican art history. Instruction is offered by local teachers.
Accommodations • Homestays. Single rooms are available. Meals are taken with host family, in local restaurants, in residences.
Program Details • Program offered once per year. Session length: 5 weeks. Departures are scheduled in May. The program is open to undergraduate students. Most participants are 18–50 years of age. Other requirements: references and approval by Director. 16–30 participants per session. Application deadline: March 1.
Costs • $2350 (includes tuition, housing, some meals, books and class materials, insurance, excursions, international airfare). A $100 deposit is required.
Contact • Ingrid Schmidt, Study Abroad Director, North Carolina State University, 2118 Pullen Hall, Box 7344, Raleigh, NC 27695-7344; 919-515-2087; Fax: 919-515-6021; E-mail: study_abroad@ncsu.edu; World Wide Web: http://www2.ncsu.edu/ncsu/chass/intstu/abroad.html

OUTDOOR ODYSSEYS, INC.

LORETO TO LA PAZ PADDLE

General Information • Wilderness/adventure program with visits to Sea of Cortez, 2 deserted off-shore islands in the Sea of Cortez. Once at the destination country, participants travel by kayak.
Learning Focus • Instruction in sea kayaking. Nature observation (whale watching, marine mamals, bird watching, flora, botany). Other activities include camping, hiking, snorkeling. Instruction is offered by naturalists, professional kayak guides. This program would appeal to people interested in whale watching, marine biology, ecotourism, wilderness, sea kayaking, botany, nature studies, adventure.
Accommodations • Hotels, campsites. Single rooms are available for an additional $40.
Program Details • Program offered 9 times per year. Session length: 6 days. Departures are scheduled in February–April. Most participants are 25–65 years of age. Participants must be 14 years or older to enroll. 10 participants per session. Reservations are recommended at least 4–6 weeks before departure.
Costs • $845 (includes housing, all meals, excursions, use of kayaks and other equipment [life jackets, tents, etc.], most camping equipment). A $422 deposit is required.
Contact • Clark Casebolt, Owner, Outdoor Odysseys, Inc., 12003 23rd Avenue, NE, Seattle, WA 98125; 800-649-4621; Fax: 206-361-0717; E-mail: ceekayaker@aol.com; World Wide Web: http://www.pacificrim.net/~bydesign/odyssey.html

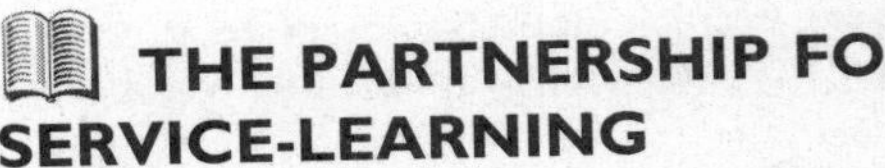

THE PARTNERSHIP FOR SERVICE-LEARNING

MEXICO

General Information • Academic study and volunteer service program in Guadalajara. Classes are held on the campus of Autonomous University of Guadalajara.
Learning Focus • Courses in Spanish language, institutions in Mexican society. Instruction is offered by local teachers.
Accommodations • Homestays. Single rooms are available. Meals are taken with host family, in residences.
Program Details • Program offered once per year. Session length: 8½ weeks. Departures are scheduled in June. The program is open to undergraduate students, graduate

students, pre-college students, adults. Most participants are 19–24 years of age. Other requirements: 1 year of college or 2 years of high school-level Spanish study. Application deadline: 2 months prior to departure.
Costs • $4400 (includes tuition, housing, some meals, excursions, service placement and supervision, pre-departure and orientation materials). A $250 deposit is required.
Contact • Maureen Lowney, Coordinator of Student Programs, The Partnership for Service-Learning, 815 Second Avenue, Suite 315, New York, NY 10960; 212-986-0989; Fax: 212-986-5039; E-mail: pslny@aol.com

SAN DIEGO STATE UNIVERSITY

SPANISH LANGUAGE IMMERSION IN CUERNAVACA, MEXICO

General Information • Language study program in Cuernavaca.
Learning Focus • Courses in language study, cultural studies. Instruction is offered by professors from the sponsoring institution.
Accommodations • Homestays. Single rooms are available. Meals are taken with host family, in residences.
Program Details • Program offered once per year. Session length: 3 weeks. Departures are scheduled in July. The program is open to undergraduate students, graduate students, pre-college students, adults. Most participants are 18–80 years of age. 25 participants per session. Application deadline: 60 days prior to departure.
Costs • $1200 (includes tuition, housing, some meals). A $400 deposit is required.
Contact • Patrick Lathrop, Travel Coordinator, San Diego State University, 5250 Campanile Drive, San Diego, CA 92115-1919; 619-594-5154; Fax: 619-594-7080

SANTA BARBARA MUSEUM OF ART

OAXACA: TRADITIONAL AND CONTEMPORARY FOLK ART

General Information • Cultural tour with visits to Oaxaca, Oaxaca, Mitla-Zapotec Settlement. Once at the destination country, participants travel by bus.
Learning Focus • Instruction in art and history of the area. Escorted travel to Monte Alban and Mitla. Museum visits (historical museums). Instruction is offered by art historians. This program would appeal to people interested in art, photography, history, crafts, culture, architecture.
Accommodations • Hotels. Single rooms are available for an additional $315.
Program Details • Program offered once per year. Session length: 6 days. Departures are scheduled in December. Most participants are 30–80 years of age. Participants must be members of the sponsoring organization (annual dues: $40). 15–20 participants per session.
Costs • $2260 including airfare, $1890 without airfare (includes housing, some meals, excursions, international airfare). A $500 deposit is required.
Contact • Shelley Ruston, Director of Special Programs, Santa Barbara Museum of Art, 1130 State Street, Santa Barbara, CA 93101; 805-963-4364, ext. 336; Fax: 805-966-6840

SEA QUEST KAYAK EXPEDITIONS/ZOETIC RESEARCH

SEA QUEST KAYAK EXPEDITIONS AND ZOETIC RESEARCH

General Information • Nature study and wilderness program with visits to Sea of Cortez. Once at the destination country, participants travel by sea kayak.
Learning Focus • Instruction in sea kayaking, snorkeling and natural history. Nature observation (whales, other marine and desert life). Other activities include camping, hiking, sea kayaking, snorkeling. Instruction is offered by naturalists, professional educators and biologists. This program would appeal to people interested in kayaking, whale watching, snorkeling, nature studies.
Accommodations • Campsites.
Program Details • Program offered 10 times per year. Session length: 5 and 7 days. Departures are scheduled in February–April. Most participants are 16–60 years of age. 6–12 participants per session. Reservations are recommended at least 2–16 weeks before departure.
Costs • $749–$899 (includes all meals, all sea kayaking equipment). A $375 deposit is required.
Contact • Mark Lewis, Expedition Director, Sea Quest Kayak Expeditions/Zoetic Research, PO Box 2424, Friday Harbor, WA 98250; 360-378-5767

SOUTHERN METHODIST UNIVERSITY

PROGRAM IN XALAPA, MEXICO

General Information • Language study program in Xalapa. Classes are held on the campus of University of Veracruz. Excursions to El Tajin, Totonacas.
Learning Focus • Courses in Spanish language, Spanish culture. Instruction is offered by professors from the sponsoring institution and local teachers.
Accommodations • Homestays. Meals are taken with host family.
Program Details • Program offered once per year. Session length: 6 weeks. Departures are scheduled in June. The program is open to undergraduate students. Most participants are 19–23 years of age. Other requirements: minimum 2.5 GPA, one year college-level Spanish and sophomore standing. 25 participants per session. Application deadline: March 1.
Costs • $3200 (includes tuition, housing, some meals, excursions). A $400 deposit is required.
Contact • Karen Westergaard, Associate Director, Southern Methodist University, Office of International Programs, Dallas, TX 75275-0391; 214-768-2338; Fax: 214-768-1051; E-mail: intipro@mail.smu.edu; World Wide Web: http://fllcjm.clements.smu.edu

STATE UNIVERSITY OF NEW YORK COLLEGE AT BROCKPORT

SPANISH LANGUAGE IMMERSION PROGRAM IN MEXICO

General Information • Language study program in Cuernavaca. Classes are held on the campus of Center for Bilingual and Multicultural Studies.

Learning Focus • Courses in Spanish language. Instruction is offered by local teachers.
Accommodations • Homestays. Single rooms are available. Meals are taken with host family.
Program Details • Program offered once per year. Session length: 5 weeks. Departures are scheduled in July. The program is open to undergraduate students. Most participants are 19–35 years of age. Other requirements: minimum 2.5 GPA. 20 participants per session. Application deadline: May 15.
Costs • $2800 (includes tuition, housing, all meals, books and class materials, international airfare). A $100 deposit is required.
Contact • Dr. John J. Perry, Director, Office of International Education, State University of New York College at Brockport, 350 New Campus Drive, Brockport, NY 14420; 716-395-2119; Fax: 716-637-3218; E-mail: jperry@acspr1.acs.brockport.e; World Wide Web: http://www.brockport.edu/study_abroad

UNIVERSAL CENTRO DE LENGUA Y COMMUNICACION SOCIAL

UNIVERSAL CENTRO DE LENGUA Y COMUNICACIÓN SOCIAL

General Information • Language study program in Cuernavaca. Excursions to Taxco, Mexico City, Teotihuacán, Tepoztlan, Acapulco.
Learning Focus • Courses in history, literature, language study, cultural studies. Instruction is offered by professors from the sponsoring institution.
Accommodations • Homestays. Single rooms are available. Meals are taken with host family.
Program Details • Session length: 1 or more weeks. Departures are scheduled in January–December. The program is open to undergraduate students, graduate students, pre-college students, adults. Most participants are 7–75 years of age. 100 participants per session. Application deadline: every Friday.
Costs • $140 per month (includes tuition). Application fee: $100. A $100 deposit is required.
Contact • Ramiro Cuéllar Hernández, Director, Universal Centro de Lengua y Communicacion Social, J.H. Preciado #171, Colonia San Antón, Cuernavaca 62020, Mexico; +52 73-18-29-04; Fax: +52 73-18-29-10; E-mail: universa@laneta.apc.org

UNIVERSIDAD DEL MAYAB

SPANISH AS A SECOND LANGUAGE THROUGH TOTAL IMMERSION

General Information • Language study program in Mérida. Classes are held on the campus of University of the Mayab. Excursions to haciendas, pueblos, archeological sites, colonial cities, beaches, colonial convents, churches.
Learning Focus • Courses in history, archaeology, literature, ethnology, art, Mayan culture, Mayan language. Instruction is offered by professors from the sponsoring institution and local teachers.
Accommodations • Homestays, locally-rented apartments, hotels, posadas. Single rooms are available. Meals are taken with host family, in residences.
Program Details • Program offered 26 times per year. Session length: 2 weeks. Departures are scheduled in January–December. The program is open to undergraduate students, graduate students, pre-college students, adults. Most participants are 19–90 years of age. 12 participants per session. Application deadline: 6 weeks prior to departure.
Costs • $720 (includes tuition, housing, all meals, books and class materials, excursions). A $100 deposit is required.
Contact • Patricia Jankiewicz-Castellanos MA, Director, Language Department, Universidad del Mayab, Apdo. Postal 92, Cordemex 97310, Mexico; +52 99-22-00-01; Fax: +52 99-22-00-06

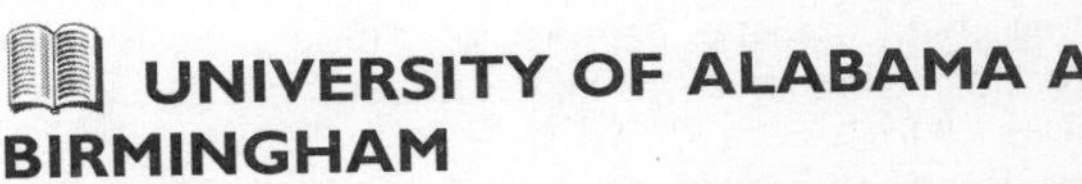

UNIVERSITY OF ALABAMA AT BIRMINGHAM

UNIVERSITY OF ALABAMA AT BIRMINGHAM IN MEXICO

General Information • Language study and cultural program in Guadalajara. Classes are held on the campus of University of Guadalajara. Excursions to Mexico City.
Learning Focus • Courses in Spanish language, literature, cultural studies. Instruction is offered by professors from the sponsoring institution and local teachers.
Accommodations • Homestays. Single rooms are available. Meals are taken with host family, in residences.
Program Details • Program offered once per year. Session length: 5 weeks. Departures are scheduled in July. The program is open to undergraduate students, graduate students. Most participants are 19–49 years of age. Other requirements: must have completed Spanish 101 and 102. 20–25 participants per session. Application deadline: May 31.
Costs • $1995 (includes tuition, housing, all meals, books and class materials, excursions, international airfare). A $200 deposit is required.
Contact • Frank Romanowicz, Study Abroad Coordinator, University of Alabama at Birmingham, 1400 University Boulevard, HUC 318, Birmingham, AL 35294-1150; 205-934-5025; Fax: 205-934-8664; E-mail: ucipØ17@larry.huc.uab.edu

UNIVERSITY OF COLORADO AT BOULDER

GUADALAJARA SUMMER LANGUAGE PROGRAM

General Information • Language study program in Guadalajara. Classes are held on the campus of University of Guadalajara.
Learning Focus • Courses in Spanish language, Mexican culture. Instruction is offered by local teachers.
Accommodations • Homestays. Meals are taken with host family.
Program Details • Program offered 2 times per year. Session length: 5 or 10 weeks. Departures are scheduled in June, July. The program is open to undergraduate students. Most participants are 19–23 years of age. Other require-

ments: minimum 2.75 GPA and Spanish recommended. 10–20 participants per session. Application deadline: March 1.
Costs • $1315 for Colorado residents, $2065 for nonresidents (includes tuition, housing, all meals, insurance). A $300 deposit is required.
Contact • Study Abroad Program, University of Colorado at Boulder, International Education, Campus Box 123, Boulder, CO 80309-0123; 303-492-7741; Fax: 303-492-5185; E-mail: studyabr@colorado.edu; World Wide Web: http://www.colorado.edu/OIE/StudyAbroad

UNIVERSITY OF DELAWARE

WINTER SESSION IN MEXICO

General Information • Language study program in Mérida. Classes are held on the campus of Mérida Institute of Technology. Excursions to Valladolid, Cobá, Chichén Itzá, Tulúm, Playa del Carmen.
Learning Focus • Courses in art history, Spanish language, Latin American studies, political science, political science. Instruction is offered by professors from the sponsoring institution.
Accommodations • Homestays. Meals are taken with host family.
Program Details • Program offered once per year. Session length: 5 weeks. Departures are scheduled in January. The program is open to undergraduate students. Most participants are 18–21 years of age. Other requirements: minimum 2.0 GPA. 25 participants per session. Application deadline: October.
Costs • $3660 (includes tuition, housing, all meals, excursions, international airfare). A $200 deposit is required.
Contact • International Programs and Special Sessions, University of Delaware, 4 Kent Way, Newark, DE 19716-1450; 888-831-4685; Fax: 302-831-6042; E-mail: studyabroad@mvs.udel.edu

UNIVERSITY OF FLORIDA

UNIVERSIDAD AUTONOMA DE YUCATÁN, MERIDA, MEXICO–LANGUAGE, SOCIETY, AND CULTURE OF MEXICO AND THE YUCATÁN

General Information • Language study program in Mérida. Classes are held on the campus of Autonomous University of Yucatán. Excursions to Mayan sites, coastal areas.
Learning Focus • Courses in Spanish language, anthropology. Instruction is offered by professors from the sponsoring institution and local teachers.
Accommodations • Homestays. Single rooms are available. Meals are taken with host family, in residences.
Program Details • Program offered 2 times per year. Session length: 6 or 12 weeks. Departures are scheduled in May, June. The program is open to undergraduate students, graduate students, adults. Most participants are 18–40 years of age. Other requirements: minimum 2.5 GPA and one year of Spanish. 20–30 participants per session. Application deadline: March 15.
Costs • $3900–$5000 depending upon session (includes tuition, housing, some meals, books and class materials, excursions, orientation). Application fee: $250.
Contact • Overseas Studies, University of Florida, 123 Tigert Hall, PO Box 113225, Gainesville, FL 32611-3225; 352-392-5206; Fax: 352-392-5575; E-mail: overseas@nervm.nerdc.ufl.edu

UNIVERSITY OF FLORIDA

UNIVERSIDAD DE YUCATÁN, MERIDA, MEXICO–ECOLOGY OF THE YUCATÁN

General Information • Academic study program in Mérida, Yucatán. Classes are held on the campus of Autonomous University of Yucatán. Excursions to rain forests, Mayan historical sites, coastal sites.
Learning Focus • Courses in ecology, Spanish language. Instruction is offered by professors from the sponsoring institution and local teachers.
Accommodations • Homestays. Single rooms are available. Meals are taken with host family, in residences.
Program Details • Program offered once per year. Session length: 6 weeks. Departures are scheduled in May. The program is open to undergraduate students, graduate students, adults. Most participants are 18–40 years of age. Other requirements: minimum 2.5 GPA. 15 participants per session. Application deadline: March 15.
Costs • $3900 (includes tuition, housing, all meals, books and class materials, excursions, orientation, administration fee). Application fee: $250.
Contact • Overseas Studies, University of Florida, 123 Tigert Hall, PO Box 113225, Gainesville, FL 32611-3225; 352-392-5206; Fax: 352-392-5575; E-mail: ovrseas@nervm.nerdc.ufl.edu

UNIVERSITY OF KANSAS

SUMMER LANGUAGE AND CULTURE INSTITUTE IN GUADALAJARA, MEXICO

General Information • Language study program in Guadalajara. Classes are held on the campus of Universidad del Valle de Atemajac (UNIVA). Excursions to Mexico City, colonial towns.
Learning Focus • Courses in Spanish language, Spanish literature, Mexican culture. Instruction is offered by professors from the sponsoring institution and local teachers.
Accommodations • Homestays. Meals are taken on one's own, with host family, in local restaurants, in residences.
Program Details • Program offered once per year. Session length: 8 weeks. Departures are scheduled in June. The program is open to undergraduate students, graduate students. Most participants are 19–26 years of age. Other requirements: 2 semesters of college-level Spanish or equivalent. 30 participants per session. Application deadline: March 1.
Costs • $1955 (includes tuition, housing, some meals). Application fee: $15. A $300 deposit is required.
Contact • Susan MacNally, Coordinator of Summer Institutes, University of Kansas, Office of Study Abroad, 203 Lippincott Hall, Lawrence, KS 66045; 913-864-3742; Fax: 913-864-5040; E-mail: osa@falcon.cc.ukans.edu; World Wide Web: http://kuhub.cc.ukans.edu/~intlstdy/osa/osamain.html

UNIVERSITY OF OREGON, INTERAMERICAN UNIVERSITY STUDIES INSTITUTE

MEXICAN STUDIES

General Information • Academic study program in Querétaro. Classes are held on the campus of Autonomous University of Querétaro. Excursions to Teotihuacán, Mexico City, Guadalajara.
Learning Focus • Courses in Mexican history, Spanish language, modern Mexican literature, art history. Instruction is offered by professors from the sponsoring institution and local teachers.
Accommodations • Homestays. Single rooms are available. Meals are taken with host family.
Program Details • Program offered once per year. Session length: 11 weeks. Departures are scheduled in August. The program is open to undergraduate students, adults. Most participants are 19–28 years of age. Other requirements: minimum 2.75 GPA and 2nd year Spanish competence. 22 participants per session. Application deadline: July 1.
Costs • $2869 (includes tuition, housing, all meals, excursions). Application fee: $50. A $100 deposit is required.
Contact • Ms. Jennifer Jewett, Program Coordinator, University of Oregon, Interamerican University Studies Institute, PO Box 10958, Eugene, OR 97440; 800-345-4874; Fax: 541-686-5947; E-mail: iusi2oregon@efn.org; World Wide Web: http://www.efn.org/~iusi

UNIVERSITY OF OREGON, INTERAMERICAN UNIVERSITY STUDIES INSTITUTE

SUMMER SPANISH

General Information • Language study program in Querétaro. Classes are held on the campus of Centro Intercultural de Querétaro. Excursions to Pátzcuaro.
Learning Focus • Courses in Spanish language, Mexican civilization. Instruction is offered by professors from the sponsoring institution and local teachers.
Accommodations • Homestays. Single rooms are available. Meals are taken with host family.
Program Details • Program offered once per year. Session length: 6 weeks. Departures are scheduled in June. The program is open to undergraduate students, graduate students, adults. Most participants are 19–45 years of age. Other requirements: minimum 2.75 GPA. 25 participants per session. Application deadline: April 1.
Costs • $1981 (includes tuition, housing, all meals, excursions). Application fee: $50. A $100 deposit is required.
Contact • Ms. Jennifer Jewett, Program Coordinator, University of Oregon, Interamerican University Studies Institute, PO Box 10958, Eugene, OR 97440; 800-345-4874; Fax: 541-686-5947; E-mail: iusi2oregon@efn.org; World Wide Web: http://www.efn.org/~iusi

UNIVERSITY OF ROCHESTER

SPANISH IN MEXICO

General Information • Language study program in Oaxaca. Classes are held on the campus of Instituto Cultural de Oaxaca.
Learning Focus • Courses in language study. Instruction is offered by professors from the sponsoring institution and local teachers.
Accommodations • Homestays. Meals are taken with host family, in residences.
Program Details • Program offered once per year. Session length: 4 weeks. Departures are scheduled in May. The program is open to undergraduate students, adults. Most participants are 18–30 years of age. Other requirements: previous Spanish language study,either 3 years high school or 1 year college. 8–10 participants per session. Application deadline: March 15.
Costs • $2700 (includes tuition, housing, some meals, excursions).
Contact • Anne Lutkus, Language Coordinator, University of Rochester, Department of Modern Languages and Cultures, Rochester, NY 14627; 716-275-4251; E-mail: adlt@db1.cc.rochester.edu; World Wide Web: http://www.rochester.edu/College/study-abroad/

UNIVERSITY OF SOUTHERN MISSISSIPPI

MEXICAN STUDIES PROGRAM

General Information • Language study program in Cuernavaca.
Learning Focus • Courses in Spanish language, geography, history, civilizations, cultural studies, Mexican studies. Instruction is offered by professors from the sponsoring institution.
Accommodations • Homestays. Meals are taken with host family.
Program Details • Program offered once per year. Session length: 4 weeks. Departures are scheduled in May. The program is open to undergraduate students, graduate students. Other requirements: minimum 2.0 GPA, good academic standing, and previous study in Spanish. 60 participants per session. Application deadline: April 3.
Costs • $1999 for undergraduates, $2149 for graduate students (includes tuition, housing, all meals, excursions, international airfare). A $100 deposit is required.
Contact • Director, Mexican Studies Program, University of Southern Mississippi, Box 10047, Hattiesburg, MS 39406-0047; 601-266-4344; Fax: 601-266-5699; E-mail: m_ravencraft@bull.cc.usm.edu

UNIVERSITY OF SOUTHERN MISSISSIPPI

YUCATÁN, MEXICO STUDIES PROGRAM

General Information • Academic study program in Cancun, Chichen Itza, Mérida.
Learning Focus • Courses in civilizations, international business, Spanish language, Mexican studies, political science, cultural studies.
Accommodations • Homestays.
Program Details • Program offered once per year. Session length: 3 weeks. Departures are scheduled in May. The program is open to undergraduate students, graduate

students. Other requirements: minimum 2.0 GPA, good academic standing, and previous study in field. Application deadline: April 5.
Costs • $1999 for undergraduates, $2299 for graduate students (includes tuition, housing, international airfare). A $100 deposit is required.
Contact • Director, Yucatán Mexico Studies Program, University of Southern Mississippi, Box 10047, Hattiesburg, MS 39406-0047; 601-266-4344; Fax: 601-266-5699; E-mail: m_ravencraft@bull.cc.usm.edu

UNIVERSITY OF TOLEDO

UNIVERSITY OF TOLEDO IN GUADALAJARA

General Information • Language study program in Guadalajara. Classes are held on the campus of Autonomous University of Guadalajara.
Learning Focus • Courses in language and culture. Instruction is offered by local teachers.
Accommodations • Homestays. Single rooms are available. Meals are taken with host family, in residences.
Program Details • Program offered 2 times per year. Session length: 6 weeks. Departures are scheduled in June, August. The program is open to undergraduate students. Most participants are 20–30 years of age. Other requirements: intermediate-level Spanish. 10–15 participants per session. Application deadline: February 28.
Costs • $2000 (includes tuition, housing, some meals, books and class materials, international airfare). Application fee: $25. A $100 deposit is required.
Contact • Joel A. Gallegos, Study Abroad Coordinator, University of Toledo, C.I.S.P. SWAC 2357, Toledo, OH 43606; 419-530-1240; Fax: 419-530-1245; E-mail: jgalleg@utnet.utoledo.edu; World Wide Web: http://www.utoledo.edu/www/cisp/study-abroad/

UNIVERSITY OF WISCONSIN–EAU CLAIRE

SUMMER PROGRAM IN MEXICO

General Information • Language study and cultural program in Cuernavaca. Classes are held on the campus of Instituto Tecnológico y de Estudios Superiores de Monterrey–Campus Morelos.
Learning Focus • Courses in Spanish language, Latin American studies. Instruction is offered by professors from the sponsoring institution and local teachers.
Accommodations • Homestays. Single rooms are available. Meals are taken with host family, in residences.
Program Details • Program offered once per year. Session length: 6 weeks. Departures are scheduled in June. The program is open to undergraduate students, adults. Most participants are 18–25 years of age. Other requirements: minimum 2.0 GPA, 2 years of college-level Spanish for Latin American Studies courses. 20–25 participants per session. Application deadline: February 15.
Costs • $1550 for Wisconsin residents, $2500 for non-residents (includes tuition, housing, all meals, books and class materials). Application fee: $30. A $200 deposit is required.
Contact • Cheryl Lochner-Wright, Study Abroad Coordinator, University of Wisconsin–Eau Claire, Center for International Education, 111 Schofield Hall, Eau Claire, WI 54702-4004; 715-836-4411; Fax: 715-836-4948; E-mail: inted@uwec.edu

UNIVERSITY OF WISCONSIN–MADISON

OAXACA, MEXICO PROGRAM

General Information • Academic study program in Oaxaca. Classes are held on the campus of Instituto Cultural de Oaxaca.
Learning Focus • Courses in Spanish language, literature. Instruction is offered by local teachers.
Accommodations • Homestays. Meals are taken with host family, in residences.
Program Details • Program offered once per year. Session length: 8 weeks. Departures are scheduled in May. The program is open to undergraduate students. Other requirements: 4 semesters Spanish and at least sophomore standing. 20–38 participants per session. Application deadline: first Friday in March.
Costs • $3605–$3705 (includes tuition, housing, all meals, books and class materials, excursions, international airfare). A $100 deposit is required.
Contact • Peer Advisors, Office of International Studies and Programs, University of Wisconsin–Madison, 261 Bascom Hall, 500 Lincoln Drive, Madison, WI 53706; 608-265-6329; Fax: 608-262-6998; E-mail: abroad@macc.wisc.edu; World Wide Web: http://www.wisc.edu/uw-oisp/

WICHITA STATE UNIVERSITY

PUEBLA SUMMER PROGRAM

General Information • Language study program in Puebla. Excursions to Oaxaca, Veracruz.
Learning Focus • Courses in Spanish language, literature, Mexican culture. Instruction is offered by professors from the sponsoring institution.
Accommodations • Homestays, hotels. Meals are taken as a group, in central dining facility.
Program Details • Program offered once per year. Session length: 6 weeks. Departures are scheduled in June. The program is open to undergraduate students, graduate students, adults. Most participants are 17–60 years of age. Other requirements: two semesters of college Spanish. 65 participants per session. Application deadline: April 1.
Costs • $1550 (includes tuition, housing, all meals, excursions). Application fee: $15. A $100 deposit is required.
Contact • John H. Koppenhaver, Associate Dean, Liberal Arts and Sciences and Puebla Program Director, Wichita State University, 1845 North Fairmount, Wichita, KS 67260-0005; 316-978-3100; Fax: 316-978-3234; E-mail: koppenha@twsuvm.uc.twsu.edu

CENTER FOR GLOBAL EDUCATION AT AUGSBURG COLLEGE

LEARNING FROM THE SOUTH: A SEMINAR IN NICARAGUA FOR WOMEN LEADERS

General Information • Academic study program with visits to Managua, rural areas.
Learning Focus • Instruction in current issues in Nicaragua. Escorted travel to local communities. Other activities include meetings with women leaders, community members. Instruction is offered by in-country coordinators. This program would appeal to people interested in social justice, third world studies, Central America, advocacy, Nicaragua.
Accommodations • Program-owned houses.
Program Details • Program offered once per year. Session length: 10 days. Departures are scheduled in June. Program is targeted to women leaders. Most participants are 20–70 years of age. Participants must be 18 years or older to enroll. 15 participants per session. Application deadline: May 20. Reservations are recommended at least 6 weeks before departure.
Costs • $1640 (includes housing, all meals, books and class materials, excursions, international airfare, translation). A $100 deposit is required.
Contact • International Travel Seminars, Center for Global Education at Augsburg College, Center for Global Education, 2211 Riverside Avenue, Minneapolis, MN 55454; 800-299-8889; Fax: 612-330-1695; E-mail: globaled@augsburg.edu; World Wide Web: http://www.augsburg.edu/global

COLLEGE CONSORTIUM FOR INTERNATIONAL STUDIES–UNIVERSITY OF MOBILE

CCIS PROGRAM IN NICARAGUA

General Information • Academic study program in San Marcos. Classes are held on the campus of University of Mobile–Latin American Campus.
Learning Focus • Courses in Latin American studies, Spanish language, business, social sciences, history, political science, natural science, archaeology. Instruction is offered by local teachers.
Accommodations • Homestays, dormitories. Meals are taken as a group, with host family, in central dining facility, in residences.
Program Details • Program offered 3 times per year. Session length: 5 weeks. Departures are scheduled in May–July. The program is open to undergraduate students, graduate students, pre-college students, adults. Most participants are 18–27 years of age. Other requirements: minimum 2.5 GPA. 7 participants per session.
Costs • $1678 (includes tuition, housing, all meals). Application fee: $50. A $200 deposit is required.
Contact • Jane C. Evans, Executive Director, College Consortium for International Studies, 2000 P Street, NW, Suite 503, Washington, DC 20036; 800-453-6956; Fax: 202-223-0999; E-mail: ccis@intr.net

GLOBAL EXCHANGE REALITY TOURS

NICARAGUA

General Information • Academic study program with visits to Managua. Once at the destination country, participants travel by bus, airplane.
Learning Focus • Instruction in current political, economic and social situations. Instruction is offered by researchers, naturalists. This program would appeal to people interested in election observation, culture, labor issues.
Accommodations • Hotels, guest houses. Single rooms are available for an additional $200–$500.
Program Details • Program offered once per year. Session length: 10 days. Departures are scheduled in October. Program is targeted to seniors, students and professionals. Participants must be 18 years or older to enroll. 10 participants per session. Application deadline: 1 month prior to departure. Reservations are recommended at least 2 months before departure.
Costs • $800 (includes housing, some meals). A $200 deposit is required.
Contact • Loreto Curti, Reality Tours Coordinator, Global Exchange Reality Tours, 2017 Mission Street, Room 303, San Francisco, CA 94110; 415-255-7296; Fax: 415-255-7498; E-mail: globalexch@igc.apc.org

PANAMA

AMERISPAN UNLIMITED

SPANISH CLASSES AND HOMESTAYS IN PANAMA

General Information • Language study program with visits to Panama City. Once at the destination country, participants travel by bus.

Learning Focus • Instruction in the Spanish language. Instruction is offered by trained Spanish teachers. This program would appeal to people interested in Spanish language, Latin America.

Accommodations • Homestays. Single rooms are available.

Program Details • Session length: 2–12 weeks. Departures are scheduled throughout the year. Most participants are 16–70 years of age. Participants must be 16 years or older to enroll. 2–3 participants per session. Reservations are recommended at least 4 weeks before departure.

Costs • $490 for 2 weeks, $980 for 4 weeks, $245 for each additional week (includes tuition, housing, some meals, books and class materials, insurance). A $100 deposit is required.

Contact • AmeriSpan Unlimited, PO Box 40513, Philadelphia, PA 19106; 800-879-6640; Fax: 215-985-4524; E-mail: info@amerispan.com; World Wide Web: http://www.amerispan.com

JOURNEYS INTERNATIONAL, INC.

DARIEN EXPLORER

General Information • Wilderness/adventure program with visits to Cana, El Real, La Palma, Lepe, Panama City, Pirre Cloud Forest. Once at the destination country, participants travel by foot, boat, airplane, hiking.

Learning Focus • Escorted travel to within Panama. Other activities include camping, hiking. Instruction is offered by naturalists, native English-speaking guides. This program would appeal to people interested in nature studies, culture, hiking, wildlife, photography.

Accommodations • Hotels, campsites, lodges. Single rooms are available.

Program Details • Program offered once per year. Session length: 14 days. Departures are scheduled in December. Program is targeted to active hikers with an interest in cultures. Most participants are 25–55 years of age. Participants must be 12 years or older to enroll. Other requirements: excellent health and physical condition. 12 participants per session. Reservations are recommended at least 60 days before departure.

Costs • $2545 (includes housing, all meals, excursions, flights in country). A $300 deposit is required.

Contact • Michelle Gervais, Latin America Sales Director, Journeys International, Inc., 4011 Jackson Road, Ann Arbor, MI 48103; 313-665-4407; Fax: 313-665-2945; E-mail: michelle@journeys-intl.com; World Wide Web: http://www.journeys-intl.com

JOURNEYS INTERNATIONAL, INC.

GOLDEN ISTHMUS WEEK

General Information • Wilderness/adventure program with visits to Aligandi Island, Boquete, Chiriqui, Panama City, San Blas Islands.

Learning Focus • Escorted travel to the Panama Canal and Kuna Indian villages. Nature observation (cloud forests, jungle life). Other activities include snorkeling. Instruction is offered by naturalists, native English-speaking guides. This program would appeal to people interested in history, culture, nature studies, wildlife.

Accommodations • Hotels, inns, lodges. Single rooms are available.

Program Details • Program offered 3 times per year. Session length: 8 days. Departures are scheduled in January, February, March. Most participants are 25–55 years of age. Participants must be 12 years or older to enroll. 2–14 participants per session. Reservations are recommended at least 60 days before departure.

Costs • $1375 (includes housing, some meals, excursions, flights in country). A $300 deposit is required.

Contact • Michelle Gervais, Latin America Sales Director, Journeys International, Inc., 4011 Jackson Road, Ann Arbor, MI 48103; 313-665-4407; Fax: 313-665-2945; E-mail: michelle@journeys-intl.com; World Wide Web: http://www.journeys-intl.com

JOURNEYS INTERNATIONAL, INC.

PANAMA FAMILY DISCOVERY

General Information • Family tour with visits to Aonistad International Park, Barro Colorado, Boquete, Panama City, San Blas Islands. Once at the destination country, participants travel by foot, boat.

Learning Focus • Escorted travel to the Panama Canal, Kuna Indian Villages and the San Blas Islands. Nature observation (cloud and rain forests). Other activities include snorkeling, birdwatching. Instruction is offered by naturalists, native English-speaking guides. This program would appeal to people interested in bird watching, nature studies, photography, culture, wildlife.

Accommodations • Hotels, lodges . Single rooms are available.

Program Details • Program offered once per year. Session length: 8 days. Departures are scheduled in December. Program is targeted to active families. Most participants are 5–70 years of age. Participants must be 5 years or older to enroll. 14 participants per session. Reservations are recommended at least 60 days before departure.

Costs • $1250 for adults, $850 for children under 12 (includes housing, some meals, excursions, flights in country). A $300 deposit is required.

Contact • Joan Weber, Family Trips Director and Owner, Journeys International, Inc., 4011 Jackson Road, Ann Arbor,

GARDEN/HORTICULTURAL TOURS

GOURMET COOKING/WINE TOURS

INTERNSHIP PROGRAMS

WESTERN HEMISPHERE

Honduras

Martinique

Mexico

NATURE STUDY TOURS

COUNTRY TO COUNTRY

AFRICA

ARCTIC AND ANTARCTIC

PERFORMING ARTS PROGRAMS

EAST ASIA AND PACIFIC

WESTERN EUROPE

PHOTOGRAPHY TOURS

AFRICA

ARCTIC AND ANTARCTIC

EAST ASIA AND PACIFIC

SPORTS PROGRAMS

VOLUNTEER SERVICE PROGRAMS

WILDERNESS/ADVENTURE PROGRAMS

PROGRAMS OFFERING COLLEGE CREDIT

FORESTER INSTITUTO INTERNACIONAL

FORUM TRAVEL INTERNATIONAL

FRENCH-AMERICAN EXCHANGE

GEORGE MASON UNIVERSITY

GEORGETOWN UNIVERSITY

GLOBAL AWARENESS THROUGH EXPERIENCE (GATE)

GLOBAL CITIZENS NETWORK

GLOBAL EXCHANGE REALITY TOURS

STATE UNIVERSITY OF NEW YORK AT NEW PALTZ

STATE UNIVERSITY OF NEW YORK COLLEGE AT BROCKPORT

STATE UNIVERSITY OF NEW YORK COLLEGE AT PLATTSBURGH

STATE UNIVERSITY OF WEST GEORGIA

STUDIO ART CENTERS INTERNATIONAL

SYRACUSE UNIVERSITY

TEMPLE UNIVERSITY

TEXAS CHRISTIAN UNIVERSITY

TRAVELEARN

TRINITY CHRISTIAN COLLEGE

TRINITY COLLEGE

PROGRAM SPONSORS

COUNCIL ON INTERNATIONAL EDUCATIONAL EXCHANGE

COUNTRY WALKERS

CRAFT WORLD TOURS

CROSS-CULTURAL SOLUTIONS

CROSS-CULTURE

CSA–CENTER FOR STUDY ABROAD

INTERNATIONAL BICYCLE FUND

INTERNATIONAL COUNCIL FOR CULTURAL EXCHANGE (ICCE)

INTERNATIONAL STUDIES ABROAD

INTERNATIONAL ZOOLOGICAL EXPEDITIONS

INTER-UNIVERSITY BOARD FOR CHINESE LANGUAGE STUDIES

IONA COLLEGE

AN IRISH SOJOURN

IVORY ISLE TRAVEL

JAMES MADISON UNIVERSITY

JAPAN-AMERICA STUDENT CONFERENCE

JAPAN CENTER FOR MICHIGAN UNIVERSITIES

JOHN CABOT UNIVERSITY

JOURNEYS EAST

JOURNEYS INTERNATIONAL, INC.

JOURNEYS THRU SCOTLAND

KCP INTERNATIONAL LANGUAGE INSTITUTE

KENTUCKY INSTITUTE FOR INTERNATIONAL STUDIES

LANGUAGE IMMERSION INSTITUTE

LANGUAGE LIAISON

LANGUAGE LINK

LANGUAGE STUDIES ABROAD

LANGUAGE STUDIES CANADA

LA SABRANENQUE

LEARNING PROGRAMS INTERNATIONAL

LEXIA EXCHANGE INTERNATIONAL

LONDON COLLEGE OF FASHION

LORENZO DE MEDICI–THE ART INSTITUTE OF FLORENCE

LOS ANGELES COMMUNITY COLLEGE DISTRICT

LOUISIANA STATE UNIVERSITY

LOUISIANA TECH UNIVERSITY

LOYOLA UNIVERSITY, NEW ORLEANS

LYNN UNIVERSITY

NATURAL HABITAT ADVENTURES

NATURAL HISTORY MUSEUM OF LOS ANGELES COUNTY

NATURE EXPEDITIONS INTERNATIONAL

OXFORD ADVANCED STUDIES PROGRAM

OXFORD ASSOCIATE STUDENT PROGRAMME

THE PARTNERSHIP FOR SERVICE-LEARNING

PEOPLE TO PEOPLE INTERNATIONAL

PHOTO ADVENTURE TOURS

PHOTO EXPLORER TOURS

PONT-AVEN SCHOOL OF ART

QUEEN'S UNIVERSITY AT KINGSTON

RADFORD UNIVERSITY

RAMAPO COLLEGE OF NEW JERSEY

RHODES COLLEGE

RICE UNIVERSITY

ROCKLAND COMMUNITY COLLEGE

ROLLINS COLLEGE

ROSARY COLLEGE

RUSSIAN AND EAST EUROPEAN PARTNERSHIPS

Options & Opportunities Around the World